Cohabitation
Law, Practice and Precedents

While every care has been taken to ensure the accuracy of this work, no responsibility for loss or damage occasioned to any person acting or refraining from action as a result of any statement in it can be accepted by the authors, editors or publishers.

Cohabitation
Law, Practice and Precedents

Eighth Edition

Helen Wood MA
District Judge

James Cook BA (Hons), LLB (Hons), TEP
Partner, Collyer Bristow LLP

Lisette Dupré, LLM
Partner, Dawson Cornwell

Ashley Murray LLB (Hons)
Barrister, Northern Circuit

David Salter MA, LLM
Deputy High Court Judge and Recorder

Emily Ward, LLB (Hons)
Barrister, Broadway House Chambers and Deputy District Judge

LexisNexis® UK & Worldwide

United Kingdom   RELX (UK) Limited trading as LexisNexis®, 1–3 Strand, London WC2N 5JR and 9–10 St Andrew Square, Edinburgh EH2 2AF

LNUK Global Partners   LexisNexis® encompasses authoritative legal publishing brands dating back to the 19th century including: Butterworths® in the United Kingdom, Canada and the Asia-Pacific region; Les Editions du Juris Classeur in France; and Matthew Bender® worldwide. Details of LexisNexis® locations worldwide can be found at www.lexisnexis.com

© 2020 RELX (UK) Ltd.
Published by LexisNexis®

All rights reserved. No part of this publication may be reproduced in any material form (including photocopying or storing it in any medium by electronic means and whether or not transiently or incidentally to some other use of this publication) without the written permission of the copyright owner except in accordance with the provisions of the Copyright, Designs and Patents Act 1988 or under the terms of a licence issued by the Copyright Licensing Agency Ltd, 5th Floor, Shackleton House, 4 Battlebridge Lane, London, SE1 2HX. Applications for the copyright owner's written permission to reproduce any part of this publication should be addressed to the publisher.

Warning: The doing of an unauthorised act in relation to a copyright work may result in both a civil claim for damages and criminal prosecution.

Crown copyright material is reproduced with the permission of the Controller of HMSO and the Queen's Printer for Scotland. Parliamentary copyright material is reproduced with the permission of the Controller of Her Majesty's Stationery Office on behalf of Parliament. Any European material in this work which has been reproduced from EUR-lex, the official European Communities legislation website, is European Communities copyright.

LexisNexis® and the Knowledge Burst logo are registered trademarks of RELX Group plc, used under license. Butterworths® and Tolley® are registered trademarks of RELX (UK) Ltd. Matthew Bender® is a registered trademark of Matthew Bender & Company Inc. Other products and services may be trademarks or registered trademarks of their respective companies.

A CIP Catalogue record for this book is available from the British Library.

ISBN 978-1-7847-3460-2

9 781784 734602

ISBN for this volume: 9781784734602

Printed and bound by CPI Group (UK) Ltd, Croydon, CR0 4YY

Visit LexisNexis at http://www.lexisnexis.co.uk

Acknowledgments

The authors wish to thank David Burrows for his contribution to the child support and enforcement section of Chapter 5, and to acknowledge his help and advice along with Nick Wikeley, Desmond Rutledge, Andy King, Jane Gordois and Carole Broadwith.

They are also indebted to Professor Rebecca Probert for providing the much needed Introduction, and to Professor Chris Barton whose idea this was.

Foreword

The ease with which a couple can opt for cohabitation, consciously or by default, belies the complexity that often attends the termination of their relationship.

In many respects legislation has provided safeguards and remedies that place cohabitants in a similar if not identical position to those who are married or in a civil partnership. In other important respects, notably property and financial provision, there has been a reluctance to do so. There are public policy arguments about the importance of marriage and the family for society, and counter arguments that point out that nearly half of all children are born outside marriage and the law should reflect the realities of family life in the 21st century.

Further attempts to legislate for inclusivity for cohabitants have been abandoned. As far as rights over property are concerned, these remain rooted in land law, equity and trusts. There is little or no discretion and the end result can often appear unfair.

The outcome of litigation can never be certain, and in disputes between cohabitants this is especially so. Many expensive arguments could be avoided if only cohabitants could be persuaded to take appropriate advice at the outset, whether as to beneficial interests on the purchase of the shared home or by the formalisation of agreed terms in a properly drafted cohabitation agreement.

The advice that cohabitants need reaches into all aspects of legal practice. This book provides a clear and authoritative exposition of the law, both contentious and non-contentious, with guidance on practice and procedure, precedents and checklists. It will be an invaluable reference for all those advising at every stage of a cohabitation relationship.

Lady Justice Eleanor King

Preface

The aim of this book is to assist practitioners when dealing with the particular requirements of those who are neither married nor in a civil partnership.

A lawyer will usually only be consulted when a relationship is either in difficulties or at an end. It is at this stage that myths as to entitlement to property and financial provision may have to be exploded. This is so especially in relation to property where there remains very little statutory protection for cohabitants and uncertainty abounds.

The approach of this book is that 'prevention is better than cure'. It is divided into ten sections. Each sets out the substantive law and, where appropriate, precedents and procedural guides. As such it is multi-disciplinary, enabling practitioners to advise clients fully at all stages of a cohabitation relationship, and on every aspect.

The law is as stated at 31 March 2020.

Helen Wood
March 2020

Contents

Acknowledgments	v
Foreword	vii
Preface	ix
Table of Abbreviations	xxxix
Table of Statutes	xli
Table of Statutory Instruments	xlix
Table of International Material	liii
Table of Cases	lv

Chapter 1   Property

Part A   Law and Practice

Section 1   Ownership of the home

Introduction	1.1
The duty of the solicitor on the purchase of a shared home	1.2
Declaring the beneficial interests on acquisition	1.4
Express declaration of trust	1.5
Effects of an express declaration of trust	1.6
Land Registry Forms; restrictions and cautions	1.7
Expressing the shares	1.9
Who owns what if there is a dispute?	1.17
Express declaration of beneficial interests	1.18
Severing the joint tenancy	1.21
No express declaration of beneficial interests	1.23
Sole legal ownership or joint legal ownership?	1.24
Implied trusts	1.25
Resulting trusts	1.27
Constructive trusts	1.32

Contents

Proprietary estoppel	1.53
Accounting for occupation rent	1.60
Applications for declaration of interest in trust property and order for sale	1.62
Applications under the Married Women's Property Act 1882	1.74
Applications under Matrimonial Proceedings and Property Act 1970	1.84

Section 2 Occupation of the home

The owner-occupied home	1.85
The rented home	1.88
Private sector tenancies	1.90
Housing associations and other registered social landlords	1.91
Local authority housing	1.100
Tenancy in joint names	1.104
Tenancy in sole name	1.105
Protecting the cohabitant in occupation	1.106
Applying to transfer the tenancy	1.109
The homeless cohabitant	1.127

Section 3 Ownership and use of chattels

Introduction	1.132
Ownership of chattels	1.133
Bank accounts	1.134
Existing property	1.135
Gifts	1.136
Cohabitation agreement	1.137
Applications for declarations of ownership and orders for sale	1.138
Injunctions	1.142
Engaged couples	1.143
The use of chattels	1.144

Part B Procedural Guides

Order under Trusts of Land and Appointment of Trustees Act 1996, s 14

Legal background	1.145

	Procedure		**1.146**
Transfer of a Tenancy under Family Law Act 1996, Pt IV, s 53 and Sch 7			
	Legal background		**1.147**
	Procedure		**1.148**
Part C	Checklists		
	Essential information where the dispute is over owner-occupied property		**1.149**
	Essential information where the dispute is over rented property		
	Acting for a cohabiting couple on the acquisition of property		
Part D	Precedents		
	How to use these precedents		**1.152**
	Section 1	Non-contentious precedents	
	A	Clauses: Commencement and recitals	
		Commencement and date	**1.153**
		Purchase of property	**1.154**
		Mortgage of property	**1.155**
		The underlying purpose of the trust	**1.156**
		Recitals of fact and intention: third party contributions	**1.157**
		Mortgage payments	**1.158**
		Co-owners intend to marry/enter into a registered civil partnership with each other: provisions of this declaration to apply despite marriage/civil partnership	**1.159**
	B	Clauses: Trusts	
		The standard trusts	**1.160**
		Co-owners to be joint tenants until severance and tenants in common in unequal shares after severance	**1.161**
		Co-owners to be tenants in common until their marriage/civil partnership and subsequently joint tenants	**1.162**
		Shares of the net proceeds of sale differ from those of the net income until sale	**1.163**
		Deferred trust of land: '*Mesher*' and '*Martin*'-type trusts	**1.164**

Contents

C Clauses: Shares

Fixed shares: expressed as fractions or percentages of the net proceeds of sale	1.165
Fixed shares: expressed as a fixed share of the sale price, less a fixed share of the amount required to redeem the mortgage, less a fixed share of the sale costs	1.166
Fixed shares: refund of original contributions: provision for abatement: fixed shares of the balance of the net proceeds of sale	1.167
Fixed shares: refund of original contributions plus interest: provision for abatement: fixed shares of the balance of the net proceeds of sale	1.168
Fixed shares: refund of original contributions expressed as a fraction or percentage of the sale price: alternative provisions for the division of the balance of the net proceeds of sale	1.169
Floating shares: in proportion to the contributions made by each co-owner throughout the duration of the trust	1.170
Floating shares: calculation of the shares: addition of contributions and apportionment of net proceeds of sale pro rata	1.171
Floating shares: calculation of the shares: introductory clause to the formulae	1.172
Floating shares: formulae for calculating floating shares: narrative form	1.173
Floating shares: formulae for calculating floating shares: tabular form	1.174
The average of two or more methods of calculating the shares	1.175
Supplemental clause providing for the gradual equalisation of the shares	1.176

D General clauses

Contingencies: introductory clause	1.177
General	1.178
Payments from lodgers	1.179
Payments from grown-up children	1.180
Separation	1.181
A co-owner's death	1.182

Contents

	Contributions towards repairs and improvements not to affect the co-owners' fixed shares	1.183
	Prohibited acts	1.184
	Positive acts	1.185
	Legal advice	1.186
	Costs of this declaration	1.187
	Sale costs	1.188
	Costs of transfer of beneficial interest	1.189
	Sale price	1.190
	Amount required to redeem the mortgage	1.191
	Incidental costs of selling the property	1.192
	Net proceeds of sale	1.193
	Open market value	1.194
	Mortgage payments	1.195
	Repairs and improvements	1.196
	Co-owners	1.197
	The nature of this declaration	1.198
	Execution in duplicate	1.199
	Attestation clause	1.200
E	Contingencies	
	If the co-owners permit any other person to reside with them in the property	1.201
	If a co-owner fails to pay his or her share of the mortgage payments	1.202
	If one co-owner wishes to sell the property and the other co-owner refuses to sell it	1.203
	If one co-owner dies and the other does not become solely and beneficially entitled to the property	1.204
	If a co-owner is declared bankrupt	1.205
	Conversion from fixed shares to floating shares	1.206
	If a co-owner is unemployed or incapable of working	1.207
	If a co-owner is unemployed or incapable of working because she is pregnant or he or she is looking after a child or children	1.208
	Mortgage payments made by the other co-owner to be treated as a loan	1.209

Conversion of fixed shares into floating shares		1.210
One co-owner to have prior rights		1.211
Rules for determining who has prior rights		1.212
If a co-owner moves out before the property is sold		1.213
If the co-owners separate shortly after they purchase the property		1.214
If a co-owner wishes to realise his or her share in the property		1.215

F Forms

Fixed shares: Short form	1.216
Fixed shares: Long form	1.217
Fixed shares: One co-owner alone to be responsible for the mortgage payments	1.218
Floating shares: Tabular form	1.219
Floating shares: Long form	1.220
Deed of surrender of any potential right to claim a beneficial interest in the property	1.221
Declaration of trust by sole owner acknowledging that the partner has acquired a beneficial interest	1.222
Another person has contributed to the purchase price	1.223
Elderly person buys his or her council house with financial assistance from his or her children	1.224
Variation of a Declaration of Trust	1.225
Checklist for ownership of the home	1.226
HM Land Registry Form TR1	1.227
HM Land Registry Form JO	1.228
HM Land Registry Form SEV	1.229
HM Land Registry Form RX1	1.230
HM Land Registry Form FR1	1.231

Section 2 Contentious precedents

Claim form for a declaration of a beneficial interest in property and an order for sale under the Trusts of Land and Appointment of Trustees Act 1996	1.232
Claimant's witness statement in support of application for declaration/order for sale	1.233
Claimant's witness statement in support of application for sale of land under the Trusts of Land and Appointment of	

Trustees Act 1996	1.234
Order for sale of property under the Trusts of Land and Appointment of Trustees Act 1996	1.235
Applicant's sworn statement in support of injunction to prevent service of Notice to Quit	1.236
Application for transfer of tenancy under Pt IV of the Family Law Act 1996	1.237
Sworn statement in support of application for transfer of tenancy under Pt IV of the Family Law Act 1996	1.238
Order for transfer of protected or secure tenancy under Pt IV of the Family Law Act 1996	1.239
Order for transfer of statutory tenancy under Pt IV of the Family Law Act 1996	1.240
Tomlin order on compromise of dispute over property	1.241
Declaration of ownership of chattels	1.242

Chapter 2 Cohabitation Agreements

Part A Law and Practice

Introduction	2.1
Advising clients	2.2
Validity of cohabitation agreements	2.3
Enforceability of cohabitation agreements	2.4
The intention to create legal relations	2.5
Consideration	2.6
Uncertainty	2.7
Duress or coercion; inequality of bargaining power	2.8
Ousting the court's jurisdiction	2.9
Contents of a cohabitation agreement	2.10

Part B Checklists

Checklist – points to consider when advising on and drafting a cohabitation agreement	
The initial interview	2.11
Drafting	2.12
Submitting the draft to the client	2.13
Checklist of matters to be contained in every cohabitation agreement	2.14

Contents

Checklist of matters that may be contained in agreement intended to regulate property and financial matters	2.15

Part C Precedents

Clauses

Acknowledgment of advice received	2.16

After-acquired property

Separate	2.17
Shared	2.18
Aims and expectations	2.19
Attestation clause incorporating legal adviser's certificate	2.20

Bank accounts

Separate	2.21
Shared	2.22
Beneficial interests: separate	2.23
Binding effect of agreement	2.24
Birth control	2.25
Business interests: separate	2.26
Cancellation of cohabitation agreement	2.27

Cars

Separate	2.28
Shared	2.29
One party to provide a car for the other	2.30
Careers	2.31

Child care

Allocation of responsibility	2.32
Support of carer	2.33
Children: statement of intentions	2.34
Commencement	2.35
Commencement date	2.36
Confidentiality	2.37
Consideration: specific	2.38
Consideration: general	2.39

Cooling-off clause

Counselling	2.40
Trial separation	2.41
Costs	
Shared equally	2.42
One party to pay all the costs	2.43
One party to pay for independent advice	2.44
Covenants relating to residential property	2.45
Credit cards	
Separate	2.46
Shared	2.47
Debts	2.48
Declaration of trust	2.49
Deed	2.50
Dispute resolution	2.51
Arbitration	2.52
Conciliation	2.53
Named mediator	2.54
Duration	
Indefinite	2.55
Fixed term	2.56
Dwelling	
Joint tenancy	2.57
Tenancy in common	2.58
One party is sole owner	2.59
Estate rights	2.60
Execution of this agreement	2.61
Fiduciary duty	2.62
Financial disclosure	
By one party only	2.63
By both cohabitants	2.64
Further assurances	2.65
Gifts between cohabitants	
Presumption that the gift is absolute	2.66

Contents

Reservation of rights	2.67
Gifts received: separate	2.68
Guests	2.69
Headings	2.70
Housekeeping allowance: fixed sum	2.71
Housework	2.72

Illness or incapacity

Attorneyship	2.73
Next of kin	2.74
Support	2.75

Income

Separate	2.76
Shared	2.77
Intention to create legal relations	2.78
Interpretation of this agreement	2.79

Joint property

Joint tenancy	2.80
Tenancy in common	2.81
Joint use: separate ownership	2.82
Legal adviser's certificate	2.83
Life insurance: agreement to take out and maintain a policy	2.84

Living expenses

To be paid from joint account	2.85
To be paid in proportion to the parties' respective incomes	2.86
Fixed percentages	2.87
One party pays all	2.88
Defined areas of responsibility	2.89

Marriage

Agreement to continue on marriage	2.90
Agreement ceases to apply on marriage	2.91
Medical insurance	2.92
Mortgage payments	2.93

Non-disclosure of agreement to third parties	2.94
Pensions and death-in-service benefits	2.95
Present property: separate	2.96
Present property and debts: separate	2.97
Proper law	2.98

Recitals

Cohabitation	2.99
Intention to create legal relations	2.100
Intention not to create legal relations	2.101
Purpose of this agreement	2.102
No duress or undue influence	2.103
Cohabitant under 18	2.104
Recitals to be legally binding	2.105
Independent legal advice	2.106
Understanding the nature and effect of the agreement	2.107
Recitals: personal information about the parties	2.108
Recitals relating to the child(ren)	2.109
Release of rights (if any) over the other's separate property	2.110
Release of right to apply to the court for an order under the Inheritance (Provision for Family and Dependants) Act 1975	2.111
Religious upbringing of child(ren)	2.112
Remedies for breach of agreement	2.113
Rent	2.114
Review: ad hoc review	2.115
Review of agreement	2.116
Revocation clause	2.117
Separation	2.118
Severance	2.119
Sexual relations	2.120

Support

Mutual support	2.121
No obligation	2.122

Contents

No promises made	2.123
Reservation of right	2.124
Waiver of rights	2.125

Surname

Each to retain their own surname	2.126
Both to be known by the same surname	2.127
End of relationship	2.128
Notice	2.129
Terminating events	2.130

Termination consequences

General introductory clause	2.131
Bank and building society accounts	2.132
Credit and charge cards	2.133
The dwelling: option to 'buy out' the other's share	2.134
Separate property	2.135
Jointly owned goods and chattels	2.136
Support	2.137
Lump sum payment	2.138
Miscellaneous cancellations	2.139
Children	2.140
The other's child(ren)	2.141
Termination of agreement on marriage: consequences	2.142
Transfers between cohabitants	2.143
Clause	2.144
Deed	2.145
Waiver of breach	2.146
Whole agreement	2.147
Wills	2.148

Forms

Cohabitation Agreements

Cohabitation Agreement - Short form	2.149
Cohabitation Agreement - Longer form	2.150
Keeping everything separate	2.151

One party supporting the other	2.152
Agreement relating to personal chattels acquired jointly by cohabitants	2.153
Agreement setting up a joint account to pay housing costs, etc	2.154

Chapter 3   Taxation of Unmarried Couples

Law and Practice

Introduction	3.1
Income tax	3.2
Married couples	3.3
Elderly married couples	3.4
Allowances for children	3.5
Universal credit, child tax credit and working tax credit	3.6
Capital gains tax	3.7
Private residence relief	3.8
Inheritance tax	
Introduction	3.9
Lifetime gifts	3.10
Gifts of residence	3.11
Gifts not intended to confer benefit	3.12
Gifts of other property	3.13
Business and agricultural reliefs	3.14
Inheritance tax on death	3.15
Stamp duty land tax	3.16

Chapter 4   Personal Protection

Part A   Law and Practice

Section 1   Family Law Act 1996, Pt IV

Introduction	4.1
The relief available	4.2
Which level of judiciary?	4.3
Applications to vary, extend or discharge an order made under Pt IV	4.4
Non-molestation orders	4.5
Procedure on an application for a non-molestation order	4.8

Contents

Application without notice for a non-molestation order	4.14
Power of arrest	4.15
Undertakings	4.16
Occupation orders	4.17
Occupation orders under s 33	4.20
Additional provision under s 40	4.24
Occupation orders under s 36	4.27
Occupation orders under s 38	4.35
Procedure on application for an occupation order	4.40
Application for an occupation order without notice to the respondent	4.42
Undertakings	4.44
Power of arrest	4.45
Enforcement of orders under Pt IV	4.48
Committal for contempt of court	4.54
The committal hearing	4.57

Section 2   Other remedies

The Protection from Harassment Act 1997	4.59
Enforcement	4.63
Other remedies in tort	4.65
Housing Act 1985	4.67

Part B   Procedural Guides

Non-molestation and/or occupation order under Family Law Act 1996, Pt IV

Legal background	4.68
Procedure	

Transfer of a Tenancy under Family Law Act 1996, Pt IV, s 53 and Sch 7

Legal background	4.70
Procedure	4.71

Claims under the Protection from Harassment Act 1997

Legal background	4.72
Injunctions under the Protection from Harassment Act 1997	4.73

Assault and battery	4.74
Procedure	4.75

Committal and arrest for disobedience of an injunctive order or breach of an undertaking in the Family Court, the High Court and the County Court

Legal background	4.76
Which rules of court	4.77
Committal proceedings begun by notice to show good reason	4.78
Committal proceedings begun by arrest under a power of arrest	4.79
Committal proceedings begun by arrest under a warrant of arrest	4.80
Remand following arrest	4.81
Conduct of committal proceedings where the respondent is before the court following an arrest – preliminaries	4.82
Conduct of committal proceedings when the respondent is before the court, whether on notice or following an arrest	4.83
Absence of respondent	4.84
Penalties	4.85
Procedure	4.86

Part C   Checklists

Checklist for first instructions for applications under Pt IV of the Family Law Act 1996	4.87
Checklist of steps for application under Pt IV of the Family Law Act 1996	4.88

Part D   Precedents

Application in Form FL401 for non-molestation or occupation order under Family Law Act 1996, s 36	4.89
Witness statement in support of application without notice for non-molestation and occupation orders under s 33 of the Family Law Act 1996	4.90
Witness statement in support of application for service by an alternative method	4.91
Letter to mortgagee/landlord of dwelling-house the subject of an application for an occupation order under s 33 or s 36 of the Family Law Act 1996	4.92

Contents

Chapter 5 Children

Part A Law and Practice

Section 1 Registration of births; parental responsibility

Introduction	5.1
Registration of births	5.2
Determination of parentage	5.3
Declaration of parentage	5.4
Evidence on an application for declaration of parentage	5.5
Refusal to submit to testing	5.6
Assisted reproduction	5.7
Parental responsibility	5.8
Acquiring parental responsibility	5.9
Jointly registering the birth	5.10
Parental responsibility agreement	5.11
Parental responsibility order	5.14
Applications for orders under s 8 of the Children Act 1989	5.19
Change of name	5.21
Appointment of a guardian	5.25

Section 2 Adoption

Introduction	5.26
The Adoption and Children Act 2002	5.27
The Adoption and Children Act 2002 and applications by cohabitants	5.28
Adoption by one person	5.29
Preliminaries to adoption	5.30
Consent to adoption	5.31
Dispensing with consent	5.32
The status of the unmarried father	5.33
Unmarried fathers and party status	5.34
The exercise of the court's discretion	5.35
Revocation of an adoption order	5.36

Section 3 Child abduction

Removal of children from the jurisdiction	5.37
The unmarried parent without parental responsibility	5.38

	Rights of custody	**5.39**
Section 4	Financial provision for children	
	Introduction	**5.42**
	Child maintenance	**5.43**
	Child support	**5.44**
	Schedule 1 to the Children Act 1989	**5.50**
	The court's approach	**5.60**
	Enforcement of financial provision orders	**5.67**
	Registration for enforcement in the Family Court	**5.74**
Part B	Procedural Guides	
	Scientific test direction	
	Legal background	**5.75**
	Procedure	**5.76**
	Parental responsibility order (or discharge of the same or parental responsibility agreement)	
	Legal background	**5.77**
	Procedure	**5.78**
	Appointment or removal of a guardian	
	Legal background	**5.79**
	Procedure	**5.80**
	Financial relief for a child under the Children Act 1989, Sch 1	
	Legal background	**5.81**
	Procedure	**5.82**
Part C	Precedents	
	Form C1: Application for an Order	**5.83**
	Parental Responsibility Agreement	**5.84**
	Application by an unmarried father for a parental responsibility order	**5.85**
	Change of name deed made by a mother on behalf of her child: not intended for enrolment	**5.86**
	Informal appointment of a guardian by one parent	**5.87**
	Informal appointment of a guardian by both parents	**5.88**
	Child maintenance agreement	**5.89**
	Notice of [intention to proceed with] a financial application to which the standard procedure applies	**5.90**

Contents

Notice of [intention to proceed with] a financial application to which the fast-track procedure applies	5.91
Financial Statement for a financial remedy (other than a financial order or financial relief after an overseas divorce or dissolution etc) in the family court or High Court	5.92

Chapter 6   Death and Succession

Part A   Law and Practice

Section 1   Making provision for death

Introduction	6.1
Wills	6.2
Describing the cohabitant	6.3
'Cohabitation' and wills	6.4
Joint property	6.5
Nominations	6.6
Lifetime gifts	6.7
Donationes mortis causa	6.8

Section 2   Death of a cohabitant

Introduction	6.9
Cohabitant leaves a valid will	6.10
Cohabitant dies intestate	6.11
Surviving spouses and civil partners and the effect of a decree of judicial separation or separation order	6.12
Children of a deceased cohabitant	6.13
Proprietary estoppel	6.14
Applications under the Inheritance (Provision for Family and Dependants) Act 1975	6.15
Application by a surviving cohabitant under Inheritance (Provision for Family and Dependants) Act 1975, s 1(1)(ba)	6.37
Application by a 'dependant' under s 1(1)(e) of the Inheritance (Provision for Family and Dependants) Act 1975	6.49
Applications under the Inheritance (Provision for Family and Dependants) Act 1975 by children	6.59
Orders that may be made	6.72
The order	6.77
Variation of orders	6.78
Transactions and dispositions intended to defeat claims	

under Inheritance (Provision for Family and Dependants) Act 1975, s 2	6.79
Interlocutory applications	6.81
Interim orders	6.83
Preservation of property	6.85
Costs	6.87
Tax implications of orders under the Inheritance (Provision for Family and Dependants) Act 1975	6.88
Claims by dependants following fatal accidents	6.89

Section 3 Illness or incapacity of a cohabitant

Introduction	6.96
Advance decisions or 'living wills'	6.97
The content of an advance decision	6.98
The legal status of an advance decision	6.99
Validity of an advance decision	6.100
Applicability of an advance decision	6.101
Lasting Powers of Attorney (LPAs)	6.102

Part B Procedural Guide

Claim for Financial Provision under the Inheritance (Provision for Family and Dependants) Act 1975

Legal background	6.103
Procedure	6.104

Part C Checklists

Checklist for first instructions on making a claim under the Inheritance (Provision for Family and Dependants) Act 1975	6.105

Part D Precedents

Section 1 Non-contentious precedents

Clauses

Combined commencement and revocation clause	6.106
Commencement including date: separate revocation clause	6.107
Will in expectation of marriage	6.108
Will in expectation of marriage: some provisions applying before marriage and others on marriage	6.109
Declaration of mutuality	6.110
Declaration of non-mutuality	6.111

Contents

Survivorship clause: General applicability	6.112
Survivorship clause: Specific to cohabitant	6.113
Funeral wishes	6.114
Appointment of cohabitant as executor	6.115
Appointment of cohabitant as sole executor and universal beneficiary	6.116
Appointment of executors and trustees including a professional charging clause	6.117
Appointment of guardians	6.118
Appointment of guardian and substitute guardian	6.119
Guardianship: Statement of wishes concerning children under 18	6.120
Guardianship: Trustees' power to lend capital to guardians	6.121
Absolute gift of (a share of) a house	6.122
Life or lesser interest in (a share of) a dwelling and its net proceeds of sale	6.123
Occupation rights restricted to a particular property: variation lifting that restriction	6.124
Option to purchase (a share of) a dwelling	6.125
Bequest of personal chattels	6.126
Bequest of personal chattels: cohabitant to choose	6.127
Jewellery	6.128
Car on hire purchase, etc	6.129
Cohabitation as a condition precedent: pecuniary legacy	6.130
Pecuniary legacy: index-linked	6.131
Release of debt	6.132
Lump sum to buy an annuity	6.133
Administration trusts and definition of residuary estate	6.134
Cohabitant entitled absolutely	6.135
Cohabitant and other adults equally entitled: no gifts over	6.136
Cohabitant and testator's children given specified shares: provisions for their 'separate families'	6.137
The 'slice system'	6.138
Cohabitant's entitlement based on the duration of the relationship	6.139
Life interest	6.140

Life interest determinable on cohabitation	6.141
Revocable life interest	6.142
Full discretionary trust	6.143
Two-year discretionary trust	6.144
Investment	6.146
Delegation of investment management	6.147
Maintenance	6.148
Advancement	6.149
Insurance	6.150
Appropriation	6.151
Remuneration	6.152
Statement for the purposes of the Inheritance (Provision for Family and Dependants) Act 1975	6.153
Definitions	6.154
Miscellaneous	6.155
Testimonium	6.156
Attestation clause	6.157
Forms	
Pension scheme: request to trustees	6.158
Codicil 'disinheriting' former cohabitant	6.159
Will: unmarried mother leaving her entire estate to her child under 18	6.160
Will: childless unmarried couple: all to the surviving partner: gift over to their respective parents	6.161
Will: unmarried couple with minor children: both parents have parental responsibility: all to the surviving partner: gift over to children: further gift over in case of a family catastrophe	6.162
Will: older unmarried couple: life interest to the survivor	6.163
Will: older unmarried couple: limited provision for the surviving partner: residue to the testator's children	6.164
Application for a standing search	6.165

Section 2   Contentious precedents

Claim form for application by surviving cohabitant for provision from the estate of a deceased cohabitant	6.166
Claim form for application by dependant for provision	

Contents

from estate and permission to proceed out of time	6.167
Witness statement in support of a claim by a surviving cohabitant for provision from estate of deceased cohabitant and application for an interim order	6.168
Witness statement of dependant in support of claim for provision from estate and application for permission to proceed outside the time-limits	6.169
Witness statement of cohabitant in support of claim for provision for herself and child of the family, for an interim payment and for the deceased's beneficial interest in jointly owned property to be treated as part of his net estate	6.170
Witness statement of adult in support of claim for provision from estate of deceased step-parent	6.171
Witness statement of personal representatives in answer to claim	6.172
Specimen directions on application for provision from estate	6.173
Order on application for interim payment	6.174
Order on application for provision from estate	6.175

Chapter 7   Pension Rights of Cohabitants

Law and Practice

Introduction	7.1
Civil partnerships	7.2
State retirement pension	
Introduction	7.3
Pensionable age	7.4
The old scheme	7.5
The new state scheme	7.6
Taxation of pension schemes	
Taxation of pension schemes	7.7
Inheritance (Provision for Family and Dependants) Act 1975	7.8
Occupational pension schemes	
Structure	7.9
Pensions for surviving dependants and nominees	7.10
Lump sum death in service benefits	7.11

Personal pension schemes	
Structure	7.12
Death benefits	7.13
Stakeholder pensions	7.14
Auto-enrolment in workplace pension schemes	7.15
Other pensions	7.16
Children	7.17
Impact of cohabitation on survivors' pensions	7.18
Conclusions	7.19

Chapter 8   Pre-nuptial Agreements

Part A   Law and Practice

Introduction	
The law of coverture	8.1
Reform	8.2
Current position	8.4
Modern relevance of the pre-nuptial agreement	8.6
A decade of development	8.8
The case law – *Hyman* to *Radmacher*	8.9
Radmacher v Granatino – the appeals	
Decision of the Court of Appeal	8.15
Decision of the Supreme Court	8.16
Case law – post *Radmacher* – a decade of interpretation	8.21
Other jurisdictions and human rights	8.32
Advising the client	8.34
The honeymoon agreement	8.36
The essentials of a pre-nuptial agreement	
Essentials	8.37
Independent legal advice	8.38
Material disclosure	8.39
Periodic review	8.40
Free will	8.41
Fairness	8.42
Checklist	8.43

Contents

   Professional liability limitation   8.44
  Statutory reform
   Ambit of reform   8.46
  The Law Commission
   The Law Commission report   8.49
   'Qualifying Nuptial Agreement' – some applications   8.51
   'Qualifying Nuptial Agreements' – legal advice guidance   8.56
   'Qualifying Nuptial Agreements' – an overview   8.57
   Need for reform – commentary   8.58
  The future   8.59
Part B   Precedents
  Pre-nuptial agreement   8.61

Chapter 9   Cohabitation and Welfare Benefits

Law and Practice
 Introduction
  'Living together as a married couple'   9.1
  Welfare benefits: a very brief introduction   9.2
  Using this chapter   9.3
 Why cohabitation is relevant in social security and tax credits law
  Differences in treatment as between couples and single people   9.8
 Cohabitation rules in the benefits system
  Which benefits and tax credits are affected by the 'living together' tests?   9.9
  Areas where cohabitation matters   9.12
  When does 'couple' *require* marriage or civil partnership?   9.13
 Social security definitions of couple
  Nine types of couple   9.14
  Types of cohabitation in social security law   9.16
  Checklist: are they married or civil partners?   9.17
  Applying the 'living together' test if marriage and civil partnership are discounted   9.18
 What constitutes living together as a married couple?
  General approach   9.19

Two checklists?	9.20
Other tests	9.24
Using the lists of factors: standing back	9.25
Members of the same household	
How to approach the question	9.26
What the Handbook said	9.27
Is the household test overriding?	9.28
Does the client share a household?	9.29
The alleged partner lives at a different address	9.30
The alleged partner stays over but it is not a shared household	9.32
They live at the same address but in separate households under the same roof	9.34
What if a shared household is proved though?	9.38
Alternative reasons	
Living together	9.39
Disability and care – and some general principles	9.40
Other reasons for living together in the same household	9.42
Future plans, intention, motive and purpose	
Why living together?	9.43
Sexual relationship	
Sex does matter – but is it a determinative factor?	9.45
What the Handbook said	9.47
The need for enquiry about sex	9.48
Claimant and alleged partner have never had sex	9.50
No sex now? No sex ever?: the evolution of the Handbook	9.54
Sleeping arrangements	9.56
Previous sexual relationship, now ceased	9.59
Faithfulness – other sex partners	9.64
Stability of the relationship	
What the Handbook said	9.65
What does stability mean?	9.66
How is time spent together?	9.67
Impermanence	9.68

Contents

- A settled relationship — 9.69
- Relationship long-term but evolving? — 9.70
- Endurance — 9.71
- Arguing stability points — 9.72

Financial support
- Introduction — 9.73
- What the Handbook said — 9.74
- What the Guidance says — 9.75
- Does either alleged partner maintain the other? — 9.76
- Shared or separated money — 9.77
- Property purchase — 9.78
- Child maintenance — 9.79
- Questions to ask — 9.80

Children
- What the Handbook said — 9.81
- What the guidance says — 9.82
- Children as proof of sexual relationship — 9.83
- Whose children are they? — 9.84
- Childcare — 9.85
- Regarding the alleged partner as a (step-)parent — 9.86
- The birth certificate — 9.87
- Inaction by the Child Support Agency or Child Maintenance Service — 9.88
- Stages of children growing up — 9.89

Public acknowledgement
- Introduction — 9.90
- What the Handbook said — 9.91
- Claimant's own description — 9.92
- Acknowledging themselves as a couple — 9.93
- Surnames — 9.94
- Socialising — 9.95
- Wider factors — 9.96

Living together in same-sex cases	
Provisions of the Civil Partnership Act 2004	9.97
Arguing for single status in alleged same-sex couple cases	9.98
Temporary separations	
Introduction	9.103
DMG guidance on the temporary absence of one party	9.104
He might come back	9.105
Multi-partner scenarios	
Rules	9.106
Unlawful or prohibited relationships	
Full list	9.107
Running a cohabitation case against the DWP, HMRC or a local authority	
How the DWP, HMRC and local authorities make adverse cohabitation decisions	9.108
Practical issues to address	9.111
Challenging the decision	9.118
Appeals procedure in 'living together' cases	9.119
Checklist of issues to address in preparing the appeal	9.126
Checklist of areas to cover in your arguments	9.127
Chapter 10 Miscellaneous	
Part A Law and practice	
Change of name	10.1
Contractual licence	10.2
Part B Precedents	
Change of name deed: not intended for enrolment	10.3
Contractual licence	10.4
Separation agreement	10.5
Family Law Protocol: Part 12 Cohabitation	10.6
Index	**813**

Table of Abbreviations

AA 1976	Adoption Act 1976
ACA 2002	Adoption and Children Act 2002
ASP	Additional State Pension
BDRA 1953	Births and Deaths Registration Act 1953
CA 1989	Children Act 1989
CCR	County Court Rules
CPA 2004	Civil Partnership Act 2004
CPR	Civil Procedure Rules 1998
CSA 1991	Child Support Act 1991
CSPSSA 2002	Child Support, Pensions and Social Security Act 2002
CTC	Child tax credit
DVMPA 1976	Domestic Violence and Matrimonial Proceedings Act 1976
DVCVA 2004	Domestic Violence, Crime and Victims Act 2004
FA	Finance Act
FLA 1996	Family Law Act 1996
FLRA 1969	Family Law Reform Act 1969
FPFO 2008	Family Proceedings Fees Order 2008
FPR	Family Procedure Rules 2010
HA	Housing Act
IA 1986	Insolvency Act 1986
IHTA 1984	Inheritance Tax Act 1984
I(PFD)A 1975	Inheritance (Provision for Family and Dependants) Act 1975
ITPA 2014	Inheritance and Trustees' Powers Act 2014

Table of Abbreviations

LPA	Lasting power of attorney
LPA 1925	Law of Property Act 1925
LRA 2002	Land Registration Act 2002
LR(MP)A 1970	Law Reform (Miscellaneous Provisions) Act 1970
LRR 2003	Land Registration Rules 2003
LTA 1927	Landlord and Tenant Act 1927
MCA 1973	Matrimonial Causes Act 1973
MPPA 1970	Matrimonial Proceedings and Property Act 1970
MWPA 1882	Married Women's Property Act 1882
PACE	Police and Criminal Evidence Act 1984
PHA 1997	Protection from Harassment Act 1997
PRAR 1991	Parental Responsibility Agreement Regulations 1991
RA 1977	Rent Act 1977
S2P	State Second Pension
SDLT	Stamp duty land tax
SERPS	State Earnings Related Pensions
SSCBA 1992	Social Security Contributions and Benefits Act 1992
TCA 2002	Tax Credits Act 2002
TOLATA 1996	Trusts of Land and Appointment of Trustees Act 1996
UC	Universal credit
WTC	Working tax credit

Table of Statutes

A

Administration of Estates Act 1925
.... 6.127
s 35 .... 6.122
41 .... 6.151
46(1) 6.11
55(1)(x) 6.126
Administration of Justice Act 1970
Sch 8 .... 5.74
Administration of Justice Act 1982
s 22 .... 6.2
Adoption Act 1976
.... 5.27, 5.29, 5.34
s 14 .... 5.28
Adoption and Children Act 2002
.... 5.18, 5.27
s 1(4) 5.32, 5.35
19 .... 5.30
(1) 5.33
21 .... 5.30
42(2) 5.30
44(3) 5.30
47 .... 5.33
49 .... 5.28
50 .... 5.28
51(2) 5.29
52(6) 5.33
69(4) 6.59
111 .... 5.8
144(4) 5.29
(5) 5.28
(6) 5.28

B

Births and Deaths Registration Act 1953
.... 5.77
s 1 .... 5.2
10 .... 2.35
10A 2.35, 5.8
14(1) 5.2
14A 5.14

C

Charging Orders Act 1979
s 1(2) 5.72
Child Abduction and Custody Act 1985
.... 5.38
Child Maintenance and Other Payments Act 2008
s 42 .... 5.45
Child Support Act 1991
. 2.35, 5.47, 5.51, 5.61, 5.71, 5.72,
5.81, 6.160, 10.5, 10.6
s 3 .... 5.43

Child Support Act 1991 – *cont.*
s 3(1) 5.45
4 .... 5.46
(5) 5.69
8(6) 5.52
–(8) 5.44, 5.48, 5.60, 5.70
9(2) 5.49
(3) 5.49, 5.89
(4) 5.49
26(2) 5.3
27 .... 5.75
ss 28–40 .... 5.68
s 44 .... 5.44, 5.65
55 .... 5.65
(1)(a) 5.45
(b) 5.45
(2) 5.45
Sch 1, para 11 .... 5.89
16 .... 5.89
(1)(b)
.... 5.65
7 .... 9.118
Child Support, Pensions and Social Security Act 2000 .... 5.5
Children Act 1989
.. 1.198, 4.10, 4.13, 4.22, 5.1, 5.45
s 1 .... 6.120
(1) 1.125, 5.16, 5.59
(3) 5.19, 5.24
(4) 5.18, 5.24
(5) 5.16
(6) 5.16
2(2) 2.35, 5.86
(5) 6.118
(9) 5.18
1(2A) 5.16, 5.18, 5.19
(2B) 5.16, 5.19
2(3) 5.9
3 .... 5.77
(1) 5.8
4 .... 5.2, 6.160
(1)(a) 2.35, 5.8, 5.9, 5.10, 5.11,
5.77
(b) 2.35, 5.9
(c) 5.14
(1A) 5.14
(2A) 2.109, 5.8, 5.10, 5.18
(3) 5.13
4ZA 5.2, 5.77
(1)(a) 5.8, 5.9, 5.10, 5.11
(b) 5.9
(c) 5.14
(5) 5.8, 5.10, 5.18
4A 5.77
5 .... 5.9, 5.79
(3) 5.88
(4) 5.88
(5) 5.87

xli

Table of Statutes

Children Act 1989 – *cont.*
- s 5(5)(a) 5.25
- (b) 5.25
- (8) 5.25
- (10) 5.88
- (13) 6.118, 6.119
- 6 .... 5.88
- (5) 6.119
- (6) 6.119
- (7) 5.79, 6.119
- 7 .... 5.20
- 8 ... 4.76, 5.9, 5.14, 5.16, 5.19, 5.20, 5.23, 5.24, 5.25, 5.35, 5.40, 5.60, 5.65
- (1) 2.35, 6.120, 10.1
- 9 .... 5.75
- 10(4) 5.19
- (9) 5.19
- 11(5) 5.19
- 12 .... 5.9
- (1) 5.16, 5.77
- (4) 5.18
- 13 .... 5.24, 5.86
- (1) 5.38, 10.1
- (a) 5.22, 5.23
- (2) 5.38
- ss 14A–14G 5.25
- s 15 .... 5.81
- 17 .... 1.130
- 20 .... 1.128, 1.129
- 23A 1.128
- 31 .... 4.22
- (11) 10.1
- 33(7) 5.86, 10.1
- (a) 5.22
- 62 .... 4.5
- 91(8) 5.13, 5.88, 6.118
- 105 .... 4.22
- (1) 10.1
- Sch 1 .... 1.6, 1.67, 1.87, 1.102, 1.109, 1.123, 1.126, 2.35, 2.141, 5.2, 5.43, 5.48, 5.50, 5.54, 5.55, 5.72, 8.23, 8.29, 8.30, 10.6
- , para 1 .... 5.81
- (1) 1.122, 5.53
- (2) 1.120, 5.51
- (5)(a) 5.51
- (b) 5.51
- 2 .... 5.62, 5.81
- (1) 5.53
- 3 .... 5.62
- (1)(a) 5.65
- (b) 5.65
- (2)(a) 5.65
- (b) 5.65
- (4) 5.43
- (5) 5.70

Children Act 1989 – *cont.*
- Sch 1, para 3(6) 5.70
- 4(2) 2.141, 5.59
- 6 .... 5.62, 5.81
- 9 .... 5.51, 5.60
- 10 .... 5.51, 5.81
- 11 .... 5.81

Children and Families Act 2014 .... 5.16
- s 11 .... 5.19

Civil Partnership Act 2004
.... 1.1, 1.94, 1.99, 9.97, 1.103, 1.111, 1.132, 1.159, 6.15, 8.46, 10.6
- s 74 .... 10.6
- (5) 10.6
- 255 .... 7.2

County Courts Act 1984
- s 38 .... 4.73

Custody Act 1883 .... 8.2

D

Debtors Act 1869 .... 4.76
Debtors Act 1878 .... 4.76
De Facto Relationships Act 1984 (New South Wales)
- s 47(d) 2.81
- (e) 2.82

Domestic Proceedings and Magistrates' Courts Act 1978
- Pt I 5.74

Domestic Violence and Matrimonial Proceedings Act 1976 .... 6.42
- s 1(2) 6.154

Domestic Violence Crime and Victims Act 2004 .... 4.11, 4.16, 4.54
- s 1 .... 4.1
- 3 .... 4.6
- 4 .... 4.1
- Sch 7, para 41(3)(a) 4.6

E

Equality Act 2010
- Sch 9, para 18(1) 7.2

F

Family Law Act 1986
- s 55A 5.4, 5.6, 5.75
- 59 .... 5.4

Family Law Act 1996
.... 4.73, 4.74
- Pt IV 1.89, 1.101, 1.105, 1.126, 2.130, 4.1, 4.2, 4.3, 4.11, 4.40, 4.45, 4.55, 4.59, 4.64, 4.65, 4.68, 4.76, 4.80, 5.62
- s 30(4) 1.109

Table of Statutes

Family Law Act 1996 – *cont.*
- s 33 .... 1.104, 1.144, 4.19, 4.20, 4.21, 4.22, 4.23, 424, 4.26, 4.32, 4.33, 4.68, 4.92
  - (4) 4.21
  - (6) 1.114, 4.23, 4.24
- 35 .... 1.144, 4.68
- 36 .... 1.109, 1.144, 4.19, 4.24, 4.27, 4.28, 4.29, 4.30, 4.32, 4.38, 4.39, 4.68, 4.92
  - (6) 1.114
- 37 .... 4.68
- 38 . 4.19, 4.35, 4.36, 4.37, 4.38, 4.39, 4.41, 4.68
- 39 .... 4.68
  - (3) 4.17
- 40 .... 4.26, 4.33, 4.68
  - (1)(c) 1.144
  - (d) 1.144
  - (e) 1.144
- 42(4) 4.6
- 42A 4.16, 4.48, 4.50, 4.68, 4.79
  - (1) 4.12
  - (2) 4.12
- 43 .... 4.68
- 45 .... 4.14
- 46 .... 4.44, 4.50
  - (1) 4.44
  - (4) 4.10
- 47 .... 4.11, 4.15
  - (3) 4.79
  - (4) 4.46
  - (7) 4.79
  - (8) 4.80
  - (9) 4.80
- 48 .... 4.81
- 53 ...... 1.109, 1.147, 4.3, 4.70, 5.62
- 54(5) 1.85
- 59 .... 4.3
- 62(3) 4.72
- 63 .... 4.20
- 63I(2) 4.79
- Sch 7 ... 1.104, 1.108, 1.109, 4.3, 4.70, 5.62
  - , Pt II 1.114, 1.119
  - para 10 .... 1.147, 4.70
    - (2) 1.119
    - (3) 1.119
    - (5) 1.119
  - 11 .... 1.119

Family Law Reform Act 1969
- s 15 .... 6.13
- 20(1) 5.75
- 21 .... 5.6
  - (1) 5.75
  - (3) 5.5, 5.75
- 23(1) 5.6, 5.75

Family Law Reform Act 1987
- s 1(2) 5.77
- 19 .... 6.13

Family Law (Scotland) Act 2006
  .... 10.6

Fatal Accidents Act 1976
  .... 2.148, 6.42
- s 1A 6.90
- 3(4) 6.89

Finance Act 1986
- s 102 .... 3.11
- 102B 3.11

Finance Act 1999 .... 3.11

Finance Act 2003
- Sch 3, para 3 .... 3.16
  - 4, para 8 .... 3.16

Finance Act 2004 .... 3.11, 7.7
- s 167 .... 7.10
- Sch 15, para 10(1)(b)
  .... 3.11
  - 11(5)(c)
  .... 3.11
  - 28, para 15(3)
  .... 7.10

Finance Act 2008
- s 10 .... 3.9
- Sch 4 .... 3.9

Finance Act 2012
- s 208 .... 3.9

Finance Act 2016
- s 128 .... 3.16

Finance Act 2020
- s 23 .... 3.8

Forfeiture Act 1982
  .... 6.36

H

Housing Act 1980 .... 1.126
Housing Act 1985 ..... 1.30, 1.100, 4.67
- s 79 .... 1.112
  - (1) 1.109
- 81 .... 1.109
- 91(3) 1.102
- 113 .... 1.102, 1.103

Housing Act 1988 .... 1.90
- Pt 1 .... 1.91, 1.112
- s 1(1)(b) 1.92
- 5(1)(b) 1.92
- 15 .... 1.93
- 17(1) 1.94
  - (4) 1.94
- Sch 2, Ground 7 .... 1.94

Housing Act 1996 .... 1.90
- s 177(1) 4.6
- 191 .... 1.128
- 202 .... 1.129
- 204 .... 1.129

Human Fertilisation and Embryology Act 1990
- s 27 .... 5.7
- 28(3) 5.7

Human Fertilisation and Embryology Act 2008 .... 5.1, 5.8
- s 33(1) 5.7

xliii

Table of Statutes

Human Fertilisation and Embryology Act 2008 – *cont.*
- s 37 .... 5.7
- 43 .... 5.2
- 44 .... 5.7

Human Rights Act 1998
.... 1.94, 1.99, 5.18, 10.6

I

Income Tax Act 2007
- s 836 .... 1.178
- 837 .... 1.178

Income Tax (Trading and Other Income) Act 2005
- s 629 .... 3.1

Infants and Child Custody Act 1839
.... 8.2

Inheritance and Trustees' Powers Act 2014
... 6.1, 6.15, 6.27, 6.50, 6.51, 6.59, 6.61
- s 3 .... 6.126

Inheritance (Family Provision) Act 1938
.... 6.15

Inheritance (Provision for Family and Dependants) Act 1975
.. 1.198, 1.204, 2.60, 2.111, 2.148, 2.151, 5.75, 6.10, 6.13, 6.19, 6.20, 6.24, 6.28, 6.46, 6.91, 6.144, 7.19, 9.19, 10.6
- s 1 .... 6.103, 10.6
  - (1) 6.17, 6.27
  - –(3) 6.53
  - (ba) . 6.29, 6.39, 6.43, 6.44, 6.45, 6.49, 6.50, 6.51, 6.52, 6.81, 6.105
  - (c) .. 6.29, 6.59, 6.62, 6.63, 6.65, 6.81
  - (d) .. 6.15, 6.29, 6.59, 6.61, 6.62, 6.63, 6.65, 6.66, 6.81
  - (e) . 2.111, 6.27, 6.29, 6.39, 6.49, 6.50, 6.51, 6.54, 6.55, 6.57, 6.61, 6.81
  - (1A) 6.17, 6.37, 6.43
    - (b) 6.41
  - (1B) 6.17, 6.37, 6.43
  - (2)(b) 6.27, 6.37, 6.153
  - (3) 2.111, 6.27, 6.50
- 2 ... 2.111, 6.1, 6.5, 6.12, 6.26, 6.27, 6.77, 6.79, 6.80, 6.83, 6.84
  - (1)(a) 6.16, 6.78
  - (b) 6.16
  - (c) 6.16, 6.85
  - (d) 6.16, 6.85
  - (e) 6.16
  - (f) 6.75
  - (h) 6.16
  - (3) 6.153
- 3 . 6.54, 6.67, 6.72, 6.78, 6.83, 6.153
  - (1) 6.30, 6.57, 6.63, 6.66, 6.68, 6.70

Inheritance (Provision for Family and Dependants) Act 1975 – *cont.*
- s 3(1)(a)–(g) 6.29, 6.45, 6.48, 6.55, 6.56, 6.58, 6.64
  - (b) 6.32
  - (c) 6.32
  - (d) 6.32
  - (g) 6.65, 6.69
  - (2) 6.29, 6.45
  - (2A) 6.29, 6.45, 6.48
  - (3) 6.29, 6.63, 6.66, 6.68
    - (a)–(c) 6.66
  - (4) 2.111, 6.29, 6.55, 6.56, 6.57, 6.58, 6.153
    - (b) 6.50
  - (5) 6.71
  - (6) 6.31
- 4 .... 6.22, 6.103
- 6 .... 6.16
  - (7) 6.78
- 7 .... 6.78
- 8(1) 6.158, 7.8
- 9 .... 1.6, 1.19, 6.1, 6.5, 6.11
- 10 .... 6.1, 6.7, 6.11, 6.16, 7.8
  - (6) 6.79
- 11 .... 6.16
- 12 .... 6.79
- 14 .... 6.12
- 14A 6.12
- 15 .... 2.111, 6.12
- 16 .... 6.16
- 17 .... 6.16
- 19(1) 6.88
- 21 .... 6.153
- 25(1)(a) 7.8
  - (c) 7.8

Inheritance Tax Act 1984
- s 7(4) 3.9
- ss 8D–8M 3.9
- s 18 .... 1.162, 6.2
- 22 .... 1.162
- 58 .... 6.143
- 64 .... 6.143
- 65 .... 6.143
- 92 .... 6.112
- 106 .... 3.14
- 120 .... 3.14
- 144 .... 3.15, 6.144
- Sch 1A 3.9

Insolvency Act 1986
.... 1.198
- s 306 .... 1.205
- 305(2) 1.205
- 336 .... 1.205
- 337 .... 1.205
- 339 .... 1.6, 1.162, 1.205
- 341 .... 1.205

J

Jobseekers Act 1995
.... 9.97

Table of Statutes

Jobseekers Act 1995 – *cont.*
- s 3 .... 9.8
  - (1) 9.9
    - (e) 9.8
  - 4 .... 9.8
  - 35 .... 9.8

L

Land Registration Act 2002
- s 4 .... 1.7
  - 33(a) 1.8
    - (i) 1.223
  - ss 40–47 .... 1.223
  - s 78 .... 1.7

Land Registration (Scotland) Act 1979
.... 1.7

Landlord and Tenant Act 1927
- s 13 .... 6.146
  - 19 .... 1.97

Latent Damages Act 1986
- s 14A 8.45
  - 14B 8.45

Law of Property Act 1925
- s 30 .... 1.62, 1.63, 1.71, 1.181, 1.204
  - 36(2) 1.21
  - 53(1)(b) 1.5, 1.6, 1.152, 1.198
    - (2) 1.5
  - 58 .... 1.225
  - 177 .... 6.108
  - 184 .... 6.112
  - 188(1) 2.153
  - 199 .... 1.21

Law of Property (Miscellaneous Provisions) Act 1989
- s 1 .... 1.198, 1.200
  - (2) 2.50
  - 2 .... 6.125

Law Reform (Miscellaneous Provisions) Act 1934
- s 1(2)(a)(ii) 6.91

Law Reform (Miscellaneous Provisions) Act 1970
- s 1 .... 2.90
  - 2 .... 1.159
  - 3(1) 10.6
  - (2) 1.136

Law Reform (Succession) Act 1995
.... 6.15
- s 3 .... 6.12

Legal Services Act 2007
.... 8.47

Legitimacy Act 1976
- s 2 .... 5.9
  - 9 .... 5.17

Limitation Act 1980
- s 2 .... 4.59
  - 11(1A) 4.59

M

Magistrates' Courts Act 1980
- s 128 .... 4.81
  - 129 .... 4.81

Maintenance Agreements Act 1957
.... 8.17

Maintenance Enforcement Act 1991
.... 5.71

Maintenance Orders Act 1958
- s 1(1) 5.74
  - 2(1) 5.74
  - 4 .... 5.74
  - 4A 5.74

Marriage (Same Sex Couples) Act 2013
.... 6.11, 9.14, 9.97

Married Women's Property Act 1882
.... 1.84, 1.143, 8.1, 8.2, 8.3, 8.60, 10.6
- s 17 ...... 1.74, 1.76, 1.78, 1.80, 8.29
  - 65 .... 10.6
  - 66 .... 10.6

Matrimonial and Family Proceedings Act 1984
- Pt III 8.23

Matrimonial Causes Act 1857
.... 8.3

Matrimonial Causes Act 1973
. 1.38, 1.68, 5.45, 6.109, 8.1, 8.32, 8.60
- Pt II 4.76
- s 22A 3.16
  - 23 .... 2.90, 5.81, 8.10
    - (1)(a) 5.43
  - 23A 3.16
  - 24 .... 1.6, 1.159, 2.90, 5.81, 8.10
  - 24A 2.90, 3.16
  - 25 ... 1.1, 1.126, 1.132, 8.5, 8.6, 8.7, 8.9, 8.10, 8.11, 8.13, 8.14, 8.15, 8.16, 8.17, 8.18, 8.21, 8.22, 8.23, 8.24, 8.26, 8.28, 8.30, 8.33, 8.35, 8.38, 8.40, 8.41, 8.42, 8.44, 8.48, 8.49, 8.57
    - (1) 1.125, 5.59, 8.19, 8.46
    - (2) 8.29, 8.46
      - (g) 8.12
    - (2A) 8.46
    - (2B) 8.46
    - (3) 1.125, 5.59
  - 27 .... 5.81
  - 32 .... 5.72
  - 34 .... 8.14, 8.17, 8.20, 8.36
  - 35 .... 5.81, 8.14, 8.17, 8.20, 8.36
  - 36 .... 5.81
  - 37(2) 5.72
    - (b) 1.107

Matrimonial Proceedings and Property Act 1970
- s 37 .... 1.84, 1.143, 1.183, 10.6

Mental Capacity Act 2005
.... 2.73
- ss 24–26 .... 6.97

xlv

Table of Statutes

P

Pensions Act 1995
  Sch 4, Pt 1 .... 7.4
Pensions Act 2004 .... 7.9, 9.13
  Pt 2 .... 7.16
Pensions Act 2007
  s 15(1) 7.5
  24 .... 7.5
  30 .... 7.5
    (1) 7.6
    (4)(a) 7.6
  Sch 4 .... 7.5
Pensions Act 2008 .... 7.15
Pensions Act 2014 .... 7.3
Perpetuities and Accumulations Act 2009
.... 6.143
Police and Criminal Evidence Act 1984
.... 9.115
Protection from Eviction Act 1977
.... 10.2
  s 3A(2) 10.2
  5(1) 1.107
Protection from Harassment Act 1997
...... 2.130, 4.58, 4.62, 4.65, 4.68,
4.73, 4.77
  s 1 .... 4.61
  3 .... 4.61
    (3) 4.72, 4.80
    (4) 4.80
    (5) 4.72, 4.80
  6 .... 4.59
  7(4) 4.61
Public Service Pensions Act 2013
.... 7.9
Public Trustee Act 1906
  s 5 .... 6.152

Q

Qualification of Women Act 1918
.... 8.3

R

Rent Act 1977 ... 1.90, 1.95, 1.106,
1.112
  Sch 1, para 2(2) 1.98, 1.99
    15, Case 5 .... 1.96
Rent (Agriculture) Act 1976
.... 1.112

S

Serious Crime Act 2015
.... 4.1
Settled Land Act 1925
.... 6.123
Sex Disqualification (Removal) Act 1919
.... 8.3
Social Security Act 1986
  s 20(11) 6.154

Social Security Administration Act 1992
  s 115A 9.116
  115C 9.116
  115D 9.116
Social Security Contributions and Benefits
Act 1992 .... 6.41
  s 36(2) 9.10
  37(4)(b) 9.10
  38(3) 9.10
    (c) 9.11
  39A 9.10
  39B 9.10
    (5)(b) 9.8
  122(1A) 9.97
  133 .... 9.3, 9.106
  137 .... 9.1
    (1) 9.15
    (1A) 9.15, 9.97
State Pension Credit Act 2002
  s 5 .... 9.9
  12 .... 9.106
Succession (Scotland) Act 1964
  s 8(1) 6.122
Supreme Court Act 1981
  s 114(1) 6.117
Supreme Court of Judicature
(Consolidation) Act 1925
.... 8.9

T

Tax Credits Act 2002
.... 9.97
  s 3(5A) 9.15
  48(2) 9.97
Taxation of Chargeable Gains Act 1992
.... 3.7
  s 58 .... 3.7
  222–224 .... 3.8
    (6) 3.8
  223(3) 3.8
  262 .... 3.8
Taxation of Pensions Act 2014
.... 7.11, 7.13, 7.19
  Sch 2, Pt 1 .... 7.10
Trustee Act 1925
  s 19(1) 6.150
    (2) 6.150
  31 .... 6.148
  32 .... 6.149
    (1), proviso (b)
.... 6.149
  34 .... 6.117
  61 .... 6.155
Trustee Act 2000 .... 6.151
  Pt IV 6.147
  s 1 .... 6.145
  3 .... 6.146
  4 .... 6.146
  8 .... 6.146
  28(4) 6.117

Trusts (Capital and Income) Act 2013
.... 6.164
Trusts of Land and Appointment of Trustees Act 1996 ..... 1.50, 1.67, 1.123, 1.203, 1.204, 5.50, 5.55, 6.123, 10.6
s 1 .... 1.160
 6(1) 1.160
  (4)(b) 6.146
  (6) 1.8
  (8) 1.8
 8 .... 1.160
 12 .... 1.60, 1.63
 13 .... 1.60, 1.63, 1.85, 1.145
  (6) 1.72
 14 . 1.60, 1.62, 1.63, 1.65, 1.69, 1.71, 1.145, 1.181, 1.205, 1.215, 5.75, 10.6
  (1) 1.64, 1.156
 15 .... 1.62, 1.63, 1.70, 1.145, 1.181
  (1) 1.60, 1.69, 1.71
  (3) 1.69
  (4) 1.71
 23(3) 1.65

U

Unfair Contract Terms Act 1977
.... 8.45

W

Welfare Reform Act 2012
 ss 1–43 .... 9.12
 s 39(1) 9.9
 57 .... 9.12
Welfare Reform and Pensions Act 1999
.... 7.1
Wills Act 1837
 s 7 .... 5.87
 9 .... 6.157
 15 .... 6.2, 6.117
 18 .... 6.2
  (1) 6.108
  (3) 6.108
 18A 6.2, 6.130, 6.159
 33 .... 6.160

Table of Statutory Instruments

A

Adoption Rules 1984 (SI 1984/611)
   r 15(3) 5.34
Allocation of Housing (England)
   Regulations 2000 (SI 2000/702)
   .... 1.128
Allocation of Housing (Wales) Regulations
   2000 (SI 2000/1080)
   .... 1.128

C

Child Support and Claims and Payments
   (Miscellaneous Amendments and
   Change to the Minimum Amount of
   Liability) Regulations 2013 (SI
   2013/1654) 5.46
Civil Partnership (Opposite-sex Couples)
   Regulations 2019 (SI 2019/1458)
   .... 7.2
Civil Procedure Rules 1998 (SI 1998/3132)
   r 1.1(2) 10.6
   PD 2B para 3.2 .... 10.6
   Pt 6 .... 1.68, 4.62, 6.20
      7 .... 1.68, 1.145, 4.73, 10.6
   PD7A 1.145
      , para 2.1 .... 10.6
   Pt 8 ..... 1.67, 1.145, 4.73, 4.78, 5.70,
                            6.20, 10.6
   r 8.1(3) 10.6
      8.8 .... 10.6
   PD 8A 1.145, 6.103
   r 16.4 .... 10.6
   PD 16 .... 6.20
   Pt 22 .... 1.67, 6.20
      23 .... 5.75
   PD 23B, para 1.1(3)
      .... 5.75
                 2.1 .... 5.75
   Pt 25 .... 10.6
   PD 25A, para 3 .... 4.73
      29, para 2.2 .... 10.6
   r 33.1(1) 5.73
   Pt 36 .... 10.6
   r 43.3(5)(a) 10.6
      44.3 .... 6.103
        (2)(a) 10.6
      44.3B(1)(c) 10.6
   Pt 57 .... 6.20, 6.103
   rr 57.14–57.16 .... 6.20
   r 57.16 .... 10.6
        (3A) 6.20
   PD 57 .... 6.103

Civil Procedure Rules 1998 (SI 1998/3132) – cont.
   r 64.3 .... 10.6
   PD 64A, para 1(1)(a)(iii)
   .... 10.6
   r 65.28 .... 4.73
      65.29 .... 4.82
   Pt 69 .... 5.73
      70 .... 5.68
   r 70.1(2) 5.73
      70.2(2)(a) 5.73
           (b) 5.73
   PD 70, para 1.1 .... 5.73
   r 71.2(1) 5.73
        (6)(a) 5.73
          (b) 5.73
          (c) 5.73
        (7) 5.73
   Pt 72 .... 5.73
      73 .... 5.68, 5.73
   r 73.10 .... 5.71
   Pt 81 .... 4.64
   r 81.5 .... 4.76
   PD 81, para 16.2 .... 4.76
   Pt 83 .... 5.73
      84 .... 5.73
      89 .... 5.73
   Sch 2, CCR Ord 4, r 3
   .... 1.66
                  29
   .... 4.49
Practice Direction (Pre-Action Conduct)
   Annex A, para A.2
   .... 10.6
Council Tax Reduction Schemes and
   Prescribed Requirements (Wales)
   Regulations 2012 (SI 2012/3144)
   reg 4 .... 9.9
Council Tax Reduction Schemes (Prescribed
   Requirements) (England) Regulations
   2012 (SI 2012/2885)
   reg 4 .... 9.9

E

Employment and Support Allowance
   Regulations 2008 (SI 2008/794)
   reg 2(1) 9.106
Enrolment of Deeds (Change of Name)
   Regulations 1983 (SI 1983/680)
   .... 10.3
   reg 8 .... 10.1
      (3) 5.22, 10.1
      (5) 5.22, 10.1

Table of Statutory Instruments

F

Family Court (Composition and Distribution of Business) Rules 2014 (SI 2014/840)
 Sch 2 .... 5.72
Family Court (Contempt of Court) (Powers) Regulations 2014 (SI 2014/833)
 .... 4.57, 4.85
Family Procedure Rules 2010 (SI 2010/2955) 1.78, 1.123
 r 2.3 .... 5.81
 3.5 .... 5.54
 3.6 .... 5.54
 3.7 .... 5.54
 3.8 .... 5.20, 5.54
 3.9 .... 5.54
 3.10 .... 5.54
 Pt 3A 4.43
 PD 3A, Annex A 5.77, 5.79
 3AA 4.43
 r 6.35 .... 4.9
 rr 8.29–8.34 .... 1.147
 Pt 9 .... 5.81
 r 9.9B 5.55
 9.14(1)–(2) 5.57
  (4) 5.57
 9.18A 5.55, 5.56
 9.19(1) 5.56
  (4) 5.56
 9.20(4) 5.58
 10.3(2) 4.9
  (b)(i) 4.8
   (ii) 4.8
 10.5 .... 4.4
 10.6 .... 4.4
 10.7 .... 4.4
 10.9 .... 4.48
 10.10(2) 4.12
  (3) 4.12
 10.11 .... 4.82
 PD 9A 5.54
  10A, para 3.1 .... 4.48
  12B, para 6.3 .... 5.20
  12F 5.38
  12J, para 4 .... 5.16
 Pt 17 .... 4.8
 18 .... 5.75
 r 19.14(4)(a) 5.58
 Pt 33 .... 4.76, 5.68, 5.70, 5.73
 r 33.2 .... 5.73
 33.3 .... 5.73
  (1)(a) 5.73
  (2)(b) 5.73
 PD 33A 4.76
 r 37.5 .... 4.76
Family Proceedings Courts (Children Act 1989) Rules 1991 (SI 1991/1395)
 .... 10.6

Family Proceedings Fees (Amendment) Order 2014 (SI 2014/877)
 .... 4.8, 4.40
Family Proceedings Rules 1991 (SI 1991/1247) 10.6

H

High Court and County Courts Jurisdiction Order 1991 (SI 1991/724)
 .... 1.65, 1.145
High Court and County Courts Jurisdiction (Amendment) Order 1996 (SI 1996/3141) 1.66
Homeless Persons (Priority Need) (Wales) Order 2001 (SI 2001/607)
 .... 1.128
Homelessness (Priority Need for Accommodation) (England) Order 2002 (SI 2002/2051)
 .... 1.128
Housing Benefit and Council Tax Benefit (Decisions and Appeals) Regulations 2001 (SI 2001/1002)
 .... 9.118
Housing Benefit (Persons who have attained the qualifying age for State Pension Credit) Regulations 2006 (SI 2006/214)
 reg 2(1) 9.106

I

Income Support (General) Regulations 1987 (SI 1987/1967)
 reg 2(1) 9.106
 5 .... 9.12
 16(1) 9.103
  (2) 9.103
  (3) 9.103
 51 .... 1.224, 6.133
 54 .... 9.12
 Sch 2, para 13(2A)
 .... 9.12

J

Jobseeker's Allowance Regulations 1996 (SI 1996/207)
 reg 1 .... 9.8
  (3) 9.106
 88 .... 9.8
 Sch 8 para 4(b) 9.8, 9.9
  5 .... 9.8, 9.9

L

Land Registration Rules 2003 (SI 2003/1417)
 r 91 .... 1.7
 92 .... 1.7

Land Registration Rules 2003 (SI 2003/1417) – cont.
- r 93 .... 1.7
- 94 .... 1.7
- 95 .... 1.7
- 96 .... 1.7
- 97 .... 1.7
- 98 .... 1.7
- 99 .... 1.7
- Sch A, Form A 10.6

M

Marriage (Same Sex Couples) Act 2013 (Consequential and Contrary Provisions and Scotland) Order 2014 (SI 2014/560) 9.14
- Sch 1, para 22(8) 9.15

N

Non-Contentious Probate Rules 1987 (SI 1987/2024)
- r 9 .... 6.106
- 43(1) 6.26

P

Parental Responsibility Agreement Regulations 1991 (SI 1991/1478) 2.109, 5.12

S

Stakeholder Pension Schemes Regulations 2000 (SI 2000/1403) 7.14

T

Tax Credits (Appeals) (No 2) Regulations 2002 (SI 2002/3196) 9.118

Tax Credits (Claims and Notifications) Regulations 2002 (SI 2002/2014) 9.118

Tax Credits (Income Thresholds and Determination of Rates) Regulations 2002 (SI 2002/2008)
- reg 8 .... 9.8

Tribunal Procedure (First-tier Tribunal) (Social Entitlement Chamber) Rules 2008 (SI 2008/2685) 9.121
- r 3 .... 5.49
- 16 .... 9.121

Tribunal Procedure (Upper Tribunal) Rules 2008 (SI 2008/2698)
- r 3 .... 5.49

U

Unfair Terms in Consumer Contracts Regulations 1999 (SI 1999/2083) 8.45

Universal Credit, Personal Independence Payment, Jobseeker's Allowance and Employment and Support Allowance (Decisions and Appeals) Regulations 2013 (SI 2013/380) 9.118

Table of International Material

C

Convention on Jurisdiction and the Recognition and Enforcement of Judgments in Civil and Commercial Matters (Lugano Convention 2007) 8.61

E

European Convention for the Protection of Human Rights and Fundamental Freedoms 1950
  Art 1 .... 7.10
    6(3) 4.57
    8 ... 1.104, 5.5, 5.34, 6.90, 7.5, 7.6
    14 . 1.98, 1.99, 6.90, 7.5, 7.6, 7.10
  Protocol 1 .... 7.10
    Art 1 .... 1.104, 8.33

H

Hague Convention on Parental Responsibility and Protection of Children 1996 .... 8.33
  Art 15 .... 5.39
    16 .... 5.39
Hague Convention on the Civil Aspects of International Child Abduction 1980
  .... 5.40, 8.33
  Art 3 .... 5.39
    6(1) 5.41
    15 .... 5.39
Hague Protocol on the Law Applicable to Maintenance Obligations 2007
  .... 8.33
  Art 8(1) 8.32
    (5) 8.32

Table of Cases

A

A (a minor) (paternity: refusal of blood test), Re [1994] 2 FLR 463, [1994] Fam Law 622, sub nom GW (blood tests), Re [1994] 2 FCR 908, CA 5.6
A (a minor) (parental responsibility), Re [1996] 1 FCR 562, 160 JP 84, [1995] Lexis Citation 1554 .... 5.14
A (a child) (change of name), Re [2003] EWCA Civ 56, [2003] 2 FLR 1, [2003] 1 FCR 493, [2003] Fam Law 555, [2003] All ER (D) 231 (Jan), sub nom Re A (a child) (change of name) [2002] 1 FCR 493 .... 5.24
A (A Child: Application for leave to apply for a child arrangements order), Re [2015] EWFC 47, [2015] All ER (D) 24 (Jun) 5.19
A (a child) (change of name). See A (a child) (change of name), Re
A v A (a minor) [1994] 1 FLR 657, [1995] 1 FCR 309, [1994] Fam Law 368 ... 5.60, 5.62
A v A [2006] EWHC 2900 (Fam), [2007] Fam Law 295, [2007] All ER (D) 41 (Jan), sub nom NA v MA [2007] 1 FLR 1760 .... 8.13
A v A [2018] EWHC 2194 .... 8.42
A v T (ancillary relief: cultural factors) [2004] EWHC 471 (Fam), [2004] 1 FLR 977, [2004] Fam Law 404, (2004) Times, 2 March, [2004] All ER (D) 238 (Mar) 8.13
A v Y (child's surname) [1999] 2 FLR 5, [1999] 1 FCR 577, [1999] Fam Law 443 .... 5.24
AB v CD. See E & F (children) (assisted reproduction: parent), Re
AB v CD (No 2) [2019] EWHC 2244 (Fam), [2019] All ER (D) 91 (Aug) 5.5
AH v PH (Scandanavian Marriage Settlement) [2013] EWHC 3878 (Fam) 8.25
AK v HMRC (TC [2016] UKUT 0098 (AAC) 9.110
Abbott v Abbott [2007] UKPC 53, 70 WIR 183, [2008] 2 LRC 511, [2008] 1 FLR 1451, [2008] Fam Law 215, [2007] All ER (D) 432 (Jul), PC 1.38
Abram, Re [1996] 2 FLR 379, [1997] 2 FCR 85, [1996] Fam Law 666, [1997] BPIR 1 .... 6.69
Adekunle v Ritchie (17 August 2007, Unreported) Leeds County Court 1.49
Ahmed v Kendrick (1987) 56 P & CR 120, [1988] 2 FLR 22, [1988] Fam Law 201, (1987) Times, 12 November, CA 1.21, 4.75
Amicus Horizon Ltd v Brand [2012] EWCA Civ 895, [2013] 3 FCR 47, [2012] HLR 666, [2012] All ER (D) 252 (May) 9.24
Andresen v Lovell [2009] EWHC 3397 (QB), [2009] All ER (D) 196 (Dec) 4.74
Annen v Rattee (1984) 273 EG 503 .... 1.201
Ansah v Ansah (1976) FLR Rep 9 .... 4.86
Ansah v Ansah [1977] Fam 138, [1977] 2 All ER 638, [1977] 2 WLR 760, 121 Sol Jo 118 .... 4.58
Aspden v Elvy [2012] EWHC 1387 (Ch), [2012] 2 FLR 807, [2012] 2 FCR 435, [2012] Fam Law 1085, [2012] 2 P & CR D41, [2012] All ER (D) 192 (May) 1.42
A-G v Holbrook (1823) 3 Y & J 114, 12 Price 407, 147 ER 761 .... 6.132
Atrill v O'Donnell (Unreported, 27 November 1998) 4.58
Australian Blue Metal Ltd v Hughes [1963] AC 74, [1962] 3 All ER 335, [1962] 3 WLR 802, 106 Sol Jo 628, PC 1.201

B

B (a minor) (abduction), Re [1994] 2 FLR 249, [1995] 2 FCR 505, [1994] Fam Law 606, (1994) Times, 12 May, CA 5.39
B (a minor) (abduction: rights of custody), Re [1997] 2 FLR 594, [1998] 2 FCR 212 .... 5.40
B (dec'd), Re [2000] Ch 662, [2000] 1 All ER 665, [2000] 2 WLR 929, [2000] 1 FCR 385, [2000] NLJR 20, (2000) Times, 1 February, [1999] All ER (D) 1458 .... 6.24, 6.50
B (Change of Names: Parental Responsibility: Evidence), Re [2017] EWHC 3250 (Fam), [2018] 4 WLR 19, [2018] 1 FLR 1471, [2018] Fam Law 269, 168 NLJ 7777, [2017] All ER (D) 73 (Dec) 5.24
B v A [2012] EWHC 3127 (Fam), [2013] 2 FLR 958, [2012] All ER (D) 87 (Dec) 4.75

lv

Table of Cases

B v B (occupation order) [1999] 1 FLR 715, [1999] 2 FCR 251, [1999] Fam Law 208, 31 HLR 1059, (1999) Times, 5 January, [1998] Lexis Citation 2926, [1998] All ER (D) 754 .... 4.23
B v S (financial remedy: marital property regime) [2012] EWHC 265 (Fam), [2012] 2 FLR 502, [2012] 2 FCR 335, [2012] All ER (D) 189 (Mar) 8.7
B v S (Financial Remedy: Marital Property Regime) [2012] EWHC 425 (Fam) ... 8.24, 8.30
B v United Kingdom (Application 39067/97) [2000] 1 FLR 1, [2000] 1 FCR 289, [2000] Fam Law 88, EctHR 5.40
B v V (Children: Financial Provision: Unmarried Parents) Current Law September 1999 .... 5.61
B-J (a child) (non-molestation order: power of arrest), Re [2001] Fam 415, [2001] 1 All ER 235, [2001] 2 WLR 1660, [2000] 2 FLR 443, [2000] 2 FCR 599, [2000] Fam Law 807, [2000] Lexis Citation 2887, [2000] All ER (D) 874 .... 4.46
BC v DE (proceedings under Children Act 1989: legal costs funding) [2016] EWHC 1806 (Fam), [2016] 1 WLR 4720, [2017] 1 FLR 1521, [2016] Fam Law 1219 .... 5.60
BN v MA (maintenance pending suit: prenuptial agreement) [2013] EWHC 4250 (Fam), [2014] Fam Law 443 .... 8.25, 8.39, 8.44
Bagum v Hafiz [2015] EWCA Civ 801, [2016] Ch 241, [2015] 3 WLR 1495, [2016] 2 FLR 337, [2015] Fam Law 1192, (2015) Times, 07 September, [2015] WTLR 1303, [2015] 2 P & CR D53, [2015] All ER (D) 249 (Jul) 1.63
Balfour v Balfour [1919] 2 KB 571, 88 LJKB 1054, [1918–19] All ER Rep 860, 63 Sol Jo 661, 121 LT 346, 35 TLR 609, CA 2.5
Banks v Banks [1999] 1 FLR 726, [1999] Fam Law 209, CC 4.23
Barnes v Phillips [2015] EWCA Civ 1056, [2016] 2 FLR 1292, [2015] Fam Law 1470, [2016] HLR 24, [2016] WTLR 1, [2016] 1 P & CR D27, [2015] All ER (D) 206 (Oct) 1.41
Basham, Re [1987] 1 All ER 405, [1986] 1 WLR 1498, [1987] 2 FLR 264, [1987] Fam Law 310, 130 Sol Jo 986, [1987] LS Gaz R 112 .... 2.60, 6.14
Bater v Greenwich London Borough Council [1999] 4 All ER 944, [1999] 2 FLR 993, [1999] 3 FCR 254, [1999] Fam Law 694, 32 HLR 127, [1999] NPC 102, [1999] 33 LS Gaz R 30, [1999] EGCS 111, (1999) Times, 28 September, [1999] Lexis Citation 2680, [1999] All ER (D) 845 .... 1.92, 1.108, 1.147, 4.70
Baynes v Hedger [2008] EWHC 1587 (Ch), 11 ITELR 71, [2008] 2 FLR 1805, [2008] 3 FCR 151, [2008] Fam Law 952, [2008] Fam Law 1087, [2008] All ER (D) 175 (Jul); affd on other grounds [2009] EWCA Civ 374, 11 ITELR 987, [2009] 2 FLR 767, [2009] 2 FCR 183, [2009] Fam Law 666, [2009] 20 LS Gaz R 19, [2009] All ER (D) 50 (May) 6.35, 6.40, 6.43, 6.50, 6.57, 9.93
Beaumont, Re, Martin v Midland Bank Trust Co Ltd [1980] Ch 444, [1980] 1 All ER 266, [1979] 3 WLR 818, 123 Sol Jo 803 .... 6.38, 6.39, 6.50, 6.51
Begum v Anam [2004] EWCA Civ 578, [2004] All ER (D) 309 (Apr) 4.84, 4.86
Benham's Will Trusts, Re, Lockhart v Harker, Read and the Royal National Lifeboat Institution [1995] STC 210 .... 6.134
Berger v Berger [2013] EWCA Civ 1305, [2013] All ER (D) 319 (Oct) 6.24
Bernard v Josephs [1982] Ch 391, [1982] 3 All ER 162, [1982] 2 WLR 1052, (1983) 4 FLR 178, 126 Sol Jo 361 .... 1.42, 1.207, 1.208, 1.209
Berry v Berry [1929] 2 KB 316, 98 LJKB 748, [1929] All ER Rep 281, 141 LT 461, 45 TLR 524 .... 2.144
Besterman, Re, Besterman v Grusin [1984] Ch 458, [1984] 2 All ER 656, [1984] 3 WLR 280, [1984] FLR 503, [1984] Fam Law 203, 128 Sol Jo 515 .... 6.74
Bhura v Bhura [2014] EWHC 727 (Fam), [2015] 1 FLR 153, [2015] 2 FCR 353, [2014] Fam Law 1116, [2014] All ER (D) 213 (Mar) 1.40
Bhusate (personal representative of the estate of Kashinath Bhusate (dec'd)) v Patel (personal representative of the estate of Kashinath Bhusate (dec'd)) [2018] EWHC 2362 (Ch), 168 NLJ 7809, [2018] All ER (D) 34 (Sep) 6.24
Borwick's Settlement, Re, Woodman v Borwick, Re Woodman [1916] 2 Ch 304, 85 LJ Ch 732, 60 Sol Jo 567, 115 LT 183, 32 TLR 583, [1916–17] All ER Rep Ext 1379 .... 6.148
Brack v Brack. See DB v PB
Brewer v Brewer [1989] 2 FLR 251, [1989] FCR 515, [1989] Fam Law 352, CA 4.58

Table of Cases

Brewster's Application for Judicial Review, Re [2017] UKSC 8, [2017] NI 326, [2017] 2 All ER 1001, [2017] 1 WLR 519, [2017] 3 LRC 320, [2017] IRLR 366, [2017] ICR 434, [2017] Fam Law 395, 167 NLJ 7734, (2017) Times, 13 February, [2017] All ER (D) 74 (Feb), SC 7.10
Brodie v Brodie [1917] P 271, 86 LJP 140, [1916–17] All ER Rep 237, 62 Sol Jo 71, 117 LT 542, 33 TLR 525, PDA 8.35, 8.36
Brough v Law (unreported) 5.43
Buchanan-Wollaston's Conveyance, Re, Curtis v Buchanan-Wollaston [1939] Ch 738, [1939] 2 All ER 302, 108 LJ Ch 281, 83 Sol Jo 376, 160 LT 399, 55 TLR 604, CA 1.156
Burchell v Clark (1876) 2 CPD 88, 42 JP 132, 46 LJQB 115, 25 WR 334, 35 LT 690, CA 1.199, 2.61
Burden v United Kingdom (Application 13378/05) [2007] STC 252, 9 ITLR 535, [2007] 1 FCR 69, (2007) Times, 19 January, [2007] SWTI 106, 21 BHRC 640, [2006] ECHR 13378/05, [2006] All ER (D) 160 (Dec), EctHR 3.9
Burnett v George [1992] 1 FLR 525, [1993] 1 FCR 1012, [1992] Fam Law 156, CA 4.65
Burns v Burns [1984] Ch 317, [1984] 1 All ER 244, [1984] 2 WLR 582, [1984] FLR 216, [1984] Fam Law 24, 128 Sol Jo 173, [1984] LS Gaz R 893 .... 1.3
Burris v Azadani [1995] 4 All ER 802, [1995] 1 WLR 1372, [1996] 1 FLR 266, [1996] 1 FCR 618, [1996] Fam Law 145, [1995] NLJR 1330, (1995) Times, 9 August . 4.65, 4.72, 4.75
Butterworth v Supplementary Benefits Commission [1982] 1 All ER 498, (1981) 2 FLR 264 .... 9.19, 9.23

C

C (a minor), Re [1986] 1 FLR 578, [1986] Fam Law 187, CA 4.86
C (minors), Re [1992] 2 All ER 86, [1992] 1 FLR 1, [1991] FCR 856, [1992] Fam Law 153, (1991) Times, 8 August, 135 Sol Jo LB 100 .... 5.16
C (leave to apply for provision), Re [1995] 2 FLR 24, [1995] Fam Law 479, sub nom W (a minor) (claim from dec'd's estate), Re [1995] 2 FCR 689 .... 6.23, 6.63, 6.65
C (minors) (change of surname), Re [1997] 2 FLR 730, [1997] 3 FCR 310, [1997] Fam Law 722 .... 5.22
C (minors) (change of surname), Re [1998] 1 FLR 549, [1998] 2 FCR 544, [1998] Fam Law 250, [1997] 48 LS Gaz R 29, (1997) Times, 8 December, [1997] Lexis Citation 4755, 142 Sol Jo LB 20 .... 5.24
C (a minor) (change of surname), Re [1998] 2 FLR 656, [1999] 1 FCR 318, [1998] Fam Law 659, (1998) Times, 2 February 5.24
C (abduction: wrongful removal), Re [1999] 2 FLR 859, [1999] 3 FCR 678, [1999] Fam Law 609 .... 5.41
C (A Child), Re [2002] EWCA Civ 446 .... 5.18
C (A Child) Schedule 1 Children Act Variation, Re [2018] Lexis Citation 63, [2018] All ER (D) 32 (Aug) 5.65
C v C (non-molestation order: jurisdiction) [1998] Fam 70, [1998] 2 WLR 599, [1998] 1 FLR 554, [1998] 1 FCR 11, [1998] Fam Law 254, [1997] 47 LS Gaz R 30, (1997) Times, 16 December, [1997] Lexis Citation 4740, 141 Sol Jo LB 236 .... 4.6
C v C (Divorce: Stay of English Proceedings) [2001] 1 FLR 624, [2000] Lexis Citation 4609 .... 8.11
C v C (Ancillary Relief: Nuptial Settlement). See Charalambous v Charalambous
C and V (minors) (parental responsibility and contact), Re [1998] 1 FLR 392, [1998] 1 FCR 52, [1998] Fam Law 10, (1997) Times, 30 June 5.14, 5.16
CF v KM [2010] EWHC 1754 (Fam), [2011] 1 FLR 208, [2010] Fam Law 1060 ..... 5.48, 5.60, 5.61
CG v Secretary of State for Work and Pensions (IS) [2011] UKUT 97 (AAC) . 9.5, 9.6, 9.85, 9.122, 9.126
CJ v Flintshire Borough Council [2010] EWCA Civ 393, [2010] 2 FLR 1224, [2010] 3 FCR 40, [2010] Fam Law 697, 154 Sol Jo (no 16) 27, [2010] All ER (D) 75 (Apr) 4.86
Cairnes, Re, Howard v Cairnes (1983) 4 FLR 225, 12 Fam Law 177 .... 6.158
Callaghan, Re [1985] Fam 1, [1984] 3 All ER 790, [1984] 3 WLR 1076, [1985] FLR 116, [1985] Fam Law 28, 128 Sol Jo 705 .... 6.61, 6.66

Table of Cases

Cameron v Treasury Solicitor [1996] 2 FLR 716, [1997] 1 FCR 188, [1996] Fam Law 723, CA 6.11, 6.29
Cantor v Cox [1975] 239 EG 121 .... 1.27
Capehorn v Harris [2015] EWCA Civ 955, [2016] 2 FLR 1026, [2015] Fam Law 1347, [2016] HLR 1, [2015] All ER (D) 384 (Jul) 1.40
Cattle v Evans [2011] EWHC 945 (Ch), [2011] 2 FLR 843, [2011] Fam Law 809, 155 Sol Jo (no 18) 31, 155 Sol Jo (no 19) 31, [2011] 2 P & CR DG27, [2011] All ER (D) 209 (Apr) 6.48
Chalmers v Johns [1999] 1 FLR 392, [1999] 2 FCR 110, [1999] Fam Law 16 ... 4.17, 4.23
Charalambous v Charalambous [2004] EWCA Civ 1030, [2005] 2 WLR 241, [2004] 2 FLR 1093, [2004] 2 FCR 721, (2004) Times, 7 September, [2004] All ER (D) 582 (Jul), sub nom C v C (Ancillary Relief: Nuptial Settlement) [2005] Fam 250 .... 8.32
Cheese v Thomas [1994] 1 All ER 35, [1994] 1 WLR 129, 69 P & CR 316, [1994] 1 FLR 118, [1995] 1 FCR 162, [1994] Fam Law 80, 26 HLR 426, [1993] NLJR 1368, (1993) Times, 24 August 2.8
Chelmsford County Court v Ramet [2014] EWHC 56 .... 4.86
Chiltern District Council v Keane [1985] 2 All ER 118, [1985] 1 WLR 619, 83 LGR 573, 129 Sol Jo 206 .... 4.86
Church Comrs for England v Al-Emarah [1997] Fam 34, [1996] 3 WLR 633, [1996] 2 FLR 544, 29 HLR 351, [1996] 22 LS Gaz R 27, (1996) Times, 13 May, 140 Sol Jo LB 129, sub nom Church Comrs v Alemarah [1996] 3 FCR 252, CA 1.119
Churchill v Roach [2002] EWHC 3230 (Ch), [2004] 2 FLR 989, [2004] 3 FCR 744, [2003] All ER (D) 348 (Apr) 6.40
City of London Building Society v Flegg [1988] AC 54, [1987] 3 All ER 435, [1987] 2 WLR 1266, 54 P & CR 337, [1988] 1 FLR 98, [1988] Fam Law 17, 19 HLR 484, 131 Sol Jo 806, [1987] LS Gaz R 1966, [1987] NLJ Rep 475, (1987) Times, 18 May, HL 1.2, 1.198
Clarke v Clarke [1990] 2 FLR 115, [1990] FCR 641, [1990] Fam Law 331, CA 4.86
Cleaver, Re, Cleaver v Insley [1981] 2 All ER 1018, [1981] 1 WLR 939, 125 Sol Jo 445 .... 6.110
Clutton v Clutton [1991] 1 All ER 340, [1991] 1 WLR 359, [1991] 1 FLR 242, [1991] FCR 265, [1991] Fam Law 304, [1990] NLJR 1682, (1990) Times, 13 November 1.164
Coats (J & P) v Chadwick [1894] 1 Ch 347, 63 LJ Ch 328, 8 R 159, 42 WR 328, 38 Sol Jo 217, 70 LT 228, 10 TLR 226 .... 4.86
Cooke v Head [1972] 2 All ER 38, [1972] 1 WLR 518, 116 Sol Jo 298 .... 1.36
Coombes v Smith [1986] 1 WLR 808, [1987] 1 FLR 352, [1987] Fam Law 123, 130 Sol Jo 482, [1986] LS Gaz R 2238 .... 6.14
Coventry, Re, Coventry v Coventry [1980] Ch 461, [1979] 3 All ER 815, [1979] 3 WLR 802, 123 Sol Jo 606 .... 6.28, 6.44, 6.54, 6.63, 6.69
Cowan v Foreman [2019] EWHC 349 (Fam), [2019] 1 FLR 1191, [2019] Fam Law 482, [2019] WTLR 441; revsd sub nom Cowan v Foreman (as executor of the estate of Michael Cowan and as trustee of the Business Property Trust and the Residuary Trust in the Will of Michael Cowan dated 24 March 2016 and as trustee of the Michael Cowan Foundation) [2019] EWCA Civ 1336, [2020] 2 WLR 61, 22 ITELR 280, [2019] WTLR 707, [2019] All ER (D) 31 (Aug) 6.25
Cowcher v Cowcher [1972] 1 All ER 943, [1972] 1 WLR 425, 116 Sol Jo 142 ... 1.3, 1.6, 1.202, 1.223
Cowley (Earl) v Countess of Cowley [1901] AC 450, 70 LJP 83, 50 WR 81, 85 LT 254, 17 TLR 725, HL 5.21, 10.1
Cox v Jones [2004] EWHC 1486 (Ch), [2004] 2 FLR 1010, [2004] 3 FCR 693, [2004] All ER (D) 281 (Jun) 1.136
Coxen, Re, McCallum v Coxen [1948] Ch 747, [1948] 2 All ER 492, [1948] LJR 1590, 92 Sol Jo 442 .... 1.213, 6.124
Crake v Supplementary Benefits Commission [1982] 1 All ER 498, (1981) 2 FLR 264 .... 9.19, 9.23
Crane v Morris [1965] 3 All ER 77, [1965] 1 WLR 1104, 109 Sol Jo 456, 194 Estates Gazette 905, CA 1.201
Crawley Borough Council v Sawyer (1987) 86 LGR 629, 20 HLR 98, (1987) Times, 16 October, CA 9.29

Crossley v Crossley [2007] EWCA Civ 1491, [2008] 1 FLR 1467, [2008] 1 FCR 323, [2008] Fam Law 395, (2008) Times, 3 January, [2007] All ER (D) 396 (Dec) 8.7, 8.8, 8.10, 8.14
Curran v Collins [2015] EWCA Civ 404, [2016] 1 FLR 505, [2015] Fam Law 780, [2016] WTLR 235, [2015] 2 P & CR D27, [2015] All ER (D) 01 (May) 1.35
Cust v CIR (1917) 91 EG 11 .... 6.125

D

D (A Child), Re [2014] EWCA Civ 315, [2015] 1 FLR 166, [2014] 3 FCR 314, [2014] Fam Law 971, [2014] All ER (D) 254 (Mar) 5.16, 5.18
DB v PB [2016] EWHC 3431 (Fam), [2017] 4 WLR 44, [2017] 2 FLR 1540, [2017] Fam Law 380, [2016] All ER (D) 120 (Dec); revsd sub nom Brack v Brack [2018] EWCA Civ 2862, [2019] 3 All ER 664, [2019] 1 WLR 3438, [2019] 2 FLR 234, [2019] Fam Law 258, [2019] All ER (D) 18 (Jan) 8.29, 8.35
DG v Her Majesty's Revenue and Customs (TC) [2013] UKUT 0631 (AAC) 9.18
DK v Secretary of State for Work and Pensions [2016] ScotCS CSIH 84 .. 9.45, 9.49, 9.57, 9.64, 9.106
Dancer v Dancer [1949] P 147, [1948] 2 All ER 731, [1949] LJR 138, 92 Sol Jo 528, 64 TLR 505, PDA 5.21, 10.1
Danish Bacon Co Ltd Staff Pension Fund, Re, Christensen v Arnett [1971] 1 All ER 486, [1971] 1 WLR 248, 115 Sol Jo 95 .... 6.158
Dart v Dart [1996] 2 FLR 286, [1997] 1 FCR 21, [1996] Fam Law 607, [1995] Lexis Citation 1675, CA 8.9
Davies v Davies [2014] EWCA Civ 568, [2014] Fam Law 1252, [2016] WTLR 1175, [2016] WTLR 1547, [2014] 2 P & CR D31 .... 1.57
Davies v Davies [2016] EWCA Civ 463, [2016] P & CR 241, [2017] 1 FLR 1286, [2016] Fam Law 815, [2016] All ER (D) 09 (Jun) 1.58
Davis (As trustee in bankruptcy of Jackson) v Jackson [2017] EWHC 698 (Ch), [2017] 1 WLR 4005, [2017] 2 FLR 1153, [2017] Fam Law 722, 167 NLJ 7745, [2017] WTLR 465, [2017] BPIR 950, [2017] All ER (D) 119 (Apr) 1.18
Davis v Smith [2011] EWCA Civ 1603, [2012] 1 FLR 1177, [2012] Fam Law 401, [2012] All ER (D) 55 (Jan) 1.22
Dawson v Wearmouth [1999] 2 AC 308, [1999] 2 All ER 353, [1999] 2 WLR 960, [1999] 1 FLR 1167, [1999] 1 FCR 625, [1999] Fam Law 378, (1999) Times, 26 March, [1999] Lexis Citation 2066, 143 Sol Jo LB 114, [1999] All ER (D) 330, HL 5.24
Dean v Dean [1987] 1 FLR 517, [1987] FCR 96, [1987] Fam Law 200, CA 4.57, 4.86
Debenham, Re [1986] 1 FLR 404, [1986] Fam Law 101 .... 6.32, 6.34
De la Rochefoucauld v Boustead. See Rochefoucauld v Boustead
de Lasala v de Lasala [1980] AC 546, [1979] 2 All ER 1146, [1979] 3 WLR 390, 123 Sol Jo 301, PC 8.33
Dennis, Re, Dennis v Lloyds Bank Ltd [1981] 2 All ER 140, 124 Sol Jo 885, 131 NLJ 210 .... 6.24, 6.28, 6.53, 6.63
Dennis v McDonald (1982) 3 FLR 398 .... 1.204, 1.209, 1.213
Densham (a bankrupt), Re, ex p trustee of bankrupt v Densham [1975] 3 All ER 726, [1975] 1 WLR 1519, 119 Sol Jo 774 .... 1.30
Deutsche Bank AG v Asia Pacific Broadband Wireless Communications Inc [2008] EWCA Civ 1091, [2009] 2 All ER (Comm) 129, [2008] 2 Lloyd's Rep 619, [2008] All ER (D) 104 (Oct) 8.29
Dickson v Rennie [2014] EWHC 4306 (Fam), [2015] 2 FLR 978, [2015] Fam Law 261, [2015] All ER (D) 49 (Jan) 5.48
Director General of Fair Trading v Smiths Concrete Ltd. See Ready Mixed Concrete (Supply of), Re
District Judge's Direction (Children: conciliation) [2004] 1 FLR 974, HC 5.20
Ditta Estasis Salotti di Colzano Aima e Giamano Colzano v RÜWA Polstereimaschinen GmbH: C-24/76 [1976] ECR 1831, [1977] 1 CMLR 345, EUCJ 8.29
Dix, Re. See Gully v Dix
Dolan v Corby [2011] EWCA Civ 1664, [2012] 2 FLR 1031, [2012] 1 FCR 276, [2012] Fam Law 400, [2012] All ER (D) 136 (Jan) 4.23

Table of Cases

Douglas Lowson v Rebecca Coombes (Lowson v Coombes) (1998) CASE No – CCRTF 98/0112/2, sub nom Lowson v Coombes [1999] Ch 373, [1999] 2 WLR 720, 77 P & CR D25, 1 ITELR 514, [1999] 1 FLR 799, [1999] 2 FCR 731, [1999] Fam Law 91, [1999] 01 LS Gaz R 23, (1998) Times, 2 December, [1998] All ER (D) 644 ..... 1.27, 1.61
Drake v Whipp [1996] 1 FLR 826, [1996] 2 FCR 296, [1996] Fam Law 472, 28 HLR 531, (1995) Times, 19 December, CA 1.25
Draper's Conveyance, Re, Nihan v Porter [1969] 1 Ch 486, [1967] 3 All ER 853, [1968] 2 WLR 166, 19 P & CR 71, 111 Sol Jo 867, 204 EG 693 .... 1.21
Du Boulay v Du Boulay (1869) LR 2 PC 430, 6 Moo PCCNS 31, 38 LJPC 35, 17 WR 594, 16 ER 638, 22 LT 228 .... 5.21, 10.1
Duranceau, Re [1952] 3 DLR 714, ONCA 6.28
Duxbury v Duxbury [1992] Fam 62n, [1990] 2 All ER 77, [1991] 3 WLR 639n, [1987] 1 FLR 7, [1987] Fam Law 13 .... 6.74

E

E (a child) (abduction: custody rights), Re [2005] EWHC 848 (Fam), [2005] 2 FLR 759, [2005] All ER (D) 451 (May) 5.39
EM v HMRC (TC) [2018] UKUT 220 (AAC) 9.41, 9.43
E-R (a child) (Child arrangements order: existence of natural parent presumption) [2015] EWCA Civ 405, [2016] 1 FLR 521, [2015] 2 FCR 385, [2015] Fam Law 633, [2015] All ER (D) 203 (Apr) 5.25
E & F (children) (assisted reproduction: parent), Re [2013] EWHC 1418 (Fam), [2013] 3 FCR 532, [2013] All ER (D) 279 (Jun), sub nom AB v CD [2013] 2 FLR 1357, [2013] Fam law 962, [2013] NLJR 19 .... 5.7
Edgar v Edgar [1980] 3 All ER 887, [1980] 1 WLR 1410, (1981) 2 FLR 19, 124 Sol Jo 809 .... 8.9, 8.14
Egan v Egan [1975] Ch 218, [1975] 2 All ER 167, [1975] 2 WLR 503, 119 Sol Jo 220 .... 1.201
Ella v Ella [2007] EWCA Civ 99, [2007] 2 FLR 35, [2007] 3 FCR 768, [2007] Fam Law 483, [2007] All ER (D) 67 (Jan) 8.13
Ely v Robson [2016] EWCA Civ 774, 20 ITELR 428, [2017] 1 FLR 1704, [2016] Fam Law 1221, [2016] WTLR 1383, [2017] 1 P & CR D1, [2016] All ER (D) 140 (Jul) 1.54
English v Western [1940] 2 KB 156, [1940] 2 All ER 515, 67 Ll L Rep 45, 109 LJKB 728, 84 Sol Jo 465, 162 LT 370, 56 TLR 680, CA 9.29
Escritt v Escritt (1982) 3 FLR 280 .... 6.24
Evers's Trust, Re, Papps v Evers [1980] 3 All ER 399, [1980] 1 WLR 1327, 10 Fam Law 245, 124 Sol Jo 562 .... 1.156
Eves v Eves [1975] 3 All ER 768, [1975] 1 WLR 1338, 119 Sol Jo 394 .... 1.36

F

F, Re [1990] 2 AC 1, [1989] 2 WLR 1025, [1989] 2 FLR 376, 133 Sol Jo 265, [1989] 10 LS Gaz R 42, [1989] NLJR 183, CA; affd [1990] 2 AC 1, [1989] 2 WLR 1025, [1990] LRC (Const) 511, [1989] 2 FLR 376, [1989] Fam Law 390, 133 Sol Jo 785, [1989] NLJR 789, sub nom F v West Berkshire Health Authority (Mental Health Act Commission intervening) [1989] 2 All ER 545, 4 BMLR 1, (1989) Times, 25 May, HL 6.96
F (Abduction: Unmarried Father: Sole Carer), Re [2002] EWHC 2896 (Fam), [2003] 1 FLR 839 .... 5.40
F (Children), Re [2007] EWCA Civ 873, (2007) Times, 6 August, [2007] All ER (D) 389 (Jul), sub nom F (paternity: jurisdiction), Re [2008] 1 FLR 225, [2007] Fam Law 984, sub nom F (Children) (paternity: jurisdiction), Re [2008] 1 FCR 382 .... 5.5
F (children)(DNA evidence), Re [2007] EWHC 3235 (Fam), [2008] 1 FLR 348, [2008] Fam Law 405, [2008] NLJR 183, [2008] All ER (D) 171 (Jan) 5.5
F (paternity: jurisdiction), Re. See F (Children), Re
F v F (ancillary relief: substantial assets) [1995] 2 FLR 45, [1996] 2 FCR 397, [1995] Fam Law 546 .... 8.9
F v F [2009] EWHC 2485 (Fam), [2010] 1 FLR 1743, [2010] Fam Law 128 .... 8.14, 8.15
F v West Berkshire Health Authority (Mental Health Act Commission intervening). See F, Re

FB v Secretary of State for Work and Pensions (IS) [2011] UKUT 335 (AAC) 9.18
FG v MBW [2011] EWHC 1729 (Fam), [2012] 1 FLR 152, [2011] All ER (D) 106 (Oct), sub nom FG v MBW (Financial remedy for child) [2011] Fam Law 1334 .... 5.60
Farrar v Lord Winterton (1842) 5 Beav 1, 6 Jur 204, 49 ER 476 .... 6.122
Fender v St John-Mildmay [1938] AC 1, 81 Sol Jo 549, 53 TLR 885, sub nom Fender v Mildmay [1937] 3 All ER 402, 106 LJKB 641, 157 LT 340, HL 2.3
First National Securities Ltd v Hegerty [1985] QB 850, [1984] 1 All ER 139, [1984] 3 WLR 769, [1985] FLR 80, 126 Sol Jo 836; affd [1985] QB 850, [1984] 3 All ER 641, [1984] 3 WLR 769, 48 P & CR 200, [1985] FLR 80, [1984] Fam Law 315, 128 Sol Jo 499 .... 1.21
Fitzpatrick v Sterling Housing Association Ltd [1998] Ch 304, [1997] 4 All ER 991, [1998] 2 WLR 225, [1998] 1 FLR 6, [1998] 1 FCR 417, 30 HLR 576, [1997] NLJR 1275, (1997) Times, 31 July; revsd [2001] 1 AC 27, [1999] 4 All ER 705, [1999] 3 WLR 1113, [2000] 3 LRC 294, 79 P & CR D4, [1999] 2 FLR 1027, [2000] 1 FLR 271, [2000] 1 FCR 21, [2000] Fam Law 14, 32 HLR 178, [1999] NPC 127, [1999] 43 LS Gaz R 34, [1999] EGCS 125, (1999) Times, 2 November, 7 BHRC 200, [1999] All ER (D) 1171, HL 1.94, 1.98, 9.24, 9.64, 9.71
Fowler v Barron [2008] EWCA Civ 377, 11 ITELR 198, [2008] 2 FLR 831, [2008] 2 FCR 1, [2008] Fam Law 636, [2008] All ER (D) 318 (Apr) 1.48
Fullard, Re, Fullard v King [1982] Fam 42, [1981] 2 All ER 796, [1981] 3 WLR 743, 11 Fam Law 116, 125 Sol Jo 747 .... 6.33, 6.87

G

G (a minor) (parental responsibility order), Re [1994] 1 FLR 504, [1994] 2 FCR 1037, [1994] Fam Law 372, CA 5.16
G (parentage: blood sample), Re [1997] 1 FLR 360, [1997] Fam Law 243, sub nom G (a minor) (paternity: blood tests), Re [1997] 2 FCR 325, CA 5.6
G (a child) (secure accommodation order), Re [2000] 2 FLR 259, [2000] 2 FCR 385 .... 1.2
G (a child) (education), Re [2006] EWCA Civ 1507, [2007] 1 FLR 1663, [2006] 40 LS Gaz R 36, 150 Sol Jo LB 1328, [2006] All ER (D) 67 (Oct) 5.24
G v F (non-molestation order: jurisdiction) [2000] Fam 186, [2000] 3 WLR 1202, [2000] 2 FCR 638, (2000) Times, 24 May, [2000] Lexis Citation 1943, [2000] All ER (D) 927, sub nom G v G (non-molestation order: jurisdiction) [2000] 2 FLR 533 .... 4.5
G v G [1990] 1 FLR 395, [1990] FCR 572, [1990] Fam Law 254, CA 4.75
G v G [2009] EWHC 2080 (Fam), [2010] 2 FLR 1264, [2010] Fam Law 919 .... 5.60
G v G (financial provision: separation agreement) [2004] 1 FLR 1011, CA 8.13
GB v London Borough of Hillingdon (HB) [2010] UKUT 11 (AAC) 9.4
GS v L (financial remedies: pre-acquired assets: needs) [2011] EWHC 1759 (Fam), [2013] 1 FLR 300, [2012] Fam Law 800, [2012] All ER (D) 178 (Mar) 8.21
GW (blood tests), Re. See Re A (a minor) (paternity: refusal of blood test)
GW v RW [2003] EWHC 611 (Fam), [2003] 2 FLR 108, [2003] 2 FCR 289, [2003] Fam Law 386, [2003] All ER (D) 40 (May) 5.60
Garland v Morris [2007] EWHC 2 (Ch), [2007] 2 FLR 528, [2007] Fam Law 585, [2007] All ER (D) 11 (Jan) 6.70
Gay v Sheeran [1999] 3 All ER 795, [2000] 1 WLR 673, [1999] 2 FLR 519, [1999] 2 FCR 705, [1999] Fam Law 619, 31 HLR 1126, [1999] 30 LS Gaz R 29, (1999) Times, 30 June, [1999] Lexis Citation 2618, [1999] All ER (D) 639 .... 1.101, 1.109
Geary v Rankine [2012] EWCA Civ 555, [2012] 2 FLR 1409, [2012] 2 FCR 461, [2012] All ER (D) 04 (Apr) 1.40
Ghaidan v Godin-Mendoza [2004] UKHL 30, [2004] 2 AC 557, [2004] 3 WLR 113, [2004] 2 FLR 600, [2004] 2 FCR 481, [2004] Fam Law 641, [2004] HLR 827, [2004] 2 EGLR 132, [2004] 27 LS Gaz R 30, [2004] NLJR 1013, (2004) Times, 24 June, 148 Sol Jo LB 792, 16 BHRC 671, [2004] All ER (D) 210 (Jun), sub nom Ghaidan v Mendoza [2004] 3 All ER 411, [2005] 1 LRC 449, HL 1.94, 1.98
Gillett v Holt [2001] Ch 210, [2000] 2 All ER 289, [2000] 3 WLR 815, [2000] 2 FLR 266, [2000] 1 FCR 705, [2000] Fam Law 714, [2000] 12 LS Gaz R 40, (2000) Times, 17 March, [2000] Lexis Citation 2694, [2000] All ER (D) 299 .... 1.57, 1.58, 6.14
Gissing v Gissing [1971] AC 886, [1970] 2 All ER 780, [1970] 3 WLR 255, 21 P & CR 702, 114 Sol Jo 550, 216 Estates Gazette 1257, HL . 1.3, 1.9, 1.12, 1.33, 1.51, 1.81, 1.140

Table of Cases

Gohil v Gohil [2015] UKSC 61, [2016] AC 849, [2016] 1 All ER 685, [2015] 3 WLR 1085, [2015] 2 FLR 1289, [2015] 3 FCR 497, [2015] Fam Law 1459, 165 NLJ 7673, (2015) Times, 03 November, [2015] All ER (D) 100 (Oct), SC 8.18, 8.23
Goldstone v Goldstone [2011] EWCA Civ 39, [2011] 1 FLR 1926, [2011] 1 FCR 324, [2011] Fam Law 340, [2011] All ER (D) 218 (Jan) 5.76
Goodchild, Re, Goodchild v Goodchild [1997] 3 All ER 63, [1997] 1 WLR 1216, [1997] 2 FLR 644, [1997] 3 FCR 601, [1997] NLJR 758, (1997) Times, 12 May 6.32, 6.69, 6.110
Goodman v Carlton [2002] EWCA Civ 545, [2002] 2 FLR 259, [2002] All ER (D) 284 (Apr) 1.3
Goodman v Gallant [1986] Fam 106, [1986] 1 All ER 311, [1986] 2 WLR 236, 52 P & CR 180, [1986] 1 FLR 513, [1986] Fam Law 159, 129 Sol Jo 891 .. 1.6, 1.18, 1.52, 1.161
Gordon v Douce [1983] 2 All ER 228, [1983] 1 WLR 563, (1983) 4 FLR 508, 13 Fam Law 149, 127 Sol Jo 324 .... 1.11
Gorman (a bankrupt), Re, ex p Trustee of the Bankrupt v Bankrupt [1990] 1 All ER 717, [1990] 1 WLR 616, [1990] 2 FLR 284, [1990] Fam Law 430, [1990] 19 LS Gaz R 41, DC 1.205
Gorringe v Mahlstedt [1907] AC 225, 76 LJ Ch 527, 51 Sol Jo 497, 97 LT 111, [1904–7] All ER Rep Ext 1110, HL 6.4
Graham v Murphy [1997] 1 FLR 860, [1997] 2 FCR 441, [1997] Fam Law 393, (1992) Times, 26 February 6.87
Graham-York v York (Personal Representative of the Estate of Norton Brian York) [2015] EWCA Civ 72, 18 ITELR 525, [2016] 1 FLR 407, [2015] Fam Law 528, [2015] 2 P & CR D1, [2015] All ER (D) 115 (Feb), sub nom Leeds Building Society v York (Personal Representative of the Estate of Norton Brian York) [2015] HLR 532 .... 1.52
Grant v Edwards [1986] Ch 638, [1986] 2 All ER 426, [1986] 3 WLR 114, [1987] 1 FLR 87, [1986] Fam Law 300, 130 Sol Jo 408, [1986] LS Gaz R 1996, [1986] NLJ Rep 439 .... 1.35
Gray v Work [2015] EWHC 834 (Fam), [2015] Fam Law 1045, [2015] All ER (D) 302 (Mar); affd sub nom Work v Gray [2017] EWCA Civ 270, [2018] Fam 35, [2017] 3 WLR 535, [2017] 2 FLR 1297, [2017] Fam Law 599, 167 NLJ 7743, (2017) Times, 20 June, [2017] All ER (D) 61 (Apr) 8.28, 8.40
Greasley v Cooke [1980] 3 All ER 710, [1980] 1 WLR 1306, 124 Sol Jo 629 .... 1.86
Grey v Grey [2009] EWCA Civ 1424, [2010] 1 FLR 1764, [2010] 1 FCR 394, [2010] Fam Law 440, [2010] All ER (D) 188 (Jul) 6.41
Griffiths v Renfree [1989] 2 FLR 167, [1989] FCR 551, [1989] Fam Law 355, 21 HLR 338, [1989] 2 EGLR 46, [1989] 32 EG 40, (1989) Times, 4 March, CA 1.92
Grosvenor, Re, Grosvenor v Grosvenor [1916] 2 Ch 375, 85 LJ Ch 735, 60 Sol Jo 681, 115 LT 298, [1916–17] All ER Rep Ext 1364 .... 6.122
Grubb v Grubb [2009] EWCA Civ 976, [2011] 1 FLR 687, [2010] Fam Law 1277 .... 4.23
Guerroudj v Rymarczyk [2015] EWCA Civ 743, [2016] 1 FLR 1349, [2015] Fam Law 1194, [2015] HLR 751, [2015] 2 P & CR D56, [2015] All ER (D) 152 (Jul) 1.114
Gully v Dix [2004] EWCA Civ 139, [2004] 1 FLR 918, [2004] 1 FCR 453, [2004] Fam Law 334, [2004] 06 LS Gaz R 32, (2004) Times, 28 January, [2004] All ER (D) 162 (Jan), sub nom Dix, Re [2004] 1 WLR 1399 .... 6.38, 6.39, 6.51, 9.29, 9.33

H

H (A Minor), Re (1976) Fam Law 172 .... 6.68
H, Re [1990] 1 FLR 441, [1990] Fam Law 175 .... 6.36
H (minors) (local authority: parental rights) (No 3), Re [1991] Fam 151, [1991] 2 All ER 185, [1991] 2 WLR 763, 89 LGR 537, 135 Sol Jo 16, (1990) Times, 21 November, sub nom H (minors) (No 2), Re [1991] 1 FLR 214, [1991] FCR 361, [1991] Fam Law 306 .... 5.16
H (a minor) (parental responsibility order), Re [1996] 1 FLR 867, [1996] 3 FCR 49, [1996] Fam Law 402, (1996) Times, 28 February, CA 5.16
H (a minor) (blood tests: parental rights), Re [1997] Fam 89, [1996] 4 All ER 28, [1996] 3 WLR 506, [1996] 2 FLR 65, [1996] 3 FCR 201, [1996] Fam Law 461, [1996] NLJR 406, (1996) Times, 12 March 5.5, 5.75, 5.76

Table of Cases

H (parental responsibility), Re [1998] 1 FLR 855, [1998] Fam Law 325, sub nom RH (a minor) (parental responsibility), Re [1998] 2 FCR 89 .... 5.16
H (child abduction: rights of custody), Re [2000] 2 AC 291, [2000] 2 All ER 1, [2000] 2 WLR 337, [2000] 1 FCR 225, [2000] Fam Law 310, [2000] 1 FLR 374, [2000] 07 LS Gaz R 40, (2000) Times, 8 February, [2000] Lexis Citation 2541, [2000] All ER (D) 120, HL 5.41
H (a child) (adoption: disclosure), Re [2001] 1 FLR 646, [2001] 1 FCR 726, (2001) Times, 5 January, [2000] All ER (D) 2046 .... 5.8, 5.34
H (child abduction: unmarried father: rights of custody), Re [2003] EWHC 492 (Fam), [2003] 2 FLR 153 .... 5.40
H v C [2009] EWHC 1527 (Fam), [2009] 2 FLR 1540, [2009] Fam Law 802 .... 5.70
H v H [2007] EWHC 459 (Fam), [2007] 2 FLR 548, [2008] 2 FCR 714, [2007] Fam Law 578, 151 Sol Jo LB 503, [2007] All ER (D) 88 (Apr) 8.5
H v H [2016] Lexis Citation 596, [2016] All ER (D) 88 (Nov) 8.29
H v M (unreported) 5.60
H v M. See Hammond v Mitchell
H v P [1993] Fam Law 515, CC 5.62
H and A (children), Re [2002] EWCA Civ 383, [2002] 1 FLR 1145, [2002] 2 FCR 469, [2002] All ER (D) 331 (Mar) 5.3
Hale v Tanner [2000] 1 WLR 2377, [2000] 2 FLR 879, [2000] 3 FCR 62, [2000] Fam Law 876, (2000) Times, 22 August, [2000] Lexis Citation 14 .... 4.58, 4.86
Hall v Hall (1982) 3 FLR 379 .... 1.213
Hammersmith and Fulham London Borough Council v Monk [1992] 1 AC 478, [1992] 1 All ER 1, [1991] 3 WLR 1144, 90 LGR 38, 63 P & CR 373, [1992] 1 FLR 465, [1992] 2 FCR 129, [1992] Fam Law 292, 24 HLR 206, [1992] 1 EGLR 65, [1992] 3 LS Gaz R 32, [1992] 09 EG 135, (1991) Times, 6 December, 136 Sol Jo LB 10, HL 1.92, 1.101, 1.104, 1.106, 1.108, 1.147, 4.70
Hammerton v Hammerton [2007] EWCA Civ 248, [2007] 2 FLR 1133, [2007] 3 FCR 107, [2007] Fam Law 664, [2007] Fam Law 798, (2007) Times, 12 April, [2007] All ER (D) 393 (Mar) 4.57, 4.76
Hammond v Mitchell [1992] 2 All ER 109, [1991] 1 WLR 1127, sub nom H v M [1992] 1 FLR 229, [1991] FCR 938, [1991] Fam Law 473, (1991) Times, 2 May 1.36, 1.67, 1.132
Hancock, Re [1998] 2 FLR 346, [1999] 1 FCR 500, [1998] Fam Law 520 ...... 6.69, 6.71
Harmsworth v Harmsworth [1987] 3 All ER 816, [1987] 1 WLR 1676, [1988] 1 FLR 349, [1988] Fam Law 169, 131 Sol Jo 1625, [1988] 1 LS Gaz R 36 .... 4.86
Haroutunian v Jennings (1980) 1 FLR 62 .... 5.60
Harris v Harris [2001] EWCA Civ 1645, [2002] Fam 253, [2002] 1 All ER 185, [2002] 2 WLR 747, [2002] 1 FLR 248, [2001] 3 FCR 640, [2002] Fam Law 93, [2002] 02 LS Gaz R 27, (2001) Times, 19 November, 145 Sol Jo LB 270, [2001] All ER (D) 99 (Nov) 4.86
Harrogate Borough Council v Simpson [1986] 2 FLR 91, [1986] Fam Law 359, 17 HLR 205, [1985] RVR 10, CA 1.94
Harrow London Borough Council v Johnstone [1997] 1 All ER 929, [1997] 1 WLR 459, 95 LGR 470, [1997] 1 FLR 887, [1997] 2 FCR 225, [1997] Fam Law 478, 29 HLR 475, [1997] 15 LS Gaz R 26, [1997] NLJR 413, (1997) Times, 14 March, HL 1.106, 1.107
Henry v Henry [2010] UKPC 3, [2010] 1 All ER 988, 75 WIR 254, [2010] 4 LRC 643, [2010] 2 P & CR D17, [2010] All ER (D) 288 (Feb), PC 1.58
Herbert v Doyle [2010] EWCA Civ 1095, 13 ITELR 561, [2011] 1 EGLR 119, [2011] NLJR 990, [2015] WTLR 1573, [2010] All ER (D) 126 (Oct) 1.54
Herron v Diack and Newlands 1973 SLT (Sh Ct) 27 .... 6.114
Holland v IRC [2003] WTLR 207 10.6
Holland v IRC [2003] ST1 62 .... 3.9
Holliday v Musa [2012] EWCA Civ 1268, [2013] 1 FLR 806, [2013] Fam Law 26, [2012] All ER (D) 140 (Oct) 6.48
Holman v Howes [2007] EWCA Civ 877, 10 ITELR 492, [2008] 1 FLR 1217, [2007] Fam Law 987, [2007] BPIR 1085, [2007] All ER (D) 449 (Jul) 1.38
Holmes-Moorhouse v Richmond-upon-Thames London Borough Council [2009] UKHL 7, [2009] 3 All ER 277, [2009] 1 WLR 413, [2009] LGR 730, [2009] PTSR 698, [2009] 1 FLR 904, [2009] 2 FCR 277, [2009] Fam Law 391, (2009) Times, 5 February, 153 Sol Jo (no 5) 28, [2009] All ER (D) 36 (Feb), HL 1.128

Table of Cases

Hopkins v Hopkins [2015] EWHC 812 .... 8.28, 8.35
Horner v Horner (1983) 4 FLR 50 .... 4.6
Horrocks v Forray [1976] 1 All ER 737, [1976] 1 WLR 230, 6 Fam Law 15, 119 Sol Jo 866 .... 10.1, 10.4
Horton v Owen [1943] KB 111, [1943] 1 All ER 159, 41 LGR 38, 107 JP 1, 112 LJKB 316, 87 Sol Jo 31, 168 LT 47, 59 TLR 36, DC 6.153
Human Fertilisation and Embryology Act 2008 (Cases A, B, C, D, E, F, G and H), Re [2015] EWHC 2602 (Fam), [2016] 1 All ER 273, [2016] 1 WLR 1325, [2017] 1 FLR 366, [2015] 3 FCR 555, [2015] Fam Law 1333, 146 BMLR 123, [2015] All ER (D) 57 (Sep) 5.7
Human Fertilisation and Embryology Act 2008 (Cases P, Q, R, S, T, U, W and X) [2017] EWHC 49 (Fam), [2017] All ER (D) 81 (Jan) 5.7
Humberside County Council v B [1993] 1 FLR 257, [1993] 1 FCR 613, [1993] Fam Law 61 .... 4.22
Hunter v Canary Wharf Ltd [1997] AC 655, [1997] 2 All ER 426, [1997] 2 WLR 684, [1997] 3 LRC 424, [1997] 2 FLR 342, [1997] Fam Law 601, 30 HLR 409, 54 ConLR 12, [1997] 19 LS Gaz R 25, [1997] NLJR 634, 84 BLR 1, (1997) Times, 25 April, 141 Sol Jo LB 108, HL 4.65
Huntingdon Life Sciences v Stop Huntingdon Animal [2003] EWHC 810 .... 4.75
Huntingford v Hobbs [1993] 1 FLR 736, [1993] 1 FCR 45, [1992] Fam Law 437, 24 HLR 652, [1992] NPC 39, [1992] EGCS 38, CA 1.30
Hussain v Hussain [1986] Fam 134, [1986] 1 All ER 961, [1986] 2 WLR 801, [1986] 2 FLR 271, [1986] Fam Law 269, 130 Sol Jo 341, [1986] NLJ Rep 358 .... 4.75, 4.86
Hyman v Hyman [1929] AC 601, 27 LGR 379, 93 JP 209, 98 LJP 81, [1929] All ER Rep 245, 73 Sol Jo 317, 141 LT 329, 45 TLR 444, HL 8.9

I

Ilott v Mitson [2011] EWCA Civ 346, [2012] 2 FLR 170, [2011] 2 FCR 1, [2011] Fam Law 798, 155 Sol Jo (no 14) 30, [2011] All ER (D) 37 (Apr) 6.70
Ilott v Mitson [2014] EWHC 542 (Fam), [2015] 1 FLR 291, [2014] Fam Law 789, [2014] WTLR 575, [2014] All ER (D) 189 (Mar); revsd [2015] EWCA Civ 797, [2016] 1 All ER 932, [2015] 2 FLR 1409, [2015] 2 FCR 547, [2015] Fam Law 1196, [2015] WTLR 1399, [2015] All ER (D) 290 (Jul); revsd sub nom Re Jackson (dec'd); Ilott v Mitson [2017] UKSC 17, [2018] AC 545, [2017] 4 All ER 545, [2017] 2 WLR 979, [2017] 4 LRC 153, 19 ITELR 1021, [2017] 1 FLR 1717, 167 NLJ 7739, [2017] WTLR 533, [2017] All ER (D) 96 (Mar), SC 6.13, 6.28, 6.29, 6.70
IRC v Arkwright [2004] EWHC 1720 (Ch), [2005] 1 WLR 1411, [2004] STC 1323, 76 TC 788, [2004] 31 LS Gaz R 26, [2005] RVR 266, (2004) Times, 4 August, [2004] All ER (D) 285 (Jul) 6.125
IRC v Holmden [1968] AC 685, [1968] 1 All ER 148, [1968] 2 WLR 300, 46 ATC 337, [1967] TR 323, 112 Sol Jo 31, HL 1.6, 1.224
Ipekçi v McConnell [2019] EWFC 19, [2019] 2 FLR 667, [2019] Fam Law 743, 169 NLJ 7837, [2019] All ER (D) 51 (Apr) 8.31, 8.39, 8.42
Ivin v Blake (1993) 67 P & CR 263, [1995] 1 FLR 70, [1994] 2 FCR 504, [1995] Fam Law 72, CA 1.36

J

J, Re [1995] 1 FLR 660, [1995] Fam Law 300 .... 9.41
J (abduction: rights of custody), Re [1999] 2 FLR 653, [1999] 3 FCR 577, [1999] Fam Law 611 .... 5.41
J (children) (contact orders: procedure), Re [2018] EWCA Civ 115, [2018] 2 FLR 998, [2018] Fam Law 530, [2018] All ER (D) 32 (Feb) 5.16
J v C (child: financial provision) [1999] 1 FLR 152, [1998] 3 FCR 79, [1999] Fam Law 78 .... 5.59, 5.61, 5.62
J v C [2006] EWHC 2837 (Fam), [2007] 1 FLR 1064, [2007] 1 FCR 365, [2006] All ER (D) 147 (Nov) 5.5
J v J [2009] EWHC 2654 (Fam), [2010] Fam Law 329 .... 8.4
J v J [2014] EWHC 3654 (Fam), [2016] 1 FCR 31, [2015] Fam Law 372, [2015] 1 Costs LO 31, [2014] All ER (D) 153 (Nov) 8.6, 8.7

J v V (disclosure: offshore corporations) [2003] EWHC 3110 (Fam), [2004] 1 FLR 1042, [2004] Fam Law 398 .... 8.13
J A Pye (Oxford) Ltd v United Kingdom (Application 44302/02) (2007) 46 EHRR 1083, [2008] 1 EGLR 111, [2007] RVR 302, (2007) Times, 1 October, 23 BHRC 405, [2007] ECHR 44302/02, [2007] All ER (D) 177 (Aug), EctHR 8.33
JB v KS [2015] EWHC 180 (Fam), [2015] 2 FLR 1180, [2015] Fam Law 376, [2015] All ER (D) 247 (Jan) 5.16
JH v HMRC (TC) [2015] UKUT 0397 (AAC) 9.25
JL v SL [2014] EWHC 3658 .... 8.4
JP v Secretary of State for Work and Pensions (IS) [2014] UKUT 0017 (AAC) .. 9.24, 9.93, 9.102
J-S (a child) (contact and parental responsibility), Re [2002] EWCA Civ 1028, [2003] 1 FLR 399, [2002] 3 FCR 433, [2003] Fam Law 81, [2002] All ER (D) 89 (Jul) 5.16
Jackson v Secretary of State for Work and Pensions [2020] EWHC 183 (Admin), [2020] 1 WLR 1441, [2020] All ER (D) 37 (Feb) 7.6, 9.2
Jackson (dec'd); Ilott v Mitson. See Ilott v Mitson
James v Thomas [2007] EWCA Civ 1212, [2008] 1 FLR 1598, [2007] 3 FCR 696, [2008] Fam Law 99, [2008] Fam Law 519, [2007] All ER (D) 373 (Nov) 1.37
Jelley v Iliffe [1981] Fam 128, [1981] 2 All ER 29, [1981] 2 WLR 801, 125 Sol Jo 355 .... 6.38, 6.39, 6.50, 6.51, 6.56, 9.29
Jennings, Re [1994] Ch 286, [1994] 3 All ER 27, [1994] 3 WLR 67, [1995] 1 FCR 257, sub nom Jennings, Re, Harlow v National Westminster Bank plc [1994] 1 FLR 536, [1994] Fam Law 439 .... 6.28, 6.32, 6.63, 6.69
Jennings v Rice [2002] EWCA Civ 159, [2003] 1 P & CR 100, [2003] 1 FCR 501, [2002] 1 FCR 501, [2002] NPC 28, [2002] WTLR 367, [2002] All ER (D) 324 (Feb) 1.58
Jessop v Jessop [1992] 1 FLR 591, [1992] 1 FCR 253, [1992] Fam Law 328, (1991) Times, 16 October, CA 6.41
Johnson v Walton [1990] 1 FLR 350, [1990] FCR 568, [1990] Fam Law 260, (1990) Times, 2 January, CA 4.6
Jones v Hipgrave [2004] EWHC 2901 (QB), [2005] 2 FLR 174, (2005) Times, 11 January, [2004] All ER (D) 217 (Dec) 4.75
Jones v Jones [2012] Fam 1, [2011] 3 WLR 582, [2011] 1 FLR 1723, [2011] 1 FCR 242, [2011] Fam Law 455, [2011] NLJR 210, (2011) Times, 28 March, [2011] EWCA Civ 41, [2011] All ER (D) 231 (Jan) 8.4
Jones v Kernott [2011] UKSC 53, [2012] 1 AC 776, [2012] 1 All ER 1265, [2011] 3 WLR 1121, 14 ITELR 491, [2012] 1 FLR 45, [2011] 3 FCR 495, [2011] Fam Law 1338, [2012] HLR 188, (2011) Times, 10 November, [2011] BPIR 1653, [2012] 1 P & CR D22, [2011] All ER (D) 64 (Nov), SC ... 1.28, 1.33, 1.40, 1.41, 1.43, 1.50, 1.51, 1.52, 10.6
Jones v Padavatton [1969] 2 All ER 616, [1969] 1 WLR 328, 112 Sol Jo 965 ... 2.5, 2.100
Jones v Roberts [1995] 2 FLR 422, [1995] Fam Law 673 .... 6.36
Joslin, Re, Joslin v Murch [1941] Ch 200, [1941] 1 All ER 302, 110 LJ Ch 65, 85 Sol Jo 105, 165 LT 171, 57 TLR 293 .... 6.33
Joyce v Barker Bros (1980) The Times, February 26 .... 1.160

K

K (specific issue order), Re [1999] 2 FLR 280, [1999] Fam Law 455 .... 5.5
K (children) (rights of custody: Spain), Re [2009] EWHC 1066 (Fam), [2010] 1 FLR 57, [2009] Fam Law 1017, [2009] All ER (D) 179 (May); affd sub nom Kennedy v Kennedy [2009] EWCA Civ 986, [2010] 1 FLR 782, [2009] Fam Law 1124, [2009] All ER (D) 06 (Nov) 5.39
K (a child) (Northern Ireland), Re [2014] UKSC 29, [2014] AC 1401, [2014] NI 315, [2014] 3 All ER 149, [2014] 2 WLR 1304, [2014] 2 FLR 629, [2014] 2 FCR 231, [2014] Fam Law 943, [2014] All ER (D) 127 (May), SC 5.39
K v JMP Co Ltd [1976] QB 85, [1975] 1 All ER 1030, [1975] 2 WLR 457, 5 Fam Law 83, 119 Sol Jo 188 .... 6.89
K v K [1992] 2 All ER 727, [1992] 1 WLR 530, [1992] 2 FLR 220, [1992] 2 FCR 253, [1992] Fam Law 336, 25 HLR 229, [1992] 16 LS Gaz R 31, (1992) Times, 21 February, 136 Sol Jo LB 69 .... 1.126, 5.62
K v K (Ancillary Relief: Pre-nuptial Agreement) [2003] 1 FLR 120 .... 8.12

Table of Cases

K v L [2011] 550 Civ 8.4
KA v MA (prenuptial agreement: needs) [2018] EWHC 499 (Fam), [2018] 2 FLR 1285, [2018] Fam Law 800, [2018] WTLR 125, [2018] All ER (D) 92 (Apr) 8.29, 8.30
KJ v SSWP (IS) [2019] UKUT 312 (AAC) 9.19
Kaur v Dhaliwal [2014] EWHC 1991 (Ch), [2015] 2 FCR 40, [2014] Fam Law 1241, [2014] WTLR 1381, [2014] All ER (D) 164 (Jun) 6.39, 6.52
Kennedy v Kennedy. See K (children) (rights of custody: Spain), Re
Kerai v Patel [2008] EWCA Civ 600, [2008] 2 FLR 2137, [2008] Fam Law 724, [2008] All ER (D) 421 (Apr) 4.86
Kerr v Department for Social Development [2004] UKHL 23, [2004] NI 397, [2004] 4 All ER 385, [2004] 1 WLR 1372, (2004) Times, 13 May, [2004] All ER (D) 65 (May), HL 9.110
Khorasandjian v Bush [1993] QB 727, [1993] 3 All ER 669, [1993] 3 WLR 476, [1993] 2 FLR 66, [1993] 2 FCR 257, [1993] Fam Law 679, 25 HLR 392, [1993] 15 LS Gaz R 40, [1993] NLJR 329, (1993) Times, 18 February, 137 Sol Jo LB 88 .... 4.65, 4.72
Kimber v Kimber [2000] 1 FLR 383 .... 6.41, 9.19
Kinch v Bullard [1998] 4 All ER 650, [1999] 1 WLR 423, 77 P & CR D1, [1999] 1 FLR 66, [1998] Fam Law 738, [1998] 3 EGLR 112, [1998] 47 EG 140, [1998] EGCS 126, (1998) Times, 16 September, [1998] All ER (D) 378 .... 1.21
King v The Chiltern Dog Rescue [2015] EWCA Civ 581, [2016] Ch 221, [2016] 2 WLR 1, [2015] WTLR 1225, [2016] 1 P & CR D9, [2015] All ER (D) 105 (Jun) 6.8
Kotke v Saffarini [2005] EWCA Civ 221, [2005] 2 FLR 517, [2005] 1 FCR 642, [2005] Fam Law 535, [2005] NLJR 414, [2005] All ER (D) 145 (Mar) 6.42, 6.89
Kourkgy v Lushe (1983) 4 FLR 65 .... 6.38, 6.39, 6.52
Kremen v Agrest (financial remedy: non-disclosure: post-nuptial agreement) [2012] EWHC 45 (Fam), [2012] 2 FLR 414, [2012] 2 FCR 472, [2012] Fam Law 519, [2012] All ER (D) 146 (Jan); sub nom Kremen v Agrest (Cheshnokov intervening) [2013] EWCA Civ 41, [2013] 2 FLR 187, [2013] 2 FCR 181, [2013] BPIR 497, [2013] All ER (D) 39 (Feb) 8.7, 8.23, 8.27, 8.28, 8.41, 8.44

L

L v C [2007] 3 HKLRD 819 .... 8.26
L v M [2014] EWHC 2220 (Fam), [2014] All ER (D) 100 (Nov) 8.28
Laskar v Laskar [2008] EWCA Civ 347, [2008] 1 WLR 2695, [2008] 2 P & CR 245, [2008] 2 FLR 589, [2008] Fam Law 638, [2008] 2 EGLR 70, [2008] 07 EG 142 (CS), [2008] All ER (D) 104 (Feb) 1.28, 1.29, 1.49
Lau v DPP [2000] 1 FLR 799, (2000) Times, 29 March, [2000] Lexis Citation 2731, [2000] All ER (D) 224, DC 4.61
Layton v Martin [1986] 2 FLR 227, [1986] Fam Law 212, [1985] Lexis Citation 291 .... 6.39, 6.52
Leach, Re, Leach v Lindeman [1986] Ch 226, [1985] 2 All ER 754, [1985] 3 WLR 413, [1985] FLR 1120, [1985] Fam Law 319, 129 Sol Jo 318 .... 6.61
Leake (formerly Bruzzi) v Bruzzi [1974] 2 All ER 1196, [1974] 1 WLR 1528, 118 Sol Jo 831 .... 1.204
Leeds Building Society v York (Personal Representative of the Estate of Norton Brian York) See Graham-York v York (Personal Representative of the Estate of Norton Brian York)
Le Foe v Le Foe and Woolwich plc, Woolwich plc v Le Foe and Le Foe [2001] 2 FLR 970, [2002] 1 FCR 107, [2001] Fam Law 739, [2001] All ER (D) 325 (Jun) 1.35
Lewis v Lewis and Metropolitan Properties Co Ltd [1984] Fam 79, [1984] 2 All ER 497, [1984] 3 WLR 45, [1984] FLR 492, [1984] Fam Law 185, 16 HLR 90, 128 Sol Jo 299, [1984] LS Gaz R 1205; affd sub nom Lewis v Lewis [1985] AC 828, [1985] 2 All ER 449, [1985] 2 WLR 962, 50 P & CR 231, [1985] FLR 994, [1985] Fam Law 328, 17 HLR 459, 129 Sol Jo 349, [1985] LS Gaz R 2167, HL 1.108
Lewis (as Executrix of the Estate of Blackwell (dec'd)) v Warner [2016] EWHC 1787 (Ch), [2017] Ch 13, [2016] 3 WLR 1545, [2017] 2 FLR 133, [2016] Fam Law 1322, [2016] Fam Law 1091, [2016] WTLR 1399, [2016] All ER (D) 104 (Jul) 6.28
Liden v Burton [2016] EWCA Civ 275, [2017] 1 FLR 310, [2016] Fam Law 687 ..... 1.59
Lindop v Agus [2009] EWHC 14 (Ch), [2009] EWHC 1795 (Ch), [2010] 1 FLR 631, [2009] Fam Law 808 .... 6.41
Lissimore v Downing [2003] 2 FLR 308 .... 1.55

Lloyd v Sadler [1978] QB 774, [1978] 2 All ER 529, [1978] 2 WLR 721, 35 P & CR 78, 122 Sol Jo 111, [1978] 1 EGLR 76, 245 Estates Gazette 479 .... 1.96
Lloyds Bank Ltd, Re, Bomze and Lederman v Bomze [1931] 1 Ch 289, 100 LJ Ch 45, [1930] All ER Rep 479, 144 LT 276, 47 TLR 38 .... 2.8
Lloyds Bank Ltd v Bundy [1975] QB 326, [1974] 3 All ER 757, [1974] 3 WLR 501, [1974] 2 Lloyd's Rep 366, 9 LDAB 365, 118 Sol Jo 714 .... 2.103
Lloyds Bank plc v Rosset [1991] 1 AC 107, [1990] 1 All ER 1111, [1990] 2 WLR 867, 60 P & CR 311, [1990] 2 FLR 155, [1990] Fam Law 395, 22 HLR 349, [1990] 16 LS Gaz R 41, [1990] NLJR 478, (1990) Times, 30 March, HL .. 1.28, 1.33, 1.34, 1.36, 1.52, 1.81, 1.140, 1.198
Lomas v Parle [2003] EWCA Civ 1804, [2004] 1 All ER 1173, [2004] 1 WLR 1642, [2004] 1 FLR 812, [2004] 1 FCR 97, (2004) Times, 13 January, [2003] All ER (D) 328 (Dec) 4.58, 4.68, 4.69, 4.75, 4.86
Longley (Dec'd), Longley and Longley v Longley [1981] CLY 2885 .... 6.24
Lowson v Coombes. See Douglas Lowson v Rebecca Coombes (Lowson v Coombes)
Luckwell v Limata [2014] EWHC 502 (Fam), [2014] 2 FLR 168, [2014] Fam Law 792 .... 8.19, 8.27, 8.30, 8.35
Lynch, Re, Lynch v Lynch [1943] 1 All ER 168, 87 Sol Jo 48, 168 LT 189, 59 TLR 130 .... 6.3, 6.4

M

M (Child Support Act: parentage), Re [1997] 2 FLR 90, [1997] 3 FCR 383, [1997] Fam Law 536 .... 5.7
M (A Child) (parental reponsibility: father's application for parental responsibility), Re [2013] EWCA Civ 969, [2014] 1 FLR 339, [2014] 2 FCR 46, [2013] Fam Law 1256, [2013] All ER (D) 12 (Aug) 5.16
M v F [2013] EWHC 1901 (Fam), [2014] 1 FLR 352, [2014] 1 FCR 456, [2013] All ER (D) 218 (Aug) 5.14
M v M (PRENUPTIAL AGREEMENT) [2002] 1 FLR 654 .... 8.11, 8.34, 8.42
M v W (non-molestation order: duration) [2000] 1 FLR 107, [2000] Fam Law 13 .... 4.13
MB v EB [2019] EWHC 1649 (Fam); [2019] EWHC 3676 (Fam) 8.31
MT v OT [2018] EWHC 868 (Fam), [2019] 1 FLR 93, [2018] Fam Law 1113, [2018] All ER (D) 136 (Apr) 5.61, 5.64
M-T v T [2006] EWHC 2494 (Fam), [2007] 2 FLR 925, [2007] Fam Law 1066 ...... 5.60
McCartney v McCartney [2008] EWHC 401 .... 8.35
McFarlane v McFarlane [1972] NI 59, CA 1.36
McFarlane v McFarlane [2006] UKHL 24, [2006] 2 AC 618, [2006] 3 All ER 1, [2006] 2 WLR 1283, [2006] 1 FLR 1186, [2006] 2 FCR 213, [2006] Fam Law 629, [2006] NLJR 916, (2006) Times, 25 May, 150 Sol Jo LB 704, [2006] All ER (D) 343 (May), HL 8.4, 8.6, 8.17, 8.43, 8.60
McHardy and Sons (a firm) v Warren [1994] 2 FLR 338, [1994] 2 FCR 1247, [1994] Fam Law 567, (1994) Times, 8 April, CA 1.35, 1.38
McIntosh v McIntosh [1990] FCR 351, (1989) Times, 12 May, [1989] Lexis Citation 2376, CA 4.58
McLaughlin's Application for Judicial Review (Northern Ireland) [2018] UKSC 48, [2019] NI 66, [2019] 1 All ER 471, [2018] 1 WLR 4250, 46 BHRC 268, [2018] All ER (D) 144 (Aug), SC 7.5, 9.2
MacLeod v MacLeod [2008] UKPC 64, [2010] 1 AC 298, [2009] 1 All ER 851, [2009] 3 WLR 437, [2009] 2 LRC 748, 11 ITELR 819, [2009] 1 FLR 641, [2009] 1 FCR 523, [2009] Fam Law 178, (2008) Times, 29 December, [2009] All ER (D) 32 (Jan), PC 8.6, 8.10, 8.14, 8.16, 8.60
Malone v Harrison [1979] 1 WLR 1353, 123 Sol Jo 804 .... 6.40, 6.56
Marr v Collie (Bahamas) [2017] UKPC 17, [2018] AC 631, [2017] 3 WLR 1507, [2017] 4 LRC 404, [2018] 1 P & CR 73, 20 ITELR 602, [2017] 2 FLR 674, [2017] Fam Law 827, PC 1.26, 1.28, 1.29, 1.32
Martin v Martin [1978] Fam 12, [1977] 3 All ER 762, [1977] 3 WLR 101, 121 Sol Jo 335 .... 1.164
Mendoza v Ghaidan [2004] UKHL 30, [2004] 2 AC 557, [2004] 2 FLR 600 .... 1.99
Mesher v Mesher [1980] 1 All ER 126 .... 1.164

Table of Cases

Midland Bank plc v Cooke [1995] 4 All ER 562, [1995] 2 FLR 915, [1996] 1 FCR 442, [1995] Fam Law 675, 27 HLR 733, [1995] 30 LS Gaz R 34, [1995] NLJR 1543, (1995) Times, 13 July, 139 Sol Jo LB 194 .... 1.35, 1.38, 1.46
Midland Bank plc v Pike [1988] 2 All ER 434 .... 1.146
Miller v Miller [2006] UKHL 24, [2006] 2 AC 618, [2006] 3 All ER 1, [2006] 2 WLR 1283, [2006] 1 FLR 1186, [2006] 2 FCR 213, [2006] Fam Law 629, [2006] NLJR 916, (2006) Times, 25 May, 150 Sol Jo LB 704, [2006] All ER (D) 343 (May), HL 8.4, 8.6, 8.17, 8.43, 8.60
Moore v Moore [2007] EWCA Civ 361, [2007] 2 FLR 339, [2007] 2 FCR 353, [2007] Fam Law 698, (2007) Times, 25 April, 151 Sol Jo LB 573, [2007] All ER (D) 158 (Apr) 8.6, 8.7
Morgan v Hill [2006] EWCA Civ 1602, [2007] 1 WLR 855, [2007] 1 FLR 1480, [2006] 3 FCR 620, (2006) Times, 8 December, [2006] All ER (D) 386 (Nov) 5.60
Mortgage Corp Ltd v Shaire, Mortgage Corp Ltd v Lewis Silkin (a firm) [2001] Ch 743, [2001] 4 All ER 364, [2001] 3 WLR 639, 80 P & CR 280, [2000] 1 FLR 973, [2000] 2 FCR 222, [2000] Fam Law 402, [2000] 3 EGLR 131, [2000] 11 LS Gaz R 37, [2000] EGCS 35, (2000) Times, 21 March, [2000] Lexis Citation 2740, [2000] BPIR 483, [2000] All ER (D) 254 .... 1.70, 1.146
Mouncer v Mouncer [1972] 1 All ER 289, [1972] 1 WLR 321, 116 Sol Jo 78 .... 6.41
Murphy v Gooch [2007] EWCA Civ 603, 10 ITELR 300, [2007] 2 FLR 934, [2007] 3 FCR 96, [2007] Fam Law 905, 151 Sol Jo LB 896, [2007] BPIR 1123, [2007] 2 P & CR D46, [2007] All ER (D) 350 (Jun) 1.60

N

N (a child) (payments for benefit of child), Re [2009] EWHC 11 (Fam), [2009] 1 WLR 1621, [2009] 1 FLR 1442, [2009] 1 FCR 606, [2009] Fam Law 389, [2009] All ER (D) 142 (Jan) 5.62
N v F (Financial Orders: Pre-Acquired Wealth) [2011] EWHC 586 (Fam), [2011] 2 FLR 533, [2012] 1 FCR 139, [2011] Fam Law 686, [2011] All ER (D) 96 (Apr) 8.4
N v N (divorce: ante-nuptial agreement) [1999] 2 FLR 745, [1999] 2 FCR 583, [1999] Fam Law 691, [1999] 31 LS Gaz R 39, [1999] NLJR 1074, (1999) Times, 12 July, [1999] Lexis Citation 2797, [1999] All ER (D) 732 .... 8.6, 8.10
N v N (foreign divorce: financial relief) [1997] 1 FLR 900, sub nom N v N (overseas divorce: financial relief) [1997] 1 FCR 573, [1997] Fam Law 396 .... 8.10
NA v MA. See A v A
NA v Secretary of State for Work and Pensions (IS) [2012] UKUT 299 (AAC) .. 9.66, 9.76, 9.96
NG v KR (pre-nuptial contract) [2008] EWHC 1532 (Fam), [2009] 1 FLR 1478, [2009] 1 FCR 35, [2008] Fam Law 1082; revsd sub nom Radmacher (formerly Granatino) v Granatino; sub nom NG v KR (prenuptial contract) [2009] EWCA Civ 649, [2009] 2 FLR 1181, [2009] 2 FCR 645, [2009] Fam Law 789, [2009] NLJR 996, (2009) Times, 13 July, 153 Sol Jo (no 27) 29, [2009] All ER (D) 31 (Jul); affd sub nom Radmacher (formerly Granatino) v Granatino (pre-nuptial contract) [2010] UKSC 42, [2011] 1 AC 534, [2011] 1 All ER 373, [2010] 3 WLR 1367, [2011] 2 LRC 660, [2010] 2 FLR 1900, [2010] 3 FCR 583, [2010] Fam Law 1263, [2010] 42 LS Gaz R 18, [2010] NLJR 1491, (2010) Times, 22 October, 154 Sol Jo (no 40) 37, [2010] ER (D) 186 (Oct), SC . 8.1, 8.4, 8.5, 8.6, 8.7, 8.8, 8.9, 8.10, 8.12, 8.13, 8.14, 8.15, 8.19, 8.20, 8.21, 8.22, 8.23, 8.24, 8.25, 8.26, 8.27, 8.28, 8.29, 8.30, 8.32, 8.33, 8.34, 8.35, 8.36, 8.37, 8.38, 8.39, 8.40, 8.41, 8.42, 8.43, 8.44, 8.46, 8.49, 8.56, 8.60, 8.61
NI v HMRC [2015] UKIT 160 (AAC 9.118
NM v SM [2017] EWHC 1294 (Fam) 5.39
Nahajec v Fowle [2017] EW Misc 11 CC 6.70
Negus v Bahouse [2007] EWHC 2628 (Ch), [2008] 1 FLR 381, [2008] 1 FCR 768, [2008] Fam Law 208, [2007] Fam Law 1132, [2007] All ER (D) 353 (Oct) 6.28
Neil v Ryan [1998] 2 FLR 1068, [1999] 1 FCR 241, [1998] Fam Law 728, (1998) Times, 1 September 4.58
Newlon Housing Trust v Alsulaimen [1999] AC 313, [1998] 4 All ER 1, [1998] 3 WLR 451, [1998] 2 FLR 690, [1998] 3 FCR 183, [1998] Fam Law 589, 30 HLR 1132, [1998] NLJR 1303, (1998) Times, 20 August, 142 Sol Jo LB 247, [1998] All ER (D) 383, HL 1.106, 1.107
Nguyen v Phung [1984] FLR 773, [1985] Fam Law 54, CA 4.86

Nicholls v Nicholls [1997] 2 All ER 97, [1997] 1 WLR 314, [1997] 1 FLR 649, [1997] 3 FCR 14, [1997] Fam Law 321, [1996] NLJR 61, (1997) Times, 21 January 4.76
Nutting v Southern Housing Group Ltd [2005] HLR 25 .... 9.24
Nwogbe v Nwogbe [2000] 2 FLR 744, [2000] 3 FCR 345, (2000) Times, 11 July, [2000] Lexis Citation 3335 .... 4.24

O

O (a minor) (abduction: custody rights), Re [1997] 2 FLR 702, [1997] 2 FCR 465, sub nom O (a minor) (child abduction: custody rights), Re [1997] 25 LS Gaz R 34, (1997) Times, 24 June 5.39
O (a child) (blood tests: constraint), Re [2000] Fam 139, [2000] 2 All ER 29, [2000] 2 WLR 1284, [2000] 1 FLR 418, [2000] 1 FCR 330, [2000] Fam Law 324, 55 BMLR 229, [2000] 06 LS Gaz R 35, 144 Sol Jo LB 85 .... 5.5
O'Kelly v Davies [2014] EWCA Civ 1606, [2015] 1 WLR 2725, [2015] 1 P & CR 340, [2015] 2 FLR 1311, [2015] Fam Law 383, [2016] WTLR 333, [2014] All ER (D) 128 (Dec) 1.43
Outram v Hyde (1875) 24 WR 268 .... 1.202
Oxley v Hiscock [2004] EWCA Civ 546, [2005] Fam 211, [2004] 3 All ER 703, [2004] 3 WLR 715, [2004] 2 P & CR D35, 6 ITELR 1091, [2004] 2 FLR 669, [2004] 2 FCR 295, [2004] Fam Law 569, [2004] 21 LS Gaz R 35, [2004] 20 EG 166 (CS), (2004) Times, 14 July, 148 Sol Jo LB 571, [2004] All ER (D) 48 (May) 1.28, 1.30, 1.33, 1.46, 1.50, 1.51, 1.52, 1.53, 1.140

P

P (a minor) (parental responsibility order), Re [1994] 1 FLR 578, [1994] Fam Law 378 .... 5.14
P (terminating parental responsibility), Re [1995] 1 FLR 1048, [1995] 3 FCR 753, [1995] Fam Law 471 .... 5.18
P (parental responsibility: change of name), Re [1997] 2 FLR 722, [1997] 3 FCR 739, [1997] Fam Law 723, CA 5.24
P (parental responsibility), Re [1998] 2 FLR 96, [1998] 3 FCR 98, [1998] Fam Law 461 .... 5.16
P (a child) (financial provision), Re [2003] EWCA Civ 837, [2003] 2 FLR 865, [2003] 2 FCR 481, [2003] Fam Law 717, [2003] 33 LS Gaz R 27, (2003) Times, 24 July, [2003] All ER (D) 312 (Jun) 5.52, 5.59, 5.60, 5.61, 5.70
P (a child)(abduction: custody rights), Re [2004] EWCA Civ 971, [2005] Fam 293, [2005] 2 WLR 201, [2004] 2 FLR 1057, [2004] 2 FCR 698, [2004] 35 LS Gaz R 33, (2004) Times, 19 August, [2004] All ER (D) 520 (Jul) 5.41
P v P (inherited property) [2004] EWHC 1364 (Fam), [2005] 1 FLR 576, [2006] 2 FCR 579, sub nom V, Re (financial relief: family farm) [2005] Fam Law 101 .... 8.4
PG v TW (No 1) (child: financial provision: legal funding) [2012] EWHC 1892 (Fam), [2014] 1 FLR 508 .... 5.60
PG v TW (No 2) (Child: Financial Provision) [2014] 1 FLR 923 .... 5.60
PK v Mr K [2015] EWHC 2316 (Fam), [2016] 2 FLR 576, [2015] Fam Law 1316, 165 NLJ 7666, [2015] All ER (D) 67 (Aug) 5.36
PP v Basildon District Council (HB) [2013] UKUT 0505 (AAC) 4.59, 9.24, 9.122
Pankhania v Chandegra (by her litigation friend, Ronald Andrew Eagle) [2012] EWCA Civ 1438, [2013] 1 P & CR 238, [2013] 3 FCR 16, [2012] PLSCS 241, [2013] 1 P & CR D11, [2012] All ER (D) 132 (Nov) 1.18
Parnall (Dec'd), Re [2003] All ER (D) 40 .... 10.6
Parrott v Parkin, The Up Yaws [2007] EWHC 210 (Admlty), [2007] 1 Lloyd's Rep 719, [2007] 3 FCR 515, [2007] Fam Law 597, [2007] 2 FLR 444, [2007] All ER (D) 145 (Feb) 1.133
Parrott, Re, Cox v Parrott [1946] Ch 183, [1946] 1 All ER 321, 115 LJ Ch 211, 90 Sol Jo 139, 175 LT 190, 62 TLR 189 .... 5.21
Pascoe v Turner [1979] 2 All ER 945, [1979] 1 WLR 431, 123 Sol Jo 164 .... 1.5, 1.54
Passee v Passee [1988] 1 FLR 263, [1988] Fam Law 132, (1987) Times, 8 August, CA 1.13
Paul v Constance [1977] 1 All ER 195, [1977] 1 WLR 527, 7 Fam Law 18, 121 Sol Jo 320 .... 1.134

Table of Cases

Pauling (No 1), Re [1965] Ch 303 .... 6.149
Perkins v Borden re Woolnough deceased [2002] WRLT 595 .... 1.21
Pettitt v Pettitt [1970] AC 777, [1969] 2 All ER 385, [1969] 2 WLR 966, 20 P & CR
    991, 113 Sol Jo 344, 211 Estates Gazette 829, HL .. 1.6, 1.9, 1.11, 1.13, 1.33, 1.81, 1.140
Phillips v Pearce [1996] 2 FLR 230, [1996] 2 FCR 237, [1996] Fam Law 603 ... 5.61, 5.62
Pickering v Ilfracombe Rly Co (1868) LR 3 CP 235, 37 LJCP 118, 16 WR 458,
    [1861–73] All ER Rep 773, 17 LT 650 .... 2.119
Pidduck v Molloy [1992] 2 FLR 202, [1992] 1 FCR 418, [1992] Fam Law 529, (1992)
    Times, 9 March, CA 4.86
Pitt v Pitt (1823) Turn & R 180, 37 ER 1065, Ct of Ch 1.202
Pounder v London Underground [1995] PIQR 217 .... 6.41, 6.89
Pounds v Pounds [1994] 4 All ER 777, [1994] 1 WLR 1535, [1994] 1 FLR 775, [1994]
    2 FCR 1055, [1994] Fam Law 436, [1994] NLJR 459, (1994) Times, 17 March 8.33
Power, Re, Public Trustee v Hastings [1947] Ch 572, [1947] 2 All ER 282, 111 JP 245,
    91 Sol Jo 409, 177 LT 245 .... 6.146
Practice Direction (Minor: Change Of Surname) [1977] 1 WLR 1065 .... 5.22, 10.1
Practice Direction (Probate: Minors' Grants) [1991] 1 WLR 1069 .... 6.26
Practice Direction (Minor: Change of surname: Deed pole) [1995] 1 All ER 832, [1995]
    1 FLR 458 .... 5.22
Practice Direction Administration of estates [1975] 3 All ER 403 .... 6.26
Practice Note – The Central Authority for England and Wales, Child Abduction and
    Custody Act 1985 – Hague Convention on the Civil Aspects of International Child
    Abduction; Applications for return orders by unmarried fathers [1998] 1 FLR 491,
    [1998] 1 FCR 253 .... 5.39
President's Guidance (Adoption: The New Law And Procedure) [2006] 1 Flr 1234
    .... 5.27

Q

Q v Q. See S v R; R v M
Quigley v Masterson [2011] EWHC 2529 (Ch), [2012] 1 All ER 1224, [2012] 1 FCR
    541, [2011] 3 EGLR 81, [2011] 49 Estates Gazette 100, [2012] 1 P & CR D19,
    [2011] All ER (D) 71 (Oct) 1.21

R

R (blood tests: constraint), Re [1998] Fam 66, [1998] 2 WLR 796, [1998] 1 FLR 745,
    [1998] 1 FCR 41, [1998] Fam Law 256 .... 5.5
R (Surname: Using Both Parents'), Re [2001] EWCA Civ 1344, [2001] 2 FLR 1358,
    [2002] 1 FCR 170, [2002] Fam Law 9, [2001] All ER (D) 241 (Oct) 5.24
R v Boness [2005] EWCA Crim 2395, [2006] 1 Cr App Rep (S) 690, 169 JP 621, [2006]
    Crim LR 160, (2005) Times, 24 October, [2005] All ER (D) 153 (Oct) 4.69
R v Clarke [1949] 2 All ER 448, 33 Cr App Rep 216 .... 8.1
R v Hills [2000] TLR 893 .... 4.59
R v Penwith District Council Housing Benefits Review Board, ex p Menear (1991) 24
    HLR 115, [1991] RVR 221, (1991) Times, 21 October 9.4
R v R (Family Court: Procedural Fairness) [2014] EWFC 48, [2015] 1 WLR 2743,
    [2015] 2 FLR 1005, [2015] Fam Law 264, [2014] All ER (D) 138 (Dec) 4.14
R v R [1992] 1 AC 599, [1991] 3 WLR 767, 94 Cr App Rep 216, [1992] 1 FLR 217,
    [1992] Fam Law 108, 155 JP 989, [1992] Crim LR 207, 135 Sol Jo LB 181, sub nom
    R v R (Rape: marital exemption) [1991] 4 All ER 481, [1992] LRC (Crim) 522, HL
    .... 8.1
R (on the application of TT) v Registrar General for England and Wales (AIRE Centre
    intervening) [2019] EWHC 2384 (Fam), [2020] Fam 45, [2020] 2 All ER 813, [2019]
    3 WLR 1195, [2020] 1 FLR 676, [2019] Fam Law 1405, [2019] All ER (D) 68 (Sep);
    affd sub nom R (on the application of McConnell) v Registrar General for England
    and Wales [2020] EWCA Civ 559, [2020] 2 All ER 813, [2020] All ER (D) 184
    (Apr) 5.1, 5.7
R (on the application of Steinfeld) v Secretary of State for International Development (in
    substitution for the Home Secretary and the Education Secretary) [2018] UKSC 32,
    [2018] 4 All ER 1, [2018] 3 WLR 415, [2018] 2 FLR 906, [2018] Fam Law 1119, 168
    NLJ 7800, 45 BHRC 169, [2018] All ER (D) 145 (Jun), SC 9.15

R (on the application of Kehoe) v Secretary of State for Work and Pensions [2005] UKHL 48, [2006] 1 AC 42, [2005] 4 All ER 905, [2005] 3 WLR 252, [2005] 2 FLR 1249, [2005] 2 FCR 683, [2005] Fam Law 850, [2005] NLJR 1123, (2005) Times, 15 July, [2005] All ER (D) 171 (Jul), HL 5.47, 5.69

R v Selby Justices, ex p Frame [1992] QB 72, [1991] 2 All ER 344, [1991] 2 WLR 965, 12 Cr App Rep (S) 434, 155 JP 333, [1991] 23 LS Gaz R 33, (1990) Times, 3 October, DC 4.86

R (on the application of Tilianu) v Social Fund Inspector [2010] EWHC 213 (Admin), [2010] 3 CMLR 246, [2010] All ER (D) 187 (Feb); affd sub nom R (on the application of Tilianu) v Secretary of State for Work and Pensions [2010] EWCA Civ 1397, [2011] 4 All ER 174, [2011] PTSR 781, [2010] NLJR 1756, (2011) Times, 22 February, [2010] All ER (D) 117 (Dec) 9.4

R v Teachers' Pensions (2018) 16 August, PO 19086 .... 7.10

RH (a minor) (parental responsibility), Re. See H (parental responsibility), Re

Radmacher (formerly Granatino) v Granatino (pre-nuptial contract). See NG v KR (pre-nuptial contract)

Radmacher (formerly Granatino) v Granatino; sub nom NG v KR (prenuptial contract). See NG v KR (pre-nuptial contract)

Ratcliffe, Re, Holmes v McMullan [1999] STC 262, [1999] 11 LS Gaz R 70, (1999) Times, 19 March, [1999] Lexis Citation 2554, 143 Sol Jo LB 82, [1999] All ER (D) 167 .... 6.134

Rawlings v Rawlings [1964] P 398, [1964] 2 All ER 804, [1964] 3 WLR 294, 108 Sol Jo 424, CA 1.156

Ready Mixed Concrete (Supply of), Re [1992] QB 213, [1991] 3 WLR 707, [1992] ICR 229, sub nom Director General of Fair Trading v Smiths Concrete Ltd [1991] 4 All ER 150, (1991) Times, 26 July 4.86

Rees v Newbery and Institute of Cancer Research [1998] 1 FLR 1041, [1998] Fam Law 320 .... 6.56

Rhodes v Dean [1996] CLY 555 .... 6.56, 6.58

Richards v Dove [1974] 1 All ER 888 .... 1.133

Robinson v Murray [2005] EWCA Civ 935, [2006] 1 FLR 365, [2005] 3 FCR 504, [2005] Fam Law 859, (2005) Times, 19 August, [2005] All ER (D) 129 (Jul) 4.58, 4.86

Robinson v Ommanney (1883) 23 Ch D 285, 52 LJ Ch 440, 31 WR 525, [1881–5] All ER Rep 265, 49 LT 19, CA 6.110

Robson v Robson [2010] EWCA Civ 1171, [2011] 1 FLR 751, [2011] 3 FCR 625, [2011] Fam Law 224, [2010] NLJR 1530, 155 Sol Jo (no 1) 30, [2010] All ER (D) 262 (Oct) 8.4

Robson v Secretary of State for Social Services (1982) 3 FLR 232 .... 9.41, 9.43

Rochefoucauld v Boustead [1897] 1 Ch 196, 66 LJ Ch 74, sub nom De la Rochefoucauld v Boustead 45 WR 272, 41 Sol Jo 156, 75 LT 502, 13 TLR 118, [1895–9] All ER Rep Ext 1911, CA 1.6

Rogers' Question, Re [1948] 1 All ER 328, CA 1.3

Ross v Caunters [1980] Ch 297, [1979] 3 All ER 580, [1979] 3 WLR 605, 123 Sol Jo 605 .... 6.2

Rowe v Prance [1999] 2 FLR 787, [1999] Fam Law 623, [1999] 21 LS Gaz R 41, [1999] EGCS 75, [1999] Lexis Citation 2564, [1999] All ER (D) 496 .... 1.133

Royal Bank of Scotland v Etridge (No 2) and other appeals, Barclays Bank plc v Coleman, Bank of Scotland v Bennett, Kenyon-Brown v Desmond Banks & Co (a firm) [2001] UKHL 44, [2002] 2 AC 773, [2001] 4 All ER 449, [2001] 3 WLR 1021, [2001] 2 All ER (Comm) 1061, [2001] 5 LRC 684, [2002] 1 P & Cr D25, [2002] 1 Lloyd's Rep 343, [2001] 2 FLR 1364, [2001] 3 FCR 481, [2001] Fam Law 880, [2001] NLJR 1538, [2001] 43 EGCS 184, (2001) Times, 17 October, [2001] All ER (D) 156 (Oct), sub nom Royal Bank of Scotland v Etridge (No 2) and other appeals, Barclays Bank plc v Coleman, Bank of Scotland v Bennett, Kenyon-Brown v Desmond Banks & Co [2001] GCCR 3105, HL 2.8

Royse, Re, Royse v Royse [1985] Ch 22, [1984] 3 All ER 339, [1984] 3 WLR 784, [1985] FLR 196, [1984] Fam Law 156, 128 Sol Jo 665, [1984] LS Gaz R 2543 .... 6.36

Ruttie, Re, Ruttie v Saul [1969] 3 All ER 1633, [1970] 1 WLR 89, 113 Sol Jo 903 .... 6.23

Table of Cases

S

S (a minor), Re [1995] 2 FLR 648, [1995] 3 FCR 225, [1995] Fam Law 596, CA 5.14, 5.16
S, Re [1996] 1 WLR 235, [1996] 1 FLR 910, [1996] 3 FCR 357, [1996] Fam Law 352 .... 6.36
S (a child) (adoption proceedings: joinder of father), Re [2001] 1 FLR 302, [2001] 1 FCR 158, [2000] Lexis Citation 3840, [2000] All ER (D) 1405 .... 5.8, 5.34
S v H [2020] EWFC B16 .... 8.31, 8.42
S v R [2008] EWHC 1874 (Fam), [2009] 1 P & CR D12, [2008] All ER (D) 146 (Aug), sub nom Q v Q 11 ITELR 748, [2009] 1 FLR 935, [2009] Fam Law 17 .... 1.53
S v S [1972] AC 24, [1970] 3 All ER 107, [1970] 3 WLR 366, 114 Sol Jo 635, HL 5.5
S v S (divorce: staying proceedings) [1997] 2 FLR 100 .... 8.10, 8.14
S v S (ancillary relief) [2008] EWHC 2038 (Fam), [2009] 1 FLR 254, [2009] 2 FCR 534, [2008] Fam Law 1182, 152 Sol Jo (no 35) 28, [2008] All ER (D) 16 (Sep) 8.10
SA v Comissions for HMRC [2017] UKUT 0090 (AAC) 9.103
SA v PA (Pre-marital agreement: Compensation) [2014] EWHC 392 (Fam), [2014] 2 FLR 1028, [2014] 3 FCR 603, [2014] Fam Law 799, [2014] All ER (D) 134 (Mar) 8.5, 8.7, 8.26, 8.41, 8.42
Salmon, Re, Coard v National Westminster Bank Ltd [1981] Ch 167, [1980] 3 All ER 532, [1980] 3 WLR 748, 124 Sol Jo 813 .... 6.23
Santos v Santos [1972] Fam 247, [1972] 2 All ER 246, [1972] 2 WLR 889, 116 Sol Jo 196 .... 9.29, 9.33
Savings and Investment Bank Ltd v Gasco Investments (Netherlands) BV (No 2) [1988] Ch 422, [1988] 1 All ER 975, [1988] 2 WLR 1212, 132 Sol Jo 790, [1987] NLJ Rep 1088 .... 4.77
Schaefer v Schuhmann [1972] AC 572, [1972] 1 All ER 621, [1972] 2 WLR 481, 116 Sol Jo 121, [1972–73] ALR 501, PC 2.148
Secretary of State for Work and Pensions v AM (IS [2010] UKUT 428 (AAC) (CIS/0384/2010 .... 9.87, 9.117, 9.122
Secretary of State for Work and Pensions v Jones [2003] EWHC 2163 (Fam), [2004] 1 FLR 282, [2003] Fam Law 881, [2003] 35 LS Gaz R 34, (2003) Times, 13 August 5.6
Sekhon v Alissa [1989] 2 FLR 94, [1989] Fam Law 355 .... 1.27, 1.157, 1.223
Sen v Headley [1991] Ch 425, [1991] 2 All ER 636, [1991] 2 WLR 1308, 62 P & CR 277, [1991] 2 FLR 449, [1996] 1 FCR 692, [1991] Fam Law 373, 135 Sol Jo 384, [1991] NLJR 384, (1991) Times, 6 March 6.8
Sharland v Sharland [2015] UKSC 60, [2016] AC 871, [2016] 1 All ER 671, [2015] 3 WLR 1070, [2015] 2 FLR 1367, [2015] 3 FCR 481, [2015] Fam Law 1461, (2015) Times, 02 November, [2015] All ER (D) 108 (Oct), SC 8.23
Sharp v Sharp [2017] EWCA Civ 408, [2018] Fam 317, [2017] 4 All ER 1046, [2018] 2 WLR 1617, [2017] 2 FLR 1095, [2017] Fam Law 821, 167 NLJ 7752, 167 NLJ 7751, [2017] All ER (D) 74 (Jun) 8.4
Sinclair, Re, Lloyds Bank plc v Imperial Cancer Research Fund [1985] Ch 446, [1985] 1 All ER 1066, [1985] 2 WLR 795, [1985] FLR 965, [1985] Fam Law 227, 129 Sol Jo 206, [1985] LS Gaz R 1567 .... 6.2, 6.159
Silverton v Gravett [2001] All ER (D) 282 .... 4.72
Singh v Bhakar [2007] 1 FLR 880 .... 4.72, 4.75
Slade v Slade [2009] EWCA Civ 748, [2010] 1 All ER 1231, [2010] 1 WLR 1262, [2010] 1 FLR 160, [2010] 1 FCR 227, [2009] Fam Law 925, [2009] NLJR 1065, (2009) Times, 20 August, [2009] All ER (D) 182 (Jul) 4.86
Smalley, Re, Smalley v Scotton [1929] 2 Ch 112, 98 LJ Ch 300, 73 Sol Jo 234, 141 LT 158, 45 TLR 396, CA 6.3
Smallwood, Re, Smallwood v Martins Bank Ltd [1951] Ch 369, [1951] 1 All ER 372, 95 Sol Jo 108, [1951] 1 TLR 331 .... 6.35
Smith v Lancashire Teaching Hospitals NHS Trust [2016] EWHC 2208 (QB), [2017] PIQR P46, [2016] All ER (D) 33 (Sep); revsd sub nom Smith (suing in her own right and as the surviving partner of Bulloch, deceased) v Lancashire Teaching Hospitals NHS Foundation Trust [2017] EWCA Civ 1916, [2018] QB 804, [2018] 2 WLR 1063, 162 BMLR 1, [2018] PIQR P73, (2018) Times, 08 January, [2018] WTLR 1469, [2017] All ER (D) 11 (Dec) 6.90
Smith v Smith (1976) 120 SJ 100 .... 1.156

Smith v Smith [2000] 3 FCR 374, [2000] Lexis Citation 2229 .... 8.11
Snoek, Re (1983) 13 Fam Law 18, [1982] Lexis Citation 553 .... 6.35
Soulsbury v Soulsbury [2007] EWCA Civ 969, [2008] Fam 1, [2008] 2 WLR 834, [2008] 1 FLR 90, [2007] 3 FCR 811, (2007) Times, 14 November, [2007] All ER (D) 132 (Oct) 8.7, 8.10, 8.33
Southwell v Blackburn [2014] EWCA Civ 1347, [2015] 2 FLR 1240, [2015] Fam Law 530, [2014] HLR 736, [2015] WTLR 147, [2015] 1 P & CR D39, [2014] All ER (D) 219 (Oct) 1.59
Spindlow v Spindlow [1979] Fam 52, [1979] 1 All ER 169, [1978] 3 WLR 777, (1980) 1 FLR 133, 9 Fam Law 22, 122 Sol Jo 556 .... 4.6
Springette v Defoe 1.30, 1.46
Stack v Dowden [2007] UKHL 17, [2007] 2 AC 432, [2007] 2 All ER 929, [2007] 2 WLR 831, [2008] 2 P & CR 56, 9 ITELR 815, [2007] 1 FLR 1858, [2007] 2 FCR 280, [2007] Fam Law 593, [2007] NLJR 634, (2007) Times, 26 April, 151 Sol Jo LB 575, [2007] BPIR 913, [2007] 2 P & CR D28, [2007] All ER (D) 208 (Apr), HL 1.18, 1.26, 1.28, 1.29, 1.31, 1.33, 1.34, 1.35, 1.37, 1.38, 1.40, 1.45, 1.46, 1.47, 1.48, 1.49, 1.50, 1.51, 1.52, 1.53, 1.60, 1.140, 1.146, 10.6
Stephens v Avery [1988] Ch 449, [1988] 2 All ER 477, [1988] 2 WLR 1280, [1988] FSR 510, 132 Sol Jo 822, [1988] NLJR 69, (1988) Times, 1 March 2.120
Stock v Brown [1994] 1 FLR 840, [1994] 2 FCR 1125, [1994] Fam Law 254 .... 6.24
Street v Mountford [1985] AC 809, [1985] 2 All ER 289, [1985] 2 WLR 877, 50 P & CR 258, 17 HLR 402, 129 Sol Jo 348, [1985] 1 EGLR 128, [1985] LS Gaz R 2087, [1985] NLJ Rep 460, 274 Estates Gazette 821, HL 1.201, 10.2, 10.4
Suttill v Graham [1977] 3 All ER 1117, [1977] 1 WLR 819, 7 Fam Law 211, 121 Sol Jo 408 .... 1.204
Sutton v Mishcon de Reya [2003] EWHC 3166 (Ch), [2004] 1 FLR 837, [2004] 3 FCR 142, (2004) Times, 28 January, [2003] All ER (D) 369 (Dec) 2.2, 2.3
Synge v Synge [1894] 1 QB 466, 58 JP 396, 63 LJQB 202, 9 R 265, 42 WR 309, [1891–4] All ER Rep 1164, 70 LT 221, 10 TLR 194, CA 2.60

T

T (a minor) (change of surname), Re [1998] 2 FLR 620, [1999] 1 FCR 476, [1998] Fam Law 531, [1998] 27 LS Gaz R 26, (1998) Times, 23 June, 142 Sol Jo LB 190 .... 5.24
T (a child) (DNA tests: paternity), Re [2001] 2 FLR 1190, [2001] 3 FCR 577, [2001] Fam Law 738, [2001] All ER (D) 82 (Jul) 5.5
T v B [2010] EWHC 1444 (Fam), [2010] Fam 193, [2011] 1 All ER 77, [2010] 3 WLR 1349, [2010] 2 FLR 1966, [2011] 1 FCR 1, [2010] Fam Law 1067, 174 CL&J 444, [2010] All ER (D) 239 (Jun) 5.53
T v S [1994] 2 FLR 883, [1994] 1 FCR 743, [1995] Fam Law 11, [1993] Lexis Citation 3808 .... 5.62
TC (Kenya) v Secretary of State for the Home Department [2008] EWCA Civ 543, [2008] All ER (D) 77 (Jun) 8.4
TS v HMRC [2015] UKUT 0507 (AAC) 9.18, 9.31
TW v TM (minors) (child maintenance: jurisdiction and departure from formula) [2015] EWHC 3054 (Fam), [2016] 2 FLR 1386, [2016] Fam Law 15, [2015] All ER (D) 237 (Oct) 5.60
Tanner v Tanner [1975] 3 All ER 776, [1975] 1 WLR 1346, 119 Sol Jo 391 ..... 1.5, 1.86
Taylor v Dickens [1998] 1 FLR 806, [1998] 3 FCR 455, [1998] Fam Law 191, (1997) Times, 24 November, [1997] Lexis Citation 4129 .... 1.58, 6.14
Taylor and Harman v Warners (unreported) 21 July 1987 .... 1.2
Thomas v Fuller-Brown [1988] 1 FLR 237, [1988] Fam Law 53, CA 1.36
Thompson v Hurst [2012] EWCA Civ 1752, [2014] 1 FLR 238, [2013] 1 FCR 522, [2013] Fam Law 396, [2012] All ER (D) 244 (Mar) 1.41
Thomson v Humphrey [2009] EWHC 3576 (Ch), [2010] 2 FLR 107, [2010] Fam Law 351, [2009] All ER (D) 280 (Jun) 1.39
Thorner v Major [2008] EWCA Civ 732, 11 ITELR 344, [2008] 2 FCR 435, 152 Sol Jo (no 27) 32, [2008] All ER (D) 17 (Jul); revsd [2009] UKHL 18, [2009] 3 All ER 945, [2009] 1 WLR 776, 12 ITELR 62, [2009] 2 FLR 405, [2009] 3 FCR 123, [2009] Fam Law 583, [2009] 2 EGLR 111, [2009] NLJR 514, [2009] 13 EG 142 (CS), (2009) Times, 26 March, 153 Sol Jo (no 12) 30, [2009] 2 P & CR D5, [2009] All ER (D) 257 (Mar), sub nom Thorner v Curtis [2009] 2 P & CR 269, HL 1.56, 1.57, 1.58, 6.14

Table of Cases

Thorpe v Thorpe [1998] 2 FLR 127, [1998] 2 FCR 384, [1998] Fam Law 320, [1998] Lexis Citation 2480 .... 4.58
Tinsley v Milligan [1994] 1 AC 340, [1993] 3 All ER 65, [1993] 3 WLR 126, [1993] 2 FLR 963, [1994] 2 FCR 65, (1993) Times, 28 June, HL 1.61
Total E & P Soudan SA v Edmonds [2007] EWCA Civ 50, [2007] All ER (D) 303 (Jan) 8.4, 8.5, 8.8, 8.59
Tribe v Tribe [1996] Ch 107, [1995] 4 All ER 236, [1995] 3 WLR 913, 71 P & CR 503, [1995] 2 FLR 966, [1996] 1 FCR 338, [1996] Fam Law 29, [1995] 32 LS Gaz R 30, [1995] NLJR 1445, (1995) Times, 14 August, 139 Sol Jo LB 203 .... 1.61
Turton v Turton [1988] Ch 542, [1987] 2 All ER 641, [1987] 3 WLR 622, 55 P & CR 88, [1988] 1 FLR 23, [1987] Fam Law 383, 131 Sol Jo 540, [1987] LS Gaz R 1492, (1987) Times, 29 April 1.11, 1.213

U

UA v HMRC (TC) [2019] UKUT 113 (AAC) 9.105, 9.121

V

V, Re (financial relief: family farm). See P v P (inherited property)
V v V (child maintenance) [2001] 2 FLR 799, [2001] Fam Law 649, (2001) Times, 16 August, [2001] All ER (D) 248 (Jun) 5.44
V v V (prenuptial agreement) [2011] EWHC 3230 (Fam), [2012] 1 FLR 1315, [2012] 2 FCR 98, [2012] Fam Law 274, [2012] 04 LS Gaz R 17, [2012] All ER (D) 18 (Jan) 8.21, 8.35
VB v JP [2008] EWHC 112 (Fam), [2008] 1 FLR 742, [2008] 2 FCR 682, [2008] All ER (D) 230 (Jan) 8.4, 8.5
VG v Secretary of State for Work and Pensions (IS) [2012] UKUT 470 (AAC) 9.28
VO v HMRC (TC) [2017] UKHT 343 (AAC) 9.118
Vaughan v Vaughan [1973] 3 All ER 449, [1973] 1 WLR 1159, 117 Sol Jo 583 .... 4.6
Versteegh v Versteegh [2018] EWCA Civ 1050, [2019] Fam 518, [2019] 2 WLR 399, [2018] 2 FLR 1417, [2018] Fam Law 966, [2018] All ER (D) 64 (May) .. 8.24, 8.30, 8.38, 8.41
Vrint, Re, Vrint v Swain [1940] Ch 920, [1940] 3 All ER 470, 109 LJ Ch 431, 84 Sol Jo 501, 163 LT 306, 56 TLR 953 .... 6.33

W

W (a minor) (adoption: homosexual adopter), Re [1998] Fam 58, [1997] 3 All ER 620, [1997] 3 WLR 768, [1997] 2 FLR 406, [1997] 3 FCR 650, [1997] Fam Law 597, [1997] 24 LS Gaz R 32, (1997) Times, 21 May, 141 Sol Jo LB 137 .... 5.28
W (minors) (abduction: father's rights), Re [1999] Fam 1, [1998] 3 WLR 1372, [1998] 2 FLR 146, [1998] 2 FCR 549, [1998] Fam Law 452, [1998] 19 LS Gaz R 24, (1998) Times, 9 April, [1998] Lexis Citation 3689, 142 Sol Jo LB 131 .... 5.39
W (children) (change of name), Re [2013] EWCA Civ 1488, [2014] 2 FLR 221, [2014] 3 FCR 175, [2014] Fam Law 147, [2013] All ER (D) 154 (Aug) 5.24
W (a child), Re, Re B (children), Re A (a child) [2001] Fam 1, [2000] 2 WLR 258, [1999] 2 FLR 930, [1999] 3 FCR 337, [1999] Fam Law 688, [1999] 33 LS Gaz R 29, (1999) Times, 5 August, [1999] Lexis Citation 4687, 143 Sol Jo LB 242, [1999] All ER (D) 907 .... 5.24
W (a minor) (claim from dec'd's estate), Re. See C (leave to apply for provision), Re
W v A (child: surname) [1981] Fam 14, [1981] 1 All ER 100, [1981] 2 WLR 124, 11 Fam Law 22, 124 Sol Jo 726 .... 5.24
W v H (Family Division: without notice orders) [2001] 1 All ER 300, [2000] 2 FLR 927, [2000] 3 FCR 481, [2000] All ER (D) 1422 .... 4.75
W v J (child: variation of financial provision) [2003] EWHC 2657 (Fam), [2004] 2 FLR 300, [2004] Fam Law 568 .... 5.60
WW v HW [2015] EWHC 1844 (Fam), [2016] 2 FLR 299, [2015] Fam Law 1060, 165 NLJ 7663, [2015] All ER (D) 167 (Jul) 8.29
Waggott v Waggott [2018] EWCA Civ 727, [2019] Fam 479, [2019] 2 WLR 297, [2018] 2 FLR 406, [2018] Fam Law 659, 168 NLJ 7790 .... 8.4, 8.5

Wales v Wadham [1977] 2 All ER 125, [1977] 1 WLR 199, 7 Fam Law 19, 121 Sol Jo
154 .... 2.63
Walker v Hall [1984] FLR 126, [1984] Fam Law 21, 127 Sol Jo 550, [1983] LS Gaz R
2139, CA 1.2, 1.30
Walker v Innospec Ltd [2017] UKSC 47, [2017] 4 All ER 1004, [2018] 1 LRC 310,
[2018] 1 CMLR 707, [2017] IRLR 928, [2017] ICR 1077, (2017) Times, 25 July,
[2017] All ER (D) 77 (Jul), SC 7.2
Wallbank v Price [2007] EWHC 3001 (Ch), [2008] 2 FLR 501, [2008] 3 FCR 444
.... 1.22
Walsh v Singh [2009] EWHC 3219 (Ch), [2010] 1 FLR 1658, [2010] 1 FCR 177, [2010]
Fam Law 247; affd [2011] EWCA Civ 80, [2011] 2 FLR 599, [2011] Fam Law 344,
[2011] 4 Costs LO 429, [2011] All ER (D) 108 (Feb) 1.39
Ward v Laverty [1925] AC 101, 94 LJPC 17, [1924] All ER Rep 319, 68 Sol Jo 629, 131
LT 614, 40 TLR 600, [1924] 2 IR 122, HL 6.120
Watson, Re [1999] 1 FLR 878, [1999] 3 FCR 595, [1999] Fam Law 211, [1999]
02 LS Gaz R 28, (1998) Times, 31 December, 143 Sol Jo LB 51 .... 6.39, 6.43, 6.45, 6.47,
6.51, 9.19, 9.28, 9.36, 9.61
Wayling v Jones (1993) 69 P & CR 170, [1995] 2 FLR 1029, [1996] 2 FCR 41, [1996]
Fam Law 88, [1995] Conv 409, CA 1.53, 6.14
Westmeath (Marquis) v Marquis of Salisbury (1831) 5 Bli NS 339, 35 RR 54, 5 ER 349,
sub nom Westmeath (Marquis) v Marchioness of Westmeath 1 Dow & Cl 519, 6 ER
619, HL 8.35
Wheeldon v Wheeldon [1998] 1 FLR 463, [1997] 3 FCR 769, [1997] Fam Law 602,
[1997] Lexis Citation 1591, CA 4.79
White v White [2003] EWCA Civ 924, [2004] 2 FLR 321, [2003] All ER (D) 252
(May) 1.67, 1.123, 5.55, 8.57, 8.60
Wicks v Wicks [1999] Fam 65, [1998] 1 All ER 977, [1998] 3 WLR 277, [1998] 1 FLR
470, [1998] 1 FCR 465, [1998] Fam Law 311, [1998] 05 LS Gaz R 29, (1997) Times,
29 December, [1997] Lexis Citation 5057, 142 Sol Jo LB 76 .... 5.72
Wight v IRC (1982) 264 ERG 935 .... 1.204, 6.125
Wild v Pensions Ombudsman [1996] 2 FLR 680, [1997] 1 FCR 248, [1996] Fam Law
667, (1996) Times, 17 April, 140 Sol Jo LB 108 .... 6.6, 7.11
Williams & Glyn's Bank Ltd v Boland [1981] AC 487, [1980] 2 All ER 408, [1980] 3
WLR 138, 40 P & CR 451, 10 LDAB 243, 124 Sol Jo 443, [1980] RVR 204, HL
.... 10.4
Wilson v Webster [1998] 1 FLR 1097, [1998] 2 FCR 575, [1998] Fam Law 391, [1998]
16 LS Gaz R 23, (1998) Times, 5 March, [1998] Lexis Citation 2391 .... 4.58
Wilson v Wilson [1969] 3 All ER 945, [1969] 1 WLR 1470, 20 P & CR 780, 113 Sol Jo
625 .... 1.6, 1.8, 1.198
Windeler v Whitehall [1990] 2 FLR 505, [1990] FCR 268, [1990] Fam Law 424 ..... 1.36,
1.136
Witkowska v Kaminski [2006] EWHC 1940 (Ch), [2007] 1 FLR 1547, [2006] 3 FCR
250, [2006] All ER (D) 357 (Jul) 6.39, 6.52
Wodzicki v Wodzicki [2017] EWCA Civ 95, [2018] 1 FLR 473, [2017] Fam Law 502,
167 NLJ 7737, [2017] All ER (D) 22 (Mar) 1.29
Woodard v Woodard [1995] 3 All ER 980, [1992] RTR 35, [1996] 1 FLR 399, [1997] 1
FCR 533, [1991] Fam Law 470, (1991) Times, 15 March 6.8
Work v Gray. See Gray v Work
Wragg, Re, Wragg v Palmer [1919] 2 Ch 58, 88 LJ Ch 269, [1918–19] All ER Rep 233,
63 Sol Jo 535, 121 LT 78 .... 6.146
Wynn's Will Trusts, Re, Public Trustee v Newborough [1952] Ch 271, [1952] 1 All ER
341, 96 Sol Jo 120, [1952] 1 TLR 278 .... 6.155

X

X (parental responsibility: children in care), Re [2000] Fam 156, [2000] 2 All ER 66,
[2000] 2 WLR 1031, [2000] 1 FLR 517, [2000] 1 FCR 379, [2000] Fam Law 244,
[2000] 01 LS Gaz R 23, (2000) Times, 19 January, [1999] Lexis Citation 4116, 144
Sol Jo LB 25, [1999] All ER (D) 1418 .... 5.11
Xydhias v Xydhias [1999] 2 All ER 386, [1999] 1 FLR 683, [1999] 1 FCR 289, [1999]
Fam Law 301, [1999] NLJR 52, (1999) Times, 13 January, [1998] All ER (D) 789
.... 8.7, 8.10, 8.33

Table of Cases

Y

Y (children) (occupation order), Re [2000] 2 FCR 470 .... 4.23
Y (Mrs) (2020) 29 January, PO-23903 .... 7.18
Y v Local Government Pension Scheme (2019) 19 September, PO-27699 .... 7.10
Y v Y (Financial Remedy: Marriage Contract) [2014] EWHC 2920 (Fam) 8.27
Yaxley v Gotts [2000] Ch 162, [2000] 1 All ER 711, [1999] 3 WLR 1217, 79 P & CR 91, 78 P & CR D33, [1999] 2 FLR 941, [1999] Fam Law 700, 32 HLR 547, [1999] NPC 76, [1999] 2 EGLR 181, [1999] EGCS 92, (1999) Times, 8 July, [1999] Lexis Citation 2625, [1999] All ER (D) 671 .... 1.54
Yemshaw v Hounslow London Borough Council [2011] UKSC 3, [2011] 1 All ER 912, [2011] 1 WLR 433, [2011] 4 LRC 191, [2011] PTSR 462, [2011] 1 FLR 1614, [2011] 1 FCR 576, [2011] Fam Law 349, [2011] HLR 251, [2011] 06 LS Gaz R 20, [2011] NLJR 174, (2011) Times, 28 January, 155 Sol Jo (no 5) 30, [2011] All ER (D) 187 (Jan), SC 4.6
Yeoman's Row Management Ltd v Cobbe [2008] UKHL 55, [2008] 4 All ER 713, [2008] 1 WLR 1752, [2009] 1 All ER (Comm) 205, 11 ITELR 530, [2008] 3 EGLR 31, (2008) Times, 8 September, 152 Sol Jo (no 31) 31, [2008] All ER (D) 419 (Jul), HL 1.54

Z

Z (Children), Re [2014] EWHC 1999 (Fam), [2014] Fam Law 1235, [2014] All ER (D) 155 (Jun); revsd sub nom Z (children) (disclosure of DNA profile), Re [2015] EWCA Civ 34, [2015] 4 All ER 205, [2015] 1 WLR 2501, [2015] 1 Cr App Rep 423, [2015] 1 FLR 1100, [2015] Fam Law 369, [2015] All ER (D) 49 (Feb) 5.6
Z v Z (no 2) (financial remedies: marriage contract) [2011] EWHC 2878 (Fam), [2012] 1 FLR 1100, [2012] Fam Law 136, [2011] All ER (D) 112 (Dec) 8.7, 8.21, 8.23, 8.35
ZX v Secretary of State for Work and Pensions (IS) [2010] UKUT 123 (AAC) 9.6
Zamet v Hyman [1961] 3 All ER 933, [1961] 1 WLR 1442, 105 Sol Jo 911, CA 2.111

Decisions of the European Court of Justice are listed below numerically. These decisions are also included in the preceding alphabetical list.

C-24/76: Ditta Estasis Salotti di Colzano Aima e Giamano Colzano v RÜWA Polstereimaschinen GmbH [1976] ECR 1831, [1977] 1 CMLR 345, EUCJ 8.29

INTRODUCTION

The need for a work that deals with the legal position of unmarried couples is greater today than ever before: the latest figures show that the number of cohabiting couples across the UK as a whole has reached 3.5 million[1]. Cohabitation has become the norm for first partnerships[2], and while many will go on to marry their partner, many others will not[3]. The context of cohabitation is also increasingly diverse, with socio-economic factors, religion and ethnic background all playing an important role in the decision whether or not to marry[4]. Some cohabitants idealise marriage and intend to marry when they can have the perfect wedding, or when the relationship itself has reached a particular state; others reject the institution of marriage – or any form of state regulation - altogether. Some may be cohabiting for pragmatic reasons, or because they see no particular advantage in formalising their relationship[5]. Others may believe that they are in fact married, having gone through a ceremony that is binding in the eyes of their religious community, only to find at a later date that the law regards their union as a 'non-qualifying marriage' and treats them as if they are merely cohabiting[6]. There are thus significant issues facing the law.

Yet the law has not as yet developed a comprehensive approach to cohabiting couples: in some contexts cohabitants are treated as if they were married, in others they are accorded lesser rights, and in yet others they have no rights at all, or at least none that are specific to their status as cohabitants[7]. The advent of opposite-sex civil partnerships may provide a solution for those who were cohabiting on account of ideological objections to marriage, but it is difficult to see why those who are cohabiting because of idealistic or pragmatic reasons would be any more likely to register a civil partnership[8].

It is clear that many cohabitants, particularly women, experience disadvantage upon relationship breakdown. Proposals for reform have proliferated in recent years, but as yet no action has been taken. Nor has there been any review of the totality of laws applicable to cohabiting couples in order to evaluate the coherence of the current approach.

In order to understand the current position – and in particular to understand how we got to where we are and why more progress has not been made – it is essential to understand something of the background. This introductory chapter sets out a brief history of the extent and legal treatment of cohabitation, and then considers the challenges facing those responsible for advising modern cohabitants.

---

[1] ONS, *Families and Households in the UK, 2019* (2019). By contrast, 12.8 million couples are married or in a civil partnership. Further data shows that married or civilly partnered couples account for 50.7% of all of those aged over 16: ONS, *Population estimates by marital status and living arrangements, England and Wales: 2018* (2019).

Introduction

2   R Probert, 'From this day forward? Pre-marital Cohabitation and the Rite of Marriage from the 1960s to the Present Day' in J Miles, P Mody and R Probert (eds), *Marriage Rites and Rights* (2015).

3   B Wilson and R Stuchbury, 'Do partnerships last? Comparing marriage and cohabitation using longitudinal census data' (2010) 139 *Population Trends* 37 found that two-fifths of their 1991 sample of cohabiting adults had married their partner by 2001, while two-fifths had split up and the remaining one-fifth were still living together.

4   See eg J Eekelaar and M Maclean, 'Marriage and the Moral Bases of Personal Relationships' (2004) 31 *Journal of Law and Society* 510; J Miles, P Pleasence and N Balmer, 'The Experience of Relationship Breakdown and Civil Law Problems by People in Different Forms of Relationship' [2009] CFLQ 47; E van Acker, *Marriage and Values in Public Policy: Conflicts in the UK, the US and Australia* (2017).

5   See eg A Barlow and J Smithson, 'Legal Assumptions, Cohabitants' Talk and the Rocky Road to Reform' [2010] CFLQ 328, who classify cohabitants into 'ideologues' who reject marriage, 'pragmatists' who would marry if they thought there were legal advantages to doing so, 'romantics' who plan to marry and 'uneven' couples where one wants to marry and the other does not.

6   The term 'non-qualifying marriage' was suggested as a replacement for 'non-marriage' in *AG v Akhter and Khan* [2020] EWCA Civ 122. For discussion see RC Akhtar, P Nash and R Probert (eds), *Cohabitation and Religious Marriages: Status, Similarities and Solutions* (2020).

7   This approach is not unique to this jurisdiction: see eg B Perelli-Harris and N Sanchez Gassen, 'The reciprocal relationship between the state and union formation across Western Europe: policy dimensions and theoretical considerations' (2010), MPIDR Working Paper, WP 2010-034; A Barlow, 'Legislating for Cohabitation in Common Law Jurisdictions in Europe: Two Steps Forward and One Step Back' in K Boele-Woelki, N Dethloff and W Gephart (eds), *Family Law and Culture in Europe: Developments, Challenges and Opportunities* (2014); J Miles, 'Unmarried cohabitation in a European perspective' in JM Scherpe (ed), *European Family Law: Vol III Family Law in a European Perspective* (2016).

8   For discussion see A Hayward, 'The Steinfeld Effect: Equal Civil Partnership and the Construction of the Cohabitant' [2019] CFLQ 283.; J Miles and R Probert, 'Civil partnership: ties that (also) bind' [2019] CFLQ 303.

9   See eg J Miles and R Probert (eds), *Sharing Lives, Dividing Assets* (2009), chs 7 and 8; G Douglas, J Pearce and H Woodward, 'Cohabitants, Property and the Law: A Study of Injustice' (2009) 72 *Modern Law Review* 24 although for a challenge to this view of disadvantage see R Auchmuty, 'The Limits of Marriage Protection in Property Allocation When a Relationship Ends' [2016] CFLQ 303.

A BRIEF HISTORY OF COHABITATION

There is a widespread but erroneous belief that cohabitation was popular in earlier centuries, in particular the late-eighteenth and early-nineteenth centuries[1], and that we are today seeing the revival of 'social marriage'[2]. In fact, rates of cohabitation were very low in this earlier period: the proportion of children born outside marriage barely edged above 5 per cent until the mid-nineteenth century[3], and only a very small proportion of such children were born within cohabiting relationships[4]. Marriage in church was almost universal even before Lord Hardwicke's Clandestine Marriages Act of 1753 put the rules governing the formation of marriage on a statutory basis for the first time[5].

Nor did the supposed strictness of the 1753 Act encourage couples to eschew legally-binding rites. The Act merely put the long-established canonical requirements for the formation of marriage on a statutory footing and gave them teeth by stipulating that a failure to comply with certain formalities would render the marriage void. Although observance of Anglican rites was therefore mandatory for all (save Jews and Quakers, who were exempted from the Act), there is little evidence that other Protestant dissenting sects had married according to their own rites before 1754, and ample evidence that they complied with the law after that date[6]. Similarly, although Catholics had shown a greater tendency to marry according to their own rites before the 1753 Act, in its wake the vast majority accepted the need to supplement the Catholic ceremony with a legally-binding Anglican marriage[7]. For the vast majority, religious nonconformity was not seen as a reason for refusing to formalise a relationship.

Of course, there were always *some* couples who flouted the conventions of the time and who lived together unmarried. And the number of such couples undoubtedly increased during the nineteenth century, as more of the population moved to or grew up in an urban setting and as traditional controls and structures weakened. The very fact that such controls were weakening led some contemporary commentators to fulminate against the perceived immorality of the times: cohabitation was seen as characteristic of 'outcast London'[8]. The journalist Henry Mayhew, writing in the 1850s, certainly discovered a number of unmarried couples during his investigation of the lives of the London poor,[9] although some street sellers were so incensed by his claim that only one-tenth of them were formally married that they held a public meeting to protest[10].

Even when marriage and the family came under increasing criticism towards the end of the nineteenth century, with radical intellectuals proposing new alternatives to formal, permanent marriage, few actually put such ideas into practice. The nascent feminist movement did not champion 'free unions': most believed that the preferable way forward was to reform the law of marriage and that cohabitation offered too little protection to women[11].

Given the stigma that continued to attach to cohabiting relationships well into the 1950s[12], it is unsurprising that cohabitation remained rare during this period. Indeed, it was not until the 1970s that cohabitation emerged as a statistically significant family form[13]; prior to this, as Mike Murphy has noted, 'under 1 per cent of women aged 18–49 were cohabiting'[14]. As the statistics set out in the introduction demonstrate, cohabitation has now 'become a normal part of the life course'[15].

What this tells us is that the current popularity of cohabitation is unprecedented, and that the English legal system has never had to deal with unformalised relationships on such a scale before. But how has English law reacted to the existence of such relationships?

[1] See eg J Gillis, *For Better, For Worse: British Marriages 1600 to the Present* (1985); K O'Donovan, *Sexual Divisions in Law* (1985), p 46; S Parker, *Informal Marriage, Cohabitation and the Law, 1754–1989* (1990), pp 14–27; A Diduck and F Kaganas, *Family Law, Gender and the State: Text, Cases and Materials* (2nd edn, 2005), pp 58–60.
[2] See eg S McRae, *Cohabiting Mothers* (1993); A Barlow, S Duncan, G James and A Park, *Cohabitation, Marriage and the Law: Social Change and Legal Reform in the 21st Century* (2005), p 53.
[3] P Laslett, 'Introduction: comparing illegitimacy over time and between cultures', ch 1 in P Laslett, K Oosterveen and R Smith, *Bastardy and its Comparative History* (1980).
[4] R Probert, *Marriage Law and Practice in the Long Eighteenth Century: A Reassessment* (2009), ch 3.
[5] R Probert and L D'Arcy Brown, 'The Impact of the Clandestine Marriages Act: Three Case-studies in Conformity' (2008) 23 *Continuity and Change* 309.
[6] See generally R Probert, *Marriage Law and Practice in the Long Eighteenth Century: A Reassessment* (2009).

Introduction

[7] R Probert and L D'Arcy Brown, 'Catholics and the Clandestine Marriages Act of 1753' (2008) *Local Population Studies* 78.
[8] A Mearns, *The Bitter Cry of Outcast London* (1883).
[9] H Mayhew, *London Labour and the London Poor* (1851).
[10] R Probert, *The Changing Legal Regulation of Cohabitation: From Fornicators to Family, 1600–2010* (2012).
[11] L Bland, *Banishing the Beast: English Feminism and Sexual Morality 1885–1914* (1995).
[12] See R Probert, 'Looking back on the overlooked: cohabitants and the law 1857–2007', in N Lowe and G Douglas (ed), *Family Law: Legacies and Prospects* (2009).
[13] See eg K Kiernan, H Land and J Lewis, *Lone Motherhood in Twentieth Century Britain* (1998), p 40; J Haskey, 'Cohabitational and marital histories of adults in Great Britain' (1999) 96 *Population Trends* 13.
[14] M Murphy, 'The evolution of cohabitation in Britain, 1960-95' (2000) 54 *Population Studies* 43.
[15] E Beaujouan and M Ní Bhrolchàin, 'Cohabitation and marriage in Britain since the 1970s' (2011) 145 *Population Trends* 35, p 35.

A BRIEF HISTORY OF COHABITATION LAW

Just as there are misunderstandings about the prevalence of cohabitation in times past, so too there is an equally widespread – and equally erroneous – belief that cohabiting couples would have enjoyed legal protection by means of a 'common-law marriage' prior to 1754. This rests on the double assumption that it was possible to marry by a simple exchange of consent before the Clandestine Marriages Act and that a cohabiting couple would be presumed to have exchanged such consent. However, given that a bare exchange of consent carried no legal rights – other than that of insisting that the marriage be solemnised in church – such a presumption would have conferred no legal protection on cohabitants[1]. There *was* a presumption that couples who had cohabited and were reputed to have married had in fact gone through a legally binding ceremony of marriage, but several points need to be noted. First, it should be borne in mind that the presumption operated against a background in which cohabitation was punishable as fornication: cohabitation gave rise to a presumption that the parties were married precisely because it was assumed that no one would cohabit unless they were married. Similarly, couples would not enjoy the reputation of married couples within the community unless there was reason to believe that they had married.

At a time when the community was responsible, through the poor law, for the support of those settled in the parish, and when children born outside marriage obtained a legal settlement in the parish of their birth, neighbours had good reason to check the marital status of any newcomers. Secondly, and vitally, the presumption only operated in certain contexts, where a child or remoter issue of the supposed marriage was claiming an interest and was unable to provide precise details. Given the unsatisfactory state of registration and record-keeping at the time, there would have been many formally-celebrated marriages of which no documentary evidence existed. The presumption was therefore an evidentiary tool to allow other means of proving a legal marriage rather than a mechanism for equating the married and the unmarried. Finally, it should be noted that the presumption does, in theory, still exist – although given the very different conditions of modern society it will rarely be appropriate for the courts to presume that a marriage has taken place where there is no formal evidence[2].

So, how *did* the law treat cohabiting couples? The practice of presenting and punishing cohabiting couples for fornication had died out almost everywhere by the late eighteenth century, and over the course of the following century the law rarely engaged with cohabitants save when they obtruded themselves on its notice[3]. There were of course a few cases in which cohabitants were involved in disputes over contracts, trusts, and wills (with varying degrees of success), but the family law of the time – known then as the law of domestic relations – was exclusively concerned with marriage.

As the state began to intervene more directly in family life, however, there was some limited recognition of cohabiting relationships. Section 17 of the Prevention of Cruelty to Children (Amendment) Act 1894 provided that rules designed to protect children against their parents should apply to step-parents and 'to any person cohabiting with the parent of the child', while under the Workman's Compensation Act of 1906 children born outside marriage could claim compensation on the same footing as legitimate children.

But it took a national emergency for rights to be extended to unmarried partners: the outbreak of the First World War saw separation allowances being extended to all dependants of soldiers – including the so-called 'unmarried wives' – and provision was also made for such women to receive a pension in the case of the soldier's death or injury[4]. Such provision was, however, less generous than that conferred on legal wives. Post-war unemployment was similarly seen as a national, short-term emergency, leading to the provision of dependants' allowances for women living with unemployed workers[5]. But there was concern about the explicit recognition of unmarried relationships, and in 1927 the law was changed to limit such allowances to women who had care of the unemployed worker's children. Of course, such a woman might well be the mother of those children, but the change in terminology allowed a veneer of respectability to be preserved. Had the original wording remained on the statute book, it might have provided a precedent for further reform, but this was not to be.

In the meantime, a more durable principle had been introduced by the Widows' Orphans' and Old Age Contributory Pensions Act, which stipulated that widows who remarried or cohabited would not be entitled to receive a pension. The application of the 'cohabitation rule' was extended to new contexts in the wake of the Second World War, as the state assumed greater responsibility for the welfare of its citizens[6]. But the growing financial burden of such provision – and increasing suspicion that women were obtaining benefits fraudulently by failing to disclose a cohabiting relationship – led to a renewed scrutiny of cohabiting relationships. After 1964, the undisclosed presence of a man in the household of a woman who was in receipt of national assistance was sufficient ground to prosecute her for fraud: it was no longer necessary to establish that he was actually supporting her.

And of course women had no legal means of securing support from cohabiting partners. It was not until the 1970s that the law began to make positive provision for cohabitants – but then, as we have seen, it was not until the 1970s that couples began to cohabit in significant numbers. The Inheritance (Provision for Family and Dependants) Act 1975 allowed a wider range of 'dependants' to claim provision from the estate of a deceased individual, the Domestic Violence and Matrimonial Proceedings Act 1976 enabled the courts

Introduction

to grant an injunction to protect cohabitants against domestic violence, and 'reputed' spouses were included as dependants under the Pneumoconiosis (Workers' Compensation) Act 1979. Cohabitants also benefited from reforms to the general law: the rejection of the 'family assets' doctrine in *Pettitt v Pettitt*[7] and *Gissing v Gissing*[8], and the reiteration that interests in the family home were to be determined by principles of trusts law, did have one benefit for cohabiting couples, in that judicial creativity was refocused on the boundaries of the constructive trust, which, unlike the earlier family assets doctrine, applied outside marital relationships[9]. Such changes were both a product of, and encouraged, a greater social acceptance of cohabitation[10].

Yet there was clearly no coherent policy of extending rights to cohabiting couples, as is evident from the fact that they were excluded from other contemporary pieces of legislation dealing with family issues[11]. The Law Commission did consider carrying out a review of the legal position of unmarried couples at this time, but decided against it on the grounds that the topic was one 'largely governed by considerations of social and financial policy'[12]. And in the 1980s there was a shift in social policy that led to limits being placed on a number of the doctrines developed in the previous decade[13].

The few reforms benefiting cohabiting couples to be passed by the Conservative administration of the time focused on the established categories of the bereaved cohabitant[14] and the victim of domestic violence (and even this was controversial, as evidenced by the reaction to the Family Homes and Domestic Violence Bill in 1995[15]). By contrast, those living with a bankrupt were – contrary to the recommendations of the Cork Report[16] – not included within the scope of new rules protecting the family home[17]. Moreover, same sex relationships were specifically stigmatised as 'pretended family relationships' by s 28 of the Local Government Act 1988.

The 1980s did, however, witness a number of developments affecting cohabitants in their role as parents. The Family Law Reform Act 1987 removed most of the negative legal consequences of being born outside marriage, while the Children Act 1989 marked a decisive shift away from marriage to parenthood as the basis for rights and responsibilities. The desirability of assisting cohabiting couples to have children was, however, a much more contested issue. The appropriate status of the male partner of a woman receiving fertility treatment was not even considered in the original draft of the Human Fertilisation and Embryology Bill, and when a clause dealing with the issue was introduced it was with the grudging message that it 'should not be seen as encouraging unmarried people to use infertility treatments'[18].

At the start of the twenty-first century the focus shifted to those who could not marry: same sex couples were accepted as members of each other's family in *Fitzpatrick v Sterling Housing Association*[19], while in *Ghaidan v Mendoza* the House of Lords was willing to accept that such couples could be described as living together 'as husband and wife'. The Civil Partnership Act 2004 provided same sex couples with a means of formalising their relationship and thereby acquiring virtually the same rights and responsibilities as married couples; and in 2014 same-sex couples were finally able to marry, following the passage of the Marriage (Same Sex Couples) Act 2013.

Yet although the Civil Partnership Act also removed differences in treatment between same-sex and opposite-sex cohabitants, the legal regime to which they were subject was far from comprehensive. The fact that no provision had been made for cohabitants provoked new calls for reform, and in 2005 the Law Commission began a project examining the legal consequences of relationship breakdown for cohabiting couples.

A substantial consultation paper was produced with impressive swiftness and thoroughness[20], and in 2007 the Law Commission set out its recommendations[21]. The key features of the recommended scheme were that cohabiting couples who had satisfied certain eligibility criteria (basically, having had a child together or having lived together for a certain period) should be able to apply for financial relief on separation unless they had specifically opted out of the scheme. The applicant would also have to prove that he or she had experienced economic disadvantage and/or that the respondent had a retained benefit as a result of the applicant's 'qualifying' contributions – these being defined as 'any contribution arising from the cohabiting relationship which is made to the parties' shared lives or to the welfare of members of their families'[22]. The level of financial relief would then be determined by the court first reversing the retained benefit and then sharing any remaining economic disadvantage, but in both cases only in so far as it deemed this 'reasonable and practicable', having regard to a list of discretionary factors (including the welfare of any minor children, the financial needs, obligations and resources of both parties, and their conduct).

In March 2008, the then Government indicated that it would examine the operation of similar principles in Scotland before deciding whether the scheme should be introduced in England and Wales[23], and in 2011, the coalition Government that had been elected in 2011 announced that it did not intend to take forward the Law Commission's recommendations for reform during its existing term in office[24]. Subsequent Conservative governments have not indicated any intention to do so either.

Subsequently, in a review of the law relating to intestacy and family provision claims, the Law Commission further recommended that a surviving cohabitant should automatically be entitled to receive a share of the deceased's estate under the intestacy rules[25]. It was proposed that a cohabitant of five years' standing should receive the same as a spouse. Where the cohabiting relationship had lasted between two and five years, the survivor would receive 50 per cent of what a spouse would have received. However, if the couple had had a child together, the surviving cohabitant should automatically receive the same as a spouse would have done, regardless of the duration of the relationship. The Cohabitants (Inheritance) Bill 2012 sought to give effect to these proposals, but failed to proceed beyond a second reading[26].

Since then there have been a number of bills introduced by private members advocating the implementation of these proposals, but in the absence of government support legislative reform seems unlikely at the present moment.

1 See R Probert, 'Common law marriage: myths and misunderstandings' [2008] CFLQ 1.
2 See further R Probert, 'The Presumptions in Favour of Marriage' (2018) 77 *Cambridge Law Journal* 375.
3 See eg G Frost, *Living in Sin* (2008), for examples of cases in which cohabiting couples were involved.
4 R Probert, '"Unmarried Wives" in War and Peace' [2005] CFLQ 1.
5 Unemployed Workers' Dependants (Temporary Provision) Act 1921, s 1(2).
6 See eg National Insurance (Industrial Injuries) Act 1946, s 88(3).
7 [1970] AC 777.

[8] [1971] AC 886.
[9] See eg *Cooke v Head* [1972] 2 All ER 38.
[10] See eg R Probert, 'Common law marriage: myths and misunderstandings' [2008] CFLQ 1.
[11] For example, the Fatal Accidents Act 1976 and the Domestic Proceedings and Magistrates' Courts Act 1978.
[12] Law Commission *Fourteenth Annual Report, 1978–79* Law Com No 97 (1980), para 2.32.
[13] R Probert, 'Cohabitation in Twentieth Century England and Wales: Law and Policy' (2004) 26 *Law and Policy* 13.
[14] See eg the Administration of Justice Act 1982, defining cohabitants as dependants for the purposes of the Fatal Accidents Act 1976; Law Reform (Succession) Act 1995, amending the Inheritance (Provision for Family and Dependants) Act and obviating the need for cohabitants to bring themselves within the concept of 'dependant'.
[15] S Doughty, 'Anger at Bill to "sabotage" marriage' (1995); W Oddie, 'How could MPs fail to spot this blow to marriage?' *Daily Mail* 23 October 1995.
[16] Cork Report, *Insolvency Law and Practice: Report of the Review Committee* Cmnd 8558 (London: HMSO, 1982).
[17] R Probert, 'The security of the home and the home as security' in R Probert (ed), *Family Life and the Law: Under One Roof* (Ashgate, 2007).
[18] Hansard (HL) 20/3/90, vol 517, col 209.
[19] [2000] 1 FLR 271.
[20] *Cohabitation: the financial consequences of relationship breakdown – A Consultation Paper* Law Com CP No 179 (2006).
[21] *Cohabitation: the financial consequences of relationship breakdown* Law Com No 307 (2007).
[22] Above, para 4.34.
[23] Ministerial Statement to Parliament, Hansard HC vol 472 col 22WS (6 March 2008). For information on the operation of the scheme in Scotland, see the briefing paper issued by the Centre for Research on Families and Relationships, 'No longer living together: how does Scots cohabitation law work in practice?' (2010).
[24] Hansard HL, vol 730, col 118; HC, vol 532, cols 15–16WS (6 September 2011).
[25] Law Commission, *Intestacy and Family Provision Claims on Death*, Consultation Paper No 191.
[26] See http://services.parliament.uk/bills/2012-13/inheritancecohabitants.html.

THE COHABITANT AS CLIENT

In the meantime, one challenge for the lawyer in this context may be the very basic one of disabusing their clients of the belief that cohabitation already entails certain legal rights and responsibilities. A survey carried out in 2000 found that 56 per cent of the general population, and 59 per cent of cohabiting couples, believed that cohabiting couples had a 'common-law marriage', which conferred the same rights as if they were married[1]. The Living Together Campaign (funded by the then Department of Constitutional Affairs) was subsequently launched to inform cohabitants of their (lack of) rights. That it enjoyed only modest success in dispelling the common law marriage myth is clear from the follow-up study carried out in 2006-7.

This found that the numbers believing in the existence of common law marriage fell slightly (to 51 per cent of the general population and 53 per cent of cohabitants), but that belief was being replaced by uncertainty rather than by knowledge of the correct legal position, the percentage who were unsure of the legal position having risen from 6 per cent in the earlier study to 10 per cent in the later one[2]. Subsequent research has confirmed 'substantial and ongoing public misunderstanding of cohabitation law'[3], and the most recent study found that almost half of the population – 46 per cent – still believe that cohabitation for a certain period of time confers the same rights as marriage[4].

Such uncertainty – and the persisting belief in common law marriage – may in part be due to the way in which cohabitation is discussed in the media. It was during the late 1970s – when discussions of the new legal rights being conferred on cohabitants regularly overstated the extent of legal protection – that the common law marriage myth emerged[5]. And today, for every article highlighting the fact that there is no such thing as common law marriage, there are many more using terms such as 'common law wife' or 'common law husband' to refer to cohabiting individuals[6]. In addition, the tendency to present proposals for reform as presaging imminent change may well lead couples to believe that, even if they do not yet enjoy legal rights, they soon will[7].

Couples who believe that they already enjoy legal rights are by definition unlikely to seek advice as to how to acquire them. But even those who do *not* believe that they are protected by a common law marriage do not always take steps to put matters on a legal footing by making contracts, declarations of trust, or wills. Many are put off by the perceived cost of legal advice; others fall prey to an 'optimism bias', believing that their relationship will endure[8]. Even those who are involved in a legal transaction – for example the purchase of a home in joint names – often misunderstand the advice that they are given or are not made aware of its potential implications for their future relationship[9].

It should also be noted that the fact that an individual does *not* believe in common law marriage does not necessarily mean that they have a correct understanding of the law. Here, again, the presentation of the issue in the media may play a part. Articles debunking the common law marriage myth tend to emphasise cohabitants' lack of legal rights and rarely draw attention to the rights that they do enjoy[10]. This may go some way to explaining why cohabitants are far less likely than married couples to seek legal advice upon relationship breakdown[11]: if they believe that they have *no* legal rights then there will be no reason for them to consult a solicitor.

For those that do make it through the doors of a solicitor's office, it is clearly essential that they obtain accurate and comprehensive advice as to the legal options that *are* available to them. It is the aim of the chapters that follow to assist in the task of providing such advice.

[1] A Barlow, S Duncan, G James and A Park, 'Just a piece of paper? Marriage and cohabitation in Britain' in A Park, J Curtice, K Thomson, L Jarvis and C Bromley (eds), *British social attitudes: the 18th report* (2001).
[2] A Barlow, C Burgoyne, E Clery and J Smithson, 'Cohabitation and the law: myths, money and the media' in A Park, J Curtice, K Thompson, M Phillips and E Clery (eds), *British social attitudes – the 24th report* (2008).
[3] P Pleasence and N J Balmer, 'Ignorance in Bliss: Modelling Knowledge of Rights in Marriage and Cohabitation' (2012) *Law & Society Review* 297, p 321.
[4] A Barlow, 'Modern Marriage Myths – the dichotomy between expectations of legal rationality and lived law' in RC Akhtar, P Nash and R Probert (eds), *Cohabitation and Religious Marriages: Status, Similarities and Solutions* (2020).
[5] R Probert, 'The evolution of the common law marriage myth' [2011] Fam Law 283.
[6] R Probert 'Why do couples still believe in common law marriage?' [2007] Fam Law 403.
[7] See eg C Dyer, 'Unmarried couples to get new rights: Reforms will cover gay relationships', *The Guardian*, 31 May 2006; M Kite, 'Unmarried couples to get rights on property: Harriet Harman announced plans to bring forward legislation', *The Sunday Telegraph*, 15 October 2006.
[8] A Barlow, C Burgoyne and J Smithson, *The Living Together Campaign – an investigation of its impact on legally aware cohabitants* (2007).
[9] See eg G Douglas, J Pearce and H Woodward, 'Cohabitation and conveyancing practice:

Introduction

problems and solutions' [2008] Conv 365; M Pawlowski and J Brown, 'Joint Purchasers and the presumption of joint beneficial ownership – a matter of informed choice?' (2013) Tru L I 3.

[10] See eg J Husband, 'Your money: not marrying is a rights thing to do', *Mirror*, 11 October 2008.

[11] S Arthur, J Lewis, M Maclean, S Finch and R Fitzgerald, *Settling Up: Making Financial Arrangements After Separation* (National Centre for Social Research, 2002).

Rebecca Probert
Professor of Law, University of Exeter

Chapter 1

PROPERTY

Part A LAW AND PRACTICE

Section 1 Ownership of the home

Introduction

1.1 As many cohabitants discover to their surprise, and often to their cost, living together does not in itself found an interest in the shared home.

When a relationship of cohabitation breaks down the court does not have the power to make orders in relation to property on the same discretionary basis as if the parties were married to one another or in a civil partnership and making application for a financial remedy[1]. Instead, cohabitants are reliant on the principles of land and trust law to determine any dispute regarding the ownership of property.

Mindful of the rise in the number of people living together without getting married or entering a civil partnership, in 2002, the Law Commission published a discussion paper 'Sharing Homes'. This concluded that:

> 'It is not possible however to devise a statutory scheme for the ascertainment and quantification of beneficial interests in the shared home which can operate fairly and evenly across the diversity of domestic circumstances which are now to be encountered.[2]'

However, in a subsequent report, *Cohabitation: The Financial Consequences of Relationship Breakdown*[3] the Law Commission recommended the provision of a new statutory scheme of financial relief for cohabitants who fulfil specific eligibility criteria, having either had a child together or lived together for a minimum period. The provision proposed was analogous to that provided to those on breakdown of a marriage or civil partnership.

Whilst the Government commended the thoroughness and quality of the report, the changes were not implemented in the 2010–15 Parliament and between 2008 and 2016 five Private Members Bills have been unsuccessful in this regard. Nevertheless, the Law Commission is hopeful that the changes will be implemented in the near future[4].

---

[1] Matrimonial Causes Act 1973 (MCA 1973), s 25; Civil Partnership Act 2004 (CPA 2004).
[2] Law Com No 278 (November 2002).
[3] Law Com No 307 (July 2007).
[4] Law Com statement on Government's response to Law Com No 307 (6 September 2011).

1.2 Property

The duty of the solicitor on the purchase of a shared home

1.2 If a solicitor is instructed in the purchase of a property by an unmarried couple, or others who intend to share the occupation of the property, the following duties arise[1]:

- to explain the differences between beneficial joint tenancies and tenancies in common[2];
- to assess and explain the advantages and disadvantages of holding the beneficial title as joint tenants as against holding as tenants in common[3];
- to assist the prospective purchasers to reach a decision as to how to deal with the beneficial interest and, if necessary, to advise one or more of the parties to obtain independent legal advice[4];
- to record how the beneficial interests are to be held[5].

A large number of cohabitants will by-pass the opportunity to have legal advice either because they move into a property which has already been acquired by the other cohabitant, or because they are simply not involved in the purchase. In the latter case, a solicitor will have a duty nonetheless to enquire whether any other person is to contribute to the purchase price or is otherwise likely to be beneficially interested in the property[6]. This duty applies even where the solicitor is not also acting for a mortgagee.

[1] In *Carlton v Goodman* [2000] 2 FLR 259 Ward LJ wearily reminded conveyancers 'that they would save their clients a great deal of later difficulty if only they would sit the purchasers down, explain the difference between a joint tenancy and a tenancy in common, ascertain what they want and then expressly declare in the conveyance or transfer how the beneficial interest is to be held because that will be conclusive and save all argument'.

[2] *Taylor and Harman v Warners* (unreported) 21 July 1987, summarised in *The Law Society's Gazette* 29 June 1988 at pp 26 and 27. Warner J said that merely to inform the purchasers of the survivorship right in a beneficial joint tenancy is 'perfunctory'.

[3] See *Taylor and Harman v Warners* (above): it is not sufficient simply to explain the difference between the two.

[4] The SRA Code of Conduct 2011, chapter 3.

[5] See **1.4** below.

[6] *City of London Building Society v Flegg* [1988] AC 54; *Walker v Hall* [1984] FLR 126.

1.3 Despite a number of stern judicial warnings as to the culpability of solicitors who fail to make pertinent enquiries and give appropriate advice to prospective purchasers, there still appears to be a reticence about declaring the beneficial interests[1]. There are a number of possible explanations for this.

- In most cases the purchasers themselves give no consideration to the question of beneficial ownership when they acquire the property[2].
- To declare the trusts might well be construed as demonstrating a lack of optimism that the relationship will succeed. It could be taken as an assumption that the relationship will fail, sooner or later, and there may be a fear that to insist on declaring the trusts could precipitate this.
- It is necessary to ask probing personal questions. To ask them can be embarrassing for the practitioner; to answer them can be embarrassing for the clients.
- Some practitioners may feel that the exercise serves little useful purpose where the couple intends eventually to marry or become civil partners, because the court will have the power to adjust the beneficial interests in the event that the marriage or civil partnership breaks down.

- There are various ways of calculating the beneficial interests[3]. It may be difficult to decide, when a couple purchases, which method of calculation will produce the fairest result when they come to sell.
- Family finances are often pooled, which can make it difficult to pinpoint the exact contributions made by either party towards the mortgage payments.
- There have been one or two judicial statements to the effect that shares can only be assessed arithmetically when the property is bought outright, and that there is no place for mathematical calculations where generally the property is purchased with the aid of a mortgage[4].
- The potential immutability of a declaration of trust is often an inhibiting factor. Having 'fixed' the beneficial interests on acquisition, what happens if the co-owners' circumstances change? In theory, another declaration of trust should be executed to record the variation, but in practice it is unlikely to happen. It may be thought to be preferable to rely upon the principles of implied trusts in the absence of an express declaration.
- There is competition between conveyancers to cut purchase costs to a minimum, particularly in the first-time buyers' market. Proper advice and documentation concerning the beneficial interests can add substantially to the costs[5].
- Sometimes there is a conflict, or a potential conflict of interests between the buyers. The need to obtain independent legal advice would further increase the costs.
- Declarations of trust do not fall completely or comfortably within the province of a conveyancer, a trust lawyer or a family lawyer. It is sometimes difficult to establish who is best suited to advise on, negotiate or draft a declaration. Having to refer to several people in the same firm could increase the costs.
- There is a mistaken belief amongst lawyers that failing to enquire about and declare the beneficial interests is not negligent.

[1] 'I ask in despair how often this court has to remind conveyancers that they would save their clients a great deal of later difficulty if only they would sit the purchasers down, explain the difference between a joint tenancy and a tenancy in common, ascertain what they want and then expressly declare in the conveyance or transfer how the beneficial interest is to be held because that will be conclusive and save all argument. When are conveyancers going to do this as a matter of invariable standard practice? This court has urged that time after time. Perhaps conveyancers do not read the law reports. I will try one more time: ALWAYS TRY TO AGREE ON AND THEN RECORD HOW THE BENEFICIAL INTEREST IS TO BE HELD. It is not very difficult to do.' Lord Justice Ward in *Carlton v Goodman* [2002] 2 FLR 259.

[2] 'When two people are about to be married and are negotiating for a matrimonial home it does not naturally enter the head of either to enquire carefully, still less to agree, what should happen to the house if the marriage comes to grief' (*Re Rogers' Question* [1948] 1 All ER 328, per Evershed LJ). 'In a great many cases, perhaps in the vast majority, no consideration will have been given by the parties . . . to the question of beneficial ownership of the home at the time that is being acquired' (*Gissing v Gissing* [1970] 2 All ER 780 at 785, per Viscount Dilhorne).

[3] See **1.9–1.15** below.

[4] 'Where the house is bought outright and not on mortgage, the extent of their respective shares will depend upon a more-or-less precise arithmetical calculation of the extent of their contributions to the purchase price. Where, on the other hand, and as is more usual nowadays, the house is bought with the aid of a mortgage, then the court has to assess each of the parties' respective contributions in a broad sense' (*Burns v Burns* [1984] FLR 216 at 241G, per May LJ).

1.3 *Property*

⁵ Compare: 'The additional costs would be insignificant' (*Cowcher v Cowcher* [1972] 1 All ER 943 at 959h, per Bagnall J).

Declaring the beneficial interests on acquisition

1.4 It will always be preferable to have a clear statement of the cohabitants' intentions with regard to the ownership of property that is recorded at the time of acquisition, than to have to rely on the courts to determine the position at a later date in the event of a dispute.

To be effective as a declaration of the beneficial interests, all the formalities must be complied with.

Express declaration of trust

1.5 An express declaration of trust in respect of land is an instrument in writing, which is signed by the person or persons competent to declare the trust and which records the beneficial interests of those who are entitled to the land, its net proceeds of sale and its net income until sale[1].

Even if the declaration of trust is not signed a draft may be evidence of intention and be upheld by the court[2].

In the absence of an express declaration of trust, it is open to anyone claiming a beneficial interest in the land to rely on the doctrines of implied trusts, resulting trusts and constructive trusts, which are exempt from the written formalities[3]. An interest could also be claimed on the basis of proprietory estoppel[4] or contract[5].

1. Law of Property Act 1925 (LPA 1925), s 53(1)(b) (see **1.6** below).
2. *Williamson v Sheikh* [2008] EWCA Civ 990.
3. Law of Property Act 1925 (LPA 1925), s 53(2).
4. As in *Pascoe v Turner* [1979] 1 WLR 431.
5. As in *Tanner v Tanner* [1975] 1 WLR 1346.

Effects of an express declaration of trust

1.6 Section 53(1)(b) of the LPA 1925 states that:

> 'a declaration of trust respecting any land or any interest therein must be manifested and proved by some writing signed by some person who is able to declare such trust or by his will.'

The trust does not need to be declared in writing at the time of its creation. A subsequent declaration will suffice, provided that it is in existence before any action is brought[1].

Although there is no legal requirement that there should be more than one deed, it is considered better practice to keep the trusts off the title[2]. So, generally, there will be two deeds: one (the transfer) vesting the legal estate in a sole owner or in the trustees of land; and the other (the declaration of trust) setting out the beneficial interests.

An express declaration of trust which comprehensively declares the beneficial interests in the property and its proceeds of sale is conclusive unless and until it is varied by those who are competent to vary it, or it is rectified or set aside on the grounds of fraud or mistake[3]. However, such a declaration is only conclusive as to the position at the time when the trust is declared[4]. Subsequent events may cause the beneficial interests to vary.

An express declaration of trust can be varied provided that the variation is manifested and proved by an instrument in writing signed by the person or persons able to vary the original trusts[5]. The new trusts will then operate by virtue of the new instrument[6]. The beneficial interests may in certain circumstances also be varied by an order of the court[7].

1. *Rochefoucauld v Boustead* [1897] 1 Ch 196 at 206.
2. 'The declaration of beneficial trusts could perfectly well have been contained in a separate document altogether off the face of the title to the land, and many conveyancers would regard that as the more proper method of proceeding' (*Wilson v Wilson* [1969] 3 All ER 945 at 948H, per Buckley J).
3. *Goodman v Gallant* [1986] 1 FLR 513 at 517C.
4. 'If that document declares not merely in whom the legal title is to vest but in whom the beneficial title is to vest, that necessarily concludes the question of title as between the (co-owners) for all time, and in the absence of fraud or mistake at the time of the transaction the parties cannot go behind it at any time thereafter even on death or the break-up of the marriage' (*Pettitt v Pettitt* [1970] AC 777 at 813E, per Lord Upjohn).
5. 'The trust and the equitable interests arising under it cannot be changed except with the consent of all interested parties' (*Cowcher v Cowcher* [1972] 1 All ER 943 at 950f, per Bagnall J).
6. *Re Holmden's Settlement Trusts* [1968] AC 685 at 713D, per Lord Wilberforce.
7. For example: Matrimonial Causes Act 1973 (MCA 1973), s 24; Inheritance (Provision for Family and Dependants) Act 1975 (I(PFD)A 1975), s 9; Insolvency Act 1986 (IA 1986), s 339; Children Act 1989 (CA 1989), Sch 1.

Land Registry Forms; restrictions and cautions

1.7 Since 1 December 1990 every district in England and Wales has been an area of compulsory registration of title[1].

The Land Registry is not interested in trusts and, as far as possible, any reference to a trust must be excluded from the registers[2].

Except where joint proprietors are beneficial joint tenants, in order to give effect to the concurrent or successive interests in the land they hold, joint proprietors should apply for the entry of the appropriate restriction on the register[3].

The standard restriction that is inserted by the Land Registry is as follows:

> **RESTRICTION:** No disposition by a sole proprietor of the registered estate (except a trust corporation) under which capital money arises is to be registered unless authorised by an order of the court.

When official copies of the entries are obtained, the presence of this restriction on the register means that the property is not held as joint tenants so that the surviving registered proprietor cannot sell the property without appointing a second trustee. It will either be held as tenants in common by the registered proprietors or on some other trusts under which the registered proprietors hold as trustees and which may also include other persons as beneficiaries. It

1.7 *Property*

is not possible to establish the trusts on which the property is held from the register and other documentation will have to be investigated.

1. Land Registration Act 2002 (LRA 2002), s 4. Registration of title to land was introduced in Scotland by the Land Registration (Scotland) Act 1979. See also, in relation to registration, Ruoff and Roper *Registered Conveyancing* (Sweet & Maxwell, Looseleaf).
2. Land Registration Act 2002, s 78.
3. The form to be used for a standard Form A restriction on severance of a joint tenancy is Form SEV and it must be signed by the applicants or their solicitors. Unless the applicants are the registered proprietors, their signed consent is required or other evidence that the applicant has sufficient interest to have a restriction registered (Land Registration Rules 2003 (LRR 2003), rr 91–95). Modifications of restrictions are made using Form RX2, cancellations Form RX3 and withdrawals RX4 in accordance with LRR 2003, rr 96–99. See generally Ruoff and Roper (above).

1.8 The standard forms of transfers (Land Registry Forms TR1 (Transfer of Whole) (see **1.227** below) TP1 (Transfer of Part) and FR1 (on first registration)[1] give three boxes to tick, depending on whether the property is to be held as joint tenants, tenants in common in equal shares or as otherwise specified by the joint proprietors. The third box can be used to indicate that the property is held as tenants in common in unequal shares, although this will not appear on the register. It can also be used to refer to another document, eg a declaration of trust or will. The transfer should also be executed by the transferees. Often it is not, particularly where no indemnity covenant is given.

In the case of a beneficial joint tenancy, it is only necessary to tick the relevant box on the transfer. In the case of a beneficial tenancy in common, it is considered best practice to declare the beneficial interests in an instrument entirely separate from the transfer itself[2]. In any event, the transfer is usually retained by the Land Registry and it may be difficult to obtain a copy.

It may be necessary for a person who is not on the Land Registry Title as a proprietor, but who believes that he or she has a beneficial interest in the property, to take steps to prevent a disposition of the property. A restriction may be registered on the Title by a non-owner to prevent a contravention of s 6(6) or (8) of the TOLATA 1996. Alternatively, a person claiming a beneficial interest in the land may register a caution. A Caution Against First Registration will be appropriate where the land is unregistered. This gives the person entering the caution the right to receive notice of any transaction affecting the property, and 14 days in which to make an objection. Cautions Against Dealings were abolished from 13 October 2003 by the Land Registration Act 2002. Rights previously protected by a Caution Against Dealings must now be protected by a notice or restriction. An interest under a trust of land or settlement cannot be protected by a notice and so the only method of protection now available is a restriction[3].

1. Land Registry form JO (Trust Information) is an alternative way for joint owners to record the nature of the trust under which land is held and it must accompany an application for registration of the disposition (forms TP1, TP2, TR1, TR2, TR5, AS1, or AS3).
2. *Wilson v Wilson* [1969] 3 All ER 945 at 948.
3. Land Registration Act 2002, s 33(a).

Expressing the shares

FIXED SHARES AND FLOATING SHARES

1.9 Usually, the co-owners' shares of the net proceeds of sale are ascertained or fixed at the time of purchase[1]. In this book, such shares are referred to as *fixed shares*.

In the absence of any deed or variation executed by those who are competent to vary the original trusts, and in the absence of any court order, fixed shares remain static throughout the duration of the trust of land[2].

Alternatively, and more unusually in practice, the ascertainment of the shares can be deferred until the property is sold, and then determined in the light of the actual contributions made by either party while the trust of land subsisted[3]. In this book, such shares are referred to as *floating shares*[4].

The effect of executing a declaration of trust which creates floating shares is much the same as expressly creating a resulting trust and a constructive trust at the outset.

[1] 'In the absence of any special circumstances . . . the time at which the beneficial interest crystallises is the time of the acquisition' (*Bernard v Josephs* (1983) 4 FLR 178 at 188F, per Griffiths LJ).
[2] *Pettitt v Pettitt* [1970] AC 777 at 813E.
[3] 'There is nothing inherently improbable in their acting on the understanding that the wife should be entitled to a share which was not quantified immediately on the acquisition of the home, but should be left to be determined when the mortgage was repaid or the property disposed of, on the basis of what would be fair having regard to the total contributions, direct or indirect, which each spouse had made by that *date*' (*Gissing v Gissing* [1970] 2 All ER 780 at 793d, per Lord Diplock).
[4] The expression 'floating shares' is not a technical term. They could be referred to as, say, 'deferred shares'. When floating shares crystallise, they become fixed.

THE ADVANTAGES OF FIXED SHARES

1.10 Ascertaining or 'fixing' the co-owners' shares of the net proceeds of sale when they purchase the property has a number of advantages[1]. They include the following.

- Certainty. The position is clear from the start.
- At any given time each co-owner can work out approximately how much he or she would be entitled to receive if the property were sold.
- Simplicity. All that is needed to work out 'who gets what' is a completion statement when the property is sold or – during the subsistence of the trust – a current valuation of the property and a mortgage redemption statement or a statement of the surrender value of any mortgage-linked insurance policy.
- Convenience. There is less paperwork needed than for floating shares. There is no need for the co-owners to keep receipts and accounts as evidence of their respective contributions.
- If the co-owners' circumstances change (eg if their contributions towards the mortgage payments vary, or if they contribute disproportionately

1.10 *Property*

towards the cost of any repairs and improvements to the property) the imbalance can be rectified by means of a supplemental declaration of trust.
- The fixed share system enables one co-owner to confer a gratuitous benefit on the other – if that is the intention[2].

[1] For the distinction between fixed shares and floating shares, see **1.9** above. For a discussion of the disadvantages of fixed shares, see **1.11** below.

[2] For example, where the co-owners declare themselves to be beneficial joint tenants or beneficial tenants in common in equal shares, and one co-owner has contributed substantially more than the other towards the purchase price or the mortgage payments.

THE DISADVANTAGES OF FIXED SHARES

1.11 The fixed share system is not without its disadvantages[1].

- Fixed shares are potentially immutable. They conclude the question of title between the co-owners for all time 'and in the absence of fraud or mistake at the time of the transaction the parties cannot go behind the declaration of trust at any time thereafter, even on death or the breakdown of their relationship'[2].
- Circumstances change. What seemed fair and reasonable when the property was purchased may be quite unconscionable when the time comes to sell it.
- Often it requires each co-owner to commit himself to paying a specified share of the mortgage payments. For various reasons such as unemployment, one or other co-owner may be unable or unwilling to keep up those payments.
- It may be necessary to keep the fixed shares under constant review. In practical terms such a review may be forgotten, producing an unfair result when the property is sold.
- In practice, it is unlikely that the co-owners will execute a supplemental declaration of trust if their contributions vary. Inviting one's partner to enter into a further declaration could create difficulties within the relationship. It may involve some expenditure on valuation fees. It will almost certainly involve legal fees.
- There are several ways of calculating fixed shares. It is not easy to decide at the outset which method will produce the fairest result when the property is sold. One method of calculation might favour one partner, while another method might favour the other. Occasionally, the differences between the various formulae can produce perverse results[3].
- Problems arise over post-separation contributions, particularly where one co-owner has abandoned the property and stopped making contributions towards the mortgage payments.
- It is not entirely clear when the fixed shares should 'crystallise' if the couple separate. Should they crystallise on the date of separation or on the date when the property is eventually sold? The Court of Appeal has experienced difficulties in answering these questions[4].

[1] For the distinction between fixed shares and floating shares, see **1.9** above.
[2] *Pettitt v Pettitt* [1970] AC 777 at 813E, per Lord Upjohn.
[3] See Precedents **1.165** and **1.170** below and the footnotes thereto.

⁴ In *Hall v Hall* (1982) 3 FLR 379, the court held that the plaintiff was entitled to a share of the equity valued at the date on which the relationship ended. This decision was explained and distinguished in *Gordon v Douce* [1983] 1 WLR 563. In *Turton v Turton* [1988] 1 FLR 23, it was held that 'unless there is some express declaration or agreement to the effect that the parties' respective beneficial shares are to be valued at the time of their separation . . . the parties' beneficial interests would always have to be regarded in the normal way under a trust for sale, with the effect that they would endure until such time as the property is sold, and that they then attach to the proceeds of sale' (at 34A, per Kerr LJ).

THE ADVANTAGES OF FLOATING SHARES

1.12 Floating shares may be considered preferable to fixed shares for the following reasons[1].

- The concept is more equitable, in theory at least because 'who gets what?' depends on 'who paid what?'.
- There should be no need to keep floating shares under constant review.
- Any variations in the co-owners' contributions will automatically be taken into account. There is no need to execute a supplemental declaration of trust.
- The contributions made by each party will be examined retrospectively from the date on which the property was sold or from the date on which the co-owners separated, in much the same way that a court is able to look back with the benefit of hindsight on all the relevant facts[2].
- There should be less difficulty over post-separation contributions[3].
- Any possible need to apply to the court for a declaration of trust to be rectified or set aside on the grounds of fraud or mistake is virtually eliminated.
- There should be less likelihood of one co-owner inadvertently conferring a gratuitous benefit on the other.
- Although it may appear that the mathematics of calculating floating shares are complex, in reality – given all the relevant information and a reliable calculator – the exercise should not take very much longer than the calculation of fixed shares[4].

[1] For the distinction between fixed shares and floating shares, see **1.9** above. For a discussion of some of the disadvantages of floating shares, see **1.13** below.
[2] *Gissing v Gissing* [1970] 2 All ER 780 at 793.
[3] For the difficulties over post-separation contributions, see **1.11** above.
[4] See Precedents **1.170–1.173** below.

THE DISADVANTAGES OF FLOATING SHARES

1.13 Floating shares have their drawbacks[1].

- There is less certainty. A co-owner may find it difficult to quantify his or her entitlement at any time.
- Co-owners must keep accounts, receipts and statements, showing who paid what and when. In many cases it is unlikely that they will do so.
- Even if they do keep accounts, the co-owners could still disagree about the contributions made, especially if they came from a joint account.
- The calculations may be more complicated than the calculation of fixed shares.

1.13 *Property*

- It is difficult to know where to draw the line with repairs and improvements, for example what repairs should affect the beneficial interests, and what repairs are so minor as to be irrelevant.
- Although floating shares reflect the direct cash contributions made by each co-owner, inflation can play havoc with the equities. For example, payment of £1,000 by co-owner A when the property was purchased in 1974 would probably, in real terms, be worth five times as much as a payment of £1,000 made by co-owner B towards improvements to the property in 1993[2].
- Cash contributions towards repairs and improvements are not always identical to the enhancement value; the co-owners might disagree about the extent to which the value of the property has been enhanced[3].
- Floating shares can only exist in the context of a beneficial tenancy in common. Accordingly, they are subject to any perceived disadvantages to which tenancies in common are themselves subject.
- There is less scope for mutual dependence. For example, floating shares would prejudice a co-owner who had left work in order to have a baby or to look after children, and who was therefore unable to make any financial contribution towards the mortgage payments or any repairs or improvements to the property.
- Two methods of calculating floating shares are described in this book. One is the simple addition of each co-owner's contributions, and an apportionment of the net proceeds of sale pro rata[4]. The other identifies the extent to which any change in the value of the property is attributable to a co-owner's lump-sum contributions and his or her mortgage-related contributions[5]. These methods will produce different (sometimes substantially different) results[6].
- An injustice might occur if one co-owner pays the mortgage (which will affect his or her beneficial interest) and the other co-owner pays other outgoings which may not affect any beneficial interests.

[1] For the distinction between fixed shares and floating shares, see **1.9** above. For a discussion of some of the advantages of floating shares, see **1.12** above.
[2] Alluded to by Nicholls LJ in *Passee v Passee* [1988] 1 FLR 263 at 271.
[3] In *Pettitt v Pettitt* [1970] AC 777 at 780, the wife was not prepared to concede that her husband's expenditure of £723.17s had increased the value of Tinker's Cottage by £1,000.
[4] See Precedent **1.171** below.
[5] See Precedent **1.173** below.
[6] See Precedent **1.173**.

FRACTIONS, PERCENTAGES AND RATIOS

1.14 Fixed shares are usually expressed as fractions or percentages of the sale price or the net proceeds of sale. Occasionally, they appear as ratios. When quoting fractions there is a tendency to reduce them to the lowest common denominator, but this could diminish the understanding of the document for the sake of visual amenity. In the final analysis, how the shares are expressed will be a compromise between strict accuracy and ease of understanding. This is best illustrated by examples:

Example: A and B buy a bungalow for £56,000. B pays £40,000, and A pays £16,000. A declaration of trust which states that B is entitled to 71.4286 per cent of the net proceeds of sale and that A is entitled to

28.5714 per cent would be entirely accurate, but rather bizarre. A declaration which states that B is entitled to 40/56ths and A 16/56ths, would be much easier to reconcile with the original contributions: probably easier to reconcile than reducing the fractions to the lowest common denominator – B 5/7ths and A 2/7ths.

Example: A and B buy a house for £73,850. A contributes £47,264, and B contributes £26,586. A declaration of trust, which provides that A is entitled to receive 47,264/73,850ths and B 26,586/73,850ths of the net proceeds of sale would be precise but a little clumsy. It would be much better to say that A will receive 64 per cent and B 36 per cent.

SHARES OF THE SALE PRICE AND SHARES OF THE NET PROCEEDS OF SALE

1.15 The sale or disposal of a property usually comprises four cash elements:

(1) the sale price itself;
(2) the amount required to redeem the mortgage;
(3) the incidental costs of the sale; and
(4) the net proceeds of the sale.

A statement in a declaration of trust to the effect that one co-owner will receive 75 per cent of the sale price and the other co-owner will receive 25 per cent of the sale price is, on its own, deficient, because it fails to take into account the co-owners' liability for the payment of the sale costs or for the redemption of the mortgage, if there is one. So, any reference to the sale price should be followed by some indication as to how the deductions are to be apportioned between the co-owners.

'The net proceeds of sale', on the other hand, generally refers to the balance of the sale price remaining after all the deductions have been made. So, in principle, the expression 'net proceeds of sale' should be preceded by some indication as to how the deductions were apportioned between the co-owners. In isolation, a statement that one co-owner will receive three-quarters, and the other co-owner one-quarter, of the net proceeds of sale, assumes that the sale costs and the amount required to redeem the mortgage have already been deducted from the sale price in those proportions.

1.16 The acquisition of a property also usually consists of four distinct cash elements:

(1) the purchase price;
(2) the mortgage advance;
(3) the incidental purchase costs; and
(4) the co-owners' down payments or cash contributions.

A common mistake is to correlate the co-owners' down payments – their cash contributions towards the purchase price – and their eventual shares of the net proceeds of sale. It is only safe to correlate the co-owners' original contributions to their shares of the net proceeds of sale where:

– there is no mortgage; or

1.16 *Property*

- there is a mortgage, but the co-owners intend to contribute towards the mortgage payments in exactly the same proportions as their down payments bear to each other; and
- they also intend to pay the sale costs in exactly the same proportions as their down payments bear to each other.

It is recommended that wherever there is a mortgage, the shares of the co-owners should be expressed as a fraction or percentage of the sale price, *less* a fraction or percentage of the amount required to redeem the mortgage, *less* a fraction or percentage of the incidental costs of selling the property.

It is important to remember both the purchase costs and the sale costs. Often they are overlooked.

Who owns what if there is a dispute?

1.17 The starting point for determining who owns what in any dispute over property will be the documents of title.

If the property was bought at the outset with the purpose of providing a home for the cohabitants, the solicitors acting at the time should have ensured that the parties' intentions were clearly recorded (see **1.1** above). In practice, this does not always happen.

There are two aspects to the ownership of property: the legal title to the property and the beneficial interests in it. Both may be vested in the same people, but this is not necessarily the case.

On the face of it, if the title documents show a person to be the legal owner, there is a presumption that he or she will also own the beneficial interest. This presumption can be rebutted by showing that the legal owner holds the beneficial interest on trust for another, whether jointly or in common with him, or absolutely.

A trust can be shown to exist either by producing a document in writing in which it is expressly set out, or where no such document exists, by asking the court to imply the existence of a trust, relying upon principles of equity.

Express declaration of beneficial interests

1.18 If there is a declaration in the conveyance or transfer of the property to the legal owner(s) as to those in whom the beneficial title will vest, then in the absence of fraud, mistake or undue influence, or the operation of proprietory estoppel that declaration will be conclusive.

This was the position in *Goodman v Gallant*[1]. In that case, Mr Goodman transferred the former matrimonial home into the names of Mrs Goodman and her cohabitant, Mr Gallant. There was an express declaration that they held the property as beneficial joint tenants. Before long, the relationship turned sour and Mrs Goodman severed the joint tenancy. In the litigation which followed she contended that the beneficial interests in the property should be

75/25 per cent in her favour on the basis of contribution. The court held that it could not disturb the express declaration that the parties were to hold the proceeds of sale as joint tenants, and following the severance of the joint tenancy, in equal shares. The equitable doctrine of implied trusts could not be invoked where there was an express declaration[2]. This was confirmed by the important decision of the House of Lords in *Stack v Dowden*[3].

In *Davis v Jackson and Another*[4] the trustee in bankruptcy of Mr Jackson applied for an order for sale in respect of the property held in the joint names of Mr Jackson and his estranged wife. Mr and Mrs Jackson had lived apart for many years. After separation, Mrs Jackson had bought a property in her sole name with the assistance of a mortgage advance. A number of years later she fell into arrears with the mortgage repayments. Mr Jackson stepped in and arranged a remortgage. The lenders required him to be a party to the mortgage deed, and the property was at that stage put into joint names. Mrs Jackson continued to make all the mortgage repayments.

In the absence of any vitiating factor, subsequent variation, or facts giving rise to an estoppel, the court held that express declaration of trust contained in the TR1 made the claim of the trustee in bankruptcy for a half share of the net proceeds unanswerable[5].

[1] [1986] 1 FLR 513.
[2] See **1.6** above. See also *Pankhania v Chandegra (by her litigation friend, Ronald Andrew Eagle)* [2012] EWCA Civ 1438.
[3] [2007] UKHL 17.
[4] [2017] 2 FLR 1153.
[5] Using the mechanism of equitable accounting however, the judge endeavoured to mitigate the situation for Mrs. Jackson see paras 30 et seq.

BENEFICIAL JOINT TENANTS

1.19 The express declaration as to the beneficial interests may provide that the parties are beneficial joint tenants. This means that unless or until the joint tenancy is severed[1] each joint tenant has an equal and identical interest in the entire property, or the net proceeds of sale thereof. Where property is held by beneficial joint tenants, on the death of a joint tenant his or her interest passes to the remaining joint tenants in equal shares by operation of the right of survivorship. A beneficial joint tenant of property cannot leave his or her share by will, nor can it be distributed on an intestacy because it will not form part of the estate for succession purposes[2].

[1] See **1.21** below.
[2] However, see **6.11** and the court's powers under s 9 of the I(PFD)A 1975 to treat a severable share as part of the net estate for the purposes of an application under that Act.

TENANTS IN COMMON

1.20 If the beneficial interests are held as tenants in common, the interest of each will be expressly specified. For example, the beneficial interests may be expressed to be held by the parties as tenants in common in equal shares or such other proportion as may be agreed. This will mean that each will own a

1.20 *Property*

specified share of the property which will form part of his or her estate on death, rather than passing to the surviving tenant(s) as would be the case if they had been joint tenants.

Severing the joint tenancy

1.21 If a joint tenancy is severed, the nature of the parties' interests in the property changes to that of tenants in common in equal shares[1]. The severed shares will then form part of each owner's estate for succession purposes.

A joint tenancy can be severed by the tenant who wishes to sever the joint tenancy serving[2] a notice of severance on the other joint tenant(s) (s 36(2) of the LPA 1925). There will be good service of the notice of severance if it is either left at or sent by registered post to the last known home *address* or business of the person to be served[3].

For registered land a restriction should be entered[4].

A severance can be brought about in other ways. For example in *Burgess v Rawnsley*[5] it was suggested that a common intention or agreement between joint tenants that the tenancy should be severed may be sufficient, even if there was nothing in writing[6].

The effect of one joint tenant making an application for an order for sale or becoming bankrupt can be to sever the joint tenancy, as can one joint tenant dealing with his interest as if it were held as a tenant in common, for example by selling, assigning or charging it[7]. In *Perkins v Borden*[8] a brother and sister owned a house as joint tenants but both gave instructions to a solicitor to prepare wills leaving each other a life interest in their share with the remainder to go to other relatives. It was held that the element of agreement present in their instructions was sufficient to sever the joint tenancy and that the pre-1926 methods of severance were still applicable; 'it is not a case of one of them acting behind the back of the other. The reference in the will to a half share makes it clear that they were treating their share as disposed by their wills'. It would not of course have amounted to severance if only one had made a will disposing of that share.

[1] For an interesting discussion on how the severed shares may be found to be held other than equally see Mark Pawlowski, 'Joint owners, severance and the family home' *Family Law* October [2016], p 1238.
[2] See *Kinch v Bullard* [1999] 1 FLR 66, in which a notice was deemed served once it arrived at the *address* of the *addressee*, even if it never came to his notice, and even though the sender had decided to withdraw it and so had destroyed it on arrival.
[3] LPA 1925, s 199.
[4] See **1.7**.
[5] [1975] Ch 429. See also *Perkins v Borden re Woolnough deceased* [2002] WRLT 595.
[6] See also *Quigley v Masterson* [2011] EWHC 2529 (Ch).
[7] *Ahmed v Kendrick* [1988] 2 FLR 22; *Re Drapers Conveyance* [1969] 1 Ch 486; *First National Securities v Hegerty* [1984] 1 All ER 139.
[8] *Perkins v Borden re Woolnough deceased* LSG 2002 (99) 24, [2002] WTLR 595.

1.22 In *Wallbank and Wallbank v Price*[1], Mr and Mrs Wallbank owned their matrimonial home as joint beneficial owners. The marriage came to an end and Mrs Wallbank signed a declaration in the following terms:

'I . . . have voluntarily agreed to vacate [the former matrimonial home] and also to forfeit any moneys or profit in anyway connected with this property, and by signing this declaration I revoke any rights in the disposal of the . . . property.'

She alleged that Mr Wallbank had exerted undue influence upon her to obtain her signature to the declaration. This was not made out, and the court held that the declaration was not only sufficient to sever the joint tenancy but also to dispose of her own beneficial interest in the property.

In *Davis v Smith*[2] the Court of Appeal upheld the decision of the judge at first instance that the joint tenancy had been severed even though there was no formal notice given. In that case there were divorce proceedings, and negotiations were in progress for the resolution of financial matters. The division of the assets was broadly accepted as being equal. To that end an endowment policy had been surrendered, and an unequal division made in favour of the husband to enable him to proceed on the purchase of a house. The intention was that the inequality would be *address*ed in the division of the proceeds of sale of the family home. The family home was already on the market and an offer had been received. Before contracts could be exchanged, an accident befell the wife, who died. The court held that whilst a joint tenancy could survive even the sale of a jointly owned property, in this case it was apparent that the parties had already expressed an intention and an expectation that the proceeds would be shared equally.

Where the relationship between joint tenants has broken down, consideration should always be given to severing the joint tenancy and appropriate advice given. Such advice was given to both parties in *Davis v Smith* but not acted upon.

[1] [2008] 2 FLR 501.
[2] [2012] 1 FLR 1177.

No express declaration of beneficial interests

1.23 If the documents of title do not disclose an express declaration as to the ownership of the beneficial interests in the property, it may be possible to establish an intention that a person not on the legal title would nonetheless have a beneficial interest, and that the legal owner holds the property on trust for them both beneficially, or indeed for the non-owner absolutely.

A beneficial interest may be established in the absence of express declaration by relying upon an implied trust, either a resulting or a constructive trust. The non-owner may alternatively be able to rely upon the equitable doctrine of proprietary estoppel.

Sole legal ownership or joint legal ownership?

1.24 In the absence of an express declaration as to beneficial ownership, for example by a tick in the appropriate box of the Land Registry Form JO, TR1 or FR1, or a separate trust deed, the route to ascertaining the beneficial interests will depend upon whether the legal title in the property is held in the sole name of one of them, or jointly.

1.24 *Property*

If the property is held in the sole name of one of the parties, the presumption is that on the basis that 'equity follows the law' the legal owner is also entitled to the entire beneficial interest. The onus is upon the non-owner to persuade the court, first that he or she has a beneficial interest, and secondly as to the extent of it.

If the legal title to the property is held in the parties' joint names, there will be a presumption that the beneficial interests will be held in the same way as the legal title, ie equally. The burden of proof will be upon the joint owner who asserts that the beneficial interests should be held in different proportions to show why they should be other than equal. However, the joint owner will not usually have to persuade the court as to the fact of the sharing of the beneficial interests as this is presumed by the registration of the title in joint names.

Implied trusts

1.25 Using the principle of implied trusts, the court is able to determine whether and if so how the beneficial interests are to be shared in cases where either the property is held in one party's sole name, or if in joint names, no express declaration of the beneficial interests has been made.

Implied trusts can take the form of either a resulting trust, or a constructive trust. The practical significance of the distinction is in quantification. Where there is a resulting trust, quantification of shares is on the basis of contributions to the purchase price. Where the court finds a constructive trust, the court is able to use a broader brush in order to ascertain the extent of each party's beneficial share.

The two approaches can often produce quite different monetary outcomes[1].

[1] See *Drake v Whipp* [1996] 1 FLR 826.

1.26 Until *Stack v Dowden*, it was not always clear from the authorities which of the two applied in any given set of circumstances. That case provided much needed clarification. The majority view of the House of Lords was that where there is a dispute about the beneficial ownership of a shared home in the *domestic context*[1], whether between cohabitants or family members, constructive trust principles should be applied. The judgment of the Privy Council in *Marr v Collie*[2] went further, suggesting that property or other assets acquired in the course of a cohabitation relationship but with 'a commercial dimension'[3] were equally susceptible to an analysis of the parties' intention following the principles of constructive trusts[4]. In so finding, the Privy Council expressly disapproved the decision in *Laskar* as authority for the proposition that a transfer into joint names indicates legal and beneficial joint ownership unless the contrary is proved[5] had application only to the domestic context. Lord Kerr said as follows[6]:

> 'Where a property is bought in the joint names[7] of a cohabiting couple, even if that is as an investment, it does not follow inexorably that the 'resulting trust solution' must provide the inevitable answer as to how its beneficial ownership is to be determined . . . It is entirely conceivable that partners in a relationship would buy, as an investment, property which is conveyed into their joint names with the intention that the beneficial ownership should be shared equally between them, even

though they contributed in different shares to the purchase. Where there is evidence to support such a conclusion, it would be both illogical and wrong to impose the resulting trust solution on the subsequent distribution of the property.'

Addressing the so-called 'clash of presumptions' evident between the majority in *Stack v Dowden*, and the judgment of Lord Neuberger, Lord Kerr said this[8]:

'If it is the unambiguous mutual wish of the parties, contributing in unequal shares to the purchase of property, that the joint beneficial ownerships should reflect their joint legal ownership, then effect should be given to that wish. If, on the other hand, that is not their wish, or if they have not formed any intention as to beneficial ownership but had, for instance, accepted advice that the property be acquired in joint names, without considering or being aware of the possible consequences of that, the resulting trust solution may provide the answer.'

[1] Baroness Hale at para 69.
[2] [2017] 2 FLR 674.
[3] At para 40.
[4] See paras [56]–[59].
[5] *Stack v Dowden*.
[6] At para 49.
[7] Ie without an express declaration as to the beneficial interests.
[8] At para 54.

Resulting trusts

1.27 A resulting trust will arise where a person whose name may not be on the legal title to the property has nonetheless provided all or part of the purchase price. In the absence of evidence as to how they intended that they should share the beneficial interests, they would be entitled in direct proportion to their financial contribution.

The presumption that the financial contributions of a non-owner were intended to be recognised by a beneficial interest in the property may be rebutted by evidence that the money was a gift or a loan, or even payment of rent. In *Sekhon v Alissa*[1] it was held that there was a resulting trust in favour of a mother who had contributed £22,500 towards her daughter's purchase of a house. The daughter could not rebut the presumption that in contributing to the purchase price it was the intention that her mother would have an interest in the house, as she could not show that the money was intended either as a gift or as a loan to her.

Equity will presume an intention to make a gift where the donor is under an equitable obligation to make provision for or support another, for example parent and child, and husband and wife, and it will apply to gifts made by the man where a man and woman are engaged to be married. However, the presumption of advancement, or gift, does not apply as between cohabitants[2].

The situation may arise where there is a dispute between the parties as to their respective intentions regarding the contributions. Generally speaking, it will be the intention of the person making the contribution that will be determinative, regardless of whether that intention was communicated to the legal owner, as long as there was no question of fraud or deceit. Very often no clear intention will be discernible. In such cases, the lack of a positive intention, either to have

1.27 *Property*

a share of the property or for the contribution to be a gift or a loan, will operate either positively to rebut the presumption of advancement if the presumption of resulting trust applies, or negatively if the presumption of advancement applies, when it will be insufficient to dislodge that presumption.

1   [1989] 2 FLR 94.
2   *Lowson v Coombes* [1999] 1 FLR 799; *Cantor v Cox* [1975] 239 EG 121.

1.28 The relevance of resulting trusts in the context of the shared home of cohabitants has been eroding gradually. In *Oxley v Hiscock*[1] the Court of Appeal said the principle of resulting trusts was likely to be largely overridden by constructive trusts in those cases in which the parties could bring themselves within one of the two categories identified by Lord Bridge in *Lloyds Bank Plc v Rosset*[2]. In other words, where the party seeking to establish a beneficial interest can rely upon a common intention that the beneficial ownership was to be shared, either expressly agreed or understood, or to be inferred from the parties' conduct. This was considered by the House of Lords in *Stack v Dowden*. Baroness Hale endorsed the suggestion of the Law Commission in the Discussion Paper, *Sharing Homes*, that an 'holistic approach to quantification, undertaking a survey of the whole course of dealing between the parties and taking account of all conduct which throws light on the question which shares were intended'[3], was preferable to a strict arithmetical approach to financial contributions to the purchase price. This was the approach that would be more likely to produce the outcome that the parties intended. It is clear from the Supreme Court decision *Jones v Kernott*[4] that the court is concerned to ascertain the parties' common intention as to the sharing of the beneficial interests and not to embark upon an accounting exercise[5].

This was endorsed by the judgment in *Marr v Collie*[6]. In that case, the Privy Council expressly determined that the decision in *Laskar v Laskar*[7] should not be seen as being authority for the proposition that a transfer into joint names indicates legal and beneficial joint ownership unless the contrary is proved[8], only in the domestic context.

1   [2004] 2 FLR 669.
2   [1990] 2 FLR 155; see **1.33** below.
3   At para 61.
4   [2011] UKSC 53.
5   See para 24.
6   [2017] 2 FLR 674.
7   [2008] 2 FLR 589.
8   *Stack v Dowden*.

1.29 In *Laskar*, a mother and daughter bought the mother's council house with the benefit of the 'Right to Buy' discount that accrued to the mother through her secure tenancy. There was a mortgage in joint names, and each contributed a small amount of cash to make up the balance of the purchase price. The property was conveyed into their joint names without a declaration as to the beneficial ownership. It had always been the plan that the mother would live with another daughter and that the property would be let to tenants. The mother managed the lettings and saw to repairs and the rent was applied to discharge the mortgage repayments. After a family disagreement the daughter sought to realise her interest in the property and claimed that after

Stack v Dowden there was a presumption that as a joint legal owner she owned the beneficial interests in equal shares with her mother.

The Court of Appeal held that the presumption applied to a family home occupied by cohabitants, but not as in that case to a property that had been purchased as an investment with a view to obtaining rental income and capital appreciation. The doctrine of resulting trusts would therefore apply and in the absence of any relevant discussions between the parties the beneficial shares would reflect the contributions to the purchase price. On this basis the daughter's share was assessed at 33 per cent taking into account the right to buy discount that was a contribution entirely from the mother.

The court went on to say that even if the presumption of joint beneficial ownership had applied, it would have been rebutted by the following factors:

– their financial affairs were always kept separate;
– the property had not been bought as a home for either or both of them;
– the property had been bought primarily as an investment;
– there was a wide disparity in contribution and it could not presumed that the mother would intend to make a gift of such a size to only one of her children;
– the daughter had joined in the purchase because otherwise the mother could not afford to exercise the right to buy.

Notwithstanding the judgment of Lord Kerr in *Marr v Collie*, on the particular facts of that case the application of resulting trust principles can be said to have been appropriate given that the co-funding was necessitated by the mother's lack of funds, and although the relationship was familial, the financial venture on which the parties had embarked was not associated with a mutual commitment to each other for the future. The investment could therefore be characterized as a purely financial one, designed to pay dividends to each of the participants but shorn of any aspiration for a future equal sharing of proceeds[1].

[1] Per Lord Kerr *Marr v Collie* para 48, see also *Wodzicki v Wodzicki* [2018] 1 FLR 473.

QUANTIFICATION AND RESULTING TRUSTS

1.30 Where one or more parties contribute cash to the purchase of a property, and there is no mortgage advance, their respective contributions will be easily ascertained, and thus the shares arising under the resulting trust.

Quite often a party will assert a beneficial interest by virtue of other contributions made, not necessarily at the time of purchase.

Expenses connected with the purchase, for example legal fees and stamp duty land tax (SDLT), have generally been treated as part of the purchase price[1].

However, furniture, soft furnishings, fittings and even improvement work have not been regarded as contributions to the purchase price[2].

Since the 'Right to Buy' was introduced by the Housing Act 1985 (HA 1985), public sector tenants have been able to buy their homes at a discount. The

1.30 *Property*

question of whether this discount, accrued over the period of the tenancy, can amount to a contribution to the purchase price of the property has been considered in a number of cases. In *Springette v Defoe*, it was held that the discount should be treated as a cash contribution. This was confirmed as good authority in *Laskar v Laskar*[3].

[1]   See *Re Densham* [1975] 1 WLR 1519; *Walker v Hall* [1984] FLR 126; *Huntingford v Hobbs* [1993] 1 FLR 736.
[2]   *Pettitt v Pettitt* [1970] AC 777.
[3]   However, the resulting trust approach taken in *Springette v Defoe* was disapproved in *Oxley v Hiscock* as it concerned co-ownership in a domestic context and to that extent it should not be followed.

1.31 Most purchases are made with the assistance of a mortgage advance. This can complicate quantification under the doctrine of resulting trusts as taking responsibility for a loan is not necessarily the same as contributing cash. Generally speaking however, moneys raised by way of a loan and applied to the purchase price of a property have been regarded as a contribution by the person who obtained the loan.

Mr Huntingford's interest in the home bought jointly with Mrs Hobbs was quantified by reference to the sum borrowed on mortgage, rather than the sum of the mortgage repayments actually made, the parties having agreed at the time of the purchase that he would be solely responsible for the repayments.

In both *Stack v Dowden* and *Laskar v Laskar* Lord Neuberger was dubious about the principle of treating liability under a mortgage as the equivalent of a cash contribution when assessing beneficial shares under a resulting trust. However, in *Laskar* he said, 'there was a strong case for apportioning the mortgage equally between the parties when it comes to assessing their respective contributions to the purchase price'[1]. In that case the parties had assumed joint responsibility for the mortgage, and the repayments were made from the rental income on the property.

[1]   At para 29.

Constructive trusts

1.32 The restrictions upon and uncertainty about what can properly be called contributions to the purchase price for the purposes of establishing a resulting trust, as well as the strictly arithmetical approach to quantification, have given way to the constructive trust in the domestic context of cohabitants and other home sharers as it more properly reflects the realities of the give and take, in financial and other terms, of close personal relationships[1].

A constructive trust may arise where two (or more) people acquire property with the common intention that it is to be shared, although the property is conveyed into the name of one (or some) of them only. To establish a beneficial interest, the non-owner also has to show that in reliance upon a common intention that the beneficial interests in the property were to be shared, he or she acted to his or her detriment. The basis for the trust is that it would be inequitable for the non-owner to be denied the share that it was the common intention that he or she should have. The same principles can be applied where a joint legal owner wishes to show that he or she is beneficially entitled to more than the half share that would otherwise be presumed from joint legal ownership.

1   See *Marr v Collie* [2017] 2 FLR 674.

ESTABLISHING A CONSTRUCTIVE TRUST

1.33 The jurisprudence in this area can be traced back to *Pettitt v Pettitt*[1] and *Gissing v Gissing*[2] and on through a succession of cases culminating in *Lloyds Bank Plc v Rosset*[3], and thereafter *Oxley v Hiscock*[4], the important decision of the House of Lords in *Stack v Dowden*[5] followed by that of the Supreme Court in *Jones v Kernott*[6].

In *Gissing v Gissing* the basic principles were set out. In order to establish a beneficial interest, a non-owner would have to persuade the court that it would be inequitable for the legal owner to claim sole beneficial ownership. To achieve this, it would be necessary to demonstrate that there was a common intention to share the beneficial interests, and that the non-owner had acted to his or her detriment in reliance upon that common intention.

The common intention could be proved by direct evidence of an agreement to this effect, or this could be inferred by the court by the parties' conduct.

This was developed further in *Lloyds Bank Plc v Rosset*[7] with Lord Bridge's helpful analysis of the approach that the court should take in a case involving a dispute between cohabitants or co-owners over their interest in property.

Lord Bridge identified a 'two-stage enquiry' for the court. The court should first establish whether there was a common intention that the beneficial interests in the property were to be shared. If not, the matter ended there. If a common intention to share the beneficial interests was established, the court would go on to consider in what proportions the beneficial interests would be shared.

1   [1970] AC 777.
2   [1971] AC 886.
3   [1990] 2 FLR 155.
4   [2004] 2 FLR 669.
5   [2007] 1 FLR 1858.
6   [2011] UKSC 53.
7   [1990] 2 FLR 155.

1.34 In a case in which the legal title is vested in joint names this will usually suffice to satisfy the court as to a common intention to share the beneficial ownership and the enquiry moves on to one of quantification.

However, where the title is registered in the sole name of one of two cohabitants, further evidence will be necessary for the court to consider whether there was a common intention that the beneficial ownership was to be shared. The court will begin by looking to see if there was an express agreement, arrangement or understanding reached between the parties as to

1.34 *Property*

the sharing of the beneficial ownership. This will be a question of fact, 'based on evidence of express discussions between the parties however imperfectly remembered or however imprecise'[1]. This highlights the importance of taking very detailed instructions at the outset in order to give advice on the merits, and to form the basis of a full witness statement if it is considered that an arguable case is made out.

In the absence of anything express, the court will then look at the conduct of the parties to see if an intention to share the beneficial ownership can be inferred[2]. Again, the taking of full and detailed instructions at an early stage is of vital importance.

The conduct that might give rise to a constructive trust in these circumstances was considered in detail by Lord Bridge in *Lloyds Bank Plc v Rosset*. He said that 'direct contributions to the purchase price by the partner who is not the legal owner, whether initially or by payment of mortgage instalments, will readily justify the inference necessary to the creation of a constructive trust. But, as I read the authorities, it is at least extremely doubtful whether anything less will do'. In that case the wife's fairly heavy involvement in the renovation and redecoration of a property purchased in her husband's sole name with funds inherited by him but used as the matrimonial home was insufficient to found a beneficial interest, in the absence of either evidence of contributions to the purchase price or of an intention to share the ownership of the property beneficially.

Although not directly concerned with the issues that arise in cases where only one party is legally entitled to property, there was support from the House of Lords in *Stack v Dowden*[3] for the proposition that the words of Lord Bridge in *Rosset* set the first hurdle, of contribution from which a common intention may be inferred, ' . . . rather too high in certain respects . . . '[4] suggesting that when dealing with this issue courts should take a broader approach. There is encouragement for the view that the court will not be restricted to direct financial contributions, but will be able to look at the parties' whole course of conduct in relation to the property in order to ascertain their shared intentions. The majority in the House of Lords was of the opinion that the law had moved on since *Rosset* and that the court could and should take 'a wide view of what is capable of counting as a contribution towards the acquisition of a residence, while remaining sceptical of the value of alleged improvements that are really insignificant, or elaborate arguments (suggestive of creative accounting) as to how the family finances were arranged'[5]. Lord Walker went on to say that he 'would include contributions in kind by way of manual labour, provided that they are significant'[6].

This reflects the views put forward in the Law Commission's Discussion Paper *Sharing Homes*[7]. Although the Law Commissioners found it impossible to devise a statutory scheme for the determination of shares in the shared home that would work fairly, they suggested that there were measures that the courts could take to assist. For example, the courts could take a broader approach both to the kinds of contribution from which a common intention may be inferred, as well as to the quantification of the share.

[1] [1990] 2 FLR 155. *Rosset No 1*.

² *Rosset No 2*.
³ For a full discussion see **1.45** below.
⁴ Baroness Hale of Richmond at para 63.
⁵ Lord Walker at para 34.
⁶ At para 36.
⁷ Published on 18 July 2002.

CONDUCT FROM WHICH A COMMON INTENTION TO SHARE THE BENEFICIAL INTERESTS MAY BE INFERRED IN SOLE NAME CASES

1.35 Cases decided before *Stack v Dowden* will still have some relevance to the question of which contributions may be sufficient to enable the court to infer an intention to share the beneficial interest. Apart from direct financial contribution to the purchase price at the time the property was acquired, for example by paying the deposit[1], financial contribution by paying the mortgage instalments, particularly if combined with expenditure of money and effort on repairs may be conduct sufficient to demonstrate an intention to share the beneficial ownership in the absence of any evidence that there was an express agreement or understanding that this would be the case. It seems clear from *Grant v Edwards*[2] that the expenditure must be referable to the acquisition of the home. In that case the court gave a 50 per cent beneficial interest to a cohabitant, Miss Grant, who made regular and substantial contributions to the outgoings. Mr Edwards had made an excuse for leaving Miss Grant's name off the legal title from which she could reasonably have concluded that she was intended to have a share, and furthermore, without her contributions to the household expenses he would not have been able to afford the mortgage repayments.

However, in *Curran v Collins*[3], the excuse given by Mr Collins, the sole owner of the property, to his cohabitant Miss Curran when she raised the question of having an interest in the property was found not to be prima facie evidence of a common intention that they should share the beneficial interests, but rather was put forward by Mr Collins in order to avoid the embarrassment of having to decline her request. Mr Collins had said that it would be too expensive to have the property in joint names as it would involve paying for two insurance policies rather than one.

In *Le Foe v Le Foe and Woolwich plc; Woolwich plc v Le Foe and Le Foe*[4], a deputy High Court judge considered that Lord Bridge in *Rosset* was not saying in absolute terms that there were no circumstances in which indirect contributions may suffice in cases where there is no express agreement to share the beneficial ownership, simply that such cases will be the exception. In determining the extent of Mrs Le Foe's beneficial interest in the former matrimonial home, held in the sole name of Mr Le Foe and subject to a mortgage, direct repayments of which were made by him, the deputy judge concluded that indirect contributions made by Mrs Le Foe to the mortgage were sufficient for him to infer a common intention that she should have a beneficial interest in the former matrimonial home. The court found that although Mr Le Foe earned more than his wife there was 'no doubt that the family economy depended for its functions on [Mrs Le Foe's] earnings. It was an arbitrary

1.35 *Property*

allocation of responsibility that [Mr Le Foe] paid the mortgage, service charge and outgoings, whereas [Mrs Le Foe] paid for day-to-day domestic expenditure'.

1   In *McHardy & Sons (A Firm) v Warren* [1994] 2 FLR 338, a wedding gift of £650 from the husband's parents used to pay the deposit on the purchase of the first matrimonial home was held to be sufficient to establish a joint intention that they should share the beneficial interest in the property. See also *Midland Bank v Cooke* [1995] 2 FLR 915 in which the wife's notional half share of the gift by the husband's parents of the deposit for the couple's first home amounted to the wife's financial contribution to the purchase price.
2   [1987] 1 FLR 87.
3   [2015] EWCA Civ 404.
4   [2001] 2 FLR 970.

1.36 In *Cooke v Head*[1] a small contribution to the mortgage repayments and a significant practical contribution to the construction of the property was found to amount to conduct from which a common intention to share the beneficial ownership could be inferred.

In *Thomas v Fuller-Brown*[2] the fact that Mr Fuller-Brown had carried out substantial improvement works to the property in which he was living with Mrs Thomas, and which was in her sole name, did not of itself entitle him to an interest in the property, in the absence of an express agreement, or a common intention to be inferred from their conduct. As Lord Justice Slade put it, 'a man who does work by way of improvement to his cohabitee's property without a clear understanding as to the financial basis on which the work is to be done does so at his own risk'[3].

In *Eves v Eves*[4] it was said that in the absence of a common intention to share the beneficial ownership, which was in fact found in that case, the female cohabitant's contribution by way of assistance with decoration and improvements to the home would have been insufficient as conduct from which the court could have inferred such an intention[5].

In *Windeler v Whitehall*[6] contributions by way of keeping the house, and business entertaining, albeit with flair and to a high standard, were insufficient to entitle Miss Windeler to a beneficial interest in the home she had shared with Mr Whitehall[7].

1   [1972] 1 WLR 518.
2   [1988] 1 FLR 237.
3   At 247B.
4   [1975] 3 All ER 768.
5   See also *Hammond v Mitchell (Property: Beneficial Interest)* [1992] 1 FLR 229.
6   [1990] 2 FLR 505.
7   See also *Lloyds Bank plc v Rosset* [1990] 2 FLR 155; *McFarlane v McFarlane* [1972] NI 59; *Ivin v Blake (Property: Beneficial Interest)* [1995] 1 FLR 70.

1.37 There have been a number of cases on the question of common intention, decided after *Stack v Dowden*. In *James v Thomas*[1], the Court of Appeal considered a case in which the shared home was in the sole name of Mr Thomas. He had acquired the property some time before he met Miss James and she later moved in with him. Miss James relied upon her contributions to Mr Thomas' agricultural contracting business in which she worked hard, and until they went into partnership together, for no remuneration. It was her case that Mr Thomas had told her that she would benefit from the success of the business and would be well provided for in the event of his death, and it was on this basis that she put all her energies into the business. Other than the contribution she made to the business through her hard work she made no direct financial contributions. Mr Thomas paid all the outgoings on the property from the profits of the business, later the partnership. The relationship broke down after 4 years and Miss James sought a declaration that she had a beneficial interest in the shared home on constructive trust principles. She was unsuccessful both at first instance and in the Court of Appeal.

In order to establish a constructive trust she had first to establish that there was either an express agreement between them that she would have a beneficial share in the house, or that such an agreement could be inferred from their conduct during the whole course of dealings in relation to the property, and that she had acted to her detriment in reliance upon that agreement.

Although the Court of Appeal acknowledged that in *Stack v Dowden* it had been made clear that it was possible for an agreement to share the beneficial interests to be made or inferred at any point after the property had been acquired, in this case it was held that where there was no evidence of an express agreement to share the beneficial interests, the court would be reluctant to infer an agreement simply from the parties' conduct. The highest Miss James could put her case was that the profits of the business, later the partnership, had been enhanced by her efforts, and those moneys had been applied to the payment of the mortgage instalments. The Court of Appeal was unable to infer an agreement that she should have a beneficial interest in the property on that basis, whilst making the point that there may be circumstances in which contributions to capital repayments by a non-owning cohabitant may evidence an agreement that the beneficial interests were to be shared.

[1] [2008] 1 FLR 1598.

1.38 *Holman v Howes*[1] concerned a couple who had formerly been married and then reconciled. They bought a house to live in together, the legal title to which was registered in Mr Howes' sole name. They each contributed roughly the same amount to the purchase price. They separated and after a brief reconciliation the parties again split up and Miss Holman remained in the house with their child for over 20 years. She took on all the responsibilities connected with the property and sought a declaration that she was entitled to the entire beneficial interest. Adopting the approach set out in the judgment of Baroness Hale in *Stack v Dowden* to find what was intended between the parties the Court of Appeal upheld the finding of the judge at first instance that the intention of the parties at the time of purchase was that it would be a joint venture. The fact that Miss Holman had taken on all the financial responsibility for the upkeep of the property after the separation could not be evidence of a common intention that she was to have the entire beneficial interest in the absence of any discussions between the parties about this either at the time of acquisition or since. What the evidence pointed to was a joint enterprise and the beneficial shares would therefore be equal.

1.38 *Property*

Abbott v Abbott[2] was a decision of the Privy Council relating to a married couple and their property in Antigua. There is no legislation in Antigua equivalent to the Matrimonial Causes Act 1973 and so property disputes fall to be dealt with on the same basis as that applying to unmarried couples in England and Wales.

The matrimonial home was in the sole name of the husband, having been built on land conveyed to him by his mother shortly after the marriage. The building costs were met in part by gifts from the husband's mother, and in part by secured borrowing for which the husband and wife were jointly and severally liable. They operated a joint bank account and pooled their resources. When the marriage broke down the wife claimed half the property. At first instance the judge adopted constructive trust principles and determined that the husband held the matrimonial home on trust for himself and his wife in equal shares. The husband appealed to the East Caribbean Court of Appeal and was successful. Reinstating the decision of the judge at first instance on the wife's appeal, the Privy Council said that the Court of Appeal had been in error in concluding from the famous words of Lord Bridge in *Rosset* that a common intention to share the beneficial ownership could not be inferred in the absence of direct financial contributions to the purchase price by the wife. Baroness Hale said that the law had moved on since then and that the approach now was to look at the entire course of dealings between the parties in relation to the property and from that ascertain their common intention as to the beneficial ownership. In the present case the factors that lent weight to a common intention to share the beneficial ownership equally were these:

– the inference to be drawn from the gifts of land and cash from the husband's mother was that it was a gift to them both, not just to the husband[3];
– the parties organised their finances jointly;
– they were jointly liable for the secured borrowing;
– the husband accepted that the wife had a beneficial share, although he disputed the extent of it.

[1] [2008] 1 FLR 1217.
[2] [2008] 1 FLR 1451.
[3] *Warren v McHardy*; *Midland Bank v Cooke*.

1.39 In *Thompson v Humphrey*[1] Warren J conducted a helpful review of the authorities on contribution. In that case the subject property was in the sole name of Mr Humphrey. His cohabitant, Mrs Thompson, claimed a beneficial interest in Church Farm, the property in which they had lived together along with the children of her former husband. Her case was put on the basis that it was intended between them that they would share the beneficial ownership equally. There was a paucity of detailed evidence about any express discussions the parties had, but at its highest the applicant could establish only that there had been a common intention that Church Farm would be a home for them and her children, and that the respondent had said that he would always look after her financially. This was insufficient for Warren J to find that there was a common intention that the applicant should have a beneficial share in the property.

Walsh v Singh[2] was a reminder that contributions alone will not establish a beneficial share in the absence of a common intention or specific representations as to beneficial ownership by the legal owner to support detrimental reliance. In that case the property had been bought by Mr Singh in his sole *name* 2 years after the parties commenced cohabitation. The mortgage was in the sole name of Mr Singh and no financial contribution was made to the purchase by the applicant. The parties became engaged to be married but they separated without marrying some 4 years later. In the meantime the applicant had assisted in the development of the property and adjoining land purchased subsequently as an equestrian centre. The land had been placed in Mr Singh's SIPP. Miss Walsh provided financial assistance for the purchase of the land but this was held by the judge to be a loan rather than a contribution to the purchase price.

In support of her claim for a beneficial half share in the property Miss Walsh relied upon the fact that she had given up a promising career at the Bar in order to focus on the equestrian business. It was her case that she would not have done this unless she had been told that 'half of everything we were doing was mine' and that this amounted to detrimental reliance. HHJ Purle QC found that the motivation for this was not a promised half share, but her commitment to Mr Singh whom she was intending to marry. The decision to give up the Bar was essentially a joint decision that suited them both, for different reasons.

In conclusion, whilst accepting that Miss Walsh had made significant contributions to the equestrian business that would have been sufficient to found a beneficial interest, the necessary common intention coupled with detrimental reliance were missing and her claim in this regard therefore failed. He identified the specific factors from the evidence that informed his decision:

- the property was purchased in Mr Singh's name and he bore all the expense of renovation and development;
- the applicant was not in a financial position at that time to make any monetary contribution;
- the applicant retained her own property which she let out, and when sold she retained the proceeds;
- the parties did not pool their finances;
- there was never any record in writing of the alleged beneficial half share – this was surprising in view of Miss Walsh's high intelligence and legal training;
- there was evidence that at the time the property was purchased the applicant told Mr Singh's bank manager that she knew that she would not have any interest in the property;
- there was evidence that subsequently the applicant had told a third party that if she and Mr Singh ever split up she would only have a few horses, the dog and the horse box;
- Mr Singh was too financially astute to promise a beneficial share when it was he putting all the money in to the project;
- an agreement drawn up after separation did not make any reference to a sharing of the beneficial interests, rather it was predicated on the express basis that Mr Singh was sole owner;

1.39 *Property*

- Miss Walsh's contributions were referable to her commitment to the relationship rather than a belief in a beneficial interest;
- although significant, her contributions were small compared with the financial and other contributions of Mr Singh.

The judge also found it 'likely that Mr Singh would have told Miss Walsh also that she could live at [the property] with him indefinitely, that he would support her, and that she should have no fears for the future, as they were to be married. This was consistent with the protestations of love and long-term commitment he expressed from an early stage of their relationship. It was in this context that he probably also told Miss Walsh from time to time that her financial future was secure. He may well have said something to that effect also at the time of the purchase of [the property] but I do not think that this was understood by Miss Walsh or could reasonably have been understood by her as promising her a beneficial interest in [the property]. She knew Mr Singh was buying that property for them both to live in, but in his own name, as he was paying both the cash element of the purchase price and the mortgage. She understood that this meant that he would be the sole owner, and went ahead because she hoped to marry him and spend the rest of her life with him. She knew that there was a risk that things would go wrong, but took that risk willingly'[3].

[1] [2010] 2 FLR 107.
[2] [2010] 1 FLR 1658.
[3] At para 43.

1.40 *Geary v Rankine*[1] was one of the first reported decisions on establishing a common intention constructive trust after *Jones v Kernott*[2]. The property in question, a guest house in Hastings, had been bought by Mr Rankine in his sole name and with his own funds as an investment. He employed a manager to run the guest house as he and Mrs Geary were living together in London. The manager proved less than satisfactory and first Mr Rankine and then Mrs Geary went to Hastings to work in the business. This state of affairs continued for around 13 years until the couple separated. Mrs Geary claimed a beneficial interest in the guest house which was rejected both at first instance and on appeal to the Court of Appeal.

Following the principles in *Jones v Kernott* and *Stack v Dowden*[3] the starting point for ascertaining beneficial entitlement was the legal title. This was in Mr Rankine's sole name giving rise to a presumption that the beneficial interest was also intended for him. The burden was upon Mrs Geary to establish that there was a different common intention.

It was conceded on behalf of Mrs Geary that a common intention at the time of purchase could not be sustained. She therefore had to satisfy the court that the position changed subsequently, either by express statement or by inference from the parties' conduct. The trial judge had found that there was no such change in Mr Rankine's intention so far as the beneficial interests were concerned. He found also that Mrs Geary had not acted to her detriment in reliance upon any assertion that she was to have a beneficial interest in the property.

It was emphasised that the court could not at the first stage, when the legal title was in a party's sole name and the court had to ascertain whether or not there was a common intention constructive trust, *impute*[4] a common intention to the parties. It was only at the second stage, when a common intention had been established, that the court was able to impute to them, from the whole course of dealings between the parties in relation to the property, what their intention was as to their respective beneficial shares[5].

The importance of the distinction was underlined in *Capehorn v Harris*[6]. In that case the Court of Appeal allowed the appeal against the decision of the district judge in which it was clear that although she had made findings as to the legal and beneficial ownership of the two properties and the business that were in issue, she had sought nevertheless to impute to the parties a different intention. In so doing, the Court of Appeal identified that she had fallen into the error of eliding the two stages of analysis. At the first stage, in the absence of any evidence of an actual agreement, the court could infer an agreement as to the sharing of the beneficial interests. The question of imputing an agreement was relevant only to the second stage where necessary in order to determine the extent of the respective shares.

[1] [2012] 2 FLR 1409.
[2] [2012] 1 FLR 45.
[3] [2007] 1 FLR 1858.
[4] Cf *infer*.
[5] Further on this point see the commentary of Rebecca Bailey-Harris on *Bhura v Bhura* [2014] EWHC 727 (Fam) reported in August [2014] Fam Law 1116.
[6] [2015] EWCA Civ 955.

1.41 *Barnes v Phillips*[1] also concerned the two stage test, and the stage at which it was appropriate to impute to the parties a shared intention. In that case, the Court of Appeal agreed that the judge at first instance had failed to make reference in his judgment to what he had undoubtedly determined by inference, namely that there had been an agreement to vary the beneficial shares in which the two cohabitants held their jointly owned property. It followed therefore that when he carried out the exercise of imputing to them the shares in which they then held the property, this was carried out as part of the second stage in the analysis, quantification, not the first stage.

However, the Court of Appeal considered that it was open to them to determine whether a common intention to vary the shares could be inferred. The conclusion was that it could. The evidence that weighed in favour of this was first, that shortly before separation Mr Barnes had received from funds raised by way of re-mortgage a sum equivalent to 25 per cent of the equity in the property, and secondly, that contributions to the mortgage thereafter were made substantially by Miss Phillips, Mr Barnes having told her at an early stage following separation that he was no longer able to pay.

In making an assessment of the equitable interests at 85 per cent for Miss Phillips and 15 per cent for Mr Barnes, the Court of Appeal expressly approved, in principle, the approach of the first instance judge in taking into account as part of the whole course of dealing in relation to the property, given the broad meaning advocated by Lord Walker and Baroness Hale in *Jones v Kernott*[2]. In particular, the judge had been entitled to take into account the lack

1.41 *Property*

of financial contributions made by Mr Barnes after the separation to the maintenance of the two children of the family who remained with Miss Phillips[3].

In *Thompson v Hurst*[4] Ms Hurst bought the council house of which she had been the tenant for a little under 20 years. She contributed the purchase price by way of the right to buy discount and a mortgage advance that was serviced by her earnings. Mr Thompson had lived with her there for all but the first 2 years and had made some contributions to the housekeeping.

The parties' relationship broke down 4 years after the purchase and Mr Thompson asked the court to determine their beneficial interests. At first instance the court found that there was a common intention constructive trust, and that in the absence of anything express as to sharing, the court finding that they did not *address* their minds to this, a fair division 10 per cent/90 per cent in favour of Ms Hurst would be fair on the basis of the whole history of the parties' relationship.

Mr Thompson appealed. The argument was advanced on his behalf that the fact that the parties had set out to own the house jointly, but were prevented from this by the mortgage lender's refusal to consider Mr Thompson suitable as a party to a mortgage deed, was sufficient for the court to find that there was an intention that they should share the beneficial interests jointly. This was roundly rejected by the Court of Appeal[5]:

> ' . . . [this] argument amounts to a submission that there should be a legal presumption of joint beneficial ownership, not merely where the parties are indeed the joint legal owners, but where there is evidence that they would have liked to be joint legal owners but for one reason or another that was not practical or desirable. Neither *Stack* nor *Jones* nor any other case, is authority for such a proposition. Indeed, the proposition is not consistent with principle nor sound policy.'

The court's task in sole name cases was succinctly set out[6]:

> 'In the case of a single legal owner . . . where there is no express declaration of trust, the claimant has first to establish some sort of implied trust, normally what is now termed a common intention constructive trust . . . The claimant must show that it was intended that he or she was to have a beneficial interest at all. That can only be achieved by evidence of the parties' actual intentions, express or inferred, objectively ascertained. If such evidence does show a common intention to share beneficial ownership, but does not show what shares were intended, then each of them is to have that share which the court considers fair, having regard to the whole of dealing in relation to the property.'

[1] [2015] EWCA Civ 1056.
[2] [2011] UKSC 53.
[3] At para 41.
[4] [2014] 1 FLR 238.
[5] Etherton LJ at para 20.
[6] Etherton LJ at para 22.

1.42 *Aspden v Elvy*[1] was an unusual case with substantial disputes of fact. Mr Aspden claimed a beneficial interest in a converted barn that in 2006, before its conversion, he had transferred to Ms Elvy. The barn had formed part of a farmhouse and associated land and buildings that he had bought in his sole name in 1986. He and Ms Elvy had commenced cohabitation shortly afterwards, by then having had a relationship for a little under a year. They went on to have two children.

In 2006 Mr Aspden had a reversal of fortunes in that he was unsuccessful in unrelated litigation. The parties had already separated, although they saw each other most days because Ms Elvy continued to run a business from the outbuildings at the farm. Mr Aspden realised that he would have to sell the farm to meet the costs of the litigation, and when in a very low state he told Ms Elvy that he proposed to divide the property, and transfer the barn and some land to her. The transfer was effected within a very short space of time. The farmhouse was sold later the same year. Mr Aspden paid his creditors from the proceeds and set up home in a static caravan on part of the land that had been transferred to Ms Elvy.

Between 2006 and 2009, the barn was converted to a dwellinghouse that was then occupied by Ms Elvy and the parties' children. The cost of conversion was in the region of £90,000. Both parties contributed financially and by assisting with the manual labour, although to what extent was in dispute. In 2009 Ms Elvy announced that she had formed a new relationship and would be selling the barn.

HHJ Behrens had to determine whether Mr Aspden had a beneficial interest, and if so, how this should be quantified.

His finding was that when the barn was purchased in 1986, as part of the larger property, Mr Aspden was the sole legal and beneficial owner. He found also that when Mr Aspden transferred his interest in the barn to Ms Elvy in 2006 there was nothing in his words or conduct at that time that would give rise to an inference that he was to retain any interest in the barn.

However, the judge accepted that Mr Aspden had contributed between £65,000 and £70,000 to the conversion costs. This represented a substantial part of his remaining assets. In the light of this he rejected Ms Elvy's assertion that his financial contributions were intended as gifts, preferring Mr Aspden's account that he hoped and expected that he would be able to move into the barn with Ms Elvy when the work was completed, and that she was aware of this.

In concluding that it was possible for there to be a change in the parties' intentions he relied upon the words of Griffiths LJ in *Bernard v Joseph*[2]:

> 'It might in exceptional circumstances be inferred that the parties agreed to alter their beneficial interests after the house was bought; an example would be if the man bought the house in the first place and the woman years later used a legacy to build an extra floor to make more room for the children. In such circumstances the obvious inference would be that the parties agreed that the woman should acquire a share in the greatly increased value of the house produced by her money . . . '

As there were no express discussions between the parties as to quantification, the judge approached this by inputing an intention by reference to what he considered fair having regard to the whole course of dealings between the parties. This resulted in a 25 per cent share for Mr Aspden on the basis of what the judge considered to be a fair return on the money he had put into the conversion, given the eventual value of the barn.

1   [2012] EWHC 1387 (Ch).
2   [1982] 3 All ER 162, at para 171.

1.43 *O'Kelly v Davies*[1] was a sole name case with unusual facts. The cohabiting couple's first home had been purchased in joint names. This was transferred to the woman's sole name 4 years later but the man continued to pay the mortgage. Although it was not part of either party's case, the judge at first instance found that this was done to enable the woman to claim state benefits for herself, and later their daughter as well, as if she were a single parent: the man worked abroad for much of the time.

Fifteen years after that, the woman sold the property to the man at market value and with the net proceeds purchased another property with a small mortgage, and banked the £30,000 that remained.

The couple continued to live in the first property and the second property was rented out until eventually it was repossessed. When the relationship broke down the man claimed a beneficial interest in the second property and this was the result at first instance. The court determined that the man did not need to rely upon the illegality of purpose in order to found his beneficial interest and so this did not affect the outcome. The woman appealed.

In dismissing the appeal, Pitchford LJ conducted a helpful review of the evolution of the area of the law when ascertaining beneficial interests in domestic property[2]. He confirmed that the starting point as required by *Jones v Kernott*[3] was that subject to common intention the beneficial interest in the first property belonged to the woman. In the absence of any express agreement between the parties as to their interests their respective contributions to the purchase by way of mortgage repayments were relevant in the search for their common intention, which the court held was that the woman would hold the beneficial interest on trust for herself and the man in equal shares.

In relation to the second property, the court found that the dealings with this property repeated the earlier pattern, being conveyed into the woman's sole name, but with the man continuing to be responsible for the majority of the household expenditure, including the mortgage repayments. Accordingly, the man was entitled to an equal beneficial interest in that property, that being fair by reference to the previous course of dealings between the parties in relation to the property.

1   [2014] EWCA Civ 1606.
2   Paras 18–29.
3   [2011] UKSC 53.

DETRIMENTAL RELIANCE

1.44 As well as establishing a common intention to share the property beneficially, a non-owner who wishes to persuade the court to impose a constructive trust must also show detrimental reliance in the belief of the shared ownership.

Law and Practice **1.46**

If a common intention has been established by inference from the non-owner's financial contributions to the property, then the same contributions can be used as evidence of detriment.

QUANTIFICATION AND CONSTRUCTIVE TRUSTS

1.45 Once the court is satisfied that a beneficial interest has been established it is necessary to quantify that beneficial share.

The beneficial interest may arise by the presumption in joint names cases, or in sole name cases by evidence either of express discussions at the time of purchase or by inference from conduct, including contributions, whether directly to the purchase price or by other contributions (financial or otherwise) together with in either case the non-owner having acted to his or her detriment.

The starting point, however, is different depending upon whether the legal title to the property is held in joint names or in one party's sole name.

In a joint names case the court starts with the presumption that the beneficial interests are held in the same way as the legal estate, that is in equal shares, and it is for the party contending for sharing in some other proportion to rebut that presumption. In other words the question for the court is whether the parties intended their beneficial interests to be different from their legal interests, and if so to what extent. The fact that the parties may have made unequal contributions to the purchase of the home will not usually be sufficient to displace the presumption.

In a sole name case the court is looking to ascertain the parties' common intention as to the sharing of the benefical interests and there is no presumption that they will be shared equally.

This exercise where a constructive trust is concerned is to be contrasted with the position where there is a resulting trust, when quantification will very largely be an accounting exercise, the beneficial interests being determined pro rata to the respective contributions to the purchase price. It will depend upon the facts of each particular case whether a resulting trust or a constructive trust analysis will provide the better outcome for the applicant, but on the basis of the decision of the majority in *Stack v Dowden* the constructive trust approach is the one that should be followed in the context of cohabitants and other home sharers.

1.46 The approach of the court to quantification of beneficial interests where there is a constructive trust in a sole name case was considered by the Court of Appeal in *Oxley v Hiscock*[1]. The decision in that case confirmed that in the absence of express agreement at the time of purchase as to how the beneficial interests were to be shared, the court should look at the entire history of the financial dealings between the parties in relation to the property from the date of purchase onwards. This is reflected in what Baroness Hale identified in *Stack v Dowden* as 'The search . . . to ascertain the parties' shared intentions, actual, inferred or imputed, with respect to the property in the light of their whole course of conduct in relation to it'. However, she cautioned that,

'... it does not enable the court to abandon that search in favour of the result which the court itself considers fair ...' and to that extent it is suggested that the Court of Appeal went too far in *Oxley v Hiscock*.

The facts of *Oxley v Hiscock* were as follows. Mr Hiscock and Mrs Oxley had met in the mid-1980s. Mr Hiscock worked abroad, but when he was in the UK they lived together at Mrs Oxley's property, in Page Close, Bean, Dartford, of which she was a secure tenant. When she had the opportunity to become the owner of that property under the 'Right to Buy' at a discount of £20,000 she did so, and Mr Hiscock provided the £25,200 needed to complete the purchase. That property was sold in 1991 and the property in dispute, in Dickens Close, Hartley, Kent, was purchased as a home for them both, and Mrs Oxley's children. The purchase was funded by the net proceeds of sale of Page Close, £61,500, borrowing of £30,000 and £35,500 from Mr Hiscock's own funds. The property was conveyed into the sole name of Mr Hiscock.

The solicitors advised Mrs Oxley that she ought to record the beneficial interests in view of the contribution she was making to the purchase of Dickens Close. Her reply was:

> '... I am quite satisfied with the present arrangements, and feel I know Mr Hiscock well enough not to need written legal protection in this matter.'

In due course, the relationship came to an end and Dickens Close was put on the market in 2001. The proceeds were divided by Mr Hiscock, substantially in his favour.

At first instance, the court found that there had been discussions between the parties at the time of purchase as to whose name should appear on the legal title in the context of a possible claim by Mrs Oxley's former husband. On this basis, the judge concluded that there was an intention that they should share the beneficial interests and there was therefore a constructive trust. In reaching a decision on quantification, the court determined that on an examination of the whole course of dealings between the parties in relation to the property, all the evidence pointed to '... an intention to share the benefit and the burden ... jointly and equally'.

Mr Hiscock appealed on the basis that in the absence of any express agreement as to how the beneficial interests were to be shared the court had to follow resulting trust principles, as in *Springette v Defoe*.

The Court of Appeal endorsed the general approach of the judge at first instance to quantification but held that on the evidence there was no basis for a finding that the parties had agreed on an equal division. Indeed, there appeared to be no agreement about the proportions in which they were to share:

> 'This must ... be seen as a case where there is no evidence of any discussion between the parties as to the amount of the share which each was to have. And on that basis, the judge asked herself the wrong question. She should not have sought, by reference to the conduct of the parties while they were living together at ... Dickens Close, to determine what intention both were then "evincing" – unless, by

that, she was able to find a common intention, communicated to each other, to determine, definitively, the shares which had been left undetermined at the time of acquisition. She might have asked herself whether their subsequent conduct, while living together at . . . Dickens Close, was consistent only with a common intention, at the time of acquisition, that their shares should be equal; but she did not. The right question, in the circumstances of this case, was "what would be a fair share for each party having regard to the whole course of dealing between them in relation to the property?"[2]'

The Court of Appeal considered that to give Mrs Oxley 50 per cent failed to take into account the substantially greater cash contribution by Mr Hiscock to the purchase price of Dickens Close, £60,700 as against £36,300, but was prepared to accept that the balance of the purchase price funded by mortgage advance was provided equally through the pooling of their resources whilst they were living together. On this basis, the beneficial interests were to be shared 60/40 in favour of Mr Hiscock.

This decision confirmed that the broad brush approach of the court in *Midland Bank v Cooke* to quantification of beneficial interests where a constructive trust is found is to be preferred to the restrictive resulting trust approach adopted in *Springette v Defoe*, at least in the domestic context.

[1] [2004] 2 FLR 669.
[2] Chadwick LJ at para 44.

1.47 In *Stack v Dowden*, the majority of the House of Lords agreed that the constructive trust approach was the appropriate approach to quantification. However, it was the unanimous view that in considering the whole course of dealings between the parties the objective was to determine what their intention had been as to the share each would have, not to impose what the court might consider to be a fair apportionment.

Stack v Dowden concerned the quantification of beneficial interests where the legal title was registered in the parties' joint names. The fact of joint legal ownership meant that the court was not troubled by the issue of whether there was an intention to share the beneficial interest. This was to be presumed. Baroness Hale identified the question for the court in joint names cases to be this: ' . . . did the parties intend their beneficial interests to be different from their legal interest . . . and if they did, in what way and to what extent?'[1].

The burden of proof is on the party who asserts that the beneficial interests are held differently from the legal interests. In determining the question on the particular facts of each case, Baroness Hale set out[2] a non-exhaustive list of factors that may be relevant:

'Many more factors than financial contributions may be relevant to divining the parties' true intentions. These include: any advice or discussions at the time of the transfer which cast light upon their intentions then; the reasons why the home was acquired in their joint names; the reasons why (if it be the case) the survivor was authorised to give a receipt for the capital moneys; the purpose for which the home was acquired; the nature of the parties' relationship; whether they had children for whom they both had responsibility to provide a home; how the purchase was financed, both initially and subsequently; how the parties arranged their finances, whether separately or together or a bit of both; how they discharged the outgoings on the property and their other household expenses. When a couple are joint owners of the home and jointly liable for the mortgage, the inferences to be drawn from who pays for what may be very different from the inferences to be drawn when only one is owner of the home. The arithmetical calculation of how much was paid by each is also likely to be less important. It will be easier to draw the inference that they intended that each should contribute as much to the household as they reasonably could and that they would share the eventual benefit or burden equally. The parties' individual characters and personalities may also be a factor in deciding where their true intentions lay. In the cohabitation context, mercenary considerations may be more to the fore than they would be in marriage, but it should not be assumed that they always take pride of place over natural love and affection.'

She concluded that 'At the end of the day, having taken all this into account, cases in which the joint legal owners are to be taken to have intended that their beneficial interest should be different from their legal interests will be very unusual'.

Notwithstanding this, the majority decision of the House of Lords was that the position in *Stack v Dowden* was indeed unusual and that the presumption of joint beneficial interests was rebutted.

In that case the parties had been together for around 30 years, and had four children. They had never married. They lived together in rented accommodation until 1983 when Ms Dowden took the opportunity to buy the house of her late Uncle Sidney at a favourable price. The property was conveyed into her sole name. The deposit came from a building society account in her sole name into which some payments had been made by Mr Stack. The balance was borrowed by way of mortgage advance for which she alone was contractually liable. Ms Dowden made the mortgage repayments and paid all the household bills. Ten years later that property was sold and the parties bought a property in Chatsworth Road, London NW2. The legal title was registered in the parties' joint names. There was no express declaration as to the beneficial interests, although there was a statement on the standard form of transfer then current to the effect that the survivor of them could give a valid receipt for the purchase money. Although this would ordinarily point to joint beneficial interests, it was held that in the absence of any evidence that the parties understood the effect of this declaration, it was ineffective to determine the beneficial ownership.

The purchase price of Chatsworth Road was found from the net sale proceeds of the first house in Ms Dowden's sole name, savings also in her sole name, and a mortgage in joint names linked to two endowment policies, one in the name of each of them. Mr Stack made the mortgage repayments and paid the premium on the policy in his name. Ms Dowden paid most of the other outgoings on the house and paid the premium on the policy in her name. Throughout their relationship the parties kept their financial arrangements quite separate and made payments referable to the property from their respective resources. This included reducing the sum outstanding on the mortgage by making capital repayments from time to time. It was accepted that Ms Dowden contributed more in this way than did Mr Stack.

A little under 10 years after the purchase of Chatsworth Road the parties separated. Ms Dowden remained in the property with the children. Mr Stack made a claim for an order for sale and an equal division of the net proceeds. At first instance he was successful and Ms Dowden appealed. The Court of Appeal substituted an apportionment of 65 per cent/35 per cent in her favour. Mr Stack appealed to the House of Lords and the appeal was dismissed.

Baroness Hale identified that the onus was upon Ms Dowden to show that the parties' common intention when the legal title to the property was put into their joint names was that they would hold the property otherwise than as beneficial joint tenants. It was her view that Ms Dowden made out her case. The following factors were identified as being relevant in rebutting the presumption of joint beneficial ownership:

– Ms Dowden had contributed far more to the acquisition of Chatsworth Road.
– Ms Dowden had contributed far more to the capital reduction of the outstanding mortgage.
– Although Mr Stack paid the mortgage interest and the premium on the joint endowment policy Ms Dowden was responsible for all the other regular expenditure, negating any suggestion that they had each agreed to contribute to their joint needs according to their means.
– The parties kept their financial affairs separate.

Since *Stack v Dowden* there have been a number of decisions in which the principles emerging from that case have been applied.

1   At para 66.
2   At para 69.

1.48 *Fowler v Barron*[1] underlined the severe burden of proof upon the party seeking to displace the presumption that the beneficial interests are shared differently from the legal title. In that case the family home was in the joint names of Mr Barron and Miss Fowler. Theirs was a 23-year relationship and they had two children. There was no express declaration as to the beneficial interests. There was a mortgage in joint names and the balance of the purchase price came from Mr Barron's resources. The mortgage repayments and all other outgoings including the weekly shop were paid by Mr Barron. Ms Fowler spent her earnings on herself and the children and paid for holidays and occasional treats. When the parties separated, Mr Barron claimed that he was sole beneficial owner and that he had agreed to the property being in joint names with the intention only that Miss Fowler would succeed to his share in the event that he pre-deceased her. He did not intend her to benefit in any other circumstances.

At first instance the case was heard before the decision in *Stack v Dowden* and the judge applied resulting trust principles to find in Mr Barron's favour. Miss Fowler appealed. The Court of Appeal had the benefit of the decision in *Stack v Dowden*. Applying constructive trust principles as required following that case, the onus was on Mr Barron to satisfy the court that the beneficial interests should be held other than in equal shares. The court said that in the absence of any express discussions between the parties it was a question of

1.48 *Property*

searching for the common intention to be inferred from 'the whole of the parties' relationship so far as it illumined their shared intentions'.

In that case it was held that it was relevant to 'consider whether the facts were inconsistent with the inference of a common intention to share the property in equal shares, to an extent to discharge the civil standard of proof on the person seeking to displace the presumption. The emphasis was on the parties' shared intentions'[2]. The factors that led the court to a conclusion that the presumption had not been rebutted and that Ms Fowler was entitled to an equal share were these. First, Mr Barron's evidence that he intended that Ms Fowler should benefit from the property only in the event of his death did not evince a common intention as he had not disclosed this to Ms Fowler. Secondly, the fact that the mortgage was joint was not inconsistent with a shared intention to share the beneficial interests equally. In relation to Ms Fowler's financial contributions the court held as follows[3]:

> 'The proper inference as to the way in which the woman had spent her income was that, with the exception of clothing for herself, her payments for gifts, school clubs and trips, holidays and special occasions, were her contributions to household expenses for which they were both responsible. The further inferences to be drawn were that the parties intended that who paid what should make no difference to their interests, and that the parties simply did not care about the respective size of each other's contributions; [they] had largely treated their incomes and asset as one pool from which household expenses would be paid.'

[1] [2008] 2 FLR 831.
[2] At p 831.
[3] At p 832.

1.49 *Adekunle v Ritchie*[1] concerned joint ownership of a property by a mother and her son. They had been living in a council property of which the mother was a secure tenant. The mother decided to exercise her right to buy but could not do this without the help of the son. They took out a joint mortgage for 100 per cent of the purchase price. The property was conveyed into their joint names but without an express declaration of the beneficial interests. Two years later the son moved out but returned after 12 years. Two years later the mother died intestate and an issue arose between the son and his nine siblings as to beneficial ownership of the property.

The approach of the judge was to apply constructive trust principles following *Stack v Dowden* and this was referred to and approved by Lord Neuberger in *Laskar v Laskar*. Although both *Laskar* and the present case concerned the purchase of a council house by a parent and child, the distinguishing features of this case were that the house had been bought as a home for the mother and the parties had enjoyed a domestic relationship. In these circumstances a resulting trust would not be appropriate.

The judge found that the mother and son had made roughly similar contributions to the mortgage and other outgoings but that it was unlikely that the mother had intended that one son should benefit so disproportionately from her estate when she had ten children altogether. Taking an holistic approach to the situation he concluded that the son was entitled to a one-third interest.

[1] Unreported, 17 August 2007, Leeds County Court.

1.50 The decision of the Supreme Court in *Jones v Kernott*[1] provided long awaited clarity in this area of the law. Ms Jones and Mr Kernott met in 1980. They had two children together but never married. In 1985 they bought a property together in their joint names. There was no express declaration of the beneficial interests. Ms Jones paid a deposit of 5 per cent of the purchase price, the balance of which was funded on an interest-only mortgage. A year later Mr Kernott built an extension which he funded almost exclusively, and also worked on himself, which increased the value of the property by about 50 per cent. They lived in the property together for around 8 years during which time they had two children. Both parties worked. From her earnings and £100 a week housekeeping money from Mr Kernott, Ms Jones paid all the household bills including the mortgage.

When the relationship broke down Ms Jones stayed at the property with the children. Using his half share of a joint endowment policy that by agreement the parties surrendered, Mr Kernott was able to put down a deposit on a house of his own.

About 12 years after the separation, by which time house price inflation had brought about an increase in the value of both properties, Mr Kernott served notice to sever the joint tenancy. Ms Jones countered this with an application under the Trusts of Land and Appointment of Trustees Act 1996 (TOLATA 1996) for a declaration that she owned the entire beneficial interest in the property in joint names or a beneficial interest in the house in Mr Kernott's sole name. In the years of their separation Ms Jones alone had maintained the joint property and Mr Kernott his own property. He had made little contribution to the upkeep of the children.

The judge at first instance found that up until Mr Kernott's purchase of his own house using the endowment moneys there was no evidence to displace the presumption that equity followed the law. However, the judge also found that 'whilst the intentions of the parties may well have been at the outset to provide them as a couple with a home for themselves and their progeny, those intentions have altered significantly over the years to the extent that [Mr Kernott] demonstrated that he had no intention until recently of availing himself of the beneficial ownership in this property, having ignored it completely by way of an investment in it or attempt to maintain or repair it whilst he had his own property on which he concentrated'.

Having made this crucial finding of fact, that the parties' intentions had changed significantly from what they had been when the property was acquired, he concluded that in the absence of any indication by words or conduct as to how they intended that the beneficial interests were thereafter to be shared, the appropriate criterion was what he considered to be fair and just. Accordingly he apportioned the beneficial interests 90/10 in Ms Jones' favour.

Ms Jones' claim for a beneficial interest in Mr Kernott's property was dismissed.

Mr Kernott appealed to the High Court arguing that the judge was wrong to infer or impute an intention that the parties' beneficial interests should change after their separation and to quantify these in a way which he considered fair. The deputy High Court judge concluded that the change in intention could readily be inferred or imputed from the parties' conduct. Mr Kernott appealed again. The Court of Appeal held that the beneficial interests in the joint property were held in equal shares. The 'ambulatory' constructive trust that the court below had invoked in order to increase Ms Jones' share from 50 per cent over the passage of time was roundly rejected. Giving the judgment of the court, Wall LJ as he then was, applied *Oxley v Hiscock*[2] and *Stack v Dowden*[3] and found that there was no basis for varying the shares in which the property was held. The presumption from the legal title was that the beneficial interests were in equal shares. The court could not depart from this unless there was evidence that the parties had expressly, or could by their conduct be inferred to have agreed or intended something other than this.

The court said that there was no evidence about what the parties intended. They did not appear to have given the matter any thought, much less discussed it. The only indicator was that in serving notice to sever the joint tenancy, Mr Kernott must have believed that he had a half share. The court felt unable to infer from the parties' conduct since separation a joint intention that over the passage of time the shares would be varied to the 90/10 split determined by the court below.

Permission was given to Ms Jones to appeal to the Supreme Court and the decision of that court was handed down on 9 November 2011. The appeal was allowed and the decision of the trial judge that the beneficial interests were held 90/10 in Ms Jones' favour restored.

[1] [2011] UKSC 53.
[2] [2004] 2 FLR 669.
[3] [2007] 1 FLR 1858.

1.51 The essential difference between the Court of Appeal and the Supreme Court was in the approach to inferences to be drawn from the parties' conduct and the extent to which their intentions as to the sharing of the beneficial interests might change over time.

The Supreme Court said that the logical inference to be drawn from the finding of the county court judge that the parties' intentions had changed significantly from what they had been when the property was acquired was that the parties intended that Mr Kernott's interest in the shared home should crystallise at the point at which he bought his own home using the endowment moneys, leaving him to benefit from any capital gain in his own home, and Ms Jones to benefit from any further capital gain in the shared home. A rough calculation on that basis produced a result so close to that achieved by the trial judge that the Supreme Court considered that it would be wrong to interfere in that decision.

The lead judgment of Lord Walker and Baroness Hale sets out a clear summary of the principles that will apply in a case between cohabiting couples where the legal title is vested in their joint names, but without any express declaration of their beneficial interests, and where both are liable for any mortgage:

(1) The starting point is that equity follows the law and they are joint tenants both in law and equity.

(2) That presumption can be displaced by showing: (a) that the parties had a different common intention at the time when they acquired the home, or (b) that they later formed the common intention that their respective shares would change.

(3) Their common intention is to be deduced objectively from their conduct: 'the relevant intention of each party is the intention which was reasonably understood by the other party to be manifested by that party's words and conduct notwithstanding that he did not consciously formulate that intention in his own mind or even acted with some different intention which he did not communicate to the other party' (Lord Diplock in *Gissing v Gissing*). Examples of the sort of evidence which might be relevant to drawing such inferences are given in *Stack v Dowden*, at para 69.

(4) In those cases where it is clear either: (a) that the parties did not intend joint tenancy at the outset, or (b) had changed their original intention, but it is not possible to ascertain by direct evidence or by inference what their actual intention was as to the shares in which they would own the property, 'the answer is that each is entitled to that share which the court considers fair having regard to the whole course of dealing between them in relation to the property': Chadwick J in *Oxley v Hiscock*, para 69. In our judgment, 'the whole course of dealing . . . in relation to the property' should be given a broad meaning, enabling a similar range of factors to be taken into account as may be relevant to ascertaining the parties' actual intentions.

(5) Each case will turn on its own facts. Financial contributions are relevant but there are many other factors which may enable the court to decide what shares were either intended (as in case (3)) or fair (as in case (4)).

Thus in joint names cases such as *Jones v Kernott* the search is to ascertain the shares in which the beneficial interests are held. This will be a question of evidence and the court is not free to impose a solution upon the parties that is different from what the evidence shows their intention to have been. However, in the absence of any evidence as to what the parties' intentions were, the court has to reach a conclusion and it will do so by posing the hypothetical question as to what their intentions as reasonable and just people would have been had they thought about it at the time[1].

In other words, the court is entitled in those circumstances to impute an intention as to the beneficial interests and give each that share which the court considers fair having regard to the whole course of dealing between them in relation to the property[2]. The 'whole course of dealing . . . in relation to the property' should be given a broad meaning, enabling a similar range of factors to be taken into account as may be relevant to ascertaining the parties' actual intentions[3].

In this case there was no need for the court to impute an intention that the parties' beneficial interests in the property would change at the point at which Mr Kernott used the joint endowment policy to fund the purchase of his own home, since the trial judge had already made that finding. However, in view of the blurring of the distinction between inference and imputation evident in the earlier authorities, notably *Pettitt v Pettit* and *Gissing v Gissing*, and the

1.51 *Property*

misgivings expressed by Lord Neuberger in *Stack v Dowden* as to the propriety of imputing to the parties an intention that could not be deduced objectively from their actions and statements, it was necessary for the Supreme Court to clarify the position.

[1] At para 47.
[2] At para 51(4) quoting from Chadwick LJ in *Oxley v Hiscock*, para 69.
[3] At para 51(4).

1.52 In *Graham-York v York & Others*[1] the court's task in ascertaining the shares in which a beneficial interest, once determined, should be held was considered. At first instance the court had found that the claimant had on constructive trust principles established a beneficial interest in the family home that had been held in the sole name of her cohabitant, now deceased. The size of that share had been assessed at 25 per cent, the trial judge imputing at this second stage in the analysis what was considered to be a fair share, having regard to the whole course of dealings between the parties relating to the property.

The claimant appealed, contending that in the absence of any express common intention as to the parties' respective interests in the property, a fair share would have been 50 per cent.

The Court of Appeal dismissed the appeal, saying that on the facts of this case there could be no question of imputing an intention to the parties that they would hold the beneficial shares equally. Although the claimant had contributed by running the household and sharing in the bringing up of the parties' child, her financial contribution was minimal. Such was the unequal nature of their relationship as it appeared from the evidence that there could be little doubt that the deceased cohabitant had no intention that there should ever have been an equal sharing.

The Court of Appeal reminded itself that the proper approach was to be found in the judgment jointly delivered by Lord Walker and Lady Hale in *Jones v Kernott*[2], and concluded as follows:

> ' . . . in deciding . . . what shares are fair, the court is not concerned with some form of redistributive justice. Thus it is irrelevant that it may be thought a "fair" outcome for a woman who has endured years of abusive conduct by her partner to be allotted a substantial interest in his property on his death. The plight of [the claimant] attracts sympathy, but it does not enable the court to redistribute property interests in a manner which right-minded people might think amounts to appropriate compensation. [The claimant] is "entitled to that share which the court considers fair having regard to the whole course of delaing between them <u>in relation to the property</u>". It is these last words, which I have emphasised, which supply the confines of the equity as to fairness.'[3]

Law and Practice 1.52

JOINT NAMES	JOINT NAMES	SOLE NAME
+ Express declaration of trust in TR1/JO/FR1 or separate trust deed	No express declaration of trust	
Conclusive as to beneficial interests in the absence of fraud or mistake	'Equity follows the law' ie there is a presumption that the registered proprietors are joint tenants in law and equity in equal shares	'Equity follows the law' ie there is a presumption that the sole legal owner is also the sole beneficial owner
		Two stage enquiry for the court[a]
Goodman v Gallant[b]	Burden of proof is on the owner seeking to show otherwise. Not to be 'lightly embarked upon' *Stack v Dowden*[c]	(1) Was there a common intention that the beneficial interests in the property were to be shared?
	Applicant has to establish either: that they had a different common intention than equal shares when the home was acquired, or that they subsequently formed a common intention that their shares would change	Was there an express agreement, arrangement or understanding reached between the parties? This is a question of fact 'based on evidence of express discussions between the parties however imperfectly remembered or however imprecise' (*Rosset No 1*)
	The parties' common intention is to be deduced (inferred) objectively from the conduct and dealings between the parties	In the absence of anything express can an intention to share the beneficial ownership be inferred?

53

1.52 Property

JOINT NAMES	JOINT NAMES	SOLE NAME
+ Express declaration of trust in TR1/JO/FR1 or separate trust deed	No express declaration of trust	
	See *Stack v Dowden* para 69 for examples of the sort of evidence that might be relevant to drawing inferences Where it is clear either that the parties did not intend joint tenancy at the outset, or had changed their original intention, but it is not possible to ascertain by direct evidence what their actual intention was, the court can impute[d] an intention to share in the way the court considers fair having regard to the whole course of dealing between them in relation to the property[e]	'direct contributions to the purchase price by the partner who is not the legal owner, whether initially or by payment of mortgage instalments, will readily justify the inference necessary . . . it is at least extremely doubtful whether anything less will do' (*Rosset No 2*) Since *Lloyds Bank v Rosset* judicial encouragement to lower the hurdle for contributions from which an inference can be drawn: The court should 'take a wide view of what is capable of counting as a contribution . . . while remaining sceptical of the value of alleged improvements that are really insignificant, or elaborate arguments (suggestive of creative accounting) as to how the family finances were arranged . . . would include contributions in kind by way of manual labour, provided that they are significant' (*Stack v Dowden*[f])
		If the answer to (1) is 'no', there is no beneficial interest
		If the answer to (1) is 'yes', establish detrimental reliance and proceed to

Law and Practice **1.53**

JOINT NAMES	JOINT NAMES	SOLE NAME
+ Express declaration of trust in TR1/JO/FR1 or separate trust deed	No express declaration of trust	
		(2) Quantification – in the absence of any discussion between the parties what would be a fair share for each party having regard to the whole course of dealing between them in relation to the property?[g]

^a *Lloyds Bank v Rosset* [1990] 2 FLR 155.
^b [1986] 1 FLR 513.
^c [2007] 1 FLR 1858.
^d *Jones v Kernott* [2011] UKSC 53.
^e *Oxley v Hiscock* [2004] 2 FLR 669.
^f [2007] 1 FLR 1858.
^g *Oxley v Hiscock* [2004] 2 FLR 669.

[1] [2015] EWCA Civ 72.
[2] [2011] UKSC 53.
[3] At para 22.

Proprietary estoppel

1.53 Similar principles to those relied upon in constructive trusts are evident when the court is asked to invoke its equitable jurisdiction to prevent one party from asserting his or her strict legal rights against another where a promise has been made to the other party, and that party has acted to his or her detriment in reliance upon the promise. However, in *Stack v Dowden*, Lord Walker cautioned against the merging of the two doctrines and specifically disapproved the suggestion in *Oxley v Hiscock* that there was little or no difference between them[1]:

> 'Proprietary estoppel typically consists of asserting an equitable claim against the conscience of the "true" owner. The claim is a "mere equity". It is to be satisfied by the minimum award necessary to do justice . . . which may sometimes lead to no more than a monetary award. A "common intention" constructive trust, by contrast, is identifying the true beneficial owner or owners, and the size of their beneficial interests.'

In *Q v Q*[2] Black J, as she then was, considered the law on proprietary estoppel and constructive trusts and the distinctions between them, particularly in relation to remedy. In a case of proprietary estoppel the court has a discretion only to do the minimum required by equity in order to effect a just outcome.

Proprietary estoppel may arise in cases where there has been no financial contribution to the purchase price by the non-owner and so no question of finding a resulting trust, and as between cohabitants and others in the domestic context where there is no common intention to share the beneficial interests. In the context of cohabitants this may have relevance where the property is

1.53 *Property*

acquired by one party before the commencement of the cohabitation and contributions are made against the background of assurances of provision.

In *Wayling v Jones*[3] the court found that the claimant had been promised the hotel in which he had worked for the deceased unstintingly and for nominal payment, and when the deceased failed to leave it to him in his will it was held that he was entitled to it under the doctrine of estoppel.

[1] At para 37.
[2] [2008] EWHC 1874 (Fam).
[3] [1995] 2 FLR 1029.

1.54 There was a similar outcome in *Pascoe v Turner*[1]. At the end of their cohabitation, Mr Pascoe told Mrs Turner that she need not trouble to move out of what had been their shared home, a property paid for by him and in his sole name, it was all hers. There was no formal transfer of the property, but Mr Pascoe was well aware that Mrs Turner subsequently spent a quarter of her modest savings on repairs, improvements and redecoration to the house. Some time later, Mr Pascoe sought unsuccessfully to determine Mrs Turner's occupation of the house. The court held that whilst there was no evidence from which the court could infer a constructive trust, there had been a clear statement by Mr Pascoe that he had given the property to her as a gift, and she had acted to her detriment in reliance upon this by spending money on the fabric of the property. Mr Pascoe was held to his promise and was ordered to transfer the house to Mrs Turner outright.

In *Yaxley v Gotts and Gotts*[2] the defendants owned several properties that they rented out. The claimant was a friend of the defendants and a self-employed builder who had worked for them from time to time. The claimant had seen a property which he thought would be a suitable investment for the defendants. They bought it, and it was agreed that in return for the claimant carrying out unpaid building work to convert the property into flats, he would become the owner of one of them. There was no formal agreement in writing. The parties fell out and the defendants denied the claimant's interest in the property. The Court of Appeal held that the defendants should be held to the agreement that the claimant was entitled to one of the flats, the claimant having fulfilled his side of the agreement and carried out the building work without payment.

Ely v Robson[3] concerned an agreement reached between former cohabitants, Mr Ely and Ms Robson. The facts were these. In 1986 the parties started to cohabit in a property owned in the sole name of Ms Robson. A year later they moved to live in a property bought in the sole name of Mr Ely at 6 Torbay Road, Poole. Two years later Ms Robson bought another property in her sole name but the parties remained at 6 Torbay Road, and in due course both Ms Robson's mother and aunt also took up residence.

Although the relationship between Mr Ely and Ms Robson broke down in 2005 they all continued to share 6 Torbay Road. Eventually in 2007 Mr Ely asked Ms Robson to move out, and when she refused he issued a claim for possession. Ms Robson defended the claim, asserting a beneficial interest in equal shares, this reflecting their common intention.

The claim and counterclaim were listed for trial in September 2007. In the August, Mr Ely and Ms Robson met in Poole Park to discuss settlement. Although the parties were in dispute about when this took place and what exactly resulted from it, on 14 August 2007 Mr Ely's solicitors wrote to Ms Robson's solicitors setting out the terms that they understood from their client had been agreed at the meeting in Poole Park. In broad terms these were that Mr Ely would hold 6 Torbay Road on trust for himself and Ms Robson as to 80 per cent/20 per cent respectively. Ms Robson would be permitted to remain at the property until the death of both her aunt and her mother.

Following this the solicitors acting for Ms Robson wrote to the court indicating that the parties were close to settlement and asking for the trial date to be vacated. The solicitors for Mr Ely consented to this course.

Although the court vacated the hearing, and listed it for a short appointment a few weeks later, there was no further action until, according to the court records, the solicitors for Ms Robson were in touch to say that the parties had now reached agreement.

By 2014 both Ms Robson's aunt and mother had died. Mr Ely issued proceedings for declaratory relief as to the parties' shares in the equitable interest in 6 Torbay Road, and an order for sale. He relied upon the agreement he said that they had reached in 2007. Ms Robson defended the claim on the basis that it had always been the parties' common intention that they would share the beneficial interests equally and that there had been no subsequent agreement to vary this.

The trial judge found that the parties had indeed met in Poole Park in August 2007 and reached clear terms for the compromise of the litigation which Mr Ely had then acted upon. On this basis he found that this raised an estoppel preventing Ms Robson from resiling from the agreement.

Ms Robson appealed. Although the findings and decision of the trial judge were upheld by the Court of Appeal, it was said that it was unclear how he had reached the conclusion that this was a case of proprietory estoppel. However, it was clear that whatever had been the position before the meeting in Poole Park, from that time Mr Ely had held 6 Torbay Road on trust for them both. The agreement of August 2007, which was in sufficiently clear terms, and which was intended to be binding on them both, confirmed their common understanding as to their respective beneficial shares from that point.

This case is a salutary reminder to legal advisers of the risks inherent in their clients apparently compromising litigation without the formalities being attended to, particularly in the domestic, context[4].

[1]   [1979] 1 WLR 431.
[2]   [1999] 2 FLR 941.
[3]   [2016] EWCA Civ 774.
[4]   *Cobbe v Yeoman's Row Management Ltd* [2008] UKHL 55; *Herbert v Doyle* [2010] EWCA Civ 1095.

1.55 In *Lissimore v Downing*[1] a former cohabitant sought to rely upon proprietary estoppel to salvage something from the 8-year relationship she

1.55 *Property*

enjoyed with a member of a rock band. Miss Lissimore's claim was that Mr Downing had made 'representations and/or promises . . . which she relied upon to her detriment, such that it would be inequitable for the defendant to resile from the said representations and/or promises'.

At their highest, the representations amounted to statements to the effect, 'I bet you never thought all of this [the estate] would be yours in a million years' and references to the claimant as the 'Lady of the Manor'. There were also general statements that Miss Lissimore would never want for anything, and that Mr Downing always looked after his girlfriends.

In terms of detriment, Miss Lissimore's case was that she had given up her job, turned down an offer of a better job, and had become financially dependent upon Mr Downing and so had not invested the modest capital she had received on her divorce. She also claimed that she invested considerable time and effort in the running of the estate.

The findings of the judge were that although Mr Downing had supported Miss Lissimore financially throughout their relationship to a high standard, and that she had taken a full part in the activities of the estate, she had voluntarily given up her modest employment to enjoy life with Mr Downing. He did not induce her with promises for the future, and she did not sacrifice anything in terms of her career. She willingly helped out on the estate but not out of any belief that she had ownership of any part of it. In any event, the statements made by Mr Downing were not sufficiently specific to enable the court to assess what was promised.

This decision has been regarded in some quarters as an unduly restrictive approach to both the nature of the representation necessary, and detriment[2].

However, what all these cases highlight is that where the court is concerned essentially to make findings about the party's usually differing accounts of events and conversations, possibly many years before, the court's assessment of the reliability of each party's evidence, and the entire history of their relationship will have considerable bearing upon the outcome.

[1]   [2003] 2 FLR 308.
[2]   See [2003] Fam Law 567, Professor Rebecca Bailey-Harris.

1.56 *Thorner v Majors*[1] was a case in point. The claimant had worked unpaid on his cousin's farm for approaching 30 years. They were both what Lord Walker called 'taciturn and undemonstrative men committed to a life of hard and unrelenting physical work'. The context for what few oblique indications there were of an assurance given by the deceased to the claimant that the farm would one day be his was therefore of critical importance.

After about 14 years of helping on the farm, the deceased handed to the claimant a Prudential Bonus Notice relating to two policies on his life saying that they were to cover his death duties. The claimant had understood this, reasonably so the court found, as confirmation of what he had privately hoped would be the case, namely that it was his cousin's intention that he would inherit the farm. Thereafter there were occasional remarks made by the deceased that reinforced the claimant's expectation. For example, the deceased pointed out to the claimant a water trough that he said would never freeze up in the cold weather. The claimant understood this, and similar casually made observations, as being intended to give him information that he would need as his successor on the farm.

That case also raised the issue of certainty in relation to the property in question. The House of Lords said that it was sufficiently clear that what the deceased had intended the claimant to have was the farm, whatever it comprised, at the date of his death. It was irrelevant that during the years since the claimant was given the Prudential Bond Notice the farm was made up of different land holdings, the deceased having bought and sold land in the intervening period.

[1] [2009] 2 FLR 405.

1.57 In another farming case, *Davies & Anor v Davies*[1] the principles of proprietary estoppel were summarised by Floyd LJ. He quoted from Lord Walker in *Thorner v Major*[2]:

' . . . the doctrine is based on three main elements . . . a representation or assurance made to the claimant; reliance on it by the claimant; and detriment to the claimant in consequence of his (reasonable) reliance . . . '

He suggested that[3]:

'Whilst these three elements are useful for the purposes of analysis and structured decision-making, they are not to be treated as watertight compartments. He quoted from Robert Walker LJ, as he then was, in *Gillett v Holt* . . . although the judgment is, for convenience divided into several sections with headings which give a rough indication of the subject-matter, it is important to note at the outset that the doctrine of proprietary estoppel cannot be treated as subdivided into three or four watertight compartments . . . the quality of the relevant assurances may influence the issue of reliance, that reliance and detriment are often intertwined, and that whether there is a distinct need for a "mutual understanding" may depend on how the other elements are formulated and understood. Moreover the fundamental principle that equity is concerned to prevent unconscionable conduct permeates all the elements of the doctrine. in the end the court must look at the matter in the round . . . the detriment need not consist of the expenditure of money or other quantifiable financial detriment, so long as it is something substantial. The requirement must be approached as part of a broad inquiry as to whether repudiation of an assurance is or is not unconscionable in all the circumstances.'

He added that[4]:

'Two further principles emerge clearly from [*Gillet v Holt*]. Firstly, whether the claimant has suffered detriment must be judged at the point where the person who gave the assurance seeks to go back on it. Secondly, whether the detriment is sufficiently substantial must be judged by whether it would be unjust or inequitable to allow the assurance to be disregarded.

Whether there is detrimental reliance in any given case is an evaluative judgment on the facts, which normally lies within the exclusive province of the trial judge.'

Applying those principles, Floyd LJ refused to interfere with the finding of the trial judge that the claimant had given up her career in reliance upon an

1.57 *Property*

assurance from her parents that if she returned to work on the family farm it would one day be hers, and that in so doing there was a net detriment to her.

The question of how that equity raised by the claimant against her parents should be satisfied was dealt with at a subsequent hearing before the same first instance judge. His decision that the claimant should receive a lump sum of £1.3m was reduced on appeal to £500,000.

[1] [2014] EWCA Civ 568.
[2] At para 29.
[3] At para 30.
[4] At para 32.

1.58 The judgment of Lewison LJ[1] sets out the legal propositions underpinning cases based on proprietory estoppel:

(i) Deciding whether an equity has been raised and, if so, how to satisfy it is a retrospective exercise looking backwards from the moment when the promise falls due to be performed and asking whether, in the circumstances which actually happened, it would be unconscionable for a promise not to be kept either wholly or in part: *Thorner v Major*[2].

(ii) The ingredients necessary to raise an equity are: (a) an assurance of sufficient clarity, (b) reliance by the claimant upon that assurance, and (c) detriment to the claimant in consequence of his reasonable reliance: *Thorner v Major* at [29].

(iii) However, no claim based on proprietary estoppel can be divided into watertight compartments. The quality of the relevant assurances may influence the issue of reliance; reliance and detriment are often intertwined, and whether there is a distinct need for a 'mutual understanding' may depend on how the other elements are formulated and understood: *Gillett v Holt*[3] at [225]; *Henry v Henry*[4] at [37].

(iv) Detriment need not consist of the expenditure of money or other quantifiable financial detriment, so long as it is something substantial. The requirement must be approached as part of a broad enquiry as to whether repudiation of an assurance is or is not unconscionable in all the circumstances: *Gillett v Holt* at [232]; *Henry v Henry* at [38].

(v) There must be a sufficient causal link between the assurance relied on and the detriment asserted. The issue of detriment must be judged at the moment when the person who has given the assurance seeks to go back on it. The question is whether (and if so to what extent) it would be unjust or inequitable to allow the person who has given the assurance to go back on it. The essential test is that of unconscionability: *Gillett v Holt* at [232].

(vi) Thus the essence of the doctrine of proprietary estoppel is to do what is necessary to avoid an unconscionable result: *Jennings v Rice*[5].

(vii) In deciding how to satisfy any equity the court must weigh the detriment suffered by the claimant in reliance on the defendant's assurances against any countervailing benefits he enjoyed in consequence of that reliance: *Henry v Henry* at [51] and [53].

(viii) Proportionality lies at the heart of the doctrine of proprietary estoppel and permeates its every application: *Henry v Henry* at [65]. In particular, there must be a proportionality between the remedy and the detriment which is its purpose to avoid: *Jennings v Rice* at [28] (citing from earlier cases) and [56]. This does not mean that the court should abandon expectations and seek only to compensate detrimental reliance, but if the expectation is disproportionate to the detriment, the court should satisfy the equity in a more limited way: *Jennings v Rice* at [50] and [51].

(ix) In deciding how to satisfy the equity the court has to exercise a broad judgmental discretion: *Jennings v Rice* at [51]. However, the discretion is not unfettered. It must be exercised on a principled basis, and does not entail what HHJ Weekes QC memorably called a 'portable palm tree': *Taylor v Dickens*[6] (a decision criticised for other reasons in *Gillett v Holt*).

In determining the outcome, Lewison LJ identified that there were two possible but fundamentally different approaches. One was to satisfy the claimant's expectation unless it would be disproportionate to do so. The other was to ensure that the claimant was compensated for such detriment as the claimant had suffered.

The latter basis appeared to be the approach taken by the defendants in formulating an offer of £350,000 based on an evaluation of the various heads of detriment.

Lewison LJ was unable to ascertain the trial judge's rationale for the award of £1.3m other than that he must have placed a value of nearly £1m on the non-financial aspects of the detrimental reliance and/or the claimant's expectation that she would inherit the farmland. Lewison LJ noted that unlike the position in *Gillett v Holt* and *Thorner v Major* the expectations were changing and uncertain. Similarly, in terms of detrimental reliance, it was not said that the claimant had set the course of her life on the basis of the assurances given. The trial judge had identified two broad strands in the detriment suffered by the claimant. First, that she had worked for long hours on the farm without full payment, and secondly that had she not worked on the farm she could have continued with the much more congenial employment that was available to her.

He could not ascribe such a large value to either head on the particular facts of this case and reduced the award accordingly.

[1] [2016] EWCA Civ 463.
[2] [2009] UKHL 18 at [57] and [101].
[3] [2001] Ch 210.
[4] [2010] UKPC, [2010] 1 All ER 988.
[5] [2002] EWCA Civ 159.
[6] [1998] 1 FLR 806.

1.59 In *Southwell v Blackburn*[1] the Court of Appeal considered the claim by Mrs Blackburn to an interest in the property she had shared with Mr Southwell. The decision of the judge at first instance to award a sum of £28,500 to Mrs Blackburn under the principles of proprietary estoppel was upheld on appeal. In that case Mrs Blackburn had left the rented home that she had established for herself and her daughters following her divorce to set up home with Mr Southwell. The property that they lived in had been bought in Mr Southwell's sole name to be their family home and they lived together there for about 9 years. Although the parties had jointly chosen the property, the purchase had been financed entirely by Mr Southwell and he paid the mortgage and most of the household outgoings. He had been scrupulous in ensuring that Mrs Blackburn was not involved in the legal and financial side of the property because, as the judge found, he was mindful of the risk that she may try to establish a beneficial interest.

It was clear however that in leaving the security of her own property to move to live with Mr Southwell, Mrs Blackburn was taking a risk. She had invested the bulk of the £25,000 that she received in her divorce settlement in fitting out and furnishing that house. Against this background the judge found that Mr Southwell had reassured her that she would always have a home and be secure, and that in making such promises as were necessary to persuade her to move to live with him, he knew that she would rely upon them.

On that basis the judge concluded, and the Court of Appeal agreed, that it would be unconscionable for him to go back on his promise. In terms of quantification, the judge considered that the appropriate figure was one that, allowing for inflation, would put Mrs Blackburn back in the position she had been in before she moved to live with Mr Southwell.

Although the elements necessary to establish a constructive trust were not present in that case, since there had been no clear promise that Mrs Blackburn would have any legal ownership of the property, the court was satisfied that Mr Southwell's promise that she would, 'always have a home and be secure in this one' was sufficient to amount to a commitment to her beyond the end of their relationship.

In relation to the necessary detrimental reliance upon the promise, whilst Mrs Blackburn had benefitted from the arrangement in terms of living rent free and additional financial support provided by Mr Southwell, so too had Mr Southwell, who had the support of Mrs Blackburn at home whilst he was furthering his career. The court concluded that making an assessment of detriment, particularly in the context of cohabitants, was not necessarily a strict accounting exercise, and should be viewed over the entire course of the relationship. In this case the direct consequence to Mrs Blackburn of the reliance upon Mr Southwell's promise was the loss of her investment in the home she left to move in with him, and this was the basis of the assessment of the relatively modest sum that Mr Southwell was ordered to pay.

The circumscribed nature of the relief that the court can give in cases of proprietary estoppel was again underlined in *Liden v Burton*[2]. The court agreed that the circumstances in which Ms Liden had paid £500 a month to Mr Burton gave rise to a promissory estoppel. The court found that he had, 'induced, encouraged or allowed Ms Liden to believe she was obtaining an interest in the property, that the monthly payments were made in reliance thereon, and that it would be unconscionable for Mr Burton to deny Ms Liden an interest in the property'[3].

Nonetheless, the order provided only for her to receive the first £33,522 of the equity that was to be held on trust for her. This amounted to no more than a refund of the contributions she had made, with some interest, to reflect the fact that if Ms Liden had known that her payments were not intended to secure for her an interest in the property, she would have invested her money elsewhere.

1   [2014] EWCA Civ 1347.
2   [2016] EWCA Civ 275.
3   At para 13.

Accounting for occupation rent

1.60 When cohabitants separate and one remains in a property in which it is agreed or determined that the other has a beneficial interest, there may have to be an account taken of occupation rent. Following *Stack v Dowden* it is clear that the statutory principles contained in TOLATA 1996[1] must be applied. In simple terms, these enable the court to order the beneficial owner in occupation to pay compensation to a beneficial owner who is out of occupation. The court must have regard to the following factors when making such an order:

– the intentions of the person(s) who created the trust;
– the purpose for which the property subject to the trust is held;
– the welfare of any minor who occupies or might reasonably be expected to occupy the property as his home; and
– the interest of any secured creditor of any beneficiary.

In *Stack v Dowden*, Mr Stack had asked the court for an order that Ms Dowden account to him for an occupation rent as she was living in the property and he had to provide separate accommodation for himself at his own expense. Applying the statutory criteria, the majority of the House of Lords considered that there should be no compensation. Lord Neuberger dissented from this view for the following reasons:

'First, both parties had the right in principle to occupy [the house], Ms Dowden was living there on her own as she wanted, she had excluded Mr. Stack against his will, and he was incurring the cost of alternative accommodation: accordingly such a payment seems appropriate in the absence of any good reason to the contrary. Secondly, the parties plainly thought it was right, when agreeing [that he should leave] that, as a quid pro quo for his exclusion from the house, Mr. Stack should be paid (or credited) at the rate of £900 per month. The circumstances of the parties do not appear to have changed [by or at the *date*] when they effectively accepted that Mr. Stack would remain excluded from the house.

Thirdly . . . the four specific matters set out in s 15(1) . . . either favour ordering a payment in favour of Mr. Stack, or they are neutral or irrelevant. Thus, . . . the purpose for which the house was bought and the purpose for which it was held, favour the conclusion, as the house was bought as a home for Mr. Stack (as well as Ms Dowden and the children) . . . the welfare of minors residing in the house . . . is neutral as there is no suggestion of prejudice to the four children whether or not he was paid . . . the interest of any secured creditor . . . is irrelevant for present purposes.'

The Court of Appeal looked at the issue of compensation in *Murphy v Gooch*[2]. In that case the property was held by Ms Murphy and Mr Gooch as tenants in common in equal shares. On the breakdown of their relationship Ms Murphy left and commenced proceedings in order to realise her beneficial share. During the period that Mr Murphy was in sole occupation he paid the mortgage and

1.60 *Property*

the rent, this being a property bought under a shared ownership scheme. It was not in issue that he should be credited with Ms Gooch's share of those payments, but he resisted the suggestion that he should pay compensation to Ms Gooch by way of occupation rent. Lightman J reviewed the statutory principles[3] and concluded that the payments made by Mr Murphy on behalf of Ms Gooch cancelled out the payments that she should receive as an occupation rent. In the context of this case the relevant factors were that the parties had bought the property as a home for them both, but that since Ms Gooch was constrained to leave at the end of their relationship Mr Murphy alone had been enjoying this[4].

[1] Sections 12–15.
[2] [2007] EWCA Civ 603, [2007] 3 FCR 96, [2007] 2 FLR 934.
[3] At para 19.
[4] The reasoning was not challenged but as to the net result see Elizabeth Cooke 'Accounting Payments: Please can we get the Maths Right?' [2007] Fam Law 1024.

ILLEGALITY OF PURPOSE

1.61 Many cohabitants may have to rely upon equity to resolve their property disputes. Will equity intervene if there is evidence of illegality in the arrangements between them?

In *Tinsley v Milligan*[1] a property was acquired jointly by two women, but was conveyed into the name of only one of them to enable the other to make fraudulent claims for State benefits. When they fell out, the legal owner tried to persuade the court that the other could not assert her beneficial interest as her name was not on the title in order that she could perpetrate a fraud. The court was not so persuaded and held that the non-owner could rely on the resulting trust that arose by virtue of her contribution to the purchase price. This case was followed in *Lowson v Coombes*[2].

The Court of Appeal considered illegality in a constructive trust case, *O'Kelly v Davies*[3]. The conclusion was that since Mr Davies did not need to rely upon the illegality behind the reason for the property being held in Miss O'Kelly's sole to establish a beneficial interest in the property, the trial judge's finding that there had been a common intention that he should have an interest would not be disturbed.

[1] [1993] 2 FLR 963.
[2] [1999] 1 FLR 799. See also *Tribe v Tribe* [1995] 2 FLR 966.
[3] [2014] EWCA Civ 1606.

Applications for declaration of interest in trust property and order for sale

1.62 Sections 14 and 15 of the Trusts of Land and Appointment of Trustees Act 1996 (TOLATA 1996) make provision for the court to order the sale of property held on trust and replaced s 30 of the LPA 1925 with effect from 1 January 1997.

Property held on trust will include all land held on either an express trust, for example where there are joint owners, or where there is a resulting or constructive trust[1].

Trust property will include the proceeds of sale of trust property, and any other property acquired with the proceeds of sale.

A trust of land can include a mixed trust of land and personalty.

[1] See **1.24** and **1.27** above.

WHAT RELIEF IS AVAILABLE?

1.63 The court's powers under ss 14 and 15 of the TOLATA 1996 are more comprehensive than those under s 30 of the LPA 1925. In addition to ordering or preventing the sale of trust property the court may declare the nature or extent of a person's interest in the trust property, and may make orders relating to the exercise of the trustees' functions. The court may also give directions as to the application of the right to occupy provisions under ss 12 and 13 of TOLATA 1996 and order the payment of an occupation rent.

Bagum v Hafiz and Another[1] confirmed the ambit of the court's jurisdiction. Whilst the court has no power under s 14 TOLATA 1996 to order or direct that one beneficiary under a trust of land sell or transfer their interest to another beneficiary, s 15 confers powers wider than those vested in the trustees. This enabled the court in this case to order a sale of the property making provision for all of the beneficial owners to make an offer if that was their wish.

[1] [2015] EWCA Civ 801.

WHO MAY APPLY?

1.64 An application under s 14 of the TOLATA 1996 may be made by any person who is a trustee of land, or has an interest in trust property[1]. This includes a secured creditor, or a creditor who has a charging order, and a trustee in bankruptcy.

[1] Section 14(1) of the TOLATA 1996.

WHICH COURT?

1.65 The county court has unlimited jurisdiction in applications under s 14 of the TOLATA 1996[1].

In the High Court, application may be made to either the Chancery Division or the Family Division. In any event, there is power to transfer between Divisions, and between the county court and High Court and vice versa.

[1] Section 23(3) of the TOLATA 1996, and the High Court and County Court Jurisdiction Order 1991 (SI 1991/724).

ISSUING THE APPLICATION

1.66 In the county court, the application must be made to the court for the district in which the respondent resides or carries on business or the district in which the property is situated[1].

1.66 *Property*

In the High Court, the application may be made to the Central Office in London or any District Registry.

[1] CPR, Sch 2, CCR Ord 4, r 3; High Court and County Courts Jurisdiction (Amendment) Order 1996 (SI 1996/3141).

PROCEDURE

1.67 The procedure is the same in the High Court and county court. CPR apply, and application should be made by claim form in Form N208 under Part 8[1]. The claim form must state:

- that Part 8 applies to the claim;
- the remedy the claimant is seeking and the legal basis for the claim;
- that the claim is brought under the TOLATA 1996; and
- if any party is acting in a representative capacity, what that capacity is.

The claim form must contain a statement of truth[2].

At the time of issue of the claim the claimant is required to file evidence in support of the claim. It may be contained within the claim form, but except for the most straightforward case it will generally be preferable for there to be a separate witness statement. A defendant to the claim is also required to file any evidence relied upon at the same time as returning the acknowledgement form, and what follows in relation to the preparation of witness statements applies to all parties.

The reported decisions in this area underline the importance that is often attached to the minutiae of the parties' financial and other history. It is worth setting out in full the closing words of the judgment of Waite J, as he then was, in *H v M (Beneficial Interest)*[3]:

> 'The primary emphasis accorded by the law in cases of this kind to express discussions between the parties ("however imperfectly remembered and however imprecise their terms") means that the tenderest exchanges of a common law courtship may assume an unforeseen significance many years later when they are brought under equity's microscope and subjected to an analysis under which many thousands of pounds of value may be liable to turn on fine questions as to whether the relevant words were spoken in earnest or in dalliance and with or without representational intent. This requires that the express discussions to which the court's initial inquiries will be *address*ed should be pleaded in the greatest detail, both as to language and as to circumstance. In the Family Division, where there is no procedure for pleadings or particulars, the degree of particularity with which the relevant discussions are asserted in the claimant's initial affidavit will be of prime importance for both sides. From the claimant's point of view, failure to achieve particularity at that stage may cause the claim to founder for vagueness at the trial, where the affidavit will stand as her evidence-in-chief, on which she will be unlikely to be allowed to enlarge orally before she is cross-examined on it. From the respondent's point of view, he must be entitled, in an area of law where the nuances of language are all-important, to know exactly what case he has to meet.
>
> Particularity will have the further advantage to both sides of enabling the strength of the claim to be assessed by the parties' advisers at an early stage, with sufficient definition to provide a fair basis for reasonable compromise. That will be an especially desirable objective in the case of separating unmarried couples, whose

distress or bitterness is often found, paradoxically, to have been increased rather than diminished by their decision not to undertake a commitment to each other in marriage.'

It is of vital importance therefore that full and detailed instructions are taken at the outset in order that a party's case is set out clearly from the start, and is focused on the issues that the court will have to determine[4].

The claim form and evidence in support, together with as many copies as there are defendants should be filed at court with the fee payable. On receipt, the court will issue the claim and return copies for service together with a response pack in Form N208C for service on each defendant. The claimant will receive Notice of Issue in Form N209.

[1] See CPR Pt 22.
[2] **1.149**, **1.233** and **1.234**. For further reading see Da Costa and Garrod 'Procedural Aspects of Cohabitation Claims' [2003] Fam Law 270.
[3] [1992] 1 FLR 229.
[4] If an application is to be made under Sch 1 CA 1989 consideration should be given to conjoining the applications. See *W v W (Joinder of Trusts of Land Act and Children Act Applications)* [2004] 2 FLR 321. Note: 'conjoin' should not be confused with 'consolidate'. See Alexander Chandler, 'Strange bedfellows: case management in Sch 1 and TOLATA' [2016] September *Family Law*.

1.68 Each defendant is required within 14 days of service of the claim form to return the acknowledgement form that will be in the response pack indicating whether the claim is contested together with any written evidence relied upon. On receipt of the acknowledgement form, or after 16 days, the court will put the papers before the district judge. The district judge will give directions which will usually include listing a hearing date for a case management conference.

At the case management conference, directions will be given. These may include provision for each defendant to file a statement of case, disclosure of documents, filing of witness statements and obtaining evidence of valuation. If the claim is disputed, as will usually be the case, the district judge will direct that it proceed under CPR Pt 7.

In terms of disclosure, in any dispute as to the beneficial ownership, it will be essential to obtain the conveyancing file, mortgage application form and any documents filed at the Land Registry.

In all cases the court, and the parties, should consider Alternative Dispute Resolution (ADR) and in an appropriate case the district judge may stay the claim to enable the parties to mediate. Some judges may direct a dispute resolution hearing similar to the Financial Dispute Resolution appointment (FDR) in applications under the Matrimonial Causes Act 1973 for a financial order.

Directions will be subject to a strict timetable which should include provision for a further case management conference so that the district judge can ensure that the case will be ready for hearing.

1.68 *Property*

In the event that any defendant fails to attend the case management conference, the claimant will have to prove service of the claim[1].

[1] CPR Pt 6.

THE EXERCISE OF THE COURT'S DISCRETION

1.69 In deciding whether to make an order for sale, or declaration of a person's interest in the trust property under s 14 of the TOLATA 1996 the court must take into account all relevant matters, including those set out in s 15(1) and (3), namely:

- s 15(1):
    (a) the intentions of the person or persons (if any) who created the trust;
    (b) the purposes for which the property subject to the trust is held (ie the current purpose rather than the original purpose);
    (c) the welfare of any minor who occupies or might reasonably be expected to occupy any land subject to the trust as his home; and
    (d) the interests of any secured creditor of any beneficiary; and
- s 15(3): the circumstances and wishes of any beneficiaries of full age and entitled to an interest in possession in property subject to the trust or (in case of dispute) of the majority (according to the value of their combined interests).

1.70 The factors set out in s 15 are not exhaustive and the court may consider any other matters that it considers relevant. *Mortgage Corporation v Shaire*[1] is an example of the court exercising its discretion in favour of families and against banks and other chargees, and is of interest also because it summarises the court's approach to the question of who owns what when there is a dispute.

The story began in 1980 with the breakdown of the marriage of Mr and Mrs Shaire. Mr Shaire moved out of the jointly-owned matrimonial home leaving Mrs Shaire in the house with their child. In 1986, Mrs Shaire began a relationship with a Mr Fox, and he moved in with her in 1987.

There were then divorce proceedings between Mr and Mrs Shaire. It was agreed as part of the divorce settlement that the house would be transferred into the joint names of Mrs Shaire and Mr Fox in exchange for a lump sum payment to Mr Shaire. This was raised by Mrs Shaire and Mr Fox by way of a mortgage advance.

The couple lived in the house with the child. Mrs Shaire worked part-time and had only modest earnings. Mr Fox paid the mortgage and the household expenses.

In 1992, Mr Fox died from a heart attack. After his death it came to light that he had forged Mrs Shaire's signature on several documents, including a mortgage to First National Bank and a charge to The Mortgage Corporation to secure a substantial sum which he had used to pay off the earlier borrowings.

In 1994, The Mortgage Corporation brought possession proceedings. Mrs Shaire was still living in the house with her son, although by this time he was an adult.

The issues raised by the possession proceedings included how the beneficial interests in the property had been shared between Mr Fox and Mrs Shaire, and whether there should be an order for sale so that The Mortgage Corporation could enforce their charge.

In relation to the beneficial share, those representing the bank said it was 50/50.

Those representing Mrs Shaire said it was a minimum of 75/25 in her favour.

The court decided that Mrs Shaire was beneficially entitled to a 75 per cent interest in the house.

The approach taken was first to decide the shares in which Mr and Mrs Shaire had owned the property. The court agreed with counsel for both sides that it was 50/50 but set out the following factors that it was to take into account:

- there was an equal contribution to the purchase price by means of a wedding present of £2,000 to them both, and the balance by mortgage in joint names;
- the house was held in joint names;
- the house was intended as a family home and the parties lived there until the marriage breakdown;
- Mrs Shaire believed that joint names meant equal shares;
- the fall back presumption is that equality is equity.

It did not affect the court's decision that it was Mr Shaire who had made the mortgage repayments and paid all household outgoings.

The question then for the court was whether Mr Fox took over Mr Shaire's share so that they held in equal shares or whether Mr Shaire's share was divided between Mr Fox and Mrs Shaire so that they held as a minimum 75/25 in Mrs Shaire's favour.

The documents of title transferring the property to Mr Fox and Mrs Shaire did not set out the shares in which they were beneficially entitled, and the court was not prepared to accept that the standard wording in the old form of HM Land Registry Transfer Form providing that the survivor could give a valid receipt for the purchase money meant that they held the property as joint tenants in equal shares. The judge said that people who were not lawyers could not possibly intend that such a clause would mean that they shared equally.

There was nothing else in writing, and so the judge concluded that there was not an express agreement between them as to how they should share the beneficial interests that would cast any light on what they had agreed, if anything.

1 [2000] 1 FLR 973.

1.71 The court therefore had to look at the parties' conduct and in so doing the court set out a number of factors that it said made the arguments in favour of 75 per cent for Mrs Shaire compelling:

- they took on equal liability for the mortgage raised to buy out Mr Shaire;
- Mr Shaire was bought out for less than the value of his interest – the element of gift should be regarded as a gift to Mrs Shaire not Mr Fox;
- Mrs Shaire gave up capital claims against Mr Shaire in the divorce settlement;
- 25 per cent was Mr Fox's contribution in terms of his shared liability for the mortgage;
- the wording of agreement on the divorce was that Mr Fox and Mrs Shaire were together buying out Mr Shaire's half share, Mr Fox therefore had a one-quarter share.

The next question was whether there should be an order for sale.

It was argued on behalf of The Mortgage Corporation that a sale should be ordered unless there were exceptional circumstances. The court rejected that argument and said that it was able to exercise its discretion on the basis of the matters set out in s 15(1).

On the facts of this case the following matters were held to be relevant to the exercise of the court's discretion:

- Mrs Shaire had a 75 per cent interest in the house, the bank only 25 per cent;
- the house had been Mrs Shaire's home since 1976;
- she still lived there and wanted to stay there;
- for her to leave would be a real and significant hardship, but not an enormous one;
- the bank was in the business of lending money and they could be compensated for failing to realise their interest by payments of interest which Mrs Shaire could afford to pay.

There would therefore be no order for sale on condition that Mrs Shaire paid either interest to the bank for the use of its share of the property, or one-quarter of what would be the fair rent for the property.

The criteria upon which an order will be made under s 14 of the TOLATA 1996 are much clearer than under s 30 of the LPA 1925. Furthermore, as the TOLATA 1996 removes the concept of the trust for sale, and the power of the trustees by agreement to postpone sale, the court is no longer approaching the dispute from the standpoint that there is a presumption in favour of sale.

Note, however, that where an application is made by a trustee in bankruptcy the factors set out in s 15 do not apply[1]. The more restrictive matters to which the court must have regard in those circumstances recognise the interests of a spouse or former spouse, or a child for the 12 months after the bankruptcy order, but not the interests of a cohabitant.

[1] Section 15(4) of the TOLATA 1996.

The order

1.72 As well as making an order for the sale of the trust property, the court may prevent the sale in order to allow one party to occupy the property. In those circumstances there is power to order compensation to the party who is thereby unable to realise his or her interest in the trust property[1]. If it is not appropriate to make an order for immediate sale, the application should be dismissed leaving the parties to come back to court should circumstances change. Conditional orders should be avoided.

Where there is also a dispute about the ownership of the beneficial interest, the court may make a declaration as to the nature or extent of a party's interest in the trust property.

[1] Section 13(6) of the TOLATA 1996.

Injunctions

1.73 The court has the power to make an order restraining the disposal of trust property pending the final hearing. Application will be made on notice (exceptionally without notice) to the judge with an affidavit in support. The affidavit will set out fully and frankly all the circumstances, and the applicant's grounds for believing that the trust property is to be disposed of or otherwise dealt with.

Applications under the Married Women's Property Act 1882

1.74 Some cohabitants may be able to use the procedure contained in s 17 of the MWPA 1882. This will only apply to those who were engaged to be married, provided that no more than 3 years has elapsed since the engagement was broken off.

What relief is available?

1.75 The court has the power to resolve any dispute over the title to or possession of property but it cannot adjust the interests in property.

Property will include personal property, and the net proceeds of sale of property, or any other property bought with the net proceeds.

Who may apply?

1.76 Apart from spouses and former spouses, s 17 of the MWPA 1882 is only available to couples who were formerly engaged to be married within 3 years of the termination of the engagement.

Which court?

1.77 Application must be made to the Family Court.

1.78 *Property*

PROCEDURE

1.78 Applications under s 17 of the MWPA 1882 are family proceedings and so the Family Procedure Rules 2010 (FPR) will apply. Application is made in Form D50 or D50B if the application is for a transfer of tenancy. The application must state what order is sought and have annexed to it a draft order.

Where the application relates to the title to or possession of land, the application must contain details of any mortgage, and state whether the title to the land is registered or unregistered, and if registered, the Title Number.

SERVICE OF THE APPLICATION

1.79 The application and any written evidence in support must be served on the respondent together with a form of acknowledgement of service in Form D50A. Where there is a mortgage, the mortgagee must be served with the application.

THE HEARING

1.80 The district judge has jurisdiction to make interim or final orders in applications under s 17 of the MWPA 1882. The hearing is in private.

THE COURT'S APPROACH

1.81 When resolving a dispute as to the ownership of property, the usual trust principles will apply as laid down in *Pettitt v Pettitt*[1] and *Gissing v Gissing*[2] and restated in *Lloyds Bank plc v Rosset*[3].

In determining the size of a party's share in property, the same principles will apply[4].

When deciding whether or not to order the sale of property in dispute the court has an unfettered discretion, but one of the factors that will be relevant in relation to a dwelling house is whether the house provides a home for any relevant children.

[1] [1970] AC 777.
[2] [1971] AC 886.
[3] [1990] 2 FLR 155. See **1.33** above.
[4] See **1.45** above.

THE ORDER

1.82 The court may make an order that is merely declaratory of a party's beneficial interest in property, real and/or personal, and it may order the sale of property.

INJUNCTIONS

1.83 The district judge may make an injunction restraining the disposal of property which is the subject of the application pending the final hearing. Application will be made on notice (in exceptional circumstances without notice), with an affidavit in support.

Applications under Matrimonial Proceedings and Property Act 1970

1.84 Like the MWPA 1882, whilst primarily of relevance to married people, s 37 of the MPPA 1970 is available to those who are or were engaged to be married. This section can be invoked where an entitled applicant has made a substantial contribution to the improvement of property (real or personal), whether or not that person has a beneficial interest in the property. If successful, the applicant is treated as acquiring a share, or increasing an existing share, by reference to the contribution.

If an application is also to be made under the MWPA 1882, the proceedings should be consolidated.

Section 2 Occupation of the home

The owner-occupied home

RIGHTS OF OCCUPATION

1.85 If a cohabitant can establish a beneficial interest in the family home, either by being a joint owner, or by virtue of a resulting or constructive trust[1], the right to occupy the property will be undeniable, unless it has been prohibited, suspended or restricted by an order under Pt IV of the Family Law Act 1996 (FLA 1996), or by the court's powers under s 13 TOLATA 1996.

Difficulties often arise where both cohabitants have rights of occupation as a result of their beneficial interests, and both choose to exercise those rights. In those cases, it may be appropriate to make application under Pt IV of the FLA 1996 for an order prohibiting, suspending or restricting the exercise of the right by the other cohabitant, or for an exclusion order under s 13 TOLATA 1996.

It is possible for a cohabitant who does not have rights of occupation to acquire them by making application under Pt IV of the FLA 1996. If all the relevant criteria for making an order are satisfied, rights of occupation may be granted, but only in cases in which the cohabitant who is the respondent to the application is 'entitled' to occupy[2].

Problems can arise where there is mortgage default, particularly where the party in possession is not a party to the mortgage. The provisions of s 54(5) of the Family Law Act 1996 enable a 'connected person' to make the mortgage repayments in respect of the home and to seek to be joined to any possession

1.85 *Property*

proceedings. For these purposes a connected person, in relation to the mortgagee, includes that person's cohabitant or former cohabitant.

[1] See **1.27** above.
[2] See **4.17** below.

LICENCES

1.86 If a cohabitant cannot establish or acquire rights of occupation, it may be possible to remain in occupation of the family home by relying on a licence to occupy.

During the subsistence of the relationship, the cohabitant with rights of occupation will have either expressly or by implication granted a licence to the other cohabitant to occupy the property. Ordinarily, a bare licence will be determinable upon reasonable notice and in these circumstances there will be no answer to a claim for possession.

However, the licence may have some contractual basis and will be enforceable if all the requirements for a valid contract are present. For example, in *Tanner v Tanner*[1] the court found that by giving up her secure rented accommodation to live in a property owned by the father of her two children a woman had given good consideration for an implied contractual licence to remain in the property until the children had finished their education.

Similarly, if an owner of property has led a person with a licence to occupy to believe that such occupation will continue, and in reliance upon that the licensee acts to his or her detriment, then the court may prevent or estop the owner from denying the right of occupation. This was the position in *Greasley v Cooke*[2].

[1] [1975] 3 All ER 776.
[2] [1980] 3 All ER 710.

ORDERS UNDER SCH 1 TO THE CHILDREN ACT 1989

1.87 A cohabitant may be able to occupy property by virtue of looking after a child of the relationship where a transfer of property order has been made under Sch 1 to the CA 1989[1].

[1] See **5.50**.

The rented home

RIGHTS OF OCCUPATION

1.88 The law relating to landlord and tenant is a complex area and the following is intended as no more than a very basic outline.

Where cohabitants are living in rented property (as their only or principal residence), the right to remain in occupation if the cohabitation ceases for any reason will be the primary concern.

The position will vary according to whether the tenancy is held in joint names or in the sole name of one of the cohabitants, and will also depend upon the nature of the tenancy under which the property is held. Different provisions apply to the different types of tenancy, for example in relation to security of tenure, rent control, assignment and succession on death.

RIGHTS OF OCCUPATION UNDER PT IV OF THE FAMILY LAW ACT 1996

1.89 An order giving a non-tenant cohabitant rights of occupation under Pt IV of the FLA 1996 is not capable of affecting the rights of third parties. Accordingly, such an order will not in itself provide a defence to possession proceedings by the landlord[1].

[1] See also **1.106** below.

Private sector tenancies

1.90 Tenancies of dwelling-houses created before 15 January 1989 are known as protected tenancies (contractual or statutory) and are governed by the Rent Act 1977 (RA 1977)[1].

Most tenancies created after 15 January 1989 will either be assured or assured shorthold tenancies, and the provisions of the Housing Act 1988 (HA 1988) will apply. Following the HA 1996, most tenancies created after 28 February 1997 will be assured shorthold tenancies unless the landlord expressly provides otherwise.

Assured shorthold tenancies are a species of tenancy lacking long-term security of tenure. Rent control and ease of recovering possession are essentially geared to commercial considerations.

[1] Private sector tenancies are those outside the local authority sector.

Housing associations and other registered social landlords

1.91 Tenancies granted by housing associations after 15 January 1989 are governed by Pt 1 of the HA 1988 and may be either assured or assured shorthold tenancies. The provisions that apply are set out at **1.92** below.

Tenancies in existence before 15 January 1989 will almost certainly be secure tenancies which are effectively the same as those granted by local authorities[1].

[1] Housing Act 1988.

ASSURED TENANCIES

Security

1.92 Assured tenancies afford greater protection to the tenant than assured shorthold tenancies. However, it should be noted that in order for a tenancy to be or remain as an assured tenancy, the tenant, or at least one of the joint tenants, must be living in the property. Thus, if cohabitants are joint tenants, the removal of one of them from the property will not of itself affect the tenancy[1]. However, if the tenancy is in the sole name of one of the cohabitants, and that cohabitant leaves the property, the tenancy will cease to be an assured tenancy, and the landlord will be able to obtain possession[2].

A fixed-term assured tenancy cannot be brought to an end by one joint tenant unilaterally as long as the fixed term has not expired. When a fixed-term assured tenancy comes to an end, for example by effluxion of time, it is replaced by a periodic tenancy on more or less the same terms as the fixed-term tenancy. Although the periodic tenancy will also be a joint tenancy, one tenant will be able to bring the tenancy to an end by serving a notice to quit. The situation could arise in which one cohabitant leaves during the currency of the periodic tenancy and serves notice to quit. This will determine the joint periodic tenancy leaving the tenant in occupation to deal with any possession proceedings brought by the landlord. There will be no answer to the landlord's claim as the court has no power to revive the tenancy[3]. However, the tenancy itself is property for as long as it remains in existence, ie before termination by notice to quit, and in *Bater v Greenwich London Borough Council and Another*[4] Thorpe LJ confirmed that the court has both statutory and inherent powers to prevent unilateral termination of a tenancy in certain circumstances[5].

[1] Section 1(1)(b) of the HA 1988.
[2] Section 5(1)(b) of the HA 1988. Compare with the situation as between husband and wife in *Griffiths v Renfree* [1989] 2 FLR 167.
[3] *Hammersmith and Fulham London Borough Council v Monk* [1992] 1 FLR 465.
[4] [1999] 2 FLR 993.
[5] See **1.108** below.

Assignment

1.93 An assured tenancy will either be for a fixed term, or a periodic tenancy determinable upon giving notice to quit. Whereas an assured tenancy for a fixed term may be assigned as long as the terms of the individual tenancy agreement do not prohibit assignment, a periodic tenancy may not be assigned without the landlord's consent unless the tenancy agreement expressly provides otherwise. There is no requirement that the landlord must not unreasonably withhold his consent[1].

[1] Section 15 of the HA 1988 implies a covenant against assignment without the landlord's consent in the absence of any provision in the tenancy agreement.

Succession

1.94 On the death of one joint tenant of an assured tenancy, the tenancy will automatically vest in the survivor.

An assured tenancy in the name of one person only is an interest in land and can be left by will, and in the absence of a valid will, it will be subject to the intestacy rules[1]. If the surviving cohabitant is specified in the deceased tenant's will as the beneficiary of the deceased's interest in the tenancy, there will be no short-term difficulty. However, Ground 7 in Sch 2 to the HA 1988 is a mandatory ground that will enable a landlord to recover possession of property subject to a periodic tenancy that has devolved under the former tenant's will, provided that the proceedings for possession are started within 12 months of the tenant's death, or if the court directs, 12 months after the landlord became aware of the death.

If there is no will, a cohabitant cannot benefit under the intestacy rules. However, where there is a periodic assured tenancy, a cohabitant can succeed to the tenancy in the sole name of the other cohabitant if they were living together as husband and wife immediately before the death, the survivor was occupying the property as his or her only or principal home and the deceased had not acquired the tenancy by succession. In these circumstances, the periodic assured tenancy will not form part of the deceased's estate[2].

The effect of this in practice is that if a person went to live with the survivor to a joint tenancy, on the death of the surviving tenant, the surviving cohabitant would have no right to succeed to the tenancy, no rights of occupation, and the landlord would be able to apply for an order for possession without having to satisfy the court as to the usual grounds for possession set out in Sch 2.

In *Harrogate Borough Council v Simpson*[3] the court held that same-sex cohabitants could not live together as 'husband and wife' for these purposes. This was confirmed in *Fitzpatrick v Sterling Housing Association Ltd*[4]. However, these decisions pre-*date*d the implementation of the Human Rights Act 1998 (HRA 1998). The decision in *Mendoza v Ghaidan*[5] removed the inherent discrimination on the basis of sexual orientation by adopting an interpretation of the domestic statute that is compatible with the Convention.

CPA 2004 extended succession rights to civil partners and those living together as civil partners.

[1] See **6.11**.
[2] Section 17(1) and (4) of the HA 1988.
[3] [1986] 2 FLR 91.
[4] [2000] 1 FLR 271.
[5] [2004] 2 FLR 600.

PROTECTED TENANCIES

1.95 Slightly different considerations apply to tenancies created before 15 January 1989 to which the provisions of the RA 1977 apply. These tenancies will either be protected contractual tenancies or statutory tenancies. A contractual tenancy is a tenancy agreement to which the provisions of the RA 1977 apply. A statutory tenancy will arise by the operation of the provisions of the RA 1977 where a contractual tenancy comes to an end by effluxion of time or service of a notice to quit, or where the tenancy is acquired by succession.

Security

1.96 One of the cohabiting parties can serve a notice to quit on the landlord which will terminate that party's obligations under the tenancy but will not jeopardise the tenancy for the remaining cohabitant as long as he or she continues to use the property as a residence¹. The remaining cohabitant will then be a statutory tenant². However, if the tenancy is in the sole name of the cohabitant who has left, the cohabitant in occupation has no rights in respect of the tenancy and no rights of occupation.

1   This is subject to the discretionary ground for possession in Case 5 of Sch 15 to the RA 1977 – where the tenant has given notice to quit and, in consequence of that notice, the landlord has contracted to sell or let the dwelling-house or has taken any other steps as the result of which he would, in the opinion of the court, be seriously prejudiced if he could not obtain possession.
2   *Lloyd v Sadler* [1978] 2 All ER 529.

Assignment

1.97 Unless the tenancy agreement contains a covenant against assignment, protected contractual tenancies can be assigned with the landlord's consent, which is not to be unreasonably withheld¹.

A statutory tenancy cannot be assigned.

1   Section 19 of the Landlord and Tenant Act 1927 (LTA 1927).

Succession

1.98 If a protected contractual or a statutory tenancy is in joint names, on the death of one of the joint tenants the survivor will automatically succeed to the tenancy. A surviving cohabitant will succeed to a protected tenancy in respect of which the deceased was the original sole tenant if the surviving cohabitant was living at the property as the husband or wife of the deceased immediately before the death and if, and for so long as, he or she occupies the property as his or her residence. In these circumstances, the surviving cohabitant will become entitled to an assured tenancy (or statutory tenancy if the succession was before 15 January 1989) of the property on the same terms as under the contractual tenancy.

Following *Ghaidan v Godin Mendoza*¹, 'living with the original tenant as his or her wife or husband' means 'as if they were his or her wife or husband'. The House of Lords upheld the decision of the Court of Appeal that sought to *address* the breach of the Convention found in the provisions of para 2(2) of Sch 1 to the Rent Act 1977. In this, the Court of Appeal had gone far beyond what at the time had seemed to be the liberal decision of the House of Lords in *Fitzpatrick v Sterling Housing Association Ltd*². In that case it was decided that although a cohabitant of the same sex could not succeed to a statutory tenancy on the death of the other cohabitant, it was possible to succeed to a lesser form of tenancy as a member of the deceased tenant's family. It was then a question of fact as to whether or not the survivor could satisfy the court as to the necessary elements of the relationship.

At first instance the trial judge had applied *Fitzpatrick v Sterling Housing Association Ltd* and found that the same-sex partner of the deceased tenant was entitled to succeed only to an assured tenancy, as a member of the tenant's family, not to the secure tenancy that a spouse of a deceased tenant would have succeeded to.

The surviving partner appealed that decision on the basis of Art 14 of the European Convention for the Protection of Human Rights and Fundamental Freedoms 1950, which provides:

> 'The enjoyment of the rights and freedoms set forth in this Convention shall be secured without discrimination on any ground such as sex, race, colour, language, religion, political or other opinion, national or social origin, association with a national minority, birth or other status.'

The facts were very similar to those in *Fitzpatrick v Sterling Housing Association Ltd*. Two men had lived together for many years in an intimate and loving relationship. The property in which they lived was subject to a secure tenancy of which the deceased partner was the sole tenant.

The issue raised in both cases was the interest in the tenancy of the surviving partner on the death of the tenant.

[1] [2004] 2 FLR 600.
[2] [2000] 1 FLR 271.

1.99 Before the implementation of the Human Rights Act 1998, the House of Lords felt unable to construe para 2(2) of Sch 1 to the Rent Act 1977 as including same-sex relationships. The Court of Appeal in *Mendoza v Ghaidan*, unable to find any objective and reasonable justification for the exclusion of same-sex relationships from the relevant Schedule, concluded that such an interpretation was an infringement of Art 14:

> '. . . to afford a statutory tenancy to the survivor of a heterosexual relationship when the survivor of an equivalent homosexual relationship was limited to the less beneficial assured tenancy constituted discrimination on grounds of sexual orientation.'

In order to remedy the breach of the Convention, the court reinterpreted the Schedule to include those living as if they were the husband or wife of the deceased tenant, so as not to discriminate on grounds of sexual orientation, and so as to render the domestic legislation compatible with the Convention. This was upheld by the House of Lords, dismissing the defendant's appeal.

If the deceased tenant was the sole tenant of an assured tenancy (or statutory tenancy pre-15 January 1989) acquired by succession, a cohabitant will not automatically qualify to succeed. Instead, the surviving cohabitant will have to establish that he or she was a member of the family of both the original tenant and the successor to the tenancy immediately before their respective deaths, and that he or she was living with the tenant who succeeded to the original tenancy at the time of death and for the 2 years immediately before the death of the successor to the tenancy. Whilst this provision may be relevant to sons and daughters and other close family members, it is difficult to imagine the sort of ménage to which it could apply!

CPA 2004 extends succession rights to civil partners and those living together as civil partners.

1.100 *Property*

Local authority housing

1.100 Tenancies granted by local authorities are known as secure tenancies and the HA 1985 applies. Tenancies granted by housing associations before 15 January 1989 will also be secure tenancies.

SECURITY

1.101 If the tenancy is in joint names, whilst the removal of one joint tenant from the property will not affect the security of tenure of the other, if either of the tenants serves a valid notice this will defeat the other tenant's interest if the tenancy is a periodic tenancy[1].

Neither tenant can unilaterally bring a fixed-term tenancy to an end by serving a notice to quit or surrendering the lease.

If the tenancy is in the sole name of the cohabitant who leaves the property, the remaining cohabitant has no interest in the tenancy and no rights of occupation unless an order is obtained under Pt IV of the FLA 1996[2].

[1] *Hammersmith and Fulham London Borough Council v Monk* [1992] 1 FLR 465.
[2] *Gay v Sheeran* [1999] 2 FLR 519, CA.

ASSIGNMENT

1.102 A secure tenancy cannot be assigned except in the specific cases mentioned in s 91(3) of the HA 1985. These include assignments pursuant to an order made under Sch 1 to the CA 1989 and the assignment of secure tenancies to a person who would have qualified to succeed on the death of the tenant. If the tenancy is in joint names, the other joint tenant will qualify. If the property is in the sole name of the cohabitant who wishes to assign the tenancy, the other cohabitant must satisfy two criteria. First, the assignee must have lived with the assignor for the entire 12-month period immediately before the assignment. Secondly, the assignee must come within the definition of 'a member of the [assignor's] family'[1].

[1] See s 113 of the HA 1985 for definition of members of a person's family.

SUCCESSION

1.103 If the tenancy is in the joint names of cohabitants, the surviving cohabitant will succeed to the tenancy automatically. If the tenancy was in the sole name of the deceased cohabitant, the survivor may succeed if he or she can satisfy two criteria. First, the survivor must have lived with the deceased for the entire 12-month period immediately before the death of the tenant. Secondly, the survivor must come within the definition of 'a member of the tenant's family'[1].

There can only be one succession to a secure tenancy. Accordingly, the survivor of joint tenants, or a person who himself succeeded to a secure tenancy, cannot pass on a tenancy.

CPA 2004 extends succession rights to civil partners and those living together as civil partners.

[1] See s 113 of the HA 1985.

Tenancy in joint names

1.104 If a tenancy is in joint names, both parties will be jointly and severally liable to pay the rent and perform all the other obligations of the tenancy, but they will both have the right to occupy and enjoy the property and cannot lawfully exclude the other except where an exclusion order is in force, for example pursuant to Pt IV of the FLA 1996.

The survivor of joint tenants will automatically succeed to the tenancy, and in view of the restrictions on succession by cohabitants that apply to some forms of tenancy, if a tenancy can be taken in joint names, or assigned into joint names by agreement, this will usually be preferable.

A joint tenant will be in a better position than a cohabitant who is not a tenant when it comes to applying for an order under Pt IV of the FLA 1996. As a joint tenant, he or she will be able to apply under s 33 and orders made under that section may last for longer than orders made in favour of a cohabitant who is not a tenant[1].

The provisions of Sch 7 to the FLA 1996 in relation to orders for the transfer of tenancies may also operate in favour of joint tenants as the criteria to be considered in the case of a cohabitant who is not a tenant (and is without rights of occupation given by the FLA 1996) are wider ranging and more discriminatory. They include, for example, the length of the cohabitation and the fact that the parties have not committed themselves to marriage or civil partnership.

It is important to be aware that although one of two joint tenants cannot determine a fixed-*date* tenancy or surrender a lease before the end of the term, the service of a valid notice to quit on the landlord by one tenant of a periodic tenancy can bring the tenancy to an end regardless of the other tenant's wish to remain in the property[2]. Furthermore, following the decision of the Supreme Court in *Sims v Dacorum Borough Council*, any challenge to this either as a violation of Art 8 ECHR rights[3] or under Art 1 of the First Protocol to the Convention[4] is likely to be unsuccessful.

The action that can be taken to prevent the termination of a joint tenancy in this way is set out at **1.108** below.

[1] See **4.26** below.
[2] *Hammersmith and Fulham London Borough Council v Monk* [1992] 1 FLR 465.
[3] Right to respect for one's home.
[4] Right to peaceful enjoyment of possessions.

Tenancy in sole name

1.105 Whilst a cohabitant who is not the tenant of a shared property has no obligation to pay rent or other charges, neither will that person have any right

1.105 *Property*

to occupy the property beyond the licence impliedly or expressly granted by the cohabitant who is the tenant[1].

If that licence is terminated on the breakdown of a cohabitation relationship, a cohabitant may only acquire rights of occupation by obtaining an order under Pt IV of the FLA 1996. This is a discretionary remedy and is likely to be available for interim protection only[2].

Even if the cohabitant who is not the tenant remains in occupation after the tenant has left, the tenant may terminate the tenancy by serving a notice to quit on the landlord or surrendering the tenancy to the landlord. Clearly, he or she will be anxious to be relieved of the responsibilities imposed by the tenancy, regardless of any other motive there may be. In these circumstances, in the absence of an order giving the non-tenant cohabitant rights of occupation, there will be no defence to possession proceedings brought by the landlord unless, exceptionally, the remaining cohabitant could establish that a new tenancy had been granted.

If the tenant has not brought the tenancy to an end and the non-tenant cohabitant remains at the property, he or she may be able to apply for an order transferring the tenancy[3].

[1] See **1.2**.
[2] See **4.35**.
[3] See further below.

Protecting the cohabitant in occupation

1.106 Whether the tenancy is in the sole name of the departing cohabitant, or in joint names, urgent action may be necessary to preserve the property for the remaining cohabitant.

Once a tenancy has been brought to an end it cannot be revived for any purposes[1], although if the landlord is co-operative a new tenancy could be granted.

The fact that a tenancy may be in joint names does not prevent one tenant from serving a notice to quit and thereby defeating the other tenant's interest in the tenancy[2].

This will not apply in the case of protected tenancies under the RA 1977.

[1] *Newlon Housing Trust v Alsulaimen* [1998] 2 FLR 690.
[2] *Hammersmith and Fulham London Borough Council v Monk* [1992] 1 FLR 465; *Harrow London Borough Council v Johnstone* [1997] 1 FLR 887.

NOTICE TO QUIT

1.107 To be valid to terminate the tenancy, a notice to quit must fulfil two basic requirements. First, it must be in writing and secondly, it must give 4 weeks' notice. Whether acting for the tenant giving notice to quit, or the unfortunate tenant or cohabitant remaining at the property, it will be as well to check that the formalities have been complied with before concluding that the notice to quit is effective[1].

Service of a notice to quit is not a 'disposition of property' that can be set aside by the court[2] and, therefore, it is of prime importance to keep the tenancy alive by preventing service of a notice to quit.

[1] Section 5(1) of the Protection from Eviction Act 1977.
[2] In *Harrow London Borough Council v Johnstone* [1997] 1 FLR 887, the concession made in *Newlon Housing Trust v Alsulaimen* [1998] 2 FLR 690 that notice of termination could be set aside as a reviewable disposition under MCA 1973, s 37(2)(b) if no injunction had been granted before service of the notice was called into question.

INJUNCTION TO PREVENT TERMINATION OF TENANCY

1.108 The only remedy open to the cohabitant remaining in the shared home who is faced with the prospect of the other cohabitant serving a notice to quit is to apply to the court for an order to prevent such service. The basis for the court's jurisdiction is the power given by Sch 7 to the FLA 1996 to transfer tenancies between cohabitants. Clearly any disposal of the tenancy before the court had determined an application to transfer would pre-empt the court's decision[1].

Any application for an injunction should ideally be within an existing application for a transfer of tenancy, but in cases of urgency, the court will generally accept an undertaking to issue the substantive application within a short timescale.

If a notice to quit is served after an application has been made for a transfer of the tenancy, this will not affect the court's powers to transfer the tenancy[2].

[1] *Bater v Greenwich London Borough Council and Another* [1999] 2 FLR 993, CA.
[2] *Hammersmith and Fulham London Borough Council v Monk* [1992] 1 FLR 465; *Lewis v Lewis and Another* [1984] FLR 492.

Applying to transfer the tenancy

1.109 In common with married parties, or those in a civil partnership, who separate, it will usually be prudent to ensure a cohabitant's continued security of tenure by making application for a transfer of the tenancy of the former shared home, whether the tenancy is in joint names or the sole name of the cohabitant who has left.

Until Sch 1 to the CA 1989 came into force, there was no jurisdiction to entertain such an application, and then application could be made only by a parent with the care of a child, with the primary intention of benefitting the child.

However, Pt IV of the FLA 1996 now gives the court wide powers to order the transfer of tenancies between cohabitants, and this will generally be the preferred route.

In the case of a secure tenancy under the HA 1985, if the remaining cohabitant is not a tenant, and the tenancy has not been brought to an end by a valid notice to quit, the remaining tenant will have to acquire rights of occupation under s 36 of the FLA 1996 before the court will have power to order a transfer of tenancy under s 53 and Sch 7. This was the position in *Gay v*

1.109 *Property*

Sheeran[1]. In that case, the tenancy was in the joint names of the departing cohabitant and his previous cohabitant. It was agreed that neither the landlord nor either of the joint tenants had brought the tenancy to an end, but it was a fact that the tenant condition was not satisfied. Section 79(1) of the HA 1985 provides that for a tenancy to be a secure tenancy, the tenant condition in s 81 has to be satisfied. In this case, that condition was not satisfied because none of the tenants was in occupation. In order to satisfy the condition, the remaining cohabitant had to acquire rights of occupation by way of an occupation order under s 36 of the FLA 1996 in order for her occupation to be treated as occupation by the departing cohabitant pursuant to s 30(4) of the FLA 1996.

The court held that even if the occupation order was sought partly with a view to obtaining a transfer order, this was not outside the scope of s 36 of the FLA 1996, although the requirements for an order under that section would have to be satisfied.

Even though the remaining cohabitant was able to put herself in a position to apply for the transfer of the tenancy, in her case the court expressed doubts as to whether there was power under Sch 7 to the FLA 1996 to transfer a tenancy that was in the name of a third party as well as the cohabitant who had left. It was considered that the words in the Schedule effectively limited a relevant tenancy to one held in a tenant's 'own right or jointly with the other spouse or cohabitant', in other words, not held jointly with a person other than the spouse or cohabitant.

[1] [1999] 2 FLR 519.

Application to transfer a tenancy under Pt IV of the Family Law Act 1996

Which court?

1.110 Application should be made to the Family Court, noting that the Lay Justices have no jurisdiction in these applications. If there are other family proceedings in a particular court it will generally be good practice to make an application to transfer the tenancy to that court.

Who may apply?

1.111 As well as a spouse or former spouse and following implementation of CPA 2004 civil partners and former civil partners, there is provision for applications to be made by a cohabitant who is no longer living with the other cohabitant.

Which tenancies may be transferred?

1.112 Not all tenancies may be the subject of an order for transfer. For example, assured shorthold tenancies are excluded.

Only a 'relevant tenancy' may be transferred. This will include:

(1) a protected tenancy or statutory tenancy to which the RA 1977 applies;
(2) a statutory tenancy under the Rent (Agriculture) Act 1976;
(3) a secure tenancy under s 79 of the HA 1985;
(4) an assured tenancy or assured agricultural occupancy to which Pt I of the HA 1988 applies.

The court may make an order only in relation to a property that was the home in which the cohabitants lived together, and only if one of the parties is entitled to occupy the home by virtue of one of the relevant tenancies.

The court can only transfer the interest that the transferor had in the tenancy immediately before the order for transfer.

Time for the application

1.113 There is no prescribed time for an application by a former cohabitant, simply a requirement that the parties are no longer living together, and the applicant's marriage or new relationship will not prevent an application being made. Having said that, the lapse of time since cohabitation, and marriage or a new relationship, whilst not a bar to relief, may be considered by the court on the exercise of its discretion.

The exercise of the court's discretion

1.114 In deciding whether or not to make what is known as a Part II order in favour of a former cohabitant, the court is to have regard to all the circumstances of the case, including:

(1) the circumstances in which the tenancy was granted, or the circumstances in which one or both of the cohabitants became tenants;
(2) the matters set out in s 33(6) of the FLA 1996, namely:
   - the housing needs and housing resources of the parties and any relevant child,
   - the financial resources of the parties, and
   - the likely effect of any order, or the refusal of an order, on the health, safety or well-being or the parties or any relevant child;
(3) if only one of the cohabitants is entitled to occupy under a relevant tenancy the matters set out in s 36(6) of the FLA 1996, namely:
   - the nature of the parties' relationship,
   - the duration of the cohabitation,
   - whether there are or have been any children who are children of both parties or for whom both parties have or have had parental responsibility, and
   - the length of time since the parties lived together; and
(4) the suitability of the parties as tenants.

In *Guerroudj v Rymarczyk*[1] the Court of Appeal upheld the decision of the court below that the joint tenancy granted by the local council to the cohabiting parties should be transferred into the name of the man alone.

1.114 *Property*

Following the breakdown of their relationship, the woman had offered a financial incentive to the man to leave the flat they shared. He had refused, and issued an application under the FLA 1996 for a transfer of tenancy into his name. The woman also applied for the tenancy to be transferred to her.

Although the judge at first instance found the matter to be very finely balanced, it was the man's debilitating back condition that tipped the balance in his favour. This factor had also weighed with the housing authority when offering the couple the flat in the first place as he had a priority need. The woman's argument that the man would by reason of that always have a priority need, whereas she would not and therefore the tenancy should be transferred to her, did not hold sway although the judge did order the man to pay to her £1,500 by way of compensation.

[1] [2015] EWCA Civ 743.

Issuing the application

1.115 The application should be made on Form D50B. It is effectively treated as if it were an application for an occupation order. A sworn statement in support should be filed. The statement should confirm the applicant's eligibility to apply, that the tenancy is a relevant tenancy, and that one or both of the parties, as the case may be, is entitled to occupy the property by reason of the tenancy. The criteria upon which the court will exercise its discretion should also be *address*ed.

To issue the application, the applicant's solicitor will attend at the court office with sufficient copies of the Form D50B and supporting statement. A fee is payable unless exemption/remission is claimed. The court will seal all documents and return copies for service on the respondent and the landlord.

Service

1.116 The application and statement in support, will be served by post on the other cohabitant and the landlord by the court unless the court directs otherwise.

What the respondent should do

1.117 The respondent will receive with the application a Notice of Proceedings and acknowledgement of service in Form D50A. This must be completed and returned to the court within 14 days of receipt. If the application is contested it will be usual for a statement setting out the reasons for this to be sent to the court and to the applicant within a further 14 days.

The hearing

1.118 Unless the court is able to make an order on the papers, a short hearing will be fixed when the parties will be required to attend.

The hearing will be in private unless the court directs otherwise.

If the court has sufficient information to make an order transferring the tenancy, or if the respondent consents, a final order can be made. Otherwise, directions will be given.

The order

1.119 Part II of Sch 7 to the FLA 1996 sets out the types of order that the court may make. These vary according to the type of tenancy, but essentially they provide for a transfer of the tenancy without the requirement for any further documentation, and confirm that the transferor takes the tenancy subject to all existing rights and obligations. This has been held to extend to the terms of a suspended order for possession of a property[1]. However, the court can mitigate the effect of this by directing that the parties are to be jointly and severally liable to discharge or perform all or any of the liabilities and obligations in respect of the property which otherwise only one of them would be liable to deal with. This power extends to liabilities and obligations in respect of the property that arise apart from the tenancy, for example payment for services, decoration and repair. If the court makes such a direction, the order may also provide for one party to indemnify the other against any such liability[2].

In addition, when the court makes an order under Pt II, there is power to award compensation to be paid by the transferee to the transferor. In deciding whether to exercise that power, the court must have regard to all the circumstances, including:

(1) whether the transfer of the tenancy will result in a financial loss to the transferor;
(2) the financial needs and resources of the parties;
(3) the financial needs and obligations which the parties have, or are likely to have in the foreseeable future, including financial obligations to each other and to any relevant child.

The court may either at the time the order is made, or at any time before the payment is due to be made in full, direct that any compensation payment may be deferred to a specified date or event, or paid by instalments, unless to do so would cause the transferee greater financial hardship than the transferor[3].

[1] *Church Commissioners for England v Emarah and Another* [1996] 2 FLR 544.
[2] Part III, para 11.
[3] Part III, para 10(2), (3) and (5).

APPLICATION UNDER SCH 1 TO THE CHILDREN ACT 1989

1.120 Paragraph 1(2) of CA 1989, Sch 1 enables the court to make a number of financial and property provisions in respect of children, including the transfer of property which will include the transfer of a tenancy.

1.121 *Property*

Which court?

1.121 Application should be made to the Family Court, noting that the Lay Justices have no jurisdiction in these applications.

Who may apply?

1.122 Paragraph 1(1) of CA 1989, Sch 1 provides that applications for the transfer of property, which will include a tenancy, may be made by the following:

- the parent of a child ('parent' includes a step-parent);
- the guardian of a child; or
- any person who has a residence order with respect to a child.

Procedure

1.123 The application is for a financial remedy and FPR apply as for any other application under Sch 1, CA 1989 for a financial remedy for a child. Where there is also to be an application under TOLATA 1996 generally speaking it will be preferable for the applications to be conjoined and heard at the same time[1].

[1] *W v W (Joinder of Trusts of Land Act and Children Act Applications)* [2004] 2 FLR 321.

Service

1.124 Service of the application need not be personal service, but 14 days' notice must be given.

There is no requirement to serve the landlord of the property, but it may be prudent for the applicant to obtain his consent to what is proposed, and to provide the court with evidence of that consent.

The exercise of the court's discretion

1.125 The matters to which the court must have regard when deciding whether or not to order a transfer of tenancy are broadly speaking the same as when the court is exercising its discretion under s 25(3) of the MCA 1973. However, there is no specific requirement that the child's welfare is to be either the court's 'first consideration'[1] or the 'paramount consideration'[2].

The court must have regard to all the circumstances, which will include:

- the financial needs of the child;
- the income, earning capacity (if any), property and other financial resources of the child;
- any physical or mental disability of the child; and
- the manner in which the child was being, or was expected to be, educated or trained.

In addition, the court will look at the income, earning capacity, property and other financial resources, and financial needs, obligations and responsibilities, at the time of the hearing and in the foreseeable future, of the child's parents, which will include a step-parent or former step-parent, and that of the applicant and any other person in whose favour the court proposes to make the order.

[1] Section 25(1) of the MCA 1973.
[2] Section 1(1) of the CA 1989.

The court's approach

1.126 Although the matters to which the court must have regard when making orders under Sch 1 to the CA 1989 are effectively the same as those in s 25 of the MCA 1973, the approach is slightly different.

The court takes the view that the provision is to be for the child during his minority, and only exceptionally will provision be carried beyond a child's 18th birthday or the completion of full-time tertiary education.

In practice, this means that any property which is transferred for the benefit of a child will usually revert to the transferor when the child reaches the age of 18, or ceases full-time education, whichever occurs first.

In the context of a tenancy, it may be unnecessary for there to be provision for the tenancy to revert to the transferor as in most cases, unlike owner-occupied property, a tenancy will have no value other than as a place in which to live. However, the position can be complicated if the transferor has the right to buy the property under the HA 1980, and will lose that right if a transfer is effected. In *K v K (Minors: Property Transfer)*[1] a transfer of tenancy was ordered despite the fact that the transferor would thereby lose benefits under the HA 1980 right to buy scheme.

There is no provision in the CA 1989 for the court to award compensation as there is in Pt IV of the FLA 1996[2].

[1] [1992] 2 FLR 220.
[2] See also S Bridge *Transferring Tenancies of the Family Home* [1998] Fam Law 26.

The homeless cohabitant

1.127 If a cohabitant is without accommodation, for example on the breakdown of the relationship, or if the family home is repossessed, there are certain limited steps that can be taken to assist. What follows is intended to be a broad outline of the position and if more detail is required a specialist text should be consulted[1].

[1] For example, Arden and Hunter *Homelessness and Allocations* (Legal Action Group, 9th edn, 2012).

APPLICATION TO THE LOCAL AUTHORITY

1.128 Local housing authorities have a statutory duty to rehouse homeless persons. This duty is limited and applied strictly.

1.128 *Property*

HA 1996, Pt VII as amended by the Homelessness Act 2002 and the regulations which supplement it[1] set out the statutory duties of the local authorities towards homeless persons. The local authorities must also have regard to the guidance issued by the Department for Communities and Local Government[2]. The basic objective of the statutory duty is to require the local housing authorities to provide accommodation for certain limited categories of homeless applicants.

To be eligible, four criteria must be satisfied. The applicant must:

(1) be eligible for assistance – this requirement effectively excludes refugees and asylum seekers;
(2) be homeless or threatened with homelessness – this will include a 28-day possession order and homelessness as a result of domestic violence;
(3) have a priority need, for example be pregnant, live with a pregnant woman, have dependent children[3], be vulnerable because of old age, mental illness, physical disability or fall within one of the categories contained in the statutory instruments[4], or be a victim of a disaster such as a fire or flood; and
(4) not be intentionally homeless – a stringent test is laid down by s 191 of the HA 1996 and is strictly interpreted by the local housing authorities.

If a homeless applicant is dissatisfied with the decision of a local housing authority, the HA 1996 makes provision for a review of the decision, and if a point of law is involved, a right of appeal to the county court. However, there are strict time-limits which cannot be extended by the court[5].

[1] Allocation of Housing (England) Regulations 2000 (SI 2000/702); Allocation of Housing (Wales) Regulations 2000 (SI 2000/1080); Homeless Persons (Priority Need) (Wales) Order 2001 (SI 2001/607); Homelessness (Priority Need for Accommodation) (England) Order 2002 (SI 2002/2051).
[2] *Homelessness prevention: a guide to good practice*, DCLG June 2006.
[3] A shared residence order under Children Act 1989 will not necessarily influence the decision of the housing authority: *Holmes-Moorhouse v Richmond-upon-Thames LBC* [2009] UKHL 7.
[4] The statutory instruments add the following additional categories. It should be noted that the situation differs between England and Wales. In Wales, the categories are:
- a person who is 18 or older but under 21 and at any time while still a child was, but no longer is, looked after, accommodated or fostered or is at particular risk of sexual or financial exploitation (it should be noted that there is no restriction in time or duration on the fostering and so a child accommodated with the parent's agreement at the age of three for 6 months will qualify as priority need);
- a person who is 16 or 17 years old;
- a person without dependent children who has been subject to domestic violence or is at risk of such violence, if he or she returns to their home;
- a person serving in the armed forces who has been homeless since leaving those forces;
- a former prisoner who has been homeless since leaving custody and who has a local connection within the area of the local housing authority.

The English provisions are more restrictive, being:
- a person aged 16 or 17 who is not either a relevant child for the purposes of s 23A of the Children Act 1989 and to whom a local authority do not owe duty to provide accommodation under s 20 of the Children Act 1989;
- a person (other than a relevant student) who is under 21 and, at any time after reaching 16, but while still under 18, was, but is no longer, looked after, accommodated or fostered;

- a person (other than a relevant student) who has reached the age of 21 and who is vulnerable as a result of having been fostered, accommodated or looked after;
- a person who is vulnerable as a result of having been a member of the armed forces;
- a person who is vulnerable as a result of having served a custodial sentence, having been committed for contempt of court or any kindred offence;
- a person who is vulnerable as a result of ceasing to occupy accommodation by reason of violence from another person or threats of violence from another person which are likely to be carried out.

5 See ss 202 and 204 of the HA 1996.

REQUEST TO LOCAL AUTHORITY UNDER S 20 OF THE CHILDREN ACT 1989

1.129 The harsh effects of the operation of the homelessness provisions of the HA 1996 are mitigated at least as far as children are concerned by s 20 of the CA 1989. This places a duty on local authorities to provide accommodation for children in need. The definition of a child in need includes a child whose carer has been prevented from providing him with suitable accommodation. However, the duty does not extend to providing accommodation for the carer as well as the child, and the reality will almost certainly be that the child will be separated from the adult members of the family.

REQUEST TO THE SOCIAL SERVICES DEPARTMENT UNDER S 17 OF THE CHILDREN ACT 1989

1.130 It is arguable that it is within the general duty imposed upon social services departments by s 17 of the CA 1989 to provide services for children in need and their families to make cash available for a deposit for private rented accommodation to avoid homelessness. Although the circumstances have to be exceptional for cash to be made available, in practice it will largely be a question of resources.

APPLICATION FOR A LOAN FROM THE SOCIAL FUND

1.131 For those in receipt of income support, there is the prospect of obtaining a loan from the social fund for the deposit on private rented accommodation[1]. Such payments are discretionary and there are strict criteria for eligibility. Although no interest is payable, the loan does have to be repaid.

1 Social Fund Directions issued by Secretary of State for Social Security.

Section 3 Ownership and use of chattels

Introduction

1.132 Disputes over chattels are notorious for the ill feeling and expense that they engender, usually to a wholly disproportionate degree.

Although the courts are reluctant to determine the ownership of chattels[1], there will be occasions when litigation will be the only way to resolve a dispute.

1.132 *Property*

However, the procedures are generally more cumbersome than for married parties or civil partners, when the court can be invited to divide chattels on the basis of the wide discretion exercisable under s 25 of the MCA 1973 or CPA 2004.

[1] See *H v M (Property: Beneficial Interest)* [1992] 1 FLR 229 at 240, and District Judge Gerlis, 'Divorce and the Counting of Spoons' [1998] Fam Law 47.

Ownership of chattels

1.133 The basis for division of the personal property of cohabitants is that of ownership, not need. The principles determining ownership are broadly the same as those applying to disputes over real property, that is trust principles[1]. This will mean that certain contributions, for example by way of housekeeping and bringing up children, will have limited if any relevance.

What will be relevant, in the case of a resulting trust, will be any contribution to the purchase price, in the case of a constructive trust, the existence of any agreement between the parties as to the ownership of a chattel, or the parties' intentions (express or implied), regardless of contribution to the purchase price.

Unlike the position where there is a disagreement about the ownership of real property, with personal property it is possible to establish an express trust without having to show that the terms were in writing. If an express trust is established, this will avoid the need for a claimant to pursue the perhaps less straightforward argument that there was a constructive trust. This was the position in *Rowe v Prance*[2]. In that case, a man and a woman had a close relationship for 14 years. They planned to buy a boat and sail around the world. The man bought a boat from the net proceeds of sale of his matrimonial home and told the woman that they would live together on the boat. He referred to the boat as 'ours' and said that the woman had an interest in it. He had not at that stage even permanently separated from his wife. The woman gave up her rented house and put her furniture into storage. The couple's plans never came to fruition, and the woman successfully claimed an interest in the boat. On the basis that equality is equity, she was held to have an equal share with the man.

The 'Up Yaws'[3] concerned two boats. The parties, Miss Parrott and Mr Parkin, bought the first boat using credit in Miss Parrott's name, although the boat was registered to Mr Parkin. He did any maintenance that was necessary and Miss Parrott paid for materials and the mooring fees. They sold the first boat and bought the second, 'Up Yaws'. They traded in the first boat and the balance of the purchase price came from a loan secured on their shared home of which Miss Parrott was the legal owner, and a small amount of cash, the bulk of which was provided by Miss Parrott. When their relationship came to an end, Miss Parrott sought to realise her interest in the second boat. This required the court to look back and consider the beneficial interests in the house and the first boat. The court held that in relation to the property a common intention to share the beneficial ownership could be inferred and that Mr. Parkin had acted to his detriment in reliance upon that common intention. In relation to the first boat, the court found that the parties had agreed that in raising a loan against the security of the house in order to buy the boat she was buying out Mr. Parkin's interest in the house with the intent that thereafter she would own the house and he would own the boat. However, the significant contribution by Miss Parrott to the purchase of the second boat raised the presumption of a resulting trust in her favour quantified in accordance with her contribution to the purchase price.

If goods are bought on credit terms, contribution by way of payment of the deposit and the instalments will be relevant. Such a situation was considered by Walton J in *Richards v Dove*[4] who concluded that certain principles could be derived from the authorities:

(1) as it is extremely tricky to define ownership by reference to disputed evidence on who paid most of the hire-purchase instalments on particular items, a broad approach is justifiable;
(2) merely paying one or two instalments on a particular item may not entitle the payer to any share; but
(3) on the other hand, it is unrealistic to suppose that substantial or regular contributions were not intended by the parties to be reflected in some corresponding beneficial interest.

[1] See **1.17** et seq.
[2] [1999] 2 FLR 787.
[3] [2007] 2 FLR 444.
[4] [1974] 1 All ER 888.

Bank accounts

1.134 There is a presumption that funds in a bank or building society account held in joint names and intended to be used as a common pool will be divided in equal shares, regardless of the source of the credits to the account, and any items bought with funds from the account will be regarded as jointly owned property. Of course, the presumption can be rebutted by evidence showing a contrary intention, either express or implied, and in those circumstances the funds will be held in proportion to the contributions made.

Conversely, trust principles may be applied to establish that the funds held in an account in the name of one of the cohabitants belong to both jointly[1].

It may be necessary to take action as soon as there is a breakdown in a cohabitation relationship to ensure that the funds in a joint account are not removed unilaterally. If the bank in question is alerted, the account will generally be frozen so that neither party may withdraw funds without the consent of the other. This may create practical difficulties in the short term if the account is the only source of living expenses, or if direct debits and standing orders are paid from it.

[1] In *Paul v Constance* [1977] 1 All ER 195 an account in the sole name of the deceased cohabitant was held to belong to the survivor absolutely rather than to form part of the deceased's estate. The funds had chiefly comprised the deceased's damages from a personal injury claim, but they had in addition paid in joint bingo winnings, and had on one occasion withdrawn monies which were shared between them equally. The deceased had told the surviving cohabitant that the money in the account was as much hers as it was his. The court held that it was the parties' intention to create an express trust for themselves in equal shares.

1.135 *Property*

Existing property

1.135 It will generally be the case that items owned by either party before the cohabitation began, or bought by one party from his or her own resources during the currency of the relationship, will remain the property of that party.

Gifts

1.136 Gifts will remain the property of the donee. It will not be uncommon for one party to give sums of money to, or pay for goods or services on behalf of, the other during the course of the relationship. The fact that the relationship subsequently comes to an end does not give the donor the automatic right to reclaim those monies from the other party. In the absence of clear evidence that the monies were a loan, any payments made will be deemed to be a gift and, therefore, not recoverable.

If it is the donee who is seeking to establish that certain items were intended as gifts, it will be necessary to show that there was an intention to transfer ownership, and that there was actual delivery.

Mere usage of items will not be sufficient to satisfy the court as to ownership. For example, in *Windeler v Whitehall*[1], Mr Whitehall had bought a dressing table for use by his cohabitant, Miss Windeler. When she moved out of Mr Whitehall's home at the end of their relationship she took the dressing table with her. Mr Whitehall claimed its return. The court drew a distinction between items bought exclusively for Miss Windeler's use, consumables such as perfume and toiletries, and items of furniture. Whilst the dressing table was bought by Mr Whitehall for Miss Windeler's exclusive use, the court required more evidence than this to find that it was a gift. Against the background of the parties' relationship in this case the court formed the view that Mr Whitehall would expect Miss Windeler to leave the dressing table in the house if she left, and accordingly ordered its return.

In the event of a dispute over ownership of an engagement ring, s 3(2) of the Law Reform (Miscellaneous Provisions) Act 1970 governs the position. The gift of an engagement ring is presumed to be an absolute gift. The presumption can be rebutted by evidence to show that the gift was expressly or by implication conditional upon the marriage taking place. In *Cox v Jones*[2] the judge rejected the evidence of Mr Jones that he had given an engagement ring to Miss Cox on the express understanding that if the engagement were broken off for any reason the ring would have to be returned. Having heard all the evidence the judge considered that this was implausible.

[1] [1990] 2 FLR 505.
[2] [2004] 2 FLR 1010.

Cohabitation agreement

1.137 If there is an enforceable cohabitation agreement[1], there may be provision in the agreement for the ownership and/or division of chattels at the end of the cohabitation. At the very least, the agreement should be evidence of the parties' intention at the outset.

[1] See **2.149**.

Applications for declarations of ownership and orders for sale

1.138 If there is really no alternative but to invite the court to decide the ownership of disputed chattels, the correct procedure is to apply for a declaration or enquiry as to the beneficial interest.

WHICH COURT?

1.139 The High Court and any county court have jurisdiction.

THE COURT'S APPROACH

1.140 When resolving a dispute as to the ownership of property, the usual trust principles will apply as laid down in *Pettit v Pettitt*[1] and *Gissing v Gissing*[2] down through *Lloyds Bank plc v Rosset*[3] to the recent cases of *Oxley v Hiscock*[4] and *Stack v Dowden*[5].

The role of the judge is to decide, on the basis of the oral evidence, and any relevant documentary evidence, whether the court's equitable jurisdiction can be invoked to assist the applicant. In practice, this may well come down to which of the two versions of events that are presented in the parties' evidence is the more plausible. It is rare for a couple's intentions as to their home to be recorded in writing, much less the contents. The nature of the parties' relationship may play a part in the judge's decision as to what is more likely to have been the intention with regard to a particular item of personal property.

The courts can be expected to take a more 'broad-brush' approach when dealing with an inventory of furniture and personal effects, than say a small number of valuable items.

In relation to determining the size of the beneficial interest, in the absence of any conclusive evidence on the point, the court will resort to the maxim, 'equality is equity'.

[1] [1970] AC 777.
[2] [1971] AC 886.
[3] [1990] 2 WLR 867.
[4] [2004] 2 FLR 669.
[5] [2007] 1 FLR 1858.

THE ORDER

1.141 The court may make an order that is merely declaratory of a party's beneficial interest in property, and it may order the sale of the property, or for one party to account to the other to the value of that beneficial interest.

Injunctions

1.142 Any judge may make an injunction restraining the disposal of property which is the subject of the application pending the final hearing. In practice, the application will generally be made to the district judge. The application will usually be made on notice, but in certain circumstances there may be merit

1.142 *Property*

in an application without notice. The application must be supported by a witness statement. In the case of an application without notice, the witness statement must set out exactly why the applicant wishes the court to consider the application without giving notice to the respondent.

Engaged couples

1.143 Some cohabitants will also be engaged to be married. If their relationship breaks down, the fact of their engagement will enable them to make application to the court under the MWPA 1882 for a declaration as to beneficial ownership of real or personal property. The application must be made within 3 years of the termination of the engagement. Although this procedure is analogous to the procedure available to cohabitants who have not been engaged to apply under the court's equitable jurisdiction for such a declaration, applications made under the MWPA 1882 benefit from the provisions of s 37 of the MPPA 1970. This will enable the court to take into account a substantial contribution in money or money's worth to the improvement of real and personal property when assessing that party's beneficial interest, unless there was an express agreement between the parties that such contributions were purely gratuitous. The total contribution must be substantial and the court must find that the only explanation for the size of the contribution must be that the applicant believed that it was founding an interest in the property.

The use of chattels

PART IV OF THE FAMILY LAW ACT 1996

1.144 When the court makes an occupation order under ss 33, 35 or 36 (only ss 33 and 36 will apply to cohabitants), it can grant either party possession or use of furniture or other contents of the shared home[1].

In deciding whether to make such provision, the court will have regard to all the circumstances of the case, including:

- the financial needs and resources of the parties; and
- the financial obligations which they have or are likely to have in the foreseeable future, including financial obligations to each other and to any relevant child.

The court may also order either party to take reasonable care of any furniture or other contents, and to keep them secure[2].

An order made under s 40 will cease to have effect when the occupation order ceases to have effect.

[1] Section 40(1)(c).
[2] Section 40(1)(d) and (e).

Part B PROCEDURAL GUIDES

Order under Trusts of Land and Appointment of Trustees Act 1996, s 14

Legal background

1.145 TOLATA 1996, s 14 entitles a trustee or a beneficiary of the proceeds of sale of land to apply for any order relating to the exercise by the trustees of any of their functions (including the power of exclusion and the power of sale), or declaring the nature and extent of a person's interest in a trust of land. Applications may be made by former cohabitants, family members or third parties such as trustees in bankruptcy wishing to establish a beneficial interest. By virtue of the HCCCJO 1991 (as amended), the county court's jurisdiction is unlimited. Section 14 of the 1996 Act is to be read together with ss 13 and 15. An application under TOLATA 1996 is governed by CPR Pt 7 or 8. See also CPR PD 7A and CPR PD 8A.

Procedure

1.146

Who may apply	A trustee, a joint legal or beneficial owner, or a judgment creditor holding a charging order	*Midland Bank v Pike*[a]
Property	Legal title owned jointly by co-owners	
Application	For an order 'declaring the nature or extent of a person's interest in [the] property'	TOLATA 1996, s 14(2)(b)
Court	High Court: Chancery Division	
	County court: if issued in a county court the claim form must be marked 'Chancery Business'	CPR PD 7A, para 2.5
Fee	For recovery of land: in High Court: £465 in county court: £175	CPFO 2008, fee 1.4
Procedure	CPR Pt 7 – normally claims will be more appropriate for issue under this procedure	
	CPR Pt 8 – traditionally claims have often been issued under the Pt 8 procedure (formerly originating summons). Pt 8 only applies where there is 'unlikely [to be] a dispute of fact'. By definition most s 14 claims involve disputed questions of fact	CPR 8.1(2)(a)

1.146 *Property*

Issue of claim: Pt 7	Issue claim in Form N1 with particulars of claim (in the form or separately)	CPR 7.1; CPR 7.4(1)(a)
Particulars of claim: served separately	Particulars of claim are likely to include the following: (1) the background facts; (2) reference to the facts which define the form of trust or equity claimed: (a) contributions; (b) any agreement with terms defined (if possible) and description of when formed; (c) detrimental reliance; (3) aspects of the claim that come within s 15(1); (4) aspects of the claim relevant to the check list at para [69] of *Stack*	TOLATA 1996, s 15; *Stack v Dowden*[b] at para [69]
Defendant	Other owner of the property	
Pt 8 claim: issue of claim	If there is little 'dispute of fact' this procedure can be used Claim issued in Form 208 with specific requirements, eg: (1) statement that Pt 8 applies; (2) remedy sought by the claimant and the 'legal basis' for it; (3) enactment for claim: ie, TOLATA 1996 (shown in the heading to the claim)	CPR 8.1(2)(a); CPR PD 8A; CPR 8.2
Pt 8 claim: evidence	(1) Claimant's evidence: served with claim form	CPR 8.5(2)
	(2) Any 'written evidence': filed with claim form	CPR 8.5(1)
	(3) Any other written evidence: only with permission	CPR 8.6(1)(b)
Defence	(1) Acknowledgement of service	CPR 8.3
	(2) Service of defendant's evidence on claimant with acknowledgement of service	CPR 8.5(3), (4)
Case management	Pt 8: treated as allocated to the multi-track	CPR 8.9(c)
	Definition of issues:	
	(1) What are the issues of fact?	CPR 1.4(2)(b)
	(2) Are there any issues of law?	CPR 3.1(2)(i), (l)

Order	Declaration as to the parties' respective holding of the beneficial interests	TOLATA 1996, s 14(2)(b)
	Under TOLATA 1996 the court may then go on to deal with other matters, such as sale of the property, provision for an occupation rent, etc	TOLATA 1996, TOLATA 1996, s 14(2)(a) (see, for example, *Mortgage Corporation v Shaire*[c])

[a] [1988] 2 All ER 434.
[b] [2007] 1 FLR 1858.
[c] [2000] 1 FLR 973.

Transfer of a Tenancy under Family Law Act 1996, Pt IV, s 53 and Sch 7

Legal background

1.147 Since the coming into force of FLA 1996, Pt IV on 1 October 1997, the court is empowered to transfer tenancies, both contractual and statutory, between cohabitants who no longer live together as husband and wife, as well as between spouses and former spouses. As set out in FLA 1996, Sch 7, para 10, the person to whom the tenancy is transferred can be ordered to pay compensation to the other party. The power to transfer the tenancy to a former spouse arises on decree nisi; the order becomes effective on decree absolute; and there is a prohibition on applying if that former spouse has remarried. If there is a decree of judicial separation, the power to transfer arises after the decree is pronounced. A tenancy in the other spouse's name, or in joint names, can be destroyed by the unilateral surrender or giving of notice to quit by one tenant without consultation with the other (*Hammersmith and Fulham London Borough Council v Monk*[1]). A party should ask for an undertaking that the tenancy will not be surrendered and then serve that undertaking on the landlord. If the undertaking is not given the applicant should apply for an injunction and serve the order on the landlord (*Bater v Greenwich London Borough Council*[2]).

An application under FLA 1996, s 53 and Sch 7 is governed by the procedure in FPR 8.29–8.34.

[1] [1992] 1 FLR 465.
[2] [1999] 2 FLR 993.

Procedure

1.148

Who may apply	Either spouse, but a decree of judicial separation must be granted before the order is made	FLA 1996, Sch 7, para 2(2)

1.148 *Property*

	Either former spouse, but a decree nisi must be granted before the order is made and the applicant must not have remarried; if application is for the transfer of a statutory tenancy or contractual tenancy containing a prohibition on assignment, it must be made before decree absolute	FLA 1996, Sch 7, para 13
	A cohabitant who is no longer living with the other cohabitant as husband and wife	FLA 1996, Sch 7, para 3
Application	To the Family Court or the same court as existing matrimonial/civil partnership proceedings	FLA 1996, Sch 7, para 2(2); FPR 8.30; PD 8A, para 1.1(a)
Fee	£75	FPFO 2008, fee 1.4
Service	The court will serve the respondent and the landlord unless the applicant is directed to serve	FPR 8.31
	A landlord may be made a party to proceedings	FPR 8.32
Respondent	The other spouse or cohabitant	
Interlocutory injunction	The court may grant an injunction if ancillary or incidental to the assistance sought; an application for an injunction must be in accordance with procedure under FPR 20.4	FPR 8.34
Orders for disclosure	Any party may apply to the court under r 21.2 for any person to attend a production appointment to produce documents specified or described in the order	FPR 8.33
Order	Transfer of tenancy or statutory tenancy	FLA 1996, Sch 7, paras 7-9
	Payment by the spouse or cohabitant to whom the tenancy is transferred, to the other; deferment of payment or payment by instalments if transferee's financial hardship greater than transferor's	FLA 1996, Sch 7, para 10

Order that both liable to discharge obligations prior to date of transfer and indemnity	FLA 1996, Sch 7, para 11

Part C   CHECKLISTS

Essential information where the dispute is over owner-occupied property

1.149 (A) About the property:

(1)   *address*;
(2)   *date* of acquisition;
(3)   solicitors who acted on acquisition (obtain file?);
(4)   what information and advice was given by the solicitors about ownership of the legal and beneficial interests (negligence claim?);
(5)   ownership of legal title (Index Map Search/apply for office copy entries/register restriction or caution? (see **1.7**)/advise on possible severance of joint tenancy? (see **1.21**));
(6)   any declaration of beneficial interests (trust deed);
(7)   purchase price and contributions to it (deposit/mortgage advance/gifts or loans from third parties/contribution to costs and disbursements);
(8)   contributions since purchase (mortgage repayments/repairs and renovations/other payments/non-financial contributions);
(9)   any agreement or understanding as to the beneficial ownership and status of financial or other contributions;
(10) valuation; and
(11) details of mortgagee and redemption figure.

(B) About the cohabitation:

(1)   *date*s of cohabitation;
(2)   *date*s of any agreement to marry (have 3 years elapsed since termination?);
(3)   details of any children of the relationship/other children;
(4)   arrangements for payment of shared outgoings;
(5)   any agreement or understanding as to the ownership of the property and the status of contributions, financial or otherwise; and
(6)   details of any acts of detriment and/or reliance pursuant to the agreement.

(C) Evidence:

(1)   file of papers from solicitors acting on the acquisition of the property;
(2)   title deeds and documents and any express declarations of trust;
(3)   documentary evidence of contributions made; and
(4)   oral or written evidence of any agreements or understandings as to the ownership of the legal and/or beneficial interests and the status of any contributions financial or otherwise.

1.150 *Property*

Essential information where the dispute is over rented property

1.150 The following information must be ascertained where there is a dispute over rented property:

(1) Address.
(2) Landlord's name and *address*/landlord's agent's name and *address*.
(3) Copy of tenancy agreement.
(4) Date of agreement.
(5) Parties to the agreement.
(6) Type of tenancy.
(7) Rent payable/arrears?
(8) Has the tenancy been determined by a valid notice to quit?
(9) Should urgent steps be taken to prevent termination of the tenancy by the other party?
(10) Who is living at the property?

Acting for a cohabiting couple on the acquisition of property

1.151 The following may act as a checklist:

(1) Who is to live at the property?
(2) How are the purchase price, costs and disbursements to be funded?
(3) In whose name(s) is the title to be registered?
(4) If in one name only, consider whether the other party/parties should be advised to take independent legal advice.
(5) If in joint names, advise on the difference between holding as tenants in common/joint tenants, and if necessary advise the parties to take independent legal advice.
(6) Consider any potential for a conflict of interest.
(7) If in joint names, consider how the beneficial interests are to be declared.
(8) Advise on the importance of making a will.
(9) Invite the parties to consider entering into a cohabitation agreement.

Part D PRECEDENTS

How to use these precedents

1.152 The following section contains a considerable number of individual clauses and comparatively few complete precedents. The individual clauses can be pieced together to form a complete declaration of trust which, when completed will assume the following structure, or something similar:

(1) commencement and *date*[1];
(2) recitals (both of fact and intention)[2];
(3) trusts[3];
(4) shares (either fixed shares[4] or floating shares[5]);
(5) a clause introducing the contingencies[6], or in other words, 'What happens if . . . ?' – it is recommended that the provisions for each

contingency are set out in a separate Schedule at the end of the declaration;
(6) general, miscellaneous clauses[7];
(7) Schedules[8]; and
(8) attestation clause[9].

There are two types of complete precedent: the short form and the long form. The short forms tend to combine the recitals, trusts and shares in the context of the co-owners jointly and each co-owner separately. In addition, the short forms do not provide for any contingencies, although Schedules setting them out could be appended to any of the short-form precedents. The long-form precedents are essentially illustrations of the effect of combining any number of individual clauses.

[1] 1.153 below.
[2] 1.154–1.159 below.
[3] 1.160–1.164 below.
[4] 1.165–1.169 below.
[5] 1.170–1.176 below.
[6] 1.177 below.
[7] 1.178–1.199 below.
[8] 1.201–1.215 below.
[9] 1.200 below.

Section 1 Non-contentious precedents

A Clauses: Commencement and recitals

1.153

Commencement and date[1]

THIS DECLARATION OF TRUST is made on (*date*)

BETWEEN 'the co-owners' (1) (*name 1*) of (*address*) ('*name*') and (2) (*name 2*) (also) of (*address*) ('*name 2*').

IT IS AGREED AND DECLARED as follows:

[1] LPA 1925, s 53(1)(b) states that 'a declaration of trust respecting any land or any interest therein must be manifested and proved by some writing signed by some person who is able to declare such trust or by his will'.
Although it is imperative that the declaration of trust be in writing, it is not essential that it should be a deed.
Stamp Duty Land Tax (SDLT) applies to land transactions and is a tax on the transaction rather than the document. A declaration of trust is not substantively registrable at HM Land Registry. It is no longer necessary to complete an SDLT 60 self-certificate if you don't need to notify HMRC about a Stamp Duty Land Tax transaction.

RECITALS OF FACT

1.154

Purchase of property[1]

Recitals

- The co-owners are the proprietors of (*address*) ('the property').

1.154 Property

- Title to the property is registered at the Land Registry under title number (*number*).
- The co-owners purchased the property on (*completion date*)[2].
- The co-owners purchased the property for £
- The incidental costs of purchasing the property came to £
- (*Name 1*) paid £   towards the purchase price and purchase costs.
- (*Name 2*) paid £   towards the purchase price and purchase costs.
- The co-owners obtained an advance of £   from and have mortgaged the property to (*lender*) ('the mortgage')[3].

[1] For the effect of recitals on the construction of an instrument, see, generally, *Halsbury's Laws of England*, Vol 32 (2012, 5th edn) at para 418.
[2] The completion date is probably preferable to the date on which contracts were exchanged.
[3] For separate recitals relating to the mortgage, see **1.155**.

1.155

Mortgage of property[1]

- The mortgage is a repayment mortgage.
- The mortgage is an endowment mortgage.
- (*Name 1*) has taken out an endowment policy on their life with (*insurance company*) numbered (*number*).
- The endowment policy is (assigned to)/(deposited with)/(neither assigned to nor deposited with) (*lender*).
- The co-owners entered into a mortgage indemnity policy for a single premium of £   (which will be added to the mortgage and repaid over the mortgage term) [OR] (of which (*name 1*) paid £   and (*name 2*) paid £   ).

[1] There are so many possible variables that only a small selection has been included here. Perhaps the facts relating to the mortgage are less important than the co-owners' intentions regarding the mortgage payments (see **1.158** below).

1.156

The underlying purpose of the trust[1]

- The co-owners purchased the property for their joint occupation[2].
- The co-owners purchased the property in order to provide a home for themselves and their (respective) children[3].
- The co-owners purchased the property as an investment.

[1] The underlying purpose of the trust for sale could be an important consideration in any possible future application to the court for an order under TOLATA 1996, s 14(1). The courts have progressively developed this theme since *Re Buchanan-Wollaston's Conveyance* [1939] Ch 738.
[2] The court is more likely to order a sale where no children are involved and the parties have simply purchased the property for their joint occupation (*Smith v Smith* (1976) 120 SJ 100).
[3] 'If there were young children, the position would be different. One of the purposes of the trust would no doubt have been to provide a home for them, and while that purpose still existed a sale would not generally be ordered' (*Rawlings v Rawlings* [1964] P 398 at 419, per Salmon LJ). See also *Re Evers' Trust* [1980] 1 WLR 1327.

1.157

Recitals of fact and intention: third party contributions[1]

- (*Name 3*) paid £   towards the purchase price and purchase costs with the intention of acquiring a beneficial interest in the property.

- (*The co-owners*) [OR] (*Name 1* and *name 2*) acknowledge that the payment of £   made by (*name 3*) towards the purchase price and purchase costs was neither a loan nor a gift to them but was made with the express intention that (*name 3*) would acquire a beneficial interest in the property.

[1] The law presumes a resulting trust in favour of the third party unless that presumption is rebutted by evidence that the third party intended to make a gift or a loan without acquiring any beneficial interest (*Sekhon v Alissa* [1989] 2 FLR 94).

RECITALS OF INTENTION

1.158

Mortgage payments[1]

- The co-owners intend to contribute equally towards the mortgage payments.

[OR]

- The co-owners intend that their contributions towards the mortgage payments will be treated as equal, regardless of any inequality that may exist at any time.

[OR]

- (*Name 1*) intends to pay   per cent of the mortgage payments.
- (*Name 2*) intends to pay   per cent of the mortgage payments.

[OR]

- The co-owners intend to contribute towards the mortgage payments in the proportions that their respective incomes bear to each other, or in such other proportions as they may from time to time agree.

[1] It is very important to ascertain the co-owners' intentions regarding the mortgage payments. Without any clear instructions in this respect, it would be unwise to channel them into holding fixed shares of the net proceeds of sale, but see **1.169** below. For a definition of 'the mortgage payments', see **1.195** below.

1.159

Co-owners intend to marry/enter into a registered civil partnership with each other: provisions of this declaration to apply despite marriage/civil partnership

- The co-owners are engaged to be married to each other/intend to enter into a registered civil partnership together[1].

[OR]

- The co-owners expect to marry each other/enter into a registered civil partnership together.

[AND]

1.159 *Property*

- The co-owners intend that the provisions of this Declaration of Trust will apply regardless of their marriage/civil partnership and its possible dissolution[2].

Warning

The effect of this clause is to turn the declaration of trust into a form of pre-nuptial agreement. See, generally, CHAPTER 8 below.

[1] For provisions relating to the property of engaged couples, or couples who have been engaged to each other within the last 3 years, see LR(MP)A 1970, s 2.
[2] For property adjustment orders in connection with dissolution of marriage or civil partnership, see MCA 1973, s 24 and CPA 2004.

B   Clauses: Trusts

1.160

The standard trusts[1]

Trusts

The co-owners (declare that they):

(1) hold the property on a trust of land[2];

(2) hold the property and its net proceeds of sale (and its net income until sale)[3] in trust for themselves (*and any third party, if appropriate*)[4] as beneficial (joint tenants)[5]/(tenants in common)[6]/(regardless of their actual contributions towards acquiring, financing and improving the property)[7].

[1] This precedent sets out the standard trust of land. It also states whether the co-owners hold as beneficial joint tenants or beneficial tenants in common.
[2] Under the TOLATA 1996 a trust of land now applies to any trust of property, including land (s 1). Trustees of land have in relation to the land all the powers of an absolute owner (s 6(1)), unless there is any provision to the contrary (s 8). The trustees therefore have both a power of sale and a power to postpone the sale.
[3] The phrase 'the net income until sale' should be deleted if the net proceeds of sale and the net income until sale are enjoyed in differing shares. See **1.163** below.
[4] The name of anyone else who is beneficially interested should be inserted, for example someone who has contributed to the purchase price with the intention of acquiring a beneficial interest, rather than with the intention of making a gift or a loan.
[5] 'Joint tenants' and 'tenants in common' are alternatives. One must be deleted. See *Joyce v Barker Bros* (1980) *The Times*, February 26, where a conveyance stated that the purchasers were joint tenants and tenants in common.
[6] This precedent assumes that in the case of a beneficial tenancy in common the shares will be set out in a separate clause. Sometimes the method of calculating the shares is lengthy and complex, and in such cases it may be preferable to separate the clauses relating to the shares and the trusts. However, if the shares are simple and straightforward (for example 'in equal shares') they could be dealt with in this clause, without the need for a separate clause.
[7] The words 'regardless of their actual contributions . . . etc' are not essential. They are unnecessary if the co-owners hold floating shares. Their inclusion may be considered useful for clarity where one co-owner is likely to confer a gratuitous benefit on the other.

1.161

Co-owners to be joint tenants until severance and tenants in common in unequal shares after severance[1]

Trusts[2]

The co-owners (declare that they):

(1) hold the property on a trust of land;

(2) hold the property and its net proceeds of sale and its net income until sale in trust for themselves as beneficial joint tenants until the beneficial joint tenancy is severed (regardless of their actual contributions towards acquiring, financing and improving the property)[3];

(3) will hold the property and its net proceeds of sale (and its net income until sale[4] in trust for themselves as beneficial tenants in common in the shares set out below[5] after the beneficial joint tenancy has been severed.

[1] This is, presumably, the sort of declaration of trust Slade LJ had in mind when he said that 'it would no doubt be possible for a trust in terms to provide that the beneficial interests of two parties should be equivalent to those of joint tenants unless and until severance occurred, but that in the event of severance their interests should be otherwise than in equal shares' (*Goodman v Gallant* [1986] 1 FLR 513 at 525C).
[2] See, generally, the footnotes to **1.160** above.
[3] See **1.160**.
[4] See **1.160**.
[5] These shares could be fixed or floating.

1.162

Co-owners to be tenants in common until their marriage/civil partnership and subsequently joint tenants[1]

Trusts[2]

The co-owners (declare that they):

(1) hold the property on a trust of land);

(2) hold the property and its net proceeds of sale (and its net income until sale)[3] in trust for themselves as beneficial tenants in common (in the shares set out below)[4] until the solemnisation of their intended marriage/the registration of their civil partnership;

(3) will hold the property and its net proceeds of sale and its net income until sale in trust for themselves as beneficial joint tenants after their intended marriage/civil partnership has been solemnised/registered(regardless of their actual contributions towards acquiring, financing and improving the property)[5].

[1] The effect of the inheritance tax exemptions must be considered, ie transfers between spouses/civil partners (Inheritance Tax Act 1984, s 18), and gifts in consideration of marriage/registration of civil partnership (Inheritance Tax Act 1984, s 22). Note also the effect of IA 1986, s 339, in respect of transactions at an undervalue.
[2] See, generally, the footnotes to **1.160** above.
[3] See the comments in **1.160**.
[4] The shares could be fixed or floating. If the co-owners hold 'in equal shares', it would be preferable to insert those words here instead of 'in the shares set out below', thus avoiding the need for an additional clause.
[5] See **1.160**.

1.163

Shares of the net proceeds of sale differ from those of the net income until sale

Trusts[1]

The co-owners (declare that they):

(1) hold the property on a trust of land;

1.163 *Property*

 (2) hold the net proceeds of sale in trust for themselves as beneficial tenants in common (in the shares set out in Clause   ) (regardless of their actual contributions towards acquiring, financing and improving the property);

 (3) hold the net income until sale in trust for themselves as beneficial tenants in common (in the shares set out in Clause   )[2] regardless of the manner in which the net proceeds of sale will be divided between them.

[1] See, generally, the footnotes to **1.160** above.
[2] See Precedent **1.178** below.

1.164

Deferred trust of land: 'Mesher' and 'Martin'-type trusts[1]

Trusts

The co-owners (declare that they):

(1) hold the property on a trust of land;

(2) will postpone the sale of the property, unless they agree otherwise or unless the court orders otherwise, until the first of these events occurs:

 (2.1) (*child's name*) [OR] (the youngest child of the family) attains the age of 18 or completes full-time secondary education, whichever is later; or

 (2.2) the co-owner with whom (*child's name*) [OR] (the youngest child of the family) lives in the property marries or cohabits[2];

(3) hold the property and its net proceeds of sale (and its net income until sale) in trust for themselves as beneficial tenants in common in the shares set out below.

[1] An order of the court whereby the sale of a family home is postponed until the youngest child of the family is aged 18, or some other age, is usually known as a '*Mesher* order' (*Mesher v Mesher* [1980] 1 All ER 126). Although it was not reported until 1980, the case was, in fact, heard by the Court of Appeal on 12 February 1973. An order of the court whereby the sale is postponed until the wife dies, remarries or cohabits, is usually known as a '*Martin* order' (*Martin v Martin* [1978] Fam 12). Mesher orders have experienced variable popularity over the years since the case and, for example, found favour after the 2007—8 global financial crisis. For a historical discussion of the rise and fall of the *Mesher* order see *Clutton v Clutton* [1991] 1 All ER 340 at 345, per Lloyd LJ.
[2] The word 'cohabits' tends to defy definition.

C Clauses: Shares

(i) Fixed shares

1.165

Fixed shares: expressed as fractions or percentages of the net proceeds of sale

Shares

When the property is sold (*name 1*) will receive (*fraction or percentage*)[1] of the net proceeds of sale and (*name 2*) will receive (*fraction or percentage*) of the net proceeds of sale[2].

Warning

Care should be taken when expressing the co-owners' shares as fractions or percentages of the net proceeds of sale. It is only safe to do so if: (a) there is no mortgage; or (b) they contribute to the mortgage payments in fractions or percentages which are identical to their respective entitlements out of the net proceeds of sale; and (c) they intend to pay the sale costs in the same fractions or percentages. See Example.

Example

A and B bought a house for £88,500. The purchase costs amounted to £1,500. A contributed £30,000, B contributed £10,000. They obtained a mortgage advance of £50,000 and contributed equally to the mortgage payments. They intended to share the sale costs equally. Five years later they sold the house for £130,000. The sale costs amounted to £4,000. The amount required to redeem the mortgage was £46,000. The net proceeds of sale came to £80,000. Who got what?

Wrong solution

A and B had executed a declaration of trust which said that A would receive 75 per cent of the net proceeds of sale and B would receive 25 per cent. These percentages reflected their original contributions to the purchase price (A £30,000 and B £10,000). It was a mistake to correlate their contributions to their entitlements from the net proceeds of sale because these percentages fail to take into account the shared responsibility for the mortgage payments and the sale costs. A ended up with £60,000, and B £20,000.

Wrong solution

A and B executed a declaration of trust which stated that A would receive 55/90ths of the net proceeds of sale and B would receive 35/90ths. In each case the denominator (90) represents £90,000 (the purchase price of £88,500 plus the purchase costs of £1,500). In A's case the numerator (55) represents £55,000 (her original contribution of £30,000 plus £25,000, half of the mortgage advance). In B's case, the numerator (35) represents £10,000 plus £25,000. On this basis, A ended up with £48,889 and B with £31,111.

This formula will only work if the mortgage debt is repaid over its full term. Say, for example, A and B had split up shortly after they bought the house, and had sold it for £93,000. The sale costs came to £3,000, and the amount required to redeem the mortgage was the same as the original advance, £50,000. The net proceeds of sale would have been £40,000 and, in effect, the couple would be back to square one in terms of the combined total of their original contributions. The application of this formula would mean that A would receive £24,444 and B £15,556.

Suggested solution

It would have been better if A and B had executed a declaration of trust which stated that A would receive 55/90ths of the sale price, *less* half of the amount required to redeem the mortgage, *less* half of the sale costs. B would receive 35/90ths of the sale price *less* half of the amount required to redeem the mortgage, *less* half of the sale costs. On this basis A would receive (£79,444—£23,000—£2,000) = £54,444. B would receive (£50,556—£23,000—£2,000) = £25,556.

Even this solution is not perfect. Problems would arise if the couple failed to pay the mortgage in equal shares, or if only one of them contributed towards repairs and improvements to the property.

[1] In the case of fractions, the combined total of the numerators must be the same as the denominator. In the case of percentages, the combined total must be 100.
[2] It may be considered prudent to define 'net proceeds of sale' (see **1.193** below).

1.166 Property

1.166

Fixed shares: expressed as a fixed share of the sale price, less a fixed share of the amount required to redeem the mortgage, less a fixed share of the sale costs[1]

Shares

When the property is sold:

(1) (name 1) will receive (fraction or percentage)[2] of the sale price[3] less:

    (1.1) (fraction or percentage)[4] of the amount required to redeem the mortgage[5]; and

    (1.2) (fraction or percentage)[6] of the incidental costs of selling the property;

(2) (name 2) will receive (fraction or percentage)[7] of the sale price[8] less:

    (2.1) (fraction or percentage)[9] of the amount required to redeem the mortgage[10]; and

    (2.2) (fraction or percentage)[11] of the incidental costs of selling the property;

(3) if the total amount to be deducted from one co-owner's share of the sale price exceeds the value of that share then the excess will be paid from the other co-owner's share[12].

Example

A and B bought a house for £57,000. The purchase costs came to £1,000. A contributed £4,000 and B contributed £10,000. They took out a mortgage of £44,000. A assumed responsibility for three-quarters of the mortgage payments and B assumed responsibility for one-quarter of the mortgage payments. Two years later they sold the house for £48,000. The amount required to redeem the mortgage was £43,500. The sale costs came to £1,500 and the net proceeds of sale were £3,000. Who got what?

They had signed a declaration of trust that said that A would receive 37/58ths of the sale price *less* three-quarters of the amount required to redeem the mortgage, *less* one half of the sale costs. It said that B would receive 21/58ths of the sale price, *less* one quarter of the amount required to redeem the mortgage, *less* one half of the sale costs.

On that basis, A would receive (£30,620—£32,625—£750). The result is a minus sum: —£2,755. B would receive (£17,380—£10,875—£750)=£5,755.

Their declaration of trust also stated that if the total amount to be deducted from one co-owner's share of the sale price exceeded the value of that share, then the excess would be paid from the other co-owner's share. So B paid A's shortfall of £2,755, and was entitled to retain all of the net proceeds of sale (£3,000).

[1] For an illustration of how this formula works, see the suggested solution at **1.165** above.
[2] The denominator will, presumably, represent the purchase price plus the purchase costs. The numerator will represent the co-owner's original contribution, plus the share of the mortgage debt for which he or she is assuming responsibility.
[3] For a definition of 'the sale price', see **1.190** below.
[4] The denominator will, presumably, represent the mortgage advance itself; and the numerator will represent the extent to which the co-owner assumes responsibility for the mortgage payments.
[5] For a definition of 'the amount required to redeem the mortgage', see **1.191** below.
[6] If the co-owners intend to share the sale costs equally, insert one-half or 50 per cent, as the case may be.
[7] The denominator will, presumably, represent the purchase price plus the purchase costs. The numerator will represent the co-owner's original contribution, plus the share of the mortgage debt for which he or she is assuming responsibility.
[8] For a definition of 'the sale price', see **1.190** below.
[9] The denominator will, presumably, represent the mortgage advance itself; and the numerator

will represent the extent to which the co-owner assumes responsibility for the mortgage payments.
10 For a definition of 'the amount required to redeem the mortgage', see **1.191** below.
11 If the co-owners intend to share the sale costs equally, insert one half or 50 per cent, as the case may be.
12 This subclause provides for the possibility that the property has gone down in value, or the mortgage debt exceeds the market value. One co-owner will be liable for the excess of the other co-owner's debt. *See Example.*

1.167

Fixed shares: refund of original contributions: provision for abatement: fixed shares of the balance of the net proceeds of sale[1]

Shares

When the property is sold:

(1) *(name 1)* will receive a refund of *(name 1's)* original contribution of £   towards the purchase price and the purchase costs;

(2) *(name 2)* will receive a refund of *(name 2's)* original contribution of £   towards the purchase price and the purchase costs;

(3) if the net proceeds of sale are insufficient to refund the co-owners' original contributions fully, the contributions will abate (in the proportions that they bear to each other)[2] [OR] (equally);

(4) when the original contributions have been refunded the remaining balance of the net proceeds of sale will be divided as to *(fraction or percentage)* for *(name 1)* and *(fraction or percentage)*[3] for *(name 2)*.

Example 1

A and B bought a house for £88,500. The purchase costs amounted to £1,500. A contributed £30,000 and B contributed £10,000. They obtained a mortgage advance of £50,000 and contributed equally to the mortgage payments. They agreed to share the sale costs equally. Five years later they sold the house for £130,000. The sale costs totalled £4,000. The amount required to redeem the mortgage was £46,000. The net proceeds of sale were £80,000. Who got what?

When they bought the house, A and B executed a declaration of trust which said that each of them would get back his or her original contribution, and that the balance of the net proceeds of sale would be divided equally between them. Therefore, A was refunded her £30,000. B was refunded his £10,000. The balance of the net proceeds (£40,000) was divided equally between them. A received, in total, £50,000 and B received £30,000.

The problem with applying this formula is more noticeable in A's case. Her original contribution has remained stationary, or stagnated. The value of the property has increased by about 47 per cent, and in real terms her original contribution of £30,000 should have grown to roughly £44,000.

Compare the suggested solution at **1.165** where the facts are identical and the example in the footnote at **1.168** below, where the original contribution is credited with interest.

Example 2

The facts are similar to those in footnote 1 above, except that the property was sold for £76,000. The amount required to redeem the mortgage was £46,000. The sale costs came to £2,000 and the net proceeds of sale were £28,000, representing an overall loss of £12,000.

The declaration of trust provided that the original contributions would abate in the proportions that they bear to each other. So, A's original contribution of £30,000 was reduced to £21,000; and B's original contribution of £10,000 was reduced to £7,000.

1.167 *Property*

If the declaration of trust had stated that their original contributions would abate equally, A would have received £24,000, and B would have ended up with £4,000. In other words, their net loss of £12,000 would have been shared by them equally.

1   For a variation of this formula, see **1.168** below. *See Example 1.*
2   A provision for abatement is necessary to cover any downturn in property values. *See Example 2.*
3   The denominator will, presumably, represent the mortgage debt and the sale costs. The numerator will reflect the extent to which each co-owner assumes responsibility for the mortgage and the sale costs.

1.168

Fixed shares: refund of original contributions plus interest: provision for abatement: fixed shares of the balance of the net proceeds of sale[1]

Shares

When the property is sold:

(1) (*name 1*) will receive a refund of (*name 1's*) original contribution of £   towards the purchase price and the purchase costs *plus* (simple) interest at a rate of (7) per cent per year from the date (on which the purchase of the property was completed) [OR] (of this Declaration of Trust) to the date on which the refund of the contribution is made;

(2) (*name 2*) will receive a refund of (*name 2's*) original contribution of £   towards the purchase price and the purchase costs *plus* (simple) interest at a rate of (7) per cent per year from the date (on which the purchase of the property was completed) [OR] (of this Declaration of Trust) to the date on which the refund of the contribution is made;

(3) if the net proceeds of sale are insufficient to refund the co-owners' original contributions plus interest, the original contributions and the interest on them will abate (in the proportions that they bear to each other) [OR] (equally);

(4) subject to the above, the remaining balance of the net proceeds of sale will be divided as to (*fraction or percentage*) for (*name 1*) and (*fraction or percentage*) for (*name 2*).

Example

The facts are identical to those in the example given at **1.167** above, except that A and B's declaration of trust said that they would be entitled to simple interest at 7 per cent a year. A receives her original contribution of £30,000, plus £10,500 in interest, plus £13,000 (half of the remaining balance): a total of £53,500. B receives a total of £26,500 (his contribution of £10,000, plus £3,500 in interest, plus £13,000 (half of the remaining balance)).

1   See the footnotes to **1.167** above. *See Example.*

1.169

Fixed shares: refund of original contributions expressed as a fraction or percentage of the sale price: alternative provisions for the division of the balance of the net proceeds of sale[1]

Shares

When the property is sold:

(1) (*name 1*) will receive (*fraction or percentage*)[2] of the sale price, representing the return on (*name 1*'s) original contribution of £   towards the purchase price and purchase costs;

(2) (*name 2*) will receive (*fraction or percentage*)[3] of the sale price, representing the return on (*name 2*'s) original contribution of £   towards the purchase price and purchase costs;

(3) the amount required to redeem the mortgage will be paid from the remaining (*fraction or percentage*)[4] of the sale price ('the mortgage share');

(4) if the amount required to redeem the mortgage exceeds the mortgage share, the excess will be paid by the co-owners (in equal shares) [OR] (as to per cent by (*name 1*) and per cent by (*name 2*)) [OR] (in the proportions that each of them has contributed towards the mortgage payments)[5];

(5) subject to the above, the remaining balance of the mortgage share will be divided between the co-owners (in equal shares) [OR] (as to per cent for (*name 1*) and per cent for (*name 2*)) [OR] (in the proportions that each of them has contributed towards the mortgage payments)[6];

(6) the co-owners will pay the incidental costs of selling the property (in equal shares) [OR] (as to per cent by (*name 1*) and per cent by (*name 2*)) [OR] (in the proportions that their respective shares of the rest of the net proceeds of sale bear to each other).

[1] This is probably the most satisfactory formula for expressing fixed shares. In principle, it is the same as the formula at **1.166** above. However, it is more flexible than in that case because it *addresse*s the possibility that, when they purchase, the co-owners may have no definite plans as to the extent to which each of them will assume responsibility for the mortgage payments.

[2] The numerator should represent the co-owner's contribution; the denominator should represent the purchase price plus the purchase costs.

[3] The numerator should represent the co-owner's contribution; the denominator should represent the purchase price plus the purchase costs.

[4] The numerator should represent the mortgage advance; the denominator should represent the purchase price plus the purchase costs. The fractions or percentages in subclauses 1, 2 and 3 should come to 100 per cent of the purchase price and purchase costs.

[5] The words 'in the proportions that each of them has contributed towards the mortgage payments' creates floating shares. In other words, those proportions will not be finally ascertained until the trust for sale comes to an end.

[6] The words 'in the proportions that each of them has contributed towards the mortgage payments' creates floating shares. In other words, those proportions will not be finally ascertained until the trust for sale comes to an end.

(ii) FLOATING SHARES

1.170

Floating shares: in proportion to the contributions made by each co-owner throughout the duration of the trust[1]

Shares

When the property is sold, the net proceeds of sale[2] will be divided between the co-owners in proportion to (the extent to which the change in the value of the property is attributable to)[3] the contributions made by each of them towards the:

(1) purchase price;

(2) incidental costs of the purchase;

(3) payment of mortgage interest;

(4) payment of mortgage endowment policy premiums;

1.170 Property

(5) repayment of mortgage capital;

(6) cost of repairs and improvements to the property;

(7) payment of interest and repayment of capital on further advances and loans taken out for repairs and improvements to the property; (and

(8) incidental costs of selling the property)[4].

[1] For the distinction between fixed shares and floating shares, see **1.9** above. For a discussion of some of the advantages and disadvantages of floating shares, see **1.10–1.13** above.

[2] For a definition of 'the net proceeds of sale', see **1.193** below.

[3] The words in brackets should be deleted if the shares are to be calculated by the addition of the contributions and the apportionment of the net proceeds of sale pro rata (see **1.171** below). The words in brackets must be included if the shares are to be calculated in accordance with the formulae set out in **1.173** (narrative form) and **1.174** (tabular form) below.

[4] For a definition of 'the incidental costs of selling the property', see **1.192** below. The sale costs should only be included here if the co-owners intend to pay the sale costs in the proportions that their respective shares bear to each other. If the co-owners intend to pay the sale costs in equal shares, or in some other fixed proportions, there should be included a separate clause to this effect (see **1.188** below).

Other items could be included in this list, for example mortgage guarantee premiums, mortgage protection policy premiums, buildings insurance premiums, rent, rentcharge, ground rent, service charges, etc.

1.171

Floating shares: calculation of the shares: addition of contributions and apportionment of net proceeds of sale pro rata[1]

Calculation of shares

The share of the net proceeds of sale to which each co-owner is entitled will be calculated by:

(1) adding together his or her contributions to produce 'the individual contribution'; and then

(2) adding together (both)/(all) of the co-owners' individual contributions to produce 'the combined contributions'; and then

(3) dividing the net proceeds of sale (plus the incidental costs of selling the property)[2] by the combined contributions to produce 'the dividend'; and finally

(4) multiplying the individual contribution by the dividend to produce the share.

Warning

This method of calculating floating shares does not take into account the extent to which the change in the value of the property can be attributed to each co-owner's lump sum contributions and mortgage-related contributions. If the change in value is to be taken into account, Precedents **1.173** and **1.174** can be used instead.

Although this method of calculating the shares is far simpler than the formulae, in certain circumstances it can produce a perverse result. For an illustration, see the example in Precedent **1.174** below.

Example

A and B bought a bungalow for £165,000. The purchase costs came to £2,500. A paid £87,500 and B paid £18,000. They took out a mortgage for £62,000. They lived together for 3 years. A paid £15,000 towards the mortgage. B paid £5,000 towards the mortgage. They carried out improvements which cost £20,000. B paid £12,000 in cash towards the improvements but A paid nothing in cash towards the improvements. They obtained a loan of £8,000 for the improvements. A paid £1,500 on the loan and B paid £500. They sold the bungalow for £197,000. The amount required to redeem the mortgage was £60,000. The amount required to repay the loan was £7,500. The sale costs came to £5,000 and the net proceeds of sale were £124,500. Who got what?

Suggested solution

A and B's individual contributions were:

	A	B
Purchase price and costs	87,500	18,000
Mortgage payments	15,000	5,000
Improvements: cash	0	12,000
Loan payments	1,500	500
	£104,000	£35,500

The method of calculating A's share is as follows:
(a) his individual contribution is £104,000;
(b) the combined contributions are £139,500;
(c) the net proceeds of sale (£124,500) are divided by the combined contributions to produce a dividend of 0.89247;
(d) A's individual contribution is multiplied by the dividend to produce his share, which is £92,817.

Applying the same method, B's share is £31,683. Incidentally, had the formulae in Precedents 1.173 and 1.174 below been used on this occasion, A would have been better off by £74.

[1] As there is more than one method of calculating floating shares, it is sensible to set out clearly the manner in which the shares will be calculated. The method of calculating A's share is as follows:
(a) A's individual contribution is £104,000; (b) the combined contributions are £139,500; (c) the net proceeds of sale (£124,500) are divided by the combined contributions to produce a dividend of 0.89247; (d) A's individual contribution is multiplied by the dividend to produce his share, which is £92,817. Applying the same method, B's share is £31,683. Incidentally, had the formulae in Precedents 1.173 and 1.174 below been used on this occasion, A would have been better off by £74.
[2] The sale costs should only be included if their payment is to be borne pro rata to the shares of the rest of the net proceeds of sale.

1.172

Floating shares: calculation of the shares[1]: introductory clause to the formulae[2]

Calculation of shares

The share of the net proceeds of sale to which each co-owner is entitled will be calculated in accordance with the provisions of Schedule (*number*).

[1] It is assumed that this clause would be immediately preceded by wording identical or similar to that contained in Precedent 1.170 above.
[2] The formulae contained in Precedents 1.173 and 1.174 below are quite complicated. It may be considered preferable to set them out in a separate schedule, rather than include them in the main body of the declaration of trust.

1.173

Floating shares: formulae for calculating floating shares[1]: narrative form

SCHEDULE *(number)*

(1) The share of the net proceeds of sale to which each co-owner is entitled ('share') before the deduction of his or her share of the incidental costs of selling the property will be calculated by adding together his or her lump sum contributions and his or her mortgage-related contributions.

Lump sum contributions

(2) Each co-owner's lump sum contributions ('lump sum') will be calculated by applying the following formula.

$$\frac{\text{Individual payments}}{\text{purchase price} + \text{improvements}} \times \text{sale price} = \text{lump sum}$$

WHERE:

(2.1) *Individual payments* is the total of the individual co-owner's lump sum payments towards:

    (a) the purchase price; and

    (b) the incidental costs of purchasing the property; and

    (c) repairs and improvements to the property.

(2.2) *Purchase price* is the total of:

    (a) (both)/(all) of the co-owners' lump sum payments towards the purchase price; and

    (b) (both)/(all) of the co-owners' lump sum payments towards the incidental costs of purchasing the property; and

    (c) the mortgage advance.

(2.3) *Improvements* is the total of:

    (a) (both)/(all) of the co-owners' lump sum payments towards repairs and improvements to the property; and

    (b) all further mortgage advances and all loans, whether secured or unsecured, taken out for the purpose of carrying out repairs and improvements to the property.

(2.4) *Sale price* is the gross sale price of the property before any deductions.

Mortgage-related contributions

(3) Each co-owner's mortgage-related contributions ('mortgage related contribution') will be calculated by applying the following formulae.

    (3.1) *First*[2]

$$\frac{\text{loans}}{\text{purchase price} + \text{improvements}} \times \text{sale price} = \text{gross mortgage share}$$

WHERE:

(3.1.1) *Loans* is the total of:
- (a) the mortgage advance; and
- (b) all further mortgage advances; and
- (c) all loans taken out for the purpose of carrying out repairs and improvements to the property; and
- (d) all improvement grants.

(3.1.2) *Purchase price* has the same meaning as it has in para (2.2) above.

(3.1.3) *Improvements* has the same meaning as it has in para (2.3) above.

(3.1.4) *Sale price* has the same meaning as it has in para (2.4) above.

(3.1.5) *Gross mortgage share* represents the extent to which the change in the value of the property can be attributed to the sums of money provided by way of mortgages, loans and grants.

(3.2) Second

gross mortgage share — redemption = net mortgage share

WHERE:

(3.2.1) *Redemption* is the total amount required to redeem or repay:
- (a) the mortgage advance; and
- (b) all further mortgage advances; and
- (c) all loans taken out for the purpose of carrying out repairs and improvements to the property; and
- (d) all improvement grants.

(3.3) Third[3]

$$\frac{\text{individual mortgage payments}}{\text{combined mortgage payments}} \times \text{net mortgage share} = \text{mortgage related contribution}$$

WHERE:

(3.3.1) *Individual mortgage payments* is the total of each individual co-owner's contributions towards the repayment or payment of capital, interest and premiums on:
- (a) the mortgage advance; and
- (b) all mortgage-linked insurance policies; and
- (c) all further mortgage advances; and
- (d) all loans taken out for the purpose of carrying out repairs and improvements to the property; and
- (e) all improvement grants.

1.173 *Property*

> (3.3.2) *Combined mortgage payments* is the total of (both)/(all) of the co-owners' individual mortgage payments.

The share[4]

(4) Lump sum + mortgage related contribution = share

Sale costs

(5) The incidental costs of selling the property will be paid by the co-owners (in equal shares) [OR] (in the proportions that each share bears to the other share or shares).

Example

A and B bought a flat for £44,000. The purchase costs came to £1,000. B paid £4,000. A paid £1,000. They took out a mortgage for £40,000. B paid £2,000 in mortgage payments. They sold the flat for £50,000. The amount required to redeem the mortgage was £39,000. The sale costs were £2,000 and the net proceeds of sale were £9,000. Who got what?

Addition of contributions: apportionment of net proceeds pro rata (wrong solution)

If A and B had executed a declaration of trust which contained the method of calculating floating shares set out in Precedent **1.171** above, the result would have been as follows.

A's contributions came to £12,000 overall — £1,000 towards the purchase and £11,000 towards the mortgage.

B's contributions came to £6,000 overall — £4,000 towards the purchase and £2,000 towards the mortgage.

The net proceeds of sale (£9,000) would be divided between them in the ratio 12:6.

A would get £6,000. B would get £3,000. A would receive twice as much as B. Even though the property has increased in value, B seems to have lost £1,000 on the original contribution of £4,000.

Suggested solution: applying the formulae

The result would have been totally different if these formulae had been applied, because they would have separated A's and B's lump sum contributions from their mortgage-related contributions.

The property went up in value, by roughly 11 per cent, from £45,000 (including purchase costs) to £50,000.

Tim's lump sum contribution of £1,000 increased by the same percentage to £1,111. B's lump sum contribution of £4,000 increased to £4,444.

The share of the property bought by the mortgage advance of £40,000 increased in value to £44,445. This is called the 'gross mortgage share'. By deducting from the gross mortgage share the amount required to redeem the mortgage (£39,000), we arrive at the 'net mortgage share' of £5,445. By virtue of A's mortgage-related contributions, A is entitled to 11/13ths of the net mortgage share (£4,607). B is entitled to 2/13ths of the net mortgage share (£838). A's lump sum contribution (£1,111) and mortgage-related contribution (£4,607) are added to produce £5,718. B's lump sum contribution (£4,444) and mortgage-related contribution (£838) are added to produce £5,282. The sale costs (£2,000) are paid pro rata. A £1,040, B £960. A ends up with £4,678. B ends up with £4,322.

Warning

The application of these formulae could cause hardship if:
(a) a large share of the property is bought by the mortgage; and

(b) one co-owner contributes substantially more than the other towards the mortgage payments; and
(c) the property goes down in value.

[1] The formulae set out in this precedent are identical to those set out in **1.174** below. The only difference is the style. Here they are described in narrative form; in **1.174** they appear in tabular form.

The formulae seek to identify and isolate the extent to which any change in the value of the property can be attributed to the lump sums provided by each co-owner and to the lump sum which they have borrowed on a mortgage. The change in value of the share purchased by the mortgage is then apportioned between the co-owners according to the sums which each has paid towards the mortgage.

In most cases, the application of these formulae will produce a more equitable result than the other method of calculating floating shares: namely the simple addition of the contributions, followed by an apportionment of the net proceeds of sale pro rata (**1.171** above). The example is an illustration.

[2] To double-check the accuracy of the calculations at this stage the co-owners' combined lump sum contributions plus the gross mortgage share should be the same as the sale price. *Note*: A calculator is necessary. The formulae require exact figures. Approximate figures will not do.

[3] To double-check the accuracy of the calculations at this stage the co-owners' combined mortgage-related contributions should be the same as the net mortgage share in para (3.2) above. *Note*: A calculator is necessary. The formulae require exact figures. Approximate figures will not do.

[4] To double-check the accuracy of the calculations at this stage the combined total of both or all shares should be the same as the net proceeds of sale plus the sale costs. *Note*: A calculator is necessary. The formulae require exact figures. Approximate figures will not do.

1.174

Floating shares: formulae for calculating floating shares[1]: tabular form

Calculation of shares

The share of the net proceeds of sale to which each co-owner is entitled will be calculated by:

(1) completing the record of contributions set out in the (first) Schedule; and then

(2) applying the formulae set out in the (second) Schedule.

FIRST SCHEDULE

RECORD OF CONTRIBUTIONS

PURCHASE		£	
NAME 1	Contribution to purchase price and costs		A
NAME 2	Contribution to purchase price and costs		B
Mortgage advance			C
Gross purchase price	[A + B + C]		D

IMPROVEMENT		£	
NAME 1	Contributions		E
NAME 2	Contributions		F
Improvement grant(s) and further mortgage advance(s) and loan(s) taken out for improvements			G

1.174 *Property*

IMPROVEMENT		£	
Combined cost of improvements	[E + F + G]		H

MORTGAGE PAYMENTS		£	
NAME 1	Contributions		I
NAME 2	Contributions		J
Combined contributions	[I + J]		K

SALE		£	
Sale price (or, if one co-owner is selling his/her share in the property to the other, the agreed current market value of the whole property)			L
Mortgage redemption and repayment of any improvement grant and loan taken out for improvements			M
Sale costs: estate agency/legal fees/apportionments of outgoings			N
Net proceeds of sale	[L - (M + N)]		O

SECOND SCHEDULE

CALCULATION OF SHARES

STAGE ONE: In which the change in the value of the property is apportioned between the contributions towards the purchase and improvement of the property made by the co-owners individually and by virtue of the mortgage advance(s)			
NAME 1	$\dfrac{A+E}{D+H} \times L =$		P
NAME 2	$\dfrac{B+F}{D+H} \times L =$		Q
Mortgage(s)	$\dfrac{C+G}{D+H} \times L =$		R
Sale price	[P + Q + R]		L

STAGE TWO: In which the increase or reduction in the value of the property attributable to the amount(s) provided by way of the mortgage(s) is apportioned between the co-owners according to their respective contribution towards repayment of the mortgage(s)			
	R − M		S
NAME 1	$\dfrac{I}{K} \times S =$		T

STAGE TWO: In which the increase or reduction in the value of the property attributable to the amount(s) provided by way of the mortgage(s) is apportioned between the co-owners according to their respective contribution towards repayment of the mortgage(s)			
NAME 2	$\frac{J}{K} \times S =$		U

STAGE THREE: In which the co-owner's entitlements from stages one and two are added together			
NAME 1	P + T		V
NAME 2	Q + U		W
Net proceeds of sale + sale costs	[O + N]		X

STAGE FOUR: In which the sale costs are apportioned between the co-owners in accordance with their entitlements in stage three			
NAME 1	$\dfrac{V}{X \times N}$		Y
NAME 2	$\dfrac{W}{X \times N}$		Z
Sale costs			N

STAGE FIVE: In which the co-owner's shares of the net proceeds of sale are ascertained			
NAME 1	V - Y		
NAME 2	W - Z		
Net proceeds of sale			O

[1] For the two Schedules containing the record of contributions and the formulae, see below. The formulae are the same as those expressed in narrative form in **1.173** above. They identify the extent to which each co-owner's lump sum contributions and mortgage-related contributions affect the value of the property.

(iii) Fixed shares or floating shares

1.175

The average of two or more methods of calculating the shares[1]

Shares

When the property is sold:

(1) (*name 1*) will receive the *average* of the sums to which (*name 1*) is entitled in Schedules (*number*) and (*number*) to this Declaration of Trust;

1.175 *Property*

(2) (*name 2*) will receive the *average* of the sums to which (*name 2*) is entitled in Schedules (*number*) and (*number*) to this Declaration of Trust.

[1] If the average of two or more methods of calculating the shares is to be used, it is probably better to set out the different methods of calculation in separate Schedules. A single clause that attempted to describe various different methods would, almost certainly, be difficult to understand and would probably be very lengthy.

1.176

Supplemental clause providing for the gradual equalisation of the shares[1]

Gradual equalisation of shares[2]

(1) The co-owners intend that on the (seventh)[3] anniversary of the date (on which the purchase of the property was completed) [*OR*] (of this Declaration of Trust) their respective shares of the net proceeds of sale will become and remain equal, and to that intent the following provisions will apply.

(2) In this Clause:

(2.1) 'the larger share' means the share of the co-owner who is entitled to the larger share of the net proceeds of sale[4];

(2.2) 'the smaller share' means the share of the co-owner who is entitled to the smaller share of the net proceeds of sale; and

(2.3) 'the difference' means the difference between the larger share and the smaller share on the date when the property is sold or either share is realised.

(3) For each complete year that has elapsed since the date (on which the purchase of the property was completed) [*OR*] (of this Declaration of Trust) the larger share will decrease by (1/14th)[5] of the difference and the smaller share will increase by (1/14th)[6] of the difference.

(4) For the avoidance of doubt:

(4.1) no apportionment will be made in respect of any period of less than a year (see *Example*);

(4.2) the calculations in this Clause will cease to have effect immediately after the (seventh)[7] anniversary of the date (on which the purchase of the property was completed) [*OR*] (of this Declaration of Trust); and

(4.3) if the co-owners separate, the calculations in this Clause will apply only in respect of each complete year that has elapsed since the date (on which the purchase of the property was completed) [*OR*] (of this Declaration of Trust) and the date on which the co-owners separated (see *Example*).

Example

A and B purchased a house and executed a declaration of trust on 20 January 1989. On 9 October 1991 they separated. On 16 March 1992 they sold the property. The net proceeds of sale came to £150,000, of which A was entitled to the 'larger share' of £110,000 and B was entitled to the 'smaller share' of £40,000. The declaration of trust provided that their respective shares should be equalised over a 7-year period. Who gets what?

The 'difference' between the larger share and the smaller share on the date when the property is sold is £70,000. A's share will decrease by 2/14ths of the difference and B's share will increase by 2/14ths of the difference. The numerator represents the two complete years from 20 January 1989 to 20 January 1991, during which time they were living together. No apportionment is made in respect of the period from 21 January 1991. So, A gets £100,000 and B gets £50,000.

1   This clause could apply equally to fixed shares and floating shares. It is recommended that this Clause should immediately follow the Clause setting out the respective shares.
2   The concept is quite simple. The co-owners 'split the difference' over a given period. Inheritance tax implications should be considered. There is certainly a transfer of value, but it is not entirely clear whether there is one transfer of value, or a series of transfers. The provisions of IA 1986, s 339, which relate to transactions at an undervalue, should also be considered.
3   Insert the appropriate anniversary.
4   This clause only envisages a gradual equalisation of the shares of two co-owners.
5   The denominator should be double the number of years. So, for a 5-year period it would be 1/10th; for 6 years, 1/12th; for 10 years, 1/20th, etc. In most cases the fraction will be more intelligible than a percentage.
6   The denominator should be double the number of years. So, for a 5-year period it would be 1/10th; for 6 years, 1/12th; for 10 years, 1/20th, etc. In most cases the fraction will be more intelligible than a percentage.
7   Insert the appropriate anniversary.

D   General clauses

1.177

Contingencies: introductory clause[1]

Contingencies

- If one of the co-owners fails to pay their share of the mortgage payments, the provisions of Schedule (*number*) will apply[2].
- If one of the co-owners wishes to sell the property and the other co-owner refuses to sell it, the provisions of Schedule (*number*) will apply[3].
- If one of the co-owners dies and the other co-owner does not become solely and beneficially entitled to the property, the provisions of Schedule (*number*) will apply[4].
- If one of the co-owners is declared bankrupt, the provisions of Schedule (*number*) will apply[5].
- If one of the co-owners ceases permanently to reside in the property and the other co-owner continues to reside in it, the provisions of Schedule (*number*) will apply[6].
- If one of the co-owners is unemployed or incapable of working, the provisions of Schedule (*number*) will apply[7].
- If one of the co-owners is unemployed or incapable of working because she is pregnant, or he or she is looking after a child or children, the provisions of Schedule (*number*) will apply[8].
- If one of the co-owners attends a full-time course of education which lasts for less than (one year), the provisions of Schedule (*number*) will apply[9].
- If one of the co-owners attends a full-time course of education which lasts for more than (one year), the provisions of Schedule (*number*) will apply[10].
- If the co-owners permit any other person to reside with them in the property, the provisions of Schedule (*number*) will apply[11].
- If the co-owners separate within a period of (12 months) after purchasing the property, the provisions of Schedule (*number*) will apply[12].
- If the co-owners are about to separate, or have recently separated, and both of them wish to keep the property, the provisions of Schedule (*number*) will apply[13].

1.177 *Property*

- If the co-owners carry out building works and contribute towards the cost of the building works disproportionately to their respective shares of the net proceeds of sale, the provisions of Schedule (*number*) will apply[14].
- If one of the co-owners wishes to realise his or her share of the property, the provisions of Schedule (*number*) will apply[15].

[1] A declaration of trust may need to *address* a number of contingencies, uncertainties or risks. It is recommended that these are briefly introduced by a single sentence in the main body of the declaration, and that the substantive provisions are, in each case, incorporated in a separate Schedule at the end of the declaration.

The contingencies included in these precedents are typical of many of the problems that arise, but are not exhaustive. They serve a variety of purposes.

In some cases they are included primarily for information purposes, for example **1.205** and **1.201**.

Some of the contingencies provide that payments made by one co-owner on the other's behalf will be treated as a loan, and that their respective beneficial interests will not be affected. Examples include the precedents at **1.202**, **1.207** and **1.209** below.

In the case of the precedent at **1.208**, the payments made by the other co-owner are treated as a gift. To a lesser degree, other precedents may contain a gift element, but generally such contingencies are designed to deal only with a temporary state of affairs.

Where there is likely to be a long-term imbalance, the contingencies provide that fixed shares will be converted into floating shares. Illustrations can be found at **1.206** and **1.210** below.

Some of the contingencies give a co-owner the opportunity to 'buy out' the other co-owner's share on favourable terms, but usually subject to a strict time limit. Examples include the precedents at **1.204** and **1.214** below.

There are also contingencies which might best be described as dispute resolution contingencies. Illustrations are the precedents at **1.211** and **1.212** below, which try to get to grips with the problem that could arise if both co-owners wish to keep the property.

Note: If more than one contingency Schedule is being used, care must be taken to ensure that they are not inconsistent with each other.

[2] See **1.202** below.
[3] See **1.203** below.
[4] See **1.204** below.
[5] See **1.205** below.
[6] See **1.213** below.
[7] See **1.207** below.
[8] See **1.208** below.
[9] See **1.209** below.
[10] See **1.210** below.
[11] See **1.201** below.
[12] See **1.214** below.
[13] See **1.211** and **1.212** below.
[14] See **1.209** below.
[15] See **1.215** below.

NET INCOME UNTIL SALE

Note that in the case of a husband and wife who are living together, special rules relate to the apportionment of income arising from property held in their joint names. These rules are contained in the Income Tax Act 2007, ss 836 and 837.

1.178

General

Regardless of the manner in which the net proceeds of sale of the property are to be divided between the co-owners (in equal shares) [OR] (as to per cent for (*name 1*) and as to per cent for (*name 2*)).

1.179

Payments from lodgers

Regardless of the manner in which the net proceeds of sale of the property are to be divided between them, any payment made to one or both of the co-owners by anyone who normally resides with them as a contribution towards his or her living and accommodation expenses will be divided between the co-owners (in equal shares) [OR] (as to per cent for (name 1) and as to per cent for (name 2)).

1.180

Payments from grown-up children

Regardless of the manner in which the net proceeds of sale of the property are to be divided between the co-owners, any payments received by (name 2) from any of (name 2's) children who normally reside in the property as a contribution towards his or her living and accommodation expenses will belong to (name 2) [OR] (the co-owners in equal shares).

CIRCUMSTANCES IN WHICH AN APPLICATION CAN BE MADE TO THE COURT FOR AN ORDER TO SELL THE PROPERTY

1.181

Separation[1]

Either co-owner can apply to the court for an order that the property be sold[2] if the co-owners have lived apart for a continuous period of at least (three) months immediately preceding the presentation of the application.

[1] If this Clause is being used in conjunction with any of the contingency schedules, there must be no inconsistency between the time-limits.
[2] LPA 1925, s 30, giving power to apply to the court where trustees for sale refuse to sell, has been replaced by ss 14 and 15 of the TOLATA 1996.

1.182

A co-owner's death[1]

After the end of a period of (6) months from the date of the death of a co-owner, his or her personal representatives, or any person who is entitled under the deceased co-owner's will or the law relating to intestacy to his or her beneficial interest in the property, can apply to the court for an order that the property be sold.

[1] If this Clause is used in conjunction with the contingency schedule at 1.204 below, there must be no inconsistency between the timespans.
It may be preferable to specify a period commencing on the death rather than on the date on which a grant of representation is first taken out, because the issue of the grant could be delayed for various reasons.

1.183

Contributions towards repairs and improvements not to affect the co-owners' fixed shares[1]

No contribution in money or money's worth which either co-owner may make towards repairs and improvements to the property will affect the size of their

1.183 *Property*

respective shares of the net proceeds of sale.

[1] If a definition of 'repairs and improvements' is considered necessary, see **1.196**. Compare MPPA 1970, s 37.

COVENANTS

1.184

Prohibited acts

Neither co-owner will do or attempt to do any of the following things without the other co-owner's consent, and if they are living apart that consent must be in writing:

(1) carry out or take out a loan for the purpose of carrying out any structural alterations or major repairs or improvements to the property;

(2) grant any tenancy or licence or allow anyone else to occupy the property;

(3) transfer his or her beneficial interest in the property other than by Will or Codicil;

(4) charge or incumber the property or any part of it or any interest in it.

1.185

Positive acts

Each co-owner will:

(1) Obligations

Always comply with the obligations imposed on the co-owners jointly and individually in:

(1.1) the registers kept at the Land Registry;

(1.2) this Declaration of Trust;

(1.3) the mortgage;

(1.4) any insurance policy that is linked to the mortgage;

(1.5) any insurance policy that affects the building or its contents;

(1.6) any order affecting the property that has been issued by a body acting on statutory authority;

(1.7) the Lease;

(1.8) the Memorandum and Articles of Association of the Management Company.

(2) Payments

Promptly pay his or her share of the mortgage payments, insurance premiums, and all other outgoings on the property.

(3) Repair

Keep and contribute towards the cost of keeping the property in reasonable repair, condition and decoration.

(4) Insure

Keep and contribute towards the cost of keeping the property adequately insured under comprehensive cover to its full re-instatement value.

(5) Keep accounts

Keep proper accounts, receipts and statements recording all the contributions made by each and both of the co-owners towards the mortgage payments and the costs of all repairs and improvements to the property.

(6) Execute further assurances

Complete, sign and execute any form, document and deed which may be required in order to transfer the legal estate and beneficial interest in the property or otherwise to implement the provisions of this Declaration of Trust.

(7) Allow access

Let any valuer have access to the property and any information about the property which may be relevant in assessing its open market value.

(8) Indemnity

Indemnify the other co-owner from and against the consequences of the failure of the co-owner giving this indemnity to comply with any of the obligations imposed on him or her.

1.186

Legal advice[1]

Each of the co-owners has received independent legal advice on the provisions and implications of this Declaration of Trust.

[1] See, generally, **1.2** and **2.2**.
Note that the effect of acting for clients with different interests is that the solicitor must act with caution as he may suddenly find that he is in the position of having a duty to one client, the effect of which if carried out will be contrary to the interest of the other client. A solicitor that continues to act for both clients in these circumstances risks proceedings for negligence being brought against him by one client or the other.

1.187

Costs of this declaration

(*Name 1*) will pay all the legal costs relating to the preparation and execution of this Declaration of Trust.

[OR]

The co-owners will pay the legal costs relating to the preparation and execution of this Declaration of Trust (in equal shares).

1.187 *Property*

[OR]

Each of the co-owners will pay the costs incurred by him or her in obtaining independent legal advice on the provisions and implications of this Declaration of Trust.

1.188

Sale costs[1]

The co-owners will pay the incidental costs of selling the property (in equal shares) [OR] (in the proportions that their respective shares of the rest of the net proceeds of sale of the property bear to each other).

[1] It is important that the co-owners clearly agree in advance how the incidental costs of selling the property will be borne between them. These costs usually include estate agents' commissions as well as legal fees, and are sometimes substantial.
There is no need to include this Clause if the method of calculating the co-owners' shares already takes the sale costs into account.

1.189

Costs of transfer of beneficial interest

Unless the co-owners agree otherwise, if one of them transfers all his or her legal estate and beneficial interest in the property to the other (or the other's nominee), the valuation fees, legal fees and other costs incurred by the transferor will be paid by the transferor, and the valuation fees, legal fees and other costs incurred by the transferee will be paid by the transferee.

DEFINITIONS

1.190

Sale price

'The sale price' means:

(1) the price for which the property is sold; and

(2) the price paid by the buyer of the property for any chattels jointly owned by the co-owners, whether or not a separate price is paid for those chattels.

1.191

Amount required to redeem the mortgage[1]

'The amount required to redeem the mortgage' means the sums of money required by the lenders to enable the co-owners to repay all mortgages, charges and loans to which the property is subject (other than a charge created by one of the co-owners affecting his or her beneficial interest alone) and to enable the co-owners to be completely released and discharged from the performance of all their obligations under such mortgages, charges and loans, and includes:

(1) all legal and administrative fees incurred or charged by any lender in connection with the repayment; and

(2) any financial penalty imposed by any lender for each repayment.

[1] In the case of an endowment mortgage or insurance-linked mortgage it may be considered

desirable to add the words 'less the surrender values of all insurance policies linked to the mortgage, whether or not those policies have been assigned to or deposited with the lenders'.

1.192

Incidental costs of selling the property[1]

'The incidental costs of selling the property' means the total sum of money (including VAT) to be paid in respect of:

(1) estate agent's commission; and

(2) legal costs and disbursements; and

(3) apportionments of rates, taxes, insurance, and other outgoings on the property; and

(4) any other costs incurred in connection with the sale or transfer of the property or any interest in it.

[1] Note that in the 'short form' complete precedents, 'the incidental costs of selling the property' has been abbreviated to 'the sale costs'.

1.193

Net proceeds of sale

'The net proceeds of sale' means the sale price[1], less:

(1) the amount required to redeem the mortgage[2]; and

(2) the incidental costs of selling the property[3].

[1] For a definition of 'the sale price', see **1.190** above.
[2] For a definition of 'the amount required to redeem the mortgage', see **1.191** above.
[3] For a definition of 'the incidental costs of selling the property', see **1.192** above.

1.194

Open market value

'The open market value' means the best price for the property that the co-owners could reasonably be expected to obtain if they sold the property on the date of the valuation, assuming that:

(1) the property is being sold with vacant possession; and

(2) there is no discount in respect of the joint ownership of the property; and

(3) a buyer, who is not connected with (either)/(any) of the co-owners, is ready, willing and able to complete the purchase of the property immediately for cash; and

(4) all carpets, curtains, fixtures and fittings which are jointly owned by the co-owners are included in the sale.

1.195

Mortgage payments

'The mortgage payments' means the sums of money paid or payable from time to time to the lender(s) in respect of all mortgages, charges and loans to which the property is subject, and includes:

(1) the payment of interest; and

1.195 *Property*

(2) the repayment of capital; and

(3) the payment of insurance premiums; and

(4) the payment of penalties imposed by the lender(s); and

(5) the payment of interest and the repayment of capital on all loans taken out, with or without security, for the purpose of carrying out repairs and improvements to the property.

1.196

Repairs and improvements[1]

'Repairs and improvements' means major repairs necessary to maintain the fabric of the property, and any of the following measures undertaken with a view to improving its fitness for occupation:

(1) installation of a fixed bath, shower, wash basin, sink or lavatory, and any necessary associated plumbing;

(2) damp proofing measures;

(3) provision or improvement of ventilation and natural lighting;

(4) provision of electric lighting and sockets;

(5) provision or improvement of drainage facilities;

(6) improvements to the structural condition of the property;

(7) improvements to the facilities for storing, preparing and cooking food;

(8) provision of heating, including central heating;

(9) provision of storage facilities for fuel and refuse;

(10) improvements to the insulation of the property; and

(11) any other major repairs analogous to those listed above[2].

[1] It is submitted that the definition of 'repairs and improvements' will depend on the age and condition of the property, and perhaps also the socio-economic backgrounds of the co-owners. For an alternative definition, see the definition of 'building works' at **1.206** below.

[2] When a couple buy a property with the intention of carrying out substantial repairs and improvements, it may be preferable to express their shares of the net proceeds of sale as floating, rather than fixed. For the distinction between fixed shares and floating shares, see **1.7** above.

1.197

Co-owners

'The co-owners' means (*name 1*) and (*name 2*) and the trustees for the time being of the property.

1.198

The nature of this declaration

This Declaration of Trust:

(1) is a deed[1] and is executed as a deed[2] by the (co-owners) [OR] (parties to it);

(2) can be varied by a subsequent Declaration of Trust executed by all the persons who are able to vary the original trusts[3];

(3) will be legally binding on the (co-owners) [OR] (parties to it) unless and until it is varied or set aside by an order of the court[4];

(4) contains the entire understanding of the (co-owners) [OR] (parties to it) and supersedes any previous agreements, representations and promises made by them in respect of the property[5].

[1] LPA 1925, s 53(1)(b) requires that 'a declaration of trust respecting any land or any interest therein must be manifested and proved by some writing signed by some person who is able to declare such trust or by his will'. Although the declaration must be in writing, it is not essential that it be executed as a deed, unless there are covenants in it.
[2] Law of Property (Miscellaneous Provisions) Act 1989, s 1.
[3] For a form of deed of variation, see **1.225** below.
[4] For example, the court could set the declaration of trust aside on the grounds of fraud or mistake (*City of London Building Society v Flegg* [1988] AC 54; *Wilson v Wilson* [1969] 1 WLR 1470). The beneficial interests may also be affected by orders under, for example the IA 1986, the CA 1989, the I(PFD)A 1975.
[5] *Lloyds Bank Plc v Rosset* [1990] 1 All ER 1111 at 1118.

1.199

Execution in duplicate[1]

This Declaration of Trust has been executed in (duplicate)/(triplicate)/(quadruplicate) so that each (co-owner) [OR] (person who has a beneficial interest in the property) may possess a copy of it, and (both)/(all) copies will be regarded as one deed, and each copy will be as efficacious as the other(s).

[1] For the effect of multiple execution of deeds see, generally, Co Litt 229a, and *Burchell v Clark* (1876) 2 CPD 88 at 96.

1.200

Attestation clause[1]

SIGNED as a Deed by (*name 1*) in the presence of:

SIGNED as a Deed by (*name 2*) in the presence of:

[1] It is usual, but not essential, for a declaration of trust to be executed as a deed. For provisions relating to deeds and their execution, see the Law of Property (Miscellaneous Provisions) Act 1989, s 1.

E *Contingencies*

1.201

If the co-owners permit any other person to reside with them in the property[1]

SCHEDULE (*number*)

(1) This Schedule applies if:

(1.1) the co-owners permit any other person to reside with them in the property; and

(1.2) there is no alternative agreement between the co-owners.

(2) In this Schedule:

(2.1) 'the licensee' means any person (aged 18 or over) who normally resides with the co-owners, whether or not he or she is related to or dependent on either of them[2], and

1.201 *Property*

- (2.2) 'the licence' means the terms and conditions on which the co-owners permit the licensee to occupy the property.
- (3) The co-owners permit the licensee to occupy the property as a bare licensee[3].
- (4) The licensee will have no right to exclusive possession of the property or any part of it[4].
- (5) The licensee will not acquire any tenancy or beneficial interest in the property despite:
  - (5.1) any payment the licensee makes to either or both of the co-owners as a contribution towards his or her living and accommodation expenses; and
  - (5.2) any repairs or improvements to the property which the licensee carries out with or without the consent of the co-owners.
- (6) The licence can be terminated by the licensee at any time[5].
- (7) The licence can be revoked by either of the co-owners at any time[6].
- (8) The licence is personal to the licensee and cannot be transferred by him or her to any other person.
- (9) The co-owners will take whatever steps are necessary to ensure that the licensee clearly understands the terms and conditions on which he or she is permitted to occupy the property.

[1] The co-owners may permit other occupants to reside with them in a variety of circumstances: for example lodgers, the grown-up child of one of the co-owners or the boyfriend or girlfriend of a co-owner. This Schedule provides that, in the absence of any contrary agreement between the co-owners, the other occupant will be a bare licensee. In many cases where the occupation of premises is shared on an informal basis, particularly if the parties are related, the non-owner will have a bare licence. If, however, an intention to create legal relations can be found together with some form of consideration, there may be a contractual licence.

[2] Although, in general, a bare licence can be revoked at any time, the licence of a child (even an adult child) to remain in the home will only be revocable in exceptional circumstances (*Egan v Egan* [1975] Ch 218).

[3] Anyone sharing residential accommodation with the consent of the owners is, at the very least, a bare licensee. The owners' consent to the sharing of accommodation prevents the licensee from being a trespasser.

[4] Without exclusive possession there cannot be a tenancy. A lodger will always be a licensee and never a tenant. 'The occupier is a lodger if the landlord provides attendance or services which require the landlord or his servants to exercise unrestricted access to and use of the premises. A lodger is entitled to live in the premises but cannot call the place his own' (*Street v Mountford* [1985] AC 809 at 818, per Lord Templeman).

[5] *Australian Blue Metal v Hughes* [1963] AC 74 at 98.

[6] The licence can be revoked by either co-owner at will and without notice (*Crane v Morris* [1965] 1 WLR 1104 at 1108). The licence can also be revoked by one co-owner without reference to the other (*Annen v Rattee* (1984) 273 EG 503, CA).

1.202

If a co-owner fails to pay his or her share of the mortgage payments[1]

SCHEDULE (number)

- (1) This Schedule applies if:
  - (1.1) there is no alternative agreement between the co-owners; and

(1.2) one of the co-owners ('the debtor') is unable or unwilling or otherwise fails to pay his or her share of the mortgage payments when it is due; and

(1.3) the other co-owner ('the creditor') pays all or part of the debtor's share of the mortgage payments on the debtor's behalf. (; and

(1.4) the provisions of Schedule(s) do not apply)[2].

(2) The payment made by the creditor on the debtor's behalf ('the loan') will be treated as a loan from the creditor to the debtor.

(3) The loan is made on the condition that:

(3.1) it must be repaid as soon as possible; and

(3.2) if it has not been repaid within (3) months from the date on which it was made, the loan, or so much of it as remains outstanding, will bear interest at a rate of (one) per cent a year above the rate of interest payable from time to time in respect of the mortgage (before)/(after) the deduction of basic rate income tax.

[1] 'Where . . . a fund is being distributed, a party cannot take anything out of the fund until he has made good what he owes to the fund' (*Re Rhodesia Goldfields Ltd* [1910] 1 Ch 239 at 247, per Swinfen Eady J). Anyone who discharges another's secured obligation, wholly or in part, is entitled to be repaid, out of the security, the amount of the sum or sums paid by him (*Pitt v Pitt* (1823) Turn & R 180; *Outram v Hyde* [1875] 24 WR 268; *Cowcher v Cowcher* [1972] 1 All ER 943 at 951).

[2] For example if a co-owner is unemployed or incapable of working (see **1.207** below), if a co-owner is unemployed or incapable of working because of pregnancy or childcare (see **1.208** below), or if a co-owner attends a full-time course of education (see **1.209** below).

1.203

If one co-owner wishes to sell the property and the other co-owner refuses to sell it

SCHEDULE (*number*)*

(1) This Schedule applies if:**

(1.1) there is no alternative agreement between the co-owners; and

(1.2) one of the co-owners ('the applicant') wishes to sell the property; and

(1.3) the other co-owner ('the objector') refuses to sell it.

(2) The applicant will give written notice to the objector of the applicant's wish to sell the property.

(3) The date on which the objector receives that notice is 'the application *date*'.

(4) After the end of a period of (12) weeks beginning on the application date the applicant can apply to the court for an order that the property be sold if:***

(4.1) the objector has not contractually agreed to purchase the applicant's estate and interest in the property; and

(4.2) the objector refuses to sell the property.

* This precedent could be used in conjunction with the precedent at **1.181**. If both precedents are used, it is essential to ensure that the *date*s on which an application can be made to the court coincide.

** The rule that it was the prime duty of trustees for sale to sell the property was abolished by the TOLATA 1996.

*** The application shall be made under the TOLATA 1996.

1.204 Property

1.204

If one co-owner dies and the other does not become solely and beneficially entitled to the property

SCHEDULE (number)

(1) This Schedule applies if:

 (1.1) one of the co-owners ('the deceased') dies; and

 (1.2) the other co-owner ('the survivor') does not become solely and beneficially entitled to the property[1].

(2) This Schedule applies subject to and without prejudice to all rights that the survivor may have under the deceased's will[2] and generally in law[3].

(3) The survivor will be primarily liable for:

 (3.1) the payment of the mortgage;

 (3.2) the payment of all outgoings on the property;

 (3.3) keeping the property adequately insured; and

 (3.4) keeping the property in reasonable repair and condition.

(4) In this Schedule:

 (4.1) 'the death' means the date on which the deceased died;

 (4.2) 'the share' means the deceased's beneficial interest in the property; and

 (4.3) 'the estate' may mean either the deceased's personal representative(s) or the person(s) entitled to the share under the deceased's will or the law relating to intestacy[4].

(5) If the survivor is asked to do so, he or she will, as soon as practicable after the death, appoint the estate to be a new trustee of the property and will register the new trustee as a joint proprietor of the property, and the costs of effecting such appointment and registration will be paid by the estate[5].

(6) When the property or the share is sold the estate will be credited with a lump sum payment by way of reimbursement of all (if any) mortgage payments it has made in respect of the property since the death.

(7) Part 1 of this Schedule applies during the period of (6) months beginning with the death ('the concessionary period')[6].

(8) Part 2 of this Schedule applies after the end of the concessionary period.

Part 1

(9) During the concessionary period the survivor can reside in the property rent-free.

(10) During the concessionary period the value of the share can be discounted by per cent, by virtue of the fact that the property is jointly owned[7].

(11) During the concessionary period the survivor's nominee can purchase the share for its value immediately after the death[8].

Part 2

(12) After the concessionary period the estate can apply to the court for an order that the property be sold[9].

(13) After the concessionary period the value of the share will not be discounted even though the property is jointly owned[10].

(14) After the concessionary period the survivor will pay an occupation rent to the estate[11].

(15) The occupation rent will be such proportion of the fair rent as the value of the share bears to the value of the whole of the net proceeds of sale of the property.

(16) The fair rent is the market rent that would be payable for the property between a willing landlord and willing tenant[12].

[1] This Schedule would not apply if the co-owners were beneficial joint tenants, or if the deceased had, by will, made an absolute gift of his or her share to the survivor.
[2] For example a life or lesser interest, or an option to purchase.
[3] For example, under the I(PFD)A 1975.
[4] The definition of 'the estate' is inevitably vague. Much will depend on the circumstances of each individual case.
[5] For the recommended procedures where registered land is held on a trust of land and it is necessary to appoint a new trustee, see Ruoff and Roper *Registered Conveyancing* (Sweet & Maxwell, Looseleaf) at para 32–18.
[6] The concessionary period is designed to safeguard the survivor's rights of occupation for a reasonable time, and to encourage the survivor to purchase the deceased's share.
[7] In *Wight and Another v IRC* (1982) 264 ERG 935, Lands Tribunal, it was held that, because it was unlikely that a purchaser would be able to obtain an order for sale under LPA 1925, s 30, the discount in the value of a half share for capital transfer tax purposes should be 15 per cent.
[8] The words 'immediately after the death' should cover the effect of the payments of any mortgage-linked insurance policy proceeds, and the valuation discount which applies during the concessionary period.
[9] The application would be made under the TOLATA 1996. See, **1.62** above.
[10] See footnote above.
[11] For 'occupation rent', see generally: *Leake v Bruzzi* [1974] 1 WLR 1528; *Suttill v Graham* [1977] 1 WLR 819; and *Dennis v McDonald* (1982) 3 FLR 398. Since the introduction of shorthold tenancies a market rent may be more appropriate.
[12] See the dicta of Sir John Arnold P in *Dennis v McDonald* (1982) 3 FLR 398 at 409.

1.205

If a co-owner is declared bankrupt[1]

SCHEDULE (number)

(1) This Schedule applies if one of the co-owners ('the bankrupt') is declared bankrupt.

(2) The provisions of this Schedule are:

(2.1) not a matter for agreement or negotiation between the co-owners;

(2.2) an abbreviated summary of the law;

(2.3) included in this Declaration of Trust for information purposes only.

(3) The bankrupt's beneficial interest in the property will automatically vest in his or her trustee in bankruptcy ('the trustee')[2].

1.205 *Property*

- (4) The trustee has a statutory duty to get in, realise and distribute the bankrupt's estate[3] and in the exercise of that duty the trustee may apply to the court for an order that the property be sold[4].

- (5) The bankrupt's rights of occupation will depend on whether a child under 18 was living with the bankrupt at:

    - (5.1) the time when the bankruptcy petition was presented; and

    - (5.2) the commencement of the bankruptcy[5].

- (6) If the bankrupt has entered into a transaction at an undervalue with anyone else in respect of his or her share of the property, the trustee may apply to the court for an order restoring the position to what it would have been if the bankrupt had not entered into that transaction[6].

[1] Note para 2. This Schedule is purely for information purposes.
[2] IA 1986, s 306.
[3] IA 1986, s 305(2) and Ch IV.
[4] An order under TOLATA 1996, s 14.
[5] IA 1986, ss 336 and 337. See *Re Gorman (A Bankrupt), ex parte Trustee of the Bankrupt v The Bankrupt* [1990] 1 WLR 616.
[6] IA 1986, s 339. For the 'relevant time' limits, see IA 1986, s 341.

IF THE CO-OWNERS EXTEND, ALTER, IMPROVE OR REPAIR THE PROPERTY

1.206

Conversion from fixed shares to floating shares[1]

SCHEDULE *(number)*

- (1) This Schedule applies if the co-owners:

    - (1.1) carry out building works (as defined below); and

    - (1.2) contribute towards the cost of the building works disproportionately to their respective shares of the net proceeds of sale; and

    - (1.3) fail to execute a further Declaration of Trust to reflect the change in circumstances.

- (2) This Schedule also applies if the co-owners:

    - (2.1) carry out building works; and

    - (2.2) take out a loan or further mortgage for that purpose; and

    - (2.3) repay or are in the process of repaying that loan or further mortgage disproportionately to the shares in which they had been making the mortgage payments before the building works commenced; and

    - (2.4) fail to execute a further Declaration of Trust to reflect the change in circumstances.

- (3) In this Schedule 'building works' means any works of a major nature which enhance or are intended to enhance the value of the property, and includes, but is not restricted to:

    - (3.1) the building of an extension to the property;

    - (3.2) major alterations to the exterior or interior of the property;

    - (3.3) the conversion of the property into separate flats or units;

(3.4) major works undertaken with a view to improving the fitness of the property for occupation;

(3.5) the purchase of additional land to be enjoyed with the property;

(3.6) the construction of a garage or outbuildings;

(3.7) major works affecting the landscape of the garden;

(3.8) major works to the boundaries;

(3.9) major works connected with the access to or exit from the property;

(3.10) all works analogous to those listed above.

(4) Immediately before the building works commence the property will be valued or will be treated as having been valued ('the unimproved value').

(5) The unimproved value will be assessed:

(5.1) by the co-owners themselves at such figure as they agree; or

(5.2) by a professionally qualified property valuer instructed by the co-owners; or

(5.3) if the co-owners fail to agree the unimproved value or on instructing a valuer, by a valuer appointed by the President of the Royal Institution of Chartered Surveyors.

(6) Immediately before the building works commence there will be a deemed sale of the property by the co-owners as if:

(6.1) it were being sold at the unimproved value; and

(6.2) each co-owner were able to realise his or her share ('the fixed share') of the net proceeds of sale calculated in accordance with the provisions of Clause (*number*) of this Declaration of Trust.

(7) Immediately after the deemed sale of the property there will be a deemed re-acquisition of it by the co-owners as if:

(7.1) they were acquiring it at the unimproved value; and

(7.2) the fixed share of each co-owner were his or her cash contribution towards the acquisition price.

(8) Immediately after the deemed re-acquisition of the property the provisions of Clause (*number*) of this Declaration of Trust relating to the calculation of the co-owners' shares of the net proceeds of sale will cease to have effect and the following provisions will apply.

(9) After the deemed re-acquisition of the property the co-owners will hold the property and its net proceeds of sale in trust for themselves as beneficial tenants in common in shares which are proportionate to the contributions made by each of them towards the deemed re-acquisition of the property and the payments made by each of them after the deemed re-acquisition towards:

(9.1) the building works;

(9.2) any subsequent building works;

(9.3) mortgage interest;

(9.4) mortgage capital;

(9.5) mortgage-linked insurance premiums;

1.206 Property

- (9.6) interest and capital on loans taken out for the purpose of carrying out the building works and any subsequent building works; and
- (9.7) the incidental costs of selling the property.
- (10) (Formulae for calculating floating shares.)[2]

Example

A and B decided to 'improve' their house. In its unimproved state it is worth £88,000. The amount required to redeem their mortgage is £48,000. When they bought the house they executed a declaration of trust which stated that A would receive 75 per cent of the net proceeds of sale, and B would receive 25 per cent.

The building works take exactly a year to complete. During that time B pays £21,000 towards the works and £1,000 towards the mortgage payments. During that time A pays £5,000 towards the works and £3,000 towards the mortgage payments.

As soon as the building works have been completed, A and B decide to move house. They sell the house for £128,000. The amount required to redeem their mortgage is still £48,000. The net proceeds of sale come to £80,000. Who gets what?

If their declaration of trust had not incorporated this Schedule, A would still be entitled to 75 per cent of the net proceeds, and B 25 per cent. On that basis A would receive £60,000 and B would receive £20,000.

The effect of this Schedule is to create a deemed sale and re-acquisition of the property when the building works begin, and to convert A's and B's shares from fixed shares to floating shares.

Since the deemed re-acquisition, A's contributions have been £30,000 (A's original 75 per cent fixed share treated as downpayment on the re-acquisition) plus £5,000 (towards the building works) plus £3,000 (A's mortgage payments). So, A's total contribution has been £38,000.

Since the deemed re-acquisition, B's contributions have been £10,000 (B's original 25 per cent fixed share treated as downpayment on the re-acquisition) plus £21,000 (towards the bulding works) plus £1,000 (B's share of the mortgage). So, B's total contribution has been £32,000.

The net proceeds of sale (£80,000) are divided between A and B in the proportions 38:52. A receives £43,429 and B receives £39,571. The incidental costs of selling the property are paid by them in the same proportions.

[1] For the distinction between fixed shares and floating shares and a discussion of their advantages and disadvantages, see **1.9** above. See *Example*.
[2] See Precedents **1.170–1.174** above.

1.207

If a co-owner is unemployed or incapable of working[1]

SCHEDULE (number)

- (1) This Schedule applies if:
- (1.1) the co-owners are living together[2]; and
- (1.2) one of the co-owners ('the unemployed co-owner') is unemployed or incapable of working; and
- (1.3) because of a reduction in his or her income the unemployed co-owner has difficulty in maintaining his or her share of the mortgage payments; and
- (1.4) the co-owners do not execute a further Declaration of Trust to reflect the change in circumstances; and
- (1.5) the provisions of Schedule (number) do not apply[3].
- (2) The unemployed co-owner will do all he or she can to contribute towards the mortgage payments from whatever resources are available to him or her[4].

(3) Subject to the above, the other co-owner will be responsible for all the mortgage payments from the date on which the unemployed co-owner ceased to be employed or his or her incapacity to work began ('the commencement *date*')[5].

(4) The mortgage payments made by the other co-owner on behalf of the unemployed co-owner:

(4.1) during the period of (6) months[6] starting on the commencement date will not affect the beneficial interests of either co-owner in the property;

(4.2) after the end of the period of (6) months starting on the commencement date will be treated as a loan from the other co-owner to the unemployed co-owner[7].

(5) The loan is made on the basis that:

(5.1) it must be repaid as soon as possible; and

(5.2) if it has not been repaid before the property is sold it, or so much of it as remains outstanding, will be repaid to the other co-owner out of the unemployed co-owner's share of the net proceeds of sale.

[1] '... the judge must look at the contributions of each to the "family" finances and determine as best he may what contribution each was making towards the purchase of the house. This is not to be carried out as a strictly mathematical exercise; for instance, if the man was ill for a time and out of work so that the woman temporarily contributed more, that temporary state of affairs should not increase her share, nor should her share be decreased if she was temporarily unable to work whilst having a baby. The contributions must be viewed broadly by the judge to guide him to the parties' unexpressed, and probably unconsidered, intentions as to the beneficial ownership of the house' (*Bernard v Josephs* (1983) 4 FLR 178 at 188, per Griffiths LJ).

[2] If the parties were not living together the temporary support obligation contained in para 4.1 of this Schedule might be considered inappropriate.

[3] For example, **1.208** and **1.209** below.

[4] For example, savings or any redundancy payment.

[5] Alternatively, the commencement date could be the date on which the unemployed co-owner is no longer able to keep up his or her agreed share of the mortgage payments.

[6] The timespan which the co-owners consider appropriate in the circumstances shold be inserted here. Note that in the passage from *Bernard v Josephs* (above), Griffiths LJ merely envisaged a 'temporary state of affairs' which should not affect the beneficial interests.

[7] If the co-owners wish to penalise 'fault', a further paragraph should be added to the effect that: 'Despite the provisions of paragraph 4 of this Schedule all mortgage payments made by the other co-owner on behalf of the unemployed co-owner will be treated as a loan (a) from the commencement date itself if the unemployed co-owner lost employment through misconduct or voluntarily left employment without good cause; or (b) from the date on which the unemployed co-owner, without good cause, refused or failed to take a reasonable opportunity to secure employment'.

1.208

If a co-owner is unemployed or incapable of working because she is pregnant or he or she is looking after a child or children[1]

SCHEDULE *(number)*

(1) This Schedule applies if:

(1.1) the co-owners are living together[2]; and

(1.2) *(name 2)* is unemployed or incapable of working because she is pregnant; and

(1.3) either of the co-owners is unemployed or incapable of working because he or she is looking after his, her or their child or children; and

(1.4) that co-owner who is unemployed or incapable of working has difficulty in maintaining his or her share of the mortgage payments because of a reduction in his or her income; and

(1.5) the co-owners fail to execute a further Declaration of Trust to reflect the change in circumstances.

(2) The co-owner who is unemployed or incapable of working will do all he or she can to contribute towards the mortgage payments from whatever resources are available[3].

(3) Subject to the above, the other co-owner will be responsible for all the mortgage payments, and the mortgage payments that he or she makes will not affect the beneficial interests of either co-owner in the property.

[1] Note the dicta of Griffiths LJ in *Bernard v Josephs* (1983) 4 FLR 178 at 188 (see fn 1 to Precedent **1.207** above). In his view the woman's share should not be decreased 'if she was temporarily unable to work whilst having a baby' (*Bernard v Josephs* (1983) 4 FLR 178 at 188B). The word 'temporarily' is significant. The implication is that if the state of affairs is anything other than 'temporary', the beneficial interests should be affected.

[2] The support obligation might be considered inappropriate if the co-owners are not living together.

[3] For example, enhanced maternity pay from an employer, statutory maternity pay or savings.

IF A CO-OWNER ATTENDS A FULL-TIME COURSE OF EDUCATION

1.209

Mortgage payments made by the other co-owner to be treated as a loan[1]

SCHEDULE (*number*)

(1) This Schedule applies if:

(1.1) one of the co-owners ('the student') attends a full-time course of education ('the course'); and

(1.2) the course does not last for more than (one year); and

(1.3) the student has difficulty in maintaining his or her share of the mortgage payments because of a reduction in his or her income; and

(1.4) the co-owners do not execute a further Declaration of Trust to reflect the change in circumstances.

(2) The student will do all that he or she can to contribute towards the mortgage payments from whatever resources are available[2].

(3) Subject to the above, the other co-owner will be responsible for the mortgage payments from the date on which the student begins the course.

(4) The mortgage payments made by the other co-owner on the student's behalf will be treated as a loan to the student from the other co-owner.

(5) The loan is made on the basis that:

(5.1) it is interest free; and

(5.2) the student will repay the loan as soon as he or she can; and

(5.3) if it has not been repaid before the property is sold, the loan, or so much of it as remains outstanding, will be repaid to the other co-owner out of the student's share of the net proceeds of sale.

[1] This precedent is intended to cover 'a temporary state of affairs' which should not materially affect the beneficial interests of either co-owner (*Bernard v Josephs* (1983) 4 FLR 178 at 188). It assumes that the course is of comparatively short duration and will last no longer than, say, one academic year. If the course is of a longer duration, perhaps the beneficial interests should be affected: in which case Precedent **1.210** may be preferred, or used in addition to this precedent. This precedent establishes that the payments made on the student's behalf by the other co-owner are to be treated as a loan, and not a gift.

Query: If the student is not living in the property during term-time, should the other co-owner be paying the student an 'occupation rent'? (*Dennis v McDonald* (1982) 3 FLR 398).

[2] For example from savings, scholarship income, a student loan or a grant.

1.210

Conversion of fixed shares into floating shares[1]

SCHEDULE (*number*)

(1) This Schedule applies if:

(1.1) one of the co-owners ('the student') attends a full-time course of education ('the course'); and

(1.2) the course lasts or is expected to last for more than (one year); and

(1.3) while the student is on the course the other co-owner pays a larger share of the mortgage payments than he or she had originally agreed to pay (in Clause of this Declaration of Trust); and

(1.4) the co-owners do not execute a further Declaration of Trust to reflect the change in circumstances.

(2) Immediately before the student begins the course:

(2.1) the property will be valued or treated as having been valued ('the pre-course value'); and

(2.2) a statement of the amount required to redeem the mortgage will be obtained or treated as having been obtained.

(3) Immediately before the student begins the course there will be a deemed sale of the property as if:

(3.1) it were being sold by the co-owners at the pre-course value; and

(3.2) each co-owner could then realise his or her fixed share of the net proceeds of sale ('the fixed share') calculated in accordance with the provisions of Clause of this Declaration of Trust.

(4) Immediately after this deemed sale of the property there will be a deemed re-acquisition of it by the co-owners as if:

(4.1) they were acquiring it at the pre-course value; and

(4.2) each co-owner's fixed share were his or her cash contribution towards the acquisition price.

(5) Immediately after the deemed re-acquisition of the property the provisions of Clause of this Declaration of Trust relating to the calculation of the fixed share of each co-owner will cease to have effect and the following provisions will apply instead.

1.210 *Property*

(6) After the deemed re-acquisition of the property the co-owners will hold the property and its net proceeds of sale in trust for themselves as beneficial tenants in common in shares which are proportionate to the contributions made by each of them towards the deemed re-acquisition of the property and the payments made by each of them after the deemed re-acquisition towards:

    (6.1) mortgage interest;

    (6.2) mortgage capital;

    (6.3) mortgage-linked insurance premiums;

    (6.4) repairs and improvements to the property;

    (6.5) interest and capital on loans taken out for the purpose of carrying out repairs and improvements to the property; and

    (6.6) the incidental costs of selling the property.

(7) The share of the net proceeds of sale to which each co-owner will be entitled will be calculated in accordance with the provisions of Schedule (*number*)[2].

Example

In July 1988, A and B bought a terraced house. They contributed more or less the same amount towards the purchase price, and agreed to share the mortgage payments equally. They executed a declaration of trust stating that they were beneficial tenants in common in equal shares. In October 1990, A began a 3-year course leading to a degree in computer studies. At that time the house was worth £45,000, and the amount required to redeem their mortgage was £30,000. While A was away studying, B remained in the house and made all the mortgage payments herself. Christmas 1991 was not a happy time for them. Each, quite rightly, suspected that the other had found a new partner. So, they decided to go their own separate ways.

In June 1992, the house was sold for £40,000. The amount required to redeem the mortgage was still £30,000. The net proceeds of sale came to £10,000. Who got what?

If they followed the 50:50 shareout in their declaration of trust, B and A would have received £5,000 each.

However, the effect of the incorporation of this Schedule into their declaration of trust meant that their fixed shares (50:50) were converted into floating shares when A began his computer studies course.

B paid the mortgage on her own for 20 months, while A paid nothing. The total mortgage payments she made came to £5,500. So, B's 'floating share' was worth a basic £13,000, which represented her cash contribution to the deemed re-acquisition of the property in October 1990 (£7,500) plus the £5,500 which B contributed towards the mortgage payments. A's 'floating share' remained stationary at £7,500, being A's cash contribution to the deemed re-acquisition.

The net proceeds of sale (£10,000) were divided between them in the ratio 13,000:7,500. B was entitled to £6,341, and A was entitled to £3,659. The incidental costs of selling the property came to £1,250. These were paid in the same ratios: B paid £793 and A £457.

[1] For the distinction between fixed shares and floating shares, see **1.9** above. For a discussion of the relative advantages and disadvantages of each type of shareholding, see **1.10–1.13** above.

This precedent is intended to cover the situation where one of the co-owners embarks on a comparatively lengthy course of further education, ie one which will last for more than, say, one year. In this case the beneficial interets of the co-owners are affected. By contrast **1.209** above is designed to deal with a more temporary state of affairs, where the course lasts for no longer than, say, one year, and the beneficial interests are not materially affected. See Example.

[2] For the formulae for calculating floating shares, see **1.170–1.174** above.

IF BOTH CO-OWNERS WISH TO KEEP THE PROPERTY

1.211

One co-owner to have prior rights

SCHEDULE (number)

(1) This schedule applies if:

    (1.1) the co-owners are about to separate or have recently separated[1]; and

    (1.2) both of them wish to keep the property; and

    (1.3) neither of them is willing to relinquish the property to the other; and

    (1.4) each of them is able to purchase the other's share.

(2) (*Name 2*) will have the right to remain in the property and to purchase (*name 1's*) share in it (because) (*state reasons, if considered appropriate*).

(3) This Schedule will not apply if:

    (3.1) the co-owners have been living apart for a continuous period of at least (2) months; and

    (3.2) (*name 1*) has been living in the property during the whole of that period.

[1] The words 'or have recently separated' are intended to cover the possibility of constructive desertion.

1.212

Rules for determining who has prior rights

SCHEDULE (number)

(1.1) The co-owners are about to separate or have recently separated; and

(1.2) both of them wish to keep the property; and

(1.3) neither of them is willing to relinquish the property to the other; and

(1.4) each of them is able to purchase the other's share.

(2) The co-owner who has the superior right to remain in the property and to purchase the other's share in it will be determined in accordance with the following order of priority, and the co-owner who is first described in this list will be preferred to the other co-owner;

    (2.1) the co-owner with whom a child under the age of 18 will live after the co-owners have separated;

    (2.2) if the preceding category applies equally to both of the co-owners, the co-owner with whom the greater number of children under 18 will live after the co-owners have separated;

    (2.3) if both of the preceding categories apply equally to both of the co-owners, the co-owner with whom the children whose school is nearest to the property will live after the co-owners have separated;

    (2.4) the co-owner whose only or principal place of business is at the property;

1.212 *Property*

- (2.5) the co-owner whose only or principal place of business or employment is nearer to the property;
- (2.6) the co-owner who is entitled to the larger share of the net proceeds of sale of the property.

(3) This Schedule will not apply if:

- (3.1) the co-owners have been living apart for a continuous period of at least (2) months; and
- (3.2) the co-owner who does not have the superior right to remain in the property has been living in the property during the whole of that period.

1.213

If a co-owner moves out before the property is sold

SCHEDULE (*number*)

(1) Applicability

This Schedule applies if:

- (1.1) one of the co-owners ('the non-resident') ceases permanently to reside in the property[1]; and
- (1.2) the other co-owner ('the occupier') continues to reside in the property; and
- (1.3) there is no alternative agreement between the co-owners. [; and
- (1.4) the provisions of Schedule (*number*) do not apply.][2]

(2) Crystallisation of shares

The co-owners' respective shares of the net proceeds of sale of the property will be quantified and will crystallise on the date on which the non-resident leaves the property with the intention of never resuming residence in it with the occupier ('the separation *date*')[3].

(3) The settlement *date*

In this Schedule 'the settlement *date*' means the date on which the non-resident:

- (3.1) receives his or her share of the net proceeds of sale of the property together with the additions but subject to the deductions mentioned below; or
- (3.2) receives such sum as he or she has agreed to accept in full and final settlement in consideration of the transfer of his or her legal estate and beneficial interest in the property; or
- (3.3) pays to the occupier such sum as the occupier has agreed to accept in full and final settlement in consideration of the transfer of the occupier's legal estate and beneficial interest in the property to the non-resident or to such other person(s) as the non-resident directs.

(4) Election

If the settlement date is more than (6) months after the separation date the non-resident can elect to have the value of his or her share on the settlement date substituted for its value on the separation *date*4.

(5) Occupier's post-separation contributions

Before the net proceeds of sale are divided, the occupier will be credited with a lump sum payment equal to all the payments that he or she has made during the period between the separation date and the settlement date towards:

(5.1) the mortgage; and

(5.2) repairs and improvements to the property.

(6) Non-resident's post-separation contributions

Before the net proceeds of sale are divided, the non-resident will be credited with a lump sum payment equal to all the payments (if any) that he or she has made during the period between the separation date and the settlement date towards:

(6.1) the mortgage; and

(6.2) repairs and improvements to the property.

(7) Occupation rent

(7.1) Before the net proceeds of sale are divided, the non-resident will be credited with a lump sum payment representing an occupation rent in respect of the occupier's occupation of the property during the period from the separation date to the settlement date or during such shorter period as the non-resident agrees;

(7.2) the occupation rent will be such proportion of the fair rent as the value of the non-resident's share bears to the value of the whole of the net proceeds of sale on the separation *date*;

(7.3) the fair rent is the market rent that would be payable for the property between a willing landlord and a willing tenant[5].

[1] For a discussion of the meanings of expressions such as 'ceases permanently to reside', see *Re Coxen* [1948] 2 All ER 492 at 500.

[2] For example the schedule in **1.214** below.

[3] Note that in *Hall v Hall* (1982) 3 FLR 379, the Court of Appeal held that the equity was to be valued when the parties separated. This decision was not followed by the same court in *Turton v Turton* [1988] 1 FLR 23 at 34A, where Kerr LJ stated that:

' . . . unless there is some express declaration or agreement to the effect that the parties' respective beneficial shares are to be valued at the time of their separation if and when this should occur, there could never be any sufficient ground for attributing any such intention to them merely by implication from the circumstances. In the result, therefore, the parties' beneficial interests would always have to be regarded in the normal way under a trust for sale, with the effect that they would until such time as the property is sold, and that they will then attach to the proceeds of sale.'.

[4] It may be sensible to include a clause to this effect in order to cover fluctuations in value during inflationary and deflationary periods.

[5] For consideration of the proper way in which an 'occupation rent' should be assessed, see *Dennis v McDonald* (1982) 3 FLR 398. Since the introduction of shorthold tenancies a market rent may be more appropriate.

1.214

If the co-owners separate shortly after they purchase the property[1]

SCHEDULE (number)

(1) This Schedule applies if:

1.214 *Property*

- (1.1) the co-owners separate within a period of (12) months from the date (on which they completed the purchase of the property) [OR] (of this Declaration of Trust); and
- (1.2) it is possible to procure the release of the non-resident (as defined below) from his or her obligations under the mortgage; and
- (1.3) there is no alternative agreement between the co-owners.

(2) In this Schedule:

- (2.1) 'the occupier' means the co-owner who continues to occupy the property;
- (2.2) 'the non-resident' means the co-owner who has ceased to reside in the property;
- (2.3) 'the non-resident's share' means all the legal estate and beneficial interest of the non-resident in the property freed and discharged from his or her obligations under the mortgage;
- (2.4) 'the separation *date*' means the date on which the non-resident left the property with the intention of never resuming residence in it with the occupier, being a date within a period of (12) months from the date (of completion of the purchase of the property) [OR] (of this Declaration of Trust).

(3) Within a period of (3) months beginning on the separation date the occupier can purchase the non-resident's share for the amount that the non-resident paid towards the purchase price of the property (and the incidental costs of purchasing it), disregarding the amounts which the non-resident has paid towards:

- (3.1) the mortgage interest;
- (3.2) the mortgage capital;
- (3.3) mortgage-linked insurance premiums;
- (3.4) repairs and improvements to the property; and
- (3.5) the incidental costs of purchasing the property[2].

(4) If at the end of a period of (3) months beginning on the separation *date*, the occupier has not purchased the non-resident's share for the amount stated above or for such lesser amount as the non-resident has agreed, the non-resident can apply to the court for an order that the property be sold.

(5) The non-resident can elect that the provisions of this Schedule will not apply, but only if:

- (5.1) their application would result in an unconscionable gain for the occupier; and
- (5.2) the circumstances are such that the occupier has effectively ousted the non-resident from the property[3].

[1] This Schedule is designed to cover the practical problems arising if the co-owners separate within, say, 12 months of completing the purchase of the property. The party remaining in occupation is given an opportunity to buy out the share of the partner who has left the property for the leaver's original cash contribution towards the purchase price, or such lesser sum as the leaver agrees.

[2] The incidental costs of the purchase must be included either in the amount for which the occupier is able to purchase the leaver's share, or as one of the payments made by the leaver

which can be disregarded. Other disregards might include the price paid towards any fitted carpets and curtains.

3   This clause is intended to avoid inequity in a case of constructive desertion. Its application is not necessarily limited to a period of inflationary property prices. The leaver might have been paying the lion's share of the mortgage payments; or could have paid a substantial amount towards repairs and improvements to the property.

1.215

If a co-owner wishes to realise his or her share in the property[1]

SCHEDULE (number)

- (1) This Schedule applies if:
    - (1.1) one of the co-owners ('the seller') wishes to realise his or her beneficial interest in the property ('the share'); and
    - (1.2) there is no alternative agreement between the co-owners.
- (2) At his or her own expense the seller will obtain the following information ('the relevant information'):
    - (2.1) a valuation of the open market value of the property prepared by a professionally qualified property valuer who is familiar with the locality of the property;
    - (2.2) an up-to-*date* statement of the amount required to redeem the mortgage and every other charge to which the property is subject;
    - (2.3) an up-to-*date* statement of the surrender value of all mortgage-linked insurance policies; and
    - (2.4) all other information which may be relevant to the valuation of the co-owners' respective shares.
- (3) The seller will give to the other co-owner ('the buyer'):
    - (3.1) the relevant information; and
    - (3.2) a written offer to sell the share ('the offer').
- (4) The date on which the buyer receives the relevant information and the offer is 'the offer *date*'.
- (5) The offer will state:
    - (5.1) the price at which the seller is willing to sell the share to the buyer or the buyer's nominee;
    - (5.2) the date on which the seller wishes to complete the transaction, being a date at least (8) weeks after the offer *date*; and
    - (5.3) all the other terms and conditions (if any) on which the seller is willing to sell the share.
- (6) At his or her own expense the buyer can obtain any further information which may be relevant to the valuation of the co-owners' respective shares.
- (7) Within a period of (4) weeks beginning on the offer date the buyer can either:
    - (7.1) accept the offer in writing and comunicate such acceptance to the seller; or
    - (7.2) give to the seller a written counter-offer ('the counter-offer').
- (8) The counter-offer will state:

(8.1) all the terms and conditions (including the price and completion *date*) on which the buyer or the buyer's nominee is willing to buy the share; or

(8.2) all the terms and conditions (including the price and completion *date*) on which the buyer is willing to sell the buyer's share in the property to the seller or the seller's nominee.

(9) All negotiations between the co-owners should be concluded within a period of (8) weeks beginning on the offer *date*.

(10) After the end of a period of (12) weeks beginning on the offer date either co-owner can apply to the court for an order that the property be sold if:

(10.1) neither co-owner has agreed to buy the other's share; and

(10.2) the other co-owner refuses to sell the property[2].

[1] With some minor adaptations to reflect their respective bargaining positions, this Schedule could be applied *mutatis mutandis* if one co-owner wishes to 'buy out' the other.
[2] The application would be made under TOLATA 1996, s 14. See **1.62** above.

F Forms

DECLARATION OF TRUST BY CO-OWNERS

1.216

Fixed shares: Short form

THIS DECLARATION OF TRUST is made on (*date*)

BETWEEN 'the co-owners' (1) (*name 1*) of (*address*) ('*name 1*') and (2) (*name 2*) also of (*address*) ('*name 2*').

IT IS AGREED AND DECLARED that:

(1) The co-owners:

(1.1) are the proprietors of (*address*) title to which is registered at the Land Registry under title number (*number*) ('the property');

(1.2) purchased the property on (*completion date*);

(1.3) purchased the property for £   (*purchase price*);

(1.4) paid incidental purchase costs of £   (*costs*);

(1.5) obtained in advance of £   from and mortgaged the property to (*lender*) ('the mortgage');

(1.6) are beneficial tenants in common.

(2) (*Name 1*):

(2.1) paid £   towards the purchase price;

(2.2) paid £   towards the incidental purchase costs;

(2.3) will pay   per cent of the mortgage payments;

(2.4) will receive   per cent of the sale price[1], less:

(a)   per cent of the amount required to redeem the mortgage[2];

and

(b)   per cent of the incidental costs of selling the property.

(3) (*Name 2*):

    (3.1) paid £   towards the purchase price;

    (3.2) paid £   towards the incidental purchase costs;

    (3.3) will pay   per cent of the mortgage payments;

    (3.4) will receive   per cent of the sale price[3], less:

        (a)   per cent of the amount required to redeem the mortgage[4];

        and

        (b)   per cent of the incidental costs of selling the property.

SIGNED as a Deed by (*name 1*) in the presence of:

SIGNED as a Deed by (*name 2*) in the presence of:

[1] Presumably (2.1 + 2.2 + (2.3 x 1.5))/(1.4 + 1.4) expressed as a percentage.
[2] Presumably the same percentage as in (2.3).
[3] Presumably (3.1 + 3.2 + (3.3 x 1.5))/(1.3 + 1.4) expressed as a percentage.
[4] Presumably the same percentage as in (3.3).

1.217

Fixed shares: Long form

THIS DECLARATION OF TRUST is made on (*date*)

BETWEEN 'the co-owners' (1) (*name 1*) of (*address*) ('*name 1*') and (2) (*name 2*) also of (*address*) ('*name 2*').

IT IS AGREED AND DECLARED that:

(1) Recitals

(1.1) The co-owners are the proprietors of (*address*) title to which is registered at the Land Registry under title number (*number*) ('the property').

(1.2) The co-owners purchased the property on (*completion date*).

(1.3) The co-owners purchased the property for £   ('the purchase price').

(1.4) The incidental costs of the purchase totalled £   ('the purchase costs').

(1.5) (*Name 1*) paid £   towards the purchase price and the purchase costs.

(1.6) (*Name 2*) paid £   towards the purchase price and the purchase costs.

(1.7) The co-owners obtained in advance of £   from and have mortgaged the property to (*lender*) ('the mortgage').

(1.8) *(Name 1)* will pay _____ per cent of the mortgage payments.

(1.9) *(Name 2)* will pay _____ per cent of the mortgage payments.

(1.10) The co-owners will pay the incidental costs of selling the property in equal shares ('the sale costs').

(1.11) The co-owners will pay the costs incurred in connection with the preparation and execution of this Declaration in equal shares.

(1.12) In the absence of any agreement to the contrary, if one of the co-owners transfers all his or her legal estate and equitable interest in the property to the other co-owner, the legal costs incurred by the transferor will be paid by the transferor and the legal costs incurred by the transferee will be paid by the transferee.

(2) Trusts

The co-owners:

(2.1) hold the property on a trust of land;

(2.2) hold the property and its net proceeds of sale and its net income until sale in trust for themselves as beneficial tenants in common.

(3) Shares

When the property is sold:

(3.1) *(Name 1)* will receive _____ per cent of the sale price, less:

(a) _____ per cent of the amount required to redeem the mortgage; and

(b) 50 per cent of the sale costs;

(3.2) *(Name 2)* will receive _____ per cent of the sale price less:

(a) _____ per cent of the amount required to redeem the mortgage; and

(b) 50 per cent of the sale costs.

(3.3) If the deductions from one co-owner's share exceed the value of the percentage of the sale price to which he or she is entitled the excess will be paid out of the other co-owner's share.

(4) Contingencies

(4.1) If one co-owner fails to pay his or her share of the mortgage payments when it is due, the provisions of Schedule 1 will apply.

(4.2) If one or both of the co-owners pay(s) for extensions, alterations, repairs or improvements to the property, the provisions of Schedule 2 will apply.

(4.3) If one co-owner is unemployed or incapable of working, the provisions of Schedule 3 will apply.

(4.4) If anyone else normally resides with the co-owners, the provisions of Schedule 4 will apply.

(5) The nature of this declaration

This Declaration of Trust:

(5.1) is a deed and is executed as a deed by the co-owners;

(5.2) can be varied by a subsequent Declaration of Trust executed by both of the co-owners or those who are able to vary the trusts contained in it;

(5.3) can be set aside or varied by the court.

SCHEDULE 1

(If a co-owner fails to pay his or her share of the mortgage payments when it is due[1].)

SCHEDULE 2

(If the co-owners pay for extensions, alterations, repairs or improvements to the property[2].)

SCHEDULE 3

(If a co-owner is unemployed or incapable of working[3].)

SCHEDULE 4

(If anyone else normally resides in the property with the co-owners[4].)

SIGNED as a Deed by (*name 1*) in the presence of:

SIGNED as a Deed by (*name 2*) in the presence of:

[1] See **1.202** above.
[2] See **1.206** above.
[3] See **1.207** above.
[4] See **1.201** above.

1.218

Fixed shares: One co-owner alone to be responsible for the mortgage payments

THIS DECLARATION OF TRUST is made on (*date*)

BETWEEN 'the co-owners' (1) (*name 1*) of (*address*) ('*name 1*') and (2) (*name 2*) also of (*address*) ('*name 2*').

IT IS AGREED AND DECLARED that:

(1) Recitals

(1.1) The co-owners are the proprietors of (*address*) ('the property').

(1.2) Title to the property is registered under title number (*number*).

1.218 *Property*

(1.3) The property is mortgaged to (*lender*) ('the mortgage').

(1.4) The co-owners purchased the property on (*date*).

(1.5) The purchase price was £   .

(1.6) The incidental costs of the purchase came to £   .

(1.7) (*Name 1*) contributed £   towards the purchase price and purchase costs.

(1.8) (*Name 2*) contributed £   towards the purchase price and purchase costs.

(1.9) The mortgage advance was £   .

(1.10) Although the mortgage is in the co-owners' joint names (*name 1*) will be primarily responsible for the mortgage payments.

(2) Trusts

The co-owners declare that they:

(2.1) hold the property on a trust of land;

(2.2) hold the property and its net proceeds of sale and its net income until sale in trust for themselves as beneficial tenants in common.

(3) Shares

When the property is sold:

(3.1) (*name 1*) will receive   per cent of the sale price, less:

    (a) 100 per cent of the amount required to redeem the mortgage; and

    (b) 50 per cent of the incidental costs of selling the property;

(3.2) (*name 2*) will receive   per cent of the sale price, less:

    (a) 0 per cent of the amount required to redeem the mortgage; and

    (b) 50 per cent of the incidental costs of selling the property;

(3.3) if the amounts to be deducted from (*name 1's*) share of the sale price exceed the value of that share, then the excess will be paid from (*name 2's*) share.

(4) Definitions

(4.1) 'The sale price' means:

    (a) the price for which the property is sold; and

    (b) the price paid by the buyer of the property for any chattels jointly owned by the co-owners, whether or not a separate price is paid for those chattels.

(4.2) 'The amount required to redeem the mortgage' means the sum of money required by the lender to enable the co-owners to repay the mortgage and be completely released and discharged from all obligations under it.

(4.3) 'The incidental costs of selling the property' means the total sum of money (including VAT) to be paid in respect of:

(a) estate agents' commission;

(b) legal costs and disbursements;

(c) apportionments of rates, taxes, insurance, and other outgoings on the property.

SIGNED as a Deed by (*name 1*) in the presence of:

SIGNED as a Deed by (*name 2*) in the presence of:

1.219

Floating shares: Tabular form

THIS DECLARATION OF TRUST is made on (*date*)

BETWEEN 'the co-owners' (1) (*name 1*) of (*address*) ('*name 1*') and (2) (*name 2*) also of (*address*) ('*name 2*').

IT IS AGREED AND DECLARED that:

(1) Recitals

(1.1) The co-owners are the proprietors of (*address*) ('the property').

(1.2) Title to the property is registered at the Land Registry under title number (*number*).

(1.3) The co-owners purchased the property on (*completion date*).

(1.4) The purchase price was £   ('the purchase price').

(1.5) The purchase costs came to £   ('the purchase costs').

(1.6) (*Name 1*) paid £   towards the purchase price and the purchase costs.

(1.7) (*Name 2*) paid £   towards the purchase price and the purchase costs.

(1.8) The co-owners obtained an advance of £   from and have mortgaged the property to (*lender*).

(1.9) The co-owners intend to contribute towards the mortgage payments in the proportions that their respective incomes bear to each other, or in such other proportions as they may from time to time agree.

(2) Trusts

The co-owners:

(2.1) hold the property on a trust of land;

(2.2) hold the property and its net proceeds of sale and its net income until sale in trust for themselves as beneficial tenants in common.

(3) Shares

When the property is sold the net proceeds of sale will be divided between the

1.219 *Property*

co-owners in proportion to the extent to which the change in value of the property can be attributed to the contributions made by each of them towards the:

(3.1) purchase price;

(3.2) purchase costs;

(3.3) mortgage payments;

(3.4) cost of repairs and improvements to the property; and

(3.5) the incidental costs of selling the property will be borne pro rata.

(4) Calculation of shares

The share of the net proceeds of sale to which each co-owner is entitled will be calculated by:

(4.1) completing the record of contributions set out in the First Schedule; and then

(4.2) applying the formulae set out in the Second Schedule.

FIRST SCHEDULE (Record of contributions)[1].

SECOND SCHEDULE (The formulae)[2].

SIGNED as a Deed by (*name 1*) in the presence of:

SIGNED as a Deed by (*name 2*) in the presence of:

[1] See **1.174** above.
[2] See **1.174** above.

1.220

Floating shares: Long form

THIS DECLARATION OF TRUST is made on (*date*)

BETWEEN 'the co-owners' (1) (*name 1*) of (*address*) ('*name 1*') and (2) (*name 2*) also of (*address*) ('*name 2*').

IT IS AGREED AND DECLARED as follows:

(1) Recitals

(1.1) The co-owners are the proprietors of (*address*) title to which is registered at the Land Registry under title number (*number*) ('the property').

(1.2) The co-owners purchased the property on (*completion date*).

(1.3) The co-owners purchased the property for £   ('the purchase price').

(1.4) The incidental costs of the purchase totalled £   ('the purchase costs').

(1.5) (*Name 1*) paid £   towards the purchase price and the purchase costs.

(1.6) (*Name 2*) paid £   towards the purchase price and the purchase costs.

(1.7) The co-owners obtained an advance of £   from and have mortgaged the property to (*lender*) ('the mortgage').

(1.8) The co-owners intend to contribute to the mortgage payments (whether they are repayments of capital or payments of interest or insurance premiums) in the proportions that their incomes bear to each other or in such other proportions as they may from time to time agree.

(1.9) Each of the co-owners has received independent legal advice on the provisions and implications of this Declaration.

(1.10) The legal costs incurred in connection with the preparation and execution of this Declaration (including the costs of obtaining independent legal advice) will be paid by the co-owners in equal shares.

(2) Trusts

The co-owners:

(2.1) hold the property on a trust of land;

(2.2) hold the property and its net proceeds of sale and its net income until sale in trust for themselves as beneficial tenants in common.

(3) Shares

When the property is sold its net proceeds of sale will be divided between the co-owners in proportion to the contributions made by each of them towards the:

(3.1) purchase price;

(3.2) purchase costs;

(3.3) mortgage payments;

(3.4) cost of repairs and improvements to the property; and

(3.5) other payments (if any) analogous to those above.

(4) Calculation of shares

The share of the net proceeds of sale to which each co-owner is entitled will be calculated by:

(4.1) adding together his or her contributions to produce 'the individual contribution'; and then

(4.2) adding together both of the co-owners' individual contributions to produce 'the combined contributions'; and then

(4.3) dividing the net proceeds of sale plus the incidental costs of selling the property by the combined contributions to produce 'the dividend'; and finally

(4.4) multiplying the individual contribution by the dividend to produce the share.

(5) Sale and transfer costs

(5.1) When the property is sold the incidental costs of selling it will be paid by the co-owners in the proportions that their respective shares bear to each other.

(5.2) In the absence of any agreement to the contrary, if one of the co-owners transfers all his or her legal estate and equitable interest in the property to

1.220 *Property*

the other co-owner or to a third party at the direction of the other co-owner, the valuation fees, legal fees and other costs incurred by the transferor will be paid by the transferor, and the valuation fees, legal fees and other costs incurred by the transferee will be paid by the transferee.

(6) Contingencies

(6.1) If one of the co-owners dies and the other does not become solely and beneficially entitled to the property, the provisions of Schedule 1 will apply.

(6.2) If one of the co-owners wishes to sell the property and the other refuses to sell it, the provisions of Schedule 2 will apply.

(6.3) If the co-owners decide to separate and both of them wish to keep the property, the provisions of Schedule 3 will apply.

(6.4) If one of the co-owners moves out of the property before it is sold, the provisions of Schedule 4 will apply.

(7) This declaration

This Declaration of Trust:

(7.1) contains the whole agreement between the co-owners and supersedes any earlier agreements, representations or promises made by either co-owner in respect of the property;

(7.2) can be varied by a subsequent Declaration of Trust executed by all the persons who are able to vary the original trusts;

(7.3) has been executed in duplicate so that each of the co-owners may possess a copy of it, and both copies will be regarded as one deed, and each copy will be as efficacious as the other.

SCHEDULE 1[1].

SCHEDULE 2[2].

SCHEDULE 3[3].

SCHEDULE 4[4].

SIGNED as a Deed by (*name 1*) in the presence of:

SIGNED as a Deed by (*name 2*) in the presence of:

[1] See **1.204** above.
[2] See **1.203** above.
[3] See **1.211** above.
[4] See **1.212** above.

THE PERSON WHO 'MOVES IN'

1.221

Deed of surrender of any potential right to claim a beneficial interest in the property

THIS DEED made on (*date*)

Precedents **1.222**

BETWEEN (1) (*name 1*) of (*address*) ('*name 1*') and (2) (*name 2*) also of (*address*) ('*name 2*') WITNESS that:

(1) Recitals

(1.1)   (*Name 1*) is the registered proprietor of (*address*) ('the property').

(1.2)   (*Name 2*) has lived in the property with (*name 1*) since (*date*).

(2) Surrender

In consideration of (*name 1*) continuing to provide (him)/(her) with accommodation (*name 2*) releases, renounces and surrenders to (*name 1*) all if any rights that (he)/(she) may have at any time to claim a beneficial interest in the property, regardless of any contributions (he)/(she) may make towards:

(2.1)   (his)/(her) living and accommodation expenses; and

(2.2)   the payment of any mortgage on the property; and

(2.3)   any repairs and improvements to the property.

(3) Reservation of right

Nothing in this Deed deprives (*name 1*) of the right at any time during (his)/(her) life or by Will to transfer all or any part of (his)/(her) legal estate and beneficial interest in the property to (*name 2*).

(4) Procedural safeguards

(*Name 2*) acknowledges that (he)/(she) understands the nature and effect of this Deed and is entering into it:

(4.1)   freely and voluntarily;

(4.2)   without any form of pressure or coercion from (*name 1*) or anyone else; and

(4.3)   after receiving independent legal advice on its provisions and implications.

SIGNED as a Deed by (*name 1*) in the presence of:

SIGNED as a Deed by (*name 2*) in the presence of:

1.222

Declaration of trust by sole owner acknowledging that the partner has acquired a beneficial interest

THIS DECLARATION OF TRUST is made on (*date*)

BETWEEN 'the parties' (1) (*name 1*) of (*address*) ('*name 1*') and (2) (*name 2*) also of (*address*) ('*name 2*).

IT IS AGREED AND DECLARED that:

(1) Recitals

(1.1)   (*Name 1*) is the sole proprietor of (*address*) ('the property').

- (1.2) Title to the property is registered at the Land Registry under title number (*number*).
- (1.3) The property is mortgaged to (*lender*) ('the mortgage').
- (1.4) (*Name 2*) moved into the property on (*date*) and has lived there with (*name 1*) ever since.
- (1.5) (*Name 2*) has been contributing towards the mortgage payments (and has paid for repairs and improvements to the property).
- (1.6) The parties intend to continue living together for an indefinite length of time.

(2) Acknowledgment, declaration and covenants

(*Name 1*):

- (2.1) acknowledges that (*name 2*) has acquired a beneficial interest in the property by virtue of (*name 2's*) contributions towards the mortgage payments (and repairs and improvements);
- (2.2) declares that (*name 1*) holds the property and its net proceeds of sale and its net income until sale in trust for (*name 2*) and (*name 2*) as beneficial tenants in common;
- (2.3) will apply to the Land Registry for a restriction to be entered in the register in order to protect (*name 2's*) beneficial interest in the property; and
- (2.4) will do all that (*name 1*) can to transfer the property and the mortgage into the parties' joint names, if (*name 2*) wishes.

(3) Valuation of prior share

When (*name 2*) moved into the property:

- (3.1) its open market value was £   ;
- (3.2) the amount required to redeem the mortgage was £   ; and
- (3.3) the equity to which (*name 1*) was then entitled was £   ('the prior share').

(4) Calculation of shares

When the property is sold:

- (4.1) (*name 1*) will receive (*fraction or percentage*) of the sale price representing the return on the prior share;
- (4.2) the remainder of the net proceeds of sale will be divided between the parties in equal shares;
- (4.3) if the incidental costs of selling the property and the amount required to redeem the mortgage exceed the remainder of the net proceeds of sale, the excess will be paid from (*name 1's*) share of the sale price representing the return on the prior share.

(5) Contingency

Unless the parties agree otherwise, if they separate or are about to separate:

(5.1) (*name 1*) will have the right to remain in the property and to purchase (*name 2's*) share in it;

(5.2) (*name 1*) will complete the purchase of (*name 2's*) share within a period of (8) weeks beginning on the date on which (*name 2*) moves out of the property;

(5.3) if at the end of that period of (8) weeks (*name 1*) has not completed the purchase of (*name 2's*) share, (*name 2*) can apply to the court for an order that the property be sold;

(5.4) (*name 1*) will pay the valuation fees, legal fees and other costs which (*name 1*) incurs; and

(5.5) (*name 2*) will pay the valuation fees, legal fees and other costs which (*name 2*) incurs.

SIGNED as a Deed by (*name 1*) in the presence of:

SIGNED as a Deed by (*name 2*) in the presence of:

DECLARATION OF TRUST BY SOLE OWNER

1.223

Another person has contributed to the purchase price[1]

THIS DECLARATION OF TRUST is made on (*date*)

BETWEEN (1) (*name 1*) of (*address*) ('*name 1*') and (2) (*name 2*) of (*address*) ('*name 2*').

IT IS AGREED AND DECLARED that:

(1) (Name 1):

(1.1) is the proprietor of (*address*) title to which is registered at the Land Registry under title number (*number*) ('the property');

(1.2) purchased the property on (*completion date*);

(1.3) purchased the property for £   ('purchase price');

(1.4) paid £   towards the purchase price;

(1.5) paid £   towards the incidental purchase costs which amounted in total to £   ('the purchase costs');

(1.6) obtained an advance of £   from and mortgaged the property to (*lender*) ('the mortgage').

(2) (Name 2)[2]:

(2.1) paid £   towards the purchase price (and the purchase costs);

(2.2) made that payment with the intention of acquiring a beneficial interest in the property[3];

(2.3) is not a registered proprietor of the property.

(3) *(Name 1):*

(3.1) acknowledges that the payment made by *(name 2)* towards the purchase price (and the purchase costs) was neither a gift nor a loan to *(name 1)*[4];

(3.2) declares that *(name 1)* holds the property and its net proceeds of sale in trust for *(name 1)* and *(name 2)* as beneficial tenants in common;

(3.3) will apply to the Land Registry for the entry of the appropriate restriction in order to protect the beneficial interest of *(name 2)*[5].

(4) When the property is sold:

(4.1) *(name 1)* will receive   per cent of the sale price from which will be deducted:

    (a) the amount required to redeem the mortgage; and

    (b) the incidental costs of selling the property;

(4.2) *(name 2)* will receive   per cent of the sale price[6].

SIGNED as a Deed by *(name 1)* in the presence of:

SIGNED as a Deed by *(name 2)* in the presence of:

---

[1] 'A resulting trust arises where a person acquires a legal estate but has not provided the consideration or the whole of the consideration for its acquisition, unless a contrary intention is proved' (*Cowcher v Cowcher* [1972] 1 All ER 943 at 949e, per Bagnall J).

[2] If necessary, the parties' relationship could be stated at this point. For example: '*(name 2)*: is the (mother)/(father) of *(name 1)*'.

[3] *Sekhon v Alissa* [1989] 2 FLR 94.

[4] 'The next question is whether the mother's contribution was to be an unsecured loan or to give her a beneficial interest. In my judgment the law presumes a resulting trust in her favour and that presumption has to be rebutted by evidence that she intended a personal loan without acquiring any interest in the property' (*Sekhon v Alissa* [1989] 2 FLR 94 at 99D, per Hoffmann J).

[5] An interest behind a trust of land is an excluded interest. It should be protected by a restriction on the register (LRA 2002, ss 40–47; LRA 2002 s 33(a)(i)).

[6] Presumably *(name 2's* contribution)/(purchase price + purchase costs) expressed as a percentage.

1.224

Elderly person buys his or her council house with financial assistance from his or her children[1]

THIS DECLARATION OF TRUST is made on *(date)*

BETWEEN (1) *(name 1)* of *(address)* ('*name 1*') and (2) *(name 2)* of *(address)* ('*name 2*').

IT IS AGREED AND DECLARED that:

(1) Recitals

(1.1) *(Name 1)* is the sole proprietor of *(address)* title to which is registered at the Land Registry under title number *(number)* ('the property').

(1.2) The property formerly belonged to *(Borough/City/County/District)* Council ('the Council').

(1.3) (Name 1) purchased the property from the Council on (date) ('completion date').

(1.4) On completion date the value of the property was £   .

(1.5) The value of the property was discounted by £   ('the discount') because (name 1) had occupied the property as a Council tenant for (number) of years.

(1.6) In the transfer to (name 1) it was stated that (name 1) had paid the Council £   for the property ('the purchase price').

(1.7) The incidental costs of purchasing the property came to £   ('the purchase costs').

(1.8) (Name 1) paid £   towards the purchase price and the purchase costs.

(1.9) (Name 2), who is (name 1's) (son)/(daughter), paid £   towards the purchase price and the purchase costs.

(1.10) (Name 2) contributed to the purchase partly as an investment and partly to enable (name 1) to live in (name 1's) own home.

(1.11) (Name 2) intends that (name 1) should continue to live in the property for as long as (name 1) wishes, rent-free.

(1.12) (Name 2) acknowledges that the discount should primarily enure for the benefit of (name 1).

(1.13) (Name 1) acknowledges that (name 1) would have been unable to purchase the property without financial assistance from (name 2).

(2) Trusts

(Name 1) declares that (name 1) holds the net proceeds of sale of the property in trust for (name 1) and (name 2) as beneficial tenants in common.

(3) Shares

When the property is sold:

(3.1) (name 1) will receive   per cent of the sale price, representing the return on the discount and (name 1's) contribution towards the purchase price and the purchase costs, less (50) per cent of the incidental costs of selling the property ('name 1's share');

(3.2) (name 2) will receive   per cent of the sale price, representing the return on (name 2's) contribution towards the purchase price and the purchase costs, less (50) per cent of the incidental costs of selling the property ('name 2's share');

(3.3) if all or any part of the discount has to be repaid to the Council, it will be paid from (name 1's) share;

(3.4) if (name 2's) share is less than (name 2's) original contribution towards the purchase price and the purchase costs, the shortfall will be paid from (name 1's) share.

1.224 Property

(4) Gradual diminution of (name 1's) share

(4.1) In consideration of the fact that (name 1) would have been unable to purchase the property without financial assistance from (name 2), and in consideration of the assurance from (name 2) that (name 1) can continue to live in the property rent-free for as long as (name 1) wishes, (name 1) agrees that the value of (name 1's) share will gradually decrease and that the value of (name 2's) share will proportionately increase, and to that intent the following provisions will apply.

(4.2) When the property is sold or when either party realises their share in it ('the disposal') (name 1's) share will be reduced by (10) per cent for each complete year that has elapsed between the (1st) anniversary of completion date and the disposal.

(4.3) The amount by which (name 1's) share is reduced will be added to (name 2's) share.

(4.4) For the avoidance of doubt:

  (a) there will be no reduction of (name 1's) share before the (1st) anniversary of completion date because of the provisions relating to the repayment of the discount to the Council; and

  (b) there will be no reduction of (name 1's) share in respect of any period of less than a complete year.

(5) Terms of continued occupation

(Name 2) agrees that (name 1) can continue to live in the property rent-free for as long as (name 1) wishes on the terms that (name 1):

(5.1) pays all the outgoings on the property;

(5.2) keeps it in reasonable repair and condition;

(5.3) keeps it insured to its full reinstatement value; and

(5.4) complies with all the covenants and conditions to which it is subject.

SIGNED as a Deed by (name 1) in the presence of:

SIGNED as a Deed by (name 2) in the presence of:

---

[1] The purchase of a council house by a tenant with financial assistance from his or her children is, potentially, fraught with difficulties and raises important policy issues. The former tenant and his or her children should receive independent legal advice. Among the questions to be asked are as follows.
  (a) Who is to have the benefit of the discount?
  (b) Who will be liable for the repayment of the discount if there is a disposal of the property within the relevant period?
  (c) To what extent should the children be allowed to benefit at the expense of their parent and, indirectly, the ratepayer and taxpayer?
  (d) How can the children be protected from losing out on the transaction?
  (e) What is the underlying purpose of the children's involvement?
  (f) What are the parties' intentions regarding the former tenant's continued occupation of the property?
  (g) Does the former tenant have other children who might reasonably be expected to benefit from his or her estate?

(h) To what extent is securing entitlement to or increasing the amount of any income-related benefits a 'significant operative purpose' behind any value-shifting exercise? See, generally, the Income Support (General) Regulations 1987 (SI 1987/1967), reg 51, and the Commissioner's decision in R (SB) 40/85.

1.225

Variation of a Declaration of Trust[1]

THIS VARIATION is made on (*date*)

BETWEEN 'the co-owners'[2] (1) (*name 1*) of (*address*) ('*name 1*') and (2) (*name 2*) (also) of (*address*) ('*name 2*').

IT IS AGREED AND DECLARED that:

(1) Recitals

(1.1) This deed is supplemental[3] to the Declaration of Trust ('the Declaration') made between the co-owners on (*date*).

(1.2) The co-owners wish to vary the Declaration as follows.

(2) Revocation

The co-owners revoke Clause(s) (*number(s)*) [AND/OR] Schedule(s) (*number(s)*) of the Declaration.

(3) Shares

From now onwards the co-owners will hold the property (as defined in the Declaration)[4] and its net proceeds of sale in trust for themselves as beneficial tenants in common in the following shares:

(set out the shares)

(4) Confirmation

The co-owners confirm the Declaration in all other respects.

SIGNED as a Deed by (*name 1*) in the presence of:

SIGNED as a Deed by (*name 2*) in the presence of:

[1] 'If all the beneficiaries are *sui iuris* they can join together with the trustees and declare different trusts which supersede those contained in the original declaration. These new trusts operate *proprio vigore* by virtue of a self-contained instrument, namely the deed of arrangement or variation. The original declaration will have lost any force or relevance' (*Re Holmden's Settlement Trusts* [1968] AC 685 at 713C, per Lord Wilberforce).

[2] This precedent assumes that the original co-owners are the parties able to vary the trusts. If the variation is being made by, say, the personal representatives of one of the co-owners, the wording should be adapted accordingly.

[3] LPA 1925, s 58: 'any instrument . . . expressed to be supplemental to a previous instrument, shall, as far as may be, be read and have effect as if the supplemental instrument contained a full recital of the previous instrument'. It would be sensible to endorse a memorandum of the variation on the original declaration of trust.

[4] The words in brackets 'as defined in the Declaration' are not, strictly speaking, necessary.

Checklist for ownership of the home

(1) Names and addresses of parties

(2) Address of property

(3) Has the property already been bought, if so:

    (3.1) Whose name(s) is it in?

    (3.2) Obtain copy of Land Registry Official Entries

    (3.3) Is there a mortgage and who pays it?

    (3.4) Is there a life policy to pay off the mortgage. Will it benefit survivor?

    (3.5) Does the title reflect what the parties want?

(4) If property is being bought

    (4.1) In whose name will the purchase be?

    (4.2) Will there be a mortgage and who will pay it?

    (4.3) Is there to be a life policy to pay off the mortgage. Will it benefit survivor?

    (4.4) Is the property to be bought in joint names?

    (4.5) If not how will the other party's share be protected.

    (4.6) If in joint names is it to be bought equally as joint tenants or as tenants in common and in what shares?

(5) Is there a conflict of interest and should parties be separately represented?

(6) Can the arrangement be reflected in the transfer to the parties or will a declaration of trust be required?

(7) Terms of Declaration of Trust

    (7.1) Contributions

    (7.2) Costs

    (7.3) Fixed shares – proportions

    (7.4) Floating shares – recording contributions

    (7.5) Provisions for contingencies

        (7.5.1) Other person residing

        (7.5.2) Failure to pay by co-owner

        (7.5.3) One co-owner wishes to sell

        (7.5.4) Death of one co-owner

        (7.5.5) Bankruptcy of co-owner

        (7.5.6) Alterations and improvements

        (7.5.7) Unemployment

        (7.5.8) Childcare

        (7.5.9) Education

(7.6) Separation

    (7.6.1) Priority if both wish to stay

    (7.6.2) One co-owner moves out

    (7.6.3) Separation shortly after purchase

    (7.6.4) One party wants to realise share

1.227 *Property*

1.227

HM Land Registry Form TR1

HM Land Registry
Transfer of whole of registered title(s)

Any parts of the form that are not typed should be completed in black ink and in block capitals.

If you need more room than is provided for in a panel, and your software allows, you can expand any panel in the form. Alternatively use continuation sheet CS and attach it to this form.

For information on how HM Land Registry processes your personal information, see our Personal Information Charter.

Leave blank if not yet registered.	1 Title number(s) of the property:
Insert address including postcode (if any) or other description of the property, for example 'land adjoining 2 Acacia Avenue'.	2 Property:
Remember to date this deed with the day of completion, but not before it has been signed and witnessed.	3 Date:
Give full name(s) of **all** the persons transferring the property.	4 Transferor:
Complete as appropriate where the transferor is a company.	For UK incorporated companies/LLPs Registered number of company or limited liability partnership including any prefix: For overseas companies (a) Territory of incorporation: (b) Registered number in the United Kingdom including any prefix:
Give full name(s) of **all** the persons to be shown as registered proprietors	5 Transferee for entry in the register:
Complete as appropriate where the transferee is a company. Also, for an overseas company, unless an arrangement with HM Land Registry exists, lodge either a certificate in Form 7 in Schedule 3 to the Land Registration Rules 2003 or a certified copy of the constitution in English or Welsh, or other evidence permitted by rule 183 of the Land Registration Rules 2003.	For UK incorporated companies/LLPs Registered number of company or limited liability partnership including any prefix: For overseas companies (a) Territory of incorporation: (b) Registered number in the United Kingdom including any prefix:
Each transferee may give up to three addresses for service, one of which must be a postal address whether or not in the UK (including the postcode, if any). The others can be any combination of a postal address, a UK DX box	6 Transferee's intended address(es) for service for entry in the register:

Precedents **1.227**

number or an electronic address.	
	7 The transferor transfers the property to the transferee
Place 'X' in the appropriate box. State the currency unit if other than sterling. If none of the boxes apply, insert an appropriate memorandum in panel 11.	8 Consideration
	☐ The transferor has received from the transferee for the property the following sum (in words and figures):
	☐ The transfer is not for money or anything that has a monetary value
	☐ Insert other receipt as appropriate:
Place 'X' in any box that applies.	9 The transferor transfers with
Add any modifications.	☐ full title guarantee
	☐ limited title guarantee
Where the transferee is more than one person, place 'X' in the appropriate box.	10 Declaration of trust. The transferee is more than one person and
	☐ they are to hold the property on trust for themselves as joint tenants
Complete as necessary.	

The registrar will enter a Form A restriction in the register *unless*:
- an 'X' is placed:
  - in the first box, or
  - in the third box and the details of the trust or of the trust instrument show that the transferees are to hold the property on trust for themselves alone as joint tenants, *or*
- it is clear from completion of a form JO lodged with this application that the transferees are to hold the property on trust for themselves alone as joint tenants.
	☐ they are to hold the property on trust for themselves as tenants in common in equal shares

	☐ they are to hold the property on trust:
Please refer to Joint property ownership and practice guide 24: private trusts of land for further guidance. These are both available on the GOV.UK website.	
Insert here any required or permitted statement, certificate or application and any agreed covenants, declarations and so on.	11 Additional provisions

Page 2 of 3

167

1.227 *Property*

The transferor must execute this transfer as a deed using the space opposite. If there is more than one transferor, all must execute. Forms of execution are given in Schedule 9 to the Land Registration Rules 2003. If the transfer contains transferee's covenants or declarations or contains an application by the transferee (such as for a restriction), it must also be executed by the transferee.

If there is more than one transferee and panel 10 has been completed, each transferee must also execute this transfer to comply with the requirements in section 53(1)(b) of the Law of Property Act 1925 relating to the declaration of a trust of land. Please refer to Joint property ownership and practice guide 24: private trusts of land for further guidance.

Examples of the correct form of execution are set out in practice guide 8: execution of deeds. Execution as a deed usually means that a witness must also sign, and add their name and address.

Remember to date this deed in panel 3.

12 Execution

Signed as a deed* by (full name of individual) in the presence of

Signature:

Signature of witness:

Name (in BLOCK CAPITALS):

Address:

(*in the case of an assent, the words ' as a deed' may be omitted)

WARNING

If you dishonestly enter information or make a statement that you know is, or might be, untrue or misleading, and intend by doing so to make a gain for yourself or another person, or to cause loss or the risk of loss to another person, you may commit the offence of fraud under section 1 of the Fraud Act 2006, the maximum penalty for which is 10 years' imprisonment or an unlimited fine, or both.

Failure to complete this form with proper care may result in a loss of protection under the Land Registration Act 2002 if, as a result, a mistake is made in the register.

Under section 66 of the Land Registration Act 2002 most documents (including this form) kept by the registrar relating to an application to the registrar or referred to in the register are open to public inspection and copying. If you believe a document contains prejudicial information, you may apply for that part of the document to be made exempt using Form EX1, under rule 136 of the Land Registration Rules 2003.

© Crown copyright (ref: LR/SC/17) 06/19

1.228

HM Land Registry Form JO

HM Land Registry
Trust Information

Any parts of the form that are not typed should be completed in black ink and in block capitals.

This form may accompany an application in Form AP1, FR1 or ADV1 where:
- panel 9 of Form FR1 or ADV1 has not been completed and the applicant is more than one person, or
- the Form AP1 relates to a transfer (in Form AS1, AS3, TP1, TP2, TR1, TR2 or TR5) or a prescribed clauses lease (within rule 58A of the Land Registration Rules 2003) of a registered estate to more than one person (the Joint Owners), and
  - the declaration of trust panel in the transfer or lease has not been completed and/or the transfer has not been executed by the Joint Owners, and
  - the estate transferred or leased is not a rentcharge, franchise, profit or manor.

Enter the same information as either in the transfer or lease to the Joint Owners or in panel 6 of Form ADV1. Leave blank if this form accompanies a Form FR1.	1	Title number(s) of the property:
Insert address including postcode (if any) or other description of the property as it appears either in the transfer or lease to the Joint Owners, in panel 3 of Form ADV1 or in panel 2 of Form FR1.	2	Property:
	3	Date:
Give full name(s) and address(es), as in either the transfer or lease to the Joint Owners, panels 6 and 7 of Forms ADV1 or panels 6 and 8 of Form FR1.	4	Joint Owners:
Complete either this or panel 6. Place an 'X' in the appropriate box. If completing the fourth box, insert details either of the trust or of the trust instrument under which the Joint Owners hold the property. The registrar will enter a Form A restriction in the register if an 'X' is placed: - in the second or third box, or - in the fourth box, unless it is clear that the Joint Owners hold on trust for themselves alone as joint tenants.	5	☐ The Joint Owners declare that they are to hold the property on trust for themselves alone as joint tenants ☐ The Joint Owners declare that they are to hold the property on trust for themselves alone as tenants in common in equal shares ☐ The Joint Owners declare that they hold the property on trust for themselves alone as tenants in common in the following unequal shares: (*complete*) ☐ The Joint Owners are to hold the property (*complete*):
If this panel is completed, each Joint Owner must sign. Please refer to *Joint property ownership* and *practice guide 24: private trusts of land* for further guidance. These are both available on the GOV.UK website.		Signature of each of the Joint Owners Date:

6	Under the term of a written declaration of trust dated (*complete*) the Joint Owners
	☐ hold the property on trust as joint tenants for themselves alone
	☐ do not hold the property on trust as joint tenants for themselves alone

If this panel is completed, a conveyancer must sign.

Signature of conveyancer _____

Date:

WARNING
If you dishonestly enter information or make a statement that you know is, or might be, untrue or misleading, and intend by doing so to make a gain for yourself or another person, or to cause loss or the risk of loss to another person, you may commit the offence of fraud under section 1 of the Fraud Act 2006, the maximum penalty for which is 10 years' imprisonment or an unlimited fine, or both.

Failure to complete this form with proper care may result in a loss of protection under the Land Registration Act 2002 if, as a result, a mistake is made in the register.

Under section 66 of the Land Registration Act 2002 most documents (including this form) kept by the registrar relating to an application to the registrar or referred to in the register are open to public inspection and copying. If you believe a document contains prejudicial information, you may apply for that part of the document to be made exempt using Form EX1, under rule 136 of the Land Registration Rules 2003.

© Crown copyright (ref: LR/HO) 04/17

1.229

HM Land Registry Form SEV

HM Land Registry
Application to enter Form A restriction on severance of joint tenancy by agreement or notice

Any parts of the form that are not typed should be completed in black ink and in block capitals.	HM LAND REGISTRY USE ONLY Record of fees paid
Form RX1 should be used for an application following severance in other circumstances.	
If you need more room than is provided for in a panel, and your software allows, you can expand any panel in the form. Alternatively use continuation sheet CS and attach it to this form.	Particulars of under/over payments
HM Land Registry is unable to give legal advice, but you can find guidance on HM Land Registry applications (including our practice guides for conveyancers) at www.gov.uk/land-registry.	
Conveyancer is a term used in this form. It is defined in rule 217A, Land Registration Rules 2003 and includes persons authorised under the Legal Services Act 2007 to provide reserved legal services relating to land registration and includes solicitors and licensed conveyancers.	Reference number Fees debited £
For information on how HM Land Registry processes your personal information, see our Personal Information Charter.	

Where there is more than one local authority serving an area, enter the one to which council tax or business rates are normally paid.	1	Local authority serving the property: Choose Local Authority
You must enter the title number(s) relating to the property otherwise we cannot accept the application.	2	Title number(s) of the property:
Insert address including postcode (if any) or other description of the property, for example 'land adjoining 2 Acacia Avenue'.	3	Property:
Currently no fee is payable for the entry of a Form A restriction.	4	Application and fee

Application	Fee paid (£)
Entry of Form A restriction	

Fee payment method
☐ cheque made payable to 'Land Registry'
☐ direct debit, under an agreement with Land Registry

Provide the full name(s) of the person(s) applying to enter the restriction. Where a conveyancer lodges the application, this must be the name(s) of the client(s), not the conveyancer.	5	The applicant:

1.229 *Property*

This panel must always be completed.	6	This application is sent to Land Registry by
A key number is only available to professional customers, such as solicitors.		Key number (if applicable):
If you are paying by direct debit, this will be the account charged.		Name: Address or UK DX box number:
This is the address to which we will normally send requisitions. However if you insert an email address, we will use this whenever possible. Where an application is lodged by e-DRS all documents and correspondence will be dealt with electronically.		
We will only issue warning of cancellation letters to conveyancers if an email address is inserted.		Email address: Reference: Phone no: Fax no:
You must place 'X' in only one box in this panel.	7	Evidence of severance
If option (A) is chosen, all joint proprietors or their conveyancers must sign panel 9.		**(A) Application is by all the registered proprietors** ☐ All registered proprietors of the title number referred to in panel 2 are applying (no further evidence required).
If you are a conveyancer the certificate is sufficient to comply with HM Land Registry's requirements for items (B) and (C). If no conveyancer is acting, you must enclose the evidence stated with this application. HM Land Registry may destroy documents after scanning.		**(B) Application is not by all the registered proprietors – severance is by document signed by all the registered proprietors** ☐ The original or a certified copy of the document is enclosed. ☐ I am the applicant's conveyancer and I certify that I hold the original or a certified copy of the document.
Although you do not need to lodge evidence of severance when all the registered proprietors are applying, the joint tenancy must have been severed before the Form A restriction is entered.		**(C) Application is not by all the registered proprietors – notice of severance has been served** ☐ The original or certified copy of the notice of severance **and** a signed acknowledgement of receipt by the other registered proprietors is enclosed.
We only need certified copies of deeds or documents you send to us with HM Land Registry application forms. Once we have made a copy of the documents you send to us, they will be destroyed, this applies to both originals and certified copies.		☐ The original or certified copy of the notice of severance **and** my certificate is enclosed, confirming that the notice was given to the other registered proprietor(s), left at their last known place of abode or business in the UK or sent by registered post or recorded delivery service to them at their last known place of abode or business and not returned undelivered.
Section 36(2) of the Law of Property Act 1925 allows one joint owner to serve a written notice on the other joint owners, severing their joint tenancy in equity. Section 196 of that Act, as modified by section 1 of the Recorded Delivery Service Act 1962, says how such a notice must be served.		☐ I am the applicant's conveyancer and I certify that I hold the original [or certified copy of] notice of severance with an acknowledgement of receipt signed by the other registered proprietors.
		☐ I am the applicant's conveyancer and I certify that I hold the original [or certified copy of] notice of severance, and that it was served on the other registered proprietors in accordance with sections 36(2) and 196 of the Law of Property Act 1925.
	8	Application
		The applicant applies for the following restriction to be entered in the register of the above title(s):
		No disposition by a sole proprietor of the registered estate (except a trust corporation) under which capital money arises is to be registered unless authorised by an order of the court.

If a conveyancer is acting for the applicant, that conveyancer must sign. If no conveyancer is acting, the applicant (and if more than one person then each of them) must sign.

9
Signature of applicant or their conveyancer: _____
Date:

WARNING
If you dishonestly enter information or make a statement that you know is, or might be, untrue or misleading, and intend by doing so to make a gain for yourself or another person, or to cause loss or the risk of loss to another person, you may commit the offence of fraud under section 1 of the Fraud Act 2006, the maximum penalty for which is 10 years' imprisonment or an unlimited fine, or both.

Failure to complete this form with proper care may result in a loss of protection under the Land Registration Act 2002 if, as a result, a mistake is made in the register.

Under section 66 of the Land Registration Act 2002 most documents (including this form) kept by the registrar relating to an application to the registrar or referred to in the register are open to public inspection and copying. If you believe a document contains prejudicial information, you may apply for that part of the document to be made exempt using Form EX1, under rule 136 of the Land Registration Rules 2003.

© Crown copyright (ref: LR/SC/17) 01/19

1.230 Property

1.230

HM Land Registry Form RX1

HM Land Registry
Application to enter a restriction

Any parts of the form that are not typed should be completed in black ink and in block capitals.

If you need more room than is provided for in a panel, and your software allows, you can expand any panel in the form. Alternatively use continuation sheet CS and attach it to this form.

HM Land Registry is unable to give legal advice, but you can find guidance on HM Land Registry applications (including our practice guides for conveyancers) at www.gov.uk/land-registry.

Conveyancer is a term used in this form. It is defined in rule 217A, Land Registration Rules 2003 and includes persons authorised under the Legal Services Act 2007 to provide reserved legal services relating to land registration and includes solicitors and licensed conveyancers.

For information on how HM Land Registry processes your personal information, see our Personal Information Charter.

HM LAND REGISTRY USE ONLY
Record of fees paid
Particulars of under/over payments
Reference number
Fees debited £

Where there is more than one local authority serving an area, enter the one to which council tax or business rates are normally paid.

1. Local authority serving the property:

2. Title number(s) of the property:

Insert address including postcode (if any) or other description of the property, for example 'land adjoining 2 Acacia Avenue'.

Place 'X' in the appropriate box.

Give a brief description of the part affected, for example 'edged red on the attached plan'.

Complete details of charge if appropriate.

3. Property:

   The restriction applied for is to affect

   ☐ the whole of the registered estate

   ☐ the part(s) of the registered estate as shown:

   ☐ the registered charge(s) dated   in
      favour of:

To find out more about our fees visit www.gov.uk/government/collections/fees-land-registry-guides

Place 'X' in the appropriate box.

The fee will be charged to the account specified in panel 7.

4. Application and fee

Application	Fee paid (£)
Entry of restriction	

   Fee payment method

   ☐ cheque made payable to 'Land Registry'

   ☐ direct debit, under an agreement with Land Registry

List the documents lodged with this form. If this application is accompanied by either Form AP1 or FR1 please only complete the corresponding panel on Form AP1 or DL (if used). Original documents are only required if your application is a first registration, when we will return the originals if a certified copy has been supplied. If your application is not a first registration then we only need certified copies of deeds or documents you send to us with HM Land Registry application forms. Once we have made a copy of the documents you send to us, they will be destroyed, this applies to both originals and certified copies.	5	Documents lodged with this form:
Provide the full name(s) of the person(s) applying to enter the restriction. Where a conveyancer lodges the application, this must be the name(s) of the client(s), not the conveyancer.	6	The applicant:
This panel must always be completed. A key number is only available to professional customers, such as solicitors. If you are paying by direct debit, this will be the account charged. This is the address to which we will normally send requisitions. However if you insert an email address, we will use this whenever possible. Where an application is lodged by e-DRS all documents and correspondence will be dealt with electronically. We will only issue warning of cancellation letters to conveyancers if an email address is inserted.	7	This application is sent to Land Registry by Key number (if applicable): Name: Address or UK DX box number: Email address: Reference: Phone no: Fax no:

1.230 *Property*

You must place 'X' in only one box in this panel. See Practice Guide 19 if you are unsure which option you need to select.

8 The applicant is entitled to apply for a restriction because

(A) Applicant is the registered proprietor

☐ The applicant is the registered proprietor of the estate/charge referred to in panel 3

If you are a conveyancer the certificate is sufficient to comply with HM Land Registry's requirements. If no conveyancer is acting, you must enclose evidence of the applicant's entitlement to be registered as proprietor with this application. HM Land Registry may destroy documents after scanning.

List any supporting documents in panel 5 or on Form AP1 or DL (if used).

(B) Applicant is entitled to be registered as the proprietor

☐ Evidence of that entitlement accompanies this application

☐ I am the applicant's conveyancer and certify that I am satisfied that the applicant is entitled to be registered as proprietor and that I hold the originals of the documents that contain evidence of the applicant's entitlement, or an application for registration of the applicant as proprietor is pending at Land Registry

If you are a conveyancer the certificate is sufficient to comply with HM Land Registry's requirements. If no conveyancer is acting, you must enclose the relevant consent with this application. HM Land Registry may destroy documents after scanning.

(C) Application made with the consent of the registered proprietor

☐ The relevant consent accompanies this application

☐ I am the applicant's conveyancer and certify that I hold the relevant consent

If you are a conveyancer the certificate is sufficient to comply with HM Land Registry's requirements. If no conveyancer is acting, you must enclose the relevant consent and evidence of entitlement to be registered as proprietor with this application. HM Land Registry may destroy documents after scanning.

(D) Application made with the consent of person entitled to be registered as proprietor

☐ The relevant consent and evidence of that entitlement accompany this application

☐ I am the applicant's conveyancer and I certify that the relevant consent accompanies this application.

I also certify that I am satisfied that the person consenting to this application is entitled to be registered as proprietor and that I hold the originals of the documents that contain evidence of that person's entitlement, or an application for registration of that person as proprietor is pending at Land Registry

List any supporting documents in panel 5 or on Form AP1 or DL (if used).

☐ I am the applicant's conveyancer and I certify that I hold the relevant consent.

I also certify that I am satisfied that the person consenting to this application is entitled to be registered as proprietor and that I hold the originals of the documents that contain evidence of that person's entitlement, or an application for registration of that person as proprietor is pending at Land Registry

(E) Other evidence in support of applicant's claim

List any supporting documents in panel 5 or on Form AP1 or DL (if used).

None of the above statements applies but the applicant has the following sufficient interest in the making of the entry of the restriction applied for in panel 9

☐ The applicant has made the statement in panel 12

☐ I am the applicant's conveyancer and I certify as to the applicant's interest in panel 13

Set out in full the wording of the restriction required. For standard form restrictions, also insert the reference letter(s) of the form. For non-standard form restrictions delete the words in square brackets. Standard forms of restriction are set out in Schedule 4 to the Land Registration Rules 2003. Further guidance is contained in Practice Guide 19. You must set out the wording of the restriction in full, unless you are applying for a standard form of restriction that has no variable content. You must include the address(es) for service where a standard form of restriction requires an address to be included or where any other restriction requires a consent or certificate to be provided, or notice to be served on the restrictioner. Each restrictioner may give up to three addresses for service, one of which must be a postal address whether or not in the UK (including the postcode, if any). The others can be any combination of a postal address, a UK DX box number or an electronic address. If the restriction refers to a registered company or limited liability partnership incorporated anywhere in the United Kingdom include the registered number (including any prefix) immediately after the name of the company. For an overseas company include the territory of incorporation and if its particulars are registered at Companies House, state the registered number in England and Wales.	9	The applicant applies to enter a restriction [in standard form] against the estate/charge referred to in panel 3 in the following words:
If a conveyancer is acting for the applicant, that conveyancer must sign. If no conveyancer is acting, the applicant (and if more than one person then each of them) must sign. The conveyancer must sign if they have given one of the certificates referred to in panel 8.	10	Signature of applicant or their conveyancer: _____ Date:
See panel 8.	11	I/We consent to the entry of the restriction specified in panel 9 against the estate or charge referred to in panel 3. Print full name Signature 1. 1. 2. 2. 3. 3. 4. 4.

Only complete this panel if you have completed option (E) in panel 8. If a conveyancer is lodging the application, the conveyancer may either complete panel 13 and leave this panel blank, or may arrange for the applicant to complete this panel. Set out the nature of the applicant's interest. Set out details of the circumstances in which the interest arose. List any supporting documents in panel 5 or on Form AP1 or DL (if used). See the warnings at the end of this form.	12	The applicant states that the applicant has a sufficient interest in the restriction being entered in the register. Nature of applicant's interest: Details of how the applicant's interest arose: Signature of applicant: _____
Only complete this panel if you have completed option (E) in panel 8 and a conveyancer is lodging the application. Set out the nature of the applicant's interest. Set out details of the circumstances in which the interest arose. List any supporting documents in panel 5 or on Form AP1 or DL (if used). See the warnings at the end of this form.	13	I certify that the applicant has a sufficient interest in the restriction being entered in the register. Nature of applicant's interest: Details of how the applicant's interest arose: Signature of conveyancer: _____ The conveyancer's full name is:

WARNING

If you dishonestly enter information or make a statement that you know is, or might be, untrue or misleading, and intend by doing so to make a gain for yourself or another person, or to cause loss or the risk of loss to another person, you may commit the offence of fraud under section 1 of the Fraud Act 2006, the maximum penalty for which is 10 years' imprisonment or an unlimited fine, or both.

Failure to complete this form with proper care may result in a loss of protection under the Land Registration Act 2002 if, as a result, a mistake is made in the register.

Under section 66 of the Land Registration Act 2002 most documents (including this form) kept by the registrar relating to an application to the registrar or referred to in the register are open to public inspection and copying. If you believe a document contains prejudicial information, you may apply for that part of the document to be made exempt using Form EX1, under rule 136 of the Land Registration Rules 2003.

Section 77 of the Land Registration Act 2002 imposes a duty not to apply for the entry of a restriction without reasonable cause; anyone in breach of this duty may be liable to damages to anyone who suffers loss in consequence.

© Crown copyright (ref: LR/SC/17) 07/19

1.231
HM Land Registry Form FR¹

HM Land Registry
Application for first registration

FR1

Any parts of the form that are not typed should be completed in black ink and in block capitals.

You must lodge the documents of title with this application; these must be listed on Form DL.

If you need more room than is provided for in a panel, and your software allows, you can expand any panel in the form. Alternatively use continuation sheet CS and attach it to this form.

HM Land Registry is unable to give legal advice, but you can find guidance on HM Land Registry applications (including our practice guides for conveyancers) at www.gov.uk/land-registry.

Conveyancer is a term used in this form. It is defined in rule 217A, Land Registration Rules 2003 and includes persons authorised under the Legal Services Act 2007 to provide reserved legal services relating to land registration and includes solicitors and licensed conveyancers.

For information on how HM Land Registry processes your personal information, see our Personal Information Charter

HM LAND REGISTRY USE ONLY
Record of fees paid
Particulars of under/over payments
Reference number
Fees debited £

Where there is more than one local authority serving an area, enter the one to which council tax or business rates are normally paid.

1 Local authority serving the property:

Insert address including postcode (if any) or other description of the property, for example 'land adjoining 2 Acacia Avenue'.

On registering a rentcharge, profit a prendre in gross or franchise, insert a description, for example 'Rentcharge (or as appropriate) over 2 Acacia Avenue'.

2 Property:

Place 'X' in the appropriate box. Only use the third option where the property has an address and is fenced on the ground.

Enter reference, for example 'edged red'.

Enter nature and date of document.

Failure to complete this panel is likely to result in the rejection of the application.

3 The extent of the land to be registered can be clearly identified on the current edition of the Ordnance Survey map from

☐ the attached plan and shown:

☐ the plan attached to the:

☐ the address shown in panel 2

Place 'X' in the appropriate box.

4 The class of title applied for is

☐ absolute freehold ☐ absolute leasehold

☐ possessory freehold ☐ good leasehold

☐ ☐ possessory leasehold

1.231 Property

To find out more about our fees visit www.gov.uk/government/collections/fees-land-registry-guides

Failure to enter the current market value of the land in this panel and/or to include a fee based on Scale 1 will result in a requisition being raised or rejection of the application.

Remember restrictions in deeds may apply to other deeds of lower priority in this list, unless you specify otherwise.

5 Application, priority and fees

Applications in priority order	Price paid/Value (£)	Fees paid (£)
First registration of the freehold/leasehold estate		
	Total fees (£)	

Place 'X' in the appropriate box.

The fee will be charged to the account specified in panel 7.

Fee payment method

☐ cheque made payable to 'Land Registry'

☐ direct debit, under an agreement with Land Registry

Provide the full name(s) of the person(s) applying for first registration. Where a conveyancer lodges the application, this must be the name(s) of the client(s), not the conveyancer.

If the application is based on adverse possession or lost deeds, you may add a telephone number and/or email address for the applicant that we can use for arranging any survey which may be needed.

Complete as appropriate where the applicant is a company. Also, for an overseas company, unless an arrangement with HM Land Registry exists, lodge either a certificate in Form 7 in Schedule 3 to the Land Registration Rules 2003 or a certified copy of the constitution in English or Welsh, or other evidence permitted by rule 183 of the Land Registration Rules 2003.

6 The applicant:

For UK incorporated companies/LLPs
Registered number of company or limited liability partnership including any prefix:

For overseas companies
(a) Territory of incorporation:

(b) Registered number in the United Kingdom including any prefix:

This panel must always be completed.

If you are paying by direct debit, this will be the account charged.

A key number is only available to professional customers, such as solicitors.

This is the address to which we will normally send requisitions and return documents. However if you insert an email address, we will use this whenever possible.

We will only issue warning of cancellation letters to conveyancers if an email address is inserted.

7 This application is sent to Land Registry by

Key number (if applicable):
Name:
Address or UK DX box number:

Email address:
Reference:
Phone no: Fax no:

Place 'X' in the appropriate box.

In this and panel 10, each proprietor may give up to three addresses for service, one of which must be a postal address whether or not in the UK (including the postcode, if any). The others can be any combination of a postal address, a UK DX box number or an electronic address.

8 The address(es) for service for each proprietor of the estate to be entered in the register is

☐ the address of the property (where this is a single postal address)

☐ the following address(es):

Where the applicant is more than one person, place 'X' in the appropriate box.	9	Where the applicant is more than one person ☐ they hold the property on trust for themselves as joint tenants ☐ they hold the property on trust for themselves as tenants in common in equal shares

Complete as necessary.
 	
The registrar will enter a Form A restriction in the register *unless*:
- an 'X' is placed:
  - in the first box, or
  - in the third box and the details of the trust or of the trust instrument show that the applicants are to hold the property on trust for themselves alone as joint tenants, *or*
- it is clear from completion of a form JO lodged with this application that the applicants are to hold the property on trust for themselves alone as joint tenants.
 	
Please refer to *Joint property ownership* and *practice guide 24: private trusts of land* for further guidance. These are both available on the GOV.UK website.
		☐ they hold the property on trust:

Where a charge has an MD reference we will ignore an address given in this panel unless the charge is in favour of a United Kingdom bank and neither the charge form nor any agreement we have with the lender specifies an address for service. For permitted addresses see note to panel 8. Complete as appropriate where the proprietor of the charge is a company. Also, for an overseas company, unless an arrangement with HM Land Registry exists, lodge either a certificate in Form 7 in Schedule 3 to the Land Registration Rules 2003 or a certified copy of the constitution in English or Welsh, or other evidence permitted by rule 183 of the Land Registration Rules 2003.	10	Name and address(es) for service for the proprietor of any charge to be entered in the register: For UK incorporated companies/LLPs Registered number of company or limited liability partnership including any prefix: For overseas companies (a) Territory of incorporation: (b) Registered number in the United Kingdom including any prefix:
If this statement applies (i) place 'X' in the box and (ii) enclose Form DI. Rule 28 of the Land Registration Rules 2003 sets out the disclosable overriding interests that you must tell us about.	11	Disclosable overriding interests ☐ Disclosable overriding interests affect the estate.

1.231 *Property*

This panel must be completed for all applications for first registration regardless of whether you are relying on title documents or only on a statutory declaration or statement of truth. Failure to complete this panel is likely to result in the rejection of the application.

If you are lodging certified copy deeds only, have you remembered to include the separate certificate?

Place 'X' in the appropriate box.

If applicable complete the second statement with details of the interest(s); for interests disclosed only by searches do not include those shown on local land charge searches. Certify any interests disclosed by searches that do not affect the estate being registered.

If you do not place 'X' in the box we will assume that you have examined the applicant's title or are satisfied that it has been examined in the usual way.

Full details of the evidence of identity that is required can be found in Practice Guide 67 and in 'Completing the evidence of identity panels on forms AP1, FR1, and DS2' both of which can be found on the GOV.UK website.

The requirement of registration is contained in section 4, Land Registration Act 2002. Further guidance is contained in Practice Guide 1.

Place 'X' in the appropriate box.

Conveyancer is defined in rule 217A, Land Registration Rules 2003 and includes persons authorised under the Legal Services Act 2007 to provide reserved legal services relating to land registration and includes solicitors and licensed conveyancers.

12 Certificate

The title is based on the title documents listed in Form DL which are all those under the control of the applicant.

Details of rights, interests and claims affecting the estate (other than non-disclosable interests falling within rule 28(2) of the Land Registration Rules 2003) known to the applicant are, where applicable, disclosed in the title documents and Form DI if accompanying this application.

☐ The applicant knows of no other such rights, interests and claims. Only the applicant is in actual possession of the property or in receipt of the rent and profits from the property.

☐ The applicant knows only of the following additional such rights, interests and claims, including those of any person (other than the applicant) in actual possession of the property or in receipt of the rent and profits from the property:

13 Examination of title

☐ I/we have not fully examined the applicant's title to the estate, including any appurtenant rights, or satisfied myself/ourselves that it has been fully examined by a conveyancer in the usual way prior to this application.

14 Confirmation of identity

When registering transfers, charges, leases and other dispositions of land, Land Registry relies on the steps that conveyancers take, where appropriate, to verify the identity of their clients. These checks reduce the risk of property fraud.

Where a person was not represented by a conveyancer, Land Registry requires 'evidence of identity' in respect of that person, except where the first alternative in panel 15(2) applies.

'Evidence of identity' is evidence provided in accordance with any current direction made by the Chief Land Registrar under section 100(4) of the Land Registration Act 2002 for the purpose of confirming a person's identity.

If this application is to register a transfer, lease or charge, dated on or after 10 November 2008 **and** the requirement of registration applies, complete one of the following

☐ I am a conveyancer, and I have completed panel 15

☐ I am not a conveyancer, and I have completed panel 16

Page 4 of 7

15 Where the application is sent to Land Registry by a conveyancer

(1) Details of conveyancer acting

If you are sending an application to register a transfer, lease or charge, for each party to each disposition that is to be registered state in the table below the details of the conveyancer (if any) who represented them.

Where a party is not represented by a conveyancer you must also complete (2) below.

Place 'X' in the box in the second column if the person or firm who is sending the application to HM Land Registry represented that party in the transaction. Otherwise complete the details in the third column. If the party is not represented insert 'none' in the third column.

A separate box is provided, or can be added, for each party, as required by panel 15(1). That includes separate boxes for attorneys and donors where appropriate.

Name of transferor, landlord, transferee, tenant, borrower or lender		Conveyancer's name, address and reference
	☐	Reference:

(2) Evidence of identity

Where any transferor, landlord, transferee, tenant, borrower or lender listed in (1) was not represented by a conveyancer

Place 'X' in the appropriate box(es).

Insert the name of each unrepresented transferor, landlord, transferee, tenant, borrower or lender for whom you give this confirmation.

☐ I confirm that I am satisfied that sufficient steps have been taken to verify the identity of

and that they are the transferor, landlord, transferee, tenant, borrower or lender listed in (1) (as appropriate)

Evidence of identity is defined in panel 14. Full details of the evidence of identity that is required can be found in Practice Guide 67 available on the GOV.UK website.

☐ I enclose evidence of identity in respect of each unrepresented transferor, landlord, transferee, tenant, borrower or lender for whom I have not provided the confirmation above

1.231 *Property*

16 Where the application is sent to Land Registry by someone who is not a conveyancer

(1) Details of conveyancer acting

If you are sending an application to register a transfer, lease or charge (ie a mortgage), for each party to each disposition that is to be registered, state in the table below the details of the conveyancer (if any) who represented them.

You must also complete (2) below.

If the party is not represented insert 'none' in the second column.

A separate box is provided, or can be added, for each party, as required by panel 16(1). That includes separate boxes for attorneys and donors where appropriate.

Name of transferor, landlord, transferee, tenant, borrower or lender	Conveyancer's name, address and reference
	Reference:
	Reference:
	Reference:
	Reference:
	Reference:

(2) Evidence of identity

Place 'X' in the appropriate box(es).

Evidence of identity is defined in panel 14. Full details of the evidence of identity that is required can be found in 'Completing the evidence of identity panels on forms AP1, FR1, and DS2' available on the GOV.UK website.

☐ for each applicant named in panel 6 is enclosed

☐ for each unrepresented transferor, landlord, transferee, tenant, borrower or lender listed in (1) is enclosed

If a conveyancer is acting for the applicant, that conveyancer must sign.

If you are lodging certified copy deeds only, have you remembered to include the separate certificate?

If no conveyancer is acting, the applicant (and if the applicant is more than one person then each of them) must sign.

17

Signature of conveyancer: ....

Date:

OR

Signature of applicant: ....

Date:

Precedents **1.231**

WARNING
If you dishonestly enter information or make a statement that you know is, or might be, untrue or misleading, and intend by doing so to make a gain for yourself or another person, or to cause loss or the risk of loss to another person, you may commit the offence of fraud under section 1 of the Fraud Act 2006, the maximum penalty for which is 10 years' imprisonment or an unlimited fine, or both.

Failure to complete this form with proper care may result in a loss of protection under the Land Registration Act 2002 if, as a result, a mistake is made in the register.

Under section 66 of the Land Registration Act 2002 most documents (including this form) kept by the registrar relating to an application to the registrar or referred to in the register are open to public inspection and copying. If you believe a document contains prejudicial information, you may apply for that part of the document to be made exempt using Form EX1, under rule 136 of the Land Registration Rules 2003.

© Crown copyright (ref: LR/SC/17) 05/19

185

1.232 *Property*

Section 2 Contentious precedents

1.232

Claim form for a declaration of a beneficial interest in property and an order for sale under the Trusts of Land and Appointment of Trustees Act 1996

Claim Form (CPR Part 8)	In the
	OAKWOOD COUNTY COURT
	Claim No. OK 12345

Claimant

JANE PLANE
66a Sycamore Road
Oakwood
Elmshire

SEAL

Defendant(s)

RICHARD HORNBEAM
6 Firs Avenue
Oakwood
Elmshire

Details of claim (see also overleaf)

In the matter of the Trusts of Land and Appointment of Trustees Act 1996

In relation to 6 Firs Avenue Oakwood: registered at HM Land Registry under Title No OAK 5432
1. An order for the sale of the property
2. A declaration that the property and the net proceeds of sale thereof belong to the Claimant and Defendant in equal shares or such other shares as the Court may decide
3. Further or other relief
4. Costs

Defendant's name and address   £

RICHARD HORNBEAM
6 Firs Avenue
Oakwood
Elmshire

Court fee	
Solicitor's costs	
Issue date	

The court office at
is open between 10 am and 4 pm Monday to Friday. When corresponding with the court, please address forms or letters to the Court Manager and quote the case number.

N208 Claim form (CPR Part 8) (4.99)   *Printed on behalf of The Court Service*

	Claim No.	

Details of claim (continued)

See witness statement attached.

Statement of Truth
*~~I believe~~ (The Claimant believes) that the facts stated in these particulars of claim are true.
*~~I am duly authorised by the claimant to sign this statement~~
Full name ___JANE PLANE_____

Name of claimant's solicitor's firm_____

signed _____ position or office held _____
*(Claimant)(~~Litigation friend~~) (~~if signing on behalf of firm or company~~)
(~~Claimant's solicitor~~)

delete as appropriate

Claimant's or claimant's solicitor's address to which documents should be sent if different from overleaf. If you are prepared to accept service by DX, fax or e-mail, please add details.

1.233 Property

1.233

Claimant's witness statement in support of application for declaration/order for sale

(1) I, [name] of [address] make this statement in support of my application for a declaration that I have a beneficial interest in [the property] and for an order for the sale of the property.

(2) In [date] I began living with the defendant at [address]. This property was in his sole name. We lived there together until [date] when [the property] was purchased. That property was also purchased in the defendant's sole name.

(3) During the time that we lived together at [address] we each put part of our earnings into a savings account in our joint names. The account was held at the High Street branch of [bank]. These savings were intended to be used for any items of joint expenditure such as holidays, replacement of furniture and appliances in the property, decoration and repair and ultimately for use in the purchase of our next house.

(4) I was not in a position to put as much as the defendant into this joint account as my earnings were about half of what he earned. As a general rule I would pay in about a third of what the defendant paid in. However, I also paid for any extras for the house, for example I would often buy food apart from the food we bought together on the shared weekly shop, and I would buy household linen and oddments for the kitchen if I saw anything that I particularly liked. I am aware that the defendant had other savings that he kept apart from the joint savings account.

(5) In [date] we started to look for another house. The defendant said that it would be better for us financially if we bought a better house as that was how people made money. We looked around for quite a long time and eventually decided to buy [the property]. We were able to sell [address] for £   . I understand that about £   was used to redeem the mortgage. We paid £   for [the property] and as far as I am aware £   from the joint account went towards the purchase price. The balance was raised by way of mortgage advance but as I was not directly involved in the financial dealings I do not know how much was borrowed, nor how much of the equity from [address] was applied to the purchase of [the property]. I have had a valuation of [the property] a copy of which is annexed to this statement. The valuation is £   .

(6) I was not involved in the financial side of the purchase of [the property]. The defendant told me that there was no need for me to be involved with the mortgage because he could raise what was needed on the strength of his own earnings. I did not think anything about this at the time, and as I remember going to see the solicitors to sign something I presumed that my name was on the deeds. As far as I was concerned the purchase of [the property] was a joint venture. Nothing that the defendant did or said ever made me think otherwise.

When we bought [the property] he said that it would help secure our financial future and he would encourage me to save in the joint account rather than spend my money on clothes, or a holiday for us, saying that we would reap the benefits.

(7) After we moved in to [the property], we started again to build up the savings in the joint account. The defendant made the mortgage repayments and paid the bills as he had done at [address], but after about 6 months he said that he would like me to contribute to the bills as the mortgage repayments were more expensive than the old house and he was finding it difficult. I agreed of

course, and took over responsibility for payment of the telephone and water bills, and one half of the council tax. These payments amounted to about £   per month. We continued to share the cost of the weekly shop.

(8) In [date] we decided that we would like to have the house decorated throughout and have beech flooring on the ground floor. The cost of this, approximately £   , was paid from the joint account.

(9) In [date] my relationship with the defendant began to deteriorate and by the end of that year we decided to separate. I suggested that he buy out my interest, or alternatively that the house be sold. It was at this stage that the defendant informed me that the house was in his sole name and that because we were not married I had no claim to it. He would not leave the house, and because of his attitude towards me I could not continue to live there and so I left and I am currently in a rented flat.

(10) I would like to realise what I believe to be my interest in [the property] and I ask the court to make a declaration as to my beneficial entitlement by virtue of my direct financial contribution to the purchase price, and my contributions to the household expenditure generally. These contributions were made in the belief that I would have an interest in the property and not be left after 6 years with nothing. If I had thought that only the defendant was entitled to the house I would not have done as he suggested and save in the joint account for expenditure to improve the house, nor would I have made contributions to the outgoings. I have acted to my detriment in this regard.

(11) I ask the court to declare that I have a beneficial interest in [the property] on the basis of the understanding that I believed the defendant and that the property was a joint venture and that I was to have an interest in it. Although I knew that only the defendant was bound by the mortgage he led me to believe that my name was on the title deeds and this is the reason he gave me for my having to go to the solicitor's office to sign a document. I have acted to my detriment in reliance upon the understanding that I believed that we shared and I ask the court to find that the defendant holds [the property] on a constructive trust for both of us in equal shares, and that if the defendant will not buy out my share that there be a sale of the property and a division of the net proceeds.

Dated this   day of

I believe that the facts stated in this witness statement are true.

....

1.234

Claimant's witness statement in support of application for sale of land under the Trusts of Land and Appointment of Trustees Act 1996

(1) I, [name] of [address] make this statement in support of my application for the sale of [the property].

(2) I lived with [name] at [the property] from [date] until [date] when I left. I had formed a relationship with another woman who I have now married. The defendant still lives at [the property] and I believe that she has her boyfriend living there on a more or less permanent basis.

(3) I had known the defendant for about 3 years before we started to live together. At first we lived in a rented place but after a short time we decided

to buy [the property]. The property was put into our joint names. We were both working in good jobs and as much as anything else regarded the purchase as an investment. We paid equal amounts towards the deposit and the property was put into joint names. We shared the mortgage repayments and other household outgoings. Generally speaking, if repairs needed to be done I would do them as I am good at DIY, but if there was anything major we would contribute to the cost equally. As far as I am concerned [the property] belongs to us jointly.

(4) When I first left, the defendant indicated that she would buy me out. She is now dragging her feet and refusing to communicate with me. I know of no good reason why if she is not prepared to buy out my interest [the property] should not be sold.

(5) Accordingly, I ask for an order for sale, and for me to receive one half of the net proceeds. I also ask the court to order that the defendant pays me an occupation rent for the period since I left until the date of sale.

Dated this   day of

I believe that the facts stated in this witness statement are true.
....

1.235

Order for sale of property under the Trusts of Land and Appointment of Trustees Act 1996

IN THE [ ] COUNTY COURT   CASE NUMBER
BETWEEN:

                                      A   Claimant

and

                                      B   Defendant

ORDER

UPON hearing counsel for the claimant and counsel for the respondent (AND BY CONSENT)

[IT IS DECLARED THAT the defendant holds the property described in the schedule hereto on trust for the claimant and the defendant as tenants in common in equal shares (or as the case may be)]

IT IS ORDERED THAT:

(1) The property described in the schedule hereto shall be sold forthwith by agents to be agreed between the parties and at a price to be agreed between the parties and in the event of disagreement to be determined by the court.

(2) The claimant's/defendant's solicitors shall have the conduct of the sale.

(3) The claimant's costs shall be the subject of a detailed assessment if not agreed and shall be paid by the defendant and charged against his share of the net proceeds of sale of the property.

THE SCHEDULE

The freehold/leasehold property known as [address] and registered at HM Land Registry under Title Number .

1.236

Applicant's sworn statement in support of injunction to prevent service of Notice to Quit

IN THE [ ] COUNTY COURT   CASE NUMBER
In the Matter of the Family
Law Act 1996, Pt IV
BETWEEN:

                                          A   Applicant

and

                                          B   Respondent

SWORN STATEMENT OF
APPLICANT

I, [name], of [address] MAKE OATH and say as follows:

(1) I make this statement in support of my application for an order that the respondent be restrained from serving a Notice to Quit of the house in which we live together, [the property].

(2) The respondent is the sole tenant [we are joint tenants] of the property, the landlords being the [landlord]. I moved into the property 6 years ago with my two children from a previous relationship aged 9 and 11. The respondent and I have two children who are aged 2 and 4.

(3) Our relationship was always a turbulent one, and the respondent would often leave the property and go and stay with friends, sometimes for days on end. The respondent's behaviour became such that a month ago after an incident that caused the respondent to leave the property again I applied for a non-molestation order and an occupation order. The respondent did not attend the hearing and so the judge made a non-molestation order, and an order that the respondent should not return. The order will remain in force for a further 5 months.

(4) After the order was served on him, the respondent came to the house and tried to persuade me into a reconciliation. I said that I would think about it. However there was a recent incident of violence following which I told the respondent that I did not want him back. He turned nasty and said that if that was the case I should find somewhere else to live because it was his house, and that if he couldn't live there then he didn't see why I should.

(5) The respondent is so unpredictable and vindictive that I am sure he will tell the landlords that he no longer wants the tenancy of the property. It is for this reason also that I ask the court to make an order without giving notice to the respondent. If he has not already thought of doing so, this application will

certainly give him the idea and I do not want anything to jeopardise my application for a transfer of the tenancy.

SWORN etc.

1.237

Application for transfer of tenancy under Pt IV of the Family Law Act 1996

See Form FL401 at 4.89.

1.238

Sworn statement in support of application for transfer of tenancy under Pt IV of the Family Law Act 1996

I, [name] of [address] MAKE OATH and say as follows:

(1) I am the applicant and I make this statement in support of my application for the transfer of the tenancy of [the property] from the sole name of the respondent into my sole name.

(2) The respondent and I have lived together at the property since [date]. The respondent moved out 2 months ago after I obtained a non-molestation injunction against him. He now lives at his mother's. I remain at the property with our two children, Jack who is five, and Emma who is three. My 8-year-old daughter from a previous relationship also lives with us.

(3) The property is a three-bedroomed semi-detached house rented from [landlord]. The respondent is the sole tenant as he was already living at the property when I met him. We never bothered to have the tenancy changed into joint names. I gave up my own council flat when I moved in with the respondent.

(4) As the tenancy is in the respondent's sole name, I assumed that he would continue to make the rent payments after he left. However, I discovered that he had not been making the payments when I had a visit from the [landlord's] housing officer. I have been paying what I can aford, which is effectively the weekly rent payments, but the [landlords] say that unless the arrears are cleared they may not allow the transfer of the tenancy to my name.

(5) As far as I am aware, the respondent is under no pressure to move from his mother's and only the two of them live in her two-bedroomed bungalow, but the respondent says he will not give up the tenancy because he says he doesn't see why I should have the benefit of it.

(6) I have a greater need for the house with three young children to care for, and the house has been their home for as long as they can remember. I could not aford to pay a deposit for private rented accommodation, whereas the respondent is in a position to save money for that purpose if he wanted to.

(7) In all the circumstances I ask the court to make an order for the transfer of the tenancy into my name, and for the respondent to pay the accrued rent arrears.

SWORN etc.

1.239

Order for transfer of protected or secure tenancy under Pt IV of the Family Law Act 1996

IN THE [ ] COUNTY COURT   CASE NUMBER
BETWEEN:

                        A   Applicant

and

                        B   Respondent

ORDER

UPON hearing the solicitor for the applicant and the respondent appearing in person (AND BY CONSENT)

IT IS ORDERED THAT:

Pursuant to the Family Law Act, s 53, with the effect from the   day of   the estate or interest which the respondent has in [the property] shall be transferred to and vested in the applicant by virtue of this order and without further assurance.

Dated this   day of

1.240

Order for transfer of statutory tenancy under Pt IV of the Family Law Act 1996

IN THE [ ] COUNTY COURT   CASE NUMBER
BETWEEN:

                        A   Applicant

and

                        B   Respondent

ORDER

UPON hearing the solicitor for the applicant and the respondent appearing in person

IT IS ORDERED THAT:

Pursuant to the Family Law Act, s 53, the respondent shall with effect from the   day of   cease by virtue of his statutory tenancy of [the

1.240 *Property*

property], to be entitled to occupy the property and the applicant shall be deemed to be the sole tenant of the property under the said statutory tenancy.

Dated this   day of

1.241

Tomlin order on compromise of dispute over property

IN THE [ ] COUNTY COURT   CASE NUMBER
BETWEEN:

                                    A   Claimant

and

                                    B   Defendant

The parties having agreed terms of settlement as set out in the Schedule

BY CONSENT IT IS ORDERED THAT:

(1) All further proceedings in this action be stayed except for the purpose of implementing the agreed terms for which purpose the parties have permission to apply to the court.

(2) The defendant shall pay the claimant's costs of the action to be the subject of a detailed assessment if not agreed.

SCHEDULE

(A) The defendant will on or before the   day of   pay or cause to be paid to the claimant the sum of £   X,000.

(B) If the defendant fails to pay all or any part of the sum of £   X,000 by the due date the following provisions shall apply:

(a) the sum outstanding shall carry interest at 4 per cent above the base rate for the time being of [bank];

(b) the property [*address*] shall be sold forthwith by public auction, the claimant's solicitors to have the conduct of the sale;

(c) the net proceeds of sale shall be applied as follows:

(i) to redeem the mortgage outstanding to [lender];

(ii) to pay the solicitors' and estate agents' costs of sale;

(iii) to pay the outstanding sum due to the claimant with accrued interest;

(iv) in satisfying any outstanding liability of the defendant for the costs ordered to be paid in paragraph 2 above;

(v) in payment of the balance to the defendant.

Dated this   day of

1.242

Declaration of ownership of chattels

IN THE [ ] COUNTY COURT CASE NUMBER
BETWEEN:

                                A   Claimant

and

                                B   Defendant

UPON HEARING the solicitors for the parties

IT IS ADJUDGED AND DECLARED THAT:

(1) The items listed in Schedule A to this order are the property of the claimant.

(2) The items listed in Schedule B to this order are the property of the defendant.

(3) The items listed in Schedule C to this order are the property of the claimant and defendant in equal shares.

IT IS ORDERED THAT:

(4) The defendant shall by 4 pm on   and at his own expense deliver up to the claimant all the items listed in Schedule A to this order.

(5) The claimant and defendant shall by 4 pm on   agree the division between them of the items listed in Schedule C to this order. In default of agreement all the items listed in Schedule C shall forthwith be sold by public auction and the net proceeds of sale after deducting the costs of removal and sale shall be divided by the claimant and defendant in equal shares.

(6) The defendant shall pay the claimant's costs assessed at £   by 4 pm on .

Dated this   day of   .

Chapter 2

COHABITATION AGREEMENTS

Part A LAW AND PRACTICE

Introduction

2.1 Despite the prevalence of couples living together in England and Wales, agreements regulating cohabitation, and more particularly its aftermath, are rarely found in practice. This is consistent with the general lack of attention to the possible consequences of transactions entered into between cohabitants. This reluctance to transform the deliberately informal into a formal arrangement is understandable. Furthermore, at the outset of a relationship, the possibility that it may come to an end is generally not given any thought.

Advising clients

2.2 Those who are cohabiting, or intending to cohabit, will rarely see a solicitor for the express purpose of entering into a cohabitation agreement. They are more likely to present themselves as prospective purchasers of a property. Clearly, the duty of the solicitor in these circumstances is to give advice about the legal implications of buying the property together, and if there is likely to be a conflict of interest, to advise one or both parties to seek separate representation[1]. Although there is no duty to give advice about cohabitation agreements, many solicitors take this opportunity to introduce the subject and to suggest how it may help to prevent difficulties in the future, should the relationship terminate for whatever reason. Although the solicitor may explain the process and implications to both parties in general terms, he or she will not be able to represent both parties if instructions are given to proceed. In order to avoid a conflict of interest it will be necessary to refer one or both parties for independent legal advice. If the parties are established clients, the solicitor may act for one of them if the other agrees.

The case of *Sutton v Mishcon de Reya and Gawor and Co*[2] went some way to clarifying the court's approach to cohabitation agreements. It is now clear that as long as the parties can establish an intention to create legal relations, that there is no express or implied provision for payment for sexual relations and the agreement complies with the necessary requirements for a valid contract, the agreement may be valid and enforceable. Even so, there can be no guarantee and it is vital that any agreement is in writing.

2.2 Cohabitation Agreements

Those advising couples proposing to enter into an agreement should emphasise that in an imperfect world they are the best that is currently available to cohabitants to record what they have agreed and to attempt to regulate their relationship whilst it is subsisting and to make provision in the event that it breaks down. It should also be emphasised that a cohabitation agreement is no substitute for properly recording the shares in which property is owned[3], and making provision by will and/or nomination to receive benefits under a policy or pension in the event of separation by death[4].

What follows in relation to the contents and drafting of cohabitation agreements must therefore be viewed against this background.

[1] See **1.2, 1.186** above.
[2] [2004] 1 FLR 837.
[3] See **1.4** above.
[4] See **6.6** below.

Validity of cohabitation agreements

2.3 Those in this jurisdiction wishing to enter into a cohabitation agreement may do so, but in the absence of any specifically applicable legislation, they have to rely upon the law of contract if they wish to take enforcement steps. This presupposes that their agreement is a valid one.

At one time, an agreement that was founded on the premise that the contracting parties would be living together in a union other than marriage would have been declared void as a matter of public policy, being sexually immoral and likely to prejudice the status of marriage[1].

Social attitudes have changed sufficiently so that today it is unlikely that a cohabitation agreement would be considered invalid on either of these grounds. Care should nonetheless be taken to ensure that the agreement is not expressed in such a way as to suggest that the cohabitation itself, or more particularly the provision of sexual services, is the consideration for entering into the agreement.

In *Sutton v Mishcon de Reya and Gawor and Co*[2] a distinction was drawn between a cohabitation agreement regulating the property and financial arrangements of a couple who were enjoying a sexual relationship and were cohabiting or intending to cohabit, and an agreement such as the one in that case the primary purpose of which was to regulate the parties' sexual relationship. The former would not be contrary to public policy, the latter would, and would therefore be invalid.

The facts of *Sutton* were unusual. Two men had agreed to enter into a cohabitation agreement. They took legal advice from the first defendants and a written agreement was concluded.

The basis of their relationship and the proposed cohabitation was the enactment of a sexual fantasy of master and slave. The agreement contained details about provision of property and income, by the 'slave' for the 'master' both during the cohabitation and in the event that the relationship came to an end. There was also a separate Statement of Trust, referred to in the cohabitation agreement, in which the details of the master/slave relationship were recorded.

Property and other assets were transferred from the claimant, the 'slave', to the 'master' pursuant to the agreement and in anticipation of the cohabitation. However, the relationship soon came to an end and the parties never cohabited. The 'slave' sought the return of property and other assets that he had transferred to the 'master'. This was resisted, and on the advice of the second defendants the 'slave' entered into a deed of separation which required the 'master' to transfer back the property, but enabled him to retain the benefit of cash and other gifts given to him during the relationship.

The claimant brought a claim in negligence against both firms of solicitors. They applied to strike out the claim and succeeded, the judge finding that the claim had no prospects of success as the solicitors had given appropriate advice.

Central to the decision to strike out the claim was the non-enforceability of the cohabitation agreement. The main reason was the public policy consideration, the judge concluding that this ' . . . was not a property contract between two people whose sexual relationship involved them in cohabitation. It was itself an attempt to express the sexual relationship in the property relations contained in the contract . . . It was an attempt to reify an unlawful ideal'.

The judgment also touched upon the question of misrepresentation, the 'master' having failed to inform the claimant that he was HIV positive, and the domination of the one by the other in the playing out of the fantasy clearly raised the issue of undue influence[3].

[1] 'The law will not enforce an immoral promise, such as a promise between a man and a woman to live together without being married . . . ' per Lord Wright in *Fender v St John-Mildmay* [1938] AC 1 at 42.
[2] [2004] 1 FLR 837.
[3] For further reading see Mark Pawlowski 'Cohabitation Contracts The Sutton Case' [2004] Fam Law 199 and Gerald Wilson 'Sutton in Practice' [2004] Fam Law 202.

Enforceability of cohabitation agreements

2.4 Even if a cohabitation agreement were valid, it could nonetheless be unenforceable if it failed to comply with the essential requirements of contract law.

The intention to create legal relations

2.5 As between those in a close personal relationship, there is a marked reluctance for courts to find that there was an intention to create a legally binding contract[1]. Entering into a formal, written agreement may have the effect of rebutting the presumption that the parties do not intend their domestic arrangements to be legally binding[2]. However, factors such as whether the parties took independent legal advice and whether there was full and frank disclosure before entering into the agreement will be relevant to this

2.5 Cohabitation Agreements

question. Similarly, the court is more likely to find that there was an intention that the agreement would be legally binding if it is confined to matters concerning property and money, rather than simply the minutiae of domestic life.

[1] For contractual intention in social and domestic arrangements generally, see G H Treitel *The Law of Contract* (Sweet & Maxwell, 8th edn), at pp 151–153; see also *Balfour v Balfour* [1919] 2 KB 571.
[2] See *Jones v Padavatton* [1969] 1 WLR 328.

Consideration

2.6 If the agreement is in the form of a deed, no consideration is necessary. This avoids the risk of inadvertently overlooking the requirement for there to be consideration, or of making the consideration the cohabitation itself, which may render the contract void for illegality.

Uncertainty

2.7 If the terms of any contract are uncertain or vague so as to be incapable of being enforced, they may jeopardise the entire agreement. The same applies to cohabitation agreements. This is a matter for the draftsman. There should be no scope for uncertainty in the interpretation of the terms of the contract, but for safety a severance clause should be included[1].

[1] See **2.119** below.

Duress or coercion; inequality of bargaining power

2.8 There is no presumption of undue influence as between cohabiting couples as there is in other close relationships, such as those between engaged couples[1], or uncle and nephew[2]. However, there is clearly the potential for one party to exploit the emotional involvement and trust of the other. It is important therefore that both parties to the agreement are separately advised and represented, and that there is full and frank disclosure of the financial position of each party.

[1] *Re Lloyds Bank Ltd, Bomze and Lederman v Bomze* [1931] 1 Ch 289; *RBS v Etridge (No 2)* [2002] 2 AC 773.
[2] *Cheese v Thomas* [1994] 1 All ER 35.

Ousting the court's jurisdiction

2.9 Provisions in the agreement that purport to oust the jurisdiction of the court will be void on public policy grounds.

Contents of a cohabitation agreement

2.10 In the interests of enforceability it will generally be preferable to confine the contents of any agreement that is intended to be legally binding to matters of land, property and money. Provisions relating to the day-to-day regulation of the relationship are better contained in a separate document, essentially for reference purposes. Checklists of matters which should be contained in every cohabitation agreement and additional matters which may be contained in agreements intended to regulate property and financial matters may be found at **2.14** and **2.15**.

Part B CHECKLISTS

Checklist – points to consider when advising on and drafting a cohabitation agreement

The initial interview

2.11 At the initial interview:

(1) Clearly explain to the couple that, if as a result of their discussions they decide to go ahead with a cohabitation agreement, you will be able to act for only one of them, and will recommend the other to obtain independent legal advice.
(2) Advise generally on the common law, equitable, and statutory rights and obligations of cohabiting partners.
(3) If necessary, explain how these rights and obligations differ from those which apply to an engaged or married couple.
(4) Discover whether their needs could be met more readily and effectively by other deeds and documents instead of, or in addition to, a cohabitation agreement.
(5) Advise on the present status of a cohabitation agreement in English law.
(6) Discuss the remedies that are available for breach of contract.
(7) Establish whether, in the light of the advice given, there is consensus that they both wish to enter into a cohabitation agreement.
(8) Clarify the extent to which they wish the agreement to be legally binding on them.
(9) Establish exactly which partner if either, you will be able to represent.
(10) Give the other party the name, address and telephone number of at least one legal practitioner who can give competent, independent advice.
(11) Extract from the client all the information required to prepare a preliminary draft contract.
(12) Find out which partner will pay your costs.

Drafting

2.12 The usual drafting rules apply to a cohabitation agreement with, perhaps, the following modifications.

(1) It may be necessary to state a lot of facts and intentions, with the result that the recitals may be lengthier than in most documents.
(2) The parties will be setting down the ground rules for a relationship which may be entirely unique to them: it is not a marriage, and it may be difficult simply to compartmentalise this relationship into a pre-existing formula, or precedent.
(3) Four copies of the draft should be prepared (for the file, the client, the client's partner, and the remaining copy for the partner's legal adviser).

2.13 Cohabitation Agreements

Submitting the draft to the client

2.13 When discussing the draft contract with the client, either in correspondence or at a further meeting, you should:

(1) inform the client once again about his or her rights and obligations in the absence of the agreement;
(2) state how those rights and obligations are or may be affected by the draft agreement;
(3) advise the client whether the draft is fair and reasonable in the circumstances;
(4) advise the client whether or not it is in his or her best interests, financially or otherwise, to enter into the agreement;
(5) establish that nothing has been erroneously omitted or admitted, and that the draft reflects the whole agreement between the parties;
(6) reiterate the advice given before, that the client's partner should seek independent legal advice;
(7) warn the client that under no circumstances should he or she:
  (a) try to 'explain' the draft agreement to his or her partner;
  (b) make any verbal promises that are not expressly included in the draft agreement; and
  (c) pressurise his or her partner into agreeing the draft and signing the agreement.

Checklist of matters to be contained in every cohabitation agreement

2.14 The cohabitation agreement should contain:

(1) an acknowledgement that each party has received independent legal advice;
(2) an expression of the intention to be legally bound by the agreement;
(3) confirmation that the agreement is freely entered into;
(4) a commencement date;
(5) the proposed duration of the agreement;
(6) any determining events;
(7) a schedule setting out the parties' respective financial positions;
(8) clarification of the status of after-acquired property;
(9) provision for variation of the agreement;
(10) a severance clause;
(11) a jurisdiction clause;
(12) provision for the document to be executed as a deed;
(13) agreement as to payment of the costs of the agreement;
(14) ADR clause.

Checklist of matters that may be contained in agreement intended to regulate property and financial matters

2.15 Land and property:

(1) purchase and beneficial interests (in addition to trust deed);
(2) liability for repayment of mortgage or other loan for purchase;

(3) liability for any negative equity;
(4) payment for repairs and improvements;
(5) payment of outgoings;
(6) non-monetary contributions;
(7) sale of property;
(8) purchase of replacement home;
(9) application of proceeds of sale.

Insurance policies:

(10) legal ownership and beneficial interests;
(11) payment of premiums;
(12) surrender;
(13) distribution on maturity;
(14) distribution of any windfalls;
(15) provision on death.

Stock exchange and other investments:

(16) ownership;
(17) sale and distribution of proceeds.

Joint bank/building society accounts:

(18) contributions to the account;
(19) withdrawals from the account;
(20) distribution of account on any separation.

Pension:

(21) nominations for death benefits.

House contents:

(22) those in sole name only;
(23) those in joint names;
(24) provision for division on separation;
(25) car purchase and running expenses;
(26) items subject to credit.

Part C   PRECEDENTS

Clauses

2.16

Acknowledgment of advice received

Each party acknowledges that he or she has been separately advised by a qualified lawyer and is aware of the rights and obligations of cohabitants generally and the manner in which those rights and obligations are or may be affected by this agreement.

2.17 *Cohabitation Agreements*

After-acquired property

2.17

Separate

Any property that is subsequently owned by one party alone (whether created by its owner, or acquired by purchase, gift, inheritance or otherwise), and any income derived from it, and any increase in its value, will remain the separate property of the party who owns it.

2.18

Shared

Any property that is subsequently acquired by either party (whether by purchase, gift, inheritance or otherwise), and any income derived from it, and any increase in its value will belong to both parties equally, unless they expressly agree otherwise in writing.

2.19

Aims and expectations

The parties' aims and expectations are:

(1) to build and maintain a relationship which is based on mutual friendship, love, loyalty, respect and trust; and

(2) to support each other not only financially but also emotionally.

Amendments (*see* 2.144 and 2.145 below).

Arbitration (*see* 2.51–2.53 below).

2.20

Attestation clause incorporating legal adviser's certificate[1]

SIGNED as a Deed[2] by (*name 1*) in my presence after I had given (him)/(her) independent legal advice on the effects and implications of this Agreement.

[1] See footnote to 2.83 below.
[2] Execution as a deed may overcome any difficulties arising from the lack of consideration.

Bank accounts

2.21

Separate

(1) Each party will maintain separate bank or building society accounts and the money in each such account will remain his or her separate property.

(2) The parties do not intend to open any joint account.

2.22

Shared

(1) The parties will (open and) maintain an account in their joint names ('the joint account') at (*name and address of bank or building society branch*).

(2) The joint account and any interest credited to it will, at all times, belong to the parties in equal shares, regardless of the actual sums which either of them may have paid into or withdrawn from the joint account.

(3) Each party may draw cheques on and withdraw cash from the joint account (up to a limit of £   , but any cheque or withdrawal exceeding that sum must be signed or made by both parties).

(4) If either party purchases goods or makes an investment in his or her sole name out of funds held in the joint account then, in the absence of any contrary agreement between the parties, the goods or the investment will belong to the person making the purchase or investment.

2.23

Beneficial interests: separate

Neither party will acquire, or seek to acquire, or claim to have acquired a beneficial interest in any present or future property owned solely by the other party.

2.24

Binding effect of agreement

This agreement is legally binding on the parties and their respective executors and administrators, estates and assigns.

2.25

Birth control

(*Name*) will be primarily responsible for birth control arrangements.

2.26

Business interests: separate

(1) The present and future business interests of (*name*) and any income derived from them, and any increase in their value are, will be and will remain (his)/(her) separate property.

(2) (*Name's*) 'business interests' include (but are not restricted to (*set out details*)) [OR] (any asset, interest, share, rights and obligations in any business, trade, profession or vocation, or any firm, partnership, company or organisation in which (he)/(she) may be engaged, employed or concerned or to which (he)/(she) may render services now or in the future).

(3) (*Name*) warrants that (his)/(her) business interests are currently worth approximately £   .

2.27

Cancellation of cohabitation agreement

THIS AGREEMENT made on (*date*)

BETWEEN (1) (*name 1*) of (*address*) and (2) (*name 2*) of (*address*).

WITNESSES that the parties now cancel and rescind in all respects and for all

2.27 Cohabitation Agreements

purposes the Cohabitation Agreement made by them on (*date*) on which this Agreement is endorsed.

SIGNED as a Deed by (*name 1*) in the presence of:

SIGNED as a Deed by (*name 2*) in the presence of:

Cars

2.28

Separate

(1) The car that each party owns now and any vehicle that may be acquired to replace it is and will remain the separate property of that party.

(2) Each party is solely responsible for the costs of acquiring, insuring, maintaining and running his or her car.

(3) Each party will permit and effect proper insurance cover to enable the other party to drive his or her car.

2.29

Shared

(1) The (*description of car*) registration number (*number*) that the parties own at present ('the car') belongs to the parties in equal shares, regardless of whose name actually appears on the vehicle registration document, and regardless of the contributions made by either party towards its acquisition.

(2) Unless the parties agree otherwise in writing, any vehicle which is subsequently acquired to replace the car will also belong to the parties in equal shares, regardless of whose name actually appears on the vehicle registration document, and regardless of the contributions made by either party towards its acquisition.

2.30

One party to provide a car for the other

(1) Until the termination of this agreement (*name 1*) will provide (*name 2*) with a car for (his)/(her) own use and enjoyment.

(2) (*Name 1*) will pay all the running expenses of the car, including vehicle excise duty, insurance, maintenance, repairs, (membership of the AA/RAC) and petrol.

(3) The car will be replaced every (3) years with another car, and each replacement will be no more than (one year) old when it is acquired, and will have an engine capacity of not less than (1600) cc.

(4) (*Name 1*) will retain ownership of the car.

(5) On the termination of this agreement (*name 2*) will deliver up possession of the car to (*name 1*).

2.31

Careers

The parties consider that (*name 1's*) career is of greater social and economic importance to them than (*name 2*'s) career and (*name 2*) agrees that if (*name 1*) is required to move elsewhere to further (his)/(her) career (*name 2*) will transfer (his)/(her) own job to the new location.

Child care

2.32

Allocation of responsibility[1]

The parties intend to share the responsibility of looking after their children and so far as practicable will take turns in staying home from work whenever a child is unwell or the children are on holiday.

[1] See also **2.34** below, to which this clause could, if considered appropriate, be added as a sub-clause.

2.33

Support of carer[1]

If one party temporarily stops working in order to stay at home to look after the children, the other party will pay him or her (one half) of his or her disposable income until the youngest child is placed in a nursery or primary school.

[1] See **2.34** below, to which this clause could, if considered appropriate, be added as a sub-clause.

2.34

Children: statement of intentions

The parties have been advised and understand that any provision in this agreement which affects their child or children may be unenforceable in law or varied by the court. Nevertheless, if the parties have a child or children, they intend:

(1)   jointly to register the child's birth[1]; or

(2)   that the child's surname will be (*surname*)[2];

(3)   that the child's forename(s) will be chosen by the parties jointly[3];

(4)   by means of a Parental Responsibility Agreement to provide for (*name 1*) to have parental responsibility for the child[4];

(5)   that any major decision about the child's health and welfare, education and upbringing will be made by the parties jointly;

(6)   to contribute financially towards the child's upbringing for as long as is necessary on the basis of their respective abilities to pay[5]; and

(7)   that if they separate, the parent with whom the child is living will use his or her best endeavours to ensure that the child maintains contact with the parent with whom he or she is no longer living[6].

[1] Births and Deaths Registration Act 1953, ss 10 and 10A (as amended); a father who jointly registers the child's birth with the child's mother will automatically acquire parental responsibility (CA 1989, s 4(1)(a)).

[2] The right to determine the child's name is vested in the parent who has parental responsibility except where a residence order or care order is in force (see **5.21**). For the position where the child's father and mother were not married to each other at the time of the child's birth, see Children Act 1989, s 2(2).

2.34 Cohabitation Agreements

³ The right to determine the child's name is vested in the parent who has parental responsibility except where a residence order or care order is in force (see **5.21**). For the position where the child's father and mother were not married to each other at the time of the child's birth, see Children Act 1989, s 2(2).
⁴ Children Act 1989, s 4(1)(b). For the prescribed form of parental responsibility agreement, see **5.86** below.
⁵ See, generally, Children Act 1989, Sch 1, and Child Support Act 1991.
⁶ For 'contact orders' see Children Act 1989, s 8(1).

2.35

Commencement

THIS COHABITATION AGREEMENT is made on (*date*)

BETWEEN 'the parties': (1) (*name 1*) of (*address*) ('*name 1*') and (2) (*name 2*) (also) of (*address*) ('*name 2*').

IT IS AGREED that:

2.36

Commencement date

This Agreement will come into force on (*date*).

2.37

Confidentiality

Each party promises never to use, disclose or divulge to the detriment or disadvantage of the other any confidential information about the other's private life, family life or business affairs which may have come to his or her knowledge during the course of their relationship.

2.38

Consideration: specific

In consideration of (*name 2*) giving up (his)/(her) present job in order to live with (*name 1*), (*name 1*) will (*set out details*).

2.39

Consideration: general

This Agreement is made in consideration of the mutual promises (and releases) it contains and for other good and valuable consideration the sufficiency of which each of the parties acknowledges.

Cooling-off clause

2.40

Counselling

If either party is seriously thinking of ending the relationship, both parties will

2.41

Trial separation

If either party is seriously thinking of ending the relationship, both parties will spend at least (7) days apart before making any final decision.

Costs

2.42

Shared equally

The legal costs relating to the preparation (negotiation) and execution of this Agreement (including the combined total of the costs incurred by each of the parties in obtaining independent advice) will be paid by the parties in equal shares.

2.43

One party to pay all the costs

(*Name 1*) will pay all the legal costs relating to the preparation (negotiation) and execution of this Agreement (including the costs incurred by (*name 2*) in obtaining independent advice and assistance).

2.44

One party to pay for independent advice

(1) (*Name 1*) will pay the legal costs relating to the preparation (negotiation) and execution of this Agreement.

(2) (*Name 2*) will pay the costs incurred by (him)/(her) in obtaining independent legal advice on the provisions and implications of this Agreement.

2.45

Covenants relating to residential property[1]

Each party promises:

(1) at all times to comply with the covenants and conditions affecting (*address*) ('the property');

(2) at all times to keep the property in good repair and condition and insured to its full reinstatement value;

(3) not to create or attempt to create any mortgage or charge over the property or any part of it or any interest in it without the other's consent; and

(4) not to create or attempt to create any tenancy, licence, agreement or any other right affecting the property without the other's consent.

---

[1] It may be sensible to include these covenants in a cohabitation agreement if they are not already incorporated in, for example, a declaration of trust.

2.46 Cohabitation Agreements

Credit cards

2.46

Separate

Each party will maintain separate credit accounts and neither party will use the other's credit.

2.47

Shared[1]

(1) (*Name 1*) will nominate (*name 2*) to use a credit card on (his)/(her) (*credit company*) account number (*account number*).

(2) Between the parties themselves (*name 2*) will be responsible for the payment for all purchases made by (him)/(her) on the account and for any interest attributable to those purchases.

(3) (*Name 2*) promises at all times to use the card with care and consideration and to indemnify (*name 1*) against any loss incurred as a result of (his)/(her) use, misuse or abuse of the card.

[1] Usually a principal cardholder can nominate one other person to be an authorised user of a credit card. The authorised user generally has to sign an acknowledgment accepting and agreeing to be bound by the conditions of use imposed by the bank or credit company. The card itself is usually the company's property. The principal cardholder is usually liable for repayment. It may be worthwhile checking each individual agreement and the terms and conditions of use.

2.48

Debts

(1) Each of the parties will remain personally liable for any current and future debts incurred in his or her sole name.

(2) The payment by one party of any part of the other's personal debts will in no way render the payer liable for or obliged to make any further payment in respect of those debts.

2.49

Declaration of trust[1]

The rights and interests of the parties in the property known as (*address*) and its net proceeds of sale are set out in a Declaration of Trust dated (*date*) and are not in any way varied or affected by this Agreement.

[1] It may be considered preferable to deal with the beneficial interests in jointly owned property in a completely separate declaration of trust rather than to include, possibly lengthy, additional clauses in the cohabitation agreement. The execution of a declaration of trust by an unmarried couple who jointly own property is now virtually a mandatory requirement.

2.50

Deed[1]

This Agreement is a deed and is executed by the parties as a deed.

[1] One of the grounds on which it is argued that a cohabitation agreement may be unenforceable

at law is lack of consideration. This problem can be overcome by executing the cohabitation agreement as a deed. To take effect as a deed the instrument must make it clear on its face that it is intended to be a deed (whether by describing itself as a deed or expressing itself to be executed as a deed) and it must be validly executed as a deed by the parties to it (Law of Property (Miscellaneous Provisions) Act 1989, s 1(2)).

Dispute resolution

2.51 For clauses referring the dispute to a conciliator or mediator, see **2.53** and **2.54**.

2.52

Arbitration

(If any attempt at conciliation or mediation is unsuccessful) any difference, disagreement or dispute arising out of or in connection with this Agreement will be referred to an Arbitrator nominated at the request of either party by the (President) of the (Area) District Law Society.

2.53

Conciliation

Any difference, disagreement or dispute arising out of or in connection with this Agreement will be referred in the first instance to (the local family mediation service) without prejudice to the right of either party to apply subsequently to the court for adjudication.

2.54

Named mediator[1]

(1) Any difference, disagreement or dispute which arises out of or in connection with this Agreement will be referred in the first instance to (*name*) who will act as a mediator.

(2) If (*name*) is unwilling or unable to act as mediator the problem will be referred to (*name B*) instead.

[1] In certain circumstances a named mediator may be preferred to, for example, the local family mediation service. Selecting a personal friend might place that friend in a difficult position. It is probably wiser to choose someone who is known to and respected by both parties but who is not a close, personal friend of either. As a courtesy to the proposed mediator, and to avoid any potential problems about acceptance of that role, the parties should obtain the consent of the proposed mediator before making such an appointment.

Duration

2.55

Indefinite

The parties plan to live together indefinitely.

2.56

Fixed term

Unless it terminates earlier in accordance with the provisions of Clause (*number*), this Agreement will terminate on (*date*).

2.57 Cohabitation Agreements

Dwelling

2.57

Joint tenancy[1]

The parties own (*address*) as beneficial joint tenants, regardless of the actual contributions made by either party towards its acquisition.

[1] See, generally, CHAPTER 1 'Property'.

2.58

Tenancy in common[1]

The parties own (*address*) as beneficial tenants in common as to   per cent of the net proceeds of sale for (*name 1*) and as to   per cent for (*name 2*), regardless of the actual contributions made by either party towards its acquisition.

[1] See, generally, CHAPTER 1 'Property'.

2.59

One party is sole owner

(*Name 1*) owns (*address*) and (*name 2*) acknowledges that (he)/(she) has not acquired, will not acquire and will not claim to have acquired any beneficial interest in that property.

2.60

Estate rights[1]

(1) Neither party is under any obligation to make financial provision for or to confer any other benefit on the surviving party on death.

(2) Neither party has agreed, promised or represented to the other that he or she will execute a will or sign any other instrument which will make financial provision for or confer any other benefit on the surviving party[2].

(3) Each party releases, renounces and surrenders to the other party and the other party's estate any right which he or she may have as a cohabitee to apply to the court for an order under s 2 of the Inheritance (Provision for Family and Dependants) Act 1975 or any statutory modification or re-enactment of it[3].

(4) Nothing in this Agreement constitutes a renunciation of the right of the surviving party (if entitled) to obtain a grant of representation to the estate of the deceased party or a disclaimer by the surviving party of any financial provision, benefit or right conferred by the deceased party in his or her will or arising otherwise as a result of his or her death.

[1] See CHAPTER 7.
[2] See *Synge v Synge* [1894] 1 QB 466, CA, where the man made an antenuptial promise in writing to leave the woman a life interest, and the woman was entitled to enforce the promise. See also *Re Basham (Deceased)* [1986] 1 WLR 1498 – deceased giving assurances as to a stepdaughter's future rights to his estate.
[3] See **2.111** below.

2.61

Execution of this agreement[1]

This Agreement has been executed in duplicate and each copy will be deemed an original and will constitute one and the same agreement between the parties.

[1] For multiple execution of deeds, see generally, Co Litt 229a; *Burchell v Clark* (1876) 2 CPD 88 at 96, CA.

2.62

Fiduciary duty

Each party promises to show the utmost good faith and to deal fairly with the other in implementing the provisions of this Agreement.

Financial disclosure

2.63

By one party only[1]

(1) (*Name 1*) has disclosed to (*name 2*) details of the income, earning capacity, property and other financial resources, and the financial needs, obligations and responsibilities which (he)/(she) has now and is likely to have in the foreseeable future.

(2) (*Name 1*) has neither asked for, nor received, nor wishes to receive similar information from (*name 2*).

[1] As a general rule, a person who is about to enter into a contract is under no duty to disclose material facts known to him but not known to the other party. A contract 'uberrimae fidei' is an exception to such general rule. It is not clear whether a cohabitation agreement would be classified as a contract 'uberrimae fidei', akin to a family arrangement. In *Wales v Wadham* [1977] 1 WLR 199 at 218, it was held that although there might be cases where there was a duty to make full and frank disclosure before there was a duty to do so by affidavit, when the jurisdiction of the court had been invoked, no such duty arose in this case because the parties had made a bargain at arm's length. On contracts 'uberrimae fidei' see, generally G H Treitel *The Law of Contract* (Sweet & Maxwell, 8th edn) at pp 349—362.

2.64

By both cohabitants

(1) (*Name 1*) estimates that (his)/(her) net capital resources are currently worth about £   and that (his)/(her) net annual income from all sources is approximately £   .

(2) (*Name 2*) estimates that (his)/(her) net capital resources are currently worth about £   and that (his)/(her) net annual income from all sources is approximately £   .

(3) Both parties acknowledge that each of them has been given the opportunity to examine the other's financial records.

2.65

Further assurances

When required to do so, each party will complete, sign and execute any deed,

2.65 Cohabitation Agreements

document or form which may be needed in order to implement the provisions of this Agreement.

Gifts between cohabitants

2.66

Presumption that the gift is absolute

Any gift from one party to the other will be presumed to be an absolute gift unless it is expressly given on the condition that it will be returned to the giver on the termination of the parties' relationship.

2.67

Reservation of rights

Nothing in this Agreement regarding the separate property and assets of the parties deprives either party of the right to give to or receive from the other property and assets of any description by way of gift, transfer or legacy.

2.68

Gifts received: separate

Any gift, inheritance or unexpected good fortune received by either party will be and will remain the separate property of that party.

2.69

Guests

Neither party will, without first obtaining the other party's consent, invite any friend, relative or guest to stay (for longer than (24 hours)).

2.70

Headings

The headings in this Agreement have been inserted for convenience and reference and must not be interpreted as defining, limiting or extending the substance and scope of the provisions above which they appear.

2.71

Housekeeping allowance: fixed sum

(1) For as long as the parties are living together (*name 1*) will pay to (*name 2*) a housekeeping allowance of £   a (week)/(month).

(2) The allowance will be adjusted at least once a year in line with the Retail Prices Index.

(3) Any property purchased by (*name 2*) from any surplus or accumulations of the allowance will belong to (*name 2*) absolutely.

2.72

Housework

The parties will share the housework equally.

[OR]

The parties will take turns in doing the housework.

[OR]

(1) (Name 1) will be primarily responsible for the following household tasks:

(2) (Name 2) will be primarily responsible for the following household tasks:

Illness or incapacity

2.73

Attorneyship[1]

Each party will as soon as practicable execute an instrument appointing the other party to be his or her attorney for the purpose of the Mental Capacity Act 2005.

[1] If either party should become seriously ill or incapacitated the other party could be treated by various authorities as a 'legal stranger'. If the cohabitee has been appointed as an attorney, he or she will have authority to act on behalf of the incapacitated party. If the parties separate, a lasting power of attorney ('LPA') can easily be revoked. If, however, the EPA has been registered in the Court of Protection, revocation must be confirmed by the court.

2.74

Next of kin

So far as it is legally possible to do so each party will nominate and appoint the other to be his or her 'next of kin' or 'nearest relative' (for contact, emergency, visiting, advocacy and representation purposes)[1].

[1] See generally **6.96–6.102**.

2.75

Support

For as long as the parties are living together each will be responsible for supporting the other.

Income

2.76

Separate

Each party's income from all sources and all accumulations of that income will be and will remain his or her separate property and will not be subject to division between the parties on the termination of their relationship.

2.77

Shared

The parties will pool and commingle their respective incomes from all sources (and

2.77 Cohabitation Agreements

will share equally all accumulations of and property acquired from their pooled incomes, regardless of the actual income earned or received by either party).

2.78

Intention to create legal relations

(1) (Part I) [OR] (Clauses   to   inclusive) of this Contract contain(s) agreements that will be legally binding on the parties and their personal representatives and estates.

(2) (Part II) [OR] (Clauses   to   inclusive) of this Contract contain(s) agreements to which the parties are bound in honour only and which give rise to no legal rights and for the breach of which no legal action will lie.

(3) (Part III) [OR] (Clauses   to   inclusive) of this Contract contain(s) provisions of general application.

2.79

Interpretation of this agreement[1]

No provision in this Agreement will be construed against one party merely because it was drafted or inserted by his or her legal adviser.

[1] This clause is designed to negate the effects of the 'contra proferentem' rule of construction, whereby the wording of a document is construed more strongly against the party putting it forward. This rule of construction is applied in cases of ambiguity, where other rules of construction fail.

Joint property

2.80

Joint tenancy[1]

Any property or asset acquired jointly by the parties while they are living together will belong to them as beneficial joint tenants, regardless of their respective contributions towards its acquisition, unless they provide otherwise in writing[2] and clearly identify their respective shares or interests in the property or asset in question.

[1] This clause relates to any jointly acquired assets, and could include investments, a dwelling and personal chattels.
[2] This clause envisages that all joint property will be held as beneficial joint tenants unless the contrary is provided in a separate declaration of trust in writing. In the case of pure personalty, an oral declaration suffices, but is hardly satisfactory.

2.81

Tenancy in common[1]

Any property or asset acquired jointly by the parties while they are living together will belong to them as beneficial tenants in common in shares corresponding to the actual contributions made by each of them towards the acquisition of the property or asset, unless they provide otherwise in writing.

[1] See footnotes to 2.80 above.

2.82

Joint use: separate ownership

The use by one party of any property which belongs to the other party will not give rise to the joint ownership of that property.

2.83

Legal adviser's certificate[1]

I (*legal adviser's name*) of (*professional address*), (a solicitor of the Supreme Court) [OR] (a Fellow of the Institute of Legal Executives) [OR] (*as the case may be*), CERTIFY that before (he)/(she) signed this Agreement I advised (*name 1*) independently of (*name 2*) on:

(1) (his)/(her) rights and responsibilities in the absence of this Agreement; and

(2) the manner in which those rights and responsibilities are or may be affected by this Agreement; and

(3) whether or not it was prudent or advantageous, financially or otherwise, to enter into this Agreement; and

(4) whether or not at that time and in the light of such circumstances as were then reasonably foreseeable the provisions of this Agreement were fair and reasonable.

Dated:

Signed:

[1] This certificate is based on the wording of the De Facto Relationships Act 1984 (New South Wales), s 47(d), which requires that the certificates be endorsed on, or annexed to, or should otherwise accompany the agreement (De Facto Relationships Act 1984 (New South Wales), s 47(e)).
For a briefer certificate incorporated as part of the attestation clause, see **2.20**.

2.84

Life insurance: agreement to take out and maintain a policy[1]

(*Name 1*) will take out a policy of insurance on (his)/(her) life in the sum of £   for the benefit of (*name 2*) and for as long as (he)/(she) has an obligation to do so under this Agreement will maintain that policy in full force and effect[2] (and will authorise the insurer to disclose to (*name 2*) any information regarding that policy that (he)/(she) may ask for).

[1] Other provisions could be added. For example: increasing the cover periodically; an undertaking not to charge or assign the policy; remedies available if the insured fails to pay the premiums, etc.

[2] This envisages that the obligation will cease on termination of the agreement or shortly afterwards. The legal adviser should ensure that there are provisions to this effect in the clauses relating to the consequences of termination.

Living expenses

2.85

To be paid from joint account[1]

The following living expenses will be paid out of the parties' joint account: mortgage payments; rent; buildings insurance; contents insurance; water; gas; electricity; telephone; groceries; cleaning materials; general toiletries; television licence; holidays; joint recreation; car insurance; car maintenance . . . [2]

[1] This clause assumes that reference is made elsewhere in the agreement to a joint bank or building society account. See **2.22** above.
[2] Delete and add as appropriate.

2.86

To be paid in proportion to the parties' respective incomes

Except for any expenses that are solely attributable to one or the other of them, the parties agree to share all living expenses[1] in proportion to their respective incomes or in such other proportions as they may from time to time agree.

[1] It would be wise to define 'living expenses'. See **2.88** below.

2.87

Fixed percentages

(Name 1) will pay   per cent of the parties' living expenses[1] and (name 2) will pay the other   per cent.

[1] It may be sensible to define 'living expenses'. See **2.88** below.

2.88

One party pays all

(1) For as long as the parties are living together (*name 1*) will pay all their living expenses.

(2) 'Living expenses' include, but are not restricted to: mortgage payments; rent; building insurance; contents insurance; water; gas; electricity; telephone; groceries; cleaning materials; toiletries; holidays; joint recreation (etc).

2.89

Defined areas of responsibility

(1) (Name 1) will be primarily responsible for paying the following living expenses: (*set out details*).

(2) (Name 2) will be primarily responsible for paying the following living expenses: (*set out details*).

(3) Both parties will contribute equally towards the payment of the following living expenses: (*set out details*).

Marriage

2.90

Agreement to continue on marriage

(1) The parties intend that their respective rights and responsibilities contained in this Agreement will not be varied or affected in any way if they marry each other.

(2) The parties also intend that, if their marriage is subsequently dissolved or annulled, the provisions of this Agreement should be one of the matters to which the court should have regard in deciding whether and how to exercise its powers[1].

(3) Despite the provisions above, nothing in this Agreement constitutes an agreement by either party to marry the other[2].

[1] In exercising its powers under ss 23, 24 and 24A of the Matrimonial Causes Act 1973, the court should have regard to, inter alia, all the circumstances of the case which might include entering into such an agreement.

[2] Law Reform (Miscellaneous Provisions) Act 1970, s 1, provides that an agreement between two persons to marry one another does not have effect as a contract giving rise to legal rights.

2.91

Agreement ceases to apply on marriage[1]

This Agreement will cease to have effect if and when the parties marry each other.

[1] See footnotes to 2.90 above.

2.92

Medical insurance

(1) (*Name 1*) will take out and maintain in full force and effect for as long as he has an obligation to do so under this Agreement[1] medical insurance with (*company*) for (*name 2*).

(2) (*Name 1*) will take out and maintain in full force and effect medical insurance with (*company*) for the parties' children until each child reaches the age of (*18*).

(3) Despite the above, (*name 1's*) obligation to take out and maintain medical insurance for (*name 2*) (*and the children*) will continue only for as long as such insurance is available under the scheme operated by (his)/(her) company, business or employer and will be limited to the coverage provided under that scheme.

[1] If this obligation is to cease on the termination of the agreement, words to that effect should be included in the clause relating to consequences of termination.

2.93

Mortgage payments[1]

(*Name 1*) will pay   per cent and (*name 2*) will pay   per cent of the mortgage payments (and these payments will not affect the parties' respective beneficial interests in the property)[2].

[1] For other permutations, see 2.85–2.89 relating to living expenses and adapt accordingly. For example: where payments are to be made from a joint account or where they paid in proportion to the parties' respective incomes or when one party pays all the mortgage payments.

[2] Include or exclude the words in brackets as appropriate.

2.94

Non-disclosure of agreement to third parties

Neither party will disclose any part of this Agreement to any third party unless compelled to do so by legal process, or unless disclosure is necessary in order to

2.94 Cohabitation Agreements

protect or enforce the terms of this Agreement.

2.95

Pensions and death-in-service benefits[1]

Each party will:
(1) nominate the other to receive (per cent of) the pension and death-in-service benefits payable under any pension scheme of which he or she may from time to time be a member;
(2) at the other's request provide written evidence that such nomination has been received and recorded by the trustees of the pension scheme to which it relates.

[1] See **6.6** below.

2.96

Present property: separate

(1) The property listed in Schedule (*number*) belongs to (*name 1*) and will at all times remain (his)/(her) separate property.
(2) The property listed in Schedule (*number*) belongs to (*name 2*) and will at all times remain (his)/(her) separate property.
(3) Neither party will acquire any right or title to or interest in the other's separate property simply by virtue of the parties' cohabitation[1].

[1] See **2.110** below.

2.97

Present property and debts: separate[1]

(1) The property listed in Part 1 of Schedule (*number*) belongs to (*name 1*) and will at all times remain (his)/(her) separate property.
(2) The debts listed in Part 2 of Schedule (*number*) have been incurred by (*name 1*) and (he)/(she) will at all times remain solely liable for their repayment.
(3) [As in 1 above, but in respect of name 2.]
(4) [As in 2 above, but in respect of name 2.]

[1] See also **2.48** above and **2.143** below.

2.98

Proper law

This Agreement will be governed and interpreted in accordance with the law of (England and Wales).

Recitals

2.99

Cohabitation

The parties (intend to) live together.

[*OR*]

The parties have been living together since (date).

2.100

Intention to create legal relations[1]

The parties intend that this Agreement will be legally binding on them and their respective personal representatives and estates.

[1] 'As a rule when arrangements are made between close relations . . . there is a presumption against an intention of creating any legal relationship. This is not a presumption of law, but of fact' (*Jones v Padavatton* [1969] 1 WLR 328 at 332, per Salmon LJ). In the absence of any statement to the *contrary, a formal written contract should in itself rebut such presumption of fact. For a clause expressly stating that no legal relationship is created, see* **2.101** below.

2.101

Intention not to create legal relations

The parties intend that this Agreement will give rise to no legal rights and that no legal action will lie for its breach.

2.102

Purpose of this agreement

The purpose of this Agreement is to define and regulate the respective rights and responsibilities of the parties both during and after their cohabitation.

2.103

No duress or undue influence[1]

Each party is entering into this Agreement freely and voluntarily and without coercion or pressure from the other party or anyone else.

[1] A contract is voidable at common law if it was made under duress. Equity will also give relief against unconscionable bargains if one party has taken advantage of the fact that there is a marked inequality of bargaining power between the parties.
'The English Law gives relief to one who, without independent advice, enters into a contract upon terms which are unfair or transfers property for a consideration which is grossly inadequate, where his bargaining power is grievously impaired by reason of his own needs or desires, or by his own ignorance or infirmity, coupled with undue influence or pressures brought to bear on him by or for the benefit of the other' (*Lloyds Bank Ltd v Bundy* [1975] QB 326 at 339, per Lord Denning MR).

2.104

Cohabitant under 18[1]

(*Name*) is a minor and understands that this Agreement will be legally binding on (him)/(her) unless and until (he)/(she) repudiates it during (his)/(her) minority or within a reasonable time after (his)/(her) eighteenth birthday.

[1] The status, in English law, of a cohabitation agreement, is uncertain (see **2.3**). A fortiori, the status of a cohabitation agreement made by a minor is highly uncertain. It is assumed that such an agreement would be voidable at the minor's option before attaining 18 or within a reasonable time after attaining 18.

2.105 Cohabitation Agreements

2.105

Recitals to be legally binding

The parties warrant that these recitals are true and accurate and intend that they will be legally binding on them.

2.106

Independent legal advice[1]

Before signing this Agreement each party received independent legal advice on its provisions and implications.

[1] See, generally, **1.2**, **1.186**, and **2.2** above.

2.107

Understanding the nature and effect of the agreement

Each party warrants that he or she understands the nature and effect of this Agreement and is entering into it after careful consideration of all the facts, circumstances and implications.

2.108

Recitals: personal information about the parties

(1) *(Name)* was born on *(date)*.

(2) *(Name)* is employed as a *(job description)*. [OR] *(Name)* is a self-employed *(job description)*. [OR] *(Name)* is unemployed. [OR] *(Name)* is a retired *(former job description)*.

(3) *(Name)* is (single)/(separate)/(divorced)/(a widow/widower).

(4) Details of *(name's)* current assets, liabilities and income are recorded in Schedule *(number)*.

2.109

Recitals relating to the child(ren)

(1) The parties are the mother and father of *(child's name)* who was born on *(date)*; *(child's name)* who was born on *(date)*.

(2) By a Parental Responsibility Agreement made between the parties and recorded in the Principal Registry of the Family Division on *(date)*[1] *(name 1)* has parental responsibility for *(child's or children's name(s))* in addition to (his)/(her)/(their) mother or the parties jointly registered the birth and both have parental responsibility, and no order has been made by the court under CA 1989, s 4(2A).

(3) *(Name 2)* is also the mother of *(number)* child(ren) by her (former marriage(s))/relationship(s)) namely: *(child's name)* who was born on *(date)*; *(child's name)* who was born on *(date)*.

(4) *(Name 1)* is also the father of *(number)* child(ren) by his (former marriage(s))/(relationship(s)) namely: *(child's name)* who was born on *(date)*; *(child's name)* who was born on *(date)*.

(5) *(Child's or children's name(s))* live with the parties.

[1] A parental responsibility agreement will not take effect until the prescribed form, duly

completed and signed, has been filed in the Principal Registry of the Family Division (Parental Responsibility Agreement Regulations 1991 (SI 1991/1478)). For the prescribed form, see **5.83**.

2.110

Release of rights (if any) over the other's separate property

Each party releases, renounces and surrenders all (if any) rights that he or she may now or subsequently have to claim any right or title to or any share or interest in any property or income now or subsequently owned or acquired by the other party alone.

2.111

Release of right to apply to the court for an order under the Inheritance (Provision for Family and Dependants) Act 1975[1]

Each of the parties releases, renounces and surrenders to the other and the other's estate any right which he or she may have as a cohabitant[2] to apply to the court for an order under s 2 of the Inheritance (Provision for Family and Dependants) Act 1975 or any statutory modification or re-enactment of it.

[1] Whether it is actually possible to 'contract out' in this way was left an open question in *Zamet v Hyman* [1961] 1 WLR 1442, CA, where a similar release was entered into for monetary consideration by an elderly woman who was shortly to be married. In any event, strict proof would be required to establish that when the parties signed the contract they 'fully understood its significance and after full, free and informed (and particularly informed) thought about it' (at 1450, per Lord Evershed MR). Compare s 15 of the Act which applies only in divorce proceedings, etc.

[2] See, generally, the Inheritance (Provision for Family and Dependants) Act 1975, ss 1(1)(e), (3) and 3(4). See also **6.37**.

2.112

Religious upbringing of child(ren)

If the parties have a child or children, he, she or they will be brought up as members of (the Roman Catholic Church; the Jewish faith; the Church of England; the Methodist Church; *or as the case may be*).

2.113

Remedies for breach of agreement[1]

If either party breaches or fails to comply with any promise or provision contained in this Agreement the other may be entitled to apply to the court for an order awarding:

(1)   damages;

(2)   specific performance;

(3)   an injunction;

(4)   costs.

[1] The inclusion of a clause of this nature puts the parties on notice as to the possible consequences of their failure to comply with any of the specific provisions of the contract.

2.114

Rent

Each party will pay one half of the rent.

[OR] (Name 1) will pay _____ per cent of the rent and (name 2) will pay _____ per cent of the rent.

[OR] (Name) will pay the rent.

2.115

Review: ad hoc review

If for any reason either party is unhappy about any provision in this Agreement he or she may request an ad hoc review of that provision after giving the other party at least (7) days' notice.

2.116

Review of agreement

(1) The parties will review the provisions of this Agreement:

    (a) at least once every year (on or about the anniversary of the date of this Agreement); and

    (b) whenever there is a major change in the personal circumstances of either or both of them.

(2) Events giving rise to a major change in the personal circumstances of either or both of the parties include, but are not restricted to:

    (a) engagement or marriage;

    (b) childbirth;

    (c) illness, injury or accident;

    (d) unemployment, re-employment or retirement;

    (e) inheritance or unexpected good fortune;

    (f) bankruptcy.

(3) The purpose of a review is to decide whether, in the light of the information available and the circumstances reasonably foreseeable at the time:

    (a) any provision of this Agreement should be deleted;

    (b) any provision of this Agreement should be varied;

    (c) any provision should be added to this Agreement;

    (d) this Agreement should be cancelled; or

    (e) this Agreement should be superseded by a new contract.

(4) If as a result of a review any deletions, variations or additions are necessary or this Agreement is to be cancelled or superseded such change must be recorded in an instrument in writing executed (as a deed) by both parties.

2.117

Revocation clause

This Agreement revokes and replaces any previous written or oral agreement between the parties.

2.118

Separation

After the termination of this Agreement neither party will:

(a) without invitation enter or occupy any premises owned or occupied by the other party;

(b) annoy, embarrass, or interfere with the other party and his or her relatives, friends, acquaintances, and business colleagues and contacts.

2.119

Severance[1]

If the court finds that any provision of this Agreement is illegal, invalid, or otherwise unenforceable, such provision may be severed from this Agreement without affecting its other provisions which will continue to have full force and effect.

(The inclusion of this clause does not imply that the parties or their legal advisers believe that any provision of this Agreement may be illegal, invalid, or otherwise unenforceable.)

[1] 'The general rule is that, where you cannot sever the illegal from the legal part of a covenant, the contract is altogether void; but where you can sever them, whether the illegality be created by statute or by the common law, you may reject the bad part and retain the good' (*Pickering v Ilfracombe Railway Co* (1868) LR 3 CP 235 at 250, per Willes J)).
The illegal term must be capable of being separate from the remainder of the contract under what is generally known as 'the blue pencil rule'.

2.120

Sexual relations[1]

Nothing in this Agreement is to be interpreted as imposing an obligation on either party to have sexual relations with the other (or to abstain from having sexual relations with anyone else).

[1] This is a clause for the ultra cautious. One of the grounds on which it is considered that cohabitation agreements generally may be illegal is that they promote sexual immorality and are, accordingly, contrary to public policy. Principles decided in 18th and 19th century case law are still binding precedents. It is unlikely, however, that a court would now strike down a typical cohabitation agreement as immoral. 'The court's function is to apply the law, not personal prejudice. Only in a case where there is still a generally accepted moral code can the court refuse to enforce rights in such a way as to offend that generally accepted code' (*Stephens v Avery* [1988] 2 All ER 477 at 481, per Sir Nicolas Browne-Wilkinson V-C). See *Sutton* 2.2 above.

Support

2.121

Mutual support

For as long as the parties are living together each will be responsible for supporting the other.

2.122

No obligation

Neither party is under any obligation to maintain, support or make any form of financial provision to or for the benefit of the other at any time during or after their cohabitation.

2.123

No promises made

Neither party has agreed, promised or represented to the other that he or she will maintain, support or make any form of financial provision to or for the benefit of the other at any time during or after their cohabitation.

2.124

Reservation of right

Nothing in this Agreement deprives either party of the right voluntarily to maintain, support or make any other form of financial provision to or for the benefit of the other.

2.125

Waiver of rights

Each party waives, releases and surrenders any right which he or she may now or subsequently have to claim or receive maintenance, support or any other form of financial provision from the other party at any time during or after their cohabitation.

Surname

2.126

Each to retain their own surname

Each party will retain his or her own surname.

2.127

Both to be known by the same surname

Both parties will use the surname (*surname*).

2.128

End of relationship[1]

Either party can terminate this Agreement at any time simply by ceasing to live with the other party.

[1] There is no fixed or uniform approach as to what constitutes a termination of cohabitation. For a more comprehensive list of terminating events, see **2.130** below.

2.129

Notice

Either party can terminate this Agreement by giving the other party at least (2) weeks' notice in writing.

2.130

Terminating events

Without prejudice to any provisions of this Agreement that come into force on or remain in force after its termination, this Agreement will terminate when the earliest of these events occurs:

(1) The death of a party.

(2) The marriage of the parties to each other[1].

(3) The parties mutually agree on its termination and sign a written instrument cancelling this Agreement[2].

(4) The expiration of a period of (4) weeks beginning on the date when one party gives to the other written notice of his or her wish to terminate this Agreement.

(5) If the parties have lived apart for a continuous period of at least (4) weeks and one party gives to the other written notice that this Agreement is terminated.

(6) If the court grants an injunction under Pt IV of the Family Law Act 1996 or the Protection from Harassment Act 1997 or any statutory modification or re-enactment of either and (either party) [OR] (the party who applies for the injunction) gives to the other party written notice that this Agreement is terminated.

(7) If one party excludes the other from (the property) without reasonable cause and the excluded party gives written notice to the excluding party that this Agreement is terminated.

(8) The court or an Arbitrator orders that this Agreement is terminated.

[1] For a clause providing that the contract will continue on marriage, see **2.90** above; for the consequences of termination on marriage, see **2.142** below.

[2] See **2.27** above.

Termination consequences

2.131

General introductory clause

If this Agreement is terminated for any reason other than the death of a party or the marriage of the parties to each other, the provisions of Schedule (*number*) will apply.

2.132

Bank and building society accounts

(If this Agreement is terminated (for any reason other than the death of a party or the marriage of the parties to each other)) the parties will:

(1) immediately close all bank accounts and building society accounts held in their joint names;

(2) immediately destroy all plastic or other cards relating to the joint account(s) and return the pieces to the bank or building society;

2.132 Cohabitation Agreements

(3) immediately destroy all unused cheques;

(4) immediately take whatever steps are necessary to ensure that their earnings and other income are no longer credited to any joint account;

(5) on receiving the closing statements, divide the balances on all joint accounts equally between themselves;

(6) continue to be jointly and severally liable for the repayment of all overdrafts, debts and interest payable in respect of the joint account(s);

(7) punctually pay their respective share of all overdrafts, debts and interest, and each party indemnifies the other from and against all actions, demands, proceedings and losses arising from his or her failure to do so.

2.133

Credit and charge cards

(If this Agreement is terminated (for any reason other than the death of a party or the marriage of the parties to each other)) the parties will:

(1) immediately close all joint credit and charge card accounts;

(2) immediately close all credit and charge card accounts in the name of one party alone where the other party is an additional cardholder or authorised user;

(3) immediately destroy all plastic or other cards relating to such accounts and return the destroyed cards to the creditor;

(4) when they receive the closing statements, allocate the debts between themselves on the basis of who will retain each specific item obtained on credit or, where an item obtained on credit has been consumed, who consumed it or who ordered it;

(5) punctually pay their respective share of all debts and interest payable on such accounts, and each party indemnifies against any consequences of his or her failure to do so.

2.134

The dwelling: option to 'buy out' the other's share

(If the Agreement is terminated (for any reason other than the death of a party or the marriage of the parties to each other)):

(1) (*Name 1*) will have the option to purchase (*name 2's*) share of (*address*) or failing which any other principal residence jointly owned by the parties ('the property').

(2) The property will be valued by the parties themselves at such figures as they agree.

(3) If the parties are unable to agree a valuation of the property, it will be formally valued by a professionally qualified valuer, and if more than one formal valuation is obtained the average of the valuations will prevail.

(4) The property will be valued on the basis that:

(a) it is being sold with vacant possession at arm's length on the open market;

(b) all fixtures, fittings, carpets and curtains which do not belong to (*name 2*) alone are included in the sale;

(c) there is no discount for joint ownership.

(5) The price that (*name 2*) will receive for (his)/(her) estate and interest in the property will be (his)/(her) share of the value of the property less (his)/(her) share of all mortgages and charges to which the property is subject.

(6) In the absence of any alternative agreement between them, the parties will observe the following time limits:

(a) within (2) weeks of the termination of this Agreement the property will be valued and a redemption statement will be obtained in respect of every mortgage and charge to which the property is subject;

(b) within (4) weeks of the termination of this Agreement (*name 1*) will give (*name 2*) written notice of (his)/(her) intention to exercise this option;

(c) within (8) weeks of the termination of this Agreement (*name 1*) will complete (his)/(her) purchase of (*name 2's*) share.

(7) If (*name 1*) is unable or unwilling to exercise this option within (4) weeks of the termination of this Agreement or within such other time limit as (*name 2*) has agreed:

(a) (his)/(her) option to purchase (*name 2's*) share will lapse;

(b) (*Name 2*) will have the option to purchase (*name 1's*) share of the property on the same terms mutatis mutandis and the following time-limits will apply in the absence of any alternative agreement between the parties;

(c) within (2) weeks of the date on which (*name 1's*) option lapsed (*name 2*) will give (*name 1*) written notice of (his)/(her) intention to exercise this option;

(d) within (4) weeks of the date on which (*name 1's*) option lapsed (*name 2*) will complete the purchase of (*name 1's*) share.

2.135

Separate property

(If this Agreement is terminated (for any reason other than the death of a party or the marriage of the parties to each other)) each party will keep his or her separate property (and each party will remain personally liable for his or her separate debts.)

2.136

Jointly owned goods and chattels[1]

If this Agreement is terminated (for any reason other than the death of a party or the marriage of the parties to each other) all goods and chattels which the parties jointly own will be divided between them as they agree, and where they fail to agree on division those goods and chattels will be sold and the proceeds of sale will be divided equally between them.

[1] For more comprehensive provisions relating to the division of chattels, see **2.150** below.

2.137

Support

(If this Agreement is terminated (for any reason other than the death of a party or the marriage of the parties to each other)) neither party will be under any continuing obligation to support or maintain the other party.

2.138

Lump sum payment

(If this Agreement is terminated (for any reason other than the death of a party or the marriage of the parties to each other)) within (4) weeks of the termination of this Agreement (*name 1*) will pay to (*name 2*) the sum of £   to enable (him)/(her) (to establish a separate household) [OR] (in full and final settlement of any possible claim for support that may have arisen while the parties were living together.)

2.139

Miscellaneous cancellations

(If this Agreement is terminated (for any reason other than the death of a party or the marriage of the parties to each other)) either party may:

(1)   cancel any nomination that names the other party as a potential recipient of any pension or other benefits arising on the nominator's death;

(2)   cancel any nomination that names the other party as the recipient of the benefits payable under any policy of insurance on the nominator's life;

(3)   revoke any (enduring) power of attorney which appoints the other party to be his or her attorney;

(4)   disclaim any appointment as the other party's attorney by giving the other party written notice of such disclaimer.

2.140

Children

(If this Agreement is terminated (for any reason other than the death of a party or the marriage of the parties to each other)) subject always to the ascertainable wishes and feelings of any child concerned considered in the light of his or her age and understanding:

(1)   the children of the parties' relationship ('the children') will live with (*name 2*);

(2)   the children can have contact with (*name 1*) and (his)/(her) family;

(3)   both parties will maintain the children according to their respective abilities to pay;

(4)   neither party will cause any of the children to be known by a new surname without the written consent of the other party or the leave of the court.

2.141

The other's child(ren)[1]

If this Agreement is terminated (for any reason other than the death of a party or the marriage of the parties to each other) neither party will be under any continuing obligation to support or maintain the other party's child or children.

[1]   But see CA 1989, Sch 1, para 4(2).

2.142

Termination of agreement on marriage: consequences[1]

If this Agreement is terminated on the marriage of the parties to each other:

(1) the separate property and debts of each party will continue to be his or her separate property and debts;

(2) any property that is jointly owned by the parties will continue to be jointly owned by them in the proportions or shares existing at the time of their marriage;

(3) any debts for which the parties are jointly liable will continue to be their joint liability in the proportions or shares existing at the time of their marriage.

[1] See footnotes to 2.90.

2.143

Transfers between cohabitants

(1) Either party can at any time transfer his or her own separate property to the other party solely or jointly, conditionally or unconditionally.

(2) Any such transfer must comply with the legal formalities governing the transfer of property of that nature.

(3) If the nature of the property is such that no specific legal formalities govern its transfer then for the avoidance of doubt such transfer will be evidenced by an instrument in writing dated and signed by the transferor and transferee.

VARIATION OF AGREEMENT

2.144

Clause

This Agreement can only be varied by an instrument in writing executed (as a Deed)[1] by both parties.

[1] In *Berry v Berry* [1929] 2 KB 316, it was held that a separation agreement which had been made by deed (even though there was no legal requirement that it should be made by deed) could be varied by a subsequent agreement which was not a deed.

2.145

Deed

THIS (DEED OF) VARIATION made on (*date*)

BETWEEN (1) (*name 1*) of (*address*) and (2) (*name 2*) also of (*address*).

WITNESSES as follows.

(1) This (Deed)/(Variation) is supplemental to a Cohabitation Agreement ('the agreement') made between the parties on (*date*).

(2) The parties now cancel and rescind Clause(s) (*number(s)*) of the agreement.

(3) The parties now add to the agreement the Clauses set out in the Schedule.

THE SCHEDULE

2.145 *Cohabitation Agreements*

(*insert new clauses*)

SIGNED as a Deed by (*name 1*) in the presence of:

SIGNED as a Deed by (*name 2*) in the presence of:

2.146

Waiver of breach

If either party fails to enforce any provision of this Agreement at any time such acquiescence will not constitute a waiver of that provision or of the right at any other time to enforce that provision and all the other provisions of this Agreement.

2.147

Whole agreement

(1) This Agreement contains the whole agreement between the parties and replaces any previous written or oral agreements between them.

(2) The parties confirm that neither of them has entered into this Agreement on the basis of any promises or representations which are not expressly included in this Agreement.

2.148

Wills

Each party is aware of the rights[1] of the survivor if one of them should die, and each party intends to execute a will as soon as practicable[2].

[1] The surviving cohabitant *may* be entitled to:
   (a) property passing by right of survivorship;
   (b) property passing under a statutory or non-statutory nomination;
   (c) claim under the Inheritance (Provision for Family and Dependants) Act 1975, or under the Fatal Accidents Act 1976.
The surviving cohabitant has no rights on intestacy. See, generally, CHAPTER 6.

[2] A will made pursuant to a contract to make a will in a particular form can be revoked, although the testator or his estate may be liable for breach of contract (*Schaefer v Schuhmann* [1972] AC 572).

Forms

Cohabitation Agreements

SHARING EVERYTHING

2.149

Cohabitation Agreement - Short form

THIS COHABITATION AGREEMENT is made on (*date*)

BETWEEN (1) (*name 1*) and (2) (*name 2*) both of (*address*).

THE PARTIES AGREE:

(1) to combine their incomes for the purpose of living together as a family unit;
(2) to support each other while they are living together;
(3) that if they separate, each party will keep his or her own separate property; and
(4) that if they separate, any property which they jointly own will be divided equally between them.

SIGNED as a Deed by (*name 1*) in the presence of:

SIGNED as a Deed by (*name 2*) in the presence of:

2.150

Cohabitation Agreement - Longer form

THIS COHABITATION AGREEMENT is made on (*date*)

BETWEEN 'the parties' (1) (*name 1*) of (*address*) ('*name 1*') and (2) (*name 2*) (also) of (*address*) ('*name 2*').

IT IS AGREED that:

1 Recitals

1.1 (*Name 1*) was born on (*date*).

1.2 (*Name 1*) is a (*job description*).

1.3 (*Name 1*) has a current net annual income of approximately £ from all sources.

1.4 (*Name 1*) has current net capital resources worth approximately £ .

1.5 (*Name 2*) was born on (*date*).

1.6 (*Name 2*) is a (*job description*).

1.7 (*Name 2*) has a current net annual income of approximately £ from all sources.

1.8 (*Name 2*) has current net capital resources worth approximately £ .

1.9 The parties (intend to) live together.

1.10 The purpose of this Agreement is to define and regulate the respective rights and responsibilities of the parties while they are living together and if they separate.

1.11 Each party has received independent legal advice on the provisions and implications of this Agreement.

1.12 Each party has had an opportunity to examine the other party's financial records.

1.13 The parties intend that this Agreement will be legally binding on them.

2 The house

2.1 The parties (intend to) live at (*address*) ('the house').

2.2 The parties (intend to) own the house as beneficial (joint tenants) [OR] (tenants in common in equal shares), regardless of the actual contributions made by either party towards its acquisition.

3 Separate property

3.1 The items listed in Schedule 1 belong to (*name 1*) and will continue to be (his)/(her) separate property.

3.2 The items listed in Schedule 2 belong to (*name 2*) and will continue to be (his)/(her) separate property.

4 Gifts

4.1 Nothing in this Agreement regarding the separate property of each party deprives either party of the right to give to or receive from the other party any property and assets by way of gift transfer or legacy.

4.2 Any gift from one party to the other will be presumed to be an absolute gift unless it is expressly given on the condition that it will be returned to the giver on the termination of the parties' relationship.

4.3 Any gift, inheritance or unexpected good fortune received by either party will be and will remain the separate property of that party.

5 Income

The parties will pool their respective incomes from all sources, except for the income received from any assets which are specified as the separate property of one party, and will share equally all accumulations of and property acquired from their pooled incomes, regardless of the actual income earned or received by either party.

6 Support

For as long as parties are living together each party will support the other.

7 Termination

This Agreement will terminate:

7.1 if and when the parties marry each other, although nothing in this Agreement constitutes an agreement by either party to marry the other; or, earlier

7.2 if and when the parties cease to live together.

8 Termination: consequences

If this Agreement terminates because the parties cease to live together:

8.1 neither party will be under any continuing obligation to support the other;

8.2 the trust for sale on which the house is held may be enforced by either party;

8.3 all bank accounts, building society accounts, credit accounts and charge card accounts held in the parties' joint names will immediately be closed and the balances and debts will be divided equally between the parties;

8.4 each party will retain his or her separate property;

8.5 all goods and chattels which are jointly owned by the parties will be divided between them as they agree, and in default of agreement the goods and chattels will be sold and the proceeds of sale will be divided equally between the parties.

9 Dispute resolution

Any difference, disagreement or dispute arising out of or in connection with this Agreement will be referred in the first instance to a Conciliator, without prejudice to the right of either party to apply subsequently to the court for adjudication.

10 Variation

This Agreement can only be varied by an instrument in writing executed as a Deed by both parties.

11 Whole agreement

This Agreement contains the whole agreement between the parties and neither of them has entered into it on the basis of any promises or representations which are not expressly included in it.

12 Severability

If the court finds that any provision of this Agreement is illegal, invalid, or otherwise unenforceable, such provision may be severed from this Agreement without affecting any other provisions which will continue to have full force and effect.

SCHEDULE 1

((*Name 1's*) separate property.)

SCHEDULE 2

((*Name 2's*) separate property.)

SIGNED as a Deed by (*name 1*) in the presence of:

SIGNED as a Deed by (*name 2*) in the presence of:

2.151

Keeping everything separate

THIS COHABITATION AGREEMENT is made on (*date*)

BETWEEN (1) 'the parties' (1) (*name 1*) of (*address*) (*name 1*) and (2) (*name 2*) (also) of (*address*) (*name 2*)

IT IS AGREED that:

2.151 Cohabitation Agreements

1 Recitals

(Similar to the recitals in 2.150 above.)

2 The house

2.1 The parties own (*address*) ('the house').

2.2 The parties bought the house on (*date*).

2.3 The purchase price of the house was (*price*).

2.4 The incidental costs of purchasing the house amounted to £   .

2.5 The house is mortgaged to (*lender*).

2.6 The mortgage advance was £   .

2.7 (*Name 1*) paid £   towards the purchase price and purchase costs.

2.8 (*Name 1*) will pay   per cent of the mortgage payments.

2.9 (*Name 1*) will pay   per cent of the sale costs.

2.10 (*Name 1*) will receive   per cent of the sale price less   per cent of the amount required to redeem the mortgage and less   per cent of the sale costs.

2.11 (*Name 2*) paid £   towards the purchase price and purchase costs.

2.12 (*Name 2*) will pay   per cent of the mortgage payments.

2.13 (*Name 2*) will pay   per cent of the sale costs.

2.14 (*Name 2*) will receive   per cent of the sale price less   per cent of the amount required to redeem the mortgage and less   per cent of the sale costs.

3 Bank accounts

3.1 Each party will maintain separate bank accounts and building society accounts and the money in each such account will remain the separate property of that party.

3.2 The parties do not intend to open a joint account.

4 Debts

4.1 Each party will remain personally liable for his or her current debts and any future debts incurred in his or her sole name.

4.2 The payment by one party of any part of the other's personal debts will in no way render the payer liable for or to make any further contribution in respect of those debts.

5 Separate property

5.1 The items listed in Schedule 1 belong to (*name 1*) and will continue to be (his)/(her) separate property.

5.2 The items listed in Schedule 2 belong to (*name 2*) and will continue to be (his)/(her) separate property.

5.3 The use by one party of any property belonging to the other party will not give rise to the joint ownership of that property.

5.4 Each party releases, renounces and surrenders all (if any) rights he or she may now or subsequently have to claim any right or title to or share or interest in any property and income which is now or subsequently owned or acquired by the other party alone.

6 Cars

Each party will permit and effect proper insurance to enable the other party to drive his or her car.

7 Gifts

(As in **2.150**, Clause 4 above.)

8 Living expenses

The parties will contribute equally towards their joint living expenses which include, but are not restricted to, payments for water, gas, electricity, telephone, food, drink, cleaning, joint recreation and holidays.

9 Support

9.1 Except for the extent to which each party is liable to contribute towards the mortgage payments and their joint living expenses, neither party is under any obligation to support or maintain the other while they are living together and after they have ceased to live together.

9.2 Each party releases, renounces and surrenders to the other and the other's estate any right which he or she may have as a cohabitee to apply to the court for an order under s 2 of the Inheritance (Provision for Family and Dependants) Act 1975 or any statutory modification or re-enactment of it.

10 Review

The parties will review the provisions of this Agreement:

10.1 at least once every year; and

10.2 whenever there is a major change in the personal circumstances of either of them.

11 Variation

This Agreement can only be varied by an instrument in writing executed as a Deed by both parties.

12 Termination

This Agreement will terminate:

2.151 Cohabitation Agreements

12.1 if and when the parties marry each other; or, earlier

12.2 if and when the parties cease to live together.

13 Termination consequences

If this Agreement is terminated on the marriage of the parties to each other:

13.1 the separate property and debts of each party will continue to be his or her separate property and debts;

13.2 any property that is jointly owned by the parties will continue to be owned by them in the proportions or shares existing at the time of their marriage;

13.3 any debts for which the parties are jointly liable will continue to be their joint liability in the proportions or shares existing at the time of their marriage.

14 Whole agreement

(As in 2.150, Clause 11 above.)

15 Severability

(As in 2.150, Clause 12 above.)

SCHEDULE 1

((*Name 1*'s) separate property.)

SCHEDULE 2

((*Name 2*'s) separate property.)

SIGNED as a Deed by (*name 1*) in the presence of:

SIGNED as a Deed by (*name 2*) in the presence of:

2.152

One party supporting the other

THIS COHABITATION AGREEMENT is made on (*date*)

BETWEEN 'the parties' (1) (*name 1*) of (*address*) ('*name 1*') and (2) (*name 2*) (also) of (*address*) ('*name 2*').

IT IS AGREED that:

1 Recitals

(The same as, or similar to, those in **2.150** above.)

2 Consideration

The promises made in this Agreement by (*name 1*) are made in consideration of:

2.1 (name 2) giving up (his)/(her) present (job)/(accommodation) in order to live with (name 1); and

2.2 the releases given by (name 2).

3 The house

3.1 The parties (intend to) live together at (address) ('the house').

3.2 (Name 1) owns the house.

3.3 (Name 2) releases, renounces and surrenders all (if any) rights (he/she) may have to claim any right or title to or any share or interest in the house and its net proceeds of sale.

4 Living expenses

While the parties are living together (name 1) will pay:

4.1 the costs of financing, maintaining and running the house;

4.2 the bills for the utilities;

4.3 the grocery bills;

4.4 for their joint recreation and holidays.

5 Housekeeping allowance

5.1 While they are living together (name 1) will pay (name 2) a (weekly)/(monthly) allowance of £   .

5.2 The allowance will be adjusted at least once a year in order to bring it in line with the cost of living.

5.3 Any property that (name 2) acquires with the allowance and any accumulations of the allowance will belong to (name 2) absolutely.

6 Car

6.1 While they are living together (name 1) will provide (name 2) with the use of a car.

6.2 (Name 1) will pay all the expenses of running the car, including vehicle excise duty, insurance, maintenance, repairs, membership of the (AA)/(RAC) and petrol.

6.3 (Name 1) will retain the ownership of the car.

6.4 On the termination of this Agreement (name 2) will deliver up possession of the car to (name 1).

7 Credit

7.1 (Name 1) will nominate (name 2) to be an additional cardholder on (his)/(her) (credit company) account.

7.2 Between themselves (name 2) will be responsible for paying for all purchases on that account made solely for (his)/(her) own use, enjoyment and benefit and will be accountable for any interest attributable to those purchases.

8 Separate property

8.1 The items listed in Schedule 1 belong to (*name 1*) and will continue to be (his)/(her) separate property.

8.2 The items listed in Schedule 2 belong to (*name 2*) and will continue to be (his)/(her) separate property.

8.3 The use by one party of any property belonging to the other will not give rise to the joint ownership of that property.

8.4 Each party releases, renounces and surrenders all (if any) rights he or she may now or subsequently have to claim any right or title to or any share or interest in any property and income which now or subsequently belongs to the other party alone.

9 Gifts

9.1 Nothing in this Agreement regarding the separate property of each party deprives either party of the right to give to or receive from the other party any property or assets by way of gift or transfer.

9.2 Any gift from one party to the other will be presumed to be an absolute gift unless it is expressly given on the understanding that it will be returned to the giver on the termination of the parties' relationship.

9.3 Any gift, inheritance or unexpected good fortune received by either party alone will be and will remain the separate property of that party.

10 Estate rights

10.1 (*Name 2*) acknowledges that (*name 1*) is under no obligation to make any financial provision for (him)/(her) or to confer any other benefits on (him)/(her) by Will or otherwise in the event of (his)/(her) death.

10.2 (*Name 1*) has not agreed, promised or represented to (*name 2*) that (he)/(she) will execute a Will or sign any other instrument which will make financial provision for or confer any benefit on (*name 2*) in the event of (his)/(her) death.

10.3 (*Name 2*) releases, renounces and surrenders to (*name 1*) and (his)/(her) estate any right which (he)/(she) may have as a cohabitee to apply to the court for an order under s 2 of the Inheritance (Provision for Family and Dependants) Act 1975 or any statutory modification or re-enactment of it.

10.4 Nothing in this Agreement constitutes a renunciation of the right of (*name 2*) (if entitled) to obtain a grant of representation to (*name 1's*) estate or a disclaimer by (*name 2*) of any benefits conferred on (him)/(her) by (*name 1*) in (his)/(her) Will or arising otherwise as a result of (his)/(her) death.

11 Confidentiality

(*Name 2*) promises never to use, disclose or divulge to the detriment or disadvantage of (*name 1*) any confidential information about (his)/(her) private life, family life or business affairs which may have come to (his)/(her) knowledge or attention during the course of their relationship.

Precedents **2.152**

12 Termination

This Agreement will terminate when the parties cease to live together.

13 Termination: rights and obligations of *(name 1)*

When this Agreement terminates *(name 1)* will:

13.1 be entitled to stop paying the (weekly)/(monthly) allowance to *(name 2)*;

13.2 pay *(name 2)* a lump sum of £   to assist (him)/(her) to establish a separate household;

13.3 pay *(name 2)* an additional lump sum of £   in respect of every complete year which has elapsed between the date of this Agreement and the date on which it terminates;

13.4 be entitled to deduct from these lump sum payments any unpaid balance on the (credit card) account which represents purchases made by *(name 2)* for (his)/(her) sole use, enjoyment or benefit together with any interest attributable to that unpaid balance;

13.5 make the above payments to *(name 2)* within a period of (4) weeks from the latest of the following dates, namely the date on which:

    (a)   this Agreement terminates;

    (b)   *(name 2)* ceases to live in the house;

    (c)   *(name 2)* removes all (his)/(her) belongings from the house;

    (d)   *(name 2)* delivers up possession of the car to (him)/(her);

    (e)   *(name 2)* returns the credit card to (him)/(her).

14 Termination: rights and obligations of *(name 2)*

When this Agreement terminates *(name 2)* will:

14.1 leave the house;

14.2 remove all (his)/(her) belongings from the house;

14.3 deliver up possession of the car to *(name 1)*;

14.4 return the credit card to *(name 1)*;

14.5 be entitled to receive the payments less deductions mentioned in the preceding clause.

15 Separation

After this Agreement has terminated neither party will:

15.1 without invitation enter or occupy any premises that are owned or occupied by the other party;

15.2 annoy, embarrass, interfere with or molest the other party and his or her relatives, friends, acquaintances, business colleagues and contacts.

16 Remedies

If either party breaches or fails to comply with any promise or provision contained in this Agreement the other may be entitled to apply to the court for an order awarding (inter alia):

16.1   damages;

16.2   specific performance;

16.3   an injunction;

16.4   costs.

17 Variation

This Agreement can only be varied by an instrument in writing executed as a deed by both parties.

18 Whole agreement

This Agreement contains the whole agreement between the parties and neither of them has entered into it on the basis of any promises or representations which are not expressly included in it.

19 Proper law

The Agreement will be governed and interpreted in accordance with the law of England and Wales.

20 Severability

If the court finds that any provision of this Agreement is illegal, invalid or otherwise unenforceable, such provision may be severed from this Agreement without affecting any other provisions which will continue to have full force and effect.

SCHEDULE 1

((*Name 1*'s) separate property.)

SCHEDULE 2

((*Name 2*'s) separate property.)

SIGNED as a Deed by (*name 1*) in the presence of:

SIGNED as a Deed by (*name 2*) in the presence of:

2.153

Agreement relating to personal chattels acquired jointly by cohabitants[1]

THIS AGREEMENT is made on (*date*)

Precedents 2.153

BETWEEN 'the parties' (1) (*name 1*) of (*address*) ('*name 1*') and (2) (*name 2*) (also) of (*address*) ('*name 2*').

THE PARTIES AGREE as follows:

(1) They bought a (*description of item*) ('the item')² at/from (shop; seller; auctioneer, etc) on (*date*) for (*price*).

(2) (*Name 1*) contributed £   and (*name 2*) contributed £   towards the purchase price.

(3) The purpose of this Agreement is to establish what will happen to the (*item*) if one party dies or if the parties separate.

(4) If the parties are living together and one of them dies the (*item*) will belong to the survivor absolutely³.

(5) If the parties separate and neither of them wishes to keep the (*item*):

    (a) it will be sold; and

    (b) its net proceeds of sale will be divided between the parties (equally) [*OR*] (in the proportions that each of them contributed towards the purchase price).

(6) If the parties separate and only one of them wishes to keep the (*item*):

    (a) it will be valued; and

    (b) the party who wishes to keep it will pay the other party (one half of its value) [*OR*] (the proportion of its value that the other party contributed towards the purchase price).

(7) If the parties separate and both of them wish to keep the (*item*) and neither of them is willing to relinquish it to the other:

    (a) the (*item*) will be valued;

    (b) the parties will (toss a coin) [*OR*] (draw lots) [*OR*] (throw a dice)⁴;

    (c) the winner will keep the (*item*); and

    (d) the winner will pay the loser (one half of its value) [*OR*] (the proportion of its value that the loser contributed towards the purchase price).

(8) For the purposes of Clauses 6 and 7 of this Agreement:

    (a) the (*item*) will be valued informally by the parties themselves at such sum they agree;

    (b) in default of agreement between the parties the (*item*) will be valued formally by one or more persons whom the parties reasonably believe to be qualified to value it;

    (c) if more than one formal valuation is obtained the average of the valuations will prevail;

    (d) the cost of a formal valuation which is requested jointly by the parties will be paid by the parties in equal shares and the cost of obtaining any other formal valuation will be paid by the party instructing the valuer.

(9) Any difference, disagreement or dispute that arises out of or in connection with this Agreement will be referred in the first instance to (*name*), who will act as a mediator between the parties, without prejudice to the right of either party to apply subsequently to the court for adjudication⁵.

2.153 Cohabitation Agreements

(10) Without prejudice to (his)/(her) role as mediator (name) may, at the parties' request, supervise and have conduct of any of the procedures set out in this Agreement.

(11) (Other clauses)[6].

SIGNED as a Deed by (name 1) in the presence of:

SIGNED as a Deed by (name 2) in the presence of:

[1] This Agreement could be adapted to provide for several joint purchases. It could also be incorporated into a 'cohabitation contract' proper.
[2] Describe the item fully and accurately, and then give it a brief but appropriate definition: eg 'the cat'; 'the DVD'; 'the Rembrandt'.
[3] Subject to the de minimis rules, the deceased's share may have to be brought into account for inheritance tax purposes.
[4] For King Solomon's solution, see 1 Kings 3, 24 and 25.
[5] See Law of Property Act 1925, s 188(1).
[6] Other clauses might include: provisions relating to payment; further assurance to effect the transfer; assumption of responsibility for future payments where the item is being acquired on HP, etc; indemnity for the other party.

2.154

Agreement setting up a joint account to pay housing costs, etc

THIS AGREEMENT is made on (date)

BETWEEN 'the parties' (1) (name 1) of (address) ('name 1') and (2) (name 2) (also) of (address) ('name 2').

IT IS AGREED that:

(1) The parties (intend to) live together at (address) ('the property').

(2) The parties (intend to) own the property as beneficial tenants in common (in equal shares) [OR] (as to   per cent of the net proceeds of sale for (name 1) and   per cent for (name 2)).

(3) On the (first) day of each month (name 1) will pay the sum of £   by standing order from (his)/(her) separate bank account.

(4) On the (first) day of each month (name 2) will pay the sum of £   by standing order from (his)/(her) separate bank account.

(5) The monthly sums paid by each party will be credited to the account held in their joint names at (name and branch of bank or building society) ('the joint account').

(6) The monthly sums payable by each party will be revised in (September) each year and each revision will take into account:

　(a) any variation in the cost of living in the property during the preceding 12 months; and

　(b) any foreseeable variation in the cost of living in the property during the next 12 months.

(7) The revised monthly sums will become payable on the (1 October) each year and before that date each party will instruct his or her bank to amend the standing order accordingly.

(8) The following payments will be made from the joint account:

- (a) the mortgage payments;
- (b) the mortgage endowment policy premiums;
- (c) buildings and contents insurance;
- (d) water services charges;
- (e) gas bills;
- (f) electricity bills;
- (g) telephone bills;
- (h) Council Tax;
- (i) repairs and improvements to the property;
- (j) any other payments that the parties jointly authorise.

(9) Either party can terminate this Agreement by giving the other party not less than (one month's) notice in writing.

(10) When one party gives the other written notice of his or her intention to terminate this Agreement, the parties will immediately:
- (a) close the joint account;
- (b) cut into pieces all plastic and other cards relating to the joint account and return the pieces to the bank (or building society);
- (c) destroy all unused cheques on the joint account;
- (d) cancel the standing orders relating to their respective monthly sums.

(11) When the joint account has been closed the parties will:
- (a) divide the balance on it between themselves (equally) [OR] (in the proportions that their respective monthly sums bear to each other);
- (b) continue to be jointly and severally liable for any overdraft, debt, interest and bank charges incurred on the joint account;
- (c) punctually pay their respective shares of any such overdraft, debt, interest and bank charges, and each party indemnifies the other against the consequences of the indemnifying party's failure to do so.

SIGNED as a Deed by (*name 1*) in the presence of:

SIGNED as a Deed by (*name 2*) in the presence of:

Chapter 3

TAXATION OF UNMARRIED COUPLES

LAW AND PRACTICE

Introduction

3.1 In general, cohabitants are taxed in exactly the same way as single people who do not live together. This contrasts with the treatment of married couples and civil partners where there are specific exemptions and reliefs, particularly for inheritance tax and capital gains tax (all references made to spouses and married couples in this text apply to civil partners as well). In some cases, the exemptions are dependent on the married couple living together. Over the years, and with the exception of a limited relief introduced in 2015 which allows married couples and civil partners to transfer 10 per cent of their personal allowance to their partner in certain circumstances, the income tax advantages of marriage have been whittled away with the result that for the purposes of that tax there are few incentives to couples to marry rather than to cohabit. There are also some tax benefits that apply to those with children.

Income tax

3.2 Both parties to a couple are entitled to a personal allowance for income tax. In the tax year 2019/20 and 2020/21 this amounts to £12,500 which will rise by CPI from then onwards. This represents the amount that can be earned before any tax is payable. For those who receive income of a higher figure, the personal allowance represents that part of their income on which no tax is payable, although the personal allowance is reduced or removed for incomes over £100,000. As everyone is entitled to a personal allowance, minor children (under the age of 18) can also benefit although there are anti-avoidance provisions to prevent parents channelling income through their children[1].

[1] Income Tax (Trading and Other Income) Act 2005, s 629.

Married couples

3.3 Married couple's allowance was abolished for most people from 6 April 2000 and was replaced in April 2001 with a new children's tax credit. Therefore, there was a gap of one year when married couples with children received no additional income tax reliefs. Children's tax credit was in turn replaced by child tax credit from 6 April 2003.

3.3 Taxation of Unmarried Couples

In order to provide some recognition of marriage/civil partnership within the income tax system, from 6 April 2015 the marriage allowance was introduced. A spouse or civil partner who is not liable to income tax above the basic rate has been able to transfer up to £1,250 in the 2018/2019 tax year (increasing to 10 per cent of the personal allowance in subsequent tax years) of their personal allowance to their spouse or civil partner provided that the recipient of the transfer is not liable to income tax above the basic rate.

Elderly married couples

3.4 A higher personal allowance (known as the 'age allowance') was available for those over the age of 65 up to the tax year 2015/2016. However, from 6 April 2016, the available personal allowance exceeded the age allowance and thus the higher personal allowance for those over 65 is no longer applicable.

The married couples allowance was retained for elderly couples after 6 April 2000, provided that the elder of the couple had reached the age of 65 before that date. It will also apply when a person born before 6 April 1935 gets married or enters a civil partnership after 6 April 2000. The calculation is different for marriages entered into before 5 December 2005, when the allowance is paid to the husband and the calculation is based upon his income. For marriages and civil partnerships after 5 December 2005, the allowance is given to the person with the highest income and the amount is based upon his or her income.

The maximum amount of married couple's allowance is £8,915 for the tax year 2019/2020. The minimum amount is £3,450 for the 2019/2020 tax year. The eligible person receives 10 per cent of the allowance amount. The allowance is reduced in respect of income over £29,600 for the 2019/20 tax year on a tapering basis.

Allowances for children

3.5 The additional personal allowance aimed at single parents was abolished with effect from 6 April 2000.

Universal credit, child tax credit and working tax credit

3.6 Universal credit (UC) is replacing a number of benefits including child tax credit (CTC) and working tax credit (WTC). It is being phased in geographically and is expected to be rolled out completely by September 2024.

There are no limits to the number of hours a week that a person can work whilst receiving UC. The payment will reduce gradually as the claimant earns more. The new system is designed to encourage people to seek work, to reduce dependency on benefits and to simplify the benefits system. UC is paid monthly to each eligible household and the system is managed online.

UC is subject to the benefit cap (although those eligible for WTC are excluded from the cap) which is designed to make it impossible for anyone to receive more on benefits than the average weekly wage after tax and national insurance. The current cap is:

- £442.31 per week (£1,916.67 per month or £23,000 per year) for couples and lone parents in Greater London.
- £384.62 per week (£1,666,67 per month or £20,000 per year) for couples and lone parents outside Greater London.

It applies to those getting the UC housing element.

CTC is payable to single parents and couples, whether married or unmarried, who have responsibility for one or more children under 16 or a child over 16 but under 20 and in approved education or training. There is a family element of £545 per annum for all who qualify. There is also a child element for each child up to a maximum of 2 eligible children from 6 April 2019, of £2,780 with enhancements for disabled and severely disabled children. The above payments relate to the 2019/2020 tax year and from 6 April 2019 the family element of CTC will only be available for those responsible for a child or children born before that date.

WTC is also available to cohabiting couples, whether married or in a civil partnership or not, who have dependent children, a mental or physical disability or where one of the couple is aged over 25. It is necessary to work a certain number of hours per week to qualify (30 hours for those aged 25 to 59 with no children and without a disability, 16 or 24 hours for most other people). Where available, WTC provides a 'basic' amount, a lone parent or couple element, an element for those in 30 hours' work or more, a disabled worker element, a severe disability element and, for single parents and some couples, a childcare element of 70 per cent of eligible childcare costs up to prescribed maximums.

Awards are calculated by adding together all the relevant elements of a family's CTC or WTC or both. Those on income support, income-based jobseeker's allowance, income-related employment and support allowance, or pension credit then receive this amount with no further means-test. Those not on any of these four benefits however have their total tax credits reduced by 41 per cent of their income above a specified income threshold.

Claims are usually based on the income for the preceding tax year. The calculation is complex and changed in April 2012 but entitlement is withdrawn at the rate of 41 per cent of income above £6,420 in cases that include any WTC elements (or less commonly, 41 per cent income above £16,105 in cases involving only CTC and *no* WTC elements).

Capital gains tax

3.7 Although married couples and civil partners are treated as separate individuals in relation to assessment for capital gains tax, special rules apply to transfers between spouses living together[1] which are beneficial and are unavailable to unmarried couples. Where a husband and wife are living together during any year of assessment, any disposals between them, except for stock in trade, are on the basis of a no gain, no loss situation. This effectively means that the receiving spouse takes the asset at the transferring spouse's acquisition date.

3.7 Taxation of Unmarried Couples

Despite the rules about transfers between spouses, each spouse has an annual exemption of £12,000 for the tax year 2019/20 (£12,300 for the tax year 2020/21) of gains like any unmarried couple.

Disposals between unmarried couples or married couples who are not living together give rise to tax on any capital gains. Tax is payable at the top rate applicable to the individual making the disposal by adding the taxable gain to their income. If the taxable gain when added to their income is within the basic Income Tax band (up to £50,000 in the tax years 2019/20 and 2020/21), capital gains tax is charged at the rate of 18 per cent on the gains from residential property and 10 per cent on all other chargeable gains. Taxable gains in excess of the basic income tax band are charged at 28 per cent on the gains from residential property and 20 per cent on all other chargeable gains.

Disposals between husband and wife who are not living together are most likely to apply on the occasion of splitting assets between them on separation or divorce and they face an additional disadvantage which an unmarried couple would not be affected by, namely that they are treated as 'connected persons' meaning that any disposal between them is treated as a transaction otherwise than by way of a bargain at arm's length. Such a disposal is deemed to be for a consideration equal to the market value of the asset and in particular any losses can only be set off against gains on other disposals to the same person and not other gains generally.

Although disposals between an unmarried couple would also be treated as being made at market value if not at arm's length, there is no automatic presumption that the transfer is not at arm's length and losses can be set against any gains.

The most common transfers between couples, whether married or not, are either those on separation or divorce or to take advantage of other tax benefits. It is common for spouses to transfer investments between themselves so that a non-working or lower earning spouse can take advantage of lower rates of tax on investment income. Likewise, a spouse may transfer assets as part of an inheritance tax planning exercise. If the transfer is of chattels, there is an exemption where the value of the consideration for each chattel does not exceed £6,000, the level that was fixed in 1989/90[2]. Special rules apply to chattels which form part of a set.

[1] Taxation of Chargeable Gains Act 1992 (TCGA 1992), s 58.
[2] TCGA 1992, s 262.

Private residence relief

3.8 Probably the most important capital gains tax relief available to couples, whether married or unmarried, is the relief available on the disposal of a private residence[1]. The exemption applies on the disposal of a dwelling-house or part of a dwelling-house or an interest in it. It must have been the person's only or main residence at any time during the period of ownership. Where the property has been the only or main residence during the whole period of ownership, the exemption applies to the whole of the gain. There is also an overlap relief, so that the whole of the gain is still exempt even if the property has not been the only or main residence during the last 9 months of ownership from 6 April 2020[2] (18 months of ownership between 6 April 2014 and 5 April 2020 and 36 months of ownership before 5 April 2014). If the property does not qualify for the whole of the period other than the last 9 months, the proportion of the gain taxable is calculated by dividing the gain by the fraction of the period when the property was the only or main residence over the whole period of ownership. If when the land or house is bought, either a house is built on it or alterations are required to an existing house, a delay of 12 months is permitted in taking up residence or 2 years where there are good reasons outside the individual's control[3].

The rules are relatively straightforward where only one property is involved. Where there are two properties, an unmarried couple can be at an advantage in that for a husband and wife living together there can be only one main residence[4]. Therefore, they cannot claim that one house is the husband's main residence and another is the wife's. However, this option may be available to an unmarried couple if one property is owned by one and the second by the other. Although the question of which of two or more properties is a person's only or main residence is decided by the Inspector of Taxes making a determination, a taxpayer can serve a notice concluding the question within 2 years of the start of the period where there is ownership of two or more properties. Thus, it would be open to an unmarried couple who had two residences to qualify for two private residence exemptions, provided that each was occupied sufficiently to qualify as a residence.

Where an unmarried couple jointly own a property, they are treated as owning an undivided share in the whole provided that they have unrestricted access to the whole. This means that they can both claim private residence relief on their own share.

The private residence exemption applies to the dwelling house and land for the occupation and enjoyment with the residence as its garden or grounds up to 0.5 hectares. Where the garden and grounds exceed 0.5 hectares, a larger area may be allowed where it is required for the reasonable enjoyment of the dwelling house as a residence, having regard to the size and character of the dwelling house. A number of cases have also come before the courts where relief has been sought for part of a property occupied by domestic staff.

Periods of absence are also allowed subject to detailed rules and in particular a general period of up to 3 years[5].

[1] TCGA 1992, ss 222–224.
[2] Finance Act 2020, s 23.
[3] Extra-statutory concession D49.
[4] TCGA 1992, s 222(6).
[5] TCGA 1992, s 223(3).

3.9 *Taxation of Unmarried Couples*

Inheritance tax

Introduction

3.9 In terms of the tax treatment of married as opposed to unmarried couples, inheritance tax is by far the most beneficial to married couples. It is primarily a tax payable on death, although certain transfers of value made during lifetime are either taxable at the time or on a subsequent death.

Transfers between spouses are exempt whether during lifetime or on death provided that both spouses are domiciled in the United Kingdom. From 5 April 2013, if the transferor spouse is UK domiciled but the transferee spouse is not, the exemption only applies to transfers up to the prevailing nil rate band for inheritance tax purposes (currently £325,000). Before 5 April 2013, the exemption only applied to transfers up to £55,000.

In *Holland v IRC*[1] the Special Commissioners rejected arguments that the spouse exemption should apply where a couple had lived together as husband and wife but unmarried for 31 years. Arguments under the Human Rights Act were also rejected.

In *Burden v United Kingdom*[2] the European Court of Human Rights rejected an application from two unmarried sisters living together that the liability to pay inheritance tax on the death of the first to die was in breach of the European Convention of Human Rights because it would not be faced by the survivor of a marriage or civil partnership.

In contrast, any transfers of value between an unmarried couple could end up being taxable. In broad terms, all transfers on death are liable to inheritance tax together with any potentially exempt transfers made within 7 years prior to the death. Certain lifetime transfers, such as those to relevant property trusts, are also taxable during lifetime.

The rate of tax is 40 per cent (or 36 per cent where 10 per cent or more of the net estate is given to charity[3]) on death on the amount of all transfers above the nil-rate band of £325,000. It is intended that the nil-rate band will be frozen until 2020/21, following which the consumer prices index will be applied for future increases[4]. The rate on taxable lifetime transfers is 20 per cent, but this could increase up to 40 per cent if the transferor dies within 7 years (with taper relief if the transferor lives at least 3 years but less than seven)[5].

In July 2015, the Conservative Government confirmed the introduction of an additional nil rate band (referred to as the 'residence nil rate band'). For deaths on or after 6 April 2017, individuals will be able to benefit from an additional nil rate band in respect of their family home providing that it is gifted to their lineal descendants on their death. The residence nil rate band will be £175,000 for the tax year 2020/21 (an increase from £150,000 in the 2019/20 tax year). The available residence nil rate band will be tapered if the deceased's estate exceeds the taper threshold of £2 million at death at the rate of £1 for every £2 over the threshold[6].

Unmarried couples are at a further disadvantage since 9 October 2007, from which date transferable nil-rate bands were introduced for spouses and civil partners. Where the survivor of spouses or civil partners dies after that date and on the death of the first to die, their nil-rate band (including the residence nil rate band from 6 April 2017 where applicable) had not been fully used, the unused proportion can be carried forward and used on the death of the survivor. The proportion unused is calculated by reference to the nil-rate bands in force on the first death but then applied to the nil-rate bands in force at the second death. Thus if the first spouse died in 2002/03 when the nil-rate band was £250,000, and left legacies of £50,000 which were not exempt, four fifths of the nil-rate band would be unused. If the survivor dies in 2019/20 when the nil-rate is £325,000, £260,000 transferable nil-rate band can be claimed in addition to the survivor's own nil-rate band of £325,000. If the second spouse died after 6 April 2017, then the unused element of the residence nil rate band may also be transferable[7].

[1] [2003] ST1 62.
[2] [2007] STC 252.
[3] IHTA 1984, Sch 1A inserted by FA 2012, Sch 33.
[4] FA 2012, s 208.
[5] IHTA 1984, s 7(4).
[6] IHTA 1984, s 8D–8M.
[7] Finance Act 2008, s 10 and Sch 4.

Lifetime gifts

3.10 The main scope for avoiding inheritance tax between persons who are not married lies in the use of lifetime gifts. As explained above, no inheritance tax is payable on a gift made more than 7 years before the death of the donor. This is known as a 'potentially exempt transfer'. To qualify, however, there must be no reservation of benefit by the donor. This means that if:

'(a) possession and enjoyment of the property is not bona fide assumed by the donee at or before the beginning of the relevant period; or
(b) at any time in the relevant period the property is not enjoyed to the entire exclusion of the donor and of any benefit to him by contract or otherwise'

the gift will not be potentially exempt and the 7-year period will not start to run until those conditions are satisfied[1].

[1] Finance Act 1986, s 102.

Gifts of residence

3.11 The most common area where the gift with reservation provisions apply is that of gifts of houses and shares in houses. In general, if a person gives away a house or a share in a house but remains living in it, there is a reservation of benefit and the gift is ineffective for inheritance tax purposes. For example, a couple might start living together in the house owned by one of them. If the owner then wished to give a half-share in the house to his partner and to remain living there, at first sight this would constitute a reservation of benefit.

In a letter dated 18 May 1997, the Inland Revenue confirmed that the estate duty practice on the treatment of gifts involving a share in a house where the

3.11 *Taxation of Unmarried Couples*

gifted property is occupied by all the joint owners including the donor will continue to apply:

> 'The donor's retention of a share in the property will not of itself amount to a reservation. If, and for so long as, all the joint owners remain in occupation, the donor's occupation will not be treated as a reservation provided the gift is itself unconditional and there is no collateral benefit to the donor. The payment by the donee of the donor's share of the running costs, for example, might be such a benefit. An arrangement will not necessarily be jeopardised merely because it involves a gift of an unequal share in a house.'

On the basis of this interpretation, a gift by one of an unmarried couple to the other of an undivided share in a house would not be a gift with a reservation provided that both continued to occupy the property and the donor continued to pay his fair share of the running costs.

This principle was given statutory force by the Finance Act 1999[1].

In Finance Act 2004, the Government introduced legislation to counteract schemes to avoid the gift with reservation provisions by introducing an income tax charge on the use of pre-owned assets such as land and chattels from 6 April 2005. There is an exemption in the legislation for transfers between spouses and former spouses by court order[2]. The pre-owned assets charge does not catch the use of assets where the transfer is still caught by the gift with reservation provisions and is therefore still treated as part of the transferor's estate for inheritance tax purposes. A specific exemption from the pre-owned assets charge is also given to arrangements that are exempt under the shared occupation provisions described in this section[3]. Great care must be taken when there is a transfer of value of land or chattels between unmarried couples and also where there is an element of gift between a couple on the purchase of a property.

[1] Finance Act 1986 (FA 1986), s 102B.
[2] Finance Act 2004, Sch 15, para 10(1)(b).
[3] Finance Act 2004, Sch 15, para 11(5).

Gifts not intended to confer benefit

3.12 A disposition that is not intended to confer any gratuitous benefit is not a transfer of value and so is not liable to inheritance tax. In establishing this principle, an unmarried couple are at an advantage in that they are not connected persons and so only have to show that the transfer was made in a transaction at arm's length. A married couple (being connected persons) would also have to establish that the transfer was such as might be expected to be made at arm's length between persons who were not connected. In other words, an objective test is substituted for a subjective test.

Gifts of other property

3.13 The gift with reservation provisions cause less of a problem with money and investments provided that the donee has the benefit of the income from the asset given. Therefore, there is scope for an unmarried couple to maximise income tax reliefs by the transfer of assets to the member of the couple with no income, or with a lower income. The pre-owned assets charge does apply to cash gifts and assets derived from them, such gifts not being caught by the reservation of benefit provisions.

Business and agricultural reliefs

3.14 Generous reliefs of up to 100 per cent are available on transfers of business and agricultural property. As transfers between spouses are exempt, most tax planning involving these assets concentrates on maximising the reliefs by transfers to children or other beneficiaries. However, married couples do benefit from rules concerning successive ownership. To qualify for business property relief, there is a minimum period of ownership of 2 years[1]. Where business property is transferred, the transferee has to hold the property for 2 years before qualifying and so is vulnerable to tax in the event of death during that period. However, where one spouse becomes entitled to business property on the death of the other spouse, the second spouse is attributed with the period of ownership of the first spouse and so in most cases will immediately be entitled on the death of the first spouse. In the case of the unmarried couple, however, the survivor inheriting on the death of a partner will have to wait 2 years before qualifying for relief on the asset inherited. Similar rules apply to agricultural property relief[2] but the problem can be greater in the case of qualification by ownership rather than occupation where the qualifying period is 7 years rather than 2 years.

[1] IHTA 1984, s 106.
[2] IHTA 1984, s 120.

Inheritance tax on death

3.15 For the unmarried couple, careful planning is required to avoid inheritance tax both on property passing between the couple and where there are children, on property subsequently passing to them. If the estate of the first to die exceeds £325,000, inheritance tax would be payable on the balance passing to the survivor and, on the death of the survivor, inheritance tax would be payable on what was left of the combined estates of the couple over and above the nil-rate band level.

Whereas a married couple can utilise their transferable nil-rate bands to pass property to their children and thereby pay no inheritance tax on £650,000 (for the tax year 2019/20), an unmarried couple can only achieve this by both leaving an amount equal to the nil-rate band direct to their children. This may leave the survivor of the couple with insufficient assets, unless he or she is wealthy in his or her own right.

It makes sense in pure taxation terms for a stable unmarried couple to try to equalise their estates between them to mitigate inheritance tax, although in terms of splitting up the couple's assets on a breakdown of the relationship such a strategy could be disastrous for the richer of the two who has passed assets to the partner.

Tax planning is also essential in the common circumstance where a couple come together who have both been in previous relationships and each have

3.15 *Taxation of Unmarried Couples*

children from those relationships. Both are likely to want to ensure that their own children eventually receive their parent's capital whilst ensuring that during the lifetime of the survivor, he or she is adequately provided for. Wills are vital for a couple in this situation.

Where the couple are married this situation is commonly catered for by each leaving the survivor a life interest in all or part of his or her estate with the capital going to his or her own children on the death or remarriage of the other spouse. Here there would be no inheritance tax on the first death, but on the second death the capital value of the life interest fund would be aggregable with the estate of the survivor provided it was an immediate post death interest and inheritance tax would be payable on the combined total.

In the case of the unmarried couple in the same situation, inheritance tax would be payable on the first death as well[1].

Until the introduction of transferable nil-rate bands, a well-known tax planning device for married couples used to be the nil-rate band discretionary trust set up by will. On the death of the first spouse, the amount of the nil-rate band was left on discretionary trusts of which the beneficiaries were the surviving spouse, children and a wider class. The rest of the estate was left to the surviving spouse. No inheritance tax was payable on the first death because the taxable part was covered by the nil-rate band and the remainder qualified for the spouse exemption. During the lifetime of the survivor, he or she could benefit from the income from the discretionary trust with access to the capital if needed. Unlike a life or absolute interest, however, on the second death the amount of the discretionary trust is not aggregated with the survivor's estate and can be distributed to the children or others with little or no inheritance tax being payable. Holdover relief is also available for capital gains tax purposes.

A similar solution may also save inheritance tax for an unmarried couple. If each of the couple leave the whole of their estate on discretionary trusts with the other as a potential beneficiary[2], inheritance tax will be payable on the first death on any balance over the nil-rate band and this will establish the rate applicable to distributions from that discretionary trust for at least the first 10 years of its existence. On the death of the second of the couple, the estate of the first held on discretionary trust will not be aggregable with the estate of the second and the overall rate of tax may be lower. *See Example.*

The 'trust rate' of tax on income and gains within relevant property trusts is not favourable and this is clearly a factor that must be taken into account. It is possible to convert the discretionary trust into a life interest trust provided this is done more than 2 years after the death and this would have the effect of lowering the tax payable on income and capital gains to the survivor's marginal rate. If it is done within the 2 year period after death then the interest would be treated as an immediate post-death interest under the reading back provision in Inheritance Tax Act 1984, s 144 and aggregated with the survivor's free estate on their death.

    EXAMPLE

    Unmarried couple A and B:

    A has estate of £650,000;

B has estate of £450,000.

A dies first leaving life interest to B.

On death of A, inheritance tax (IHT) is £130,000.

On death of B, the IHT is payable on combined estates of £450,000 plus £650,000 (less IHT on first death £130,000) = £970,000 and amounts to £258,000.

Total IHT (£130,000 + £258,000) = £388,000.

If, instead, A left whole of estate on discretionary trusts:

On death of A, IHT £130,000 as before.

On death of B, tax on B's estate would be £50,000. The tax on distribution of discretionary trust of £520,000 within 10 years would be at a maximum rate of 3.00 per cent amounting to £15,600, a total of £65,600.

Total IHT (£130,000 + £65,600) = £195,600, a saving of £192,400.

In contrast, on the same figures, the IHT on a married couple still using a nil-rate band discretionary trust would be £180,000.

[1] Precedents for life interests under wills are included at **6.140** and **6.141**.
[2] Precedent at **6.144**.

Stamp duty land tax

3.16 Stamp duty land tax replaced stamp duty on transactions involving land after 1 December 2003[1]. Stamp duty land tax is a tax on transactions. An unmarried couple buying a house pay exactly the same stamp duty land tax as a married couple[2]. Likewise, gifts between unmarried couples are free of stamp duty land tax as transactions for no chargeable consideration in just the same way as gifts between spouses.

The only instance where married couples have an advantage for stamp duty land tax purposes is where property is transferred from one party of a marriage to another in pursuance of an order of a court made on the grant of a decree of divorce, nullity of marriage or judicial separation either on the occasion of the order or in connection with it. The exemption also applies to orders made under ss 22A, 23A or 24A of the MCA 1973 and to transfers made at any time in pursuance of an agreement made by the parties to a marriage in contemplation of the dissolution or annulment of the marriage or the judicial separation or making of a separation order[3]. This replicates the similar exemption for stamp duty.

As with stamp duty, there can be a charge to stamp duty land tax where there is an assumption of debt on a transfer of land. Thus, if one of an unmarried couple transfers a share in a house to the other subject to a mortgage, stamp duty land tax will be payable on the amount of the debt assumed by the transferee[4].

[1] Please note that in the Chancellor of the Exchequer's summer statement of 8 July 2020 in response to the Covid-19 pandemic, temporary reduced rates of stamp duty land tax will apply for residential properties purchased from 8 July 2020 until 31 March 2021 inclusive.
[2] FA 2016, s 128. From 6 April 2016, a higher rate of stamp duty land tax applies to the purchase of additional residential properties (eg second homes and buy-to-let properties) for

3.16 *Taxation of Unmarried Couples*

consideration in excess of £40,000.
3   FA 2003, Sch 3, para 3.
4   FA 2003, Sch 4, para 8.

Chapter 4

PERSONAL PROTECTION

Part A   LAW AND PRACTICE

Section 1 Family Law Act 1996, Pt IV

Introduction

4.1 The Family Law Act 1996 (FLA 1996), Pt IV governs applications for personal protection in the Family Court. This legislation was the outcome of the recommendations in The Law Commission's Report *Domestic Violence and Occupation of the Family Home*, published in 1992 (Law Com No 207). The Law Commission was asked to produce a report as a response to the growing recognition of domestic abuse as a huge social problem. It was evident that the earlier legislation was inadequate and reform was needed. Although FLA 1996, Pt IV was a significant step in the right direction, before long it became clear that further reform was necessary. Accordingly, in 2003 the Government introduced the Domestic Violence, Crime and Victims Bill which received royal assent on 15 November 2004. Sections 1 and 4 of the Domestic Violence, Crime and Victims Act 2004 (DVCVA 2004) came into force on 1 July 2007 and made important amendments to FLA 1996, Pt IV.

The most significant amendment was the new s 42A that made it a criminal offence, punishable by up to 5 years' imprisonment, to breach a non-molestation order without reasonable excuse. As a result, it is no longer permissible to attach a power of arrest to a non-molestation order although the power of arrest is retained for occupation orders. Apart from that, the existing enforcement provisions remain and the applicant may elect to pursue the civil route and an application for committal for contempt of court, rather than leave the matter to be dealt with in the criminal courts. However, the civil court will not be able to punish for contempt of court when a person has been convicted of an offence of breaching a non-molestation order, and vice versa.

The DVCVA 2004 also extended the category of associated persons eligible to apply for relief under FLA 1996, Pt IV by including same-sex couples in the definition of cohabitants and those in an intimate personal relationship which is, or was, of significant duration.

The Serious Crime Act 2015 came into force on 29 December of that year and introduced a new criminal offence of coercive and controlling behaviour. This recognises that abuse in an intimate or family relationship can go beyond physical abuse to include emotional abuse and other means of control[1].

4.1 Personal Protection

The Domestic Abuse Bill 2020 promises to further recognise the need to transform the response to domestic abuse by raising awareness of the devastating impact it has on victims and their families, strengthening the support provided by statutory agencies, and improving the effectiveness of the justice system in providing protection to victims, and bringing perpetrators to justice. The Bill completed its Third Reading in the House of Commons on 6 July 2020 and there appears to be the necessary commitment to ensure that it receives Royal Assent in due course. The Bill provides for domestic abuse protection notices to be issued by the police when attending to a domestic incident ('DAPNs') and domestic abuse protection orders ('DAPOs') that can be made by the court in various circumstances, broadly analogous to those made currently under s 42 FLA 1996.

[1] See **4.6** below.

The relief available

4.2 Under FLA 1996, Pt IV, the court may make orders between associated persons. Associated persons include cohabitants and former cohabitants, which definition now includes those of the same sex in an equivalent relationship, and *those who have or have had an intimate personal relationship with each other which is or was of significant duration*. Orders may restrain the use and threatened use of violence, intimidation, pestering, harassment or other specified forms of molestation. There is also power to make orders relating to the occupation of a home that is, was, or was intended to be a home shared by the associated persons. When making an occupation order, the court has the power to make additional provision, which includes the imposition of terms in the order as to payment of an occupation rent, payment of outgoings, and the use and care of chattels.

A power of arrest may be attached to an occupation order, but since 1 July 2007 not to a non-molestation order. Breach of both non-molestation and occupation orders remains a contempt of court but breach of a non-molestation order without reasonable excuse is now also a criminal offence.

Which level of judiciary?

4.3 Part IV of the FLA 1996 gives the Family Court the power to make orders for protection between associated persons and relevant children and occupation orders in respect of the shared home.

All levels of judiciary in the Family Court may deal with these matters[1], save that an application made by a child under 18 cannot be dealt with by lay justices[2]. A child under 16 requires the permission of the court to make an application. Lay Justices cannot deal with transfers of tenancies under s 53 of and Sch 7 to FLA 1996 and do not have jurisdiction where there is a dispute over a party's right to occupy the home[3]. Otherwise the powers and provision in FLA 1996, Pt IV are the same for all levels of judiciary.

If an application is made within existing proceedings the court will allocate it to the same level of judge as in the existing proceedings[4].

[1] FC (CDB) R 2014.

² FC (CDB) R 2014, r 16.
³ FLA 1996, s 59.
⁴ FC (CDB) R 2014, r 17.

Applications to vary, extend or discharge an order made under Pt IV

4.4 These applications must be made to the same court which made the order. FPR 10.5–10.7 apply. These provide for service of the application and any order in essentially the same way as the initial order that was made.

Non-molestation orders

WHO MAY APPLY FOR A NON-MOLESTATION ORDER?

4.5 Part IV provides that orders may be made between persons who are associated.

For the purposes of Pt IV, people are associated if:

(a) they are or have been married to each other or they are or have been civil partners of each other;
(b) they are cohabitants or former cohabitants or if of the same sex in an equivalent relationship¹;
(c) they live or have lived in the same household, otherwise than merely by reason of one of them being the employee, tenant, lodger or boarder of the other;
(d) they are relatives²;
(e) they have agreed to marry one another, even if the engagement has been broken off³;
(ea) they have or have had an intimate personal relationship with each other which is or was of significant duration⁴;
(f) in relation to any child, they are both either parents of the child or one or both has or has had parental responsibility for the child;
(g) they are parties to the same family proceedings;
(h) in the case of an adopted child or a child freed for adoption, two people are associated with each other if one is a natural parent or grandparent of the child and the other is either an adoptive parent or a person with whom the child has at any time been placed for adoption.

For the purposes of Pt IV, a relevant child is any person under the age of 18 years who is living with, or might reasonably be expected to live with, either party to the proceedings, any child who is the subject of adoption proceedings, or proceedings under the Children Act 1989, and any other child whose interests the court considers relevant.

A notable omission from the definition of associated persons has now been addressed up to a point by the amendment made to s 62 that broadens the definition of 'associated persons' to include those who 'have or have had an intimate personal relationship with each other which is or was of significant duration'. There is the potential for difficulties to arise in the interpretation of

4.5 Personal Protection

significant duration, but it is to be expected that the court will aim to take a purposive approach where personal safety is at stake.

1 *G v G (Non-Molestation Order: Jurisdiction)* [2000] 2 FLR 533. FLA 1996, s 62(3) should not be narrowly construed so as to exclude borderline cases where swift and effective protection is required for the victims of domestic violence. The category of former cohabitants will not include cohabitants who cease to be cohabitants by reason of their marriage to one another. The Domestic Violence, Crime and Victims Act 2004 amends the definition of cohabitants to 'two persons who although not married to each other, are living together as husband and wife or (if not the same sex) in an equivalent relationship': DVCVA 2004, s 3.
2 This is broadly defined to include members of earlier and later generations of the whole and half blood and, in the case of cohabitants, those who would be so related if the parties were married to one another. It now also includes first cousins: Sch 7, para 41(3)(a).
3 The fact of the engagement must be proved by documentary evidence (eg engagement notice in the newspaper or wedding invitation) or other evidence (eg giving of an engagement ring). In the case of applications for a non-molestation order, no application may be brought after the end of the period of 3 years beginning on the day on which the agreement to marry was terminated (FLA 1996, s 42(4)).
4 Additional category of associated person inserted by DVCVA 2004, s 4.

WHAT IS MOLESTATION?

4.6 There is no guidance in Pt IV, nor, as yet, any statutory definition, as to what amounts to molestation. If there is any doubt about this, case law provides examples of behaviour that the courts have restrained by making a non-molestation order[1].

In practice, the professional adviser and the courts will use common sense, but *molestation*, for the purposes of the current legislation, is clearly widely construed. It will include violence and threats of violence, but will also include more subtle acts of intimidation and harassment. In *Johnson v Walton*[2] the applicant was entitled to restrain the respondent from publishing intimate personal information and photographs in the national press, the court finding that it was done with the intention of causing distress to the applicant. However, in *C v C*[3] revelations by the wife in the tabloid press of her marriage to a well-known sports personality were held not to amount to molestation: 'the term implied quite deliberate conduct which was aimed at a high degree of harassment of the other party so as to justify the intervention of the court'. The Law Commission Report *Domestic Violence and Occupation of the Family Home*[4] offered the following definition of domestic violence:

> 'Domestic violence can take many forms . . . In its narrower meaning it describes the use or threat of physical force against a victim in the form of assault or battery. But in the context of the family, there is also a wider meaning which extends to abuse beyond the more typical instances of physical assaults to include any form of physical, sexual or psychological molestation or harassment which has a serious detrimental effect upon the health and well-being of the victim, albeit that there is no "violence" involved in the sense of physical force. Examples of such "non-violent" harassment or molestation cover a very wide range of behaviour. Common instances include persistent pestering and intimidation through shouting, denigration, threats or arguments, nuisance telephone calls, damaging property, following the applicant about and repeatedly calling at her home or place of work . . . The degree of severity of such behaviour depends less upon its intrinsic nature than upon it being part of a pattern and upon its effect upon the victim . . .'

Support for an expansive definition of violence was evident in *Yemshaw v London Borough of Hounslow*[5]. Although that case concerned the definition of violence in the context of s 177(1) of the Housing Act 1996, the judgments of Baroness Hale and Lord Rodger make it clear that a proper understanding of violence, domestic or otherwise, must include threatening or intimidating behaviour and any other form of abuse which, directly or indirectly, may give rise to the risk of harm. In that case the housing authority had rejected an application for local authority accommodation on the basis that although the applicant had found it necessary to leave the family home with the two children because of her husband's behaviour, this had not included any violence or even threats of violence. The applicant appealed and the unanimous decision of the Supreme Court was that the case should be sent back to the local authority to be reconsidered.

In March 2013 the Government definition of domestic violence and/or domestic abuse was revised.

Domestic violence and abuse is defined as:

'Any incident or pattern of incidents of controlling, coercive or threatening behaviour, violence or abuse between those aged 16 or over who are or have been intimate partners or family members, regardless of gender or sexuality. This can encompass, but is not limited to, the following types of abuse: psychological, physical, sexual, financial and emotional . . . Coercive behaviour is an act or a pattern of acts of assault, threats, humiliation and intimidation or other abuse that is used to harm, punish, or frighten their victim . . . Controlling behaviour is a range of acts designed to make a person subordinate and/or dependant by isolating them from their sources of support, exploiting their resources and capabilities for personal gain, depriving them of the means needed for independence, resistance and escape and regulating their everyday behaviour.'

There can be no doubt that any definition of 'molestation' will include any or all of the above.

The Domestic Abuse Bill 2020 (cl 1) proposes for the first time a statutory definition of domestic abuse as follows:

'(2) Behaviour of a person ("A") towards another person ("B") is "domestic abuse" if—
    (a) A and B are aged 16 or over and are personally connected to each other, and
    (b) the behaviour is abusive.
(3) Behaviour is "abusive" if it consists of any of the following—
    (a) physical or sexual abuse;
    (b) violent or threatening behaviour;
    (c) controlling or coercive behaviour;
    (d) economic abuse (see subsection (4));
    (e) psychological, emotional or other abuse;
and it does not matter whether the behaviour consists of a single incident or a course of conduct.
(4) "Economic abuse" means any behaviour that has a substantial adverse effect on B's ability to—
    (a) acquire, use or maintain money or other property, or
    (b) obtain goods or services.

4.6 *Personal Protection*

(5) For the purposes of this Act A's behaviour may be behaviour "towards" B despite the fact that it consists of conduct directed at another person (for example, B's child).'

This definition reflects the multiplicity of means by which domestic abuse may be perpetrated within close relationships. As and when it has legislative force it will replace the rather outdated concept of 'molestation'.

[1] *Spindlow v Spindlow* [1979] 1 All ER 169: merely pushing the applicant onto the sofa and threatening to smack her child was not sufficient to amount to molestation. *Vaughan v Vaughan* [1973] 3 All ER 449: there was a history of violence, but the court made a non-molestation order on the basis of the respondent pestering the applicant and making a nuisance of himself. *Horner v Horner* (1983) 4 FLR 50: threatening letters and intercepting the applicant on the way to the station, 'the kind of conduct that makes life extremely difficult', was sufficient for an order.
[2] [1990] 1 FLR 350.
[3] [1998] 1 FLR 554.
[4] Law Com No 207.
[5] [2011] 1 FLR 1614.

THE EXERCISE OF THE COURT'S DISCRETION

4.7 The court has a discretion whether to make a non-molestation order. In deciding whether or not to make an order, the court is required to look at all the circumstances, including the health, safety and well-being of the applicant and any relevant child. 'Health' includes mental as well as physical health.

Procedure on an application for a non-molestation order

ISSUING THE APPLICATION

4.8 Non-molestation orders may be made on a free-standing application, as well as in existing family proceedings. Note also that the court has the power to make a non-molestation order of its own motion in family proceedings in which the respondent is a party, if it would be for the benefit of any other party to the proceedings.

Application is made in Form FL401 whether in existing family proceedings or free-standing. The application must be fully completed and signed and must indicate the relationship between the applicant and respondent and the type of order sought. If the application is based on an agreement to marry, the date of the agreement and of the termination of the agreement must be stated.

No fee is payable[1].

Every application must be supported by a witness statement setting out the evidence in support. The witness statement must contain a statement of truth[2].

An application may be made without notice to the respondent. In that case, the witness statement must set out the reasons why the relief sought should be granted without giving the respondent the opportunity to be heard.

To issue the application, the applicant's solicitor will attend at the court office with sufficient copies of the application in Form FL401 and the witness statement for the court and every party to be served. The court will seal all documents and issue Notice of Proceedings in Form FL402. If the application is urgent, arrangements will be made to see the judge as soon as possible.

If the application is on notice, a hearing date will be given with no less than 2 clear days' notice[3] unless an order has been made by the judge abridging time for service[4].

[1] Family Proceedings Fees (Amendment) Order 2014 (SI 2014/877).
[2] FPR Pt 17.
[3] FPR 10.3(b)(i).
[4] FPR 10.3(b)(ii).

SERVICE

4.9 Where the application is not made without notice, an application in Form FL401, witness statement in support and the Notice of Proceedings endorsed with the return date must be served personally on the respondent not less than 2 clear days before the hearing date, unless the court abridges time for service or makes an order for service by an alternative method.

An application for service by an alternative method may be made where service cannot be effected by the prescribed means[1]. The application is to the judge without notice to the respondent by way of a witness statement setting out the circumstances. Service by the court is only available on request by an applicant acting in person[2].

A Certificate of Service in Form FL415 confirming service on all relevant parties must be filed by the applicant's solicitor.

[1] FPR 6.35.
[2] FPR 10.3(2).

THE HEARING

4.10 The hearing will be in private unless the court directs otherwise and the court will keep a record of the hearing in Form FL405.

There is a duty upon the court and all the parties to identify any party or witness who is a vulnerable person at the earliest stage of any family proceedings[1]. Consideration should therefore be given to making an application for participation directions either before or at the commencement of any hearing. This might include the provision of a separate entrance and waiting room for the vulnerable party or witness, or the provision of screens in the court room.

At a hearing on notice, if the respondent does not appear, the court will need to have proof of personal service of the application and supporting documents in order for the matter to proceed. In the absence of this, the hearing will usually be adjourned to another date.

If the respondent attends a hearing on notice but is not represented and the court considers that the interests of justice require that he has an opportunity

4.10 Personal Protection

to seek advice and representation, the hearing may be adjourned to another date. To avoid having to serve the respondent personally with notice of the new hearing date, the court has power to fix the date and time there and then, and communicate it to the respondent, or to ask the respondent if he is prepared to accept service of the notice of hearing by ordinary first-class post.

If the respondent appears at the hearing on notice and is represented but denies the allegations, the hearing will usually have to be adjourned and re-listed with an adequate time estimate to enable evidence to be heard from both sides. Directions will be given for filing of witness statements.

If the respondent denies the allegations but does not wish to have a fully contested hearing, in an appropriate case the court may accept an undertaking. DVCVA 2004 amended FLA 1996 s 46 in relation to the court's power to accept an undertaking in place of making a non-molestation order although the practical effect is much the same as before. The court must not accept an undertaking instead of making a non-molestation order where the respondent has used or threatened violence towards the applicant or a relevant child, and it is necessary for the protection of the applicant or child that an order is made so that any breach may be punishable under s 42A, that is as a criminal offence.

The position is unchanged when the court is considering accepting an undertaking in place of making an occupation order.

Section 46(4) of the FLA 1996 was amended by DVCVA 2004 to make provision for an application to be made for a warrant of arrest if an undertaking is alleged to have been breached.

If the court is not prepared to accept an undertaking, and the applicant does not wish to pursue his or her application to a contested hearing, he or she will have to withdraw the application or have it dismissed.

In practice, as the court's discretion in relation to non-molestation orders is so wide, unless the applicant's sworn statement is a complete fabrication it will rarely be productive for there to be a contested hearing. Courts tend to take the view that there is generally no excuse for using or threatening violence, or intimidating, harassing or pestering another person, and even if only a fraction of the allegations is made out, a non-molestation order will usually be made. However, where there is a concurrent dispute concerning contact to a child it may be necessary to hear evidence in order to make findings of fact for the purposes of the Children Act 1989 proceedings.

[1] FPR Pt 3A and PD 3AA.

The order

4.11 Before DVCVA 2004 it was possible for the court to make one order containing both non-molestation and occupation provisions. The position now is that the provisions must be contained in separate orders. This is because breach of a non-molestation order without reasonable excuse is a criminal offence and therefore has serious consequences.

A non-molestation order will be drawn on Form FL404a. This contains a form of penal notice that sets out that breach of the order without reasonable excuse may be punishable as a criminal offence or as a contempt of court. It is not permissible to attach a power of arrest to a non-molestation order.

An occupation order, made under FLA 1996, Pt IV, ss 33–38, will be drawn on Form FL404 bearing a penal notice. A power of arrest may still be attached to an occupation order if the criteria in FLA 1996, Pt IV, s 47 are fulfilled.

As the consequences of breach of a non-molestation order are potentially very severe, it is important that these orders are drafted so that it is clear to the respondent, and to any court having to deal with an alleged breach, exactly what forms of behaviour are prohibited. For this reason it will usually be preferable for non-molestation orders to be expressed in specific rather than in general terms. Whether in the context of a criminal prosecution or committal proceedings, if the order is not clear as to what can and cannot be done before a breach occurs enforcement of the order will be ineffective.

The form of words used in general non-molestation orders, not to intimidate, harass or pester, is not sufficiently clear. It is good practice for non-molestation orders to be specifically directed to those aspects of the respondent's behaviour that it is sought to curb, for example telephone calls or other direct forms of communication, sending text messages or making contact via social media, or coming within a certain distance of a particular address.

SERVICE OF ORDERS

4.12 Unless the court has made any other order as to service, orders must be served personally on the respondent.

No enforcement by committal proceedings may be taken in respect of any breach of the order before service has been effected. However s 42A(1), when read in conjunction with s 42A(2), suggests that even if the respondent has not been served with the order, if he is aware of its terms a breach may leave him open to prosecution.

When the court makes a non-molestation order a copy of the order must be sent to the applicant's local police station. This is the duty of the applicant, or the court if the applicant is acting in person and so requests[1]. The order must be accompanied by a statement showing that the respondent has been served with the order or informed of its terms[2].

The Domestic Abuse Committee of the Family Justice Council has issued a Protocol for Process servers that should be followed in every case[3].

[1] FPR 10.10(3).
[2] FPR 10.10(2).
[3] *Protocol of November 2011 for Process servers: non-molestation orders* (Family Court Practice, Part V).

4.13 *Personal Protection*

DURATION OF ORDERS

4.13 A non-molestation order may be made for a specified period or until further order. An order made by the court of its own motion in other family proceedings ceases to have effect if those proceedings are withdrawn or dismissed.

Non-molestation orders made after a hearing on notice are generally made for a fixed period, rather than expressed as lasting until further order. Orders should be made to last for as long as is necessary in each particular case.

Non-molestation orders are now generally made for an initial period of up to 6 months or for a longer period if it is likely that ancillary issues such as finances or Children Act 1989 applications are likely to continue to bring the parties into conflict. Orders will not usually last for longer than 12 months, but they may if the particular circumstances warrant it.

Non-molestation orders should be open-ended ('until further order') in only exceptional or unusual circumstances[1].

In view of the potential for criminal liability if a non-molestation order is breached, it will be good practice for the time as well as the date of expiry to be stated on the face of the order.

[1] *M v W (Non-Molestation Order: Duration)* [2000] 1 FLR 107.

Application without notice for a non-molestation order

4.14 There is power to make a non-molestation order without notice to the respondent in any case in which the court considers it is just and convenient to do so[1]. Alternatively, the court may abridge time for service of the application so that it may be heard without giving the requisite 2 clear working days' notice to the respondent.

Where an application is made without notice, the witness statement in support must state the grounds for making the application without giving the respondent an opportunity to be heard. The judge will check the statement for this information and if it is not included the statement will have to be amended before the application may proceed. When drafting the witness statement, consider the criteria to be applied by the court under Pt IV[2], namely all the circumstances, including:

(a) any risk of significant harm to the applicant or a relevant child attributable to the conduct of the respondent if an order is not made immediately;
(b) the likelihood of the applicant being deterred from pursuing the application if an order is not made immediately; and
(c) whether there is reason to believe that the respondent is evading service, and the delay in effecting service, in the case of an application in the family proceedings court, or in effecting service by an alternative method, will cause serious prejudice to the applicant or a relevant child.

Although the court staff will produce the order, it will be helpful for the judge to have a draft of the specific terms sought in a non-molestation order.

In January 2017 the President of the Family Division issued important Practice Guidance[3]. This supersedes the previous Guidance issued in 2013. It sets out the principles with which compliance is essential whenever an application is made without notice for an injunctive order. This includes the following:

(1) an ex parte injunctive order must always have a fixed end date: the date and time of its expiry must be clearly stated on the face of the order.
(2) A hearing on notice must be fixed and the date, time and place of the hearing set out in the order. This will normally be no more than 14 days after the order was made.
(3) Careful consideration needs to be given to the duration of any order made ex parte. Although many orders will be of short duration, typically no more than 14 days, in appropriate cases involving personal protection the order can be for a longer period, such as 6 or even 12 months, provided that the order specifies a return day within no more than 14 days. This must be a matter for the discretion of the judge, but a period of longer than 6 months is likely to be appropriate only where the allegation is of long term abuse or where some other good reason is shown. Conversely, a shorter period than 6 months may be appropriate in a case where there appears to be a one-off problem that may subside in weeks rather than months.
(4) The order must make it clear that: (a) it was made in the absence of the respondent and that the court has considered only the evidence of the applicant, and (b) the court has made no finding of fact. The written evidence considered must be identified in the order, and where, exceptionally, the court has received oral or other evidence (eg a photograph) that evidence should be recorded on the face of the order.
(5) The order must contain a clear statement of the respondent's right to apply to set aside or vary the order under r 18.11 before the hearing on notice. It is not sufficient that the order gives 'liberty to apply'.
(6) Any such application must be listed for hearing as a matter of urgency.

At the same time as the Practice Guidance was issued there were released omnibuses of draft non-molestation and occupation orders prepared by the Family Orders Project Team. Both the Practice Guidance and the draft orders are available on the Family Law website[4].

The risk of procedural unfairness when orders are made ex parte was underlined in *R v R (FC: Procedural Fairness)*[5]. In that case an ex parte order was made that included an exclusion zone around the family home where the respondent was still resident. Thus, although the judge had declined to make an occupation order without giving the respondent notice, the zonal order had the same effect. The respondent appeared at the return date to oppose the order which was continued without further consideration until the final hearing. Case management directions were given that included the filing of witness statements. In the meantime, the respondent had been arrested for the alleged breach of that part of the non-molestation order than prevented him from contacting the applicant. As a result, he missed the deadline for filing his statement and was debarred from giving evidence at the hearing.

4.14 Personal Protection

In allowing his appeal and setting aside all the previous orders made against him, Peter Jackson J said per curiam:

'(1) The default position of a judge faced with a without notice application should always be "Why?", not "Why not?" . . . without notice orders could only be made in exceptional circumstances and with proper consideration for the right of the absent party.

(2) The court should use its sweeping powers under FLA 1996 with caution, particularly at a one-sided hearing. Where an order was made, it was the responsibility of the court (and, where applicable, the lawyers) to ensure that it was accurately drafted. This consideration applied with special force when a breach of the order would amount to a criminal offence.

(3) Extra injunctive provisions such as exclusion areas and orders prohibiting any direct communication between parties should not be routinely included in non-molestation orders. They were serious infringements of a person's freedom of action and required specific evidence to justify them.'

[1] FLA 1996, s 45.
[2] See s 45 and FPR 10.2(4).
[3] *Practice Guidance: Family Court – Duration of Ex Parte (Without Notice) Orders* 18 January 2017.
[4] See www.familylaw.co.uk.
[5] [2015] 2 FLR 1005.

Power of arrest

4.15 Since 1 July 2007 it has no longer been possible to attach a power of arrest to a non-molestation order. This is because breach of a non-molestation order without reasonable excuse is a criminal offence.

Section 47 does still apply to occupation orders.

Undertakings

4.16 Although DVCVA 2004 amended the provisions of Pt IV of the FLA 1996 in relation to undertakings, there is little, if any, practical difference. The position remains unchanged when the court is considering accepting an undertaking instead of making an occupation order. Where an undertaking is offered in place of a non-molestation order, the court will also have to specifically consider whether there has been the use or threat of violence to the applicant or a relevant child, and whether for the protection of the applicant or the child it is necessary to make an order so that any breach may be punishable as a criminal offence under s 42A.

If an undertaking is accepted, a power of arrest may not be attached to it. However, although breach of an undertaking is not a criminal offence under s 42A, it is possible to apply for a warrant of arrest in the event of any alleged breach of an undertaking and for this to be dealt with in committal proceedings.

An undertaking will be in Form N117 and should set out in clear terms what the party giving the undertaking is promising to the court. Before the court accepts the undertaking, the judge must be satisfied that its terms and the consequences of breach are fully understood. The undertaking should be signed by the person giving it to confirm that understanding. A copy of the undertaking must be given to the person who has given the undertaking, ideally by hand immediately after the hearing.

Occupation orders

WHO MAY APPLY FOR AN OCCUPATION ORDER?

4.17 The parties to an application for an occupation order, as for a non-molestation order, must be associated persons. In addition they must share, have shared, or have intended to share, a dwelling-house as their home. 'Dwelling-house' is construed widely to include any structure which is or has been a shared home, or which was intended to be a shared home[1]. It is important to know the respective rights and interests, if any, in the shared home of the associated persons, as this will determine the s of Pt IV of the FLA 1996 under which the application may be made, and thus the court's powers.

If an application is made under the incorrect section, the court may remedy the defect using its powers under s 39(3).

It will be common in practice for one application to be made for both non-molestation and occupation orders.

An order that excludes one party from the shared home is regarded as a serious remedy[2].

[1] FLA 1996, s 63.
[2] *Chalmers v Johns* [1999] 1 FLR 392, CA.

WHICH LEVEL OF JUDICIARY?

4.18 An application may be made to the same level of judiciary as for a non-molestation order, but it should be borne in mind that the Lay Justices have no power to deal with any application or make any order where there is a dispute as to a party's entitlement to occupy the subject property, unless it is unnecessary to determine the dispute in order to deal with the application.

WHICH SECTION WILL APPLY?

4.19 Occupation orders in relation to associated persons who are not and who never have been married can be made under ss 33, 36 and 38 of the FLA 1996. The decision as to which section to use is determined by whether or not the applicant and/or respondent is entitled to occupy the home. A party is entitled to occupy the home if he or she has a beneficial interest in it, or some contractual or statutory right to occupy, for example a tenancy or licence.

If the applicant is entitled to occupy, then regardless of whether the respondent is so entitled, s 33 applies.

Section 33 is open to all within the definition of associated persons. However, ss 36 and 38 apply only to cohabitants or former cohabitants. Section 36

4.19 *Personal Protection*

applies where the applicant is not entitled to occupy but the respondent is. Section 38 applies where neither the applicant nor the respondent is entitled to occupy.

The court's powers and the exercise of its discretion are slightly different for each section.

Occupation orders under s 33

WHO MAY APPLY?

4.20 An application may be made under s 33 by a person who is entitled to occupy the home against any person with whom he or she is associated.

THE COURT'S POWERS UNDER S 33

4.21 In relation to parties to proceedings who are not and have never been married to one another the court may make an occupation order in respect of a dwelling-house that they share or shared, or intended to share, and include any of the following provisions:

- declare the applicant's entitlement to[1] occupy;
- enforce the applicant's entitlement to remain in occupation as against the respondent;
- require the respondent to allow the applicant to enter and remain in the home or part of it;
- regulate the occupation of the home by either the applicant and/or the respondent;
- prohibit, suspend or restrict the respondent's exercise of any right to occupy;
- require the respondent to leave the home or part of it;
- exclude the respondent from a defined area around the home.

An occupation order cannot be made in respect of a property occupied by the applicant, at which the respondent is an unwelcome visitor, if the parties never lived there together, or never intended to do so. This situation is encountered quite frequently in practice where, for example the applicant moves out of the shared house at the end of the period of cohabitation, but continues to be pestered by the respondent. The court can make an order restraining the molestation, but cannot exclude the respondent from the applicant's new home or the immediate area. One solution in this type of situation is to ask the court to make a specific non-molestation order which expressly prohibits the respondent from attending at the applicant's new address[2].

[1] See s 33(4).
[2] For example: 'The respondent is forbidden to intimidate, harass or pester the applicant by entering or attempting to enter or going within 25 metres of (*applicant's new address*)'.

THE BALANCE OF HARM TEST UNDER S 33

4.22 Before making an occupation order under s 33 of the FLA 1996 and deciding what (if any) provision to make, the court must first decide whether the applicant has established that there is a likelihood of significant harm to him or her or to a relevant child attributable to the conduct of the respondent. This is a duty imposed on the court. Harm in relation to an adult means ill-treatment or impairment of health. In relation to a child it also includes impairment of development. Ill-treatment includes non-physical ill-treatment, and in relation to a child includes sexual abuse. Health includes mental as well as physical well-being. Significant harm is construed in the same way as it is for the purposes of the CA 1989[1].

If it appears to the court that the applicant or a relevant child is likely to suffer significant harm attributable to the respondent if an occupation order is not made, then an order must be made, unless it appears that the respondent or a relevant child is likely to suffer significant harm if an order is made, and such harm is as great or greater than the harm attributable to the respondent that the applicant or a relevant child would suffer if an order were not made. If the respondent makes out significant harm, the court has to weigh up the relative positions of the applicant and respondent and make an order only if on balance there will be greater harm to the applicant if an order is not made.

In relation to the respondent, the harm alleged may emanate from any source, ie the source does not have to be the applicant. In the case of the applicant, the harm in question must be attributable to the respondent.

[1] CA 1989, ss 31 and 105, interpreted in *Humberside County Council v B* [1993] 1 FLR 257 by Booth J as, 'considerable, noteworthy or important'.

THE EXERCISE OF THE COURT'S DISCRETION UNDER S 33

4.23 If the 'balance of harm' test results in the court finding that the harm to the respondent or a relevant child if an order were made would be as great or greater than that to the applicant or a relevant child if an order were not made, or where there is no finding of significant harm to either applicant or respondent, the court must look at all the circumstances to decide whether or not an order should be made[1].

All the circumstances, for the purposes of s 33 of the FLA 1996, will include:

– the housing needs and resources of each of the parties and any relevant child;
– the financial resources of each of the parties;
– the likely effect of any order, or the refusal of an order, on the health, safety or well-being of the parties and of any relevant child; and
– the conduct of the parties to one another and otherwise.

In *G v G*[2] the Court of Appeal refused a respondent husband permission to appeal against the making of an occupation order. Whilst recognising that it was a serious order to make, it was relevant to the exercise of the court's discretion under s 33(6) that the respondent had alternative accommodation that was available to him, and although there had not been any findings of violence, his bullying behaviour made it imperative that the parties should live separately.

4.23 Personal Protection

In *Dolan v Corby*[3] the Court of Appeal again emphasised the breadth of the court's discretion when conducting the balance of harm test under s 33(6). The use or threat of violence was not of itself determinative. It was for the judge *to identify and weigh up all the relevant features of the case whatever their nature*[4]. In that case the poor state of the applicant's psychiatric health carried great weight with the judge at first instance. The judge found the respondent to be of a dominating disposition and to have verbally abused the applicant and frequently belittled her. His decision to exclude the respondent from the property was held to be well within the ambit of his discretion even though the respondent was himself disabled. His conclusion was that of the two of them the respondent was better equipped to find alternative accommodation.

[1] See *Chalmers v Johns* [1999] 1 FLR 392, CA, as to the relationship between s 33(6) and (7); see also *Banks v Banks* [1999] 1 FLR 726, *B v B (Occupation Order)* [1999] 1 FLR 715 and *Re Y (Children) (Occupation Order)* [2000] 2 FCR 470, for the exercise of the balance of harm test.
[2] [2011] 1 FLR 687.
[3] [2012] 2 FLR 1031.
[4] Per Black LJ at para 27 p 1039.

Additional provision under s 40

4.24 The court may at any time on or after making an occupation order under s 33 (and s 36) of the FLA 1996:

- impose on either party obligations to repair and maintain the home, or pay the rent, mortgage subscription or other outgoings of the home;
- require a party in occupation to pay an occupation rent to the party out of occupation if that party was, but for the terms of the occupation order, entitled to occupy;
- allow either party use of furniture or other contents;
- require either party to take reasonable care of any furniture or other contents; and
- require either party to keep the home and contents secure.

Note, however, that there are currently no statutory provisions for enforcement of these additional provisions[1].

[1] See *Nwogbe v Nwogbe* [2000] 2 FLR 744.

EXERCISE OF ADDITIONAL POWERS WHEN AN OCCUPATION ORDER IS MADE UNDER S 33

4.25 In deciding whether and if so how to exercise its additional powers the court must have regard to all the circumstances, including:

- the financial needs and financial resources of the parties; and
- the financial obligations which they have or are likely to have in the foreseeable future, including financial obligations to each other and to any relevant child.

Law and Practice **4.30**

DURATION OF ORDERS UNDER S 33

4.26 Occupation orders made under s 33 of the FLA 1996 will be expressed to last for a specified period, until a specified event (eg until the determination of any application for transfer of tenancy) or until further order. There will not be a final order, but orders need not be limited in duration. Any additional provision made under s 40 of the FLA 1996 will come to an end when the occupation order to which it relates comes to an end.

Occupation orders under s 36

WHO MAY APPLY?

4.27 This section applies only to cohabitants or former cohabitants who share, shared or intended to share a home, where the applicant is not entitled to occupy the home but the respondent is.

THE COURT'S POWERS UNDER S 36

4.28 If the court decides to make an occupation order under s 36 of the FLA 1996, it must contain similar provisions to the home rights:

– giving the applicant the right not to be evicted or excluded from the home or part of it by the respondent or if he or she is out of occupation the right to return and remain; and
– prohibiting the respondent from evicting or excluding the applicant or if he or she is given the right to return and remain, from interfering with that right.

If an occupation order is made, it may also contain any of the following provisions:

– to regulate the occupation of the home by either or both of the parties;
– to require the respondent to leave all or part of the home;
– to exclude the respondent from a defined area around the home; and
– to prohibit, suspend or restrict the respondent's rights of occupation.

THE EXERCISE OF THE COURT'S DISCRETION UNDER S 36

4.29 The court's discretion is exercised in two stages. In the first stage, the court decides whether or not to make an occupation order, and if an order is made, the court must give the applicant what amount to rights of occupation. In the second stage, the court considers whether to make any further provision. The criteria for each stage are different.

FIRST STAGE IN THE EXERCISE OF THE COURT'S DISCRETION UNDER S 36

4.30 Before the court can make an occupation order under s 36 of the FLA 1996 in favour of the cohabitant or former cohabitant who is not entitled to occupy the home, it must have regard to all the circumstances, including:

4.30 *Personal Protection*

- the housing needs and resources of each of the parties and of any relevant child;
- the financial resources of each of the parties;
- the likely effect of any order, or the refusal of an order, on the health, safety or well-being of either of parties and any relevant child;
- the conduct of the parties towards one another and otherwise;
- the nature of the parties' relationship and in particular the level of commitment involved in it;
- the length of time they have cohabited;
- whether they have any children in common;
- the length of time that has elapsed since they last lived together; and
- the existence of any pending proceedings relating to financial relief or the legal or beneficial ownership of the home.

If, after considering all the circumstances, the court makes an occupation order, it must give the applicant rights of occupation.

SECOND STAGE IN THE EXERCISE OF THE COURT'S DISCRETION UNDER S 36

4.31 In deciding whether to make any further provisions, for example in relation to the regulation of the occupation of the home or restricting the respondent's right to occupy, the court must take into account all the circumstances, including:

- the housing needs and resources of each of the parties and of any relevant child;
- the financial resources of each of the parties;
- the likely effect of any order or the refusal of an order on the health, safety or well-being of either of the parties or any relevant child; and
- the conduct of the parties towards one another and otherwise.

THE BALANCE OF HARM TEST UNDER S 36

4.32 In addition to the considerations outlined above, the court must carry out a balance of harm test by asking two questions.

The first question is whether the applicant or any relevant child is likely to suffer significant harm attributable to the conduct of the respondent if the additional provision (eg to exclude the respondent) is not included in the order.

The second question is whether the harm likely to be suffered by the respondent or a child if such provision is included is likely to be as great or greater than the harm attributable to the conduct of the respondent which is likely to be suffered by the applicant or a child if the provision is not included.

Unlike the balance of harm test under s 33 of the FLA 1996, this test is not overriding. The court retains its discretion regardless of the outcome of the balance of harm test.

ADDITIONAL PROVISION UNDER S 40

4.33 The court may make additional provision pursuant to s 40 and the provision the court may make, and the criteria to be considered are identical to those under s 33 of the FLA 1996[1].

[1] See 4.25 above.

DURATION OF ORDERS UNDER S 36

4.34 An occupation order made under s 36 of the FLA 1996 cannot last longer than 6 months in the first instance, and can be renewed on one occasion only, again for a period not exceeding 6 months. Therefore the maximum duration possible is 12 months.

Occupation orders under s 38

WHO MAY APPLY?

4.35 Cohabitants and former cohabitants, neither of which is entitled to occupy the home, may apply under s 38 of the FLA 1996 for an occupation order. For the court to have jurisdiction at least one of the parties must be in occupation of the home. So if the applicant leaves the home because of the respondent's violence, and the respondent then leaves the home and the applicant remains out, there is apparently no power to make an occupation order under Pt IV of the FLA 1996.

THE COURT'S POWERS UNDER S 38

4.36 Where the court makes an occupation order under s 38 of the FLA 1996 in favour of an applicant with no entitlement to occupy, and the respondent is also not entitled to occupy, the court may make the following provisions:

- to regulate the occupation of the home;
- to require the respondent to allow the applicant to occupy the home and afford him or her peaceful occupation;
- to exclude the respondent from the home (or part of it) and a defined area around it; and
- to prohibit respondent from returning to the home and a defined area around it.

THE EXERCISE OF THE COURT'S DISCRETION UNDER S 38

4.37 Before the court can make an occupation order under s 38, it must have regard to all the circumstances, including:

- the housing needs and housing resources of each of the parties and of any relevant child;
- the financial resources of each of the parties;
- the likely effect of any order, or the refusal of an order, on the health, safety, or well-being of either of the parties and of any relevant child;
- the conduct of the parties towards one another and otherwise; and

4.37 Personal Protection

– the balance of harm.

THE BALANCE OF HARM TEST UNDER S 38

4.38 The court must ask the two questions it would ask for the purposes of s 36 of the FLA 1996.

The first question is whether the applicant or any relevant child is likely to suffer significant harm attributable to the conduct of the respondent if the additional provision (eg to exclude the respondent) is not included in the order.

The second question is whether the harm likely to be suffered by the respondent or a child if provision is included is likely to be as great, or greater than the harm attributable to conduct of the respondent which is likely to be suffered by the applicant or a child if the provision is not included.

As is the case with s 36 of the FLA 1996, the balance of harm test is not overriding.

DURATION OF ORDERS UNDER S 38

4.39 An order under s 38 of the FLA 1996 may be made for a period not exceeding 6 months in the first instance and may be renewed on one occasion only for a further period not exceeding 6 months. Therefore, like orders under s 36, orders under s 38 may not last for longer than 12 months in total.

Procedure on application for an occupation order

ISSUING THE APPLICATION

4.40 The procedure for occupation orders is the same as that for applications for non-molestation orders save that the application in Form FL401 must:

– specify that an occupation order is sought;
– give the section of Pt IV of the FLA 1996 that is relied upon; and
– give details of the property in question and of the interest that the applicant and respondent have in it.

The application in Form FL401 must be supported by a witness statement.

In practice, it will be common for one application to be made for both an occupation order and a non-molestation order. If an application is made for both, only one Form FL 401 and witness statement in support is required.

On being presented with the Form FL401, the witness statement (with sufficient copies for the court and service on all parties) the court will issue the Notice of Proceedings endorsed with a return date. A fee is no longer payable[1].

---

[1] Family Proceedings Fees (Amendment) Order 2014 (SI 2014/877).

SERVICE

4.41 Copies of Form FL401, the witness statement in support and Notice of Proceedings must be served on the respondent personally no less than 2 clear days before the return date, unless the application is made without notice to the respondent or the court has ordered that time for service be abridged.

In addition, copies must be served by the applicant on the mortgagee or landlord of the home, except in the case of applications under s 38 of the FLA 1996. Service is effected by ordinary first-class post.

A Certificate of Service in Form FL415, recording service on all relevant persons, must be filed after service.

Application for an occupation order without notice to the respondent

4.42 Application may be made for an occupation order without giving notice to the respondent, but because occupation orders are potentially more significant and more likely to interfere with the respondent's personal or property rights than a non-molestation order, these orders will generally be made without notice only in the most extreme cases. If it is felt that an application without notice is justified, the procedure to be followed and the criteria to be considered by the court are the same as for applications for non-molestation orders without notice.

THE HEARING

4.43 The hearing will be in private unless the court directs otherwise and the court will keep a record of the hearing in Form FL405.

There is a duty upon the court and all the parties to identify any party or witness who is a vulnerable person at the earliest stage of any family proceedings[1]. Consideration should therefore be given to making an application for participation directions either before or at the commencement of any hearing. This might include the provision of a separate entrance and waiting room for the vulnerable party or witness, or the provision of screens in the court room.

At a hearing on notice, if the respondent does not appear, the judge will need to have proof of personal service of the application and supporting documents in order for the matter to proceed. In the absence of this, the hearing will usually be adjourned to another date.

If the respondent attends a hearing on notice but is not represented and the court considers that the interests of justice require that he has an opportunity to seek advice and representation, the hearing may be adjourned to another date. To avoid having to serve the respondent personally with the new hearing date, the court has the power to fix the date and time there and then and communicate it to the respondent or to ask the respondent if he is prepared to accept service of the notice of hearing by ordinary first-class post.

4.43 *Personal Protection*

If the respondent appears at the hearing and is represented but denies the allegations against him, the hearing will have to be adjourned for a hearing on another date with an adequate time estimate to enable evidence to be heard from both sides. Directions will usually be given as to filing of witness statements.

[1] FPR Pt 3A and PD 3AA.

Undertakings

4.44 If the respondent denies the matters alleged but does not wish to have a fully contested hearing, he may offer to give an undertaking to the court, for example not to return to the home or within 25 metres of it. Although Pt IV of the FLA 1996 provides that the court has power to accept an undertaking in order to dispose of an application[1], the circumstances in which it may do so have led to a difference of judicial opinion as to whether it is an appropriate way of proceeding. FLA 1996, s 46 provides that the court may only accept an undertaking when, if it were a case in which an occupation order would be made, the mandatory power of arrest would not attach. In other words, the use of undertakings in place of occupation orders is restricted to those cases in which there has not been the use of or threat of violence, unless the court is satisfied that if in that particular case it were making an occupation order following admissions or findings of violence, used or threatened, it would not attach a power of arrest because it could be satisfied that the applicant would be adequately protected without it[2].

If an undertaking is accepted, a power of arrest may not be attached to it.

If the court will not accept an undertaking, it may make an order on the basis that the respondent has offered no evidence.

If the court is not prepared to accept an undertaking, and the applicant does not wish to pursue his or her application to a contested hearing he or she will have to withdraw her application or have it dismissed.

[1] See s 46(1).
[2] See also **4.45** below.

Power of arrest

4.45 Part IV of the FLA 1996 evidenced a change in attitude to the power of arrest.

This was in response to research findings that the majority of applicants wanted the court to make an order with a power of arrest attached to it, rather than to accept an undertaking. Under the previous legislation, powers of arrest were used sparingly. Part IV imposed a duty to attach a power of arrest to one or more provisions of a non-molestation or occupation order made on notice if it appeared to the court that the respondent had used or threatened violence against the applicant or a relevant child, unless the court was satisfied that the applicant or child will be adequately protected without it.

Following the amendments made to Pt IV FLA 1996 by DVCVA 2004, it is no longer possible to attach a power of arrest to a non-molestation order.

However, the position in relation to occupation orders has not changed. Where an occupation order is made without notice, a power of arrest may be attached if the court finds actual or threatened violence on the part of the respondent and there is a risk that significant harm will result to the respondent or a relevant child.

Whether the application is made with notice to the respondent or without, the violence or threats of violence complained of generally will have to be within the timescale of the events immediately leading up to the application for it to be considered in the context of attaching a power of arrest.

Duration of power of arrest

4.46 Section 47(4) of the FLA 1996 provides that where a power of arrest is attached to any provisions of an occupation order made without notice to the respondent under Pt IV, it may have effect for a shorter period of time than the order itself. The court has a similar discretion when a power of arrest is attached to an order made on notice[1].

[1] *Re B-J (Power of Arrest)* [2000] 2 FLR 443.

Procedure for power of arrest

4.47 Where the court makes an order with a power of arrest attached, and the respondent was either not given notice of the hearing or was not present at the hearing this must be announced by a judge in open court at the earliest opportunity[1].

Where the court makes an occupation order containing one or more provisions to which a power of arrest is attached, each provision to which a power of arrest attaches must be set out in a separate paragraph. A provision to which a power of arrest is attached must not be contained in the same paragraph as a provision to which a power of arrest has not been attached[2].

The power of arrest is issued in Form FL406. When the occupation order has been served on the respondent, a copy of Form FL406 and the order must be sent to the applicant's local police so that they are aware of it. This is the duty of the applicant unless the applicant is acting in person and has requested that the court do so. A statement must accompany those documents, which confirms that the respondent has been served with the order or informed of its terms, whether by being present when the order was made, by telephone or otherwise. If the local police operate a domestic violence unit, generally it will be better to send the Form FL406 and order there as it is more likely to be acted upon should the need arise. Check the practice in your area.

[1] FPR PD 10A, para 3.1.
[2] FPR 10.9.

4.48 *Personal Protection*

Enforcement of orders under Pt IV

ENFORCEMENT AS A CRIMINAL OFFENCE UNDER S 42A

4.48 Since 1 July 2007, breach of a non-molestation order without reasonable excuse has been a criminal offence. The penalty on conviction is a term of imprisonment of up to 5 years. However, the sentencing options are much wider than those available to a court punishing for contempt of court. They include community penalties that can, for example, require attendance at an anger management course. This may be more appropriate than imprisonment for less serious cases, and is more likely to promote a change in behaviour for the better.

Subject to the views of the police and the CPS, an applicant has the choice of pursuing a remedy either in the criminal courts or as before, in the civil courts, in committal proceedings for contempt of court. It is not every applicant that wishes to see the respondent criminalised.

A respondent cannot be punished twice for the same breach, and the civil court has no jurisdiction to entertain committal proceedings when a respondent has been convicted in the criminal courts of an offence arising out of the same breach, and vice versa.

ENFORCEMENT BY POWER OF ARREST

4.49 If a power of arrest has been attached to any provision in an occupation order that the respondent is believed to have breached, the applicant will call the police at the office holding the copy of the order. If on investigation the police officer has reasonable cause to suspect that the respondent has breached the part of the order to which a power of arrest has been attached, the respondent may be arrested. Note that this is only a power, not a duty.

Where there has been an arrest pursuant to a power of arrest, the respondent must be brought to the court that made the order within 24 hours of the arrest. Only Sundays, Christmas Day and Good Friday are excluded from the reckoning. The effect of this is that where the arrest was made on a Friday evening, a court will have to be convened on a Saturday. As it is unlikely that the respondent will be legally represented at the first hearing, the proceedings will usually be adjourned, and the respondent released or remanded on bail or in custody depending upon the gravity of the alleged breach and any other relevant circumstances. The resumed hearing must take place within 14 days of the day of the arrest, and the respondent must have at least 2 clear days' notice of the hearing.

If the respondent is not brought to court within the required timescale, or there has not been personal service of the order before the alleged breaches, the court will have no power to deal with a committal pursuant to the power of arrest. The applicant will not be able to apply for a warrant of arrest[1], and it seems that the only procedure open to the applicant will be to apply to show cause why the respondent should not be committed under CPR, Sch 2, CCR Ord 29.

The procedure at the committal hearing is dealt with at **4.57** below.

[1] See **4.50** below.

APPLICATION FOR A WARRANT OF ARREST

4.50 An application for a warrant of arrest may be made at any time after the respondent has been served with either a non-molestation or occupation order if the applicant considers that the respondent has breached the order or part of it, provided that a power of arrest was not attached to the order or to that part of the order that the applicant considers that the respondent has breached. In the case of a non-molestation order no power of arrest can be attached, but it will be important to know whether or not the respondent has already pleaded or been found guilty of an offence under s 42A before proceeding as the respondent cannot be punished both in the criminal courts and in the civil courts for contempt of court for the same breach.

An application may also be made for a warrant of arrest where it is alleged that the terms of an undertaking given under s 46 have been breached.

Which court?

4.51 Application must be made to the same level of judiciary that made the order. Any judge apart from a deputy district judge has jurisdiction to deal with the application.

Procedure

4.52 Application is made on Form FL407 detailing the terms of the order alleged to have been breached and how it is alleged that the respondent is in breach.

A sworn statement must be filed in support[1].

[1] FPR PD 4.1.

The exercise of the court's discretion

4.53 The court considers the application and sworn statement and if there are reasonable grounds for believing that the respondent has failed to comply with the order, a warrant for arrest in Form FL408 is issued and will be executed by the court bailiff or in the case of lay justices the police.

Where a respondent is arrested pursuant to a warrant of arrest, he must be brought before the court immediately, and in any event within 24 hours of his arrest. Sundays, Christmas Day and Good Friday are excluded from the reckoning.

The procedure for the committal hearing is set out at **4.57** below.

4.54 *Personal Protection*

Committal for contempt of court

4.54 Breach of a non-molestation[1] and/or an occupation order or an undertaking is a contempt of court and can be dealt with by committal proceedings. FPR Pt 37 applies. This procedure will only be followed:

(a) where an undertaking has been broken;
(b) where a power of arrest was attached to the term of the order breached, but the police declined to exercise the power of arrest;
(c) where a power of arrest was attached to the term of the order breached but the respondent was either not brought before the court within 24 hours of his arrest or not brought back to court following an adjournment within 14 days; and
(d) where there was no power of arrest attached to the term of the order breached and the court declined to issue a warrant of arrest.

[1] Since DVCVA 2004 it is expected that most alleged breaches of a non-molestation order will follow the criminal route.

WHICH COURT?

4.55 Application is made to the court which made the order that is alleged to have been breached. Judges at every level have the power to commit for breach of orders made under Pt IV of the FLA 1996, but deputy district judges do not have any jurisdiction in enforcement of Pt IV orders.

PROCEDURE ON APPLICATION TO COMMIT

4.56 The applicant issues Form N78 (Notice to Show Cause why the respondent should not be committed), listing the breaches alleged, and files a witness statement in support, setting out all the circumstances. Form N78 endorsed with a return date and copy affidavit is served personally on the respondent.

The procedure at the committal hearing is set out at **4.57** below.

The committal hearing

4.57 Whether the respondent is arrested and brought to court under a power of arrest, pursuant to a warrant of arrest or comes to court following issue of a Form N78 Notice to show cause or the similar procedure in the family proceedings court, the procedure thereafter is the same.

Any judge apart from a deputy district judge may deal with the alleged breach. A district judge may deal with the alleged breach of an order made by a circuit judge. The hearing is in public[1].

The applicant and his or her solicitor should be present at the hearing, and the respondent should have the opportunity of having legal representation. If the respondent is not legally represented, the proceedings will almost certainly be adjourned to enable him or her to be represented. The court will be mindful that if the breaches are proved, the respondent may be deprived of his or her liberty, and so the proceedings must comply with Art 6(3) of the European Convention for the Protection of Human Rights and Fundamental Freedoms 1950[2]. This gives the respondent the right to be legally represented, if necessary at the public expense.

At the first hearing, the following courses are open to the court:

(1) To determine after hearing evidence/admissions whether the order has been breached and to decide upon the appropriate penalty for the breach. This course is only likely if the respondent is represented.
(2) To adjourn the hearing to another date and remand the respondent in custody for a maximum of 8 days. If the remand is for more than 3 days, the court will have to arrange for the respondent to be escorted to prison, otherwise the respondent may be detained in custody by the local police. The court will issue a remand order in Form FL409.
(3) To adjourn the hearing to another date and remand the respondent on bail with or without sureties/recognisances. The court will issue a remand order in Form FL409 and bail notice in Form FL412, together with Recognisance/Surety Forms FL410/FL411 as appropriate.
(4) To release the respondent and adjourn the hearing to a date no more than 14 days from the date of the arrest. The respondent must be given at least 2 clear days' notice of the adjourned hearing date.

When the court deals with the alleged breach of the order, either immediately following arrest or at an adjourned hearing, the procedure is as follows.

(1) The judge will need to be satisfied that the court had jurisdiction to make the order in the first place, that it was served on the respondent before the alleged breach and that the arrest was lawful. For example, the arrest will be unlawful if made pursuant to a power of arrest that did not attach to the part of the order in respect of which a breach is alleged.
(2) The judge will want to be satisfied that the applicant can establish each of the breaches alleged, and unless admissions are made by the respondent, oral evidence will be heard.
(3) The judge will record his finding in respect of each alleged breach and give reasons. The standard of proof is the criminal standard ie he must be sure[3]. The breach will be proved only if the respondent is in breach of the terms of the order literally construed and the respondent's conduct was deliberate.
(4) The judge will give a punishment for each breach proved, having given the respondent an opportunity to address him on any mitigating factors, and having heard the applicant's views on the appropriate punishment. A separate penalty should be imposed for each breach proved, and these can be expressed to be concurrent or consecutive. The court's powers are limited. Lay justices may not impose a term of imprisonment exceeding 2 months whereas District or Circuit judges may imprison for up to 2 years. In either case any fine must not exceed level 5 on the standard scale[4].

[1] See *Practice Guidance 3 May 2013 and 4 June 2013 (Committal for Contempt of Court) Family Court Practice* Part V.
[2] *Hammerton v Hammerton* [2007] EWCA Civ 248, [2007] 2 FLR 1133.

4.57 Personal Protection

[3] *Dean v Dean* [1987] 1 FLR 517.
[4] Family Court (Contempt of Court) (Powers) Regulations 2014 (SI 2014/833).

SENTENCING

4.58 The options are as follows:

(1) an immediate prison sentence of up to 2 years;
(2) a new order coupled with a custodial sentence suspended on strict compliance with the new order until it expires;
(3) a new order coupled with an adjournment of sentence until the expiry of the new order with liberty to the applicant to restore for sentence to be imposed before then. In the absence of an application to restore before the expiry of the new order the respondent to be relieved of his liability to be punished for the breach;
(4) a fine, on its own or in combination with any of the above. As a matter of practice, a fine is an unlikely punishment as most respondents to applications of this nature will be without the means to pay; or
(5) a stern warning but no penalty.

The sentence should reflect the frequency and severity of the breach, whether the respondent is an habitual offender against court orders, and his personal circumstances.

A first offender need not consider that he may not be imprisoned. There has been a move away from the tacit acceptance of 'one free strike'[1].

In *Wilson v Webster*[2], on the applicant's appeal, the Court of Appeal substituted a sentence of 3 months' imprisonment for that of 14 days imposed by the court below. The respondent had broken an undertaking within one month of giving it by attacking the applicant in the street, knocking her to the ground and punching her in the face.

Similarly, in *Neil v Ryan*[3] the Court of Appeal allowed an appeal by an applicant against a suspended sentence for the first breach of a non-molestation order:

> ' . . . When all is said and done, here was a woman in her own home, the victim of a serious attack when she, not unreasonably, would have believed that the court's order had given her a measure of protection from violence. If this sort of attack is not met by an immediate committal to prison, the likely message will be that the first attack in breach of an order of the court in effect will attract no immediate consequences . . . If that were the message then the protection which the court order is meant to provide would be illusory. The whole point of the order is that it should bite immediately, and that the person in serious breach of it should understand that there will be immediate punishment.'

In *Atrill v O'Donnell*[4], a 2-month sentence of imprisonment for the first breach of an undertaking was upheld on appeal. In *Hale v Tanner*[5] Hale LJ (as she then was) took the opportunity to give some guidance as to the length of sentence that should be contemplated for breaches of orders in family cases. In that case, she emphasised that the approach to punishing a breach of an order in a family case would be quite different from any other type of case, because of 'the heightened emotional tensions that arise between family members and often the need for those family members to continue to be in contact with one another because they have children together'. The judgment of Hale LJ also sets out the various factors that the courts should take into account when sentencing for contempt for breach of a non-molestation order. Among these are the following:

- If imprisonment was appropriate, the length of the committal should be considered without reference to whether or not the committal was to be suspended.
- The length of the committal depended on the two objectives in contempt proceedings:
    (a) marking the court's disapproval of disobedience to its orders, and
    (b) securing future compliance.
- The length had to bear some relationship to the maximum of 2 years available.
- Suspension was available in a much wider range of circumstances than in the criminal justice system.
- The length of any suspension required a separate consideration, although it would often be linked to continued compliance with the underlying order.
- The context in which the breach had occurred had to be borne in mind, for example, the emotions involved in family break-ups.
- In many cases, the court would have to bear in mind that there were concurrent proceedings in another court based on the same or substantially the same facts. The court could not ignore those proceedings and might have to take their outcome into account. A court would not want to cause a contemnor to suffer punishment twice.
- It would usually be desirable for the court to explain why it was making the order it was making.

In *Lomas v Parle*[6] this guidance was supplemented. That case concerned the appeal by an applicant against the sentence imposed for the admitted breach of two non-molestation orders. The two concurrent sentences of 4 months' imprisonment were substituted with sentences of 9 months' imprisonment concurrent by the Court of Appeal. There was a background of persistent intimidation and threats of violence. The respondent was also the subject of criminal proceedings and proceedings under the Protection from Harassment Act 1997 arising out of the incident that gave rise to the breach of the injunction and the Court of Appeal also dealt with the sentencing considerations in these circumstances.

In *Murray v Robinson*[7], a sentence of 8 months for each of three breaches of a non-molestation order, to run concurrently, was upheld by the Court of Appeal. There had been no actual violence to the victim, but the court took a serious view of the great distress and anxiety caused by the respondent's behaviour.

Notwithstanding the courts' increasingly tough approach, it is as well to remember that the court is punishing the respondent's contempt of court in breaching the order, not for the behaviour resulting in the breach.

4.58 Personal Protection

Whenever a punishment is imposed for being in contempt of court, it is open to the contemnor to apply to the court to purge his contempt.

Since 1 July 2007 breach of a non-molestation order without reasonable excuse has been a criminal offence and so many alleged breaches of a non-molestation order without reasonable excuse will be dealt with in the criminal jurisdiction. This will be the better course for the more serious breaches where the full sentencing powers of the criminal courts will provide a more effective sanction.

[1] *Brewer v Brewer* [1989] Fam Law 352; *Ansah v Ansah* [1977] 2 All ER 638; *McIntosh v McIntosh* [1990] FCR 351; and *Thorpe v Thorpe* [1998] 2 FLR 127.
[2] [1998] 1 FLR 1097.
[3] [1998] 2 FLR 1068.
[4] Unreported, 27 November 1998.
[5] [2000] 2 FLR 879.
[6] [2004] 1 FLR 812.
[7] [2006] 1 FLR 365.

Section 2 Other remedies

The Protection from Harassment Act 1997

4.59 The PHA 1997 creates civil (and criminal) remedies to protect individuals from 'stalking', which can cover a wide range of anti-social behaviour, including that between cohabitants.

There is no requirement for parties to be associated, unlike Pt IV of the FLA 1996, nor even for there to be or to have been a relationship between them[1].

The PHA 1997 creates a statutory tort of harassment, and for the purposes of the Act the 3-year primary period of limitation of actions that applies to torts resulting in personal injury is disapplied[2]. The usual tortious limitation period under s 2 of the Limitation Act 1980 will apply, that is 6 years.

[1] *R v Hills* [2000] TLR 893.
[2] PHA 1997, s 6 and Limitation Act 1980, s 11(1A).

Which court?

4.60 As with any action in tort, the proceedings may be commenced in any county court or in the High Court and the same procedural requirements apply as to actions in tort generally.

Prohibition of harassment

4.61 Section 1 of the PHA 1997 prohibits harassment and provides that a person must not pursue a course of conduct:

(a) which amounts to harassment of another; and
(b) which he knows or ought to know amounts to the harassment of the other.

It amounts to harassment of another if a reasonable person in possession of the same information would think the course of conduct amounted to harassment of the other, ie it is an objective test.

Section 3 provides for a cause of action in damages for an actual or apprehended breach of s 1.

Damages may be awarded for anxiety caused by the harassment and financial loss resulting from the harassment.

The right to apply for an injunction to restrain harassment is not mentioned in the PHA 1997, but the court's inherent jurisdiction to grant an injunction is not affected.

There is no definition of harassment but references to harassing a person include alarming the person or causing distress.

A course of conduct must involve conduct on at least two occasions.

Conduct includes speech[1]. However, the fewer the incidents relied upon, and the farther apart in time they are, the less likely it is that it will be reasonable to describe them as a course of conduct[2].

The prohibition of harassment does not apply to a course of conduct if the person who pursued it shows that:

(a) it was pursued for the purpose of preventing or detecting crime;
(b) it was pursued under any enactment or rule of law or to comply with any condition or requirement imposed by any person under any enactment; or
(c) in the particular circumstances, the pursuit of the course of conduct was reasonable.

[1] See s 7(4).
[2] *Lau v DPP* [2000] 1 FLR 799.

PROCEDURE

4.62 Proceedings under PHA 1997 are civil proceedings and are governed by CPR Pt 65.

The claim will usually be issued in the county court[1] although the High Court does have jurisdiction. The claimant issues a claim form under Pt 7. The nature of the claim must be set out concisely and the remedy sought must be specified. If personal injury damages are claimed, the claim form must contain a statement as to whether the claimant expects to recover more than £1,000 under that heading.

Separate particulars of claim may be served and, if this course is followed, the claim form must indicate that they are to follow.

If, as is likely, an injunction is required, a separate application must be made which is supported by a witness statement. Application may be made without

4.62 *Personal Protection*

notice to the defendant in an appropriate case, but the witness statement must set out why the claimant is asking the court to make an order without giving notice to the defendant.

The claim must be served on each of the defendants in accordance with CPR Pt 6. Personal service of an application for an injunction will be necessary.

As well as the claim form and any particulars of claim, the defendant will receive a response pack from the court in Form N1C. This includes an acknowledgement form which should be returned within 14 days of service indicating whether or not the claim is contested. Any defence should be filed and served 28 days after service of the particulars of claim if the defendant has filed an acknowledgement form, otherwise the defence must be filed and served within 14 days of service of the claim.

In practice, most claims will merely be the vehicle for obtaining an injunction to restrain the harassment and if the matter is disposed of at the injunction hearing (as is usually the case), the balance of the claim will be adjourned generally, requiring the defendant to do nothing further.

However, if the damages claim is pursued, the claim will be allocated to a track and case managed to a trial or disposal hearing.

[1] Any county court, as these are not family proceedings.

Enforcement

CRIMINAL LIABILITY

4.63 Breach of an injunction granted by the High Court or county court to restrain conduct which amounts to harassment without reasonable excuse is an offence with a remedy under the criminal law.

CONTEMPT OF COURT

4.64 Alternatively, if the defendant has done anything which the claimant believes is prohibited by the injunction and is thereby in contempt of court, the claimant may apply for the issue of an arrest warrant. There is no provision for a power of arrest to be attached to an order made under PHA 1997.

CPR Pt 81 applies. The application for a warrant must be substantiated on oath and a warrant must not be issued unless the judge/district judge has reasonable grounds for believing that the defendant has breached the terms of the injunction.

Following arrest the defendant must be brought to court immediately[1]. Only a circuit judge or recorder has the power to commit, and there is no provision for remanding the defendant in custody or on bail. This means that the committal must either be dealt with immediately or adjourned to a later date.

[1] Contrast this with the position under Pt IV FLA 1996, ie within 24 hours.

Other remedies in tort

4.65 Despite the powers given to the courts by Pt IV of the FLA 1996 and the PHA 1997 to deal with personal protection, there are still occasions when it may be necessary to make an application for relief under the common law tort jurisdiction to deal with assault, battery, trespass to the person or to land, or nuisance. Before the PHA 1997 was enacted, the case law had evolved to the extent that it was possible to bring an action in nuisance for behaviour that amounted to harassment, thereby avoiding the need for there to be physical violence before a cause of action arose.

In *Burnett v George*[1] it was held to be sufficient to warrant the granting of an injunction restraining the defendant from 'molesting or otherwise interfering with the claimant by doing acts calculated to do her harm' that the defendant had been making persistent telephone calls to her in the middle of the night that had a harmful effect on the claimant's mental health.

In *Khorasandjian v Bush*[2] the court took the view that harassment by telephone could amount to private nuisance where it interfered with the use and enjoyment of property. However, since *Hunter v London Docklands Development Corporation* and *Hunter v Canary Wharf Limited*[3] and *Burris v Azadani*[4] it has been clear that a licensee may not sue in private nuisance, and to this extent *Khorasandjian v Bush* has been overruled.

[1] [1992] 1 FLR 525.
[2] [1993] 3 All ER 669.
[3] [1997] 2 All ER 426.
[4] [1996] 1 FLR 266.

Procedure

4.66 The procedure for bringing an action in the common law tort jurisdiction is the same as for bringing an action in the statutory tort of harassment. The action may be commenced in any county court, save for actions relating to trespass to land or nuisance relating to land which must be commenced in the court for the district in which the land or property is situated.

A Pt 7 Claim Form must be issued and, if injunctive relief is sought, an application for an injunction must be issued supported by an affidavit.

Housing Act 1985

4.67 The Housing Act 1985 (HA 1985), as amended by the HA 1996, provides a discretionary ground for possession of a dwelling-house let under a secure tenancy where one partner in a marriage, civil partnership or cohabitation relationship has left the property as a result of the violence of the other and the court is satisfied that he or she is unlikely to return.

Part B PROCEDURAL GUIDES

Non-molestation and/or occupation order under Family Law Act 1996, Pt IV

Legal background

4.68 An application under FLA 1996, Pt IV can be made to the Family Court either as a freestanding application or within existing proceedings. By FC(CDB)R 2014, r 17, an application within existing proceedings will be allocated to the level of judge dealing with the existing proceedings.

An application by a person under the age of 18, or for leave under s 43 (applications by children under 16) will be allocated to the first available judge other than a lay justice (FC(CDB)R 2014, r 16).

Personal protection in the form of a 'non-molestation order' is available to 'associated persons', a term widely defined in s 62(3). 'Molestation' is not defined in the Act. It includes violence and threats of violence but is not confined to such acts (see s 42). It includes controlling, coercive or threatening behaviour and all forms of abuse.

'Occupation orders' are available under ss 33, 35, 36, 37 and 38. Each section is self-contained, setting out who may apply and the court's powers. In practice, most applications will be under s 33. If an application is made under the wrong section, the court can make an order under another section (s 39). The court can include ancillary provisions (s 40).

Power of arrest may be attached to an occupation order. However, it is not possible to attach a power of arrest to a non-molestation order (s 42A). A breach of a non-molestation order is a criminal offence.

Where injunctive relief from harassment within the meaning of PHA 1997 is sought, see **4.72** below. Thus a person who is not an 'associated person' within FLA 1996, Pt IV may need to sue under PHA 1997. Compensatory damages can be awarded under PHA 1997 and thus that Act (and/or proceedings in tort for, eg, assault) should be used where such a claim is pursued. Concurrent proceedings under the FLA 1996 and PHA 1997 can be brought and should be consolidated (see *Lomas v Parle*[1]).

[1] [2004] 1 FLR 812.

Procedure

4.69

What is a 'non-molestation' order?	An order prohibiting the respondent from molesting another person who is associated with the respondent and/or a relevant child	FLA 1996, s 42(1)

Who may apply for a 'non-molestation' order?	An associated person; a person is associated with another person if:	FLA 1996, s 62(3)
	they are or have been married to each other	
	they are or have been civil partners of each other	
	they are cohabitants or former cohabitants	
	they live or have lived in the same household, otherwise than merely by reason of one of them being the other's employee, tenant, lodger or boarder	
	they are relatives (as defined)	FLA 1996, s 63(1)
	they have agreed to marry one another (whether or not that agreement has been terminated)	
	they have entered into a civil partnership agreement (whether or not that agreement has been terminated)	CPA 2004, s 73
	they have or have had an intimate personal relationship with each other which is or was of significant duration	FLA 1996, s 62(3)
	in relation to a child both persons are parents or have or have had parental responsibility for the child	FLA 1996, s 62(4)
	they are parties to the same family proceedings	FLA 1996, s 63(1), (2)
Who may apply for an 'occupation order' under s 33?	An applicant who is entitled to occupy a dwelling-house by virtue of a beneficial estate or interest or contract or by virtue of any enactment giving him the right to remain in occupation or who has home rights	FLA 1996, s 30
	The respondent is an 'associated person'	FLA 1996, s 62(3)
	The dwelling-house must be, have been, or have been intended to be, the home of the applicant and respondent	FLA 1996, s 33

4.69 *Personal Protection*

Who may apply for an 'occupation order' under s 35?	An applicant former spouse or former civil partner who is not entitled to occupy; the respondent is entitled to occupy; the dwelling-house was or was intended to be their home	FLA 1996, s 35
Who may apply for an 'occupation order' under s 36?	An applicant cohabitant or former cohabitant who is not entitled to occupy; the respondent is entitled to occupy; the dwelling-house is, was, or was intended to be the home where they live(d) together	FLA 1996, s 36
Who may apply for an 'occupation order' under s 37?	An applicant spouse former spouse, civil partner or former civil partner where neither applicant nor respondent is entitled to occupy; the dwelling-house must be or have been their home	FLA 1996, s 37
Who may apply for an 'occupation order' under s 38?	An applicant cohabitant or former cohabitant where neither applicant nor respondent is entitled to occupy. The dwelling-house must be or have been the home in which they live(d) together	FLA 1996, s 38
How is the application made?	In all cases, on Form FL401 supported by a witness statement (which must state the grounds)	FPR 10.2
Fee	No fee is payable on an application for a non-molestation or occupation order	
Ex parte applications	In any case where it considers it is 'just and convenient' to do so the court can make a non-molestation order or an occupation order on an ex parte basis. The court must have regard to 'all the circumstances', including the criteria in s 45(2)	FLA 1996, s 45(1), (2)
	The witness statement must state the reasons why notice was not given	FPR 10.2(4)
	If an ex parte order is made there must be a 'full hearing' as soon as just and convenient	FLA 1996, s 45(3)

Form of order	An occupation order is in Form FL404. A non-molestation order is in Form FL404a	
Service of ex parte order	Respondent must be personally served with: a copy of the order made a copy of the application in Form FL401 a copy of the witness statement in support of the application notice of the date of the full hearing in Form FL402.	FPR 10.6; FJC Protocol of November 2011: *Process Servers: Non-Molestation Orders*
Application on notice	Notice in Form FL402, together with a copy of the application in Form FL401 and the witness statement in support must be served on the respondent personally not less than 2 days before the application is to be heard	FPR 10.3
	Before the application is served, the court can abridge time for service	FPR 10.3(1)(b)(ii)
	If the application is for an occupation order under ss 33, 35 or 36 a copy of the application and notice in Form FL416 must be served by first class post on the mortgagee or landlord	FPR 10.3(3)
Proof of service	After service, the applicant must file a statement in Form FL415	FPR r 6.37
Response	Respondent may, but is not required to, serve a statement in reply and/or make a cross-application	
Hearing	An application for a non-molestation order or an occupation order is dealt with in private unless the court otherwise directs	FPR 10.5
	The application in the County Court is heard by a district judge or circuit judge The court keeps a record of the hearing in Form FL405	FP(AJ)D 2009

4.69 *Personal Protection*

Orders available	*Non-molestation order* An order may forbid molestation in general or particular acts of molestation or both	FLA 1996, s 42(6)
	The better modern practice is to make the order as specific as is appropriate whether or not it also contains a clause forbidding molestation in general. In particular, an order can require the respondent to 'keep-away' from a specified address (but not to 'get out', which needs to be part of an occupation order).	*Boness v R*[a]
	Occupation order under s 33 An order may: enforce the applicant's entitlement to remain in occupation as against the respondent	
	require the respondent to permit the applicant to enter and remain in the dwelling-house or part of the dwelling-house	
	regulate the occupation of the dwelling-house by either or both of the parties	
	if the respondent is entitled to occupy, prohibit, suspend or restrict the exercise by him of his right to occupy the dwelling-house	
	if the respondent has home rights in relation to the dwelling-house, restrict or terminate those rights	
	require the respondent to leave the dwelling-house or part of the dwelling-house	
	exclude the respondent from a defined area in which the dwelling-house is included	
	For additional provisions, see s 40	
	Occupation orders under ss 35, 36 Mandatory provisions are set out in ss 35(3), (4), 36(3), (4), and discretionary provisions in ss 35(5), 36(6)	

Procedural Guides 4.69

	For additional provisions, see s 40	
	Occupation orders under ss 37, 38 See ss 37(3), 38(3)	
Duration of non-molestation orders	For a specified period or until further order	FLA 1996, s 42(7)
	Application for extension of the order is made in Form FL403	FPR 10.8
Duration of occupation orders	*Applicant with estate or interest etc or with home rights* for a specified period	
	until the occurrence of a specified event	
	or until further order	FLA 1996, s 33(10)
	Application for extension of the order is made in Form FL403	FPR 10.8
	Spouse, former spouse, civil partner or former civil partner not entitled to an interest for a maximum of 6 months, but can be renewed any number of times	FLA 1996, ss 35(10), 37(5)
	Application for extension of the order is made in Form FL403	FPR 10.8
	Cohabitant or former cohabitant not entitled to an interest for a maximum of 6 months, but can be renewed only once	FLA 1996, ss 36(10), 38(6)
	Application for extension of the order is made in Form FL403	FPR 10.8
Penal notice	A penal notice must be endorsed on an order before it can be enforced by committal	FPR 10.12, 37.9, PD 37A

4.69 *Personal Protection*

	The prescribed forms of order (FL404 and FL404a) include an appropriately worded penal notice. Because the sanction for breach is different, the wording of the penal notice for breach of a non-molestation order is unique to that form of order. Thus two separate orders are required if the court makes both types of order	FPR 10.12, PD 37A
Power of arrest	The court '*shall* attach a power of arrest to one or more provisions of an occupation order unless satisfied that . . . the applicant . . . will be adequately protected without [it]' if the respondent has used or threatened violence	FLA 1996, s 47(2)
	If the order is made ex parte, the court *may* attach a power of arrest to an occupation order if 'the respondent has used or threatened violence . . . ' and 'there is a risk of significant harm . . . if the power of arrest is not attached . . . '	FLA 1996, s 47(3)
	It is not possible to attach a power of arrest to a non-molestation order. Breach of such an order is a criminal offence	FLA 1996, s 42A
Undertakings	The court may accept an undertaking. The court 'shall not accept an undertaking . . . instead of making an occupation order in any case where . . . a power of arrest would be attached' nor instead of making a non-molestation order where 'it is necessary . . . that any breach may be punishable under s 42A'	FLA 1996, s 46(1), (3), (3A)
	The court must deliver a copy of the undertaking to the party giving the undertaking	FPR 37.7
	A warrant of arrest can be issued to enforce an undertaking	FLA 1996, s 46(4)

Damages	It is not possible to claim damages under the FLA 1996. However, damages can be claimed under PHA 1997, s 3. If concurrent proceedings are brought they should be consolidated	*Lomas v Parle*[b]
Service of injunction	Personal service of an order is required	FPR 10.6; FJC Protocol of November 2011: *Process Servers: Non-Molestation Orders*
	The applicant's solicitor should endeavour to effect service as soon as possible	
	An injunction directing an act to be done cannot be enforced unless it is served before the time within which the act is to be done has expired; an injunction cannot be enforced unless the respondent knows about it. Service should be effected in accordance with the terms of the Protocol	FPR 37.5; FJC Protocol of November 2011: *Process Servers: Non-Molestation Orders*
	Form 404a (non-molestation order) and/or Form FL406 (containing only those provisions of the occupation order to which a power of arrest has been attached) must be delivered to the officer in charge of any police station for the applicant's address or such other police station as the court may specify. The form must be served together with a statement showing that the respondent has been served with the order(s) or otherwise informed of its terms	FPR 10.10
	A copy of an occupation order made under s 33, 35 or 36 must be served by the applicant by first class post on the mortgagee or landlord	FPR 10.6(3)

[1] [2005] EWCA Crim 2395.
[2] [2004] 1 FLR 812.

4.70 *Personal Protection*

Transfer of a Tenancy under Family Law Act 1996, Pt IV, s 53 and Sch 7

Legal background

4.70 Since the coming into force of FLA 1996, Pt IV on 1 October 1997, the court is empowered to transfer tenancies, both contractual and statutory, between cohabitants who no longer live together as husband and wife, as well as between spouses and former spouses. As set out in FLA 1996, Sch 7, para 10, the person to whom the tenancy is transferred can be ordered to pay compensation to the other party. The power to transfer the tenancy to a former spouse arises on decree nisi; the order becomes effective on decree absolute; and there is a prohibition on applying if that former spouse has remarried. If there is a decree of judicial separation, the power to transfer arises after the decree is pronounced. A tenancy in the other spouse's name, or in joint names, can be destroyed by the unilateral surrender or giving of notice to quit by one tenant without consultation with the other (*Hammersmith and Fulham London Borough Council v Monk*[1]). A party should ask for an undertaking that the tenancy will not be surrendered and then serve that undertaking on the landlord. If the undertaking is not given the applicant should apply for an injunction and serve the order on the landlord (*Bater v Greenwich London Borough Council*[2]).

An application under FLA 1996, s 53 and Sch 7 is governed by the procedure in FPR 8.29–8.34.

[1] [1992] 1 AC 478, [1992] 1 FLR 465.
[2] [1999] 2 FLR 993.

Procedure

4.71

Who may apply	Either spouse, but a matrimonial/civil partnership order must be granted before the order is made	FLA 1996, Sch 7, para 2(2)
	Either former spouse, but a decree nisi must be granted before the order is made and the applicant must not have remarried; if application is for the transfer of a statutory tenancy or contractual tenancy containing a prohibition on assignment, it must be made before decree absolute	FLA 1996, Sch 7, para 13
	A cohabitant who is no longer living with the other cohabitant as husband and wife	FLA 1996, Sch 7, para 3
Application	To the Family Court or the same court as existing matrimonial/civil partnership proceedings	FLA 1996, Sch 7, para 2(2); FPR 8.30, PD 8A, para 1.1(a)

Fee	£75	FPFO 2008, fee 1.4
Service	The court will serve the respondent and the landlord unless the applicant is directed to serve	FPR 8.31
	A landlord may be made a party to proceedings	FPR 8.32
Respondent	The other spouse or cohabitant	
Interlocutory injunction	The court may grant an injunction if ancillary or incidental to the assistance sought; an application for an injunction must be in accordance with procedure under FPR 20.4	FPR 8.34
Orders for disclosure	Any party may apply to the court under r 21.2 for any person to attend a production appointment to produce documents specified or described in the order	FPR 8.33
Order	Transfer of tenancy or statutory tenancy	FLA 1996, Sch 7, paras 7–9
	Payment by the spouse or cohabitant to whom the tenancy is transferred, to the other; deferment of payment or payment by instalments if transferee's financial hardship greater than transferor's	FLA 1996, Sch 7, para 10
	Order that both liable to discharge obligations prior to date of transfer and indemnity	FLA 1996, Sch 7, para 11

Claims under the Protection from Harassment Act 1997

Legal background

4.72 The High Court and the County Court have jurisdiction to grant an injunction for personal protection by forbidding harassment under PHA 1997 or any conduct which amounts to a recognised form of tort (*Khorasandjian v Bush*[1]). Such proceedings are not 'family proceedings'; however, a warrant of arrest can be granted in respect of a breach (PHA 1997, s 3(3), (5)). Unlike FLA 1996, the court can award damages under the PHA 1997 (see *Singh v Bhakar*[2], where damages of £35,000 were awarded). In *Burris v Azadani*[3], the Court of Appeal held that, where it is necessary to make the injunction effective for the protection of the applicant, an 'exclusion zone' can be ordered

4.72 *Personal Protection*

forbidding the defendant to go within a specified area around the applicant's home. In *Silverton v Gravett*[4], the 'exclusion zone' included also the claimant's place of work.

Where the victim and the perpetrator of harassment or molestation are 'associated persons' within FLA 1996, s 62(3), the remedies under that Act are more comprehensive, particularly if occupation of the family home is an issue.

For precedents, see *Emergency Remedies in the Family Courts* (Family Law).

[1]   [1993] 2 FLR 66.
[2]   [2007] 1 FLR 880.
[3]   [1996] 1 FLR 266.
[4]   [2001] All ER (D) 282.

Injunctions under the Protection from Harassment Act 1997

4.73 An injunction can be granted in the County Court (as in the High Court) without a claim for damages or other relief, by virtue of CCA 1984, s 38. Whereas an injunction under FLA 1996 is applied for by way of an application in Form FL401 under FPR Pt 10, an application for an injunction under PHA 1997 is governed by CPR Pt 65 which requires the claim to be brought under CPR Pt 8.

Under the CPR, proceedings are commenced by 'claim form'. Claims under the PHA 1997 must be brought under the Pt 8 procedure (see r 65.28 and CPR Pt 8). Generally, a Pt 8 claim form (N208) should not contain the same amount of detail as in a Pt 7 claim. A Pt 8 claim form should set out in summary form the issue which the claimant wants the court to decide and the remedy sought. If an interim remedy is also sought (eg a without notice injunction) see also CPR Pt 25 and in particular CPR PD 25A (see Pt III) which supplements Pt 25. Best practice for making a free-standing application is to file N208 incorporating short particulars of claim, which can, but need not, include a claim for damages, together with an application in Form N16A (County Court) or Application Notice in Form N244 (High Court), provided that the evidence setting out the relevant facts is given in Form N16A or N244, or in witness statement(s), verified by a statement of truth (see para 3 of PD 25A).

Assault and battery

4.74 If protection is required but is not available under the FLA 1996 (eg because the parties are not 'associated persons') nor under the PHA 1997 (eg because there is no 'course of conduct': in *Andreson v Lovell*[1] a 'one-off unwanted grope' was an isolated incident and not harassment, but it would be an assault) it may be possible to sue in tort and seek an injunction in those proceedings.

[1]   [2009] EWHC 3397 (QB).

Procedure

4.75

Who may apply	A person who is or may be the victim of a course of conduct prohibited by PHA 1997, s 1	PHA 1997, s 3(1)
	Application for an interim injunction may be made by the defendant to the claim	*Huntingdon Life Sciences v Stop Huntingdon Animal Cruelty*[a]; CPR 25.1(1)(a), 25.2(1)
Which court?	High Court or the County Court at the hearing centre for the area where the claimant or defendant resides A district judge has jurisdiction to deal with all claims under PHA 1997	PHA 1997, s 3(3); CPR 65.28
Application	Claim Form N208 must be issued, unless the court allows the application to be made before proceedings are started because the matter is urgent or there are good reasons for not giving notice A claimant must file any written evidence on which he intends to rely when he files his claim form. A claimant may rely on the matters set out in the claim form if it is verified by a statement of truth.	CPR 65.28, 25.2(1) (2), 25.3(1); PD 25A, para 4.4 CPR 8.5 and 8.6
	An urgent application for an injunction should be made as an interim application in pending proceedings by application notice in Form N16A (County Court) or Form N244 (High Court)	CPR Pt 23; PD 23A; CPR 25.1(1)(a); PD 25A, para 2.1
	A form of acknowledgement of service (N210) must be served with the claim form. The defendant must file an acknowledgement of service. If he does not do so, he may attend the hearing but may not take part unless the court gives permission	PD 8, para 3; CPR 8.3 and 8.4

	Damages can be claimed, but need not be	PHA 1997, s 3; CCA 1984, s 38; CPR PD 2, para 8.1(d)(ii)
	An application for an interim injunction must be supported by evidence, ie a witness statement, unless the court orders otherwise	CPR 25.3(2)
Fee	High Court: £480 County Court: £280	
	(non-money claim) payable on issue of application in Form N16A or N244 together with Claim Form N208	CPFO 2008 (as amended), fee 1.5
Oral application without documents	The court can dispense with the requirement for an application notice and in cases of extreme urgency can grant an interim injunction by telephone. However, the court should be expected to require an undertaking to file evidence, verified by a statement of truth, notice of application and, if not yet done, to issue a claim form	CPR 23.3(2)(b); PD 25A, paras 4.2, 4.5, 5.1(2)
	Such an undertaking must be strictly complied with	*Re S (A Child) (Family Division: Without Notice Orders)*[b]
Application begun without notice	An interim injunction can be granted without notice of the application having been given, where the matter is urgent and the court considers that there are good reasons for not giving notice	CPR 25.2(1), (2), 25.3(1)
	Any applicant without notice is under a duty to give full and frank disclosure of all relevant facts	*W v H*[c]; *B v A (Wasted Costs Order)*[d]
	In an urgent case informal notice, ie short notice, of application for a personal protection injunction is better practice than no notice, unless the circumstances require secrecy	CPR PD 23A, para 4.2

Procedural Guides **4.75**

	If a claim form has already been served, the applicant should take steps to tell the respondent that the application is being made without full notice unless secrecy is essential	CPR PD 25A, para 4.3
	The reasons for not giving notice must be stated in the evidence in support	CPR 25.3(3); PD 25A, para 3.4
	If the application is made before the application notice has been issued, the notice and evidence in support and fee must be filed on the same or next working day (or as ordered by the court), as should the claim form and fee, if not already issued	CPR PD 25A, paras 4.4(3), 5.1(4), (5)
	The respondent against whom an interim injunction is granted may apply to have it set aside or varied, but must apply within 7 days after it is served or at the return date provided in the order	CPR 23.10(1), (2); PD 25A, para 5.1(3)
Evidence	Applications for interim injunctions must be supported by evidence, ie set out in a document verified by a statement of truth, which may be in a witness statement or the statement of case or the application itself	CPR 25.3(2); PD 25, para 3.2
	The evidence must set out the facts on which the applicant relies for the claim including all material facts of which the court should be made aware	CPR PD 25A, para 3.3
	The witness statement must be verified by a statement of truth	CPR 8.2 and 22.1(1)
Service of notice	The application and evidence in support must be served as soon as practicable after it is filed and at least 3 working days before the hearing to give valid notice, unless the court shortens the time	CPR 2.8, 3.1(2)(a), 23.7(1)(a); PD 25A, para 2.2

4.75 *Personal Protection*

	Informal notice (ie less than 3 days) is better than no notice	*G v G*[e]
	Where proceedings have commenced, informal notice should be given unless secrecy is essential	CPR PD 25A, para 4.3(3)
Response	The defendant must file an acknowledgment of service. A defendant who intends to rely on written evidence must file it when he files his acknowledgment of service. (A claimant may file further written evidence in reply.) If the defendant fails to acknowledge service, he may attend the hearing but may not take part unless the court gives permission	CPR 8.3–8.5; PD 8A, para 3,
	Respondent to application for injunction may: (i) elect not to oppose (ii) oppose in whole or in part by filing and serving evidence (iii) make his own application in like form	CPR 23.11(1)
Hearing	CPR do not require the hearing of an interim application to be conducted in open court in public	CPR 23.8, 25.1, 25.2, 39.2(1)
	The applicant should submit a draft of the injunction in typescript (in Form N16 in the County Court) and on disk (in a format compatible with the word processing format used by the court) if he has not filed one already	CPR 23.7(3)(b); PD 25A, paras 2.4, 4.3
	Breach of an order under PHA 1997, s 3 is both a crime and a contempt of court. The facts on which the order is obtained need to be proven to the civil standard	*Hipgrave and Hipgrave v Jones*[f]
Orders available	The court may grant an injunction restraining the defendant from pursuing any conduct which amounts to harassment. The order may prohibit specific conduct and/or harassment in general.	

	Where necessary for the protection of the applicant, an exclusion zone can be provided around her home or her place of work	*Burris v Azadani*[g]; *Silverton v Gravett*[h]
	Power of arrest is not available (though a warrant of arrest can be granted after the event)	PHA 1997, s 3(3), (4)
Order made without notice: duration and review	If an injunction is granted at a hearing of which the respondent has not been given notice:	
	a return date must (unless the court orders otherwise) be given for a hearing at which the respondent can be present	CPR PD 25A, para 5.1(3)
	the respondent is in any event entitled within 7 days of service on him to apply to have the order set aside	CPR 23.10; Form N16
	Where an injunction is granted without notice having been given, it is good practice for the court to order that it runs to a date later than the return date, so that there is no hiatus until an injunction granted on notice can be served.	
Damages	The court can award damages under the PHA 1997	PHA 1997, s 3, eg, *Singh v Bhakar*[i]
	Concurrent proceedings under the FLA 1996 and the PHA 1997 should be consolidated and tried together	*Lomas v Parle*[j]
Undertakings	An enforceable undertaking can be accepted by the court	*Hussain v Hussain*[k]; CPR 81.4–81.11
Form of injunction order or undertaking: penal notice and clear instructions	To be enforceable, when served an injunction order must have prominently displayed on the front a warning notice of the consequences of disobedience	CPR PD 81, paras 1, 2; Form N16A
	Any order for an injunction must set out clearly what the respondent must do or not do (in the County Court the injunction should be issued in Form N138)	CPR PD 25A, para 5.2

4.75 *Personal Protection*

	An undertaking given to a county court must be recorded in Form N117	
Service of injunction or delivery of form of undertaking	Before an injunction can be enforced it must have been personally served on the respondent, before any alleged breach, unless the court has dispensed with service or he was present when the order was made or he has been notified of the terms of the order. Service should be effected in accordance with the Protocol (see 'Introduction' in the Protocol, which extends it to 'harassment')	CPR 81.5; Family Justice Council *Protocol for Process Servers*, November 2011
	An undertaking becomes enforceable when and because it is given to the court; however, unless a record of it is given to the person who gave it, difficulties can arise on enforcement proceedings, and in the County Court a copy is required to be delivered to the giver by the court or, failing that, served by the applicant	CPR 81.7; *Hussain v Hussain*[1]
Duration of interim injunction made on notice	An interim injunction granted on notice can be ordered to last until a fixed date or trial or further order	CPR PD 25A, para 5.2
	If the claim is stayed other than by agreement between the parties, an interim injunction shall be set aside unless the court orders that it should continue to have effect	CPR 25.10
Warrant for arrest	Application for a warrant of arrest in respect of disobedience of an injunction prohibiting harassment should be made in the High Court if the order was made there or, if the order was made in the County Court, the application may be made in any County Court office	PHA 1997, s 3(4), (5)
	The formal requirements upon making application for a warrant are provided by rules	CPR 65.29

ᵃ [2003] EWHC 810.
ᵇ [2001] 1 All ER 362.
ᶜ [2001] 1 All ER 300.
ᵈ [2013] 2 FLR 958.
ᵉ [1990] 1 FLR 395.
ᶠ [2005] 2 FLR 174.
ᵍ [1996] 1 FLR 266.
ʰ [2001] All ER (D) 282.
ⁱ [2007] 1 FLR 880.
ʲ [2004] 1 FLR 812.
ᵏ [1986] 2 FLR 271.
ˡ [1986] 2 FLR 271.

Committal and arrest for disobedience of an injunctive order or breach of an undertaking in the Family Court, the High Court and the County Court

Legal background

4.76 An injunctive order (including a non-molestation order or occupation order under FLA 1996, Pt IV; a CA 1989, s 8 order to which a penal notice has been attached; and an order under PHA 1997) directing a person to do an act at or within a specified time, or to abstain from doing an act, or an undertaking to like effect which incorporates a penal warning notice, may be enforced by committal proceedings initiated by the person entitled to the benefit of the direction or undertaking. Any undertaking for the payment of money that has effect as if it was an order under Matrimonial Causes Act 1973, Pt II may be enforced as if it was an order and FPR Pt 33 applies (FPR PD 33A). Some money orders may be enforceable by judgment summons under the Debtors Acts 1869 and 1878. Personal service of an injunctive order is required by CPR 81.5 and FPR 37.5. The court can dispense with service or provide for some other form of service, but an injunction cannot be enforced unless it can be proved that the person to whom it was directed knew about the order and, where an act is directed to be done, the order must have been served before the time set for the act to be done. 'Any procedural defect in the commencement or conduct by the applicant of a committal application may be waived by the court if satisfied that no injustice has been caused to the respondent by the defect' (*Nicholls v Nicholls*[1]; CPR PD 81, para 16.2). However, grave procedural errors will result in the findings and sentences being quashed (*Hammerton v Hammerton*[2]).

The President issued Practice Guidance on 3 May 2013 on 'Committal for Contempt of Court'. Although it is described as 'guidance' rather than a 'direction', it should be followed because 'liberty of the subject' is so important. No one is to be committed by the Family Court (whether sentence is immediate or suspended) without (a) the name of the contemnor, (b) proper details of the contempt and (c) reasons for the committal being made publicly available in a judgment published on the BAILII website.

[1] [1997] 1 FLR 649.
[2] [2007] 2 FLR 1133.

4.77 *Personal Protection*

Which rules of court

4.77 Applications for committal in respect of injunctive orders are interlocutory in nature (*Savings and Investment Bank v Gasco Investments (Netherlands) BV (No 2)*[1]). Consequently, if the injunctive order was made in family proceedings an application for committal is made in family proceedings and is now governed by FPR Pt 37. In civil proceedings, committal proceedings are governed by CPR Pt 81. However, Pt 81 does not apply to family proceedings. If the injunctive order was made in non-family civil proceedings, eg under the PHA 1997, then the CPR apply. In family cases, see generally FPR PD 37A.

[1] [1988] Ch 422.

Committal proceedings begun by notice to show good reason

4.78 The standard procedure for beginning proceedings for committal for enforcement of an injunction or an undertaking is by way of notice to show good reason why an order for committal should not be made, begun by application notice or Pt 8 claim form (High Court), Form N78 (County Court) or FL418 (magistrates' court).

Committal proceedings begun by arrest under a power of arrest

4.79 The power to arrest, for breach of an occupation order granted under FLA 1996, s 47(3) or for breach of a forced marriage protection order granted under FLA 1996, s 63I(2), provides the police with authority to intervene and stop a breach while it is happening or where they have reason to believe that such a breach has occurred. A power of arrest can also be exercised after the disobedience has ended and after an arrest for a criminal offence (*Wheeldon v Wheeldon*[1]). Where the police use the civil power of arrest the arrested person must be brought before the civil court within 24 hours (FLA 1996, s 47(7)). Breach of a non-molestation order in Form 404a made after 30 June 2007 is a criminal offence in respect of which the police may use their criminal powers of arrest.

There is no power to attach a power of arrest to an injunction under the PHA 1997 or at common law. Further, as from 1 July 2007, the power of arrest is abolished for non-molestation orders (see now FLA 1996, s 42A).

[1] [1998] 1 FLR 463.

Committal proceedings begun by arrest under a warrant of arrest

4.80 FLA 1996, s 47(8), (9) extended to the High Court and County Court a power to issue a warrant of arrest. This power is available where no power of arrest was attached to the breached direction (s 47(8)). The court can issue a warrant for the arrest of a person where the court has reasonable grounds, substantiated on oath (s 47(9)), to believe that he has failed to comply with a non-molestation or occupation order made under FLA 1996, Pt IV.

PHA 1997, s 3(3)–(5) provides the High Court and County Court with the power to issue a warrant of arrest where the court has reasonable grounds, substantiated on oath (s 3(5)), to believe that the respondent has failed to comply with an injunction which forbids harassment.

Remand following arrest

4.81 Once an arrested respondent is before the court, the court can immediately deal with the breach for which he has been arrested or adjourn (whether or not upon enlarged injunctive provisions). If adjourning, the court may remand. In FLA 1996 cases the power to remand is given to the High Court and County Court by s 47(11) and Sch 5, and exists in a magistrates' court by virtue of MCA 1980, ss 128 and 129. The remand can be in custody or on bail. Under FLA 1996, s 48, the power to remand can be exercised to enable a medical report to be made on the respondent.

There is no power to remand under PHA 1997.

Conduct of committal proceedings where the respondent is before the court following an arrest – preliminaries

4.82 Where a respondent is before the court for an alleged breach of an injunction, in order to ensure a fair trial there are essential preliminaries which the judge will consider. Is the respondent before the court within 24 hours of the arrest and is a lawful arrest admitted or proved? Is there proof of service of the injunction? Have the alleged breaches been reduced to writing and is Form N78 required? Is the respondent represented and, if not, does he seek an adjournment to obtain it or require time to prepare? Does he appreciate that he may be entitled to legal aid? Is the applicant present or represented and, if not, is an adjournment required? If adjourning, what directions are required and should the respondent be remanded? If remanded, should it be on bail or in custody?

An arrest is effected on the basis of a particular alleged breach. Earlier breaches cannot be dealt with unless Form N78 is also served (see FPR 10.11 and, in the case of the PHA 1997, CPR 65.29).

Conduct of committal proceedings when the respondent is before the court, whether on notice or following an arrest

4.83 Whether the respondent appears on notice in answer to a notice to show good reason, or following an arrest, the procedure to be followed for the determination of whether the respondent has disobeyed an order or breached an undertaking, and the disposal powers of the court, are the same. The breach must be proved to the criminal standard of proof. Thus, if not admitted, the applicant's evidence is heard first.

Absence of respondent

4.84 Provided that the court is satisfied that the respondent has been duly served, and has had the opportunity to obtain legal advice, the court can proceed in his absence. In *Begum v Anam*[1] a committal order was set aside as

4.84 *Personal Protection*

the respondent had not had the opportunity to obtain legal representation nor to arrange a production warrant to secure his attendance from prison.

[1] [2004] EWCA Civ 578.

Penalties

4.85 The court can order imprisonment (immediate or suspended) and/or a fine, or adjourn consideration of penalty for a fixed period and/or extend or enlarge the injunction. The common disposal orders are set out in County Court Form N79 and family proceedings court Form FL419. For the differing powers of judges of the Family Court, see the Family Court (Contempt of Court) (Powers) Regulations 2014.

Procedure

4.86

Preliminary matters	An injunctive order must be served personally on the person to whom it is directed, unless there has been an order for substituted service or dispensing with service	CPR 81.5 (civil); FPR 37.5 (family)
	However, pending service, if the respondent disobeys an injunctive order which requires him to abstain from doing an act, the court can impose a penalty if it is satisfied that he knew about the terms of the order	CPR 81.8 (civil); FPR 37.8 (family)
	Proof of service of the order is required. In all courts this is usually by Form FL415. Service should be effected in accordance with the Protocol	Family Justice Council *Protocol for Process Servers*, November 2011
	A mandatory injunctive order directing a person to do an act cannot be enforced unless it was served before the time at or by which the act was directed to be done	CPR 81.5 (civil); FPR 37.5 (family)
	An undertaking becomes enforceable on being given to and accepted by the court; however the court can require the giver to sign a statement to the effect that he understands the terms of his undertaking and the consequences of failure to comply with it	*Hussain v Hussain*[a]; CPR PD 81, para 2.2

	A copy of the undertaking in Form N117 in the County Court, D787 in the Principal Registry or FL422 in a family proceedings court, is required to be delivered to the giver of the undertaking, but the giver is bound even if he does not receive a copy	CPR 81.7 (civil); FPR 37.7 (family)
Who may apply for committal or enforcement?	Person in whose favour the injunctive order was granted or the undertaking was given	CPR 81.3 (civil); FPR 37.3 (family)
Which court?	The court which granted the injunctive order or undertaking	CPR PD 81, para 10 (civil); FPR 37.10 (family)
	The powers of the County Court to deal with disobedience or breach are the same as the High Court	Contempt of Court Act 1981; CCA 1984, s 38
	Lay justices' statutory powers to deal with disobedience or breach are limited to imposing immediate or suspended committal, fine or adjourning consideration of penalty	Family Court (Contempt of Court) (Powers) Regulations 2014
Committal applications (general)	The affidavit or statement in support should narrate the facts relied on, but the list of alleged breaches must be given in the application notice	CPR 81.10 (civil); FPR 37.10 (family); *Harmsworth v Harmsworth*[b]
	Fee on application in the Family Court: £155	FPFO 2008, fee 5.3
Application for warrant of arrest under FLA 1996, s 47(8) or s 63J	Application is made, without notice to the respondent, in Form FL408, to 'the relevant judicial authority', ie the convenient hearing centre in whichever tier of court the injunctive order was granted	FLA 1996, ss 47(8), 63(1) and 63J
	The application must be substantiated on oath and the court must have reasonable grounds for believing that the respondent has failed to comply with an order, or part of an order to which no power of arrest had been attached	FLA 1996, s 47(9), s 63J

4.86 *Personal Protection*

	Breach of a non-molestation order is a criminal offence. However, the respondent cannot be both punished for a criminal offence and a contempt of court for the same breach. An application for a warrant of arrest to a civil court should confirm that there is no conviction	FLA 1996, s 42A(3), (4)
	The warrant is executed in the High Court by the Tipstaff, in the County Court by the bailiffs (or, in each case, by the police on request), and in the magistrates' court by the police	Form FL408
	In the magistrates' court the justices' clerk is responsible for delivering the warrant to the police	
Application for warrant of arrest under PHA 1997, s 3(3)	Application must be made in accordance with CPR Pt 23 and may be made without notice	PHA 1997, s 3(4); CPR 65.29
	The application must be supported by affidavit evidence setting out the grounds for the application and state whether the claimant has informed the police and whether criminal proceedings are being pursued	PHA 1997, s 3(5); CPR 65.29
Production in court following arrest under FLA 1996, s 47 or s 63I	A person arrested under a power of arrest must be brought before the relevant judicial authority within 24 hours not including Sunday, Christmas Day or Good Friday	FLA 1996, s 47(7), s 63I
	Neither FLA 1996 nor the rules prescribe how soon a person arrested under a warrant of arrest must be brought before the court. Nevertheless it must be as soon as practicable	FLA 1996, s 47(8)–(10), s 63J

Procedural Guides 4.86

Procedures open to court under FLA 1996, ss 47, 48 when arrested person produced in court and under ss 63I–63M	The court may hear the facts upon which the arrest was based, and decide penalty or adjourn, in which case the respondent must be given not less than 2 days' notice of the adjourned hearing, or	FLA 1996, s 47(7)(*b*), (10); FPR 10.11(3)
	remand in custody for a period not exceeding 8 days, or	FLA 1996, ss 47(11), 63K, Sch 5 para 2(5)
	remand on bail on conditions and/or recognisances	FLA 1996, s 47(11), (12), Sch 5 para 2(5)
	where the court has reason to suspect mental illness or severe mental impairment, the court may remand, to enable a medical examination and report, for not more than 3 weeks if in custody, or 4 weeks if on bail	FLA 1996, s 48, s 63L
Powers of court under PHA 1997, s 3(5) when arrested person produced in court	The court may hear the facts upon which the arrest was based, and decide penalty, or adjourn for not more than 28 days, in which case the defendant must be given not less than 2 days' notice of the adjourned hearing	CPR 65.30
Hearing without notice to the respondent	In exceptional circumstances, the court may, without notice having been given to the respondent, deal with an application begun by notice to show good reason, by dispensing with service of the summons or notice	CPR 39.3, 81.28 (civil); FPR 37.27 (family)
	It is not appropriate for a court to proceed without notice where arrest under a power or warrant can be achieved under FLA 1996, s 47, or under PHA 1997, s 3(5). However, where a power or warrant of arrest is not available, proceeding without notice may exceptionally be appropriate. When the court takes this exceptional step and imposes imprisonment, the court should fix a date and time for the contemnor to be brought before the court	CPR 81.28 (civil); FPR 37.27 (family)

4.86 *Personal Protection*

Service of application to commit	Personal service of the application is required	FPR 37.27
	In both family and civil proceedings a period of 14 clear days after service is required unless the court directs otherwise by using its powers to abridge time for service	CPR PD 81, para 15.2 (civil); FPR PD 37A, para 12.1 (family)
	In exceptional cases, the court can dispense with service	see Hearing without notice to the respondent (above)
Service of notice of adjourned hearing	Where a hearing is adjourned, personal service of notice of the adjourned hearing is required, unless the respondent was present in court and was told when and where the adjourned hearing would resume and/or was remanded under FLA 1996, s 47(7),(10), Sch 5 or MCA 1980, ss 128, 129	*Chiltern DC v Keane*[c]
Case management	The court can make directions at any time as to service of evidence and conduct of the proceedings, or strike out an inappropriate application	CPR PD 81, paras 15 and 16 (civil); FPR PD 37A, para 12.3 (family)
The hearing	District judges as well as High Court and circuit judges have power to hear committal proceedings under FLA 1996, Pts 4 and 4A	FLA 1996, ss 58, 63(1), 63O, 63S
	However district judges do not have power to hear committal proceedings under PHA 1997	PHA 1997, s 3(3), (4) only gives power to issue a warrant; CPR PD Committal, para 11
	Normally held in open court	CPR 39.2, 81.28 (civil); President's Guidance of 3 May 2013 (family)
	If it is just to do so, the court can proceed if the respondent, having been duly served, fails to attend	*Begum v Anam*[d]; CPR 39.3

	Committal proceedings, although technically civil proceedings, are treated as criminal proceedings for the purposes of ECHR, Art 6. Consequently, persons in danger of losing their liberty are, subject to means, eligible for legal aid. (Contempt in the face of the court is separately dealt with in LASPOA 2012, s 14(g))	LASPOA 2012, Schs 1 and 3; *Chelmsford County Court v Ramet*[c]
	Procedure is akin to criminal trial. The criminal standard of proof ('beyond reasonable doubt') applies	*Dean v Dean*[f]
	An application notice can be amended with the permission of the court but not otherwise	CPR PD 81, paras 12(2), 13.2(2) (civil); FPR 37.27 (family)
	An alleged contemnor cannot be directed or compelled to give information	CPR 81.28 (civil); FPR 37.27(3) (family)
	A deliberate act or failure to act (actus reus) with knowledge of the terms of the order (mens rea) must be proved	*DG of Fair Trading v Smiths Concrete*[g]
Powers of court	The disposal must be proportionate to the seriousness of the contempt, reflect the court's disapproval and be designed to secure compliance in future. The principles of sentencing in the CJA 2003 apply. The judge cannot sentence again for matters already dealt with by the criminal court. The court should briefly explain its reasons for the choice of disposal	*Murray v Robinson*[h] *Hale v Tanner*[i]; *Lomas v Parle*[j]; *Slade v Slade*[k]
	Committal to prison is appropriate only where no reasonable alternative exists	*Hale v Tanner*[l]
	Imprisonment is restricted to total of 2 years in the High Court or a county court, 2 months in a magistrates' court, and must be for a fixed term	CCA 1981, s 14; MCA 1980, s 63(3)
	Sentence can be suspended or adjourned on terms	CPR 81.29 (civil); FPR 37.28 (family)

4.86 *Personal Protection*

	Any time spent on remand in custody must be taken into account in the sentence	*Kerai v Patel*[m]
	Person under the age of 21 can be detained under Powers of Criminal Courts (Sentencing) Act 2000, s 96	*R v Selby Justices ex parte Frame*[n]
	Person under the age of 18 cannot be committed to any form of detention for contempt of court (but could be prosecuted for breach of a non-molestation order)	*R v Selby Justices*[o]; FLA 1996, s 42A
	MHA powers are available	CCA 1981, s 14; MHA 1983, ss 35, 37, 38
	Fine can be imposed	*Hale v Tanner*[p]
	A fresh injunction can be granted	*Coats v Chadwick*[q]
	A power of arrest can be attached, if available, to the injunctive order	*Ansah v Ansah*[r]; FLA 1996, s 47
	Sequestration is available only in the High Court	CPR 81.19–81.27 (civil); FPR 37.25 (family)
Form of order	The order must specify 'exact details' of each contempt found proved and specify the disposal ordered	*Nguyen v Phung*[s]; *Re C (A Minor) (Contempt)*[t]
	Where sentence is suspended or adjourned, the period of suspension or adjournment and the precise terms for activation must be specified	*Pidduck v Molloy*[u]; CPR 81.29 (civil); FPR 37.28 (family)
	In the High Court, the order is issued in Form A85 and warrant in Form PF303. In the County Court, Form N79 and warrant in Form N80. In a magistrates' court, Form FL419 and warrant in Form FL420	
Service of order	Where immediate imprisonment or detention is imposed, the court serves the order	CPR 81.30 (civil); FPR 37.29 (family); *Clarke v Clarke*[v]
	Where sentence is suspended, the applicant must serve the order, unless the court directs otherwise	CPR 81.29(2) (civil); FPR 37.28 (family)

Review by Official Solicitor	The court sends a copy of every committal order and relevant details to the Official Solicitor, who reviews the case and may apply or appeal of his own motion or at the contemnor's request	*Lord Chancellor's Direction of 29 May 1963; Secretary's Circular of 28 September 1981*
Discharge of contemnor	A contemnor is entitled to apply to purge his contempt and be discharged from prison	CPR 81.31 (civil); FPR 37.30 (family)
	The application should be made in accordance with CPR Pt 23 or FPR Pt 18 but in practice a letter from the contemnor usually suffices	*CJ v Flintshire Borough Council*[w]
	If the committal was made in civil proceedings, the application notice must be served as soon as practicable after it is filed and at least 3 days before the hearing. If made in family proceedings, the application must be served at least 7 days before the hearing	CPR 23.7(1) (civil); FPR 18.8 (family)
	The contemnor should be in court	*PD of 25 July 1983*
	On an application to purge, the court can say 'yes', 'no' or 'not yet'	*Harris v Harris*[x]

[a] [1986] 2 FLR 271.
[b] [1988] 1 FLR 349 at 354D-355B.
[c] [1985] 1 WLR 619 at 622H-623C.
[d] [2004] EWCA Civ 578.
[e] [2014] EWHC 56.
[f] [1987] 1 FLR 517.
[g] [1992] QB 213.
[h] [2006] 1 FLR 365.
[i] [2000] 2 FLR 879.
[j] [2003] EWCA Civ 1804.
[k] [2009] EWCA Civ 748.
[l] [2000] 2 FLR 879.
[m] [2008] EWCA (Civ) 600.
[n] [1991] 2 WLR 965.
[o] [1991] 2 WLR 965.
[p] [2000] 2 FLR 879.
[q] [1894] 1 Ch 347.
[r] (1976) FLR Rep 9.
[s] [1984] FLR 773 at 778C.
[t] [1986] 1 FLR 578 at 585A.
[u] [1992] 2 FLR 202.
[v] [1990] 2 FLR 115.
[w] [2010] 2 FLR 1224.
[x] [2001] EWCA Civ 1645, [2002] 1 FLR 248.

4.87 *Personal Protection*

Part C   CHECKLISTS

Checklist for first instructions for applications under Pt IV of the Family Law Act 1996

4.87 A General:
(1) full name and date of birth of client;
(2) full name and date of birth/age of respondent;
(3) names and dates of birth of any relevant children and relationship to each party;
(4) client's permanent address;
(5) client's temporary address;
(6) should an application be made not to disclose present address?
(7) client's contact telephone numbers;
(8) are the parties associated persons?
  – have they cohabited? and/or
  – do they have a child? and/or
  – do they or have they had an intimate personal relationship with each other of significant duration?
  – do they fall within any of the other categories within s 62 of the FLA 1996? (See **4.1** above);
(9) are there any 'relevant' children within s 62(2) of the FLA 1996?
(10) period of cohabitation;
(11) duration of relationship;
(12) parties' financial position.

B Non-molestation order:
(1) history of behaviour complained of;
(2) recent incidents;
(3) final incident;
(4) effect of behaviour on applicant;
(5) effect of behaviour on any relevant children;
(6) behaviour directed at any relevant children;
(7) any witnesses?
(8) client's own behaviour;
(9) police intervention?
(10) has either party any criminal convictions?
(11) hospital or medical treatment required?
(12) obtain consent for release of medical records/to obtain medical report;
(13) are social services involved? And if so details of office and officer concerned;
(14) any previous injunctions?
(15) with whom are the children currently living?
(16) are any urgent steps necessary under the CA 1989?
(17) description/photograph of respondent, and where most likely to be found, for process server;
(18) advise that breach of non-molestation order without reasonable excuse can be an offence and lead to criminal liability.

C Occupation order:

(1) address of property;
(2) property is/was intended to be shared home?
(3) if client has left does he/she wish to return?
(4) if so, as a temporary measure/long term?
(5) is property rented/owner-occupied?
(6) name and address of landlord/mortgagee;
(7) in whose name is tenancy/title?
(8) if rented, should an application be made to restrain service of notice to quit?
(9) make application for transfer of tenancy?
(10) if property is owner-occupied or other property in issue, see checklists at **1.149** and **1.150**.

Checklist of steps for application under Pt IV of the Family Law Act 1996

4.88 The following steps for applications are as follows:

(1) public funding;
(2) warning letter, if appropriate;
(3) application for non-molestation and/or occupation order; prepare schedule of specific behaviour to be prohibited by non-molestation order;
(4) with/without a power of arrest in the case of an occupation order?
(5) Form FL401 and sworn statement in support;
(6) application without notice to respondent, if appropriate;
(7) contact court if urgent hearing without notice required;
(8) arrange to meet client at court;
(9) application for transfer of tenancy?
(10) application for injunction to restrain service of notice to quit?
(11) contact process server;
(12) service on landlord/mortgagee of application for occupation order (including transfer of tenancy) by first-class post;
(13) arrange personal service on respondent of application/order;
(14) file statement of service in Form FL415;
(15) police provided with any power of arrest attached to an occupation order (after respondent served);
(16) client notified about return date.

4.89 Personal Protection

Part D PRECEDENTS

4.89

Application in Form FL401 for non-molestation or occupation order under Family Law Act 1996, s 36

Application for:	To be completed by the court
a non-molestation order	Date issued
an occupation order	
Family Law Act 1996 (Part IV)	Case number
The court	

Please read the accompanying notes as you complete this form.

1 About you (the applicant)

State your title (Mr, Mrs etc), full name, address, telephone number and date of birth (if under 18):

Ms MARY HAWTHORN
19 POPLAR COURT
OAKWOOD
ELMSHIRE   01213 641633

State your solicitor's name, address, reference, telephone, FAX and DX numbers:

PLANE & PARTNERS
LAW CHAMBERS
HIGH STREET
OAKWOOD
DX 12345 OAKWOOD
Tel: 01213 613000   Ref: J Shaw

2 About the respondent

State the respondent's name, address and date of birth (if known):

PETER ROWAN
c/o MAPLE ENTERPRISES
OAKWOOD INDUSTRIAL ESTATE
OAKWOOD
ELMSHIRE

3 The Order(s) for which you are applying

This application is for:

☑ a non-molestation order

☑ an occupation order

☐ Tick this box if you wish the court to hear your application without notice being given to the respondent. The reasons relied on for an application being heard without notice must be stated in the statement in support.

4 Your relationship to the respondent (the person to be served with this application)

Your relationship to the respondent is:
(Please tick only one of the following)

1 ☐ Married

2 ☐ Civil Partners

3 ☐ Were married

4 ☐ Former civil partners

5 ☐ Cohabiting

6 ☑ Were cohabiting

7 ☐ Both of you live or have lived in the same household

8 ☐ Relative
State how related:

9 ☐ Agreed to marry.
Give the date the agreement was made.
If the agreement has ended, state when.

10 ☐ Agreed to form a civil partnership.
Give the date the agreement was made.
If the agreement has ended, state when.

11 ☐ Both of you are parents of, or have parental responsibility for, a child

12 ☐ One of you is a parent of a child and the other has parental responsibility for that child

4.89 *Personal Protection*

13 ☐ One of you is the natural parent or grandparent of a child adopted, placed or freed for adoption, and the other is:

    (i) the adoptive parent

  or (ii) a person who has applied for an adoption order for the child

  or (iii) a person with whom the child has been placed for adoption

  or (iv) the child who has been adopted, placed or freed for adoption.

State whether (i), (ii), (iii) or (iv):

14 ☐ Both of you are the parties to the same family proceedings (see also Section 11 below).

5 Application for a non-molestation order

If you wish to apply for a non-molestation order, state briefly in this section the order you want.

Give full details in support of your application in your supporting evidence.

I want the respondent to stop making threats and being violent. I want him to stop ringing my mobile and sending me text messages.

6 Application for an occupation order

If you do not wish to apply for an occupation order, please go to section 9 of this form.

(A) State the address of the dwelling-house to which your application relates:

19 Poplar Court
Oakwood
Elmshire

(B) State whether it is occupied by you or the respondent now or in the past, or whether it was intended to be occupied by you or the respondent:

I am living in the flat now.
I asked the respondent to leave.
We lived there together before that.
I have a licence to occupy but the respondent now wants me out.

(C) State whether you are entitled to occupy the dwelling-house: ☐ Yes ☑ No

If yes, explain why:

(D) State whether the respondent is entitled to occupy the dwelling-house: ☑ Yes ☐ No

If yes, explain why:

He owns it.

On the basis of your answers to (C) and (D) above, tick one of the boxes 1 to 6 below to show the category into which you fit

1 ☐ a spouse or civil partner who has home rights in the dwelling-house, or a person who is entitled to occupy it by virtue of a beneficial estate or interest or contract or by virtue of any enactment giving him or her the right to remain in occupation.

If you tick box 1, state whether there is a dispute or pending proceedings between you and the respondent about your right to occupy the dwelling-house.

2 ☐ a former spouse or former civil partner with no existing right to occupy, where the respondent spouse or civil partner is so entitled.

3 ☑ a cohabitant or former cohabitant with no existing right to occupy, where the respondent cohabitant or former cohabitant is so entitled.

4 ☐ a spouse or former spouse who is not entitled to occupy, where the respondent spouse or former spouse is also not entitled.

5 ☐ a civil partner or former civil partner who is not entitled to occupy, where the respondent civil partner or former civil partner is also not entitled.

6 ☐ a cohabitant or former cohabitant who is not entitled to occupy, where the respondent cohabitant or former cohabitant is also not entitled.

4.89 *Personal Protection*

Home Rights

If you do have home rights please:

State whether the title to the land is registered or unregistered (if known):

If registered, state the Land Registry title number (if known):

If you wish to apply for an occupation order, state briefly here the order you want. Give full details in support of your application in your supporting evidence:

I want to be able to stay in the flat and for the respondent to be excluded

7 Application for additional order(s) about the dwelling-house

If you want to apply for any of the orders listed in the notes to this section, state what order you would like the court to make:

I want an order making the respondent pay all the outgoings on the flat. I also want the use of the furniture in the flat.

8 Mortgage and rent

Is the dwelling-house subject to a mortgage?

☑ Yes ☐ No

If yes, please provide the name and address of the mortgagee:

*Elmsfield Building Society
Construction House
Oakwood
Elmshire*

Is the dwelling-house rented?

☐ Yes ☑ No

If yes, please provide the name and address of the landlord:

5

9 At the court

Will you need an interpreter at court?

☐ Yes ☑ No

If yes, specify the language:

If you require an interpreter, you must notify the court immediately so that one can be arranged.

If you have a disability for which you require special assistance or special facilities, please state what your needs are. The court staff will get in touch with you about your requirements.

10 Other information

State the name and date of birth of any child living with or staying with, or likely to live with or stay with, you or the respondent: N/A

State the name of any other person living in the same household as you and the respondent, and say why they live there: N/A

11 Other Proceedings and Orders

If there are any other current family proceedings or orders in force involving you and the respondent, state the type of proceedings or orders, the court and the case number. This includes any application for an occupation order or non-molestation order against you by the respondent. N/A

This application is to be served upon the respondent

Signed: Date:

4.89 *Personal Protection*

Application for non-molestation order or occupation order
Notes for guidance

Section 1

If you do not wish your address to be made known to the respondent, leave the space on the form blank and complete Confidential Address Form C8. The court can give you this form.

If you are under 18, someone over 18 must help you make this application. That person, who might be one of your parents, is called a 'next friend'.

If you are under 16, you need permission to make this application. You must apply to the High Court for permission, using this form. If the High Court gives you permission to make this application, it will then either hear the application itself or transfer it to a county court.

Section 3

An urgent order made by the court before the notice of the application is served on the respondent is called an ex-parte order. In deciding whether to make an ex-parte order the court will consider all the circumstances of the case, including:

- any risk of significant harm to the applicant or a relevant child, attributable to conduct of the respondent, if the order is not made immediately
- whether it is likely that the applicant will be deterred or prevented from pursuing the application if an order is not made immediately
- whether there is reason to believe that the respondent is aware of the proceedings but is deliberately evading service and that the applicant or a relevant child will be seriously prejudiced by the delay involved.

If the court makes an ex-parte order, it must give the respondent an opportunity to make representations about the order as soon as just and convenient at a full hearing.

'Harm' in relation to a person who has reached the age of 18 means ill-treatment or the impairment of health, and in relation to a child means ill-treatment or the impairment of health and development.

'Ill-treatment' includes forms of ill-treatment which are not physical and, in relation to a child, includes sexual abuse. The court will require evidence of any harm which you allege in support of your application.

Section 4

For you to be able to apply for an order you must be related to the respondent in one of the ways listed in this section of the form. If you are not related in one of these ways you should seek legal advice.

Cohabitants are two persons who, although not married to each other, nor civil partners of each other, are living together as husband and wife or civil partners. People who have cohabited, but have then married or formed a civil partnership will not fall within this category but will fall within the category of married people or people who are civil partners of each other.

Those who live or have lived in the same household do not include people who share the same household because one of them is the other's employee, tenant, lodger or boarder.

You will only be able to apply as a relative of the respondent if you are:

(A) the father, mother, stepfather, stepmother, son, daughter, stepson, stepdaughter, grandmother, grandfather, grandson, granddaughter of the respondent or of the respondent's spouse, former spouse, civil partner or former civil partner.

(B) the brother, sister, uncle, aunt, niece, nephew or first cousin (whether of the full blood or of the half blood or by marriage or by civil partnership) of the respondent or of the respondent's spouse, former spouse, civil partner or former civil partner.

This includes, in relation to a person who is living or has lived with another person as husband and wife or as civil partners, any person who would fall within (A) or (B) if the parties were married to, or civil partners of, each other (for example, your cohabitee's father or brother).

Agreements to marry: You will fall within this category only if you make this application within three years of the termination of the agreement. The court will require the following evidence of the agreement:

    evidence in writing

or the gift of an engagement ring in contemplation of marriage

or evidence that a ceremony has been entered into in the presence of one or more other persons assembled for the purpose of witnessing it.

Agreements to form a civil partnership: You will fall within this category only if you make this application within three years of the termination of the agreement. The court will require the following evidence of the agreement:

    evidence in writing

or a gift from one party to the agreement to the other as a token of the agreement

or evidence that a ceremony has been entered into in the presence of one or more other persons assembled for the purpose of witnessing it.

Section 4 continued

Parents and parental responsibility:
You will fall within this category if

- both you and the respondent are either the parents of the child or have parental responsibility for that child
- **or** if one of you is the parent and the other has parental responsibility.

Under the Children Act 1989, parental responsibility is held automatically by a child's mother, and by the child's father if he and the mother were married to each other at the time of the child's birth or have married subsequently. Where, a child's father and mother are not married to each other at the time of the child's birth, the father may also acquire parental responsibility for that child, if he registers the birth after 1st December 2003, in accordance with section 4(1)(a) of the Children Act 1989. Where neither of these circumstances apply, the father, in accordance with the provisions of the Children Act 1989, can acquire parental responsibility.

From 30 December 2005, where a person who is not the child's parent ("the step-parent") is married to, or a civil partner of, a parent who has parental responsibility for that child, he or she may also acquire parental responsibility for the child in accordance with the provisions of the Children Act 1989.

Section 5

A non-molestation order can forbid the respondent from molesting you or a relevant child. Molestation can include, for example, violence, threats, pestering and other forms of harassment. The court can forbid particular acts of the respondent, molestation in general, or both.

Section 6

If you wish to apply for an occupation order but you are uncertain about your answer to any question in this part of the application form, you should seek legal advice.

(A) A dwelling-house includes any building or part of a building which is occupied as a dwelling; any caravan, houseboat or structure which is occupied as a dwelling; and any yard, garden, garage or outhouse belonging to it and occupied with it.

(C) & (D) The following questions give examples to help you to decide if you or the respondent, or both of you, are entitled to occupy the dwelling-house:

(a) Are you the sole legal owner of the dwelling-house?
(b) Are you and the respondent joint legal owners of the dwelling-house?
(c) Is the respondent the sole legal owner of the dwelling-house?
(d) Do you rent the dwelling-house as a sole tenant?
(e) Do you and the respondent rent the dwelling-house as joint tenants?
(f) Does the respondent rent the dwelling-house as a sole tenant?

If you answer

- **Yes** to (a), (b), (d) or (e) you are likely to be entitled to occupy the dwelling-house
- **Yes** to (c) or (f) you may not be entitled (unless, for example, you are a spouse or civil partner and have home rights – see notes under 'Home Rights' below)
- **Yes** to (b), (c), (e) or (f), the respondent is likely to be entitled to occupy the dwelling-house
- **Yes** to (a) or (d) the respondent may not be entitled (unless, for example, he or she is a spouse or civil partner and has home rights).

Box 1 For example, if you are sole owner, joint owner or if you rent the property. If you are not a spouse, former spouse, civil partner, former civil partner, cohabitant or former cohabitant of the respondent, you will only be able to apply for an occupation order if you fall within this category.

If you answer yes to this question, it will not be possible for a magistrates' court to deal with the application, unless the court decides that it is unnecessary for it to decide this question in order to deal with the application or make the order. If the court decides that it cannot deal with the application, it will transfer the application to a county court.

Box 2 For example, if the respondent is or was married to you, or if you and the respondent are or were civil partners, and he or she is sole owner or rents the property.

Box 3 For example, if the respondent is or was cohabiting with you and is sole owner or rents the property.

Home Rights

Where one spouse or civil partner "(A)" is entitled to occupy the dwelling-house by virtue of a beneficial estate or interest or contract or by virtue of any enactment giving him or her the right to remain in occupation, and the other spouse or civil partner "(B)" is not so entitled, then B (who is not entitled) has home rights.

The rights are

(a) if **B** is in occupation, not to be evicted or excluded from the dwelling-house except with the leave of the court; and
(b) if **B** is not in occupation, the right, with the leave of the court, to enter into and occupy the dwelling-house.

Note: Home Rights do not exist if the dwelling-house has never been, and was never intended to be, the matrimonial or civil partnership home of the two spouses or civil partners. If the marriage or civil partnership has come to an end, home rights will also have ceased, unless a court order has been made during the marriage or civil partnership for the rights to continue after the end of that relationship.

4.89 Personal Protection

Section 6 (continued)

Occupation Orders
The possible orders are:

If you have ticked box 1 above, an order under section 33 of the Act may:

- enforce the applicant's entitlement to remain in occupation as against the respondent
- require the respondent to permit the applicant to enter and remain in the dwelling-house or part of it
- regulate the occupation of the dwelling-house by either or both parties
- if the respondent is also entitled to occupy, the order may prohibit, suspend or restrict the exercise by him, of that right
- restrict or terminate any home rights of the respondent
- require the respondent to leave the dwelling-house or part of it
- exclude the respondent from a defined area around the dwelling-house
- declare that the applicant is entitled to occupy the dwelling-house or has home rights in it
- provide that the home rights of the applicant are not brought to an end by the death of the other spouse or civil partner or termination of the marriage or civil partnership.

If you have ticked box 2 or box 3 above, an order under section 35 or 36 of the Act may:

- give the applicant the right not to be evicted or excluded from the dwelling-house or any part of it by the respondent for a specified period
- prohibit the respondent from evicting or excluding the applicant during that period
- give the applicant the right to enter and occupy the dwelling-house for a specified period
- require the respondent to permit the exercise of that right
- regulate the occupation of the dwelling-house by either or both of the parties
- prohibit, suspend or restrict the exercise by the respondent of his right to occupy
- require the respondent to leave the dwelling-house or part of it
- exclude the respondent from a defined area around the dwelling-house.

If you have ticked box 4 or box 5 above, an order under section 37 or 38 of the Act may:

- require the respondent to permit the applicant to enter and remain in the dwelling-house or part of it
- regulate the occupation of the dwelling-house by either or both of the parties
- require the respondent to leave the dwelling-house or part of it
- exclude the respondent from a defined area around the dwelling-house.

You should provide any evidence which you have on the following matters in your evidence in support of this application. If necessary, further statements may be submitted after the application has been issued.

If you have ticked box 1, box 4 or box 5 above, the court will need any available evidence of the following:

- the housing needs and resources of you, the respondent and any relevant child
- the financial needs of you and the respondent
- the likely effect of any order, or any decision not to make an order, on the health, safety and well-being of you, the respondent and any relevant child
- the conduct of you and the respondent in relation to each other and otherwise.

If you have ticked box 2 above, the court will need any available evidence of:

- the housing needs and resources of you, the respondent and any relevant child
- the financial resources of you and the respondent
- the likely effect of any order, or of any decision not to make an order on the health, safety and well-being of you, the respondent and any relevant child
- the conduct of you and the respondent in relation to each other and otherwise
- the length of time that has elapsed since you and the respondent ceased to live together
- where you and the respondent were married, the length of time that has elapsed since the marriage was dissolved or annulled
- where you and the respondent were civil partners, the length of time that has elapsed since the dissolution or annulment of the civil partnership

Section 6 (continued)

- the existence of any pending proceedings between you and the respondent:
  - under section 23A of the Matrimonial Causes Act 1973 (property adjustment orders in connection with divorce proceedings etc.)
  - or under Part 2 of Schedule 5 to the Civil Partnership Act 2004 (property adjustment on or after dissolution, nullity or separation)
  - or under Schedule 1 para 1(2)(d) or (e) of the Children Act 1989 (orders for financial relief against parents)
  - or relating to the legal or beneficial ownership of the dwelling-house.

If you have ticked box 3 above, the court will need any available evidence of:

- the housing needs and resources of you, the respondent and any relevant child
- the financial resources of you and the respondent
- the likely effect of any order, or of any decision not to make an order, on the health, safety and well-being of you, the respondent and any relevant child
- the conduct of you and the respondent in relation to each other and otherwise
- the nature of your and the respondent's relationship
- the length of time during which you have lived together as husband and wife or civil partners
- whether you and the respondent have had any children, or have both had parental responsibility for any children
- the length of time that has elapsed since you and the respondent ceased to live together
- the existence of any pending proceedings between you and the respondent under Schedule 1 para 1(2)(d) or (e) of the Children Act 1989 or relating to the legal or beneficial ownership of the dwelling-house.

Section 7

Under section 40 of the Act the court may make the following additional orders when making an occupation order:

- impose on either party obligations as to the repair and maintenance of the dwelling-house
- impose on either party obligations as to the payment of rent, mortgage or other outgoings affecting it
- order a party occupying the dwelling-house to make periodical payments to the other party in respect of the accommodation, if the other party would (but for the order) be entitled to occupy it
- grant either party possession or use of furniture or other contents
- order either party to take reasonable care of any furniture or other contents
- order either party to take reasonable steps to keep the dwelling-house and any furniture or other contents secure.

Section 8

If the dwelling-house is rented or subject to a mortgage, the landlord or mortgagee must be served with notice of the proceedings in Form FL416. He or she will then be able to make representations to the court regarding the rent or mortgage.

Section 10

A person living in the same household may, for example, be a member of the family or a tenant or employee of you or the respondent.

4.90

Witness statement in support of application without notice for non-molestation and occupation orders under s 33 of the Family Law Act 1996

1st statement
made by applicant
on [date]

IN THE FAMILY COURT AT [ ]   CASE NUMBER

BETWEEN:

                            A   Applicant

And

                            B   Respondent

STATEMENT OF APPLICANT IN SUPPORT OF APPLICATION FOR NON-MOLESTATION AND OCCUPATION ORDERS

(1) I, [name], of [address] make this affidavit in support of my applications for a non-molestation order against the respondent and an order that he be restrained from coming within 50 metres of [address]. This is a property that I rent from the local council, and which used to be the home that I shared with the respondent until he left in [date].

(2) My relationship with the respondent began in [date] and he moved in with me in [date]. We have a child, [name], who was born on [date] and who is now [age] years old. [name] remained living with me after the respondent moved out.

(3) Throughout our relationship the respondent was violent towards me and it was his violence that brought our relationship to an end. He would think nothing of pushing and shoving me around the bedroom, or pulling me across the room by my hair when he came home from the pub the worse for drink. He would also go into very bad moods and his temper then was uncontrollable. On one occasion [date] he came home from work having had a disagreement with his foreman. The first thing he did when he came in was to take it out on me, shouting abuse at me, calling me fat and lazy, and asking me why I was serving up a meal that he said was only fit for a dog to eat. When I protested at this he responded by throwing his plate of food across the room at me. Fortunately I ducked out of the way and the plate and its contents landed in a great mess on the kitchen worktop. However the respondent then came charging across the kitchen towards me and grabbed me by the throat. I thought he was going to strangle me and I am sure he would have done had a neighbour not called round to see what was going on, having heard all the shouting and commotion. Incidents like this would take place at least once every couple of months, and eventually I became so tired of it that in [date] I asked the respondent to leave, and to my surprise he did.

(4) After the respondent moved out I would see him every week when he came to the house to see [name] and we remained on reasonable terms. However, earlier this year I started a relationship with another man and although we do not have any plans to live together the respondent turned very nasty about it. He started off by making snide comments and then he started threatening that he would take [child] away from me because he said I was an unfit mother. On another occasion he came round to see [child] and wanted to take him out for the afternoon. It was clear to me that the respondent had been drinking and so I refused, whereupon the respondent slapped me round the face, called me a slag, and would only leave when I enlisted the help of a friend to physically remove him from the house.

(5) On [date] things came to a head. He came to the house and walked in without knocking. He walked straight upstairs and into my bedroom and without saying a word grabbed the first thing that was to hand, a table lamp. He smashed this against the wall. I had followed him upstairs and ordered him out of the house. He refused to leave and so I went downstairs to telephone the police. He followed me, grabbed the telephone from me and then grabbed me by the throat with great force. He then pushed me onto the sofa and held me down, shouting abuse at me. Eventually he calmed down and he left but not before saying that he would kill me if he saw my boyfriend anywhere near [child]. I am very concerned that he will carry out this threat. Certainly he has shown himself capable of inflicting extreme violence on me in the past and I am very much in fear of him and what he may do next time he comes to the house. He has sent me a large number of threatening text messages and has called me on my mobile 'phone telling me that he is going to get me.

(6) In view of the history of violence towards me and the respondent's unpredictability I would like the protection of an order made without giving notice to the respondent. I am sure that if the respondent were to have notice of my application he would fly into a rage and come round straight away and harm me[1].

(7) In the circumstances I seek an order that the respondent be restrained from using or threatening violence against me, and from contacting me by telephone or by sending text messages. I also seek an order that the respondent having left the home we used to share at [address], he be forbidden to return to it or go within 50 metres of it.

I believe that the facts stated in this witness statement are true.

[1] See **4.14**.

4.91

Witness statement in support of application for service by an alternative method

1st statement
Made by [name]
On behalf of the applicant
On [date]

IN THE FAMILY COURT AT [ ]   CASE NUMBER

BETWEEN:

A   Applicant

And

B   Respondent

STATEMENT IN SUPPORT OF APPLICATION for SERVICE BY AN ALTERNATIVE METHOD

4.91 Personal Protection

(1) I, [name], of [address], say as follows:

(2) I have the conduct of this matter on behalf of the applicant and I am authorised by her to make this statement in support of an application for an order for service of the application herein on the respondent by an alternative method.

(3) In these proceedings the applicant seeks relief under Pt IV of the Family Law Act 1996, in particular a non-molestation order against the respondent. The grounds of her application are set out in her statement dated [. . .] to which I shall refer.

(4) It will be apparent from the applicant's statement that although the respondent has left the property in which they were living together, he retains a key to the property and has on a number of occasions returned there unannounced. If the applicant has been out he has ransacked the place, and if she has been in he has subjected her to verbal and sometimes physical abuse.

(5) The problem in relation to service of the application and supporting documents is that the applicant has no idea where the respondent is living. She believes that he is staying with friends, but is not certain which friends. She is aware however that the respondent is still working at [address], and I duly made arrangements for a process server to attend at those premises in order to serve the respondent. However, the respondent had obviously been tipped off that a process server was looking for him, and several attempts to effect personal service of the respondent at his work address have been blocked by the receptionist who refuses to co-operate with the process server. The process server did confirm to me that on each of his visits to the [address] he saw that the respondent's motor vehicle as described to him by the applicant was in the car park leading him to believe that the respondent was there and was evading service.

(6) In the circumstances, I believe that the respondent would receive the documents to be served on him if they were posted to him by ordinary first-class mail at his work address, alternatively by email to him at his e mail address as follows [ ], or by text message to his mobile number as follows [ ] and I ask for an order that this method of service be substituted for personal service.

I believe that the facts stated in this witness statement are true.

4.92

Letter to mortgagee/landlord of dwelling-house the subject of an application for an occupation order under s 33 or s 36 of the Family Law Act 1996

FIRST-CLASS POST

Dear Sir/Madam,

Address of Property

Roll Number (in the case of mortgaged property)

Names of Mortgagors/Tenants

We act for   who is (one of) the mortgagor(s)/tenant(s) of the above-mentioned property.

Pursuant to Rule 10.3(3) of the Family Procedure Rules 2010, we enclose a copy of our client's application for an occupation order in respect of the property.

We also enclose notice in the prescribed Form FL416 informing you of your right to make representations in writing, or at any hearing.

Please acknowledge receipt of this letter within 7 days.

Yours faithfully,

Chapter 5
CHILDREN

Part A LAW AND PRACTICE

Section 1 Registration of births; parental responsibility

Introduction

5.1 It has been some time since marriage was universally accepted as the only appropriate relationship within which to bring up children. Over 48 per cent of all children in the UK are now born outside marriage[1], and some 2.2 million children now live with cohabiting couples, including an increasing number of children living with same sex cohabitants[2].

Over the years, legislation has slowly removed the distinction between children born within marriage and those born outside it. First, references to legitimate and illegitimate children were largely removed from family law legislation and replaced with a description of their parents as either married to one another or not. In 2003 changes were made to the CA 1989 so that fathers named on the birth certificate would automatically acquire parental responsibility even if not married to the mother.

More recently, the HFEA 2008 updated the definitions of parenthood for parents undergoing assisted reproduction treatment and provided a mechanism under which a female partner could, in certain circumstances, acquire parental responsibility on registration in the same way as her male counterpart.

A further important common law development is Sir Andrew McFarlane P's decision in 2019 in *R (TT) v Registrar General for England and Wales*[3]. He defines the term 'mother' in this way at para 279:

> 'There is a material difference between a person's gender and their status as a parent. Being a "mother", while, hitherto, always associated with being female, was the status afforded to a person who underwent the physical and biological process of carrying a pregnancy and giving birth. It was now medically and legally possible for an individual, whose gender was recognised in law as male, to become pregnant and give birth to their child. While that person's gender was "male", their parental status, which derived from their biological role in giving birth, was that of "mother".'

5.1 Children

Families may now be constituted in any number of ways, and individuals may choose their gender, marry or form civil partnerships as they feel best suits them.

In light if these developments and for simplicity, references in this section are generally to the 'mother' and the 'other parent' except in situations where the law could only possibly apply to a male second parent.

[1] Births in England and Wales 2018, Office for National Statistics.
[2] Families and Households in the UK 2016, Office for National Statistics.
[3] *R (on the application of TT) v Registrar General for England and Wales (AIRE Centre intervening)* [2019] All ER (D) 68 (Sep). It is understood this case may be appealed.

Registration of births

5.2 Every birth within England and Wales must be registered with the registrar of births and deaths for the sub-district in which the child was born[1].

A 'qualified informant' must provide the required information within 42 days of the date of birth. In the case of parents who are not married to one another at the time of the birth, the mother has a duty to register the birth, although the other parent[2] will be a 'qualified informant' and may register it.

If both parents sign the birth register together they will both be recorded as parents on the child's birth certificate. If the other parent does not attend then only the mother will be recorded as a parent unless she provides one of the following:

- a statutory declaration from the other parent confirming parentage;
- a parental responsibility order or agreement in relation to the child and makes a statutory declaration that any agreement complies with s 4 or s 4ZA of the CA 1989, and that there is no order bringing the order or agreement to an end; or
- an order made under Sch 1 to the CA 1989 for financial provision to be made by the other parent, and makes a statutory declaration that the order has not been discharged.

If the parent of a child who is not married[3] to the mother of the child wishes to be named as the parent on the child's birth certificate, in the absence of a joint request for his or her name to be registered, that parent may apply for registration of their details in any one of the following circumstances:

- they produce statutory declarations from themselves and from the mother that they are the parent of the child;
- they produce a parental responsibility order or agreement in relation to the child and make a statutory declaration that the agreement complies with the requirements of s 4 or s 4ZA of the CA 1989 and that there is no order bringing the order or agreement to an end;
- they produce an order requiring them to make financial provision for the child under Sch 1 to the CA 1989 and make a statutory declaration that the order has not been discharged.

In practice, since the introduction of the Child Support Agency[4], there will be relatively few cases in which either parent will be able to produce a financial provision order within the first 42 days of a child's life. It is also unlikely that a court would be in a position to make a parental responsibility order on a contested application within 6 weeks of the birth of the child, and so the opportunity for one or other parent to register the parent's details where there is no agreement between them will be limited.

If the parents of a child born outside marriage[5] subsequently marry[6] one another the child becomes legitimated and the birth should be re-registered[7].

[1] BDRA 1953, s 1.
[2] Usually the father, but the same rules apply to a second female parent pursuant to an agreement under HFEA 2008, s 43.
[3] Or in a civil partnership.
[4] And its successors, the Child Maintenance and Enforcement Commission (CMEC) and most recently the Child Maintenance Service (CMS).
[5] Or civil partnership.
[6] Or enter into.
[7] BDRA 1953, s 14(1) (one of the few remaining references to 'legitimacy' in the legislation).

Determination of parentage

5.3 Where a child is born to a woman who is married, there is a presumption that her husband is the father of the child, provided that the parties were married at the estimated date of conception[1]. There is no such presumption of paternity even where the unmarried parents of a child were living together in a stable relationship at the time of the birth.

However, if a man's name is recorded in the Register of Births as the father of a child this is *prima facie* evidence of paternity and therefore the burden of proof will be on the father if he subsequently disputes it.

CSA 1991, s 26(2), sets out circumstances in which the Child Maintenance Service may assume that a man is the father of a child in the face of his denial of paternity, in which situations the burden of proof falls on him to prove he is not the father. These circumstances include a case in which the man is named as the father on the child's birth certificate, and where he refuses to submit to scientific testing to establish paternity.

As well as being an issue for parents who may wish to avoid or confirm paternity (whether for reasons connected with parental responsibility, contact and living arrangements, or financial support), parentage may also be a matter that a child may wish to bring before the court.

[1] Although the relevance of such a presumption in the age of DNA testing has been questioned, see for example the comments of Thorpe LJ in *Re H and A (Paternity: Blood Tests)* [2002] 1 FLR 1145.

Declaration of parentage

5.4 In any case in which parentage is disputed a declaration of parentage can be sought from the court under FLA 1986, s 55A.

A parent (or alleged parent), the child or anyone else with sufficient personal interest may apply for a declaration of parentage (including the Secretary

5.4 Children

of State in circumstances where an alleged parent objects to a child maintenance calculation on the basis that they are not a parent of the child). The alleged parents and the person whose parentage is in issue must be respondents to the application. There is provision for the Attorney General to intervene[1] to minimise the incidence of fraudulent applications proceeding unopposed.

[1] FLA 1986, s 59.

Evidence on an application for declaration of parentage

5.5 CSPSSA 2000 effected an important change to the court's powers under FLRA 1969 to order testing in order to establish paternity. Before CSPSSA 2000 the position was that if the parent of a child aged under 16 years refused to allow the child to be subjected to tests the court could not compel the taking of a sample[1]. The position now is that where the parent refuses to allow testing when directed by the court, the court may consent to a test if it is in the best interests of the child to do so[2].

The approach of the court was considered in *Re T (Paternity: Ordering Blood Tests)*[3]. In that case the child's mother and her husband agreed that as they were unable to conceive together the mother would have a sexual relationship with a family friend with a view to conceiving a child that would be brought up by the mother and her husband. She did not conceive. However, some years later she resumed her sexual relationship with the family friend. She became pregnant and she brought up the child with her husband. The family friend saw the child in the normal course of events, but before long the mother took the view that he was overstepping the mark and brought an end to his visits. He applied for parental responsibility and contact but was unsuccessful. Subsequently, he made it known publicly that he believed himself to be the father of the child and the judge found that there was a significant risk that the child would learn of the situation sooner rather than later. He made a further application to the court 6 years later for a direction for DNA testing to establish paternity[4].

Confirming that the earlier authorities of *S v S; W v Official Solicitor*[5] and *Re H (Paternity: Blood Test)*[6] remained good law, Bodey J held that:

> 'Under domestic law the child's best interests were to be weighed against the competing interests of the adults affected. In most cases it was likely to be in the child's best interests that the truth about paternity was known and under Art 8 ECPHRFF 1950 all parties had the right to respect for private and family life. The child had a right to know his true identity and to have the possibility of contact with each of his natural parents; also a competing right to have the current stability of his family life protected. Similarly the mother and her husband, and the applicant . . . had conflicting rights. When the various Convention rights pulled in different directions, the rights and best interests of the child concerned fell particularly to be considered, and in this case the child's right to know, perhaps with certainty, his true identity, emerged as the weightiest consideration. The interference with other rights which would result from going ahead with the tests was proportionate to the legitimate aim of providing the child with the possibility of certainty as to his real paternity.'[7]

[1] See *Re O (A Minor) (Blood Tests: Constraint)* [2000] 1 FLR 418 in which Wall J, as he then was, disagreed with the approach of Hale J, as she then was, in *Re R (Blood Test; Constraint)* [1998] 1 FLR 745 where she had given temporary care and control of the child to the Official Solicitor to enable him to consent to the taking of samples.

² FLRA 1969, s 21(3).
³ [2001] 2 FLR 1190.
⁴ See *Re F (Children) DNA Evidence* [2008] 1 FLR 348 for guidelines for orders for DNA testing and *AB and CD and C (a child) (No 2)* [2019] EWHC 2244 (Fam) for how the court deals with informing a child about the results of a DNA test.
⁵ [1972] AC 24.
⁶ [1996] 2 FLR 65.
⁷ For the circumstances in which the court may decline to make an order requiring the mother to disclose to a child the identity of his father see *Re K (Specific Issue Order)* [1999] 2 FLR 280; *Re J (Paternity: Welfare of Child)* [2007] 1 FLR 1064; *Re F (Paternity: Jurisdiction)* [2008] 1 FLR 225.

Refusal to submit to testing

5.6 The refusal of a parent to consent to the scientific testing of a child no longer creates evidential difficulties in view of the court's powers under FLRA 1969, s 21 to give consent in appropriate cases. Where a man against whom a declaration of parentage is sought fails to submit to testing directed by the court he cannot be compelled to take part in testing, but the court is entitled to draw an adverse inference¹ from his reluctance to do so.

In *Secretary of State for Work and Pensions v Jones*² an application was made by the Secretary of State for Work and Pensions for a declaration of parentage under FLA 1986, s 55A. An application for a maintenance calculation had been made to the Child Support Agency naming Mr Jones as the child's father. He denied paternity. A direction was made by the family proceedings court that Mr Jones should submit to a DNA test to establish paternity. He refused to do so.

The President of the Family Division at that time held that on the subsequent hearing on the issue of paternity the magistrates had been wrong not to follow the authority of the Court of Appeal in *Re A (A Minor) (Paternity: Refusal of Blood Test)*³ and *Re G (Parentage: Blood Sample)*⁴ and draw the inference from Mr Jones' refusal to be tested that he was the father of the child⁵.

Following a pilot scheme in 2016, CAFCASS may now meet the cost of DNA testing in such applications. This is to help remove any objections from alleged fathers, to a DNA test on the basis of costs and allow for a simplified and streamlined process.

¹ The court may draw such inferences, if any, from that fact as appear proper in the circumstances. FLRA 1969, s 23(1).
² [2004] 1 FLR 282.
³ [1994] 2 FLR 463.
⁴ [1997] 1 FLR 360.
⁵ The interesting question of what inference to draw when a refusal accompanies an assertion of paternity, rather than a denial, was raised but not answered by the current President in *Re Z (Children)* [2014] EWHC 1999 (Fam).

Assisted reproduction

5.7 A woman¹ who has carried a child as a result of the placing in her of an embryo or of sperm and eggs is treated as the child's mother regardless of whether her eggs or donor eggs were used². At common law, the genetic father

5.7 Children

is considered to be the legal father. Where an unmarried couple have undergone in vitro fertilisation using their own sperm they will both be the child's parents (regardless of whether a donor egg was used).

The situation becomes more complicated where donor sperm is used. Since the coming into force of HFEA 2008 on 1 April 2009, the mother's unmarried partner (whether male or female) will be treated with the mother as the child's parent where, at the time the treatment takes place[3]:

- the mother was not married or in a civil partnership (or, if they were, their husband/wife/civil partner did not consent to the treatment);
- both the mother and their partner provided the appropriate notices under s 37 (male) or s 44 (female) of the HFEA 2008;
- the treatment is provided by an appropriately licensed clinic; and
- the partner is still alive.

HFEA 2008 did not apply retrospectively, and earlier treatments (between 1 August 1991 and 31 March 2009) are still determined by HFEA 1990. Under that Act the requirements for unmarried fathers were similar to the 2008 regime, except that there was no equivalent to s 37 requiring formal notice to be given[4]. There was no equivalent provision for a female partner.

The case of *AB v CD and the Z Fertility Clinic*[5] concerned a situation where the course of fertility treatment straddled the cross-over between the 1990 and 2008 regimes. When the new regime came into force the clinic did not ensure that the appropriate consent forms were completed and, in particular, did not ensure that both partners received the necessary counselling required by the terms of its licence. As a result, the mother's female partner was deemed not to be the children's parent. In light of this case and other similar situations, the Human Fertility and Embryology Authority has instructed all clinics to conduct a complete audit of patient records since April 2009 for unmarried couples[6]. The outcome of that audit found that 51 of the 109 clinics had 'anomalies' on their records. At the time of writing, nearly 30 cases had been brought to court in the hope of remedying failures by clinics to observe the formal requirements of HFEA 2008. In each case so far, the court has been able to find (often creative) means of justifying the decision to make a declaration of parentage notwithstanding the strict wording of the statute[7]. Many more cases, however, remain in the pipeline.

A child born by donor insemination before 1 August 1991 will not be regarded as the child of the donor, whether married to the mother or not[8].

[1] This also means an individual who is recognized as male in law. See *R (on the application of TT) v Registrar General for England and Wales (AIRE Centre intervening)* [2019] All ER (D) 68 (Sep) at 165.
[2] HFEA 2008, s 33(1), also HFEA 1990, s 27.
[3] Specifically, at the time the embryo or the sperm and eggs are placed in the mother, or at which she is artificially inseminated.
[4] HFEA 1990, s 28(3).
[5] [2013] 2 FLR 1357.
[6] HFEA (CE(14)01, 2014).
[7] See, in particular, *Re Human Fertilisation and Embryology Act 2008 (Cases A, B, C, D, E, F, G and H)* [2017] 1 FLR 366; *Re the Human Fertilisation and Embryology Act 2008 (Case O)* [2016] EHWC 2273 (Fam) and *In the Matter of the Human Fertilisation and Embryology Act*

2008 (Cases P, Q, R, S, T, U, V, W and X) [2017] EWHC 49 (Fam).
[8] Re M (Child Support Act: Parentage) [1997] 2 FLR 90.

Parental responsibility

5.8 CA 1989, s 3(1) defines parental responsibility as 'all the rights, powers, responsibilities and authority which by law a parent of a child has in relation to the child and his property'.

Until CA 1989 was amended by the ACA 2002[1], if the parents of a child were not married[2] to one another at the time of the birth the mother would automatically have parental responsibility but the father would not.

The effect of this was that an unmarried father without parental responsibility was potentially disadvantaged. They may not have been consulted in adoption proceedings[3] or if the mother wished to change the child's name, nor would they be entitled to receive information from the child's doctor or school, or give consent for medical treatment.

CA 1989, s 4(1)(a)[4] now provides that[5] a parent[6] who registers the child's birth jointly with the child's mother will have parental responsibility. Where circumstances at the time of the birth do not make this possible, the procedure for entering into a parental responsibility agreement is retained, and a parent without parental responsibility may still apply for a parental responsibility order.

It is also possible for a parent's name to be placed on the birth certificate by making an application to re-register the birth[7].

These measures go some way to removing the discrimination between unmarried mothers and the other parent but it should be noted that whereas a mother may lose parental responsibility only if an adoption order is made in respect of the child, the other parent may also lose the parental responsibility if the court orders it under CA 1989, s 4(2A)[8].

[1] Adoption and Children Act 2002, s 111.
[2] Since 2 December 2019 parents who are in a civil partnership or married automatically have parental responsibility. CA 1989, s 4(1).
[3] Re R (Adoption: Father's Involvement) [2001] 1 FLR 302; Re H; Re G (Adoption: Consultation of Unmarried Fathers) [2001] 1 FLR 646.
[4] And, since 1 April 2009, s 4ZA(1)(a) for second female parents.
[5] For children born on or after 1 December 2003.
[6] Either a biological father or, since the enactment of HFEA 2008, either a man or woman who is a legal parent by virtue of being the partner of a woman who has undergone licensed assisted reproduction treatment, see *Assisted Reproduction* at 5.7.
[7] Births and Deaths Registration Act 1953, s 10A.
[8] Section 4ZA(5) in respect of second female parents.

Acquiring parental responsibility

5.9 An unmarried father or second female parent may acquire parental responsibility for their child by any one of the following means:

– jointly registering the child's birth with the child's mother[1];

5.9 Children

- marrying (or entering into a civil partnership with) the child's mother[2];
- entering into a parental responsibility agreement with the child's mother[3];
- obtaining a parental responsibility order[4];
- being appointed as the child's guardian[5];
- being named in a child arrangements order as a person with whom the child shall live[6]; or
- having an adoption order made in their favour.

More than one person may have parental responsibility for the same child.

[1] CA 1989, ss 4(1)(a) and 4ZA(1)(a).
[2] CA 1989, s 2(3) indirectly recognises the effect of the LA 1976, s 2.
[3] CA 1989, ss 4(1)(b) and 4ZA(1)(b).
[4] CA 1989, ss 4(1)(a) and 4ZA(1)(a).
[5] CA 1989, s 5.
[6] CA 1989, ss 8 and 12.

Jointly registering the birth

5.10 CA 1989, ss 4(1)(a) and 4ZA(1)(a) provide that a parent who jointly registers the child's birth with the child's mother or re-registers it will have parental responsibility. The birth certificate will be evidence of this. However, such a parent may lose parental responsibility acquired under s 4(1)(a) or s 4ZA(1)(a) if the court orders it under CA 1989, s 4(2A) or s 4ZA(5). Re-registration of a child born to unmarried parents can be effected at any time subject to the requirements that if the child has reached the age of 16 the child's written consent must be given. Furthermore, an amendment to the birth certificate made automatically following a declaration of parentage will not impart parental responsibility on the other parent.

It follows from this that a birth certificate is not necessarily conclusive evidence of a father or second female parent's parental responsibility since the birth may have been re-registered subsequently, or indeed superseded by an order removing parental responsibility, or an adoption order.

Parental responsibility agreement

5.11 If the parents of a child who are not married to one another at the time of the birth agree, they can enter into a parental responsibility agreement which, if all the formalities are complied with, will mean that they will then both have parental responsibility for the child. There is nothing to prevent unmarried parents from entering into a parental responsibility agreement even where a care order in respect of the child has been granted in favour of a local authority[1].

A parental responsibility agreement is not necessary if both parents jointly register the child's birth[2].

[1] *Re X (Parental Responsibility Agreement: Children in Care)* [2000] 1 FLR 517.
[2] CA 1989, ss 4(1)(a) and 4ZA(1)(a).

Procedure

5.12 The form for a parental responsibility agreement is prescribed by the PRAR 1991[1], as amended, and available as court forms C(PRA1) and C(PRA3). The parents' signatures must be witnessed by a Justice of the Peace or an officer of the court[2] and filed (with sufficient copies for each parent) at the Central Family Court. On receipt, the copy agreements will be sealed and one sent to each parent. There must be a separate agreement for each child. The original agreement remains at the Central Family Court and is a public document. Unless all the formalities are observed, the agreement will not take effect.

In view of the cumbersome procedure, and a tendency not to have recourse to the law before it is absolutely necessary, it is hardly surprising that the number of parental responsibility agreements registered each year accounts for little more than 1 per cent of all live births outside marriage.

[1] SI 1991/1478.
[2] This does not include solicitors.

Duration of agreements

5.13 A parental responsibility agreement will automatically come to an end on the child's 18th birthday[1].

An agreement cannot be revoked unilaterally, and can only be brought to an end before the child's 18th birthday by an order of the court[2].

An application to terminate a parental responsibility agreement may be made by either party to the agreement or any other person with parental responsibility for the child. With the court's leave, the child may apply to terminate the agreement.

[1] CA 1989, s 91(8).
[2] CA 1989, s 4(3).

Parental responsibility order

5.14 If parents of a child who are not married to one another (or in a civil partnership) at the time of the birth, and who have not jointly registered the birth, cannot agree that the father (or second female parent) should have parental responsibility that parent can apply to the court under s 4(1)(c) or s 4ZA(1)(c) of CA 1989 for an order giving them parental responsibility[1]. A parental responsibility order is intended to confer status on an unmarried parent so that they are in no worse position than a married parent would be. The effect of a parental responsibility order is not to give the parent a right to interfere in what the person with day-to-day care of the child is doing[2].

The issue of parental responsibility is quite separate from those of where the child should live and who they should spend time with, and different considerations apply[3].

The effect of a parental responsibility order was summarised by the Court of Appeal in *Re S (Parental Responsibility)*[4]:

'... The granting of a parental responsibility order was the granting of a status ... It was wrong to place undue and false emphasis on the rights and duties and powers comprised in "parental responsibility" and not to concentrate on the fact that what was at issue was the conferring on a committed father of the status of parenthood for which nature had already ordained that he must bear responsibility, and there was all too frequently a failure to appreciate that any abuse of the exercise of parental responsibility which was adverse to the welfare of the child could be controlled by the wide exercise of s 8 orders ...'

[1] If the father or second female parent is not named on the birth certificate then, in the absence of agreement from the mother, they cannot simply circumvent the need for a parental responsibility order by obtaining a declaration of parentage and subsequent amendment of the birth certificate as re-registration under BDRA 1953, s 14A is not one of the specified enactments under CA 1989, s 4(1A) – see *M v F and H (Legal Paternity)* [2014] 1 FLR 352 at para 31.
[2] *Re P (A Minor) (Parental Responsibility Order)* [1994] 1 FLR 578 and *Re A (A Minor) (Parental Responsibility)* [1996] 1 FCR 562.
[3] *Re C and V (Contact and Parental Responsibility)* [1998] 1 FLR 392.
[4] [1995] 2 FLR 648 at 648F.

Procedure

5.15 The application is made in Form C1 (accompanied by a Form FM1) to the Family Court.

The respondent(s) to the application will be the mother and any other person having parental responsibility for the child, or having the day-to-day care of the child. They will need to be served with notice of the application.

The exercise of the court's discretion

5.16 When deciding whether or not to make an order for parental responsibility in favour of a parent, the court will apply the principle that the child's welfare is the paramount consideration[1]. Additionally, CFA 2014 introduced a presumption that involvement of a parent in its life will further the child's welfare[2]. The presumption applies to all cases commenced on or after 22 October 2014, but not those commenced prior to that date[3]. In addition, the court will have regard to the general principle that unless it considers that it would be better for the child that an order be made, no order should be made on any application under the CA 1989[4].

These considerations apart, the CA 1989 does not prescribe any matters to which the court must have specific regard. However, reported cases suggest that the factors that will guide the court include:

– the reasons for the parent's application;
– the degree of commitment shown by the parent to the child;
– the degree of attachment between the parent and the child[5];
– the nature of the relationship between the mother and the other parent of the child.

The fact that a parent may not be able to exercise one or more of the parental rights that a parental responsibility order would confer upon him should not necessarily deter the court from making an order in his favour[6].

The presumption of parental involvement added at CA 1989, ss 1(2A) and (2B) has 'long been part of the bedrock of family law'[7]. However, awareness about the many forms of domestic violence has increased significantly in recent years and more protective measures are filtering into the family justice system. Further changes[8] to Practice Direction 12J to FPR direct that the court must now in 'every case consider carefully whether the presumption applies, having particular regard to any allegations or admissions of harm by domestic abuse to the child or the parent'[9]. 'Harm' is defined as 'ill-treatment or the impairment of health or development'. The Court of Appeal looked at the interplay between PD 12J and the presumption in *J (children) (contact orders: procedure)*[10]. McFarlane LJ said that given the statutory default position established by CA 1989, s 1(6) is that a parent is not to be treated as a risk of harm to a child unless there is some evidence of risk 'before the court', it is important to consider any evidence expediently so as to determine whether the presumption applies. In that case there were serious allegations made by both parents.

A parental responsibility order can be made in favour of the other parent even where the child is in the care of the local authority, thereby giving him the right to be heard in the care proceedings[11].

In *Re S (Parental Responsibility)*[12] it followed from the fact that a parental responsibility order did no more than confer status that the judge at first instance had been wrong to refuse a parental responsibility order to the father of a 6-year-old girl who although he had been convicted of being in possession of paedophilic material was nonetheless a genuine, attached and committed father.

In reaching his decision, Ward LJ's review of the authorities up to that point remains the leading exposition on how to apply the welfare test in CA 1989, s 1 to the question of parental responsibility. In *Re M (Parental Responsibility Order)*[13] Ryder LJ condensed this into a list of non-exhaustive factors which he described as the '*Re S (Parental Responsibility)* factors':

(1) The court should take into account the degree of commitment which the father has shown towards the child, the degree of attachment which exists between the father and the child and the reasons of the father for applying for the court order.
(2) It is a relevant but not an overriding consideration that the court considers the prospective enforceability of parental rights.
(3) It is important to observe the interrelation between the rights and the status and the exercise of those rights and the restrictions upon the exercise of those rights that exists or can be imposed. One of the examples given of this was the 'cruel and callous' behaviour of a father who abducted a child from her mother for a few days who was not granted parental responsibility and other circumstances where a misuse of 'rights' could be controlled by a specific issue or prohibited steps

5.16 Children

order or in the last resort the discharge of a parental responsibility order.
(4) While not wholly irrelevant to each other, the s 8 welfare decision and a decision whether to grant a father parental responsibility are separate and distinct questions to be examined from different perspectives.
(5) Where a concerned though absent father has established a degree of commitment to a child, there is a degree of attachment between them and his reasons for applying for parental responsibility are neither demonstrably improper or wrong, then prima facie, it would be in the interests of the child for a parental responsibility order to be made and the court will need cogent evidence that the child's welfare would be adversely affected before considering otherwise.

In *Re H (Parental Responsibility)*[14] a father appealed against the refusal of a parental responsibility order on the basis that he had demonstrated commitment to the child, the child was attached to him, and the motivation behind his application was genuine. The Court of Appeal held that those factors[15]:

' . . . though a starting-point, were not intended to be exhaustive. Notwithstanding that parental responsibility was a question of status and different in concept from orders made under s 8 . . . the court had a duty to take into account all the relevant circumstances bearing in mind that s 1 applied, under which the welfare of the child was paramount. If the judge considered that there were factors adverse to the father sufficient to tip the balance . . . it would not be right to make the order even though the three requirements could be shown by the father.'

What concerned the court in that case was that the father was unable to accept responsibility for his actions, having inflicted injuries on the 4-year-old child that the court considered could only have been caused deliberately and sadistically.

In *Re J-S (Contact: Parental Responsibility)*[16] it was held by the Court of Appeal that the case for granting parental responsibility to a father who had, until the parents separated, played an important part in the child's life and whose devotion to him was overwhelming, despite findings by the trial judge of violence and harassment of the mother by the father. The father easily established the recognised criteria of commitment, attachment and appropriate motivation as set out in *Re H (Parental Responsibility)*.

In *Re C and V (Contact and Parental Responsibility)*[17] the court confirmed that a parental responsibility order did no more than confer on a natural father the state of fatherhood enjoyed by a father who was married to the child's mother.

JB v KS and E (A Child Acting by his Children's Guardian)[18] concerned a child conceived through an informal sperm donation arrangement. Although it would be wrong to treat the situation as equivalent to one where a child had been born in the context of a loving heterosexual relationship, in this case the court found that there had been a relationship between the mother and the donor which was respectful, intimate and enduring. This was another case which demonstrated the difficulties that arise in informal arrangements where parties may avoid having difficult conversations about the reality of life after the child's birth and may, as a result, have incompatible expectations about the second parent's involvement.

In *Re P (Parental Responsibility)*[19] the court exercised its discretion to refuse a parental responsibility order having found that the father would use the status if conferred to try to interfere with and possibly undermine the mother's care of the child. The Court of Appeal upheld the judge's decision, holding that it was not sufficient to say that the father's potential for interference could be controlled by orders that could be made under s 8 of the CA 1989.

It will be inappropriate for the court to withhold a parental responsibility order until the applicant has demonstrated his commitment by assisting in the financial upkeep of the child[20].

Where the purpose of the father's application was to obtain the precise information that a child (of sufficient age and understanding) wished to conceal then the application should be refused. Also, parental responsibility is not to be 'automatically conferred' if the father poses a risk to the child or if his reasons for applying were 'demonstrably wrong'. Case law is clear that the likely misuse of parental responsibility could lead to it being refused[21].

Parental responsibility has also been removed in situations where a parent has been held to have inflicted devastating emotional harm on the whole family including the child, such as in *Re D (Withdrawal of Parental Responsibility)*[22] where the father had pleaded guilty to sexual offices committed against the mother's two other daughters.

Note that a parent will acquire parental responsibility where an order is made that the child is to live with them[23]. This is true even if the application is made without notice to the mother, for example in a situation in which the other parent contends that the court should intervene in an emergency situation. It may be that the order regarding who the child is to live with is discharged when the mother has had an opportunity to be heard, and yet the other parent has still acquired parental responsibility by default.

[1] CA 1989, s 1(1).
[2] CA 1989, ss 1(2A) and (2B).
[3] Although FPR PD 12J was amended as early as April 2014 to include the words: 'the Family Court presumes that the involvement of a parent in a child's life will further a child's welfare, so long as the parent can be involved in a way that does not put the child or other parent at risk of suffering harm' (at para 4).
[4] CA 1989, s 1(5).
[5] Re H (Illegitimate Children: Father: Parental Rights) (No 2) [1991] 1 FLR 214.
[6] Re C (Minors) (Parental Rights) [1992] 1 FLR 1.
[7] J (children) (contact orders: procedure) [2018] EWCA Civ 115, at para 48.
[8] Came into force on 2 October 2017.
[9] See para 7. Any order made must not expose the parent to risk of harm, as well as the child.
[10] [2018] EWCA Civ 115.
[11] Re G (A Minor) (Parental Responsibility Order) [1994] 1 FLR 504.
[12] [1995] 2 FLR 648.
[13] [2014] 1 FLR 339.
[14] [1998] 1 FLR 855; followed in Re P (Parental Responsibility) [1998] 2 FLR 96.
[15] At p 855F.
[16] [2002] EWCA Civ 1028.
[17] [1998] 1 FLR 392.
[18] [2015] 2 FLR 1180.

[19] [1998] 2 FLR 96.
[20] Re H (Parental Responsibility: Maintenance) [1996] 1 FLR 867.
[21] Re M (Parental Responsibility Order) [2014] 1 FLR 339.
[22] [2015] 1 FLR 166.
[23] CA 1989, s 12(1).

Duration of order

5.17 An order giving a parent parental responsibility will automatically end on the child's 18th birthday, the marriage or civil partnership of the parties[1], adoption, or the child's death but otherwise it cannot be discharged except by a further order of the court.

[1] The parties re required to re-register the birth within 3 months of the marriage or civil partnership. Legitimacy Act 1976, s 9.

Discharge of order

5.18 Any person with parental responsibility may apply to discharge the order, and with leave the child may also apply. The welfare principle does not technically apply to applications to terminate parental responsibility[1], however CA 1989 s 1(2A) does. It has been noted that courts should be slow to terminate a parental responsibility order ' . . . not least because they can only do so in the case of unmarried fathers'[2].

In *Re P (Terminating Parental Responsibility)*[3] a father was said to have forfeited his parental responsibility by causing serious injuries to his child for which he was convicted and imprisoned. The court noted that the welfare of the child is paramount and that an order terminating parental responsibility should only be used as an appropriate step in the regulation of the child's life where the circumstances really do warrant it and not otherwise. *Re D (A Child)*[4] confirmed that the introduction of ACA 2002 and HRA 1998 had not changed the test as expounded in *Re P*. Although in this case the court did terminate the father's parental responsibility, Ryder LJ was clear that the case should not be construed as making it easier to remove an unmarried parent's parental responsibility.

No order can be made to discharge a parental responsibility order where the father also has a residence order (or child arrangements order that the child live with him) in his favour[5].

The discharge of a residence or child arrangements order does not automatically revoke the parental responsibility order, which has to be considered separately.

Parental responsibility, once acquired, cannot be given up or transferred to any other person[6]. The mother of a child can only lose parental responsibility through adoption or a freeing order, likewise the other parent if they were married to or in a civil partnership with the mother at the time of the child's birth, or later marry or enters a civil partnership.

A parent who acquires parental responsibility by jointly registering the child's birth with the mother can lose that status by court order under CA 1989, s 4(2A) and s 4ZA(5).

1   CA 1989, s 1(4).
2   Re C (A Child) [2002] EWCA Civ 446, para 13.
3   [1995] 1 FLR 1048.
4   [2014] EWCA Civ 315.
5   CA 1989, s 12(4).
6   CA 1989, s 2(9).

Applications for orders under s 8 of the Children Act 1989

5.19 Whether the parent of a child has parental responsibility or not, he or she may apply to the court without leave for a child arrangements order[1] (regulating who the child is to live, spend time or otherwise have contact with), for the determination of a specific issue or to prohibit certain steps being taken.

Quite often in practice an application for a child arrangements order for contact will be combined with an application for a parental responsibility order where the parent has not already acquired it.

The same principles will guide the court when deciding whether to make an order under s 8, regardless of whether a parent was married to (or in a civil partnership with) the child's mother at the time of the birth or not, namely that the welfare of the child is the paramount consideration. The court will have regard in particular to the matters set out in s 1(3) of the CA 1989 (the 'welfare checklist'):

(a)   the ascertainable wishes and feelings of the child concerned (considered in the light of the child's age and understanding);
(b)   his physical, emotional and educational needs;
(c)   the likely effect on the child of any change in his or her circumstances;
(d)   the child's age, sex, background and any characteristics the court considers relevant;
(e)   any harm which the child has suffered or is at risk of suffering;
(f)   how capable each of the child's parents, and any other person in relation to whom the court considers the question to be relevant, is of meeting the child's needs; and
(g)   the range of powers available to the court under the CA 1989 in the proceedings in question.

The court will also have regard to the general principle that any delay is likely to prejudice the child, and that it will not make an order unless it would be better for the child than making no order at all.

In addition, for cases that commenced on or after 22 October 2014, CFA 2014, s 11 introduced a presumption[2] that involvement of a parent in its life will further the child's welfare.

If an order is made that a child should live with a parent without parental responsibility, even if that order is made on an interim basis, the court must also make a parental responsibility order in that parent's favour[3].

If an order is made that the child should live with one parent where both parents have parental responsibility, and if those parents subsequently cohabit for a continuous period exceeding 6 months, the child arrangements order will cease to have effect[4]. This will not operate to deprive a parent of the benefit of parental responsibility when that parental responsibility was acquired as a result of a child arrangements order specifying them as a person with whom the child was to live.

Notice of an application under CA 1989, s 8 must be given to any person with parental responsibility, any person caring for the child at the time the application is made, any person who is believed by the applicant to be named in a current relevant court order affecting the child, and any person with whom the child has lived for at least 3 years prior to the application. There will be circumstances, therefore, where a s 8 application could be sought without an unmarried parent having to be notified. In relation to care proceedings, however, notice must be given to any person whom the applicant believes to be a parent of the child, whether or not that person has parental responsibility.

In the context of a relationship breakdown, grandparents and other relatives apart from a child's parents may wish to apply for s 8 orders. Unless they (unusually) fall within the categories of persons specified in s 10 of the CA 1989, they will need the permission of the court to bring an application.

Section 10(9) sets out the matters to which the court will have particular regard when deciding whether or not to give permission:

(a) the nature of the proposed application for the s 8 order;
(b) the applicant's connection with the child; and
(c) any risk there might be of the proposed application disrupting the child's life to such an extent that he or she would be harmed by it.

The above factors are not criteria nor an exhaustive list of matters the court may consider in deciding whether to grant leave. All material facts of the case may be considered, as well as the welfare checklist and the likely prospects of success of the proposed substantive application[5].

[1] CA 1989, s 10(4).
[2] At CA 1989, ss 1(2A) and (2B).
[3] See 5.16 above.
[4] CA 1989, s 11(5).
[5] *Re A (A Child: Application for leave to apply for a child arrangements order)* [2015] EWFC 47.

PROCEDURE

5.20 The procedure for applying for and dealing with s 8 applications after 22 April 2014 is set out in the Child Arrangements Programme, which was incorporated into FPR PD 12B on the same date.

Applications for a child arrangements order are made on Form C100. Where there are allegations of harm or domestic violence a Form C1A should accompany the application together with a C8 should an address need to be confidential.

Parents are expected to consider whether dispute resolution services, including mediation, would be appropriate and can be safely attempted before issuing an application for a s 8 order. Other than in exceptional circumstances[1] the applicant will be expected to have attended a Mediation Information and Assessment Meeting (MIAM) to obtain information about mediation and consider the suitability of mediation as a way of resolving the dispute. The mediator will sign the C100 to confirm their attendance. Where a judge considers that the parties have not taken sufficient steps to explore alternative forms of dispute resolution the court may direct that proceedings, or a hearing in the proceedings, be adjourned to enable the parties to obtain further information about non-court dispute resolution and, if the parties agree, to enable such dispute resolution to be attempted[2].

Where an application is made for a child arrangements order, Cafcass[3] or CAFCASS Cymru will be notified and carry out initial safeguarding enquiries, including seeking information from local authorities and carrying out police checks on the parties. Where possible, they will also undertake telephone risk identification interviews with the parties. Any safety issues identified will be reported to the court in a safeguarding letter.

A First Hearing Dispute Resolution Appointment (FHDRA) should ordinarily be listed 5 to 6 weeks after the application is filed at court. All parties should attend. Local practices vary as to whether children should attend this first meeting but should be made clear on the notice of hearing provided by the court[4].

The FHDRA provides an opportunity for the parties to be helped to an understanding of the issues between them and to reach an agreement. If an agreement can be reached the court will be able to make an order reflecting that agreement. If not, the court will make directions for the future conduct of the case – this may include the preparation of a welfare report under CA 1989, s 7, fact-finding and/or dispute resolution hearings and detailed statements from the parties.

Orders made at the FHDRA should be made on an order CAP02.

[1] Set out in full at FPR 3.8 but essentially in cases where the application is urgent, where there is a history of domestic violence or there are child protection concerns.
[2] FPR PD 12B, para 6.3.
[3] The Children and Family Court Advisory and Support Service.
[4] The District Judge's Direction: Children: Conciliation [2004] 1 FLR 974 stated that the practice in the Principal Registry of the Family Division from 22 April 2004 was for 'any child aged 9 or over to whom the conciliation appointment relates *must* attend (unless otherwise directed) and that when a child of 9 or over attends, any younger child to whom the application relates *may* also attend. This direction related to the PRFD conciliation program, and continued in practice even though no subsequent guidance was issued after that program was superseded first by the Private Law Programme (November 2004), then the Revised Private Law Programme (April 2010) and most recently the Child Arrangements Programme (April 2014).

Change of name

5.21 The issue of the surname by which a child is to be known is one that can frequently arise where the parents of a child are not married and so do not

5.21 Children

share the same surname, unless one of them has chosen formally to adopt the surname of the other[1]. Similarly, the name of the mother may change on marriage or remarriage, or she may choose to revert to a former surname on divorce, raising the question of whether the name of the child should be changed as well. Understandably, both parents may hold strong opinions about why their own surname should be used, and the courts have viewed any application to change a child's name as a matter of utmost importance and have shown a reluctance to accede to such a request lightly.

[1] See, generally, Nasreen Pearce *Name-changing: A Practical Guide* (Fourmat Publishing, 1990). Broadly speaking, a person can be called by whatever name he or she chooses. This is provided he does not do so for any fraudulent purpose or in order to deceive and inflict economic loss on another (*Du Boulay v Du Boulay* (1869) LR 2 PC 430; *Cowley v Cowley* [1901] AC 450) or for purely frivolous reasons such as 'Pudsey Bear' in the infamous case of Eileen De Bont. No formalities are necessary, and a name can be acquired simply by habit and repute. See *Dancer v Dancer* [1949] P 147. It was stated by Justice Harry Vaisey in *re Parrott, Cox and Parrott* [1946] Ch 183 that a Christian name given to a person on baptism cannot be changed by deed poll and can therefore only be changed on confirmation, by Act of Parliament or by adding a name when a child is adopted. In a few cases authority to take a new forename has been given by royal licence.

WHO MAY CHANGE THE SURNAME OF A CHILD?

5.22 Except where there has been a clerical error or a mistake, the entry of a child's name in the Register of Births cannot be changed. However, the name by which a child is known can be changed, and if a child's parents are in agreement they may execute a change of name deed to record this[1].

However, the birth may be re-registered to include the father's surname on the birth certificate if the mother consents, if there is an order or agreement giving the father parental responsibility or if there is a court order for the father to maintain the child. This procedure cannot be used to change the child's name[2].

In cases in which a child arrangements order regulating where a child is to live or a care order is in force in respect of any child, the permission of the court is required before a child may be known by a new surname unless the written consent of every person with parental responsibility has been obtained[3].

A Practice Direction governs the formal procedure for changing a child's surname by deed poll[4].

Re PC (Change of Surname)[5] concerned three legitimate children whose mother effected a change of their surname by deed poll following her remarriage. The children lived with the mother and her new husband and, initially, there was contact with the father. The father discovered the change of name from the headmaster of the children's school who had rightly refused to register the change of name without evidence of the consent of every person with parental responsibility. The mother applied for a specific issue order to compel the school to register the change of name. The mother's argument that she could exercise her parental responsibility unilaterally and so change the children's names without reference to any other person with parental responsibility, ie their father, was rejected. For the avoidance of doubt in the future, the court set out as follows who might apply to change a child's surname:

Law and Practice 5.23

(1) Where only one person has parental responsibility for a child (eg a surviving parent after the death of the other, or the mother of a child born outside marriage where there has been no order or agreement for parental responsibility), that person has the right and power lawfully to cause a change of surname without any other permission or consent.

(2) Where two or more people have parental responsibility for a child, one of those people can lawfully cause a change of surname only if all other people having parental responsibility consent or agree. Subject to (3) below, there is no necessary requirement that that consent be in writing.

(3) Where two or more people have parental responsibility for a child and either a residence or a care order is in force, then one of those people can lawfully cause a change of surname only if all other people having parental responsibility consent in writing.

(4) In any other situation an appropriate order of the court is required.

The court also pointed out that in the case of children over 16 none of the above may apply as generally their wishes and feelings would prevail.

[1] At some stage somebody is likely to require evidence of the change of name, and so it is usual practice to document a change of name by means of one of the more formal procedures, such as executing a deed or making a statutory declaration. Other methods include Notarial Instrument, Royal Licence, and even a private Act of Parliament. Where a change of name deed is to be enrolled in the Central Office of the Supreme Court, the enrolment regulations distinguish between children who have attained the age of 16, and those who have not (Enrolment of Deeds (Change of Name) Regulations 1983 (SI 1983/680), reg 8). A child of 16 or over can either execute the deed poll himself or endorse his consent on the deed executed by his parent or guardian on his behalf. (See Enrolment of Deeds (Change of Name) Regulations 1983, reg 8(3).) Where a child is under 16 the deed poll must be executed by his parent or guardian, and the application for enrolment must be supported by an affidavit showing that the change of name is for the child's benefit (1983 Regulations, reg 8(5); see also Practice Direction of 24 May 1976 [1977] 1 WLR 1065).
[2] BDRA 1953.
[3] CA 1989, ss 13(1)(a) and 33(7)(a).
[4] *Practice Direction of 20 December 1994 (Child: Change of Surname)* [1995] 1 FLR 458.
[5] [1997] 2 FLR 730.

PROCEDURE

5.23 It is clear from the authorities that one parent wishing to change a child's name against the wishes of the other will be well advised to bring the matter to court for determination.

If there is a residence order in force, a free-standing application should be made for leave to cause the child to be known by a new surname under the jurisdiction given by CA 1989, s 13. In any other case, an application should be made for a specific issue order under CA 1989, s 8.

Where the change of name has already been effected unilaterally, application by a concerned parent or party with parental responsibility should be made under s 8 for an order requiring the name to be changed back, and a prohibition against any future change. The court might also be invited to make a living arrangements order, thereby invoking the general prohibition in s 13(1)(a) against a unilateral change.

5.23 *Children*

As a matter of practice, any application to change a child's name back following a unilateral change should be made as swiftly as possible because any delay may lend support to the 'status quo' argument.

Exercise of the court's discretion

5.24 If an application is made under s 8 of the CA 1989 for a specific issue order relating to a child's surname, the court will have to apply the criteria in s 1 of the CA 1989, including the 'welfare checklist'. Although technically CA 1989, s 1(4) does not make it mandatory for the court to have regard to the 'welfare checklist' set out at s 1(3) when considering an application under s 13 it is clear that the court will consider all the factors in the welfare checklist in the exercise of its discretion. Indeed, in reviewing the authorities of *Dawson v Wearmouth* and *Re W, Re A, Re B (Change of Name)* (both set out below) Ryder LJ went so far as to say 'The test is welfare, pure and simple'[1].

In *Dawson v Wearmouth*[2] the House of Lords dealt with the criteria to be applied in determining an application to change a child's surname. In that case, a child born to unmarried parents was registered by the mother with the surname used by her and the child's half siblings. The father objected and applied for an order that the child should be known by his surname instead. At first instance, the judge had made an order that the child should be known by the father's surname. The mother appealed. The Court of Appeal said that the judge at first instance had failed to give sufficient weight to the fact the child was registered with the mother's surname, albeit also that of her former husband, but one shared by her other children. The father's appeal to the House of Lords was dismissed. The salient points of the decision of the House of Lords were that:

(1) changing a child's name was a serious matter, and not one for unilateral action;
(2) the welfare checklist applied to the exercise of discretion;
(3) the name in which the child was registered was a factor to be taken into account but was not necessarily decisive in each case; and
(4) any change of name should lead to an improvement from the point of view of the welfare of the child.

Further guidance was given in *Re W, Re A, Re B (Change of Name)*[3] as follows:

(1) If the parents were married, they both had the power and duty to register their child's name.
(2) If they were not married, the mother had the sole duty and power to do so.
(3) After the registration of the child's name, the grant of a residence order obliged any person wishing to change the surname to obtain the leave of the court or the written consent of all those who had parental responsibility.
(4) In the absence of a residence order, the person wishing to change the surname from the registered name had to obtain the relevant written consent or the leave of the court by making an application for a specific issue order.

(5) On any application, the welfare of the child was paramount.
(6) Among the factors to which the court should have regard was the registered surname of the child and the reasons for the registration, for instance recognition of the biological link with the child's father. Registration was always a relevant and important consideration, but it was not in itself decisive.
(7) Relevant considerations should include factors which could arise in the future as well as the present.
(8) Reasons given for changing or seeking to change a child's name based on the fact that the child's name was not the same as the parent making the application did not generally carry much weight.
(9) The reasons for an earlier unilateral decision to change a child's name might be relevant.
(10) Any change of circumstances of the child since the original registration might be relevant.
(11) In the case of a child whose parents were married to each other, the fact of the marriage was important and there would have to be strong reasons to change the name from the father's surname if the child was so registered.
(12) Where the child's parents were not married to each other, the mother had control over registration. Consequently, on an application to change the surname of the child, the degree of commitment of the father to the child, the quality of contact, if it occurred, between father and child, and the existence or absence of parental responsibility were all relevant factors to take into account.

In *Re P (Parental Responsibility)*[4] two children born outside marriage had been registered with the father's surname. After the breakdown of the parents' relationship, largely as a result of the father persistently committing criminal offences and serving long terms of imprisonment, the mother moved to a new area for a fresh start, and she and the children assumed her maiden surname. The father's appeal against the decision of the circuit judge that they should continue to be known by their new surname was dismissed. The Court of Appeal said that the judge at first instance had applied the correct criteria. In addition to the requirement that the court must consider the welfare of the child to be paramount, these were identified as those set out in the judgment of Dunn LJ in *W v A (Minors: Surname)*[5]:

'When considering the question of a change of name, that is to be regarded as an important matter . . . It is a matter for the discretion of the individual judge hearing the case, seeing the witnesses, seeing the parents, possibly seeing the children, to decide whether or not it is in the interests of the child in the particular circumstances of the case that his surname should or should not be changed; and the judge will take into account all the circumstances of the case, including no doubt where appropriate any embarrassment which may be caused to the child by not changing his name and, on the other hand, the long-term interests of the child, the importance of maintaining the child's links with his paternal family, and the stability or otherwise of the mother's remarriage. I only mention those as typical examples of the kind of considerations which arise in these cases, but the judge will take into account all the relevant circumstances in the particular case before him.'

In *Re C (Change of Surname)*[6] the question of preserving family ties by the use of a parent's surname was considered. In that case, two children born outside marriage lived with their father. There was a residence order in force. The children had been registered at birth with their mother's maiden name, and ignorant of the prohibition against it the father had caused the children to be known by his own surname. He had by then started to live with another woman and she and her three children also adopted his surname. The mother had remarried and so no longer used the surname with which the children had been registered. The court granted the father's application for leave for the children to be known formally by his surname, and the Court of Appeal refused the mother's application for leave to appeal. The basis of the decision was that, although it was important to recognise the link with their mother that their official surname gave them, in this case, as the mother acknowledged that they would be known by their father's name on a day-to-day basis in any event, and she no longer used the original surname herself, it was hard to see how keeping her name would assist in preserving the link.

In *Re C (Change of Surname)*[7] the Court of Appeal considered that it was not in the child's best interests for her surname to be changed back to the father's name 3 years after the mother had changed her surname to her own by deed poll. Nonetheless the mother's actions were wrong and it was emphasised that there was:

> '. . . a heavy responsibility on those who seek to effect a change of name, as a matter of prudence if not of direct law, to take the issue of dispute to the court and to appreciate that good reasons have to be shown before the judge will allow such a change in the future.'

In *Re T (Change of Surname)*[8], however, the Court of Appeal held that the children's surname should be changed back to that of their father. The convenience to the mother of having the same surname for all her children was of slight weight against the strength of the father's application to check the mother's ill-considered act.

In *A v Y (Child's Surname)*[9] an application by a father to change the surname of a 4-year-old child was dismissed. The child had been known by the mother's surname since birth and a change to the father's surname would cause confusion. The delay in making the application was relevant. Further, there would be no benefit in giving the child a double surname as suggested by the father.

However, in *Re R (Surname: Using Both Parents')*[10] the use of both surnames was adopted by the Court of Appeal as a pragmatic solution to disputes between parents over the use of surnames. In that case the children of unmarried parents were to be removed by the mother to live in Spain. Although initially opposed by the father, he subsequently agreed to this, leaving only the issue as to the surname by which the children were to be known. The mother had changed the names unilaterally by deed poll to her own surname. Thorpe LJ proposed that as the children were to live in Spain, the Spanish custom of combining maternal and paternal surnames should be adopted. Hale LJ, as she then was, agreed but went further and proposed that in appropriate cases the use of both parental surnames was to be encouraged so as to make the child's parentage transparent.

In *Re F (Contact)*[11] and more recently in *Re B and another (Change of Names: Parental Responsibility: Evidence)*[12] a change of name was allowed on the basis that it would provide some extra protection against the threat of abduction by the children's father.

In some cases cultural issues will be relevant to the court's decision. In *Re A (Change of Name)*[13], it was held that with the child's welfare being the paramount consideration it was appropriate to the cultural mores of the society into which he was born that his names should protect his mother from the loss of dignity and prestige in the community of acknowledging her adultery, even if this meant that his names did not reflect his true parentage.

[1] *Re W (Change of Name)* [2014] 2 FLR 221.
[2] [1999] 1 FLR 1167.
[3] [1999] 2 FLR 930.
[4] [1997] 2 FLR 722.
[5] [1981] Fam 14 at p 21.
[6] [1998] 1 FLR 549.
[7] [1998] 2 FLR 656.
[8] [1998] 2 FLR 620.
[9] [1999] 2 FLR 5.
[10] [2001] 2 FLR 1358.
[11] [2007] 1 FLR 1663.
[12] [2017] EWHC 3250 (Fam).
[13] [2003] 2 FLR 1.

Appointment of a guardian

5.25 There is provision in the CA 1989[1] for any parent having parental responsibility for a child, or the court, to appoint a guardian of that child to take over parental responsibility for the child on the parent's death.

The appointment usually takes effect when there is no parent with parental responsibility for the child by reason of death. So, for example, if the mother of the child dies having appointed her mother as guardian of the child, if the other parent of the child had parental responsibility the mother's appointment of a guardian would not be operative until after that parent's death or such other time as he or she might cease to have parental responsibility for the child.

A parent of a child who was not married to the mother of the child at the time of birth will not have power to appoint a guardian unless he or she has parental responsibility, although the child's mother could appoint them to be the child's guardian in the event of her death. In this event, the other parent would then have parental responsibility for the child on the mother's death, and would have the power to appoint a guardian to act after his or her own death.

Should the mother of a child appoint as guardian any person other than the other parent (without parental responsibility), any dispute over who should bring up the child will be resolved by way of proceedings under s 8 of the CA 1989. The other parent may wish to apply for an order that the child live with them, for example, or may simply wish to have some specific issue determined. In such circumstances, the court will be guided by the normal welfare principles – there is no presumption in favour of the 'natural' parent, and though this is 'undoubtedly an important and significant factor' it forms only part of the court's assessment of what is in the best interest of the child[2].

Where, immediately before her death, there is an order in place that the child should live with the mother, even if the other parent has parental responsibility, the appointment of any other person as the child's guardian will take effect from her death. However, where the mother does not have a residence order and the other parent has parental responsibility, any appointment of a guardian by the mother will not take effect upon her death, but on the death of both parents[3]. If the person appointed as guardian wishes to act as such an application must be made to court for a special guardianship order[4].

To be effective the appointment of a guardian must be in writing and, except in certain specified circumstances[5], must be dated and signed by the person making the appointment. The most convenient way to appoint a guardian is by will, but this is not essential if the formalities are complied with.

[1] Section 5.
[2] *Re E-R (Child Arrangements Order)* [2016] 1 FLR 521.
[3] CA 1989, s 5(8).
[4] CA 1989, ss 14A–14G.
[5] CA 1989, s 5(5)(a) and (b).

Section 2 Adoption

Introduction

5.26 Adoption is a specialist topic and it is intended merely to highlight those areas of particular concern to the unmarried family.

The Adoption and Children Act 2002

5.27 The ACA 2002 replaced the AA 1976. ACA 2002 made significant changes to adoption generally, and, in particular, how adoption affects unmarried adopters[1].

One of the main aims of the legislation was to increase the pool of those eligible to apply for adoption orders and so reduce the numbers of children caught up in the care system.

In addition to adoption orders, the court may make special guardianship orders. This stops short of severing the child's legal ties with his birth family, but provides a degree of stability and permanence. Parental responsibility can also be granted to step-parents.

[1] For an outline to the key changes brought about by ACA 2002 see *President's Guidance (Adoption: The New Law And Procedure)* March 2006 [2006] 1 FLR 1234.

The Adoption and Children Act 2002 and applications by cohabitants

5.28 Section 14 of the AA 1976 precluded a joint application to adopt a child except where the applicants were married to one another. This did not prevent

Law and Practice **5.30**

one of the parties from applying for an adoption order, and if successful asking the court to make a residence order in favour of the other. It was also possible for couples of the same sex to use this procedure[1]. This less than satisfactory and discriminatory situation was remedied by ss 49 and 50 of the ACA 2002. These provide that an application for an adoption order may be made by either a couple, or one person, while s 144 defined 'a couple' as either a married couple or 'two people (whether of different sexes or the same sex) living as partners in an enduring family relationship'[2].

[1] *Re W (Adoption: Homosexual Adopter)* [1997] 2 FLR 406.
[2] Those with close blood ties are excluded from the definition of 'couple' – ACA 2002, s 144(5) and (6).

Adoption by one person

5.29 Whilst AA 1976 allowed a single unmarried person to apply for an adoption order, ACA 2002 extended this to include a person who the court is satisfied is the partner of a parent of the child who is the subject of the application[1]. A partner is one of a couple as defined by ACA 2002, s 144(4) who is not the child's parent.

This provision enables a step-parent to adopt the child of his or her spouse or civil partner without the need for there to be a joint application with the child's parent, as had been the case under AA 1976, and allows one member of a cohabiting couple to adopt his or her partner's child.

[1] ACA 2002, s 51(2).

Preliminaries to adoption

5.30 A child may be placed for adoption either voluntarily by a parent[1] or by order of the court on the application of a local authority in circumstances in which the local authority is satisfied that the child should be adopted but either the parents do not consent or have withdrawn their consent[2]. There will of course be circumstances in which adoption is an agreed course between private individuals, for example where one of a couple applies to adopt the child of the other. In such cases the applicant is required to give written notice to the local authority of their intention to apply to adopt the child, at least 3 months but no more than 2 years before the application[3].

Before an application for an adoption order is made conditions as to residence must be met.

Where the child is placed for adoption by an adoption agency the child must have had his home with the applicant(s) for at least 10 weeks before an order can be made[4]. Where the application is by a step-parent or partner of the child's parent the child must have had his home with the applicant for a continuous period of at least 6 months preceding the application. In the case of local authority foster parents the period is 12 months, and in all other non-agency cases for 3 years out of the 5 years preceding the application, unless the court gives leave to make an application before the condition is met.

5.30 *Children*

The relevant adoption agency or local authority will provide a report for the court that deals with the suitability of the applicant(s), issues of the child's welfare, and in the case of unmarried couples whether or not they have an 'enduring family relationship'.

[1] ACA 2002, s 19.
[2] ACA 2002, s 21.
[3] ACA 2002, s 44(3).
[4] ACA 2002, s 42(2).

Consent to adoption

5.31 The court cannot make an adoption order without the consent of the child's parent or guardian unless the court is satisfied that in the interests of the child such consent should be dispensed with.

Dispensing with consent

5.32 The giving of parental consent is always subject to the court's powers to dispense with consent in cases in which either the parent cannot be found or is incapable of giving consent, or the welfare of the child requires it. This is determined by reference to the welfare checklist contained in s 1(4).

The status of the unmarried father

5.33 The father of a child who was not married to the child's mother at the time of the birth is not a 'parent' for the purposes of the ACA 2002 unless he has parental responsibility for the child[1].

The practical effect of this is that unless he has parental responsibility his consent will not be required before a placement or an adoption order can be made[2].

ACA 2002 provides for a child's father who was not married to the child's mother at the time of the birth to register the birth jointly with the mother and so acquire parental responsibility. This is in addition to the routes to parental responsibility that existed before ACA 2002 (see **5.8** above).

Although a father with parental responsibility will have the right to give, or withhold, his consent to adoption, a father who acquires parental responsibility after the mother has given her consent to the child being placed for adoption will be deemed to have given his consent. This is subject to the provisions for withdrawing consent to the placement only. However, once an application has been made for an adoption order the making of an order can be opposed only with the permission of the court if the court is satisfied that there has been a change of circumstances since the consent was given or the placement order made[3].

[1] ACA 2002, s 52(6).
[2] ACA 2002, s 19(1).
[3] ACA 2002, s 47.

Unmarried fathers and party status

5.34 Although for the purposes of AA 1976 a father without parental responsibility had no right to consent to freeing for adoption or the making of an adoption order, nor any right under the AR 1984 to be given notice of the proceedings, AR 1984, r 15(3) allowed the court to direct that any person be made a respondent. Largely as a result of the impact of the ECHR and the acknowledgement that such fathers had a right to respect for family life under Art 8 where there had been a significant relationship with the child, it became established that fathers without parental responsibility would be informed of the proceedings unless there was good reason not to do so. In *Re R (Adoption: Father's Involvement)*[1] the President of the Family Division at that time said that each case will:

> '. . . have to be decided on its merits as to whether or not it is appropriate that [the father] should be joined as a respondent . . . there will be extreme cases such as rape where it would be wholly inappropriate for such a father to be joined. There is a spectrum and the question is: at what point does each father without parental responsibility stand on that spectrum?'

The considerations that would weigh in favour of the involvement in adoption proceedings of a father without parental responsibility were developed further by the President in *Re H; Re G (Adoption: Consultation of Unmarried Fathers)*[2] in which he held that as a matter of general principle judges giving directions in adoption applications would be expected to inform such fathers of the proceedings unless, for good reason, it was inappropriate to do so.

[1] [2001] 1 FLR 302.
[2] [2001] 1 FLR 646.

The exercise of the court's discretion

5.35 ACA 2002 brought adoption proceedings in line with CA 1989 in making the child's welfare the paramount consideration for the courts when deciding whether to make an adoption order. Furthermore, it is the child's welfare throughout his or her life that must be considered, and the principles of delay, and non-intervention apply as they do in CA 1989. A comprehensive welfare checklist is set out in ACA 2002, s 1(4).

Increasingly, the making of adoption orders has not been considered incompatible with the child maintaining links with his or her birth family and it was possible for concurrent contact orders to be made under CA 1989, s 8. ACA 2002 imposes a duty on the court before making an adoption order to consider whether there should be any arrangements for allowing any person to have contact with the child.

Revocation of an adoption order

5.36 Adoption extinguishes all legal ties a child has with their birth family and creates new ties that are intended to be lifelong, with their adoptive family. Revocation is however possible in very exceptional circumstances[1] and jurisdiction lies in the inherent jurisdiction of the High Court.

[1] See *PK v Mr K and another* [2015] EWHC 2316 (Fam).

5.37 Children

Section 3 Child abduction

Removal of children from the jurisdiction

5.37 The detailed provisions of the law relating to child abduction are outside the scope of this book, and specialist publications should be consulted. This section is designed to serve as a brief introduction to this complex area and to highlight the importance to an unmarried parent of having parental responsibility.

The unmarried parent without parental responsibility

5.38 Where more than one person has parental responsibility for a child who is habitually resident in the UK, the removal of that child from the jurisdiction by one parent without the consent of the other may be unlawful. In particular, if there is a child arrangements order in force concerning who a child is to live with, then under CA 1989, s 13(1) the child may not be removed from the UK unless everyone with parental responsibility for the child consents, or the court gives permission (save that a parent with an order that the child is to live with them may remove them from the jurisdiction for a period of less than one month)[1].

Where the mother is the only parent with parental responsibility, however, there will generally be nothing in English civil law to prevent her from removing the child from the UK. In cases where there is no child arrangements order, the Child Abduction and Custody Act 1985 provides a remedy only to those with parental responsibility.

Detailed guidance on the form and requirements of court applications relating to wrongful removal (both to prevent unlawful removal and to secure the return of a child taken away unlawfully) is provided in FPR PD 12F and the President's guidance dated 13 March 2018[2].

[1] CA 1989, s 13(2).
[2] Practice Guidance: Case Management and Mediation of International Child Abduction Proceedings, 13 March 2018.

Rights of custody

5.39 Where a parent does not have parental responsibility, it may be possible to argue that there has been 'wrongful removal' or 'wrongful retention' under the terms of the Hague Convention on the Civil Aspects of International Child Abduction (the Hague Convention) if the removal or retention was in breach of that parent's 'rights of custody'.

'Rights of custody' is a concept to be determined within the context of the Hague Convention and not with reference to any particular domestic definition. However, it will include rights relating to the care of the child, and the decision as to where the child should live.

On 17 October 1997 the Lord Chancellor's Child Abduction Unit issued a practice note[1] setting out the policies at that time in respect of the acceptance of applications by fathers for the return of children for whom they do not have parental responsibility.

The importance of the practice note was the recognition that in certain circumstances a parent of a child who does not have parental responsibility may nonetheless have 'rights of custody' for the purposes of the Hague Convention.

The 1996 Hague Convention on Parental Responsibility came into force on 1 November 2012. Under Art 16, if a parent has acquired parental responsibility abroad (including under mechanisms that do not require judicial or administrative involvement, eg by agreement or unilateral act), that parent will retain parental responsibility when the child's habitual residence changes to the UK[2].

In *Re B (A Minor) (Abduction)*[3] and *Re O (Child Abduction: Custody Rights)*[4] it was held that a father who was exercising parental functions over a substantial period of time may have 'inchoate' rights of custody sufficient to amount to 'rights of custody' for the purposes of the Hague Convention. This was also seen in a matter of a removal of a child from Lithuania to Northern Ireland, determined by the UK Supreme Court, in *Re K (A child) (Northern Ireland)*[5].

There are cases in which a mere application to the local family court has 'vested' rights of custody in the court, which has allowed an applicant who otherwise had no rights of custody to mount an application for a child's return. This was seen in the case of *Re M*[6]. Separately, in *Re W; Re B (Child Abduction: Unmarried Father)*[7] Hale J, as she then was, considered applications by two unmarried fathers for declarations under Art 15 of the Hague Convention that the removal of their respective children from England and Wales was wrongful within the meaning of Art 3 on the ground that the removal was in breach of the rights of custody held by the father in one case, and the court in the other[8].

[1] [1998] 1 FLR 491.
[2] Whether parental responsibility has been so acquired is a question to be referred to the foreign court under Art 15, see *Re K (Rights of Custody: Spain)* [2010] 1 FLR 57 and *Kennedy v Kennedy* [2010] 1 FLR 782.
[3] [1994] 2 FLR 249.
[4] [1997] 2 FLR 702.
[5] (2014) UKSC 29.
[6] [2017] EWHC 1294 (Fam) [2017] 4 WLUK 216.
[7] [1998] 2 FLR 146.
[8] See also *Re E (Abduction Rights of Custody)* [2005] 2 FLR 759 regarding the court's right of custody while seised of the right to determine the child's place of residence.

5.40 In *Re W*, there were pending proceedings before the family proceedings court for parental responsibility and contact orders. Indeed, the children were removed from the jurisdiction only a matter of days before the final hearing at which orders were granted in favour of the father. Hale J held that the removal of the child from the jurisdiction was a breach of the rights of custody attributable to the court, and made the declaration sought.

No such declaration was given in *Re B (Abduction: Rights of Custody)*[1]. The father had never applied for parental responsibility, and his application for a prohibited steps order preventing the removal of the children from the jurisdiction was ultimately compromised and a residence order made in favour of the mother[2].

It was stated by Hale J, *per curiam*, that unmarried parents should be advised that removal by the mother of a child who is habitually resident here will be wrongful under the Hague Convention if:

(a) the father has parental responsibility either by agreement or court order or by jointly registering the birth;
(b) there is a court order in force prohibiting it;
(c) there are relevant proceedings pending in a court in England and Wales; or
(d) where the father is currently the primary carer for the child, at least if the mother has delegated such care to him.

In *Re H (Child Abduction) (Unmarried Father: Rights of Custody)*[3] Holman J held that removal from the jurisdiction was a breach of rights of custody of a father without parental responsibility on the basis that correspondence between the parents' solicitors concerning the child's proposed removal from the jurisdiction established the father's inchoate right to determine the child's place of residence. The mother's solicitors had written to those acting for the father stating that it was not the mother's intention, as was believed by the father, to remove the child to Spain. Holman J regarded this as amounting to an undertaking that this was the case, and observed:

> 'The practice was that when responsible and reputable solicitors wrote to each other in these sorts of terms, their letters could be relied upon. The mother's solicitors could have responded that the father had no parental responsibility and that the question of the child's residence was therefore none of his business, but they did not do so. The positive terms in which the mother's solicitors in fact wrote involved a determination of the child's place of residence into the foreseeable future at the request of the father. For so long as the terms of the letter of the mother's solicitors remained operative and not withdrawn, the father clearly had a right of custody in relation to the child.'

In *Re F (Abduction: Unmarried Father: Sole Carer)*[4] the mother of four children had moved to Australia taking all but the youngest child with her. The youngest child remained with the man who believed himself to be the father and he applied for a residence order. He was the father of and had parental responsibility for the other children. All the children had been substantially in his care, the mother having lived with them only intermittently. The mother did not initially dispute the man's paternity as far as the youngest child was concerned but subsequently denied it and it was agreed that there would be paternity tests. Before the outcome of the tests was known and the application for a residence order processed, the mother was party to the abduction of the youngest child to join her and her siblings in Australia. Following the abduction, the father made an application for the child's return under the Hague Convention and an order was made on an ex parte basis. The mother applied to set aside the order but was unsuccessful. The court held that:

> '(1) There were circumstances in which a person who was not related by blood to a child, but who fell into a quasi-parental role and had exclusive care of the child,

might be found to have inchoate rights of custody in relation to the child for the purposes of making an application under the Hague Convention.

(2) Inchoate rights of custody were those which were capable of being affected by court applications in which there was a reasonable prospect of success. The father here, even if he were not the natural father, had good prospects of obtaining a residence order under s 8 of the Children Act 1989 and consequently had inchoate rights of custody which were capable of being perfected.'

A parent without parental responsibility whether or not they are the primary carer of the child may be well advised not to delay in making an application to the court to prevent the removal of the child from the jurisdiction if they believe they have sufficient evidence of the mother's intention to remove the child[5].

[1] [1997] 2 FLR 594.
[2] See also *B v UK* [2000] 1 FLR 1, ECHR.
[3] [2003] 2 FLR 153.
[4] [2003] 1 FLR 839.
[5] See Helen L Conway 'Feared Abduction – Jumping the Gun?' [2000] Fam Law 272.

5.41 It is increasingly the case that the court will consider that if it is seised of proceedings to determine rights of custody, removal of the child from the jurisdiction without the court's permission while the proceedings are pending is a breach of the rights of custody attributable to the court. This was the case in *Re J (Abduction: Declaration of Wrongful Removal)*[1], *Re C (Abduction: Wrongful Removal)*[2] and *Re H (Abduction: Rights of Custody)*[3]. In the latter case, the House of Lords held that the court acquired rights of custody if its jurisdiction had been invoked in respect of matters of custody within the meaning of the Hague Convention. Proceedings which called upon the court to determine a child's place of residence gave the court a right of custody. The date on which the court's jurisdiction was invoked was, at the latest, the date on which proceedings raising matters of custody were served; in special cases, the court's jurisdiction might be invoked before service of such an application.

This raises the question of whether a hearing without notice to the mother deprives her of her right to a fair trial under Art 6(1) of the Convention. This was considered in *Re J (Abduction: Wrongful Removal)*[4]. The Court of Appeal considered whether in making an order without notice to the mother, as Hale J, as she then was, had done in this case, she had deprived the mother of a fair trial. It was held that the mother had not been deprived of a fair trial. Cases concerning children often had to be dealt with as a matter of great urgency, and in the circumstances of that case the father had been entitled to make both applications without notice to the mother. It was certainly possible that there might be a breach of the right to a fair trial if no opportunity were provided by the law to challenge an order made without notice, but it was always open to a party against whom an order had been made without notice to apply to the court to have it set aside.

A recital in a court order that a child is not to be removed from the jurisdiction without prior written agreement of the parties or a court order confers rights of custody on the other parent[5].

[1] [1999] 2 FLR 653.

5.41 *Children*

² [1999] 2 FLR 859.
³ [2000] 1 FLR 374.
⁴ [2000] 1 FLR 78.
⁵ *Re P (Abduction: Consent)* [2004] 2 FLR 1057.

Section 4 Financial provision for children

Introduction

5.42 A parent's obligation to maintain his or her child will not depend upon whether he or she has parental responsibility. It is an absolute obligation and the only circumstances in which this obligation will be removed is on the making of an adoption order in respect of the child.

Child maintenance

TERMINOLOGY

5.43 Discussions of maintenance for children generally include the following:

(1) 'Child periodical payments' refers to orders made by the court (including consent orders) for regular (usually monthly) payments to one parent by the other, typically under CA 1989, Sch 1 or (in the case of married parents) MCA 1973, s 23(1)(a).
(2) 'Child support' under CSA 1991 pursuant to a decision by the Child Maintenance Service (CMS)[1].
(3) 'Child maintenance' as a catch-all phrase for both child periodical payments and child support, as well as private agreements reached between parents.

In each case there is no distinction between whether parents are married or unmarried or of the same or opposite sex. In most cases parentage, and not cohabitation, is the pre-requisite for financial provision.

Cohabitation can prevent one parent from seeking maintenance from the other under any statutory scheme. Where there has been a separation and child support or a periodical payments order is in place, if cohabitation is resumed it will terminate continuing payments after 6 months of cohabitation[2].

In *Brough v Law and CMEC*, Lewison LJ suggested that during the period of resumed cohabitation and until the 6 months has expired the surviving duty to pay child maintenance would be 'suspended . . . and cease at the expiry of 6 months'.

[1] Or one of its predecessors: the Child Support Agency (CSA) and the Child Maintenance and Enforcement Commission (CMEC).
[2] CSA 1991, s 3, CA 1989, Sch 1, para 3(4).

Child support

5.44 The child support scheme was set up in 1993 (under the CSA 1991) to provide an administrative means whereby maintenance could be quantified and then be payable by a separated parent (the 'non-resident parent' or 'NRP') to the main carer (the 'parent with care' or 'PWC') for their qualifying children; and to set up a scheme for enforcement of unpaid maintenance.

Under CSA 1991, s 8, the parents of a qualifying child (one who is eligible to be paid child support maintenance) are prevented from seeking a court order for child periodical payments save:

(1) By consent order.
(2) 'Top-up order's under s 8(6)–(8).

Application can be made to court where, for example, there is a step-child; one or more of the parents or qualifying children are habitually outside the[1] UK; or to vary an existing court order[2].

Nothing in CSA 1991 is intended to prevent parents reaching agreement if they are able to do so; and indeed the £20 application fee that was introduced in June 2014 was designed primarily to give applicants cause to consider whether it would be better to reach agreement directly with the other parent[3].

[1] CSA 1991, s 44.
[2] See, for example, *V v V (Child Maintenance)* [2001] 2 FLR 799.
[3] Application fees are not payable by applicants who are under 19 or who are victims of domestic violence or abuse.

QUALIFYING CHILD: MEANING OF 'CHILD'

5.45 Child support is payable in respect of one or more 'qualifying children', who are defined as children, both of whose natural parents are living apart, or are living apart from the qualifying child[1]. It cannot therefore apply to step-children whose periodical payments are covered by MCA 1973 or CA 1989 (who may also be entitled to child support maintenance from their natural parent).

Child support maintenance is payable whilst the qualifying child is a 'child' within the terms of CSA 1991, s 55, that is:

(a) Under 16[2];
(b) Under 20[3] and in full-time education (but not advanced education)[4]; nor if he or she is married or formerly married[5].

[1] CSA 1991, s 3(1).
[2] CSA 1991, s 55(1)(a).
[3] The maximum age was increased from 'has not attained the age of 19' to 'has not attained the age of 20' by CMOPA 2008, s 42 on 10 December 2012.
[4] CSA 1991, s 55(1)(b).
[5] CSA 1991, s 55(2).

THE CHILD SUPPORT CALCULATION

5.46 An application for child support maintenance is made under CSA 1991, s 4 by either parent or a person with care (a non-parent looking after the qualifying child). This triggers a calculation which produces a figure for child support maintenance.

5.46 Children

Since the CSA was established in 1991 there have been three mechanisms for calculating the required level of child support. The initial scheme (colloquially known now as 'CS1' or the 'old' scheme) was heavily criticised for being overcomplicated but continued to operate from enactment until March 2003. Plans to move existing cases from the old scheme to 'CS2' (the 'net income' scheme) never materialised.

Calculations under CS2 were based on a percentage of the payer's net income, and most existing child maintenance calculations will have been made under this scheme. This scheme was gradually phased out for new applicants in December 2012. All existing cases started under CS1 and CS2 operate through the CSA as a department within the Department for Work and Pensions. It was intended, however, that all existing cases would be closed by the end of 2018. Whilst the ongoing liability to pay under the CS1 and CS2 schemes has stopped, the 493,600[1] cases that remain open primarily concern arrears. There was no automatic transition onto 'CS3', meaning parents who wished to continue to use the CSA/CMS had to apply under the new scheme, incurring an application fee and becoming liable for collection charges in the process.

All applications since 25 November 2013 have been operated under CS3 (the 'gross income' scheme).

Stage 1: The new, gross income, calculation is as follows:

(1) A 'nil rate' for payers who fall into certain categories, such as students and those with an income of less than £5 per week;
(2) A 'flat rate' of £7 per week for paying parents with a gross income of less than £100 per week or in receipt of certain prescribed benefits;
(3) A 'reduced rate' for paying parents with a gross income of between £100 and £200 per[2] week;
(4) The 'basic rate':
    (a) for income up to £800 per week:
        (i) 12% for one qualifying child;
        (ii) 16% for two qualifying children;
        (iii) 19% for three or more qualifying children;
    (b) and for further income between £800 and £3,000 per week:
        (i) 9% for one qualifying child;
        (ii) 12% for two qualifying children;
        (iii) 15% for three or more qualifying children.

Stage 2: Where the NRP is living in a household where there are other dependent children his income will be reduced in the following proportion before the calculation is carried out:

(1) 11% for one other relevant child;
(2) 14% for two other relevant children;
(3) 16% for three other relevant children.

Stage 3: Where the NRP shares the care of the children, his payments will be (further) reduced by the following proportions based on the number of nights the children spend with him:

(1) 1/7 for 52 to 103 nights per year;

(2) 2/7 for 104 to 155 nights per year;
(3) 3/7 for 156 to 174 nights per year; and
(4) 1/2 plus a further £7 for 175+ nights per year.

Once an initial calculation has been carried out, either parent may make a variation application to the CMS, at which point the CMS will also be able to incorporate into their calculation the following:

(1) 'Special expenses' (including the costs of contact, costs relating to the illness or disability of another child and the maintenance (but not educational) element of boarding school fees);
(2) Unearned income of more than £2,500 pa;
(3) Income that, in the opinion of the Secretary of State, has been unreasonably diverted to other destinations in order to reduce his liability to pay maintenance.

[1] As at December 2018.
[2] Set out in the Child Support and Claims and Payments (Miscellaneous Amendments and Change to the Minimum Amount of Liability) Regulations 2013 (SI 2013/1654) but designed to achieve a straight line increase from £7 for those earning £100 per week to the basic rate for those earning £200 per week. The precise calculation can perhaps be carried out most easily using the government's child maintenance calculator at https://www.gov.uk/calculate-your-child-maintenance.

Variation, collection and enforcement

5.47 Once a child support calculation has been carried out it is possible for either parent to apply for a 'variation' inviting the CMS to consider a wider range of financial circumstances other than simply the NRP's declared income. The categories of assets considered under CS3 were more limited that those under CS2. However changes were made in December 2018 meaning they are now similar[1].

Once an assessment has been made, parties are encouraged to make private 'direct pay' arrangements for the calculated maintenance to be paid. If either party insists on using the CMS's 'Collect and Pay' service administration fees will be added to every amount collected. This results in a 20% increase in the amount paid by the payer and a 4% deduction from the amount received by the recipient, so that for every £100 assessed the NRP will pay £120 and the PWC will receive £96[2].

Other than referring the matter to the Collect and Pay service, the PWC is not permitted to control enforcement of collection of arrears for the children: this is left to the administrators[3]. There is almost no remedy for the PWC if CMS fails to enforce payments.

[1] Under CS2 the CSA was entitled to look at an NRP's capital (excluding his home, business and a few other exceptions). Any such capital over £65,000 under CS2 was treated as being capable of achieving a notional return of 8% pa which was then added to their income for the purpose of the calculation. Similarly, under CS2 the CSA was able to look at the NRP's lifestyle and increase its award if that lifestyle was not consistent with that parent's declared income. Under CS3 there is no provision to look at the NRP's lifestyle but since December 2018 it is possible to look at the NRP's capital over £31,250.

² On the face of it there is a clear opportunity here for a PWC to inflict financial pain on the NRP at limited cost to herself. It remains to be seen whether this will be used tactically by vindictive PWCs. Notwithstanding the forced closure of CS1 and CS1 cases, applications for CS3 have been dropping since March 2017. This may be because of the £20 charge or because more parents are entering into family based arrangements. As at September 2019 there were 724,200 CS3 arrangements.
³ *R (Kehoe) v Secretary of State for Work and Pensions* [2005] UKHL 48, [2005] 3 WLR 252.

TOP-UP ORDERS: DISCRETIONARY PRINCIPLES

5.48 CSA 1991, ss 8(6)–(8) provides for orders to be made in financial remedy proceedings in terms that 'shall not prevent a court from exercising any power . . . to make a [child] maintenance order' where:

(1) a maintenance calculation has been carried out and the NRP's gross weekly income exceeds £3,000 per week (s 8(6))¹;
(2) for educational expenses 'for the instruction or training of the child'²; and
(3) where disability living allowance or a personal independence payment is paid for a child or is otherwise disabled, to cover 'expenses attributable' to that disability.

Such an application is made in existing or free-standing CA 1989, Sch 1 proceedings (see **5.50** below).

¹ It now appears to be settled (notwithstanding a contrary indication in CF v KM (Financial Provision for Child: Costs of Legal Proceedings) [2011] 1 FLR 208) that the top-up jurisdiction for child support cannot be engaged unless and until the CMS has made a maximum assessment: Dickson v Rennie [2015] 2 FLR 978.
² CSA 1991, s 8(7).

AGREEMENTS AND CHILD MAINTENANCE

5.49 Nothing in CSA 1991 is intended to prevent parents from agreeing their own figure for child periodical payments¹ with each other – whether with or without advice or through dispute resolution; though their agreement may not in any way exclude operation of the child support scheme² in the event that either parent later wishes to apply³. Such an application will override any terms previously agreed between the parents.

At the same time as introducing the latest scheme for child support, the government has also been keen to encourage parents to reach their own agreements if possible. To this end its Child Maintenance Options website⁴ includes a 'Family Based Arrangements Form' that parents are encouraged to complete together (albeit that the document specifically states that it is not a legal document). As noted at **5.44** above, the introduction of the application fee for applications to the CMS was primarily to give applicants cause to consider whether it would be better to reach agreement directly with the other parent.

Tribunal rules⁵ require the respective tribunals to 'bring to the attention of parties [before them] the availability of any appropriate' dispute resolution scheme and 'to facilitate the use of the (*sic*) procedure'.

¹ CSA 1991, s 9(2).

[2] CSA 1991, s 9(4).
[3] CSA 1991, s 9(3).
[4] See www.cmoptions.org.
[5] Tribunal Procedure (First-tier Tribunal) (Social Entitlement Chamber) Rules 2008, r 3 and the Tribunal Procedure (Upper Tribunal) Rules 2008, r 3.

Schedule 1 to the Children Act 1989

5.50 Although the CMS will be the starting point for those asked to advise anyone with children in their care following the breakdown of a relationship with the other parent, generally it will be necessary to consider the financial provision in addition to periodical payments that can be made for children under CA 1989, Sch 1. Cohabiting parents should consider whether there might be a claim under the TOLATA 1996 at the outset.

WHAT RELIEF IS AVAILABLE?

5.51 The court has the power to make the following orders in respect of children[1]:

- periodical payments;
- secured periodical payments[2];
- lump sum;
- settlement of property; and
- transfer of property.

Although only one substantive order can be made for settlement or transfer of property[3], there is no bar to multiple applications for lump sum payments[4].

In addition, the court may make orders for interim periodical payments, subject to the CSA 1991[5], and has power to alter the provision contained in a maintenance agreement[6].

[1] CA 1989, Sch 1, para 1(2).
[2] The court's jurisdiction to make a periodical payments order, secured or otherwise, will be subject to the operation of the CSA 1991, as amended by CSPSSA 2000, see 5.51.
[3] CA 1989, Sch 1, para 1(5)(b).
[4] CA 1989, Sch 1, para 1(5)(a).
[5] CA 1989, Sch 1, para 9.
[6] CA 1989, Sch 1, para 10.

WHICH COURT?

5.52 An application should be made to the Family Court, who will then allocate it to the appropriate level of judge[1].

[1] Applications for a top-up order where the maximum calculation following a maximum assessment (CSA, s 8(6)) should generally be listed at High Court level: *Re P (Child: Financial Provision)* [2003] 2 FLR 865.

WHO MAY APPLY?

5.53 An application may be made by[1]:

- the parent of a child ('parent' includes a step-parent);

5.53 Children

- the guardian of a child;
- the special guardian of a child;
- any person named in a child arrangements order as a person with whom a child is to live; or
- in certain limited circumstances a child over 18[2].

With the exception of those in the latter category, the court has jurisdiction to make orders for children under the age of 18, although an order for periodical payments will usually be expressed to last until a child's 17th birthday unless he or she is in full-time education or training, or has a disability.

There is no definition of 'parent' in CA 1989 and in *T v B (Parental Responsibility: Financial Provision)*[3] Moylan J held that for the purposes of Sch 1 it should be strictly interpreted to include only a legal parent. In that case a child was born to a lesbian couple as a result of their joint application for treatment by way of artificial insemination by donor. They had not entered into a civil partnership. On the breakdown of their relationship a shared residence order was made which had the effect of conferring parental responsibility also upon the woman who had not borne the child. The other applied for financial provision for the child under Sch 1. The court rejected the submissions of the applicant that the definition of 'parent' could extend to a social and psychological parent as the respondent clearly was in that case.

[1] CA 1989, Sch 1, para 1(1).
[2] CA 1989, Sch 1, para 2(1). Where the child is or will be undergoing education or training or where there are special circumstances, and a periodical payments order was not in force immediately before the child's 16th birthday, and the child's parents are not living together.
[3] [2010] 2 FLR 1966.

Pre-application protocol

5.54 The pre-application protocol[1] introduced by the FPR is intended to apply to all applications for a financial remedy, including applications under CA 1989, Sch 1, however straightforward or complex.

The aim is to exchange financial and other relevant information at an early stage to assist the parties to identify and resolve their differences speedily and fairly, or at least narrow the issues. This is with a view to saving costs and is in line with the overriding objective.

Even if the parties are unable to reach agreement, adherence to the protocol will assist the court in dealing justly with the case and as speedily and cost-effectively as possible. The court will therefore expect the parties to comply with the terms of the protocol.

Since 22 April 2014, prior to issuing a court application, the prospective applicant must[2] attend a mediation, information and assessment meeting ('MIAM')[3].

[1] FPR PD 9A.
[2] Unless an exemption an applies.
[3] FPR 3.5–3.10.

Law and Practice **5.56**

PROCEDURE IN THE FAMILY COURT

5.55 Also, since 22 April 2014 applications under CA 1989, Sch 1 have been dealt with under the shortened procedure (the 'fast-track') set out at Chapter 5 of FPR 9 and not the full procedure used for other financial remedies (such as financial division on divorce). This can provide faster access to a final contested hearing but may not include the opportunity to attempt a Financial Dispute Resolution hearing ('FDR') (which is generally considered to be a useful opportunity to bring about a settlement using 'early neutral evaluation' from a judge). However, since 4 June 2018 the fast track procedure has applied only to applications for, and variation of[1], periodical payments[2]. Parties who may like their application to be dealt with under the full procedure ('standard procedure') must make a specific application for this[3]. All other applications under CA 1989, Sch 1 will follow the standard procedure set out at Chapter 4 of FPR 9.

The application for an order under CA 1989, Sch 1 is in Form A1 (for fast track cases) or Form A (for standard procedure cases) together with any documents stated to be required or referred to in the application. A copy of the Form A1/A with sufficient copies for service on the respondent, together with the court fee, must be sent to court for issue. On receipt, the court will endorse the date of the first hearing. Under the fast track the first hearing shall be listed not less than 6 weeks and not more than 10 weeks after the date of filing of the application. Under the standard procedure, this will be 12 and 16 weeks. The court will then either effect service of the application upon the respondent within 4 days, or send the papers to the applicant's solicitors for service by them within 4 days of receipt. If service is not effected by the court a certificate of service must be filed at court before the date fixed for the first appointment.

Where there is also to be an application under TOLATA 1996 generally speaking it will be preferable for the application to be conjoined (not consolidated) and case managed together[4].

[1] Save in some circumstances.
[2] FPR 9.9B.
[3] FPR 9.18A.
[4] *W v W (Joinder of Trusts of Land Act and Children Act Applications)* [2004] 2 FLR 321.

PROCEDURE AFTER ISSUE

Fast track

5.56 Not more than 21 days after the issue of the application the parties must simultaneously exchange a financial statement in Form E1, accompanied by the prescribed documents only[1].

No additional disclosure or inspection of documents may be given until the court has given its approval[2].

Should the respondent wish to seek a direction that the standard procedure apply, such an application must be made within 7 days of service of the

5.56 Children

application. The applicant would make their request with the original application[3].

[1] FPR 9.19(1).
[2] FPR 9.19(4).
[3] FPR 9.18A.

Standard procedure

5.57 35 days before the first appointment, each party must simultaneously file and serve a statement of financial circumstances in Form E1, verified by a statement of truth and accompanied by specified documents only[1]. No disclosure or inspection of documents may be requested or given between the filing of the application for a financial remedy and the first appointment[2].

Not less than 14 days before the first appointment parties must file and serve concise statement of issues, chronologies, questionnaires and Forms G.

[1] FPR 9.14(1)–(2).
[2] FPR 9.14(4).

Procedure at first hearing

5.58 The first appointment must be conducted with the aim of defining the issues and saving costs in pursuance of the overriding objective. Under either procedure the court may use the first hearing or part of it as a FDR appointment[1].

Both parties must personally attend the first hearing unless the court directs otherwise.

If the court is able to determine the application at the first hearing it may do so, otherwise it will direct that further evidence be filed and a date set for a directions hearing or appointment, FDR (under the standard procedure) or final hearing[2].

[1] FPR 9.20 (4) and 19.14(4)(a).
[2] FPR 9.20.

The exercise of the court's discretion

5.59 The matters to which the court must have regard when deciding whether or not to make one or more orders for financial relief are similar to those considered when the court is exercising its discretion under MCA 1973, s 25(3). However, there is no explicit requirement that the child's welfare is to be either the court's 'first consideration'[1], or the 'paramount consideration'[2]. Nonetheless it is apparent from *J v C*[3] and *Re P*[4] that the child's welfare will assume a greater importance in the exercise of the court's discretion than simply being one of the relevant circumstances. It will be 'in the generality of cases, a constant influence on the discretionary outcome', as Thorpe LJ put it in *Re P*.

The court must have regard to all the circumstances, including:

- the financial needs of the child;
- the income, earning capacity (if any), property and other financial resources of the child;
- any physical or mental disability of the child; and
- the manner in which the child was being, or was expected to be, educated or trained.

In addition, the court will look at income, earning capacity, property and other financial resources, and financial needs, obligations and responsibilities, at the time of the hearing and in the foreseeable future, in the following cases:

- when the court is considering an application made by a parent, special guardian, or guardian of the child, or someone named in a child arrangements order as someone with whom the child is to live, it will look at the financial position of the child's parents, which definition will include a step-parent or former step-parent, and that of the applicant and any other person in whose favour the court proposes to make the order, for example a person with such a child arrangements order;
- when the court is considering an application made by a child over 18, it will look at the financial position of the parents of the child as well the applicant for the order; and
- when the court is asked to make an order against a person who is not the parent of the child, for example a step-parent or former step-parent, it will in addition have regard to matters set out in Sch 1, para 4(2). These concern the degree of the assumption of responsibility, whether this was in the knowledge that the child was not his, and the liability of any other person to maintain the child.

Note that the definition of 'parent' for these purposes, will include any party to a marriage, whether or not that marriage is still subsisting, in relation to whom the child is or was a child of the family. It will not include parties who cohabit, and so under Sch 1 one cohabitant will have no liability for the children of the other cohabitant alone.

[1] MCA 1973, s 25(1).
[2] CA 1989, s 1(1).
[3] [1999] 1 FLR 152.
[4] [2003] 2 FLR 865.

The court's approach

PERIODICAL PAYMENTS

5.60 An order for periodical payments will only be made if the CMS does not have jurisdiction, or where the court retains a residual jurisdiction under CSA 1991, ss 8(6)–(8) and so in practice such applications tend to be limited either to cases where the paying party is particularly affluent, or special circumstances apply.

An order in favour of a child can reflect the contribution of the parent with care to the child's upbringing by including an allowance for that parent[1].

5.60 *Children*

The starting point in any top-up application is the calculation under the child support formula. Any departure from that formula must be justified[2].

In *W v J (Child: variation of financial provision)*[3] Bennett J held that there was no jurisdiction to make an allowance for the legal fees of one parent in an order for periodical payments, even though the application had been brought for the benefit of the child. However, since then the courts have begun to recognise the need for there to be equality of arms between parties to these applications.

In *MT v T*[4] Charles J made an allowance for legal costs in an application for interim periodical payments. This was on the basis that since the application was brought by the mother effectively on behalf of and for the benefit of the child, she was acting in a quasi-fiduciary or representative capacity and should not have to bear the costs personally.

In *G v G*[5] Moylan J made an award of interim periodical payments of £40,000 as a contribution to the costs of the applicant mother. The court held that there was jurisdiction to make such an order under Sch 1 if it was considered appropriate to do so for the benefit of the children. In that case Moylan J took the view that it would be of benefit to the children if the mother were properly represented. It was relevant to his decision that there was a significant financial imbalance between the parents, the applicant was conducting the litigation in an entirely responsible way, and the respondent could well afford to pay.

In *CF v KM*[6] the question arose as to whether the court had the jurisdiction to make interim provision for legal costs where there had as yet been no determination by CMEC as to the non-resident parent's liability to pay the maximum assessment. In practice, applications for periodical payments, interim or otherwise, and for costs allowances within such provision, will be confined to those cases in which the court retains jurisdiction, generally where there is power to make a top-up order. In this case Charles J determined the issue by making a lump sum order sufficient to cover the applicant's legal costs. The basis for the decision was that there was nothing in Sch 1, para 9 to prevent the court from making a lump sum order other than on a final basis in cases in which the court did not retain the jurisdiction to make a periodical payments order. It was of course necessary for the court to find, which it did in that case, that on a balance of probabilities it would benefit the child if the mother had legal representation in both the Sch 1 and s 8 proceedings.

In *PG v TW (No 1)*[7] Theis J ordered interim provision for costs of £80,000, together with a further £27,000 which would only fall to be paid if the father did not withdraw his strike out application. It is interesting to note that in the substantive hearing that followed (*PG v TW (No 2)*[8]) HHJ Horowicz ordered that the mother's costs be met by the father in full on an indemnity basis because to leave the mother with unpaid legal fees would have had an impact on the child's welfare[9].

In *BC v DE*[10] the issue before the court was whether the extremely wealthy father should be ordered to pay outstanding costs for the mother's Sch 1 and s 8 proceedings amounting to £141,269.18, in addition to prospective costs of

£154,245. Cobb J was concerned with achieving equality of arms. He took the view that significant outstanding legal costs results in solicitor and client becoming 'beholden' to one another and may well [22] 'impact on the freedom of, and relative strengths within, their professional relationship . . . Further, the debt may materially influence the client's stance on possible settlement, and the solicitor's advice in relation to the same'. The father was ordered to pay £212,438.78.

Although a principle has therefore been established that the court has power under Sch 1 to make an allowance for costs by way of an interim periodical payments or lump sum order, in exercising its discretion the court will always be mindful that the pursuit of the substantive claim must be for the benefit of the child and not to satisfy the applicant's desire to litigate.

[1] *Haroutunian v Jennings* (1980) 1 FLR 62, followed in *A v A* [1994] 1 FLR 657; *P (a child) (financial provision)* [2003] EWCA Civ 837; *FG v MBW (Financial Remedy for Child)* [2012] 1 FLR 152.
[2] *GW v RW (Financial Provision: Departure from Equality)* [2003] 2 FLR 108; *Re: TW & TM (Minors)* [2015] EWHC 3054 (Fam).
[3] [2004] 2 FLR 300.
[4] [2007] 2 FLR 925.
[5] [2009] EWHC 2080 (Fam).
[6] [2011] 1 FLR 208.
[7] [2014] 1 FLR 508.
[8] [2014] 1 FLR 923.
[9] So following the approach of Peter Hughes QC in *H v M* (unreported) which went unchallenged when the case reached the Court of Appeal as *Morgan v Hill* [2007] 1 FLR 1480.
[10] [2016] EWHC 1806 (Fam).

LUMP SUM

5.61 There is no limit to the size, or indeed number, of lump sum orders that may be made in the Family Court[1].

A lump sum order may be payable by instalments, and although the size of the lump sum cannot be varied, the size and frequency of the instalments may be.

It is not possible to order a lump sum payable by instalments as a back door route to a periodical payments order[2].

In *Phillips v Peace*[3] although the court could not make an order for income provision for the child against the very rich father who had arranged his financial affairs so that the assessment of the Child Support Agency (as it was then) was nil, the court made a lump sum order that took into account the medical costs associated with the birth, the equipping of the nursery and the cost of furnishing a new flat for the mother and child to live in. The total lump sum awarded was just short of £25,000. In addition, a settlement of £90,000 was ordered to enable a suitable flat to be purchased on trust, the terms of the trust being to provide a home for the child until she finished university, and thereafter the mother to have the right to buy the property from the trustees at the market value. Although the lump sum included a small sum to reimburse the mother for the cost of registering the child at a private school, the mother's claim for the cost of private education was rejected on the basis that it was too early at that stage to make any decision about what would best suit the child's needs. This would not preclude a further application for lump sum provision to cover school fees at a later stage.

In reaching his decision as to the level of provision, Johnson J took into account that whilst the child was the daughter of a rich and successful businessman and would have had a certain standard of living commensurate with that had her parents lived together, her mother with whom she would live was of modest means, claiming income support.

In *J v C (Child: Financial Provision)*[4] the father of a child born after the breakdown of his relationship with the mother to whom he was never married, won £1.4m on the national lottery. The mother applied for lump sum, transfer and settlement of property orders to benefit the child.

The court made it clear that it attached little weight to the length or the quality of the parents' relationship (short and turbulent), nor to the fact that the windfall was received over a year after the relationship ended[5]:

> 'Parents are responsible for their children throughout their dependency. The fact that such riches as they have came after the breakup of the relationship cannot affect that. This case is not the same as Phillips v Peace where the parents came from two very different backgrounds, or what in the olden days used to be called "stations in life". These two parents are reasonably equivalent . . . There is a further point of public policy that, where resources allow, the family obligation should be respected in such a way as to reduce, or even eliminate, the need for children to be supported by public funds.'

Accordingly an order was made requiring the father to buy a four-bedroomed house for the child to live in with her mother and half sisters. The property would be held on trust for the child's benefit during her dependency and would revert to her father thereafter. The mother's cohabitation or remarriage would not affect the situation. There was also lump sum provision to enable the mother to buy a car and furnish the new property.

The court was at pains to ensure that no element of the child's income needs was reflected in the lump sum, as this would offend against the principle of the CSA 1991.

In *B v V (Children: Financial Provision: Unmarried Parents)*[6] the parties had cohabited for 3 years and had a child, aged four at the date of the hearing. The father's income was about £38,000 and he had capital assets of about £174,000. The mother had the care of the child. She did not work, but the judge found that she had a part-time earning capacity. The mother had no assets. The judge ordered payment of a lump sum of £55,000 to enable the mother to purchase a small flat, leaving it up to her to improve on that by fulfilling her earning capacity. The property was to be held on trust until the child reached 21 years or finished full-time education, whichever was later, at which point the proportion contributed by the father would revert to him.

In *Re P (Child: Financial Provision)*[7] the parents of a 2 year-old child were not married and had not lived together. The father had unlimited resources and a

Law and Practice **5.62**

lifestyle that reflected this. He had told the trial judge that he could afford to pay £10m if required to do so. The mother came from an affluent background but had little or no earning capacity.

The court at first instance made an order for an allowance of £450,000 for a house, a lump sum of £30,000 for furnishings, £20,000 for a car and periodical payments of £35,360 per annum, to be reduced by £9,333 on the child's 7th birthday.

The mother's appeal against the housing allowance and periodical payments was allowed and an order was made for a housing fund of £1m, £100,000 for interior decoration and periodical payments of £70,000 per annum.

Thorpe LJ set out his view as to the approach the court should take where both of the parents were affluent, although similar principles would apply in other cases. The starting point would be the provision and equipping of a home, then any lump sum and finally a 'broad common-sense assessment' of the budget that the applicant would need to maintain the home and lifestyle. He acknowledged that in cases in which there was sufficient money available to take into account the parent's needs as the carer of the child, this set up a tension between the parents, the paying party tending to resist any payment that may confer an incidental benefit on the carer. In determining all these matters Thorpe LJ expressed the view that it was necessary to[8]:

> 'recognise the responsibility, and often the sacrifice, of the unmarried parent (generally the mother) who is to be the primary carer for the child . . . In order to discharge this responsibility the carer must have control of a budget that reflects her position and the position of the father, both social and financial. On the one hand she should not be burdened with unnecessary financial anxiety or have to resort to parsimony when the other parent chooses to live lavishly. On the other hand whatever is provided is to be spent at the expiration of the year . . . There can be no slack to . . . fund a pension . . . or otherwise to put money away for a rainy day.'

In *MT v OT*[9] the mother made a second application for twins aged 17. The father ran the 'millionaires defence'. It was ordered that further lump sums be paid to enable the mother to move house and pay off her debts. In additional the father was ordered to increase the sums secured for periodical payments, school fees, tertiary education and legal fees.

1   *CF v KM* [2011] 1 FLR 208.
2   *Phillips v Peace* [1996] 2 FLR 230.
3   [1996] 2 FLR 230.
4   [1999] 1 FLR 152.
5   Per Hale J at 160B–D.
6   Current Law September 1999, para 248.
7   [2003] 2 FLR 865.
8   At para 49.
9   [2018] EWHC 868 (Fam).

TRANSFER OR SETTLEMENT OF PROPERTY

5.62 In many cases the main purpose of an application under Sch 1 will be to secure a home for the benefit of the child and the applicant. Where provision

5.62 *Children*

for a child under Sch 1 includes an allowance for housing, the court tends to take the view that the provision is to be for the child during his minority, and only exceptionally will provision be carried beyond a child's 18th birthday or the completion of full-time tertiary education.

In practice, this means that any property that is transferred for the benefit of a child will usually revert to the transferor when the child reaches 18, or ceases full-time education, whichever occurs first[1].

The question of how long property could be settled for the benefit of a child was considered by Munby J, as he then was, in *Re N (Payments for benefit of child)*[2]. In that case the respondent father successfully appealed the decision of the district judge to settle property until the child was 21. The court held that in the absence of the circumstances set out in Sch 1[3], orders for financial provision for children cannot extend beyond their minority. This means the child's 18th birthday, in the absence of special circumstances or completion of the child's tertiary education. The latter could include a gap year either before or after university.

The definition of 'property' will include a tenancy. Before Pt IV of the FLA 1996 came into force, applications for the transfer of a tenancy for the benefit of a child were frequently used as an incidental means of securing accommodation for the parent with care[4].

However, whilst there may remain cases to which Sch 1 to the CA 1989 will be appropriate, it is likely that most cohabitants will now seek an outright transfer of tenancy under the provisions of s 53 of and Sch 7 to the FLA 1996[5].

Alternatively, in appropriate circumstances, an occupation order may be made under Pt IV of the FLA 1996[6].

1   *H v P (Illegitimate Child: Capital Provision)* [1993] Fam Law 515; *A v A (A Minor: Financial Provision)* [1994] 1 FLR 657; *T v S (Financial Provision for Children)* [1994] 2 FLR 883; *Phillips v Peace* [1996] 2 FLR 230; *J v C (Child: Financial Provision)* [1999] 1 FLR 152.
2   [2009] 1 FLR 1442.
3   Schedule 1, paras 2, 3 and 6.
4   *K v K (Minors: Property Transfer)* [1992] 2 FLR 220.
5   See **1.209**.
6   See **4.18**.

INTERIM ORDERS

5.63 The court has power to make an interim order for periodical payments that will expire no later than the final determination of the substantive application.

VARIATION OF ORDERS

5.64 Orders for periodical payments, secured or otherwise, may be varied on the application of the payer or payee.

The amount of a lump sum order may not be varied, but where the lump sum is payable by instalments the frequency and amount of the instalments may be varied.

However, there is no prohibition on subsequent applications for further lump sum orders[1].

[1] See *MT v OT* [2018] EWCH 868 (Fam).

TERMINATION OF PAYMENTS

5.65 Dependency of a child is the likely arbiter of termination of payments in private agreements or where an order has been made under CA 1989, Sch 1. Each agreement should have its own terms incorporated into it.

Dependency is expressed in statutory terms as not extending past the child's seventeenth birthday 'unless the court thinks it right in the circumstances'[1]; and in any event not beyond the child's eighteenth birthday (para 3(1)(b))[2]. It can be extended beyond 18, however, in the case of a child's continuing in education or training[3] or in 'special circumstances'[4].

Child support maintenance terminates when the qualifying child ceases to be a 'child' under s 55 (see above) or in a variety of more or less technical circumstances set out in CSA 1991, Sch 1, para 16. Some para 16 conditions beg the question in issue: for example, para 16(1)(b) provides for termination where there are no longer any qualifying children; but this demands the reader's ability to detect, say, that where jurisdiction of the CMS ceases under s 44 (habitual residence of one or more of qualifying children, PWC or NRP outside UK) then the child is no longer a qualifying child.

A change to a child's living arrangements may warrant termination of payments. In *Re C (A child: Schedule 1 Children Act variation)*[5] the judge terminated an order of payments of £5,500 per month to the mother and reduced the settlement of property order from £700,000 plus SDLT to £200,000 plus SDLT. The child shared his time between his father in Canada and mother in England. However, he was diagnosed with autistic spectrum disorder following the first set of Sch 1 proceedings. In s 8 proceedings the court ordered the child live with the father and spend time with the mother in Canada (at the father's expense) and England.

[1] CA 1989, Sch 1 para 3(1)(a).
[2] CA 1989, Sch 1 para 3(1)(b).
[3] CA 1989, Sch 1 para 3(2)(a).
[4] CA 1989, Sch 1 para 3(2)(b).
[5] [2018] All ER (D) 32 (Aug).

TERMINATION BY RESUMPTION OF COHABITATION

5.66 As mentioned above maintenance terminates on resumption of cohabitation by operation of law; and by operation of any agreement in the case of a private agreement. As far as is known, the common law does not imply a term for duration of cohabitation to cause termination by resumption of cohabitation.

5.67 *Children*

Enforcement of financial provision orders

5.67 This book can deal only briefly with the subject of enforcement of orders and agreements (mostly, though not exclusively, for child maintenance). More detail and appropriate references can be found in *The Family Court Practice*.

ENFORCEMENT OF PAYMENT OF CHILD MAINTENANCE ARREARS AND OTHER FINANCIAL PROVISION

5.68 Enforcement of arrears and other payments as between cohabitants may be under three schemes according to the nature of the underlying statutory basis for payment:

(1) by civil claim in restitution or contract where there is a private agreement;
(2) by statutory enforcement of statutory provision and orders under Family Procedure Rules 2010 Pt 33 (with Civil Procedure Rules 1998 Pts 70 to 73); and
(3) by the CSA or CMS only under CSA 1991, ss 28–40 (this part of the 1991 Act was extensively amended and extended by CMOPA 2008).

The schemes for enforcement are divided irreconcilably (in procedural terms) between the private law remedies available at (1) and (2) and the public or administrative law scheme under (3).

The introduction of the single Family Court in April 2014 went some way towards simplifying the process for applicants wishing to enforce child maintenance orders, with a new single point of entry for all family law applications. Nevertheless, the options and complexity can remain overwhelming. The Law Commission report on the enforcement of family financial orders was issued on 15 December 2016 and in August 2018 the Government committed to introducing a free-standing comprehensive procedure for enforcement within the FPR.

ENFORCEMENT OF ARREARS OF CHILD SUPPORT MAINTENANCE FOLLOWING AN ASSESSMENT BY CMS

5.69 Arrears of child support maintenance can be pursued only by the CSA/CMS and the recipient parent has no involvement in the process. As a very last resort any serious failure on the part of the CSA or CMS may be addressed by an application for judicial review and/or a claim for maladministration.

A parent with care who wishes to sidestep the CSA enforcement machinery must dispense altogether with the child support scheme. However, the arrears that have accrued under the CSA maintenance liability can never be the subject of the enforcement proceedings brought by the parent with care. Only those arrears that have accrued from the date of any request 'to cease acting' (CSA 1991, s 4(5)) and payments thereafter can be enforced outside the statutory regime. In *Kehoe*[1] the House of Lords made it clear that there can be no cross-over between the private and the administrative schemes.

[1] R *(on the application of Kehoe) v Secretary of State for Work and Pensions* [2005] UKHL 48, [2006] 1 AC 42, [2005] 4 All ER 905, [2005] 3 WLR 252.

ENFORCEMENT OF CHILD PERIODICAL PAYMENTS

5.70 By contrast with payments due under a CMS assessment, there are no restrictions upon the payee of an order made under CA 1989, Sch 1 to take any necessary enforcement steps.

These orders may be for substantive provision or a top-up order[1]. In the latter case the Family Court has jurisdiction to back-date the payment of that order according to the earlier of the first effective date of the calculation (which can be many months, even years before) or 6 months prior to the CA 1989, Sch 1 application[2]. This in itself creates potential for arrears which may remain unpaid[3]:

(1) Civil Procedure Rules 1998 – where there is an agreement (oral or written) a parent must first obtain an order by the CPR Pt 8 procedure before that order can be enforced. The usual civil means of enforcement are then available upon application (see Tables below).
(2) Family Procedure Rules 2010 – for orders made under CA 1989, Sch 1 the applicant has the range of enforcement methods available under FPR Pt 33 (see tables and enforcement in the Family Court below).

[1] CSA 1991, s 8(6)–(8).
[2] CA 1989, Sch 1, para 3(5) and (6); and see *Re P (Child; Financial Provision)* [2003] 2 FLR 865, CA.
[3] See eg *H v C* [2009] 2 FLR 1540.

ENFORCEMENT PROCEDURES FOR FINANCIAL PROVISION AND CHILD MAINTENANCE

5.71 Tables 1 and 2 list the main forms of application for enforcement (including reference to the MEA 1991) arising in proceedings between cohabitants. Parallel child support maintenance enforcement under CSA 1991 is referred to; and reference to lump sum and capital orders (charging orders and orders for sale) is included briefly. Enforcement of arrears of child periodical payments may become necessary by charging order and sale of property (CPR 73.10).

USING THE TABLES

5.72 Table 1 lists the main forms of financial provision likely to be covered by agreements and orders in this book. It then lists in reference figures codes for the forms of enforcement available in respect of each. Parallel forms of child support maintenance enforcement (CSA 1991) are also given.

Table 2 lists each of the codes referred to in Table 1 and sets out the source reference for the form of enforcement, the procedural rules reference and the

5.72 Children

court in which enforcement is available. Some levels of the judiciary have limited powers to order enforcement remedies[1].

Table 1 – Enforceable forms of agreement and order: child maintenance and lump sums: procedure under which enforcement proceeds

Enforceable order	Family proceedings (covered by FPR)	Family proceedings (covered by CPR)	Child support maintenance (CSA 1991)
Agreed child maintenance		(2)(3)	
Periodical payments order (no default)	(1)(1A)(1B)		
Periodical payments orders (default)	(1)(1A)(1B)(3)		(3A)(3B)
(1) Lump sum; and (2) Arrears of periodical payments (accumulated)[a]	(4)(5)(6)(7)(8)	(4)(5)(6)(7)(8)	(4A)(4B)(5A)(6A)(7)(8A)
Enforcement of charging order by foreclosure and order for sale	(9)	(9)	(9)

[a] In the case of periodical payments orders under MCA 1973 and CA 1989, Sch 1 permission is needed to enforce arrears more than a year old (MCA 1973, s 32: there appears to be no equivalent provision in CA 1989, Sch 1).

Table 2 – Main forms of enforcement of orders for payments of child maintenance and for payment of lump sums or accumulated arrears of child maintenance

	Form of enforcement	Statutory or other source	Procedure	Court for issue of enforcement proceedings
1	Payment by standing order or direct debit on nominated bank account	Maintenance Enforcement Act 1991	(1) By consent (as part of order); or (2) as FPR Pt 18 application	High court or family court
1A	Payment into court	Maintenance Enforcement Act 1991	FPR Pt 18 application	Family court
1B	Collection through CMS/CSA	Maintenance Enforcement Act 1991	FPR Pt 18 application	Family court
2	Breach of contract	Common law	CPR Pt 8	County court

Law and Practice 5.72

	Form of enforcement	Statutory or other source	Procedure	Court for issue of enforcement proceedings
3	Attachment of earnings	Attachment of Earnings Act 1971	County Court Rules 1981, Order 27 (found in CPR, Sch 2); in family proceedings as applied by FPR 33.19A	High court (for high court orders) or family court (for high court or family court orders)
3A	Deduction from earnings order(+)a	CSA 1991, s 31	Appeal: Child Support (Collection and Enforcement) Regulations 1992, reg 22	Appeal: family court
3B	Regular deduction order (+)	CSA 1991, s 32A	Appeal: Child Support (Collection and Enforcement) Regulations 1992, reg 25AB	Appeal: family court
4	Charging order	Charging Orders Act 1979	CPR Pt 73 (in FPR proceedings per and as amended by FPR 33.25)	High court, family court or county courtb
4A	Charging order: child support maintenance only	CSA 1991, s 36	CPR Pt 73	County court
4B	Lump sum deduction order (+);	CSA 1991, ss 32E–32H	Appeal: Child Support (Collection and Enforcement) Regulations 1992, reg 25AB	Appeal: family court
5	Third party debt order	Common law (and see Senior Courts Act, s 40)	CPR Pt 72 (in FPR proceedings: per and as amended by FPR 33.24)	As for 4 Charging order above
5A	Third party debt order: child support maintenance only	CSA 1991, s 36	CPR Pt 72	County court

387

5.72 *Children*

	Form of enforcement	Statutory or other source	Procedure	Court for issue of enforcement proceedings
6	*Parasitic enforcement orders* Avoidance of disposition Restraint of disposal Freezing (*Mareva*) orders	(a) MCA 1973, s 37(2)(a) and (c)^c; (b) MCA 1973, s 37(2)(b) (c) Common law; and see Civil Procedure Act 1997, s 7	CPR Pts 23 and 25; FPR Pts 18 and 20	Court where order made
6A	Orders preventing avoidance	CSA 1991, s 32L	FPR 8.35–40	High court or family court
7	Taking control of goods	Powers in civil courts and under CSA 1991, s 35		
8	Judgment summons	Debtors Act 1869, s 5	FPR 33.9–33.18	High court or family court
8A	Committal	CSA 1991, ss 39A and 40	Child Support (Collection and Enforcement) Regulations 1992	Magistrates court (civil proceedings)
9	Foreclosure and sale	Common law	CPR 73.10C	Originating application (CPR Pt 8) in court where order made.

^a These 'orders' (indicated by (+)) are imposed by administrative direction, and are not orders in the conventional 'court order' sense of the word in the rest of this table: they are appealed against to the court: DEO – to a magistrates' court (or by judicial review); RDO and LSDO – to the county court.

^b Which one is prescribed at COA 1979, s 1(2).

^c There is no equivalent power to MCA, s 37(2) in CA 1989, Sch 1; and in the light of such cases as *Wicks v Wicks* [1998] 1 FLR 470, CA it is unlikely the court would assume an inherent jurisdiction. In certain circumstances a freezing order may be available; but it may be necessary to transfer to the High Court if this remedy is sought.

[1] Family Court (Composition and Distribution of Business) Rules 2014 (SI 2014/840), Sch 2.

PROCEDURES AVAILABLE IN THE HIGH COURT AND FAMILY COURT FOR ENFORCEMENT

5.73 FPR 33.3 has provided a procedure, new to family proceedings, which enables an applicant in the High Court or Family Court[1] to opt in his or her application to leave it to the court to decide on 'such method of enforcement as the court may consider appropriate'. The rules use the term 'judgment creditor' for the person 'entitled to enforce a judgment or order'; and 'judgement debtor' is the person against whom the order was made[2]. FPR 33.2 applies CPR Pt 70 to family proceedings. This rule applies throughout Pt 33 where application is made for enforcement of an order for payment of money.

Law and Practice 5.73

The CPR Practice Direction 70 – Enforcement of judgments and orders at para 1.1 summarises the forms of enforcement as follows:

'A judgment creditor may enforce a judgment or order for the payment of money by any of the following methods:
(1) a writ of *control* or warrant of control (see Part 83 and Part 84);
(2) a third party debt order (see Part 72);
(3) a charging order, stop order or stop notice (see Part 73);
(4) in a county court, an attachment of earnings order (see Part 89);
(5) the appointment of a receiver (see Part 69).'

Of these, (2), (3) and (4) will be considered here. Application for enforcement of an order for payment of money is made as follows:

(1) By any means of enforcement available to him/her[3] from the list set out above (either as specified in the application or by such means as 'the court may consider appropriate')[4].
(2) By appropriate notice of application.
(3) Accompanied by a statement (verified by a statement of truth) which shows the amount due under the order and how that amount is calculated[5].

A judgment creditor who applies for enforcement by one of these means can apply by more than one means of enforcement and do so 'either at the same time or [by one means] after another'[6]. Plainly a judgment creditor can only be paid once; but cumulatively that can be by more than one method of enforcement.

Rule 33.3(2)(b) leaves it open to a judgment creditor to apply for enforcement, but leaves it to the court to decide by what means enforcement should proceed. Thus, if a judgment creditor asks the court to decide what method of enforcement the court considers appropriate:

(1) 'An order to attend court will be issued' and CPR 71.2(6) and (7)[7] apply.
(2) The order to attend will be endorsed with a penal notice[8], and, though the rules do not say so, it will presumably have to be served personally (the rules do not give any indication as to by whom or at whose expense).
(3) The judgment debtor will be required to attend court and to produce there such 'documents in his control [as] are described in the order [to attend court]'[9].
(4) The judgment debtor will be required at court to answer such questions on oath as are put to him by the court[10].

There appears to be no requirement that the judgment creditor attend nor that s/he can ask questions or make submissions as to the means of enforcement once evidence has been heard. Presumably questions could be put through the judge in any event; and the court would not refuse to hear how enforcement could be achieved in the view of the creditor. The final decision is for the court[11]: a novel departure leaving the court, in effect, to advise on disposal and

5.73 Children

then to dispose of the case (no adjudication is involved, since no issue is before the court) on the basis of its own advice.

1. FPR 33.1(1).
2. CPR 70.1(2).
3. CPR 70.2(2)(a).
4. FPR 33.3(2)(b): see below.
5. FPR 33.3(1)(a).
6. CPR 70.2(2)(b).
7. CPR 71.2 as a whole applies where a judgment creditor applies for a judgment debtor to attend court to give information as to his means or about his ability to pay a judgment (r 71.2(1)). This para of r 71.2 has not been applied to family proceedings.
8. CPR 71.2(7).
9. CPR 71.2(6)(a) and (b).
10. CPR 71.2(6)(c).
11. FPR 33.3(2)(b).

Registration for enforcement in the Family Court

5.74 The Maintenance Orders Act 1958 (MOA 1958) aims to enable certain orders[1] to be registered in the Family Court for enforcement purposes. Application is made in the originating court which, if it so decides, may order registration in the payer's court[2].

Application for enforcement proceeds in the Family Court; and any variation of maintenance application can be dealt with there[3]. Collection of arrears and current payments can be arranged through the Family Court.

1. Primarily orders made in the High Court, but the list does include orders made in the magistrates' court under DPMCA 1978, Pt I, see AJA 1970, Sch 8.
2. MOA 1958, s 2(1).
3. MOA 1958, ss 1(1), 4 and 4A.

Part B   PROCEDURAL GUIDES

Scientific test direction

Legal background

5.75 In any civil proceedings in which an issue as to parentage arises, a party may apply to the court for a direction for the use of scientific tests or bodily samples to determine the issue, or the court may, on its own initiative, issue such a direction (FLRA 1969, s 20(1)). An application cannot be made on a freestanding basis but only in existing proceedings (eg FLA 1986, s 55A, CA 1989, s 9 or CSA 1991, s 27, TOLATA 1996, s 14 or under I(PFD)A 1975). The court issues a direction (see also *Re H (Paternity: Blood Test)*[1]). No sample can be taken without consent (FLRA 1969, s 21(1)) or by direction of the court where a person having care and control of a child refuses consent (FLRA 1969, s 21(3)): failure to comply with a direction enables the court to draw such inferences as appear proper in the circumstances of the particular case (FLRA 1969, s 23(1)). Procedure is governed by CPR PD 23B imported into family proceedings by the FPR PD that describes those practice directions relating to family proceedings in force before 6 April 2011 that support the FPR,

Procedural Guides 5.76

para 2.1: although no procedure is prescribed by CPR PD 23B the fact that it accompanies CPR Pt 23 implies that in family proceedings its equivalent, Pt 18, would apply.

A child under 16 or who lacks capacity acts by a 'responsible adult' as defined in CPR PD 23B, para 1.1(3).

1   [1996] 2 FLR 65, CA.

Procedure

5.76

Who may apply	Any party to the proceedings; or the court on own initiative	FLRA 1969, s 20(1)
The proceedings	Any civil proceedings in which parentage is in issue	FLRA 1969, s 20(1)
The application	By FPR Pt 18 procedure application notice (Form D11)	FPR 18.1(2)(a)
	The application must specify who is to carry out the tests	FLRA 1969, s 20(1A)
	If application is regarding (1) a person under 16 or (2) who is a protected party (per FPR Pt 15), the name and address of the responsible adult must be given	CPR PD 23B, para 1.2
Respondent/Other parties	(1) All other parties to the existing proceedings (2) Anyone else from whom samples may be required	See, for example, FPR 8.20 for declarations under r 8.18
Notice	(1) FPR proceedings: 7 days before hearing	FPR 18.8(1)(b)(ii)
	(2) CPR proceedings: 3 days before hearing	CPR 23.7(1)(b)
Joinder	Application for joinder in proceedings: (1) FPR proceedings	No procedure: quaere on analogy with CPR procedure (per *Goldstone v Goldstone & ors*[a])
	(2) CPR proceedings	CPR 19.2
Direction	Court gives a direction in form proposed in *Re H*	*Re H*[b]
	The name of the tester must be included in the direction	
Service of direction	By the court (1) on parties to proceedings	CPR PD 23B, para 1.4(1)
	(2) anyone from whom sample is to be taken	CPR PD 23B, para 1.4(2)
Report	Made to the court by the tester	FLRA 1969, s 20(2)

	Report in form prescribed by Blood Tests (Evidence of Paternity) Regs 1971	FLRA 1969, ss 20(3), 22
	Served by the court on (1) parties to proceedings, (2) responsible adult (as applicable) and (3) anyone from whom sample to be taken	CPR PD 23B, para 1.5
Fees and costs	Fee for report payable by applicant for direction; but treated as costs in the main proceedings	FLRA 1969, s 20(6)

a [2011] EWCA Civ 39.
b [1996] 2 FLR 65 at 83.

Parental responsibility order (or discharge of the same or parental responsibility agreement)

Legal background

5.77 Parental responsibility comprises all the rights, duties, powers, responsibilities and authority which, by law, a parent has in relation to a child and his property, or which a guardian of a child's estate has in relation to his property (CA 1989, s 3).

A child's mother always has parental responsibility for the child; however, if they were not married to (or in a civil partnership with) the child's father at the time of the birth, the father will only acquire parental responsibility by marrying (or entering an civil partnership with) the mother, by making a formal parental responsibility agreement with them (using Form C(PRA1)) or by obtaining an order from the court (CA 1989, s 4, to be read in conjunction with FLRA 1987, s 1(2)) or if his name is placed on the birth certificate at registration or re-registration of the birth under the Births and Deaths Registration Act 1953 (see CA 1989, s 4(1)(a)). A step-parent may acquire parental responsibility for a child of his spouse or civil partner by agreement (using Form C(PRA2)), or by order of the court (CA 1989, s 4A). A second female parent (if not married to or in civil partnership with the mother, or later marries or enters a civil partnership with them) may acquire responsibility for a child by agreement (using Form C(PRA3)) or by order of the court (CA 1989, s 4ZA). The court must make such an order where it makes a residence order in favour of the father or second female parent (CA 1989, s 12(1)) and care should therefore be taken to consider this requirement when making or opposing an interim residence application; otherwise, it is in the court's discretion whether to grant a specific application under CA 1989, s 4 and s 4ZA.

On making an application to the court, the applicant should also file a completed Form FM1 confirming attendance at a mediation information and assessment meeting or giving reasons for not attending (FPR PD 3A, Annex A).

The court may subsequently revoke such an order and also a parental responsibility agreement (which may not be revoked merely by agreement).

Procedure

5.78

Who may apply	Father without parental responsibility	CA 1989, s 4(1)(c)
	The spouse or civil partner of a parent with parental responsibility	CA 1989, s 4A
	The second female parent of a child	CA 1989, s 4ZA; HFEA 2008, s 43
Which court	Family court (lay justices) if none of the criteria in the schedule to the *Guidance* apply	CA 1989, s 10(1); FC(CDB)R 2014; President's Guidance *Allocation and Gatekeeping*
	Proceedings can be transferred sideways, upwards or downwards, using order in Form C49	FC(CDB)R 2014
Which proceedings	Freestanding application	CA 1989, s 4(1), s 4ZA(1)
	Court must make order on making a child arrangements order that the child shall live with the second parent without parental responsibility even if no specific application is made; it has a discretion whether or not to make a parental responsibility order where the child is to have contact with the second parent	CA 1989, s 12(1)
Application	On Form C1 (or Forms C(PRA1), C(PRA2) or C(PRA3) as appropriate), together with Form FM1, with sufficient copies for each respondent. Where it is alleged that the child who is the subject of the application has suffered, or is at risk of suffering, any harm from (*a*) any form of domestic abuse; (*b*) violence within the household; (*c*) child abduction; or (*d*) other conduct or behaviour, supplemental Form C1A must also be completed	FPR PD 3A, PD 5A, PD 12B
	Fee: £215	FPFO 2008, Sch 1, fee 2.1(*a*), (*b*);

Respondents	Notice to be served in Form C6 on every person with parental responsibility and on every person with parental responsibility before care order	FPR 12.3
Additional persons to be served with notice of the proceedings	Notice to be served in Form C6A on local authority, if providing accommodation, and on person caring for child or providing refuge	FPR PD 12C, para 3.1
Service	Applicant must serve a copy of the application, together with Form C6 (endorsed with date fixed for hearing), on each respondent at least 14 days before the hearing; notice of the proceedings must be served in Form C6A (endorsed with date fixed for hearing) on other persons to be served at least 14 days before the hearing	FPR PD 12B, para 8.8; FPR PD 12C, para 2.1
	At or before first directions appointment or hearing, applicant must file statement in Form C9 to prove that requirements for service have been complied with	FPR 12.8
Answer to application	Respondent to an application must file a written answer and serve it on the other parties to the proceedings within 14 days of the date on which the application is served	FPR 12.32
Joinder or removal of parties	By court order, of its own initiative or on written request on Form C2 together with Form C1A if necessary (see under 'Application' above)	FPR 4.3, 12.3(3)
Directions	As to applications for directions, see —	FPR 12.12
	NB A written request for directions must be made on Form C2 and C1A if necessary (see under 'Application' above)	
	Directions which may be given (eg timetable for the proceedings, submission of evidence or transfer of proceedings to another court)	FPR 12.12

	Timing of proceedings	FPR 12.13
	Attendance at the directions hearing	FPR 12.14
Order	Conferring parental responsibility on the father, spouse, civil partner or second female parent, Form C45	CA 1989, ss 4(1)(*a*), 12(1); FPR PD 12B
	Form C45, for termination of parental responsibility order or parental responsibility agreement	
Transitional arrangements	Implementation of CFA 2014	Children and Families Act 2014 (Transitional Proceedings) Order 2014

Appointment or removal of a guardian

Legal background

5.79 A guardian usually stands in the shoes of a parent when a child no longer has a parent with parental responsibility living (although one may also be appointed where a parent who had the benefit of a CAO dies regardless of whether the non-resident parent survives).

Under CA 1989, s 5, a guardian may be appointed in writing by a parent with parental responsibility, the appointment to take effect when he dies (if he has a CAO 'live with' order) or when the last surviving parent with parental responsibility dies. In default (or in addition), the court has a concurrent right of appointment. The court may also terminate (under CA 1989, s 6(7)) the appointment of a guardian, whether he had been appointed by the court or a parent.

On making an application to the court, the applicant should also file a completed Form FM1 confirming attendance at a mediation information and assessment meeting or giving reasons for not attending (FPR PD 3A, Annex A).

Procedure

5.80

Who may apply	*Appointment* Any person (the proposed guardian)	CA 1989, s 5(1)
	Removal Any person with parental responsibility or, with permission, the child	CA 1989, s 6(7)

5.80 Children

Which court	Family court (lay justices) if none of the criteria in the schedule to the *Guidance* apply	CA 1989, s 10(1); FC(CDB)R 2014; President's Guidance *Allocation and Gatekeeping*
	Proceedings can be transferred sideways, upwards or downwards, using order in Form C49	FC(CDB)R 2014
Which proceedings	Freestanding application; own initiative order in any family proceedings	CA 1989, s 5(1), (2), 6(7)
Application	*Appointment* On Form C1, together with Form FM1	FPR PD 3A, PD 5A
	Fee: £215	FPFO 2008, Sch 1, para 2.1(c);
	Removal On Form C1, together with Form FM1, with sufficient copies for each respondent	FPR 5.1; PD 3A, PD 5A, PD 12B
	Fee: £215	FPFO 2008, Sch 1, para 2.1(c);
Respondents	Notice to be served in Form C6 on every person with parental responsibility, every person with parental responsibility before a care order, and (on application to discharge court-appointed guardian) parties to the original proceedings	FPR 12.3
Additional persons to whom notice in Form C6A is to be given	Local authority, if providing accommodation Person caring for child or providing refuge If application is for appointment, father without parental responsibility	FPR PD 12C, para 3.1
Service	Applicant must serve a copy of the application, together with Form C6 (endorsed with date fixed for hearing), on each respondent at least 14 days before the hearing; notice of the proceedings must be served in Form C6A (endorsed with date fixed for hearing) on other persons to be served at least 14 days before the hearing	FPR PD 12C

	At or before first directions appointment or hearing, applicant must file statement in Form C9 to prove that requirements for service have been complied with	FPR 12.8, FPR PD 5A
Joinder of parties	By court order, of its own initiative or on written request on Form C2	FPR 4.3, 12.3(3)
Answer to application	Respondent must file a written answer and serve it on the other parties to the proceedings within 14 days of the date on which the application is served	FPR 12.32
Directions	Applications for directions	FPR 5.1; PD 5A, PD 12B
	NB A written request for directions must be made on Form C2	
	Directions which may be given (eg as to timetable for the proceedings, submission of evidence or transfer of proceedings to another court)	FPR 12.12
	Timing of proceedings	FPR 12.13
	Attendance at the directions hearing	FPR 12.14
Order	On Form C46, appointing a guardian, in which case the appointee assumes parental responsibility until the appointment is brought to an end by the court	CA 1989, ss 5(1), (6), 6(7); FPR PD 12B
	On Form C46, bringing to an end the appointment of a guardian under CA 1989, s 5 (whether made by the court or not)	CA 1989, s 6(7); FPR PD 12B
Transitional arrangements	Implementation of CFA 2014	Children and Families Act 2014 (Transitional Proceedings) Order 2014

Financial relief for a child under the Children Act 1989, Sch 1

Legal background

5.81 Subject to the provisions of CSA 1991, which leave the court with a limited role in ordering maintenance or variation of maintenance agreements in respect of children, CA 1989, Sch 1 provides three forms of financial relief for a child: first, para 1 enables a maintenance order, settlement and transfer of property order to be made in favour of a child against either or both of its parents; secondly, para 2 enables a periodical payments order and lump sum order to be made in favour of a child who has reached 18 where: (i) the child's parents are not living with each other, (ii) there was not in force a periodical payments order for the child immediately before he reached 16, and (iii) he is undergoing education or training or there are special circumstances (orders under both paras 1 and 2 may be varied or extended under para 6); and, thirdly, by paras 10 and 11, the court may vary a maintenance agreement containing financial arrangements for the child either during the lifetime of the parent or after the death of one of them. For the reasons set out under s 15, if a child's parents are married, the greater procedural powers that are available make it more advantageous for an application for financial relief against a parent by a child to be brought under MCA 1973, ss 23, 24 and 27 and for an alteration of a maintenance agreement to be brought under MCA 1973, ss 35 and 36; however, where the parents are not married, there is no jurisdiction apart from CA 1989, Sch 1.

An application under CA 1989, Sch 1 is defined as a financial remedy under FPR 2.3. The procedure under Pt 9 applies. The application may be made to the Family Court.

Procedure

5.82

Who may apply	*Application for child under 18*	CA 1989, Sch 1, para 1(1); FPR 9.10
	Parent or guardian or special guardian of child or person named in a child arrangements order as a person with whom a child is to live	
	The order will be made either on the application of the above or without an application on the making, varying or discharging of a child arrangements order	CA 1989, Sch 1, para 1(6)
	Application by child over 18 The child who is over 18 and:	
	who is or will be undergoing education or training or where there are special circumstances	CA 1989, Sch 1, para 2(1)(a), (b)
	who has not had in force a periodical payments order immediately before he was 16	CA 1989, Sch 1, para 2(3), (6)
	whose parents are not living together	CA 1989, Sch 1, para 2(4)

	Variation application Any of the persons set out above, with, additionally on an application under CA 1989, Sch 1, para 1, the child himself if he has reached 16	CA 1989, Sch 1, para 6(4)
	Application to alter maintenance agreement Either party to the agreement or a personal representative	CA 1989, Sch 1, paras 10(2), 11(1)
Application	Preliminary requirement for proposed parties to attend a MIAM before application, subject to exemptions.	CFA 2014, s 10(1); FPR 3.6, PD 3A
	To the Family Court	FPR 5.4
	The application is on Form A1/A together with any documents stated to be required or referred to in the application. Proceedings start when a court officer issues an application, and are issued on that date	FPR 5.1–5.3, PD 5A
	The application on Form A1 is dealt with under the 'fast-track' procedure in FPR Pt 9, Ch 5	FPR 9.18–9.20, PD 9A
	Either may seek a direction that the standard procedure in FPR Pt 9, Ch 4 is followed, for example where there are contested issues about the settlement of property. This is determined on paper without notice to the parties before the first hearing	FPR 9.18A
	The application on Form A is dealt with under the standard procedure in FPR Pt 9, Ch 4.	FPR 9.12–9.17, PD 9A
Fee	£215	FPFO 2008, fee 2.1(v)
Service	Within 4 days of the date on which the application was filed, a court officer will serve a copy of the application on the respondent and give notice of the date of the first hearing to both parties.	

5.82 *Children*

	Alternatively, the applicant must serve the respondent within 4 days, beginning with the date on which the copy of the application was received from the court, and file a certificate of service on or before the first appointment	FPR 9.12(1), (2) and r 9.18
Respondents	Any parent who is not an applicant, or both parents, where the holder of a residence order or special guardianship order applies	CA 1989, Sch 1, para 1(2)
Directions/Interim orders	The court may make an interim order for periodical payments. FPR Pt 18 procedure applies to applications for interim orders	CA 1989, Sch 1, para 9; FPR 9.7(2)
Procedure	Where the fast-track procedure under FPR Pt 9, Ch 5 applies	FPR 9.18A
	The court will fix a first appointment not less than 6 weeks and not more than 10 weeks after the filing of the application	FPR 9.18(1)(a)
	Not more than 21 days after the issue of the application, the parties must simultaneously exchange a financial statement on Form E1, accompanied by a limited category of documents. No disclosure or inspection of the parties' documents may be given between the filing of the application and the first appointment, save as laid down in FPR 9.19(4)	FPR PD 5A; FPR 9.19(1)
	Unless the court is able to determine the application at the first hearing, the court may direct further evidence and set a date for a directions hearing or final hearing	FPR 9.20
	Where the standard procedure under FPR Pt 9, Ch 4 applies	FPR 9.12–9.17

	The court will fix a first appointment not less than 12 weeks and not more than 16 weeks after the filing of the application	FPR 9.12(1)(a)
	Not less than 35 days before the first appointment both parties must simultaneously exchange a financial statement on Form E1, accompanied by a limited category of documents. No disclosure or inspection of the parties' documents may be given between the filing of the application and the first appointment, save as laid down in FPR 9.14(4)	FPR PD 5A; FPR 9.14(1)
	Not less than 14 days before the first appointment, each party must file and serve (i) statement of issues, chronology, questionnaire and Form G	FPR 9.14(5)
Order	*Application for child under 18* Periodical payments Secured periodical payments Lump sum Settlement of property or transfer of property *Application by child over 18* Periodical payments Lump sum *Application to alter maintenance agreement* Varying or revoking any financial arrangements contained in the maintenance agreement, including inserting provision for periodical payments or for security for increasing or decreasing the level of periodical payments	

5.83 Children

Part C PRECEDENTS

5.83

Form C1: Application for an Order

Application for an order   Form C1

Children Act 1989 except care and supervision orders, Section 8 orders and orders related to enforcement of a contact order.

If you are applying for a section 8 order or an order related to enforcement of a contact order you will need to use a different application form (Form C100 for Section 8 orders and Form C79 for enforcement). Booklet 'CB1 - Making an application - children and the family courts' gives more information. These leaflets are available from your local court or online at hmctsformfinder.justice.gov.uk.

If you are applying for one of the following private law Children Act 1989 orders you **must** file a separate completed FM1 form with this application:

- A parental responsibility order (sections 4(1)(c), 4ZA(1)(c) or 4A(1)(b) of the Children Act 1989) or an order terminating parental responsibility (sections 4(2A), 4ZA(5) or 4A(3) of that Act).
- An order appointing a child's guardian (section 5(1) of the Children Act 1989) or an order terminating the appointment (section 6(7) of that Act).
- An order giving permission to change a child's surname or remove a child from the United Kingdom (sections 13(1) or 14C of the Children Act 1989).
- A special guardianship order or an order varying or discharging such an order (section 14D of the Children Act 1989).

If you are applying for a care or supervision order, you will need to use Form C110A, which is available online at hmctsformfinder.justice.gov.uk.

Cafcass/CAFCASS CYMRU will carry out checks as it considers necessary.
Cafcass - Children and Family Court Advisory and Support Service (in England); CAFCASS CYMRU - Children and Family Court Advisory and Support Service Wales.

The family court sitting at	**To be completed by the court**
The full name(s) of the child(ren)	Date issued
	Case number
	Child(ren)'s number(s)

Important Note
You should only answer question 7 if you are applying for a Parental Responsibility Order.

1 About you (the person completing this form known as 'the applicant')

If you do not wish your address or telephone number to be made known to the respondent, leave the address details blank and complete Confidential contact details form C8. You can get a copy of this form from any family court office or from our website at hmctsformfinder.justice.gov.uk Please ensure that any documents submitted with this form or at a later date, do not include the confidential contact details you wish to withhold.

State:

- your title, full name, address, telephone number, date of birth and relationship to each child above
- your solicitor's name, address, reference, telephone, FAX and DX numbers.
  Solicitor's fee
  account no.

2 The child(ren) and the order(s) you are applying for

For each child state:
- the full name, date of birth and sex
- the type of order(s) you are applying for (for example, Parental Responsibility Order).

3 Other cases which concern the child(ren)

If there have ever been, or there are pending, any court cases which concern:
- a child whose name you have put in paragraph 2
- a full, half or step brother or sister of a child whose name you have put in paragraph 2
- a person in this case who is or has been, involved in caring for a child whose name you have put in paragraph 2

attach a copy of the relevant order and give:
- the name of the court
- the name and contact address (if known) of the children's guardian, if appointed
- the name and contact address (if known) of the children and family reporter, if appointed
- the name and contact address (if known) of the welfare officer, if appointed
- the name and contact address (if known) of the solicitor appointed for the child(ren).

4 The respondent(s)

Family Procedure Rules 2010, SI 2010/2955, 12.3

For each respondent state:
- the title, full name and address
- the date of birth (if known) or the age
- the relationship to each child.

5 Others to whom notice is to be given

Practice Direction 12c to the Family Procedure Rules 2010 - Service of application in certain proceedings relating to children

For each person state:
- the title, full name and address
- the date of birth (if known) or the age
- the relationship to each child.

6 The care of the child(ren)

For each child in paragraph 2 state:
- the child's current address and how long the child has lived there
- whether it is the child's usual address and who cares for the child there
- the child's relationship to the other children (if any).

5.83 Children

7   Domestic abuse, violence or harm

Do you believe that the child(ren) named above have suffered or are at risk of suffering any harm from any of the following:
- *any form of domestic abuse*
- *violence within the household*
- *child abduction*
- *other conduct or behaviour*

by any person who is or has been involved in caring for the child(ren) or lives with, or has contact with, the child(ren)?

Please tick the box which applies   ☐ Yes   ☐ No

If you tick the Yes box, you must also fill in Supplemental Information Form (form C1A). You can obtain a copy of this from a court office if one has not been enclosed with the papers served on you.

8   Social Services

For each child in paragraph 2 state:
- *whether the child is known to the Social Services. If so, give the name of the social worker and the address of the Social Services department.*
- *whether the child is, or has been, on the Child Protection Register. If so, give details of registration.*

9   The education and health of the child(ren)

For each child state:
- *the name of the school, college or place of training which the child attends*
- *whether the child is in good health. Give details of any serious disabilities or ill health.*
- *whether the child has any special needs.*

10   The parents of the child(ren)

For each child state:
- *the full name of the child's parents*
- *whether the parents are, or have been, married to each other or civil partners of each other*
- *whether the parents live together. If so, where.*
- *whether, to your knowledge, either of the parents have been involved in a court case concerning a child. If so, give the date and the name of the court.*

11   The family of the child(ren) (other children)

For any other child not already mentioned in the family (for example, a brother or half sister) state:
- *the full name and address*
- *the date of birth (if known) or age*
- *the relationship of the child to you.*

Precedents 5.83

12   Other adults
State:
- the full name of any other adults (for example, lodgers) who live at the same address as any child named in paragraph 2
- whether they live there all the time
- whether, to your knowledge, the adult has been involved in a court case concerning a child. If so, give the date and the name of the court.

13   Your reason(s) for applying and any plans for the child(ren)
State briefly your reasons for applying and what you want the court to order.
- ***Do not*** *complete this section if this form is accompanied by a supplementary form.*

14   Attending the court
State:
- whether you will need an interpreter at court. If so, please indicate what language and dialect you will use. If you require an interpreter you must notify the court immediately so that one can be arranged.
- whether you have a disability for which you require special assistance or special facilities. If so, please say what your needs are. The court staff will get in touch with you about your requirements.

15 Parenting Information - Arrangements after Separation

	Yes	No
Have you received a Parenting Plan booklet? *(If No, you may obtain a copy from a court office, a citizen's advice bureau or other family advice service.)*	☐	☐
Have you agreed to a Parenting Plan? *(If Yes, please include a copy of the Plan when you send your application to the court)*	☐	☐
If you did agree a Parenting Plan, has the Plan broken down?	☐	☐
If Yes, please explain briefly why the Plan broke down -		

Signed _____   Date _____

(Applicant)

[Sign and Lock >]

C1   Page 4 of 4

405

5.84 Children

5.84

Parental Responsibility Agreement

Parental Responsibility Agreement
Section 4(1)(b) Children Act 1989

Keep this form in a safe place
Date recorded at the Principal Registry of the Family Division:

Read the notes on the other side before you make this agreement.

This is a Parental Responsibility Agreement regarding

the Child   *Full name*

Gender   *Date of birth*   *Date of 18th birthday*

Between

the Mother   *Name*

Address

and   the Father   *Name*

Address

We declare that we are the mother and father of the above child and we agree that the child's father shall have parental responsibility for the child (in addition to the mother having parental responsibility).

Signed **(Mother)**   Signed **(Father)**

Date   Date

Certificate of witness

The following evidence of identity was produced by the person signing above:

The following evidence of identity was produced by the person signing above:

Signed in the presence of:
Name of Witness

Signed in the presence of:
Name of Witness

Address   Address

Signature of Witness   Signature of Witness

[A Justice of the Peace] [Justices' Clerk] [An assistant to a justices' clerk][An officer of the court authorised by the judge to administer oaths]

[A Justice of the Peace] [Justices' Clerk] [An assistant to a justices' clerk][An officer of the court authorised by the judge to administer oaths]

C(PRA1) (04.14)   www.justice.gov.uk   © Crown Copyright   Published by LexisNexis 2014 under the Open Government Licence   Page 1 of 2

Precedents 5.84

Notes about the Parental Responsibility Agreement

Read these notes before you make the agreement.

About the Parental Responsibility Agreement

The making of this agreement will affect the legal position of the mother and the father. You should both seek legal advice before you make the Agreement. You can obtain the name and address of a solicitor from the Children Panel (020 7242 1222)

or from
- a local office of the family court
- a Citizens Advice Bureau
- a Law Centre
- a local library.

You may be eligible for legal aid.

When you fill in the Agreement

Please use black ink (the Agreement will be copied). Put the name of one child only. If the father is to have parental responsibility for more than one child, fill in a separate form for each child. **Do not sign the Agreement.**

When you have filled in the Agreement

Take it to a local office of the family court, or the Principal Registry of the Family Division (the address is below).

A justice of the peace, a justices' clerk, an assistant to a justices' clerk, or a court official who is authorised by the judge to administer oaths, will witness your signature and he or she will sign the certificate of the witness. **A solicitor cannot witness your signature.**

To the mother: When you make the declaration you will have to prove that you are the child's mother so take to the court the child's full birth certificate.

You will also need evidence of your identity showing a photograph and signature (for example, a photocard, official pass or passport). **Please note that the child's birth certificate cannot be accepted as sufficient proof of your identity.**

To the father: You will need evidence of your identity showing a photograph and signature (for example, a photocard, official pass or passport).

When the Certificate has been signed and witnessed

Make 2 copies of the Agreement form. You do not need to copy these notes.

Take, or send, this form and the copies to **The Principal Registry of the Family Division, First Avenue House, 42-49 High Holborn, London, WC1V 6NP.**

The Registry will record the Agreement and keep this form. The copies will be stamped and sent back to each parent at the address on the Agreement. The Agreement will not take effect until it has been received and recorded at the Principal Registry of the Family Division.

Ending the Agreement

Once a parental responsibility agreement has been made it can only end
- by an order of the court made on the application of any person who has parental responsibility for the child
- by an order of the court made on the application of the child with permission of the court
- when the child reaches the age of 18.

407

5.84 *Children*

Step-Parent Parental Responsibility Agreement

Section 4A(1)(a) Children Act 1989

Keep this form in a safe place Date recorded at The Central Family Court:

Read the notes on the other side before you make this agreement.

This is a Step-Parent Parental Responsibility Agreement regarding

the Child	Full name		
	Gender	Date of birth	Date of 18th birthday
Between Parent A	Name		
	Address		
and *the other parent (with parental responsibility)	Name		
	Address		
and the step-parent	Name		
	Address		
We declare that	we are the parents and step-parent of the above child and we agree that the above mentioned step-parent shall have parental responsibility for the child (in addition to those already having parental responsibility).		

	Signed **(Parent A)**	*Signed **(Other Parent)**	Signed **(Step-Parent)**
	Date	Date	Date
Certificate of witness	The following evidence of identity was produced by the person signing above:	The following evidence of identity was produced by the person signing above:	The following evidence of identity was produced by the person signing above:
	Signed in the presence of: Name of Witness	Signed in the presence of: Name of Witness	Signed in the presence of: Name of Witness
	Address	Address	Address
	Signature of Witness	Signature of Witness	Signature of Witness
*If there is only one parent with parental responsibility, please delete this section.	[A Justice of the Peace] [Justices' Clerk][An assistant to a justices' clerk] [An officer of the court authorised by the judge to administer oaths]	[A Justice of the Peace] [Justices' Clerk] [An assistant to a justices' clerk][An Officer of the Court authorised by the judge to administer oaths]	[A Justice of the Peace] [Justices' Clerk][An assistant to a justices' clerk][An officer of the court authorised by the judge to administer oaths]

C(PRA2) (08.14)   www.justice.gov.uk   © Crown Copyright   Published by LexisNexis 2013 under the Open Government Licence   Page 1 of 2

Precedents 5.84

Notes about the Step-Parent Parental Responsibility Form

Read these notes before you make the Agreement

The making of this agreement will affect the legal position of the parent(s) and the step-parent. You should seek legal advice before you make the Agreement. You can obtain the name and address of a solicitor from the Children Panel (020 7242 1222) or from:

- a local office of the family court,
- a Citizens Advice Bureau,
- a Law Centre,
- a local library.

You may be eligible for legal aid.

When you fill in the Agreement

Please use black ink (the Agreement will be copied). Put the name of one child only. If the step-parent is to have parental responsibility for more than one child, fill in a separate form for each child. **Do not sign the Agreement.**

When you have filled in the Agreement

Take it to a local office of the family ourt, or The Central Family Court (the address is below).

A justice of the peace, a justices' clerk, an assistant to a justices' clerk, or a court official who is authorised by the judge to administer oaths, will witness your signature and he or she will sign the certificate of the witness. **A solicitor cannot witness your signature.**

To Parent A and the Other Parent with parental responsibility:

When you make the declaration you will have to prove that you have parental responsibility for the child. You should therefore take with you to the court one of the following documents:

- the child's full birth certificate and a marriage certificate or civil partnership certificate to show that the parents were married to each other or were in a civil partnership with each other at the time of birth or subsequently,
- a court order granting parental responsibility,
- a registered Parental Responsibility Agreement Form between the child's mother and father or other parent
- if the birth was registered after the 1 December 2003, the child's full birth certificate showing that the parents jointly registered the child's birth.

You will also require evidence of your (both parents') identity showing a photograph and signature (for example, a photocard, official pass or passport) **(Please note that the child's birth certificate cannot be accepted as sufficient proof of your identity.)**

To the step-parent: When you make the declaration you will have to prove that you are married to, or the civil partner of, a parent of the child so take to the court your marriage certificate or certificate of civil partnership.

You will also need evidence of your identity showing a photograph and signature (for example, a photocard, official pass or passport).

When the Certificate has been signed and witnessed

Make sufficient copies of the Agreement Form for each person who has signed the form. You do not need to copy these notes.

Take, or send, this form and the copies to **The Central Family Court, First Avenue House, 42-49 High Holborn, London, WC1V 6NP.**

The Court will record the Agreement and keep this form. The copies will be stamped and sent back to each parent at the address on the Agreement. The Agreement will not take effect until it has been received and recorded at The Central Family Court.

Ending the Agreement

Once a step-parent parental responsibility agreement has been made it can only end:

- by an order of the court made on the application of any person who has parental responsibility for the child,
- by an order of the court made on the application of the child with permission of the court,
- when the child reaches the age of 18.

Sign and Lock >

C(PRA2) (08.14)

5.85 Children

5.85

Application by an unmarried father for a parental responsibility order

Application for an order	Form C1
Children Act 1989	
The court	To be completed by the court
	Date issued
	Case number
The full name(s) of the child(ren)	Child(ren)'s number(s)

Important Note
You should only answer question 7 if you are asking the court to make one of the following orders: a Contact Order, a Residence Order, a Prohibited Steps Order, a Specific Issue Order or a Parental Responsibility Order.

1 About you (the person completing this form known as 'the applicant')

State:
- *your title, full name, address, telephone number, date of birth and relationship to each child above*
- *your solicitor's name, address, reference, telephone, FAX and DX numbers.*

2 The child(ren) and the order(s) you are applying for

For each child state:
- *the full name, date of birth and sex*
- *the type of order(s) you are applying for (for example, residence order, contact order, supervision order).*

C1 (12.05)　　　　　　　　　　　　　　　　　　　　　　　　　　　　　HMCS

3 Other cases which concern the child(ren)

If there have ever been, or there are pending, any court cases which concern:
- *a child whose name you have put in paragraph 2*
- *a full, half or step brother or sister of a child whose name you have put in paragraph 2*
- *a person in this case who is or has been, involved in caring for a child whose name you have put in paragraph 2*

attach a copy of the relevant order and give:
- *the name of the court*
- *the name and contact address (if known) of the children's guardian, if appointed*
- *the name and contact address (if known) of the children and family reporter, if appointed*
- *the name and contact address (if known) of the welfare officer, if appointed*
- *the name and contact address (if known) of the solicitor appointed for the child(ren).*

4 The respondent(s)

Appendix 3 Family Proceedings Rules 1991; Schedule 2 Family Proceedings Courts (Children Act 1989) Rules 1991

For each respondent state:
- *the title, full name and address*
- *the date of birth (if known) or the age*
- *the relationship to each child.*

C1

5.85 Children

5 Others to whom notice is to be given

Appendix 3 Family Proceedings Rules 1991; Schedule 2 Family Proceedings Courts (Children Act 1989) Rules 1991

For each person state:
- the title, full name and address
- the date of birth (if known) or the age
- the relationship to each child.

6 The care of the child(ren)

For each child in paragraph 2 state:
- the child's current address and how long the child has lived there
- whether it is the child's usual address and who cares for the child there
- the child's relationship to the other children (if any).

7 Domestic abuse, violence or harm

Do you believe that the child(ren) named above have suffered or are at risk of suffering any harm from any of the following:
- any form of domestic abuse
- violence within the household
- child abduction
- other conduct or behaviour

by any person who is or has been involved in caring for the child(ren) or lives with, or has contact with, the child(ren)?

Please tick the box which applies   Yes ☐   No ☐

If you tick the Yes box, you must also fill in Supplemental Information Form (form C1A). You can obtain a copy of this from a court office if one has not been enclosed with the papers served on you.

C1

8 Social Services

For each child in paragraph 2 state:
- whether the child is known to the Social Services. If so, give the name of the social worker and the address of the Social Services department.
- whether the child is, or has been, on the Child Protection Register. If so, give details of registration.

9 The education and health of the child(ren)

For each child state:
- the name of the school, college or place of training which the child attends
- whether the child is in good health. Give details of any serious disabilities or ill health.
- whether the child has any special needs.

10 The parents of the child(ren)

For each child state:
- the full name of the child's parents
- whether the parents are, or have been, married to each other or civil partners of each other
- whether the parents live together. If so, where.
- whether, to your knowledge, either of the parents have been involved in a court case concerning a child. If so, give the date and the name of the court.

5.85 Children

11 The family of the child(ren) (other children)

For any other child not already mentioned in the family (for example, a brother or half sister) state:
- *the full name and address*
- *the date of birth (if known) or age*
- *the relationship of the child to you.*

12 Other adults

State:
- *the full name of any other adults (for example, lodgers) who live at the same address as any child named in paragraph 2*
- *whether they live there all the time*
- *whether, to your knowledge, the adult has been involved in a court case concerning a child. If so, give the date and the name of the court.*

13 Your reason(s) for applying and any plans for the child(ren)

State briefly your reasons for applying and what you want the court to order.
- ***Do not** give a full statement if you are applying for an order under Section 8 of Children Act 1989. You may be asked to provide a full statement later.*
- ***Do not** complete this section if this form is accompanied by a supplementary form.*

C1

14 Attending the court

State:
- whether you will need an interpreter at court. If so, please indicate what language interpreter you will use. If you require an interpreter you must notify the court immediately so that one can be arranged.
- whether you have a disability for which you require special assistance or special facilities. If so, please say what your needs are. The court staff will get in touch with you about your requirements.

15 Parenting Information – Arrangements after Separation

	Yes	No
Have you received a Parenting Plan booklet? (If No, you may obtain a copy from a court office, a citizen's advice bureau or other family advice service.)	☐	☐
Have you agreed to a Parenting Plan? (If Yes, please include a copy of the Plan when you send your application to the court)	☐	☐
If you did agree a Parenting Plan, has the Plan broken down?	☐	☐

If Yes, please explain briefly why the Plan broke down –

Signed   Date
(Applicant)

C1

5.86

Change of name deed made by a mother on behalf of her child: not intended for enrolment[1]

THIS CHANGE OF NAME DEED made on (*date*)
BY me (*mother's name*) of (*address*).
WITNESSES that:

1   I am

5.86 Children

(1.1) the mother of (*child's forename(s) and old surname*) ('*child*')[2] who was born on (*date*); and

(1.2) the only person who has parental responsibility for (*child*)[3].

2 On (*child's*) behalf:

(2.1) I completely renounce and abandon the use of (his)/(her) surname (*old surname*); and

(2.2) I now adopt and assume for (him)/(her) the surname (*new surname*); and

(2.3) I ask and authorise all persons at all times when addressing, describing and identifying (*child*) to use (his)/(her) new surname (*new surname*).

3 From now onwards (*child*) will be known as (*child's forename(s) and new surname*):

(3.1) in all deeds, documents, forms, records and other written instruments; and

(3.2) in all actions and proceedings; and

(3.3) in all dealings and transactions; and

(3.4) on all occasions.

SIGNED as a Deed by me (*mother's name*) on behalf of my (son)/(daughter) (*child's forename(s) and new surname*) in the presence of:

[1] For changing a child's name generally, see Nasreen Pearce *Name-changing: A Practical Guide* (Fourmat Publishing, 1990) at Chapter 3. See also **5.21** et seq.
[2] Insert the child's usual forename for future reference in the deed.
[3] See CA 1989, s 2(2). If the mother is not the only person with parental responsibility, see CA 1989, ss 13 and 33(7).

[1] For changing a child's name generally, see Nasreen Pearce Name-changing: A Practical Guide (Fourmat Publishing, 1990) at Chapter 3. See also **5.21** et seq.

5.87

Informal appointment of a guardian by one parent[1]

Children Act 1989, s 5

I (*name*) of (*address*) APPOINT (*name*) of (*address*) to be the guardian of my (son)/(daughter) (*child's name*) in the event of my death.

Dated

Signed

[1] Informal insofar as it is not contained in a will or deed. CA 1989, s 5(5) allows a parent or guardian to appoint a guardian provided that the appointment 'is made in writing, is dated and is signed by the person making the appointment'. This form of appointment would be particularly suitable for a parent under the age of 18, who, by virtue of the Wills Act 1837, s 7 (as amended), would not be able to execute a valid will.

5.88

Informal appointment of a guardian by both parents

Children Act 1989, s 5

WE (*father's name*) and (*mother's name*) of (*address*) JOINTLY APPOINT[1] (*name*) of (address) to be the guardian of our (son)/(daughter) (child's name) in the event that both of us die before (he)/(she) reaches the age of eighteen[2].

Dated

Signed

Signed

[1] CA 1989, s 5(10): 'Nothing in this section shall be taken to prevent an appointment under sub-s (3) or (4) being made by two or more persons acting jointly'.
[2] Unless it is brought to an end earlier in accordance with the provisions of s 6, the appointment of the guardian will continue until the child reaches 18 (CA 1989, s 91(8)).

5.89

Child maintenance agreement[1]

THIS MAINTENANCE AGREEMENT made on (date)

BETWEEN (1) (father's name) of (address) ('name 1') and (2) (mother's name) of (address) ('name 2')

WITNESSES as follows:

(1) Recitals

(1.1) On (date) (name 2) gave birth to a (son)/(daughter) whose name is (child's name) ('name 3').

(1.2) (Name 1) acknowledges that he is (name 3's) father.

(2) Maintenance agreement

(Name 1) agrees that:

(2.1) he will pay to (name 2) maintenance for (name 3's) benefit;

(2.2) the maintenance payable will start at £   a year;

(2.3) the maintenance payable each year will be paid in 12 equal monthly instalments;

(2.4) each instalment will be paid in advance by standing order on the (first) day of each month;

(2.5) the first instalment will be paid on (date);

(2.6) the maintenance payable will be reviewed in (April) each year when:

    (a) the amount of maintenance payable until then will be multiplied by the extent to which the Retail Prices Index has changed during the year which ended on (31 March) immediately before the review; and

    (b) the revised amount of maintenance payable will take effect with the payment of the instalment due on (1 May) immediately after the review and will continue to be payable at the same rate until it is reviewed again immediately after the payment of the instalment due on the following (1 April)

(2.7) he will continue to pay maintenance in accordance with the terms of this Agreement until the date on which a maintenance assessment made under the Child Support Act 1991 with respect to (name 3):

(a) takes effect[2]; or

(b) would, if a maintenance assessment had been made, cease to have effect[3].

(3) Right to apply for maintenance assessment

The existence of this Agreement does not prevent either party, or any other person, from applying to the Secretary of State for a maintenance assessment to be made with respect to (*name 3*)[4].

SIGNED as a Deed by (*name 1*) in the presence of:

SIGNED as a Deed by (*name 2*) in the presence of:

[1] See, generally, **5.39** above.
[2] For the effective date of the maintenance assessment, see CSA 1991, Sch 1, para 11. A maintenance assessment will take effect on such date as may be determined in accordance with regulations made by the Secretary of State (which date may be earlier than the date on which the assessment is made).
[3] For the termination of maintenance assessments, see CSA 1991, Sch 1, para 16.
[4] CSA 1991, s 9(3).

5.90

Notice of [intention to proceed with] a financial application to which the standard procedure applies

Notice of [intention to proceed with] a financial application to which the standard procedure applies

To be completed by the Applicant	
The Family Court sitting at	Case No.
Help with Fees - Ref no. (if applicable) HWF - ▢▢▢▢ - ▢▢▢▢	

This form should be completed if you are applying for financial provision (a financial order or other financial remedy) **except** an application:

- for a periodical payments order **only**, under section 23 of the Matrimonial Causes Act 1973, paragraph 2 of Schedule 5 to the Civil Partnership Act 2004 or paragraphs 1 or 2 of Schedule 1 to the Children Act 1989 - please complete Form A1.
- to vary or to discharge a periodical payments order **only** - please complete Form A1.
- for financial provision under Part 1 of the Domestic Proceedings and Magistrates' Courts Act 1978 or Schedule 6 to the Civil Partnership Act 2004 - please complete Form A1.
- after an overseas divorce etc (Form D50F) or for neglect or failure to maintain a party or child (Form D50C) or for alteration of a maintenance agreement during the lifetime of the parties (Form D50H)

Full name of applicant

Full name of respondent(s)

Nature of application

This application is for financial provision, including provision to be made to or for the benefit of the child(ren):

▢ in connection with matrimonial or civil partnership proceedings (divorce, dissolution etc), **or**

▢ under paragraphs 1 or 2 of Schedule 1 to the Children Act 1989

tick the statement that applies	and	tick one of the following orders

The applicant intends:
▢ **to apply** to the Court for

or

▢ **to proceed with** the application in the

[divorce] [dissolution] [nullity] [annulment] [(judicial) separation]
application for

or

▢ **to apply to vary**

▢ an order for maintenance pending suit/outcome of proceedings
▢ a lump sum order
▢ a property adjustment order
▢ a settlement or a transfer of property for the benefit of the child(ren)
▢ a periodical payments order **together with** other financial provision
▢ a pension sharing order
▢ a pension compensation sharing order

▢ **to apply to discharge** a periodical payments order **and** to substitute for it one or more orders opposite

▢ a lump sum order
▢ a property adjustment order
▢ a pension sharing order
▢ a pension compensation sharing order

Form A Notice of [intention to proceed with] an application for a financial provision to which the standard procedure applies (06.18)

© Crown Copyright Published by LexisNexis 2018 under the Open Government Licence

5.90 *Children*

Additional information required

Are you applying for an order by consent in terms of written agreement (a consent order)? ☐ Yes ☐ No If Yes, **attach the draft order to this form**

[Add file attachment]

1. Further details of the financial application

If your application includes an application for a property adjustment order in relation to land, please give the following details, if applicable

Address(es) of the property or properties

Name(s) and address(es) of any mortgagee(s)

If an application is made for any periodical payments or secured periodical payments for children, please complete this section.

☐ there is a written agreement made before 5 April 1993 about maintenance for the benefit of children

☐ there is a written agreement made on or after 5 April 1993 about maintenance for the benefit of children

☐ there is no agreement, but the applicant is applying for payments:

☐ for a stepchild or stepchildren

☐ in addition to child support maintenance already paid under a Child Support Agency assessment

☐ to meet expenses arising from a child's disability

☐ to meet expenses incurred by a child in being educated or training for work

☐ when either the child **or** the person with care of the child **or** the absent parent of the child is not habitually resident in the United Kingdom

If none of the above applies, the court may not have jurisdiction to hear the application for periodical payments.

Has the Child Support Agency made any calculation of maintenance in respect of the child(ren)

☐ Yes ☐ No

If Yes, state briefly your reasons for making this application to the court including any reasons why the Child Support Agency is no longer dealing with your claim or any reasons why you need additional maintenance to top up payments made through the Child Support Agency:

If your application includes an application in relation to one or more children, please complete the tables below for each child, continuing on additional sheets if necessary

Name of child 1

Date of birth

Gender ☐ Male ☐ Female

Relationship to Applicant

Relationship to Respondent

Country of residence (if not England or Wales)

[Add child]

Service details

☐ I am not represented by a solicitor in these proceedings

☐ I am not represented by a solicitor in these proceedings but am receiving advice from a solicitor

☐ I am represented by a solicitor in these proceedings, who has signed Section 5, and all documents for my attention should be sent to my solicitor whose details are as follows:

Solicitor's details

Name of solicitor			
Name of firm			
Address to which all documents should be sent for service:		Telephone no.	
		Fax no.	
		DX no.	
		Your ref.	
Postcode		Solicitor's fee account no.	

E-mail	

Respondent's address for service

Address (including postcode)

Postcode

5.90 Children

2. Requirement to attend a Mediation, Information and Assessment Meeting (MIAM)

Before making an application for a financial order you must first attend a Mediation, Information and Assessment Meeting (MIAM). At the MIAM an authorised family mediator will consider with you (and the other party if present) whether family mediation, or another form of non-court dispute resolution, would be a more appropriate alternative to court. The mediator will also be able to sign post you to other help and support services.

You **must** have attended a MIAM before making this application **unless** the requirement to attend a MIAM does not apply because the financial order you are applying for:

- is for a consent order; **or**
- you are exempt from the requirement to attend a MIAM. (Some exemptions you can claim for yourself, others must be certified by an authorised family mediator).

In special circumstances such as where domestic violence is involved - you may not need to attend a MIAM. However, you will be asked to provide the judge with evidence (such as a police report to prove domestic violence has taken place) and should bring it to the first hearing.

All applicants must complete sections 1 and 2 and complete and sign section 5 of this form. **In addition**, you must tick one of the boxes below and ensure that you, your legal adviser or a family mediator completes and signs the relevant section(s) of this form as shown.

2a. Are you claiming exemption from the requirement to attend a MIAM? ☐ Yes ☐ No

If Yes, complete section 3.

If No, please **answer question 2b**.

2b. Has a family mediator informed you that a mediator's exemption applies, and you do not need to attend a MIAM? ☐ Yes ☐ No

If Yes, you must ensure that the family mediator completes and signs section 4a.

If No, please **answer question 2c**.

2c. Have you attended a MIAM? ☐ Yes ☐ No

If Yes, you must ensure that the **family mediator completes and signs section 4b**.

If No, you cannot make this application.

3. Applicant claims exemption(s) from attendance at a Mediation, Information and Assessment Meeting (MIAM)

(To be completed by the person intending to make a court application or their legal representative)

The applicant has not attended a MIAM because the following MIAM exemption(s) applies:

☐ Domestic violence (you must complete **section 3a**)

☐ Urgency (you must complete **section 3b**)

☐ Previous MIAM attendance or previous MIAM exemption (you must complete **section 3c**)

☐ Other (you must complete **section 3d**)

Now complete the relevant section 3a, b, c, or d by ticking the appropriate box(es)

Further details of MIAM exemption(s) claimed by the applicant

If you have claimed a MIAM exemption above you must also tick the relevant box(es), as shown below to confirm that you have the necessary evidence to support your ground(s) for exemption and should bring it to the first hearing. Where you are asked to provide additional details you must do so.

Section 3a - Domestic violence evidence

The applicant confirms that there is evidence of domestic violence, as specified below:

☐ evidence that a prospective party has been arrested for a relevant domestic violence offence;

☐ evidence of a relevant police caution for a domestic violence offence;

☐ evidence of relevant criminal proceedings for a domestic violence offence which have not concluded;

☐ evidence of a relevant conviction for a domestic violence offence;

☐ a court order binding a prospective party over in connection with a domestic violence offence;

☐ a domestic violence protection notice issued under section 24 of the Crime and Security Act 2010 against a prospective party;

☐ a relevant protective injunction;

☐ an undertaking given in England and Wales under section 46 or 63E of the Family Law Act 1996 (or given in Scotland or Northern Ireland in place of a protective injunction) by a prospective party, provided that a cross-undertaking relating to domestic violence was not given by another prospective party;

☐ a copy of a finding of fact, made in proceedings in the United Kingdom, that there has been domestic violence by a prospective party;

☐ an expert report produced as evidence in proceedings in the United Kingdom for the benefit of a court or tribunal confirming that a person with whom a prospective party is or was in a family relationship, was assessed as being, or at risk of being, a victim of domestic violence by that prospective party;

5.90 Children

Section 3a - Domestic violence evidence - **continued**

☐ a letter or report from an appropriate health professional confirming that-

    (i) that professional, or another appropriate health professional, has examined a prospective party in person; and

    (ii) in the reasonable professional judgment of the author or the examining appropriate health professional, that prospective party has, or has had, injuries or a condition consistent with being a victim of domestic violence;

☐ a letter or report from-

    (i) the appropriate health professional who made the referral described below;

    (ii) an appropriate health professional who has access to the medical records of the prospective party referred to below; or

    (iii) the person to whom the referral described below was made;

confirming that there was a referral by an appropriate health professional of a prospective party to a person who provides specialist support or assistance for victims of, or those at risk of, domestic violence;

☐ a letter from any person who is a member of a multi-agency risk assessment conference (or other suitable local safeguarding forum) confirming that a prospective party, or a person with whom that prospective party is in a family relationship, is or has been at risk of harm from domestic violence by another prospective party;

☐ a letter from an independent domestic violence advisor confirming that they are providing support to a prospective party;

☐ a letter from an independent sexual violence advisor confirming that they are providing support to a prospective party relating to sexual violence by another prospective party;

☐ a letter from an officer employed by a local authority or housing association (or their equivalent in Scotland or Northern Ireland) for the purpose of supporting tenants containing-

    (i) a statement to the effect that, in their reasonable professional judgment, a person with whom a prospective party is or has been in a family relationship is, or is at risk of being, a victim of domestic violence by that prospective party;

    (ii) a description of the specific matters relied upon to support that judgment; and

    (iii) a description of the support they provided to the victim of domestic violence or the person at risk of domestic violence by that prospective party;

☐ a letter which-

    (i) is from an organisation providing domestic violence support services, or a registered charity, which letter confirms that it-

        (a) is situated in England and Wales,

        (b) has been operating for an uninterrupted period of six months or more; and

        (c) provided a prospective party with support in relation to that person's needs as a victim, or a person at risk, of domestic violence; and

    (ii) contains-

        (a) a statement to the effect that, in the reasonable professional judgment of the author of the letter, the prospective party is, or is at risk of being, a victim of domestic violence;

Section 3a – Domestic violence evidence - **continued**	(b) a description of the specific matters relied upon to support that judgment;
	(c) a description of the support provided to the prospective party; and
	(d) a statement of the reasons why the prospective party needed that support;
	☐ a letter or report from an organisation providing domestic violence support services in the United Kingdom confirming-
	(i) that a person with whom a prospective party is or was in a family relationship was refused admission to a refuge;
	(ii) the date on which they were refused admission to the refuge; and
	(iii) they sought admission to the refuge because of allegations of domestic violence by the prospective party referred to in paragraph (i);
	☐ a letter from a public authority confirming that a person with whom a prospective party is or was in a family relationship, was assessed as being, or at risk of being, a victim of domestic violence by that prospective party (or a copy of that assessment);
	☐ a letter from the Secretary of State for the Home Department confirming that a prospective party has been granted leave to remain in the United Kingdom under paragraph 289B of the Rules made by the Home Secretary under section 3(2) of the Immigration Act 1971, which can be found at https://www.gov.uk/guidance/immigration-rules/immigration-rules-index;
	☐ evidence which demonstrates that a prospective party has been, or is at risk of being, the victim of domestic violence by another prospective party in the form of abuse which relates to financial matters.
Section 3b – Urgency	**The applicant confirms that the application must be made urgently because:**
	☐ there is risk to the life, liberty or physical safety of the prospective applicant or his or her family or his or her home; or
	☐ any delay caused by attending a MIAM would cause—
	☐ a significant risk of a miscarriage of justice; or
	☐ unreasonable hardship to the prospective applicant; or
	☐ irretrievable problems in dealing with the dispute (including the irretrievable loss of significant evidence); or
	☐ there is a significant risk that in the period necessary to schedule and attend a MIAM, proceedings relating to the dispute will be brought in another state in which a valid claim to jurisdiction may exist, such that a court in that other State would be seized of the dispute before a court in England and Wales.
Section 3c – Previous MIAM attendance or MIAM exemption	**The applicant confirms that one of the following applies:**
	☐ in the 4 months prior to making the application, the person attended a MIAM or participated in another form of non-court dispute resolution relating to the same or substantially the same dispute; or
	☐ at the time of making the application, the person is participating in another form of non-court dispute resolution relating to the same or substantially the same dispute; or
	☐ in the 4 months prior to making the application, the person filed a relevant family application confirming that a MIAM exemption applied and that application related to the same or substantially the same dispute; or

5.90 Children

Section 3c - Previous MIAM attendance or MIAM exemption - continued

☐ the application would be made in existing proceedings which are continuing and the prospective applicant attended a MIAM before initiating those proceedings; or

☐ the application would be made in existing proceedings which are continuing and a MIAM exemption applied to the application for those proceedings.

Section 3d - Other exemptions

The applicant confirms that one of the following other grounds for exemption applies:

☐ evidence that the prospective applicant is bankrupt exists in one of the following forms:

  ☐ application by the prospective applicant for a bankruptcy order;
  ☐ petition by a creditor of the prospective applicant for a bankruptcy order; or
  ☐ a bankruptcy order in respect of the prospective applicant.

☐ the prospective applicant does not have sufficient contact details for any of the prospective respondents to enable a family mediator to contact any of the prospective respondents for the purpose of scheduling the MIAM.

☐ the application would be made without notice (Paragraph 5.1 of Practice Direction 18A sets out the circumstances in which applications may be made without notice.)

☐ (i) the prospective applicant is or all of the prospective respondents are subject to a disability or other inability that would prevent attendance at a MIAM unless appropriate facilities can be offered by an authorised mediator; (ii) the prospective applicant has contacted as many authorised family mediators as have an office within fifteen miles of his or her home (or three of them if there are three or more), and all have stated that they are unable to provide such facilities; and (iii) the names, postal addresses and telephone numbers or e-mail addresses for such authorised family mediators, and the dates of contact, can be provided to the court if requested.

☐ the prospective applicant or all of the prospective respondents cannot attend a MIAM because he or she is, or they are, as the case may be (i) in prison or any other institution in which he or she is or they are required to be detained; (ii) subject to conditions of bail that prevent contact with the other person; or (iii) subject to a licence with a prohibited contact requirement in relation to the other person.

☐ the prospective applicant or all of the prospective respondents are not habitually resident in England and Wales.

☐ a child is one of the prospective parties by virtue of Rule 12.3(1).

☐ (i) the prospective applicant has contacted as many authorised family mediators as have an office within fifteen miles of his or her home (or three of them if there are three or more), and all of them have stated that they are not available to conduct a MIAM within fifteen business days of the date of contact; and (ii) the names, postal addresses and telephone numbers or e-mail addresses for such authorised family mediators, and the dates of contact, can be provided to the court if requested.

☐ there is no authorised family mediator with an office within fifteen miles of the prospective applicant's home.

Now complete Section 5.

Precedents 5.90

4.	Mediator certifies that the prospective applicant is exempt from attendance at Mediation Information and Assessment Meeting (MIAM) or confirms MIAM attendance

(To be completed and signed by the authorised family mediator)
(tick the boxes that apply)

4a.   **The following MIAM exemption(s) applies:**

☐ An authorised family mediator confirms that he or she is satisfied that -

     ☐ (a) mediation is not suitable as a means of resolving the dispute because none of the respondents is willing to attend a MIAM; or

     ☐ (b) mediation is not suitable as a means of resolving the dispute because all of the respondents failed without good reason to attend a MIAM appointment; or

     ☐ (c) mediation is otherwise not suitable as a means of resolving the dispute.

4b.   **The prospective applicant attended a MIAM:**

☐ The prospective applicant only attended a MIAM.

☐ The prospective applicant and respondent party(s) attended the MIAM together.

☐ The prospective applicant and respondent(s) have each attended a separate MIAM.

☐ The prospective respondent party(s) has/have made or is/are making arrangements to attend a separate MIAM.

Mediation or other form of Dispute Resolution is not proceeding because:

☐ The applicant has attended a MIAM alone and
- the applicant does not wish to start or continue mediation; or
- the mediator has determined that mediation is unsuitable; or
- the respondent did not wish to attend a MIAM

☐ Both the applicant and respondent have attended a MIAM (separately or together) and
- the applicant does not wish to start or continue mediation; or
- the respondent does not wish to start or continue mediation; or
- the mediator has determined that mediation is unsuitable

☐ Mediation has started, but has:
- broken down; or
- concluded with some or all issues unresolved

Signed	

Authorised Family Mediator
(a family mediator who is authorised to undertake MIAMs)

FMC Registration no.	
Family Mediation Service name	
Sole trader name	
Address	
Dated	

5. Signature

I am duly authorised by the applicant to sign this statement.

Print full name

Name of applicant solicitors firm

Address of solicitor's firm

Signed   Dated

*delete as appropriate   *(Applicant) (Litigation friend) (Applicant's solicitor)

Position or office held
(If signing on behalf of firm or company)

Checklist for completing Form A

Page 1
- Write in your full name
- Tick the nature of the financial application you are making and the type(s) or order you are seeking
- Tick if you are applying for an order by consent in the terms of a written agreement (a consent order).

Page 2 and 3
- Tick the relevant box(es) to provide further details about the order you are applying for, and provide additional information where shown.

Page 4
- Complete the details for service.

Page 5
- Answer questions 2a to 2c about whether a MIAM exemption applies or whether you have attended a MIAM.

- If you answered question 2a on page 5 with "yes" you must tick one of the first four boxes in section 3 to indicate the category of MIAM exemption that you are claiming. You must then complete section 3a, b, c or d as shown.

Page 10
- If a family mediator needs to certify that a mediator's exemption applies you must ask them to complete section 4a of this form and sign where shown.

- If you have attended a MIAM you must ask the family mediator who conducted it to complete section 4b of the form and sign where shown.

Page 11
- Check that you (or your solicitor if relevant) have completed and signed section 5.

What you do next

You should normally make your application to the Designated Family Centre for your area. You can find this, and a full list of courts and what type of work they do online at courttribunalfinder.service.gov.uk

Fees

You may need to pay a fee with your application. You should read leaflet **EX50 Civil and family court fees** to find out what fee, if any, you need to pay. This leaflet is available from your local court or online at hmctsformfinder.justice.gov.uk

General information for completing this form

1. You need to complete this form if you want to ask the court to make one or more of the orders shown on page 1. You must tick the relevant boxes on page 1 to indicate the nature of your application and the type(s) of order you are seeking.

2. Pages 1 to 3 set out the core information you need to provide if you wish to make an application to the court. You or your solicitor must also sign and date Section 5 of this form.

3. If you are applying for an order by consent you should tick the box on page 1 to make this clear and attach the draft order with this application.

Requirement to attend a Mediation, Information and Assessment Meeting

4. It is now a legal requirement that, unless an exemption applies, a person who wishes to apply to court for a financial order must first attend a Mediation, Information and Assessment Meeting (a MIAM). At the stage before proceedings the other party (the respondent) is expected to attend either the same MIAM or a separate MIAM.

5. At the MIAM, a trained family mediator will give you (the applicant) and the other person if present (the respondent) information about family mediation and other types of non-court dispute resolution. They will consider with you whether non-court dispute resolution would be an appropriate way to resolve the dispute. It is then for the applicant and respondent to decide whether or not to do so.

6. The requirement for the applicant to attend a MIAM does not apply if a financial order is being applied for and the other person (respondent) is in agreement about what you are asking the court to order (the order is a "consent order").

7. You or your solicitor must tick the relevant box in Section 2 of this form so that the court knows whether the MIAM requirement applies, whether an exemption applies (and why) or whether you have attended a MIAM.

MIAM exemptions and MIAM attendance

8. As the applicant you are expected to have contacted an authorised family mediator in order to make arrangements to attend a MIAM unless:
   - the MIAM requirement does not apply for the reason explained at paragraph 6 of these notes, or
   - you are claiming a MIAM exemption, or a family mediator certifies that a mediator's exemption applies.

9. You can find an authorised family mediator by using the 'Find your local mediator' search facility available at: www.familymediationcouncil.org.uk

10. You should give the mediator the contact details of the other person so that the family mediator can contact them to check their willingness to attend a MIAM. If the other persons (or none of the other persons if there is more than one respondent) are unwilling to attend a MIAM this is a ground for the family mediator to exempt you from attending a MIAM.

11. If you or your solicitor believe that you have grounds for claiming exemption from MIAM attendance you or your solicitor must tick the relevant box in Section 2 of this form and complete Section 3.

12. If a family mediator wishes to certify that a mediator's exemption applies, so that you do not need to attend a MIAM, you must ask the family mediator to complete Section 4a of this form and sign it where shown.

13. If you have attended a MIAM you must ask the family mediator who conducted the MIAM to complete Section 4b of this form and sign it where shown.

14. If you claim a MIAM exemption and make an application to the court, the court will inquire into the grounds for exemption. The court may ask you to produce written evidence (see Section 3 of this form for details against each exemption shown).

15. If the court determines that the exemption was not validly claimed it may direct you, or you and the other party, to attend a MIAM and, if the case has already progressed to the first hearing, may adjourn the case to enable you to make arrangements to attend a MIAM.

16. The detailed procedure relating to the MIAM requirement and MIAM exemptions and attendance is set out in Part 3 of the Family Procedure Rules and in supporting Practice Direction 3A (judicial guidance). These are available online at: www.justice.gov.uk/courts/procedure-rules/family/practice_directions/pd_part_03a

Paying for MIAM attendance or for family mediation

17. Legal aid is available for MIAMs and for family mediation. If you are eligible for legal aid you could receive both the MIAM and mediation sessions free of charge, as well as some advice from a solicitor to support you in the mediation process.

5.90 Children

18. If you, or the prospective respondent, is eligible for Legal Aid then the total cost of MIAM attendance can be met by the Legal Aid Agency, whether you and the prospective respondent attend the same MIAM or separate MIAMs.
19. If neither you nor the respective respondent is eligible for Legal Aid then the mediator will agree with you how the cost of MIAM attendance is to be met.
20. Please refer to paragraph 29 for further details on how you can find out whether you are eligible for Legal Aid by using the calculator tool available at www.gov.uk/legal-aid

Safety and MIAM attendance

21. Please note: the family mediator will discuss with you and with the other person whether you wish to attend the MIAM separately or together. Family mediators have a responsibility to ensure the safety and security of all concerned and will always check with each of you that attending together is your individual choice and is safe.

Information about mediation

22. If suitable, mediation can be a better way of resolving issues about financial arrangements when you or your partner petition for a matrimonial or civil partnership order. Mediation can be less expensive than going to court and much less stressful for all the family.
23. Family Mediation is an impartial process that involves an independent third person who assists both parties involved in a family dispute to reach a resolution. Family mediation can be used to settle any or all of the following issues:

    - Financial arrangements and dividing up property
    - Arrangements for children
    - Any combination of these
    - Any other disputes to do with separation and divorce.

24. The family mediator helps the process of negotiation between the parties to agree their own arrangements by way of a Memorandum of Understanding. You can ask a solicitor, if you have one, to check the Memorandum of Understanding.
25. If both parties agree, you can ask the court to endorse what you have agreed by issuing a consent order. The mediator will help you to decide whether your case is complicated and does in fact need the court to consider your situation and make an order. The mediator should also tell you about other local services and options for resolving your dispute.
26. A statutory Mediation Information and Assessment Meeting (MIAM) is reserved for "authorised mediators" under the Family Procedure Rules. "Authorised family mediator" means a person identified by the Family Mediation Council as qualified to conduct a MIAM. "Qualified to conduct a MIAM" is interpreted as holding current Family Mediation Council accreditation (FMCA). FMCA mediators are issued with a unique FMC registration number. Authorised mediators are requested to enter this number in the box provided.

Further information and sources of help

27. General information about family mediation is available from the Family Mediation Council website at: www.familymediationcouncil.org.uk
28. The family mediator who undertakes the MIAM for you must be a member of a national mediation organisation which adheres to the Family Mediation Council's Code of Conduct and the mediator must be authorised to conduct MIAMs. The service finder will help you find such a local mediator.
29. You can find out more about legal aid for family matters, including whether you may eligible for legal aid on the Legal Aid Information Service on the Gov. UK site at: www.gov.uk/check-legal-aid or you can telephone the Civil Legal Advice direct helpline 0345 345 4345.
30. For general advice on separation services and options for resolving disputes: www.sortingoutseparation.org.uk
31. For help with taking a case to court without a lawyer, the Personal Support Unit: www.thepsu.org/
32. For guidance on representing yourself at court, including a list of commonly used terms that you may come across: http://www.barcouncil.org.uk/using-a-barrister/representing-yourself-in-court/
33. For advice about finding and using a family law solicitor see: Law Society www.lawsociety.org.uk, and Resolution (family law solicitors): www.resolution.org.uk
34. For advice about finding a family law barrister: see http://www.barcouncil.org.uk/using-a-barrister/find-a-barrister/ and for arrangements for using a barrister directly see http://www.barcouncil.org.uk/using-a-barrister/ how-to-instruct-a-barrister/

5.91

Notice of [intention to proceed with] a financial application to which the fast-track procedure applies

Notice of [intention to proceed with] a financial application to which the fast-track procedure applies	To be completed by the Applicant	
	The Family Court sitting at	Case No.
	To be completed by the court	
	Fee charged/Remission ID	

This form should **only** be completed if you are applying for one of the following orders for financial provision (a financial order or other financial remedy) to which the fast-track procedure applies:
- an application for a periodical payments order **only** (under section 23 of the Matrimonial Causes Act 1973, paragraph 2 of Schedule 5 to the Civil Partnership Act 2004 or paragraphs 1 or 2 of Schedule 1 to the Children Act 1989)
- financial provision under Part 1 of the Domestic Proceedings and Magistrates' Courts Act 1978 or Schedule 6 to the Civil Partnership Act 2004
- an application to vary or discharge a periodical payments order, **except** where you seek to discharge it and to substitute for it one or more of the following orders: a lump sum order, a property adjustment order, a pension sharing order or a pension compensation sharing order – use Form A in these circumstances.

If you are applying for:
- a periodical payments order **together with** another type of financial order or financial remedy – please complete Form A.
- financial provision after an overseas divorce etc (use Form D50F) or on the ground of failure to maintain a party or child (use Form D50C) or for alteration of a maintenance agreement during the parties' lifetime (use Form D50H)

Full name of applicant

Full name of respondent(s)

Nature of application

This application is for financial provision, including provision to be made to or for the benefit of the child(ren):
- ☐ in connection with matrimonial or civil partnership proceedings (divorce, dissolution etc), **or**
- ☐ under paragraphs 1 or 2 of Schedule 1 to the Children Act 1989, **or**
- ☐ under Part 1 of the Domestic Proceedings and Magistrates' Courts Act 1978 or Schedule 6 to the Civil Partnership Act 2004

tick the statement that applies	and	tick one of the following orders
The applicant intends: ☐ **to apply** to the Court for, **or:** ☐ **to proceed with** the application in the [divorce][dissolution][nullity][annulment][(judicial) separation] application for, **or** ☐ **to apply to vary,** or ☐ **to apply to discharge**		☐ a periodical payments order **only** ☐ a periodical payments order or lump sum order under Part 1 of the Domestic Proceedings and Magistrates' Courts Act 1978 or Schedule 6 to the Civil Partnership Act 2004
Are you applying for an order by consent in the terms of a written agreement (a consent order)?	☐ Yes ☐ No	If Yes, **attach the draft order to this form**

Form A1 Notice of [intention to proceed with] a financial application to which the fast-track procedure applies (06.18)

Page 1 of 15

© Crown Copyright Published by LexisNexis 2018 under the Open Government Licence

5.91 Children

1. Further details of the financial application

If an application is made for any periodical payments or secured periodical payments for children please complete this section:

☐ there is a written agreement made before 5 April 1993 about maintenance for the benefit of children;

☐ there is a written agreement made on or after 5 April 1993 about maintenance for the benefit of children; or

☐ there is no agreement, but the applicant is applying for payment:

　☐ for a stepchild or stepchildren

　☐ in addition to child support maintenance already paid under a Child Support Agency assessment

　☐ to meet expenses arising from a child's disability

　☐ to meet expenses incurred by a child in being educated or training for work

　☐ when either the child **or** the person with care of the child **or** the absent parent of the child is not habitually resident in the United Kingdom

If none of the above applies, the court may not have jurisdiction to hear the application for periodical payments.

Has the Child Support Agency made any calculation of maintenance in respect of the child(ren)

☐ Yes　　　☐ No

If Yes, state briefly your reasons for making this application to the court including any reasons why the Child Support Agency is no longer dealing with your claim or any reasons why you need additional maintenance to top up payments made through the Child Support Agency:

If you are making a financial application for a child please complete the tables below for each child continuing on additional sheets if necessary, and then complete the statement of truth.

Name of child 1	
Date of birth	
Gender	☐ Male　　☐ Female
Relationship to Applicant	
Relationship to Respondent	
Country of residence (if not England or Wales)	

Precedents **5.91**

Service details

☐ I am not represented by a solicitor in these proceedings

☐ I am not represented by a solicitor in these proceedings but am receiving advice from a solicitor

☐ I am represented by a solicitor in these proceedings, who has signed Section 6, and all documents for my attention should be sent to my solicitor whose details are as follows:

Solicitor's details

Name of solicitor	
Name of firm	

Address to which all documents should be sent for service:		Telephone no.	
		Fax no.	
		DX no.	
Postcode		Your ref.	

E-mail	

Respondent's address for service

Address (including postcode)
Postcode

433

5.91 *Children*

2. Applicant and Respondent details

Applicant's details 1

Name of Applicant

Applicant's address (including postcode)

Postcode

Telephone no.

Ref.

Email address

Respondent's details 1

Name of Respondent

Respondent's address (including postcode)

Postcode

Telephone no.

Ref.

Email address

Have there been any previous court orders or written agreements regarding financial provision?

☐ Yes   ☐ No

If Yes, please attach a copy of the order or written agreement. If the order is not available, please state the date, the terms, the parties and the court below:

Precedents 5.91

3. Requirement to attend a Mediation, Information and Assessment Meeting (MIAM)

Before making an application for a financial remedy you must first attend a Mediation, Information and Assessment Meeting (MIAM). At the MIAM an authorised family mediator will consider with you (and the other party if present) whether family mediation, or another form of non-court dispute resolution, would be a more appropriate alternative to court. The mediator will also be able to sign post you to other help and support services.

You **must** have attended a MIAM before making this application **unless** the requirement to attend a MIAM does not apply because the financial order you are applying for:
- is for a consent order; **or**
- you are exempt from the requirement to attend a MIAM. (Some exemptions you can claim for yourself, others must be certified by an authorised family mediator).

In special circumstances such as where domestic violence is involved, you may not need to attend a MIAM. However, you will be asked to provide the judge with evidence (such as a police report to prove domestic violence has taken place) and should bring it to the first hearing.

All applicants must complete sections 1 and 2 and complete and sign section 6 of this form. **In addition**, you must tick one of the boxes below and ensure that you, your legal adviser or a family mediator completes (and where indicated signs) the relevant section(s) of this form as shown.

3a.	Are you claiming exemption from the requirement to attend a MIAM?	☐ Yes	☐ No	**If Yes, complete section 4.** **If No, please answer question 3b.**
3b.	Has a family mediator informed you that a mediator's exemption applies, and you do not need to attend a MIAM?	☐ Yes	☐ No	**If Yes, you must ensure that the family mediator completes and signs section 5a.** **If No, please answer question 3c.**
3c.	Have you attended a MIAM?	☐ Yes	☐ No	**If Yes, you must ensure that the family mediator completes and signs section 5b.** **If No, you cannot make this application.**

4. Applicant claims exemption(s) from attendance at a Mediation, Information and Assessment Meeting (MIAM)

(To be completed by the person intending to make a court application or their legal representative)

The applicant has not attended a MIAM because the following MIAM exemption(s) applies:

- ☐ Domestic violence (you must complete **section 4a**)
- ☐ Urgency (you must complete **section 4b**)
- ☐ Previous MIAM attendance or previous MIAM exemption (you must complete **section 4c**)
- ☐ Other (you must complete **section 4d**)

Now complete the relevant section 4a, b, c or d by ticking the appropriate box(s)

Further details of MIAM exemption(s) claimed by the applicant

If you have claimed a MIAM exemption above you must also tick the relevant box(s), as shown below to confirm that you have the necessary evidence to support your ground(s) for exemption and should bring it to the first hearing. Where you are asked to provide additional details you must do so.

Section 4a - Domestic violence evidence

The applicant confirms that there is evidence of domestic violence, as specified below:

- ☐ evidence that a prospective party has been arrested for a relevant domestic violence offence;
- ☐ evidence of a relevant police caution for a domestic violence offence;
- ☐ evidence of relevant criminal proceedings for a domestic violence offence which have not concluded;
- ☐ evidence of a relevant conviction for a domestic violence offence;
- ☐ a court order binding a prospective party over in connection with a domestic violence offence;
- ☐ a domestic violence protection notice issued under section 24 of the Crime and Security Act 2010 against a prospective party;
- ☐ a relevant protective injunction;
- ☐ an undertaking given in England and Wales under section 46 or 63E of the Family Law Act 1996 (or given in Scotland or Northern Ireland in place of a protective injunction) by a prospective party, provided that a cross-undertaking relating to domestic violence was not given by another prospective party;
- ☐ a copy of a finding of fact, made in proceedings in the United Kingdom, that there has been domestic violence by a prospective party;
- ☐ an expert report produced as evidence in proceedings in the United Kingdom for the benefit of a court or tribunal confirming that a person with whom a prospective party is or was in a family relationship, was assessed as being, or at risk of being, a victim of domestic violence by that prospective party;

Precedents **5.91**

Section 4a - Domestic violence evidence - **continued**

☐ a letter or report from an appropriate health professional confirming that-
    (i) that professional, or another appropriate health professional, has examined a prospective party in person; and
    (ii) in the reasonable professional judgment of the author or the examining appropriate health professional, that prospective party has, or has had, injuries or a condition consistent with being a victim of domestic violence;

a letter or report from-
☐ (i) the appropriate health professional who made the referral described below;
    (ii) an appropriate health professional who has access to the medical records of the prospective party referred to below; or
    (iii) the person to whom the referral described below was made;

confirming that there was a referral by an appropriate health professional of a prospective party to a person who provides specialist support or assistance for victims of, or those at risk of, domestic violence;

☐ a letter from any person who is a member of a multi-agency risk assessment conference (or other suitable local safeguarding forum) confirming that a prospective party, or a person with whom that prospective party is in a family relationship, is or has been at risk of harm from domestic violence by another prospective party;

☐ a letter from an independent domestic violence advisor confirming that they are providing support to a prospective party;

☐ a letter from an independent sexual violence advisor confirming that they are providing support to a prospective party relating to sexual violence by another prospective party;

☐ a letter from an officer employed by a local authority or housing association (or their equivalent in Scotland or Northern Ireland) for the purpose of supporting tenants containing-
    (i) a statement to the effect that, in their reasonable professional judgment, a person with whom a prospective party is or has been in a family relationship is, or is at risk of being, a victim of domestic violence by that prospective party;
    (ii) a description of the specific matters relied upon to support that judgment; and
    (iii) a description of the support they provided to the victim of domestic violence or the person at risk of domestic violence by that prospective party;

5.91 Children

Section 4a - Domestic violence evidence - **continued**

☐ a letter which-
  (i) is from an organisation providing domestic violence support services, or a registered charity, which letter confirms that it-
    (a) is situated in England and Wales,
    (b) has been operating for an uninterrupted period of six months or more; and
    (c) provided a prospective party with support in relation to that person's needs as a victim, or a person at risk, of domestic violence; and
  (ii) contains-
    (a) a statement to the effect that, in the reasonable professional judgment of the author of the letter, the prospective party is, or is at risk of being, a victim of domestic violence;
    (b) a description of the specific matters relied upon to support that judgment;
    (c) a description of the support provided to the prospective party; and
    (d) a statement of the reasons why the prospective party needed that support;

☐ a letter or report from an organisation providing domestic violence support services in the United Kingdom confirming-

  (i) that a person with whom a prospective party is or was in a family relationship was refused admission to a refuge;

  (ii) the date on which they were refused admission to the refuge; and

  (iii) they sought admission to the refuge because of allegations of domestic violence by the prospective party referred to in paragraph (i);

☐ a letter from a public authority confirming that a person with whom a prospective party is or was in a family relationship, was assessed as being, or at risk of being, a victim of domestic violence by that prospective party (or a copy of that assessment);

☐ a letter from the Secretary of State for the Home Department confirming that a prospective party has been granted leave to remain in the United Kingdom under paragraph 289B of the Rules made by the Home Secretary under section 3(2) of the Immigration Act 1971, which can be found at https://www.gov.uk/guidance/immigration-rules/immigration-rules-index;

☐ evidence which demonstrates that a prospective party has been, or is at risk of being, the victim of domestic violence by another prospective party in the form of abuse which relates to financial matters.

Section 4b – Urgency

The applicant confirms that the application must be made urgently because:

☐ there is risk to the life, liberty or physical safety of the prospective applicant or his or her family or his or her home; or

☐ any delay caused by attending a MIAM would cause—

  ☐ a significant risk of a miscarriage of justice; or

  ☐ unreasonable hardship to the prospective applicant; or

Precedents **5.91**

Section 4b – Urgency - continued

☐ irretrievable problems in dealing with the dispute (including the irretrievable loss of significant evidence); or

☐ there is a significant risk that in the period necessary to schedule and attend a MIAM, proceedings relating to the dispute will be brought in another state in which a valid claim to jurisdiction may exist, such that a court in that other State would be seized of the dispute before a court in England and Wales.

Section 4c – Previous MIAM attendance or MIAM exemption

The applicant confirms that one of the following applies:

☐ in the 4 months prior to making the application, the person attended a MIAM or participated in another form of non-court dispute resolution relating to the same or substantially the same dispute; or

☐ at the time of making the application, the person is participating in another form of non-court dispute resolution relating to the same or substantially the same dispute; or

☐ in the 4 months prior to making the application, the person filed a relevant family application confirming that a MIAM exemption applied and that application related to the same or substantially the same dispute; or

☐ the application would be made in existing proceedings which are continuing and the prospective applicant attended a MIAM before initiating those proceedings; or

☐ the application would be made in existing proceedings which are continuing and a MIAM exemption applied to the application for those proceedings.

Section 4d – Other exemptions

The applicant confirms that one of the following other grounds for exemption applies:

☐ evidence that the prospective applicant is bankrupt exists in one of the following forms:

  ☐ application by the prospective applicant for a bankruptcy order;

  ☐ petition by a creditor of the prospective applicant for a bankruptcy order; or

  ☐ a bankruptcy order in respect of the prospective applicant.

☐ the prospective applicant does not have sufficient contact details for any of the prospective respondents to enable a family mediator to contact any of the prospective respondents for the purpose of scheduling the MIAM.

☐ the application would be made without notice (Paragraph 5.1 of Practice Direction 18A sets out the circumstances in which applications may be made without notice.)

5.91 *Children*

☐ (i) the prospective applicant is or all of the prospective respondents are subject to a disability or other inability that would prevent attendance at a MIAM unless appropriate facilities can be offered by an authorised mediator;
(ii) the prospective applicant has contacted as many authorised family mediators as have an office within fifteen miles of his or her home (or three of them if there are three or more), and all have stated that they are unable to provide such facilities; and
(iii) the names, postal addresses and telephone numbers or e-mail addresses for such authorised family mediators, and the dates of contact, can be provided to the court if requested.

☐ the prospective applicant or all of the prospective respondents cannot attend a MIAM because he or she is, or they are, as the case may be
(i) in prison or any other institution in which he or she is or they are required to be detained;
(ii) subject to conditions of bail that prevent contact with the other person; or
(iii) subject to a licence with a prohibited contact requirement in relation to the other person.

☐ the prospective applicant or all of the prospective respondents are not habitually resident in England and Wales.

☐ a child is one of the prospective parties by virtue of Rule 12.3(1).

☐ (i) the prospective applicant has contacted as many authorised family mediators as have an office within fifteen miles of his or her home (or three of them if there are three or more), and all of them have stated that they are not available to conduct a MIAM within fifteen business days of the date of contact; and
(ii) the names, postal addresses and telephone numbers or e-mail addresses for such authorised family mediators, and the dates of contact, can be provided to the court if requested.

☐ there is no authorised family mediator with an office within fifteen miles of the prospective applicant's home.

Now complete Section 6.

5. Mediator certifies that the prospective applicant is exempt from attendance at Mediation Information and Assessment Meeting (MIAM) or confirms MIAM attendance

(To be completed and signed by the authorised family mediator)
(tick the boxes that apply)

5a. The following MIAM exemption(s) applies:

☐ An authorised family mediator confirms that he or she is satisfied that -

    ☐ (a) mediation is not suitable as a means of resolving the dispute because none of the respondents is willing to attend a MIAM; or

    ☐ (b) mediation is not suitable as a means of resolving the dispute because all of the respondents failed without good reason to attend a MIAM appointment; or

    ☐ (c) mediation is otherwise not suitable as a means of resolving the dispute.

5b. The prospective applicant attended a MIAM:

☐ The prospective applicant only attended a MIAM.

☐ The prospective applicant and respondent party(s) attended the MIAM together.

☐ The prospective and respondent(s) have each attended separate MIAM.

☐ The prospective respondent party(s) has/have made or is/are making arrangements to attend a separate MIAM.

Mediation or other form of Dispute Resolution is not proceeding because:

☐ The applicant has attended a MIAM alone and
- the applicant does not wish to start or continue mediation; or
- the mediator has determined that mediation is unsuitable; or
- the respondent did not wish to attend a MIAM

☐ Both the applicant and respondent have attended a MIAM (separately or together) and
- the applicant does not wish to start or continue mediation; or
- the respondent does not wish to start or continue mediation;
- the mediator has determined that mediation is unsuitable

☐ Mediation has started, but has:
- broken down; or
- concluded with some or all issues unresolved

Signed	
	Authorised Family Mediator (a family mediator who is authorised to undertake MIAMs)
FMC Registration no.	
Family Mediation Service name	
Sole trader name	
Address	
Dated	

6. Statement of truth

*delete as appropriate

*[I believe] [the Applicant believes] that the facts stated in this application are true

*I am duly authorised by the applicant to sign this statement.

Print full name	
Name of applicant solicitors firm	
Address of solicitor's firm	
Signed	
	(Applicant) (Litigation friend) (Applicant's solicitor)
Dated	
Position or office held (If signing on behalf of firm or company)	

Proceedings for contempt of court may be brought against a person who makes or causes to be made, a false statement in a document verified by a statement of truth.

Precedents **5.91**

Checklist for completing Form A1

Page 1
- ☐ Write in your full name and the full name of the respondent.
- ☐ Tick the nature of financial application you are making and the type(s) of order you are seeking
- ☐ Tick if you are applying for an order by consent in the terms of a written agreement (a consent order).

Page 2 and 3
- ☐ Tick the relevant box(es) to provide further details about the financial provision you are applying for, and provide additional information where shown.

Page 3
- ☐ Complete the details for service.

Page 4
- ☐ Complete the applicant and respondent details.

Page 5
- ☐ Answer questions 3a to 3c about whether a MIAM exemption applies or whether you have attended a MIAM.

Page 6
- ☐ If you answered question 3a on page 5 with "yes" you must tick one of the first four boxes box in section 4 to indicate the category of MIAM exemption that you are claiming. You must then complete section 4a, b, c, or d as shown.

Page 10
- ☐ If a family mediator needs to certify that a mediator's exemption applies you must ask them to complete section 5a of this form and sign where shown.

- ☐ If you have attended a MIAM you must ask the family mediator who conducted it to complete section 5b of the form and sign where shown.

Page 11
- ☐ Check that you (or your solicitor if relevant) have completed and signed section 6.

What you do next
You should normally make your application to the Designated Family Centre for your area. You can find this, and a full list of courts and what type of work they do online at courttribunalfinder.service.gov.uk

Fees
You may need to pay a fee with your application. You should read leaflet EX50 Civil and family court fees to find out what fee, if any, you need to pay. This leaflet is available from your local court or online at hmctsformfinder.justice.gov.uk

5.91 Children

General information for completing this form

1. You need to complete this form if you want to ask the court to make one of the orders shown on page 1. You must tick the relevant boxes on page 1 to indicate the nature of your application and the type of order you are seeking.

2. Pages 1 to 3 set out the core information you need to provide if you wish to make an application to the court. You or your solicitor must also sign and date the Section 6 of this form.

3. If you are applying for an order by consent you should tick the box on page 1 to make this clear and attach the draft order with this application

Requirement to attend a Mediation, Information and Assessment Meeting

4. It is now a legal requirement that, unless an exemption applies, a person who wishes to apply to court for a financial order must first attend a Mediation, Information and Assessment Meeting (a MIAM). At the stage before proceedings the other party (the respondent) is expected to attend either the same MIAM or a separate MIAM.

5. At the MIAM, a trained family mediator will give you (the applicant) and the other person if present (the respondent) information about family mediation and other types of non-court dispute resolution. They will consider with you whether non-court dispute resolution would be an appropriate way to resolve the dispute. It is then for the applicant and respondent to decide whether or not to do so.

6. The requirement for the applicant to attend a MIAM does not apply if a financial order is being applied for and the other person (respondent) is in agreement about what you are asking the court to order (the order is a "consent order").

7. You or your solicitor must tick the relevant box in Section 3 of this form so that the court knows whether the MIAM requirement applies, whether an exemption applies (and why) or whether you have attended a MIAM.

MIAM exemptions and MIAM attendance

8. As the applicant you are expected to have contacted an authorised family mediator in order to make arrangements to attend a MIAM unless:
    - the MIAM requirement does not apply for the reason explained at paragraph 6 of these notes, or
    - you are claiming a MIAM exemption, or a family mediator certifies that a mediator's exemption applies.

9. You can find an authorised family mediator by using the 'Find your local mediator' search facility available at: www.familymediationcouncil.org.uk

10. You should give the mediator the contact details of the other person so that the family mediator can contact them to check their willingness to attend a MIAM. If the other persons (or none of the other persons if there is more than one respondent) are unwilling to attend a MIAM this is a ground for the family mediator to exempt you from attending a MIAM.

11. If you or your solicitor believe that you have grounds for claiming exemption from MIAM attendance you or your solicitor must tick the relevant box in Section 3 of this form and complete Section 4.

12. If a family mediator wishes to certify that a mediator's exemption applies, so that you do not need to attend a MIAM, you must ask the family mediator to complete Section 5a of this form and sign it where shown.

13. If you have attended a MIAM you must ask the family mediator who conducted the MIAM to complete Section 5b of this form and sign it where shown.

14. If you claim a MIAM exemption and make an application to the court, the court will inquire into the grounds for exemption. The court may ask you to produce written evidence (see Section 4 of this form for details against each exemption shown).

15. If the court determines that the exemption was not validly claimed it may direct you, or you and the other party, to attend a MIAM and, if the case has already progressed to the first hearing, may adjourn the case to enable you to make arrangements to attend a MIAM.

16. The detailed procedure relating to the MIAM requirement and MIAM exemptions and attendance is set out in Part 3 of the Family Procedure Rules and in supporting Practice Direction 3A (judicial guidance). These are available online at: www.justice.gov.uk/courts/ procedure-rules/family/practice_directions/pd_ part_03a

Paying for MIAM attendance or for family mediation

17. Legal aid is available for MIAMs and for family mediation. If you are eligible for legal aid you could receive both the MIAM and mediation sessions free of charge, as well as some advice from a solicitor to support you in the mediation process.

18. If you, or the prospective respondent, is eligible for Legal Aid then the total cost of MIAM attendance can be met by the Legal Aid Agency, whether you and the prospective respondent attend the same MIAM or separate MIAMs.

19. If neither you nor the respective respondent is eligible for Legal Aid then the mediator will agree with you how the cost of MIAM attendance is to be met.

20. Please refer to paragraph 29 for further details on how you can find out whether you are eligible for Legal Aid by using the calculator tool available at www.gov.uk/legal-aid

Safety and MIAM attendance

21. Please note: the family mediator will discuss with you and with the other person whether you wish to attend the MIAM separately or together. Family mediators have a responsibility to ensure the safety and security of all concerned and will always check with each of you that attending together is your individual choice and is safe.

Information about mediation

22. If suitable, mediation can be a better way of resolving issues about financial arrangements when you or your partner petition for a matrimonial or civil partnership order. Mediation can be less expensive than going to court and much less stressful for all the family.

23. Family Mediation is an impartial process that involves an independent third person who assists both parties involved in a family dispute to reach a resolution. Family mediation can be used to settle any or all of the following issues:

    - Financial arrangements and dividing up property
    - Arrangements for children
    - Any combination of these
    - Any other disputes to do with separation and divorce.

24. The family mediator helps the process of negotiation between the parties to agree their own arrangements by way of a Memorandum of Understanding. You can ask a solicitor, if you have one, to check the Memorandum of Understanding.

25. If both parties agree, you can ask the court to endorse what you have agreed by issuing a consent order. The mediator will help you to decide whether your case is complicated and does in fact need the court to consider your situation and make an order. The mediator should also tell you about other local services and options for resolving your dispute.

26. A statutory Mediation Information and Assessment Meeting (MIAM) is reserved for "authorised mediators" under the Family Procedure Rules. "Authorised family mediator" means a person identified by the Family Mediation Council as qualified to conduct a MIAM. "Qualified to conduct a MIAM" is interpreted as holding current Family Mediation Council accreditation (FMCA). FMCA mediators are issued with a unique FMC registration number. This number should be entered by the authorised mediator in the box provided.

Further information and sources of help

27. General information about family mediation is available from the Family Mediation Council website at: www.familymediationcouncil.org.uk

28. The family mediator who undertakes the MIAM for you must be a member of a national mediation organisation which adheres to the Family Mediation Council's Code of Conduct and the mediator must be authorised to conduct MIAMs. The service finder will help you find such a local mediator.

29. You can find out more about legal aid for family matters, including whether you may eligible for legal aid on the Legal Aid Information Service on the Gov. UK site at: www.gov.uk/check-legal-aid or you can telephone the Civil Legal Advice direct helpline 0345 345 4345.

30. For general advice on separation services and options for resolving disputes: www.sortingoutseparation.org.uk

31. For help with taking a case to court without a lawyer, the Personal Support Unit: www.thepsu.org/

32. For guidance on representing yourself at court, including a list of commonly used terms that you may come across: www.barcouncil.org.uk/instructing-a-barrister/representing-yourself-in-court/

33. For advice about finding and using a family law solicitor see: Law Society www.lawsociety.org.uk, and Resolution (family law solicitors): www.resolution.org.uk

34. For advice about finding using a family law barrister: see www.barcouncil.org.uk/about-the-bar/find-abarrister/ and for arrangements for using a barrister directly see www.barcouncil.org.uk/using-a-barrister/how-to-instruct-a-barrister/

5.92 Children

5.92

Financial Statement for a financial remedy (other than a financial order or financial relief after an overseas divorce or dissolution etc) in the family court or High Court

Financial Statement for a financial remedy (other than a financial order or financial relief after an overseas divorce or dissolution etc) in the family court or High Court

Name of Court	
Case No.	
Name of Applicant	
Name of Respondent	

(please tick appropriate boxes)

This is the Financial Statement of the

☐ Applicant
☐ Respondent

in this application

This form should only be completed if you are applying for a financial remedy other than a financial order or financial relief after an overseas divorce or dissolution etc. in the family court or high court.

If you are applying for a financial order (which can only be applied for as part of a divorce, dissolution, annulment or (judicial) separation in the High Court or family court in England and Wales) or for financial relief after an overseas divorce or dissolution etc. you should complete Form E.

If you are applying for a financial remedy in the magistrates' court you should complete Form E2.

Please fill in this form fully and accurately. Where any box is not applicable, write 'N/A'.

You have a duty to the court to give a full, frank and clear disclosure of all your financial and other relevant circumstances.

A failure to give full and accurate disclosure may result in any order the court makes being set aside.

If you are found to have been deliberately untruthful, criminal proceedings may be brought against you for fraud under the Fraud Act 2006.

The information given in this form must be confirmed by a statement of truth. **Proceedings for contempt of court may be brought against a person who makes or causes to be made, a false statement in a document verified by a statement of truth.**

You must attach documents to the form where they are specifically sought and you may attach other documents where it is necessary to explain or clarify any of the information that you give.

If there is not enough room on the form for any particular piece of information, you may continue on an attached sheet of paper.

If you are in doubt about how to complete any part of this form you should seek legal advice.

This statement is filed by

Solicitor's fee account no.

Name and address of solicitor

Form E1 Financial Statement for a financial remedy in the family court or High Court (11.14)
http://www.hmcourts-service.gov.uk/cms/index.htm © Crown Copyright Published by LexisNexis 2015 under the Open Government Licence

1. General information

1.1 Full name

1.2 Date of birth DD \ MM \ YYYY 1.2A Occupation

1.3 Are you married/in a civil partnership? ☐ Yes ☐ No

1.4 If you are not married or in a civil partnership are you living with a partner? ☐ Yes ☐ No

1.5 Your present residence and the occupants of it and on what terms you occupy it (e.g. tenant, owner-occupier).

Address	Occupants	Terms of occupation

1.6 Children living with you

Names	Date of birth
	DD \ MM \ YYYY

1.7 Children not living with you

Names	Date of birth
	DD \ MM \ YYYY

Amount of any maintenance being paid £ _____

5.92 Children

1.8 Other dependents
(Give details – including whether you have these responsibilities on a permanent basis).

Names	Details

1.9 Details of the state of health of yourself and the children if you think this should be taken into account.

Yourself	Children

1.10 Details of the present and proposed future educational arrangements for the children.

Present arrangements	Future arrangements

1.11 Details of any child support maintenance calculation or any maintenance order or agreement made in respect of any children of the family. If no calculation, order or agreement has been made, give an estimate of the liability of the non-resident parent in respect of the children of the family under the Child Support Act 1991.

1.12 Details of any other court cases between you and your spouse/civil partner, whether in relation to money, property, children or anything else.

Case No.	Court	Type of proceedings

2. Employment

2.1 I am ☐ employed (complete 2.2)
☐ self employed (complete 2.3)
☐ unemployed (go to 3.)
☐ a pensioner (go to 3.)

5.92 Children

2.2 Details of earned income from employment. Complete one page for each employment

> Documentation required for attachment to this section:
> a) P60 for the last financial year (you should have received this from your employer shortly after the last 5th April)
> b) Your last three payslips
> c) Your last Form P11D if you have been issued with one

Name and address of your employer	
Job title and brief details of the type of work you do	
Hours worked per week in this employment	
How long have you been with this employer?	
Explain the basis of your income i.e. state whether it is based on an annual salary or an hourly rate of pay and whether it includes commissions or bonuses	
Gross income for the last financial year as shown on your P60	
Net income for the last financial year i.e. gross income less income tax and national insurance	
Average net income for the last three months i.e. total income less income tax and national insurance divided by three	
Briefly explain any other entries on the attached payslips other than basic income, income tax and national insurance	
If the payslips attached for the last three months are not an accurate reflection of your normal income briefly explain why	
Details and value of any bonuses or other occasional payments that you receive from this employment not otherwise already shown, including the basis upon which they are paid	
Details and value of any benefits in kind, perks or other remuneration received from this employer in the last year (e.g. provision of a car, payment of travel, accommodation, meal expenses, etc.	
Your estimate of your net income from this employment for the next 12 months.	
Estimated TOTAL of ALL net earned income from employment for the next 12 months: Total A £	

2.3 Income from self-employment or partnership

Complete this section giving details of your income from your business. Complete one page for each business.

> Documentation required for attachment to this section:
> a) Copies of your business accounts for the last 2 years
> b) A copy of your last tax assessment or, if that is not available, a letter from your accountant confirming your tax liability
> c) If net income from the last financial year and estimated net income for the next 12 months is significantly different, a copy of management accounts for the period since your last account

Name of the business	
Date to which your last accounts were completed	
Your share of gross business profit from the last completed accounts	
Income tax and national insurance payable on your share of gross business profit above	
Net income for that year (using the two figures directly above, gross business profit less income tax and national insurance payable)	
Details and value of any benefits in kind, perks or other remuneration received from this business in the last year e.g. provision of a car, payment of travel, accommodation, meal expenses, etc.	
Amount of any regular monthly or other drawings that you take from this business	
If the estimated figure directly below is different from the net income as at the end date of the last completed accounts, briefly explain the reason(s)	
Your estimate of your net annual income for the next 12 months	

Estimated TOTAL of ALL net income from self-employment or partnership for the next 12 months: Total B   £   0.00

5.92 *Children*

3. Other income

3.1 Details of income from investments (e.g. dividends, interest or rental income) received in the last financial year (the year ended last 5th April), and your estimate of your income for the current financial year. Indicate whether the income was paid gross or net of income tax. You are not required to calculate any tax payable that may arise.

Nature of income and the asset from which it derived	Paid gross or net	Income received in the last financial year	Estimated income for the next 12 months
	Estimated TOTAL investment income for the next 12 months:	Total C £	

3.2 Details of all state benefits (including state pension and child benefit) that you are currently receiving.

Name of benefit	Amount paid	Frequency of payment	Estimated income for the next 12 months
	Estimated TOTAL benefit income for the next 12 months:	Total D £	

3.3 Details of any other income not disclosed above.
INCLUDE:
Any source including a Pension (excluding State Pension), and Pension Protection Fund (PPF) compensation
- from which income has been received during the last 12 months (even if it has now ceased)
- from which income is likely to be received during the next 12 months

You are reminded of your obligation to give full disclosure of your financial circumstances.

Nature of income	Paid gross or net	Income received in the last financial year	Estimated income for the next 12 months
	Estimated TOTAL other income for the next 12 months:	Total E £	

Form E1

Precedents **5.92**

4. Capital

4.1 Details of your interest in property, land or buildings. Complete one page for each property you have an interest in.

> Documentation required for attachment to this section:
> a) A copy of any valuation of the property obtained within the last six months. If you cannot provide this document, please give your own realistic estimate of the current market value
> b) A recent mortgage statement confirming the sum outstanding on each mortgage

Property name and address	
Land Registry title number	
Mortgage company name(s) and address(es) and account number(s)	
Type of mortgage	
Details of who owns the property and the extent of your legal and beneficial interest in it (i.e. state if it is owned by you solely or jointly owned with your spouse/civil partner or with others)	
If you consider that the legal ownership as recorded at the Land Registry does not reflect the true position, state why	
State your percentage interest in the property	% 100
Current market value of the property	
Balance outstanding on any mortgage(s)	
If a sale at this stage would result in penalties payable under the mortgage, state amount	
Estimate the costs of sale of the property	
Total equity in the property (i.e. market value less outstanding mortgage(s), penalties if any and the costs of sale)	
TOTAL value of your interest in ALL other property: Total F £	0.00

Form E1

5.92 Children

4.2 Details of all personal bank, building society and National Savings Accounts that you hold or have held at any time in the last twelve months and which are or were either in your own name or in which you have or have had any interest. This applies whether any such account is in credit or in debit. For joint accounts give your interest and the name of the other account holder. If the account is overdrawn, show a minus figure.

Documentation required for attachment to this section:
For each account listed, all statements covering the last 12 months.

Name of bank or building society, including branch name	Type of account (e.g. current)	Account number	Name of other account holder (if applicable)	Balance at the date of this statement	Total current value of your interest
			TOTAL value of your interest in ALL accounts: (G1) £		

4.3 Details of all investments, including shares, PEPs, ISAs, TESSAs, National Savings Investments (other than already shown above), bonds, stocks, unit trusts, investment trusts, gilts and other quoted securities that you hold or have an interest in. (Do not include dividend income as this will be dealt with separately later on.)

Documentation required for attachment to this section:
Latest statement or dividend counterfoil relating to each investment.

Name	Type of Investment	Size of holding	Current value	Name of any other account holder (if applicable)	Total current value of your interest
			TOTAL value of your interest in ALL holdings: (G2) £		

Form E1

4.4 Details of all life insurance policies including endowment policies that you hold or have an interest in. Include those that do not have a surrender value. Complete one page for each policy.

> Documentation required for attachment to this section:
> A surrender valuation of each policy that has a surrender value.

Name of company	
Policy type	
Policy number	
If policy is assigned, state in whose favour and amount of charge	
Name of any other owner and the extent of your interest in the policy	
Maturity date (if applicable)	D D \ M M \ Y Y Y Y
Current surrender value (if applicable)	
If policy includes life insurance, the amount of the insurance and the name of the person whose life is insured	
Total current surrender value of your interest in this policy	

TOTAL value of your interest in ALL policies: (G3) £

Add together the totals of G1 to G3 to give TOTAL G £

5.92 Children

4.5 Give details of any other assets not listed above.
INCLUDE (the following list is not exhaustive):
- Any personal or business assets not yet disclosed
- Any monies owed to you
- Any cash sums held in excess of £500
- Any other personal belonging individually worth more than £500
- Trust interests (including interests under a discretionary trust), stating your estimate of the value of the interest and when it is likely to become realisable. If you say it will never be realisable, or has no value, give your reasons
- Any asset that is likely to be received in the foreseeable future
- Any asset held on your behalf by a third party
- Any asset not disclosed elsewhere on this form even if held outside England and Wales
- You are reminded of your obligation to disclose all your financial assets and interests of ANY nature.

Type of asset	Value	Total NET value of your interest
TOTAL value of ALL your other assets: Total H	£	

4.6 Details of any liabilities you have.
EXCLUDE liabilities already shown such as:
Mortgages
Any overdrawn bank, building society or National Savings accounts
INCLUDE:
Money owed on credit cards and store cards
Bank loans
Hire purchase agreements
List all credit and store cards held including those with a nil or positive balance. Where the liability is not solely your own, give the name(s) of the other account holder(s) and the amount of your share of the liability.

Liability	Name(s) of other account holder(s) (if applicable)	Total liability	Total current value of your interest in the liability
TOTAL value of your interest in ALL liabilities: Total I		£	

Form E1

Precedents **5.92**

5. Income needs
(Do not include any payments made by other members of the household out of their own income)

5.1 I have regular expenses as follows:
(do not include payments on any arrears)

Amounts are per
☐ week
☐ month

	Amount
Mortgage	
Rent	
Council Tax	
Gas	
Electricity	
Water charges	
TV rental/licence	
HP repayments	
Mail order	
Housekeeping, food, school meals	
Travelling expenses	
Children's clothing and pocket money	
Maintenance Payments	
Car Expenses	
Insurance – House	
Insurance – Other (please give details)	
Others	
Total payments £	

5.2 Income needs for children living with you or provided for by you.
INCLUDE:
• Only those income needs that are different to those of your household shown above

Item	Current cost	Estimated future cost
SUB-TOTAL children's income needs: £		

TOTAL of ALL income needs: £

Form E1   Page 12 of 15

5.92 *Children*

6. Financial resources of child(ren)

Income	Property	Other
TOTAL:	TOTAL:	TOTAL:

7. Financial Details *Summaries*

7.1 Summary of your estimated income for the next 12 months (Parts 2 to 3).

Description	Reference of the section on this statement	Value
Estimated net total of income from employment	A	
Estimated net total of income from self-employment or partnership	B	
Estimated net total of investment income	C	
Estimated state benefit receipts	D	
Estimated net total of all other income	E	
Estimated TOTAL income for the next 12 months (Totals A to E):	£	

7.2 Summary of your capital (Part 4).

Description	Reference of the section on this statement	Value
Current value of your interest in property	F	
Current value of personal assets	G	
Current value of all your other assets	H	
Current value of your liabilities	I	
TOTAL value of your assets (Totals F to H minus I):	£	

Form E1

Statement of Truth

*delete as appropriate

*[I believe] [the Applicant/Respondent believes] that the facts stated in this statement are true

*I am duly authorised by the Applicant/Respondent to sign this statement

and confirm that the information given above is a full, frank, clear and accurate disclosure of my financial and other relevant circumstances.

Print full name

Address for service

Postcode

Name of Applicant's/ Respondent's solicitor's firm

Signed

Dated D D \ M M \ Y Y Y Y

*(Applicant/Respondent) (Litigation friend)
*(Applicant's/Respondent's solicitor)

Position or office held (if signing on behalf of firm or company)

Proceedings for contempt of court may be brought against a person who makes or causes to be made, a false statement in a document verified by a statement of truth.

Address all communications to the Court Manager of the Court and quote the case number. If you do not quote this number, your correspondence may be returned.

Sign and Lock >

Form E1

5.92 *Children*

Schedule of Documents to accompany Form E1

The following list shows the documents you must attach to your Form E1 if applicable. You may attach other documents where it is necessary to explain or clarify any of the information that you give in the Form E1.

Form E1 paragraph	Document	Please tick		
		Attached	Not applicable	To follow
2.2	**Employment income:** your P60 for the last financial year in respect of each employment that you have.	☐	☐	☐
2.2	**Employment income:** your last three payslips in respect of each employment that you have.	☐	☐	☐
2.2	**Employment income:** your last form P11D if you have been issued with one.	☐	☐	☐
2.3	**Self-employment or partnership income:** a copy of your last tax assessment or if that is not available, a letter from your accountant confirming your tax liability and business accounts for the last 2 years.	☐	☐	☐
2.3	**Self-employment or partnership income:** if net income from the last financial year and the estimated income for the next twelve months is significantly different, a copy of the management accounts for the period since your last accounts.	☐	☐	☐
4.1	a copy of any valuation relating to each other property disclosed that has been obtained in the last six months.	☐	☐	☐
4.1	a recent mortgage statement in respect of each mortgage on each other property disclosed confirming the amount outstanding.	☐	☐	☐
4.2	**Personal bank, building society and National Savings accounts:** copies of statements for the last 12 months for each account that has been held in the last twelve months, either in your own name or in which you have or have had any interest.	☐	☐	☐
4.3	**Other investments:** the latest statement or dividend counterfoil relating to each investment as disclosed in paragraph 4.3.	☐	☐	☐
4.4	**Life insurance (including endowment) policies:** a surrender valuation for each policy that has a surrender value as disclosed under paragraph 4.4.	☐	☐	☐
State relevant Form E1 paragraph	Description of other documents attached:			

Form E1

Chapter 6
DEATH AND SUCCESSION

Part A LAW AND PRACTICE

Section 1 Making provision for death

Introduction

6.1 Cohabitants are not able to benefit under the rules that govern intestacy, and so if it is intended that provision should be made for one cohabitant on the death of another, positive steps must be taken during the lifetime of both parties.

If cohabitants wish to make provision for one another after death, they may do one or more of the following:

- make a will in favour of the other;
- hold property in joint names so that on death the survivor will automatically succeed to ownership;
- nominate the surviving cohabitant to receive benefits payable on death under the terms of a life assurance policy or pension scheme;
- make a lifetime gift of property.

However, all of the above are subject to the powers of the court under the Inheritance (Provision for Family and Dependants) Act 1975 (I(PFD)A 1975) to set aside transactions, deem jointly owned property part of the deceased's net estate, and make orders for financial provision out of the estate[1].

The Law Commission published a Consultation Paper on 28 October 2009 asking (inter alia) whether certain cohabitants should have a place in the intestacy rules, the conditions which have to be met, and how much of the estate they should receive. That project is now complete and certain of the recommendations have been enacted in the Inheritance and Trustees' Powers Act 2014 (ITPA 2014) that received Royal Assent on 14 May 2014. This includes reforms that amend the legal rules which had disadvantaged unmarried fathers when a child died intestate, and remove arbitrary obstacles to family provision claims by dependants of the deceased and anyone treated by the deceased as a child of his or her family outside the context of a marriage or civil partnership.

However, the reforms made little improvement to the law for cohabitants in the case of an intestacy and the recommendations set out in Part 8 of the

6.1 Death and Succession

Law Commissions report are unlikely to be implemented in the foreseeable future.

[1] I(PFD)A 1975, ss 10, 9 and 2.

Wills

6.2 In principle there should be no difference between the contents of the wills of those who are married or in a civil partnership and those who are not, and, with the notable exception of inheritance tax planning, there is little difference in practice. However, the law itself distinguishes between those who are married or in a civil partnership and those who are not in a number of ways. Among them are the following:

(1) *Wills Act 1837, s 15*[1] states that a gift to a beneficiary is void if the will is witnessed by the beneficiary or his or her spouse or civil partner[2]. However, if a cohabitant were to witness a will conferring a benefit on his or her partner, the gift would be valid.

(2) *Wills Act 1837, s 18* provides that, except in certain circumstances, a will is revoked if the testator subsequently marries or enters in to a civil partnership[3]. Subsequent cohabitation outside the marriage or civil partnership will not revoke an existing will.

(3) *Wills Act 1837, s 18A*[4] provides that on the dissolution or annulment of a marriage or civil partnership, a will takes effect as if the appointment of the former spouse or former civil partner as an executor or trustee were omitted, and any devise or bequest to the former spouse or former civil partner lapses[5]. These provisions apply automatically, unless a contrary intention appears by the will. The section does not apply on the termination of the relationship of a couple who are not married or in a civil partnership[6].

(4) *Administration of Justice Act 1982, s 22* states a presumption. Unless a contrary intention is shown, it is presumed that where a testator gives property to his spouse in terms which in themselves would give an absolute interest to the spouse, but also purports to give his issue an interest in the same property, the gift to the spouse is absolute notwithstanding the purported gift to the issue. The presumption does not apply in the case of an unmarried couple. So, if the testator were to say, 'I give all my property to (*cohabitant*) and after their death to my children', the surviving partner would receive only a life interest, not an absolute interest. This has significant disadvantages for inheritance tax purposes.

(5) *Inheritance Tax Act 1984, s 18 (as amended)* generally speaking, transfers of value between spouses and civil partners are wholly exempt[7]. This exemption does not apply to unmarried couples.

[1] As amended by CPA 2004.
[2] This was the problem in the well-known negligence case of *Ross v Caunters* [1980] Ch 297.
[3] The main exception is where the will is expressly made in expectation of marriage.
[4] Added by the Administration of Justice Act 1982, ss 18(2) and 73(6), with effect from 1 January 1983.
[5] It is unfortunate that s 18A did not provide that for all the purposes of the testator's will the former spouse should be treated as having predeceased him (*Re Sinclair* [1985] Ch 446). The Law Commission has published an informal consultation paper: 'The Effect of Divorce on Wills' (November 1992).

[6] A new will or codicil should be executed (see Precedent **6.159** below).
[7] As amended by ss 177 and 178 of the Finance Act 2013. If the transferor/deceased is domiciled in the UK and the spouse is domiciled outside the UK, the exemption is limited to the value of the nil rate band at the time of transfer. However, in order to benefit from the unlimited exemption the non UK domiciled spouse does have the option to elect to be treated as UK domiciled for UK inheritance tax purposes. The election can be made during the lifetime of the deceased or within 2 years of the date of death.

Describing the cohabitant

6.3 A testator should describe his partner clearly, accurately and unambiguously. The best course of action is simply to state the cohabitant's full and correct forenames and surname (and any alias) and his or her address. To abbreviate any later references in the will, the partner's forename, or some other concise and accurate description, can be placed in brackets immediately after the first occurrence of the full name. For example: Mary Jane Smith ('Mary').

A description on its own – 'my partner', 'my cohabitant', 'my boyfriend' – must never be used. However, where it is stated in addition to the full and correct name it will probably be innocuous. Several reported decisions reveal a tendency among some unmarried couples to refer to each other as 'my husband' or 'my wife'[1]. When it comes to making their wills, these terms should be avoided for the obvious reason that they have led, and could continue to lead, to litigation. However, in most cases where the inaccurate or euphemistic expression 'my wife' has been used in addition to the partner's full and correct name, the courts have applied the *falsa demonstratio* rule[2], and the gift has not been invalidated.

[1] For example: *Re Smalley* [1929] 2 Ch 112; and *Re Lynch* [1943] 1 All ER 168.
[2] In this context, the full maxim is *falsa demonstratio non nocet dummodo constet de persona* (a false description does no harm provided that it is clear who the person is). The ambiguity can be cured by extrinsic evidence.

'Cohabitation' and wills

6.4 The words used in a will are given their ordinary grammatical meaning[1]. However, it is the testator's privilege to be able to use 'his own dictionary' and make words mean whatever they wish[2]: 'He can make "black" mean "white" if he makes the dictionary sufficiently clear in his will'[3]. References in a will to 'cohabitation' are likely to occur in two sets of circumstances. First, in the context of the testator's own relationship, where a gift to the surviving cohabitant is made subject to the condition that the couple are still living together when the testator dies[4]. The second, and more usual, occurrence is where a life interest is given to the surviving cohabitant and it is expressed to be determinable on cohabitation[5]. The underlying purpose is usually economic. If the survivor enters into a new relationship, the testator – or his estate – will no longer be responsible for maintaining her or him.

Where a life interest is determinable on cohabitation, the very act of cohabiting, whatever that may be (and this could be loosely defined in the will), will operate as a disqualification. The burden of proof is on those who are seeking to disqualify. It is notoriously difficult to establish whether or not

6.4 Death and Succession

a couple are cohabiting⁶. Sometimes the couple are uncertain themselves. By referring to 'cohabitation' in his will the testator is asking someone – primarily the executors and trustees, but perhaps also the remaindermen, the surviving cohabitant, and the court – to make a value judgment as to which incidents of such a relationship are to be treated as essential, and which incidents can be discarded as superfluous. In order to shield the trustees it has become common practice to impose a discretionary trust, which probably makes their evidential burden lighter, extends their immunities, and circumscribes the scope for any appeal against their decision⁷. Although a discretionary trust has its uses, the testator must still make his intentions clear to the trustees, perhaps by way of a letter of wishes. But neither the trust nor the memorandum will resolve the underlying difficulties in answering the question of whether a couple is cohabiting. In addition, consideration must be given to the tax treatment of the ongoing trust.

1. *Gorringe v Mahlstedt* [1907] AC 225 at 227.
2. *Re Lynch* [1943] 1 All ER 168.
3. Parry and Kerridge *The Law of Succession* (Sweet & Maxwell, 13th edn).
4. For an example and further comment, see **6.130** below.
5. For examples, see **6.123** and **6.141** below.
6. See the DWP Guidance for Decision-Makers, Vol 3, Ch 11: Living together as husband and wife or as civil partners.
7. For a discretionary trust, see **6.143** below; for a 2-year discretionary trust, see **6.144** below; for a life interest subject to the trustees' power of revocation, see **6.142** below.

Joint property

6.5 If property, whether real or personal, is held in the joint names of cohabitants as beneficial joint tenants, on the death of one of them the survivor will automatically succeed to the ownership of the property. Jointly owned property will not ordinarily¹ form part of the deceased's estate.

In the case of land, care must be taken when the property is acquired to ensure that the beneficial interests are expressly declared, and not left open to interpretation².

The contents of bank accounts in joint names will belong to the survivor and will be immediately accessible without the need to produce a grant of representation in respect of the estate.

1. Subject to I(PFD)A 1975, s 9, where application is made for an order under s 2 of the Act.
2. See **1.4**.

Nominations

6.6 There is no provision in the state pension scheme for benefits to be paid to a surviving cohabitant, but many occupational and private schemes will enable the trustees or fund managers to make payments to a person with whom the deceased was living as spouse or civil partner at the date of death, as well as to dependants, within which category a cohabitant may be included. The rules of each scheme will be different, and it is prudent to establish what benefits will be payable in the event of death in service or death after retirement (usually very limited) and who will be eligible to receive them.

Most schemes, whilst giving the trustees or fund managers unfettered discretion to distribute certain benefits payable on death as they see fit between those eligible, will also allow them to take into account any expression by the scheme member of a preference as to how the discretion should be exercised. Such schemes will generally have a standard form 'Expression of wishes', which can be completed by the scheme member and kept on file by the pension provider.

Trustees are not obliged to take into account any expression of wishes by the scheme member, but they do have to exercise their discretion in accordance with the rules of the scheme. In *Wild v Pensions Ombudsman*[1] a complaint about the decision of the trustees to exercise their discretion in favour of a woman with whom the deceased had been living before his death was upheld on the basis that she was not in fact dependent upon the deceased and so could not be brought within the category of persons eligible to be considered for provision, namely, 'dependants, relatives or legal representatives of the member'.

[1] [1996] 2 FLR 680.

Lifetime gifts

6.7 Subject to taxation considerations (for example capital gains tax, the annual gift exemption limit of £3,000 and inheritance tax on gifts made within 7 years of death) cohabitants are free to make gifts to one another of property during their joint lives. It is important to bear in mind the court's powers to set aside transactions that were intended to defeat a claim for provision under the I(PFD)A 1975[1]. For this reason, the more time that has elapsed between the gift and death the better.

[1] I(PFD)A 1975, s 10.

Donationes mortis causa

6.8 In some cases a person who is approaching death, and who has not made formal provision for another, may seek to remedy this by making a gift in contemplation of his or her death, and conditional upon it. Certain formalities have to be complied with for the gift to be effective to transfer ownership, but in one case it was held that a cohabitant was entitled to land that was given to her by her dying cohabitant merely by his handing to her the keys to the box in which the title deeds to the land were kept, and his clear statement to her that she was to have the land as a gift[1].

In *Woodard v Woodard*[2] it was held by the Court of Appeal that the act of the deceased, who was then within days of dying from leukemia, of handing to his son the keys to his car, together with his words that he could, 'keep the keys, I won't be driving it any more', was sufficient to satisfy the requirements for a valid *donatio mortis causa*. However, the case law on the doctrine has since been reviewed by the Court of Appeal who confirmed the strict limits in which this doctrine should be used and highlighted that it should not be relied upon in substitution of a valid Will[3].

6.8 Death and Succession

The Law Commission published a recent consultation on the law of wills and it was accepted that the doctrine of *donatio mortis causa* should be retained but with greater clarity in the terms of its use[4].

1   *Sen v Headley* [1991] 2 FLR 449.
2   [1996] 1 FLR 399.
3   *King v The Chiltern Dog Rescue and others* [2015] EWCA Civ 581.
4   https://s3-eu-west-2.amazonaws.com/lawcom-prod-storage-11jsxou24uy7q/uploads/2017/07/Making-a-will-consultation.pdf.

Section 2 Death of a cohabitant

Introduction

6.9 On the death of a cohabitant, a number of situations may arise, depending upon whether there are children of the parties or a previous marriage or relationship, or even a surviving spouse or civil partner, and whether the cohabitant dies intestate, or leaves a valid will.

Cohabitant leaves a valid will

6.10 If a deceased cohabitant has left a valid will, the estate should be administered in accordance with the will subject to any question of interpretation[1] and to any order that may be made by the court where application is made for provision under the I(PFD)A 1975.

1   See **6.4**.

Cohabitant dies intestate

6.11 If there is an intestacy, the distribution of the estate is dealt with in accordance with the provisions of s 46 of the Administration of Estates Act 1925, as amended by the Intestates' Estates Act 1952, the Family Provision Act 1966, successive Family Provision (Intestate Succession) Orders and the Inheritance and Trustees' Powers Act 2014.

The latest rules governing intestacy were introduced by the ITPA 2014 in respect of deaths on or after 1 October 2014[1]. The effect of the latest rules are as follows:

–   If there is a surviving spouse or civil partner but no children, the entire estate will pass to the surviving spouse or civil partner.
–   If there is a surviving spouse or civil partner and children and the value of the estate does not exceed £270,000, the surviving spouse or civil partner will receive everything.
–   If there is a surviving spouse or civil partner and children and the value of the estate exceeds £270,000, the surviving spouse or civil partner will receive all the personal chattels, the statutory legacy of £270,000 free of inheritance tax and costs, and one half the of the remainder. The other half of the remainder will be divided between the children in equal shares (and on statutory trusts if they are minors). If any of the children predecease their deceased parent, but leave children who survive them, those children will take the share their deceased parent would otherwise have taken.

There is no provision for a surviving cohabitant if there is an intestacy and it is therefore important that cohabitants are encouraged to make a will. However, it should be borne in mind that certain property will not form part of the deceased's estate for the purposes of any will or intestacy in any event. Jointly owned property, such as a house or bank account in joint names, will pass to the surviving joint owner automatically on death. Similarly, certain benefits from insurance and pension policies can be the subject of a nomination in favour of a particular beneficiary or beneficiaries that will exclude those assets from the deceased's estate[2].

It should be borne in mind however, that where an application is made for provision under the I(PFD)A 1975, the court has power to deem certain property which otherwise would be excluded from the estate to be part of the net estate for the purposes of that Act[3] or set aside lifetime transactions[4]. This may mean for example that an attempt by the deceased to provide for the surviving cohabitant by a lifetime gift may prove ineffective.

If no provision has been made outside the estate for a surviving cohabitant, then the only course where there has been an intestacy is to make application under the I(PFD)A 1975.

In very rare cases where there are no eligible beneficiaries under an intestacy, a surviving cohabitant may apply to the Crown to whom the estate will have passed *bona vacantia* for provision as someone 'for whom the intestate may reasonably have been expected to make provision'[5].

[1] Intestacy rules apply to same sex married couples from 13 March 2014 via the Marriage (Same Sex Couples) Act 2013.
[2] See **6.6**.
[3] I(PFD)A 1975, s 9.
[4] I(PFD)A 1975, s 10.
[5] Administration of Estates Act 1925, s 46(1); *Cameron v Treasury Solicitor* [1996] 2 FLR 716.

Surviving spouses and civil partners and the effect of a decree of judicial separation or separation order

6.12 Cohabitants may find themselves in the position of living with a person who is married to, or in a civil partnership with, someone else. If a cohabitant dies intestate and there is a surviving spouse or civil partner, the spouse or civil partner will benefit unless, in the case of married parties, there has been a decree of judicial separation or in the case of civil partners, a separation order.

If there is a decree of judicial separation or separation order and the separation was continuing at the date of death, the deceased's estate will devolve as if the other party to the proceedings were dead. Therefore, there will be no provision for the spouse or civil partner on intestacy and any testamentary provision in his or her favour will lapse.

Note, however, the power of the court under I(PFD)A 1975, s 14 and s 14A[1] on an application for provision under s 2, to disregard a decree of divorce or judicial separation, or in the case of a civil partnership a dissolution order, nullity order, separation order or presumption of death order, in circumstances

6.12 *Death and Succession*

in which the death of one of the parties occurred within 12 months of the decree or order and a financial provision order had not been made.

If there is a failure to change the terms of any will following dissolution or annulment of a marriage or civil partnership, in the case of individuals who have died on or after 1 January 1996, Law Reform (Succession) Act 1995, s 3 provides that where an appointment of a former spouse or civil partner as an executor or trustee exists, that former spouse or civil partner shall be treated as having died on the date the marriage or civil partnership was dissolved or annulled and the same applies to any provision made in a will for a former spouse or civil partner.

A former spouse or civil partner who has not remarried or entered into another civil partnership may be a potential applicant under the I(PFD)A 1975. Enquiry should be made as to whether any order was made in the dissolution proceedings which precludes such an application[2].

[1] Inserted by CPA 2004.
[2] I(PFD)A 1975, s 15.

Children of a deceased cohabitant

6.13 There is no difference between the treatment of the illegitimate children of a deceased cohabitant and the legitimate children for succession purposes.

If there is an intestacy, they are included in the category of children, without discrimination[1].

If their deceased parent leaves a valid will, they are similarly included in the general category of children unless children are referred to specifically by name and unless the will specifies that only legitimate children may benefit.

Whether or not they benefit from the will or any intestacy, children of parents who are not married or in a civil partnership may apply to the court under the I(PFD)A 1975 for reasonable financial provision out of the estate. Even a child who is not a natural child of the deceased cohabitant could make a claim against the estate if he or she was being maintained, wholly or in part by the deceased immediately before the death.

Applicants may be minor or adult children although there is a reluctance on the part of the courts to make significant awards to adult children who are independent and self-supporting[2].

The definition of 'child' will also include a child *en ventre sa mère* at the date of the death of the deceased parent.

Children who have been adopted by the deceased are eligible to apply, but not the natural children of parents where there is an adoption order in favour of another party as this operates to sever all legal obligations.

[1] FLRA 1969, s 15; FLRA 1987, s 19.
[2] See, for example, *Ilott v Mitson & Others* [2014] EWHC 542 (Fam).

Proprietary estoppel

6.14 A surviving cohabitant may find that, on the death of the other cohabitant, provision that was promised has not been made. The omission may have been deliberate or merely neglectful. In certain situations, equity will step in to assist the disappointed party. See the discussion at **1.53**.

The essentials for an application for relief in reliance upon the equitable doctrine of estoppel are that the applicant must have acted to his or her detriment in reliance upon a promise that he or she would be given an interest in property, subject to there being sufficient connection between the promise and the detrimental conduct. There should also be knowledge on the part of the promisor that the other party was relying upon the promise and acting detrimentally as a result, yet taking no steps to disabuse him or her, thereby making it unconscionable for the promisor to go back on his word[1].

In *Wayling v Jones*[2] the parties lived together in a homosexual relationship. The deceased was the owner of an hotel and the applicant had worked in the hotel for pocket money and expenses alone. The applicant, a much younger man, went along with this on the basis that the deceased had promised that he would leave him the hotel in his will. In the event he did not, and the applicant claimed against the estate. He was unsuccessful at first instance, but on appeal the Court of Appeal held that[3]:

' . . . On the facts it was clear that the promises had been made, that the plaintiff's conduct was such that inducement might be inferred, and that since the plaintiff had stated in examination-in-chief that he would have left the deceased if the promises had been withdrawn, the defendants had not discharged the burden of establishing that the plaintiff had not relied on the promises . . . '

An order was made for the applicant to receive the net proceeds of sale of the hotel which by that time had been sold, and so the estate was held to the promise made by the deceased[4].

[1] *Gillett v Holt and Another* [2000] 2 All ER 289, CA.
[2] [1995] 2 FLR 1029.
[3] At 1029G.
[4] See also *Re Basham (Deceased)* [1987] 2 FLR 264, not followed in *Taylor v Dickens* [1998] 1 FLR 806: ' . . . there was a difference between saying you will make a will and saying you will not revoke a will . . . ' (at 806G). This stricter approach was also evident in *Coombes v Smith* [1987] 1 FLR 352. See also *Thorner v Major* [2008] EWCA Civ 732.

Applications under the Inheritance (Provision for Family and Dependants) Act 1975

INTRODUCTION

6.15 Although a testator's freedom to dispose of his property by will remains a fundamental right, since the introduction of the Inheritance (Family Provision) Act 1938 this has been subject to the power of the court in statutorily prescribed circumstances to alter the provision that has been made. The categories of applicant were extended in the I(PFD)A 1975 to include children of the family, and further extended to cohabitants of at least 2 years' standing by an amendment to the I(PFD)A 1975 following the Law Reform

6.15 Death and Succession

(Succession) Act 1995. The Civil Partnership Act 2004 contained provision for the categories of applicant to be extended to include civil partners. Further amendments have been made by the Inheritance and Trustees' Powers Act 2014 (ITPA 2014) that include extending the category of potential applicants in s 1(1)(d) from children of the family in the context of marriage and civil partnership to any child in respect of whom the deceased stood in the role of parent.

The emphasis in the successive legislation and its interpretation has remained the same. The legislation is not intended to give the court *carte blanche* to rewrite the terms of the will or interfere with the operation of the intestacy rules.

What relief is available?

6.16 Certain categories of applicant may apply to the court for financial provision if the deceased's estate failed to make 'reasonable financial provision', either directly by will or indirectly by the operation of the law relating to intestacy. If so satisfied, the court may exercise its discretion to make one or more of the following orders in favour of the applicant:

- periodical payments[1];
- variation, discharge, suspension, revival of periodical payments order[2];
- lump sum[3];
- transfer of property[4];
- settlement of property[5];
- variation of settlement[6];
- variation of trusts[7];
- variation or discharge of secured periodical payments[8];
- variation or revocation of maintenance agreements[9];
- setting aside a disposition intended to defeat a claim[10];
- interim relief[11].

[1] I(PFD)A 1975, s 2(1)(a).
[2] I(PFD)A 1975, s 6.
[3] I(PFD)A 1975, s 2(1)(b).
[4] I(PFD)A 1975, s 2(1)(c).
[5] I(PFD)A 1975, s 2(1)(d).
[6] I(PFD)A 1975, s 2(1)(e).
[7] I(PFD)A 1975, s 2(1)(h).
[8] I(PFD)A 1975, s 16.
[9] I(PFD)A 1975, s 17.
[10] I(PFD)A 1975, ss 10 and 11.
[11] I(PFD)A 1975, s 10.

Who may apply?

6.17 According to s 1(1) of the I(PFD)A 1975, the potential applicants are:

(a) a surviving spouse or civil partner;
(b) a former spouse who has not remarried, or a former civil partner who has not entered into another civil partnership;

(ba) a surviving cohabitant whether someone living with the deceased as spouse or civil partner who had lived with the deceased throughout the whole of the period of at least 2 years immediately before the death[1];
(c) a child of the deceased;
(d) any person other than a child of the deceased who was treated by the deceased as a child of the family within the context of a marriage or civil partnership[2], or in relation to any family in which the deceased stood in the role of parent, any person who was treated by the deceased as a child of the family; and
(e) any person not included in categories (a)–(d) above who was being maintained in whole or in part by the deceased immediately before the death.

[1] CPA 2004 inserted s 1(1A) and s 1(1B) to further define a surviving cohabitant as a person who has lived in the same household as the deceased for the whole of the period of 2 years ending immediately before the deceased died, either as husband and wife (s 1(1A)) or as civil partner s 1(1B) of the deceased.
[2] Ie a step-child.

THE PARTIES TO THE APPLICATION

6.18 If there is more than one applicant and there is no conflict of interest between them, they may make an application jointly. Otherwise there will have to be separate applications which may then be consolidated.

The personal representatives should always be named as respondents to the application together with any significant beneficiary under a will or intestacy, ie a person who is likely to be affected financially by any order made, or any other person affected by the claim.

The court may direct that other persons who are not already parties be joined in the proceedings.

WHICH COURT?

6.19 The High Court and any county court have unlimited jurisdiction to hear claims under the I(PFD)A 1975. In practice, most claims will be dealt with in the county court.

In the High Court, application may be made to either the Chancery Division or the Family Division. The choice of Division in the High Court will depend largely on the issues involved. For example, if there will be detailed accounts to be taken the Chancery Division may be preferred, but the broader issues generally raised by these cases may, as a rule, be better suited to the Family Division.

In any event, the court has power to transfer between Divisions, and between the county court and High Court and vice versa.

In the county court the application may be made to the county court local to the deceased's residence at the date of death. If the deceased was resident abroad, the application may be filed at the county court local to a respondent to the application, or where the estate or part of it is situated.

6.19 Death and Succession

In the High Court, application may be made in London or any district registry.

Note that although the place of death is irrelevant, the deceased must have been habitually resident in England and Wales at the date of death for the court to have jurisdiction under the I(PFD)A 1975.

PROCEDURE

6.20 Proceedings under the I(PFD)A 1975 are not family proceedings and are governed by the CPR. The claim is made under CPR Pt 8. CPR 57.14–57.16 and the accompanying Practice Direction contain additional provisions for claims under the I(PFD)A 1975 in both the county court and High Court.

The application is made by Part 8 Claim Form N208 which gives details of the claim and contains a statement of truth. Where a grant has been taken out, the claim form must be accompanied by a witness statement that exhibits an office copy of the grant of representation and any relevant will. Although not specifically required by CPR, it will be good practice to include:

(a) the name of the deceased, the date of death and country of domicile at that time;
(b) the category or categories of potential applicant to which the applicant claims to belong;
(c) the date of the grant of representation and the names and addresses of the personal representatives;
(d) whether any provision is made for the applicant by will or the law of intestacy, and if so, the nature of that provision;
(e) any other persons interested in the estate, and the nature of that interest;
(f) particulars of the applicant's financial resources at the time of the application and in the foreseeable future; and
(g) the nature of the provision sought.

In addition, the death certificate should be exhibited together with any other relevant documentation. Where a child is applying, the child's birth certificate should be exhibited.

Following amendments made to I(PFD)A by ITPA 2014 it is possible to make a claim before a grant is taken out. In those circumstances CPR 57.16(3A) provides that the evidence in support must explain the reasons why it has not been possible for a grant to be obtained, exhibit a copy of the will if available and set out brief details of the estate and those interested in it.

In either case the witness statement must also comply with the requirements of the CPR Pt 22 and contain a statement of truth.

When the court issues the claim, it will provide a response pack for service on the defendants along with sealed copies of the claim form and witness statement. The claimant will receive Notice of Issue.

CPR Pt 57 provides that within 21 days of service of the claim form, inclusive of the day of service, a defendant must acknowledge service and a defendant who is a personal representative must, and any other category of defendant may, file and serve a statement in answer to the claim.

If a defendant is a personal representative, the statement must contain the following information to the best of that person's ability[1]:

(a) the full particulars of the estate;
(b) the names and addresses of all the beneficiaries of the estate, and the extent of their interest in the estate;
(c) the name of any beneficiary who is a child or who lacks mental capacity; and
(d) any facts that may affect the exercise of the court's discretion.

On receipt of the acknowledgement, or after the time for doing so has expired, the papers are put before the district judge. The district judge will usually direct a hearing when case management directions will be given. These will include provision for allocation, usually to the multi-track, disclosure of documents, filing of further evidence, and there will be consideration given to transfer of proceedings, joinder of parties, and whether certain parties should have separate representation because of a potential conflict of interest. The directions given will be subject to a strict timetable which will have to be adhered to. This will usually include provision for a further case management conference so that the district judge can ensure that the case will be ready for trial.

If there is an application for permission to bring a claim out of time, or for interim provision, a further interlocutory hearing will be fixed.

In the event that one or more defendants do not appear at the case management conference it will be necessary for the claimant to prove service of the claim[2].

[1] CPR Pt 57, PD 16.
[2] CPR Pt 6.

TIME FOR MAKING THE APPLICATION

6.21 The application must be made within 6 months of the date of the grant of representation. In calculating the 6-month period, the day on which the grant of representation was issued is included. However, nothing now prevents the making of an application before the grant of representation is first taken out[1].

[1] Inserted by ITPA 2014, s 6, Sch 2.

APPLICATION FOR PERMISSION TO APPLY OUT OF TIME

6.22 There is provision for the court to allow applications made outside the time-limit imposed by I(PFD)A 1975, s 4, but permission must be expressly requested in the claim form. The claimant's witness statement/affidavit must set out the grounds for the application and give a full explanation as to why the application was not made within the time-limit. A defendant wishing to oppose the application will signify as much in the acknowledgement form.

6.22 Death and Succession

The application for permission will be dealt with as a preliminary issue and the district judge will give directions at the first hearing if it is not possible to dispose of it on that occasion.

The exercise of the court's discretion on an application for permission

6.23 The court's power to allow the application to proceed notwithstanding that it was issued out of time is discretionary. The matters to which the court will have regard in the exercise of its discretion, as well as all the circumstances of the case and the interests of justice will include:

- the length of the delay;
- the reason for the delay, and in particular whether any fault rests with the claimant or the claimant's solicitors;
- whether the defendant was aware of the potential claim before proceedings commenced;
- whether negotiations were on foot when the time-limit expired;
- whether the estate has already been distributed;
- whether the claim stands any real prospect of success; and
- whether the claimant could pursue a claim against his or her solicitors in the event that permission were not given.

These general guidelines can be found in the judgments in *Re Salmon, Coard v National Westminster Bank Limited*[1]. That case also made it clear that it is for the claimant to establish sufficient grounds for disapplying the time-limit, as to do so necessarily deprives the defendant of the benefit of it.

The exercise of the judge's discretion is unfettered, but it must be exercised with regard to the interests of justice.

There are cases in which the court has exercised its discretion in favour of the applicant. For example, in *Re Ruttie; Ruttie v Saul*[2] an application made 6 weeks out of time was allowed where negotiations were well advanced and there would have been serious hardship to the impecunious applicant and no prejudice to the defendant save for the loss of advantage of the expiry of the time-limit. In *Re C (Deceased) (Leave to Apply for Provision)*[3] a claim was made on behalf of the deceased's illegitimate daughter, by her mother. The claim was made 4 years after the death and 2 years after the grant of probate was taken out. At the hearing before the district judge no explanation was given for the delay and leave to proceed with the claim was refused. Allowing the mother's appeal, Wilson J, as he then was, said that 'the task is to determine whether the net weight of the relevant factors is such as to justify permission to claim outside the normal period'[4].

Whilst pointing out that there was no general principle that applications on behalf of minors to bring claims out of time should be treated more sympathetically, he said that a significant factor in the balance was the fact that if leave was not allowed the child in this case would be left without any remedy. He was guided by the judgments given in *Re Salmon* and suggested that other relevant factors in the exercise of the court's discretion were the extent of and reasons for the delay, any prejudice there may be to beneficiaries, for example where the estate has already been distributed, and the merits of the application. In this case, the merits were very good and the estate had not been distributed.

[1] [1980] 3 All ER 532.
[2] [1969] 3 All ER 1633.
[3] [1995] 2 FLR 24; also reported as *Re W (A Minor) (Claim from Deceased's Estate)* [1995] 2 FCR 689.
[4] At 29E.

6.24 *Stock v Brown*[1] was described as an exceptional case in which leave was given to a very elderly widow to make a claim in respect of her late husband's estate nearly 6 years out of time. The provision in the will gave her a life interest in his estate. For some years this provided her with an adequate income and she was content. However, interest rates then fell dramatically and her income was insufficient. On appeal, leave was given to bring a claim out of time. The court took the view that the exceptional delay was more than offset by the 'combination of extenuating circumstances and meritorious need'[2]. See also *Re B (Deceased)*[3].

Even more exceptional was the recent decision in *Bhusate v Patel and Others*[4] in which permission was given for an application to be made nearly 26 years out of time. In that case, Chief Master Marsh was guided by the principles set out in *Re Salmon*, as refined by Black LJ in *Berger v Berger*[5]. Central to his decision to allow the application to proceed were the following factors: the merits of the claim were very strong, the applicant had given a satisfactory explanation for the delay in making the application, and there would be no remedy open to the applicant if the application was not granted. The Chief Master also took the view that the conduct of the applicant's step-children, who were defendants to the application, was an important consideration.

The court refused an application to proceed out of time in *Re Dennis (Deceased)*[6]. Following the guidelines set down in *Re Salmon*, the court said that in addition to the 19-month delay in bringing the claim that was partly unexplained, the case was not an arguable one. A son of the deceased, described by the judge as something of a 'rolling stone', claimed a lump sum by way of provision from the large estate to meet the capital transfer tax he had to pay on substantial lifetime gifts from his father. The court held that as this need was not in the nature of maintenance, and this was the only provision that could be made to a child of the deceased, his claim had little or no prospect of success and he should not have leave to proceed.

In *Re Longley (Deceased), Longley and Longley v Longley*[7] the court took the view that as the estate had been distributed by the time an application was made, long after the time-limit had expired, the disappointed claimant could sue her solicitors against whom she had a good claim. It was not the duty of the court to protect negligent solicitors.

After taking legal advice, the claimant in *Escritt v Escritt*[8] decided against making application for provision within the time-limit, but did make an application 3 years later after a slight change in her circumstances. Leave was not granted and the application was struck out.

In *Berger v Berger*[9] permission to make a claim 6 and a half years after the deceased's death was refused. The Court of Appeal disagreed with the trial judge that the claim had no prospects of success because the will did make reasonable financial provision for the claimant, the widow of the deceased. However, it agreed that the main factor in the exercise of his discretion to refuse permission was the very significant delay in commencing proceedings. Even though the claimant was elderly and had not been in particularly good health, the factors that ultimately led her to seek advice had been evident from an early stage and she had enlisted professional help at that time. Nothing changed, but it took another 4 or 5 years before she contemplated a claim under I(PFD)A 1975. It was the absence of the 'extraneous circumstances' in *Stock v Brown*, namely the dramatic fall in interest rates that distinguished this case and failed to provide a sufficient excuse for the delay.

[1] [1994] 1 FLR 840.
[2] At 842.
[3] [2000] 1 All ER 665 at 668.
[4] [2018] EWHC 2362 (Ch).
[5] [2013] EWCA Civ 1305.
[6] [1981] 2 All ER 140.
[7] [1981] CLY 2885.
[8] (1982) 3 FLR 280.
[9] [2013] EWCA Civ 1305.

6.25 The more recent decision of Mostyn J in *Cowan v Foreman & Others*[1] saw the court taking a strict approach to the question of limitation periods, invoking the overriding objective and the emphasis in the civil jurisdiction upon the imposition of sanctions.

As to the approach to be taken by the court, Mostyn J doubted whether this was a discretionary exercise at all. In his judgment the court was concerned to be satisfied that the applicant had provided good reasons justifying the delay, and that the claim was of sufficient merit to be allowed to proceed. He described this as *the making of a qualitative decision or a value judgment*[2].

In that case the applicant had delayed for around 13 months. The court was not persuaded, on the evidence, that she was not aware of the 6-month time limit for bringing a claim. The applicant failed the merits test as well, given that generous provision had already been made for the applicant by the deceased's will. The importance of the principle of testamentary freedom was reinforced, the court roundly rejecting the applicant's argument as amounting to *a form of forced spousal heirship unknown to the law*[3].

[1] [2019] EWHC 349 (Fam).
[2] At para 6.
[3] At para 21.

Standing search

6.26 Although it is now possible to make a claim before the issue of a grant, to avoid falling foul of the time-limit imposed by I(PFD)A 1975, s 2, there is a facility to set up a standing search at the Central Probate Registry or any

District Registry or sub-registry which ensures that notice is given of any application for a grant. Application is made on Form PA1S, accompanied by the fee payable[1].

On receipt, the court will supply a copy of any grant fitting the details given on Form PA1S that was issued not more than 12 months before the receipt of the application for the search or within 6 months thereafter. If necessary, the search can be extended by submitting the appropriate request and fee to the court within the last month of the 6-month period[2].

[1] See **6.165**.
[2] Non-Contentious Probate Rules 1987, r 43(1), *Practice Direction (Probate: Standing Search for Grant of Representation)* [1975] 3 All ER 403 and *Practice Direction (Probate: Minors' Grants)* [1991] 1 WLR 1069.

THE GROUND FOR THE APPLICATION

6.27 I(PFD)A 1975, s 1(1) provides that for every category of applicant the ground for making an application for an order under s 2 is 'that the disposition of the deceased's estate effected by his will or the law relating to intestacy, or the combination of his will and that law, is not such as to make reasonable financial provision for the applicant'.

In the case of applicants other than a spouse or civil partner, this is qualified by s 1(2)(b) which provides that 'reasonable financial provision' shall mean 'such financial provision as it would be reasonable in all the circumstances of the case for the applicant to receive for his maintenance'. This imports a requirement on the part of a claimant to satisfy the court that he or she has a need for maintenance that should be satisfied from the estate of the deceased. This is a necessary condition for an order, but may not in itself be sufficient for provision to be made.

The ITPA 2014 has slightly altered the position regarding those falling into the residuary category 1(1)(e), namely any person not included in the other categories who was being maintained in whole or in part by the deceased immediately before the death. Previously s 1(3) stated that a person shall be treated as being maintained by the deceased if the deceased was, otherwise than for full valuable consideration, making a substantial contribution towards that person's reasonable needs. The courts therefore balanced the contribution made by the deceased towards the needs of the applicant against any benefits flowing from the applicant to the deceased. This was the case even if the applicant and the deceased were living in an interdependent domestic relationship without any commercial aspect. The new wording of s 1(3) still requires the deceased to have been making a substantial contribution towards the reasonable needs of the applicant but the words 'otherwise than for full valuable consideration' are omitted. Instead, there is a narrower exception for any contribution that was made for full valuable consideration pursuant to an arrangement of a commercial nature. This means that contributions made between people in a domestic context should not now be weighed against one another.

Reasonable financial provision for applicant to receive for maintenance

6.28 Reasonable financial provision for the applicant to receive for maintenance has been variously defined:

> 'What is proper maintenance depends on all the facts and circumstances of the case being considered; but although it does not mean just enough to enable an applicant to get by on, neither does it mean anything which it may be regarded as reasonably desirable for the applicant's general benefit or welfare.[1]'

> '[reasonable financial provision] is the provision sufficient to enable the dependent to live neither luxuriously nor miserably, but decently and comfortably according to his or her station in life.[2]'

> '. . . only payments which would, directly or indirectly, enable the applicant to discharge the recurring costs of his living expenses . . .[3]'

> '. . . only those payments which will directly or indirectly enable the applicant in the future to discharge the cost of his daily living at whatever standard is appropriate to him . . .[4]'

In *Negus v Bahouse*[5] Goff LJ whilst acknowledging that *maintenance is the touchstone*[6] took into account the lifestyle that the claimant had enjoyed with the deceased over the 8 years they were together in assessing what it was appropriate for her to receive for her maintenance.

Further guidance upon what might constitute maintenance was provided by the Supreme Court in *Ilott v The Blue Cross & Others*[7]. Essentially it was a flexible concept dependent upon the facts of each case but would not be limited to provision at subsistence level. It may extend to the provision of housing, but more likely in the form of a life interest than by capital for outright purchase.

As to the manner in which provision for maintenance may be made, it need not be restricted to periodical payments but could be provided by way of a *Duxbury* lump sum. In *Ilott v Blue Cross & Others* the lump sum awarded of £50,000 was expressed to be for the purpose of enabling the claimant to replace worn out household items. It was suggested that a reliable car and even a holiday might fall into the category of *similar necessities*[8].

The question of maintenance was considered in *Lewis v Warner*[9]. In that case the applicant, aged 91, and the deceased had been cohabiting for 20 years in the deceased's property. After her death, the deceased's daughter took steps to secure possession of the property in order to sell it. The applicant had more than sufficient assets to buy the house himself and at first instance it was held that the applicant should be given an option to purchase at a price fixed by reference to a valuation obtained by the deceased's daughter.

She appealed, and in dismissing the appeal Newey J concluded that maintenance under I(PFD)A 1975 does not have to be:

> 'confined to support with the "cost of . . . daily living" (to quote from the *Dennis* case). It is capable . . . of referring to other forms of assistance with the requirements of daily life. If therefore, a person is in want of a particular thing to sustain a reasonable quality of life, the provision of it could possibly represent "maintenance" regardless of his financial means. In other words, a person can potentially (albeit only very rarely) be in need of "financial provision" for his

"maintenance" without being in any way short of money: his money may not be able to secure him what he requires. As a result, there appears to me to be no absolute bar on the provision of something for full consideration representing "financial provision" for a person's "maintenance".[10]'

On the particular facts of that case the threshold was crossed as the deceased had failed to make provision for the applicant's continued occupation of the property that they had shared and had been his home for 20 years, in an area where he had lived all his life. During that time he had built up a network of support that was necessary to enable him to live independently. Whilst he could afford to buy another property, in the circumstances, and at his time of life, what he needed was what money could not buy him without the intervention of the court, namely the opportunity to remain in his home.

1 Per curiam in *Re Coventry (Deceased)* [1979] 3 All ER 815 at 816D.
2 *Re Duranceau* [1952] 3 DLR 714 at 720.
3 *Re Dennis (Deceased)* [1981] 2 All ER 140 at 140H.
4 *Re Jennings (Deceased)* [1994] 3 All ER 27 at 35J.
5 [2008] 1 FLR 381.
6 At para 88.
7 [2017] UKSC 17.
8 At para 40.
9 [2016] EWHC 1787 (Ch).
10 At para 26.

THE COURT'S APPROACH TO WHETHER REASONABLE FINANCIAL PROVISION HAS BEEN MADE

6.29 Before the court can decide what, if any, order to make in favour of the applicant, it has to make a finding that the provision that has been made following the death does not make such financial provision as it would be reasonable in all the circumstances of the case for the applicant to receive for his or her maintenance.

This is an objective test. In other words, the question is not whether the deceased acted unreasonably in the provision that was made, but whether the effect of the devolution of the deceased's estate is to produce an unreasonable result in terms of provision for the maintenance of the applicant. Notwithstanding this, the reasonableness or otherwise of the deceased's actions concerning his estate may be a relevant factor for consideration in ss 3(1)(g) and 3(1)(d)[1].

It does not necessarily follow that if no provision is made, the provision, or lack of it, is unreasonable. If the deceased had not in his or her lifetime assumed any financial responsibility for the applicant, it is unlikely that a failure to make provision after death would be found to be unreasonable.

It is implicit in this that the applicant must satisfy the court that there is some kind of obligation on the estate to provide for his or her maintenance.

The applicant's dire financial circumstances or need for maintenance are not in themselves sufficient to establish a claim[2].

6.29 *Death and Succession*

In determining this question, which is essentially a question of fact, the court must have regard to the matters set out in s 3 of the I(PFD)A 1975. As well as the matters set out in s 3(1)(a)–(g) to which regard must be had in every case, the court must look at the additional matters set out in s 3. The subsection that will apply depends upon the particular category of applicant. Section 3(2A) applies to applications by cohabitants under s 1(1)(ba); s 3(3) applies to applications by children under s 1(1)(c) and (d); and s 3(4) to applications under s 1(1)(e) by dependants. Section 3(2) applies to claims by a spouse or former spouse who has not remarried or civil partner or former civil partner who has not entered into another civil partnership. These additional requirements are considered at **6.37–6.70** below.

[1] *Ilott v The Blue Cross & Others* [2017] UKSC 17 at paras 16 and 17.
[2] *Cameron v Treasury Solicitor* [1996] 2 FLR 716.

MATTERS TO WHICH THE COURT MUST HAVE REGARD IN EVERY CASE IN DETERMINING WHETHER REASONABLE FINANCIAL PROVISION HAS BEEN MADE FOR THE APPLICANT

6.30 Section 3(1) of the I(PFD)A 1975 states that the court must have regard to:

(a) the financial needs and resources of the applicant at the date of the hearing and in the foreseeable future;
(b) the financial needs and resources of any other applicant at the date of the hearing and in the foreseeable future;
(c) the financial needs and resources of any beneficiary of the estate at the date of the hearing and in the foreseeable future;
(d) any obligations and responsibilities of the deceased towards any applicant or beneficiary of the estate;
(e) the size and nature of the estate;
(f) any physical or mental deficiency of the applicant or any beneficiary of the estate; and
(g) any other matter, including the conduct of the applicant or any other person, which in the circumstances of the case the court may consider relevant.

Financial resources and financial needs

6.31 These require consideration of earning capacity and financial obligations and responsibilities[1].

The court will be able to ascribe earnings in cases in which a party's true earning capacity is not being maximised.

The court may take into account contingent resources such as the possibility of an inheritance, unless it is very remote.

Although financial needs means reasonable requirements, the assessment of a party's financial needs can take into account the standard of living enjoyed during the deceased's lifetime.

[1] I(PFD)A 1975, s 3(6).

Obligations and responsibilities

6.32 What constitutes reasonable financial provision for the applicant must be viewed in the light of the deceased's obligations and responsibilities to any other applicant or beneficiary and his or her financial position[1].

However generally only those obligations that the deceased had immediately before death will be relevant. As a rule, mere blood ties without obligations will not suffice[2].

Obligations will include moral as well as legal obligations[3].

[1] I(PFD)A 1975, s 3(1)(b), (c) and (d).
[2] *Re Jennings (Deceased)* [1994] 3 All ER 27.
[3] *Re Goodchild (Deceased) and Another* [1997] 2 FLR 644; and *Re Debenham (Deceased)* [1986] 1 FLR 404.

Size and nature of the net estate - I(PFD)A 1975, s 3(1)(e)

6.33 The courts discourage claims against estates where the assets are small on the basis that the costs of the proceedings will make significant inroads into what is available to satisfy the competing interests in the estate.

Although, generally, the costs will be met out of the estate, the court will have no hesitation in making an order for costs against an unsuccessful applicant who has pursued an unmeritorious claim. In *Re Vrint*[1] the estate was valued at a little over £138[2] and the claim by the deceased's estranged widow was dismissed with costs. The court said that given the size of the estate, the claim ought never to have been brought[3].

It was held in *Re Fullard*[4] that before making an order that the estate pay the costs of an unsuccessful applicant, the court should look closely at the merits of the application.

However, the fact that an estate is large enough to make adequate provision for all interested parties, whilst making the balancing exercise easier, does not remove the need for the applicant to satisfy the court that reasonable financial provision has not been made and that it should have been.

[1] [1940] 3 All ER 470.
[2] Present day value approximately £3,600.
[3] See also *Re Joslin* [1941] 1 All ER 302.
[4] [1981] 2 All ER 796.

Any physical or mental disability of an applicant or a beneficiary - I(PFD)A 1975, s 3(1)(f)

6.34 In *Re Debenham*[1] the court awarded provision for an adult daughter of the deceased even though there was no legal obligation towards her. The deceased had abandoned her at birth and thereafter heartlessly rejected all her attempts to establish a relationship. The court said that although the deceased had made no effort during her lifetime to help the applicant, because of her health problems there was nonetheless a moral obligation on the estate to make provision for her.

[1]   [1986] 1 FLR 404.

Any other relevant matter, including conduct

6.35 The court will admit evidence of facts from which can be inferred the deceased's reasons for disposing of his estate as he did[1].

In *Re Snoek (Deceased)*[2] it was held that the vicious and atrocious behaviour of the applicant in the later years of her marriage to the deceased did not entirely cancel out her earlier contribution to the home and family, and provision was made for her.

In *Baynes v Hedger*[3] the court considered that the conduct of one of the claimants in pressurising, if not bullying, the deceased into baling her out of a succession of financial crises was an important factor in the case.

[1]   *Re Smallwood, Smallwood v Martins Bank* [1951] 1 All ER 372.
[2]   (1983) 13 Fam Law 18.
[3]   [2008] 3 FCR 151.

THE FORFEITURE ACT 1982

6.36 The Forfeiture Act 1982 gives the court discretion to modify the application of the forfeiture rule if it takes the view that, bearing in mind the extent of the applicant's moral culpability, it would be unjust to deny him or her any benefit as a result of unlawfully killing the deceased. In *Royse v Royse*[1] Mrs Royse was convicted of killing her husband. The forfeiture rule prevented her from benefiting under his will of which she was the sole beneficiary. The Forfeiture Act 1982 was not in force when Mrs Royse made her application for provision from the estate which the court said should fail for the same reasons, namely that she should not be able to profit from her unlawful act in killing her husband.

In *Jones v Roberts*[2] the decision in *Royse* was followed, and there are very few decisions in which the court has exercised its discretion to modify the operation of the forfeiture rule[3].

In *Re S*[4] a husband murdered his wife. On her death, the proceeds of a joint policy became payable. The insurance company did not oppose the modification of the forfeiture rule to enable the deceased's estate, which was effectively the proceeds of the policy, to be held in trust for the parties' young son.

[1]   [1984] 3 All ER 339.
[2]   [1995] 2 FLR 422.
[3]   *Re H (Deceased)* [1990] 1 FLR 441.
[4]   [1996] 1 FLR 910.

Application by a surviving cohabitant under Inheritance (Provision for Family and Dependants) Act 1975, s 1(1)(ba)

6.37 The requirements for an application under the section are set out in s 1(1A)[1] and s 1(1B)[2]. Whilst recognising the existence of cohabitation, the threshold criteria are less generous than for a surviving spouse or civil partner. Although cohabitants of at least 2 years' standing no longer have to establish dependency on the deceased, I(PFD)A 1975, s 1(2)(b) makes a clear distinction between applications made by a surviving spouse or civil partner and all other categories of applicant. The question of whether or not reasonable financial provision has been made for a surviving spouse or civil partner is determined without regard to whether that provision is required for his or her maintenance. The other categories of applicant are restricted by the requirement to show that reasonable provision for their maintenance has not been made.

[1] Inserted by the Law Reform (Succession) Act 1995 in respect of those living together as spouses.
[2] Inserted by CPA 2004 in relation to those living together as civil partners.

WHO IS ELIGIBLE TO APPLY?

6.38 To qualify to make an application under the category of a cohabitant of at least 2 years' standing the following criteria must be satisfied:

(a) the deceased must have died on or after 1 January 1996; and
(b) for the whole of the 2 years immediately preceding the death of the deceased, the applicant and the deceased must have:
 – lived in the same household;
 – as spouse or civil partner.

These requirements raise questions of interpretation.

For the whole of the 2 years immediately preceding the death of the deceased

6.39 Until *Re Watson (Deceased)*[1] there had been no reported decisions for guidance on how strictly the courts may construe this requirement. Although in that case it was not argued that the application should fail because the deceased had spent the last 3 weeks of his life in hospital, Neuberger J, as he then was, commented that it was[2]:

'. . . not an argument which could respectably have been advanced. In the first place, as a matter of ordinary language, the fact that someone is in hospital for a period, possibly for a long period, at the end of which he dies, does not mean that, before his death, he ceased to be part of the household of which he was part, until he was forced by illness to go to hospital, and to which he would have returned had he not died.'

This approach reflects the case law in related areas. For example, when considering whether for the purposes of applications under I(PFD)A 1975, s 1(1)(e) the applicant was being maintained by the deceased 'immediately before the death', the courts have tended to look at the general arrangement between the parties up to the date of death rather than construe the section so as to exclude applications where the dependency had as a matter of fact ceased before the date of death[3].

It was held in *Re Beaumont (Deceased)* that the court should look, 'not at the *de facto* state of maintenance existing at the moment of death, but at the settled and enduring basis or arrangement then generally existing between the parties, using the date of death as the day on which that arrangement was to be considered'[4].

That case was referred to in *Jelley v Iliffe and Others*[5] in which it was said that 'a relationship of dependence which has persisted for years will not be defeated by its termination during a few weeks of mortal sickness'[6].

In *Re Dix*[7], the Court of Appeal held that notwithstanding that the claimant had lived apart from the deceased for the last 3 months of his life, she was entitled to claim against his estate under s 1(1)(ba) and s 1(1)(e). In that case the parties had lived together in a settled relationship for 27 years in spite of the problems that resulted from the deceased's alcoholism. Eventually, the situation became intolerable for the claimant and she left with a suitcase of clothes to stay with her daughter. The question for the court was whether the relationship was at an end or merely suspended. The Court of Appeal said that the judge at first instance was right to conclude on the evidence that the parties did not regard their relationship at an end. The judge had accepted the claimant's case that she was forced by a combination of the deceased's behaviour and her own ill health to leave, but that she always intended to return. It was likely that she would have returned, as she had following previous separations, had the claimant's daughter not deliberately failed to tell her of the deceased's attempts to contact her to plead for her return.

In *Kourkgy v Lusher*[8] the court found that the applicant was not being maintained by the deceased immediately before his death. The deceased had only a matter of days before his death returned to live with his wife, although there had been cohabitation with the applicant for some 6 years immediately preceding that. The court took the view on the evidence that the deceased had been moving towards a position of divesting himself of responsibility for the applicant for some months before his death, and this was finally achieved when he returned to live with his wife, albeit days before his death.

In *Layton v Martin*[9] it was held that a former cohabitant had no claim under the I(PFD)A 1975 as she had ceased to live with the deceased about 2 years before his death.

In *Witkowska v Kaminski*[10] the claimant was a Polish national. She had originally entered the United Kingdom on a tourist visa and, when that expired, she became an illegal overstayer. Shortly after they met, the claimant moved in to live with the deceased. Over the 5 years they were together, the pattern was that she would return to Poland on frequent visits, and during this time the deceased would send money for her support. The claimant was in Poland on a 14-week visit when the deceased had an accident as a result of which he shortly thereafter died. When she heard of the accident she returned to the United Kingdom but arrived just too late. It was not in issue that the claimant and the deceased had lived together in the same household as spouses, but it was in dispute that the cohabitation had subsisted up to the deceased's death. The case of the defendant, the deceased's son, was that there was evidence that the claimant had decided not to return to live with the deceased. However, the court considered that evidence of payments sent by the deceased to the claimant in Poland up to 7 weeks before his death, correspondence and telephone calls between them during her absence and the fact that she had left some of her possessions at the deceased's home all pointed to the relationship continuing up to the time of his death.

In *Kaur v Dhaliwal*[11] the Court of Appeal dismissed the appeal by the sons of the deceased from a decision that the deceased and the applicant had lived together for the requisite period. Although the applicant and the deceased had cohabited for just short of 2 years immediately preceding the deceased's death, they had a settled relationship that continued until the deceased's death, and the interruption in their living arrangements was for reasons unconnected with the state of their relationship.

[1] [1999] 1 FLR 878.
[2] At 882H–883A.
[3] *Re Beaumont (Deceased)* [1980] 1 All ER 266.
[4] At 267E.
[5] [1981] 2 All ER 29.
[6] Per Stephenson LJ at 35A.
[7] [2004] 1 FLR 918, [2004] 1 WLR 1339.
[8] (1983) 4 FLR 65.
[9] [1986] 2 FLR 227.
[10] [2007] 1 FLR 1547.
[11] [2014] EWHC 1991 (Ch).

Living in the same household

6.40 Even if there is an intimate relationship and the parties spent periods of time together on holidays and the like, without a shared household there can be no basis for an application under this section[1].

In the Law Commission's report, *Cohabitation: The Financial Consequences of Relationship Breakdown*[2] it is recommended that for the purposes of the legislation then proposed that cohabitants should be defined as those who *are living as a couple in a joint household*.

Reference is made in the Report to the 'six signposts' currently used in the social security context[3] as a starting point for the central factors that a court may have in mind when deciding the issue. These factors are:

(1) existence of a joint household;
(2) financial arrangements;
(3) stability of the relationship;
(4) responsibility for children;
(5) sexual relationship;
(6) public recognition of the relationship.

6.40 *Death and Succession*

In *Churchill v Roach*[4] the court found that the claimant and the deceased were not living in the same household at the material time but were maintaining two separate households. The judge did not consider that it was necessarily fatal to the application that there were two houses, and he accepted that there was a degree of sharing when the parties met at weekends and for more extended periods of time, but on the facts of that case the claimant failed to satisfy the criteria as he understood it to be:

> '... living in the same household ... seems to me to have elements of permanence, to involve a consideration of the frequency and intimacy of contact, to contain an element of mutual support, to require some consideration of the degree of voluntary restraint upon personal freedom which each party undertakes, and to involve an element of community of resources. None of these factors is of itself sufficient, but each may provide an indicator.'

This question was considered by Lewison J, as he then was, in *Baynes v Hedger*[5] in relation to one of the two claimants whose application was not the subject of the later appeal to the Court of Appeal. In that case it was held[6] that:

> 'Whether two people lived together in the same household was a question of fact. It was not simply a matter of living under the same roof but of the public and private acknowledgement of their society and the mutual protection and support that bound them together. Nor did two people living in the same household cease to do so because they became physically separated.'

It was determinative of the court's finding in *Baynes v Hedger* that one of the applicants and the deceased had not shared a household for the requisite period, that although historically they had lived together in a same-sex relationship, there had for at least the 30 years before the death of the deceased, been a settled pattern whereby they each maintained their own households and only 'stayed' with or 'visited' the other periodically.

1. *Malone v Harrison* [1979] 1 WLR 1353.
2. Law Com No 307.
3. See also CHAPTER 9.
4. [2004] 2 FLR 989.
5. [2008] 3 FCR 151.
6. At p 152.

6.41 There may be a dispute as to whether the applicant and the deceased lived in the same household, even if they lived under the same roof. However, if the court finds that the applicant satisfied the requirements for living together as spouse or civil partner[1], it will generally be the case that this requirement will be satisfied.

Brief periods of separation will not necessarily prevent a finding that the parties were living in the same household[2], nor will the fact that one party had another household as well as the shared household[3].

HHJ Behrens provided a helpful review of the authorities in *Lindop v Agus, Bass and Hedley*[4]. In that case he concluded that although it ran counter to the applicant's case that she retained her father's address for correspondence and for the purposes of the electoral roll, on the totality of the evidence she and the deceased had lived together as husband and wife openly and her claim under s 1(1A) was made out.

Cases decided in other jurisdictions may also be of relevance here.

For the purposes of establishing separation in the context of divorce proceedings, the parties in *Mouncer v Mouncer*[5] were held not to be living in a separate household because although they slept in separate rooms and the wife no longer did the husband's washing, they shared the cleaning and continued to take meals together.

In *Kimber v Kimber*[6] HHJ Tyrer concluded that whilst it was impossible to draw up an exhaustive list of the criteria for determining the existence of cohabitation, certain factors were relevant derived from the authorities, and the Social Security Contributions and Benefits Act 1992. The judge's approach was approved by the Court of Appeal in *Grey v Grey*[7].

[1] I(PFD)A 1975, s 1(1A)(b), see **6.43** below.
[2] *Pounder v London Underground Limited and Others* [1995] PIQR 217.
[3] *Jessop v Jessop* [1992] 1 FLR 591.
[4] [2010] 1 FLR 631.
[5] [1972] 1 All ER 289.
[6] [2000] 1 FLR 383.
[7] [2010] 1 FLR 1764.

6.42 In proceedings under the DVMPA 1976 the parties were held to be living together even where they had completely severed their living arrangements but were still under the same roof[1].

Kotke v Saffarini[2] concerned a claim under the Fatal Accidents Act 1976 for loss of dependency. An issue arose as to whether the claimant and the deceased had been living in the same household as spouses for at least 2 years before the death. The Court of Appeal upheld the decision of the trial judge that, although the claimant and the deceased were living together as spouses at the date of his death, the claimant had not made out her case that they had done so for at least 2 years before the date of death. The court held that whilst the retention of a separate property by the deceased would not in itself prevent a finding that the parties were living in one household, on the facts of this case, '. . . the extent to which . . . the deceased maintained and made use of it and treated himself as still resident there, indicated that he and the claimant had not [2 years before the date of death] reached the position of treating [the claimant's house] as their mutual home'.

[1] *Adeoso (otherwise Ametepe) v Adeoso* [1981] 1 All ER 107.
[2] [2005] 2 FLR 517.

Living together as spouse or civil partner

6.43 This was an issue in *Re Watson (Deceased)*[1], a case decided before the amendment to I(PFD)A 1975 made by CPA 2004. The parties had shared the home of the deceased for the last 11 years of his life. Although they had known one another for over 30 years, and in their younger days had enjoyed an intimate relationship, they had never married. During the time that they shared a home the deceased had worked long hours outside the home, and the applicant had worked long hours in the home, cooking, washing, cleaning and the like. They had separate bedrooms, but shared the other accommodation,

6.43 Death and Succession

took meals together and were otherwise companionable. Although the applicant owned her own home elsewhere and had a small income, the deceased provided the accommodation without charge, and the outgoings were shared on an informal basis. In finding that the applicant satisfied the requirements of s 1(1)(ba) of the I(PFD)A 1975 as a person living in the same household as the deceased, and as his wife, Neuberger J, as he then was, said that:

> '. . . when considering that question, one must beware of indulging in too much over-analysis. Anyone who reads newspapers or law reports does not need to be told that marriages, like, perhaps even more than, other human relationships, can vary from each other in multifarious ways. However, in my judgment, when considering whether two people are living together as husband and wife, it would be wrong to conclude that they do so simply because their relationship is one which a husband and wife could have. If the test were as wide as that, then, bearing in mind the enormous variety of relationships that can exist between husband and wife, virtually every relationship between a man and a woman living in the same household would fall within s 1(1A). It seems to me that, when considering the question, the court should ask itself whether, in the opinion of a reasonable person with normal perceptions, it could be said that the two people in question were living together as husband and wife; but, when considering that question, one should not ignore the multifarious nature of marital relationships[2].

In what is thought to be the first reported decision of a claim under s 1(1B), it was the view of Lewison J, as he then was, in *Baynes v Hedger* in relation to one of two claimants whose application was not subject to a later appeal to the Court of Appeal that "it is not possible to establish that two persons have lived together as civil partners unless their relationship as a couple is an acknowledged one"[3]. In that case the deceased and one of the claimants had formed an intimate relationship and had lived together as a family with the claimant's children. This continued for some years until they established their own households after which they would visit one another from time to time. As the judge observed they, "were of a generation for whom a same-sex relationship was not an acceptable lifestyle, and their relationship was not openly acknowledged" and although he found that initially they shared a bedroom and probably had a sexual relationship, he concluded that later when they had each their own house this may not have been the case. Although he was satisfied that they were emotionally committed to one another right up until the deceased's death, he concluded that their relationship was a private one, and they did not themselves acknowledge that they were a couple.'

[1] [1999] 1 FLR 878.
[2] At 883E–G.
[3] At para 150.

Making out the ground for the application

6.44 If the court is satisfied that the applicant fulfils the criteria for eligibility under s 1(1)(ba), it will go on to consider whether or not the ground for applying for provision is made out, namely that the disposition of the deceased's estate does not make reasonable financial provision for the maintenance of the surviving cohabitant.

This is essentially a question of fact for the court, but one that it was held in *Re Coventry (Deceased)*[1] involved ' . . . the judge making a value judgment (or qualitative decision) whether in the circumstances, looked at objectively, it was unreasonable that the provisions governing the estate did not provide for the applicant['s maintenance], and not merely by deciding whether the deceased had acted unreasonably or unfairly in leaving his estate as he had'[2].

[1]   [1979] 3 All ER 815.
[2]   At p 815J.

MATTERS TO WHICH THE COURT MUST HAVE REGARD

6.45 The matters to which the court must have regard when making a finding about the provision that has been made are those set out in I(PFD)A 1975, s 3. As well as the matters set out in s 3(1)(a)–(g), which are common to all applicants and which are considered at **6.30** above, in the case of applications by a cohabitant under s 1(1)(ba), s 3(2A) requires the court to have regard to:

'(a)   the age of the applicant and the length of the period during which the applicant lived as the spouse or civil partner of the deceased and in the same household as the deceased;
(b)   the contribution made by the applicant to the welfare of the family of the deceased, including any contribution made by looking after the home or caring for the family.'

These matters mirror those which the court must consider under s 3(2) of the I(PFD)A 1975 when exercising its powers in favour of a spouse or former spouse who has not remarried or civil partner or former civil partner who has not entered into another civil partnership. They were considered in *Re Watson (Deceased)*[1].

[1]   [1999] 1 FLR 878.

Age of the applicant and length of cohabitation

6.46 Clearly the older the applicant, and the longer he or she has put the family's interests first, the less likely it is that he or she will be able to achieve financial independence.

In the case of elderly applicants, the court will bear in mind that the purpose of the I(PFD)A 1975 is to make provision for the applicant, and so any order made will be geared to the applicant's life expectancy so as not to provide a windfall for the applicant's survivors.

Applicant's contribution to the welfare of the family

6.47 There would appear to be no reason why, when considering this matter in a claim by a surviving cohabitant, the court should not look at it in the same way as when considering an application by a surviving spouse or former spouse who has not remarried, or surviving civil partner or former civil partner who has not entered into another civil partnership. This is subject to the proviso that the question of whether reasonable financial provision has been made must be decided on the basis of what is reasonable for the applicant to receive for his or her maintenance.

In *Re Watson (Deceased)*[1] the applicant's contribution by taking on and discharging the responsibility for all aspects of the day-to-day running and management of the household for the 11 years the parties lived together was regarded as substantial.

[1] [1999] 1 FLR 878.

THE EXERCISE OF THE COURT'S DISCRETION

6.48 If, after considering all the matters in s 3(1) and (2A) of the I(PFD)A 1975, the court has found as a fact that reasonable provision has not been made for the applicant's maintenance, it must then go on to decide what, if any, provision to make. It does not necessarily follow from a finding that reasonable provision has not been made that the court will make a substantive order. The court must exercise its discretion at this second stage and, in so doing, is required by s 3 to take into account once again all the matters set out in s 3(1)(a)–(g) and (2A).

In *Musa v Holliday*[1] the Court of Appeal upheld the first instance decision to award the transfer to the deceased's cohabitant of the bulk of the deceased's UK property. The Court of Appeal found that on the unusual facts of that case HHJ Kushner had correctly made a determination that the applicant needed a home outright and sufficient income to maintain the mortgage repayments and other outgoings, and to provide for the income needs of herself and her son. The income could only be provided by the transfer to the applicant of the deceased's business in the UK. Although by this award the applicant received most of the UK assets of the estate, the judge was satisfied that the six competing beneficiaries had sufficient to meet their needs from the deceased's assets in Northern Cyprus. It is unlikely that a surviving spouse could have done better but there is little doubt that the result owes a good deal to the bad blood evident between the parties, and the need for all financial ties to be severed.

In *Cattle v Evans*[2] the parties had been together for around 18 years but had lived together for only the last 5 years. They bought a property in Spain in joint names as their shared home using funds from the sale of the property owned by the deceased. The applicant used the sale proceeds of her own property to buy a property to rent out, and she contributed to renovation work at the Spanish property. They subsequently decided to sell the Spanish property and live in Wales but before the purchase of the property in Wales could be completed, the deceased received a diagnosis of terminal cancer. He proceeded with the purchase in his sole name using his half share of the proceeds of sale of the Spanish property and the parties lived there until his death shortly afterwards. He died intestate.

In awarding the applicant a life interest in a modest property to be purchased by the estate the court took into account that apart from the Spanish property the parties had kept their property and finances separate and the property in Wales had been funded almost entirely by the deceased.

[1] [2013] 1 FLR 806.
[2] [2011] 2 FLR 843.

Application by a 'dependant' under s 1(1)(e) of the Inheritance (Provision for Family and Dependants) Act 1975

6.49 If a surviving cohabitant is not eligible to apply under s 1(1)(ba) because there has not been the required cohabitation for 2 years immediately preceding the death, or the other conditions of eligibility cannot be satisfied, the only alternative is to make an application under s 1(1)(e).

WHO IS ELIGIBLE TO APPLY?

6.50 Applications under this section are not limited to those living together as spouse or civil partner who do not qualify to apply under s 1(1)(ba). Any person who can claim dependency upon the deceased may apply. This category will include, for example, friends and family members[1].

From 1 October 2014 ITPA 2014 has made important changes to claims made under this section. First, the definition of a dependant for the purposes of s 1(1)(e) is now qualified as follows[2]:

' . . . a person is to be treated as being maintained by the deceased (either wholly or partly, as the case may be) only if the deceased was making a substantial contribution in money or money's worth towards the reasonable needs of that person, other than a contribution made for full valuable consideration pursuant to an agreement of a commercial nature.'

Before this amendment, the court was required to balance the respective contributions of the applicant and the deceased up to the date of death and only if there was a net contribution by the deceased to the applicant would the applicant be eligible to make a claim. The balancing exercise is no longer required, and the only vitiating factor will be the payment of money by the deceased to the applicant for full valuable consideration pursuant to an arrangement of a commercial nature.

This will exclude, for example, claims where there has been a landlord/lodger relationship where the rental paid is the full commercial value. However, it allows for a situation in which the consideration falls short of that either from the outset, or over time.

The amendments also deal with the difficulty that had arisen whereby the courts had tended to interpret the eligibility criteria as requiring the applicant to prove that the deceased had assumed responsibility for his or her maintenance[3]. This was specifically addressed by the Law Commission in the report that gave rise to ITPA 2014[4]. The consequent amendment to s 3(4), specifically sub-s (b), admits the possibility of the deceased having maintained the applicant as required by s 1(1)(e) without there being any assumption of responsibility, thereby making it clear that no such evaluation is required for the purposes of determining eligibility.

[1] See *Re B (Deceased)* [2000] 1 All ER 665, in which a mother with the full-time care of a severely disabled child was held to fall into this category by virtue of the incidental benefits received by the mother from payments made from the child's personal injury damages for the child's maintenance.
[2] IPFDA 1975, s 1(3).

6.50 *Death and Succession*

[3] *Jelley v Iliffe* [1981] Fam 128; *Bouette v Rose* [1999] All ER (D) 1458; *Martin v Midland Bank Trust Co Ltd* [1980] 1 Ch 444; [1980] 1 All ER 266; *Baynes v Hedger* [2009] EWCA Civ 374, [2009] 2 FLR 767.
[4] *Intestacy and Family Provisions Claims on Death* Law Com 331 (TSO), 2011.

Immediately before the death

6.51 The requirement for the maintenance of the applicant by the deceased to be current at the time of death is not changed by ITPA 2014. However, courts have tended to look at the general arrangement between the parties up to the date of death rather than construe the section so as to exclude applications where the dependency had as a matter of fact ceased before the date of death. In *Re Beaumont (Deceased)*[1] it was held that the court should look 'not at the *de facto* state of maintenance existing at the moment of death, but at the settled and enduring basis or arrangement then generally existing between the parties, using the date of death as the day on which that arrangement was to be considered'[2].

That case was referred to in *Jelley v Iliffe and Others*[3], in which it was said that 'a relationship of dependence which has persisted for years will not be defeated by its termination during a few weeks of mortal sickness'[4].

In *Re Dix*[5], the Court of Appeal held that notwithstanding that the claimant had lived apart from the deceased for the last 3 months of his life, she came within s 1(1)(e) and was also entitled to claim against his estate under s 1(1)(ba). In that case the parties had lived together in a settled relationship for 27 years in spite of the problems that resulted from the deceased's alcoholism. Eventually, the situation became intolerable for the claimant and she left with a suitcase of clothes to stay with her daughter. The question for the court was whether the relationship was at an end or merely suspended. The Court of Appeal said that the judge at first instance was right to conclude on the evidence that the parties did not regard their relationship at an end. The judge had accepted the claimant's case that she was forced by a combination of the deceased's behaviour and her own ill health to leave, but that she always intended to return. It was likely that she would have returned, as she had following previous separations, had the claimant's daughter not deliberately failed to tell her of the deceased's attempts to contact her to plead for her return.

[1] [1980] 1 All ER 266.
[2] At 267E.
[3] [1981] 2 All ER 29.
[4] Per Stephenson LJ at 35A; see also *Re Watson* [1999] 1 FLR 878.
[5] [2004] 1 FLR 918.

6.52 In *Kourkgy v Lusher*[1], however, the court found that the applicant was not being maintained by the deceased immediately before his death. The deceased had returned to live with his wife only a matter of days before his death, although there had been cohabitation with the applicant for some 6 years immediately preceding that. The court took the view on the evidence that the deceased had been moving towards a position of divesting himself of responsibility for the applicant for some months before his death, and this was finally achieved when he returned to live with his wife, albeit days before his death.

In *Layton v Martin*[2] it was held that the former cohabitant had no claim under the I(PFD)A 1975, as she had ceased to live with the deceased about 2 years before his death.

In *Witkowska v Kaminski*[3] the claimant was a Polish national. She had originally entered the United Kingdom on a tourist visa and when that expired she became an illegal overstayer. Shortly after they met, the claimant moved in to live with the deceased. Over the 5 years they were together, the pattern was that she would return to Poland on frequent visits, and during this time the deceased would send money for her support. The claimant was in Poland on a 14-week visit when the deceased had an accident as a result of which he shortly thereafter died. When she heard of the accident she returned to the United Kingdom but arrived just too late. It was not in issue that the claimant and the deceased had lived together in the same household as spouses, but it was in dispute that the cohabitation had subsisted up to the deceased's death. The case of the defendant, the deceased's son, was that there was evidence that the claimant had decided not to return to live with the deceased. However, the court considered that evidence of payments sent by the deceased to the claimant in Poland up to 7 weeks before his death, correspondence and telephone calls between them during her absence and the fact that she had left some of her possessions at the deceased's home all pointed to the relationship continuing up to the time of his death.

In *Kaur v Dhaliwal*[4], a claim made under s 1(1)(ba), the Court of Appeal dismissed the appeal by the sons of the deceased from a decision that the deceased and the applicant had lived together for the requisite period. Although the applicant and the deceased had cohabited for just short of 2 years immediately preceding the deceased's death, they had a settled relationship that continued until the deceased's death, and the interruption in their living arrangements was for reasons unconnected with the state of their own relationship.

[1]   (1983) 4 FLR 65.
[2]   [1986] 2 FLR 227.
[3]   [2007] 1 FLR 1547.
[4]   [2014] EWHC 1991 (Ch).

Being maintained

6.53 Following the amendment to s 1(1)–(3) I(PFD)A 1975 the court will no longer have to balance the respective contributions in order to ascertain whether there is a net gain to the applicant. The only matter for the court will be whether there is a substantial contribution, in cash or in kind, other than by way of a commercial arrangement.

It is possible that an arrangement that began on a business footing may in time evolve to become one in which there is a degree of dependency.

There is no statutory definition to assist the court in deciding whether any sums paid to the applicant by the deceased can be regarded as maintenance sufficient to satisfy the eligibility criteria. The case law suggests that such sums should enable the applicant directly or indirectly to *discharge the cost of his daily living at whatever standard of living is appropriate to him*[1].

[1] Re Dennis (deceased) [1981] 2 All ER 140.

MAKING OUT THE GROUND FOR THE APPLICATION

6.54 If the applicant has satisfied the court that he or she is within the category eligible to apply for provision under s 1(1)(e) of the I(PFD)A 1975, the court will then look at the provision that has been made and whether in the light of the evidence and the matters referred to in s 3 that provision is such as it would be reasonable in all the circumstances of the case for the applicant to receive for his or her maintenance. This is essentially a question of fact for the court, but one that it was held in *Re Coventry (Deceased)*[1] involved 'the judge making a value judgment (or qualitative decision) whether in the circumstances, looked at objectively, it was unreasonable that the provisions governing the estate did not provide for the applicant, and not merely by deciding whether the deceased had acted unreasonably or unfairly in leaving his estate as he had'[2].

[1] [1979] 3 All ER 815.
[2] At 815J.

MATTERS TO WHICH THE COURT MUST HAVE REGARD

6.55 The matters to which the court must have regard when making a finding about the provision that has been made are those set out in s 3(1) of the I(PFD)A 1975. As well as the matters set out in s 3(1)(a)–(g) which are common to all applicants and which are considered at **6.30** above, in the case of applications under s 1(1)(e), s 3(4), as amended by IPTA, requires the court to have regard to 'the length of time for which and basis on which the deceased maintained the applicant, and to the extent of the contribution made by way of maintenance, and to whether and, if so, to what extent the deceased assumed responsibility for the maintenance of the applicant'.

Assumption of responsibility for maintenance by the deceased

6.56 Although much of the existing case law looks at the assumption of responsibility in the context of eligibility, the decided cases may offer some assistance when the court is considering the assumption of responsibility for the purposes of s 3.

In *Jelley v Iliffe and Others*[1] the court determined that:

> 'The bare fact that the applicant was being maintained by the deceased under an agreement subsisting at the deceased's death was sufficient to, and generally did, raise a presumption that the deceased had assumed responsibility for [the applicant's] maintenance . . . and it was unnecessary to prove any other overt act demonstrating the assumption of responsibility because . . . the words "assumed responsibility for" in s 3(4) meant "had undertaken" to provide maintenance.

Moreover it was not necessary for an applicant to prove that the deceased had intended to maintain [the applicant] after his or her death, and it was sufficient if the deceased's conduct was such that the applicant had been made wholly or partially dependent on the deceased for his maintenance during the deceased's lifetime . . .'

This approach was confirmed in *Rees v Newbery and the Institute of Cancer Research*[2]. The assumption of maintenance could be inferred from the fact that the deceased in his lifetime undertook such maintenance[3]. In *Malone v Harrison and Another*[4], although the applicant and the deceased had never lived together, for 12 years they took holidays together that were paid for by the deceased, and for the rest of the time the applicant made herself available to the deceased. He discouraged her from working so that she could be at his beck and call. He bought a flat in joint names for her occupation, and a flat in Malta for their holidays, also in joint names. He gave her a car and some shares. The deceased made no provision in his will for the applicant, but before his death had brought to her attention that she may be able to make a claim against his estate. It was held that the deceased had assumed full responsibility for the applicant for the last 12 years of his life.

However, in *Rhodes v Dean*[5], despite satisfying the court that she had been maintained by the deceased, the Court of Appeal considered that the trial judge had correctly applied the provisions of s 3(1)(a)–(g) and in particular s 3(4) in finding that the deceased had not assumed responsibility for the applicant's maintenance. The deceased had provided the applicant with accommodation for 2 years and 2 months, but had not assumed financial responsibility for all her maintenance needs. Bearing in mind the sum of £36,000 that the applicant had received from a joint bank account on the death of the deceased, the judge had been right to conclude that it was not unreasonable that no provision had been made for the applicant in the deceased's will.

[1] [1981] 2 All ER 29.
[2] [1998] 1 FLR 1041.
[3] The applicant, a 50-year-old actor with modest earnings, applied for financial provision out of the deceased's £700,000 estate. The two had become friends through their work. The basis for the application was that for nearly 10 years the applicant had been living in a flat owned by the deceased at substantially less than the market rent. The deceased's motives appeared to have been entirely philanthropic. The deceased had intended to make a new will to make continued provision after his death, but died before the will was executed. The court held, granting the application, that the provision of accommodation at less than the market rent amounted to maintenance of the applicant, and by inference that the deceased had assumed responsibility for the applicant.
[4] [1979] 1 WLR 1353.
[5] [1996] CLY 555.

6.57 In *Baynes v Hedger*[1] the deceased had become closely involved with the first claimant and her family, including a daughter, the second claimant, who was also her goddaughter. Over the course of many years the deceased generously provided financial help. In relation to the first claimant, the deceased had some 30 years before provided her with a large sum of money with which to buy a house, and made her a beneficiary of a trust fund that gave her an income. Since then she had made occasional one-off payments and some much smaller payments on a more regular basis.

6.57 *Death and Succession*

At first instance Lewison J, as he then was, decided that this claimant could not satisfy the requirements of s 1(1)(e) as there was no evidence that she had been maintained by the deceased immediately before the death. He rejected the argument that the fact that the source of the first claimant's home and major part of her income was the deceased pointed to dependency. She did not fall within the category and her claim must fail. However, the judge went on expressly to consider in the context of s 3(4) the extent to which the deceased had assumed responsibility for her maintenance. He concluded that a one off gift of money for a house in the distant past did not show any assumption of responsibility for future maintenance. The creation of the settlement indicated the clear extent of the responsibility assumed and that it was this, rather than the deceased's free assets, that was to be the source of the maintenance.

The second claimant had been the recipient of very generous financial support from the deceased throughout her adult life that continued up to a few months before her death. Latterly the financial assistance had been at the second claimant's request, if not insistence, as a result of the precarious state of her finances. Some of the payments were gifts, others were expressed to be 'soft' loans that it was doubtful would be repaid in full. On this basis the judge held that she qualified to make a claim under s 1(1)(e).

In the exercise of his discretion under s 3(1) and 3(4) the judge went on to determine that the financial arrangements between the second claimant and the deceased did not amount to an assumption of responsibility for her continued support. Her primary concern was to help the second claimant to pay off her debts so that she could then support herself on her own earnings. For this and other reasons he concluded that the second claimant had failed to establish that the deceased's will had failed to make reasonable provision for her and so her claim failed.

[1] [2008] 3 FCR 151, [2009] 2 FLR 767.

THE EXERCISE OF THE COURT'S DISCRETION

6.58 If after considering all the matters in s 3(1)(a)–(g) and s 3(4) of the I(PFD)A 1975 the court is satisfied that reasonable provision has not been made for the applicant's maintenance, it must go on to decide what if, any provision, to make. It does not follow from a finding that reasonable provision has not been made that the court will make a substantive order[1]. This stage also involves the court in the exercise of its discretion, and in so doing it must take into account once again all the matters set out in s 3(1)(a)–(g) and s 3(4).

[1] *Rhodes v Dean* [1996] CLY 555.

Applications under the Inheritance (Provision for Family and Dependants) Act 1975 by children

6.59 The amendments to IPFDA by ITPA 2014 introduce a new category of applicant, namely any person towards whom the deceased has stood in the role of parent. There is no requirement for any blood or family tie.

Children may therefore qualify to apply for an order under the I(PFD)A 1975 by virtue of being either the natural child of the deceased[1], a person treated by the deceased as a child of the family in relation to any marriage or civil partnership[2], or a child who in relation to any family in which the deceased at any time stood in the role of a parent, was treated by the deceased as a child of the family[3]. A child claiming under s 1(1)(d) could be the child of a spouse or former spouse, civil partner or former civil partner, who had been treated by the deceased as a child of the family in relation to that marriage or civil partnership. A claimant could also be someone with no connection to any marriage or cohabitation to which the deceased may have been a party[4] as long as the deceased had stood in the role of parent to that child.

The definition of 'child' for the purposes of the I(PFD)A 1975 will not preclude applications by adult children.

A child in respect of whom an adoption order has been made cannot claim against the estate of a biological parent, unless the child has a contingent interest in the deceased parent's estate immediately before the adoption[5].

A child will include a child *en ventre sa mère* at the date of the deceased parent's death.

There is no distinction made between a legitimate child and an illegitimate child.

[1] Section 1(1)(c).
[2] Ie a step-child.
[3] Section 1(1)(d) as amended by ITPA 2014.
[4] And since the implementation of ITPA 2014, the child of a surviving cohabitant.
[5] Section 69(4) ACA 2002 as amended by ITPA 2014.

Who is eligible to apply under s 1(1)(c)?

6.60 This section applies only to the natural children of the deceased, be they minor children or adults. Unlike other categories of applicant, the question of the eligibility of a natural child to apply under this section should be easily determined.

Who is eligible to apply under s 1(1)(d)?

6.61 The enactment of ITPA 2014 extends the category of applicant under this subsection to include not only children of the family in the context of marriage and civil partnership, but also a child with no connection to any marriage or cohabitation to which the deceased may have been a party[1] as long as the deceased had stood in the role of parent to that child.

In its report, *Intestacy and Family Provisions Claims on Death*[2], The Law Commission rejected views gathered during the consultation process that extending the potential applicants under s 1(1)(d) would create problems[3]:

> '. . . A court would not find that a child who was simply sponsored by the deceased or with whom the deceased undertook voluntary work was treated as a child of the family, unless the quality and intensity of that help could be characterized as parental. Nor would simply helping an elderly neighbour, without much more, merit such a description . . . There may be a risk of speculative,

ill-judged litigation to test the boundaries of this new category but this is no reason not to cure what appears to us . . . as an undesirable anomaly in the law[4] . . . Nothing has emerged from consultation which alters our preliminary view that section 1(1)(d) is outdated and may operate in an arbitrary and unfair manner. Applicants with the same quality of relationship with the deceased may be treated quite differently from one another depending on whether the deceased was married or in a civil partnership, cohabiting, or single. It is . . . no answer to say that some children of the family excluded because of the wording of section 1(1)(d) may have standing to apply . . . as dependants under section 1(1)(e). That subsection imposes a quite different set of threshold requirements and sets a much higher hurdle.'

The definition of a child treated as a child of the family in the context of marriage or civil partnership has been given a wide interpretation by the courts, and the case law will be relevant to the assessment of the relationship in other contexts.

In *Re Leach, Leach v Lindeman*[5] the 55-year-old stepdaughter of the deceased was eligible to apply under s 1(1)(d). The basis for this decision was that, even though the deceased had married the applicant's father late in life, and at a time when the applicant was living independently, the relationship between them was in the nature of a close mother/daughter relationship, and this continued even after the death of the applicant's father. It was held that the applicant had been treated by the deceased as a child of the family that was formed when she married the applicant's father.

Re Callaghan (Deceased)[6] concerned an application by the adult stepson of the deceased. In that case, the deceased had come into the applicant's life when he was about 13, although he had not married the applicant's mother until long after the applicant had himself married and left home. Nonetheless, Booth J found on the particular facts of the case that:

' . . . the acknowledgement by the deceased of his own role of grandfather to the plaintiff's children, the confidences as to his property and financial affairs which he placed in the plaintiff and his dependence on the plaintiff to care for him in his last illness are examples of the deceased's treatment of the plaintiff as a child, albeit an adult child, of the family. All these things are part of the privileges and duties of two persons who, in regard to each other, stand in the relationship of parent and child; it is the existence of that relationship that enables the plaintiff to apply under s 1(1)(d) of [the I(PFD)A 1975].'

[1] And since the implementation of ITPA 2014, the child of a surviving cohabitant.
[2] Law Com 331 (TSO, 2011).
[3] At para **6.40**.
[4] At para **6.38**.
[5] [1985] 2 All ER 754.
[6] [1984] 3 All ER 790.

WHO IS ELIGIBLE TO APPLY UNDER S 1(1)(E)?

6.62 Children who are not eligible to apply under s 1(1)(c) or (d) may be able to make a claim against the deceased's estate on the basis of dependency.

The ground for the application

6.63 As with the other categories of applicant, apart from a surviving spouse, the ground for making the application as a child under s 1(1)(c), or (d)[1] is that the disposition of the deceased's estate does not make such financial provision as it would be reasonable in all the circumstances of the case for the applicant to receive for his or her maintenance.

The effect of this in relation to claims by infant children is that provision is considered on the basis that it is designed to last until the child's majority, or at the latest until he or she has finished higher education.

Provision for a child's maintenance can include the cost of private education, although in view of the wording of s 3(1) and (3) it is unlikely that a court will view provision to cover the cost of school fees as reasonable if private education would not have been considered in the lifetime of the deceased parent or it would otherwise be inappropriate for the child in question[2].

In relation to claims by adult children, the applicant's financial circumstances will be of great significance. The definition of 'maintenance' will not extend to payment of capital debts incurred by an adult child[3] nor topping up the pension fund of an adult child who in every other respect, including income, was well provided for[4].

It will be one of the prerequisites for a successful claim that the applicant is in need of maintenance from the estate, although the existence of that need will not of itself lead to provision being made[5].

[1] Or possibly (e) if very unusual circumstances exist.
[2] *Re W (A Minor) (Claim from Deceased's Estate)* [1995] 2 FLR 24.
[3] *Re Dennis (Deceased)* [1981] 2 All ER 140.
[4] *Re Jennings (Deceased)* [1994] 3 All ER 27.
[5] *Re Coventry* [1979] 3 All ER 815; *Re Dennis (Deceased)* (above).

Matters to which the court must have regard

6.64 The matters to which the court must have regard when making a finding about the provision that has been made are those set out in s 3 of the I(PFD)A 1975. As well as the matters set out in s 3(1)(a)–(g) which are common to all applicants and which are considered at **6.30** above, in the case of applications by children there are additional matters to which the court must have regard.

Additional matters to which the court must have regard in applications under s 1(1)(c) and s 1(1)(d): Education and training

6.65 In the case of a claim by a natural child of the deceased under s 1(1)(c) or a child eligible to apply under s 1(1)(d), the court must also, without prejudice to the generality of s 3(1)(g), have regard to the manner in which the applicant was being or in which he might expect to be educated or trained.

This will only be a matter of relevance to claims by infant children or at least those still undergoing full-time education or training. The fact that there are

6.65 Death and Succession

sufficient funds in the estate to provide for private education will not of itself mean that any order will take such an expense into account. As the wording of the subsection suggests, it will depend upon whether the applicant was in fact receiving private education or could expect to by reason of his family circumstances[1].

[1] Re C (Deceased) (Leave to Apply for Provision) [1995] 2 FLR 24.

Additional matters to which the court must have regard in an application under s 1(1)(d): Assumption of responsibility by deceased/liability of another to maintain

6.66 In the case of applications by a child under this section, in addition to the matters to be considered under s 3(1) of the I(PFD)A 1975, the court must also have regard to s 3(3)[1], namely:

(a) to whether the deceased maintained the applicant and, if so, to the length of time for which and basis on which the deceased did so, and to the extent of the contribution made by way of maintenance;
(b) (aa) to whether and, if so, to what extent the deceased assumed responsibility for the maintenance of the applicant;
(c) to whether in maintaining or assuming responsibility for maintaining the applicant the deceased did so knowing that the applicant was not his own child;
(d) to the liability of any other person to maintain the applicant.

These subsections do not qualify or limit the scope of s 1(1)(d)[2]. In other words, the matters referred to in s 3(3)(a)–(c) are not preconditions to eligibility under s 1(1)(d).

[1] As amended by ITPA 2014.
[2] Re Callaghan [1985] FLR 116.

THE EXERCISE OF THE COURT'S DISCRETION

6.67 If after considering all the relevant matters in s 3 of the I(PFD)A 1975 the court has found as a fact that the disposition of the deceased's estate failed to make reasonable financial provision for the applicant's maintenance, it will go on to the second stage and decide whether an order should be made.

Even if the court has found the ground for the application made out, it does not follow that a substantive order will be made. It is subject to discretion, which is exercised by looking once again at the matters set out in s 3.

Generally speaking, the court will take a broad view on the facts of each particular case and try to balance the applicant's claim with the interests of the beneficiaries and any other applicants.

APPROACH OF THE COURT TO CLAIMS BY MINOR CHILDREN

6.68 Minor children, in particular a natural or adopted child of the deceased, will generally be in a very strong position when making a claim for provision out of the deceased's estate. After all, unless they are fortunate enough to be of independent means, they will look to their parents or the adults with whom they are living for financial support, and morally and in the case of parents as a matter of law[1], they are under an obligation to provide such support. They clearly fall into the category of individual that the I(PFD)A 1975 is designed to assist, namely those who are placed in a position of dependence by the deceased but are not adequately provided for on his or her death.

The matters to which the court must have regard under s 3(1) and s 3(3) are unlikely to present any difficulty to an applicant who is the natural infant child of the deceased, save that there may be competing claims. For example, the natural child of the deceased's spouse or former spouse may be in competition with the cohabitant and illegitimate child of the deceased. In such a situation, it is likely that the court will also look at the financial situation of each surviving parent, and their relative ability to make provision for the child in their care[2].

[1] CSA 1991 and CSA 1995.
[2] *Re H (A Minor)* (1976) Fam Law 172.

APPROACH OF THE COURT TO CLAIMS BY ADULT CHILDREN

6.69 Since the decision of the Court of Appeal in *Re Jennings (Deceased)*[1], the circumstances in which a claim by an adult child will succeed were considered to be relatively limited. That case endorsed the rationale of Oliver J at first instance in *Re Coventry (Deceased)*[2]. His decision to dismiss the applicant's claim for provision from the estate of his late father was upheld by the Court of Appeal, quoting approvingly from the judgment in the court below[3]:

> 'It cannot be enough to say, "Here is a son of the deceased, he is in necessitous circumstances, there is property of the deceased which could be made available to assist him but which is not available if the deceased's dispositions stand; therefore those dispositions do not make reasonable provision for the applicant". There must . . . be established some sort of moral claim by the applicant to be maintained by the deceased or at the expense of his estate beyond the mere fact of a blood relationship, some reason why it can be said that, in the circumstances, it is unreasonable that no or no greater provision was made.'

In *Re Jennings (Deceased)* the Court of Appeal overturned Wall J's finding that the deceased father's failure to support his son, the applicant, during his minority, produced a moral obligation that would make a failure to make provision for the applicant on his death unreasonable: 'An Act intended to facilitate the making of reasonable financial provision cannot have been intended to revive defunct obligations and responsibilities as a basis for making it'[4]. 'It is not the purpose of [the I(PFD)A 1975] to punish or redress past bad or unfeeling parental behaviour where that behaviour does not still impinge on the applicant's present financial situation'[5].

It was affirmed in *Re Jennings (Deceased)* that for an able-bodied adult child of the deceased to succeed in an application for provision from the estate, 'there must be some special circumstance, typically a moral obligation of the deceased towards [the child]'[6]. This is not to import into the statute a moral obligation as a pre-condition to a successful application by an adult child, rather to underline that an adult child who does not demonstrate a financial need for provision is likely to have to show some special circumstance, such as a moral obligation, in order to succeed.

In *Re Abram (Deceased)*[7] the court found a special circumstance leading to the conclusion that the deceased mother's failure to make provision in her will for her adult son who was clearly in need of maintenance was unreasonable. The facts were that the son had for most of his working life worked for his mother in the family business. He had worked for a very low wage on the basis that in due course the business would be his. In the event, he could no longer support his family on the wages he received and he had no alternative but to leave the business. This led to a rift between mother and son and although this was repaired before her death, she never revoked the will that she had made when they were estranged that left her estate elsewhere. Looking at all the circumstances of the case, the court found that the applicant had established a moral claim to provision from the estate.

In *Re Goodchild (Deceased) and Another*[8], decided at first instance before *Re Abrams*, the Court of Appeal upheld a finding that the applicant's father owed him a moral obligation to ensure that as much of the estate of his late mother would devolve to him on his father's death as it would have done if he had not changed his will in favour of his new wife on his remarriage. This decision was based on the mutual intention of the applicant's parents in the wills they prepared that the survivor of them would succeed to the estate of the first to die and on the death of the survivor the estate would devolve on the applicant.

In *Re Hancock (Deceased)*[9] Butler-Sloss LJ indicated that it may not be necessary in every case for an adult child to show moral obligation or some other special circumstance. In that case, no provision had been made for the deceased's eldest daughter from a relatively modest estate. However, a parcel of land comprised in the estate had realised over six times its probate value and, therefore, there was scope to make provision for her. The court found on the evidence that the deceased was well-disposed towards his daughter and would have made provision for her if his means had allowed, and this was considered to be a matter that could be taken into account under s 3(1)(g). It was held by the House of Lords that, in view of the windfall, the Court of Appeal had been right to uphold the decision of the court at first instance to make provision for the applicant daughter, even though the court had found that it was not unreasonable for no provision to have been made for her.

[1] [1994] 3 All ER 27.
[2] [1979] 3 All ER 815.
[3] At 822A.
[4] Per Nourse LJ at 34G.
[5] Per Henry LJ at 39F.
[6] Per Nourse LJ at 33J.
[7] [1996] 2 FLR 379.
[8] [1997] 2 FLR 644.
[9] [1998] 2 FLR 346.

6.70 In *Garland v Morris*[1], the judge weighed in the balance the factors set out in s 3(1) and concluded that the claimant, one of two daughters of the deceased, had failed to establish that it was unreasonable in all the circumstances for her father to fail to make any provision for her in his will. In that case, following her parents' divorce, the claimant had severed all links with her father and aligned herself with her mother. Her mother committed suicide and left her small estate entirely to the claimant. Her sister remained on good terms with their father and he gave financial assistance to her and her family during his lifetime and left the bulk of his estate to her on his death. The judge found that, although the claimant was in very difficult financial circumstances, her sister was also in genuine need of the benefit that she had received under the will and the claimant had already had the benefit of receiving the mother's estate. It was also relevant that there had been no effort by the claimant to speak to or contact the deceased for the last 15 years of his life, whereas he had enjoyed a close relationship with his other daughter and had helped her out financially. Against this background it was not unreasonable for the father to consider that he had no further obligations towards the claimant.

Ilott v Mitson[2] also concerned an estranged daughter. In that case the deceased had cut her daughter off when at the age of 17 and without her approval she left home to live with her boyfriend, whom she later married. Although there were some attempts at reconciliation, they remained estranged for the remaining 26 years of the deceased's life. Two years before her death, the deceased made a will leaving her estate of a little under £500,000 between three charities. She left a letter of wishes explaining her reasons for making no provision for her daughter.

At the date of the hearing before DJ Million, the circumstances of the daughter were that she remained married to Mr Ilott with whom she had five children. They lived in a council property and were heavily reliant upon means tested benefits. Even though they had limited resources they managed their finances satisfactorily and were not in debt. However, they had a very basic standard of living, being unable to afford holidays or to replace household items when they were at the end of their useful life.

At first instance, DJ Million determined that the deceased's will did not make reasonable financial provision for Mrs Ilott. In awarding the sum of £50,000 for Mrs Ilott's maintenance he took into account the estrangement and the consequent lack of expectation of any inheritance as limiting factors on the award.

Both parties appealed. Mrs Ilott appealed on the basis that £50,000 was not reasonable provision not least because it did not properly take into account her housing need, and failed to consider the impact of receiving a lump sum upon her continued receipt of certain of her state benefits. The charities cross-appealed on the threshold issue, that is that the court should not have found that the will did not make reasonable provision.

Eleanor King J, as she then was, determined the cross-appeal in favour of the charities. They appealed and the Court of Appeal overturned her decision.

Parker J heard the appeal as to quantum and dismissed it. On Mrs Ilott's appeal to the Court of Appeal, the original award was set aside and an award

6.70 *Death and Succession*

was made of £143,000 to enable her to purchase the family home under the Right to Buy scheme, together with a lump sum of £20,000. The rationale was that in order to meet the objective of the legislation and provide for Mrs Ilott's maintenance she had to have sufficient to purchase her house otherwise her right to benefits would be lost. If she were deprived of her benefits there would be no financial provision for maintenance at all.

The charities were given permission to appeal the quantum decision, and the appeal was heard by the Supreme Court on 12 December 2016. The judgment was handed down on 15 March 2017[3]. It was the first time that an appeal under I(PFD)A 1975 or its predecessor legislation had reached the highest appellate court.

The Supreme Court restored the order of DJ Million, concluding that he had not made the errors upon which basis the Court of Appeal had revisited his award.

[1] [2007] 2 FLR 528.
[2] [2011] EWCA Civ 346.
[3] [2017] UKSC 17, reported as *Ilott v Blue Cross & Others*. See also *Nahajec v Fowle* [2017] EW Misc 11 CC.

CIRCUMSTANCES AT THE DATE OF THE HEARING

6.71 When the court is considering the matters to which it is required to have regard under s 3 of the I(PFD)A 1975, it will be the circumstances at the date of the hearing that will be relevant, not those at the date of death or at any other time[1].

In *Re Hancock (Deceased)*[2] a parcel of land comprised in the estate was sold for £663,000 net as against its earlier valuation for probate at £100,000. The appropriate figure for the court to take into account was the later figure.

[1] I(PFD)A 1975, s 3(5).
[2] [1998] 2 FLR 346.

Orders that may be made

6.72 If the court, after consideration of the matters referred to in s 3 of the I(PFD)A 1975, concludes that reasonable financial provision has not been made for the applicant from the deceased's estate, it will then decide what if any provision should be made, again by reference to the factors in s 3.

The applicant will already have made out a need for maintenance from the estate in order to reach this second stage, and the question will therefore be whether any provision is appropriate in the light of the s 3 factors, and if so what form it should take.

The court has power to make any one or more of the following orders in order to make reasonable financial provision for the maintenance of an applicant.

Periodical payments

6.73 A periodical payments order will usually be expressed to have commenced at the date of the deceased's death as the provision made by the order is intended to have effect as a substitution for the actual disposition of the deceased's estate. However, if the applicant has delayed excessively in making or pursuing the application, the court may exercise its discretion to order the payments to begin on the date of the application, or even from the date of the order.

If there has been an interim order, this may affect the timing of the final order.

Unless an earlier date is specified, a periodical payments order will terminate on the death of the applicant, or in the case of a spouse or former spouse, on remarriage.

The duration of the order will be intended to reflect the extent of the deceased's obligations towards the applicant. So, for example, periodical payments to a minor child will generally cease when the child attains his or her majority or ceases full-time education or training.

Lump sum

6.74 An order for a lump sum payment out of the net estate will be the order that is most commonly encountered, even where the applicant is limited to receiving provision for his or her maintenance only. The lump sum may represent capitalised periodical payments calculated on the basis of the approach used in *Duxbury v Duxbury*[1]. Alternatively, a lump sum may be provided to enable the applicant to be rehoused during his or her lifetime, or to pay for such other expenditure that the court deems appropriate for the applicant's maintenance. In *Re Besterman (Deceased)*[2] a capital sum was awarded to provide a 'financial cushion'.

There is no power to vary a lump sum order except as to the terms of a lump sum payable by instalments, and it has been held that the court therefore must take into account the effects of inflation and other variables when considering the appropriate amount of a lump sum order.

[1] [1987] 1 FLR 7.
[2] [1984] 2 All ER 656.

Transfer of property

Settlement of property

6.75 The provision of a home for the lifetime of the applicant will be regarded as a legitimate maintenance requirement. This may be achieved either by the outright transfer of property or as part of a settlement. If there is no property or no property that is suitable already comprised in the net estate, s 2(1)(f) of the I(PFD)A 1975 allows property to be acquired for the purpose out of the net estate.

Variation of settlement

6.76 Children of a marriage or children treated as a child of the family in relation to any marriage or civil partnership (or a surviving spouse or civil partner) may benefit from an order varying a settlement made by the deceased.

The order

6.77 A copy of every order made on an application under s 2 of the I(PFD)A 1975 must be sent to the Principal Registry of the Family Division for filing, and a memorandum of the order should be endorsed on the grant of representation of the estate.

Variation of orders

6.78 An order for periodical payments under s 2(1)(a) of the I(PFD)A 1975 can be varied on application by the applicant who has the benefit of the order, or by the personal representatives of the deceased, any beneficiary of the estate, or any other person who did or could have applied for an order under s 2.

The court has power to vary the order upwards or downwards, temporarily suspend any part of it, discharge the order, or make a lump sum or transfer of property order instead.

In exercising its powers of variation, the court must have regard to all the circumstances of the case, including any change in the factors to which the court had regard under s 3 when making the original order[1].

A lump sum order can be varied only if it was ordered to be paid by instalments, and the variation can only be as to the terms of the instalment payments, whether the amount, or the time for payment[2].

[1] I(PFD)A 1975, s 6(7).
[2] I(PFD)A 1975, s 7.

Transactions and dispositions intended to defeat claims under Inheritance (Provision for Family and Dependants) Act 1975, s 2

6.79 When an application is made for provision under I(PFD)A 1975, s 2, the court has power to set aside transactions or dispositions made less than 6 years before the deceased's death if they were made other than for full valuable consideration and with the intention of defeating an applicant's claim for provision, if to do so would facilitate the making of financial provision for the applicant.

Section 12 provides that when deciding whether or not the deceased intended to defeat the operation of the I(PFD)A 1975, either by making it impossible to make an order or by reducing the amount of any order, the court has to be satisfied on a balance of probabilities that this was the intention, although it need not have been the sole intention.

Section 10(6) provides that when deciding whether and if so how to exercise its powers to set aside transactions and dispositions, the court must have regard to the circumstances in which the disposition was made, any consideration that was given for it, the relationship between the deceased and the donee, the financial resources of the donee and all the circumstances of the case.

A disposition for the purposes of s 10 will not include any *donatio mortis causa*.

PROCEDURE

6.80 An application to set aside a transaction or disposition will be made in the application for an order under s 2, the applicant setting out as much information about the matter as possible.

Interlocutory applications

STRIKING OUT A CLAIM AS DISCLOSING NO REASONABLE CAUSE OF ACTION

6.81 Many of the reported cases concern applications made at the interlocutory stage to strike out a claim as disclosing no reasonable cause of action.

The making of such applications as a purely tactical measure should be avoided because of the cost, but there will be occasions when it is entirely appropriate to make an application, which if successful will almost certainly result in a saving of costs to the estate.

Where an application is made under either s 1(1)(ba) or (e) there may be scope for arguing that the applicant does not satisfy the eligibility criteria.

An application by an adult child under s 1(1)(c) or (d) may be struck out if it is clear that the applicant has no need for provision out of the estate for his or her maintenance.

PROCEDURE

6.82 As soon as possible after the claim has been issued, any respondent wishing to make application to strike out the claim should issue an application notice and file and serve a witness statement or affidavit in support. On issue, the application should be listed for a short appointment before the district judge when directions can be given as to the filing of further evidence and listing for the hearing of the application.

Interim orders

6.83 The court has power to make an order for interim provision from the deceased's net estate for an applicant for an order under s 2 of the I(PFD)A 1975. The criteria to be satisfied are that the applicant is in immediate need of financial assistance and there are funds available from the net estate to meet that need.

Although interim orders have of necessity to be made before the court has decided the merits of the application, the court is required to have regard to the factors set out in s 3, 'so far as the urgency of the case admits' before making an order.

There is scope for a payment or payments of capital and/or income to be made on an interim basis, and these can be expressed to be on account of any sums received when the application under s 2 is finally determined. Any sum or sums awarded on an interim basis must be 'reasonable'.

There is no explicit provision for the court to order repayment of sums paid on account if no substantive order is made at the end of the day, but this could be imposed as one of the conditions or restrictions that the court may include in any interim order.

PROCEDURE

6.84 An applicant who is in immediate need of financial assistance by way of an interim order should make an application as soon as possible after the issue of the application for an order under s 2. The application should be supported by a witness statement or affidavit setting out details of the applicant's financial position so as to illustrate the urgency of the need for financial assistance. Details of the deceased's estate should be provided so far as they are known to the applicant. Insofar as it is not apparent from the claim form, the applicant should deal with the merits of the substantive claim as an interim order is unlikely if there is any prospect that the claim under s 2 may fail.

The application will be listed for a short appointment before the district judge so that directions can be given as to filing of evidence by the respondents, and the matter listed for hearing with an appropriate time estimate.

Respondents wishing to defend an application for an interim order will need to address the merits of the substantive claim and, if appropriate, challenge the financial grounds for the application. The court will expect the respondents to give as much detail as possible of the size and nature of the net estate, and how much of it, if any, would be available to meet any interim order that was made.

Preservation of property

6.85 As the court has power under the I(PFD)A 1975 to make orders relating to specific property comprised in the estate[1], it is possible for orders to be made under the court's inherent jurisdiction to safeguard such property pending the final determination of an application under s 2.

[1] See s 2(1)(c) and (d).

PROCEDURE

6.86 An application for an injunction will be made in the usual way, accompanied by a witness statement or affidavit setting out the background, the grounds for the application and the relief sought. Except in very exceptional cases, the application should be on notice in the first instance. If the matter cannot be resolved on the return date, directions will be given for evidence to be filed by the respondent to the application and a date fixed for the resumed hearing.

Costs

6.87 As is generally the case, the costs of an application will be at the discretion of the court.

Whilst there is no reason why costs should not follow the event, it is not unusual in cases in which the applicant has been unsuccessful for an order to be made for each side to bear its own costs. Indeed, it was the practice for an order for costs against an unsuccessful applicant to be made in only exceptional cases[1].

In *Re Fullard (Deceased)*[2] a former wife unsuccessfully applied for provision from the estate of her deceased former husband. Ormrod LJ enjoined judges to 'reconsider the practice of ordering the costs of both sides to be paid out of the estate'[3], but upheld the decision of the court below to dismiss her claim with her costs to be paid out of the estate.

In *Graham v Murphy and Another*[4] a *Calderbank* offer was made on behalf of the estate that came very close to the order that was made. In order to do justice between the parties, the judge made an order for the estate to pay one-third of the successful applicant's costs on the standard basis, as well as the costs of the estate's administrators, on an indemnity basis.

[1] See **6.33** above.
[2] [1981] 2 All ER 796.
[3] At 799C.
[4] [1997] 1 FLR 860.

Tax implications of orders under the Inheritance (Provision for Family and Dependants) Act 1975

6.88 Orders for provision made by the court have the same effect as if the provision had been made direct to the applicant by will or on intestacy, that is, they are treated as operating from death[1].

As between cohabitants, and parents and children there are no inheritance tax exemptions that will apply to gifts on death.

[1] I(PFD)A) 1975, s 19(1).

Claims by dependants following fatal accidents

FATAL ACCIDENTS ACT 1976

Damages for loss of dependency

6.89 If death has been caused by the tortious act of a third party, such that if the deceased had lived there would have been a right of action against the tortfeasor, the tortfeasor can be liable at the suit of a dependant of the deceased.

6.89 Death and Succession

The category of dependants includes spouses, civil partners and former spouses or civil partners of the deceased, parents and other ascendants, children (whether natural or merely treated as the deceased's children) and children of the family of any marriage, siblings, aunts, uncles and cousins of the deceased.

In addition, any person who was living with the deceased as husband and wife in the same household immediately before, and for at least 2 years before the death[1], may apply. It has been held that brief interruptions in the period of 2 years will not be fatal to a claim[2].

In relation to the question of eligibility there is no requirement to prove dependency as such, but unless the applicant can show a loss as a result of the deceased's death there can be no claim.

When the court is assessing the dependency claim of a cohabitant, it is required by the FAA 1976 to take into account ' . . . (together with any other matter that appears to the court to be relevant to the action) the fact that the dependant [cohabitant] had no enforceable right to financial support by the deceased as a result of their living together'[3]. In other words, the court must be aware that the relationship of dependency could have been brought to an end by either party without obligation, unlike a married relationship.

It will be appropriate for the court to hear evidence about the nature and duration of the relationship in order that it may assess its stability, and apply the appropriate multiplier.

This situation could be affected by the provisions of any cohabitation agreement[4].

The fact that a cohabitant may not be eligible to make a claim for damages under the FAA 1976 may not necessarily mean that his or her dependency is not taken into account. In *K v JMP Co Ltd*[5] a claim was made by the children of the deceased. They had been living with him immediately before his death, together with their mother, the deceased's cohabitant. The court took into account expenses of the cohabitant that had been paid by the deceased when assessing the multiplicand. This increased the value of the claim and indirectly benefitted the cohabitant.

1 *Kotke v Saffarrini* [2005] 2 FLR 517.
2 *Pounder v London Underground* [1995] PIQR 217.
3 FAA 1976, s 3(4).
4 See generally CHAPTER 2.
5 [1975] 1 All ER 1030.

Bereavement damages

6.90 There is an anomaly in the FAA 1976 in relation to the treatment of cohabitants, who are not within the limited class of persons entitled to claim bereavement damages. This is a relatively modest fixed sum, currently £12,980, that may be claimed by a spouse or civil partner of the deceased, or where the deceased was a minor child, by that child's parents.

This situation was highlighted by the decision of Edis J in *Smith v Lancashire Teaching Hospitals NHS Trust and Another*[1]. In that case, Ms Smith had been the long-standing cohabitant of the deceased. She claimed that the provisions of the FAA 1976 that excluded her from bereavement damages were incompatible with her rights under the European Convention, in particular Arts 8 and 14, and she sought a declaration to that effect.

The judge concluded that Art 8 was not engaged, as bereavement damages could not be said to be payments to promote the continuation of family life, and the small sum of money involved was below the threshold of seriousness for the purposes of Art 8. It followed that Art 14 was not engaged.

Although the judge accepted Ms Smith's argument that there appeared to be no legitimate reason for the exclusion of cohabitants from claiming bereavement damages, and that the legislation was in need of reform, he was unable to grant Ms Smith the remedy she sought.

Ms Smith successfully appealed that decision. The Court of Appeal set aside the order of Edis J and made a declaration of incompatibility with Art 14 in conjunction with Art 8 in respect of s 1A of the FAA 1976 in that it excluded cohabitants of 2 years or more[2].

Until the legislation is changed however, the position of cohabitants remains the same as it was before this decision.

[1] [2016] EWHC 2208 (QB).
[2] *Smith v Lancashire Teaching Hospitals NHS Foundation Trust & Others (Rev 2)* [2017] EWCA Civ 1916.

LAW REFORM (MISCELLANEOUS PROVISIONS) ACT 1934

6.91 Damages can be claimed for the benefit of the estate of the deceased in respect of pain and suffering between the date of the tortious act and the death. However, there can be no claim for loss of earnings beyond the date of death[1].

A cohabitant who is entitled to share in the estate on death or following a claim under the I(PFD)A 1975 clearly will benefit if the estate is enlarged by an award of damages.

[1] LR(MP)A 1934, s 1(2)(a)(ii).

CRIMINAL INJURIES COMPENSATION SCHEME

6.92 In fatal cases, dependants or relatives of someone who died as a result of a criminal injury, or someone who was criminally injured but died from some other cause, are eligible to apply for compensation.

Who may apply?

6.93 The categories of applicant include a person who at the time of the deceased's death had been living together as husband or wife or as same-sex partner in the same household as the deceased and for the 2 years immediately

6.93 Death and Succession

leading up to the death. An exception is made if for reasons of infirmity or ill health physical proximity in the same house is not possible.

Time-limit for application

6.94 A claim must be submitted to the Criminal Injuries Compensation Authority within 2 years of the date of death.

Procedure

6.95 Application should be made in Form TS14, which can be obtained by request from the Criminal Injuries Compensation Authority or online[1]. Details of the Criminal Injuries Compensation Scheme (Form TS1) and a Guide to the Criminal Injuries Compensation Scheme set out the procedure for application and assessment.

Where death has occurred as a result of a criminal injury, the Criminal Injuries Compensation Authority will assess eligibility for compensation in the form of a fatal injury award and/or a dependants award and/or an award for loss of parental services.

An application may be made notwithstanding that an award was made to the victim before death.

If death follows but is not the result of a criminal injury, an award of supplementary compensation may be made to an applicant who was financially dependent upon the deceased. This is intended to cover loss of earnings, expenses and liabilities incurred by the victim as a result of the crime of violence.

[1] Tay House, 300 Bath Street, Glasgow G2 4JZ, tel: 0141 331 2726, fax: 0141 331 2287.

Section 3 Illness or incapacity of a cohabitant

Introduction

6.96 When one cohabitant falls ill, or is diagnosed as having a terminal illness, there may be uncertainty as to the status of the other cohabitant when it comes to consent to medical treatment, especially if there are family members who have differing views as to how the patient should be treated and cared for. On admission to hospital, a patient will be asked to give the name of his or her 'next of kin', or contact in the event of an emergency.

A little thought and forward planning can help to minimise any tension between relatives and cohabitants when these situations arise.

The questions of consent to medical treatment and who should be allowed to have information and be consulted about the patient are matters for the patient himself. However, necessity may justify medical intervention without consent. If a patient is unable to give consent, then in the absence of an advance decision, it will be a matter for the clinical judgment of the medical team, subject to the jurisdiction of the High Court to make a declaration that the proposed treatment is in the best interests of the patient[1].

As a matter of law, therefore, a cohabitant is in no different position than a civil partner, spouse or relative, when it comes to consultation and decision-making about a patient. However, from a practical point of view, the hospital staff will generally limit the people involved to close family, unless they are aware of any request from the patient to consult, for example, a cohabitant.

[1] Re F (Sterilisation: Mental Patient) [1989] 2 FLR 376.

Advance decisions or 'living wills'

6.97 Advance decisions to refuse medical treatment were given legal effect for the first time by the MCA 2005[1]. An advance decision, also referred to as a living will, is a means by which a person of full capacity may specify that if in the future he should lack the capacity to make a decision about medical treatment, the advance decision is to be acted upon by the relevant health care professionals. Such documents often include wishes regarding the refusal of life-sustaining treatment in situations where the person is in a coma or has very little quality of life. Advance decisions are likely to be considered if a person is diagnosed as suffering from a terminal illness, or is to undergo a course of medical treatment.

Those in cohabitation relationships, in particular, may wish to make provision in this way, especially if there is scope for differences of opinion between the relatives of the patient and the other cohabitant.

[1] MCA 2005, ss 24–26.

THE CONTENT OF AN ADVANCE DECISION

6.98 An advance decision may only relate to the refusal of specified treatment. It cannot require particular treatment or care to be given.

Except where the advance decision relates to life-sustaining treatment, there is no prescribed form of words, and it may even be an oral statement.

In the case of an advance decision that relates to life-sustaining treatment the following formalities must be observed. It must:

– be in writing;
– be signed by the person making it, or by another person in his presence and at his direction;
– be witnessed;
– set out that it is to apply to the specified treatment even if life is at risk.

Euthanasia is outside the scope of advance decisions.

THE LEGAL STATUS OF AN ADVANCE DECISION

6.99 To be effective, an advance decision must be both valid, and applicable.

6.99 Death and Succession

If both valid and applicable, an advance decision has the same effect as if the maker of it had capacity to make that decision at the time the question of refusing medical treatment arises.

If there is any doubt about the existence, validity or applicability of an advance decision application may be made to the Court of Protection for a declaration.

VALIDITY OF AN ADVANCE DECISION

6.100 An advance decision will not be valid in the following circumstances:

- the person who made the advance decision has withdrawn it at a time when he had the capacity to do so;
- the advance decision has been overtaken by a lasting power of attorney that gives the donee the power to give or refuse consent to the specified treatment;
- the person who made the advance decision has acted in way that is clearly inconsistent with the advance decision remaining his fixed position.

APPLICABILITY OF AN ADVANCE DECISION

6.101 For an advance decision to be applicable the following must apply:

- the person who made the advance decision must lack capacity at the time it is sought to act upon it;
- the treatment specified in the advance decision must be that which it is proposed to carry out;
- any circumstances specified in the advance decision must be present.

In addition, if there are reasonable grounds for believing that circumstances exist that were not anticipated at the time the advance decision was made and that would have affected the decision had they been anticipated, the advance decision will not be applicable.

Lasting Powers of Attorney (LPAs)

6.102 There are two types of LPA. One is for Health and Welfare and the other is for Property and Financial Affairs.

Cohabitees can grant each other LPAs for Health and Welfare as an alternative to an advance decision as the document enables the attorney to make decisions relating to the health and welfare of the donor. This type of LPA can specifically give power to the attorney to give or refuse consent to life-sustaining treatment. The documents can cover any decision about healthcare and medical treatment as well as day to day decisions about personal welfare.

The LPA for Property and Financial Affairs replaced Enduring Powers of Attorney from 1 October 2007 and it gives an attorney power to make decisions about the donor's money and property including managing bank accounts and selling property.

Both types of LPA have to be registered with the Office of the Public Guardian before they can be used. For more information on LPAs and procedures see *Elderly Clients – A Precedent Manual* (Jordan Publishing 2013).

Part B   PROCEDURAL GUIDE

Claim for Financial Provision under the Inheritance (Provision for Family and Dependants) Act 1975

Legal background

6.103 A claim may be made against the estate of a deceased person by certain members of the deceased's family and dependants categorised in the I(PFD)A 1975, s 1 (as amended by the Law Reform (Succession) Act 1995) and CPA 2004 for financial provision out of the net estate of the deceased, on the ground that the disposition of the deceased's estate effected by his will and/or under the laws of intestacy is not such as to make reasonable financial provision for the applicant. Unless the court gives permission extending the time limit, the application must be made within 6 months of the date on which representation is first granted (s 4) although nothing prevents the application being made before the grant is taken out.

The procedure for both the High Court and County Court is governed by CPR Pt 57. See also CPR PD 57 and CPR PD 8A. Before issuing proceedings practitioners must comply with the CPR Protocol. Non-compliance could result in the court making an order for costs against the non-complying party (CPR 44.3).

Procedure

6.104

Who may apply	The spouse of the deceased	I(PFD)A 1975, s 1(a)
	The registered civil partner of the deceased	I(PFD)A 1975, s 1(a); CPA 2004, s 71, Sch 4
	The former spouse of the deceased who has not remarried	I(PFD)A 1975, s 1(b)
	The former civil partner of the deceased who has not formed a subsequent civil partnership	I(PFD)A 1975, s 1(b); CPA 2004, s 71, Sch 4
	A cohabitant of the deceased	I(PFD)A 1975, s 1(ba), s 1A as amended by the Law Reform (Succession) Act 1995

6.104 *Death and Succession*

	A person who lived in the same household as the deceased as his/her civil partner	I(PFD)A 1975, s 1(ba), s 1B; CPA 2004, s 71, Sch 4
	A child of the deceased	I(PFD)A 1975, s 1(c)
	Any person who was treated as a child of the family by the deceased	I(PFD)A 1975, s 1(d)
	Any other person who immediately before the death of the deceased was being maintained by him	I(PFD)A 1975, s 1(e); CPA 2004
Which court	High Court (Chancery or Family Division) or county court	CPR 57.15; CCA 1984, s 25
	District judges (including district judges of the Principal Registry of the Family Division) have jurisdiction to hear such applications	CPR 57.15; I(PFD)A 1975, s 22
Application	*High Court/county court* By Pt 8 claim form which should be entitled 'In the estate of . . . deceased' and 'In the matter of I(PFD)A 1975'	CPR 57.16, 8.2
Time limit	The claim must be issued either before or within 6 months of the date on which representation is taken out (unless extended by the court). Application to extend the time limit must be included in the claim form	I(PFD)A 1975, s 4
Documents	The applicant must file with the claim form a witness statement/affidavit in support exhibiting an official copy of the grant of representation and of every testamentary document admitted to proof	CPR 57.16(3), 8.5(1), (2)
Defendants	Personal representativesBeneficiariesOther persons affected by the claimAny other person directed by the court to be added	CPR r 19.7
Service	The claim form must be served within 4 months after date of issue	
	Extension of time must be sought under CPR 7.6	

Procedural Guide **6.104**

	Acknowledgement of service must be filed within 21 days after service of the claim form and served on the claimant and other parties if served within the jurisdictionIf served outside the jurisdiction extended period is permitted by CPR 57.16(4A)	CPR 57.16(4), 6.19, 6.22, 8.3(1), 10.3(1)
	For service on children and patients see CPR 6.6	
	otherwise, in accordance with CPR 10.3(2)	CPR 10.3(2)
Statement/Affidavit in answer	Must be filed by the personal representatives within 21 days after service of the claim form (it should include the matters set out in CPR PD 57, para 16)	CPR 57.16(4),(5); PD 57, para 16
	May be filed by other defendants within 21 days after service of the claim form	CPR 57.16(4)
Service of answer	Every defendant who files any written evidence within 21 days in answer must serve a copy on the claimant and every other defendant who is not represented by the same solicitor	CPR 57.16(4)
Reply	A claimant may serve a statement in reply on all other parties within 14 days of service of the defendant's evidence on him	CPR 8.5(5), (6)
Directions/case management conference pre-trial hearing	At the same time as issuing the claim form a directions hearing may be requested	CPR PD 8A, para 4.1
	The court will in any event give directions after the defendant has filed the acknowledgement of service or after the time for filing it has expired. Parties must complete the listing questionnaire in Form N170 and provide an estimate of costs, following which the court will consider whether to hold a pre-trial review, set a timetable and fix the date for the trial	CPR PD 8A, para 4.2 CPR 29.6-29.8

Fee	High Court: £480	CPFO 2008, fee 1.5
	County court: £280	CPFO 2008, fee 1.5
Order	Periodical payments	I(PFD)A 1975, s 2(1)(a)
	Lump sum	I(PFD)A 1975, s 2(1)(b)
	Transfer of property	I(PFD)A 1975, s 2(1)(c)
	Settlement of property	I(PFD)A 1975, s 2(1)(d)
	Acquisition, transfer and settlement of property	I(PFD)A 1975, s 2(1)(e)
	Variation of ante-nuptial and post-nuptial settlement	I(PFD)A 1975, s 2(1)(f)
	Variation of trusts of the estate	
	Variation or discharge of secured periodical payments	I(PFD)A 1975, s 16
	Variation or revocation of maintenance agreements	I(PFD)A 1975, s 17
	Order setting aside disposition intended to defeat a claim under the Act	I(PFD)A 1975, ss 10, 11
	Treatment of deceased's former beneficial interest in joint property as part of his estate and not passing by survivorship	I(PFD)A 1975, s 9
	Interim order	I(PFD)A 1975, s 5
	Consequential orders	I(PFD)A 1975, s 2(4)

Part C CHECKLISTS

Checklist for first instructions on making a claim under the Inheritance (Provision for Family and Dependants) Act 1975

6.105 The following should be considered when taking first instructions in respect of a claim under the I(PFD)A 1975:

- Deceased habitually resident in England and Wales?
- Full name of deceased.
- Address at date of death.
- Date and place of death.
- In the event of an application by a cohabitant under s 1(1)(ba), was the date of death after January 1996?
- Is there a valid will?
- If so, who are the executors and beneficiaries?

- What provision, if any, has been made for the surviving cohabitant?
- If no provision has been made, did the deceased make any promises to make provision after his death?
- If there is no valid will, who will benefit under the statutory trusts?
- Has a Grant of Representation been taken out, and if so, by whom?
- Date of the issue of the Grant.
- If more than 6 months has elapsed since the date of the Grant, why were steps not taken to issue an application before the expiry of the 6 months?
- Date cohabitation with deceased commenced.
- Was the period of cohabitation unbroken – if not, dates and reasons for break in cohabitation.
- Was cohabitation continuing right up to the date of death (subject to deceased ending life in hospital/hospice)?
- Does the cohabitation exceed 2 years?
- Does surviving cohabitant remain living in the shared home?
- Details of acquisition and ownership of the shared home.
- Details of assets and liabilities of deceased, ie the likely value of the estate.
- Details of any joint assets/liabilities.
- Details of any nominations in respect of insurance policies/pensions.
- Details of deceased's pension arrangements.
- Details of financial circumstances of surviving cohabitant.
- If cohabitation less than 2 years immediately preceding the date of death, can dependency be established? In particular, did the deceased provide a home and/or financial support, and what did the surviving cohabitant give in return? Full details required.
- What other financial obligations and responsibilities did the deceased have?
- Are there likely to be conflicting claims?

Part D PRECEDENTS

Section 1 Non-contentious precedents

Clauses

6.106

Combined commencement and revocation clause[1]

I (*name*)[2] of (*address*) DECLARE that this is my Will[3] and that it revokes[4] my earlier Wills.

[1] For separate commencement and revocation clauses, see **6.107** below.
[2] The testator's full and correct forenames and surname should be stated. If any assets are registered in another name, it may be sensible to add after the full and correct name '(also known as   )'. This would facilitate the inclusion of the other name in the grant of representation. See, generally, Non-Contentious Probate Rules 1987 (SI 1987/2024), r 9.
[3] The words 'last will', which are often used, are probably of no significance.
[4] It is usual practice to revoke all earlier wills, even when it is clear that there are none to revoke.

6.107

Commencement including date: separate revocation clause[1]

THIS WILL is made on (date)[2] by me (name)[3] of (address).

I REVOKE my earlier Wills[4].

[1] For a combined commencement and revocation clause, see 6.106 above.
[2] If the date is not included in the commencement it is usually stated in the testimonium at the end of the will.
[3] See footnote 2 at **6.106** above.
[4] See footnote 4 at **6.106** above.

6.108

Will in expectation of marriage[1]

THIS WILL will not be revoked by my expected marriage to (cohabitant).

[1] Except in certain cases, a will is revoked by the testator's marriage or civil partnership (Wills Act 1837, s 18(1), as amended). Section 18(3) states that 'where it appears from a will that at the time it was made the testator was expecting to be married to a particular person and that he intended that the will should not be revoked by the marriage, the will shall not be revoked by his marriage to that person'. Until s 18 was substituted by the Administration of Justice Act 1982, such wills were known as 'wills in contemplation of marriage', by virtue of the wording of LPA 1925, s 177.

6.109

Will in expectation of marriage: some provisions applying before marriage and others on marriage[1]

(1) THIS WILL will not be revoked by my expected marriage to (cohabitant).

(2) PART I[2] of this Will applies at all times.

(3) PART II will apply until my expected marriage is solemnised.

(4) PART III will apply when my expected marriage has been solemnised.

PART I

(Insert the provisions which will apply regardless of whether or not the marriage has been solemnised, for example funeral wishes, specific bequests, trustee powers, etc.)

PART II

(Insert provisions which apply immediately.)

PART III

(Insert the provisions which will apply on the solemnisation of the expected marriage.)

[1] For wills made in expectation of marriage, see footnote 1 to **6.108** above.
[2] Division into 'parts' may be considered preferable to division into 'schedules' as it enables each clause of the will to continue in numerical order (cf MCA 1973, etc).

6.110

Declaration of mutuality[1]

I HAVE AGREED with (cohabitant) that if I survive (him)/(her) I will not revoke or change this Will.

[1] **Warning.** A 'mutual will' is made when testators contractually agree that neither of them will revoke or alter his will. If, after the first death, the survivor revokes the mutual will, equity will enforce the original agreement by imposing a constructive trust on the survivor's death. The disadvantages of a mutual will are: (a) the will is revoked on marriage; (b) it is very difficult to identify the assets which are subject to the constructive trust; and (c) the agreement can be frustrated by lifetime alienation or dissipation of the assets. The advantages of a mutual will are that the survivor's ability to renege on the agreement is curtailed, and the survivor is free to enjoy the assets without being subject to a trust. Mutual wills can cause many practical difficulties and should be used with caution. A mutual will, made by an unmarried person, may be contrary to public policy because it acts in restraint of marriage (*Robinson v Ommanney* (1883) 23 Ch D 285, CA).

See, generally, *Williams on Wills* (Lexis Nexis Butterworths, 10th edn, 2014); A J Oakley *Constructive Trusts* (Sweet & Maxwell, 3rd edn, 1996); Law Reform Committee's 22nd Report (1980), 'The making and revocation of wills', at paras 3.50–3.52; and the articles by Professor C E F Rickett 'Mutual Wills and the Law of Restitution' (1989) 105 LQR 534, and 'Extending Equity's Reach through the Mutual Wills Doctrine' (1991) MLR 581. See also *Cleaver (Deceased)* [1981] 1 WLR 939; *Re Goodchild* [1997] 1 WLR 1216.

6.111

Declaration of non-mutuality[1]

ALTHOUGH (*cohabitant*) and I are making Wills in similar terms they are not 'Mutual Wills' and each of us can alter or revoke his or her Will at any time.

[1] See footnotes to **6.110** above. It is important to distinguish between 'mutual wills' in the lay sense and 'mutual wills' in the legal sense.

6.112

Survivorship clause[1]: General applicability

ANYONE who does not survive me by (14) days[2] will be treated as having died before me for all the purposes of this Will.

[1] The object of a survivorship clause is to stop the assets of both partners passing to the parents or relatives of the second to die in cases of not quite simultaneous death, usually in accidents. See also the statutory presumption that where uncertainty exists as to the order in which two or more persons have died, 'the younger shall be deemed to have survived the elder' (LPA 1925, s 184). There may also be inheritance tax advantages in including a survivorship clause in a will (Inheritance Tax Act 1984, s 92).

[2] Law Com No 187, para 57 in relation to Inheritance on an intestacy states: 'We consider that an appropriate length for such a survivorship clause is 14 days. Any longer might lead to unacceptable delays in the administration of estates'.

6.113

Survivorship clause: Specific to cohabitant[1]

IF (*cohabitant*) does not survive me by (14) days (he)/(she) will be treated as having died before me for all the purposes of this Will.

[1] See footnotes at **6.112** above.

6.114

Funeral wishes[1]

If possible and practicable I would like:

- any part of my body which may be of use to others to be made available for treatment or transplantation[2];
- my (kidneys)/(corneas)/(heart)/(lungs)/(liver)/(pancreas) to be used for transplantation[3];

- (*name of firm*) to be my funeral directors;
- an obituary notice to be inserted in (*name of newspaper, journal, etc*);
- my funeral service to be conducted in accordance with the (*rites*)/(*usages*) of (*name of faith or denomination*);
- my funeral service to be held at (*location*);
- there to be no religious formalities at my funeral;
- (*hymns, songs, tunes, music, etc*) to be played or sung at my funeral;
- (*scriptural, poetry or other readings*) to be read at my funeral;
- family flowers only;
- donations, if desired, to be made to (*Charity*);
- to be cremated;
- my ashes to be scattered (in the grounds of the Crematorium [OR] (*wherever*);
- my ashes to be interred in (*location*);
- to be buried;
- to be buried in (*location*) [OR] (wherever is most convenient)/(at sea)4;
- a headstone to be placed on my grave;
- (*cohabitant*) to decide what wording should be inscribed on the headstone;
- refreshments to be provided for those attending my funeral;
- my funeral arrangements to be as simple (and inexpensive) as possible;
- (*cohabitant*) to decide on any other funeral arrangements;
- the expenses incurred in carrying out these wishes (and *cohabitant's* wishes) to be paid out of my estate.

[1] A binding disposition of the body of the deceased cannot be made by will so as to oust the executors' rights and duties as to its disposal. Many precedent books suggest that it is unnecessary or even undesirable to incorporate funeral wishes in a will. The main arguments for excluding such wishes include:
    (a) the will might not be found until it is too late;
    (b) the wishes are generally not binding; and
    (c) it adds to the cost of preparing the will, or having to prepare another will or codicil if the testator changes his mind about any of these wishes.
Reasons for *including* funeral wishes in a will include:
    (a) they require the testator to make his wishes known;
    (b) others are relieved of the duty of making such decisions;
    (c) there is less likelihood of conflict between executors, relatives, beneficiaries, etc;
    (d) such wishes are usually honoured and rarely changed; and
    (e) expenditure can be formally authorised.
[2] This sub-clause is based on the wording of the standard 'Donor Card'.
[3] This sub-clause is based on the wording of the standard 'Donor Card'.
[4] Those with an appetite for black comedy might enjoy the Scottish case *Herron v Diack and Newlands* 1973 SLT (Sh Ct) 27 which involved an unsuccessful burial at sea.

6.115

Appointment of cohabitant as executor[1]

I APPOINT (*cohabitant*) of (*address*) to be the Executor of this Will but if (he)/(she) dies before me or is unwilling or unable to act as Executor I APPOINT (*name*) of (*address*) (and (*name*) of (*address*)) to be the Executor(s) (and Trustees)[2] of this Will instead.

[1] If the cohabitant is also the universal beneficiary use **6.116** instead.
[2] It is only necessary to appoint trustees where there is or could be an ongoing trust.

6.116

Appointment of cohabitant as sole executor and universal beneficiary[1]

IF (he)/(she) survives me by (14) days[2] I GIVE all of my estate[3] to (*cohabitant*) of (*address*) AND APPOINT (him)/(her) to be my Executor[4] but if (he)/(she) fails to survive me by (14) days the following clauses will apply[5].

[1] The sole executor and universal beneficiary must be an adult.
[2] A survivorship clause is not essential but advisable.
[3] For the meaning of 'estate' see, generally, *Williams on Wills* (Lexis Nexis Butterworths, 8th edn 2008).
[4] As the sole executor and universal beneficiary has all the powers needed to administer the estate, no further powers or provisions are necessary. There is no continuing trust, so there is no need to appoint the executor as a trustee.
[5] It is virtually essential to include substitutionary gifts, appointments and provisions.

6.117

Appointment of executors and trustees including a professional charging clause[1]

1   I APPOINT (*name*) of (*address*) and (*name*) of (*address*)[2] to be the Executors and Trustees of this Will.

2   In this Will 'my trustees' means my personal representatives and the persons who at any time are the trustees of any trusts created by this Will.

3   A professionally qualified trustee can charge and be paid in priority to the gifts in this Will for all the work done by him or his firm in obtaining probate, administering my estate, and acting as a trustee, even though some of the work could have been done by a person who is not professionally qualified[3].

[1] It seems logical to include a professional charging clause (where appropriate) in the appointment itself. This generally happens where trust corporations are appointed. Despite the Trustee Act 2000, it is still desirable to include such a clause.
[2] The maximum number that can be appointed is four (Trustee Act 1925, s 34; Supreme Court Act 1981, s 114(1)).
[3] Trustee Act 2000, s 28 now allows a trustee who is a trust corporation or is acting in a professional capacity to receive payment in respect of services, even if they are services which are capable of being provided by a lay trustee. This applies except where excluded by the trust instrument. Section 28(4) provides that any payment is to be treated as remuneration for services for the purposes of s 15 of the Wills Act 1837, so a professional trustee who witnesses the will no longer forfeits the right to payment for services, which was previously treated as a general legacy.

6.118

Appointment of guardians[1]

I APPOINT (*name*) of (*address*) (and (*name*) of (*address*))[2] to be the guardian(s) of my children under eighteen[3].

[1] A guardian can only be appointed in accordance with the provisions of s 5 of the CA 1989 (s 5(13)). See, generally, 'Appointment of a Guardian' at **5.25** above.
[2] More than one person may have parental responsibility for the same child at the same time (CA 1989, s 2(5)).
[3] Unless it is brought to an end earlier, the appointment of a guardian continues until the child reaches the age of 18 (CA 1989, s 91(8)).

6.119

Appointment of guardian and substitute guardian[1]

I APPOINT (*name*) of (*address*) to be the guardian of my children under eighteen but if this appointment fails for any reason[2] I APPOINT (*name*) of (*address*) to be the guardian instead.

[1] A guardian can only be appointed in accordance with the provisions of CA 1989, s 5(13). See, generally, 'Appointment of a Guardian' at **5.25** above.
[2] For example, the guardian could predecease the testator; the guardian could die before the child reaches 18; the guardian could disclaim; or the appointment could be brought to an end by order of the court. See, generally, CA 1989, s 6(5), (6) and (7).

6.120

Guardianship: Statement of wishes concerning children under 18[1]

IT IS MY WISH that, as far as circumstances and finances permit, my children will be:

– kept together;
– allowed to retain their present surname(s)[2];
– encouraged to keep in contact with their (grandparents, uncles, aunts, cousins, godparents, etc as the case may be)[3];
– brought up in the (Christian) faith[4];
– educated at (a single sex)/(an independent) school;
– (other wishes, as appropriate).

[1] The wishes of the parent are only permitted to prevail if they are not inconsistent with other considerations relating to the child's welfare (*Ward v Laverty* [1925] AC 101). See also CA 1989, s 1.
[2] See, generally, Nasreen Pearce *Change of Name – The Law & Practice*, Caliph Publishing.
[3] For 'contact orders', see CA 1989, s 8(1).
[4] 'In accordance with the *Gillick* principle, the parent's wishes over religious upbringing yield to the child's right to make his own decision once he has reached sufficient intellect and understanding to be capable of doing so' (H K Bevan *Child Law* (Butterworths, 1989), at para 11.06).

6.121

Guardianship: Trustees' power to lend capital to guardians[1]

MY TRUSTEES can at any time raise capital from my residuary estate and lend it to the guardian(s) of any child of mine:

– on such terms and conditions (including repayment, interest, and security) as they consider appropriate in the circumstances;
– even if they exhaust my residuary estate in the process;
– even if one of the guardians is also a trustee of this Will;
– without being liable for any loss incurred;
– but only if they consider that doing so would be better for the child than not doing so.

[1] If the children are the beneficiaries under the will, the cost of looking after them will generally be met (so far as funds are available) by the trustees under their statutory powers of advancement. There may be circumstances in which it would be helpful for the trustees to

have power to lend capital to the guardians, for example the guardians may need to acquire a larger house in order to accommodate the children. For potential inheritance tax difficulties with such a power, see *Butterworth's Wills, Probate and Administration Service* (Butterworths) at paras A[1027]–[1030].

6.122

Absolute gift of (a share of) a house

(1) I GIVE to (*cohabitant*) my (share of the) property known as (*address*) or failing which the property that is my principal residence at the time of my death ('the property')[1].

(2) IF when I die:

    (a) there is any doubt as to which of two or more properties is my principal residence the decision of my Trustees will be final[2];

    (b) the property is subject to a binding but uncompleted contract of sale then this gift will take effect as a gift of (my share of) its net proceeds of sale[3];

    (c) the property has been sold then I GIVE to (*cohabitant*) the sum of pounds (£   ) (free of tax) instead.

(3) THIS GIFT is subject to any legal or equitable charge affecting the property immediately before my death AND I GIVE to (*cohabitant*) (free of tax) the full benefit of and all sums payable under any policies of insurance on my life which have been given as security for the repayment of such charges[4].

[OR]

(3) ANY legal or equitable charge affecting the property immediately before my death will (if not automatically discharged by any policies of insurance on my life given as security for this purpose) be paid and discharged from my residuary estate in exoneration of the property[5].

(4) THIS GIFT will bear its own share of any tax which is payable on or by reason of my death[6].

[OR]

(4) ANY tax attributable to the property which is payable on or by reason of my death will be paid and discharged from my residuary estate in exoneration of the property[7].

(5) ALL expenses incurred in transferring the property to (*cohabitant*) and registering (his)/(her) title at the Land Registry will be paid by (*cohabitant*)8.

[OR]

(5) ALL expenses incurred in transferring the property to (*cohabitant*) and registering (his)/(her) title at the Land Registry will be paid from my residuary estate[9].

[1] A specific devise or specific legacy will fail by ademption if its subject-matter has ceased to form part of the testator's estate at the time of his death. If the testator sells the property, the disappointed devisee is not entitled to the traceable net proceeds of sale (*Re Bagot's Settlement* (1862) 31 LJ Ch 772 at 774).

[2] If there is any doubt about which of two or more residences is 'the principal residence', it may be considered preferable that the surviving partner should choose, rather than the trustees. For example: 'If (*address*) has been sold in my lifetime and if there is any doubt as to which of two or more properties is my principal residence at the time of my death this gift will apply only to the one property that (*cohabitee*) selects within (6 weeks) of my death'. Compare the prior

6.122 Death and Succession

rights of a surviving spouse on an intestacy in the dwelling house in Scottish Law (Succession (Scotland) Act 1964, s 8(1)).
3   A binding contract for sale will effect an ademption (*Farrar v Earl of Winterton* (1842) 5 Beav 1).
4   In the absence of any provision to the contrary the specific devisee would be primarily liable for any money charged on the property (AEA 1925, s 35).
5   In the absence of any provision to the contrary the specific devisee would be primarily liable for any money charged on the property (AEA 1925, s 35).
6   See, generally, *Butterworth's Wills, Probate and Administration Service* (Butterworths), Vol 1, at paras 1031–1035, 'Tax Free or Not Tax Free'.
7   See, generally, *Butterworth's Wills, Probate and Administration Service* (Butterworths), Vol 1, at paras 1031–1035, 'Tax Free or Not Tax Free'.
8   In the absence of a direction to the contrary, the expense incurred in vesting a specific devise in the devisee is borne by the devisee personally (*Re Grosvenor* [1916] 2 Ch 375).
9   In the absence of a direction to the contrary, the expense incurred in vesting a specific devise in the devisee is borne by the devisee personally (*Re Grosvenor* [1916] 2 Ch 375).

6.123

Life or lesser interest in (a share of) a dwelling and its net proceeds of sale[1]

(1)   I GIVE my (share of the) property known as (*address*) or failing which the property that is my principal residence at the time of my death[2] to my Trustees on a trust of land[3].

(2)   MY TRUSTEES can invest the net proceeds of sale of that property as freely as if it were their own money and can purchase and improve any replacement property or a share in any replacement property for (*cohabitant*) to live in[4].

(3)   ANY property which is subject to these trusts is referred to as 'the property', and the property and any cash or investments representing it are referred to as 'the property fund'.

(4)   MY TRUSTEES will allow (*cohabitant*) live in the property on the terms mentioned below and will pay any income from the property fund to (him)/(her) during (his)/(her) lifetime until (he)/(she) cohabits[5] ('the termination of these trusts').

(5)   UNTIL the termination of these trusts (*cohabitant*) can live in the property rent free on the terms that (he)/(she):

   (a)   pays the outgoings;

   (b)   keeps it in reasonable repair and condition;

   (c)   keeps it insured to its full reinstatement value;

   (d)   complies with the covenants and conditions to which it is subject.

(6)   MY TRUSTEES will not:

   (a)   exercise their trust for sale without reasonable cause before the termination of these trusts;

   (b)   be personally liable for the failure of (*cohabitant*) to comply with any of the obligations imposed on (him)/(her);

   (c)   be personally liable for paying any income from the property fund to (*cohabitant*) after the termination of these trusts unless they have knowledge of the event causing the termination.

(7)   SUBJECT to these provisions my Trustees will hold the property fund (as part of my residuary estate)/(on trust for   )/(for   ).

[1] Contrast this clause with a clause giving the surviving partner a life or lesser interest in the whole of the estate (**6.140** below) and a clause conferring mere occupation rights that do not extend to an interest in the proceeds of sale (**6.124** below).
[2] This wording is designed to avoid the problem of abatement.
[3] Trustees of land have power under the Trusts of Land and Appointment of Trustees Act 1996 to delegate any of their functions as trustees to any beneficiary entitled to an interest in possession. Such delegation can be used to give a life tenant powers equivalent to those of a life tenant under the Settled Land Act 1925. Since that Act, it has no longer been possible to create a strict settlement.
[4] For the powers of trustees to purchase and improve land for occupation by a beneficiary, see the footnotes to **6.145** below.
[5] For difficulties which arise when a life interest is terminable on cohabitation, see **6.4**.

6.124

Occupation rights restricted to a particular property: variation lifting that restriction

(1) I GIVE my (share of the) property known as (*address*) or failing which the property that is my principal residence at the time of my death ('the property') to my Trustees on a trust of land.

(2) MY TRUSTEES will allow (*cohabitant*) live in the property for as long as (he)/(she) wishes on the terms that (he)/(she):

(a) pays the outgoings;

(b) keeps it in reasonable repair and condition;

(c) keeps it insured to its full reinstatement value;

(d) complies with the covenants and conditions to which it is subject.

(IF (*cohabitant*) wishes to live elsewhere my Trustees can sell the property and apply the proceeds in or towards the purchase of another property or a share in another property which will be held on exactly the same trusts as the property itself (but if the purchase price of the other property or a share in it is less than the net proceeds of sale of the property itself the surplus cash will immediately (form part of my residuary estate)/(be paid by my Trustees to   ))).

(3) MY TRUSTEES will not:

(a) require (*cohabitant*) to pay an occupation rent;

(b) require (*cohabitant*) to share the property with anyone else;

(c) be personally liable for the failure of (*cohabitant*) to comply with any of the obligations imposed on (him)/(her);

(d) exercise their power of sale without reasonable cause unless or until (*cohabitant*) ceases to occupy the property on a permanent basis[1] or fails to comply with any of the obligations imposed on (him)/(her).

(4) SUBJECT to these provisions my Trustees will hold (my share of) the property and its net proceeds of sale (as part of my residuary estate)/(on trust for   )/(for   ).

[1] For consideration of the meaning of expressions such as 'permanently ceases to reside', see *Re Coxen* [1948] 2 All ER 492 at 500.

6.125

Option to purchase (a share of) a dwelling[1]

(1) I GIVE to:

    (a) my Trustees my (share of the) property known as (*address*) or failing which the property that is my principal residence at the time of my death ('the property') on a trust of land.

    (b) (*cohabitant*) the option to purchase the property from my Trustees at the price and on the terms and conditions stated below.

(2) THE PROPERTY will be valued on the basis that:

    (a) it is being sold at arm's length on the open market with vacant possession;

    (b) all the fixtures and fittings and carpets and curtains are included in the sale;

    (c) there is no discount for joint ownership[2].

(3) THE PRICE will be (75% of) the value of (my share of) the property.

(4) FROM the date of my death, within a period of:

    (a) (4) weeks the property will be valued by a professionally qualified valuer appointed by my Trustees;

    (b) (6) weeks my Trustees will give written notice of this option to (*cohabitant*);

    (c) (8) weeks (*cohabitant*) will give written notice to my Trustees exercising this option;

    (d) (12) weeks (*cohabitant*) will complete the purchase of the property.

(5) MY TRUSTEES can:

    (a) compromise on the price if (*cohabitant*) obtains a valuation of the property which differs from that obtained by them;

    (b) let (*cohabitant*) live in the property rent free until it is sold provided that (he)/(she) pays all the outgoings and keeps it insured to its full reinstatement value;

    (c) enforce their trust for sale after the end of the period of (12) weeks from the date of my death;

    (d) extend any of the time-limits set out in this clause if they consider that such an extension is reasonable in the circumstances.

(6) MY ESTATE will pay:

    (a) the cost of obtaining the valuation;

    (b) the costs of transferring the property to (*cohabitant*); including Stamp Duty Land Tax, Land Registry fees and legal fees;

    (c) any inheritance tax payable because the price is less than the open market value.

(7) THIS OPTION:

    (a) is personal to (*cohabitant*) and cannot be exercised by anyone else;

- (b) can be exercised by (*cohabitant*) even though (he)/(she) is one of my Trustees;
- (c) will lapse if it has not been exercised by (*cohabitant*) within (8) weeks from the date of my death or within such later period as my Trustees consider to be reasonable in the circumstances.

(8) SUBJECT to these provisions my Trustees will hold (my share of) the net proceeds of sale of the property (as part of my residuary estate)/(on trust for   )/(for   ).

[1] An option to purchase can be very useful. It allows the surviving partner to buy the whole property and, where the testator permits his partner to purchase at an undervalue, there is an added incentive to buy. It frees the property from an ongoing trust of land, and it releases cash for distribution to other beneficiaries. Note the Law of Property (Miscellaneous Provisions) Act 1989, s 2.

[2] See *Wight and Another v IRC* (1982) 264 EG 935, Lands Tribunal, which related to the valuation of a property held as tenants in common. It was held that for capital transfer tax purposes the discount for joint ownership should be 15%, rather than the 10% which had become customary following the earlier decision in *Cust v CIR* (1917) 91 EG 11. See also *Arkwright v IRC* [2004] STC 1323.

6.126

Bequest of personal chattels

I GIVE free of tax to (*cohabitant*) all my personal chattels (as defined in the Administration of Estates Act 1925)[1] that have not been specifically bequeathed to others.

[1] Until 1 October 2014 'Personal chattels' were defined under s 55(1)(x) Administration of Estates Act 1925 as carriages, horses, stable furniture and effects (not used for business purposes), motor cars and accessories (not used for business purposes), garden effects, domestic animals, plate, plated articles, linen, china, glass, books, pictures, prints, furniture, jewellery, articles of household or personal use or ornament, musical and scientific instruments and apparatus, wines, liquors and consumable stores, but do not include any chattels used at the death of the intestate for business purposes nor money or securities for money'). For wills executed after 1 October 2014 or on an intestacy after that date, 'Personal chattels' are defined under s 3 ITPA 2014 as tangible movable property, other than any such property which consists of money or securities for money, or was used at the death of the intestate solely or mainly for business purposes, or was held at the death of the intestate solely as an investment. The above definition may need to be adapted slightly to suit the testator's requirements. For example ' . . . and this gift includes any car and accessories used for business purposes'.

6.127

Bequest of personal chattels: cohabitant to choose

(1) I GIVE free of tax to (*cohabitant*) such of my personal chattels (as defined in the Administration of Estates Act 1925)[1] that have not been specifically bequeathed to others as (he)/(she) may choose within the period of (6) weeks beginning with the date of my death.

(2) Any personal chattels that (he)/(she) has not chosen within that period will form part of my residuary estate.

[1] For definition of personal chattels, see footnote to **6.126** (above).

Specific bequest

6.128

Jewellery[1]

I GIVE all my jewellery including watches[2] to my daughter (*name*) free of tax (and my Trustees can let her wear my jewellery when she reaches the age of (14)).

[1] Unless they are particularly valuable, it is usually preferable that specific chattels vest in a minor immediately, rather than be made contingent on the child reaching 18. Strictly speaking, the chattels should be kept until the child is 18 and can give a valid receipt for them.
[2] D T Davies *Will Precedents and Inheritance Tax* (Butterworths, 4th edn) at p 176, contains a more comprehensive definition: 'all my jewellery and all other articles of a like nature including tiaras, rings, necklaces, earrings, brooches, pendants, bracelets and watches'.

6.129

Car on hire purchase, etc[1]

I GIVE to (*cohabitant*) (free of tax) any car I own or lawfully have in my possession at the time of my death.

IF the car is subject to a hire purchase or conditional sale agreement . . . [2] I GIVE to (*cohabitant*) all my rights under that agreement on condition that (he)/(she) pays all sums, performs all obligations and indemnifies my estate against all liabilities arising under it.

[OR]

. . . my Trustees will do what they can to complete the purchase of the car and to transfer it to (*cohabitant*) at the expense of my residuary estate.

[1] Although this clause relates to a car, the same principles would apply in respect of other goods being acquired on HP. Clauses of this nature are fraught with difficulties and, wherever possible, the practitioner should inspect the HP, etc, agreement. For comments and precedents on goods subject to a credit sale agreement and leasing agreement, see *Butterworth's Wills, Probate and Administration Service* (Butterworths) Vol 1.
[2] The ownership of goods under an HP agreement is not vested in the testator (compare credit sale agreements).

6.130

Cohabitation as a condition precedent[1]: pecuniary legacy[2]

IF (*cohabitant*) and I are still living together at the time of my death, I GIVE (him)/(her) the sum of   pounds (£   ) free of tax.

[1] Wills Act 1837, s 18A contains provisions relating to the effect on wills of a decree of dissolution or annulment of marriage. Nothing comparable exists in respect of the end of an unmarried couple's relationship. If the couple split up, it is imperative that they review their wills as soon as possible. For example, see **6.160** below. If a testator specifically wishes to make a gift to the cohabitee conditional on their still living together, he should appoint independent executors who could apply to the court for directions if there were any problems over compliance with the condition precedent.
[2] The pecuniary legacy is merely an illustration of the condition precedent. The same rules would apply in respect of other gifts. If the cohabitee does not satisfy the condition specified, the pecuniary legacy will fail.

6.131

Pecuniary legacy: index-linked[1]

(1)   I GIVE to (*cohabitant*) the sum of £   free of tax ('this legacy').

(2) This legacy will be index-linked by reference to the extent by which the Retail Prices Index has changed between the month in which I sign this Will and the month in which I die.

(3) If the Retail Prices Index no longer exists at the time of my death my trustees may apply whatever formula they consider appropriate to ensure that the value of this legacy is the same at my death as it was when I signed this Will[2].

[1] The Retail Prices Index (RPI) is designed to measure the changes in the prices of good and services purchased by householders from their net income, and is, therefore, indicative of the purchasing power of money. The figures are published by the Office of National Statistics monthly.

[2] This sub-clause is probably unnecessarily cautious. The original 'Cost-of-Living Index' was introduced in 1914, and was superseded by the RPI in June 1947. A new base for the RPI was set in January 1987.

6.132

Release of debt[1]

I RELEASE (*cohabitant*) free of tax from any debt and the interest on any debt which (he)/(she) may owe me at the time of my death.

[1] The release of a debt constitutes a pecuniary legacy to the debtor (*Attorney-General v Holbrook* (1823) 3 Y & J 114). If the debtor dies before the testator, the release will lapse like any other legacy, unless the will contains express provisions against lapse, for example: ' . . . but if (he)/(she) dies before me (his)/(her) personal representatives will have the benefit of this release'. Cohabitants often make loans to each other, with varying degrees of formality, and it is sensible to ascertain exactly what the testator's wishes are in order to avoid any misunderstanding. A declaration in the will that moneys advanced by the testator were gifts, not loans, to the cohabitee would, in theory, produce the same result, but there are constructional difficulties in such a declaration. The clause would 'speak' from the date of the will, rather than from the date of death.

6.133

Lump sum to buy an annuity[1]

I GIVE free of tax to (*cohabitant*) the sum that my Trustees consider sufficient to enable (him)/(her) to purchase from a reputable insurance company a gross annuity of £   payable quarterly from the date of my death AND I HOPE that (*cohabitant*) will use the sum to purchase such an annuity.

[1] This is probably the easiest way of providing the surviving cohabitant with an annuity. More complicated provisions, including index-linking, can be found in the standard will precedent books. If the surviving cohabitee is or is likely to be receiving income-related benefits from the DSS, the notional capital rule under reg 51 of the Income Support (General) Regulations 1987 (SI 1987/1967) must be considered.

6.134

Administration trusts and definition of residuary estate[1]

I GIVE all (the rest)[2] of my estate to my Trustees on trust to:

(1) sell or retain;

(2) pay my debts, funeral expenses, testamentary expenses, and any inheritance tax (that is not charged on or primarily payable out of other property)[3], and

(3) hold what remains ('my residuary estate') on the following trusts.

[1] It may be considered preferable to separate the administration trusts from the trusts of

residue. Compare, Statutory Will Forms 1925, Form 8 'Administration Trusts'.
2   The words 'the rest' should be included if this clause is preceded by a legacy or legacies.
3   In the absence of a direction to the contrary, the residue will bear the inheritance tax. The testator may prefer to state 'pay . . . any inheritance tax attributable to property which I hold as a joint tenant'. Care should be taken where part of the residue is exempt from inheritance tax (eg a gift to charity) and part is not to make it clear whether the division into shares is before or after deduction of inheritance tax. See *Re Benham's Will Trusts* [1995] STC 210; *Re Ratcliffe* [1999] STC 262.

RESIDUARY ESTATE

6.135

Cohabitant entitled absolutely[1]

MY TRUSTEES will pay or transfer any residuary estate to (*cohabitant*) absolutely.

IF (*cohabitant*) dies before me, my Trustees will pay or transfer my residuary estate to (or hold it on trust for) . . . [2]

1   This clause assumes that 'my residuary estate' has already been defined (see **6.134** above).
2   It is advisable to include a gift over.

6.136

Cohabitant and other adults equally entitled: no gifts over[1]

MY TRUSTEES will pay or transfer my residuary estate to (*cohabitant*) and (*name*) and (*name*) in equal shares or to the survivor of them absolutely.

1   This clause assumes that 'my residuary estate' has already been defined. The words 'pay or transfer' are probably preferable to, and less misleading than, 'hold on trust for' where there is no on-going trust.

6.137

Cohabitant and testator's children given specified shares: provisions for their 'separate families'[1]

MY TRUSTEES will divide my residuary estate into (*number*) equal shares which they will hold as follows:

(1)   (*number*) shares ('the (*cohabitant's family name*) Fund' for (*cohabitant*);

(2)   (*number*) shares ('the (*testator's family name*) Fund' for my children (*name*) and (*name*) in equal shares or for the survivor absolutely;

(3)   if (*cohabitant*) dies before me my Trustees will hold the (*cohabitant's family name*) Fund for (his)/(her) children (*name*) in equal shares or for the survivor absolutely;

(4)   if any of my children or (*cohabitant's*) children dies before me leaving a child or children living at my death, that child or those children on reaching the age of (18) will take, and if more than one in equal shares, the share of my residuary estate which his, her or their parent would have taken if he or she had survived me;

(5)   if the trusts affecting either Fund completely fail that Fund will be added to the other Fund.

1   This clause assumes that 'my residuary estate' has already been defined. It is designed to cover 'funds' of equal or unequal size.

6.138

The 'slice system'

MY TRUSTEES will pay or transfer to (cohabitant):

(1)   (75) % of the first (£100,000) of my residuary estate; and

(2)   (50) % of my residuary estate in so far as it exceeds (£100,000)[1].

IN DEFAULT of and subject to this gift my Trustees will hold my residuary estate (on trust) for (names).

[1] The percentages and figures can be adapted to suit the testator's requirements; those quoted are merely illustrative. The clause can be adapted to provide alternatives where the testator is survived by the cohabitee and issue, and where the testator dies without issue and is survived by the cohabitee. For example: 'If I die without issue and (cohabitant) survives me . . . '; and 'If I die leaving issue and (cohabitant) survives me . . . '.

6.139

Cohabitant's entitlement based on the duration of the relationship[1]

MY TRUSTEES will pay or transfer to (cohabitant) (10) % of my residuary estate[2] for each complete year which has elapsed between (date) [OR] (the date of this Will)[3] and the date of my death[4] and no apportionment will be made in respect of any period of less than a year.

IN DEFAULT of and subject to this gift my Trustees will hold my residuary estate (on trust) for (names).

[1] The same concept could be applied to a pecuniary legacy.
[2] The percentage can be adapted to suit the testator's requirements.
[3] If any date other than the date of the will is stated it must be precise: eg day, month, year.
[4] If it is considered necessary, the following words could be added: ' . . . so that if I die on or after (date), (cohabitant) will be entitled to all of my residuary estate . . . '.

6.140

Life interest

(1)   MY TRUSTEES will hold my residuary estate on trust to pay its income[1] to (cohabitant) during (his)/(her) lifetime.

(2)   AFTER the death of (cohabitant) my Trustees will hold the capital and income of my residuary estate on trust for those of my children who survive me[2] and reach the age of (18) and if more than one in equal shares.

(3)   IF any of my children dies before me[3] or before reaching the age of (18) leaving a child or children who do reach that age that child or those children equally will take the share of my residuary estate that his, her or their parent would otherwise have taken.

[1] The income may be insufficient for the surviving partner's needs. Consider whether the trustees should have power to advance capital or make loans.
[2] Note that the interests of the remaindermen are contingent on their surviving the testator, not the life tenant. If the alternative is preferred, delete the word 'me' and replace it with the life tenant's name or description.
[3] Note that the interests of the remaindermen are contingent on their surviving the testator, not the life tenant. If the alternative is preferred, delete the word 'me' and replace it with the life tenant's name or description.

6.141

Life interest determinable on cohabitation[1]

(1) MY TRUSTEES will hold my residuary estate on trust to pay its income to (*cohabitant*) during (his)/(her) lifetime until (he)/(she) cohabits[2].

(2) SUBJECT to the above trust my Trustees will hold my residuary estate (on trust) for [   ].

[1] For a brief discussion of the definition of 'cohabits' and the evidential problems experienced in trying to establish whether a couple are cohabiting, see **6.155** below.
For alternative provisions in respect of the residuary estate, consider a revocable life interest (**6.142** below), and a discretionary trust (**6.143** below).

[2] It is considered that the word 'marries' in the expression 'until (he)/(she) marries or cohabits (whichever happens first)' is probably otiose.

6.142

Revocable life interest[1]

(1) MY TRUSTEES will hold my residuary estate on trust to pay the income from it to (*cohabitant*) during (his)/(her) lifetime subject to the powers and provisions that follow.

(2) MY TRUSTEES can revoke the life interest of (*cohabitant*) and hold my residuary estate as if (he)/(she) had died on the date of revocation.

(3) THE REVOCATION can only be made:

 (a) by my Trustees, provided that they are at least two in number or a trust corporation;

 (b) by deed.

(4) THE REVOCATION can be made:

 (a) in respect of (*cohabitant's*) interest in all of my residuary estate or any asset comprised in it;

 (b) before Probate of this Will has been granted;

 (c) before the administration of my estate has been completed;

 (d) at any time during the lifetime of (*cohabitant*).

(5) IN EXERCISING their power of revocation:

 (a) my Trustees will have absolute discretion;

 (b) my Trustees can have regard to, or disregard, any wishes I may have communicated to them;

 (c) the decision of my Trustees will be final and binding.

(6) MY TRUSTEES can:

 (a) appoint any person, professional trustee or trust corporation to be a new trustee of all or any part of my residuary estate and, where appropriate, provide for their remuneration;

 (b) provided that they are at least two in number or a trust corporation, execute any deed or deeds extinguishing or restricting the future exercise of their power of revocation.

(7) SUBJECT to the above trusts, powers and provisions my Trustees will hold the capital and income of my residuary estate (on trust) for.

[1] A revocable life interest is one of the devices used by some practitioners to overcome some of the difficulties that arise when a testator wishes to give his partner a life interest, but also wishes it to terminate as soon as she enters into a new relationship. It is not entirely clear how successful such a clause is in practical and human terms.

6.143

Full discretionary trust[1]

(1) MY TRUSTEES will hold the capital and income of my residuary estate on trust for any one or more of the Beneficiaries whom they appoint.

(2) THE BENEFICIARIES are:

    (a) *(cohabitant)*;

    (b) anyone with whom I am living at the time of my death;

    (c) my (husband)/(wife), if any;

    (d) my former (husband)/(wife), if any;

    (e) my children and remoter issue;

    (f) my parents;

    (g) my brothers and sisters and their children and remoter issue;

    (h) the children and remoter issue of *(cohabitant)*, anyone with whom I am living at the time of my death, my (husband)/(wife) and my former (husband)/(wife).

(3) THE APPOINTMENT(S) can only be made:

    (a) by my Trustees, provided that they are at least two in number or a trust corporation;

    (b) by deed;

    (c) within the period of 125² years (less 3 days) beginning with the date of my death ('the 125-year period').

(4) THE APPOINTMENT(S) can be made:

    (a) as one appointment or as several appointments;

    (b) at any time during the 125-year period;

    (c) before Probate of this Will has been granted;

    (d) before the administration of my estate has been completed;

    (e) revocably or irrevocably;

    (f) even though one or more of my Trustees stands to benefit personally from the appointment(s).

(5) IN MAKING any appointment my Trustees:

    (a) have total discretion;

    (b) have the same powers that they would have if my residuary estate belonged to them personally;

    (c) may have regard to, or disregard, any wishes I may have communicated to them;

    (d) are under no obligation to ensure equality among the Beneficiaries or any class of Beneficiaries;

6.143 *Death and Succession*

- (e) can create interests that are free from any trust;
- (f) can create any kind of trust;
- (g) can stipulate any age or date at which a Beneficiary may be entitled;
- (h) can confer any powers and discretions they think fit;
- (i) can impose any restrictions, limitations, terms and conditions they think fit;
- (j) can make any provisions they think fit;
- (k) will not invalidate any earlier payment or application of any part(s) of the capital or income of my residuary estate.

(6) MY TRUSTEES can:

- (a) appoint any person, professional trustee or trust corporation to be a new trustee of the whole or any part of my residuary estate and, where appropriate, provide for their remuneration;
- (b) provided that they are at least two in number or a trust corporation, execute at any time(s) a deed or deeds extinguishing or restricting the future exercise of their powers.

(7) IN DEFAULT of any appointment and subject to any appointment the following provisions apply.

(8) DURING the 125-year period my Trustees:

- (a) will pay all or any part of the income of my residuary estate to any one or more of the Beneficiaries or apply it for his, her or their benefit, education, maintenance and support in whatever manner they think fit;
- (b) can pay or apply any accumulations of income from past years as if they were the income of the present year.

(9) AT THE END of the 125-year period my Trustees will hold the capital and income of my residuary estate for my children and remoter issue who are alive at that time and if more than one in equal shares according to their stocks, so that no issue whose parent is still alive will be entitled.

---

[1] Discretionary trusts allow the trustees great flexibility, enabling them to react to changing family and tax circumstances. In the context of cohabitation they are occasionally used for the purpose of varying the financial provision made for the surviving partner according to any changes in his or her personal circumstances. The trustees have extremely wide-ranging powers. It is essential to establish whether the testator really wishes to leave his family's welfare and finances in the hands of trustees on a long-term basis.

A discretionary trust gives no qualifying interest in possession for the purposes of the Inheritance Tax Act 1984, s 58. No inheritance tax arises on the death of any of the potential beneficiaries, but the trust is subject to a 10-yearly charge and exit charges (Inheritance Tax Act 1984, ss 64 and 65).

For a full discussion of the tax implications and the advantages and disadvantages of these trusts, see D T Davies *Wills Precedents and Inheritance Tax* (Butterworths, 4th edn) and *Butterworth's Wills, Probate and Administration Service* (Butterworths).

[2] The Perpetuities and Accumulations Act 2009 increased the perpetuity period from 80 to 125 years for all purposes and no other period can now be specified. It also abolished the rule against excessive accumulations of income which was previously restricted to 21 years but can now last for the whole of the trust period specified.

6.144

Two-year discretionary trust[1]

(1) MY TRUSTEES will hold the capital and income of my residuary estate on trust for any one or more of the Beneficiaries whom they appoint.

(2) THE BENEFICIARIES are:
- (a) (cohabitant);
- (b) anyone with whom I am living at the time of my death;
- (c) my (husband)/(wife), if any;
- (d) my former (husband)/(wife), if any;
- (e) my children and remoter issue;
- (f) my parents;
- (g) my brothers and sisters and their children and remoter issue;
- (h) the children and remoter issue of (cohabitant), anyone with whom I am living at the time of my death, my (husband)/(wife) and my former (husband)/(wife).

(3) THE APPOINTMENT(S) can only be made:
- (a) by my Trustees, provided that they are at least two in number or a trust corporation;
- (b) by deed;
- (c) within the period of 2 years (less 3 days) beginning with the date of my death ('the 2-year period').

(4) THE APPOINTMENT(S) can be made:
- (a) as one appointment or as several appointments;
- (b) at any time during the 2-year period;
- (c) before Probate of this Will has been granted;
- (d) before the administration of my estate has been completed;
- (e) revocably or irrevocably;
- (f) even though one or more of my Trustees stands to benefit personally from the appointment(s).

(5) IN MAKING any appointment my Trustees:
- (a) have total discretion;
- (b) have the same powers that they would have if my residuary estate belonged to them personally;
- (c) may have regard to, or disregard, any wishes I may have communicated to them;
- (d) are under no obligation to ensure equality among the Beneficiaries or any class of Beneficiaries;
- (e) can create interests that are free from any trust;
- (f) can create any kind of trust;
- (g) can stipulate any age or date at which a Beneficiary may be entitled;

6.144 Death and Succession

- (h) can confer any powers and discretions they think fit;
- (i) can impose any restrictions, limitations, terms and conditions they think fit;
- (j) can make any provisions they think fit;
- (k) will not invalidate any earlier payment or application of any part(s) of the capital or income of my residuary estate.

(6) MY TRUSTEES can:
- (a) appoint any person, professional trustee or trust corporation to be a new trustee of the whole or any part of my residuary estate and, where appropriate, provide for their remuneration;
- (b) provided that they are at least two in number or a trust corporation, execute at any time(s) a deed or deeds extinguishing or restricting the future exercise of their powers.

(7) IN DEFAULT of any appointment and subject to any appointment the following provisions apply.

(8) DURING the 2-year period my Trustees:
- (a) will pay all or any part of the income of my residuary estate to any one or more of the Beneficiaries or apply it for his, her or their benefit, education, maintenance and support in whatever manner they think fit;
- (b) can accumulate the income;
- (c) can add accumulations of income to the capital of my residuary estate.

(9) AT THE END of the 2-year period my Trustees will hold the capital and income of my residuary estate (on trust) for . . .

---

[1] A 2-year discretionary trust is widely used as an inheritance tax planning device, and takes advantage of the provisions of the Inheritance Tax Act 1984, s 144. For a fuller discussion see *Butterworth's Wills, Probate and Administration Service* (Butterworths) at paras A[967–970].

In the context of cohabitation a 'mini discretionary trust' might be regarded as a useful 'wait and see' vehicle, where the testator wishes to make provision for the surviving partner, but also wishes to withdraw such provision as soon as the survivor has entered into a new, stable relationship.

The testator should make his wishes clear to his trustees, preferably in a written 'off-the-record' memorandum.

The interaction of 'mini discretionary trusts' and the I(PFD)A 1975 has not yet been fully explored by the courts.

TRUSTEE'S POWER

6.145 Note that the Trustee Act 2000, s 1 now lays down a statutory duty of care for trustees.

6.146

Investment[1]

(MY TRUSTEES can) invest as freely as if the assets of my residuary estate were their own and can acquire assets which produce no income[2] and can purchase[3] and improve[4] any property for the purpose of providing a home for a beneficiary[5].

1   Trustee Act 2000, s 3 now contains wide investment powers. It is, however, recommended that a specific power be included for the benefit of the testator. Even where the investment power is express, the trustees must have regard to the standard investment criteria laid down in s 4 of the Trustee Act 2000.
2   Assets which produce no income are not 'investments', and are, therefore, unauthorised (*Re Wragg* [1919] 2 Ch 58).
3   Although trustees of land can now purchase land for occupation by a beneficiary (Trusts of Land and Appointment of Trustees Act 1996, s 6(4)(b)), it is still advisable to include these powers.
4   A very limited power to raise money for improvements is conferred by LTA 1927, s 13.
5   A power to invest in the purchase of land did not automatically authorise the trustees to acquire a vacant freehold house for occupation by the testator's family; because it produced no income it was not an investment (*Re Power's Will Trusts* [1947] Ch 572). Trustee Act 2000, s 8 now allows the acquisition of freehold or leasehold land in the United Kingdom for occupation by a beneficiary.

6.147

Delegation of investment management[1]

(MY TRUSTEES can) delegate their powers of investing, managing and administering trust assets to any person or company (whether UK resident or not) and allow trust assets to be held in the name of that person or company as their nominee on whatever terms (including remuneration) they think appropriate.

1   Trustee Act 2000, Pt IV allows the appointment of agents, nominees and custodians and lays down the criteria and conditions applicable.

6.148

Maintenance[1]

(MY TRUSTEES can) apply all or any part of the income of that share of my residuary estate to which a beneficiary is or may in future be entitled for that beneficiary's maintenance, education or benefit in whatever manner they in their absolute discretion think fit, regardless of whether other funds are available for these purposes, and regardless of whether anyone has a legal duty to provide for that beneficiary's maintenance or education[2].

1   The statutory power to apply income for maintenance and to accumulate surplus income during a minority is contained in Trustee Act 1925, s 31 as amended by ITPA 2014, s 8. It is submitted that the standard will clauses which refer to this section and amend it are unintelligible to the ordinary testator.
2   If necessary, the clause could prohibit any payment being made while the father has anything to do with the child's education or upbringing (*Re Borwicks Settlement* [1916] 2 Ch 304).

6.149

Advancement[1]

(MY TRUSTEES can) apply all or any part of the capital of that share of my residuary estate to which a beneficiary is or may in future be entitled for that beneficiary's advancement or benefit[2] in whatever manner they in their absolute discretion think fit[3].

1   The statutory power of advancement is contained in Trustee Act 1925, s 32 as amended by ITPA 2014, s 9. It is submitted that the widely used type of clause which refers to the section and amends it is unintelligible to the ordinary testator.
2   'Advancement' suggests establishing the beneficiary in life. The wider-term 'benefit' includes (*inter alia*) payments for the beneficiary's maintenance or education. The trustees must have good reason for making the advance, and must see that its purpose is carried out (*Re Pauling (No 1)* [1965] Ch 303).

6.149 Death and Succession

³ Trustee Act 1925, s 32(1), proviso (b), which requires that the advances be brought into account, will apply unless specifically excluded.

6.150

Insurance¹

(MY TRUSTEES can):

(1) insure any asset in my estate against any insurable risk² and for any amount even though a beneficiary is absolutely entitled to³ it;

(2) pay insurance premiums out of income or capital⁴ in whatever manner they think fit;

(3) use any insurance money they receive to restore the asset or alternatively treat that money as if it were the net proceeds of sale of the asset insured.

¹ For the existing statutory powers, see the Trustee Act 1925, s 19 as amended by the Trustee Act 2000.
² The statutory power now applies to 'loss or damage due to any event' (Trustee Act 1925, s 19(1)).
³ Trustee Act 1925, s 19(2) includes the trustees' statutory power of insurance where they hold on a bare trust subject to directions by the beneficiaries.
⁴ The statutory power is exercised at the expense of income (Trustee Act 1925, s 19(1)).

6.151

Appropriation¹

(MY TRUSTEES can) appropriate any part of my estate in its then actual condition or state of investment in or towards the satisfaction of any legacy, interest or share in my estate without having to obtain any consent and regardless of whether they are acting as personal representatives or trustees².

¹ See, generally, AEA 1925, s 41.
² The statutory power applies only to personal representatives. It does not apply to trustees. For comment and proposed reform see the Law Commission Report LC 260, published 21 July 1999. No amendments were made to this power in the Trustee Act 2000.

6.152

Remuneration

(MY TRUSTEES can) if they are professionally qualified trustees or a trust corporation¹ charge and be paid for all the work they do in obtaining probate, administering my estate and acting as trustees, even though some of that work could have been done by a person who is not professionally qualified.

¹ Express authorisation to charge is not required where the Public Trustee takes on the appointment (Public Trustee Act 1906, s 5).

6.153

Statement for the purposes of the Inheritance (Provision for Family and Dependants) Act 1975¹

I HAVE NOT MADE (greater)/(any) provision² in this Will for (*cohabitant*) (not through any lack of love or affection for (him)/(her) but) because:

(a) I consider that (he)/(she) already has adequate financial resources³;

(b) (he)/(she) is not maintained by me or financially dependent on me⁴;

(c) our relationship has been of a comparatively short duration⁵;

(d) I believe that my (children) have a greater claim on my estate;

(e) (other reasons, if any)[6].

[1] For the admissibility as evidence of statements made by the deceased, see I(PFD)A 1975, s 21. If the statement is defamatory, objectionable, or distressing to 'the family' it will be excluded from the probate (*In the Estate of Hall* [1943] 1 All ER 159).

[2] For anyone other than a spouse 'reasonable financial provision' means 'such financial provision as it would be reasonable in all the circumstances of the case for the applicant to receive for his maintenance' (I(PFD)A 1975, s 1(2)(b)).

[3] See I(PFD)A 1975, s 3.

[4] See I(PFD)A 1975, s 2(3). However, the situation could change between the date of the will and the testator's death.

[5] See I(PFD)A 1975, s 3(4). Likewise, the situation could change between the date of the will and the testator's death.

[6] For example: there could be a nomination in the cohabitant's favour; various assets could pass to the cohabitant by the *ius accrescendi*; the testator may have made lifetime gifts to the cohabitant; the cohabitant may have expectations under the will of someone else; the origin of the deceased's assets may be relevant; the couple might even have signed a cohabitation contract waiving the right to apply to the court for an order under the Act. See **2.111** above. See also clause 10 at **6.164** below.

THE WORD 'COHABITS' IN WILLS

6.154

Definitions

For the purposes of this Will 'cohabitation' exists where two people who are not married to each other or in a civil partnership together live together in the same household as spouses or civil partners, and 'cohabits' will be interpreted accordingly[1]. [OR]

For the purposes of this Will 'cohabitation' exists where two people who are not married to each other or in civil partnership together live together in the same household as spouses or civil partners for a period of (*number*) months in any (*number*) month period, and 'cohabits' will be interpreted accordingly[2]. [OR]

For the purposes of this Will (*cohabitant*) will be treated as cohabiting if (he)/(she) lives in the same household with a person of either sex who is not a blood relative of (his)/(hers) or mine[3]. [OR]

For the purposes of this Will 'cohabits' means 'has sexual relations'[4].

[1] This definition is based partly on the wording of the DVMPA 1976, s 1(2) and the Social Security Act 1986, s 20(11).

[2] This definition is based partly on the Solicitors' Family Law Association *Precedents for Consent Orders* (5th edn), Precedent 32. Cf Barton, above, at p 3: 'sharing a bedroom during at least four nights per week during at least three consecutive months with someone of the opposite sex'.

[3] This definition could include those living with friends.

[4] Cf the euphemistic expression 'dum casta vixerit'. It is submitted that some testators would construe 'cohabits' in exactly this way.

6.155

Miscellaneous

– For the purposes of deciding whether or not (*cohabitant*) is cohabiting, my Trustees may have regard to the criteria applied by the Department of Work and Pensions for the purposes of deciding whether or not a claimant is cohabiting[1].

6.155 *Death and Succession*

- The fact that (*cohabitant*) is living in the same household with someone who is not (his)/(her) or my blood relative will give rise to a presumption that they are cohabiting and the burden of proving that (he)/(she) is not cohabiting will lie with (*cohabitant*).

- My Trustees will not be liable for paying the income from (my residuary estate) to (*cohabitant*) after (his)/(her) interest in it has terminated unless they have knowledge of the event causing the termination[2].

- The decision of my Trustees as to whether or not (*cohabitant*) is cohabiting will be final and binding[3].

[1] See Guidance for Decision-Makers Vol 3 Ch 11: Living together as husband and wife or as civil partners.

[2] Trustee Act 1925, s 61 provides that 'if it appears to the court that a trustee . . . is or may be personally liable for any breach of trust . . . but has acted honestly and reasonably, and ought fairly to be excused . . . the court may relieve him either wholly or partly from personal liability'. This relief may also be extended to executors.

[3] Any clause in a will which purports to make the trustees' decision final and binding is invalid (*Re Wynn* [1952] 1 All ER 341). The reason for this is that the court exercises a general controlling influence over all trustees, and a clause which attempts to oust its jurisdiction is thereby repugnant and contrary to public policy.

6.156

Testimonium[1]

AS WITNESS my hand on (*date*)

[OR]

SIGNED by me on (*date*).

[1] The testimonium will be needed if the date does not appear in the commencement of the will.

6.157

Attestation clause[1]

SIGNED by (*testator*) in our joint presence and then by us in (his)/(hers).

[1] The formal requirements for the execution of a valid will are set out in the Wills Act 1837, s 9 (as substituted by the Administration of Justice Act 1982, s 17). This section ends with the statement that 'no form of attestation shall be necessary'.
This clause is for use in normal cases. For attestation clauses where the testator is unable to read or write, or is visually handicapped, or when another person signs on the testator's behalf, see the standard will precedent books.

Forms

6.158

Pension scheme: request to trustees[1]

(*Full Name and Address of Member*)

(*date*)

To: The Trustees

The (*name*) Pension Scheme

(address)

Dear Sirs,

Statement of wishes concerning death benefits

Although I am aware that you have an absolute discretion in respect of the payment of any lump sum and other benefits on my death, I would be grateful if you could have regard to my wishes, as stated below, until you receive a further statement from me.

I would like the following people to receive the following shares:

Name	Relationship	Address	Percentage

Yours faithfully,

(member's signature)[2]

[1] It would be sensible to check the terms of the scheme to see whether or not such a nomination is possible.
As this is a 'non-statutory' nomination, the benefits do not form part of the deceased's estate for the purposes of an order under the I(PFD)A 1975 (s 8(1)). See also *Re Cairnes* (1983) 4 FLR 225, 12 Fam Law 177.

[2] A nomination of this kind is not a 'testamentary disposition' (*Re Danish Bacon Co Staff Pension Fund* [1971] 1 All ER 486).
The member should send the letter to the trustees in a sealed envelope stating his full name, the date, and the words 'Statement of Wishes relating to the (*name*) Pension Scheme'.

6.159

Codicil 'disinheriting' former cohabitant[1]

THIS (SECOND) CODICIL is made by me (*testator*) of (*address*) on (*date*) and is supplemental to my Will dated (*date*) (and the Codicil(s) to it dated   ).

(1) I REVOKE the appointment of (*cohabitant*) as an Executor and Trustee of my Will.

(2) I REVOKE every devise, bequest, legacy, benefit and privilege given to or conferred on (*cohabitant*) in my Will.

(3) I INTEND that my Will will be interpreted and take effect as if (*cohabitant*) had died before me[2].

(4) I CONFIRM my Will (and Codicil(s)) in all other respects.

SIGNED by (*testator*) in our joint presence and then by us in (his)/(hers).

[1] For unmarried couples there is no equivalent to Wills Act 1837, s 18A, which describes the effect on a will of a decree of dissolution or annulment of marriage. Therefore, if cohabitants split up, it is vitally important that they should review their respective wills immediately. A codicil of this nature should only be executed if the will contains suitable alternative

appointments and gifts unless, of course, the testator consciously wishes to bring about a potential intestacy or partial intestacy. A codicil of this nature could also be executed by a married person in the throes of a divorce but where no decree of the court has yet been made.

[2] Cf *Re Sinclair* [1985] Ch 446.

6.160

Will: unmarried mother leaving her entire estate to her child under 18

THIS WILL is made on (*date*) by me (*testatrix*) of (*address*).

(1) I REVOKE my earlier Wills.

(2) I WOULD LIKE to be (cremated).

(3) I APPOINT my parents (*name*) and (*name*) of (*address*) ('my Trustees') to be my Executors and Trustees and the guardians of my (son)/(daughter) (*child's name*)[1].

(4) I GIVE all my estate to my Trustees on trust to:

    (a) sell or retain;

    (b) pay my debts, funeral expenses and testamentary expenses; and

    (c) hold what remains ('my residuary estate') as follows.

(5) MY TRUSTEES will hold my residuary estate on trust for my (son)/(daughter) (*child's name*) if and when (he)/(she) reaches the age of (18).

(6) IF my (son)/(daughter) dies before me or before (he)/(she) reaches (18) leaving issue, my Trustees will hold my residuary estate on trust for such issue who reach (18) and if more than one in equal shares[2].

(7) IF all of the above trusts fail, my Trustees will pay or transfer my residuary estate to my parents in equal shares or to the survivor of them absolutely.

(8) MY TRUSTEES can:

    (a) invest as freely as if the assets of my residuary estate were their own and can acquire assets which produce no income and can purchase and improve any property for the purpose of providing a home for a beneficiary;

    (b) apply all or any part of the income of that share of my residuary estate to which a beneficiary is or may in future be entitled for that beneficiary's maintenance, education or benefit in whatever manner they in their absolute discretion think fit, regardless of whether other funds are available for these purposes, and regardless of whether anyone has a legal duty to provide for the beneficiary's maintenance or[3] education;

    (c) apply all or any part of the capital of that share of my residuary estate to which a beneficiary is or may in future be entitled for that beneficiary's advancement or benefit in whatever manner they in their absolute discretion think fit.

SIGNED by (*testatrix*) in our joint presence and then by us in hers.

[1] It is assumed that the child's father has not acquired parental responsibility. See, generally, CA 1989, s 4.

[2] Although the reference to the testatrix's grandchildren may seem completely inappropriate, it would not be possible in these circumstances to rely on the provisions of Wills Act 1837, s 33. In order for that section to apply, the son or daughter would have to die before the testatrix, leaving issue living at her death. Furthermore, the gift over to the parents, which is probably

sensible, could be construed as 'a contrary intention' for the purposes of s 33.

[3] For example, a maintenance assessment may have been made under the CSA 1991, requiring the absent parent to make periodical payments.

6.161

Will: childless unmarried couple: all to the surviving partner: gift over to their respective parents

THIS WILL is made on (*date*) by me (*testator*) of (*address*).

(1) I REVOKE my earlier Wills.

(2) I WOULD LIKE:

    (a) any part of my body which may be of use to others to be made available for treatment or transplantation;

    (b) to be cremated;

    (c) donations to be made to (Charity).

(3) IF (he)/(she) survives me by (7) days I GIVE my estate to (*cohabitant*) of (*address*) AND I APPOINT (him)/(her) to be my Executor, but if (he)/(she) fails to survive me by (7) days the following clauses will apply.

(4) I APPOINT (*name*) of (*address*) and (*name*) of (*address*) ('my Trustees') to be the Executors and Trustees of this Will.

(5) I GIVE my estate to my Trustees on trust to:

    (a) sell or retain;

    (b) pay my debts, funeral expenses, testamentary expenses and Inheritance Tax; and

    (c) hold what remains ('my residuary estate') as follows.

(6) MY TRUSTEES will divide my residuary estate into two equal shares and if the trusts of one of these shares fail, that share will be added to the other share.

(7) MY TRUSTEES will pay or transfer one share to my parents (*name*) and (*name*) of (*address*) equally or to the survivor of them.

(8) MY TRUSTEES will pay or transfer the other share to (*cohabitant's*) parents (*name*) and (*name*) of (*address*) equally or to the survivor of them.

SIGNED by (*testator*) in our joint presence and then by us in (his)/(hers).

6.162

Will: unmarried couple with minor children: both parents have parental responsibility: all to the surviving partner: gift over to children: further gift over in case of a family catastrophe

THIS WILL is made on (*date*) by me (*testator*) of (*address*).

(1) I REVOKE my earlier Wills.

(2) I WOULD LIKE to be (cremated)1.

(3) IF (he)/(she) survives me by (7) days I GIVE my estate to (*cohabitant*) of (*address*) AND I APPOINT (him)/(her) to be my Executor, but if (he)/(she) fails to survive me by (7) days the following clauses will apply.

6.162 Death and Succession

(4) I APPOINT (*name*) of (*address*) and (*name*) of (*address*) ('my Trustees') to be the Executors and Trustees of this Will.

(5) I APPOINT (*name*) of (*address*) to be the guardian of my children.

(6) I GIVE all my estate to my Trustees on trust to:

    (a) sell or retain;

    (b) pay my debts, funeral expenses, testamentary expenses and Inheritance Tax; and

    (c) hold what remains ('my residuary estate') as follows.

(7) MY TRUSTEES will hold my residuary estate on trust for my children who survive me and reach the age of (18) and if more than one in equal shares.

(8) IF a child of mine dies before me or before reaching (18) leaving a child or children who do reach that age that child or those children equally will take the share of my residuary estate that his, her or their parent would otherwise have taken.

(9) IF all the above trusts fail my Trustees will divide my residuary estate into two equal shares and if the trusts of one of these shares fail that share will be added to the other share.

(10) MY TRUSTEES will pay or transfer one share:

    (a) to my parents (*name*) and (*name*) equally or to the survivor of them; or

    (b) if both of my parents die before me, to my brothers and sisters (names) equally or to the survivor of them.

(11) MY TRUSTEES will pay or transfer the other share:

    (a) to (*cohabitant's*) parents (*name*) and (*name*) equally or to the survivor of them; or

    (b) if both of (*cohabitant's*) parents die before me, to (his)/(her) brothers and sisters (names) equally or to the survivor of them.

(12) (Trustees' powers.)

SIGNED by (*testator*) in our joint presence and then by us in (his)/(hers).

[1] If this is the woman's will, and the man does not have parental responsibility for the child(ren), insert a guardianship appointment at this stage. For example, 'I APPOINT (*cohabitant*) to be the guardian of our children'.

6.163

Will: older unmarried couple: life interest to the survivor

THIS WILL is made on (*date*) by me (*testator*) of (*address*).

(1) I REVOKE my earlier Wills.

(2) I WOULD LIKE to be cremated.

(3) I APPOINT (*name*) of (*address*) and (*name*) of (*address*) ('my Trustees') to be my Executors and Trustees.

(4) I GIVE all my personal chattels (as defined in the Administration of Estates Act 1925) to (*cohabitant*) free of tax.

(5) I GIVE the rest of my estate to my Trustees on trust to:

    (a) sell or retain;

(b) pay my debts, funeral expenses, testamentary expenses and inheritance tax; and

(c) hold what remains ('my residuary estate') as follows.

(6) MY TRUSTEES will hold my residuary estate on trust to pay its income to (*cohabitant*) during (his)/(her) lifetime.

(7) AFTER the death of (*cohabitant*) my Trustees will pay or transfer the capital and income of my residuary estate to those of my children (*name*), (*name*) and (*name*) who survive me and if more than one in equal shares.

(8) IF any of my children dies before me leaving a child or children living at my death that child or those children equally on reaching the age of (18) will take the share of my residuary estate that his, her or their parent would otherwise have taken.

(9) (Trustees' powers, including a clause excluding the operation of the apportionment rules.)

SIGNED by (*testator*) in our joint presence and then by us in (his)/(hers).

6.164

Will: older unmarried couple: limited provision for the surviving partner: residue to the testator's children

THIS WILL is made on (*date*) by me (*testator*) of (*address*).

(1) I REVOKE my earlier Wills.

(2) I WOULD LIKE:

(a) to be cremated;

(b) my ashes to be scattered;

(c) (*cohabitant*) to decide what other funeral arrangements should be made;

(d) the expenses incurred in carrying out these wishes to be paid out of my estate.

(3) I APPOINT my children (*name*) of (*address*) and (*name*) of (*address*) ('my Trustees') to be the Executors and Trustees of this Will.

(4) I GIVE to (*cohabitant*) free of tax all my personal chattels (as defined in the Administration of Estates Act 1925) and without imposing an obligation or creating a trust I would like (him)/(her), either by Will or lifetime gifts, to pass on to my children and grandchildren any articles which have particular associations with my family.

(5) I GIVE to (*cohabitant*)   pounds (£   ) free of tax.

(6) I RELEASE (*cohabitant*), free of tax, from any sum of money that (he)/(she) may owe me at the time of my death.

(7) I GIVE the rest of my estate to my Trustees on trust to:

(a) sell or retain;

(b) pay my debts, funeral expenses, testamentary expenses and inheritance tax including the tax attributable to property that I hold as a joint tenant; and

(c) hold what remains ('my residuary estate') as follows.

6.164 Death and Succession

(8) MY TRUSTEES will pay or transfer my residuary estate to my children (*name*) and (*name*) equally or to the survivor of them but if either of them dies before me leaving a child or children who reach the age of (18) that child or those children equally will take the share of my residuary estate that (his)/(her)/(their) parent would otherwise have taken.

(9) (Trustees' powers, including a clause excluding the operation of the apportionment rules[1].)

(10) I HAVE NOT MADE greater provision for (*cohabitant*) in this Will because:

  (a) the house and bank accounts that we hold as joint tenants will automatically pass to (him)/(her) by right of survivorship;

  (b) I am satisfied that (he)/(she) has adequate resources to enable (him)/(her) to live comfortably for the rest of (his)/(her) life;

  (c) of the possibility that if I had left the whole of my estate to (him)/(her) my family could be disinherited and (his)/(her) family commensurately enriched.

SIGNED by (*testator*) in our joint presence and then by us in (his)/(hers).

[1] Bearing in mind that the Trusts (Capital and Income) Act 2013 excluded the majority of the rules of apportionment.

6.165

Application for a standing search

(NCPR 43(1))

In the High Court of Justice

Family Division

The Principal [or   District Probate] Registry

I/We apply for the entry of a standing search so that there shall be sent to me/us an office copy of every grant of representation in England and Wales in the estate of—

Full name of deceased:

Full address:

Alternative or alias names:

Exact date of death:

which either has issued not more than 12 months before the entry of this application or issues within 6 months thereafter.

Signed:

Name in block letters:

Full address:

Precedents **6.165**

Reference No. (if any):

(NCPR 1988, Form 2.)

Alternatively, a standing search is more commonly made by using the online using the government portal[1] or via post using form PA1S[2].

[1] https://www.gov.uk/search-will-probate.
[2] https://www.gov.uk/government/publications/find-a-will-or-probate-document-form-pa1s.

6.166 Death and Succession

Section 2 Contentious precedents

6.166

Claim form for application by surviving cohabitant for provision from the estate of a deceased cohabitant

Claim Form (CPR Part 8)	In the OAKWOOD COUNTY COURT
	Claim No.

Claimant

JENNY PINE

SEAL

Defendant(s) ROBERT FOREST and JOHN BEECH, the
personal representatives of PAUL BEECH,
deceased (1)
RICHARD BEECH (2)
MARY OAK (3)
JAMES BEECH (4)

Details of claim (see also overleaf)

Pursuant to the Inheritance (Provision for Family and Dependants) Act 1975 the claimant claims:
1. Financial provision from the net estate of Paul Beech, deceased
2. The costs of the claim to be paid out of the estate

Defendant's name and address   £

ROBERT FOREST &
JOHN BEECH of
RICHARD BEECH of
MARY OAK of
JAMES BEECH of

Court fee	
Solicitor's costs	
Issue date	

The court office at
is open between 10 am and 4 pm Monday to Friday. When corresponding with the court, please address forms or letters to the Court Manager and quote the case number.

N208 Claim form (CPR Part 8) (4.99)   *Printed on behalf of The Court Service*

	Claim No.	

Details of claim (continued)

See witness statement attached.

Statement of Truth
*~~I believe~~ (The Claimant believes) that the facts stated in these particulars of claim are true.
*~~I am duly authorised by the claimant to sign this statement~~

Full name ___JANE PLANE_____

Name of claimant's solicitor's firm_____

signed _____ position or office held _____
*(Claimant)(~~Litigation friend~~) (if signing on behalf of firm or company)
(~~Claimant's solicitor~~)

delete as appropriate

Claimant's or claimant's solicitor's address to which documents should be sent if different from overleaf. If you are prepared to accept service by DX, fax or e-mail, please add details.

6.167

Claim form for application by dependant for provision from estate and permission to proceed out of time

	Claim Form (CPR Part 8)	In the OAKWOOD COUNTY COURT
		Claim No.

Claimant

JONATHAN CHERRY

(SEAL)

Defendant(s)   JOHN HAZEL, Administrator of the Estate
of Mary Hazel, deceased   (1)
DORIS HAZEL   (2)
JOHN HAZEL   (3)

Details of claim (see also overleaf)

Pursuant to the Inheritance (Provision for Family and Dependants) Act 1975 the claimant claims:
1. Financial provision from the net estate of Mary Hazel deceased
2. The costs of the claim to be paid out of the estate
3. Permission to proceed with the claim notwithstanding that the time for doing so has expired, on the grounds set out in the witness statement served herewith.

Defendant's name and address		£
JOHN HAZEL of . . .	Court fee	
	Solicitor's costs	
DORIS HAZEL of . . .	Issue date	

The court office at
is open between 10 am and 4 pm Monday to Friday. When corresponding with the court, please address forms or letters to the Court Manager and quote the case number.
N208 Claim form (CPR Part 8) (4.99)   *Printed on behalf of The Court Service*

	Claim No.	

Details of claim (continued)

Statement of Truth
*I believe(The Claimant believes) that the facts stated in these particulars of claim are true.
*I am duly authorised by the claimant to sign this statement

Full name ____JONATHAN CHERRY_____

Name of claimant's solicitor's firm____PLANE & PARTNERS_____

signed ___*Jonathan Cherry*___ position or office held _____
*(Claimant)(Litigation friend) (if signing on behalf of firm or company)
(Claimant's solicitor)

delete as appropriate

PLANE & PARTNERS

Claimant's or claimant's solicitor's address to which documents should be sent if different from overleaf. If you are prepared to accept service by DX, fax or e-mail, please add details.

6.167 Death and Succession

Notes for claimant on completing a Part 8 claim form

- Please read all of these guidance notes before you begin completing the claim form. The notes follow the order in which information is required on the form.
- Court staff can help you fill in the claim form and give information about procedure once it has been issued. But they cannot give legal advice. If you need legal advice, for example, about the likely success of your claim or the evidence you need to prove it, you should contact a solicitor or a Citizens Advice Bureau.
- If you are filling in the claim form by hand, please use black ink and write in block capitals.
- You must file any written evidence to support your claim either in or with the claim form. Your written evidence must be verified by a statement of truth.
- Copy the completed claim form, the defendant's notes for guidance and your written evidence so that you have one copy for yourself, one copy for the court and one copy for each defendant. Send or take the forms and evidence to the court office with the appropriate fee. The court will tell you how much this is.

Notes on completing the claim form

Heading

You must fill in the heading of the form to indicate whether you want the claim to be issued in a county court or in the High Court (The High Court means either a District Registry (attached to a county court) or the Royal Courts of Justice in London).

Use whichever of the following is appropriate:

'In the .... County Court'
(inserting the name of the court)

or

'In the High Court of Justice .... Division'
(inserting eg. 'Queen's Bench' or 'Chancery' as appropriate)
'..................... District Registry'
(inserting the name of the District Registry)

or

'In the High Court of Justice .... Division,
(inserting eg. 'Queen's Bench' or 'Chancery' as appropriate)
Royal Courts of Justice'

Claimant and defendant details

As the person issuing the claim, you are called the 'claimant'; the person you are suing is called the 'defendant'. Claimants who are under 18 years old (unless otherwise permitted by the court) and patients within the meaning of the Mental Health Act 1983 must have a litigation friend to issue and conduct court proceedings on their behalf. Court staff will tell you more about what you need to do if this applies to you.

You must provide the following information about yourself **and** the defendant according to the capacity in which you are suing and in which the defendant is being sued. When suing or being sued as:-

an individual:

All known forenames and surname, whether Mr, Mrs, Miss, Ms or other (e.g. Dr) and residential address (**including** postcode and telephone and any fax or e-mail number) in England and Wales. Where the defendant is a proprietor of a business, a partner in a firm or an individual sued in the name of a club or other unincorporated association, the address for service should be the usual or last known place of residence **or** principal place of business of the company, firm or club or other unincorporated association.

Where the individual is:

under 18 write '(a child by Mr Joe Bloggs his litigation friend)' after the child's name.

a patient within the meaning of the Mental Health Act 1983 write '(by Mr Joe Bloggs his litigation friend)' after the patient's name.

trading under another name

you must add the words 'trading as' and the trading name e.g. 'Mr John Smith trading as Smith's Groceries'.

suing or being sued in a representative capacity

you must say what that capacity is e.g. 'Mr Joe Bloggs as the representative of Mrs Sharon Bloggs (deceased)'.

suing or being sued in the name of a club or other unincorporated association

add the words 'suing/sued on behalf of' followed by the name of the club or other unincorporated association.

a firm

enter the name of the firm followed by the words 'a firm' e.g. 'Bankbox – a firm' and an address for service which is either a partner's residential address or the principal or last known place of business.

a corporation (other than a company)

enter the full name of the corporation and the address which is either its principal office or any other place where the corporation carries on activities and which has a real connection with the claim.

a company registered in England and Wales

enter the name of the company and an address which is either the company's registered office **or** any place of business that has a real, or the most, connection with the claim e.g. the shop where the goods were bought.

an overseas company (defined by s744 of the Companies Act 1985)

Enter the name of the company and either the address registered under s691 of the Act **or** the address of the place of business having a real, or the most, connection with the claim.

N208A Notes for claimant (CPR Part 8) (4.99) Printed on behalf of The Court Service

Details of claim

Under this heading you must set out either
- the question(s) you wish the court ot decide; **or**
- the remedy you are seeking and the legal basis for your claim; **and**
- if your claim is being made under a specific CPR Part or practice direction, you must state which.

Defendant's name and address

Enter in this box the full name and address of the defendant to be served with the claim form (i.e. one claim form for each defendant). If the defendant is to be served outside England and Wales, you may need to obtain the court's permission.

Address for documents

Insert in this box the address at which you wish to receive documents, if different from the address you have already given under the heading 'Claimant'. The address you give must be either that of your solicitors or your residential or business address and must be in England or Wales. If you live or carry on business outside England and Wales, you can give some other address within England and Wales.

Statement of truth

This must be signed by you, by your solicitor or your litigation friend, as appropriate.

Where the claimant is a registered company or a corporation the claim must be signed by either the director, treasurer, secretary, chief executive, manager or other officer of the company or (in the case of a corporation) the mayor, chairman, president or town clerk.

6.167 Death and Succession

Notes for defendant (Part 8 claim form)

Please read these notes carefully – they will help you to decide what to do about this claim.

- You have 14 days from the date on which you were served with the claim form (see below) in which to respond to the claim by completing and returning the acknowledgment of service enclosed with this claim form.
- If you **do not return** the acknowledgment of service, you will be allowed to attend any hearing of this claim but you will **not** be allowed to take part in the hearing unless the court gives you permission to do so.

Court staff can tell you about procedures but they cannot give legal advice. If you need legal advice, you should contact a solicitor or Citizens Advice Bureau immediately

Responding to this claim

Time for responding

The completed acknowledgment of service must be returned to the court office within 14 days of the date on which the claim form was served on you. If the claim form was

- sent by post, the 14 days begins 2 days from the date of the postmark on the envelope.
- delivered or left at your address, the 14 days begins the day after it was delivered.
- handed to you personally, the 14 days begins on the day it was given to you.

Completing the acknowledgment of service

You should complete section A, B, **or** C as appropriate **and all** of section D.

Section A – contesting the claim

If you wish to contest the remedy sought by the claimant in the claim form, you should complete section A. If you seek a remedy different from that sought by the claimant, you should give full details in the space provided.

Section B – disputing the court's jurisdiction

You should indicate your intention by completing section B and filing an application disputing the courts jurisdiction within 14 days of filing of your acknowledgment of service at the court. The court will arrange a hearing date for the application and tell you and the claimant when and where to attend.

Section C – objecting to use of procedure

If you believe that the claimant should not have issued the claim under Part 8 because:

- there **is** a substantial dispute of fact involved and
- you do not agree that the rule or practice direction stated does provide for the claimant to use this procedure

you should complete section C setting out your reasons in the space provided.

Written evidence

If you wish to file written evidence in reply to the claimant's written evidence, you must send it to the court with your acknowledgment of service. Your written evidence must be verified by a statement of truth or the court may disallow it.

Serving other parties

At the same time as you file your completed acknowledgment of service (and any written evidence) with the court, you must also send copies of both the form and any written evidence to any other party named on the claim form.

What happens next

The claimant may, within 14 days of receiving any written evidence from you, file further evidence in reply. On receipt of your acknowledgment of service and any evidence from the claimant in reply, the court file will be referred to the judge for directions for the disposal of the claim. The court will contact you and tell you what to do next.

Note: The court may already have given directions or arranged a hearing. If so, you will have received a copy with the claim form. You should comply with any directions and attend any hearing in addition to completing, filing and serving your acknowledgment of service.

Statement of truth

This must be signed by you, by your solicitor or your litigation friend, as appropriate.

Where the claimant is a registered company or a corporation the claim must be signed by either the director, treasurer, secretary, chief executive, manager or other officer of the company or (in the case of a corporation) the mayor, chairman, president or town clerk.

N208C Notes for defendant (CPR Part 8) (4-99) *Printed on behalf of The Court Service*

6.168

Witness statement in support of a claim by a surviving cohabitant for provision from estate of deceased cohabitant and application for an interim order

IN THE [ ] COUNTY COURT   CLAIM NUMBER
IN THE MATTER OF

An application under s 1 of the Inheritance (Provision for Family and Dependants) Act 1975
AND IN THE MATTER OF

The estate of [name] deceased
BETWEEN:

	[name]	Claimant
And		
	[name(s)] Personal Representatives of [name], deceased	1st Defendants
And		
	[name]	2nd Defendant
And		
	[name]	3rd Defendant
And		
	[name]	4th Defendant

WITNESS STATEMENT OF [name]

I, [name], of [address] say as follows:

(1) I make this statement in support of my claim for provision from the estate of [name] ('the deceased') and in support of my application for an interim payment from the estate.

(2) The deceased and I began to cohabit 6 years ago when I moved into his home. We continued to cohabit right up until his death [date]. We had known one another for about 2 years before we began to live together. The deceased was 59 at the date of his death. I am 42.

(3) A Grant of Probate of the deceased's will was taken out on [date] and the personal representatives are the deceased's brother and his solicitor.

(4) The will of the deceased made no provision for me apart from a small legacy of £5,000. The will provides for the deceased's residuary estate to be shared between his three adult children, who are defendants to this claim.

(5) The deceased made his will on [date], about a year after we met, and before we started to live together. I believe that the provision that he made in his will recognised the depth of our friendship. Although he talked about changing his will after we began to live together this is something he did not get round to doing.

6.168 *Death and Succession*

(6) When I first met the deceased I was working as a personal assistant earning enough to live in a comfortable way. Like the deceased, I had recently been divorced and had a lump sum of £125,000 as my share of the matrimonial assets. I intended to buy my own house, but as the relationship developed with the deceased it looked as though it may be a lasting relationship and so I continued to live in rented accommodation. Eventually we decided to live together and as the deceased owned his own home it was agreed that I would move in with him. Over the years that we lived together I was very happy to use my savings to pay for holidays and other treats, and to improve the deceased's home. For example, 4 years ago I paid £30,000 to have the kitchen and bathroom refitted. Although the deceased earned far more than I did, we shared the household outgoings. The deceased would pay all the bills, and I would buy the food and pay for dry cleaning, newspapers and the like. I was not able to save anything from my earnings and I now have only £48,000 remaining of my lump sum. I have no other assets apart from the car that the deceased bought for me 2 years ago that is now worth about £4,500. My net monthly income is £1,300 and I exhibit to this statement a schedule setting out my income needs.

(7) I believe the deceased's house to be worth in the region of £350,000. I am unsure as to the extent of the other assets in the estate, but I know that there is a share portfolio, and a car worth about £9,000. The deceased was a member of his employer's pension scheme.

(8) Given the settled and committed nature of my relationship with the deceased, my contribution in looking after the deceased and the home for 6 years, I ask the court to find that in all the circumstances it is unreasonable for there to be no provision for me from the deceased's estate apart from the legacy of £5,000. The beneficiaries of the residuary estate are all over 25 years and have good jobs and own their own homes. I am left after 6 years with very little capital. Had I invested my lump sum in a property as I had initially intended I would have been in a much better financial position than I am now. Although my earnings are sufficient to live on in a modest way, since living with the deceased I have become accustomed to living to a much higher standard.

(9) I therefore ask for sufficient financial provision to be made for me from the estate by way of a lump sum payment to enable me to rehouse myself and provide a financial cushion.

DATED this   day of

Statement of Truth

The claimant believes that the facts stated in this witness statement are true.

Signed . . . .

6.169

Witness statement of dependant in support of claim for provision from estate and application for permission to proceed outside the time-limits

IN THE [ ] COUNTY COURT   CLAIM NUMBER
IN THE MATTER OF

Precedents **6.169**

An application under s 1 of the Inheritance (Provision for Family and Dependants) Act 1975
AND IN THE MATTER OF

The estate of [name] deceased
BETWEEN:

	[name]	Claimant
And		
	[name] Administrator of [name], deceased	1st Defendant
And		
	[name]	2nd Defendant
And		
	[name]	3rd Defendant

WITNESS STATEMENT OF [name]

I, [name], of [name] say as follows:

(1) I make this statement in support of my claim for provision from the estate of [name] ('the deceased') and in support of my application for permission to proceed with my claim notwithstanding that the time-limit for bringing a claim has expired.

(2) The deceased died on [date] and a Grant of Letters of Administration was taken out by the deceased's brother, [name] on [date]. The deceased's mother, [name] and her brother are the only beneficiaries of the estate. To my knowledge they are both very comfortable financially and have no particular need of the windfall that the deceased's death will bring them.

(3) I believe that the deceased's estate to be valued at a figure in the region of £850,000.

(4) The deceased and I had known each other from our schooldays, and after leaving school had always kept in touch. About 5 years ago we began to see one another on a more serious basis, and although we never lived together, we had a very close relationship. I am now 38 and the deceased was 36 when she died from cancer.

(5) The deceased had a very successful career as an actuary and had never married. She had very high earnings and had also amassed savings. I was at that time, and I still am trying to make a living as an artist. Initially I was fortunate to be able to use rooms rent free in a friend's office as a studio, but about 4 years ago my friend sold the offices and I had nowhere to go. I could not afford to pay a market rent. The deceased offered to pay the rent on a studio for me and so I signed a 7-year lease and every month since then until her death she gave me £650 for this purpose. This was paid by standing order direct to the landlord's bank account. She was very generous in other ways as well because she was aware that I was always struggling financially. She would frequently write out cheques to pay my bills when she knew that I did not have enough to pay them and she bought most of my clothes. The deceased invariably paid when we went out for meals and she always paid for a holiday for the two of us twice a year.

(6) As will be apparent from my trading accounts for the last two financial years, copies of which are exhibited to this statement as [ ], my income from my business is not sufficient to discharge all my outgoings that are set out on the schedule exhibited as [ ]. The plain fact is that I was unable to make ends meet without the considerable cash injections I received from the deceased, which I would estimate at about £900 per month taking into account everything that the deceased paid for on my behalf. I am now very heavily overdrawn at the bank having had to meet the cost of my studio myself for several months as well as having to pay for many things that the deceased would have helped me with had she been alive.

(7) In these circumstances I ask the court to find that the deceased was maintaining me at the date of her death and that it is unreasonable that I receive no provision from her estate.

(8) I am aware that my claim is brought outside the time-limit but for the reasons set out below I ask the court to give me permission to proceed with my claim.

(9) The deceased was diagnosed with cancer and died within a very short space of time. When she knew she was ill, her mother moved into her home to be with her. I visited her every day, and did what I could to make her final days comfortable.

(10) I was not sure whether or not her mother knew the extent to which the deceased supported me and I did not mention it until after her death when I felt I had to say something about the standing order for the rent for my studio. The deceased's mother discussed it with her brother and they agreed that they would continue to pay it for a few months until I could make other arrangements. This they did for 3 months.

(11) The deceased's brother then wrote to me to say that the payments would end with immediate effect. I was grateful to them for continuing the payments for as long as they had so I did not say anything. However, a few months later when I realised that I was getting into a mess financially, I went to see my bank manager.

(12) He advised me to see a solicitor which I did. He said I should get Counsel's opinion on whether I could make a claim against the estate. I was rather put off by the cost of this, and also I felt it was rather distasteful. However, after another interview with my bank manager I decided that I had no alternative and I instructed my solicitor to proceed.

(13) By this time the Grant had been taken out and 8 months had elapsed. I realise that I should have taken action sooner, but I was reluctant to do so largely because it seemed rather grasping. However, the reality is that for over 3 years the deceased subsidised my living expenses to a very large degree, and I find it impossible to make ends meet without that financial help.

(14) Furthermore, I would not have taken on the commitment of rented studio accommodation if the deceased had not offered to pay for it.

(15) In the circumstances I ask the court to accept that I have a good claim for provision from the deceased's estate and that it would be unjust to prevent me from proceeding with that claim because for good reasons I did not start my claim until 2 months after the expiry of the time-limit.

DATED this   day of

Statement of Truth

The claimant believes that the facts stated in this witness statement are true.

Signed ....

6.170

Witness statement of cohabitant in support of claim for provision for herself and child of the family, for an interim payment and for the deceased's beneficial interest in jointly owned property to be treated as part of his net estate

IN THE [ ] COUNTY COURT   CLAIM NUMBER
IN THE MATTER OF

An application under s 1 of the Inheritance (Provision for Family and Dependants) Act 1975
AND IN THE MATTER OF

The estate of [name], deceased
BETWEEN:

                                      A   Claimant

And

                     Personal Representative(s) of [name], deceased   1st Defendants

And

                                      B   2nd Defendant

WITNESS STATEMENT OF [name]

I, [name], of [address] say as follows:

(1) I make this statement in support of my claim for provision from the estate of [name] ('the deceased').

(2) The deceased and I began to cohabit 8 years ago, when he moved into my house. We continued to live together until the deceased was killed in a road traffic accident on [date]. There are two children of our relationship, C born on [date] who is five and D born on [date] who is three. I am 36 years old and the deceased was 48 when he died.

(3) A Grant of Probate of the deceased's will was taken out by his wife, B, and his solicitor on [date].

(4) As far as I am aware, the estate comprises savings and investments of about £280,000. The deceased's beneficial interest in his former matrimonial home passed to B as the surviving joint owner on his death. I estimate the value of that interest at £230,000 and I ask the court to direct that this be treated as part of the deceased's net estate. If this is not treated as part of the deceased's net estate I would say that the net estate will not be of sufficient size to make reasonable provision for myself and the children.

(5) The deceased remained married to B up until his death. They did not have any children. He had left her in order to live with me and she has never

agreed to a divorce. Even though he could have divorced her after 5 years' separation he said that he could not be bothered getting involved with solicitors and he did not want to have an argument with her over the financial side of things. We never discussed the question of a will. I simply took it that he had made provision for me and the children. As it was, he had made a will soon after he was married to B in which he left everything to her, and he had clearly forgotten to revise it in the light of his changed circumstances.

(6) The house in which I live is in my sole name. It is worth about £275,000 and is subject to a mortgage. The equity in the property is about £140,000. I had bought the property with my divorce settlement before I met the deceased. At the time I met the deceased I was working and earning enough to pay the mortgage and live in a modest way. I continued to work after the deceased came to live with me, but because we then pooled our resources we lived to a much better standard.

(7) When C was born, I gave up work and the deceased then had to support us entirely from his earnings. D was born a couple of years later and I have not returned to work. I would find it difficult to earn enough to keep the family afloat because of my limited earning capacity and the cost of child care. As at the date of his death, the deceased was earning £5,300 net per month and he paid £2,250 per month into my bank account for the mortgage and housekeeping. I doubt that I could earn much more than £800 per month in a full-time job. As will be seen from the schedule of outgoings exhibited at [ ] the mortgage repayments alone are £525 and the shortfall of my present income from State benefits over routine expenditure is considerable. I exhibit to this statement marked SB2, a letter from my bank manager dated [*date*] warning me that I have exceeded my overdraft limit, together with my bank statements since the death of the deceased. It will be apparent that I am getting very heavily into debt simply by discharging the routine household accounts without the standing order payment of £2,250 that was paid into my account every month by the deceased.

(8) I am in a desperate financial situation. I have no capital other than the equity in my house, and no prospect of being able to earn enough to support myself and the two children. B has a good job and was not in need of maintenance from the deceased. I am aware that the former matrimonial home has a small mortgage and that it is larger than is necessary for one person. B could rehouse herself in a suitable property mortgage free with her own share of the former matrimonial home.

(9) In the circumstances, I ask for provision to be made for me and the children from the deceased's estate, for the deceased's share of his former matrimonial home to be treated as part of his net estate, and for interim provision to be made for me from the estate so that the children and I can pay the bills as they fall due and repay my overdraft.

DATED this   day of

Statement of Truth

The claimant believes that the facts stated in this witness statement are true.

Signed . . . .

6.171

Witness statement of adult in support of claim for provision from estate of deceased step-parent

IN THE [ ] COUNTY COURT CLAIM NUMBER
IN THE MATTER OF

An application under s 1 of the Inheritance (Provision for Family and Dependants) Act 1975
AND IN THE MATTER OF

The estate of [name], deceased
BETWEEN:

	A	Claimant
and		
	AB and CD the personal representatives of the estate of [name], deceased	1st Defendants
and		
	B	2nd Defendant

STATEMENT OF [name]

I, [name], of [address] make this statement in support of my claim for provision from the estate of my late step-father, [name] ('the deceased').

(1) The deceased died on [date] aged 83. A Grant of Probate was taken out by the executors of his will, the first defendants. The sole beneficiary of the will, as my mother pre-deceased him, is his daughter, my step-sister, B.

(2) I am 53 years of age. My mother and the deceased were married when I was 3 years of age. B was born 8 years after their marriage. She is 45 and for the past 20 years has lived in New Zealand.

(3) My mother was never married to my father and I have never had any knowledge of his identity or whereabouts. The deceased treated me as his own child, but once B was born I did not feel that our relationship was quite the same as it had been before. He clearly preferred B to me, and this obviously had implications for my own relationship with my half-sister.

(4) I have never moved out of Oakwood. I have a job working at the local library. I have never married. About 15 years ago my mother's health began to fail. I took on the shopping and household chores which the deceased was not inclined to do himself and effectively ran the house for them. In addition, I took my mother to medical appointments, and generally ran them both about as the deceased could not drive.

(5) My mother died 3 years ago. She left her estate to the deceased. After her death I continued to look after the deceased and his house, and to do the garden and such other chores as I could manage. About a year before his death the deceased agreed that I could stay in the house with him so that I would be there if he needed any help in the night. The deceased was never

one for spending money on outside help if someone would do it for him for nothing. I kept my own home although I did not live there, and I paid my own way in terms of food. Even though I know that the deceased was grateful for what I did, my impression was that he saw me as doing my duty, effectively repaying his kindness in bringing me up as his daughter.

(6) I have not been as fortunate in life as my half-sister. She has married well and has no particular need of the deceased's estate. I have always put my mother and the deceased first, and have attended to their needs selflessly. I own a modest home, and have earnings of £1,250 per month net. Otherwise I have no assets or income. Had the deceased pre-deceased my mother, I would have inherited half the combined estates on her death, and it seems grossly unfair that I should now inherit nothing, particularly bearing in mind the contribution I made in caring for them both.

(7) I therefore ask the court to find that it is unreasonable for no provision to have been made for me from the deceased's estate and to make provision for me by way of a lump sum.

DATED this   day of

Statement of Truth

The claimant believes that the facts stated in this witness statement are true.

Signed . . . .

6.172

Witness statement of personal representatives in answer to claim

IN THE [ ] COUNTY COURT   CLAIM NUMBER
IN THE MATTER OF

An application under s 1 of the Inheritance (Provision for Family and Dependants) Act 1975
AND IN THE MATTER OF

The estate of [name], deceased
BETWEEN:

A	Claimant
and	
Personal Representatives of [name], deceased	1st Defendant(s)
and	
B	2nd Defendant

WITNESS STATEMENT OF 1st DEFENDANTS

I/WE, [name(s)] of [address]

Make this statement in answer to the application by A for provision from the estate of [name], deceased ('the deceased').

(1) We are the personal representatives of the deceased.

(2) The grant of probate was granted to us out of the [ ] District Registry on [date]. Exhibited to this statement as PR1 is a true copy of the grant of probate.

(3) The gross value of the deceased's estate for probate purposes was £280,245 consisting of the following:

Cash at	£6,500
Cash at	£3,400
Shares per schedule PR2	£270,345

(4) The deceased was in addition entitled to receive a death benefit from his employers under the terms of the company pension scheme. No nomination was made in respect of this and the payment will be made at the discretion of the trustees of the scheme. The death benefit amounts to £144,000.

(5) The liabilities of the deceased at the date of his death, including funeral expenses, are set out in the schedule marked PR3 annexed hereto.

(6) The estate has not yet been fully administered.

(7) The sole beneficiary of the estate in accordance with the deceased's will is his widow, B. A copy of the deceased's will dated [date] is exhibited and marked PR4.

(8) The following matters are relevant to the exercise of the court's discretion:

[give details]

DATED this   day of

Statement of Truth

The first defendants believe that the facts stated in this witness statement are true.

Signed ....

6.173

Specimen directions on application for provision from estate

IN THE [ ] COUNTY COURT   CLAIM NUMBER

IN THE MATTER OF

An application under s 1 of the Inheritance (Provision for Family and Dependants) Act 1975
AND IN THE MATTER OF

The estate of [name], deceased
BETWEEN:

                              A   Claimant

and

	Personal Representative(s) of [name], deceased	1st Defendant(s)

and

	B	2nd Defendant

UPON HEARING the solicitors for all parties

IT IS ORDERED THAT:

(1) The application for an interim payment will be heard on the first available date after 28 days with a time estimate of one hour.

(2) The 2nd defendant shall by 4pm on [date] file and serve a witness statement in answer to the application for provision from the estate.

(3) The claimant shall by 4pm on [date] file and serve a witness statement in reply, if so advised.

(4) The claim for provision from the estate will be heard on the first available date after 56 days with a time estimate of one day.

(5) Costs in the case.

6.174

Order on application for interim payment

IN THE [ ] COUNTY COURT   CLAIM NUMBER
IN THE MATTER OF

An application under s 1 of the Inheritance (Provision for Family and Dependants) Act 1975
AND IN THE MATTER OF

The estate of [name], deceased
BETWEEN:

	A	Claimant

and

	Personal Representative(s) of [name], deceased	1st Defendant(s)

and

	B	2nd Defendant

UPON HEARING the solicitors for both parties

IT IS ORDERED THAT

(1) [name] and [name] as the executors of the will of [name] deceased shall pay to the claimant from the net estate of the deceased

(a) a lump sum payment of £2,500 by 4 pm on [date]
(b) periodical payments at the rate of £750 per month payable monthly in advance from the date of this order until the final hearing of the claim or further order.

(2) The payments ordered to be made by paragraph (1) of this order shall be made on condition that they are accounted for by the claimant following the making of a final order herein.

(3) The costs of this application shall be reserved to the final hearing.

DATED this   day of

6.175

Order on application for provision from estate

IN THE [ ] COUNTY COURT   CLAIM NUMBER
IN THE MATTER OF

An application under s 1 of the Inheritance (Provision for Family and Dependants) Act 1975
AND IN THE MATTER OF

The estate of [name], deceased
BETWEEN:

	A	Claimant
and		
	Personal Representative(s) of [name], deceased	1st Defendant(s)
and		
	B	2nd Defendant

UPON HEARING COUNSEL FOR ALL PARTIES

AND UPON the court being satisfied that the disposition of the deceased's estate by his will dated [date] is not such as to make reasonable provision for the claimant and the children of the deceased [name] d.o.b. [date] and [name] d.o.b. [date].

IT IS ORDERED THAT:

(1) The beneficial half share of the deceased in the property [address] shall be treated as part of the net estate of the deceased.

(2) [name] and [name], the executors of the will of the deceased dated [date] shall pay the claimant a lump sum of £120,000, payable as to £50,000 by 4pm on [date] And as to the balance, less the sums to be accounted for by the claimant pursuant to the order dated [date], by 4pm on [date].

(3) The will of the deceased shall have effect and shall be deemed to have had such effect as from the death of the deceased.

6.175 Death and Succession

(4) The costs of the claimant shall be subject to a detailed assessment in default of agreement and paid out of the net estate of the deceased.

DATED this   day of

Chapter 7
PENSION RIGHTS OF COHABITANTS

LAW AND PRACTICE

Introduction

7.1 Individuals may acquire rights to pensions benefits during their lifetimes. If the individual lives to pension age, a pension becomes payable until death. However, there are benefits which are paid to other persons on the basis of the individual's contributions and entitlement. In some cases, these benefits are restricted to pensions for widows and widowers and dependent children. However, there are circumstances under which dependants or other persons who are not married to the person entitled to the pension can benefit. The purpose of this chapter is to look at the circumstances in which a cohabitant may benefit from the pension arrangements of his or her partner. For ease of reference, the person having the primary pension rights is referred to as 'the pension holder'.

The position of a married couple who are divorced has been altered radically over the past three decades in relation to pension benefits. 'Earmarking' (or 'pension attachment' as it is more formally termed), under which a divorced spouse may be awarded a lump sum or pension benefits out of the pension entitlement of the other spouse when that benefit becomes payable, was introduced by the Pensions Act 1995.

The Welfare Reform and Pensions Act 1999 introduced pension sharing on divorce (or nullity, but not judicial separation), under which courts have the power on the breakdown of a marriage to split existing pension benefits between the spouses. The non-pension holder may be awarded a pension credit which creates an indefeasible pension for that person and can (depending on the circumstances) either be left in the existing scheme as specific benefits for that former spouse ('internal transfer') or transferred out to other permitted pension arrangements ('external transfer').

None of these provisions apply to cohabitants, who are not married or in a civil partnership.

Civil partnerships

7.2 The Civil Partnership Act 2004[1], as well as the extending pension attachment and pension sharing to civil partners on relationship breakdown,

7.2 *Pension Rights of Cohabitants*

enabled amendments to be made to pensions legislation by statutory instrument to implement the changes necessary for civil partners to be treated in the same way as married couples. Civil partnership was extended to opposite-sex couples from 2 December 2019 by the Civil Partnerships, Marriages and Deaths (Registration etc) Act 2019 and the Civil Partnership (Opposite-sex Couples) Regulations 2019[2]. State pension rights have been extended to civil partners under the old state scheme (see **7.5**) so that civil partners were able to claim a basic state pension using their civil partner's NI contribution record, where the contributing civil partner was born on or after 5 April 1950 and had attained state pension age prior to 6 April 2016. Under the new state pension scheme (see **7.6**) for those who reach state pension age from 6 April 2016, entitlement is based on the individual's own National Insurance record only and eligibility to inherit a state pension has ended.

Surviving civil partners of members of contracted-out schemes are eligible for survivors' benefits based on contracted-out rights earned by service from 6 April 1988. Additionally, they were eligible for survivors' benefits based upon non-contracted out pensionable service from 5 December 2005. Civil partners did not, therefore, enjoy full equality with married couples in relation to survivors' benefits. Survivors' benefits in respect of pre-5 December 2005 non-contracted-out service depended upon an amendment to the relevant scheme rules[3]. This provision was found to be incompatible with EU law by the Supreme Court in *Walker v Innospec Ltd*[4] and had to be disapplied, ensuring in broad terms that survivors' benefits are provided based on pre-5 December 2005 service.

[1] Civil Partnership Act 2004, c 33, s 255.
[2] SI 2019/1458.
[3] Equality Act 2010, Sch 9, para 18(1).
[4] [2017] UKSC 47.

State retirement pension

Introduction

7.3 The state retirement pension (SRP) is a state benefit payable on reaching pensionable age to those with a sufficient National Insurance record. The old state scheme applies to those who reached pensionable age prior to 6 April 2016 (regardless of whether they took their pension by this date or deferred taking it). The Pensions Act 2014 introduced a new state pension scheme for those who reach pensionable age on or after 6 April 2016. The state pensions of individuals already in the old scheme will not be affected by the changes contained in the 2014 Act. Transitional arrangements apply to those who have qualifying years of National Insurance contributions before 6 April 2016, but who attain pensionable age after that date.

Pensionable age

7.4 Pensionable age is currently 65 for men born before 6 December 1953. The age at which women can claim their SRP was 60 until April 2010. The age was equalised at 65 for both men and women by November 2018, having been gradually phased in. Women born before 6 April 1950 have not been affected by the change; women born after 6 December 1953 have a new pensionable age of 65. Further changes mean that the age at which a person will be able to claim their SRP will reach (a) age 66 for both men and women by October 2020; (b) age 67 by between 2026 and 2028; (c) age 68 by between 2037 and 2039[1].

A state pension age calculator can be found at https://www.gov.uk/state-pension-age.

[1] Pensions Act 1995, Sch 4, Part 1 as amended by the Pensions Act 2007, the Pensions Act 2011 and the Pensions Act 2014, ss 26 and 27.

The old scheme

7.5 Category A SRP, a flat rate basic pension, was payable on a person's own NIC record, a full record being 30 years' worth for those who reached pensionable age on or after 6 April 2016. Those who were divorced or former civil partners, however, could combine their own NICs, if insufficient alone, with those of their former spouse or former civil partner to produce a Category A SRP. Subsequent re-partnering as cohabitants does not interfere with such an entitlement; marriage or civil partnership post-divorce/dissolution and prior to the SRP claim, however, did prevent the entitlement based on joint NICs.

Married people and civil partners could also become entitled to a Category B SRP pension by virtue of their spouse's or civil partner's contributions, if they did not have sufficient contributions to get a full basic state pension. Widows, widowers and surviving civil partners can also claim a category B pension (or an increase in their own category A pension) based on their late spouse's or late civil partner's NICs, where the widowed spouse or civil partner has reached pensionable age before 6 April 2016. These rules are complex. However, for cohabitants, no such claim can be made: there is no provision to base an SRP entitlement on the NICs of a cohabitant.

Bereavement benefits could be claimed by widow(er)s and surviving civil partners who are bereaved under pension age. Where the deceased died before 6 April 2017, the benefits included a bereavement payment (a one-off payment), a bereavement allowance (a monthly payment previously referred to as widow's pension) and a widowed parent's allowance[1] (where the applicant was entitled to child benefit for at least one child and the deceased was the child's parent). In respect of deaths after 6 April 2017, these benefits have been grouped together as bereavement support payment (see **7.6**).

It was possible to defer a SRP claim so as to enhance its value (or receive a lump sum). Whilst spouses and civil partners can inherit the benefits of such deferral should their spouse or civil partner die whilst deferring, this inheritance was not available to cohabitants: for them, the value of the late partner's deferral is lost.

The Additional State Pension (ASP) was a component of the old state scheme and consisted of the State Second Pension (S2P) and the State Earnings Related Pension Scheme (SERPS), which S2P replaced as from April 2002. However, existing SERPS entitlements were preserved. ASP was payable as an addition

7.5 Pension Rights of Cohabitants

to the SRP. The use of a former spouse's contributions to increase state pension applied only to the basic state pension and not to ASP. ASP closed on 5 April 2016 on the introduction of the new state scheme. Employees generally paid additional contributions to qualify for ASP, unless they were a member of an occupational pension scheme and their employment was contracted out of ASP. Contracting out for defined contribution pension schemes (both occupational and personal pension schemes) was abolished from 6 April 2012[2]. Members of such schemes were contracted back into ASP. Contracting out of defined benefit pension schemes was abolished when the new state scheme was brought into effect on 6 April 2016[3].

In the case of married couples and civil partners, it was possible to make a pension sharing order in respect of ASP. This is still possible where the transferor is in the old scheme (ie reached pensionable age before 6 April 2016). It is also possible where the transferor is in the new scheme (having reached pensionable age on or after 6 April 2016), if the proceedings for divorce or dissolution were commenced prior to this date. Where proceedings are commenced on or after 6 April 2016, pension sharing in respect of the state pension of the person in the new scheme is limited to their 'protected payments' only, ie their weekly transitional rate pension to the extent that it exceeds the full rate of the new single tier pension. These provisions do not benefit cohabitants.

Provisions which allowed widow(er)s and surviving civil partners to inherit a proportion of their late spouse's or late civil partner's ASP did _not_ benefit cohabitants who are not married or civil partners.

[1] It was held in *Re McLaughlin's Application for Judicial Review (Northern Ireland)* [2018] UKSC 48 that the preclusion of entitlement to widowed parent's allowance by a surviving unmarried partner of the deceased was incompatible with art 14 of the ECHR read with art 8.
[2] Pensions Act 2007, s 15(1) and Sch 4.
[3] Pensions Act 2014, s 24.

The new state scheme

7.6 The new state single tier pension (STP) was introduced by the Pensions Act 2014 and came into force on 6 April 2016. It applies to those who reach pensionable age on or after 6 April 2016, ie men who were born on or after 6 April 1951 and women who were born on or after 6 April 1953. There is now a qualifying period of 35 years of NI contributions in order to qualify for the full rate as compared with the 30 year qualifying period under the old state scheme. STP is a single, flat rate payment with no ASP. A person who has fewer than 35 qualifying years (but not less than 10 qualifying years) is entitled to a reduced rate of STP. Contributions made after a person has already accrued 35 qualifying years will not provide any increased pension (in contrast with the old state scheme). A transitional rate of STP is payable to a person falling within the new scheme, who has at least the minimum number of qualifying years and at least one qualifying year attributable to tax years prior to the introduction of STP. Such a person will be entitled to a 'foundation amount' representing the higher of their entitlement under the new scheme or under the current scheme. A person may opt to defer claiming his/her state pension under the new state scheme to provide an increase in their weekly pension. There is, however, no lump sum option now available. There is no equivalent (with very limited exceptions) to the category B pension under the current scheme, whereby a person may obtain a pension in reliance on their spouse's/civil partner's contributions record. Similarly, it is no longer possible to rely under the new state scheme on the contributions of a former spouse or civil partner on death or on divorce/dissolution. As a result of this change, cohabitants are not now as adversely treated as was the case prior to 6 April 2016.

Bereavement support payment is payable under the Pensions Act 2014, s 30 in place of the bereavement benefits discussed at **7.5** where the deceased died on or after 6 April 2017, where the claimant was the spouse or civil partner of the deceased and where he/she is under state pension age. It is payable at a higher rate if the claimant is entitled to child benefit or pregnant when the deceased died. In *Jackson v Secretary of State for Work and Pensions*[1], it was held that the Pensions Act, s 30(4)(a), read with s 30(1), was incompatible with art 14, read with art 8, of the ECHR in so far as it empowered the Secretary of State to order by regulations that bereavement support payment be paid at a higher rate in the case of a person who was pregnant or entitled to child benefit only if they were the spouse or civil partner of the deceased.

[1] [2020] EWHC 183 (Admin) applying *McLaughlin* (see fn 6 above).

Taxation of pension schemes

Taxation of pension schemes

7.7 The taxation of pension schemes is a complex area, a detailed discussion of which is outside the scope of this work. The Finance Act 2004 introduced provisions intended to simplify the taxation of pension schemes as from April 2006. There are two limits on pension contributions: the lifetime allowance and the annual allowance. For 2020/21, the lifetime allowance (the total amount of pension savings that can benefit from tax relief) is £1,073,100. The annual allowance (the annual limit of tax relief on contributions) is £40,000 for 2020/21. Significant changes to the access to money purchase pension funds were introduced by the Taxation of Pensions Act 2014 with effect from 6 April 2015. They permit an individual with defined contribution arrangements, who is above the minimum pension age (currently age 55: see below), to take an unlimited amount of income from their pension fund by what is known as 'flexi access drawdown'. Under flexi access drawdown, 25% is available tax-free with the balance being taxed at the individual's marginal rate of income tax. Those who take an income from their pension by way of flexi access drawdown have their further pension contributions restricted to a money purchase annual allowance of £4,000 per annum (2020/21) aimed at restricting the ability to recycle income into a new pension arrangement to take further tax-free lump sum payments. For funds not in drawdown, it is possible to offer an uncrystallised funds pension lump sum, which may be in the form of a single payment representing all benefits within the scheme or by way of stage payments. Each payment is considered as part tax-free cash (25%) and the remainder (75%) is taxed at the individual's marginal rate.

Changes were also made in relation to the tax charge on defined contribution pension funds on death. Prior to 6 April 2015, where death occurred before

7.7 Pension Rights of Cohabitants

age 75, the pension fund, when crystallised (that is, already in a drawdown account), was subject to a 55% tax charge if paid as a lump sum or at the dependant's marginal rate, if drawn down. If the fund was uncrystallised, it could be taken tax-free as a lump sum or at the dependant's marginal rate, if drawn down. Where death occurred at age 75 or over, the position was – in the case of both crystallised and uncrystallised benefits – that there was a tax charge of 55% if the funds were paid as a lump sum or at the dependant's marginal rate, if drawn down.

Under the system in relation to payments made on or after 6 April 2015 (rather than in respect of deaths occurring on or after that date), where death occurs before age 75, the fund (whether crystallised or uncrystallised) may be taken tax-free either as a lump sum or as a drawn down pension by any beneficiary.

Where death occurs at age 75 or over, there is a tax charge of the recipient's marginal rate from 2016/17 whether paid as a lump sum or drawn down. These changes may increase the flexibility available to cohabitants in their financial planning.

Currently, individuals cannot commence taking their pensions before age 55, unless they have a 'protected retirement age'[1]. There are also some other exceptions, most notably, the uniformed services schemes and those suffering from a terminal illness. The minimum pension age will increase from age 55 to age 57 in 2028. It will then remain 10 years below the state pension age.

The payment of a pension may be guaranteed for a fixed period. Where the pension holder dies before the end of that period and payments continue to be paid to the estate, they will be subject to inheritance tax. However, pension payments made to the deceased's widow, widower or surviving civil partner are not subject to inheritance tax. If a lump sum death benefit is payable to the deceased pension holder's personal representatives either by right or because there is no-one else who qualifies for the payment, or if the deceased could, up until death, have signed a nomination, which bound the trustees of a pension scheme to make payment to a person named by the deceased, the lump sum will be an asset of the deceased's estate liable to inheritance tax. A binding nomination is different from a letter of wishes (see Precedent at 6.158). A letter of wishes records what the deceased would like to happen with the death benefit and does not bind the trustees of a pension scheme. Many pension schemes and policies provide a form referred to as a nomination, but which usually contains a statement that the trustees are not bound to follow the deceased's wishes. If this is the case, the form is a letter of wishes and not a binding nomination. Most pension schemes and personal pension policies allow a member to dispose of the death benefits and to make changes to the benefits that they are entitled to. Usually, the member can nominate or appoint the death benefits to someone else, assign the death benefits into a trust, or make changes to the pension benefits they intend to take and when they intend to take them. If the deceased made a nomination, appointment or assignment or made any changes to the pension benefits in the 2 years prior to death, a liability to inheritance tax may have arisen. Where the death benefits are assigned into a trust, the pension scheme trustees will not exercise any discretion and are obliged to make payment to the trustees appointed by the pension holder, who also nominates the potential beneficiaries who may be considered by those trustees. In order to keep the lump sum death benefits outside the pension holder's estate for inheritance tax purposes, the trust needs to provide for the distribution of the lump sum death benefits to someone other than the policy holder's estate. This mechanism does give the policy holder greater certainty over the distribution of the lump sum death benefits. The policy holder may normally alter the trustees and preferred beneficiaries at a later stage.

[1] Ie those who had unqualified rights, as at 5 April 2006, to take a pension before the normal minimum pension age.

Inheritance (Provision for Family and Dependants) Act 1975

7.8 Where a cohabitant is able to make a claim under the Inheritance (Provision for Family and Dependants) Act 1975 (see **6.15–6.88**), death benefits payable under a pension scheme will not normally form part of the deceased's net estate, unless a lump sum death benefit was paid as of right to the deceased's personal representatives as opposed to a sum paid to a beneficiary pursuant to an exercise of discretion by the trustees (1975 Act, s 25(1)(a)). It should, however, be noted that the definition of 'net estate' in s 25(1)(c) of the 1975 Act includes any sum of money . . . which is to be treated for the purposes of the 1975 Act as part of the deceased's net estate by virtue of any enactment under s 8(1) of the 1975 Act; this could include a payment derived from a statutory public sector pension scheme. Furthermore, s 10 of the 1975 Act confers on the court the power to recover money disposed of by the deceased in the 7 years prior to death otherwise than for full valuable consideration and with the intention of defeating an application under the 1975 Act. This might include excessive contributions made to a pension scheme. Any monies recovered under s 10 of the 1975 Act form part of the deceased's net estate for the purposes of a claim.

Occupational pension schemes

Structure

7.9 Occupational pension schemes are schemes that are provided by employers and in the private sector are set up under a trust deed so that the assets are independent of the employer. There are also various schemes for public sector workers (eg the police, the civil service and the armed forces), which are statutorily based and have their own regulations[1].

The vast majority of private sector occupational pension schemes qualify for income tax relief on contributions and the scheme itself is exempt from income tax and capital gains tax so that the fund accumulates tax free[2].

As the benefits from registered schemes are limited both as to contributions and benefits, it is possible for employers to top up or replace these schemes with unregistered schemes which do not qualify for tax relief and so are not restricted as to the benefits that they can provide. Such schemes are usually set

7.9 Pension Rights of Cohabitants

up for individuals or small groups of employees and there is no reason why their rules should not include benefits for unmarried couples.

[1] Such schemes were the subject of major reforms contained in the Public Service Pensions Act 2013, which took effect (other than in relation to the Local Government Pension Scheme where the reforms took effect in April 2014) from April 2015.
[2] Pensions Act 2004, c 35.

Pensions for surviving dependants and nominees

7.10 The statutory framework for these schemes[1] formerly restricted all benefits that could be paid to persons other than the pension holder. In the case of the death in service of the pension holder in a final salary scheme, pensions can only be paid to the pension holder's (former) widow or widower, (former) civil partner or for children and dependants. The widow or widower's or civil partner's pension is restricted to two-thirds of the maximum pension that the pension holder would have been entitled to at pension age. Benefits will depend upon whether the member died whilst an active member (ie one who was still contributing), a deferred member (ie a member who is no longer an active member, but had still to draw benefits) or was already drawing retirement benefits.

Cohabitants or their children may qualify for a death in service pension as *dependants* of the pension holder. A dependant is a person who was financially dependent on the employee, was mutually financially dependent[2] or dependent by virtue of physical or mental impairment[3]. Although the regulations allow pensions to be paid to adult dependants in these circumstances, some company schemes restrict pensions to widows and widowers or civil partners and this would need to be checked in the scheme's booklet issued to members. Some schemes restrict dependant's pension for a surviving cohabitant to those who have, for example, lived together as a couple (whether married or in a civil partnership) for, say, 2 years or more. Much will depend upon the terms of the individual scheme. The provision of incorrect information by a scheme as to entitlement to a survivor's pension will not override the terms of the scheme[4]. In the case of another local government pension scheme[5], the Supreme Court in *Re Brewster* disapplied the requirement in the relevant Regulations for a nomination, enabling a survivor's pension to be paid to a cohabitant of 10 years' standing (and fiancé) of the deceased member. It was held that the requirement for the nomination of a cohabiting partner in the Regulations was incompatible with ECHR, art 14 (prohibition of discrimination) read together with art 1, Protocol 1 (peaceful enjoyment of possessions). This decision does not prevent pension schemes from introducing and enforcing criteria that properly distinguish between different categories of beneficiaries such that a cohabitant would automatically qualify for a widower's pension[6].

Pensions for children have to cease when the child ceases to be dependent, eg ceases full-time education, or reaches the age of 23. If a child is dependent because of physical or mental impairment, dependence can be indefinite. The age 23 limit is also relaxed from 16 September 2016 in certain circumstances, in the case of a money purchase arrangement, to enable a child of a member to receive income from flexi-access drawdown regardless of age. Natural and adopted children qualify automatically, but other children, such as those of a partner from a previous relationship, only qualify if they were dependent financially or by reason of physical or mental impairment at the date of death of the pension holder.

Under the provisions of the Taxation of Pensions Act 2014, Sch 2, Pt 1 (see 7.7), it is possible, in the case of money purchase schemes, from 6 April 2015, for death benefits from a drawdown fund to be paid to *any* beneficiary, eg adult children, a non-dependant cohabitant, a former cohabitant or other non-dependants. Such death benefits may be paid either to a 'nominee' or a 'successor'. Nominees can receive a nominee's drawdown pension and a successor can receive a successor's drawdown pension. A nominee is any individual other than a dependant who is nominated by a member or, where there are no dependants and no individual or charity has been nominated by the member, any individual nominated by the scheme administrator. A successor is someone who inherits any unused drawdown funds on the death of a dependant or nominee or a successor. A successor can be nominated by the previous beneficiary or, where no nomination has been made by the previous beneficiary, by the scheme administrator.

1   Finance Act 2004, s 167 (pension death benefit rules).
2   This can include an unmarried partner of the same or opposite sex who relies on the other's income to maintain a standard of living that depended on the joint income.
3   Finance Act 2004, Sch 28 para 15(3).
4   *Miss Y v Local Government Pension Scheme* (2019) 19 September, PO-27699, Pensions Ombudsman (a survivor's pension for cohabiting partners under the LGPS only became applicable from 1 April 2008; although the scheme had provided incorrect information, it did not have a discretionary power to make an award out the scope of the scheme. Such information may give rise to compensation for distress and inconvenience).
5   *Re Brewster (Northern Ireland)* [2017] UKSC 8.
6   *Mr R v Teachers' Pensions* (2018) 16 August, PO 19086, Pensions Ombudsman (widower's pensions were added to the Teachers' Pension Scheme with effect from 6 April 1988; nominated partners' pensions were added from 1 January 2007. The complainant, who had cohabited with the deceased member for many years, had been formally nominated to receive a surviving partner's pension. He relied upon the decision in *Re Brewster* arguing that the pension he would receive was much less than that payable to a widower and that the requirement for the deceased to pay increased contributions as a requirement for a widower's pension was discriminatory).

Lump sum death in service benefits

7.11 In addition to pensions for surviving dependants and, in the case of money purchase schemes, nominees and successors, registered schemes can also provide lump sum benefits in the event of the death in service of the pension holder. From April 2006, the limits are calculated by reference to the individual's lifetime allowance. If the maximum is payable under the scheme, it can amount to a substantial amount. As discussed at 7.7, the taxation position changed significantly under the provisions contained in the Taxation of Pensions Act 2014.

To avoid the sum being liable to inheritance tax on the death of the employee, the lump sum death benefit is invariably subject to discretionary trusts exercisable by the trustees of the pension scheme. Under the HMRC guidelines[1], tax rules do not set any conditions on who is able to receive lump sum death in service benefits. However, the pension scheme rules may do so.

7.11 Pension Rights of Cohabitants

Beneficiaries of the lump sum can include the employee's personal representatives, potential beneficiaries in the employee's will or a nominated beneficiary as well as dependants. See, further, 7.7.

Therefore, it is essential that where a pension holder wishes to benefit his/her cohabitant in the event of death in service, he/she should complete a letter of wishes form provided by the pension scheme or, if none is provided, a letter of wishes (see **6.158**). This should be sent to the trustees of the pension scheme. It will not bind the trustees; however, they are unlikely to exercise their discretion in favour of an unmarried partner if no letter of wishes has been signed and there are other competing beneficiaries. The jurisdiction of the Pensions Ombudsman may be invoked to overturn the exercise of the trustees' discretion[2]. The trustees have 2 years in which to distribute the lump sum[3]. Where there are competing beneficiaries, trustees often pay the lump sum over to the personal representatives of the employee's estate where it will be dealt with under his will or intestacy. This again underlines the importance of cohabitants making wills if they wish to benefit each other.

Most pension schemes allow lump sums to be paid to a trust for eligible beneficiaries. This is primarily to allow minor children to be provided for, but also gives scope for tax planning through the use of a discretionary trust with the cohabitant as one of the beneficiaries. See, further, 7.7.

[1] Registered Pension Schemes Manual.
[2] See, for example, *Wild v Pensions Ombudsman* [1996] 2 FLR 680 (see **6.6**) and *McGurk v Royal Mail Pension Trustees Limited* (2009) 7 July, ref 74946/2, where the exercise of discretion by the trustee to pay part of a lump sum benefit to a cohabitant was upheld, notwithstanding the existence of a separated spouse and children, as the trustee had all the relevant information that the cohabitant satisfied the criteria for financial dependency.
[3] If the lump sum is distributed after this period, it is an unauthorised payment and a tax charge will be payable.

Personal pension schemes

Structure

7.12 Personal pension schemes were introduced in 1988 (replacing retirement annuity contracts for the self-employed) to encourage mobility of pensions for employees and also to provide a vehicle for the self-employed and those with no company pension scheme. A group personal pension is a collection of personal pensions provided by an employer for employees. Contributions are made to an insurance company or other pension provider with similar tax reliefs to those available to company schemes. On retirement, the fund accumulated may be accessed by the purchase of an annuity (which is currently unusual because of the poor rates now on offer) or by various means of income drawdown, which were liberalised under the Taxation of Pensions Act 2014 (see 7.7). There is no longer any requirement to purchase an annuity at age 75.

A self-invested personal pension (SIPP) is a type of personal pension, in which the member has some control over the underlying investments.

Death benefits

7.13 The position in relation to death benefits derived from personal pensions changed fundamentally from 6 April 2015 under the Taxation of Pensions Act 2014. Before 6 April 2015, the benefits that could be paid depended on whether the funds were crystallised or not. From 6 April 2015, the type of benefits payable depends upon the age of the pension holder as at the date of death.

In the case of death before age 75, the funds can be paid to any beneficiary tax-free as a lump sum, an annuity or as a drawdown pension. A fund which has already been drawn down may be used to purchase an annuity at any time. In the event of death after age 75, the fund may be paid to any beneficiary (taxed at that beneficiary's marginal rate) as a lump sum, annuity or as a drawdown pension. The fund can be paid to a trust (so as not to be subject to inheritance tax as part of the pension holder's estate: see, further, 7.7) as a lump sum subject to a 45% tax charge.

The restriction that income may only be paid to a 'dependant' no longer applies (see **7.10**). Where an individual has been nominated as a beneficiary by the pension holder, they are able to receive pension benefits. Any beneficiary can elect to take an income (including in the form of drawdown) with the advantage that on their death any remaining funds may be passed on to a successor until the fund is eventually exhausted.

Joint-life annuities may also be paid out to any beneficiary.

In the context of cohabitation, it is essential that the pension holder either sets up a trust to receive the return of fund or other benefit with the cohabitant as a beneficiary or nominates their cohabitant as a beneficiary. If the fund becomes payable to the pension holder's personal representatives, it will form part of his or her estate and be liable to inheritance tax because, of course, there is no spouse exemption applicable in the case of cohabitants.

Stakeholder pensions

7.14 Stakeholder pensions were introduced by the Welfare Reform and Pensions Act 1999. They are a type of money purchase/defined contribution pension scheme. The intention was to provide a system of low-cost money purchase pension provision from 6 April 2001. Charges on stakeholder pensions are limited. Stakeholder pensions are available to both employees and the self-employed. Employers had to facilitate access to such schemes by their employees from 8 October 2001. This applied to all employers with more than five employees. Thus, employers have to have at least one designated scheme to which their employees can contribute. Take up since the introduction has been particularly poor and many companies have set up schemes that have not attracted any members. Because of the introduction of auto-enrolment (see **7.15**) with effect from 1 October 2012, the requirement to designate access to a stakeholder pension was removed, although employers may still choose to offer a stakeholder pension, if they so wish, to meet their automatic enrolment obligations, or as an additional savings option.

7.14 Pension Rights of Cohabitants

Contributions are limited to £3,600 gross per annum. Non-earners are able to make contributions up to this limit. Stakeholder pensions have, therefore, been used as a vehicle for tax planning by enabling a non-working cohabitant to build up a pension. Furthermore, on relationship breakdown, a non-working cohabitant may be able to set up a stakeholder pension with contributions funded by voluntary maintenance.

Stakeholder schemes can be set up either under trust in the same way as an occupational scheme or under contract like a personal pension scheme.

The regulations introducing stakeholder pensions[1] did not introduce any new provisions relating to HMRC approval and so schemes have to achieve approval either as a registered scheme if written under trust or as personal pension schemes if under contract.

Therefore, the rules on who can benefit are the same as described above for those two types of scheme. Any cohabitant who contributes to a stakeholder pension will have to establish which type of scheme he or she is joining and how he or she can best ensure that any benefits accrue to his or her partner in the event of his or her death.

[1] Stakeholder Pension Schemes Regulations 2000 (SI 2000/1403).

Auto-enrolment in workplace pension schemes

7.15 A new compulsory pension scheme for employees came into force on 1 October 2012 under the Pensions Act 2008 as amended by the Pensions Act 2011. All eligible employees (but not the self-employed) must be enrolled by their employer in an automatic enrolment (auto-enrolment) scheme, which may be either their employer's pension scheme or a new national pension scheme called NEST (National Employment Savings Trust). These are commonly referred to as 'workplace pensions'. The requirement to enrol employees applies to workers who are aged 22 or over, but under state pension age, who have earnings of more than £10,000 per annum and who work or ordinarily work in the UK. Employees' contributions are supplemented by contributions from employers (a minimum of 3%) and tax relief from the government. Employees must make a specific choice to opt out, if they do not wish to be enrolled in the scheme. NEST is intended to offer low-cost, simple pension provision for those on low to moderate earnings. It is capable of being subject to a pension sharing order in the case of married couples or civil partners.

Other pensions

7.16 Pensions come in all shapes and sizes. The main types of pensions available have been discussed above. However, an awareness when advising cohabitants is required of other types of pensions which may be encountered. For example, small self-administered schemes (SSAS) are a form of occupational pension scheme limited to 12 or fewer members frequently encountered in family businesses.

The Pension Protection Fund (PPF) was established in 2005 by the Pensions Act 2004, Pt 2 to act as a form of insurance to ensure the payment of certain defined benefit occupational pension scheme benefits up to a certain level, if a scheme is underfunded and of insufficient funds to pay liabilities, where the employer is insolvent. Increasingly, given the modern trend towards mobility of employment, foreign pensions are encountered, such as international pension plans established by multi-national companies, Qualifying Recognised Overseas Pensions Schemes (QROPS), Qualifying Non-UK Pension Schemes (QNUPS) and Off-Shore Employer Finance Retirement Benefits Schemes (EFRBS). Specialist advice from an independent financial adviser will be required, when such pensions are encountered.

Children

7.17 Pensions may not be an obvious consideration for cohabitants planning for the future of their children. However, it is possible to put £2,880 per annum into a pension (for example, a stakeholder pension (see **7.14**) or other personal pension (see **7.12**)), which with automatic tax relief will equate to a gross contribution of £3,600 per annum. The child will not be able to access the pension until minimum pension age and will not, therefore, be able to use the funds to purchase a house or to fund education. It is, nonetheless, a savings option for cohabitants alongside, for example, a Junior ISA or premium bonds.

Impact of cohabitation on survivors' pensions

7.18 It is important that a survivor check the impact of cohabitation on any survivor's pension already payable to him/her as this may be lost on cohabitation (as well as on remarriage or the formation of a civil partnership). Until the mid-2000s, most public sector pension schemes provided for a surviving partners' pension to be lost on remarriage or cohabitation. However, reforms at this time included changes to survivors' pensions to reflect changes in social patterns of behaviour, under which the rules providing for a survivor's pension to be removed on remarriage or cohabitation were removed. In general, these changes were not made retrospective[1] with limited exceptions applying to the armed forces, police officers and firefighters. The new public sector pension schemes introduced from April 2015 provide for lifetime survivors' pension schemes.

[1] See, for example, *Mrs Y* (2020) 29 January, PO-23903, Pensions Ombudsman (where a widow's pension terminated on cohabitation; a change to the rules of the Teachers' Pension Scheme applied only in relation to members in pensionable employment after 31 December 2006).

Conclusions

7.19 Pensions are a complex area both for cohabitants and the lawyers advising them. Whether on the formation of a relationship or on the breakdown of cohabitation, the advice of an independent financial adviser will be useful and, in many instances, essential, particularly in the light of the flexibilities now available under the Taxation of Pensions Act 2014. It is

7.19 Pension Rights of Cohabitants

always important with such advice to check the particular terms of the pension scheme or policy involved and, where possible, to sign a letter of wishes or make a nomination in favour of the cohabitant intended to benefit. Without such action, there is no automatic entitlement to benefit from the deceased's partner's pension and it may be necessary to resort to an application under the Inheritance (Provision for Family and Dependants) Act 1975. Any such letter of wishes/nomination needs to be kept under review (eg on the birth of a child). Where cohabitation breaks down during the lifetimes of both parties, the party without (or with lesser) pension rights may be left with little in the way of a remedy in the absence of voluntary off-setting, perhaps provided for by a cohabitation contract. Cohabitants need to view pensions in the wider context of financial planning for retirement and on death alongside other savings and wills.

Chapter 8
PRE-NUPTIAL AGREEMENTS

Part A   LAW AND PRACTICE

Introduction

The law of coverture

8.1

> 'The law supposes that your wife acts under your direction'. Mr. Bumble: 'If the law supposes that, the law is an ass — a idiot. If that's the eye of the law, the law is a bachelor; and the worst I wish the law is that his eye may be opened by experience — by experience.' (Charles Dickens, *Oliver Twist*)

This statement to the parish beadle in the 1838 novel following the confession by his wife that she had, for personal gain, disposed of another's jewellery, whilst provoking the memorable response, reflected an accurate summary of the law of coverture up to that time, whereby the married woman or 'feme covert' was not recognised, in most situations, as having legal rights and obligations separate from those of her husband.

The Bible had proclaimed woman's subservient role to man as punishment for her beguilement by the Devil into the sinful eating of the forbidden fruit:

> 'I will greatly multiply your pain in childbearing; in pain you shall bring forth children, yet your desire shall be for your husband, and he shall rule over you.'[1]

Hence, marriage was the legal embodiment of this scriptural command of man and woman having become one flesh[2]. As Blackstone observed:

> ' . . . the very being of legal existence of the woman is suspended during marriage, or at least is incorporated and consolidated into that of the husband under whose wing, protection and cover, she performs everything . . . '[3]

From the Norman invasion of 1066 until the Married Women's Property Act 1882 came into force, the wife's existence became one with that of her husband and such property as she might be possessed of upon her marriage or became possessed of during the marriage belonged, by the *ius mariti*, to him.

Prior to 1066, the Vikings had first started their forays into Britain in 789AD and, thereafter, over time their influence ensured a growing diminution in the role of women in society from that which it had been under the Anglo-Saxons, who had, in some respects, followed the example of their Roman predecessors[4]

8.1 Pre-nuptial Agreements

and permitted women to hold certain positions of authority[5], to own property, as single women to decide whether or not to enter into marriage and on entering marriage to receive a dowry from their husbands, which they were permitted to keep[6]. The Norman invasion, however, somewhat uniquely when compared with the rest of Europe where, mostly, a 'law of community of property' applied, introduced the Law of Normandy, under which the woman's role in marriage was little more than one of servitude to her husband with the woman regarded as a 'subservient chattel' with no independent legal personality, no rights to own property and on breakdown of the marital relationship only limited rights to maintenance[7].

This role for women under the law in England was to continue for many centuries, so that by the start of Victoria's reign in 1837, married women's rights were few[8]. Accordingly, in the face of the husband's right upon marriage to his wife's property and her earnings, if any, pre-nuptial or ante-nuptial[9] settlements, whereby a woman of a wealthy family as the bride-to-be transferred her property to trustees to hold on her behalf, were, therefore, commonly used by wealthier families as a means of, at the very least, protecting the woman's pre-marital assets.

[1] Genesis ch 3, v 16.
[2] Genesis 2, v 24.
[3] Under Roman Law free born women, albeit not permitted to hold political office or to vote,.were recognised as equal citizens with men.
[4] Blackstone, *Commentaries on the Laws of England* (23rd edn, 1854), Vol 1.
[5] Hilda of Whitby (c 614–680) a Christian saint and the original abbess of Whitby monastery, whose counsel was sought by kings, according to The Venerable Bede in his 'The Ecclesiastical History of the English'.
[6] The 'law of dower' see Cnut's law post 1016. Divorce too was permitted, although only officially recorded if occasioned by adultery and if the wife left with the children of the union then she was entitled to half of the couple's assets.
[7] 'What is Marriage? What should it be?' Mostyn J's speech to the All Party Parliamentary Group on Family Law (2010).
[8] Even sexual relations were at the demand of husbands and a charge of marital rape was not permissible until exceptions to the established rule were allowed from 1949 (*R v Clarke* [1949] 2 All ER 448) onwards and the rule as to implied consent of a wife to sexual intercourse with her husband itself only finally overturned as late as *R v R* [1991] 3 WLR 767 by the House of Lords. Hence, whilst the Law had upheld convictions of assault against husbands for the violent attack on their wives leading up to a rape, the Law had until the later 20th century, continued to deem lawful within such an assault the husband's final and violent last act of penetration.
[9] 'Ante-nuptial' – '131. The issue in this case is simple: what weight should the court hearing a claim for ancillary relief under the Matrimonial Causes Act 1973 give to an agreement entered into between the parties before they got married which purported to determine the result? I propose to call these "ante-nuptial agreements" because our legislation already uses the term "ante-nuptial" to refer to things done before a marriage' – Lady Hale: *Radmacher (formerly Granatino) v Granatino* [2010] UKSC 42.

Reform

8.2 The 1882 Married Womens' Property Act was a milestone in the gathering, albeit tortuous, campaign for women's rights.

Of course, that piece of legislation was very much towards the end of a half century of Victorian zeal by a small army of women protesters whose fervor for the cause of their rights was to revolutionise both the rights of women within the family and in property ownership and within a couple of decades thereafter to wrestle into their possession also the right to vote.

In 1839, the Infants and Child Custody Act had allowed wives to take custody of their children under the age of seven (later extended to 16 in the 1883 Custody Act), if divorced or separated; albeit they could not take custody if they had been found to be adulterous. This legislation was very much the result of the campaigning zeal of one woman, Lady Caroline Norton, who with the use of pamphlets[1] and in conjunction with the MP, Sir Thomas Taulford, obtained Parliamentary support for this reforming measure[2].

Caroline Norton, the granddaughter of the famous playwright, Richard Sheridan, was born on 22 March 1808 and was one of three beautiful yet penniless sisters of society known as 'the three graces'. Caroline was no feminist or suffragette by nature, but as a gifted poet, writer of popular fiction and a society beauty, who had caught the eye of the rising political star of the day, Lord Melbourne, the future Whig prime minister, she was well placed to assert her independent and liberal views about the role of women before the law. Poignantly, this was to be at her personal cost since she was herself the victim of domestic violence by her own husband, George Norton, the MP for Guildford. Indeed, Caroline separated from her husband on two occasions by reason of his regular beatings of her, only to return for the sake of her three children. In 1836, Norton's jealous and spurious accusation of Caroline's infidelity with Lord Melbourne caused a political scandal of its day. An allegation, which the jury in the subsequent criminal conversation court action was to reject, without even retiring to consider its verdict, as entirely false[3].

Caroline's reward, however, was first to be ejected by her husband from the family home without any basis at that time for pursuing her own divorce and no right to claim the custody of the children, as the law then stood[4]. Her second was to be temporarily shunned within the social circles she moved in. Added to this, The Government fell, despite the trial outcome, as a result of the scandal involving Melbourne.

[1] A form of written social media of the day – 'Observations on the Natural Claim of a Mother to the Custody of her Children as affected by the Common Law Right of the Father', 'Separation of Mother and Child by the Laws of Custody of Infants Considered' and 'A Plain Letter to the Lord Chancellor on the Infant Custody Bill' – sent to figures in Government together with the sympathy of a few individual MPs.

[2] 'As it stands at present, the law is entirely in favour of the husband and oppressive to the wife. A man who may be drunken, immoral, vicious, and utterly brutalized, may place his wife, who seeks to live separately from him, in this cruel dilemma – "You shall either continue to live with me, or you shall be deprived of your children." The wife, in such a case, has no redress.' Sir Thomas Taulford; House of Commons debate 1839.

[3] An observer in court at the time was the young reporter Charles Dickens and this trial was later to inspire his writing subsequently of Pickwick Papers within which he ridiculed court actions for breach of promise.

[4] Married parties under the rule of the Ecclesiastical Courts, could gain 'a separation' upon proof of adultery, sodomy or physical violence, but thereafter they could not remarry, albeit their separation was permanent. The reasoning being that their marriage had been a promise made before God which no man could put asunder. Divorce with the right to remarry was only possible (as on offshoot from King Henry's Protest) before 1857 by a private Act of Parliament on the grounds of adultery, if prosecuted by the husband or if sought by the wife but then the adultery by the husband had also to be accompanied with proof of life threatening cruelty. Unsurprisingly, only the very wealthy could pursue this course of action and for 150 years after 1700 only 314 such Acts were successfully obtained, almost all by men.

8.3 Pre-nuptial Agreements

8.3 In 1857, again after a period of further pamphleteering[1] by Caroline Norton and others, secular divorce was established in England and Wales through the Matrimonial Causes Act of that year. That Act established, free, for the first time, of the control of the Ecclesiastical Court, a new civil court system, which was a forerunner of today's Family Court; and again for the first time, both men and women were permitted to obtain divorce with the right to remarry on the ground of adultery, albeit, the woman had to also establish her husband had, in addition, committed incest, rape, sodomy, bestiality, bigamy or 2 years' desertion. In addition, women gained the right to separate 'needs' based maintenance for themselves – the forerunner of the 'needs' based test today. Caroline's further campaigning was also to secure by 1870 the passing of the Married Women's Property Act whereby wives gained their first autonomy in financial matters, being permitted in marriage to retain any monies received by inheritance or investments, albeit everything else (subject to the outmoded 'law of dower' and 'paraphernalia') still belonged to the husband, whether the wife had acquired it before or after marriage.

For Caroline Norton, ironically, none of these legislative achievements were to assist her personal plight. As a result of her assumed improper association with Lord Melbourne, Norton had had their three children removed out of the jurisdiction to the care of his appointed guardian in Scotland and only in 1842, upon the death of the youngest boy (8) in a riding accident at the time, did he eventually relent and permit the remaining children to return to their mother's care. His unrequited jealousy for his wife meant that when Melbourne died in 1848 leaving Caroline a small legacy, Norton then claimed that gift for himself as her husband. He further refused her maintenance support for the children when they returned to her and being envious of her literary success, he also claimed her publishing earnings as his own, as in law he was entitled to do. His last denial of her was to refuse to instigate divorce proceedings himself. Not long after her last legislative triumphs, as above, Caroline was to suffer the tragic loss of her eldest son aged 30 from tuberculosis and was left bereft with her only remaining son, who himself was disabled. When eventually Norton died in 1875, Caroline was in 1877 able to marry her companion of 25 years Sir William Stirling-Maxwell, but this was just 3 months before her own demise.

Caroline's legacy was undoubtedly the titanic shift in public opinion, particularly towards married women's rights. Just 5 years after her death and following the efforts of Ursula Bright and others and a manifesto promise of the incoming Gladstone Government (1880), by the passage of the Married Women's Property Act 1882, a woman was, finally, permitted to keep all personal and real property, which she had obtained before or gained during her marriage. This meant that marriage no longer affected the woman's property rights[2] and as soon as married women became entitled to hold property in their own right, the need for pre-nuptial settlements, at that stage, diminished. Of course, it was only to be after a World War (1914—18) that women aged 30 and over would also be able to wrestle into their possession also their entitlement to equal suffrage with men[3] and in 1919 to be permitted to enter public office, including the judiciary and the professions[4].

[1] Addressed directly to Queen Victoria entitled 'A Letter to the Queen on Lord Chancellor Cranworth's Marriage & Divorce Bill' in which Caroline Norton spoke openly about the domestic violence of her own marriage and against the wrongs inflicted by marriage upon women generally under the Law – where they could not be deemed a party or be represented in court, they could not make a will, their belongings down to their under-clothes were legally their husband's as were all their earnings in marriage; if they left the marital home without their husband's permission their husbands could lawfully without invitation enter the home of another and return their wives over their shoulders using such force as was necessary in doing so and should their wives claim to separate because of cruelty then without proof that the cruelty in question was against 'life or limb' then theirs was deemed by Law a desertion without right to any financial support thereafter.

[2] Most of the rest of Europe as well as some US states operated the 'community of property' regime, where marriage did affect the parties' property ownership rights creating thereby a pool of jointly owned assets which provided the non-earning spouse with some financial security.

[3] Qualification of Women Act 1918. Women aged over 21 secured their voting rights in 1928.

[4] Sex Disqualification (Removal) Act 1919.

Current position

8.4 Now in the twenty-first century, there should be cause for reflection that it has only been in the last 138 years that Parliament has been prepared to recognise the entitlement of a married woman to retain her own property. Many would recognise that the struggle for full recognition of women's rights in society in general and of the rights of wives on divorce in this area of the law, in particular, continues unabated.

However, some progress has been made and following the House of Lords decision in *White v White*[1], reference back to the pre-*White* case law in regard to distribution of the resources of spouses on divorce makes uncomfortable reading against the now familiar post-*White* signposts of 'fairness without discrimination' and the rationales of 'needs, compensation and sharing'. Despite this, neither *White* nor the conjoined appeal decisions of *Miller v Miller: McFarlane v McFarlane*[2] have yet completed the task of full recognition of the wife's equal entitlement to that of the husband. Indeed, some would say that such an endeavour is not the responsibility of the judiciary in any event, but rather the role of democratic debate within Parliament[3].

However, pending legislative reform, lip-service to a non-discriminatory approach upon divorce has continued in certain respects and some may still detect in the High Court decision of *VB v JP*[4] and the Court of Appeal decision in *B v B*[5], and, again, most recently in *Waggott v Waggott*[6] a lingering intellectual reluctance against full acknowledgment of the wife's equal contribution and, thereby, her entitlement to an equal share. After early signs in *Charman v Charman*[7], with the promotion of the 'principle of equality', that the then[8] newly appointed President (Sir Mark Potter) may have been willing to champion real equality of approach for women in divorce, his later judgment in *VB v JP*[9] and his, curiously, concurring judgment in *B v B*[10] gave every sign of the gears in this area being put into reverse or, at the very least, into neutral. Certainly, the judgment of Wall LJ, as he then was, in *B v B*[11] denying the existence of a 'principle' of equality, was an ominous indication of the re-emergence of the more historic judicial approach to such issues.

8.4 Pre-nuptial Agreements

Inherited land[12], family business contributions[13] and an exceptional wealth creative ability of a spouse (almost invariably husbands)[14] are still paraded as three of the more obvious bases for departure from equality. Others, such as 'non matrimonial' property[15] needs 'generously interpreted'[16], the parties' 'autonomy and personal choices in a relationship'[17] and again, most recently, the re-introduction of the distinction of 'unilateral assets'[18] have, almost predictably, developed as areas for further veiled discrimination against wives.

[1] [2000] UKHL 54.
[2] [2006] UKHL 24.
[3] See Lady Hale in *Radmacher (formerly Granatino) v Granatino* [2010] UKSC 42 and 'What is Marriage? What should it be?' and see Mostyn J's address to the All Party Parliamentary Group on Family Law (2010).
[4] [2008] EWHC 112 (Fam).
[5] [2008] EWCA Civ 543.
[6] [2018] EWCA Civ 527.
[7] [2007] EWCA Civ 50.
[8] Sir Mark Potter.
[9] [2008] EWHC 112 (Fam).
[10] [2008] EWCA Civ 543.
[11] [2008] EWCA Civ 543.
[12] *P v P (Inherited Property)* [2005] 1 FLR 576, Munby J and *Robson v Robson* [2010] EWCA 1171, Ward LJ.
[13] *Miller v Miller: McFarlane v McFarlane* [2006] UKHL 24.
[14] *Charman* [2007] EWCA Civ 50.
[15] [2006] UKHL 24; *Jones v Jones* [2011] EWCA 41 Civ, *K v L* [2011] 550 Civ and *N v F* [2011] EWHC 586 Fam; *JL v SL* [2014] EWHC 3658.
[16] *VB v JP* above, but see Ward LJ in *Robson v Robson* [2010] EWCA 1171 disapproving of the phraseology.
[17] *Charman's* case [2007] EWCA Civ 50 and *J v J* [2009] EWHC 2654 (Fam), Charles J in relation to ancillary relief applications and *Radmacher's* case ([2010] UKSC 42) in relation to ante-nuptial agreements.
[18] *Sharp v Sharp* [2017] EWCA Civ 408.

8.5 Given that the historical development of our society in regard to women's rights has within it an in-built discrimination against women attaining positions of landed wealth or commercial influence even to this day, then the present approach of our law still inherently continues to perpetuate a discrimination against the woman's role within marriage generally. For it remains the woman, who is the less likely spouse to have developed a career by the start of the marriage and the more likely by its end to have given up her chance for the same level of earnings potential in order to care for the children of a marriage. Sir Mark Potter's promised development of the 'yardstick of equality' into 'the sharing principle' in *Charman*[1] has proved, as yet, to be a false dawn for the belief that, finally, the law had, within nearly a century and a half of reforms and development, reached the position where each spouse could stand 'shoulder to shoulder' at the beginning of the statutory exercise under s 25 of the 1973 Matrimonial Causes Act. At the same time, wives have also suffered the double blow of a diminishment by the courts of their chances of compensation after, again, earlier signs of advancement (cf *Miller v Miller: McFarlane v McFarlane, H v H*[2] and *VB v JP*[3] and most recently, Mostyn J in *SA v PA (Pre-marital agreement: Compensation)*[4] and in *Waggott v Waggott*[5] the Court of Appeal's rejection of any sharing upon divorce of the higher spouse's earning capacity as enhanced by marriage and at the same time the courts acceptance that the weaker financial spouse (usually the wife) may be required to amortise capital held in order to mitigate income needs).

Against such a background, the content of the Majority decision of the extraordinary assembly of some nine[6] Justices of the Supreme Court in the *Radmacher (formerly Granatino) v Granatino* appeal[7] and the delivery of the Minority dissenting judgment by the only woman Justice sitting, who was also, at that time, the only family law specialist of the court, did little to dispel the impression that the determined direction of the law of England and Wales in relation to marital breakdown was again moving away from a position of securing complete equality for women in this area.

The subsequent publication of the long awaited Law Commission's report entitled 'Matrimonial Property Needs and Agreements'[8] was expected to suggest not only reforms to the law following the Supreme Court's decision in *Radmacher's*[9] case upon pre-nuptial agreements, but also to better define the use of the concepts of spousal 'needs' and 'non matrimonial' property within divorce financial remedy law and, possibly, to advance a percentage formulae to assist spouses to better predict the likely outcome of such matrimonial applications. The anticipation was, in parts, fulfilled, but in other respects left unsatisfied[10]. However, the principal recommendation of the Law Commission was that, for the first time within this jurisdiction, by statutory reform, there should be introduced into the law of England and Wales the concept of 'Qualifying Nuptial Agreements' to enable couples, including those contemplating marriage, to contract out of the court's discretionary powers within financial remedy applications upon divorce.

[1] [2007] EWCA Civ 50.
[2] [2007] EWHC 459 (Fam), Charles J.
[3] [2008] EWHC 112 (Fam).
[4] [2014] EWHC 392.
[5] [2018] EWCA Civ 527.
[6] Historically, the former Appellate Committee of the House of Lords rarely sat with more than five Law Lords and the few exceptions related mainly to appeals involving terrorism/constitutional cases.
[7] [2010] UKSC 42.
[8] Published February 2014 – Commission Terms of Reference set out in its Tenth Program of Law Reform (2007) Law Comm No 317. The project was commenced in 2009, the consultation opened in January 2011 and extended in 2012 in agreement with the Ministry of Justice to include 'needs' and 'non matrimonial' property with a supplementary consultation which itself opened in September 2012.
[9] Published February 2014 – Commission Terms of Reference set out in its Tenth Program of Law Reform (2007) Law Comm No 317. The project was commenced in 2009, the consultation opened in January 2011 and extended in 2012 in agreement with the Ministry of Justice to include 'needs' and 'non matrimonial' property with a supplementary consultation which itself opened in September 2012.
[10] The Commission referred the question of what is meant by 'needs' to the Family Justice Council for guidance suggesting that to develop any formulae will require considerable further research to be undertaken. This resulted in the Family Justice Council producing under a committee chaired by Roberts J, the 'Guidance on Financial Needs on Divorce' (June 2016).

8.6 Pre-nuptial Agreements

Modern relevance of the pre-nuptial agreement

8.6 Prior to the Supreme Court's decision[1] pre-nuptial agreements had remained contractually unenforceable in the courts of England and Wales. This position had been based on the grounds of public policy that such agreements undermined 'the concept of marriage as a lifelong union'[2] or, where it applied, that the terms of the same purported to oust the court's jurisdiction on an application for ancillary relief (now financial remedy). However, as set out later, the courts have, progressively, over the last two decades, shown themselves to be more willing to take such agreements into account under 'all the circumstances of the case' or as 'conduct' within the s 25 exercise under the Matrimonial Causes Act 1973 when redistributing resources between parties upon a divorce.

The increasing incidence of cohabitation, as opposed to marriage, between couples and the effects of the court's more liberal and non-discriminatory approach to the exercise of its redistributive powers on divorce have led to the increasing re-emergence of pre-nuptial agreements in a more modern form designed to protect the separate property of either or both of the spouses on the dissolution of their marriage.

Ironically, against such a historical backdrop, the pre-nuptial agreement, which was, initially, intended to shield the wife-to-be's property from the full rigour of the husband's coverture rights in marriage, is now, almost invariably, being used to attempt to shield the husband's property rights against the wife's entitlement upon a divorce. As the use and greater recognition of such a device has increased in this modern context, so the ground gained by women in financial remedy relief upon divorce prior to 2006[3] has continued to be at risk of being progressively and systematically eroded[4].

This is because the modern use of the pre-nuptial agreement is almost invariably an attempt by the male and/or his family to ensure that the wife-to-be's full rights against him upon a divorce are more restricted than the law would otherwise permit under the 'statutory exercise' of s 25 of the Matrimonial Causes Act 1973, as it stands presently, before any legislative reform consequent upon the Law Commission's Report, is sanctioned by Parliament. The wife-to-be may be persuaded in such pre-marriage discussions that there is something in it for her, whereas the reality is, almost invariably, that there will be far more in it for her future husband. Indeed, Lady Hale in *Radmacher*'s case expressed concern that the provisions of some pre-nuptial agreements in use are such that they seek to limit the wife's claim to a pre-determined sum based upon buying her wifely services by the year[5].

As 'fairness' is the approach to the present law concerning financial redistribution upon divorce, then the only justification for a pre-nuptial agreement between a couple preparing to marry is that it is an attempt by the parties to shield any pre-accrued family resources of one of the parties, to introduce in advance certainty of distribution and provision between them in order to reduce the risk of litigation and to mitigate the costs attendant upon a subsequent divorce[6] and further that the same reflects the autonomy of the parties to regulate their own financial affairs in the event that their marital relationship fails. These are, of course, at first sight, laudable objectives, but, again, in reality, such considerations are likely to be less influential in the creation of a pre-nuptial agreement at the beginning of a married life together than the concern of the financially stronger party, with present wealth or an expectation of the same, of securing, in advance, a damage limitation outcome should 'wedded bliss' descend into disharmony.

[1] [2010] UKSC 42.
[2] Per Wall J in *N v N (Jurisdiction: Pre-Nuptial Agreement)* [1999] 2 FLR 745 at 752.
[3] See *Miller v Miller: McFarlane v McFarlane* [2006] 1 FLR 1186.
[4] See Baroness Hale in *Macleod v Macleod* [2008] UKPC 64 and Baron J in *NG v KR* [2008] below.
[5] See [2010] UKSC 42, at para 137. 'Would any self-respecting young woman sign up to an agreement which assumed that she would be the only one who might otherwise have a claim, thus placing no limit on the claims that might be made against her, and then limit her claim to a pre-determined sum for each year of marriage regardless of the circumstances, as if her wifely services were being bought by the year? Yet that is what these precedents do. In short, there is a gender dimension to the issue which some may think ill-suited to decision by a court consisting of eight men and one woman'. See also 'The effect of *Radmacher* on the average person' Penny Booth, 20 October, 2010, Fam Law Week.
[6] Eg in the case of *Moore v Moore* [2007] EWCA Civ 361, approximately £1.6m had been expended on the wife's endeavours to achieve a London award, rather than a 'Marbella' award, despite the application of the Regulations of Brussels II and see *J v J* [2014] EWHC 3654 (Fam) Mostyn J, where parties had spent c £920k on legal and expert witness costs representing some 32% of the value of the assets under consideration.

8.7 In addition, of course, within the context of saving future litigation costs, the existence of a pre-nuptial agreement may, in a given case, be a 'magnetic factor' indicative of an obvious outcome[1], but cannot, as yet (and without eg the legislative introduction of 'a Qualifying Nuptial Agreement'), prevent the court process, within which the imprimatur of the court is required to authorise any financial arrangement between the parties following a divorce[2]. In this context, the notion that the law would adopt a 'presumptively dispositive' approach to the existence of a pre-nuptial agreement upon divorce following the Supreme Court's decision in *Radmacher*'s case, has, subsequently, received progressive encouragement by a number of judgments, including by Mostyn J in a trilogy of cases *Kremen v Agrest (No 11)*[3], *B v S*[4] and *SA v PA (Pre-marital agreement: Compensation)*[5].

When advising a female client, who is being pressed by her husband-to-be or his family to enter into a pre-nuptial agreement, the advice must, almost invariably, be first to suggest that she resists and says 'no' and, when advising a male client wishing to press for such an agreement, he should be cautioned, under the present law, that, if he wishes to give himself the best chance of securing the approval of the other lawyer involved, he should first seek to ensure that the proposed agreement is as generous as possible, without losing its underlying purpose of restricting the other's eventual recovery otherwise according to the law[6].

Is the effort worth it? Following the Supreme Court's decision, undoubtedly, it is for any spouse-to-be with significant prospects or substantial property/asset worth. Indeed, even before the *Radmacher* appeal, the courts had, clearly, shown themselves more prepared to have regard to the contents of such an agreement in determining what is 'fair' in any given case. The Supreme Court has now strongly signalled that the entry into a pre-nuptial agreement,

8.7 Pre-nuptial Agreements

following their decision, will in future be a compelling factor in the s 25 exercise; post *Radmacher*, it being natural to infer that parties who enter into a pre-nuptial agreement to which English law is likely to be applied intend that effect should be given to it[7]. The subsequent case law[8] has further emphasised the 'magnetic factor' of such an agreement, unless the court considers its provisions attempt to leave the other spouse with less than a 'needs' level of resources. Furthermore and in any event, the court's approach under the present developed case law to what is fair under the s 25 exercise is likely to be significantly affected by the terms of any pre-nuptial agreement in existence, which reflects the parties' prevailing circumstances upon divorce, whether or not, ultimately, its provisions are precisely adhered to by the court within the s 25 statutory exercise[9].

For the financially weaker spouse-to-be, unless the terms struck are sufficiently generous and she (as it usually is) fears that a short marriage may be the reality, then the answer as to whether the effort is worth it, is, in terms of legal and financial benefit to her, that she would, having regard to the usual contents of such an agreement, be better off upon a divorce without such an agreement in place.

Of course, these observations also assume that both male and female regard the priority of securing the certainty of such financial benefits as foremost in the decision to marry in the first place – an assumption, which, certainly, many women would, undoubtedly, challenge as false; advocating instead the importance of the wider family and emotional benefits of marriage as opposed to financial self-interest as one of their primary motivations[10].

However, pending the now imminently awaited legislative intervention on divorce distribution, the development of case law over the last few years relating to the impact of pre-nuptial agreements upon such divorce distribution has proved stubbornly resistant to giving such agreements an entirely free run to dictating the outcome of the court's order on divorce, especially where questions arise concerning the sufficiency of the needs provision effected thereby. In addition, the weight the courts have attached to such agreements within the s 25 exercise has not always been entirely predictable and, currently, the range of judicial interpretation of such agreements lacks the conformity previously anticipated.

[1] See *Crossley v Crossley* [2007] EWCA Civ 1491.
[2] *Xydhias v Xydhias* [1999] 1 FLR 683 CA, but cf Ward LJ in *Soulsbury v Soulsbury* [2007] EWCA Civ 969. See also *NG v KR (pre-nuptial contract)* [2008] EWHC 1532 (Fam) below.
[3] [2012] EWHC 45 (Fam), [2012] 2 FLR 414.
[4] [2012] EWHC 265 (Fam), [2012] 2 FLR 502.
[5] [2014] EWHC 392 (Fam).
[6] See Emma Hitchings *From Pre-Nups to Post-Nups: Dealing with Marital Property Agreements*, School of Law, Bristol University, [2009] Fam Law 1056.
[7] See Lord Phillips at para 70 of decision.
[8] See footnotes 45 to 47 above.
[9] '*Radmacher* – Fettering but not ousting' Sandra Davis, 20 October 2010, Fam Law; see now below *Z v Z* [2011] 2878 Moor J and more recently *AH v PH ((Scandinavian Marriage Settlement)* [2013] EWHC 3873 (Fam) and *Luckwell v Limata* [2014] EWHC 502 (Fam).
[10] A viewpoint which it is submitted was (inevitably) rejected by an all male Court of Appeal and the eight male Justices of the nine Justices of the Supreme Court sitting on the appeals in *Radmacher*'s case.

A decade of development

8.8 Despite the recommendation of the Government's 1998 Consultation Document, 'Supporting Families'[1], to make pre-nuptial agreements relating to property binding, legislative reform was deferred following the initial lukewarm *Response of the Judges of the Family Division* (1999) which expressed a 'unanimous lack of enthusiasm for the pre-nuptial agreement'; a sentiment also echoed by the legal profession to the proposal.

However, there followed gathering support for such a change, 'unless significant injustice would be caused', in the report of the SFLA Law Reform Committee ((22 November 2004) *A More Certain Future – Recognition of Prenuptial Contracts in England and Wales*) and, again, in 2005 and 2009 Resolution published well-argued reports urging the Government to give statutory force to nuptial contracts[2]. The latter report was, subsequently, fully supported by the Money and Property Sub-Committee of the Family Justice Council.

Sir Mark Potter, as the then President of the Family Division, added his weight to this recommendation in the Court of Appeal decision in *Charman*[3] and Thorpe LJ, as a late convert to the cause, repeated such a call in *Crossley v Crossley*[4].

With mounting media coverage and discussion of the topic, the Law Commission in 2008 announced[5] its intention to examine the status and enforceability of marital property and finance agreements made either before or during the course of a marriage with the aim of presenting draft legislation by 2012.

With little attempt at concealing the politics of their decision, the three man[6] Court of Appeal in the *Radmacher* case by their judgments on the appeal, somewhat blatantly, sought to force the hand of the newly formed Supreme Court to judicially legislate in advance of the Law Commission's recommendations upon the status of pre-nuptial agreements and the weight to be given to them upon divorce. Diplomatically, however, the Supreme Court's decision avoided an outcome which wholly undermined the Law Commission's brief upon the subject, but, in the process, gave further impetus to the primacy of the parties' right to autonomy by being able to self-determine in advance the outcome of the division of their resources upon divorce by marital agreement and thus, in the experienced view of Lady Hale, the decision of the Majority, further diminished the prospect, in that exercise, of achieving 'fairness' for the financially weaker spouse.

[1] *Supporting Families* (Stationery Office, October 1998) at p 31. This view did not receive any immediate support from the judiciary or the profession. There were 157 responses to the Consultation Document, 80 were in favour of allowing the agreements and 77 against: see *The Response of the Judges of the Family Division to Government Proposals* (made by way of submission to Chancellor's Ancillary Relief Advisory Group) [1999] Fam Law 159 and the Law Society's Report (May 2003) *Financial Provision on Divorce – Clarity and fairness – Proposals for Reform;* the latter recommending that there could be 'significant unfairness' if the law was changed to make pre-nuptial contracts binding and that in financial provision on divorce the same should remain as one of the factors only: para 312–315. However, the SFLA's Law Reform Committee's report (22 November 2004) *A More Certain Future – Recognition of Pre-marital Contracts in England and Wales* recommended that pre-nuptial

8.8 *Pre-nuptial Agreements*

contracts should be made binding unless significant injustice would be caused. See also S Bruce 'Pre-marital Agreements Following *White v White*' and 'Introduction to Precedents for Pre-marital Contracts' and Professor Barton 'The SFLA and Pre-marital Agreements: A More Lucrative Future?' Fam Law [2005] 47.
2 In 2009, the Centre for Social Justice 'Every Family Matters' suggested a similar reform with the courts being able to intervene where the terms of the agreement would cause 'significant injustice' with safeguards imposed of disclosure, advice and a minimum 28 day pre-marriage period. Resolution echoed these suggestions in a further report 'Family Agreements – Seeking Certainty to Reduce Disputes' of the same year suggesting a 42 day pre-marriage period.
3 [2007] EWCA Civ 50.
4 [2008] EWCH Civ 1491.
5 [2008] June Law Comm 311; Tenth Programme of Law Reform.
6 Thorpe, Rix, Wilson LJJ.

The case law – *Hyman* to *Radmacher*

8.9 The Supreme Court, clearly, stated that in future cases involving English pre-nuptial agreements entered into after the *Radmacher* case, it will now be natural for a court to infer that the parties to such an agreement intended that effect should be given to terms of the same.

However, in regard to the progressively diminishing number of pre-nuptial agreements, which pre-date the decision, there remains the real possibility that one or both parties may have been advised that such agreements were void or would carry little weight with the court. In those cases, therefore, the parties' intentions will not be subject to the same inference and it will remain important in such pre *Radmacher* agreements for the court still to determine if the parties intended the pre-nuptial agreement in question to be given effect. Accordingly, it will remain necessary, in such instances to have an understanding of the development of the law concerning pre-nuptial agreements pre-*Radmacher*.

The modern development of the law concerning pre-nuptial agreements since the start of the last century is to be traced in the following cases:

In *Hyman v Hyman*[1], a wife by a deed of separation (as opposed to a pre-nuptial agreement) had covenanted not to take proceedings against her husband to provide her with maintenance beyond the provision made for her by the deed. When, subsequently, she obtained a decree of divorce on the grounds of her husband's adultery, it was held that she was not prevented by her covenant from applying for maintenance. The House of Lords decided that, on public policy grounds, parties could not by agreement preclude the divorce court from exercising its jurisdiction in financial matters. In the speech of Lord Hailsham LC, the fact that there had been such an agreement remained relevant to the 'conduct of the parties' within the statutory exercise (then under s 190 of the Supreme Court of Judicature (Consolidation) Act 1925) that the court had to undertake in determining what provision was reasonable.

Thereafter, it was not until, a half century later, in 1981 and *Edgar v Edgar*[2] that the status and effect of agreements between parties to a marriage was, effectively, developed within the modern context. In that case, the Court of Appeal, in upholding the effect of an agreement (made upon separation and which did not seek to oust the court's jurisdiction) between two married parties, who had each received the benefit of independent legal advice, made it plain that, whilst the court retained its overriding discretion under the s 25 exercise of the 1973 Act, the terms reached would not be avoided in such a case, unless justice demanded. In a well-known extract from the judgment, Ormrod LJ stated[3]:

> ' . . . formal agreements, properly and fairly arrived at with competent legal advice, should not be displaced unless there are good and substantial grounds for concluding that an injustice will be done by holding the parties to the terms of their agreement.' (see note for fuller extract).

Of course, these words were directed towards a settlement reached at court between spouses already separated and pursuing an outcome to a financial relief application already brought; but they served, by analogy, to highlight the potential advantages of seeking to reach terms of agreement, more generally, either before or after marriage, as well as after an eventual separation.

In 1995, in *F v F (Ancillary Relief: Substantial Assets)*[4], which involved pre-nuptial agreements governed by the laws of Germany and Austria, the husband had made his application for financial relief within this jurisdiction, following his petition for divorce in England. Thorpe J, as he was then, expressed himself, in the particular circumstances of the case, as unwilling to attach much significance to the agreements reached, stating[5]:

> 'In this jurisdiction [pre-nuptial agreements] must be of very limited significance. The rights and responsibilities of those whose financial affairs are regulated by statute cannot be much influenced by contractual terms which were devised for the control and limitation of standards that are intended to be of universal application throughout our society.'

However, these comments (repeated as they were, obiter, the following year by the same judge in *Dart v Dart*)[6], have to be set against the facts of the case, where the provision made in the agreements for the wife was (although, apparently, as was stated in the judgment, then comparable to the salary of a German judge) almost negligible, when contrasted to the fact that it was to be made out of some £200m of assets held by the husband.

---

[1] [1929] AC 601.
[2] (1981) 2 FLR 19. 'To decide what weight should be given, in order to reach a just result, to a prior agreement not to claim a lump sum, regard must be had to the conduct of both parties leading up to the prior agreement, and to their subsequent conduct in consequence of it. It is not necessary in this connection to think in formal legal terms, such as misrepresentation or estoppel; all the circumstances as they affect each of two human beings must be considered in the complex relationship of marriage. So the circumstances surrounding the making of the agreement are relevant. Undue pressure by one side, exploitation of a dominant position to secure an unreasonable advantage, inadequate knowledge, possibly bad legal advice, an important change of circumstances, unforeseen or overlooked at the time of making the agreement, are all relevant to the question of justice between the parties. Important, too, is the general proposition that, formal agreements, properly and fairly arrived at with competent legal advice, should not be displaced unless there are good and substantial grounds for concluding that an injustice will be done by holding the parties to the terms of their agreement. There may well be other considerations which affect the justice of this case; the above list is not intended to be an exclusive catalogue' – per Ormrod LJ at 893.
[3] (1981) 2 FLR 19.
[4] [1995] 2 FLR 45.
[5] [1995] 2 FLR 45 at 66.

8.9 Pre-nuptial Agreements

[6] [1996] 2 FLR 286.

8.10 The next year, in 1997, Cazalet J in *N v N (Foreign Divorce: Financial Relief)*[1] considered that a pre-nuptial agreement, which would have been binding in Sweden, was to be treated 'as being no more than a material consideration for the court under the statutory exercise'.

In the same year, in *S v S (Divorce: Staying Proceedings)*[2], Wilson J, as he then was, effectively opened the stable door to such agreements, when, after reviewing the earlier dicta of Thorpe J, he said[3]:

> 'I am aware of the growing belief that, in the dispatch of a claim for ancillary relief in this jurisdiction, no significant weight will be afforded to a pre-nuptial agreement, whatever the circumstances. I would like to sound a cautionary note, in that respect . . . but there will come a case . . . where the circumstances surrounding the pre-nuptial agreement and the provision therein contained might, when viewed in the context of the other circumstances of the case, prove influential or even crucial. Where other jurisdictions, both in the US and in the European Community, have been persuaded that there are cases where justice can only be served by confining the parties to their rights under pre-nuptial agreements, we should be cautious about too categorically asserting the contrary. I can find nothing in [the Matrimonial Causes Act 1973] s 25 to compel a conclusion, so much at odds with personal freedoms to make arrangements for ourselves, that escape from solemn bargains, carefully struck by informed adults, is readily available here . . . The matter must be left open.'

By 1999, Wall J, as he then was, in *N v N (divorce: pre-nuptial agreement)*[4], accepted that, whilst pre-nuptial agreements were, at that time, unenforceable, they could be taken into account, where justice required it, in the s 25 exercise. He stated:

> 'However, the fact that a pre nuptial agreement, or an agreement between spouses, that neither will make a claim for ancillary relief in future divorce proceedings is unenforceable does not mean that the court will not, in appropriate circumstances, hold the parties to that agreement, provided it is just to do so: see, for example, *Edgar v Edgar* . . . The existence of the agreement, and the weight to be given to it, are both factors to be taken into account in the overall balance when the court is deciding (on the facts of the individual case) whether or not to exercise its discretion under s 25 of the Matrimonial Causes Act 1973 to make orders for financial provision under ss 23 and 24.'

Of course, in 1999, in *Xydhias v Xydhias*[5] Thorpe LJ, concluded that, as within the matrimonial jurisdiction post separation agreements were not specifically enforceable without the approval of the court, ordinary contractual principles did not apply to such agreements (a view not fully shared by Ward LJ in the case of *Soulsbury v Soulsbury*[6] and now further explained and developed by Lord Phillips in the *Radmacher* case[7]). Instead, he held that the court would carry out a discretionary review of the negotiations and surrounding circumstances in order to determine whether the parties had reached an agreement or 'an accord' to which they should be held, requiring the court to determine only those matters that remain outstanding.

Following this decision, applications were made, increasingly in practice, within ancillary relief applications, whenever there existed evidence of a concluded separation agreement (*Edgar*) or a final hearing compromise agreement (akin to the *Xydhias* case facts), for the other party to show cause why a final order should not be made in the terms of the agreement alleged to have been reached. This position also served to strengthen the status and effect of other post marital agreements reached between the parties and also that of pre-nuptial agreements within the statutory exercise upon divorce. The paradigm example of this process, where even a pre-nuptial agreement could be accepted by a court as wholly determinative of the parties' divorce distribution, arose, eventually, in *Crossley v Crossley*[8] (see below and see also *S v S*[9] and Baroness Hale in *Macleod v Macleod*[10]).

1 [1997] 1 FLR 900.
2 [1997] 2 FLR 100.
3 [1997] 2 FLR 100 at 103.
4 [1999] 2 FLR 745 at 751–755.
5 [1999] 1 FLR 683 CA.
6 [2007] EWCA Civ 969. See also Baron J in *NG v KR (pre-nuptial contract)* [2008] EWHC 1532 (Fam) below.
7 *Radmacher (formerly Granatino) v Granatino* [2010] UKSC 42.
8 [2007] EWCA Civ 1491.
9 [2008] EWHC 2038 (Fam), [2008] All ER (D) 16 (Sep).
10 [2008] UKPC 64.

8.11 In 2000 in *Smith v Smith*[1], the parties' pre-nuptial agreement provided for a lump sum payment to the wife of £16k in full settlement. The judge, at first instance, in reliance, dismissed the wife's claim. The Court of Appeal stated that the judge had been wrong to dismiss her claim on this basis. The existence of a prior agreement between the parties for a lump sum payment in full and final settlement was said to be only one of the considerations to which a judge had to give weight on an application for ancillary relief.

The following year, Johnson J, in *C v C (Divorce: Stay of English Proceedings)*[2] held that the existence of a French pre-nuptial agreement was a 'significant factor' in deciding to stay the English proceedings.

In 2002 in *M v M (Pre-nuptial Agreement)*[3] Connell J stated:

'I do bear the (pre-nuptial) agreement in mind as one of the more relevant circumstances of this case, but the court's over-riding duty remains to attempt to arrive at a solution that is fair in all the circumstances, applying s 25 of the Act.'

In the event, his award then provided the wife with a lump sum payment of £875,000, compared with the provision in the agreement of just £275,000. It had been a short 5-year marriage and there was a 5-year-old child. Overall, the husband's worth was a net £6.5m; the wife had an asset worth of £300,000. It was acknowledged that the court's award was more than the pre-nuptial agreement provision, but was much less than if there had been no agreement at all.

1 [2000] 3 FCR 374.
2 [2001] 1 FLR 624.
3 [2002] 1 FLR 654.

8.12 *K v K (Ancillary Relief: Pre-nuptial Agreement)*[1] in 2002 was the first of the more modern court decisions in which the party seeking to avoid the pre-nuptial agreement entered into was held to its terms. The parties had entered into a pre-nuptial agreement, which the wife wanted to avoid. Rodger

8.12 Pre-nuptial Agreements

Hayward-Smith QC, sitting as a deputy High Court judge, accepted that the husband had been pressurised to marry on the understanding that the wife's capital claims, in the event of an early breakdown, would be as provided for in the pre-nuptial agreement. In the event, the marriage lasted 14 months. The wife already had trust assets of £1m and she was held to the agreement's capital provision of £120,000, although she had claimed £1.6m. The husband had, at least, £25m. The court's approach was that entry into the agreement should be considered as 'conduct which it would be inequitable to disregard' under MCA 1973, s 25(2)(g). By the pre-nuptial agreement, provision was made that, in the event of the separation of the parties for a period of 6 months or more or the dissolution of the marriage within 5 calendar years of the date of the agreement, the husband would pay to the wife £100,000, to be increased by 10 per cent compound interest per annum. This provision and the nature of the negotiations preceding the agreement made it apparent that the parties intended the agreement to have effect only in the event of a short marriage. However, as the agreement provided for reasonable financial provision for any children, but made no income provision for the wife, the court concluded that the agreement did not prevent an order for periodical payments for the wife, and, in any event, such a prohibition, in the circumstances, would be unjust to the wife.

Whilst the wife had signed the pre-nuptial agreement just 3 days before the marriage, she was, nevertheless, to be held to its terms having fully understood the agreement and having been properly advised as to its terms, at the time. Specifically, it was found that she had not been put under pressure to sign the agreement nor had she felt under any other pressure at the time. The court found she exercised her own free will and the husband had not exploited a dominant position. Again, whilst there had not been full disclosure, it had been the wife, as advised, who had decided not to pursue any valuation of the assets disclosed. She was, however, fully aware that the husband was very wealthy. Furthermore, the agreement had been entered into in the knowledge that there would be a child and there had, therefore, been no unforeseen circumstances, which had arisen since the agreement to make it unjust to hold the wife to it.

Upon a review of the law, the judge distilled therefrom a number of questions that he considered were important in determining whether the pre-nuptial agreement was binding or influential. These still may remain helpful pointers for the legal advisor as to the approach of a court whenever a pre-nuptial agreement pre dating *Radmacher*'s case is involved and are, therefore, summarised below:

	Question	Answer
1.	Did she understand the agreement?	Yes.
2.	Was she properly advised as to its terms?	Yes.
3.	Did the husband put her under any pressure to sign?	No.

	Question	*Answer*
4.	Was there full disclosure?	No. There was disclosure of assets, but the wife decided not to press for values and she was aware that the husband was very wealthy.
5.	Was the wife under any other pressure?	Yes from the circumstances she found herself in and from her family; but whilst she had signed the day before the marriage, she had discussed the terms before and had had plenty of time and had felt no pressure when she actually signed.
6.	Did she willingly sign the agreement?	Yes.
7.	Did the husband exploit a dominant position, either financially or otherwise?	No.
8.	Was the agreement entered into in the knowledge that there would be a child?	Yes.
9.	Has any unforeseen circumstance arisen since the agreement was made that would make it unjust to hold the parties to it?	No.
10.	What does the agreement mean?	The agreement is clear as to the capital provision to be made for the wife if the marriage broke down within 5 years and the provision for the child was to be either agreed or adjudicated upon by the court.
11.	Does the agreement preclude an order for periodical payments for the wife?	No. It does not say so.
12.	Are there any grounds for concluding that an injustice would be done by holding the parties to the terms of the agreement?	No. Indeed, an injustice would be done to the husband if the agreement was ignored.
13.	Is the agreement one of the circumstances of the case to be considered under s 25?	Yes.
14.	Does the entry into this agreement constitute conduct which it would be inequitable to disregard under s 25(2)(g)?	Yes.
15.	Am I breaking new ground by holding the wife to the capital terms of the agreement?	No. See previous cases.

8.12 *Pre-nuptial Agreements*

	Question	Answer
16.	If the agreement does preclude a maintenance claim, would it be unjust to hold the parties to that aspect of the agreement?	Yes to the wife because of her continuing contribution for the child and the effect thereof upon her earning capacity.

¹ [2003] 1 FLR 120. See also *NG v KR (pre-nuptial contract)* [2008] EWHC 1532 (Fam).

8.13 In 2003 in *J v V (Disclosure: Offshore Corporations)*[1], where the agreement was made on the wedding night and where there was no disclosure, no legal advice and no provision for the arrival of children, despite what had happened in *K v K*, Coleridge J stated that 'Nowadays [pre-nuptial agreements] can be of some significance, but not in this case'. By contrast and it should be said somewhat exceptionally, the lack of independent legal advice and disclosure in the subsequent *Radmacher* case[2] were not found by the Supreme Court to have been *material* in the husband's decision in that case to sign up to such an agreement.

In 2004, Baron J in *A v T (ancillary relief: cultural factors)*[3], under 'all the circumstances of the case', decided that the English court should also take into consideration cultural factors, where the parties are from an ethnic background and, within this process, the court may have regard to the manner in which the case would be dealt with by courts of a foreign country where such a reference is relevant. In consequence, it was relevant to consider a pre-nuptial agreement that had been made under Sharia law. Again, in *Radmacher's* case, the fact that each of the parties' own national legal systems (German and French) would, in the circumstances, have upheld the pre-nuptial agreement entered into was an important factor in the decision of both appeal courts concluding that it was not unfair to keep the husband to the agreement he had signed.

In the same year in *G v G (financial provision: separation agreement)*[4], the Court of Appeal held that the judge was right to give weight to both the pre-nuptial and separation agreements, since both parties had intentionally chosen to regulate their marital affairs by agreement in the light of their individual experiences of previous marital breakdowns.

In 2007 in *Ella v Ella*[5], where the two spouses had dual nationality in this jurisdiction and in Israel, the Court of Appeal stayed the English proceedings commenced by the wife, who was then living in London, in favour of the Israeli court jurisdiction on the basis of the then existing parallel Israeli proceedings brought by the husband and the existence of a pre-nuptial agreement between the parties, which, clearly, provided for the law of Israel to apply.

Again, that same year, Baron J in *A v A*[6], considered a post-nuptial agreement where the parties, having separated, entered into the agreement, at the insistence of the husband, as a pre-condition of their reconciliation, following the wife's earlier adultery. The case is helpful in the analysis of the court's approach to the effect of duress or undue pressure, which has resulted in an agreement between the parties to resume their marital cohabitation. The husband had during their marriage come into an inheritance and the agreement sought to limit the wife's claims. The wife signed when the husband gave her the ultimatum that she was to leave the family home if she had not signed by a given date. The husband then discovered she had renewed the adulterous relationship and divorce proceedings followed. The wife claimed in the ancillary relief proceedings that she had been put under pressure to sign and the agreement should not be relied upon.

The court acknowledged the greater use of pre-nuptial agreements than before and that the same were much more likely to be accepted by the courts in governing the parties' financial affairs on breakdown. Their effectiveness, however, it was stated, depended upon fairness and how the parties had come to enter into the agreement. To render the agreement ineffective, it would be necessary to show the husband had exercised undue pressure or influence, by which the wife's free will had been overborne. It was held that, in the circumstances, her will had, indeed, been overborne and the post-nuptial agreement, therefore, would not be determinative and the s 25 exercise would be undertaken in the ordinary way.

1   [2003] EWHC 3110 (Fam).
2   [2010] UKSC 42.
3   [2004] 1 FLR 977.
4   [2004] 1 FLR 1011, CA.
5   [2007] 2 FLR 35.
6   [2007] 1 FLR 1760.

8.14 Thereafter, in 2008, the Court of Appeal in *Crossley v Crossley*[1] held that the 'overriding objective' enables the court in exceptional circumstances to follow the proportionate approach of rejecting a hearing upon full disclosure where spouses of significant personal wealth (H £45m and W £18m) had entered into a pre-marital agreement some 7 weeks before a childless marriage that lasted just 14 months. The pre-nuptial agreement had provided that only jointly acquired assets would be divided (there were none) and each party would retain assets they had introduced. The judge, hearing the ancillary relief application, had set aside the requirement for full disclosure and adjourned the First Appointment and listed the matter for a hearing of the issue of the effect of the pre-nuptial agreement directing bare Form E's and a solicitors letter, in place of questionnaires, setting out the wife's case as to whether there had been relevant non-disclosure upon entering the pre-nuptial agreement. On the facts of the case, the existence of the pre-nuptial agreement was considered to be a 'magnetic factor' in all the circumstances under the statutory exercise and the agreement's terms represented the fair outcome. The example of robust case management given by this case was later followed in relation to where an *Edgar* agreement had been entered into in the case of *S v S*[2].

It has transpired that the most significant judgment in this area of the law was, in hindsight, that given by Baron J in 2008 in the *NG v KR (pre-nuptial contract)*[3], now known to all upon appeal as *Radmacher v Granatino*[4]. In this case, it was the wife, who held vast wealth (c £100m), derived from her family in Germany. She sought to have the nil provision pre-nuptial agreement enforced within the husband's applications for financial relief upon divorce after an 8-year marriage in which two children, then aged nine and six, had been born and who were the subject of a shared residence order. In contrast, at first instance, the husband, Nicholas Granatino, claimed relief of over

8.14 *Pre-nuptial Agreements*

£6.9m. The High Court, finally, awarded him over £5.56m, within which were provisions for a home in the United Kingdom, use of a home in Germany and certain capital awards, including capitalised maintenance.

In what was then seen as a welcomed development, the court's more structured approach to the content and effect of the pre-nuptial agreement was to ask whether the agreement satisfied the six safeguards set out in the Government's 1998 Consultation Document, Supporting Families[5] (see below). In what many saw as an astute judgment by this highly experienced family judge, Baron J, whilst clear that the agreement failed the safeguard test in several regards, was equally clear that the husband, nevertheless, was fully aware that he was signing an agreement which was intended to deny him any provision upon a divorce and, accordingly, concluded that the existence of the agreement, which would have been, she found, enforceable in the birthplaces of both of the parties, namely Germany and France, was an important factor that should limit the husband's claim overall when carrying out the s 25 statutory exercise. Had the agreement satisfied the six safeguard test, the learned judge considered that the existence of the agreement would have become 'a magnetic factor' within the discretionary exercise under 'all the circumstances of the case' and the result and the court order, in that event, would more likely have mirrored its provisions.

Before, the Court of Appeal heard the first appeal from Baron J's decision. The Privy Council in *Macleod v Macleod*[6], dealt with an appeal by a husband from an award in ancillary relief made by the Manx courts under mirror legislation to s 25 in a case where the parties had entered into a post-nuptial agreement, which, in part, contained provisions from an earlier pre-nuptial agreement. The Board expressly resisted the temptation to attempt a judicial reform of the then current developed approach of the courts, as latterly reflected in NG's case, to pre-nuptial agreements. Lady Hale, in delivering the decision of the Board, specifically, stated that such a task was for Parliament in the light of the Law Commission's announced review[7] of this area. However, when laying down guidance as to a more uniform approach to be adopted in ancillary relief to the existence and, in appropriate cases, paramountcy of marital agreements between parties, whether in the form of a post nuptial, an *Edgar* separation or a *Xydhias* compromise agreement, her Ladyship sought to emphasise the importance of the existing statutory review powers under ss 34 and 35 of the 1973 Act in relation to such marital (post as opposed to pre-nuptial) agreements as the 'starting point' for the court's s 25 exercise and further suggested that in any future legislative reform, which may validate pre-nuptial agreements, it was essential that the court should retain a similar review power.

Her Ladyship's suggestion that all post-nuptial agreements were merely 'maintenance agreements' under another name and that even the Court of Appeal in *Edgar v Edgar*[8] (and, of significance, presided over by Ormrod LJ) had missed the significance of ss 34 and 35 of the 1973 Act in dealing with the weight to be given to post-nuptial agreements within the s 25 exercise[9], was a surprise to many practitioners in the field of ancillary relief. This gauntlet of interpretation was not to be left unchallenged long and, subsequently, the Court of Appeal and, in particular, Wilson LJ, as he then was, upon the hearing of the first appeal in *Radmacher's* case, took issue with her Ladyship's approach, suggesting, obiter, that ss 34 and 35 had been 'dead letters' in ancillary relief law for many years and their resurrection in such a context was now inappropriate[10].

Again, in 2009, before the Supreme Court's decision, Eleanor King J dealt, in *F v F*[11], with a husband's appeal from a district judge's decision, which itself had relied upon the Court of Appeal's decision in *Radmacher*. On the facts, the parties had, before their wedding, travelled to France where they had signed a separation of property agreement. The district judge had decided that the parties had only entered into the agreement because, on their understanding, it was required by French law. In fact, the signed document was entirely in French as drafted by a French lawyer. The parties had never previously met with the lawyer in question. In addition, the agreement referred to parts of the French Code Civil with which the parties had no previous knowledge. In the circumstances, after signature, neither party gave any further thought to the agreement whilst they remained married. King J, therefore, found that the circumstances leading to the signing of the agreement were fundamentally different to those in *Radmacher v Granatino*. She found that, accordingly, the parties' understanding had been that their signatures were required as some form of administrative obligation imposed upon them in France. The agreement was, in consequence, neither decisive nor magnetic as a factor in the case.

1   [2007] EWCA Civ 1491.
2   [1997] 2 FLR 100.
3   [2008] EWHC 1532 (Fam).
4   [2010] UKSC 42 (Supreme Court) and [2009] EWCA Civ 649 (Court of Appeal).
5   *Supporting Families* (Stationery Office, October 1998).
6   [2008] UKPC 64.
7   Law Commission: [2008] June; Tenth Programme of Law Reform.
8   [1980] 3 All ER 887, [1980] 1 WLR 1410, 2 FLR 19.
9   See Baroness Hale's speech in *Macleod's* case [2008] UKPC 64.
10 Such a debate, which was continued, obiter, in the Supreme Court in *Radmacher's* case as to the applicability of ss 34 and 35 to post nuptial agreements is of interest in the present context in the limited sense that strictly, the same remains persuasive as to the current approach to be adopted to post nuptial agreements. However, the Privy Council decision in *Macleod* was in relation to a post nuptial agreement whereas *Radmacher's* case was, clearly, a decision, on its facts, dealing with a pre-nuptial agreement. Whilst a Privy Council decision is also of persuasive authority, the Board's decision was delivered by Lady Hale, who in delivering the Minority speech in *Radmacher's* case in the Supreme Court, clearly considered that the Majority's expressed view in relation to post-nuptial agreements was indeed strictly obiter (but cf the criticism of the *Macleod* decision in [2015] CFLQ 63 The draft Nuptial Agreements Bill and the abolition of the common law rule: 'swept away' or swept under the carpet? Marie Parker). This suggests that *Macleod* should, until clarification is provided by a subsequent case, continue to be the principal authority dealing with the approach to post-nuptial agreements under the s 25 exercise. Indeed, the Majority in *Radmacher's* case expressly approved the approach in *Macleod* whenever the post nuptial agreement being considered was either an *Edgar* or *Xydhias* type agreement dealing with an imminent or actual separation between the parties.
11 [2009] EWHC 2485 (Fam).

8.15 Pre-nuptial Agreements

Radmacher v Granatino – the appeals

Decision of the Court of Appeal

8.15 The first appeal by the wife[1] came before Thorpe, Rix and Wilson LJJ as he then was. The appeal was successful.

Thorpe LJ in delivering the leading judgment, considered that the primary problem was the difficulty in reconciling the civil law and common law jurisdictions of Europe and the UK. The former applying formulaic property outcomes to marriage and divorce and the latter applying, in contrast, a broad judicial discretion to property distribution upon divorce. By example, he contrasted the outcomes of these two regimes on the facts of the case, where in the parties' birthplaces (Germany and France) the pre-nuptial agreement entered into would have resulted in no award to the husband, whereas under the English system of law, the husband had received £5.6m.

His Lordship acknowledged the change in judicial attitude from his own decision in *F v F* in 1995 in which he had suggested that the statutory exercise under s 25 'cannot be much influenced by contractual terms . . . ' to the decision in *Crossley* in 2008, where, again, in giving judgment, he had accepted that especially in short childless marriages of independently wealthy individuals, a pre-nuptial agreement would be regarded as a factor of magnetic importance.

Thorpe LJ considered that this movement had been necessary to modernise the law from that reflecting the laws and morals of earlier generations to the current position of recognising the autonomy of adults to govern their future financial relationship by agreement in an age when divorce had become commonplace. By such a process, also, the distinctions between the law in this jurisdiction would be reduced from those applying in the majority of the member states of Europe and the wider common law world.

His Lordship recognised that in regard to pre-nuptial agreements there still needed to be appropriate safeguards, which should be that:

(1) any term which purported to oust the court's jurisdiction would be void, albeit severable;
(2) where the appropriate safeguards had not been followed or under contractual principles there were grounds which vitiated an agreement, then the agreement would be voidable;
(3) a pre-nuptial agreement would remain, under the s 25 exercise, subject to the judge's discretionary review where it was contended that its terms were unfair.

Against such considerations, whilst the judge at first instance had directed herself appropriately in relation to her reference to the 'safeguards' set out in the 1998 Government Green Paper and the previous case law, Thorpe LJ, along with the other judges sitting, did not accept her findings that, as measured against such criteria, the pre-nuptial agreement signed was 'flawed', as she had found it to be. Nor, in the light of her findings that she would take into account in limiting his recovery the fact that the husband had entered into the 'flawed' agreement, was the Court of Appeal satisfied that the judge had properly reflected such an approach in the level of award she made.

In consequence, Thorpe LJ considered that the appropriate approach on the facts of the case was to adopt the methodology of the award made by Baron J, but to limit its duration only to the period whilst the children were dependent and they enjoyed the shared care arrangement reached between the parties. Hence, the provision made over to the husband for a home for himself and the children and the other capital provision made for him as a father and part time carer of the children would continue, but only in regard to the latter until the youngest child attained 22 years of age. As a result, in the light of the agreement reached, the husband received no capital provision for himself as a husband.

The Court of Appeal directly addressed the approach to be adopted to those matters previously considered as safeguards or pre-conditions to a pre-nuptial agreement being taken into consideration by the court (ie independent legal advice, prior full and frank disclosure, needs or the absence of provision for children).

Thorpe LJ emphasised the husband's experience in international banking and Wilson LJ considered that s 25 enabled the court to apply common sense to the facts of any given situation and, therefore, as the husband had, clearly, understood the effect of the pre-nuptial agreement and had had the chance to seek independent legal advice, but had chosen not to do so, then the absence of such advice would not enable him to escape the impact of the agreement.

As to disclosure, neither party had made specific disclosure to the other before the pre-nuptial agreement was signed, albeit the wife had deliberately ensured that her finances were kept secret. However, the husband was well aware the wife was from a very wealthy family and the Court of Appeal stated that would be sufficient in the circumstances. Wilson LJ considered that lack of disclosure alone would not be a sufficient 'flaw' and any party so relying on such an alleged failure would need to show that the effect of any non-disclosure would have been material eg as to reaching the agreement or entering into the marriage.

In regard to needs, Wilson LJ was, plainly, of the view that a pre-nuptial agreement, which purported to exclude recovery by a claimant spouse on divorce with basic needs unmet, could not, without more, be said to be unfair, if the same had been agreed to with full knowledge of such consequential effect. At the very least, His Lordship considered that a court should, in such circumstances, only allow such a party to claim to the extent necessary for the service of that 'real need'. In this respect, the husband in *Radmacher's* case was seen as having received an award at first instance as 'home maker' for the children, which more than provided for his own basic needs and fairness in the light of the agreement entered into and the court should, instead, have limited his award to that period only and not have permitted an extension covering his statistical lifetime following the independence of the children, when it was unlikely that he would have been in 'real need'.

8.15 Pre-nuptial Agreements

As to the absence of any provision for children within a pre-nuptial agreement, the Court of Appeal remained untroubled and because any children's provision could not be limited by agreement, Wilson LJ did not regard the absence or express limitation of such provision as a 'flaw' which would significantly affect the weight to be ascribed to the pre-nuptial agreement, subsequently, upon a divorce etc. Indeed, in *Radmacher's* case, such an absence of written provision, permitted the court, in the event, to make very substantial provision for the husband as the children's shared carer.

[1] [2009] EWCA Civ 649.

Decision of the Supreme Court

8.16 The Supreme Court had in the hearing before them in 2010 an appeal by the husband in which the questions for them to decide were whether the Court of Appeal:

(1) had erred in finding that a freely entered into pre-nuptial agreement ought to be given decisive weight under the s 25 assessment; and
(2) in coming to its decision, had, in error, judicially legislated in contravention of the decision of *Macleod*[1].

[1] [2008] UKPC 64.

THE MAJORITY

8.17 The Supreme Court's decision by a majority of 8 to 1 was that the Court of Appeal had correctly found that on the facts of the case it was not unfair under s 25 to hold the husband to the pre-nuptial agreement. The President of the court, Lord Phillips gave the majority judgment with Lord Mance adding further commentary in support and Lady Hale, as the sole experienced family judge sitting, delivering the only dissenting judgment.

In a review of the current law of division of assets upon divorce, Lord Phillips, specifically, highlighted the fact that in *Miller*[1] it had been recognised that assets may be treated differently where the parties during the marriage had themselves treated the same as separate property and that this had been seen as a cautious ' . . . movement in the law towards a more frequent distribution of property upon divorce in accordance with what, by words or conduct, the parties appear previously to have agreed' (see para 30).

His Lordship noted that it had been contrary to public policy for a married couple, who were living together or a couple about to get married, to make an agreement that provided for the contingency that they might separate. Such agreements had, therefore, been treated as void and the court would pay no regard to them. But this rule had not applied to an actual agreement to separate or an agreement that governed a separation that had already taken place (see *Hyman*[2]). Subsequently, the Maintenance Agreements Act 1957, which, as a prelude to ss 34 and 35 of the later Matrimonial Causes Act 1973 had advanced this situation, so that the court could determine the validity of an agreement to separate ('maintenance agreement') and whether there was a need to alter the terms of the same and the existence of such an agreement to separate could have a considerable effect upon the court's exercise of the discretionary powers under s 25 upon a divorce.

However, the approach to other post nuptial and pre-nuptial agreements had remained that they were void and the courts had only been prepared to give their terms limited weight within the statutory exercise under s 25 (see paras 35–42). Progressively, this position had changed, so that the situation had now been reached whereby in *Crossley*[3] the court had been prepared to regard the existence of a pre-nuptial agreement as a factor of 'magnetic importance' when determining the fair division of resources upon divorce (see paras 45–46).

Lord Phillips agreed with the Board in *Macleod*'s case that the old public policy rule against agreements providing for future separations was now obsolete and should be swept away; but, unlike the Board's view that this did not apply to pre-nuptial agreements, the Majority of the Supreme Court considered that such an approach applied to all nuptial agreements whether pre or post nuptial, all of which should and could, in His Lordship's opinion, be equally enforced as contracts (see para 52). This was for two reasons, namely that it was doubtful that ss 34 and 35 applied to all nuptial agreements as opposed to only *Edgar* type separation agreements and *Xydhias* type compromise agreements and there was no material distinction between the nature of pre and post nuptial agreements as contracts (see paras 53–63).

There may be good reason why a court should start with the agreement and consider initially whether any changes had occurred. In relation to both *Edgar* and *Xydhias* type agreements, by their nature and timing, they were likely to be more contemporary with the circumstances prevailing at the time of ancillary relief proceedings and therefore more relevant. Whereas, by contrast, the terms of a pre-nuptial or other early post nuptial agreement may not be as relevant. Hence, whilst the Board's approach in *Macleod* may be appropriate in relation to *Edgar* or *Xydhias* type agreements, it would not be so in relation to pre-nuptial and such other post nuptial agreements (paras 64–66).

Lord Phillips identified three issues for the court's decision (para 67). They were:

(1) Did circumstances attending the making of the agreement exist that detracted from the weight to be accorded to it?
(2) Did circumstances attending the making of the agreement exist that enhanced the weight to be accorded to it; ie the foreign element?
(3) Did the circumstances prevailing when the court's order was made make it fair or just to depart from the agreement?

[1] [2006] UKHL 24
[2] [1929] AC 601. See also the debate as to whether the court in both the *Macleod* and *Radmacher* cases correctly interpreted the common law rule in relation to agreements which anticipated the separation of the parties in [2015] CFLQ 63 'The draft Nuptial Agreements Bill and the abolition of the common law rule: 'swept away' or swept under the carpet?', Marie Parker.
[3] [2007] EWCA Civ 1491.

8.18 *As to (1) (weight)*: The court considered, under the s 25 exercise, that a pre or post nuptial agreement would only carry full weight if both parties

8.18 *Pre-nuptial Agreements*

entered it with free will, without undue influence or pressure and informed of its implications (see 3rd, 5th and 6th safeguards in Government's Green Paper (1998)). Whilst the court accepted that the six safeguards of the Green Paper would, in most cases, be highly relevant considerations, the real question for a court in this context was whether there was any material lack of disclosure, information or advice[1]. If it is clear that a party is fully aware of the implications of a pre-nuptial agreement and yet indifferent to detailed particulars of the other party's assets, there will be no need to accord the agreement reduced weight because he or she is unaware of those particulars. What is essential is that each party should have all the information that is material to his or her decision and should intend that the agreement should govern the financial consequences of the marriage coming to an end (paras 68–69).

Lord Phillips considered that it must follow that, whilst before this appeal decision it may not have been right to infer from an agreement's existence alone that the parties had intended it to take effect; in future, it will be natural to infer that parties who enter into a pre-nuptial agreement to which English law is likely to be applied intend that effect should be given to it (para 70).

Guidance as to the future approach included:

(i) asking first the question, whether there are any of the standard vitiating factors, being duress, fraud or misrepresentation, present. Such factors will negate any effect the agreement might otherwise have, whether contractually enforceable or not. Akin to *Edgar*, unconscionable conduct such as undue pressure (falling short of duress) will also be likely to eliminate the weight to be attached to the agreement and other unworthy conduct eg exploitation of a dominant position to secure an unfair advantage, would reduce or eliminate it (para 71).

(ii) taking account of a party's emotional state, and what pressures he or she was under to agree. However, this should not be in isolation from what would have happened had he or she not been under those pressures. All the circumstances of the parties at the time of the agreement will be relevant, including eg their age and maturity, and whether previously married or in long-term relationships. Such previous relationships may explain the terms of the agreement, and reveal what they foresaw when they entered into the agreement. Matters not foreseeable for less mature couples may well be fully in contemplation of more mature couples. It may be an important factor, either way, that the marriage would still have gone ahead without an agreement or without certain of the terms agreed (para 72).

(iii) an unfair agreement at inception will reduce its weight, albeit, in practice, this question will be subsumed within the wider question under s 25 whether the agreement operates unfairly, having regard to the circumstances prevailing at the time of the breakdown of the marriage (para 73).

As to (2) (foreign element): Lord Phillips, whilst noting the foreign element of the case, with the husband being French and the wife German and the agreement having a German law jurisdiction clause, commented that in future it was unlikely, with agreements made contemporaneously and, a fortiori, any made after the judgment, that there would be any live issue between the parties that they intended to be bound by the agreement and, therefore, foreign law would not need to be considered in such cases. However, when dealing with agreements concluded in the past (here 1998), such foreign elements may continue to bear on the important question of whether or not the parties intended their agreement to be effective (para 74).

As to (3) (fairness): Following *White and Miller*, under the s 25 exercise, where the pre-nuptial agreement's provisions conflict with what the court would otherwise consider to be the requirements of fairness, then the fact of the agreement is an important factor to be weighed in the balance and is capable of altering what is fair. The proposition, in substitution for the previous approach of Macleod, should be in both pre and post-nuptial agreement cases that:

> 'The court should give effect to a nuptial agreement that is freely entered into by each party with a full appreciation of its implications *unless in the circumstances prevailing it would not be fair to hold the parties to their agreement*' (para 75).

What is fair is fact sensitive to the particular facts of the case under consideration, but any nuptial agreement cannot be allowed to prejudice the reasonable requirements of any children of the family.

Respect for individual autonomy and the right to determine the division of their resources on divorce is a good reason why it would be fair to give weight to a nuptial agreement reached between parties, especially if the agreement addresses existing circumstances and not merely the contingencies of an uncertain future. Another good reason may be where parties wish to make provision for existing property owned by one or other, or property that one or other anticipates receiving from a third party. Another may be where the nuptial agreement makes provision for what is termed non matrimonial and matrimonial property, as distinguished in *White and Miller* (paras 76–80).

Lord Phillips considered, however, that where the pre-nuptial agreement attempts to address contingencies, unknown and unforeseen, of the couple's future relationship, there is more scope for events over the years to make it unfair to hold them to their agreement. The longer the marriage, the more likely it is that this will be the case, eg where a pre-nuptial agreement made no provision on divorce and the parties started their marriage with no particular wealth and, over time, by mutual contribution, one of them has accumulated significant wealth.

In His Lordship's view, 'need' and/or 'compensation' are the most likely of the three strands of fairness to make it unfair to hold the parties to a pre-nuptial agreement and the parties to such an agreement are unlikely to have intended that their agreement should result, upon marital breakdown, in one partner being left in a predicament of 'real need', while the other enjoys a sufficiency or more, and such an outcome is likely to render it unfair to hold the parties to their agreement. Similarly where the devotion of one partner to looking after the family and the home has left the other free to accumulate wealth, then again, it is likely to be unfair to hold them to an agreement that entitles the latter to retain all that he or she has earned.

8.18 Pre-nuptial Agreements

In contrast, where each can meet his or her needs, fairness may well not require a departure from their agreement in the circumstances that have come to pass. Hence, it is in regard to the third strand of 'sharing', that the court will be most likely to make an order in the terms of the nuptial agreement in place of the order that it would otherwise have made. However, a court will now be more willing to ascribe the appropriate weight to the agreement under 'all the circumstances of the case' under s 25 and, in the right case, the existence of the agreement will be the most compelling factor (see paras 81–83).

[1] See commentary within note 106 below in relation to the impact of the subsequent decision of the Supreme Court in *Gohil v Golhil* [2015] UKSC 61.

8.19 Lord Phillips highlighted certain facts of the appeal case, which resulted in the majority upholding the decision of the Court of Appeal. These were:

(1) that whilst the husband had not taken independent legal advice, he had well understood the effect of the agreement, had had the opportunity to take independent advice, but had failed to do so and, in such circumstances, he could not rely on the fact that he had not taken independent legal advice;

(2) that whilst the wife had failed to disclose the approximate value of her assets, the husband knew she had substantial wealth and had shown no interest in ascertaining its approximate extent and he had never suggested that this would have had any effect on his readiness to enter into the agreement;

(3) that whilst there had been no negotiation, it was unclear why this should be a vitiating factor as Baron J had maintained and it merely reflected the fact that the background of the parties rendered the entry into such an agreement commonplace;

(4) that it was not apparent that Baron J had made any significant reduction in her award to reflect the fact of the agreement.

However, Lord Phillips was not prepared to endorse the stance of Wilson LJ that there was nothing unfair about an absence of provision within the agreement for the possibility that the husband might be reduced to circumstances of 'real need'. If the husband had been incapacitated in the course of the marriage, affecting his ability to meet his needs, then, in the interests of fairness, it may have been unfair to hold him to the full rigours of the pre-nuptial agreement. On the facts, this was, in the prevailing circumstances, far from the case. The husband was a very able and well qualified individual and had received generous relief given to meet the needs of the two children, which would indirectly provide in large measure for his own need until his children reached independence and further the court orders had provided separately for the discharge of his personal debts.

There was no compensation factor in the case as the husband's decision to abandon his lucrative career in the city for the fields of academia was not motivated by the demands of his family, but reflected his own choice. In the light of the husband's initial agreement that he should have no part in the wife's family wealth and the fact that the same had been acquired mainly before the marriage and/or independently of any contribution by the husband, it was fair that he should be held to the pre-nuptial agreement and unfair to depart from it (paras 120–122).

It is suggested that a succinct summary of the consequences of the Supreme Court's decision upon the court's approach to pre-nuptial agreements is to be found in the later High Court case of *Luckwell v Limata*[1], where Holman J endorsed the following joint statement by leading counsel before him of the law in this area post *Radmacher* as follows:

'129. There is no doubt that the decision of the Supreme Court in *Granatino v Radmacher* [2010] UKSC 42, [2011] 1 AC 534 represented, and now requires, a significant shift in the approach to, and weight to be given to, negotiated, drafted and freely signed nuptial agreements of the kinds in the present case when there is no vitiating factor.

130. I said at the outset of this judgment that the law is not difficult to state. Such agreements must always be given weight, and often decisive weight as part of the circumstances of the case. They may affect not only whether to make any award at all, but also the size and the structure of any award. I could at this point cite passages from the majority judgment in *Granatino v Radmacher* but, helpfully, all three counsel have agreed the following propositions of law which are drawn from *Granatino v Radmacher* and which I gratefully adopt. (They were first drafted by Mr Marks and Miss Faggionato, but I quote them with the additions made by Mr Howard.)

1. It is the court, and not the parties, that decides the ultimate question of what provision is to be made;
2. The over-arching criterion remains the search for "fairness", in accordance with section 25 as explained by the House of Lords in Miller/McFarlane (ie needs, sharing and compensation). But an agreement is capable of altering what is fair, including in relation to "need";
3. An agreement (assuming it is not "impugned" for procedural unfairness, such as duress) should be given weight in that process, although that weight may be anything from slight to decisive in an appropriate case;
4. The weight to be given to an agreement may be enhanced or reduced by a variety of factors;
5. Effect should be given to an agreement that is entered into freely with full appreciation of the implications unless in the circumstances prevailing it would not be fair to hold the parties to that agreement. ie There is, at least, a burden on the [the other spouse] to show that the agreement should not prevail;
6. Whether it will "not be fair to hold the parties to the agreement" will necessarily depend on the facts, but some guidance can be given:
    i) A nuptial agreement cannot be allowed to prejudice the reasonable requirements of any children;
    ii) Respect for autonomy, including a decision as to the manner in which their financial affairs should be regulated, may be particularly relevant where the agreement addresses the existing circumstances and not merely the contingencies of an uncertain future;
    iii) There is nothing inherently unfair in an agreement making provision dealing with existing non-marital property, including anticipated future receipts, and there may be good objective justifications for it, such as obligations towards family members;
    iv) The longer the marriage has lasted the more likely it is that events have rendered what might have seemed fair at the time of the making of the agreement unfair now, particularly if the position is not as envisaged;
    v) It is unlikely to be fair that one party is left in a predicament of 'real need' while the other has "a sufficiency or more";

8.19 *Pre-nuptial Agreements*

> vi) Where each party is able to meet his or her needs, fairness may well not require a departure from the agreement.

131. In elaboration of proposition 6(i) above, I should stress that part of the express statutory duty of the court under section 25(1) is to give first consideration to the welfare while a minor of any child of the family, who has not attained the age of eighteen. As in *Granatino v Radmacher*, the children in the present case spend time with each of their parents, and the financial circumstances of each of their parents are likely to impact upon their welfare. The facts of the two cases differ markedly – Mrs Radmacher was far, far richer than is [the wife in this case] – but in *Granatino v Radmacher* quite significant financial provision was made for the husband, in his role as father, until the younger child attained 22. In that case, however, the children were broadly evenly residing with each of the parents.

132. To counsel's propositions of law, I add one other, which needs no citation of authority. The court must be scrupulous to avoid gender discrimination or gender bias[2]. Of course, gender may, and often does, impact heavily on outcome. If in fact a wife, in her role as mother, is the primary carer for the children, then her need for secure and suitable accommodation may outweigh that of the husband. If a wife, due to her commitments to caring for the children, is less able to work than is the husband, then that is likely to impact upon maintenance needs. So, too, if it is a fact of a case that a wife has lower earning capacity because of gender discrimination in the relevant employment markets. But there must be no discrimination or bias based on gender alone, nor on any stereo–typical view that a wife may be dependent upon her husband but not vice versa.'

[1] [2014] EWHC 502 (Fam).
[2] But cf 'Nuptial agreements: does the gender of the wealthy spouse affect the award?' Louise Spitz, Laura Rowley and Rebecca Dziobon, Penningtons Manches LLP [2016] Fam Law 1147 September 2016 where the authors suggest that husbands as opposed to wives have consistently received lower awards, post *Radmacher* where a marital agreement has been involved.

THE MINORITY

8.20 Lady Hale in her minority judgment, repeated her view, as in *Macleod*, that modern marriage still holds an 'irreducible minimum', including a couple's mutual duty to support each other and their children. In her view, the issue was how far individuals should be free to rewrite that essential feature of the marital relationship. She considered that it remained for Parliament to achieve comprehensive and principled reform following the Law Commission's report (see paras 132 to 135). She accepted that the Board's decision in *Macleod* had gone too far in referring to 'manifestly unjust' as opposed to 'unjust', which was the wording of ss 34 and 35 of the 1973 Act and in applying the test under ss 34 and 35 to all post nuptial agreements without adjustment. However, she confirmed that in relation to *Edgar* and *Xydhias* type agreements, *Macleod* remained good law.

Her Ladyship differed (para 138 and following) from the majority decision in a number of respects, being that:

(1) she rejected the view that pre-nuptial agreements are legally enforceable contracts;
(2) she rejected the view that it is open to the Supreme Court to hold that they are;

(3) she also rejected the upholding of the Court of Appeal's decision on the facts of the case; since the Court of Appeal had appeared to treat the parties as cohabitees as opposed to married partners and had failed to recognise the expectation of many parents of continuing to be a resource for their grown-up children. Hence, whilst the first instance decision should have given more weight to the fact of the pre-nuptial agreement, the majority's lack of additional provision to the husband was not, in Her Ladyship's view, generous enough and should have included the retention by him of the home for his lifetime and not just the dependency of the children;
(4) in her view, policy considerations justified a different approach for agreements made before and after a marriage;
(5) she considered that the test to be applied by the court when approaching a pre-nuptial agreement should not be to introduce the 'impermissible gloss' on the statute of a presumption or starting point in favour of holding the parties to the agreement;
(6) she considered also that the approach of the Court of Appeal and the majority decision did not give sufficient importance to the status of marriage in English law;
(7) she believed that reform of this area should be in regard to both pre and post-nuptial agreements and not limited to pre-nuptial agreements alone;
(8) in her view, fairness should be the sole touchstone in the light of the actual and foreseeable circumstances at the time when the court comes to make its order. No pre-nuptial agreement should prevent the court reaching a fair outcome on divorce (see para 168).

Case law – post Radmacher – a decade of interpretation

8.21 A decade on from the Supreme Court's decision in the *Radmacher* case, there has been a wide body of case law, which has directly interpreted and applied the guidance provided.

The first to be reported was $Z \ v \ Z^1$, a judgment in 2011 of Moor J. This decision served to emphasise two aspects of the current law pending any legislative reform. The first is that whatever the terms of a pre-nuptial agreement between the parties, the court will not countenance a distribution under the s 25 exercise, which fails to meet either parties' 'needs' level for accommodation and income (or for that matter any entitlement to 'compensation'). Secondly, the existence of a valid pre-nuptial agreement which remains 'material to the prevailing circumstances' and which seeks to limit or extinguish a party's entitlement under the 'sharing principle' is likely to be considered as fair and followed by the court upon divorce.

In the *Z v Z* case, the parties aged 53 (H) and 50 (W) had three dependent children. They had cohabited for 4 years and thereafter been married for 14 years before their final separation. As French nationals they had in 1994 signed a separation of property pre-nuptial agreement in Paris before two Notaries in which they opted out of the community of property default system. During the marriage, the parties had moved around with H's employment and latterly, as the marriage was failing, they had moved to London, having already consulted

8.21 Pre-nuptial Agreements

lawyers over their possible separation. Following a trial separation, H finally left W in their family home in London and W issued divorce proceedings in the UK.

Ryder J granted permission to proceed in the UK, determining that the parties' habitual residence had, latterly, been in the jurisdiction. Accordingly, upon the pursuit of W's claims for financial orders, the fact of the pre-nuptial agreement became a focal issue. W claimed H had promised orally not to enforce the same and maintained it was fair under s 25 to divide a marital pot then of £15m equally between the parties. H contended that it was fair to apply the terms of the pre-nuptial agreement, but accepted that as the same did not include maintenance he was vulnerable to W claiming, at least, a recovery to meet her 'reasonable requirements' (a la pre *White* [2000]).

Moor J considered that the Supreme Court in *Radmacher* had brought about a 'seismic change' in the Law pending any further review by the Law Commission or Parliament in cases where a pre-nuptial agreement had been signed. Such agreements would be followed ' . . . unless in the prevailing circumstances, it would not be fair to hold the parties to the agreement' (see Lord Phillips in *Radmacher*). Accordingly, whilst in other circumstances this was a case of equal contributions and, therefore, equal sharing between the parties, the presence of the agreement allowed the court to depart from the 'sharing principle' to the extent that only W's needs for accommodation and her *Duxbury* capitalised income needs would be met together with child maintenance, resulting in a clean break upon W recovering around £6m or 40 per cent plus child maintenance (assuming H met the risk of certain unlikely but possible contingent tax liabilities).

[1] [2011] EWHC 2878 (Fam).

8.22 In the same year (2011), Charles J considered the case of *V v V*[1]. This was an appeal by H against a district judge's order in the ancillary relief proceedings in which, before the marriage, a 'marriage settlement' (ie pre-nuptial agreement) had been signed. The settlement provided for H to keep all of his pre-marital property (c £1 million).

The district judge had ordered a charge back in favour of H on the home to be bought by W with the lump sum that she was awarded as part of the settlement. The appeal centered upon whether the court had been right to make such an order. Charles J, decided that the district judge had wrongly approached the settlement as if the case had been determined before the *Radmacher* decision in holding that because the settlement did not specify what was to happen upon divorce, then the weight to be attached to it was limited. On the contrary, Charles J emphasised the decision of the Supreme Court required a significant change to the approach to be taken now in relation to such agreements. The priority, on the same level of importance as the established principles of 'need, compensation and sharing', was the need to recognise the weight to be given to autonomy and the choices and agreements made by the parties to a marriage. Hence, autonomous agreements and choices made by the parties could alter an award that would otherwise have been made.

Charles J decided that, in view of the lower court's findings that the parties had intended the settlement to be effective, both were fully aware of its obvious purpose despite W not having legal advice prior to signing and that W had been unconcerned as to the precise value of the H's property, there had, therefore, been no material non-disclosure and the terms of the settlement, taken together with the district judge's findings, did not justify a conclusion that the agreement was to be given limited weight.

Charles J further considered that whilst the district judge found that the wife had been in the weaker bargaining position, this factor was not sufficient to give only limited weight to the marriage settlement. Without more, the agreement had been willingly and honestly entered into by both sides. Accordingly, the district judge had been wrong in law in her approach to the assessment of the weight to be given to the marriage settlement and in concluding that it should only be given little weight in the s 25 exercise. Incorrectly, she had adopted a pre-*Radmacher* approach to the pre-nuptial agreement under consideration.

By contrast, Charles J concluded that the agreement was a factor that should be given weight to reflect the autonomy of both parties, who had freely and knowingly entered into it and in the circumstances it provided a good reason for departing from an equal division of the available assets which in His Lordship's judgment should by fresh assessment under the statutory exercise result in a chargeback of 33.3% of the value of the wife's property in favour of the husband and this percentage was increased to 35.8% when accounting for the wife's liability to pay the husbands costs on appeal.

[1] [2011] EWHC 3230 (Fam). See also *GS v L* [2011] EWHC 1759 (Fam), King J. Financial remedies application where H sought ring fencing of £1.49m of assets as pre-acquired or subject to a community of property agreement signed in Spain in 2002. Parties married 10 years with two children and now all living in Spain. Their foremost intention had been to give W financial security in the event of H's death. In addition, the impact of the existence of the agreement in Spanish law was itself controversial and uncertain and, accordingly, Her Ladyship considered the same provided the court with scant assistance in the s 25 exercise. Save for H's pension, this was a needs case which required all the assets to be considered and which would be equally divided with W's maintenance capitalized on top £4m. King J found that neither party had a full appreciation of the implications of the community of property agreement.

8.23 In a trilogy of cases determined by Mostyn J between 2012 and 2013, the impact of a pre-nuptial agreement post *Radmacher* was further considered.

The first of these was *Kremen v Agrest (No 11) (Financial Remedy: Non-Disclosure: Post-Nuptial Agreement)*[1] In this case, there had been a number of proceedings in this jurisdiction and abroad, including Israel. W was seeking financial orders under Pt III of the Matrimonial and Family Proceedings Act 1984. Both parties were Russian and their marriage had been in Moscow in 1991. In 2001, they had signed a post-nuptial agreement in Israel in which W's entitlement was limited to $1.5m. This agreement was to be approved by the court in Israel and such approval was reaffirmed upon the parties' divorce in Israel in 2003. In fact, belatedly, H claimed the marriage and the agreement were invalid as he had been married to another at the time and in 2010 on this basis the court in Russia granted him a marriage annulment. In the proceedings brought by W in this jurisdiction, Mostyn J found H to have failed to disclose

8.23 Pre-nuptial Agreements

assets and he also found that W had been subjected to undue pressure and that she had had no independent legal advice and, therefore, His Lordship concluded that no reliance could be placed upon a post nuptial agreement signed by the parties in 2001. Assessing H's wealth at circa £20m to £30m, he awarded W £12.5m, being the court's assessment of her housing and maintenance needs and reflecting her contribution and her overall fair share. In reaching his judgment, he summarised the impact of the *Radmacher* case in relation to the approach to be adopted to nuptial agreements, as follows (see para 72 of judgment):

(1) A nuptial agreement freely entered into by each party with a full appreciation of its implications should be followed by the court unless in the circumstances prevailing it would not be fair to hold the parties to their agreement.

(2) There is no absolute rule for what amounts to full disclosure or independent legal advice – instead, the question is there has been a *material lack* of disclosure, information or advice. Each party must have all the information that is *material* to his or her decision that the agreement should govern the financial consequences of the marriage coming to an end. There may now be some qualification to this guidance as to the level of *material* disclosure following the conjoined appeal decisions of the Supreme Court in *Sharland v Sharland* and *Gohil v Gohil*[2].

(3) The presence of any of the standard vitiating factors of duress, fraud or misrepresentation will negate any effect the agreement might otherwise have. Further, unconscionable conduct such as undue pressure (falling short of duress) will likely eliminate the weight to be attached to the agreement (ibid). Other unworthy conduct, such as exploitation of a dominant position to secure an unfair advantage, will reduce or eliminate the weight to be attached to the agreement (ibid). The court may take into account a party's emotional state, and what pressures he or she was under to agree, as well as their age and maturity, and whether either or both had been married or been in long-term relationships before. The court may take into account foreign elements to determine whether or not the parties intended their agreement to be effective.

(4) In determining whether 'in the circumstances prevailing it would not be fair to hold the parties to their agreement':

    (a) The agreement cannot be allowed to prejudice the reasonable requirements of any children of the family.

    (b) Respect should be accorded to the decision of a married couple as to the manner in which their financial affairs should be regulated, particularly where the agreement addresses existing circumstances and not merely the contingencies of an uncertain future. This is likely to be so where the agreement seeks to protect pre-marital property. By contrast, it is less likely to be so where the agreement leaves in the hands of one spouse rather than the other the most part of a fortune which each spouse has played an equal role in their different ways in creating. If the devotion of one partner to looking after the family and the home has left the other free to accumulate wealth, it is likely to be

(c) unfair to hold the parties to an agreement that entitles the latter to retain all that he or she has earned.

(c) It is likely to be unfair to hold the parties to an agreement which leaves one spouse in a predicament of *real need*, while the other enjoys a sufficiency or more. However, 'need' may be interpreted as being that minimum amount required to keep a spouse from destitution. For example, if the claimant spouse had been incapacitated in the course of the marriage, so that he or she was incapable of earning a living, this might well justify, in the interests of fairness, not holding him or her to the full rigours of the pre-nuptial agreement.

His Lordship added at para 73 of the judgment:

'73. It seems to me that it will only be in an unusual case where it can be said that, absent independent legal advice and full disclosure, a party can be taken to have freely entered into a marital agreement with a full appreciation of its implications. After all, almost every common law country that has legislated in this field has as a key pre-condition these requirements as well as a safety-net where the agreement is judged to be "unfair" (eg British Columbia) or "unjust" (eg New Zealand) or "unconscionable" (eg Australia). It would surely have to be shown that the spouse, like Mr Granatino, had a high degree of financial and legal sophistication in order to have a full appreciation of what legal rights he or she is signing away. Equally, it seems to me that there would have to be clear evidence of significant economic capacity on the part of the claimant spouse before the assessment of needs was suppressed to that minimal level imposed on Mr Granatino. There would surely have to be an equivalent finding to that in para 119 viz "on the evidence he is extremely able, and has added to his qualifications by pursuing a D Phil in biotechnology". I have noted that in the recent decision of *Z v Z (No. 2)* [2011] EWHC 2878 (Fam), which concerned a French pre-nuptial agreement, Moor J generously assessed the wife's needs to include the outright ownership of valuable property and a Duxbury fund to provide a high level of income for the remainder of her life. There was no question of imposing on her an arrangement akin to an award under Schedule 1 Children Act 1989.'

---

[1] [2012] EWHC 45 (Fam).

[2] It should be noted that post the Supreme Court's decision in *Gohil v Gohil* [2015] UKSC 61, which along with the conjoined appeal of *Sharland v Sharland* [2015] UKSC 60, dealt with the impact of fraudulent disclosure upon a subsequent financial consent order, there is reason to exercise caution both in relation to the potential width of Mostyn J's guidance as to the *materiality* of the disclosure required and the effectiveness of any provision in a pre-nuptial agreement, whereby one party waives the right to appropriate disclosure for the purposes of the agreement. In *Gohil*'s case, Lord Wilson stated that a recital in a final financial order recording a party's belief that the other party had not provided full and frank disclosure had no legal effect. Instead, under the statutory exercise of s 25, the court is charged with 'a duty' to determine the fairness of a divorce distribution upon the parties' present and foreseeable financial circumstances and as such one party could not exonerate the other party from compliance with their duty of full and frank disclosure to the court. In consequence, whilst, of course, the cases of *Sharland* and *Gohil* dealt with fraudulent disclosure resulting in final orders where the duty of disclosure is to the court as well as the other party, it is suggested that incomplete disclosure resulting from one party's fraud which results in the other entering into a pre-nuptial agreement may well be seen subsequently by a court upon any challenge to a pre-nuptial's provision for the weaker financial party on a divorce as a very relevant factor when a court is determining whether it is fair to uphold the agreement's terms – see and cf 'Set-aside orders and the wider implications: Sharland and Gohil' Claire Blakemore, Partner, Withers, Natalie O'Shea [2015] Fam Law 1479.

8.24 Pre-nuptial Agreements

8.24 In the second of these cases, in *B v S (Financial Remedy: Marital Property Regime)*[1] the parties had been married for 14 years and there were two children aged 10 and 12. W, who was Spanish had made an application for financial remedy orders against H, a national of another country. The family had been in the UK since 2004 and divorce proceedings had commenced in 2009. Mostyn J had to consider what weight was to be attached, first to an alleged tacit agreement between the parties whereby they had adopted a default matrimonial property regime of 'separate property' upon their marriage in Catalonia as endorsed also by a second 'separation of property' agreement made in 2000 in another country, the identity of which could not be reported because of the requirement of anonymity. The second agreement having come into existence to deal specifically with certain property of W's, which would otherwise have fallen under the default 'community of property' regime of the other country.

H had established a widget company in 2000, which was now under a discretionary trust of which the parties and their children were beneficiaries and, therefore, the agreement was a 'nuptial settlement' and, plainly, a resource of H – however, the company was sited in a failed state where the parties security could not be guaranteed and the company profits had been very volatile. It was contended that the company had $9.5m in accessible assets and that H had had access to over £8m in company loans in recent years. Mostyn J determined, having rejected the applicability of either agreement ventured, that W should have £3m (being half of the value of the company assets value found), payable by instalments with a capitalised maintenance sum of £344k paid on the last instalment when the decreasing interim spousal maintenance for W would then terminate.

Mostyn J considered that as the law of England and Wales applied to all issues engaged, the only relevance of the foreign law involved was as to the evidence it provided as to the parties' intentions when they entered into the agreements. In a review of the *Radmacher* decision and the cases determined since in respect of pre and post-nuptial agreements, His Lordship's view was that the established requirement of 'a full appreciation of [the agreement's] implications' did not carry with it a requirement to have received specific advice as to the operation of English law on the agreement in question. If it were otherwise then many nuptial agreements would fall at that hurdle. Rather, for the agreement entered into to have a relevance to the court's decision as to what was fair under the s 25 exercise on divorce, the reference to a 'full appreciation . . . etc' must mean more than having a mere understanding that the agreement would just govern in the country in which it was made – indeed, the parties must have intended the agreement to have effect, wherever they might be divorced and, most particularly, were they to be divorced in a jurisdiction that operated a system of discretionary equitable distribution[2]. However, this strict view has subsequently been rejected by the Court of Appeal in *Versteegh v Verstreegh* (see more below).

His Lordship rejected H's case that the parties had tacitly adopted the Catalan default system of 'separation of property', without more; but rather, he found, they had intended the Catalan system to apply but subject to its 'lax judicial discretionary adjustment (powers) to effect compensatory redress for resultant economic inequality' – akin to that operated within this jurisdiction. He also found that the parties when entering into the second 'separation of property' agreement had simply intended only that the general Catalan law, as described above, would be applied thereby and in relation to neither agreement had the parties been advised whether the same may apply should they be divorced elsewhere or whether either agreement may restrict their rights to seek the statutory exercise of discretion under an equitable distribution jurisdiction such as that of England and Wales. Accordingly, neither party had entered either agreement with a full appreciation of the implications.

1   [2012] EWHC 425 (Fam).
2   See now King LJ in *Versteegh v Versteegh* [2018] EWCA Civ 1050.

8.25 In the last of these cases, in *BN v MA*[1], the parties with international backgrounds had had a relationship since 2002 and a child in 2005 and they had become committed to one another by 2007. They eventually married in 2012 and by 2013 a second child was expected by W, but then there was a separation after a violent incident occurred. W issued full applications for financial remedies upon filing her petition for divorce. In 2010, however, whilst both were abroad albeit living in different countries, they signed a comprehensive pre-nuptial agreement which was headed with an enlarged caution not to sign unless they wished to be bound by its terms and in which the terms provided a set amount for W and any children dependent upon the length of the marriage capped at 30% of H's wealth.

Mostyn J found that the law adopts 'a strict policy of requiring the demonstration of something unfair before it will open the Pandora's Box of litigation' after an agreement of this nature. He queried on what legal basis W had supposed it appropriate to file application for financial relief, including interim remedial relief, after signing such an agreement just 15 months before.

His Lordship considered post *Radmacher* that there was only one approach to apply (to all nuptial agreements no matter if signed before or after a marriage), namely to give effect to such agreements, unless, in circumstances prevailing, it would be unfair to do so. In His Lordship's view, the autonomy of the parties, especially where, as here, they were of some sophistication and independently advised, was of particular importance and that particular weight should be given to agreements, which addressed present circumstances and sought to protect pre-owned property; although, he acknowledged that no provision could overreach basic need. (Of course, it is to be noted that the Law Commission's proposals for reform relating to the effect of a duly signed Qualifying Nuptial Agreement would make all, but the issue of the parties 'needs', irrelevant as to the implementation of the terms of the agreement.)

In Mostyn J's judgment, under the current law, all that was needed was that there should have been such 'material' disclosure and legal advice that was enough to enable the parties to have understood what was being given up and to have given their free consent. Accordingly, His Lordship found in this case there was nothing to suggest it would be unfair to uphold the terms of the pre-nuptial agreement, which would be applied as closely as possible.

8.25 *Pre-nuptial Agreements*

In 2013, Moor J in *AH v PH (Scandanavian Marriage Settlement)*[2], dealt with two spouses of Scandanavian origin. Their marriage was relatively short, just over 4 years, although they had two young children. H's wealth of c £76m was mainly inherited. There had been a marriage settlement with the benefit of legal advice signed in the parties' home country and providing W with c £850,000 to buy a home upon a separation, but with no spousal or child maintenance provision. W wanted over £12m on a clean break and H submitted £4.6m to her was appropriate.

Moor J approached the case on the basis that as all the assets were essentially 'non matrimonial' in origin then he should address W's claims on the basis of her 'reasonable needs' only.

His Lordship acknowledged that the *Radmacher* decision had altered the court's previous approach to the existence of a nuptial settlement, which had been entered into by parties with a full appreciation of the implications and, even if the court considered after analysis of the circumstances that the agreement should not be binding, the fact of its existence would still be relevant within 'all the circumstances of the case'.

In His Lordship's judgment, the agreement had a number of failings. It would not, on the basis of expert evidence received by the court, be binding in Scandinavia, it did not provide for English housing or maintenance, the parties had not obtained legal advice as to its effect in this jurisdiction before signing and it did not relinquish all of W's claims in any event. Overall, W, therefore, entered into the same without a full appreciation of its implications and, therefore, the agreement would carry little weight, save only to have regard to the intention to protect H's inherited wealth, subject to W's reasonable needs – however, as Moor J observed, because of the shortness of the marriage, this would have been the approach in any event. Moor J, therefore, awarded W £5m of housing needs and her annual maintenance was to be capitalised on the basis of 17 years of child care to tertiary education and not on the basis of her lifetime.

[1] [2013] EWHC 4250 (Fam).
[2] [2013] EWHC 3878 (Fam).

8.26 In 2014, Mostyn J gave judgment in *SA v PA (Pre-Marital Agreement: Compensation)*[1]. In this case the parties (H, a Dutch solicitor aged 50 and earning £600k pa net who intended to retire at 55 and W, who was English aged 48 and not employed, although a qualified lawyer) had been married 18 years and had four children aged 13 to 19. They had signed a pre-nuptial agreement before a notary the day before their marriage in Amsterdam, the purpose of which had been to provide that there would on separation be an equal division of jointly created capital and a separate entitlement to any capital acquired by each party post-marriage from outside sources to be kept separate. There was no provision in the agreement for spousal maintenance. In the event, H had received family gifts of over £363k out of non-pension asset values of £3.8m and pension asset value held by H of £1.14m.

His Lordship determined that he should transfer the family home (value £2.2m subject to (£600k) mortgage) to W plus a lump sum of £120k, with H to be responsible for the joint debts and there to be an equal split by pension share of the pension funds with over £10k pm periodical payments for W and with child support and education costs paid by H.

In the court's view, W had had sufficient advice as to the implications of the agreement and had known exactly what she was agreeing to and the parties had intended that the agreement should cover a divorce in whatever jurisdiction that might take place. Because the agreement did not cover maintenance, the court adjudicated upon that aspect, but otherwise W was to be held to the bargain she had struck, it being determined that her claim that this was a compensation case of a lost career had not been made out. However, because under both the law of this jurisdiction and that of Holland a pre-nuptial agreement was subject to adjustment for the parties' needs, there would be provision to W, which permitted her to build up a Duxbury fund from enhanced maintenance payments for a period and it was reasonable for her to live in the former martial home, without a sale, for a further 5 years.

Mostyn J again set out the applicable current law, as he had done in the *BN v MA* case and his previous decisions in this area, as above. He laid particular emphasis, however, in the circumstances of this case, upon the meaning of the requirement that parties to a pre-nuptial agreement should have been given within the independent legal advice they received upon the agreement, 'a full appreciation of its implications'. In His Lordship's view, to have effect within the jurisdiction of England and Wales, parties who entered into a pre-nuptial agreement abroad must have had advice not specifically about the law as it applied to divorce and inheritance distribution within this jurisdiction, but, at least, to the effect that the agreement would apply wherever they might be divorced including, in particular, in a regime that operated a system of 'discretionary equitable distribution' and it would be wise to insert a clause dealing with this in the agreement (see also Moor J in the *AH v PH (Scandinavian Marriage Settlement)* case above[2].

Again, Mostyn J further emphasised the fact that a marital agreement does not have to deal with all aspects of the parties' resources in order to be presumptively binding over the assets or resources which it addresses (see *L v C*[3]). Hence, for example, an agreement under current law may deal with the capital, whilst leaving maintenance at large or it may deal with certain assets, which each party wished to retain and ringfence from the eventual pot. In this event, the court would ordinarily give effect to such an intention, albeit that would not prevent a court, upon the s 25 exercise, taking the values of those excluded assets into account overall in the assessment of the fairness of the division of the remaining resources[4].

[1] [2014] EWHC 392 (Fam).
[2] By way of comment, in this respect, it is to be noted that the Law Commission's proposals for reform as set out below have avoided a requirement which stipulates the content of the advice upon the effect of the agreement which is to be given. Accordingly, the Commission is of the view that this would remain the judgment of the individual lawyer who advises. However, clearly it would include advising what may be the outcome on divorce without a Qualifying

8.26 *Pre-nuptial Agreements*

Nuptial Agreement in place, emphasis upon the fact that by the time of a divorce etc the nature of the parties' resources may be wholly different to when the agreement was signed and, of course, the potential, as in the present case, of either party commencing divorce proceedings in another jurisdiction .

3   [2007] 3 HKLRD 819, Hong Kong CA.
4   Again by comment, under the Law Commission's proposals for reform, where a duly signed Qualifying Nuptial Agreement is in existence, there would no longer be a need in the court to consider the fairness of the same, subject to the condition that the terms of that agreement are not inconsistent with the financial needs of a party to it or the interests of any child of the family.

8.27 In the same year, Holman J in *Luckwell v Limata*[1] had to consider a case where there were not just one but several pre and post-nuptial agreements signed by the parties with independent legal advice and all with the express purpose of limiting/excluding the recovery to be made upon any future divorce by H. The parties had been married 8 years (H 45 and W 37) and there were 3 children (aged 2 to 8). The pre-nuptial signed excluded H from claiming against W's separate property of gifts to her. Two further post-nuptial agreements between the parties on the same basis followed at times when W's family were to make specific advances to her. It was accepted that had these agreements not been in place then neither the marriage nor the advances would have occurred. At the time of the divorce the only asset, the former marital home, which had been a parental gift to W in her sole name was valued at £6.7m and the family were supported by £100k pa from W's parents. H was in debt to the tune of £226k and had been unemployed since his redundancy 2 years before and was studying for an Open University degree.

Holman J considered that, whilst very great weight had to be given to the agreements freely entered into by H as a mature man after expert legal advice and where there had been a realisation of the implications of doing so, the factor of H's present and future needs would have the effect that the agreements should not be applied rigorously. Whilst 'need' is not a trump card it can outweigh the fact of an agreement in a particular case, especially as here where the agreements made no provision at all for H in any circumstances and where it was clear he was in a predicament of real need having no home, no current income, no capital, considerable debts and no borrowing capacity. Furthermore, His Lordship, considered that it was in the children's welfare interests that each parent should have appropriate homes in which the children could visit and stay with each parent (see Radmacher's case).

Holman J, therefore, directed a sale of the former marital home, even though her father had said in evidence that if this was done he would withdraw all further support for his daughter. In His Lordship's judgment, W's mother would still provide her with some support. In any event, the sale was required so that W could specifically buy a house for £900k for H's use and in which H could be provided with a home under lease at a peppercorn rent to be sold only when the youngest child reached 22 at which time 45% of the net sale proceeds of the property would return to W and H would retain the balance to acquire a more modest home based on his reasonably predicted needs then. W was ordered also to pay H a lump sum of £292k to buy furniture, a car and to pay his debts[2].

Again in 2014, Roberts J gave judgment in *Y v Y (Financial Remedy – Marriage Contract)*[3], which involved W's application for financial remedy orders upon divorce, where H and W, as French nationals, had 2 days before the marriage entered into a marriage contract under French law in which the parties elected to apply to their marriage the *separation de biens* regime, in which they retained their own separate property. In France, such an agreement would be binding upon divorce. Instead, W now sought her equal share of their marital acquest. H contended that the choice made by the parties of the applicable marital property regime was equivalent in effect to a pre-nuptial agreement and, therefore, this agreement should be determinative in excluding assets the parties accrued in marriage.

Roberts J found that W had appreciated that the agreement she was signing would determine how the parties would conduct their marital financial dealings together. Whilst the judge did not accept the W had been confronted with the contract just 2 weeks before the marriage ceremony, as she claimed, she did accept the guidance of Mostyn J in *Kremen v Agrest* (as further explained by His Lordship in *B v S*) (above), namely:

> 'Each party must have all the information that is material to his or her decision that the agreement should govern the financial consequences of the marriage coming to an end.'

Accordingly, Her Ladyship accepted, in the circumstances, that, in the absence of independent legal advice, W, on the facts of the case, would not have had all the information she needed to fully understand all of the legal consequences which her entering the contract would have upon divorce or the entitlements which she would be surrendering as a result. In particular, she would not have appreciated that whatever their financial circumstances upon divorce, she was agreeing to a financial recovery substantially less than equality. However, that did not mean that the contract was irrelevant to the outcome; but rather the weight to be attributed to its terms was to the effect that fairness required that, subject to the wife's needs, the non-matrimonial property owned by each of the parties should be excluded from the sharing exercise to be conducted.

[1] [2014] EWHC 502 (Fam).
[2] By way of comment, the Law Commission's proposals for reform (see more below) would not have altered this position in view of the Commission's recognition that 'needs' must take precedence and on this the Commission was not in favour of any distinction being made between 'needs' and 'real needs', which has been otherwise canvassed in some of the above post *Radmacher* cases.
[3] [2014] EWHC 2920 (Fam).

8.28 In *L v M*[1], Bruce Blair QC, sitting as a Deputy High Court judge, considered, in particular, the impact of both the guidance and approach adopted to independent legal advice as set out in both the *Edgar* and *Radmacher* cases, when determining a notice to show cause whether to hold a husband to the terms of a separation agreement signed by both parties and incorporated in the terms of a draft consent order.

The H had been represented within the enforcement proceedings until disengaging and the hearing before His Lordship was undertaken over 5 days in the H's absence. Email evidence from the husband before the court when the W had been contemplating taking divorce proceedings indicated that he had

8.28 *Pre-nuptial Agreements*

had some legal advice about what would happen if there was a divorce and had met with a Zimbabwean lawyer and wanted to engage in settlement negotiations. There had then been discussions and again the H revealed he had been in contact with London solicitors and eventually there was a draft agreement drawn with the assistance of a mutual lawyer friend which then became the basis of the separation agreement signed by both parties.

The H was to pay the wife a lump sum of £2,000,000 in four instalments and global maintenance on a decreasing scale until the child completed university or attained the age of 25, whichever occurred earlier. He paid £100,000 towards the lump sum and a period of reducing maintenance before fully defaulting. He claimed a number of factors should enable him to resile, including lack of full disclosure, failing funds and lack of independent legal advice.

The court rejected the H's contentions as to disclosure as he had not pursued any such allegation during the exchanges of information between the parties, he was himself in breach of disclosure orders and had expressly agreed the settlement acknowledging limited disclosure on both sides. As to lack of independent advice, His Lordship found that pursuant to *Radmacher's* case, the H had had some legal advice and had had ample opportunity to obtain more and even if that was wrong, the lack of advice would have been the H's decision 'uncontaminated by any lack of knowledge, inequality of bargaining power or other vitiating factor' (see *Edgar*), and the agreement was, in any event, freely entered into by the H with a full appreciation of its implications. The court ordered the H was to be held to the main terms of the agreement.

In 2015, the court in *Hopkins v Hopkins*[2] considered a post-nuptial agreement involving H and W aged 66 and 62 and where it was alleged there had been duress and undue pressure by the H inducing W's signature. The parties had had a long lasting and sometimes turbulent relationship before their marriage together. W was now seeking upon divorce to secure a significant provision above that provided for her in the agreement.

The court found that W before signing the post nuptial agreement had been advised by her lawyers not to enter into the agreement, her solicitor had provided her with a 21 page legal analysis, she had taken counsel's advice and eventually she had signed a disclaimer for her solicitor who fundamentally was opposed to her entering into the agreement.

Nicholas Cusworth QC, sitting as a High Court judge, determined therefore that a number of factors existed which were in favour of upholding the agreement, being not least the parties' ages, maturity and experience at the relevant time and the fact that W had been duly legally advised. The court determined that any pressure from H, if it existed, had not been such, especially in view of the information obtained from her own solicitor of W's demeanour at the time, to justify any finding that at the time of signing the agreement W had been under any undue influence or duress.

On that basis the court was required to decide whether in upholding the 'needs based' agreement, W would be left in real need. The court emphasised that 'real need' in the *Radmacher* sense was not the same as 'reasonable need' (but the court did not agree it was one step above destitution as per Mostyn J in *Kremen v Agrest*). The assessment had to be case specific and it was important that much of the agreement terms had been expressly required by W. The court determined it was fair to keep W to the provision she had agreed to and unfair to require H in the circumstances of the case to make any different provision for her.

In the same year, Holman J in *Gray v Work*[3] dealt with a 20 year relationship divorce in which post nuptial agreements drawn by Texan lawyers had been signed by the parties when H had garnered wealth of c £5m. By the time of the divorce, H's wealth, derived as it was from entirely matrimonial endeavour, was now estimated at c £144m and he offered W just £5m. The post nuptials had essentially excluded the community of property regimes existing under Texan law and provided for separation of property and income between H and W. The parties had renounced their US citizenships for tax reasons. They had eventually moved to the UK in 2008 and separated in 2013. W had made a full contribution as wife and mother.

His Lordship concluded that the agreements had specifically preserved W's right to pursue her claim for financial relief as an alternative to the provision within the agreements and in the light of that election the terms of the agreements were no longer relevant to the s 25 exercise being undertaken. If, however, that was incorrect then Holman J found that W had entered into the agreements without a full appreciation of the implications of doing so. W had received no legal advice at the time of the legal implications of the agreements outside Texas. In addition, the parties' financial position had subsequently changed significantly in the intervening 14 years so that it would not be fair to hold her to the same. It was important not to discriminate against a homemaker in such circumstances and accordingly, W was entitled to equality of division of the parties' resources.

[1] [2014] EWHC 2220 (Fam).
[2] [2015] EWHC 812 (Fam).
[3] [2015] EWHC 834 (Fam).

8.29 Again in 2015, in *WW v HW (Pre-Nuptial Agreement: Needs: Conduct)*[1], Nicholas Cusworth QC sitting as a Deputy High Court judge, following an 11 year marriage where W held the wealth, H was limited on the subsequent divorce to a housing provision for his lifetime by the parties' signed agreement, with a stepdown of 45% when the youngest child reached 23. The court found that the purpose of the agreement had been to protect W's inherited property from a sharing claim which was seen as an entirely reasonable ambition and the signing of the agreement had been a pre-condition to the parties' marriage. It was relevant to the court's determination that in order to encourage the marriage taking place H had deliberately inflated the value of his resources in disclosure to W at the time of the agreement. In addition, he had acted dishonestly in relation to a tax liability incurred by W relating to a valuable painting sale. Both parties' evidence were found in parts

8.29 *Pre-nuptial Agreements*

to be less than frank, but His Lordship substantially accepted W's evidence, whilst holding H only told the truth when it served his best interests to do so before the court.

The court determined there was, 'no obvious basis for any generosity in the interpretation of the husband's needs' and it was relevant he had lied about the extent of his pre-marital resources and the tax issues which constituted financial conduct under s 25 and the uncertainties about his future financial future had thereby been self-induced. The court found H had been offered the opportunity to take detailed advice from his solicitor about the agreement he was signing as evidenced by a retained contemporaneous letter from the solicitor shown to the judge and H had understood the agreement's consequences and therefore 'significant weight' should now be given to the same, thereby restricting his claims to his needs only. As a result, in addition to the housing provision above, which reflected the shares in the marital home based on the parties' contributions as provided for in the agreement, H was restricted to an income level incorporating his own earnings and pension subject to the prospect of variable recovery being made from him by HMRC.

In 2016 *H v H*[2] the parties' marriage lasted only for a matter of 12 weeks. The parties had entered a pre-nuptial agreement and the agreement had been signed by W against the advice of her solicitors. The pre-nuptial excluded any recovery by the W in the event of divorce. The case involved investigation into an allegation of conduct by rape of W by H which had been preceded by criminal proceedings. HHJ Booth rejected the conduct allegation and held that W had previous experience of marriage and divorce and therefore knew what she was doing when she signed the agreement. There had been no time even if the parties' 12 weeks cohabitation was included for any financial changes to occur. W's counsel argued that W would be thrown upon the state, but the court considered that in the circumstances of the case, whilst that had to be weighed in the balance, the parties had been entitled to regulate their relationship in the way that they had. Accordingly, the exceptions identified by the Supreme Court in *Radmacher* did not arise and the case was a paradigm example where the court should uphold the terms of the pre-nuptial agreement.

Also in 2016, in *DB v PB*[3], Francis J determined the W's applications for financial remedy, provision under Sch 1 of the Children Act 1989 and H's application for sale of the former matrimonial home pursuant to s 17 of the MWPA 1882. This mixture of applications was the result of the core issues arising from the parties, who were Swedish nationals, having signed three pre-nuptial agreements each containing clauses conferring exclusive jurisdiction on the Stockholm city court and declaring the parties were to retain their separate property on divorce. H maintained that the W should simply retain a half share of their marital home, leaving her after debt with c £560,000. W argued that she should equally share in the near £11m value of assets held on the basis that H had misrepresented to her that despite entering into the pre-nuptial agreements, on divorce he would not implement the agreements and she would obtain sufficient to maintain her standard of living. In addition, W argued that the effect of the pre-nuptials on her and the children was so unfair that they should be disregarded altogether. It was clear the W had received legal advice for, at least, one of the American agreements and had ultimately been quite content to enter into a pre-nuptial agreement in such terms and Francis J rejected the contention that the H had seriously misrepresented the position concerning the agreements to her.

In considering the impact of the Maintenance Regulation (EC No 4/2009), Art 4(1) and (2) which enabled parties to enter into a prorogation clause concerning a maintenance obligation, His Lordship concluded that the prorogation clause in the agreements was fully compliant and, therefore, it was clear that the Swedish court had exclusive jurisdiction over such matters and that aspect of the W's claims would be stayed until the Swedish court either consider the matter or declined to do so. Accordingly, Francis J considered that he had to avoid any outcome in dealing with W's financial remedy application which engaged consideration of her needs since this would trespass onto maintenance matters. However, the prorogation clause did not include or affect the provision in the agreements signed otherwise dealing with the separation of property held and as the family home was held in the parties' joint names he retained the jurisdiction to divide the same equally.

His Lordship's view was that by reason of the existence of valid pre-nuptial agreements he would be obliged to deal with the W's claims on a needs basis only and thereby such an approach would invade the needs provision for the W which he had determined was within the exclusive jurisdiction of the Swedish court.

In this event, Francis J found, as above, the ambit of his jurisdiction to deal with maintenance matters was, for the time being, circumscribed and, accordingly, he was forced in dealing with the W's claims, to fall back on the Sch 1 claim brought by W to provide adequate housing provision for the children of £2m on the usual basis within such a claim, whereby the property acquired would be held in trust for this purpose whilst the children remained dependent with a carer's allowance of £95,000 pa for the W.

W appealed, arguing that there was no valid prorogation clause and that Francis J had been wrong to restrict his discretion in applying the s 25(2) MCA 1973 factors after finding that there was a valid, yet unfair, prenuptial agreement.

The Court of Appeal found the prorogation clause in the 'Ohio agreement' to be invalid as it was not sufficiently complete or clear to meet the requirements of Art 4 of Council Regulation (EC) No 4/2009 (the Maintenance Regulation)[4]. In addition, The Court of Appeal found that Francis J had been unduly restrictive in his approach where valid pre-nuptial agreements had been found to exist. In giving the lead judgment, King LJ stated:

> 'In my judgment, in the ordinary course of events, where there is a valid prenuptial agreement, the terms of which amount to the wife having contracted out of a division of the assets based on sharing, a court is likely to regard fairness as demanding that she receives a settlement that is limited to that which provides for her needs. But whilst such an outcome may be considered to be more likely than not, that does not prescribe the outcome in every case. Even where there is an effective prenuptial agreement, the court remains under an obligation to take into account all the factors found in s 25(2) MCA 1973, together with a proper consideration of all

8.29 Pre-nuptial Agreements

the circumstances, the first consideration being the welfare of any children. Such an approach may, albeit unusually, lead the court in its search for a fair outcome, to make an order which, contrary to the terms of an agreement, provides a settlement for the wife in excess of her needs. It should also be recognised that even in a case where the court considers a needs-based approach to be fair, the court will as in *KA v MA*, retain a degree of latitude when it comes to deciding on the level of generosity or frugality which should appropriately be brought to the assessment of those needs.⁵'

1   [2015] EWHC 1844 (Fam).
2   [2016] Lexis Citation 596.
3   [2016] EWHC 3431 (Fam). On appeal *Brack v Brack* see below.
4   *Brack v Brack* [2018] EWCA Civ 2862 (sub nom *DB v PB*). In reaching this conclusion, the court reviewed two authorities which considered unequivocal and exclusive jurisdiction clauses, *Estasis Salotti di Colzani v Ruwa* [1976] ECR 1831 and *Deutsche Bank AG & Ors v Asia Pacific Broadband Wireless Communications & Anr* [2008] EWCA Civ 1091.
5   Para 103.

8.30 In 2018 Roberts J in *KA v MA (Pre-Nuptial Agreement – Needs)*¹ the case involved cross-applications of W and H. W's application was for financial remedies orders seeking £6m for 'reasonable needs', whereby H had applied for a notice to show cause why an order should not be made pursuant to the provisions of a pre-nuptial agreement signed by the parties 3 weeks before their marriage in 2008, providing W with an outcome of £1.6m from an agreed asset base of between £22m and £33m, much of it, as accepted by W, pre-accrued wealth of H.

Roberts J in dealing with circumstances surrounding the parties' entry into the pre-nuptial agreement, found both parties had accepted the pre-nuptial agreement as a pre-condition to the marriage. Whilst, the parties had one child together, the W was fully aware of H's wish to provide for his children by his first marriage.

Her Ladyship concluded that each had received legal advice and had intended to be bound by the agreement terms. In particular, W's solicitors had specifically advised her that she would be better off under the general provisions of the MCA 1973 and/or the provisions of Sch 1 of the Children Act 1989. Yet, the W had signed the agreement, despite being 'extremely uneasy' about doing so and whilst 'under immense pressure to do so', even to the point where there had been disagreements between the parties over the agreement until just a short time before the agreement was finally signed.

Roberts J in deciding if it would be unfair to hold the W to the agreement (pursuant to the principles set out in *Radmacher's* case), rejected the submission that H's position requiring the pre-marital agreement as a pre-condition to marriage was tantamount to duress or exploitation of a dominant position in the circumstances prevailing in this case. Both parties were mature and consenting individuals, who had been previously married. Her Ladyship rejected further the W's counsel's suggestion that W should not be bound by the agreement terms in the light of the evidence that her solicitor had advised her that the agreement was unenforceable in law. That advice, Her Ladyship determined, had to be seen in the context of several notes of attendance from which it was clear that W understood that should she sign the agreement the same might well be enforced in the event of a marriage breakdown. Accordingly, the court's view on the W's evidence, was that, whilst distressed at the dilemma she had found herself in, she ultimately had decided to reject the advice she had been given and intentionally signed the agreement.

Following the law as summarised in the *Luckwell v Limata* case above, Roberts J proceeded to assess the W's housing and income needs under the s 25 exercise within which the terms of the pre-nuptial agreement W had entered into remained a limiting factor. Her Ladyship stated:

> 'I am satisfied that a fair outcome in the assessment of both housing and income needs in this case must reflect the fact that this wife agreed to restrict the ambit of her financial claims should the marriage end in divorce.[2]'

In consequence, W's needs were assessed as a housing fund of £1.35m and a Duxbury capitalised fund of almost £1.6m.

In the same year, the Court of Appeal gave judgment in *Versteegh v Versteegh*[3] concerning the validity and impact of a Swedish pre-nuptial agreement signed one day before the marriage.

H and W, both Swedish nationals, had by their pre-nuptial agreement adopted a separation of property regime which would 'encompass and keep inviolate' the H's pre-marital accrued assets and anything he acquired solely thereafter. Twenty-one years later, the parties' separated in England, where they had spent their married life.

W's case was that, she had been without any legal advice when entering into the pre-nuptial agreement. In addition, she claimed that she had understood only that the proposed agreement would apply only to H's non-marital assets gained from family wealth and she submitted she not appreciated the potential effect of the agreement, particularly in light of the English discretionary system to dividing finances upon divorce. Accordingly, W maintained the agreement signed should not be given any effect and instead a sharing approach should be followed.

The judge at first instance held W had been aware of the effect of the agreement. As a result, reflecting the agreement terms, W was awarded half of the non-business assets (of £51.4 million) and a 23.41% interest in H's business shares.

On W's appeal, the Court of Appeal also accepted W had understood the pre-nuptial agreement terms. Indeed, W had attempted in the marriage to improve her prospects under the same during the marriage. Following the *Radmacher* guidance that where a party has a full appreciation of a nuptial agreement's implications, the agreement should be given effect unless it would be unfair to do so, the Court of Appeal considered that when assessing a party's 'full appreciation' legal advice, whilst desirable, is not essential especially where the agreement entered into is simple and signed in a country where such agreements are commonplace. King LJ stated:

> 'The desirability of legal advice forms part of the miscellany of factors which a judge considers before concluding that a party did (or did not) have a full appreciation of

the implications of the PMA. Doubtless in some cases its presence or absence will be critical. In the present case, the judge was fully aware that the wife had not received legal advice but, having seen her give evidence, made the clear finding that the wife knew "full well" the effect of the agreement. The judge said that he was able to "reach a firm and clear conclusion" and to "find as a fact that throughout the marriage the wife has known and understood the impact of the PMA" [183]. On the judge's findings there can be no doubt but that the wife clearly felt herself to be bound by the PMA in England and acted to ameliorate its effect.⁴'

Specifically, the Court of Appeal rejected Mostyn J's earlier suggestion as a general proposition in *B v S* above that a party to a pre-nuptial agreement will be taken as having lacked the necessary appreciation of the implications of an agreement where they had not received the minimum legal advice to the effect that some countries where they may live whilst married may operate under a discretionary system of equitable distribution of resources upon divorce. Again, King LJ stated:

'It cannot be right that a couple have to take legal advice of the type envisaged by Mostyn J "just in case" in ten years' time they move to live in the UK or, that they have to in some way "refresh" their PMA by the wife receiving legal advice prior to relocating . . . In my judgment, when an English court is presented with a PMA such as the present one; signed in a country where they are commonplace, simply drafted and generally signed without legal advice or indeed disclosure, it cannot be right to add a gloss to *Radmacher* to the effect that such a spouse will be regarded as having lacked the necessary appreciation of the consequence absent legal advice to the effect that some of the countries, in which they may choose to live during their married life, may operate a discretionary system.⁵'

In his judgment, Lewison LJ considered that the 'key points' from Radmacher's case were:

'i) Whether a PMA (pre-marital agreement) is contractually binding or not is irrelevant. The court should apply the same principles whether or not a binding contract has been made: [63]

ii) There is no need for black and white rules about the process leading up to the making of a PMA. What matters is whether each party has all the information material to his or her decision, and that each should intend that the agreement should govern the financial consequences of the marriage coming to an end: [69]

iii) Factors which would vitiate a contract will negate any effect that the PMA might otherwise have had: [71]. But factors falling short of those which would vitiate a contract may reduce, rather than eliminate, the weight to be given to the PMA: [72]

iv) If the terms of the PMA are unfair from the start this will reduce (not eliminate) the weight to be given to it: [73]

v) If the parties to the PMA are nationals of a state in which PMAs are common and binding, that will increase the weight to be given to the PMA: [74]

vi) In principle, if parties have made a PMA there is no reason why they should not be entitled to enforce it: [52]

vii) Thus, the court should give effect to a PMA that is freely entered into by each party with a full appreciation of its implications unless in the circumstances prevailing it would not be fair to hold the parties to their agreement: [75]

viii) Typically, it would not be fair to hold the parties to their agreement if it would prejudice the reasonable requirements of any children of the family

ix)	[77]; or if holding them to the agreement would leave one spouse in a "predicament of real need": [81]
	But in relation to the sharing principle the court is likely to make an order reflecting the terms of the PMA: [82], [177]–[178]'[6]

The W's appeal was, accordingly, rejected on all points.

[1] [2018] EWHC 499 (Fam).
[2] Para 110.
[3] [2018] EWCA Civ 1050.
[4] Para 110.
[5] Paras 64 and 65.
[6] Para 178.

8.31 In 2019, Mostyn J., dealt with an application for financial remedy brought by H against his wealthy W in *Ipekci v McConnell*[1]. H had been a New York hotel concierge in 2003 when the parties had met. W had been living in London and had been previously married. After a period of cohabitation, the parties married in 2005 and had two children. They separated in 2016.

Both parties were 45 at the date of the hearing. H continued on a modest concierge income with limited capital and debts. W was by contrast a wealthy heiress and beneficiary of trusts with a value of at least $65m. The court found W would receive distributions if she reasonably required it. The parties had signed a New York pre-nuptial agreement which made no provision for H. Mostyn J found it would be unfair to attribute any weight to the agreement for the following reasons[2]:

'i)	The parties specifically contracted that the agreement will be governed by New York law. The evidence of the single joint expert is that the agreement suffers from a fatal defect under New York law. This is because the agreement was not accompanied by a duly authenticated certificate that it conformed with the local law in its attestation. The opinion of the single joint expert was crystal clear. This defect would mean that the agreement would, in New York, have "minimal weight, if any". She cited a case on comparable facts where the New York Appeal Court held that the document would carry "no legal force save for the minor impact of its historical voice"
ii)	It seems to me that, speaking metaphorically, if the parties have made their bed in New York they must lie in it. In my judgment it would be wholly unjust to attribute weight to this agreement when under the law that the parties elected it would be afforded no weight.
iii)	Further, it is plain to me that the husband cannot be said to have had a full appreciation of the implications of the agreement when he had no legal advice at all about the impact of New York law. Further still, I am not satisfied that the solicitor who gave the advice was not compromised by virtue of having acted previously for the wife in her first divorce. It was, so it seems to me, a clear situation of apparent bias.
iv)	The agreement does not meet any needs of the husband. I do not take the language used by the Supreme Court, namely "predicament of real need" as signifying that needs when assessed in circumstances where there is a valid prenuptial agreement in play should be markedly less than needs assessed in ordinary circumstances. If you have reasonable needs which you cannot meet from your own resources, then you are in a predicament. Those needs are real needs.

8.31 *Pre-nuptial Agreements*

v) In the circumstances of this case I attribute therefore no weight to the prenuptial agreement.'

As all the parties' assets were or had their origin in non-marital wealth, His Lordship proceeded to determine the award based on the principle of needs. The court, therefore, awarded H a lump sum of c £1.3m inclusive of a Duxbury fund of £445.5k and £750k to buy a house, of which £375k was to be subject to charge-back.

Again in 2019, Cohen J in *MB v EB*[3] considered the like approach under *Radmacher* and *Veersteegh* in respect of the weight to be given to a separation deed of agreement in which H and W had concluded in 2011 a full and final end to their financial claims against each other when both were represented by experienced solicitors and where that process had been initiated by H.

The case facts were unusual, but, in essence, H was 59 and W 63 and had met 20 years before and there were no children of the relationship. W came from a very wealthy family and she had at trial access to a value of c£50m, whereas H had, when she met him, been a struggling artist and part time model with mental health problems. They had married in 2000, but shortly after H suffered a fall and was briefly in a coma. In recovery, H had moved with W to Vienna to live with her father. The parties lived together on and off and W became embroiled in Austrian residency issues resulting in her being placed into custody for a period and thereafter not being able to leave Austria. Meanwhile H had been to the UK and met another woman and eventually asked W for a divorce which she refused. W then followed H to London where their dysfunctional relationship continued. The effect of their deed of separation in 2011 was to allow the parties' marriage to continue with a view to enabling W to apply for British citizenship whilst providing H with a lump sum enabling him also to obtain some form of accommodation. By 2017, however, the parties were in dispute and H, despite the provisions of the separation agreement, had commenced financial remedy proceedings.

In extended hearings first to determine preliminary issues and then to give the substantive judgment Cohen J determined the marriage had actually failed back in 2004 and there had been no marital acquest subsequently. However, His Lordship concluded there were no grounds to undermine the deed of separation signed as both parties had been legally represented, there was no evidence W had put H under any undue pressure and H had intentionally entered the agreement without full disclosure of the true extent of W's wealth and both had intended there should be no further claim. In essence, H got the agreement he had wanted. However, the agreement reached did 'on a fine balance' of factors fall short, in His Lordship's view, in providing for H's real needs since it left a deficit of income of c £15k against his necessary annual expenditure. Cohen J considered in particular that W had been aware throughout the agreement negotiations of H's health problems and he could not provide for himself being dependent upon her provision to him. In addition, despite H having got what he had wanted from the settlement agreement, in the circumstances of these parties, where after a short marriage there had been a continuing co-dependence, it was not satisfactory for H to be in the shortfall position he found himself. The finances required to meet

H's need would be have a very minor impact on W's wealth. Accordingly, His Lordship awarded H £325k to generate (Duxbury Tables) an income of £25k pa and purchase a car.

In 2020 in *S v H*[4], W 56 and H 69 with children by previous marriages had married in 2010 and separated after 6 ½ years in 2016. The decree absolute was obtained in 2019. Some 5 days before their wedding abroad they had signed a short prenuptial agreement before a notary there without any independent legal advice or full disclosure process. They intended their married life would be in the UK where W's twin daughters were being educated and where W held a professional position. H's role in the marriage had been to substantially look after W's daughters whilst she worked.

Following separation, W issued financial remedy proceedings in 2017 and by the time of the hearing H was bankrupt and H's continued pursuit of his claims within the proceedings had been authorised by the trustee in bankruptcy. W sought a dismissal of all claims pursuant to the terms of the retained separation of all property prenuptial. Ultimately, she offered H a life interest in a flat she owned out a of total asset values of over £3m net and pension funds of £¼ m with income sources of £100k pa. H sought £739k lump sum sufficient to discharge his bankruptcy (£171k) and his costs (£76k) and provide a home. At the outset of the marriage, H, an accountant, had misled W as to his asset worth and prospects, when in fact such property as he had was the basis of secured borrowing and he was without an income.

HHJ Booth considered the circumstances of the prenuptial were such that no weight should be given to it in the situation in which H found himself on divorce. H had no earning capacity at his age and a need to discharge his bankruptcy, costs and required a home. The solution was he was awarded a first £270k lump sum, 60%v of W's pension thus providing c £17k pa income with his existing UK pension and a second lump sum to acquire a home for £375k but subject to reversion to W when H died or no longer needed a housing fund.

[1] [2019] EWFC 19.
[2] Para 27.
[3] [2019] EWHC 1649 (Fam) and [2019] EWHC 3676 (Fam).
[4] [2020] EWFC B16.

Other jurisdictions and human rights

8.32 Irrespective of the nationality or domicile of the parties, or their habitual residence at the time of or during the marriage, or their making of a pre or post nuptial agreement or any choice of law clause within it, the position remains after *Radmacher's* case that an English court seised of the matter on divorce and making an order for financial relief under the Matrimonial Causes Act 1973 will apply English law[1].

As will be apparent from what has been set out above, the relevance of any foreign element in any pre-nuptial agreement in the case will, therefore, be, primarily, in respect of the intention of the parties that the terms of the agreement would apply[2].

8.32 Pre-nuptial Agreements

The position prior to Brexit and the leaving of the United Kingdom from the European Union has been that the United Kingdom made a policy decision not to participate in the results of the work done by the European Community and the Hague Conference on Private International Law to apply uniform rules of private international law in relation to 'maintenance' obligations. Although, the United Kingdom Government opted into Council Regulation (EC) No 4/2009 of 18 December, 2008 on jurisdiction, applicable law and enforcement of decisions and co-operation in matters relating to 'maintenance' obligations, the rules relating to 'applicable law' will not apply in the United Kingdom. This is the result of the effect of Art 15 of the Council Regulation in that the law applicable to 'maintenance' obligations is to be determined in accordance with the 2007 Hague Protocol, but only in those Member States bound by the Hague Protocol. The United Kingdom has not been bound by the Hague Protocol, because it agreed to participate in the Council Regulation only on the basis that it would not be obliged to join in accession to the Hague Protocol by the European Union.

The United Kingdom Government's position was that there was very little application of foreign law in family matters within the United Kingdom and in 'maintenance' cases, in particular, and the expense of proving the content of that law would be disproportionate to the low value of the vast majority of maintenance claims.

In *Radmacher's* case, the Majority noted that had the Hague Protocol applied, its terms not only allowed the parties to designate the law applicable to a 'maintenance' obligation, but also provided that, unless at the time of the designation, the parties were fully informed and aware of the consequences of their designation, the law designated by the parties would not apply where the application of that law would lead to manifestly unfair or unreasonable consequences for any of the parties (Art 8(1) and (5)).

[1] See Dicey, Morris and Collins, *Conflict of Laws*, vol 2, (14th edn, 2006), Rule 9 1(7), and eg *C v C (Ancillary Relief: Nuptial Settlement)* [2004] EWCA Civ 1030, [2005] Fam 250, at para 31. Note has to be taken however of the EU Regulations of Matrimonial Property Regimes (2016/1103 24 June) which came into force on 29 January 2019 where subsequent to a marriage in relation to which the parties signed a pre-nuptial agreement they have taken up residence in another country which is a signatory to the Regulation, being at that time Belgium, Bulgaria, Germany, Finland, France, Greece, Italy, Croatia, Luxembourg, Malta, Netherlands, Austria, Portugal, Sweden, Slovenia, Spain, Czech Republic with Cyprus and Estonia expected to join imminently (see more below). Whilst the UK had not, due to its intended departure from the European Union, become a co-signatory, nevertheless the Regulation could have consequences on the recognition of a pre-nuptial agreement within the named countries (see more below).

[2] It should be noted that from 17 August 2015, under European Union law, it became possible to choose the applicable law of nationality to apply as regards an individual's assets on death. In default succession laws will apply dependant upon the location and nature of the asset: (see the EU Succession Regulation 650/2012 (Regulation (EU) No 650/2012 of the European Parliament and of the Council of 4 July 2012 on jurisdiction, applicable law, recognition and enforcement of decisions and acceptance and enforcement of authentic instruments in matters of succession and on the creation of a European Certificate of Succession). Whilst the UK did not opt in, UK nationals and the wording of any marital agreement as to applicable law in such a context will need to be compatible with the Regulation.

8.33 Following the re-election of the Conservative Government in December 2019 and Brexit on 31 January 2020, the British Government has, at the date of this Edition, entered into transitional negotiations aimed at reaching a comprehensive agreement with the European Union as to the terms of their future political and trade relationship. With the fall back of the 1996, 1980 and 2007 Hague Conventions, it is not currently anticipated that the outcome of those negotiations will affect the approach of the courts of England and Wales as presently developed in the case law highlighted above[1].

In most other countries in Europe, the North American states and Canada, as well as South Africa, Australia, New Zealand and many other nations in the civilised world, including China, have statutory as opposed to common law provision for the recognition of some form of pre-nuptial agreements upon divorce[2]. Many of these countries operate under a community of property regime and, by the pre-nuptial agreement process, parties will exercise an opt out of the consequences of such a regime in relation to certain identified assets, which they each hold.

The approach of the courts of England and Wales, even after the Supreme Court's decision in the *Radmacher* case, of leaving the relevance and weight upon divorce of such an agreement to the discretion of the individual judge in the circumstances of the particular case is almost exceptional. Of course, short of legislation, the Supreme Court's decision has, at least, ensured, for now, that the presence of a pre-nuptial agreement will be taken into account under 'all the circumstances of the case' and, where its terms remain relevant to the parties' prevailing circumstances and do not attempt to impede the rights of any dependent children, the same will have significant, if not compelling weight in the s 25 exercise and it will be for the party seeking to avoid the terms of the signed agreement to establish that it would be unfair to be bound to that agreement[3].

This element of uncertainty of outcome was one of the aspects of the challenge under the Human Rights Act and the Article of the First Protocol (protection of property rights etc) mounted on behalf of the wife in the first instance decision of the *Radmacher* case, *NG v KR (pre-nuptial contract)*[4] against the husband's claims for financial relief brought in the face of the nil provision pre-nuptial agreement signed by the parties. It was argued that the wife, under the pre-nuptial agreement signed by the parties, had a valid contractual right that should be protected as 'property' under the Protocol by the courts and, thereby, the agreement should be the central and inescapable focus of the s 25 statutory exercise.

By Article 1 of Protocol 1:

'Every natural person is entitled to the peaceful enjoyment of his possessions. No one shall be deprived of his possessions except in the public interest and subject to the conditions provided for by law and by the general principles of international law.

The preceding provisions shall not, however, in any way impair the right of a State to enforce such laws as it deems necessary, to control the use of property in accordance with the general interest or to secure the payment of taxes or other contributions or penalties.'[5]

In a comprehensive review of the law in this area up to that point, Baron J concluded that it remained the position in English matrimonial law that neither party could sue upon a pre-nuptial agreement since the enforceability

8.33 Pre-nuptial Agreements

of any such agreement, in the absence of statutory exceptions, depended not upon the agreement but upon the subsequent court order incorporating its terms (*de Lasala v de Lasala*[6], *Xydhias v Xydhias*[7] and *Soulsbury v Soulsbury*[8]) and, accordingly, the pre-nuptial agreement was not a binding legal contract and the Protocol, therefore, had no application. Further, there was, stated Baron J, no 'arbitrary' uncertainty of outcome within the s 25 exercise that might infringe the Protocol, but rather 'a fair balance between existing property rights and the entitlement of the claiming party to share, to receive compensation or have his needs met. This fair balance was well within "the margin of appreciation" afforded to this country'.

Of course, the Supreme Court has since, in the same case on appeal, held that pre-nuptial agreements are, indeed, legally enforceable and accordingly, Baron J's first stance against the application of the Protocol may not apply. However, Lady Hale was in no doubt in her Minority judgment that such dicta of the Majority relating to the contractual status of a pre-nuptial agreement was obiter to the issues of the case, in any event. In addition, the Majority had recognised that in practice such an enforceable contractual status is nevertheless illusory in the face of the fact that whenever a party thereto seeks to challenge the terms of the agreement, the inevitable step taken will be the issue of an application for financial relief invoking the court's discretionary jurisdiction under the s 25 process as to whether it is fair to make all, part or none of the agreement into a court order[9].

[1] See fn 1 at **8.32**.
[2] For a comprehensive survey of the approach of different jurisdictions; see Resolutions 2010 Report 'Family Agreements: Seeking Certainty to Reduce Disputes' Annex 1 – Jurisdictions other than England and Wales.
[3] See, by contrast, the pre-*Radmacher* position as criticised by Hoffmann LJ in *Pounds v Pounds* [1994] 1 WLR 1535, 1550–1551.
[4] [2008] EWHC 1532 (Fam).
[5] *JA Pye (Oxford) Ltd v United Kingdom* (Application No 44302/02) [2007] ECHR 44302/02 at para 52: 'Article 1 of Protocol No 1, which guarantees the right to the protection of property, contains three distinct rules: "the first rule, set out in the first sentence of the first paragraph, is of a general nature and enunciates the principle of the peaceful enjoyment of property; the second rule, contained in the second sentence of the first paragraph, covers deprivation of possessions and subjects it to certain conditions; the third rule, stated in the second paragraph, recognises that the Contracting States are entitled, amongst other things, to control the use of property in accordance with the general interest . . . The three rules are not, however, 'distinct' in the sense of being unconnected. The second and third rules are concerned with particular instances of interference with the right to peaceful enjoyment of property and should therefore be construed in the light of the general principle enunciated in the first rule."'.
[6] [1980] AC 546.
[7] [1999] 1 FLR 683 CA.
[8] [2007] EWCA Civ 969. But now see Baron J in *NG v KR (pre-nuptial contract)* [2008] EWHC 1532 (Fam) below.
[9] See Lord Phillips [2010] UKSC 42.

Advising the client

8.34 Notwithstanding the Law Commission's report and recommendations, Parliament has, at the date of this Edition, still to determine the form and content of any proposed future legislation incorporating specific recognition upon divorce of the pre-nuptial agreement or the suggestions for such legislative reform in this area as set out in the report.

A different proposal to that advised by the Law Commissions' report, as originally advanced by Baroness Deech which failed to get through the Parliamentary process before the 2019 general election and the end of the last Parliamentary session[1], has now been re-introduced by Baroness Shackleton into the House of Lords[2]. This Bill is considered below and has already received tentative support from the Her Majesty's Opposition. Its fate is still uncertain as three previous attempts to introduce like legislation failed. However, until Parliament approves substantive changes in regard to the primacy and weight to be given to pre-nuptial agreements upon divorce, practitioners will need to continue to be aware of both the approach of the courts before and after *Radmacher's* case.

In regard to the pre-*Radmacher* position, such pre 2010 case law will, for now, remain important in advising a client as to the likely effect of a pre-nuptial agreement entered into before the Supreme Court's judgment upon the eventual divorce distribution. In such cases, because the parties may have been advised at the time that such agreements were not binding and in the absence of strict compliance with 'the six safeguards'[3] that the agreement entered into may be disregarded altogether by a court, not only the weight of such an agreement upon the eventual outcome may be in issue, but also primarily whether it was the parties' intention that the agreement itself should have any effect.

With this situation in mind, the pre-*Radmacher* position could not be better summarised than by reference to the following extract from Connell J's judgment in *M v M*[4]:

> 'In my view, it matters not whether the court bears such an agreement in mind as part of the circumstances of the case (a very important factor) or as an aspect of the parties' conduct. Under either approach the court should look at any such agreement and decide in the particular circumstances what weight should, in justice, be attached to it. Given that a significant percentage of marriages these days end in divorce, it is understandable that mature adults, and in particular those who have been married before, might wish to agree what should happen in the event of a breakdown. The desire for certainty, or the wish to know where you stand, is not unusual. It is clear, of course, that the existence of such an agreement does not oust the jurisdiction of the court . . . The public policy objection to such agreements, namely that they tend to diminish the importance of the marriage contract, seems to me to be of less importance now that divorce is so commonplace. However the manner in which the courts should treat such agreements will vary from case to case.'

Following the decision in *M v M*[5], *K v K*[6] and later *NG v KR*[7], it clearly became the case that clients wishing to enter into a pre-nuptial agreement could no longer be advised that such an agreement would have little or no effect on the court's decision on a subsequent application for ancillary relief.

It was clear that if the wife in *K v K* and the husband in *NG v KR*[8] had not entered into the pre-nuptial agreement, both would have fared better on their applications for ancillary relief. The legal advice given to the wife in *K v K* at

8.34 *Pre-nuptial Agreements*

the time the agreement was signed was that it would not be binding, and, particularly so, if there were children. This advice, at the specific time that it was given, cannot be criticised, but, following *K v K*, the same advice now given to clients would be negligent.

1. The Divorce (Financial Provision) Bill (HL 21) introduced in May 2016.
2. The Divorce (Financial Provision) Bill (HL39). First reading received in January 2020.
3. Labour Government's 1998 Consultation Document: *Supporting Families* (Stationery Office, October 1998).
4. [2002] 1 FLR 654. Connell J at para [21]. Albeit, along with other cases, criticised by Lord Phillips (at para 45 of the *Radmacher* decision) for having referred to the approach adopted in *Edgar* in relation to pre-nuptial agreement cases, when the *Edgar* decision had been in the very different context of a separation post nuptial agreement.
5. [2002] 1 FLR 654.
6. [2003] 1 FLR 120.
7. [2008] EWHC 1532 (Fam) – *Radmacher's* case at first instance.
8. [2008] EWHC 1532 (Fam).

8.35 Since such time and at present, if the marriage has been of short duration and the necessary formalities surrounding the pre-nuptial agreement have been complied with, the agreement is likely to be 'the magnetic factor' in the exercise. Where the marriage has subsisted for longer and there have been events that have materially altered the respective positions of the parties impacting upon their financial circumstances, then the relevance of such an agreement and its effect on the eventual court order on divorce will depend upon the extent to which, as projected, the same meets the needs of the weaker party and any children or, since its agreed review date, has remained sufficiently contemporaneous to the financial position of the parties prevailing at the time of their divorce.

If the agreement does by either route remain relevant to the prevailing financial circumstances, then it is likely to be treated by the court as compelling and its terms substantially endorsed by the final order of the court on the divorce. Indeed, even where the provision made in a pre-nuptial is deemed ultimately by the court to be unfair in the prevailing financial circumstances on divorce, the agreement's existence and the fact the parties had agreed to its terms are still factors which are likely to have a limiting effect on the financially weaker party's eventual share in division.

The majority in the Supreme Court in *Radmacher's case*, clearly, however, remained unwilling to adopt, without statutory reform, the position where the terms of a pre-nuptial agreement and, particularly one with a nil or decidedly unfair provision, should be regarded as 'presumptively dispositive' of the financial outcome of a divorce. Indeed, Lady Hale, in her minority judgment, was prepared to reject such a notion without reservation. Accordingly, it remains, without further legislative change, the position that the agreement's provision will be only one of the features of a given case that the court will weigh in the balance in determining the fair distribution between the parties, albeit, as stated above, the more relevant the agreement remains to the prevailing financial circumstances upon divorce, the more compelling or 'magnetic' its effect will be by reason of the parties' autonomous choices within a marriage being regarded now as a guiding 'rationale' to the court's approach upon divorce distribution post the *Radmacher* decision (see *V v V*, Charles J above).

Pre- or post-*Radmacher*, the acknowledged underlying statutory intention that spousal 'needs' should, wherever possible, be met within the s 25 exercise remains the overarching focus of the court's approach in this area of law. The Law Commission endorsed this position in its recommendations as to the 'Qualifying Nuptial Agreement' (see more below), which if adopted would still, upon such proposals, remain open to challenge where the financially weaker spouse's needs have not been provided for.

This historical perspective to the 'needs' provision being the recognised basement of judicial divorce provision was, particularly, highlighted in the pre-*Radmacher* high profile and 'huge money' case of *McCartney v McCartney*[1], in which, as Bennett J found, despite the almost meritless case presented by the wife in regard to her contribution to the creation of wealth under consideration, she still recovered millions of pounds to cover her 'reasonable needs'. In this context, it is, instructive to consider that had there been in existence a pre-nuptial agreement in that case purporting to limit the wife's entitlement to less than her eventual recovery, the impact of the same, where there was a child and where the court concluded that the 'needs' of the wife, including those as carer, were themselves to be seen as a 'magnetic' factor in the decision, would, probably, have resulted in the court being only modestly less generous in the evaluation of what those 'needs' were.

Indeed, immediately post *Radmacher*, Moor J in the case of *Z v Z*[2] above, further emphasised that this remained the position, in circumstances where, although the pre-nuptial agreement in existence there reflected an agreed 'separation of property' between the parties, the court nevertheless, whilst acknowledging the validity of the agreement signed, was unwilling to adjust the wife's recovery below her 'reasonable needs generously assessed', resulting in a modest departure from equality and the 'sharing principle' from 50 per cent to 40 per cent on a clean break. This emphasis upon meeting the 'needs' provision of the other spouse irrespective of there being a more limited pre-nuptial agreement provision in place, has since the *Z v Z* case been refined further by distinguishing 'reasonable needs' in favour of the more restrictive 'real needs' phraseology used in *Radmacher's* case. However, the preservation of 'needs' as an 'irreducible minimum' provision continues to prevail and was the approach vividly endorsed in both the *Luckwell v Limata* case and subsequently applied in *Hopkins v Hopkins* above. Most recently in *Ipekci v McConnell*[3], as above referred to, Mostyn J has stated:

' . . . If you have reasonable needs which you cannot meet from your own resources, then you are in a predicament. Those needs are real needs.'

Without a fresh Parliamentary steer prioritising the parties' pre-nuptial provision and autonomy, it seems the courts will continue to exercise their historic paternalistic approach in this area where they deem the 'needs' of a party requires it.

[1] [2008] EWHC 401. See also King LJ in *Brack v Brack* CA [2018] above, where the importance of evaluating the fairness of a pre-nuptial agreement within the s 25 exercise was further emphasised.

8.35 *Pre-nuptial Agreements*

² [2011] EWHC 2878 (Fam).
³ [2019] EWFC 19.

The honeymoon agreement

8.36 Following on from the last section, the first instance and the Court of Appeal decisions in *Radmacher's* case, in the light of the *Macleod* decision, gave rise to the trend of parties-to-be-married agreeing not only to sign up to a pre-nuptial agreement, but also, in identical terms, to another agreement shortly after the wedding ceremony. The second or 'honeymoon' agreement, arguably under ss 34 and 35 as a 'maintenance agreement', pursuant to *Macleod*, potentially placed the greater limitation upon the court's discretionary powers as defined in those sections of the Matrimonial Causes Act 1973 in the event of a subsequent divorce.

In *Westmeath v Westmeath*¹, a distinction had been drawn between those agreements which provided for the consequences of an actual separation, which had already occurred and an agreement providing for the consequences of a future separation; the latter agreement was, as already referred to earlier, null and void. Loyal to that principle, in *Brodie v Brodie*², a pre-nuptial agreement which provided for the parties to live apart and which was re-signed immediately after marriage was held void.

Of course, following the Supreme Court's decision, this public policy objection to a pre-nuptial agreement has now been removed and so a 'honeymoon' post-nuptial agreement, which mirrors the financial provision made in the pre-nuptial agreement should not now offend the rule in *Brodie*³.

However, in the light of the Supreme Court Justices' decision in *Radmacher*, it is now apparent that this device will not be any more effective against an attempt by one of the parties subsequently to seek to 'water down' the impact of the agreement upon divorce where fairness requires.

Clearly, the Majority decision of the Supreme Court in *Radmacher's* case has substantially reduced, if not removed entirely, any previous perception of a difference of approach by a court on divorce to the contents of a pre-nuptial agreement and a post nuptial agreement, including one signed, possibly, immediately after the wedding ceremony itself. Indeed, the Minority speech of Lady Hale appeared to accept that agreements, which were signed immediately after a wedding, may well bear little distinction from the pre-nuptial agreement signed before. Indeed, there remains deep scepticism amongst many lawyers that Lady Hale was correct in applying the provisions of ss 34 and 35 of the 1973 Act to this situation at all and Mostyn J in a number of his decisions (as above) upon pre-nuptial agreements post-*Radmacher* has repeatedly asserted that the outcome of the Supreme Court's decision is that all nuptial agreements, whether made pre or post marriage, are, within the statutory exercise upon divorce, to be given effect unless shown to be unfair pursuant to the Lord Phillips test.

¹ (1830) 1 Dow & Cl 519.
² [1917] P 271.
³ See and cf [2009] CFLQ 513 1 December 2009, *Radmacher v Granatino* [2009] EWCA Civ 649: 'Upping the ante-nuptial agreement': Case Commentary Joanna Miles Trinity College, Cambridge.

The essentials of a pre-nuptial agreement

Essentials

8.37 The central focus of the Labour Government's 1998 Consultation Paper, *Supporting Families*[1], was upon ways of strengthening the family. Amongst a number of measures canvassed, it was suggested that making pre-nuptial agreements legally binding may well be a way in which parties, about to be married, would be able to exercise more choice and responsibility in considering their future as married partners and the financial consequences before they got married.

Within the process of reaching an agreement about their financial future together, it was submitted that parties may be caused to feel more secure in entering marriage as opposed to cohabitation and, with legislative protection, the rights of the financially weaker party and any children of the relationship could be protected. It was suggested that should any one of some six safeguards be found not to exist then a pre-nuptial agreement should be held not to be legally binding on the parties to the agreement. Accordingly, it was recommended that a pre-nuptial agreement would not be legally binding:

(1) where there is a child of the family, whether or not that child was alive or a child of the family at the time the agreement was made;

(2) where under the general law of contract, the agreement is unenforceable, including if the contract attempted to lay an obligation on a third party, who had not agreed to the same in advance;

(3) where one or both parties did not receive independent legal advice before entering into the agreement;

(4) where the court considers that the enforcement of the agreement would cause significant injustice (to one or both of the parties or a child of the marriage);

(5) where one or both of the parties have failed to give full disclosure of assets and property before the agreement was made;

(6) where the agreement was made fewer than 21 days prior to the marriage (this would prevent a nuptial agreement being forced on a party shortly before the wedding day, when there may be less inclination to resist).

It was previously thought that this list, particularly in the light of its adoption, initially, at first instance, by Baron J in *Radmacher's* case, contained the essential checklist of conditions, which should be in place if a pre-nuptial agreement was to be of pivotal relevance whenever a court was exercising its distributive powers upon a divorce etc. The discussion of this checklist by the Justices of the Supreme Court in the *Radmacher* appeal and the further development of this area by the subsequent case law, together with now the publication of the Law Commission's report, have, in reality, further narrowed this field of essential conditions required for the court's recognition of the terms of a pre-nuptial agreement, pending statutory reform, down to ensuring that there has been independent legal advice, material disclosure, the agreement remains financially relevant, there has been no undue pressure and that the agreement is fair, including that it meets the 'needs' of the financially weaker spouse.

8.37 Pre-nuptial Agreements

Clearly, upon the current law before any reform, whether or not the agreement appropriately provides for any child of the parties (safeguard (1) above) will not prevent the court from giving, upon a divorce, due weight, decisive or otherwise, to the terms of a pre-nuptial agreement, if fairness dictates, whilst making express provision for the child in question. In addition, in any given case, following the Supreme Court's decision and as very much demonstrated by the facts of the *Radmacher* case itself, the issue, where any one or more of such conditions have not been met, will, nevertheless, be whether the failure to do so renders it unfair in the prevailing circumstances to hold the parties to the agreement.

[1] *Supporting Families* (Stationery Office, October 1998).

Independent legal advice

8.38 The process should start by each party taking such advice and, preferably, although by no means an obligation, each should preferably pay for the same from their own resources[1]. In *Radmacher v Granatino*[2], there had been objectively insufficient opportunity for the husband to take independent legal advice within the time frame that had existed of some 7 days from delivery of the final draft to signing and where he had had no input as to the contents of the agreement up to that point and where such explanation as he had received of the terms of the document versed in a language (German), which was not his own (French), had been given by a notary paid by the wife's family and who himself had expressed dissatisfaction as to the inadequate information afforded to the husband. Nevertheless, the husband, who had a commercial background and was thereby said to be familiar with such forms of contract, realised the agreement made no provision for him under German law on divorce.

Of course, at first instance, Baron J had stated, however, that ' . . . neither that knowledge, his background nor the information he was given are the same as understanding the full legal consequences of his decision or its later enforceability'.

By contrast, neither the Court of Appeal or the Supreme Court supported Baron J's approach on such matters and adopted what has been called 'a functional rather than formal, or de facto rather than de jure, approach to the formalities issue'[3]. In short, the approved approach, under current law before any reform, is that independent legal advice is 'necessary in most cases and desirable in all', but under the s 25 exercise, because the court must consider 'all the circumstances of the case' in seeking a fair resource division between parties, a pre-nuptial agreement, knowingly and voluntarily made by the parties, cannot be ignored by the court simply on the basis that the usual formalities, the requirements for which are not yet prescribed by statute, were not followed.

This has been again highlighted by the Court of Appeal in *Versteegh's case*[4] where emphasis was made of the Supreme Court's requirement for a 'full appreciation' of the implications and effect of the agreement entered into. As King LJ stated:

'The desirability of legal advice forms part of the miscellany of factors which a judge considers before concluding that a party did (or did not) have a full appreciation of the implications of the PMA. Doubtless in some cases its presence or absence will be critical . . . '

This approach may well be justifiable under the purist's view of the wide discretion afforded to the courts by the s 25 statutory exercise, but it wholly fails to meet the desirability of injecting any certainty into the professional's ability to advise his or her client where such an agreement is in existence upon a divorce as to the likely judicial approach to be taken ultimately. In consequence, such an approach also in many cases only serves to add to the parties' costs of litigation in leaving open potential arguments on both sides which can only be finally resolved by a judicial determination.

On a wider scale such criticisms are equally applicable to the absence of any statutory starting point of equality on divorce under the 1973 Act. It is suggested that any forthcoming amendment of the legislation which introduces the suggested reforms requiring recognition of the parties' autonomy on divorce division in regard to pre-nuptial agreements must be part of more wide-ranging changes in which the starting point is an equality of division unless the same would be unjust on the facts of the particular case including, of course, the existence of a signed pre or post nuptial agreement setting out a different agreed provision.

[1] [2009] Fam Law 1056 'From Pre-Nups to Post-Nups: Dealing with Marital Property Agreements' *Independent Legal Advice*: Emma Hitchings School of Law, Bristol University, in which it is suggested that in practice, where one of the parties pays for the advice, a cap on the expense may be incurred giving rise to the problem that the extent of the advice given may have been limited and its effect less effective as a result. The client paying in this instance should be advised against imposing such a limit lest in the final analysis the advice given is deemed to have been inadequate. Equally the paying party's solicitor should be cautious in insisting upon a full breakdown of the other solicitor's bill lest this is later interpreted as unreasonable control of the advice being provided. In any event the costs arrangement reached should be fully explained in the eventual pre-nuptial agreement.
[2] [2010] UKSC 42.
[3] See [2009] CFLQ 513 *Radmacher v Granatino* [2009] EWCA Civ 649: 'Upping the ante-nuptial agreement' *Case Commentary* Joanna Miles, Trinity College, Cambridge.
[4] [2018] EWCA Civ 1050.

Material disclosure

8.39 Whatever the form chosen, in order for there to be a fully informed consent to the signing of a pre-nuptial agreement there should be material disclosure of the nature and net value of assets, pension worth and incomes. Clearly, there is no prescribed form. Practice has differed. Some practitioners present draft Forms Es – others advise that all the required copy documents should be attached. However, it is apparent that a detailed list of the net worth of capital, pension and income resources held, identifying any supporting documentation should, in the majority of cases, be sufficient, as long as the other party is expressly offered facilities for full inspection, if required. Baron J in the first instance decision of *Radmacher's* case[1], stated that where there has been inadequate disclosure, it is impossible for a party to make a fully informed decision. Despite this, Mostyn J in *BN v MA*[2] said this at para 30:

8.39 Pre-nuptial Agreements

'What then did the Supreme Court say about how to determine whether an agreement has been freely entered into with a full appreciation of its implications? In paragraph 69 it was stated that there is no rule at all that full disclosure, or full legal advice, is a necessary pre-condition for the satisfaction of this criterion. On the contrary, the question is in the individual case whether there has been a material lack of disclosure, or a material lack of information, or a material lack of legal advice. I venture the opinion that usually -- and that is in the usual run of cases and not a case when one is dealing with such a highly intelligent sophisticate as Mr. Granatino – a full appreciation of the implications will normally carry with it a requirement of having at least enough legal advice to appreciate what one is giving up . . . '[3]

Of course, in *Radmacher's* case, the wife deliberately withheld disclosure from the husband, but the fact that he was well aware that she was very wealthy and irrespective of disclosure would have signed the pre-nuptial agreement anyway, meant exceptionally that the wife's deliberate non disclosure was not material on the facts of that case. The position, as to the sufficiency of disclosure will be, in every case where a pre-nuptial agreement exists upon divorce etc, whether each party had all the information which was material to his or her decision to enter into the agreement. Currently, indifference to the detailed provision of information by either party at the time of entering into a pre-nuptial agreement is likely to deny that party any basis for contending later that inadequate disclosure was afforded.

However, as has already been canvassed above[4], since the Supreme Court's decisions in both the *Sharland* and *Gohil* cases, there is reason to suggest that a fraudulent failure to provide material disclosure by one party in advance of the signing of a pre-nuptial agreement would now, at least, result in that party having, in a reversal of the usual *Radmacher* evidential burden, to persuade a court that it was fair to place any weight upon the agreement entered into irrespective of the other party's indifference, if it existed, to any disclosure having been afforded.

[1] NG v KR [2008] EWHC 1532 (Fam).
[2] BN v MA [2013] EWHC 4250 (Fam).
[3] Cf also Mostyn J's findings of a lack of appreciation in *Ipekci v McConnell* [2019] EWFC 19.
[4] See fn 1 at **8.16**.

Periodic review

8.40 There is no magic in the period to be chosen. The convention of current practice ranges from 3 years to a maximum of 5 years. However, the pre-nuptial agreement may additionally provide for a number of significant situations each of which will trigger the need to review the terms of the agreement, whether the same be the birth of a child or the disability of either party etc. Again, in the first instance decision of *Radmacher's* case[1], it was considered relevant to enforceability that there was no provision for a review for either party in the event of the birth of a child. Such an event, it was observed by Baron J at first instance, altered the relationships and priorities of both sexes and was in that case one reason for the husband wanting to change career so as to spend more time with his family and, of course, thereby, impacted upon his income potential. The complete absence of consideration of such an event, her Ladyship considered 'flawed' that agreement and made it, so the court found, prima facie unfair.

Once again, the Court of Appeal and the Supreme Court adopted the opposite position. The relevance of the terms of a pre-nuptial and for that matter a post-nuptial agreement (other than an *Edgar* or *Xydhias* type) would be judged at the breakdown of the marriage irrespective of whether there had been any provision for or an actual review. However, both appeal courts considered that it was more likely that the longer the period of time which had elapsed since the pre-or post nuptial agreement had been entered into without adjustment of its terms, then the less likely the predictions as to the parties' financial futures and needs made therein would remain relevant to the 'prevailing circumstances' before the court under the s 25 exercise upon divorce and, thereby, the lesser the weight, which would be ascribed to the terms of the agreement in such circumstances[2].

The absence of a review clause in a pre-nuptial agreement will not under current law be fatal to an otherwise valid agreement's enforceability but it is highly desirable that such a clause be included to reflect both parties' awareness that regular review was necessary to ensure the relevance of the provisions to prevailing circumstances in the event of a divorce etc.

[1] See *NG v KR* above.
[2] See *Gray v Work* above.

Free will

8.41 There will, invariably, be some form of pressure in any discussion between couples concerning the making of a pre-nuptial agreement, even if it comes only from the fact that one of the parties holds the wealth and seeks to limit any future claim against such asset value in the event of a marriage breakdown. The extent of this consideration of pressure is not limited to the classic contractual issue of duress, which has overborne the free will of the other, but extends to any 'unconscionable' or 'unworthy' conduct.

> 'The presence of any of the standard vitiating factors of duress, fraud or misrepresentation will negate any effect the agreement might otherwise have (para 71). Further, unconscionable conduct such as undue pressure (falling short of duress) will likely eliminate the weight to be attached to the agreement (ibid). Other unworthy conduct, such as exploitation of a dominant position to secure an unfair advantage, will reduce or eliminate the weight to be attached to the agreement (ibid). The court may take into account a party's emotional state, and what pressures he or she was under to agree, as well as their age and maturity, and whether either or both had been married or been in long-term relationships before (para 72). The court may take into account foreign elements to determine whether or not the parties intended their agreement to be effective (para 74).[1]'

It will remain pivotal in most cases, therefore, to allow sufficient time before the marriage occurs and/or the final draft agreement is signed for negotiation and discussion to take place as to the terms of the pre-nuptial proposals. The estimate of time required for this purpose is frequently under estimated by the lay parties. Whilst, the Law Commission would with legislative reform require for validation of a 'Qualifying Nuptial Agreement' that the latest time to reach agreement should be 28 days before the marriage ceremony, this has been demonstrated under the present law, as above, in *K v K*, again in *Radmacher's* case and, subsequently, in *SA v PA*[2], to be, currently, no more than best practice.

8.41 *Pre-nuptial Agreements*

'63. Although it is true that the agreement was entered into on the very eve of the marriage, at a time when the wife was pregnant, and where she had only the impartial but not strictly independent advice of the notary I am satisfied that the wife freely entered into it with a sufficiency of advice to enable her to appreciate its implications.' Mostyn J in *SA v PA* [2014][3]

However, evidentially, the burden of proof will be different upon such an issue, dependent upon whether the agreement was signed pre- or post-*Radmacher*. For pre-*Radmacher* agreements, what the court will continue to look for within the s 25 exercise, upon any subsequent assessment of the fairness of the agreement, is that both parties had a reasonable time to consider its provisions and to take appropriate advice upon the same before agreeing to be bound to the agreement (see the Majority decision in *Radmacher's* case)[4]. This is because, in such cases, the intention of the parties to be bound by the terms of the pre-nuptial agreement will still need to be established as a primary evidential position.

In contrast, in post *Radmacher* agreements, assuming no contractual vitiating factor exists, it will be natural to infer from the very existence of a pre-nuptial agreement that both parties intended to be bound by the terms of the same and it will be for the party, who is seeking to persuade the court not to rely upon the terms of a pre-nuptial agreement, to rebut such an inference.

[1] *Kremen v Agrest (No 11)* [2012] EWHC 45 (Fam) at para 11 per Mostyn J.
[2] *SA v PA* [2014] EWHC 392 (Fam), Mostyn J at para 63. In Western Australia, for example, the suggestion that even 28 days cut off before the marriage ceremony is a sufficiently appropriate protective period for the financially weaker party is viewed with some considerable degree of professional scepticism amongst family solicitors there.
[3] See also *Versteegh v Versteeegh* [2018] EWCA Civ 1050, where the signing was just one day before.
[4] See [2010] UKSC 42 per Lord Phillips, paras 70–73.

Fairness

8.42 At all times, the fairness of what is being proposed is at the heart of the drafting exercise of a pre-nuptial agreement, whilst s 25 of the Matrimonial Causes Act 1973, as amended, in its present form, remains the law. If the provisions within the drafted agreement appear unfair, the other party is likely to be advised against the 'deal'. Indeed, even assuming the agreement upon such terms is entered into, should such unfairness of provision still be reflected against the prevailing circumstances upon divorce, then the court will be unwilling, in most cases under current law and post-*Radmacher*, to adhere fully to the terms struck.

What appears fair at the time of the drafting of the pre-nuptial agreement before the marital union has even commenced, is unlikely, without a wide element of generosity in the agreement's original provision and/or without subsequent periodic adjustment, to be seen as a fair measure of the needs of the financially weaker spouse many years later

This fact should be what any client hears first when seeking advice as to the merits and contents of a pre-nuptial agreement and what should be emphasised, thereafter, within any follow up client care letter.

Both pre- and post-*Radmacher*, it is clear that the existence of a pre-nuptial agreement can alter what the court would have considered fair upon the breakdown of the marriage had such an agreement not been in place[1]. Subject to this consideration, it is likely that the pre-nuptial agreement will have to address, principally, the issues of the parties' predictable 'needs' and any element of 'compensation' which may arise[2], where applicable, if the same is, currently, to satisfy the court upon divorce that its provisions are fair. It follows that it is in the sphere of the third strand of fairness, namely 'sharing' that the existence of a pre-nuptial agreement is likely to have the greatest impact.

There will be cases, however, where a nil provision within a pre-nuptial agreement will suffice, if the parties' respective financial positions prevailing at the time of the breakdown of the marriage when set against the fact that they have chosen to enter into a pre-nuptial agreement, can be said to meet their existing and future foreseeable individual requirements.

The advice in most cases, pending any legislative reform, for the client, who wishes there to be no provision for the other party in a pre-nuptial agreement must still be that, as the law currently stands, such an absence of provision considerably increases the likelihood that the agreement, after anything but a classic short childless marriage (up to 6 years), will be rejected by a court as having made fair provision for that other party in the event of a divorce etc. Of course, the fact that the parties did actually enter into an otherwise valid agreement, whether deemed fair or unfair, will still be a factor in the eventual s 25 exercise balance and it is submitted that where such a pre-nuptial agreement is challenged as unfair in eventual financial remedy proceedings, the party seeking to rely upon such an agreement will still strategically be able to make an 'open offer' of an additional 'top up' provision, at that stage, on the back of the argument that the existence of the agreement itself evidences the parties' intention that the other party's provision should, in any event, be more limited than their 'reasonable needs' provision which would have been the court's approach had there been no agreement at all.

However, the cases of *Ipekci v McConnell*[3] and *S v H*[4] which is a recent example of a nil provision pre-nuptial agreement for a husband may serve as a warning overall to such an approach – since ultimately, albeit other factors were involved, the court placed no reliance at all upon the agreement signed.

The Law Commission's report has, notwithstanding the above, clearly signalled that its proposals for statutory reform in this area would not be in favour of any hierarchy of 'need' levels, differentiating between 'reasonable/real needs' and any perceived lower form of 'basic' or 'essential' needs. Indeed, a primary condition of the enforceability of any 'Qualifying Nuptial Agreement' as submitted in the Commission's report, remains that the same must provide, at least, for the financially weaker spouse's reasonable needs[5]. However until such recommendations are enacted upon by amending legislation[6], currently it is arguably the position that there remains a continuing disconnect between the Law Commission's proposals and the approach of the judiciary post *Radmacher* in that, dependent upon the particular circumstances in any given case, some judges remain willing to endorse as fair the

8.42 Pre-nuptial Agreements

terms of an otherwise valid pre-nuptial agreement which provides, at least, for the weaker financial party's 'real needs' as opposed to their arguably higher 'reasonable needs'.

In *A v A*[7], Cohen J., faced with an agreement between parties (not a pre-nuptial agreement) enshrined by a court order (attracting an approach as to the fairness of the agreement akin to the guidance given in *Radmacher's* case) and which, subject to the court's appraisal of fairness, obligated W to repay a substantial loan owed by her to H, His Lordship observed:

> '40. I do not find that "real needs" is a helpful alternative test to that of "needs". Needs as a concept is elastic enough to encompass a situation where they have to be judged in the circumstances that pertain to the particular case. In this case they are judged against a pre-existing agreement and thus will be more rigorously assessed than they will be absent that agreement. In addition, the meeting of those needs may lead to a formula which is different to that which would apply in a case where there was not such an agreement.'

This should be contrasted with the comments of Mostyn J in *Ipeckci v McConnell*:

> 'iv) The agreement does not meet any needs of the husband. I do not take the language used by the Supreme Court, namely "predicament of real need" as signifying that needs when assessed in circumstances where there is a valid prenuptial agreement in play should be markedly less than needs assessed in ordinary circumstances. If you have reasonable needs which you cannot meet from your own resources, then you are in a predicament. Those needs are real needs.[8]'

[1] *M v M (Prenuptial Agreement)* [2002] 1 FLR 654. Connell J pared the wife's needs down because she had signed a pre-nuptial agreement (see para 44) and in *Radmacher's* case the existence of the pre-nuptial agreement to preserve non-matrimonial property had the effect of the court assessing need more conservatively than would have been the case absent that factor.
[2] Albeit in *SA v PA* above, Mostyn J has sought to limit the principle of compensation to the rare and exceptional case.
[3] [2019] EWFC 19.
[4] [2020] EWFC B9.
[5] See definition of 'Financial Needs' and generally in Family Justice Council's 'Guidance on Financial Needs on Divorce' (June 2016).
[6] See also Divorce (Financial Provision) Bill (HL 21) committee stage (Jan 2017) and further commentary on any such proposed legislative changes below.
[7] [2018] EWHC 2194.
[8] [2019] EWFC 19.

Checklist

8.43 A checklist for preparing and drafting a pre-nuptial agreement should:

(1) Provide the client with a general overview of the likely process and the time needed to reach a signed final draft and the probable costs involved[1].

(2) Having obtained a broad understanding of the client's requirements, obtain from Professional Insurers the required and appropriate level of professional indemnity cover for such work and subject thereto, advise the client as to the limited level of your professional indemnity cover for the work to be undertaken and make that level the limitation of your liability as a written pre-condition of accepting instructions in the

matter after advising the client of the potential of instructing other lawyers who may undertake the work without such a limitation and giving the client a reasonable time and opportunity of considering the written terms of such limitation including advising that the client may without commitment also seek separate advice upon such a written limitation document.

(3) Subject to the above, obtain the client's signed consent to such limitation of liability.
(4) Advise, at least that:
    (i) the current law has been subject to the published report by the Law Commission and it has been proposed that a 'Qualifying Nuptial Agreement', subject to various minimum conditions, will, if the parties' financial needs are met, be a binding agreement and that statutory reform by Parliament introducing such agreements may follow in this area; and
    (ii) (if still applicable) there has been progress within Parliament of alternative draft legislation now represented by Divorce (Financial Provision) Bill (HL 39) and explain the content thereof in relation to the proposed statutory recognition of pre-nuptial agreements as being binding within divorce financial distribution subject to certain specified exceptions (see more below); and
    (iii) subject to such reform, under current law, entry into a pre-nuptial agreement will give rise to a rebuttable presumption that the parties intended that the court would enforce the division of resources/liabilities as provided for in the agreement on dissolution of marriage and the agreement is likely to be reflected in the order of the court unless in the circumstances prevailing it would not be fair to hold the parties to their agreement, eg the weaker financial party's needs are not met; and
    (iv) it is important that each party in advance of agreement is provided with the necessary information as to the current and foreseeable extent of respective resources/incomes with, where applicable, due accountancy and tax advice; and
    (v) it is important that each party to an agreement has the opportunity to seek and does obtain independent legal advice upon the content and natural and legal meaning of the agreement and the implications and effect of the same upon the rights (and obligations) at law of the client; and
    (vi) there must be no threat or undue pressure exerted or untruthful, dishonest or misleading information provided to persuade the other party to enter an agreement; and
    (vii) any agreement, once entered into, should be kept up to date periodically and/or reviewed where there are significant changes to the parties' circumstances to ensure that should the marriage break down, the agreement deals with the prevailing financial circumstances of the parties; and
    (viii) no term in a pre-nuptial agreement can currently, as the law stands, prevent the court from deciding upon divorce that there should be a different provision ordered to that set out in the agreement; and

8.43 Pre-nuptial Agreements

- (ix) no term in a pre-nuptial agreement can affect or limit the entitlement of any child of the parties or either of them; and
- (x) no term in a pre-nuptial agreement will be sanctioned by a court of which the effect is to place the burden of maintenance of either spouse or any children of the parties onto the State where the parties hold resources otherwise sufficient to meet such an obligation; and
- (xi) it is likely that under current law any provision, which leaves either party with less than they need for adequate housing and income support to meet their then existing and/or foreseeable financial needs or which after a significant length of committed marital relationship leaves only one spouse with a significant 'surfeit' of capital or earning capacity gained by parties' mutual efforts in that relationship above that spouse's own needs will be seen as unfair and the court being unwilling to follow the agreement reached fully or at all; and
- (xii) there can be no certainty at present without legislative change that a court will fully endorse the terms of a pre-nuptial agreement between the parties on a divorce, albeit that there is an increasing incidence of the court being prepared to do so; and
- (xiii) in the event that either party is a foreign national, the court will nevertheless apply the law of England and Wales within any divorce proceedings in regard to the terms of any pre-nuptial agreement entered into between the parties notwithstanding any foreign choice of law clause within that agreement. However, as has been referred to above[2], the implementation from 29 January 2019 of the European Union Regulations on Matrimonial Property Regimes (2016/1103) may impact on the recognition of signed pre-nuptial agreements for marriages celebrated after the January 2019 implementation date in those countries which are signatories to the Regulation. The Regulation attempts to provide some uniformity of approach in the signatory countries to matrimonial property and in this process provides for recognition of the formalities in the countries involved relating to pre-nuptial agreements, including those effecting a choice of law. Whilst the UK has not been a signatory to this Regulation, the same will be relevant should either party be habitually resident within one of the named member states[3].
- (xiv) should either party envisage moving abroad it is essential that they obtain appropriate legal advice from foreign lawyers as to the enforceability of a pre-nuptial agreement within that prospective jurisdiction and any additional wording to be inserted as a result, where relevant.

(5) Schedule a number of initial meetings to take details and assemble the necessary supporting documentation that will be required.

(6) Issue the client with a pro-forma document in advance of the scheduled meetings to complete with details to be expanded upon in the meetings to reduce the time to be taken.

(7) Take a very detailed preliminary statement of instructions from the client which upon completion should be read, dated and then signed by the client. The statement should cover:

Law and Practice **8.43**

(i) the client's and his/her partner's and any of their children's full names, dates of birth, current addresses and address of their intended matrimonial home, if known; and
(ii) the client's expected date of marriage to the partner; and
(iii) the client's and his partner's previous relationship history/chronology; and
(iv) the client's and his partner's current and anticipated income, capital, chattels and pension resources and liabilities detail; and
(v) the details of any third party joint holder of any resources identified together with their address/telephone/email; and
(vi) the account numbers and address/telephone/email of identified banks or building societies, insurance companies/investments/pension fund schemes/trusts and trustees/mortgagees and loans; and
(vii) details of any recent valuations of resources and any recent statement of credit/debit account balances held; and
(viii) provisional details of any suggested valuers appropriate to value resources held; and
(ix) where businesses or trusts are involved, details of the last accounts created/company search obtained and the identity and address/telephone/email of the relevant accountants to the same; and
(x) where land/property is involved, the Land Registry details etc; and
(xi) the potential taxation upon disposal of any resource held and the identity and contact details of an accountant/financial advisor to ascertain the same; and
(xii) the contribution to date which either the client or his partner has made to such resources/liabilities; and
(xiii) the potential for further acquisition of such resources in the foreseeable future, including the identity of any expected inheritance and/or any beneficiary receipt under any trusts involved; and
(xiv) where trusts are involved, the history of distribution to date to the client or his partner or any children or any other beneficiary involved; and
(xv) the client's and/or his partner's reasons advanced for wanting a pre-nuptial agreement; and
(xvi) the provisional division of resources/income/pension/liabilities desired in the event of a divorce etc; and
(xvii) the extent to which the parties have already discussed/agreed to the need for and/or the content of provisions and/or the desired division of resources/income/pensions/liabilities within a pre-nuptial agreement; and
(xviii) any plans held to have/adopt children after marriage; and
(xix) any current agreement/concerns of the client's partner concerning a pre-nuptial agreement; and
(xx) the identity and address/telephone/email of any other lawyer/financial advisor/accountant already engaged; and
(xxi) the provision of a list of family law solicitors local to the client's partner's address, if required and whether it will be

8.43 *Pre-nuptial Agreements*

necessary for the client to fund the partner's instruction and to what extent.

(8) Discuss with the client what it is intended should be achieved by a pre-nuptial agreement and whether there may be other ways to address the concerns highlighted before the marriage takes place such as by gift or trust etc.

(9) Consider with the client the need to have a number of preliminary meetings with an accountant or financial advisor, to look at the available alternatives and/or to secure the detail of disclosure required.

(10) Consider whether Counsel is to be instructed to draft the agreement and discuss with the client the advantages and costs of involving such Counsel at an early stage.

(11) Consider any expressed concerns of the other party and, if at that stage there are none, what is the likely reaction of that other party? Eg, will introduction of the issue undermine the relationship and has this been fully thought through?

(12) Caution the client against not disclosing to the other party the real reason why he or she wants the pre-nuptial agreement in place, since lack of frankness at this stage upon such an issue will undermine the agreement's effect later.

(13) Caution the client of the effect on the other party and their advisor of seeking too much protection and the likely advice the other party will get from his or her own lawyer.

(14) Advise in the light of the protection desired by the client within a pre-nuptial agreement of the likely effect of the same under the current law of divorce etc and if the current proposals for reform become law. In particular:

   (i) what is likely to be seen as fair in any pre-nuptial agreement in addressing the predicted future needs of the parties and of any children (and potential compensation issues) in order both to persuade the other legal advisor and, eventually, should there be a marital breakdown, a court to follow the terms reached. In particular, highlight that where a pre-nuptial agreement is in place which is challenged on divorce as not adequately providing for the weaker financial spouse's reasonable needs, the court will be determining whether (following *Radmacher's* case) the provision within the agreement struck meets the 'real needs' of that party which could arguably be lower than 'reasonable needs'; and

   (ii) to what extent the client's canvassed plan to protect present or future resource worth is likely to fall on one side or the other of the line of fairness and, therefore, whether, realistically, the proposed pre-nuptial can fully, or in part only, meet the protection required; and

   (iii) in this context and purely as a general summary following the *McFarlane/Miller*[4] cases, that there is a greater likelihood of a pre-nuptial agreement effecting protection to a party with the greater ownership of pre-marital accrued property the shorter the time between the initial signing or any subsequent review of the agreement's terms and the breakdown of the marriage and where otherwise the provisions of the agreement still meet the

Law and Practice **8.43**

reasonable anticipated compensation needs of the other spouse on a divorce. Carefully worded, such protection can extend to where a child is already on the scene or contemplated. The longer the marriage may last, the more generous the provision within the agreement must be to meet the likely needs of the other party and any relevant child and any compensation factor; and

(iv) it should be pointed out that, realistically, that providing too little initially, with too much reliance upon the inclusion of a review clause within the agreement to adapt, in the future, the terms of the provision made to changing circumstances and the financial position of the parties may be short sighted against the practical likelihood that the agreement will not be returned to by most parties once their marriage has taken place until a breakdown occurs, maybe many years ahead; and

(v) warn the client that silence within the agreement as to any obvious area of provision, such as that sufficient to meet the other party's likely need for accommodation or maintenance or the possible arrival of a child, will not be viewed as neutral in effect when a court has, eventually, to determine whether the agreement overall was fair overall. Experience teaches that such silence in such areas emboldens the court to justify holding the agreement as unfair where the provision otherwise made appears too limited.

(15) Once it is clear that a pre-nuptial agreement will be required, ascertain from the client the extent to which the other party is aware of the client's wish for a pre-nuptial agreement and ensure that the client has made that other party aware of the imminent contact to be received from a solicitor concerning such a matter.

(16) Against such knowledge write to the other party in amicable terms inviting information as to their present position and advising if not already undertaken that the other party should instruct a solicitor to be advised as to the terms of such an agreement and to supply the name and address of the solicitor concerned.

(17) Write in amicable terms to the solicitor instructed by the other party and give a broad outline, as approved by the client, of the reasons for a pre-nuptial agreement being required, indicating the desire to provide as much assistance to the other solicitor within the process as possible.

(18) Agree with the other solicitor an ample time framework to ensure that the process can be completed after the provision of the first draft of the agreement within a reasonable timescale before the marriage is to take place.

(19) (Following conference with counsel if required) provide the first draft (ensuring that the language in the agreement is kept simple and avoid using over legalistic terms, wherever possible) and invite discussion of any problems, preferably by face to face meeting, where possible, between the solicitors first and then, if need be, with clients present.

(20) Agree the extent of disclosure required and the format for dealing with reference to the same within the agreement and also the extent of any professional accountancy advice etc required.

8.43 *Pre-nuptial Agreements*

(21) Where delays result in the terms of the agreement not being reached until shortly before the marriage date, expressly refer to this position within the agreement and the reasons for the delay occurring and confirm therein that despite that delay each party is content that they each have a full appreciation of the implications and effect of the agreement reached and the same fully reflects their individual intentions that the terms thereof should determine in fairness the division of their assets/income upon a marital breakdown.

(22) Draw up and have signed and witnessed in deed form the agreed terms of the pre-nuptial agreement, which must also exhibit any signed certificate(s) by each legal and other advisor involved that the appropriate independent advices for the purposes of the pre-nuptial agreement have been given.

(23) Ensure where a 'honeymoon' agreement is to be entered into after the marriage that again before such an agreement is signed etc each party's advisors have provided like advice to each party and signed separate certificate(s) to this effect.

(24) Ensure that the whole file on the case is maintained in tact indefinitely in the event of subsequent complaint or enquiry.

---

[1] This is likely to be in the region of, at least, 6 months before the wedding ceremony date and longer if there are complex financial interests to be disclosed. The professional costs of pre-nuptial drafting and negotiation are notoriously difficult to predict accurately and commercially. However, as was apparent from the Law Commission's investigations undertaken by Emma Hitchins in preparation for their report, the range of professional fees given by a limited number of correspondents questioned of between £200 and £25,000 for pre-nuptial drafts in 2011 indicated a wildly different level of charging within the profession in this area which clearly indicates the need for better evaluation and self-regulation. The lay client is entitled to know at the outset the probable cost of such work and a fixed fee cost range should be provided.

[2] See fn 1 at **8.32**.

[3] See eg European Union Regulations Matrimonial Property Regimes clauses 47 and 48A. Note also following Brexit, the Maintenance Regulation ceases to apply and a choice of law agreement for child maintenance would be possible and, therefore, the inclusion should be considered of a provision electing England and Wales as the jurisdiction of choice to settle child maintenance claims in the event the Lugano Convention 2007 is subsequently ratified by the UK.

[4] [2006] UKHL 24.

Professional liability limitation

8.44 Family lawyers in practice have failed within this jurisdiction to seriously consider the extent of their own exposure to liability in the event that the advice given to clients contemplating a pre-nuptial agreement and/or the drafting of the agreement is later shown to have been negligent. Clearly, in the general run of family work practice such considerations would not be a priority, but in accepting pre-nuptial instructions, family lawyers are exposing themselves and/or their firm to potentially huge levels of liability at some indeterminate date in the future.

The decision of the Supreme Court in *Radmacher's* case has made it clear that to be bound to the terms of a pre-nuptial agreement under the current law a party has to have freely entered into the agreement 'with a full appreciation' of the implications. The Law Commission have in their published report (see more below) put forward that for any 'Qualifying Nuptial Agreement', if introduced, one of the pre-requisites should be that the parties to the same have received independent legal advice and that this condition should not be capable of waiver. There are clearly, including the *Radmacher* case itself on its facts and a number of more recent decisions of the High Court, examples of where, despite the absence of independent legal advice being obtained, an agreement entered into has been subsequently given considerable weight upon the financial distribution considered as fair by the court upon divorce. Whilst this may be the case, each of those decisions were very much to be justified upon their particular facts and should not be taken as undermining the obtaining of independent legal advice as being, save in exceptional circumstances, an essential requirement when considering the fairness of the terms of a pre-nuptial agreement signed by the parties when undertaking the s 25 statutory exercise[1].

The Law Commission has suggested that the nature of that independent advice in relation to the proposed 'Qualifying Nuptial Agreement' that the client is advised that such an agreement will, subject to the parties' financial needs being provided for, prevent a court making an order inconsistent with the Qualifying Nuptial Agreement and also in relation to the likely effect of the Agreement upon the rights of that party. If this guidance is to be taken as an indication of the basic required standard, then applying the same to advice under the current law, there should, at least, be advice given to the client in relation to a pre-nuptial agreement, which explains the ordinary and legal meaning of its terms and its effect at law and on the rights (and obligations) of the party being advised. The Law Commission also suggested that other matters may (as opposed to must) also be covered in any such advice given to a client and these are further considered under sub para (i)–(ix) inclusive in the next section ('Qualifying Nuptial Agreements' – legal advice guidance).

Of course, there has been a practice for some time of legal advisors signing an appropriate certificate which is then attached to the signed agreement and which confirms that the requisite advice has been provided to the party concerned. However, it should be emphasised that prior to the Law Commission's suggested ambit for such advice, the form and content of these certificates has been very much a matter of individual judgment of the advisor concerned. It is of concern that some examples of the certificates currently in use have included references to the legal advisor providing advice as to the merits 'financially or otherwise' of the party entering into the agreement – such references to financial advice plainly fall outside the expertise of the legal advisor and should not be used in such a certificate.

[1] Eg, *Kremen v Agrest (No 11)* [2012] EWHC 45 (Fam) and *BN v MA* [2013] EWHC 4250 (Fam) Mostyn J.

8.45 The Law Commission in its consultation stage highlighted the recent experience of the Australian legal profession in this area of law. The account must serve as a cautionary tale to the almost relaxed approach presently shown by the legal professions in this country to the acceptance of instructions, without more, in relation to pre-nuptial agreements[1].

> '5.42 . . . . Binding Financial Agreements in Australia have already had an extraordinary legislative history, with the relevant provisions being amended several times as problems with their pre-requisites have become apparent. More relevant

8.45 *Pre-nuptial Agreements*

here is the fact that Binding Financial Agreements are regarded with great caution by lawyers where the parties have not already separated.

5.43 In other words, Binding Financial Agreements are popular and effective as substitutes for separation agreements; once finalised, no consent order is required and the Binding Financial Agreement itself has the same force as a court order. But there is great reluctance among Australian lawyers to advise clients to take the risk of entering into a binding agreement to provide for a future separation, where the circumstances are unknown. One Australian lawyer based in New South Wales has remarked to us that:

> "Many solicitors refuse to even advise parties [before marriage]. It is felt that the chance of overlooking something, changes in the circumstances of the parties, changes in the law itself, changes in the values of assets and the like make the issue very problematic."[1]

The basic advice standard required, as suggested above, still imposes on the legal advisor a duty to explain not only the meaning of the terms of any proposed agreement, but also what, in the circumstances of the client's case, the effect of those terms may be both under the present law and any potential future changes to the law which reasonably may occur. This requires both care and studious attention to note keeping to deal with and fully record the advice given concerning potential changes which may present themselves in the client's future married life with his new partner based upon reasonable predictions from his or her known present circumstances.

Of course, legal advice based upon predictions as to the future could well be ripe territory for professional liability. The client and his fiancée could be a budding Mr and Mrs Bill Gates and their modest expectations and the draft pre-nuptial agreement drawn recording the same could in a few years of married life be set against a transformation to huge wealth against which an ill termed provision or lack of provision in their pre-nuptial agreement may become the basis for a negligence action against either one or both of the lawyers involved for a not inconsiderable claim in damages. The limitation period for professional negligence of 6 years from when the loss is incurred could be longer if it is determined that 'latent' damage is present[2].

It is, therefore, essential that practitioners in this arena should take such steps to attempt to limit their liability to such potential liability levels as is feasible. The cost of indemnity insurance enhancement can be prohibitive, especially, if, as in most practices, such pre-nuptial work is not the main source of revenue and, in any event, even with a significant enhancement of insurance level may still be below the level of claim eventually pursued. Indeed, solicitors' firms in this country are, it is suggested, on average by comparison with many of their counterparts elsewhere around the world and for example in Western Australia significantly underinsured in respect of their exposure to liability for pre-nuptial work.

Even in Western Australia where such work is commonly covered by indemnity cover of AUD$12,000,000 or more, the view taken by experienced practitioners in such work is that there is concern that the protection provided at that level remains insufficient[3]. By comparison, many counsel in England and Wales who undertake pre-nuptial work continue to do so on their standard Bar Mutual Indemnity cover for work as family practitioners which currently amounts to c £2,500,000 and in consequence their personal exposure is significant without further measures being undertaken, such as obtaining Bar Standard Board approval as a limited liability entity.

Of course, obtaining the client's signed acceptance of a limitation to the legal advisor's liability in the form of a maximum level of damages recovery in the event of professional negligence as part of the retainer is a route which itself is beset with problems. There will need to be compliance with the requirements of fairness of any liability limiting term pursuant to the Unfair Contract Terms Act 1977 and also in certain respects the Unfair Terms in Consumer Contracts Regulations 1999 and, if the limitation, effectively, sets a maximum damages limit, then the level of that limit may itself be deemed as unfairly restrictive in the circumstances.

These difficulties, however, should not dissuade the practitioner from obtaining the client's acceptance to such a limitation. The alternatives are, of course, not to accept instructions in such work at all or simply to take the risk – albeit, the latter route is not recommended.

[1] Law Commission *Marital Property Agreements: A Consultation Paper* (2011).
[2] Up to 15 years: see s 14A and 14B Latent Damages Act 1986.
[3] Information obtained from senior partners of solicitors' firms practising in Perth, Western Australia.

Statutory reform

Ambit of reform

8.46 The Law Commission announced in June 2008[1] that it was to consider nuptial agreements with the aim of drawing up draft parliamentary legislation by 2012. Subsequently, the Law Commission announced that it would issue a consultation paper in the summer of 2010 (in the event, the first was in 2011 followed by a supplementary consultation paper in 2012) and consider the required timetable for further steps thereafter[2].

In 2010, in parallel, Resolution published its report 'Family Agreements: Seeking Certainty to Reduce Disputes'[3]. The Report recommended change by substantial legislation amendment. The basis of the Resolution Report suggested that the right to choice of the parties to pre-determine the division of their resources upon divorce by a pre-nuptial agreement should be the central focus of such legislative intervention.

The Resolution report proposed new sub-ss 25(2A) and 25(2B) of the Matrimonial Causes Act 1973 (and a new provision to the same effect in the Civil Partnership Act 2004) in these terms:

'(2A) The court shall regard any agreement in writing entered into between the parties to the marriage in contemplation of or after the marriage for the purpose of regulating their affairs on the breakdown of their marriage as binding upon the parties and shall make an order in the terms of the agreement unless:
(a) the agreement was entered into as a result of unfair pressure or unfair influence;
(b) one or both parties did not have a reasonable opportunity to receive

(c) independent legal advice about the terms and effect of the agreement;
(c) one or both parties failed to provide substantially full and frank financial disclosure before the agreement was made;
(d) the agreement was made fewer than 42 days before the marriage;
(e) enforcing the agreement would cause substantial hardship to either party or to any minor child of the family.

(2B) If one or more of the factors in paragraphs (a) to (e) of subsection 25(2A) applies, the court shall give the agreement such weight as it thinks fit taking into account:
(a) all the facts surrounding the agreement;
(b) the matters in section 25(1) and (2).'

Set against such amendments, Resolution further recommended that it would also be necessary to make a consequential amendment to s 25(2) of the Act, in order to add to the list of factors in that subsection to which the court is required to have regard, 'any agreement within the new s 25(2A)'.

It is suggested, however, that Resolution's approach would still fail to adequately safeguard the rights of the weaker financial party entering marriage from the manipulation of emotional pressures inherent at the start of any relationship and which often lead to an agreement. If such an agreement effectively binds the parties to its terms upon divorce, then this is likely to result, in such circumstances, in an outcome which a court under the present law's search for a fair outcome would not have otherwise sanctioned. The phrase 'substantial hardship', which is, obviously, intended to protect in these circumstances, echoes the similar current s 25 phrase of 'undue hardship', which Parliament intended to be a check to the court's automatic dismissal of future maintenance claims, but in practice has failed to stem the tide to the adoption of a clean break approach in a significant number of divorces, with the result that Lady Hale in *McFarlane/Miller* considered it necessary to expressly remind the courts that such a result should not under the existing legislation be the automatic outcome.

Some possible areas of reform include:

(1) simply amending the current s 25(2) list of particular factors to be taken into account to include, specifically, any agreements reached between the parties as described in the proposed s 25(2A) of the Resolution amendment above. Whilst some say this is little more than formalising the current position; in fact, it would for the first time identify within the legislation, the 'parties' agreements' as a specific factor in the s 25 exercise and would reflect the current state of the case law by acknowledging the relevance of such agreements in the process to be undertaken, whilst also endorsing the status of the pre-nuptial agreement within the public's perception of those issues upon the 'ordinary' divorce which matter;
(2) inserting a new sub clause within s 25, to provide that, where a pre-nuptial agreement is in place then, upon divorce etc, the terms of the same are to apply, unless it would be unfair to either party or any of the children of the family to do so. (This, actually, reflects the approach of the minority in the *Judges Response* of 1998[4] and now the approach of the Supreme Court in *Radmacher*'s case);

(3) again, inserting a new sub clause within s 25, enabling the court to give first consideration, along with the existing provision as to the welfare of any relevant child of the family, to the terms of a pre-nuptial agreement.
(4) the creation of a pre-approved form of pre-nuptial agreement, the signing of which entitles the parties to avoid entering into the s 25 process altogether upon divorce as long as their 'needs' are met. As will be seen below this, in part, at least, is the route favoured by the Law Commission's report. However, the recommendations made have fallen short of suggesting that the 'principle of autonomy' should dominate the process as, in the Commission's view, the 'needs' of the financially weaker spouse should still be the bottom line condition of the spousal entitlement to being permitted to enforce the terms of any such agreement reached[5].

[1] [2008] June; Tenth Programme of Law Reform and now see the comprehensive Law Commission Consultation Paper No 198 entitled 'Marital Property Agreements – A Consultation Paper'. The supporting research of E Hitchings, 'From Pre-nups to Post-nups: Dealing with Marital Property Agreements' [2009] Family Law 1056 and her 2010 Supplementary Report provide the current approach and practice of the Profession when dealing with clients who require pre-nuptial agreements.
[2] 'The Law Commission's review following *Radmacher*' Antonia Mee, 21 October 2010, Fam Law Week.
[3] 'Family Agreements: Seeking Certainty to Reduce Disputes' Resolution 2010.
[4] N Wilson 'Ancillary Relief Reform: Response of the Judges of the Family Division to the Government Proposals (made by way of submission to the Lord Chancellor's Ancillary Relief Advisory Group)' (1999) 29 Family Law 159, 162.
[5] The view that the financially weaker spouse who has had independent legal advice yet requires special protection in the pre-nuptial process is not one shared by a majority of experienced family practitioners in Perth, Western Australia where for substantially more than a decade the binding nature of the pre-nuptial agreement has been enshrined in legislation and where the view of the profession is strongly expressed that the pre-nuptial agreement is to be enforced like any other commercial agreement.

8.47 The Divorce (Financial Provision) Bill (HL 21) introduced in May 2016 by cross-bencher Baroness Deech in the House of Lords and which by December 2018 reached its first reading in the Commons failed to proceed in the light of the 2019 general election. Its provisions have now been re-introduced (Divorce (Financial Provision) Bill (HL 39) to the House of Lords by Baroness Shackleton and by January 2020 had received a first reading. Its further progress cannot yet be assured, as the Government has to date favoured taking more time to assess the nature of any reform of the current law including the changes needed to reflect pre-marital and marital agreements as recommended by the Law Commission. In addition, of course, the Covid-19 lockdown in 2020 has further interfered with Parliamentary business schedules. However, the Bill's provisions[1] overall seek to effect a wider reform of the current divorce law approach to financial remedy division focusing on the fair division of the parties' 'matrimonial' as opposed to 'non matrimonial' property upon a divorce and more limited access to long term maintenance. In particular, it is provided that:

'1. Amendment of the Matrimonial Causes Act 1973
(1) . . .
(3) . . .

8.47 Pre-nuptial Agreements

"pre-nuptial agreement" means an agreement entered into in contemplation of marriage for the purpose of regulating the affairs of the parties should their marriage break down;

"post-nuptial agreement" means an agreement entered into after marriage, by the parties to the marriage, for the purpose of regulating their affairs should the marriage break down;

And

3. Pre-nuptial and post-nuptial agreements

(1) For the purposes of any proceedings to which this section applies, a pre-nuptial or post-nuptial agreement in writing and signed by both parties to the marriage is to be treated as binding on them unless—
   (a) the agreement attempts to impose an obligation on a third party who has not agreed in advance to be bound by it (in which case the Divorce (Financial Provision) Bill agreement is not binding on the parties insofar as it attempts to impose that obligation);
   (b) a party neither received independent legal advice, nor had an adequate opportunity to do so, before the agreement was made;
   (c) in the case of a pre-nuptial agreement, the agreement was made less than 21 days before the marriage;
   (d) one or both parties failed to make proper disclosure of that party's assets before the agreement was made; or
   (e) the agreement is unenforceable under any rule of law relating to the validity or enforceability of contracts generally.

(2) Any non-compliance with subsection (1)(b) or (d) may be relied on only by the party disadvantaged by such non-compliance.

(3) For the purposes of subsection (1)(b), where a person authorised to carry out reserved legal activities (within the meaning of the Legal Services Act 2007) has given a party independent legal advice about the proposed entry into a pre-nuptial or post-nuptial agreement, the certificate of that person to that effect is to be treated as conclusive evidence of the giving of that advice.

(4) Where a pre-nuptial or post-nuptial agreement is to be treated as binding, the court may make a relevant financial order only to the extent to which the agreement does not deal with the matter.

And . . .

4. Matrimonial property

(1) The net value of the matrimonial property is to be shared fairly between the parties to the marriage.

(2) In applying the principle set out in subsection (1), the net value of the matrimonial property shall be taken to be shared fairly between the parties when it is shared equally, unless subsection (5) applies.

(3) The net value of the property is the value of the property at the date of the relevant financial order, after deduction of any debts incurred by one or both of the parties to the marriage:
   (a) before the marriage so far as they relate to the matrimonial property; or
   (b) during the marriage,
   which are outstanding at that date.

(4) The amount of any order for lump sum provision in favour of a party to a marriage shall be taken into account as part of the equal sharing of the matrimonial property (irrespective of what assets are actually resorted to by the other party in compliance with the order).

(5) The court may make an order involving an unequal sharing of the net value of the matrimonial property to the extent to which it is satisfied that to do so would be fair, having regard to any of the following matters—
  (a) the terms of any agreement between the parties relating to the ownership or division of any of the matrimonial property;
  (b) any destruction, dissipation or alienation of matrimonial property by either party;
  (c) the needs of any children of the family aged under 21; and
  (d) actual or prospective liability for any expenses of valuation or transfer of property in connection with the divorce.'

[1] Baroness Hale has suggested this Bill will contain less safeguards than the Law Commissions proposals -see Four Jurisdictions Family Law Conference [2018] Fam Law 377.

8.48 It will be observed that the Bill adopts a hybrid approach between the canvassed nature of the reforms which have been hitherto suggested.

It suggests (at s 3(1)) that the parties are to be bound to the agreement they have signed subject to certain exceptions. The court on a divorce faced with the existence of a valid pre-nuptial agreement can (see s 3(4)) make any financial remedy order 'only to the extent to which the agreement does not deal with the matter'.

The exceptions (see s 3(1)(a) to (e)) permitting the court to step outside the terms of any signed agreement when carrying out the s 25 exercise, are (a) where the agreement attempts to impose an obligation on a third party who has otherwise not agreed to undertake that obligation; or (b) the party has not had independent legal advice before the agreement was signed or 'an adequate opportunity' to receive such advice; or (c) the pre-nuptial agreement was made less than 21 days before the marriage; or (d) at least one party has failed to make 'proper' disclosure before the agreement was made; or (e) the agreement is invalid or unenforceable on contractual grounds.

By s 4 of the Bill, any unequal sharing of matrimonial property can only be justified as being fair by the court if it is satisfied it is so, having regard to just four specified criteria of which the terms of an agreement relating to the 'the ownership or division of any of the matrimonial property' is one.

In its present form the Bill would approach any pre-nuptial agreement in writing as a contractual document between the parties with its terms binding in effect upon the parties in regard to divorce division in so far as it deals with the parties' assets and as long as the pre-conditions for the agreement's validity were in place. Of particular interest, is the fact that there is no bottom line escape provision from the agreement's terms by reason of the same failing to provide for either party's needs (as opposed to any of their children's needs as minors under contract law) – which would be the first departure from such a 'needs' related provision since the civil jurisdiction of divorce was introduced back in 1857.

8.49 Pre-nuptial Agreements

The Law Commission

The Law Commission report

8.49 'In this Consultation Paper we ask .... Should pre-nuptial and post-nuptial agreements continue to be enforced by the courts at their discretion – governed by the principles enunciated by the Supreme Court – within ancillary relief proceedings? The Supreme Court's restatement of the law in *Radmacher v Granatino* arguably takes the law as far towards an enforceable status for marital property agreements as is possible within the current statutory framework. Our consultation asks whether there should be legislative reform to enable couples effectively to contract out of ancillary relief, and out of the court's discretion, by entering into an agreement in a prescribed form and subject to appropriate safeguards.'¹

Following on from the consultation, the Commission's published report, *Matrimonial Property, Needs and Agreements*, sought to address three specific areas, being financial needs following divorce etc, marital property agreements and non-matrimonial property. The Commission's stated intention was to render the law in the area more certain and predictable, whilst not sacrificing the protection under the law afforded to those made vulnerable by the breakdown of marriage.

The current law relating to the responsibility of former spouses upon divorce to meet each other's 'financial needs', the Commission concluded, did not at this time require reform. The Commission was satisfied that in practice the approach of the courts was such that the correct balance continued to be struck in the s 25 discretionary exercise and the same tended towards a measured outcome of financial independence for divorcing couples. However, there was evidence of some inconsistency within the court system itself as well as amongst mediators and litigants in person as to application of what is understood as the parties' financial needs' and, accordingly, the Commission considered that the meaning of that phrase should be clarified by guidance from the Family Justice Council. It was the Commission's hope that in so doing this would make clearer the kind of outcome which a judge would aim for so as to achieve a realistic level of support, which recognised the needs and responsibilities that each party had for the future whilst working towards independence where that is practicable.

The Commission was of the view that the advocating of set formulae to predict the appropriate payments to be made by one spouse to another may be of assistance and recommended Government funding for the research that would be required. However, the Commission cautioned that it should be remembered that such jurisdictions where such formulae are presently employed are very different legal systems to that of England and Wales. In any event, such guidance as could be given should not be seen as an alternative the court's discretionary exercise but a discrete aid to the parties to better negotiate an informed outcome wherever possible. Such guidance should be non-statutory and present a range of outcomes within which parties could negotiate.

As to 'marital property agreements', the Commission was clear that the presence of a discretion within the court's adjudication to the application or otherwise of such agreements was contrary to the wishes of many couples who wished to base their marriage on a 'shared understanding of the financial consequences of any future separation'. Accordingly, the Commission's central recommendation was that a 'Qualifying Nuptial Agreement' should be introduced. Such an agreement would be an enforceable contract between the parties, which could not subsequently be interfered with by the court, save and except where the same failed to meet the 'financial needs' of a party[2]. The availability of such agreements, the Commission considered, would assist the predictability of outcome for parties as well as strengthening their autonomy in comparison with the present system, whilst at the same time the preservation of the protection of a party's 'financial needs' would be both consistent with the European protection of 'maintenance' rights and a necessary limitation to prevent potentially very damaging consequences for the financially weaker spouse[3].

The Commission was clear that to constitute a 'Qualifying Nuptial Agreement', some five essential conditions would have to be met. These were that:

(a) The agreement must be contractually valid (and able to withstand challenge of undue influence or misrepresentation, for example) and any variation to the same must comply with the same requirements as the original agreement.

(b) The agreement must have been made by deed and must contain a statement signed by both parties that he or she understands that the agreement is a Qualifying Nuptial Agreement that will partially remove the court's discretion to make financial orders.

(c) The agreement must not have been made within the 28 days immediately before the wedding or the celebration of civil partnership.

(d) Both parties to the agreement must have received, at the time of the making of the agreement, disclosure of *material* information about the other party's financial situation and the Commission considered that neither party should be able to waive this requirement.

(e) Both parties must have received at the time that the agreement was formed legal advice from separate lawyers, which includes advice that the agreement is a Qualifying Nuptial Agreement that will prevent the court from making financial orders inconsistent with the agreement, save so far as financial needs are concerned and as to the effect of the agreement on the rights of the party being advised. Again, this requirement should not be capable of waiver.

The correct approach to 'non matrimonial property' proved more controversial and elusive for the Commission. Initially, it had been hoped to address what should and should not be included as 'non matrimonial' property by statutory reform providing specifically for those areas which were still undecided or unresolved by the case law. In the final analysis, it was not possible to achieve a consensus for statutory intervention and the recommendation of the 'Qualifying Nuptial Agreement' was seen as being the vehicle by which the parties could best provide for themselves what should be the outcome on divorce for such property, if specific statutory definitions were not to be made available.

[1] Paragraph 1.11 'Matrimonial Property Agreements': Law Commission Consultation Paper No 198.

8.49 *Pre-nuptial Agreements*

2   The Commission rejected the proposition that there should be different considerations for spouses of certain religious beliefs as basically discriminatory – see para 1.36 of Consultation Paper.

3   The Law Commission noted that a Green Paper, published in 2007 entitled 'Commission of the European Communities, Green Paper: On conflict of laws in matters concerning matrimonial property regimes, including the question of jurisdiction and mutual recognition', COM (2006) 400 final; envisaged a rule that determines the applicable law, which will be the same no matter where the financial consequences of divorce are determined. This involves the courts of one country applying the law of another. It was not, of course, known at this stage if the UK would opt in to such conformity if introduced. Cf also paras 4.6–4.29 of the Law Commission's Consultation Paper considering the different jurisdictional approaches of Europe and the rest of the world. Also see now the references above to the European Union Regulations on Matrimonial Property Regimes (2016/1103) implemented on 29 January 2019.

8.50 The Family Justice Council acting on the requests of the Law Commission have now under the committee set up under Roberts J provided in the 'Guidance on Financial Needs on Divorce' in June 2016 answers to what are 'needs' and how they are to be measured, which are:

'Housing and Income

The main needs in most cases are housing and present and future income

Future income typically includes a need for income in retirement

The court will assess the level and duration of need as a question of fact

The court will decide whether the needs can be best met from capital or income provision

Measuring Need

Need will be measured by assessing available financial resources

The court will strive to stretch finite resources and where resources are modest the children's needs may predominate

Need will be measured by assessing the standard of living during the relationship, generally the longer the relationship's duration the more important this factor will be

A party may be expected to suffer some reduction in standard of living having regard to the overall objective of a transition to independence

To measure need, and the ability to meet it, both parties will be expected to present appropriately detailed budgets to the court.

Assets from which needs may be met

Needs may be met from non-matrimonial resources

A court in a needs case should not focus on the marital acquest, but should instead consider all the available assets

The needs of both parties

The court will assess the needs of both parties

Before requiring payments to meet need the court will stand back and consider what portion of the payer's resources should fairly go to the payee

Where resources are modest the children's need for a home with their primary carer may predominate but, if possible, the court will strive to stretch resources to provide a home for children with each of their parents

The court will consider the detrimental impact of requiring one party to remain on the mortgage of the other's home for an indefinite period.'

'Qualifying Nuptial Agreement' – some applications

8.51 The Law Commission's Report canvassed a number of non-exhaustive working examples in which a Qualifying Nuptial Agreement ('QNP') may be of use, as follows[1]:

[1] See paras 7.12–7.33 of the Report.

(i) WHEN PROTECTING ANTICIPATED FAMILY GIFTS AND INHERITANCES:

8.52 Where parties are expecting future gifts and inheritances from their families and/or have pre-accrued assets which they would wish to keep separate from being shared by the other. Such receipts/possessions under the current law would be seen as 'non matrimonial' and as long as their respective needs were otherwise met in the event of a divorce, such assets would be unlikely to be shared. However, this could not be guaranteed, whereas if there was a QNP in place effectively declaring that such assets were not to be shared, then subject to the issue of the needs of the other spouse and any children of the family, a court would endorse the terms of the QNP and, therefore, the wishes of the parties would be secured.

(ii) WHEN PROTECTING SPECIFIC PROPERTY:

8.53 This may arise where, although both parties are content to share equally their assets on a divorce, one party already has a home which that party wishes to ensure is, in the event of divorce, retained for his or her individual use and disposal. By use of the QNP in this case, again subject to needs , that provision can be secured for that party and the QNP can go on to provide what would happen to the proceeds of sale of that property if disposed before any divorce and invested in another property asset. Indeed, the QNP could also provide for what is to happen should the needs of the parties not be met without recourse to the property or there may be a number of pre-accrued properties catered for in this way. The QNP could provide for the order in which such properties are to be used to meet any spousal need.

(iii) WHEN PROVIDING FOR A CLEAN BREAK BETWEEN WEALTHY PARTIES:

8.54 Here the parties who are independently wealthy may wish to ensure as far as possible that no claims arise from the other upon divorce because they envisage each will have more than sufficient resources. Of course, without more, upon a divorce there may be a substantial amount of asset wealth, which will have been gained by the couple as a marital acquest and which without the terms of an appropriate QNP signed it would have been seen as fair to share equally – whereas, although one party may be left with substantially less comparative wealth than the other on a subsequent divorce, the QNP spelling

8.54 Pre-nuptial Agreements

out the reason for 'nil provision' would prevent any investigation as to the position, assuming the parties' needs were otherwise met.

(iv) WHEN PROVIDING CERTAINTY AND EXCLUDING SHARING:

8.55 The parties may have substantially different levels of wealth at the outset so that it is reasonably predictable that the one will have to meet the other's needs should there be a divorce. Whilst employment of the QNP could not again guarantee the absence of scrutiny by a court in that event in due course, it could in excluding in general the sharing of assets between the parties, spell out the type of provision, including rehousing and/or term and level of maintenance that the parties considered reasonable. Such terms, as long as the circumstances were not wholly different at the divorce, would be likely to dictate the level of provision to be made as long as it was seen as meeting those needs, albeit not as generously, as without the agreement, the court may have done.

'Qualifying Nuptial Agreements' – legal advice guidance

8.56 The Law Commission recommended certain pre-requisites, as above, that needed to be included in any advice to ensure the validity of a 'Qualifying Nuptial Agreement' ('QNA'). In addition, the Report also set out some additional matters, which the Law Commission considered should, in good practice, be dealt with in any advice given, namely[1]:

(1) The advantages and disadvantages, at the time that the advice is provided, to that party of making the agreement, including what he or she might receive on a divorce without a QNA.
(2) The provision for the party's needs, out of which the parties cannot contract by using a QNA (including any uncertainty as to the form, level and duration of such provision).
(3) The need for *material* disclosure from the other party.
(4) The need, if any, to make provision in the agreement about the effect of sale and replacement of any assets specifically mentioned in it, and about the consequences of one party investing in or contributing to property during the marriage or civil partnership;
(5) That the agreement will hold regardless of changes over time, such as the birth of children.
(6) If the couple, or one of them, is a foreign national or is domiciled overseas, or has property outside England and Wales, whether it would be advisable to obtain advice from a foreign lawyer with appropriate expertise. If such foreign advice has been obtained, advice should be given about its effect on, and inter-relationship with, the English advice.
(7) An agreement that is no longer a QNA nor valid as a contract is still a marital property agreement capable of being taken into account under *Radmacher* although its effect may be limited, depending on the reason why it does not meet the requirements for a QNA.
(8) in the event that one party is paying the costs of advice for the other party, a costs ceiling imposed must not be perceived as limiting the advice reasonably required in the particular case.

(9) the above is not to be seen as exhaustive of the matters for which advice is to be given and the requirements in this respect of each case will differ. See generally the 'Checklist' set out in the previous section.

[1] See paras 7.59–7.63 of the Report.

'Qualifying Nuptial Agreements' – an overview

8.57 There will be many who will consider the recommendations of the Law Commission as disappointing and not radical enough[1]. The concept of Qualifying Nuptial Agreements ('QNA') may appear to offer the prospect of removing the distribution of parties' resources upon divorce etc entirely out of the s 25 process. However, in practice, because the strength or weakness of such an agreement will depend upon whether or not the financially weaker party's needs have been met, it is debatable to what extent this proposed model will actually reduce the number of disputes before the court where such an agreement is in place.

Whether parties have signed up to a QNA or the present conventional pre-nuptial form of agreement, it will remain open to the spouse who regards his or her interests as unfairly prejudiced by the agreement terms to challenge the provision made upon divorce. The only difference may well be that the debate upon such disputes where a QNA is involved may, if the essential formation conditions have been met, be restricted to the level of the need provision in place, whereas with any other form of pre-nuptial agreement the dispute may, as now, be wider and not limited to the same extent to the level of need as opposed to the level of fair provision overall under the s 25 exercise.

The Law Commission was clearly unwilling to envisage a completely unlimited autonomy of choice of the parties to agree terms, which could result in the State effectively being burdened with the continuing support of the financially weaker spouse where the other spouse's resources were otherwise capable of meeting those needs[2]. This approach is entirely consistent with the history of legislative spousal support within this jurisdiction since the nineteenth century.

Of course, those who would argue that the pendulum within the s 25 statutory exercise has swung too far against the interests of the married woman, in any event, by the post *White v White* developments or the greater recognition afforded to pre-marital agreements may be relieved at this outcome. If so, it must be observed that the forces which led to the Commission's review of the weight to be attached to Marital Agreements were in the end frustrated on this occasion not by any sense of concern for the gender discrimination still present in divorce distribution but rather the potential cost to the taxpayer.

[1] See Professor Barton's 'Matrimonial Property, Needs and Agreements' [2014] Fam Law [1124].
[2] Cf and contrast, (see more above) the provisions of Baroness Deech's Divorce (Financial Provisions) Bill (HL 21), where this consideration in the Bill's present form is effectively overridden.

8.58 Pre-nuptial Agreements

Need for reform – commentary

8.58 It is, at least, debatable whether the arguments which have been advanced for greater recognition of the parties' autonomy in this arena are truly reflective of the actual concerns of the vast majority of ordinary men and women, who, following the breakdown of their marriage, make use of the court's divorce process within this jurisdiction[1].

It is also doubtful that Parliament's intervention by any future legislative change in this area to enhance the status and effect of a pre-nuptial agreement upon divorce will actually result in a lesser cost burden to the average petitioner or respondent in divorce proceedings, in the absence of a wholesale change in the broader approach to distribution of resources upon dissolution of marriage.

The whole promotion of pre-nuptial agreements in the modern context, of course, has been driven by those divorcing couples whose individual or family wealth was the reason for there being a pre-nuptial agreement in the first place. The demands for the greater use and recognition of pre-nuptial agreements made on behalf of this small but influential minority of individuals have been wholly out of proportion to the real priorities for change in this area of family law, especially when measured against the impact that such changes would have upon the majority of divorcees.

The introduction of a QNA, in due course, if it occurred, would potentially result in many more couples feeling under pressure to engage a professional to draw up such an agreement or, at least, to confirm an overview of the parties' own completion of a standardised 'one size fits all' version as part of their marriage preparations. Thereafter, only a small number of these couples, once married, would keep the same under periodic review and the agreement document would be likely then to gather dust in some drawer in the matrimonial home alongside the marriage certificate or some other such documentation. Only years later upon a marital breakdown, would that by then outdated agreement re-emerge to be used by the spouse, who insisted on the agreement in the first place, against the other in an attempt to ensure a recovery based upon, not what would be fair after many years of marriage, but either the limited provision made at the outset of the marriage or that other spouse's 'real' or 'basic' needs upon divorce.

It is argued that this is the just recognition of the autonomous choices of parties about to enter matrimony. Certainly, there are marriage arrangements where there will be very respectable reasons for formalising outcomes in advance by such agreements. However, there will be many more where the very idea of a limited liability agreement between a couple entering marriage speaks far more about the absence of a true mutual commitment in the relationship.

However ornate the legal language used in a pre-nuptial agreement, the same is little more than a hard-headed commercial agreement intended in most instances to limit one spouse's recovery to less and in many cases much less than the law would have otherwise provided. It is likely to be entered into by one of the two parties with a serious underestimate as to its likely future relevance and with little or certainly significantly less financial awareness than their partner. There is highly likely, too, to be a wholly different perception between the parties as to the pre-marriage arrangement priorities within which the signing of such an agreement has become part. Unless, the parties have been in other long term relationships previously, neither and certainly not the financially weaker spouse-to-be can be expected to properly evaluate before marriage what with maturity and experience of married life their view of fairness of division on an eventual divorce will be[2].

It is unlikely, therefore, that a change of the current approach of the law wherein the weight of a pre-nuptial agreement remains within the discretionary judgment of the court, by the introduction of a 'Qualifying Nuptial Agreement' as envisaged by the Law Commission will either be a reflection of the parties' true autonomous choices or provide a fairer outcome.

[1] See more below.
[2] See the critique advanced as to the current law and proposals for reform as expounded in Procedural Fairness in Prenuptial Agreements: Inconsistent and Inadequate: Kamilia Khairul Anuar Oxford University Undergraduate Law Journal 2017) 6 OUULJ 45–55.

The future

8.59 In *Charman*[1], the former President, Sir Mark Potter said:

> 'The difficulty of harmonising our law concerning the property consequences of marriage and divorce and the law of the Civilian Member States is exacerbated by the fact that our law has so far given little status to pre-nuptial contracts. If, unlike the rest of Europe, the property consequences of divorce are to be regulated by the principles of needs, compensation and sharing, should not the parties to the marriage, or the projected marriage, have, at the least, the opportunity to order their own affairs otherwise by a nuptial contract?'

Of course, since those remarks, there has been a Supreme Court decision and now a Law Commission report. However, as referred to previously, our current law's position in divorce remains, at least for the time being, that of leaving the relevance and weight to be attached to a pre-nuptial agreement reached by the parties entirely to the discretion of the individual judge in any given case and such a position remains exceptional amongst our European partners and, as set out above, is an isolated position against the law applicable in many other parts of the world.

However, it remains to the purist unsatisfactory that, amongst a number of other anomalies created by the present position, the most obvious one is that had the parties to the pre-nuptial agreement not married at all, there would have been less room for judicial interference in implementing the identical terms of such a cohabitation agreement.

For better or for worse, society has moved on from when in 1929 the House of Lords considered pre-nuptial agreements to be contrary to the sanctity of marriage and when divorce was exceptional and there was no power in a divorce court to transfer capital. Today, both parties in entering a marriage will be more aware of the fact and possibility of divorce and are more readily seen as entering into a partnership of equals. There is clearly gathered evidence, no

8.59 Pre-nuptial Agreements

doubt the result of the greater recent publicity upon the subject, that parties about to cohabit or marry are far more interested in formalising from the outset their financial arrangements in advance of any breakdown[2].

However, there is also evidence that there has existed a gender divide within the judiciary in this jurisdiction not only as to the appropriate weight to be given to the existence of a pre-nuptial agreement within the statutory exercise on divorce, but, of greater concern, also as to whether the parties can be taken as having intended that the pre-nuptial agreement should apply in the first place in the event of a later divorce. As to this, Lady Hale made her views very clear in *Radmacher's* case when she stated:

> '137. Above all, perhaps, the court hearing a particular case can all too easily lose sight of the fact that, unlike a separation agreement, the object of an ante-nuptial agreement is to deny the economically weaker spouse the provision to which she – it is usually although by no means invariably she – would otherwise be entitled (see, for example, G F Brod, "Premarital Agreements and Gender Justice" (1994) 6 Yale Journal of Law and Feminism 229). This is amply borne out by the precedents available in recent text-books (see, for example, I Harris and R Spicer, Prenuptial Agreements: A Practical Guide (2008, Appendix D), or H Wood, D Lush, D Bishop, and A Murray, Cohabitation: Law, Practice and Precedents (2009, 4th ed, pp 583–592)). Would any self-respecting young woman sign up to an agreement which assumed that she would be the only one who might otherwise have a claim, thus placing no limit on the claims that might be made against her, and then limited her claim to a pre-determined sum for each year of marriage regardless of the circumstances, as if her wifely services were being bought by the year? Yet that is what these precedents do. In short, there is a gender dimension to the issue which some may think ill-suited to decision by a court consisting of eight men and one woman.'

[1] [2007] EWCA Civ 50.
[2] Catherine Baksi 'Pre-nuptials booming' *Law Gazette*, 17 August 2008 (www. https://www.l awgazette.co.uk/news/pre-nuptials-booming/46710.article) and 'Family Agreements: Seeking Certainty to Reduce Disputes' Resolution 2010 and Matrimonial Property Needs and Agreements: Law Commission Report [2014] Feb.

8.60 Whilst the authors of this edition have, obviously, taken note of her Ladyship's observations upon the earlier pre-nuptial precedent published up to and including the 4th edition and, in due recognition, have made certain amendments thereto in the later editions of this work, including the precedent which now appears in this current 8th edition to reflect the same; the fact of the matter is that, despite her Ladyship's comments, there have been and no doubt will continue to be many individuals, who are willing to sign such one sided agreements as previously appeared. Equally, it is anticipated that her Ladyship would acknowledge that the last several editions of this work have fully and consistently advocated and supported the position in this area of the law as reflected by the concerns which she strongly expressed in both *Macleod* and later in *Radmacher*.

Those who may yet debate the course of any future statutory amendment to the current law relating to pre-nuptial agreements may be well advised to adopt as the foreword to their preliminary considerations, the following perceptive appraisal of Baron J, at first instance, in the *Radmacher* case[1] as to the state of the law concerning pre-nuptial agreements, when she said:

'129. It is understandable that English society in general (therefore the state) regards court supervision as a necessary safeguard. To my mind, independent scrutiny of these agreements remains as necessary in modern times as it was in the last century because of the vulnerability of parties involved at times of high emotion where inequality of bargaining power may exist between them. Although civilization has made much progress over the centuries and the roles of men and women have altered so that, in some cultures, equality has been achieved that does not mean that fundamental human nature has changed. Whilst the court must permit of current mores and will take full account of contemporary morality, it should not be blind to human frailty and susceptibility when love and separation are involved. The need for careful safeguards to protect the weaker party and ensure fairness remains.'

These are incisive words of a much respected and much missed female judge whose own journey within a historically male dominated profession would have undoubtedly witnessed gender discrimination along the way and sensitised her to the position of other women in far less privileged positions than her own.

In the event, women should remain sceptical that the increasing pressure for legislative changes to give formal recognition to pre-nuptial agreements within ancillary relief proceedings is indeed a gender benevolent movement singularly motivated by an intention to complete the circle of changes, pioneered by the Married Women's Property Act 1882, or truly intended to achieve their equal entitlement with men in this area of the law. As was said by Lady Hale in *Macleod's* case[2]:

'33. It is said that calls for the legislative recognition of ante-nuptial agreements appear to have increased with the development of more egalitarian principles of financial and property adjustment on divorce, following the decisions of the House of Lords in *White v White* . . . and *Miller v Miller, McFarlane v McFarlane* . . . If such calls are motivated by a perception that equality within marriage is wrong in principle, the more logical solution would be to examine the principles applicable to ascertaining the fair result of a claim for ancillary relief, rather than the pre-marital attempt to predict what the fair result will be long before the event. If such calls are motivated by a fear that people who feel threatened by what might happen in the event of divorce will not get married at all, there is a need for serious research and consideration of the extent of and reasons for the reduction in marriage rates over recent decades. It certainly cannot be demonstrated that the lack of enforceable pre-nuptial agreements in this country is depressing the marriage rate here as compared with other countries where such agreements can be made.'

As a former Law Commissioner herself, Lady Hale's consistent call has been that any development of the status and effect of nuptial agreements upon divorce should be the business of the Law Commission and Parliament and not that of the judiciary.

The issue as to the status of the pre-nuptial agreement within the discretionary exercise upon divorce etc is in truth just one part of the wider and more pressing debate required as to the need for a complete review of the court's powers of financial remedy provision under the Matrimonial Causes Act 1973. Much in society has altered over almost half a decade since Parliament approved this legislation. The landmark cases of *White*, *Miller/McFarlane* and even *Radmacher v Granantino* have all been instances,

8.60 Pre-nuptial Agreements

in the absence of a comprehensive legislative review, of substantive re-interpretation of the law by a judiciary, many of whom were themselves from privileged backgrounds with a predictably narrow and limited outlook on society's values and mores.

As divorce affects substantially more than one in three marriages within this jurisdiction the need for a Parliamentary re-evaluation of the current law including the status of the principle of autonomy has become paramount. Coleridge J in an address in 2014 to the Family Law Conference put it this way[3]:

> 'I am convinced that the judges, at whatever level, cannot sensibly take the matter any further without making matters worse and more uncertain. Government simply has to grasp the nettle and get on with it. In the end we are of course doing the classic British thing of reform by inertia, stealth, common sense and the laws of cricket. That may in the end not be too disturbing in fact and from the point of view of the family lawyer trying to earn an honest shilling, endlessly fascinating and rewarding, in more ways than one. But it is not the way to run a railway or a modern family justice system.'

[1] [2008] EWHC 1532 (Fam).
[2] [2008] UKPC 64.
[3] 'Lobbing a few pebbles in the pond: the funeral of a dead parrot' [2014] Fam Law.

Part B   PRECEDENTS

8.61

Pre-nuptial agreement[1]

Dated 201

Deed of Pre-nuptial Agreement

Between

(1) AB

and

(2) BB

Precedents **8.61**

> **WARNING TO AB AND BB**
> THIS AGREEMENT IS INTENDED TO CREATE LEGAL RELATIONS BETWEEN YOU, AB AND YOU, BB AND TO BE LEGALLY BINDING UPON EACH OF YOU AND TO DETERMINE THE OWNERSHIP AND DIVISION BETWEEN YOU BOTH OF ANY CAPITAL, PENSION AND INCOME RESOURCES AND LIABILITIES REFERRED TO WITHIN ITS TERMS, INCLUDING YOUR INDIVIDUAL SEPARATE PROPERTY IN THE EVENT OF THE BREAKDOWN OF THE MARRIAGE AND/OR ANY CLAIM/PROCEEDINGS ARISING IN RELATION TO THE SAME AND/OR IN THE EVENT OF THE PRIOR DEATH OF EITHER OF YOU.
> YOU MUST NOT SIGN THIS AGREEMENT UNLESS YOU INTEND TO BE BOUND BY ITS TERMS.
> YOU MUST NOT SIGN THIS AGREEMENT UNLESS YOU HAVE EACH HAD INDEPENDENT LEGAL ADVICE UPON ITS TERMS, MEANING AND EFFECT AND YOU HAVE FULLY UNDERSTOOD SUCH ADVICE AND ARE FULLY SATISFIED YOU HAVE HAD ADEQUATE INFORMATION ABOUT EACH OTHER'S FINANCES AND INTENTIONS AND HAD SUFFICIENT TIME TO CONSIDER THE SITUATION AND YOU ARE CONTENT TO ENTER INTO THIS AGREEMENT.

[SOLICITORS NAMES AND ADDRESSES]

DEED OF AGREEMENT dated *[date]*

PARTIES:

(1) AB of [address] ('**A**').

(2) BB [address] ('**B**').

DEFINITIONS:

(3) The definitions which apply to this Agreement are set out in **Schedule 1**

INTRODUCTION:

(4) A and B agree that:

(i) This Agreement is made in contemplation of, and is conditional upon, the intended marriage of A and B on [date] or such other date as A and B agree.

(ii) They have cohabited together since [date] and that the fact of such cohabitation and their respective present and future needs have been fully accounted for as set out in this Agreement in the provision to be made following upon the Breakdown of the Marriage and/or in the event of the prior death of either of them.

(iii) They have each had adequate time to take appropriate independent legal advice and with such advice to consider and understand the terms of this Agreement and their meaning.

(iv) The first draft of this Agreement was seen by A on [date] and by B on [date].

[(*if desired*) **Marital Agreement**:

A and B agree within 28 days [or such other period] of the date of their marriage to enter by further Deed into a marital agreement ('Deed of Marital Agreement') in the

673

8.61 Pre-nuptial Agreements

terms of the document annexed to this Deed of Agreement].

AGREEMENT PURPOSE:

(5) A and B agree that:

(i) This Agreement is made with the intention of promoting the Marriage and in the expectation that the Marriage will continue during their joint lives together and each intends to enter their marriage vows to each other with full commitment and solemnity.

(ii) Should there be a Breakdown of the Marriage or either should pre-decease the other, then in order to avoid the distress and costs of any dispute as to the appropriate financial division between them, the terms of this Agreement should determine absolutely any financial claims they may have against one another or the other's estate.

(iii) The terms of this Agreement shall determine all rights, claims and entitlement which either may have in law or otherwise against the Property of the other as a result of the Marriage and upon the Breakdown of the Marriage and/or in the event of the prior death of the other.

(iv) Having been duly advised as to the approach of the law in regard to claims for financial remedy upon the Breakdown of the marriage and/or of reasonable provision upon death, they set out within this Agreement the provision they consider to be fair between them in the event of such breakdown or death whatever the circumstances or jurisdiction.

(iv) They enter into this Agreement following [donee name] having gifted to A [describe asset etc] (as identified at Schedule 3 and Schedule 5) and A holding [eg beneficial interests in certain trust assets] as set out in this Agreement.

(vi) There is at present a substantial disparity in the Property they each hold and one aspect of this Agreement is intended to protect the more substantial Property interests held by A following upon the Breakdown of the Marriage and/or in the event of the prior death of either party, save as otherwise agreed in writing between A and B or provided herein.

BIRTHPLACE, HABITUAL RESIDENCE AND DOMICILE:

(6) A and B agree that:

(i) A was born on [date] in [town/city and country] and is habitually resident in England and Wales and domiciled in England and Wales.

(ii) B was born on [date] in [town/city and country] and is habitually resident in England and Wales and domiciled in England and Wales.

AGREEMENT APPLICATION:

(7) A and B agree that the terms of this Agreement shall be fully binding and enforceable upon themselves and any other acting on their behalf in whatever circumstance and/or capacity and/or jurisdiction.

PARTIES' DETAILS:

(8) A and B agree that:

    (i) A is presently employed by [employment and address];

    (ii) B is presently employed by [employment and address];

    (iii) they have been in a relationship since [date] and they purchased their first home together on [date].

CHILDREN:

(9) A and B agree that[2]:

    (i) they presently have no children of their relationship;

    (ii) they intend to have children together and have taken account of this intention in terms of this Agreement;

    (iii) the terms of this Agreement cannot limit the rights and entitlement of any child they may have;

    (iv) any financial provision of any kind for any Child they have at the time of the Breakdown of the Marriage, will be determined in accordance with the law taking account of all the circumstances and all their respective resources and liabilities at the relevant time including for the avoidance of any doubt their resources and share of Joint Property and Separate Property;

    (v) upon the Breakdown of the Marriage, they shall each be responsible for the reasonable needs (and/or upon the prior death of either of them the reasonable provision by their estate), whilst dependent, of any such Child or Children herein as required of them by the Law of England and Wales.

    (vi) to endeavor to determine and reach agreement upon the level of any needs/provision required for any Child or Children herein on the Breakdown of the Marriage, all reasonable steps will be taken to jointly appoint a duly accredited family law mediator, collaboratively trained lawyer or independent arbitrator for the purpose.

CURRENT HOME:

(10) A and B agree that:

    (i) they presently reside at [address] which was purchased on [date] and the legal and beneficial title is owned by [name(s)] as [insert]; and

    (ii) they intend to live in this property at the start of the Marriage.

INDEPENDENT LEGAL ADVICE:

(11) A and B agree that:

    (i) each has instructed separate and independent legal advisors to advise them upon the terms and effect of this Agreement and the applicable law;

8.61 *Pre-nuptial Agreements*

(ii) A has received advice from [solicitor and address] and from Counsel [name and address] who have signed the attached Certificate at **Schedule 7**;

(iii) B has received advice from [solicitor and address] and from Counsel [name and address who have signed the attached Certificate at **Schedule 8**];

(iv) having received and understood the advice above referred to and made such enquiries of the other as required, they have each signed the attached Certificate marked Declaration Statements at **Schedules 9 and 10**.

(v) they regard the terms of this Agreement herein as entirely fair and each is entering into this Agreement free of any pressure, undue influence or duress and neither is relying upon any collateral promise or representation from any individual or source whatsoever;

(vi) they have fully understood in relation to this Agreement, in particular:

 (a) the terms and effect under the law of England and Wales;

 (b) the rights each is surrendering;

 (c) the advantages and disadvantages to each of them;

 (d) the terms are intended to satisfy the requirements of the Law Commission Report on Matrimonial Property, Needs and Agreements (2014) in regard to a qualifying nuptial agreement and that, if implemented by legislation the same will prevent the court from making financial orders inconsistent with the Agreement, subject to the parties' financial needs or the interests of any Child as referred to herein.

(vii) nothing in this Agreement is capable of limiting the jurisdiction of the court in any way otherwise than is permitted by the law.

DISCLOSURE OF FINANCIAL POSITIONS:

(12) A and B agree that:

(i) following the enquiries each has chosen to make of the other's financial circumstances and otherwise, each is satisfied that they have appropriate knowledge and understanding of all such matters to be able to determine that the terms of this Agreement herein are fair.

(ii) each has fully disclosed to the other all material detail of their capital, pensions, income and/or other financial resources and liabilities held currently or which the other may have prospect of obtaining;

(iii) A's disclosed financial position is set out in Schedule 3 of this Agreement;

(iv) B's disclosed financial position is set out in Schedule 4 of this Agreement;

(v) each has offered to make available to the other such further disclosure as may be requested and each confirms the disclosure provided as identified herein is sufficient to enable the terms this Agreement to be implemented;

(vi) whilst the values of any assets/investments/liabilities may by market movements be subject to daily variation and some assets/investments/liabilities may by their nature be difficult to value, the values set out in Schedule 3 and Schedule 4 of this Agreement shall be the values taken for the purposes and at the date of this Agreement.

SEPARATE PROPERTY ACQUISITION:

(13) A and B respectively agree:

(i) Save where specified in Schedule 5, A has acquired all of her Separate Property independently of and without contribution from B.

(ii) Save where specified in Schedule 6, B has acquired all of his Separate Property independently of and without contribution from A.

INTENTION TO BE BOUND BY THIS AGREEMENT/JURISDICTION:

(14) A and B agree:

(i) upon the Breakdown of the Marriage, their respective financial entitlements and responsibilities will to the extent permitted by law be governed solely by this Agreement;

(ii) whilst in certain jurisdictions, as in England and Wales, it may not be possible to limit the court's powers/discretionary equitable distribution in relation to the terms of this Agreement, their intention is that they should each be bound by this Agreement in whatever jurisdiction they may reside;

(iii) to put into effect the terms of this Agreement and, if the jurisdiction permits, to make its terms into an order of the court fully binding upon them and any other acting on their behalf or their estate in any capacity whatsoever;

(iv) to request their trustees (if any) to take the terms of this Agreement into account and exercise their powers as necessary to ensure that the obligations herein under this Agreement are met following the Breakdown of the Marriage;

(v) should the law of England and Wales make pre-nuptial agreements legally enforceable to prevent the court from making financial orders inconsistent with the Agreement, subject to their financial needs or the interests of a Child of the Parties, then they intend this Agreement to remain in full force and effect and to be subject to the law in such circumstances;

(vi) in the circumstances last set out to immediately take any steps required to make this Agreement fully enforceable under the law and in the absence of such steps being taken or not being legally effective, this Agreement will continue to have full force according to the law;

(vii) this agreement is being entered into by them following each having received full advice concerning the meaning and effect of the decision of the Supreme Court in *Radmacher v Granatino*[3] and the publication of Matrimonial Property Needs and Agreements: Law Commission Report [2014];

(viii) they intend by this Agreement to enter into legal relations with one another and, should there be a change of the current law as above, for this Agreement to be considered as equivalent to a qualifying nuptial

8.61 Pre-nuptial Agreements

agreement thereby preventing the court from making financial provision orders inconsistent with the terms of this Agreement in the event of the Breakdown of the Marriage save and except where their financial needs or the interests of any Child so necessitate;

(ix) neither would have proceeded with the Marriage without this Agreement having been entered into.

COMMENCEMENT OF AGREEMENT:

(15) A and B agree that this Agreement will commence upon their Marriage to one another provided that the same takes place within 12 months of the date of this Agreement and in default this Agreement shall stand discharged unless revived by a supplemental agreement executed by deed by them.

SEPARATE PROPERTY:

(16) A and B agree:

(i) neither will make any claim against the other's Separate Property, whatsoever the circumstances or jurisdiction.

(ii) Subject to the terms of this Agreement, each will hold and have full control over their own Separate Property absolutely and neither will at any time acquire any interest, or right to compensation or control of any kind at law or otherwise in or over or in regard to the other's Separate Property whatsoever the contribution, financial or otherwise, of that other or any third party in relation thereto and/or whatever the circumstances or jurisdiction unless otherwise agreed by the Parties in writing and by Deed in accordance with clause 26 below.

JOINT PROPERTY:

(17) A and B agree that:

(i) Subject to the terms of this Agreement, the beneficial interest in any Joint Property will be owned by the Parties in equal shares whatsoever the contribution of that other in relation thereto or whatever the circumstances or jurisdiction unless otherwise agreed by the Parties in writing and by Deed in accordance with clause 26 below.

(ii) Subject to the terms of this Agreement, neither will deal with, charge or otherwise dispose of any Joint Property without the consent of the other Party in writing and by Deed in accordance with clause 26 below.

(iii) Subject to sub-clauses (iv)–(viii) below, forthwith (or as otherwise agreed by the Parties in writing and by Deed in accordance with clause 26 below) following upon the Breakdown of the Marriage and/or prior death of either of the Parties, any Joint Property shall be distributed between them or their estates in equal shares or in such shares as have been otherwise agreed by the Parties in writing and by Deed in accordance with clause 26 below.

(iv) Subject to sub-clause (v)–(viii) below, the distribution referred to above, where the Joint Property in question is held in other than an account and/or money form, shall (unless otherwise agreed by the Parties in writing and by Deed in accordance with clause 26 below) be effected by their or their estate's joint instruction to sell the same on the open market with an agreed agent and at a price advised by that agent (the agreement by either party as to choice of agent not to be unreasonably withheld) within 28 days of the Breakdown of the Marriage and/or the prior death of either of the Parties, unless the Joint Property is in the form of land and/or buildings in which case the joint instruction as above shall be instead within 6 months.

(v) Subject to sub-clause (vi)–(viii) below, in the event that a sale as last referred to is not secured within a period of 4 months, or if land and/or buildings, 9 months of the joint instruction, then distribution as above shall be effected forthwith upon joint instruction by sale by auction.

(vi) The gross proceeds of any sale less the discharge/account made for any consequential expenses of sale, being selling agents' and legal costs of sale, any consequential commission and tax arising and the payment of any secured charge (and any other disbursement otherwise agreed by the Parties in writing and by Deed in accordance with clause 26 below), shall be distributed between the Parties or their estates as provided for in sub-clause iii) above.

(vii) Subject to viii) below, in the event of an auction being effected as above, either party shall have the right to bid at such auction for the item/property in question.

(viii) Where upon the event of the Breakdown of the Marriage and/or the prior death of either of the Parties, the Matrimonial Home remains the sole residence of one Party, that Party shall have the right to exercise the option, (unless otherwise agreed by the Parties in writing and by Deed in accordance with clause 26 below) in lieu of the property being sold to any third party or entered for any auction as above, to forthwith buy out the share of the other Party as above based on a value agreed between them (or with that other Party's estate) less any consequential (notional or actual) expenses of sale as above or in default of agreement as determined on the basis of the value of the property in question (less such consequential expenses of sale) ascertained by the median of at least two jointly instructed valuations of chartered surveyors engaged for the purpose; the cost of such instruction being borne by the party exercising the option.

LIABILITIES:

(18) A and B agree that:

(i) Each will be responsible when and howsoever arising for any liabilities connected with his or her Separate Property and will indemnify the other against any such liability and such liabilities of either shall reduce the value of that party's Separate Property.

(ii) Subject to (iii) below, each will be jointly and severally liable when and howsoever arising for any liabilities connected with their Joint Property and, as required, each Party shall indemnify the other in respect of his/her individual liability therefor and the value of any such individual liability shall reduce the value of that party's share of the Joint Property.

(iii) In the event either incurs a liability against any Joint Property without the consent of the other in writing, he or she will be solely responsible for that liability and will indemnify the other in respect of his/her individual liability therefor and the value of such individual liability shall reduce the value of that party's Separate Property.

8.61 *Pre-nuptial Agreements*

FINANCIAL APPLICATION DURING THE MARRIAGE:

(19) A and B agree that:

Any use of their Separate Property and/or Joint Property during the Marriage for the benefit or greater benefit of the other shall not be taken to be altering the effect and/or nature of the terms of this Agreement in relation to such Separate Property and/or Joint Property whatsoever unless otherwise agreed by the Parties in writing and by Deed in accordance with clause 26 below.

BREAKDOWN OF THE MARRIAGE ETC FINANCIAL PROVISION/GOVERNING JURISDICTION:

(20) A and B agree that:

(i) Upon the Breakdown of the Marriage, and/or the prior death of either of the Parties, the provisions set out in Schedule 2 of this Agreement will apply.

(ii) This Agreement and all matters relating to its interpretation, subject matter, formation or enforcement shall be governed by and subject to the law of England and Wales and in the event of the courts of any other legal jurisdiction also having jurisdiction, the intention of the Parties is that the courts of England and Wales shall have exclusive jurisdiction over any application or claim made in connection with or relating to this Agreement.

(iii) Upon the Breakdown of the Marriage and/or the prior death of either Party and unless otherwise agreed by the Parties in writing and by Deed in accordance with clause 26 below no proceedings in connection with the termination of the marriage (or the deceased's estate) and/or this Agreement shall be commenced by either of them other than in the jurisdiction of England and Wales, subject to a court in England and Wales having the power to deal with the proceedings.

(iv) Each shall be fully bound by the terms of this Agreement, to the maximum extent permitted by law, even where such proceedings are required to be brought in another jurisdiction in circumstances where England and Wales does not have jurisdiction.

(v) Where either shall reside and/or become domiciled in a jurisdiction other than England and Wales, each shall immediately take independent legal advice from suitably qualified lawyers in that other jurisdiction and shall take such steps as are advised to make this Agreement as effective as possible at law in that jurisdiction, if necessary, by entering into any further agreement.

(vi) Upon the Breakdown of the Marriage and/or the prior death of either Party, they or their estates will forthwith take all steps and sign all necessary documents as required to give effect to the terms of this Agreement including obtaining an order by consent within any proceedings if required. Save and except to give effect to this Agreement, any consent order will provide for a dismissal of all claims whatsoever each has or may have against the other in whatever jurisdiction.

(vii) In the event that either Party applies to a court for financial provision other than for the purpose of obtaining a consent order in the terms set out at Schedule 2, the court is to be requested upon such an application being made to approve the terms of this Agreement and, in the making of any order required, to reflect the contents of this Agreement, where appropriate to do so and to have regard to the conduct of the Party making that application in relation to the making of any costs order therein.

JOINT GIFTS

(21) A and B agree that:

Upon the Breakdown of the Marriage and/or the prior death of either Party:

(i) Unless otherwise agreed by the Parties by Deed in accordance with clause 26 below, any gift made to them jointly by a third party will within 28 days (or such period otherwise agreed by the Parties in writing and by Deed in accordance with clause 26 below) be divided equally between them (or their estates) and where those gifts are in the form of chattels and/or contents and capable of being so dealt with, such distribution will be by rotation with each Party (or their estate) choosing in turn and with AB having the first choice of item.

(ii) If, subject to the above, neither can agree within the 28 day period (or such period otherwise agreed by the Parties in writing and by Deed in accordance with clause 26 below) which of them should own a particular joint gift not otherwise dealt with as above, that gift will be sold by auction forthwith on the expiry of the 28 days or such other agreed period as above and the proceeds of sale less consequential expenses of sale (being selling agents and legal costs of sale, any consequential commission and tax arising and the payment of any secured charge as appropriate) divided equally between them.

(iii) Nothing in this Agreement will prevent, whatever the circumstances, either Party from making any gift or transfer to the other or receiving the same from the other or from making provision for the other by will/settlement/trust or otherwise and whilst such gift/transfer/receipt or provision shall become the receiving party's Separate Property the same shall not constitute any waiver or alteration of the terms of this Agreement unless agreed otherwise by the Parties by Deed in accordance with clause 26 below.

FINANCIAL PROVISION ON DEATH:

(22) A and B agree that:

(i) Subject to provision being duly made as referred to in (iii) below, in the event of the prior death of the other, the surviving Party will not make any claim against the deceased's estate nor make an application to the court for an order requiring financial provision from the estate in his or her favour save only as is consistent with the terms of this Agreement.

(ii) In the event that either Party makes any claim/application as last referred to, the court is to be invited to make only such provision, if any, as reflects the terms of this Agreement.

(iii) Each will forthwith make a will that makes provision on his or her death for the other upon that other's survival which, at least, reflects the provision for that other Party made in this Agreement.

CONFIDENTIALITY:

(23) A and B agree that (subject to disclosure to any professional lawyer required for the purposes of obtaining legal advice or to a court in compliance with a court order or as agreed to in writing and signed by the Parties):

    (iv) Nothing in the preceding sub-clauses is intended to oust the jurisdiction of the court to make such provision as is permitted by the law having regard to the terms of this Agreement.

    (i) neither shall cause or permit the disclosure to any third party including publication by the Press or other media or otherwise of any confidential information disclosed leading to the making of or for the purposes of this Agreement or in this Agreement; and

    (ii) every effort shall be made by each of them to take all steps necessary to prevent any such confidential information being disclosed as in (i) above.

PERIODIC REVIEW:

(24) A and B agree that:

    (i) The terms of this Agreement will be reviewed with the benefit of independent legal advice and material disclosure as necessary, upon:

        (a) the occurrence of an event which has a significant impact upon their individual or combined financial circumstances, including:

            (i) the birth or adoption of a Child of the Parties;

            (ii) the inability of either of the Parties to continue in employment for a period in excess of 6 months;

            (iii) the Parties moving permanently to a jurisdiction outside England and Wales; or

        (b) Five years from the date of the Marriage and on every subsequent fifth anniversary unless a review has taken place in the preceding 5 years by reason of an event referred to in (a) above in which case any subsequent 5 year review will occur on the fifth anniversary of that event review.

    (ii) In the event that the Parties are unable on any review to reach agreement over any proposed amendments to this Agreement, they will in an attempt to resolve the position forthwith:

        (a) attend mediation with an accredited family law mediator who is a member of the Law Society's Mediation Panel and who is included on Resolution's List of Mediators and who will be jointly appointed by the Parties; or

        (b) each appoint a collaboratively trained lawyer and engage in the collaborative law process,

    (iii) In default of the Parties being unable to reach agreement over any proposed amendments to this Agreement or in the absence of a review taking place as referred to in (i) above, the terms of the Agreement shall continue to apply and to be fully enforceable.

    (iv) Any amendments to this Agreement as a result of any review will be evidenced in writing and executed as a deed.

(v) To each be responsible for their own costs of any review of the Agreement.

ENTIRE AGREEMENT:

(25) A and B agree that this Agreement and its Schedules and attachments, constitutes the entire agreement between the Parties and is in full substitution for any earlier agreements, including any warranties, representations and understandings between them, whether written or oral, relating to its subject matter.

FORM OF VARIATION ETC:

(26) A and B agree that no variation, alteration, waiver or termination of this Agreement will be valid unless made by them in writing and executed as a Deed.

TERMINATION OF AGREEMENT:

(27) A and B agree that the terms of this Agreement will continue in force notwithstanding the Breakdown of the Marriage or the permanent separation of the Parties or prior death of either Party and this Agreement will not be terminated until, whichever be the earliest, there is either a Deed effecting such termination as last referred to in clause (26) above, or where a court retains jurisdiction under the law to do so, that court makes a final order resolving the financial claims (if any) of the Parties referred to in this Agreement.

IMPLEMENTATION OF THE AGREEMENT:

(28) A and B agree that:

(i) each of them will take such steps as may be necessary as soon as possible to implement the terms of this Agreement; and

(ii) in the event that either fails to comply with the sub-clause last referred to without reasonable excuse, that Party will pay to the other Party such consequential legal fees, costs, and other expenses incurred by that other as a result.

SEVERANCE:

(29) A and B agree that in the event that any part of this Agreement is found by any court to be invalid or unenforceable, the same will not affect the other provisions of this Agreement which will remain in full force and effect and any invalid/unenforceable part will be severed as appropriate.

INCIDENTAL COSTS:

(30) A and B agree that:

(i) A will meet B's costs arising in relation and incidental to this Agreement initially limited to £[insert amount] plus VAT; and

(ii) no reasonable request for necessary additional funds will be refused by A;

8.61 Pre-nuptial Agreements

    (iii)   payment by A of such costs as above is accepted by B as having exercised no influence over B or B's advisors or the manner in which they have advised B.

This document has been executed as a deed and is delivered and takes effect on the date stated at the beginning of it.

Signed as a deed by AB in the presence of:

[SIGNATURE OF WITNESS]
[NAME, ADDRESS [AND OCCUPATION] OF WITNESS]
Signed as a deed by BB in the presence of:

[SIGNATURE OF WITNESS]
[NAME, ADDRESS [AND OCCUPATION] OF WITNESS]

[Also – *if desired* – ATTACHED MARITAL AGREEMENT:
THIS DEED OF MARITAL AGREEMENT is made on the [day] of [month] [year]
BETWEEN
(1) AB of [insert address] ('A') and
(2) BB of [insert address] ('B')
Introduction:
1. This Deed of Marital Agreement is made further to the marriage of A (who was born on [insert date] and B (who was born on [insert date] ('the Marriage') and the Deed of Agreement between the same parties dated [insert date].]
[The reader should then repeat the contents of the Deed of Agreement above with the appropriate exclusions and amendments to the paragraph numbering].

Schedule 1: DEFINITIONS AND INTERPRETATION

1. DEFINITIONS

    Agreement: shall mean this Agreement including its Schedules and annexes and any variations/alterations etc executed by Deed by the Parties.

    Capital Claim(s): shall mean a claim for capital (including an order or orders for lump sum by instalments or otherwise, property adjustment, variation of settlement, pension sharing/attachment/compensation and including a claim for the purposes of capitalising income) following the Breakdown of the Marriage and/or the prior death of the other Party whether under the Matrimonial Causes Act 1973, the Inheritance (Provision for Family and Dependents) Act 1975, s 17 of the Married Women's Property Act 1882, the Law of Property Act 1925 or s 14 of the Trusts of Land and Appointment of Trustees Act 1996 or otherwise, including any replacement legislation or equivalent legislation in any jurisdiction.

    Capital Clean Break: a dismissal of all Capital Claims.

    Child of the Parties: any child who is a child born to or adopted by the Parties or been treated by them as a child of their family and who at the time of the Breakdown of the Marriage and/or the prior death of either Party is either under 18 years old, or under 23 years old receiving full time education or training up to first degree level or its equivalent, or disabled.

Clean Break: a dismissal of all claims, whether Capital Claims, Income Claims, Pension Claims or otherwise.

Confidential Information: information which is private to the Parties or any child of the Parties, including that relating to personal, marital, educational, financial or business matters.

IFLA: Institute of Family Law Arbitrators.

Income Claim: shall mean a claim for income (including a claim for periodical payments, secured periodical payments, or a pension attachment order) following the Breakdown of the Marriage and/or the prior death of the other Party whether under the Matrimonial Causes Act 1973, the Inheritance (Provision for Family and Dependents) Act 1975, s 17 of the Married Women's Property Act 1882, the Law of Property Act 1925 or s 14 of the Trusts of Land and Appointment of Trustees Act 1996 or otherwise, including any replacement legislation or equivalent legislation in any jurisdiction.

Joint Property: any Property that is not Separate Property.

Marriage: the legally valid ceremony of marriage between the Parties.

Matrimonial Home: the main home last occupied in the marriage by the Parties and any Child of the Parties.

Party: one of the Parties (not being a third party).

Parties: AB and BB.

Breakdown of the Marriage: the commencement by the filing of the relevant petition at court by either of the Parties of proceedings for divorce or annulment of the Marriage or for judicial separation which are subsequently concluded by a decree of divorce, annulment, or judicial separation (or would have been had one of the Parties not died before a decree being pronounced).

Property: any legal or beneficial interest in any asset or resource of whatever nature and wherever held, including any capital and/or income and/or pension and/or other benefit entitlement therefrom and whether derived from a trust fund (save as held for a third party), and any income or benefit derived or receivable from any form of remunerative employment or other source whatsoever.

Income Needs: a Party's income needs taking into account the division of Separate Property and Joint Property set out in and the other provisions of this Agreement and the financial responsibilities of a Party towards any Child of the Parties and taking into account all relevant factors under s 25 of the Matrimonial Causes Act 1973 or any replacement/equivalent legislation.

Housing Needs: a home necessary, if appropriate, to accommodate any Child of the

8.61 Pre-nuptial Agreements

Parties (whether or not the child's main base is with that Party) taking into account all relevant factors under s 25 of the Matrimonial Causes Act 1973 or any replacement/equivalent legislation and in particular the existence and content of this Agreement.

Separate Property: in respect of each Party:

(a) Property that is set out at Schedule 7 and Schedule 8 of this Agreement.

(b) after the date of this Agreement save and except if subsequently gifted to the other Party:
- (i) the sole Property of that Party;
- (ii) joint Property of that Party with any third party;
- (iii) Property held by a nominee on behalf of that Party;
- (iv) Property received by that Party as a gift (including from the other Party) or joint gifts (which are to be dealt with as provided for at clause 21 of the Agreement);
- (v) Property received by that Party by way of inheritance;
- (vi) Property subject to a trust wheresoever established or administered and to which that Party is a beneficiary or potential beneficiary;
- (vii) Property in that Party's sole personal use, including but not limited to jewellery and clothing;

(c) Property deriving from one Party's Separate Property including by way of capital or accumulated income appreciation or otherwise save and to the extent that the Separate Property was used to acquire or improve Joint Property or was gifted to the other Party;

2. INTERPRETATIONS

2.1 The Schedules and annexes form part of this Agreement and have effect as if set out in full in the body of this Agreement.

2.2 Unless the context otherwise requires, a reference to one gender includes a reference to the other genders and a reference to words in the singular include the plural and in the plural include the singular.

Schedule 2: BREAKDOWN OF THE MARRIAGE ETC FINANCIAL PROVISION

1. CLEAN BREAK

On the Breakdown of the Marriage and/or in the event of the prior death of either Party, the following provision is to be made:

1.1 Each Party will retain his or her Separate Property, subject to any gift of such Property to the other Party.

1.2 Unless otherwise agreed between the Parties in writing and signed in accordance with clause 26, Joint Property will be divided between the Parties equally in accordance with clause 17, save and except that any Joint Gifts which will be dealt with in accordance with clause 21.

1.3 Except as to give effect to paragraphs 1.1 and 1.2 above and paragraphs 1.4 and 1.5, below, neither Party will be entitled to any payment or provision from the other Party, whether of an income, capital, pension or other nature.

1.4 Notwithstanding, as set out in the Agreement, that each Party intends at the time of the Breakdown of the Marriage and/or in the event of the prior death of either that neither shall have any continuing claim against the other or that other's estate or otherwise, should either party seek before there is a consent clean break order obtained (as provided for in the Agreement) to claim that following the Breakdown of the Marriage and/or the prior death of other Party:

(a) his/her share of the Joint Property, combined with his/her Separate Property, is insufficient to meet his/her essential Housing Needs;

And

(b) the Parties agree in writing; or

(c) a court with jurisdiction to consider such a claim considers there is in law any basis for making some provision for such a shortfall payment to the claimant Party to meet his/her essential Housing Needs,

then the Parties agree that any such shortfall ('shortfall') will be met from the other Party's Separate Property and/or share of the Joint Property, subject to the following terms:

(i) the amount of such shortfall will be determined as at the Breakdown of the Marriage and/or the prior death in question, and;

(ii) that in making provision for such shortfall, the combined value of the Separate Property and the Joint Property left to the Party ('the paying Party') providing for/contributing to the shortfall will not be less than the amount required to enable his or her own (essential) Housing Needs to be met, and;

(iii) the sum representing the shortfall will be provided on trust on terms that the sum will be returned/immediately repayable to the paying Party (or his or her estate) on the death of either of the Parties or, if earlier:

a. on a date on which the Parties agree in writing; or

b. the remarriage (or the permanent cohabitation with another for a continuous period of 6 months) of the Party receiving the shortfall; or

c. the voluntary cessation of occupation as the principal residence by the Party receiving the shortfall of the property acquired for his/her essential housing need (subject to any agreement in writing between the Parties otherwise); or

d. a court seized with jurisdiction to consider such a claim considers the Party receiving the shortfall is reasonably able to repay all or part of the same.

1.5 Notwithstanding, as set out in the Agreement, that each Party intends at the time of the Breakdown of the Marriage and/or in the event of the prior death that neither shall have any continuing claim against the other or that other's estate or otherwise, should either party seek before there is a consent clean break order obtained (as provided for in the Agreement) to claim that following the Breakdown of the Marriage and/or the prior death of the other Party, having taken account of the provisions of paragraph 1.4 above:

8.61 *Pre-nuptial Agreements*

(a) his/her actual and/or potential income/capital resources will prove insufficient to meet his/her essential Income Needs and;

(b) the Parties agree in writing; or

(c) a court with jurisdiction to consider such a claim considers there is in law any basis for making some provision for such essential income shortfall to the claimant Party then the Parties agree that such shortfall will be met by the other Party ('the paying Party') from his/her income resources, as appropriate, subject to the following terms:

(i) in the event of provision for such shortfall being made, the income resources left to the paying Party will not be less than the amount required to enable his or her own (essential) Income Needs to be met; and

(ii) such provision for such shortfall, if still payable, shall not exceed in the event of the prior death of the paying Party, the claimant/receiving Party's reasonable provision from that paying Party's estate; and

(iii) shall otherwise cease without right to extend the period (sec 28 MCA 1973 or equivalent in relation to a civil partnership) on the earliest of the death of either Party or the claimant's spouse's remarriage or an order of the court terminating the provision; and

(iv) such provision shall in any event only be for such minimum term as is considered necessary having regard in particular to the existence and content of this Agreement.

Schedule 3: A's FINANCIAL DISCLOSURE

PROPERTIES

Real Property	Date of purchase or acquisition	Estimated value £	Mortgage £	Loan due to £	A's interest %	Net of costs of sale at 3% and mortgage (but not net of tax)
TOTAL		£	£	£	%	£

BANK ACCOUNTS

Precedents **8.61**

INVESTMENTS

Type of investment	Balance or value	A's interest
	£	
TOTAL	£	

LIFE INSURANCE

Provider	Policy type	Policy number	Maturity date	Surrender value	Death benefit	Lives assured

BUSINESS INTERESTS

Company	Type of interest	Estimated current value of A's interest
TOTAL	% shareholder	

PERSONAL POSSESSIONS VALUED AT OVER £500

Item	Date of purchase or acquisition	Estimated value	A's interest %
TOTAL		£	

PENSIONS

Provider	Type of policy and plan number	Whether in payment	Cash equivalent value
			£

MONIES OWED TO A

Description of money owed and by whom	Balance owed	Date debt due to be discharged
None	N/A	N/A

8.61 *Pre-nuptial Agreements*

TRUST INTERESTS

Name of trust	A's Family Settlement
Sub Trust: A Nature of A's interest	Potential % Beneficiary
Total value of trust capital	£ as at
Gross value of A's interest (estimate discretionary and contingent interests)	£ as at
Estimated Gross income to be received by A in the current financial year	
Gross income received by A in the last financial year	
Estimated gross] capital to be received by A in the current financial year	
Gross capital received by A in the last financial year	

ASSETS HELD ON TRUST FOR A THIRD PARTY (IF NOT DETAILED ELSEWHERE)

Type of asset	Beneficiary	Value of asset	A's interest

INCOME

Source	Received 2014/2015 - £	Received 2015/2016 - £	Estimated income for current tax year 2016/2017 - £

LIABILITIES

Creditor's details and description of liability	Date liability incurred	Total liability	Balance outstanding	Date liability due to be discharged

FUTURE PROPERTY

Type of Property	Estimated current value of Property – £	Details of potential interest in Property – %
TOTAL	£	%

Further Information:

Schedule 4: B's FINANCIAL DISCLOSURE

PROPERTIES

Real Property	Date of purchase or acquisition	Estimated value £	Mortgage £	Loan due to £	B's interest %	Net of costs of sale at 3% and mortgage (but not net of tax)
TOTAL		£	£	£	%	£

BANK ACCOUNTS

Name of bank and type of account	Account number	Balance £	B's interest %
TOTAL		£	%

INVESTMENTS

Type of investment	Balance or value	B's interest
	£	
TOTAL	£	

8.61 *Pre-nuptial Agreements*

LIFE INSURANCE

Provider	Policy type	Policy number	Maturity date	Surrender value	Death benefit	Lives assured

BUSINESS INTERESTS

Company	Type of interest	Estimated current value of B's interest
TOTAL	% shareholder	

PERSONAL POSSESSIONS VALUED AT OVER £500

Item	Date of purchase or acquisition	Estimated value	B's interest %
TOTAL		£	

PENSIONS

Provider	Type of policy and plan number	Whether in payment	Cash equivalent value
			£

MONIES OWED TO A

Description of money owed and by whom	Balance owed	Date debt due to be discharged
None	N/A	N/A

TRUST INTERESTS

Name of trust	B's Family Settlement Sub Trust:
Nature of B's interest	Potential % Beneficiary
Total value of trust capital	£ as at

Gross value of B's interest (estimate discretionary and contingent interests)	£ as at
Estimated Gross income to be received by B in the current financial year	
Gross income received by B in the last financial year	
Estimated gross] capital to be received by B in the current financial year	
Gross capital received by B in the last financial year	

ASSETS HELD ON TRUST FOR B THIRD PARTY (IF NOT DETAILED ELSEWHERE)

Type of asset	Beneficiary	Value of asset	B's interest

INCOME

Source	Received 2014/2015 - £	Received 2015/2016 - £	Estimated income for current tax year 2016/2017 - £

LIABILITIES

Creditor's details and description of liability	Date liability incurred	Total liability	Balance outstanding	Date liability due to be discharged

FUTURE PROPERTY

Type of Property	Estimated current value of Property – £	Details of potential interest in Property – %
TOTAL	£	%

8.61 *Pre-nuptial Agreements*

Further Information:

Schedule 5: SEPARATE PROPERTY BELONGING TO A

PROPERTIES

Real Property	Date of purchase or acquisition	Estimated value	Mortgage	A's interest %	Net of costs of sale at 3% and mortgage (but not net of tax) – £
TOTAL		£	£	%	£

BANK ACCOUNTS

Name of bank and type of account	Account number	Balance – £	A's interest – %
TOTAL		£	£

BUSINESS INTERESTS

Company	Type of interest	Estimated current value of A's interest
TOTAL	% shareholder	£

PERSONAL POSSESSIONS VALUED AT OVER £500

Item	Date of purchase or acquisition	Estimated value – £	A's interest – %
TOTAL		£	

PENSIONS

Provider	Type of policy and plan number	Whether in payment	Cash equivalent value – £

TRUST INTERESTS

Name of trust	The Family Settlement Sub Trust: A
Nature of A's interest	Potential % Beneficiary
Total value of trust capital	£ as at
Gross value of A's interest (estimate discretionary and contingent interests)	£ as at
Estimated Gross income to be received by A in the current financial year	
Gross income received by A in the last financial year	
Estimated gross] capital to be received by A in the current financial year	
Gross capital received by A in the last financial year	

INCOME

Source	Received 2014/2015 - £	Received 2015/2016 - £	Estimated income for current tax year 2016/2017 - £

FUTURE PROPERTY

Type of Property	Estimated current value of Property – £	Details of potential interest in Property – %

8.61 Pre-nuptial Agreements

Further Information:

Schedule 6: SEPARATE PROPERTY BELONGING TO B

PROPERTIES

Real Property	Date of purchase or acquisition	Estimated value	Mortgage	B's interest %	Net of costs of sale at 3% and mortgage (but not net of tax) – £
TOTAL		£	£	%	£

BANK ACCOUNTS

Name of bank and type of account	Account number	Balance – £	A's interest – %
TOTAL		£	£

BUSINESS INTERESTS

Company	Type of interest	Estimated current value of A's interest
TOTAL	% shareholder	TOTAL

PERSONAL POSSESSIONS VALUED AT OVER £500

Item	Date of purchase or acquisition	Estimated value – £	A's interest – %
TOTAL		£	

PENSIONS

Provider	Type of policy and plan number	Whether in payment	Cash equivalent value – £

TRUST INTERESTS

Name of trust	The Family Settlement Sub Trust: B
Nature of B's interest	Potential % Beneficiary
Total value of trust capital	£ as at
Gross value of B's interest (estimate discretionary and contingent interests)	£ as at
Estimated Gross income to be received by B in the current financial year	
Gross income received by B in the last financial year	
Estimated gross] capital to be received by B in the current financial year	
Gross capital received by B in the last financial year	

INCOME

Source	Received 2014/2015 -£	Received 2015/2016 -£	Estimated income for current tax year 2016/2017 -£

FUTURE PROPERTY

Type of Property	Estimated current value of Property – £	Details of potential interest in Property – %
TOTAL	£	

8.61 *Pre-nuptial Agreements*

Further Information:

Schedule 7: CERTIFICATE OF A's INDEPENDENT SPECIALIST LEGAL ADVISER

I, [insert name and address of solicitor] certify as follows:

1. I am a duly qualified solicitor of the Senior Courts of England and Wales.
2. I confirm that prior to A entering into the Agreement between A and B to which this certificate is annexed, I have provided to A independent legal advice about the nature and terms of the Agreement, including the following matters:

    • the effect of the Agreement on his/her rights including the effect of its intended potential status as a qualifying nuptial agreement

    • whether, at the time my advice was given, it was to his/her legal advantage/disadvantage to enter into the Agreement;

    • whether, at that time, and in light of the circumstances that were then reasonably foreseeable, the provisions of the Agreement were fair and reasonable.

3. A has also received additional advice from Counsel [insert name and address of Counsel]

Dated

....

[insert name of solicitor] Solicitor of the Senior Courts of England and Wales

Schedule 8: CERTIFICATE OF B's INDEPENDENT SPECIALIST LEGAL ADVISER

I, [insert name and address of solicitor] certify as follows:

1. I am a duly qualified solicitor of the Senior Courts of England and Wales.
2. I confirm that prior to B entering into the Agreement between A and B to which this certificate is annexed, I have provided to B independent legal advice about the nature and terms of the Agreement, including the following matters:

    • the effect of the Agreement on his/her rights including the effect of its intended potential status as a qualifying nuptial agreement

    • whether, at the time my advice was given, it was to his/her legal advantage/disadvantage to enter into the Agreement;

    • whether, at that time, and in light of the circumstances that were then reasonably foreseeable, the provisions of the Agreement were fair and reasonable.

3. B has also received additional advice from Counsel [insert name and address of Counsel]

Dated

....

[insert name of solicitor] Solicitor of the Senior Courts of England and Wales

Schedule 9: DECLARATION STATEMENT OF A

I, AB of [enter address], state as follows:

I confirm that prior to entering into the Agreement to which this statement is annexed, I have received independent legal advice from [insert name and address of solicitor] and I understand the following:

- The terms of the Agreement.
- The effect of the Agreement on my rights under the law of England and Wales.
- The legal advantages and disadvantages to me in making this Agreement.
- That this Agreement must meet my financial needs and the financial needs of B.

Prior to entering into the Agreement to which this statement is annexed, I have also received independent specialist legal advice from Counsel [insert name and address of counsel]. I confirm that I understand the implications of that advice and intend this Agreement to be binding and enforceable in any jurisdiction.

I am aware of the proposals for reform of nuptial agreements contained in Law Commission Report on Matrimonial Property, Needs and Agreements (2014) and I intend this Agreement to be a qualifying nuptial agreement. I understand this means that under the law of England and Wales, the court will be prevented from making financial orders inconsistent with the Agreement in the event of the Breakdown of the Marriage or prior death of either Party, except:

- To meet my financial needs.
- To meet the financial needs of B.
- In the interests of a child who meets the definition contained in this Agreement of a Child of the Parties.

Dated

AB

Schedule 10: DECLARATION STATEMENT OF B

I, BB of [enter address], state as follows:

I confirm that prior to entering into the Agreement to which this statement is annexed, I have received independent legal advice from [insert name and address of solicitor] and I understand the following:

- The terms of the Agreement.
- The effect of the Agreement on my rights under the law of England and Wales.
- The legal advantages and disadvantages to me in making this Agreement.

8.61 Pre-nuptial Agreements

- That this Agreement must meet my financial needs and the financial needs of A.

Prior to entering into the Agreement to which this statement is annexed, I have also received independent specialist legal advice from Counsel [insert name and address of counsel]. I confirm that I understand the implications of that advice and intend this Agreement to be binding and enforceable in any jurisdiction.

I am aware of the proposals for reform of nuptial agreements contained in Law Commission Report on Matrimonial Property, Needs and Agreements (2014) and I intend this Agreement to be a qualifying nuptial agreement. I understand this means that under the law of England and Wales, the court will be prevented from making financial orders inconsistent with the Agreement in the event of the Breakdown of the Marriage or prior death of either Party, except:

- To meet my financial needs.
- To meet the financial needs of A.
- In the interests of a child who meets the definition contained in this Agreement of a Child of the Parties.

Dated

BB

Limitation of Counsel's [adapt where appropriate for a Solicitor only] Liability for all Advices and Work undertaken in relation to Ante/Pre-/Post Nuptial Agreement Instructions

I, AB, of, fully understand and agree that all Advices and other Work undertaken by [insert name and address of counsel] in regard to instructions provided to him by me and/or on my behalf by my solicitors [insert name and address of solicitor in respect of an Ante/Pre-Nuptial Agreement between myself will be limited to his Terms of Liability as set out below

And

I, [insert name and address of solicitor] agree to the terms of limitation as appear below in relation to all Advices and other Work undertaken by [insert name and address of counsel], in regard to instructions provided to him/her by [insert name and address of solicitor] and/or on behalf of **AB** in respect of an Ante/Pre-/Post Nuptial Agreement between **AB** and **BB**.

The Terms of Limitation are:

1. That any liability for negligence or any other default or omission, howsoever arising, in the provision of Advices and/or other work undertaken by [insert name and address of counsel], in the relation to and/or in connection with the instructions provided to him in regard to an Ante/Pre-/Post Nuptial Agreement between **AB** and **BB** will at all times be strictly limited to his Professional Indemnity insurance maximum cover (currently of £[insert]) as provided to him/her by the Bar Mutual Indemnity Fund or its successors.

2. That it is fully understood that the instructions to [insert name and address of counsel] are only accepted by him/her on the basis of the strict application of the limitation of liability referred to herein.

3. That it is acknowledged by the signing of this document that the signatories are fully aware and understand the terms of the limitation which apply hereby and that should he/she/they not agree to such terms he/she/they should not sign this document and if he/she/they wish before signing to obtain further advice on the terms herein and/or to instruct other counsel on different terms of instruction/liability each is at liberty to do so and to decline to sign this document and to forthwith suspend/withdraw any instructions provided to Counsel [insert name of counsel] without incurring any fee.

AB

[insert solicitor's name and address]

[insert Counsel's name]

. DATED [insert date].

---

[1] This is an example of an agreement where upon a breakdown of the marriage etc, the parties wish, subject to any housing/payment need required by the weaker financial party, to retain their exclusive ownership of their individual assets whenever acquired, any received inheritance, any gifts from each other and from third parties to themselves as individuals and personal belongings, whilst sharing equally assets, furniture and other chattels of both of them acquired jointly during the marriage, on the basis of a clean break. The agreement seeks, pending any alternative legislative change, to anticipate the introduction of a QNA regime as proposed by the Law Commission and to line up the agreement's terms and conditions with the conditions required of a QNA to attempt to attract an approach in effect as near equivalent as possible to this proposed statutory model. In doing so, it also recognises the potential provision to the weaker financial party at the time of the breakdown of the marriage etc of additional funds to meet that party's essential housing or income need at that time otherwise not provided for by the parties' retention of assets and resources as provided for under the agreement's other terms. It is imperative to appreciate that every case is different and whilst the Precedent herewith reflects the particular approach to the drafting required in the given example, the same can never be a blue print for every such case. Lay clients often make the mistake in believing that the solicitor is simply going to press a button on the computer and the necessary draft will be produced at minimum cost, whereas in most cases quite the opposite is the case, especially in the field of drafting where much is 'crystal ball gazing'. Clearly, careful instructions must be taken to ensure in each case that the particular requirements of the client are embraced in the terms of the agreement drawn and it is essential that consideration is given by the professional advisor to the terms of his professional insurance cover. The Precedent has been significantly amended from a previous version which appeared in the fourth edition in the light of the comments of Lady Hale in the *Radmacher* case that 'no self respecting' woman would sign up to such (previous) one sided ante-nuptial agreements, which evaluated her contribution to the marriage in terms of time alone. Unfortunately, the truth remains that many 'self respecting' women have and continue to sign up to these type of agreements as, indeed, in the opposite gender, did Nicholas Granatino in *Radmacher's* case. Clearly, as was expressed in previous editions, the authors have considerable sympathy with the Minority view expressed by Lady Hale as to the gender divide apparent in the judicial approach to pre-nuptial agreements; sentiments which fully echoed many of the previous and current edition's concerns as to the present law in this area. Finally, if appropriate, the provision of advice and the drafting of the pre-nuptial agreement should, specifically, be made the subject of a written limitation of liability signed by the client – a copy of one such example also being provided in these Precedents below. Whatever the reliability of this form of attempted limitation to potential liability, experience in the United States, Australia and elsewhere has shown this area to be fertile territory for professional negligence actions and it would be advisable for this reason to ensure, at the very least, that the files relating to such work are preserved indefinitely.

[2] Note also following Brexit, the Maintenance Regulation ceases to apply and a choice of law

8.61 *Pre-nuptial Agreements*

agreement for child maintenance would be possible and, therefore, the inclusion should be considered of a provision electing England and Wales as the jurisdiction of choice to settle child maintenance claims in the event the Lugano Convention 2007 is subsequently ratified by the UK.

3   [2010] UKSC 42.

Chapter 9
COHABITATION AND WELFARE BENEFITS

LAW AND PRACTICE

Introduction

'Living together as a married couple'

9.1 'Cohabitation' is not a term that has been officially used in modern social security law since 1977. Benefits legislation now refers instead to the status of *living together as a married couple*[1]. This is now gender-neutral. Before 13 March 2014 it was split into the two alternatives of *living together as husband and wife*[2] and *living together as if civil partners*[3].

Nonetheless, departmental officials, judges, practitioners and claimants themselves will often use the term 'cohabitation' as shorthand for the 'living together' concepts; DWP guidance on the other hand prefers the acronym LTAMC. Either way, practitioners must understand what the concept comprises. The law on their meaning is amorphous and difficult to pin down, a difficulty recognised in many of the judgments. Mr Commissioner Howell QC in *CP/8001/1995* described it as:

'one of the most difficult problems of definition there could be, since it involves investigating and analysing the nature of a human relationship between two people and this is inevitably a complex and sensitive thing.'

He later observed, in the same case, that:

'a true relationship of cohabitation is probably easier to recognise when one comes across it than to define exhaustively in the abstract.'

This chapter addresses the status of a couple, outside of marriage or civil partnership, insofar as it relates to welfare benefits and tax credits.

[1] Social Security Contributions and Benefits Act 1992, s 137.
[2] Since 4 April 1977.
[3] Since 5 December 2005.

Welfare benefits: a very brief introduction

9.2 Before focusing on the detailed issues of how 'living together' decisions impact on entitlement and how to challenge them, it may be useful to review

9.2 Cohabitation and Welfare Benefits

the range of benefits and tax credits available, so as to put in context those areas of the system where cohabitation is an issue, and to clarify where it is not. This chapter is not, however, aimed to provide a detailed discussion and dissection of the current benefits available.

Type of benefit	Benefit	Typical client-group and purpose	Relevance of cohabitation
Means-tested benefits: for claimants of various categories, but only if on low or zero incomes.	Universal credit (which is replacing income-based Jobseeker's Allowance, income-related Employment Support Allowance, Income Support, Child Tax Credit, Working Tax Credit, most Housing Benefit and some aspects of the Social Fund). (see also 3.6)	Working age people on low incomes: low-paid workers, parents, unemployed people, carers, those with limited capacity for work, those with savings less then £16,000.	Cohabitation and couple status is particularly important in all these benefits and tax credits as they are assessed differently depending on whether the claimant is single or a member of a couple.
	Income support*	Single parents with a child under 5 yrs, carers, some young people at school – who are not in 16 hours' work or more.	Couples' income – including cohabiting couples' – is aggregated for the purpose of means-testing both capital and income.
	Income-based job-seeker's allowance*	For claimants who sign on at the Job-Centre and are available for, and actively seeking, work – cannot be in 16 hours' work or more.	Couples (including cohabitants) not eligible for universal credit.

Type of benefit	Benefit	Typical client-group and purpose	Relevance of cohabitation
	Income-related employment and support allowance* (Most new claims are for 'new style' JSA)	Paid to those who satisfy the work capability assessment as having limited capability for work – cannot be in 16 hours' work or more.	In the case of single parents with a young child, Income Support is *only* available if they are single; cohabitation negates this. In relation to pension credit, applicants can start to get Pension Credit if either they and their partner have reached State Pension age, or one of the applicants is receiving Housing Benefit for people over State Pension age. For those who were receiving Pension Credit before 15 May 2019, Pension Credit will continue even if the applicant's partner is under the State Pension age, however if entitlement stops for any reason, Pension Credit cannot start again unless the applicant (and their partner) are eligible under the new rules. Pension credit will also stop if a person starts to live with a partner who is under State Pension age, but this can be re-started when the partner reaches State Pension age.
	Pension credit (income-related benefit made up two parts – guarantee credit and savings credit)	Paid to claimants who have reached State Pension age.	
	Housing Benefit*	Paid in respect of rent to those on low incomes whether in or out of work.	

9.2 Cohabitation and Welfare Benefits

Type of benefit	Benefit	Typical client-group and purpose	Relevance of cohabitation
	Local council tax reduction schemes	Paid in respect of council tax to those on low incomes whether in or out of work.	
Tax credits	Child tax credit* (see also **3.6**)	Paid in respect of dependent children/young persons to those on low to middle incomes whether in or out of work.	
	Working tax credit* (see also **3.6**)	Paid to those in at least 16 hours' work (number of hours is different for different categories of applicant) and on low incomes.	

*for those of working age, these benefits and tax credits are only applicable in cases where Universal Credit has not yet commenced. These benefits are still available for some, including (in respect of most) where the claimant (i) gets the severe disability premium, or is entitled to it, or (ii) got or was entitled to the severe disability premium in the last month, and they are still eligible for it.

Type of benefit	Benefit	Typical client-group and purpose	Relevance of cohabitation
Contributory benefits	Retirement pension	Paid upon reaching pensionable age to those who have paid or been credited with enough NI contributions during their working life – or their spouse or civil partner has. A 'new version' RP applies to those reaching pensionable age on or after 6 April 2016.	Paid individually so cohabiting does not affect entitlement. But note that cohabiting couples do not have the same advantages here as married couples and civil partners.

706

Type of benefit	Benefit	Typical client-group and purpose	Relevance of cohabitation
			Cohabitants cannot claim Category B RP on their partner's NI contributions, nor can they inherit the benefits of a deferred claim for RP. Cohabiting with another person does not interfere with a person's right to RP based on their current, late or former spouse's or civil partner's NI contributions.
	Employment and support allowance (contributory)	For people who satisfy the work capability assessment as having limited capability for work – and who have paid enough NI contributions in the 2–3 years before stopping work.	This is paid on an individual basis so cohabiting does not affect entitlement. Two cohabitants could each get a full entitlement unaffected by the other.
	Jobseeker's allowance (contributory) (Called 'new style' JSA if claims with UC)	For people who sign on as jobseekers actively seeking and available for work – and who have paid enough NI contributions in the 2–3 years before becoming unemployed.	This is paid on an individual basis so cohabiting does not affect entitlement. Two cohabitants could each get a full entitlement unaffected by the other.

9.2 Cohabitation and Welfare Benefits

Type of benefit	Benefit	Typical client-group and purpose	Relevance of cohabitation
	Bereavement Support Payment.	Payable for a limited time to surviving spouses and surviving civil partners over 45 whose late spouse or civil partner paid enough NI prior to their death	Bereavement Support Payment is unaffected by remarriage or re-partnering. Widowed Parent's Allowance is affected by remarriage or cohabitation. They are not available to cohabitants whose partner dies. Although note the case of *Jackson and others v Secretary of State for Work and Pensions*[a] in which Holman J held that the Pensions Act 2014 s 30(4)(a), read with s 30(1), was incompatible with Art 14, read with Art 8, of the Convention, in so far as it empowered the defendant Secretary of State to order by regulations that bereavement support payment be paid at a higher rate in the case of a person who was pregnant or entitled to child benefit, only if they were a spouse or civil partner of the deceased.
	Widowed parent's allowance (if spouse or civil partner died before 6 April 2017).	Payable for a limited time to surviving spouses and surviving civil partners who have dependent children or young persons and whose late spouse or late civil partner paid enough NI prior to their death.	Also note the case of *Re McLaughlin's Application for Judicial Review (Northern Ireland)*[b] in which it was declared that s 39A of the 1992 Act was incompatible with Art 14, read with Art 8, of the Convention, in so far as it precluded any entitlement to widowed parent's allowance by a surviving unmarried partner of the deceased.

708

Type of benefit	Benefit	Typical client-group and purpose	Relevance of cohabitation
	Incapacity benefit (which is being replaced by ESA)	Payable to those who satisfied the personal capability assessment as being incapable of work – for claims prior to October 2008 – most such existing claims have now switched to ESA.	This is paid on an individual basis so cohabiting does not affect entitlement. Two cohabitants could each get a full entitlement unaffected by the other's.
Other benefits neither means-tested nor contributory	Carer's allowance	For those who are caring regularly and substantially for a disabled person who is on Attendance Allowance, Personal Independence Payment Daily Living Component, or middle/highest rate of Disability Living Allowance Care Component.	Cohabitation does not affect this; it can be claimed by a cohabitant in respect of looking after the person they are cohabiting with.
	Personal independence payment	Paid to disabled claimants who have either significant care needs or mobility difficulties or both, and who claim before they reach age 65 (rising to 66 by 2018).	Unaffected by cohabitation. Two qualifying cohabitants could each get a full entitlement unaffected by the other's.
	Disability living allowance (which is being replaced by personal independence payment)	Paid to disabled claimants with significant care needs or mobility difficulties or both, and who claimed before age 65 and before April 2013. Still available to under-16s making a new claim. DLA is now being replaced by PIP.	Unaffected by cohabitation. Two qualifying cohabitants could each get a full entitlement unaffected by the other's.
	Attendance allowance	Paid to disabled claimants of state pension age who have significant care needs.	Unaffected by cohabitation. Two qualifying cohabitants could each get a full entitlement unaffected by the other's.

9.2 Cohabitation and Welfare Benefits

Type of benefit	Benefit	Typical client-group and purpose	Relevance of cohabitation
	Child benefit	Paid to those who live with and are responsible for a child or dependent young person.	Largely unaffected by cohabitation except that only one person may claim in respect of a given child, and rules govern who has priority in certain cases where two cohabitants both qualify but only one may succeed in their CB claim. Also rules in respect of income and thresholds.
	Guardian's Allowance	Claimed by a Child Benefit claimant in addition to the Child Benefit where a child is without parents.	
	Maternity allowance	Claimed during the maternity period by a woman who has recently worked but not enough to qualify for statutory maternity pay.	Unaffected by cohabitation: the claimant may claim whether single or not.
	Industrial injuries disablement benefit	Paid in respect of disablement caused by industrial injuries or a prescribed industrial disease.	Unaffected by cohabitation: the claimant may claim whether single or not. Note that entitlement to a death benefit under this scheme (for deaths prior to April 1988 only) would only accrue to a late *spouse*, and not if a cohabitant's partner died.
Employer-paid benefits	Statutory maternity pay	Paid during the statutory maternity period to claimants who have recently worked for a sufficient time for the same employer.	Unaffected by cohabitation: a claimant may claim whether single or not.
	Statutory paternity pay	Paid to a father, or the partner of a mother, with some upbringing responsibility, during prescribed periods following a birth or following a partner's return to work from maternity leave.	To qualify other than as a father, the person must be the mother's husband or partner (whether cohabiting or married or civil partners), the child's adopter, or intended parent (if via a surrogacy arrangement).

Type of benefit	Benefit	Typical client-group and purpose	Relevance of cohabitation
	Statutory adoption pay	Payable to adopters or surrogate parents or partners of adopters.	May be claimed whether the adopter is single or a member of a couple, and in the case of a couple, including a cohabiting couple, one partner may claim longer-term SAP and the other may claim a version of SPP, whether they are jointly adopting or only one partner is adopting.
	Statutory Shared Parental Pay	Payable for fathers or partners of new mothers/adopters.	To be eligible for Shared parental Leave and Statutory Shared Parental Pay both parents must share responsibility for the child at birth and meet work and pay criteria (which are different depending on which parents want to use the shared parental leave and pay). There are different rules in relation to the mother's partner wanting to take SPL and ShPP, the mother wanting to take the SPL and ShPP.
	Statutory sick pay	Payable as a minimum entitlement during periods when an employee is off work through inability to work caused by illness or disability.	Unaffected by cohabitation: a person may claim whether single or not. Two qualifying cohabitants could each be entitled, unaffected by the other's claim.

9.2 Cohabitation and Welfare Benefits

Type of benefit	Benefit	Typical client-group and purpose	Relevance of cohabitation
Single payments and grants	Social fund: budgeting loans	Discretionary repayable loans to assist with one-off needs in certain circumstances.	Eligibility to apply for these payments largely depends on entitlement to a qualifying benefit – mostly this means IS, income-based JSA, income-related ESA, income-based JSA, UC, CTC, WTV or PC. Consequently the circumstances put forward as justifying the payment, eg for budgeting loans, are assessed on a couple basis where two people are cohabiting.
	Social fund: Surestart maternity grant	Single non-discretionary lump sum paid at time of birth.	
	Social fund: funeral grants	Single non-discretionary lump sum paid to cover some funeral costs for a person who is responsible for a funeral.	
	Winter fuel payment	Single payment per Winter per household for those who have reached women's pensionable age.	Only one payment is made to a couple – including cohabiting couples.

a [2020] EWHC 183 (Admin).
b [2018] UKSC 48.

Using this chapter

YOUR CLIENT

9.3 Most of this chapter assumes that you will be representing or advising a client who has encountered a problem (disqualification or reduction) in their benefits or tax credits because they are considered to be a member of a couple, and feel this has been wrongly decided. Or they may be seeking advice on how to manage their relationship in order legitimately to avoid falling foul of the living together rules.

If the latter applies, there is nothing fraudulent about avoidance manoeuvres that deliberately set up a *bona fide* non-cohabiting relationship, as long as that will be a genuine one. Needless to say, what practitioners must not do is collude with any falsification of the facts in a case. Practitioners need not be reminded of their relevant duties and codes of conduct, including their duties to the court and/or tribunal. The advice in this chapter should not be seen as encouraging or condoning any kind of misrepresentation of the character of your client's relationship.

Social security law tells us what a *couple* is; it does not define *single* status. Yet it is 'single' status that is often contended for by the client. Generally if a person is not a member of a couple, they must be assumed to be single[1]. The tactical relevance in social security cases of knowing how to define 'couple' is typically that your client will want to argue that they are single and *not* a member of a couple. Their welfare benefits position will nearly always be better as a single person.

[1] The exception to this is the recognition in s 133 of SSCBA of legally-contracted polygamous marriages.

WHO IS YOUR OPPONENT?

9.4 The decision-maker who has adversely decided any living-together point against your client will most likely be an official of:

(a) for most welfare benefits, the **Department for Work and Pensions** (DWP), which comprises the Jobcentre Plus, the Pension Service, and other sections;
(b) for housing benefit and council tax reduction, the **local authority**; or
(c) for tax credits, **Her Majesty's Revenue and Customs** (HMRC).

For all these, this chapter usually adopts the generic term 'the department'.

Increasingly those departments work together to collect evidence, rely on one another's evidence, and base their decisions on each other's decisions. In general this is lawful and correct. Where a fraud is suspected, the Single Benefit Fraud Investigation Service will investigate. Their evidence may be produced in cohabitation cases even where no fraud is alleged.

In areas where statute creates a passported entitlement from one benefit to another, the decision-maker dealing with the passported benefit is probably bound by the decision-maker who decided the qualifying benefit. Where, for example, an Income Support decision finds a claimant to be single, the decision in respect of the person's Housing Benefit should not go behind this[1], unless there is an indication of fraud. It is submitted, however, that the position is less clear where there is no statutory link, such as where an HMRC decision on couple status dissents from a pre-existing couple status decision made by the DWP in respect of Income Support. The judgment in *R (on the application of Tilianu) v Secretary of State for Work and Pensions*[2] gives some support for the proposition that the second decision-making authority is not so bound. In this case it was held by Christopher Symonds QC, sitting as a Deputy High Court judge, that the Social Fund Inspector was not bound to follow the Secretary of State's decision. The position is equally unclear where, say, an Income Support decision-maker takes a different view as to couple status to a decision-maker in the Child Maintenance and Enforcement Commission.

In cases where it is known that a decision incorporating a determination on LTAMC may have been made on a claim for another benefit DMG guidance states that DMs should obtain the papers on that earlier claim, before giving a determination. DMs should consider the facts of the current claim and the points at DMG para 11104 (Chapter 11) and para E4094 (Chapter E4) (all factors of the relationship, including the *Fitzpatrick v Sterling Housing Association* factors) and DMG para 11106 (Chapter 11) and para E4095 (Chapter E4) (the sexual relationship of the two people[3], the relationship of the two people concerning money and the general relationship of the two people) before determining whether two people are LTAMC. The Guidance makes

713

9.4 *Cohabitation and Welfare Benefits*

clear that DMs should do this even though a different determination may be made on the same facts as those in an earlier claim and to ensure that the circumstances in which the determination is made show the burden of proof. The DMG guidance on this point concludes by stating that 'there would have to be a good reason for a DM to reach a different determination on LTAM, based on the same facts. If the DM reaches a different determination it may be necessary to consider revision of supersession of the outcome decision on the other benefit'[4].

[1] *R v Housing Benefits Review Board of Penwith District Council ex parte Menear* (1992) 24 HLR 115; *GB v London Borough of Hillingdon (HB)* [2010] UKUT 11 (AAC).
[2] [2010] EWHC 213 (Admin) (see in particular paras [54], [57] and [58] of the judgment).
[3] This factor appears to be missing from para E4095 (Chapter E4), but discussion in relation to sexual orientation and sexual relationship is covered at para E4097 and is referred to in the checklist of matters at para E4094.
[4] DMG, para 11185–11187 (Chapter 11) and also E4155–4157 (Chapter E4).

BENEFIT FRAUD

9.5 The incursion of criminal law into the living-together realm is largely outside the scope of this chapter. However, the reality is that many lone parents find themselves accused of benefit fraud, sometimes based on a living-together allegation. People who find themselves in situations where criminal proceedings are being considered or instigated should seek specialist advice.*CG v Secretary of State for Work and Pensions (IS)*[1] contains a sobering account of the seizure of items, later used as evidence, in a police raid on the claimant's home, including 'holiday receipts, family photos and letters written to the claimant by her husband from prison' . The underlying law on whether there is or has been cohabitation is no different; indeed it is submitted that a proper hearing of that issue within the benefits adjudication framework should certainly precede the prosecution of a criminal case by the department. That is not always the case, nor does the law say it must be. This is unfortunate because the magistrates' court is arguably not perhaps the best forum in which to ventilate the finer points of living together.

[1] [2011] UKUT 97 (AAC).

USING SOCIAL SECURITY CASE LAW

9.6 This chapter cites a number of social security cases. These are useful not only for the precedents some of them set, but also because they illustrate examples of the judicial approach and response to a wide variety of factual situations. For that reason the facts in quite a number of the cases are outlined here. That a decided case has similar facts to your client's scenario is *not* a reason to expect the same outcome however. Producing and citing cases with similar facts to your client's case should be done with care, and with no suggestion that the tribunal is bound to reach the same result. An analogy between a decided case and your fact-matrix may be drawn, bearing in mind that the outcome on a given set of facts is very rarely binding, given that the subtleties of factual variation are so finely shaded.

Most social security case law consists of decisions of the Upper Tribunal, which hears cases on appeal on a point of law from the First-tier Tribunal.

Before 3 November 2008, the equivalent arrangement was that Tribunals Service social security tribunal decisions were appealable to the Social Security and Child Support Commissioners. They were equivalent to the Upper Tribunal, and their case law is as binding as the Upper Tribunal's is now.

- Many cases here predate 3 November 2008 and their citations follow the pattern **CIS/1234/2002** – where 'C' means Commissioners' File; 'IS' denotes the benefit – here Income Support – and a number and four-digit year is applied.
- Reported cases follow the format **R(IS)3/07** where 'R' means Reported, followed by which benefit, a number and two-digit year.
- Where the benefit in question is signified by a 'G', this stands for 'general' and covers bereavement benefits, and the like.
- An intervening 'S' between the 'C' and the benefit initials means the case is a Scottish case, and equally binding in England and Wales. The Northern Ireland system used different citations, and such cases are highly persuasive in Great Britain.
- Since 3 November 2008, the citation format in Great Britain is *ZX v Secretary of State for Work and Pensions (IS)*[1]: 'UKUT' denotes UK Upper Tribunal, and 'AAC' is the Administrative Appeals Chamber.

Useful sources for downloading decisions of the Upper Tribunal and Social Security Commissioners include:

(a) https://www.gov.uk/administrative-appeals-tribunal.
(b) www.osscsc.gov.uk/Decisions/decisions.htm.
(c) www.bailii.org.
(d) www.rightsnet.org.uk.

[1] [2010] UKUT 123 (AAC).

USING DEPARTMENTAL GUIDANCE

9.7 The Decision Makers' Guide is published at www.gov.uk/government/collections/decision-makers-guide-staff-guide. This guidance is for DWP staff who make decisions about benefits and pensions. It helps them make decisions that are accurate and consistent. The introduction of Universal Credit and Personal Independence Payment affects the guidance DWP staff use. DWP decision makers now use 'Advice' for decision making (instead of the DMG) for decisions that involve: Universal Credit, Personal Independence Payment, contribution-based Jobseeker's Allowance and contribution-based Employment and Support Allowance for people who are eligible for Universal Credit. This guidance is published at https://www.gov.uk/government/publications/advice-for-decision-making-staff-guide. Chapter E4 'Universal Credit – Living together as a married couple' guidance is published here: https://assets.publishing.service.gov.uk/government/uploads/system/uploads/attachment_data/file/661551/adme4.pdf. The content of Chapter E4 is very smiliar to DMG Chapter 11, the few relevant differences are highlighted where appropriate in this chapter.

The guides provide a very useful insight into why a decision has been made in the way it has. The guidance is carefully and moderately written, and cites useful legal authority. However, practitioners should remember at all times

9.7 Cohabitation and Welfare Benefits

that it is **not** law. By all means quote it where it assists your client, but where it is invoked against your client's case, it should be rebutted with the correct position in law, and it should be argued that it carries no legal authority at all.

Why cohabitation is relevant in social security and tax credits law

Differences in treatment as between couples and single people

9.8 Here are five examples of situations in which a client may be affected by the cohabitation rules; in these first four cases, one will hope to argue – depending on the facts – that the client is single.

Case 1: disqualified from universal credit: Andrea is separating from her partner Adrian. They both still live in the same property, with their children, aged 10 and 13, but have separated out their households within the home. Adrian is in full-time, well-paid work; Andrea is not. She needs to claim benefits as she is not working (and has not worked as a employee in the last 3 years) and is fairly sure that she will be the main childcarer. If they are treated as a couple then she cannot get any universal credit. Also, if they are treated as a couple[1] then she cannot get any Jobseeker's Allowance (she can't claim contribution-based JSA ('new-style' JSA if claimed with universal credit), she is disqualified by Adrian's full-time work[2] as well as by their aggregated joint income[3], ie his sizeable earnings). Even if eligible to apply, as a member of the couple she is also ineligible for child tax credit if the joint income exceeds approximately £16,105 (two or more children)[4].

Case 2: less JSA: Bereket shares a flat with his friend Mariam; they are not married. Both are in their 30s, unemployed and claiming income-based Jobseeker's Allowance. If seen as a couple they are entitled to £116.80 per week[5] between them; if regarded as two single people they will receive £74.35 per week each – £31.90 more in total.

Case 3: access to income support: Chloe is a single parent with two children aged two and four. She claims income support, child benefit and child tax credit. Her eligibility for Income Support depends on her lone parent status. If she begins a relationship with a new partner and this relationship gradually becomes more serious, then at some point the DWP may decide she is no longer a single parent, so her eligibility for income support stops[6]. She might still be able to claim universal credit or jobseeker's allowance (depending on her new partner's status and income), but getting income support *as a lone parent* is no longer an option once she is a member of a couple. Sadly, cases like this can all too readily produce fraud prosecutions. Arguing against couple status matters doubly in such cases.

Case 4: bereavement benefits: Danny claims bereavement allowance after the death of his wife Joyce. When he begins cohabiting with a new partner 8 months after his bereavement, his bereavement allowance is suspended[7].

However, in other circumstances, admittedly rarer, it is in the client's interest for the relationship to be seen as a stronger one.

Case 5: capital value of a former shared home: Eldon moves out of the home he used to share with his partner. She remains in the home, valued at £1.2m, which they continue to own jointly. There are no children. Because DWP take the view that they are 'estranged', the value of his share in the jointly owned property starts to count as his capital 26 weeks after he moves out[8], disqualifying him from jobseeker's allowance. Were they not 'estranged' the value of his share would be disregarded as capital indefinitely.

[1] Jobseekers Act 1995, ss 3, 4, 35; JSA Regulations 1996 (SI 1996/207), reg 1.
[2] Jobseekers Act 1995, s 3(1)(e).
[3] JSA Regulations 1996, reg 88.
[4] Tax Credits (Income Thresholds and Determination of Rates) Regulations 2002 (SI 2002/2008), reg 8 as amended. Approximate amounts applicable in 2015–2016 tax year.
[5] Weekly amounts are for 2019–2020.
[6] Income Support (General) Regulations 1987 (SI 1987/1967), Sch 1B.
[7] Social Security Contributions and Benefits Act 1992, s 39B(5)(b).
[8] Jobseeker's Allowance Regulations 1996 (SI 1996/207), Sch 8 paras 4(b) and 5.

Cohabitation rules in the benefits system

Which benefits and tax credits are affected by the 'living together' tests?

BENEFITS AND TAX CREDITS AFFECTED: I – FOR THE PURPOSES OF APPLYING A MEANS-TEST

9.9 Claims for the following benefit and tax credits are made on a couple basis for cohabitees – with both partners as *joint claimants*:

(a) Universal credit[1].
(b) Working tax credit.
(c) Child tax credit.

Claims for the following means-tested benefits and support are also made on a couple basis for cohabitees – one partner being the *claimant* and the other the *partner*:

  (d) Income support[2].
  (e) Income-based jobseeker's allowance[3].
  (d) Income-related employment and support allowance[4].
  (f) State pension credit[5].
  (g) Housing benefit.
  (h) Local council tax reduction schemes[6].

[1] Welfare Reform Act 2012, s 39(1).
[2] SSCBA 1992, s 124(1).
[3] Jobseekers Act 1995, s 3(1).
[4] Welfare Reform Act 2007, Sch 1, para 6(1).
[5] State Pension Credit Act 2002, s 5.
[6] Council Tax Reduction Schemes (Prescribed Requirements) (England) Regulations 2012 (SI 2012/2885), reg 4 and Council Tax Reduction Schemes and Prescribed Requirements (Wales) Regulations 2012 (SI 2012/3144 (W 316)), reg 4.

9.10 Cohabitation and Welfare Benefits

BENEFITS AFFECTED: II – FOR THE PURPOSE OF DISQUALIFICATION WHERE COHABITATION EXISTS

9.10 Benefits affected are:

(a) Bereavement allowance[1].
(b) Widowed parent's allowance[2].
(c) Widow's pension[3].
(d) Widowed mother's allowance[4].
(e) Bereavement payment[5].
(f) Bereavement support payment.

[1] SSCBA 1992, s 39B.
[2] SSCBA 1992, s 39A.
[3] SSCBA 1992, s 38(3).
[4] SSCBA 1992, s 37(4)(b).
[5] SSCBA 1992, s 36(2): not payable if the claimant is cohabiting with someone other than their spouse or civil partner at the time of the spouse's or civil partner's death.

IS THE DEFINITION THE SAME FOR THESE TWO LISTS?

9.11 According to Mr Commissioner Rice, the definition of 'living together' is the same for means-tested and widows' (now *bereavement*) benefits: *R(SB)17/81*. But Mr Commissioner Goodman entered a proviso in *CIS/317/94* at least in respect of the burden of proof:

'Mr Wright cited a passage at page 25 of the 1994 edition of Mesher and Wood on "Income Related Benefits: The Legislation" as follows:

"what these points come to [the criteria for determining whether a couple are living together as husband and wife] is that the so called 'objective facts' of a relationship may be capable of being interpreted either way. This, then, leaves the authority in difficulty, although it is clear that the burden of proof, since the rule operates as a disqualification, is on the DSS."

However, although living together as husband and wife does operate as a disqualification for widow's benefit (SSCBA 1992, s 38(3)(c)), it does not in my view so operate for income support. What is involved here is the whole gamut of facts leading to the question of whether a particular claimant is entitled to Income Support by reason of his or her financial position and if so its amount.'

The distinction between a disqualifying factor and a determining factor is subtle but important. The stakes are evidently more stark in bereavement benefits. But for practical purposes it is submitted that practitioners may safely treat the definition as the same for the two types of benefit.

Areas where cohabitation matters

9.12 Thus, cohabitation is raised specifically in rules which prescribe that:

(a) in order to claim income support as a lone parent, the client must indeed be considered single and the parent of a child under 5 years[1];
(b) the income and capital of a couple are aggregated for the purposes of calculating all means-tested benefits and tax credits;
(c) universal credit, is a means tested benefit to replace income-based jobseeker's allowance, income-related employment and support allowance,

income support and child tax credit, working tax credit and most housing benefit. All new claims including those due to a change of circumstance must now be for universal credit. All existing benefit claims are to start a managed migration to universal credit from July 2019. Pt 1 (ss 1–43) of the Welfare Reform Act 2012 provides that the scheme, unsurprisingly, adopts the same wide approach to aggregation of income and capital in couples as previously: it is possible for clients to be treated as a couple despite the absence of a marriage or civil partnership. Moreover s 39 of the Act mirrors exactly the existing legislation's couple definitions for means-tested benefits. For universal credit therefore, different rules about disregarding income apply, according to whether the claim is a couple claim or a single claim;

(d) a claimant whose partner is in full-time work is not entitled to income support, income-based JSA and income-related employment and support allowance;

(e) bereavement benefits (bereavement allowance, widowed parent's allowance, widow's pension and widowed mother's allowance) are suspended when a widow, widower or surviving civil partner starts cohabiting with a new partner[2];

(f) past cohabitation can interfere[3] with current housing benefit entitlement where a claim is made for rent paid to a former partner on a property that was previously occupied by the tenant and the landlord as a couple;

(g) that where a person from abroad, in the UK subject to a prohibition on recourse to public funds, joins their family in the UK who do not have that prohibition, the newly arrived person may inadvertently end up being deemed to have claimed on public funds if s/he cohabits with a claimant partner whose housing benefit or help from the council tax reduction scheme increases due to the arrival of the new partner. If they are not regarded as partners, and the new arrival refrains from making their own housing benefit/council tax reduction claim, there is no such problem;

(h) a member of a couple purporting *both* to get a severe disability premium as part of their income support, income-related employment and support allowance etc, can only do so if the other member of the couple also receives a qualifying benefit or is blind[4];

(i) in JSA claims made by couples without children, the partner as well as the claimant must sign on at the Jobcentre Plus;

(k) a person – often in practice a former cohabiting partner though this is not necessary – who de facto pays maintenance in respect of a claimant's children, may because of this be treated as the children's father so as to make him a 'liable relative' in the Income Support (et al) Regulations[5], meaning that any additional maintenance he pays not to the children but to the mother will be treated as a liable relative payment and will punitively reduce or extinguish her income support payments;

[1] Welfare Reform Act 2012, s 57.
[2] The 'living together' criteria are the same in bereavement benefits as for means-tested benefits: R(SB)17/81.
[3] Housing Benefit Regulations 2006 (SI 2006/216), reg 9(1)(c).
[4] eg for Income Support, Income Support (General) Regulations 1987 (SI 1987/1967), Sch 2, para 13(2A). *CIS/2900/1998* dealt with such a case, though this concerned a married couple.
[5] For Income Support, Income Support (General) Regulations 1987 (SI 1987/1967), reg 5 (for example: 'liable relative' (c)).

When does 'couple' require marriage or civil partnership?

9.13 On the other hand, a different, more restrictive view of 'couple' obtains in other areas of the social security system. In particular, for example, it should be noted that:

9.13 *Cohabitation and Welfare Benefits*

(a) in retirement pension, entitlement to Category B state pension based on the national insurance contribution conditions of a spouse, civil partner, deceased spouse or deceased civil partner only arises where there is or was indeed a marriage or civil partnership – in other words, mere cohabitation will not suffice[1];
(b) similarly there is no entitlement to bereavement benefits (bereavement allowance, widowed parent's allowance and bereavement payment) and bereavement support payment unless a spouse or civil partner (not a cohabitee) has died;
(c) other areas of retirement pension also require there to be (or have been) a marriage or civil partnership; and
(d) corresponding provisions apply in the war pensions and (for deaths before April 1988) industrial injuries schemes wherever the claimant is a surviving spouse or surviving civil partner.

[1] Pensions Act 2004.

Social security definitions of couple

Nine types of couple

9.14 Legislation prescribes a number of alternative definitions of couple status, depending on whether married/civil partners or not. The gender-mix is now less important though. The Marriage (Same Sex Couples) Act 2013 prescribed changes to many instances in social security law so that from 13 March 2014, references to 'a man and a woman' were replaced by a simpler reference to 'two people'[1]. However, some relevant couple definitions appear to have missed out on this amending process: tax credits law in particular would appear to have remained unchanged, leaving an unsatisfactory level of inconsistency.

[1] Marriage (Same Sex Couples) Act 2013 (Consequential and Contrary Provisions and Scotland) Order 2014 (SI 2014/560).

SOCIAL SECURITY DEFINITIONS OF COUPLE

9.15

	Married or civil partners	*Cohabiting: not married or civil partners*
Rules applying from 13 March 2014		
New wording: regardless of whether same-sex or opposite-sex	*benefits:* two people who are married to, or civil partners of, each other and are members of the same household[a].	*benefits:* two people who are not married to, or civil partners of, each other but are living together as a married couple[b].
	tax credits: at the time of writing, the tax credits rules have not changed so as to expressly reflect the possibility of same-sex marriage, or indeed opposite sex civil partners[c]. See below for the position, pending any change.	

Law and Practice **9.16**

	Married or civil partners	*Cohabiting: not married or civil partners*
	Existing rules before 13 March 2014	
Opposite-sex couple	*benefits:* a man and a woman who are married to each other and are members of the same household[d].	*benefits and tax credits:* a man and a woman who are not married to each other but are living together as husband and wife[e].
	tax credits: a man and a woman who are married to each other and are neither separated under a court order nor separated in circumstances in which the separation is likely to be permanent[f].	
Same-sex couple[g]	benefits: two people of the same sex who are civil partners of each other and are members of the same household[h].	*benefits and tax credits:* two people of the same sex who are not civil partners of each other but are living together as if they were civil partners[i] – if, but only if, they would be regarded as living together as husband and wife were they instead two people of the opposite sex[j].
	tax credits: two people of the same sex who are civil partners of each other and are neither separated under a court order nor separated in circumstances in which the separation is likely to be permanent[k].	

a   Marriage (Same Sex Couples) Act 2013 (Consequential and Contrary Provisions and Scotland) Order 2014 (SI 2014/560), Sch 1, para 22(8).
b   Marriage (Same Sex Couples) Act 2013 (Consequential and Contrary Provisions and Scotland) Order 2014 (SI 2014/560), Sch 1, para 22(8).
c   Following the declaration of incompatibility in the case of R *(on the application of Steinfeld and Keidan) (Appellants) v Secretary of State for International Development (in substitution for the Home Secretary and the Education Secretary) (Respondent)* [2018] UKSC 32 (the Supreme Court made a declaration that ss 1 and 3 of the CPA, to the extent that they preclude a different-sex couple from entering into a civil partnership, are incompatible with art 14 taken in conjunction with art 8 of the ECHR) and the consequent legislative changes, including by The Civil Partnership (Opposite-sex Couples) Regulations 2019.
d   SSCBA 1992, s 137(1).
e   SSCBA 1992, s 137(1) and TCA 2002, s 3(5A) – added by the Civil Partnership Act 2004, Sch 24, para 144(3).
f   TCA 2002, s 3(5A) – added by the Civil Partnership Act 2004, Sch 24, para 144(3).
g   Since 5 December 2005, Civil Partnership Act 2004.
h   SSCBA 1992, s 137(1).
i   SSCBA 1992, s 137 and s 122(1A), and TCA 2002, s 3(5A) – added by the Civil Partnership Act, Sch 24, para 144(3).
j   SSCBA 1992, s 137(1A) – added by Civil Partnership Act 2004, Sch 24(3), para 46(5).
k   TCA 2002, s 3(5A).

Types of cohabitation in social security law

9.16 Traditionally the cohabitation test was whether two people, a man and a woman, were 'living together as husband and wife' (LTAHAW).

9.16 Cohabitation and Welfare Benefits

From 2004 that expanded to also cover same-sex couples, with 'living together as if civil partners' (LTACP) added to the legislation.

The current wording, effective from 13 March 2014, is **'living together as a married couple'** (LTAMC). Like its predecessors, it can only apply if there is no marriage or civil partnership. For decisions after 12 March 2014, there can be no test of whether two people are 'living together as if civil partners' (LTACP) except in tax credits decisions. Time will tell whether the new concept of *living together as a married couple* produces any different result than the old LTAHAW. It is submitted it is unlikely to be interpreted very differently.

Sexual orientation does not, strictly speaking, play any part. Nor, now, does gender. There should now be no need to focus on whether it is an opposite-sex couple or a same-sex couple, much less whether the parties are, for example, heterosexual or homosexual. It does not strictly matter. In the case of one or both partners being transgender, it is reasonable to assume that the provisions of the Gender Recognition Act 2003 apply.

From 2004 to 2014 the legislation sought (tortuously some might argue) to keep parity of definition as between same-sex and opposite-sex cohabiting couples. Only belatedly did some difference start to emerge in the caselaw as to the norms to be expected in a civil partnership compared to a marriage. Judge Levenson discussed some of the characteristics of civil partnership in *JP v Secretary of State for Work and Pensions (IS)*[1]. But now, for alleged cohabitants, *married couple* is the only comparator, except in tax credit cases.

The rule also presupposes that the relationship is not prohibited, unlawful or criminal[2]. In other words, for example, it cannot be said that somebody under 16 is a member of a couple, or that a relationship between siblings can constitute a couple (however couple-like it is).

[1] [2014] UKUT 0017 (AAC).
[2] DMG, paras 11005–11006 and 11081–11082and Appendices to DMG Chapter 11.

Checklist: are they married or civil partners?

9.17 The first step in any case involving couple or single status is to determine whether your client and the alleged partner are married to each other or civil partners of each other:

(a) if they are married or civil partners, the only test that then applies is whether they are members of the same household (or, for tax credits, whether they are not separated)[1].
(b) if they are not married or civil partners, then the more complex tests described in this chapter will apply.

This distinction should be borne clearly in mind at the outset.

[1] This is clear in the legislation but made even clearer by Miss Commissioner Fellner in CIS/2900/1998, paras 17–18.

Applying the 'living together' test if marriage and civil partnership are discounted

9.18 In benefits cases, where two people are married or civil partners, and it is decided they share a household, then they are a 'couple'. Where two people are married or civil partners, and it is decided they *do not* share a household, then they are not a 'couple', and cannot be assessed under the LTAMC test just because they are married or are civil partners[1].

In tax credits cases, this can appear less clear because the criteria for being assessed as a couple for marriages and civil partnerships do not refer to 'household' in the tax credits rules. Consider a former couple, a man and a woman, still married, who consider themselves permanently separated from one another, but who have not (or not yet) moved to different accommodation. They should fall outside the tax credits married couple test in that they are 'a man and a woman who are married to each other' and are 'separated in circumstances in which the separation is likely to be permanent'. If so, they are home and dry in the quest to be considered single. It is not open to HMRC to assess them as possibly living together as husband and wife (as the tax credits cohabitation test remains), *because* they are married. LTAHAW does not allow for that. That disinction was underlined in similar circumstances by Judge Ovey in *TS v HMRC (TC)*[2].

On the 'legal separation' limb of the tax credits rule concerning marriage and civil partnership, the decision by Judge Wikeley in *DG v Her Majesty's Revenue and Customs (TC)*[3] should be noted for its observation that separation here must be judged in the round on all the evidence available, and there was no absolute requirement of legal documentation.

In other cases, it may be that despite appearances, there never was a marriage. These cases may well permit application of the LTAMC rule instead. Issues can arise as to the validity of a marriage that the parties maintain is genuine. These often concern the validity in the UK of a marriage contracted outside the UK under different national rules. If a purported marriage turns out to be invalid, the couple fall to be assessed under the LTAMC rule as possible cohabitants. In *CIS/11304/1995* Mr Commissioner Goodman ruled on the validity of a marriage contracted by the claimant in the UK under Islamic rules though she was already legally married to another man. The purported marriage was invalid and so the relationship had to be assessed on the basis of the 'living together' rules. Where the validity of a marriage is questioned, it is important to hold the respondent, and the Tribunal, to a logical legal framework, in other words to make sure that it deals with validity first, and only if it finds the marriage unproven goes on to assess LTAMC. Failure to adhere to that sequence had been the error of law committed by the First-tier Tribunal in *FB v Secretary of State for Work and Pensions (IS)*[4].

[1] For example, see DMG, para 11005–11006 (Chapter 11) and para E4005–4005 (Chapter E4).
[2] [2015] UKUT 0507 (AAC).
[3] [2013] UKUT 0631 (AAC).
[4] [2011] UKUT 335 (AAC).

9.19 *Cohabitation and Welfare Benefits*

What constitutes living together as a married couple?

General approach

9.19 LTAMC is not defined in the legislation, so it is for the DWP or other benefit-paying agency initially to decide whether 'the whole relationship of two people who are not married to each other is comparable to that of a couple who are married to each other'[1]. The courts have been reluctant to impose a fixed view of what LTAHAW (and now LTAMC) comprises: Woolf J, as he then was, made this clear in an early living-together case, *Crake v Supplementary Benefits Commission; Butterworth v Supplementary Benefits Commission*[2]:

> 'I am not suggesting that it is any function of this court to try and put some gloss on the wording of the paragraph, of general application. Indeed, it would be very undesirable for this court to seek to do that.'

Each case should be assessed on its merits. But there is a structure within which this can usefully be done: the authorities of the last 40 years or so have adumbrated at least two if not three structures for the assessment of 'living together' status. However, they have been equally at pains to warn against a 'checklist' approach, suggesting that there is indeed something intangible, some perhaps almost indefinable characteristic, that will often distinguish two people living together as a married couple from two people living together in some other way. It is possible to trace a strong jurisprudential counterpoint of refusal to approve any absolute test, running alongside a considerable degree of deference to Woolf J's apparent endorsement of a six-factor test; such tension as there is between these two approaches must be understood and factored in to arguments about living together.

In a widow's case, *CP/8001/1995*, Mr Commissioner Howell QC commented that:

> 'the legislation presents adjudication officers and tribunals with one of the most difficult problems of definition there could be, since it involves investigating and analysing the nature of a human relationship between two people and this is inevitably a complex and sensitive thing. An adjudication officer or tribunal faced with such a problem is unlikely to achieve a satisfactory result by simply regarding the task as ticking off items on a checklist, without also standing back and asking itself whether having looked at all the detailed evidence about individual aspects of the claimant's living arrangements in the case before them, the relationship between her and the man she is alleged to be living with can fairly and justly be described in normal parlance as that of two people living together in the manner of husband and wife.'

Mr Commissioner Jacobs, in *CIS/443/1998*, cited Neuberger J in *Re Watson (Deceased)*[3], in the context of the Inheritance (Provision for Family and Dependants) Act 1975:

> 'When considering the question, the court should ask itself whether, in the opinion of a reasonable person with normal perceptions, it could be said that the two people in question were living together as husband and wife: but, when considering that question, one should not ignore the multifarious nature of marital relationships.'

It is submitted then that an unquestioning and rigid adherence to either of the two main checklists (see below) is to be avoided. Arguments against couple status can be well-served by a degree of non-compliance with any prescriptive factors.

The Departmental Guidance states some fairly unequivocal principles, helpful insofar as they set the threshold quite high:

> 'To be treated as LTAMC the relationship has to be the same as that of a married couple. Marriage is where two people join together with the intention of sharing the rest of their lives. There is no single template of what the relationship of a married couple is. It is a stable partnership, not just based on economic dependency but also an emotional relationship of lifetime commitment rather than one for convenience, friendship, companionship or the living together of livers. If the evidence does not suggest that it is more likely than not that the relationship between the two people has the particular emotional quality that characterizes a married couple's partnership, the DM should find that they are not LTAMC.[4]'

But the 'no single template' view is very consonant with the key authorities.

The traditional test since *Crake & Butterworth* has been the six key factors or 'admirable signposts' (dealt with below, these comprise: household, stability, sex, children, finances, public acknowledgement) which originally appeared in the Supplementary Benefits Handbook[5] and were later endorsed by Woolf J in *Crake & Butterworth* at p 505. Many practitioners, and not a few tribunals, have been led astray by this endorsement, however, and it cannot be stressed too highly that, much as the six signposts provide a useful framework, they do not tell the whole story.

This much was made clear by Deputy Judge Najib in *KJ v SSWP (IS)*[6], in addition to the point that there is no requirement in every case for there to be a 'finding' on each 'signpost'. Thus:

> 'The use of the word "criteria" by Mr Power when describing the "signposts" demonstrates the flaw in the Appellant's argument. The Appellant seeks to treat the "signposts" as a set criteria or checklist by which the FtT ought to have made its decision. This is precisely what Woolf J considered to be the wrong approach and why he chose to describe them as "signposts". This is also why the Upper Tribunal in PP and the Inner House in DK were keen to stress that (i) the "signposts" were not exhaustive; (ii) no single fact or "signpost" is decisive; (iii) there need not be a detailed analysis of every piece of evidence "divided into discrete components"; (iv) individual pieces of evidence "do not require to be assessed individually for their probability"; (v) there is no requirement in every case for there to be a "finding" on each "signpost"; and (vi) the question was not whether a particular "signpost" was or was not established but rather, whether taking all the evidence into account, the primary question, namely whether two people were "living as a married couple", was established on a balance of probabilities.'[7]

---

[1] *R(G)3/71*; DMG, para 11101 (Chapter 11) and para E4091 (Chapter E4).
[2] [1982] 1 All ER 498 at 501, which was considered in the Family Division of the High Court in *Kimber v Kimber* [2000] 1 FLR 383 at 389.
[3] [1999] 1 FLR 878, at p 883.
[4] DMG, para 11103 (Chapter 11) and para E4093 Chapter E4).
[5] Mr Commissioner Edwards-Jones in *R(SB)35/85* thought that Woolf J was using the 1979 revision of this guidance.
[6] [2019] UKUT 312 (AAC).

9.19 *Cohabitation and Welfare Benefits*

⁷ *KJ v SSWP (IS)* [2019] UKUT 312 (AAC) para 23.

Two checklists?

9.20 Despite the sensible resistance to a mechanistic checklist approach, the case law has also been unable to resist imposing structure to the LTAMC test. Two key tests tend to emerge, and practitioners are advised to utilise these where they favour the client's position, and to feel free to move outside the tests when they are unhelpful. It is moreover reassuring to know that the tests are to some extent regarded as interchangeable[1].

¹ *R(SB)17/81*.

THE THREE FACTORS

9.21 The three-part assessment looks at three areas of a relationship[1]:

(a) sexual;
(b) financial; and
(c) general.

In *R(G)3/71* Mr Commissioner Shewan heard a case under the old pre-1977 'cohabitation' rules involving a widow whose alleged partner, her lodger, was admittedly the father of her child and had left his wife to go to live with the claimant. In deciding that this *was* cohabitation, and so disqualified the claimant from her Widowed Mother's Allowance, the Commissioner set out his test as follows:

> 'it is generally accepted that the question whether a woman is cohabiting with a man as his wife, within the meaning of the statute, requires an examination of three main matters:
> (1) their relationship in relation to sex;
> (2) their relationship in relation to money; and
> (3) their general relationship.
>
> Although all three are as a rule relevant, no single one of them is necessarily conclusive.'

The claimant's case was then analysed according to these factors. It is significant that sex comes first here. Its importance cannot be denied. But even with that structure there is immediately a problem of the subtle shades of distinction available as to what (ie how much sex) amounts to a sexual relationship. On the facts of that case, the alleged couple had had sex once only, resulting in a child. Although registering scepticism about the 'once only' claim, the Commissioner felt obliged to combine the evidence about intercourse with evidence about the subsequent nature of their living together in order for that factor to carry weight against the claimant; held: there *was* cohabitation.

The financial factor was framed very much in terms of distinguishing between the way a husband would support his wife and the commercial nature of the landlady/lodger relationship. The fact that the alleged partner paid the claimant variable amounts of money according to his means pushed this situation closer to a husband-wife relationship – even though to some extent his contributions represented a form of maintenance to his child. Argued differently in more modern terms, the claimant might have suggested that if voluntary child maintenance was involved, that spoke of a separation rather than a cohabitation.

The general relationship factor covers issues like time spent together, mutual assistance with household tasks, shared childcare, shared socialising and intentions for the future. The degree of mutual assistance around the house and the level of social life ('If she could get someone in to look after the children she and S "had a night out"') persuaded the Commissioner that this was akin to the behaviour of a husband rather than a lodger.

The three factors do not in terms address whether there was a shared household, yet the rules then required this for cohabitation. It is somewhat presupposed – here the admitted facts of a landlady/lodger arrangement were rather assumed to fall within the definition of household. It is nowadays still sensible to regard the existence of a household almost as a prerequisite for a living together finding.

[1] DMG, para 11106.

USING THE THREE FACTORS

9.22 Naturally, where your client truthfully denies any sexual relationship, that fact should be stressed, along with the primacy of this factor in Commissioner Shewan's judgment and later cases. Financial arrangements which differ in some way from whatever it might be said is the 'norm' in married couples need to be emphasised. The true usefulness of these factors arguably lies in factor number 3, the 'general' relationship, which is so vague in reality that any relevant circumstances can be adduced in support of single status, and yet has been elevated to 'paramount importance'[1].

[1] By Mr Commissioner Jacobs in *CIS/443/1998*.

THE SIX SIGNPOSTS

9.23 In *Crake v Supplementary Benefits Commission; Butterworth v Supplementary Benefits Commission*[1] Woolf J was referred to the Supplementary Benefits Handbook published by the then DHSS and labelled the guidance 'admirable signposts', creating a presumed doctrine in a move that has dominated – some would say burdened – the assessment of couples ever since. The 'six admirable signposts' are employed so universally as a checklist that it is easy to imagine they constitute the long and short of 'living together' law; they do not. The six factors elaborated by the Handbook were:

(a) membership of the same household;
(b) stability;
(c) financial support;
(d) sexual relationship;
(e) children; and
(f) public acknowledgement.

9.23 *Cohabitation and Welfare Benefits*

Woolf J felt they could not be faulted. It is submitted that despite caveats against the need to demonstrate systematic compliance with these factors, these are still a very useful and well-understood starting point, provided it is remembered that other factors may well come into play, and that, as with the three-factor test, where the signposts do not favour the facts in your client's case, they can be summarily dropped from the argument.

The departmental attitude to the signposts has since *Crake & Butterworth* been reverential (after all, these started as mere internal guidance and then gained judicial assent). Submissions to tribunals on behalf of the Secretary of State or local authorities still typically frame the matter on the same six-part basis. For that reason alone their contents need to be unpacked and examined for their potential in arguing your client's case. Anachronistic though it may seem, the Handbook is quoted in places in this chapter because it still throws light on how to read the still-seminal case of *Crake & Butterworth*.

[1] [1982] 1 All ER 498.

Other tests

9.24 Mr Commissioner Jacobs in *CIS/443/1998* was not the first authority to doubt the comprehensiveness of the six signposts:

[The six signposts] 'must be considered, but they must not be considered in isolation from their context. There is more to living together as husband and wife than these cold, observable facts. This is shown by some of the characteristics to be expected of a relationship of husband and wife listed by Lord Justice Waite *in Fitzpatrick v Sterling Housing Association* [1998] 1 FLR 6 at p 19:

- mutual love;
- faithfulness;
- public acknowledgement;
- sexual relations;
- shared surname;
- children;
- endurance;
- stability;
- interdependence; and
- devotion.

It is only when the external aspects of the relationship are viewed in the context of the more emotional and less tangible side of the relationship that their proper significance can be determined. I believe that this is what the Commissioner meant in CIS/87/1993, para 11 when he said:

"In my view the 'admirable signposts' place a wholly inadequate emphasis on the significance of the parties' 'general relationship'. Indeed, it is arguable that it is the parties' 'general relationship' that is of paramount importance and that their sexual relationship and their financial relationship are only relevant for the light they throw upon the general relationship."

If this is what the Commissioner had in mind, I respectfully agree. Of course, this does not mean that all of these characteristics must be present and it must be remembered that a couple may be living as husband and wife even though their relationship is unsatisfactory and unhappy.'

Practitioners will see the usefulness of expanding the list along the lines of *Fitzpatrick* if only to deny such factors are present in a given case. Helpfully, the DMG cites the case and the factors as set above, stating that 'there is more to the determination than the cold, observable facts'[1], though the DMG also observes that not all these factors need to be present for there to be a couple, further noting that 'a couple may be treated as LTAMC even though the relationship is unsatisfactory or unhappy'[2].

It is one of the very few instances in which *love* is mentioned in the case law. Perhaps that goes to the elusiveness of love, where evidence is concerned – a difficulty implicitly recognised by Mr Commissioner Jacobs in *CIS/443/1998* in which he considered whether the tribunal below should have scrutinised emotions more carefully:

> 'The tribunal did not refer to the emotional side of the relationship. I have considered whether this shows that the tribunal failed to take into account a relevant consideration or applied the wrong principle. There is a limit to which it is possible to explain how a tribunal exercised its judgment to assess the overall significance of a combination of factors. There is a limit to which it is possible for the members themselves to understand the mental processes involved. It is not realistic to expect every single factor to be set out and its contribution to the decision explained. The law recognises this and does not require every process of reasoning to be set out.'

Notwithstanding the Commissioner's generosity around the Tribunal's failure to refer to emotion, it should be stressed here that the emotional dimension may well be exactly that ingredient that is somehow missing in an empirical enquiry, and there is good reason to adduce evidence (most usefully done orally) about such matters.

More recently, the same Commissioner, now Judge Jacobs, has pursued the very same focus on areas outside the six signposts, citing *Fitzpatrick* again in *PP v Basildon District Council (HB)*[3] and defending its relevance despite being a Rent Act case concerning a gay couple, and notwithstanding the outcome in the House of Lords. Developing the theme further, Judge Jacobs also cited *Nutting v Southern Housing Group Ltd*[4] in which, on appeal, the two questions the recorder had posed were endorsed by Evans-Lombe J as entirely adequate; they were:

> '(b) Is the relationship an emotional one of mutual lifetime commitment rather than simply one of convenience, friendship, companionship or the living together of lovers?
> (c) Is the relationship one which has been presented to the outside world openly and unequivocally so that society considers it to be of permanent intent – the words "till death us do part" being apposite?'

Mention of *lifetime commitment* in contrast to the *living together of lovers* would seem to set the test very high for the benefit-paying agencies, usefully for appellants. Judge Jacobs' view in *PP v Basildon* was strongly endorsed soon after by Judge Levenson in *JP v Secretary of State for Work and Pensions (IS)*[5], a case concerning whether an alleged same-sex couple met the LTACP test. Judge Levenson also cited the Court of Appeal in *Amicus Horizon Ltd v The Estate of Miss Judy Mabbott (Deceased) and Another*[6], and found that:

> 'the very fact that a party denies that there is an emotional relationship in itself severely undermines the notion that there is such a relationship and in my opinion

9.24 *Cohabitation and Welfare Benefits*

it would require very strong evidence indeed (and more than just disbelieving the claimant or witness) to displace that denial'.

1   DMG, para 11104 (Chapter 11) and also para E4094 (Chapter E4).
2   DMG, para 11105 (Chapter 11) and also para E4094 (Chapter E4).
3   [2013] UKUT 0505 (AAC).
4   [2005] HLR 25.
5   [2014] UKUT 0017 (AAC).
6   [2012] EWCA Civ 895 (see para 31).

Using the lists of factors: standing back

9.25 In *R(SB)17/81* Mr Commissioner Rice skillfully dovetailed the *R(G)3/71* 'three factors' with the *Crake & Butterworth* 'six signposts' so as to determine that the two tests are not at odds, they do correspond, and are essentially the same criteria. Clearly, the Commissioner suggested, a *household* test is an essential requirement. Also clearly, the tests relating to *financial relationship* and *sexual relationship* correspond precisely. Of the remainder of the 'signposts', *children* goes to both *sexual* and *general relationship* in the Shewan scheme, and *stability* and *public acknowledgement* go to *general relationship*.

More recently the trend in the authorities has been to look outside of the strict criteria, or more accurately to recognise that Woolf J had never intended them to be more than a starting point. Overturning a tribunal decision in which the six signposts had been used, Mr Deputy Commissioner Wikeley judged in *CIS/4156/2006* that the tribunal 'had erred in law by relying too heavily on the checklist of indicators'; the Deputy Commissioner drew approvingly on the decision by Mr Commissioner Goodman in *CP/8001/1995*:

'An adjudication officer or tribunal faced with such a problem is unlikely to achieve a satisfactory result by simply regarding the task as ticking off items on a checklist, without also standing back and asking itself whether having looked at all the detailed evidence about individual aspects of the claimant's living arrangements in the case before them, the relationship between her and the man she is alleged to be living with can fairly and justly be described in normal parlance as that of two people living together in the manner of husband and wife.'

Deputy Commissioner Wikeley essentially agreed, when it was argued before him:

'that the relationship between the appellant and Mr W was and is one of mutual support, being more similar to one of brother and sister than husband and wife, and that the tribunal should have looked at the totality of the relationship, rather than using the signposts as a checklist.'

There is no doubt that whichever set of factors is used as a starting point, by the practitioner or the DWP, there is ample authority for going beyond their limits. They should not be regarded as conveying the totality of a relationship. That said, if, as is likely, the DWP's submission is based on the six signposts, any factual or logical issues contained therein do need to be addressed in submissions for the client. Further, it is probably unwise to eschew the checklists altogether: note how Mr Commissioner Ward held a tribunal to have been in error of law for its failure to look at either set of factors or checklist. In *CIS/2074/2008* he held:

'There are two ways by which one can approach the point, but both of them lead to the conclusion that the tribunal erred in law: either, because they failed to consider the issue of whether a sexual relationship existed, thereby failing to consider, as they should have done, a potentially relevant "admirable signpost", or because they failed to apply the test in R(G)3/71, at very least in order to determine what significance any sexual aspect might have for the categorisation of the general relationship.'

But it is arguably the omission of potentially relevant points that was at fault, not the mere failure to have regard to the checklist. In other words, a submission that takes into account the right factors will not be penalised for its failure to cite the checklists.

Where one or other of the checklists is deployed in argument, it is equally important to argue, where this assists, that no single factor can be overriding, and in fact it is legitimate to argue that they have equal status, where this suits the client's factual circumstances. On this point however, a proviso follows below in relation to the 'household' factor. Tribunals should not 'stand back' too much though: in *JH v HMRC (TC)*[1] Judge Markus enjoined them not to apply any reasonableness test in order to decide the plausibility of a given arrangement:

'9. [. . .] it will generally be inappropriate for a tribunal to appraise evidence by reference to what a reasonable person would have done. The question for the tribunal is what the individual in question is likely to have done, not what some other (hypothetical or actual) person would have done. As both Sedley LJ and Pill LJ said in Gheisari, the fact-finder should appraise the person giving the evidence (paragraphs [13] and [21] respectively).

10. Judged by reference to this guidance, the tribunal's decision in the present appeal was made in error of law. The tribunal did not accept the appellant's evidence because it considered that it was improbable. It did so on the basis of what the tribunal would have expected a person in her position to have done, and in one instance the tribunal expressly applied the test of a "reasonable" person in the appellant's position. The tribunal did not, whether as part of a single fact-finding process or by considering the evidence in stages, consider whether the appellant's account was true rather than improbable. Had it done so, the tribunal would have had to consider matters such as the appellant's particular circumstances and her explanation for her actions or those of Mr W, and would have had to assess what it was likely that she or he would have done. Unfortunately, because of the underlying error in the tribunal's approach, in a number of respects it either did not ask the appellant to provide an explanation for her actions and choices.'

It is very important to urge tribunal judges to avoid such an approach, especially in regard to childcare choices parents have made, and arrangements that might be thought unorthodox by a socially conservative person.

With that firmly in mind, practitioners are advised to adduce evidence, insofar as relevant, on all the following sections.

[1] [2015] UKUT 0397 (AAC).

9.26 *Cohabitation and Welfare Benefits*

Members of the same household

How to approach the question

9.26 There is a hierarchy of persuasiveness as to the household factor. In order of the strength of argument they generate, possible scenarios are:

(a) there is no such person as the alleged partner (this option is passed over here as being one unlikely to produce a realistic challenge by the department);
(b) there does exist such a person but they live elsewhere: the strongest position in the household argument (see **9.30**);
(c) the alleged partner does stay over sometimes but still mainly lives elsewhere (see **9.32**);
(d) the alleged partner lives at the same address but there is no shared household: harder still but not impossible to argue (see **9.34**);
(e) there is a shared household with the alleged partner: here one must concede defeat on the household factor and move on to alternative supporting factors, for example the non-spousal purpose of the relationship (see **9.37**).

What the Handbook said

9.27 The Supplementary Benefit Handbook – endorsed in *Crake & Butterworth*, stated:

> '*Members of the same household.* The man must be living in the same household as the woman and will usually have no other home where he normally lives. This implies that the couple live together wholly, apart from absences necessary for the man's employment, visits to relatives etc.'

Is the household test overriding?

9.28 In applying the six signposts or any other chosen combination of factors, the household test *is* largely over-riding in the sense that if they do not share a household (and cannot be deemed to), they probably cannot be a couple. But where there is some kind of a shared household, or this is unclear, then the other factors come into play and will need to be addressed by your client.

That this is a necessary but not sufficient characteristic of the circumstances is confirmed by a number of authorities. In *R(SB)17/81* Mr Commissioner Rice held at para 11 that:

> 'it is axiomatic that the man and woman concerned must be living in the same household. This requirement is not spelt out specifically in Decision *R(G)3/71*, but only, in my judgment, because it is self-evident.'

Lest this be seen as a principle confined to the pre-1977 rules (which *were* more explicit on the point), Mr Commissioner Jacobs confirmed this in *CIS/443/1998* at para 11:

> 'Many factors have to be considered when determining if parties are living together as husband and wife. Few are capable of being decisive on their own. One is whether the parties live in the same household.

11.1 It is only in the most unusual circumstances that parties who are not living in the same household can be living as husband and wife: see the judgment of Neuberger J in *Re Watson (Deceased)* [1999] 1 FLR 878 at page 883. So, **the fact that parties are not living in the same household is likely to be decisive.** However, temporary absences from the shared accommodation do not necessarily show that the common household has been disbanded: see Neuberger J at pages 882–882 and the decision of the Commissioner in *R(SB)19/85*, paragraph 11.' (author's emphasis)

In *CIS/7249/1999* the Secretary of State appeared to concede that a shared household is a prerequisite:

'the first step is to determine as a separate issue whether the parties are members of the same household. Only if the answer is "yes" can the tribunal go on to consider whether the parties are living together as husband and wife.'

and Miss Deputy Commissioner Ovey, hearing the case, appeared to agree, though with a reservation:

'[W]hile it seems clear that an essential element of any decision that the parties are living together as husband and wife is that that they should be living in the same household, it may not be helpful to describe that as a wholly separate issue. It is not a distinct statutory requirement and is one of the six factors set out in *R(SB)17/81*; [. . .].

I make [that] point because the submission points towards a completely isolated approach to the question whether the parties are living in the same household, and I am not persuaded that that is correct.'

The necessity of sharing a household was plainly accepted by Judge Williams in *VG v Secretary of State for Work and Pensions (IS)*[1]: that 'there must be a common household' had been emphasised from the start in the *Supplementary Benefits Handbook* even if not in *R(SB)17/81* which endorsed the Handbook. However, the language in *R(SB)17/81* had given rise to an issue when it stated the test as being whether the couple were *wholly* living together. Here they were not wholly living together as the partner was prevented from sleeping by one of the children and as he needed his sleep because of his job, he slept elsewhere when working. *Normally* or *ordinarily* might be better qualifiers than *wholly*, thought Judge Williams; it was a question of probabilities.

So where the client does *not* share a household with the alleged partner it should be strenuously argued – and evidenced – that this is the case and that the issue is conclusive as to the client's single status. If decided in his or her favour then (ie the finding is that there is no shared household) it ought to be determinative and the other factors should drop away as irrelevant and the case won. However, the other factors must still be addressed, just in case the tribunal or decision-maker consider the rare possibility of a cohabitation finding despite absence of a shared household.

[1] [2012] UKUT 470 (AAC).

Does the client share a household?

9.29 Unlike other factors, defining 'household' is assisted in cohabitation cases by case law concerning married couples just as much as by those relating

9.29 *Cohabitation and Welfare Benefits*

to unmarried couples, because the question bears heavily on married cases. The early social security cases involving marriage rely in turn on family law case law to a great extent.

The existence of a shared household may or may not be obvious. The legislation does not define 'household': this much was clear to Mr Commissioner Powell when deciding *R(IS)1/99*, in which the issue was whether couples living in residential care homes were capable of being treated as living in the same household. The five joined cases all concerned married couples, but the issue was clear: was there in each case a household? Drawing on the judgments of Mr Commissioner Sanders in both *CIS/671/1992* and *CIS/081/1993*, Commissioner Powell held that a domestic establishment was an 'essential attribute' of a 'household', and that such a domestic establishment must 'involve a group of two or more persons living together as a unit where that group enjoys a reasonable level of independence and self-sufficiency'. Perhaps this gives more guidance where the distinction must be made within the residential care home context of that case than in situations in which the client is arguing that she alone runs her own household and the alleged partner is not part of it.

Notwithstanding housing case law such as *Crawley Borough Council v Sawyer*[1], a person cannot be part of two households at the same time: *R(SB)8/85*, confirmed by Mr Commissioner Rice in *CIS/11304/1995*, though in that case the alleged partner did have two households but did not occupy them at the same time (he was occupying one for half the year, and the other for the other half of the year).

In relation to matrimonial cases, Sachs LJ, giving judgment for the Court of Appeal in *Santos v Santos*[2], distinguished between 'house' relating to 'something physical', and 'household', 'a word which essentially refers to people held together by a particular kind of tie', noting too that 'household' 'connotes being in the same family: *English v Western*[3]'.

In *Re Dix*[4] Ward LJ approved the approach taken by the Court of Appeal in *Santos v Santos*:

> 'The relevant word is "household" not "house", and "household" bears the meaning given to it by Sachs LJ. Thus they will be in the same household if they are tied by their relationship. The tie of that relationship may be made manifest by various elements, not simply their living under the same roof, but the public and private acknowledgment of their mutual society, and the mutual protection and support that binds them together. In former days one would possibly say one should look at the whole consortium vitae. For present purposes it is sufficient to ask whether either has demonstrated a settled acceptance or recognition that the relationship is in truth at an end. If the circumstances show an irretrievable breakdown of the relationship, then they no longer live in the same household and the Act is not satisfied. If, however, the interruption is transitory, serving as a pause for reflection about the future of a relationship going through difficult times but still recognised to be subsisting, then they will be living in the same household and the claim will lie. Just as the arrangements for maintenance may fluctuate, using Stephenson LJ's expression in *Jelley v Illiffe* [1981] Fam 128, 136, [. . .] so the steadfastness of a commitment to live together may wax and wane, but so long

as it is not extinguished, it survives. These notions are succinctly encapsulated in the judge's test, which was to ask whether the relationship was merely suspended, and I see no error in his approach.'

The particular kind of tie needs to be specified by the party alleging cohabitation then, and if it is not, the client must highlight the absence of this part of the department's argument. Alternatively, s/he will need to rebut such 'ties' as are contended for by the department, or show that such an arrangement is temporary only.

[1]   (1988) 20 HLR 98.
[2]   [1972] 2 WLR 889, [1972] Fam 247.
[3]   [1940] 2 KB 156.
[4]   Also reported as *Gully v Dix* [2004] EWCA Civ 139, [2004] 1 WLR 1399.

The alleged partner lives at a different address

9.30 The strongest arguments against the existence of a shared household usually show that the alleged partner lives altogether elsewhere. Living together must on the whole mean that neither alleged partner has some household elsewhere at the same time where s/he normally lives. If it can be shown that your client's alleged partner has another address where he lives, that will often make the most conclusive case for the client's single status. Your client's ignorance of his address will undermine her case.

CHECKLIST: POINTS TO ADDUCE ON ALTERNATIVE ADDRESS

9.31 Evidence will be needed as to the reality of his/her living at the other address, and should be adduced in regard to whether he/she:

(a)   can provide an actual address;
(b)   pays rent or a mortgage on the other property (produce documentary evidence eg tenancy agreement or mortgage statement) or is otherwise allowed to live there (eg as a non-dependent: if this applies, is the main householder there subject to non-dependent deductions from their Housing Benefit, Council Tax reduction scheme or benefit for mortgage interest?);
(c)   is liable for council tax there as a resident (council tax bills will assist);
(d)   receives mail there (best if examples can be produced);
(e)   is based there as far as other authorities or agencies are concerned (utility bills are always useful evidence);
(f)   spends time there;
(g)   sleeps there (mostly);
(h)   eats there;
(i)   does domestic tasks like washing clothes there;
(j)   is regarded as living there by friends and relatives;
(k)   knows his neighbours there;
(l)   receives other friends, family, relations, his children, as guests there;
(m)   is registered there for the purpose of the electoral register (see 'public acknowledgement' below); and
(n)   keeps some, most or all of his belongings there[1].

9.31 *Cohabitation and Welfare Benefits*

There will be other factors that practitioners can add in as circumstances permit. An inability to produce such evidence is likely seriously to damage your client's credibility. But documents may not always suffice. The tribunal below in *CIS/3655/2007* had been unconvinced that documents merely showing another address for the alleged partner (at which he was registered in respect of various agencies) amounted to proof that he was living there. Though it is not the main ratio of the case, Mr Commissioner Jacobs held that it was rational for the tribunal to have found the documents did not prove where he was living. That can cut both ways though; documents appearing to place the alleged partner clearly as living at your client's address do not inevitably establish him as living there. Sometimes the department's own evidence, especially when it comes from credit references agencies like Experian, will actually show one or more alternative addresses for the alleged partner, and if so these should be seized upon as possible pointers to him living elsewhere: this was a determinative point in *SW v Secretary of State for Work and Pensions (TC)*[2].

Also, in *TS v HMRC (TC)*[3] Judge Ovey expressed that caution should be exercised in relation to reliance upon the 'financial footprint'. There may be many reasons why, for people who have had joint finances and other arrangement (for example in relation to a mortgage, rent, payment of bills, bank accounts), names remain and have not been altered. It does not mean that there has been a lack of separation.

[1] Mr Commissioner Ward urged that the tribunal below in *CIS/2074/2008* should have asked about whether the claimant's daughter-in-law noticed 'evidence of Mr Tripp's belongings' when she visited her mother-in-law.
[2] [2015] UKUT 0394 (AAC).
[3] [2015] UKUT 507 (AAC).

The alleged partner stays over but it is not a shared household

9.32 There is a commonly-held belief in the existence of a 'three-night rule' or sometimes, a 'four-night rule'. These 'rules', though often propagated by claimants, advisers and departmental officials alike, do not actually exist, however. The gist of the belief is that if an alleged partner stays overnight with the claimant for so many nights a week, this is taken to prove the sharing of a household and hence a living together arrangement; by the same token a client will often assume that if he stays with her only two or three nights a week she is exempt from the living together rule. Though it contains a grain of truth, it must be resisted as any kind of satisfactory test: staying over may be one pertinent factor but it does not of itself prove or disprove a shared household, far less a cohabitation arrangement.

Evidence on this is sometimes sourced from one of the benefit fraud hotlines, and if factually wrong it must of course be corrected and rebutted where possible.

CHECKLIST ON STAYING OVER

9.33 If it is true that the alleged partner sometimes stays, the arguments must be that:

(a) the alleged partner's other address is his/her main residence;
(b) the staying-over pattern is variable;
(c) the purpose of the stay-over is:
 (i) social (TV, drinking, playing cards);
 (ii) not connected with sex;
 (iii) connected with childcare in respect of a mutual (or not) child;
 (iv) to do with support for a friend;
 (v) for company;
 (vi) for work reasons; or
 (vii) to provide overnight care in respect of a person with disabilities or illness.
(d) even if the argument as to main residence is lost (ie it is found that the number of times of staying over amounts to living there and therefore that the household is shared): that the sharing of the household is not conclusive as to cohabitation – ie the other factors come into play so as to eclipse the importance of shared household;
(e) apply *Re Dix* and *Santos v Santos*.

Some of the arguments in this list also go to the question of whether any agreed relationship actually has a different purpose from that of living like spouses or civil partners: see **9.39**.

Of some concern is Miss Commissioner Fellner's logic in *CIS/2900/1998* (a marriage case admittedly) in which the argument that the parties were not members of the same household foundered not least on the basis that the appellant received the highest rate of Disability Living Allowance Care Component; the onerous day and night-time care conditions for this entitlement 'did not support the assertion of separate households' in the Commissioner's view. Note that this case concerned two people who were married to each other, who had separated and then the wife moved back in order to fulfill a carer role in respect of the husband. Disproving a household was all important therefore. It is submitted that on the same facts in an unmarried case, such a claimant would have had some prospect of success.

The self-evident sexual overtones of the three-nights/four-nights allegation cannot be ignored: any such insinuation must be confronted head-on, and the department asked for a full submission on what precisely is being alleged, and the matter resisted, even in the face of scepticism, if untrue: see below at **9.45**.

They live at the same address but in separate households under the same roof

Separating the households out

9.34 The facts may be that the alleged partners do indeed live at the same address but maintain separate households under one roof. The issue is still more likely to arise outside of cohabitation territory – ie in cases where the parties are still married or civil partners, are about to divorce or dissolve the civil partnership, still live under the same roof, but are arguing they no longer share the same household. But it can still be important in alleged cohabitation cases; sometimes this will be where the alleged partners *were* married or civil

9.34 *Cohabitation and Welfare Benefits*

partners but are now divorced or the civil partnership dissolved. Or they may have had an admitted cohabitation relationship, as in *CIS/443/1998*, which they say is now at an end, though they are still in the same dwelling. The more general arguments as to household tend to be similar, whether marriage or civil partnership is/was involved or not.

CHECKLIST FOR 'SAME DWELLING – SEPARATE HOUSEHOLD' CASES

9.35 The case is stronger if your client and the alleged partner:

(a) have separate food storage areas in the kitchen, including the refrigerator;
(b) do not eat together, share meals (even at separate times) or make drinks for each other;
(c) spend leisure time in different rooms of the house;
(d) do not share family activities like outings, watching television, DIY or gardening;
(e) undertake childcare separately;
(f) separate their finances as much as possible (this is difficult given that your client is presumably on such a low income that their successful benefit claim is imperative);
(g) discontinue any sexual relationship;
(h) agree that the situation will not stay the same indefinitely: there is an intention that one of them will leave – whether before or after actual divorce/dissolution.

Sharing such things is not necessarily fatal to an argument that there is no shared household, however. In *CIS/72/1994*, as cited by Miss Commissioner Fellner in *CIS/2900/1998*:

> 'the only thing the wife was still doing for the husband was wash his shirts (in order to stop him running up electricity bills by using the washing machine for one shirt). He did his own catering, took the rest of his washing home to his mother, and sometimes at least contributed nothing to household expenses. The wife was doing everything she could to obtain separate accommodation for herself and the children.'

Such separation of households will often be investigated by a DWP visiting officer, or may be asked about in writing. If there is a home visit from the DWP, it can be important to seek the former spouse's/former civil partner's/former cohabitee's co-operation in corroborating these facts, should s/he be at home at the time of the visit. Alternatively, if s/he is likely to be uncooperative, the visit should be arranged when s/he is out. Unhelpfully for the appellant in *CTC/3864/2004* her alleged partner, in his evidence as to contributions to childcare, clearly credited himself with more involvement than did her version of the arrangements.

DMG notes that the DM should consider evidence relating to the following when making a finding as to whether a household exists[1]:

(a) The circumstances in which the two people came to be living in the same house;
(b) The arrangements for payment for the accommodation;

(c) The arrangements for the storage and cooking of food;
(d) The eating arrangements (whether separate or not);
(e) The domestic arrangements such as cooking, cleaning, gardening and minor household maintenance;
(f) The financial arrangements (who pays which bills? Is there a joint account? Whose name is shown on utility bills?);
(g) Evidence of family life.

[1] DMG, para 11055 (Chapter 11) and also para E4035 (Chapter E4).

9.36 DMG may assist here. One example at para 22016 of the Guidance may prove to be a useful template:

> 'Andy and Aniza are estranged and continue to live in the same house. They do not financially support each other or share domestic and social activities. One partner is reluctant to leave, until a satisfactory financial agreement has been reached with the other partner. **They each have separate households.**' (author's emphasis)

And also, a further example at chapter 11 para 11056 of the DMG:

> 'Louise had always lived with her mother, Carol. Andy was the son of Carol's oldest school friend, Maggie and was known to Louise since childhood. Andy had been injured in an accident some years ago and was confined to a wheelchair. Maggie was his carer. Carol went to live abroad and Louise remained in her mother's house alone. When Maggie died, Andy was faced with the need to find another carer. After talking over the situation, Louise agreed to become Andy's carer. As Louise and Andy lived 75 miles away from each other, it was decided that Louise would move into Andy's home which had been specially adapted for his needs. The agreement was that Louise would help Andy with dressing and cook his meals. Andy would pay Louise £100 per week for this but she would not be required to contribute to the cost of the rent. They maintained separate financial arrangements and the LA provided assistance to Andy with cleaning, gardening and household maintenance. Louise would take 3 weeks off during the year to visit her mother, whilst Andy remained at home. Louise and Andy did not socialise together. *The DM decided that Louise and Andy were living in a shared household but were not LTAMC and therefore, not a couple.*' (Author's emphasis)

Paragraph 11054 (Chapter 11) of the DMG and para E4034 (Chapter E4) enjoins decision-makers to recognise that:

> 'However, examples of two people living in one dwelling but not necessarily living together in the same household include:
> (a) lodgers or students who necessarily share a single gas/electricity supply etc. and may have an arrangement to share costs for items such as food and cleaning materials; or
> (b) two people who are married to each other or who are a civil partner of each other who separate and/but refuse to leave the home.'

It is instructive to note the types of scenarios which, in married couple cases, have produced a finding that there was **no** shared household:

(a) living separately under the same roof but the husband financially maintaining the wife;
(b) exclusive occupation of separate rooms within the same dwelling[1];
(c) sharing a room but living separately in other respects[2];
(d) husband and wife with dementia sharing a room in a residential care home but unaware that they were married[3];

(e) husband and wife sharing a double room in residential care accommodation, taking main meals in the dining room, giving mutual assistance with self-care but not living together as an independent and self-sufficient unit which would constitute a domestic establishment[4];

(f) a 30-year attachment living together for companionship but without a sexual relationship[5].

These examples may be invoked in cohabitation cases, bearing in mind that factual similarities are not binding, much less a guarantee of a similar outcome. The existence of two households under the same roof was well illustrated in *R(SB)4/83* in which the 67-year-old widower claimant was in poor health with relapsing acute bronchitis, and let out two rooms in his council house to a Mrs P partly with the purpose of her attending to him in emergencies. Mr Commissioner Mitchell took the view that

> 'a person who has, and lives in, his own separate home cannot reasonably be regarded as being a member of someone else's household. In the case under appeal, Mrs P clearly had a home of her own. She had the exclusive occupation of two rooms, which she herself had furnished. She bore her own costs in respect of lighting and heating. She bought and cooked her own food and provided for herself such other household goods as she required. **All this is quite incompatible with her having been, at the same time, a member of the claimant's household.**' (author's emphasis)

[1] *R(SB)4/83*.
[2] *CSB/463/1986*.
[3] *CIS/671/1992*.
[4] *R(IS)1/99*.
[5] *Re Watson (deceased)* [1999] 1 FLR 878.

SHARING A DEGREE OF FAMILY LIFE – BUT PERHAPS NOT AS A COUPLE

9.37 Such advice is borne out by the cautionary story in *CIS/443/1998*, in which the facts bear some detailed scrutiny in this regard.

Although the alleged partners had never been married, they had had a relationship between 1969 and 1979, during which time they had a daughter. They remained living in the same house, and had done so continuously since 1979. He had claimed Income Support in 1988 and Housing Benefit in 1995, stating on both claims that she was his partner. Their latest home was rented in joint names; they had separate bedrooms and had not had a sexual relationship since 1979. The furniture was owned by both. They ate together if they were both at home. The claimant did the decorating, small repairs and the gardening. She did the laundry and the shopping, although he sometimes came to the shops with her. They shared the housework, cooking and washing up. She paid for the food and household items, and he paid the other bills. He also said that he bought his own toiletries. Although he enjoyed painting, they watched television together and went together for a drink or to visit relatives. He said that they shared accommodation for convenience and because it was cheaper than living separately. She wished to retain her independence and her separate finances, which was one reason why their relationship had foundered in 1979.

The tribunal had found they were living together as husband and wife, and the claimant appealed.

Confining his judgment carefully to his reviewing jurisdiction (had the tribunal below erred in law in the way it undertook a balancing exercise as to the various factors?), Mr Commissioner Jacobs held in his determination that there had been no error of law; the facts which were largely agreed were capable of a living-together conclusion, and the tribunal had been entitled to reach this view. As to the absence of sex since 1979, see below under that section.

By contrast, in tax credits case *CTC/3864/2004* Mr Commissioner Mark agreed that the tribunal had erred in law in finding that the appellant was a member of a couple, and remitted the case for a fresh hearing, in the following circumstances:

The appellant and the alleged partner had also been living in the same household, since 1993, they had two children and both helped to run the household and look after the children. The evidence tended to show that they led separate lives even though, as father of the children, he had a relationship with them. There was evidence to support their leading separate lives, eg the claimant stated that he washed his own clothes, bought and cooked his own food (save for the occasional Sunday roast). There was no evidence that they represented themselves to other people as husband and wife, or that they socialised together, or had a family life together.

What if a shared household is proved though?

9.38 The argument will then shift to the other factors (which it does not where the parties are married or civil partners). Evidence on the other factors should be adduced not only to prove them in their own right, but as a means of revisiting the household issue so as to instil in the tribunal's or decision-maker's mind the possibility that the strength of the household finding at least requires some re-evaluation. As Mr Commissioner Edwards-Jones in *R(SB)35/85* observed:

> 'the existence of a common household – the fact as to which was not in dispute – was only one ingredient in the complex evaluation properly falling to be made.'

It is submitted that even a clear finding that there is a household may still disclose shades of meaning such that its importance as a factor supporting a couple finding is diminished. The closing comments of Mr Commissioner Edwards-Jones also help, where he exhorted (in vain as it happened) the then DHSS to reflect in its guidance the gist of Woolf J's view in *Crake & Butterworth* 'as to a couple "living together" being rather a starting point than a finishing point in the required evaluation, and as to what inquiry lay next'.

Miss Deputy Commissioner Ovey's decision in *CIS/7249/1999* provided an interesting matrix of facts in which the claimant lived with her former husband in his home. Since they were divorced, fortunately the full panoply of cohabitation criteria (here largely based around the 'six signposts') fell to be applied. The Deputy Commissioner found that there had been inadequate

9.38 Cohabitation and Welfare Benefits

findings and remitted the case for a fresh hearing. The known facts in the case are instructive though, insofar as they illustrate the evolution of a relationship from marriage to something rather different over some 30 years. On these facts however, there *was* a household so the issue shifted to whether other factors would disclose a living together relationship.

More recently the point was freshly endorsed (if that were necessary) by Deputy Commissioner Green in *CTC/3864/2004* who held:

> 'The main reason given by the tribunal for reaching th[e] conclusion [that on the facts of the case there was a couple] was that they had been living in the same household since 1993, they had two children and both helped to run the household and look after the children. The tribunal have erred in seeming to equate living in the same household as living as husband and wife. Living in the same household is obviously a significant factor, but there were other matters that the tribunal should have considered.'

Underlying this finding, like those in many other judgments, then, is the salient question of whether, where two people do share a household, they do so for some reason other than pursuing a life together as if spouses or civil partners. This is discussed next.

Alternative reasons

Living together

9.39 If the existence of a household shared by both the claimant and the alleged partner is proved, or indeed conceded, your argument must shift first to whether there can be an alternative explanation for the sharing of the household, preferably one that overrides any hint of a spousal or civil partnership-like couple arrangement.

Disability and care – and some general principles

9.40 Woolf J provided a useful principle in *Crake & Butterworth* before deciding favourably the case of Mrs Butterworth, a single parent with some disability following a car accident who, whilst divorcing her husband, had taken in a Mr Jones to perform household tasks and assist with looking after her:

> 'It is not sufficient, to establish that a man and woman are living together as husband and wife, to show that they are living in the same household. If there is the fact that they are living together in the same household, that may raise the question whether they are living together as man and wife, and, indeed, in many circumstances may be strong evidence to show that they are living together as man and wife; but in each case *it is necessary to go on and ascertain, in so far as this is possible, the manner in which and why they are living together in the same household*; and if there is an explanation which indicates that they are not there because they are living together as man and wife, then they [. . .] are not two persons living together as husband and wife.' (author's emphasis)
>
> It is impossible to categorise all the explanations which would result in [a finding that they are not cohabiting] but it seems to me that if the reason for someone living in the same household as another person is to look after that person because they are

ill or incapable for some other reason of managing their affairs, then that in ordinary parlance is not what one would describe as living together as husband and wife [. . .].

Quite clearly if that were not the position, housekeepers performing no other functions, other than those of housekeepers, could be regarded as falling within this paragraph. A couple who live together because of some blood relationship could be treated as falling within this paragraph. In my view it was not the intention of Parliament that they should.'

Practitioners are encouraged to ask clients in detail about the caring responsibilities taken on by co-householders alleged to be couples.

The approach was roundly endorsed by Mr Commissioner Edwards-Jones in *R(SB)35/85*, whose logic also went to the issue of sharing a household as a matter of expediency for a person with disabilities. In this case Mr W the alleged partner suffered from a war injury causing him pain, depression and memory lapses, and affecting his co-ordination; he went to live with the appellant and her brother as an admitted member of their household. Meals were taken together by both alleged partners; the appellant and her brother provided Mr W with help and care. The tribunal below had decided that there was cohabitation, because they were living in the same household and it was a stable and caring relationship, adding reassuringly, 'No moral judgment is being made and the tribunal hope the relationship and caring will continue'. The *moral judgment* point was well-made, if it meant they had not found that there was a sexual relationship, but ultimately the relationship was a bit too asexual for Commissioner Edwards-Jones to confirm the tribunal's conclusion as to couple status: in allowing the appeal he noted that:

'What one can [. . .] conclude with confidence is that such element of care as there was, together with elements of companionship and mutual convenience, explain why the claimant and Mr W were living together in the same household and in the context of the circumstances of the case as a whole constitute "an explanation which indicates that they are not there because they are living together as man [sic] and wife". And that, to my mind, is as far as one has to go.'

'As far as one has to go' creates a fairly untraversable line in the sand: once the non-cohabitation 'explanation' for the client's household is established, the case is won. If not, then at the very least the burden would appear to shift.

9.41 By way of example, in *EM v HMRC (TC)*[1], when re-making a decision in which an appeal was allowed, Judge Wikeley, after looking at the evidence in the round concluded that the appellant and Mr A were not a couple LTAHAW at the relevant time. They were a couple, and had a child. After moving out for a period of time the appellant returned to the home and resumed living under the same roof as Mr A. This was found not to be a step taken in order to revive the previous relationship, as there were a number of reasons why the appellant was 'driven back', including financial pressures, and Mr A's health. Judge Wikeley concluded 'rather as in *Butterworth*, this was a relationship which had the hallmark of one between a carer and a disabled person being cared for, rather than one that was like husband and wife'.

In these early cases it is hard to avoid an underlying presumption (useful to those claimants) that disability and a sexual relationship had to be mutually

9.41 *Cohabitation and Welfare Benefits*

exclusive, and it is submitted that this partly explains the dichotomy between the favourable treatment in cases such as *Robson* (see below), *Butterworth* and *R(SB)35/85* compared with the tougher line taken in the sexually more active cases of *R(G)3/71* and the bed-sharing pair of students in *R(SB)17/81*. Underlying *that* assumption was the understated acknowledgment that in defining a 'couple', sex matters: more of which below. In practice the absence of a sexual relationship does need to be made clear; practitioners should be more careful nowadays, in the author's view, to underline the facts in scenarios where the carer relationship is a primary, but not the sole, characteristic of the relationship. Perhaps evidence such as that concerning the locks on the bedroom doors of both Mrs Butterworth and the gentleman alleged to be her partner will be decidedly helpful.

Robson v Secretary of State for Social Services[2] held to the pattern, if such it be, on facts also involving bereaved and disabled claimants:

> 'In November 1979 the appellant, a widow aged 45, and Mr Williams, a widower aged 65, moved into a two-bedroomed council flat. They were both severely disabled and each required the use of a wheelchair and invalid car. They had been long-standing friends before the deaths of their respective spouses but there had never been any kind of sexual relationship between them. Although they were free to marry each other they had no intention of doing so.'

And:

> 'It is not alleged that they are now sharing a bedroom or ever have been.'

Allowing the appeal and remitting for a fresh hearing, Webster J gave the new tribunal a strong steer:

> 'There is not, and never has been, any sort of sexual relationship; they moved into the same house, on the face of it, because they were advised so to do by a social worker for the purpose of sharing, and therefore reducing, their expenditure; they are both free to marry and have not done so; there is no suggestion that they either regarded themselves as husband and wife or that they have been regarded or treated as husband and wife; and, most importantly, they are both very severely handicapped, a fact that provides a wholly understandable motive for their wishing to live together other than as husband and wife.'

The references to intention, motive and purpose are issues to which this chapter returns below at **9.43**.

Can receipt of a disability benefit reinforce *caring* as the main reason for sharing a household so as to displace the living-together as husband and wife reason? It is submitted that in theory it could. But the limited treatment of the matter in the case law is not that encouraging. The fact that the claimant in *CIS/087/1993*[3] received only the lowest rate of Disability Living Allowance Care Component seems to have caused Mr Commissioner Rowland to doubt the primacy of a carer/patient relationship, though in the context of a dearth of findings on sex, which might have been determinative in the re-hearing that he ordered. Further, Miss Commissioner Fellner's take on the receipt of highest rate DLA Care Component in *CIS/2900/1998* has already been cited above at

9.33; it merely added weight to a shared household finding in her view (in a marriage case, however).

1   [2018] UKUT 220 (AAC).
2   (1982) 3 FLR 232.
3   Also reported as *Re J (income support: cohabitation)* [1995] 1 FLR 660.

Other reasons for living together in the same household

9.42 The cases overall (including some married couple cases) disclose plenty of engaging obiter comment on, or just examples of, scenarios which it is sometimes suggested Parliament could not possibly have intended to catch in the living-together net. Though not amounting to binding authority, useful examples include:

(a) saving money[1];
(b) housekeeper[2];
(c) lodger and landlady;
(d) patient and carer[3];
(e) attending to a person in case of emergency connected with acute bronchitic attacks[4];
(f) companionship – the presence of another human being in an otherwise lonely establishment[5];
(g) elderly widow and elderly widower choosing for companionship in old age to live together, pool resources and care for each other[6];
(h) circumstances akin to a brother and sister who happen to live together in a close and affectionate relationship[7];
(i) mutual support[8];
(j) grown-up students sharing a household and living expenses[9];
(k) adult brothers and sisters living together;
(l) retired people living as friends;
(m) living with an 'old family friend'[10];
(n) living together prior to marriage and prohibited from having pre-marital sexual relationship by religious beliefs[11];
(o) convenience and absence of other resources[12];
(p) in order to comply with a curfew order[13].

The assessment exercise of whether Parliament can have intended such-and-such a case to be caught by cohabitation rules is admittedly a risky one, but perhaps it translates usefully into a criterion for testing the *reasonableness* of deciding that a given pair of people are a couple on a par with a married couple or a civil partnership.

Practitioners are strongly advised to consider very carefully the evidential issues that arise in such claims. In the absence of an intrusive degree of evidence, claimants alleged to be members of a couple will be hard-pressed to show that the 'mutual support' they claim as the sole basis of the relationship is no more than that. And yet again, these issues remind us that what seems to matter more than other indicators (even if this is often disclosed only in the authorities' subtext), is sex.

1   *Robson*.
2   *Crake & Butterworth*.
3   *CIS/087/1993*.

4 R(SB)4/83.
5 R(G)3/81.
6 R(SB)35/85.
7 CP/8001/1995.
8 CIS/4156/2006.
9 CP/8001/1995.
10 CIS/2599/2002.
11 CSB/150/1985.
12 CIS/7249/1999.
13 CIS/1243/2007.

Future plans, intention, motive and purpose

Why living together?

9.43 Clients may find the question 'why do you live together?' strange and unnatural. But it is a question worth asking them. The replies may disclose a 'purpose' that is somewhere outside the sphere of why two people get married or enter a civil partnership, and if so that is a useful building block and part of the evidential picture in contending for 'single status'.

To some extent this notion overlaps with alternative reasons for living together, discussed above at **9.39**. But it may be that a less tangible purpose exists in the relationship that, whilst hard to specify or define, is enough to displace a cohabitation finding.

Mr Commissioner Rowland in *CIS/087/93* equated the 'general aspects' of a relationship with *why* the parties live together:

> '14. In any event, I accept the submissions of both the claimant and Mr Connolly [for the department] to the effect that the tribunal have erred in failing to record adequate findings in respect of the general relationship between the claimant and Mrs B. They should consider why the parties are living together.'

The question of *why* two people live together was explored in more depth by Mr Deputy Commissioner Wikeley, drawing on principles in *Robson v Secretary of State for Social Services*; in *CIS/4156/2006* the Deputy Commissioner held that:

> '[The tribunal] failed adequately to address the more fundamental question identified by Mr Commissioner Howell QC in *CP/8001/1995*. That question is this – why were the two parties living together?

> In *Robson* Webster J observed that:

>> "usually the intention of the parties is either unascertainable, or, if ascertainable, is not to be regarded as reliable. But if it is established to the satisfaction of the tribunal that the two persons concerned did not intend to live together as husband and wife and still do not intend to do so, in my judgment it would be a very strong case indeed sufficient to justify a decision that they are, or ought to be treated as if they are, husband and wife" (at p 236).

> In my judgment the tribunal in this case failed to deal with the question of the parties' intentions. This was because the appellant's evidence as to the circumstances in which she and Mr W came to share the same house again was not adequately

dealt with by the tribunal. The tribunal should have examined those circumstances more closely, and indeed whether matters had changed at all during the period since 1997.'

The Deputy Commissioner thus regarded the question *why* as leading inexorably to an inquiry about *intention*, and though they are not the same thing, practitioners should address both. Any evidence as to intentions may be important, though it must be said that a relationship in which a settled status quo obtains may not disclose any intention: it just subsists as it is.

9.44 Judge Wikeley in *EM v HMRC (TC)*[1] allowed an appeal against a living together finding (and re-made the decision) on the basis, amongst other matters, that the tribunal failed properly to engage with the arguments that the appellant had advanced as to *why* she and Mr A were no longer LTAHAW by the time of the 2013/14 tax year, despite living at the same address. He said:

> 'The moral of this case is that in cases in which it is alleged that a man and a woman have been living together as husband and wife it may be necessary to "drill down" into the facts to arrive at a decision that can be properly sustained on all of the evidence. It is not necessarily enough to ask: are they living together? In order to decide whether they are living together as husband and wife, one must also ask: if they are living together, why are they living together.'

WebsterJ had observed in *Robson* that intention is usually either unascertainable or unreliable. Evidence is often to be deduced from the observable facts in any case. Conduct matters insofar as it throws light on intention: per Mr Commissioner Rice in *R(G)3/81*, 'regard should be paid to the conduct of the people concerned since their intention cannot be ascertained without regard to that'.

It is submitted nevertheless that intention *can* also be ascertained by hearing the clients' evidence. Adducing their own statements as to intention will make a difference.

Lack of intention (of taking the relationship further for example), however, may assist the argument, where it can be substantiated somehow: it was indeed a salient factor in *R(G)3/81*. The appellant was a widow who had moved in with a man who provided her with free accommodation in return for her services as a housekeeper; she paid only a £5 per week contribution to the bills; they did not have a sexual relationship. Mr Commissioner Rice, allowing the appeal, found both parties were:

> 'at pains to point out that the relationship was totally different from that which they had previously enjoyed with their respected [sic] spouses, and they certainly had no intention of marrying, nor did they entertain any serious thought about it.'

And the disabled widow in *Robson* also had no intention of marrying.

Perhaps 35 years ago the lack of intention to marry carried more weight than now; but even then this feature did not assist another appellant whose case, *R(SB)17/81*, was determined by the same Commissioner the following day. This concerned two students at Sheffield University who had started living in a one-bedroom flat but returned to their parents during vacations, the arrangement continuing for a time after they completed their degrees. The Commissioner was not persuaded by the agreed lack of marital intention; disallowing the appeal, he held:

> 'In particular, the fact that they did not intend to marry – and I was told this was a feature of many student relationships of the kind under consideration – does not mean that they did not intend to live together as though they were married.'

It is not clear whether intentionality here relates to the future, or rather to what the intentions had been upon starting to share a household. It is submitted that the ambiguity persists to this day, though Deputy Commissioner Wikeley in *CIS/4156/2006* saw they were not identical and implied that both matter, in accordance with Webster J in *Robson*.

Practitioners are advised to address the intentions the client and the alleged partner had at the beginning of the relationship, at the beginning of the sharing of a household, and as to the future. A clear commitment to moving out and living separately will assist in proving single status. That the parties, on starting to share a household, had made some decision that they would live together as a couple, like the Sheffield students, will damage their case.

The client and alleged partner may be wholly without conscious – or any – motives. That itself should be plausible – people do drift into and out of relationships – and it may be useful to adduce their oral evidence that this is the case as a way of heading off the imputation of a marital-type intention. A client's visible bewilderment at the question 'why are you living in the same household?' need not damage the case at all.

Intention is *not* the same as why the parties share a household, and even once a clear view of intention is formed, the question *why* may still linger. A well-worded statement from the appellant, and perhaps the alleged partner too, may convince a tribunal judge that the purpose of living together makes your client's relationship unlike a married couple or civil partners.

1   [2018] UKUT 220 (AAC).

Sexual relationship

Sex does matter – but is it a determinative factor?

9.45 Ever since Mr Commissioner Shewan boldly placed sex at number one of his three-part list of factors in *R(G)3/71*, one jurisprudential fault line has been clear: between the obvious and undeniable fact that sex is a hugely important determinant of couple status in our society, and the equally powerful inhibition as to enquiring too deeply – some of the latter being mere unfounded reserve, but there being also a justified disquiet about state bureaucracies knowing what goes on between adults in the privacy of their bedroom (or elsewhere).

DWP sensitivity to accusations of intrusiveness has led to decision-makers being reluctant to even ask about this. Where your client does not have a sexual relationship with the alleged partner (and especially if they never have had) then this information should be volunteered, and must go into the whole equation.

Sex matters: as Miss Deputy Commissioner Ovey observed in *CIS/7249/1999*:

> 'Although the nature of the relationship between husband and wife will differ widely according to the enormous variety of circumstances in which married couples live, it seems to me undoubtedly the case that as a matter of general usage the expression "living together as husband and wife" is used when the meaning intended is that the relationship between the parties extends to a sexual relationship, and that the general expectation is that a significant element of the relationship between a married couple will be the sexual relationship.'

More recently the Court of Session has rowed back from that view a little in *DK v Secretary of State for Work and Pensions*[1], considering that the existence of a sexual relationship could not be determinative, and that none of the relevant cases indicated that a sexual element was an essential component of living together as husband and wife. Thus at para 18:

> 'The critical question in the present case is whether the appellant and GO were living together as husband and wife during the period from 1999 to 2012. For the reasons discussed above, the sexuality of GO cannot be determinative of that question. Nor can the existence or otherwise of a sexual relationship between the appellant and GO. These are no more than factors that may be relevant to the critical question.'

[1] [2016] ScotCS CSIH 84.

WHAT KIND OF SEX?

9.46 It had been argued that sex was so determinative that the test should be applied first, and that only then and if there was a sexual relationship should the inquiry turn to the other five 'admirable signposts'. Miss Deputy Commissioner Ovey resisted this approach, noting that sex is not so wholly determinative as all that, and that in any case there was a need to be more nuanced about sex than to bluntly determine its existence or otherwise: the question that had to follow, if there was a sexual relationship, was whether:

> 'the sexual relationship [was] one of a committed, faithful nature such as might be thought to be traditionally expected of married couples (as may be inferred from the continued status of adultery as a fact evidencing the irretrievable breakdown of a marriage), or was it of a more casual kind, in which the parties took advantage from time to time of the opportunities which their common household offered?'

Despite the Deputy Commissioner's reservations about the delicacy of investigating this detail, she appeared, obiter, to expand the possibility that a sexual relationship of a casual kind need not automatically result in a couple finding.

Sex, then, is not determinative as such. The existence or otherwise of a sexual relationship, important though it is to the couple concept, has never been absolutely conclusive, and it should remain open to alleged partners to argue that despite occasional sex they are not a couple.

What the Handbook said

9.47 The Supplementary Benefits Handbook endorsed in *Crake & Butterworth* stated:

> '*Sexual Relationship*. A sexual relationship is a normal and important part of a marriage and therefore of living together as husband and wife. But its absence does

9.47 Cohabitation and Welfare Benefits

not necessarily prove that a couple are not living as husband and wife, nor does its presence prove that they are. The Commission's officers are instructed not to question claimants upon the physical aspect of their relationship, though claimants may choose to make statements about it.'

The wisdom of departmental 'don't ask' policy in this respect has been called into question more than once, but it appears to remain in force. Whilst that hampers the tribunal's full fact-finding exercise, it is valuable for the claimant in one sense, in that it is hard for the department to argue for the existence of a sexual relationship as they will usually have no evidence, unless the claimant or the alleged partner volunteer this; moreover it is always open to the claimant to give oral evidence (if true) that there is no sexual relationship.

The judicial approach to the policy is discussed below; it is submitted that there is little mileage in practitioners seeking to challenge its lawfulness or arguing that it invalidates an adverse decision because it is irrational. Instead, focus should be placed on the low evidential weight of any departmental submission that relies on inference (eg 'They admit to sharing a bed') or guesswork.

The need for enquiry about sex

9.48 Mr Commissioner Shewan may have sought to avoid too much detail when he said in *R(G)3/71*:

> 'But there is no need to speculate on the extent to which intercourse took place. The fact that there was sexual intercourse [inter alia] goes a very long way, in my view, to establishing "cohabitation" within the meaning of the Act.'

Enquiring as to 'the extent to which intercourse took place' might now be considered appropriate, if not a duty. Repeated Commissioners have lamented the lacuna in the evidence that results from the 'don't ask' policy.

Most notably in *CIS/087/1993* Mr Commissioner Rowland expressed disapproval, and noted that the consequence might be tribunals paying more attention to sex in their questioning:

> 'I asked Mr Connolly how, if, as he accepted, the parties' relationship as to sex was an important consideration when determining whether they were living together as husband and wife, those charged with investigating the facts could properly be instructed not to ask about the physical aspects of the relationship. Mr Connolly said that a policy decision had been taken although he conceded that the instruction was, to use his words, "detrimental to the administration of the law". **In my view, the instruction is inappropriate in an inquisitorial system** and, where relevant – information is not volunteered, questions may have to be asked by the Department's officers and, on appeal, by tribunals.' (author's emphasis)

Eight years later the same Commissioner was lamenting in *CIS/2599/2002* how his words had gone unheeded:

> '3. On granting leave in the present case, I observed that the documents in this case showed that the instruction was still in force and that the evidence that the claimant and her friend had separate bedrooms seemed to have been regarded as irrelevant. I also asked whether, on the facts relied upon by the Secretary of State, there was

anything that suggested that the claimant and her friend were living together as husband and wife, rather than just living together in the same household.

4. In an otherwise very full and helpful response, the Secretary of State's representative has skirted round the question of the instruction not to ask a claimant whether he or she has ever had a sexual relationship with a suspected partner.'

Like the DWP decision-maker, the tribunal had not addressed:

'the question whether the claimant had ever had any sexual relationship with the man in whose house she was living and whether, if not, there was any reason to regard the claimant and her friend as living together as husband and wife rather than as friends.'

Mr Commissioner Jacobs was still noting the avoidance of the topic by 2007, stating in *CIS/3655/2007*:

'Other than reciting that the [sex] factor formed one of the "admirable signposts", the tribunal avoided the topic. Even without asking questions or information being volunteered, there was material known to it (such as the categorisation of the relationship as "common law" on the finance application form) from which the tribunal might or might not have seen fit to draw inferences on this point, but it did not appear to have considered the topic.'

Mr Commissioner Ward's subtly different take on the issue was expressed in *CIS/2074/2008* [2008] UKUT 8 (AAC):

'[The new tribunal's enquiry] will include a need to address by questioning and inference from other known facts the question of whether there is or has been a sexual relationship. Such questioning generally need not be unduly intrusive and should as a minimum give Mrs Jackson the chance to indicate whether she has never had a sexual relationship with Mr Tripp.'

9.49 The Commissioner considered the necessity or otherwise of asking those questions:

'In *CIS/2599/2002* Mr Commissioner Rowland stated that questions "may" have to be asked not that they "must" be asked. I do not regard this as a point of substance. In my view, the wording is concerned with ensuring that a particular "admirable signpost" could be addressed. It would not have been appropriate to lay down a hard and fast rule applicable to every case: for instance, even if information had not been volunteered, other information might have become available from which a tribunal could draw inferences on the point, without the need to ask questions.'

The consequence of this is that practitioners are unlikely to succeed in any attempt to rule sexual issues inadmissible. Even a degree of sexual detail is fair game. However, the corollary is that your client is entitled to adduce detailed evidence on the *lack* of any sexual contact (if that be the case) or on the non-sexual character of the otherwise close and even apparently intimate relationship. Where a tribunal makes an adverse decision based on speculation without a full ventilation of the sexual issues, an appeal to the Upper Tribunal may well lie on that point of law, if the matter would have been material. Noted already above is the case of *CIS/2074/2008* in which Mrs Commissioner Ward found an error of law in the sense that neither the *R(G)3/71* three-part test nor the 'six signposts' had been applied.

9.49 *Cohabitation and Welfare Benefits*

> 'There are two ways by which one can approach the point, but both of them lead to the conclusion that the tribunal erred in law: either, because they failed to consider the issue of whether a sexual relationship existed, thereby failing to consider, as they should have done, a potentially relevant "admirable signpost", or because they failed to apply the test in *R(G)3/71*, at very least in order to determine what significance any sexual aspect might have for the categorisation of the general relationship.'

Hence the problem, for the Commissioner, was that sex had been ignored, as had its relevance within the wider test of 'general relationship'. In a case, *DK v Secretary of State for Work and Pensions*[1], in which the appellant argued that she was not a member of a couple because her alleged male partner was gay, the Court of Session rejected the need for detailed enquiry about either his sexuality or whether it had any bearing on the appellant's couple relationship with him:

> '[22] Furthermore, we note that, if it were necessary for Tribunal to make detailed investigations about either a person's sexuality or the existence of a sexual relationship between two persons, an intrusive inquiry would be involved. It would often be difficult to reach any conclusion, because contradictory evidence on such matters would be unlikely. Thus the evidence in question would have to be assessed against any evidence pointing in the opposite direction, such as that the persons involved behaved towards others as if they were a couple. That is of course precisely the sort of evidence that the Tribunal treated as decisive in the present case. Consequently, in cases where sexuality or sexual relations are put forward as a reason for concluding that persons are not living as husband and wife, the practical difficulties of challenging that evidence directly make it particularly important that the tribunal should focus on the totality of the evidence rather than individual components. Those difficulties also indicate why it would be quite unreasonable to expect a detailed assessment of the particular evidence given about such matters.'

[1] [2016] ScotCS CSIH 84.

Claimant and alleged partner have never had sex

NO SEX EVER – YET COHABITATION A POSSIBILITY

9.50 The fact that the client and the alleged partner have never had sex is in practice a strong argument that they are not a couple. The DMG acknowledges this, thus: 'if two people have **never** had a sexual relationship, that is often strong evidence that they are not LTAMC'[1]. The authorities are however at pains to point out that this fact is not determinative: thus Mr Commissioner Rowland held in *CIS/87/1993* that:

> '18. It will also be relevant for the tribunal to ask whether the claimant and Mrs B have *ever* had a sexual relationship. However, even if the tribunal finds that the claimant has never had a sexual relationship with Mrs B, this may be one of those cases where the absence of such a relationship is not fatal to the adjudication officer's case.'

That proviso was connected with the sleeping arrangements: see below.

[1] DMG, para 11108 (Chapter 11) and also para E4097 (Chapter E4).

No sex ever – appeals allowed

9.51 Mr Commissioner Howell QC found in *CP/8001/1995* there had been no 'living together as husband and wife' – or at least not sufficiently that the claimant had any duty to report her living arrangements, in circumstances in which she, a policeman's widow, had let a room in her council house to a male lodger either 13 or 22 years younger than her (it is not clear), who had recently separated from his wife; they had met playing darts, he had moved in, and now they had a settled relationship. The word 'stable' is not used but it could well have described the scenario. They 'did not share finances', although interestingly he had allowed her, 'for convenience', to draw cheques on the account into which his wages were paid. By 1993, 13 years into this arrangement, they were going on holiday, took meals and watched TV together. There was no sexual relationship between them. It was in this case that the tribunal had:

> 'failed to "stand back" and consider whether the evidence really did show a relationship of the kind that exists between a husband and wife, over the whole or any part of the period at issue, or whether the arrangement might be equally explainable in some other terms such as that between a brother and sister.'

However, it seems to have been assumed by the tribunal (perhaps because the department had not really disputed it) – and this was not doubted by the Commissioner – that there had never been a sexual relationship; this does seem to have influenced the judgment.

More explicitly, there was not, and never had been, any sort of sexual relationship in *Robson*, in which the alleged couple were both severely disabled, lived together partly for cost reasons but to provide mutual care as well, and it was this inter alia that led Webster J to such an unequivocal conclusion as to the intention of the parties in moving in together: there was no cohabitation.

Also in *R(G)3/81* Mr Commissioner Rice made abundantly clear how determinative the sex question was in circumstances in which the 61-year-old widowed claimant had moved in with a man in what seems to have been a very 'proper' relationship. He was anxious to have companionship, it is true; but broadly she was his housekeeper in return for free accommodation:

> 'The relations between the claimant and Mr H seemed to have been somewhat formal, in that normally they would refer to each other by their respective surnames prefixed by "Mr" or "Mrs", as the case might be. Nearly every Saturday morning the claimant went to stay with her son or daughter until Sunday evening, and she had no dealings other than of a purely formal nature with Mr H's two daughters. Furthermore, Mr H had never visited the homes of the claimant's daughter or son.'

But even more to the point,

> 'Mr De Freitas [for the claimant] submitted that on the facts of the case the claimant and Mr H did not satisfy the criteria for concluding that they were living together as man and wife. He pointed out that there was no sexual relationship whatsoever. Indeed, they did not even kiss or hold hands, and on his putting the suggestion to them in turn when they came to give evidence, they rejected the suggestion with something approaching abhorrence. **I am fully satisfied that there was no sexual relationship whatsoever.**' (author's emphasis)

9.51 Cohabitation and Welfare Benefits

The appeal was allowed. Sex had been addressed head-on, even at the risk of causing abhorrence. This was right and proper: it mattered. Practitioners will note the value of 'something approaching abhorrence' in the course of oral evidence on this point; the facial language was no doubt persuasive and does seem to have carried the day.

ENGAGED TO BE MARRIED – BUT NO SEX YET

9.52 Clients refraining from sex prior to getting married, even though their pre-marital shared household resembles in most other respects the household they hope to maintain once married, may derive a degree of protection from the judgment in *CSB/150/1985*[1] which concerned an engaged couple sharing a household who did not have, and had never so far had, sex. They were prohibited from having a pre-marital sexual relationship by their shared religious beliefs. In those circumstances the judgment was that they were not living together as husband and wife, the logic being that the pre-marital relationship was being differentiated from the forthcoming marriage very unequivocally by their behaviour. The words 'as husband and wife' assumed even greater significance in such circumstances.

[1] Cited in *CIS/7249/1999*.

NO SEX EVER – FAILURE TO INVESTIGATE

9.53 Clients should be advised to distinguish carefully between different meanings of the word 'partner' in their dealings with the department. In a Pension Credit case, *CPC/3891/2004*, Mr Commissioner Mesher berated the department for its misunderstanding or falsification in relation to circumstances where:

> 'On the claim form [the claimant] said that he lived rent-free at R Boarding Kennels in return for assistance with the work of the kennels. He declared capital of £5,222.04 and stated that he did not have a partner. It appears that the Department already had some information that the claimant had ceased self-employment on selling a public house in 2002, so that a visit was carried out on 18 March 2004 to check the proceeds of sale and what had happened to the money. On the visit, an officer was informed by an employee of the owner of the kennels that the claimant and "his partner", the owner Mrs G, had had to go to America suddenly to deal with a family matter. A note was made for further investigation of whether they were business partners or partners in the sense of an unmarried couple.'

Despite an apparently inadequate investigation of what he might have meant by 'partner', the facts eventually emerged that there had never been a sexual relationship and that there was a credible explanation of the sharing of a household other than that the claimant and Mrs G were living together as husband and wife.

No sex now? No sex ever?: the evolution of the Handbook

9.54 In *R(SB)35/85* Mr Commissioner Edwards-Jones undertook a brief historical analysis of the changes made to the Supplementary Benefits Handbook through the early 1980s. He suggested that the version that Woolf J had

had in mind in *Crake & Butterworth* when endorsing the 'six signposts' was that of 1979 as cited above, and including the sentence:

> 'But [the] absence [of a sexual relationship] does not necessarily prove that a couple are not living as husband and wife, nor does its presence prove that they are.'

It is submitted that this version must be the one that is taken to be approved. But as the Commissioner noted, the revisions are of interest: by 1982 that sentence was supplemented by another that said:

> 'However, if a couple have *never* had such a relationship it is most unlikely that they should be regarded as living together as husband and wife.'

By 1983 this read:

> 'If a couple have never had such a relationship it may be wrong to regard them as living together as husband and wife.'

In 1984 the point was omitted altogether.

Mr Commissioner Edwards-Jones acknowledged that he had no judicial authority over the contents of the Handbook, but suggested it ought to reflect the real flavour of Woolf J's endorsement, that the 'signposts' were a starting point only. However his analysis of the amendments also reflected the Handbook's real engagement with how to deal with relationships that are and always have been non-sexual.

The publication of the Handbook expired altogether with the abolition of Supplementary Benefit in 1988, so the Handbook may seem to be history of a very dull kind now, but the very present potency of the 'six signposts' does mean its content still attracts regular scrutiny. Mr Commissioner Rowland was still grappling with its 'sex' advice in *CIS/087/1993*:

> 'It is arguable that the 1983 Edition of the Supplementary Benefits Handbook more accurately reflected what Woolf J actually said than the 1982 Edition did. Nevertheless, it does seem to me **that there must be strong alternative grounds for holding a relationship to be akin to be that of a husband and wife when there has never been a sexual relationship**, because the absence of such a relationship in the past does suggest that the parties may be living together for reasons other than a particularly strong personal relationship.' (author's emphasis)

And Ms Deputy Commissioner Green adopted the Handbook's approach directly, without any reference to *Crake & Butterworth* when she decided the tax credits case *CTC/3864/2004*:

> 'It seems that [the tribunal] did consider the sort of criteria [. . .] identified in the Supplementary Benefits Handbook, which although not of legal force, have been found helpful when considering whether people are living as man [sic] and wife in the social security field [. . .]. They may provide a useful starting point when considering this issue in the tax credits field.'

NO SEX AT THE MATERIAL TIME – COULD THEY STILL BE A COUPLE?

9.55 Essentially, the answer is yes. Mr Deputy Commissioner Wikeley considered the matter at length in *CIS/4156/2006* in which it had been contended

9.55 Cohabitation and Welfare Benefits

that a finding of no sexual relationship must be determinative. However, the Deputy Commissioner held:

> 'A finding that there was a sexual relationship at the material time **is not an essential stepping-stone** to a finding that two people were living together as husband and wife. It is, however, an important feature of such a relationship and this tribunal did not explain why it had discounted other highly relevant evidence on this point.' (author's emphasis).

This was consonant with Woolf J's opinion in *Crake & Butterworth* as to the essentiality of sex for a 'couple' finding:

> 'I should also make it clear that [the cohabitation finding] does not involve a finding that Mr Watts and Mrs Crake are having sexual relations. Neither counsel have suggested, for the purposes of the paragraph, that that is necessary and the tribunal in no way indicated that that was the conclusion which they had come to, and I certainly do not draw any inference as to that.'

Sleeping arrangements

9.56 Traditionally the sharing of a bed was, and perhaps still is, a proxy test for whether there is a sexual relationship; and 'sleeping together' of course has both a literal meaning and a euphemistic one. In *R(SB)17/81*, for example, the claimant and Miss G had moved into a 1-bedroom flat, and it was not in dispute that from that point on they had been 'sleeping together'. They were found to be living together as husband and wife.

SHARING A BED BUT NO SEX EVER

9.57 But clients who admittedly sleep in the same bed but never together, will not necessarily escape a 'couple' finding. It is axiomatic anyway that absence of sex does not necessarily indicate the parties are not living together as husband and wife (see, below, the discussion of *CIS/4156/2006* for example, and *DK v Secretary of State for Work and Pensions*)[1]. In *CIS/087/1993* Commissioner Rowland recorded the findings of the tribunal below, that:

> '[The claimant] volunteered the information that they had no intimate sexual relationship. He accepted that they slept in the same bed. However, he said that Mrs [B] goes early to bed and he then goes to bed at about 3am. When he goes to bed she gets up and sleeps in the living room.'

Taking no view on the plausibility of this account, the Commissioner continued:

> 'The claimant has not disputed the accuracy of that note. He tells me that he and Mrs B had been trying to move to a two bedroomed accommodation but only since shortly before the tribunal hearing. It seems to me that, in this day and age, **sharing a bed even at different times, does suggest a degree of intimacy or a surrender of dignity that could, when taken with other evidence, properly be regarded as connoting a relationship akin to that of husband and wife.** Obviously, the sharing of a bed as a very short term expedient might be viewed differently, but this was an arrangement that had been going on for years. It is the sort of situation that might give rise to the "unlikely" finding that a couple are living together as husband and

wife despite never having had a sexual relationship. That would be a matter for the tribunal to consider when they have heard any explanation offered by the claimant.'

[1] [2016] ScotCS CSIH 84.

SEPARATE BEDROOMS

9.58 If your client can truthfully claim to be sleeping in a different bedroom that is useful evidence to adduce. It goes to 'sexual relationship' but also to the intimacy alluded to by Mr Commissioner Rowland in *CIS/087/1993*. 'Separate bedrooms' occupy an important place in the range of factors militating towards single status.

Practitioners will recall Mrs Butterworth, in *Crake & Butterworth*, who had given evidence that:

> 'by arrangement with her daughter-in-law, Mr Jones moved into her home in about January 1979. She said that that gentleman **had his own bedroom with a lock on the door**; she had her bedroom also with a lock on its door.'

Similarly, though we are not told about locks, Mr W in *R(SB)35/85* 'had his own separate bedroom in the bungalow, and some of his own furniture there'. So too did the claimants and alleged partners in *CIS/2599/2002* (in which the single parent claimant had moved in rent-free with a man) and *Robson*. In none of those cases there was a 'living together as husband and wife' finding.

However, the claimant in *R(G)3/71* had less success in persuading Mr Commissioner Shewan that separate sleeping arrangements obtained, or, that if they did, this meant the parties must be single:

> 'The claimant said S slept on a couch in the living room. Whether one accepts the claimant's evidence as to the sleeping arrangements or not, it is obvious that sexual intercourse took place between the claimant and S; because on 10 July 1970 the claimant gave birth to a child of which S was admittedly the father.'

The Commissioner's robust scepticism did not serve the claimant well, and it is noteworthy that the possibility of sex outside the bedroom could be envisaged as early as 1971.

Previous sexual relationship, now ceased

ONE SINGLE INTERCOURSE ONLY

9.59 The case cited immediately above, *R(G)3/71*, is a cautionary example of why clients should not expect to rely on a once-active sexual relationship having diminished to sexual inactivity. That a single instance of intercourse might suffice to then colour the whole tenor of the subsequent relationship, is salutary. But Mr Commissioner Shewan's analysis bears scrutiny:

> '6. The claimant asserts that the birth of the child Elizabeth, of whom S is the father, resulted from an isolated act of intercourse. This may be thought improbable, in view of the fact that the overt association between her and S continued, apparently unchanged, after that admitted act took place. But there is no need to speculate on the extent to which intercourse took place. The fact that there was sexual

intercourse, which must have taken place just about the time when S came to live at the claimant's address, and that he thereafter continued to live at that address and to associate with the claimant in the manner hereafter to be described, goes a very long way, in my view, to establishing "cohabitation" within the meaning of the Act.'

Of course, the Commissioner struggled with the witnesses' credibility here – and that too remains instructive today. But even accepting the parties' account at its highest, his logic suggested it was not just the single act of intercourse that defeated the 'single status' claim; it was the way this fact acted upon the subsequent living-together arrangements. Even applying the Commissioner's own three-part test, two of the indicators ('sex' and 'general relationship') appeared to be capable of intertwining.

So where clients' evidence is that a previously sexually active relationship is now sexually dormant, such accounts must be handled with some care so as to avoid merely creating an impression that the relationship is similar to a sexually quiescent marriage. The unspoken question is whether it would be usual for a married couple to have allowed their sexual activity to diminish to the same degree.

NO SEX FOR 20 YEARS

9.60 The same advice is indicated by another case where there had been a previous sexual relationship. In *CIS/443/1998*, the facts were that:

'The couple had lived together continuously since 1979, despite having moved house. The claimant had described the lady as his partner when he claimed Income Support in 1988 and when he claimed Housing Benefit in 1995. In 1995 he had also told the Department of Social Security that she had ceased work and had no income. Their latest home was rented in joint names. They had separate bedrooms and had not had a sexual relationship since 1979.'

Mr Commissioner Jacobs held that the tribunal below had not been in error when it found that they were living together as husband and wife.

NO SEX FOR 10 YEARS

9.61 However, the shorter period (10 years) over which sexual activity had been discontinued (or at least 'not enjoyed': one assumes this is not a qualitative assessment) by the unmarried couple in *Re Watson (Deceased)*[1], was not enough, in Neuberger J's view, to cancel the existence of a cohabiting relationship – though that case concerned inheritance provision not social security and the claimant G had sought to argue that there *had* been cohabitation.

[1] [1999] 1 FLR 878, [1999] 3 FCR 595.

NO SEX SINCE ACCIDENT

9.62 In *Crake & Butterworth* the facts giving rise to Woolf J's finding that Mrs Butterworth was not cohabiting with her alleged partner Mr Jones may be distinguished from both the foregoing unsuccessful appeals, *R(G)3/71* and

CIS/443/1998. The evidence implied, rather than made wholly clear, that there had been a sexual relationship, but that following her car accident Mrs Butterworth:

> 'had suffered from amnesia and that she did not recognise Mr Jones when he moved into the house, and she says that there has been no sexual relationship whatsoever since that time.'

The basis of any pre-existing relationship had changed: this is an important qualifier, and clients arguing the diminution of a previous sexually active relationship should be advised to consider whether any factual circumstances have had a bearing on the level of sexual activity.

PREVIOUS SEXUAL RELATIONSHIP NOW CEASED: LOSS OF LIBIDO

9.63 It is therefore not just a question of how long the sexual element of a relationship has lain dormant. It is a question of *why*. Practitioners will need to enquire of clients why a sexual relationship became non-sexual, if that is what has happened. Mr Deputy Commissioner Wikeley addressed in detail the factually difficult case of *CIS/4156/2006*. The alleged couple in that case had never married but they had admittedly cohabited previously. The relationship had changed however. The facts superficially appeared to ground a strong case for a cohabitation finding:

> '[T]he appellant and Mr W have known each other for over 30 years. They lived together as cohabitants between 1975 and 1983. Mr W stayed intermittently with the appellant between 1995 and 1997. In 1997 Mr W moved in permanently to the appellant's house (a different property to the one they had jointly occupied between 1975 and 1983). Mr W has been in full-time employment throughout this period while the appellant has been receiving income support. In September 2005 the appellant bought her house from the local authority, under the "right to buy" scheme, using funds supplied by Mr W.'

That funding of the house looked almost conclusive. As the departmental submission writer had argued:

> 'How many carers would purchase a property for the person they are caring for? The mutual support and trust displayed by this action is more akin to a couple than to carers or friends.'

The pattern of facts was nuanced but not unusual in that:

> 'Mr W had assisted the appellant financially, had done DIY, bought furniture and shared bills 50:50, trusting her to tell him what his contribution is. He had helped her physically as her medical condition had required. Although he slept in a separate bedroom, he also used the kitchen, toilet and lounge. Mr W's work commitments and their different interests meant that they were not together continuously when in the house. They went out socially and Mr W "occasionally" went shopping with the appellant. The fact that they did not watch TV together or always eat their meals together was accounted for by their different interests and was not inconsistent with living together as husband and wife. The appellant helped him with his paperwork and cooked for him.'

It was also salient that 'The tribunal also found that Mr W "sleeps separately in a bedroom on the top floor of the house"', that Mr W had said 'that the fact

9.63 *Cohabitation and Welfare Benefits*

that they don't now sleep together is the only difference from the relationship they had had when they previously lived together between 1975 and 1983', and that she had said 'since their cohabitation ended in 1983 "we never slept together except once in 1986" [. . .] but 'that she had "not had much sexual feeling" since a hysterectomy in 1987'.

Confirming the tribunal's view that 'a finding of a sexual relationship was not an *essential* prerequisite for a conclusion that a couple were living together as husband and wife', the Deputy Commissioner nevertheless considered that inadequate findings had been made, and other evidence before it had been given too little – or no – weight; there was a positive finding that:

> 'Mr W had "stayed the odd night with the appellant" after his aunt died in 1994 and for a fortnight after the appellant had been admitted to hospital in 1995, followed by "occasional nights" until 1997',

but the tribunal failed to address the *capacity* in which he stayed. This was material; it went to the issue of:

> 'whether a previous sexual relationship evolved into one of abstinence or whether the parties embarked on an entirely different type of relationship after a gap of over a decade.'

The absence of sex following a period in which there had been a sexual element to the relationship needs explaining. The suggestion is that embarking on a completely different type of (non-sexual) relationship would give greater credence to a claimant's single status than the evolution into abstinence which could justifiably still be seen as living together as husband and wife. Mr Deputy Commissioner Wikeley drew in part on the reasoning, cited with approval, in the commentary in *Social Security Legislation 2006, Vol I: Non means tested benefits* at p 79 where it states that the current departmental guidance on living together:

> 'is correct in asserting that the absence of a sexual relationship at any particular time does not prove that the parties are not cohabiting – a 'common law marriage' may evolve into a state of abstinence from sexual relations just as easily as a marriage may, and the parties will not thereby cease to live together as man and wife . . .
> It should be repeated that the question is whether the parties' relationship sufficiently approximates to marriage, and in that the possibility of, or a history of, a sexual relationship is important.'

'Evolution into abstinence' then is a concept that must be dealt with: there is a potential pitfall here. Such a diminution in sexual activity, over the years, is arguably considered too close to what can happen in a marriage for the parties to be able to argue otherwise. But where it can be argued that your client and the alleged partner have indeed embarked on an entirely new kind of relationship, the scope for demonstrating a convincing single status is greater.

Once again the criticism the claimant sought to make of the way the tribunal below had handled the case was based inter alia on their failure to investigate.

Faithfulness – other sex partners

9.64 The concept of faithfulness was raised, though not analysed, by Mr Commissioner Jacobs when he cited the *Fitzpatrick v Sterling Housing Association*[1] test. Presumably it means refraining from sexual relations with somebody other than the other member of the couple, also known as adultery, whether secretly or openly. It is submitted that this must matter.

Little attention has been paid in the case law to the effect on the living together analysis where the alleged partner has a sexual relationship with another person, not the claimant. It will be hard to corroborate, unless the third party partner is called to give evidence. In practice, where the evidence on this is persuasive then this creates a very strong argument against couple status (as between the claimant and the alleged partner).

Mr Deputy Commissioner Wikeley suggested a clear approach to this in *CIS/4156/2006*, in which the appellant's evidence had been:

> 'that "he's been out with a few other females but he's not brought them back as far as I'm aware. I told him to be discreet as it's right above my bedroom". If an accurate account, and it does not appear to have been put to Mr W, the only relationship this is akin to is a so-called open marriage. Adultery and a lack of faithfulness between partners may be facts of married and unmarried life, and the statutory expression "living together as husband and wife" may be an elastic term, but I do not think that it can be stretched that far.'

'Committed' and 'faithful' were characteristics accorded to a traditional couple relationship by Miss Deputy Commissioner Ovey in *CIS/7249/1999*.

In *DK v Secretary of State for Work and Pensions*[2] the Court of Session did not find that there was any fatal tension between a finding of living together and the evidence from the female appellant's boyfriend that he was in fact gay. But that was in a context in which she had been unhappy with a failure by the tribunal to make findings on the boyfriend's sexuality (an argument rejected by the court). Her understated logic – that if he was gay that meant it was less likely he was in a sexual relationship with her – did not persuade the court.

The existence of another relationship, between the alleged partner and another, must be useful evidence to undermine a couple finding in relation to the claimant. Evidence on this – notably a statement from the third person – will be needed where the argument is run, and it is submitted that the other relationship must be in some way serious rather than a fleeting infidelity which might not suffice to undermine couple status.

[1] In *CIS/443/1998*.
[2] [2016] ScotCS CSIH 84.

Stability of the relationship

What the Handbook said

9.65 Stability. Living together as a married couple clearly implies more than an occasional or very brief association. When a couple first live together, it may be clear from the start that the relationship is similar to that of a married couple, eg the woman has taken the man's name and has borne his child.

What does stability mean?

9.66 It is sometimes hard to know what precisely is meant by the word 'stability' – one can legitimately read it as meaning:

(a) long-term, established, settled, changeless or constant etc, or alternatively as suggesting in some way:
(b) harmonious, congenial, like-minded etc.

If so, the arguments against 'stability' would tend to major either on features like brevity, transience, the uncommitted nature of an involvement, or on the degree of disagreement, argument and friction that exists between the alleged partners.

The original Handbook entry suggests that the notion is meant to exclude occasional, brief or fleeting relationships. That is useful, where it fits your client's fact-pattern. But it will not necessarily exclude relationships that are brand new yet with a clear intention, eg marriage.

It is submitted that the concept is a very loose one, and if used in a way that is unfavourable to your client, it may be worth querying the premise, ie suggesting that the meaning of 'stability' is not established beyond doubt, and may inadvertently import a number of value judgements, which should be removed from the equation.

However, it may be that the presence of other factors over time can embed the notion of stability: that was an obiter view suggested in *NA v Secretary of State for Work and Pensions (IS)*[1], as regards an extended period of living together and a sexual relationship.

Arguments might follow the logical pattern that if the clients truly were in a stable relationship as contended by the department, then one would not see evidence such as is adduced, eg, of:

(a) disharmony;
(b) lack of commitment;
(c) frequently changing intentions;
(d) arguing;
(e) intercalation of other relationships;

and there *would* by contrast be some evidence of:

(f) commitment;
(g) unanimity;
(h) faithfulness;
(i) endurance;
(j) mutual promises.

[1] [2012] UKUT 299 (AAC).

How is time spent together?

9.67 The DMG seems to prefer a different interpretation of the word 'stability', instructing decision-makers at para 11113, in order to ascertain the degree of stability, to have regard to 'the important signs' of:

> 'the way in which two people spend their time together and the way that this has changed while they have been together.[1]'

The Guidance then goes on to address[2], under the *Stability* heading, issues as to whether the two people do certain 'activities together or for one another: providing meals and shopping; cleaning and laundry; caring for the members of the household during sickness; decorating; gardening; caring for children; [. . .] DMs should also consider the way in which two people spend their leisure time and whether they take their holidays together'.

It is submitted that this advice is logically deficient and is possibly under the wrong heading ('General relationship' might have been a better section for it) in that there is no sensible connection between those activities and the degree of stability. They may well be proxy indicators of a relationship akin to marriage or civil partnership who live together, but they certainly do not suggest, even at a merely indicative level, stability as such.

Practitioners should therefore be ready to counter any suggestion by the department that such activities either necessarily or probably denote stability. Instability in a relationship may co-exist with decorating, gardening, childcare etc done on a mutual basis. The activities listed suggest a degree of interest in the home and in living together, but in reality they get us no closer to the core of what a couple is.

[1] Which is mirrored in Chapter E4 at para E4102.
[2] At para 11114 (Chapter 11) and also at Chapter E4 para E4103.

Impermanence

9.68 The impermanence of the student relationship in *R(SB)17/81* was no bar to a 'stability' finding by Mr Commissioner Rice:

> 'Account may be taken of the stability of the relationship but the absence of an intention to marry does not mean that the couple have no intention to live together as though they are married.'

He noted too the submission that 'in particular there had never been anything permanent about the relationship'. Nevertheless, this did not avail the claimant:

> 'having heard the evidence including the claimant's statement to the above effect the tribunal took the view that the claimant and Miss G were living together within the meaning of the relevant statutory provisions. I am satisfied on the evidence that the tribunal could properly have come to that conclusion. In particular, the fact that they did not intend to marry – and I was told that this was a feature of many student relationships of the kind under consideration – does not mean that they did not intend to live together as though they were married.'

Addressing, it is submitted much more pertinently than para 11114 (above), the temporal interpretation of Stability, the Guidance suggests at para 11116 that:

> 'It is for DMs to determine at what point a relationship should be regarded as LTAMC. The length of time two people have been together is not proof of the stability of a relationship. There is no specified time limit in determining the stability of the relationship and DMs should consider the following questions: (1) is there strong evidence that they have been LTAMC from the time they began living together, that would enable DMs to determine that LTAMC existed from the outset?; (2) are they living together as a temporary arrangement without commitment on either side? If so, DMs might determine they are not LTAMC; and (3) to what extent do they both take responsibility for the activities listed at DMG 11114? Where there is doubt about the stability, DMs might determine two people were not LTAMC.'

And at 11117:

> 'DMs should not assume a stable relationship exists just because two people have been LTAMC on a previous occasion.'

Here, the DMG advice is appropriate, and as has already been seen, relationships may evolve from something akin to marriage or to civil partnership into something else, remaining ostensibly 'stable' the whole time, yet further enquiry into the facts in such cases may reveal some erosion of the claimed stability taking place.

A settled relationship

9.69 *R(SB)35/85* is one of the few other cases to address stability, at least in passing. The context was one in which the disabled Mr W had come to live with the claimant, a widow, and her brother, contributing in cash and kind to the running expenses of the household, occupying his own separate bedroom with his own furniture. They ate together; she cared for him. Notably the arrangement had subsisted for 10 years at the time of the appeal.

> 'The claimant's case being that she and Mr W who though living in a common household and having a stable relationship were *not* living together as husband and wife, the tribunal needed to concentrate closely both in arriving at and in expressing reasons for decision upon what constituted as [sic] living together as husband and wife.'

And evidence accepted by the tribunal had included that:

> 'It is a stable and caring relationship.'

The degree of 'stability' here was still not enough on its own to persuade the Commissioner that the claimant and Mr W were living together as husband and wife (even though it was a perfectly sustainable argument to say that a married relationship might eventually look identical).

Relationship long-term but evolving?

9.70 That stability and longevity in a relationship are not necessarily the same is shown in the tax credits case *CTC/3864/2004* in which Ms Deputy Commissioner Green sought to mark out a distinction:

'The tribunal's reasoning that "clearly they have a stable and longstanding relationship" was flawed in that they seemed to place undue weight on the length of time they had shared a house, but failed to give adequate weight to the evidence that the relationship had changed from about six years earlier when they ceased having a sexual relationship and started sleeping in separate rooms.'

The degree of stability, if it is prayed in aid of a 'couple' finding by the department, can perhaps only carry weight insofar as the other living-together characteristics evince stability; it is of far less – if any – consequence if stability, however solid, attaches only to a non-LTAMC period during the relationship. Somewhat circular though this logic may be, practitioners are encouraged to argue that stability is not a feature that can usefully be imputed to any portion of time in which the relationship is claimed to have evolved into something less than a cohabiting one.

In *CIS/4156/2006*, one of the factors that might have influenced the tribunal below was the finding confirming the 'stability of the relationship since 1997 and the mutual support, which was "much more than simply mutual carers"'; in this case the tribunal had been less than balanced in its findings (for many other reasons besides the stability point though) and Mr Deputy Commissioner Wikeley remitted the case for re-hearing.

Endurance

9.71 This is one of the factors listed by Lord Justice Waite in *Fitzpatrick v Sterling Housing Association*[1] and approved for the living together test by Mr Commissioner Jacobs in *CIS/443/1998*. It is not addressed directly by either authority, but it is submitted here that the quality of endurance is not only a measure of time elapsed (which would better be described as 'duration') but rather it connotes some moral quality of stability and even a stolid toleration of an adverse conjugal situation. That is not a happy concept in the context of a relationship, but once again, the argument adopted for your client may be that this is indeed lacking: if the relationship has not broken down yet, then it will, 'endurance' being missing from both the client's and the alleged partner's attitude to each other and the situation.

[1] [1998] 1 FLR 6.

Arguing stability points

9.72 Stability is never the sole determinant and is unlikely even to be particularly significant. The key is to argue whatever nuance suits the case best. In a relationship that has lasted a long time one might be saying that it is so unsettled and stormy that the stability factor is not satisfied. Or the argument may be run that such stability as can be discerned is to be disregarded, being stability of the 'wrong kind' – ie stability in a carer/patient, householder/housekeeper relationship, or that which is necessary where ex-partners still share childcare in the interests of their child(ren).

Alternatively a noticeably harmonious relationship that nevertheless began only recently could equally be argued to fall outside the definition of 'stable' due to its short duration. This will chime comfortably with question 2 that is urged upon decision-makers in para 11116 (see **9.68** above) of their Guidance, especially where linked evidence can be shown of lack of any intention to marry, enter a civil partnership, stay together or live together as a married couple.

Financial support

Introduction

9.73 This is a problematic test, because traditionally the DWP have tried to argue both corners: substantial support means they're a couple; lack of support means it's a couple because it's not solely a financial relationship. On the whole though, a lack of financial support is marginally advantageous when arguing for single status. But it produces a catch-22 position in which caution must be exercised if you argue that she is financially independent of him: remember that she is trying to claim means-tested benefit or tax credits on the basis of low income.

What the Handbook said

9.74 Financial Support. In most married couple relationships one would expect to find financial support of one party by the other, or sharing of household expenses, but the absence of any such arrangements is not conclusive.

What the Guidance says

9.75 DMG poses some pertinent questions which can be usefully asked of the client, as a starting point. They are[1]:

(1) Is one person supported by the other?
(2) How is the household income shared or used?
(3) Are their resources pooled in a common fund? Is this all their income or only the money for eg shopping or bills?
(4) Is one person bearing the major share of the household expenses, for example mortgage, rent, gas, electricity? Whose name is on the bills?
(5) Is there a joint purchase of the property or other mortgage arrangements?
(6) Have these financial arrangements always been the same or have they changed? If so how and when?
(7) If there are no financial arrangements why not?

'If any of the above applies over the long term, it could be an indication of LTAMC. However, two people may be LTAMC even if they keep their finances completely separate. The relationship of two people concerning money has to be looked at in the context of the whole relationship.'

[1] DMG, para 11109 (Chapter 11) and also para E4098 (Chapter E4).

Does either alleged partner maintain the other?

9.76 Support or maintenance is certainly an indicator. That money changes hands is not enough to prove that it is maintenance, however, and practitioners are advised to take note of the need to distinguish support from something more commercial.

Unsurprisingly in the earlier widow and lodger cases like *R(G)3/81* and *R(G)3/71* the distinction was rather critical. It assisted the appellant's case in *R(G)3/81* that as regards their financial relations:

> 'their evidence showed that they divided the cost of food equally, and that as regards other bills they provided a box, into which the claimant put £5 a week and Mr H somewhat more. In the event Mr H discharged all the bills with the exception of the telephone account, for which the claimant assumed sole responsibility – she had had the telephone installed in her bedroom on her arrival at the bungalow-and, to the extent that the claimant's contribution to these bills was inadequate, the shortfall was made up by Mr H.'

This rather informal arrangement was not so relaxed as to damage the case for singe status. By contrast the appellant in *R(G)3/71* failed to make a strong enough case that the lack of maintenance by the alleged partner took them outside the cohabitation definition. In discussing the point, in the context of the second point in his three-part test, Mr Commissioner Shewan had regard to the married norms as he then saw them, acknowledging they could be wide-ranging and various:

> 'The claimant strongly contends that she was not cohabiting with S because he was not maintaining the household as a husband does. In relying so strongly on this matter, the claimant in my view unduly stresses only one aspect of the situation: whereas the situation must be considered in a number of aspects. There are great variations in the way husbands maintain their households. In some cases they do not maintain them at all. If there is any generalisation that can be ventured, it is probably that as a rule husbands maintain their households to the extent that they – with or without consultation with their wives – consider they can reasonably afford. This was very much the basis of S's contributions in the present case. To start with, he paid nothing: because apparently he satisfied the claimant that in view of his obligations to his own wife he could not afford anything. Later he paid £5 a week, plus (as a rule) some 30 or 40 shillings [£1.50 to £2] a week; the fact that the 30s or 40s was not always paid indicates that what he paid was being represented as the limit which he could afford. This is not indicative of the status of a lodger. What a lodger pays is generally determined on a commercial basis, as a reasonable counterpart to what he is to receive by way of accommodation, meals and services. A person who cannot afford to pay the stipulated charge does not become a lodger. If on the other hand he has ample means and could well afford to pay more, that is no concern of the landlady; it does not determine what the charge is to be. On the admissions of the claimant and S, their financial relationship was much more indicative of that of husband and wife than that of land lady and lodger.'

The voluntary quality of the contributions struck the Commissioner as characteristic of a non-commercial relationship.

In *R(SB)17/81* the fact that Sheffield students:

> 'had shared the expenses, although Miss G had to lend the claimant something like £10 a week in order to enable him to meet his proper share.'

did not assist their case. And for Mrs Crake (the unsuccessful of the two claimants in *Crake & Butterworth*), who had left her husband to go and live with Mr Watts, evidence was adduced, with a view to establishing some commerciality to the relationship, that:

> 'Mr Watts could not keep her; that they led completely separate lives [. . .]; the representative repeated that she was a **housekeeper** and got her board and **money** for some meals; and that she was being **paid in kind for the services which she** performed.' (author's emphasis).

The inability of the alleged partner to maintain the claimant did not avail her then.

To suggest that one partner needs to be shown to be categorically supporting the other would be inaccurate though. In *NA v Secretary of State for Work and Pensions (IS)*[1] Judge Ward noted the tribunal below had found relevant evidence of the alleged partner participating in the financial life of the household via payment of insurance bills, phone bills, the Sky subscription and the TV licence.

[1] [2012] UKUT 299 (AAC).

Shared or separated money

9.77 In another key widow case, *CP/8001/1995* (the darts-playing widow of a policeman: appeal allowed), Mr Commissioner Goodman took a very relaxed view even of the claimant's free access to the alleged partner's bank account, noting that:

> 'He paid her a rent and a contribution to expenses; and although for convenience she was given the right to draw cheques on the bank account his wages were paid into, they did not in any sense pool their resources or have joint finances of the kind that married people commonly do.'

The Commissioner noted the general importance of money in arriving at an overall view of the relationship:

> '[the] complex problem of identifying when a whole concatenation of basic facts, such as who sleeps where, who does the housework and **whose money is used for expenses**, together come to add up to a state of affairs.' (author's emphasis)

It will be recalled that *CIS/443/1998* concerned a former cohabiting couple who now argued their relationship had changed into one of non-cohabitation. The evidence they adduced in support of this included that:

> 'Their latest home was rented in joint names.'

> 'She paid for the food and household items, and he paid the other bills. He also said that he bought his own toiletries.'

> 'He said that they shared accommodation for convenience and because it was cheaper than living separately. She wished to retain her independence and her separate finances, which was one reason why their relationship had foundered in 1979.'

That too failed to persuade the Commissioner that they were not living together as husband and wife.

Property purchase

9.78 The purchase of a property in *CIS/4156/2006* struck Mr Deputy Commissioner Wikeley as strongly suggestive prima facie of a cohabiting relationship: the tribunal below had:

> 'accepted the presenting officer's submission to the effect that Mr W's investment in the purchase of the property was "striking . . . It's a financial commitment + more friendship than a caring relationship. Not been a significant diversion from the old relationship other than sexual point of view".'

But the Deputy Commissioner was careful to ensure that this was not seen as conclusive.

Child maintenance

9.79 Properly dealt with under the head of 'Children' (see **9.81** below), the question of maintaining children is important. If it is a case of a cohabitee who pays money towards the children under some kind of duty (whether court-ordered, or arising under the liable relative rules, as a parent, or deemed liable relative who was formerly the partner of the parent/claimant and took on that responsibility by virtue of time previously spent living with and raising them) this should be explained and should not undermine a 'single status' argument. After all, the payment of maintenance – identified as such – as between ex-spouses is far from being a sign of the relationship's strength; rather it is an indication that the marriage is over.

But where maintenance payments are genuinely voluntary in the sense that the payer has undertaken, in the absence of any duty, moral or legal, whatsoever to pay maintenance to the children, that might well add up with other factors to indicate a cohabiting relationship. Where a lone parent client is accused of having a new relationship, the new alleged partner's relations with the child(ren) need to be assessed generally, but if he is supporting them financially, the single status argument is severely weakened.

Questions to ask

9.80 It is hard to discern any really firm principle threading the authorities together as regards financial affairs. But the distinctive, always unique textures of the way two people handle their money affairs in relation to each other is clearly very relevant.

The DMG questions are a good starting point, but the reasoning behind a given arrangement also matters. If the 'rent' in payment is unduly low, is there a reason for that? If one party subsidises the other as to living expenses, education costs, childcare, why has that arrangement come about? Would the level and type of subsidy between the alleged partners be out of place in a non-couple relationship or would it normally only arise in a marriage type of relationship?

9.81 *Cohabitation and Welfare Benefits*

Children

What the Handbook said

9.81 Children. When a couple are caring for a child or children of their union, there is a strong presumption that they are living as a married couple.

What the guidance says

9.82 At para 11118, the DMG majors on children who are *not* those of both the two alleged partners. It suggests that

'When two people are caring for a child they have had together, there is strong evidence that they are LTAMC. DMs can also consider:
(1) a man acting as father to a woman's children; or
(2) the woman acting as mother to the man's children; or
(3) one of two people of the same sex caring for the other person's children; or
(4) two people of the same sex caring for a child(ren) under a court order that gives them parental responsibility

as evidence that they are LTAMC.'

And in previous DMG editions, and the current Chapter E4 in relation to universal credit, mention was, and is, made of situations where two people of the same sex were caring for a child they had adopted together[1].

[1] Chapter E4 para E4107 (point 4).

Children as proof of sexual relationship

9.83 The first point is that this goes straightaway to another of the factors, sex, and has often been inseparable from that in the thinking of the judiciary. We have already seen the view taken by Mr Commissioner Shewan in *R(G)3/71* in relation to there having been one single instance of intercourse, in which the child was conceived. The child was proof of sex:

'it is obvious that sexual intercourse took place between the claimant and S; because on 10 July 1970 the claimant gave birth to a child of which S was admittedly the father.'

Mr Commissioner Rice takes us through the same logic in R(G)3/81 in relation to reconciling the two tests (three-part and six signposts) relevance to the tests:

'The existence of children is indicative of a sexual relationship and/or the general relationship of the man and woman.'

Whose children are they?

9.84 This rule has tended to work most adversely where any children are the biological offspring of both members of the alleged couple. That is not possible in same-sex couples of course. However, even where this is the case in a heterosexual alleged couple, common sense should remind the DWP that having once been a couple does not mean the two parents still are. Far from it. It is even harder for DWP to build a case on this point where the child is, for example, biologically or adoptively of only one of the alleged partners. On the whole then this factor must fail if applied adversely in isolation from the other five factors.

However, given the seemingly disproportionate deployment of the living together rule against lone parents, it is the four co-parenting scenarios in DMG 11118 above that create real pitfalls.

Childcare

9.85 It was salient in *R(G)3/71* that:

> '[The claimant] thought of him as the man she was to marry as soon as he was free to marry. When he came back to stay with her after the birth of the child Elizabeth, he did so at her request because "there was nobody else she could think of who could look after and control the children" (ie **her** children, not simply **his** child Elizabeth).'

Thus the caring responsibilities taken on by an alleged partner may also play a part in the analysis. In *CTC/3864/2004* it was nevertheless his own children that the alleged partner was (in his evidence) looking after:

> 'The claimant made a single parent claim for tax credits on 4 December 2002 on behalf of herself and her two dependent children. [. . .] It came to light that the father of the claimant's children was also living in her home.
>
> The main reason given by the tribunal for reaching [the] conclusion [that they were a couple] was that they had been living in the same household since 1993, they had two children and both helped to run the household and look after the children. [. . .] They led separate lives even though, as father of the children, he had a relationship with them. [. . .] The tribunal stated that they both helped to run the household and look after the children. However, the claimant's evidence was that, despite the fact that he was unemployed, she paid a child minder to look after the children after school.'

Remitting the case for re-hearing, Ms Deputy Commissioner Green clearly did not find the pre-existence of couple status and the bearing of joint offspring to be determinative in the slightest, if subsequent developments in the relationship meant that the couple relationship had changed, even if there was strong evidence that some shared childcare was undertaken.

The claimant in *CG v Secretary of State for Work and Pensions (IS)*[1] contended that her alleged partner had not behaved competently in relation to the childcare that he was being alleged to share with her; this informed her:

> 'account of the reason for her accompanying her husband on holiday (namely that on one occasion, while under the influence of alcohol, he had managed to lose their disabled son when abroad).'

It seems sensible to adduce such evidence where the department's evidence is that shared childcare evidences living together.

[1] [2011] UKUT 97 (AAC).

9.86 *Cohabitation and Welfare Benefits*

Regarding the alleged partner as a (step-)parent

9.86 In a Scottish case[1] in which the main ratio was not central to the present topic (it was chiefly concerned with the existence or otherwise of a marriage by cohabitation with habit and repute under Scots law), it is submitted that one part of the test applied by Deputy Commissioner Sir Crispin Agnew of Lochnaw BT QC could arguably be deployed in a living-together case:

> '[H] and [the claimant] both had children who knew that they were not legally married but [the claimant's] daughters referred to [H] as dad and treated [H] and [the claimant] for all purposes as if they were a married couple.'

That point too goes to public acknowledgment (see below).

[1] CSG/681/2003.

The birth certificate

9.87 This may be material, especially in terms of findings as to who is the father. However, even there, appearances may be deceptive. A claim made by the respondent single parent in *Secretary of State for Work and Pensions v AM (IS)*[1] which 'stretched credulity' concerned:

> 'the circumstances surrounding the registrations (and re-registrations) of the births of the older two of her four children (the younger two had no father registered). The older two children were both originally registered by the claimant alone. In May 1999, however, the claimant and Mr S re-registered the details of both children identifying Mr S as the father of both children. The DWP, unsurprisingly, relied on this as a factor showing that they were living together as husband and wife.'

However, the tribunal below had found in the single parent's favour, and in the light of her explanation involving protecting herself from domestic violence from another former partner, Judge Wikeley saw no reason to disturb that conclusion. But it is another cautionary tale in that an explicit move like registration which asserts paternity, combined with other living together features, is bound to cause difficulties when and if the relationship changes. The tribunal had been entitled not to regard the claimant's admitted deception of the Registrar of Births as undermining her evidence.

In *CIS/1243/2007*, the birth certificates of the children appeared to assist the case, in that they had disclosed different addresses for the two parents.

The facts in *R(IS)13/05* also illustrate a scenario in which a lone parent was alleged to be living with the admitted father of her children.

[1] [2010] UKUT 428 (AAC) (CIS/0384/2010).

Inaction by the Child Support Agency or Child Maintenance Service

9.88 In the same case, *CIS/1243/2007*, Miss Deputy Commissioner Ovey found that the tribunal below had erred in its couple finding when the principle plank of its reasoning had been that the Child Support Agency had written to the father of the child (ie the alleged partner) at the mother's (ie the claimant's) address; moreover since it had not followed up this letter by way of further action to recover Child Support, it had been inferred that the likely explanation for this was that he had moved in with her (and so was no longer a non-resident parent liable to pay Child Support). Yet the tribunal had no evidence as to why the CSA had failed to follow the case up. In those circumstances it was:

> 'in the absence of further reasoning, a step too far to conclude from the absence of further signs of activity by the Child Support Agency that the father moved in with the mother by 1 July 2002 and that for some reason which is not spelt out in terms that led the Child Support Agency not to pursue the maintenance claim. In this respect, then, I decide that the tribunal erred in law.'

This must amount to a useful line of argument, or at least a caution that the department is not entitled to rely on such non-sequiturs as informed it here.

Stages of children growing up

9.89 Whilst the child in *CIS/443/1998* had now grown up and by the time of the appeal was adult, her effect lingered insofar as Mr Commissioner Jacobs did allude to the stages in a couple relationship as they adjust to parenting growing children:

> 'Relationships are not static. All relationships have a beginning. Some have an end. Most that last for any length of time go through stages of development. The significance of a particular factor may vary according to the stage which the relationship has reached. For example: the financial contribution of the parties to the household may vary as children are born, go to school, grow up and eventually leave home. It is necessary to take account of how the relationship has developed to the stage that it has reached and how it appears to be developing. A change from one stage of a relationship to another does not necessarily involve that relationship ceasing to be equivalent to that of husband and wife.'

The point being made was a general one, but clearly there is a need for practitioners to be ready to counter arguments by the department that the diminution in given aspects of the relationship (here it will be recalled that the alleged partners had not had sex since 1979) is a factor of the stages in the child(ren)'s development.

Public acknowledgement

Introduction

9.90 This vague and subjective test is hard to pinpoint. It concerns the way the alleged partners present themselves publicly, as evidenced – according to the DWP in DMG para 11119[1] – by representations they may have made:

(a) on the electoral register;
(b) in claiming benefits;
(c) in obtaining accommodation;
(d) if their friends and neighbours accept them as a married couple or civil partners and that the relationship is one of permanent intent;
(e) if one person has assumed the other person's surname.

9.90 *Cohabitation and Welfare Benefits*

Previously the now-expunged para 11060 cited a wider range of matters, like whether they

(a) use the same surname and titling themselves Mr and Mrs;
(b) spend major festivals like Christmas together;
(c) go on holiday;
(d) socialise together;
(e) go shopping together.

In the end, it is difficult to identify what it is 'normal' for couples to do by way of showing that they are a couple. But all such allegations are often capable of a strong rebuttal, and once again no single piece of evidence as to public presentation will alone be enough to make the DWP case.

A recurring ambiguity, still unresolved, is whether the acknowledgement in question is:

(a) acknowledgement *by the public* of the relationship (do people think they are a couple, no matter what the parties say about it?); or
(b) the acknowledgement *by the couple* of their relationship before the eyes the public (do they hold themselves out to be a couple, no matter what people end up thinking about it?).

Both perspectives arise equally.

[1] And Chapter E4 para E4108.

What the Handbook said

9.91 The Handbook favoured the 'holding out' perspective:

> '*Public Acknowledgement.* Whether the couple have represented themselves to other parties as husband and wife is relevant, but many couples living together do not wish to pretend that they are actually married, and the fact that they retain their identity publicly as unmarried persons does not mean they cannot be regarded as living together as husband and wife.'

DMG states:

> 'If two people have presented themselves openly and unequivocally to others as spouses, this is an indication that they are LTAMC.[1]'

Arguably that is the approach to take then; and factors relating to how they are seen by others relegated to secondary importance. If so, that may well be useful where the department adduces evidence from neighbours and even acquaintances that the parties are 'considered' to be a couple.

[1] DMG, para 11119 (Chapter 11) and also para E4108 (Chapter E4).

Claimant's own description

9.92 In *CIS/443/1998* it was material that:

> 'the claimant had described the lady as his partner when he claimed Income Support in 1988 and when he claimed Housing Benefit in 1995.'

He had also:

'completed the Income Support claim form identifying the lady as his partner without being forced to do so and despite the clear definition of that word on the form. The tribunal was entitled to reject his evidence [that he had always maintained "that we do not live as man and wife"].'

Thus it is possible for the description a claimant applies to the relationship in the course of their benefit claim to be later held against them; clients should be warned that when they describe someone as a partner in any official capacity it may be hard later on to disavow that label.

The appellant in *Robson* had created similar difficulties for herself:

'evidence [was] adduced by, or on behalf of, the Commission, namely that at one time, specifically on 31 October 1979, the appellant said "Mr Williams is my common-law husband".'

On that point alone Webster J remained neutral, preferring to allow the freshly convened tribunal to make findings on that point. So it was not determinative, there being a possibility, it seemed in *Robson*, that such a self-description need not be fatal to her case.

Acknowledging themselves as a couple

9.93 There was certainly no public acknowledgement of any relationship as a married couple as between Mr H and the claimant in *R(G)3/81* and this had to go in their favour; and, in *Robson*, despite Mrs Robson's slip of the tongue in describing Mr Williams as her common-law husband, the:

'fact is that there was no suggestion before the tribunal either that they acknowledged themselves publicly as man and wife or that anyone in the community thought of them as man and wife.'

However, the students in *R(SB)17/81* had also 'not acknowledged themselves as husband and wife' (and incidentally 'visited parents separately') but were held to be a couple despite that.

More recently, Judge Levenson considered the public acknowledgment test in a case, *JP v Secretary of State for Work and Pensions (IS)*[1], that concerned an alleged same-sex couple who denied they were a couple – an unacknowledged relationship, as he put it. Applying the then-current LTACP test, it seemed to the judge that if the relationship were truly denied, then that ran counter to the key characteristic of marriage and civil partnership – these were in their very nature a 'public acknowledgement of an emotional relationship'. Mr Justice Lewison had held in *Baynes v Hedger and Others*[2], a case concerning inheritance provisions, that such a 'relationship must be openly and unequivocally displayed to the outside world'.

[1] [2014] UKUT 0017 (AAC).
[2] [2008] EWHC 1587 (Ch).

Surnames

9.94 This may traditionally have been something of an indicator, but it probably mattered more in the past than now.

9.94 *Cohabitation and Welfare Benefits*

Back in the 1980s, it can have done the parties no harm in *R(SB)35/85* that:

> 'In public they were known respectively by his name of Mr W and her married name of Mrs T.'

Similarly the claimant's case was helped in *R(G)3/81* by the finding that:

> 'normally they would refer to each other by their respective surnames prefixed by "Mr" or "Mrs", as the case might be.'

Presumably others did the same when speaking to them.

However, it must be accepted that nowadays using different surnames comes nowhere near a safeguard as regards the public acknowledgement factor.

Socialising

9.95 Again the social meaning of sharing a social life has changed. In this respect the change may be helpful, in that a shared social life may indicate far less conclusively that two people are a couple.

The living together finding in *R(G)3/71* was not uninfluenced by the evidence that:

> 'If [the claimant] could get someone in to look after the children she and S "had a night out".'

And once again the widow who did not socialise with the alleged partner in *R(G)3/81* already had a strong case. We have already seen how Mrs Crake (the live-in housekeeper) claimed (contradictorily?) that she and her alleged partner:

> 'led completely separate lives; [. . .] the only time they could go out together was on a Sunday night'

and Woolf J in her case found there was cohabitation.

We have also seen though that the social life factor could be elastic, as in *CP/8001/1995* in which Mr Commissioner Goodman held that:

> '18. In the present case, although there was evidence that the claimant and her lodger engaged in social activities together, and once or twice went halves on a twin bedded room when staying at a hotel in a group of friends, these factors together with the other aspects of the living arrangements and their friendship as it developed over the years fall short of showing with sufficient clarity that [. . .] their relationship had deepened into that of a cohabiting couple.'

Also in *R(SB)17/81* the students 'socialised together'.

Wider factors

9.96 Being on record as a contact person in relation to the children's schooling was noted, obiter, by Judge Ward as indicating a degree of public acknowledgement in *NA v Secretary of State for Work and Pensions (IS)*[1].

[1] [2012] UKUT 299 (AAC).

Law and Practice **9.98**

Living together in same-sex cases

Provisions of the Civil Partnership Act 2004

9.97 Until 5 December 2005 it was not possible for two people of the same sex to be treated as a couple in social security law: even if they *were* clearly a couple, they would be regarded as two single people. The Civil Partnership Act 2004 changed this, by inserting new definitions, as in the table at **9.14**, for same-sex couples, into SSCBA 1992, Tax Credits Act 2002 and Jobseekers Act 1995. The Civil Partnership Act also required that the LTACP ('living together as if civil partners') concept be defined by going back to the (now also obsolete except for tax credits) *living together as husband and wife* test after all. It added a further gloss ostensibly to assist in defining LTACP[1]:

> 'For the purposes of this paragraph, two adults of the same sex are to be regarded as living together in the same household as if they were civil partners if, but only if, they would be regarded as living together as husband and wife were they instead two adults of the opposite sex.'

That strange subsection has now disappeared, at least for benefits, as opposed to tax credits, since the coming into force of the Marriage (Same Sex Couples) Act 2013, because all couples who are not married or civil partners must be compared now to the gender-neutral 'married couple' comparator, carrying, as it now does, no assumptions as to whether such a couple is a man and a woman, two men or two women.

So the need to pretend, per s 137(1A), that one member of a same-sex couple has temporarily switched gender – surely an inelegant approach that at worst could cause offence – is now obviated.

There is no escaping the fact that in each case of alleged same-sex cohabitation, the decision-maker must first determine the 'living together as a married couple' definition whilst bearing clearly in mind the nature of marriage.

With the Civil Partnership Act 2004, clearly Parliament had gone out of its way to head off the risk that case law on couple status should develop two separate lines of jurisprudence, one for heterosexual couples and another in same-sex cases. That is now easier to achieve, by referring only to that gender-neutral 'married couple'.

[1] For example at SSCBA 1992, s 122(1A) (bereavement benefits) and s 137(1A) (means-tested benefits); also Tax Credits Act 2002, s 48(2).

Arguing for single status in alleged same-sex couple cases

9.98 Despite the legislation's adoption of a clear gender-agnostic 'living together as a married couple' test, and the very clear steer given to decision-makers that they must be totally even-handed, it is entirely possible that for same-sex couples different standards will continue to develop as to the application of some of the key indicative factors. It may be said that the weight of a historically ingrained culture of opposite-sex marriage has created a very different set of assumptions to any that are brought to the relatively new concept of same-sex marriage, which will be writing its own 'definition' for years to come. In a same-sex case, can it be argued that the married couple comparator ought only to be that in a same-sex marriage? Or must one look at all types and genders of marriage to see whether the one in question matches up to some 'average' married couple? Probably the latter must be the correct approach.

MEMBERS OF THE SAME HOUSEHOLD

9.99 Can it be argued that any different factors should apply in same-sex cases? In other words is there anything fundamentally different about sharing a household in a same-sex marriage as compared with an opposite-sex marriage? The question may need to be put, and differences highlighted if the same-sex relationship your clients have differs fundamentally, and will benefit from the comparison.

SEXUAL RELATIONSHIP

9.100 DWP sensitivity to accusations of intrusiveness has led to decision-makers being doubly reluctant to ask about this in same-sex cases in the time so far when it has mattered. Where your client does not have a sexual relationship with the alleged partner (and especially if s/he has never had) then this information should be volunteered, and must go into the whole equation. But as with heterosexual cases, important though it is to the couple concept, sex is not absolutely determinative, and it should remain open to same-sex alleged partners to argue that despite occasional sex they are not a couple.

CHILDREN

9.101 Given that it is impossible[1] for a child to be biologically the offspring of both members of a same-sex couple, this factor must surely have a reduced impact in same-sex cases, since traditionally in heterosexual cases it has tended to work most adversely where any children are biologically of both members of the alleged couple. Nevertheless, the existence of a resident child adopted by both members of an alleged same-sex couple will be a factor suggesting couple status. And also so in situations where two people of the same sex are caring for a child under a parental order, or a court order which gives them parental responsibility.

[1] Except in cases where one has had a gender change.

PUBLIC ACKNOWLEDGEMENT

9.102 This vague and subjective test may be even harder to apply in same-sex cases than in heterosexual ones. What is 'normal' for couples to do by way of showing that they are a couple, is difficult to identify, and in a society where homophobia still exists it may be said that a greater reticence is necessary for many same-sex couples than for heterosexual couples. This could have an adverse effect on the adjudication of same-sex cases.

That an alleged same-sex couple have not married or entered a civil partnership, and deny the relationship anyway, may be strongly suggestive that whatever their relationship is *like*, it is *unlike* that of a married couple: *JP v Secretary of State for Work and Pensions (IS)*[1].

[1]   [2014] UKUT 0017 (AAC).

Temporary separations

Introduction

9.103 Notwithstanding the SSCBA definitions of couple, regulations[1] deem there still to be a couple even though one member is 'temporarily living away from the other members of his family'. Situations where one has moved out and the other – your client – remains in the cohabitation home not quite knowing what will happen next can be caught by this, where the department decide to invoke it adversely. Framed in terms of exceptions, the deeming will, however, not bite where:

(a)   the alleged partner 'does not intend to resume living with' the client; or
(b)   his absence is likely to exceed 52 weeks.

In the tax credits legislation, it is necessary in the case of married couples or civil partnerships to show that any separation is 'likely to be permanent'[2], but there is no formal deeming provision.

[1]   Regulation 16(1)–(3), IS (General) Regulations 1987 (SI 1987/1967); the other means-tested benefits have similar equivalents.
[2]   Judge Jacobs dealt with this issue in SA v Comissions for HMRC [2017] UKUT 0090 (AAC).

DMG guidance on the temporary absence of one party

9.104 DMG[1] suggests that:

'A couple should not automatically be regarded as having stopped LTAMC just because of the temporary absence of one of the parties. When DMs determine whether LTAMC[2] continues during a temporary absence, the reason for the absence is an important factor. Absences for the following reasons would not normally mean that the couple have stopped LTAMC:
(a)   work;
(b)   a period as a hospital in-patient;
(c)   holiday;
(d)   a visit to a relative(s);
(e)   higher education.[3]'

In relation to cases to which Chapter E4 guidance applies, eg Universal Credit, where a claimant is a member of a couple and the other member is temporarily absent from the claimant's household, they cease to be treated as a couple if that absence is expected to, or exceeds, 6 months[4].

Examples, to assist, as set out at Chapter E4 para E4152, include:

'Huw and Isobel are LTAMC and in receipt of UC. Isobel is involved in a road accident and is admitted to hospital with life-threatening injuries. She needs prolonged treatment and rehabilitation and is expected to be in hospital for about 8 months. The DM treats Huw and Isobel as no longer LTAMC from the date of Isobel's admission to hospital.

9.104 Cohabitation and Welfare Benefits

Louie and David are LTAMC and in receipt of UC. David obtains work abroad and has a contract of employment for 18 months. The DM treats Louie and David as no longer LTAMC from the date that David goes abroad.

Ed and Melanie are LTAMC and in receipt of UC. Melanie's mother, Cathy, lives in Spain and Melanie hasn't seen her for 2 years. Cathy receives an inheritance and tells Melanie that she will buy her a plane ticket, if she would like to pay a visit. Melanie accepts her mother's offer and leaves the UK for a 4 week period. As the absence is for less than 6 months, Ed and Melanie continue to be treated as a couple whilst Melanie is in Spain.'

[1] At para DM, para 11151 (Chapter 11) and also para E4151 Chapter E4).
[2] R(G)11/59; R(SB)19/85.
[3] R(SB)30/83.
[4] Universal Credit Regulations, reg 3(6); Chapter E4, para E4152.

They might come back

9.105 In the light of the deeming provisions, the impression your client gives about a former partner who 'has left', and the circumstances in which they left, can make a crucial difference to the success of their benefit claim. For tax credits, the following points may help to establish 'permanence'. In cases involving both benefits and tax credits, it will assist your client's case for being regarded as single if:

(a) the departing party said that – or your client was given to understand that – he would not come back;
(b) she does not wish him to return;
(c) she told him or asked him not to come back;
(d) there is agreement between them that the relationship is over;
(e) they were married but are now divorced;
(f) they were civil partners but the civil partnership is now dissolved;
(g) she can separate out her hopes (eg *I'm hoping he'll be back one day soon*) from the reality (ie, he is simply not coming back);
(h) there are no previous examples of his having 'left' and then returned some time later – a history of splits and reconciliations is decidedly unhelpful;
(i) he has gone on to some different situation (perhaps a new relationship) which appears permanent as far as can be ascertained;
(j) there are no other strong reasons why he has left (eg work, a holiday, visiting relatives, undertaking higher education)[1].

Naturally, where the client is upset by his leaving and would like to repair and resume the relationship, it can be extremely painful for her to point out these factors. Discussion as to how to approach the case needs to be done with great sensitivity.

In the tax credits case of *UA v HMRC (TC)*[2], in which an error of law was found, Judge Wikeley stressed that when assessing evidence about a parties' living arrangements it is important that tribunals make appropriate findings while viewing the facts through the prism of any relevant cultural context. This observation applies not only in relation to this case, but has, it is submitted, wider application. The examples highlighted by Judge Wikeley illustrate the importance of interpreting evidence about an alleged separation with an awareness of its cultural context.

DWP should only investigate these cases where there is a prima facie reason for doubt, in accordance with their own guidance[3]. If they appear to be investigating in detail on a routine fishing basis, they should be asked if they will discontinue such investigation. As for tax credits, it is less likely that there would be a detailed investigation of these circumstances.

Where your client is in an admitted cohabitation relationship, then she must be careful in relation to claiming benefit if it is only temporary (eg a female partner claiming Income Support as a lone parent whilst her male partner spends a year working in the family business abroad in the country of origin). In such circumstances her claim will of course be tested as to its permanence and as to its falling outwith the deeming provisions, by the department, but it is still wise to ensure the client does not put herself in a position where the claim could later be viewed to have been fraudulent.

[1] DMG, para 11151 (Chapter 11) and also para E4151 (Chapter E4).
[2] [2019] UKUT 113 (AAC).
[3] DMG, para 11152 (Chapter 11) and also para E4153 (Chapter E4).

Multi-partner scenarios

Rules

9.106 In social security law the following rules are applied:

(a) marriage is usually only between *two* spouses; polygamy is the exception;
(b) civil partnership is always between only two civil partners;
(c) living together as a married couple always applies to only two partners.

Polygamous marriages (a husband with more than one wife) are provided for – but only if such a marriage was legally contracted in a country where polygamous marriages are available[1]. In a case where a man claims to be married to more than one woman, but the finding on the facts is that he is actually married to only one of them, he cannot be held in social security law to be living together as a married couple with his subsequent alleged wife or wives. If he is found to be married to none of them, any finding of living together as a married couple can only be made in relation to one of them. In other words there is no polygamous version of the LTAMC concept.

There is also no equivalent provision for polyandrous marriages (one wife with more than one husband). A finding of marriage could be made in respect of one of the husbands, or of living together as a married couple with one of them.

The guidance at Chapter E4 helpfully sets out a number of examples, relevant to universal credit cases[2].

The Court of Session implicitly accepted in *DK v Secretary of State for Work and Pensions*[3], that sex with another, third party, would not automatically

9.106 *Cohabitation and Welfare Benefits*

negate the relationship in question – here in the light of a suggestion, with evidence, that the female appellant's alleged boyfriend-partner was gay.

1   See definitions of 'partner' and 'polygamous marriage' in Income Support (General) Regulations 1987 (SI 1987/1967) reg 2(1); Jobseeker's Allowance Regulations 1996 (SI 1996/207), reg 1(3); Employment and Support Allowance Regulations 2008 (SI 2008/794), reg 2(1); State Pension Credit Act 2002, s 12; Housing Benefit Regulations 2006 (SI 2006/213), reg 2(1); Housing Benefit (Persons who have attained the qualifying age for State Pension Credit) Regulations 2006 (SI 2006/214), reg 2(1); for Council Tax Benefit, see SSCBA 1992, s 133.
2   Chapter E4, para E4064.
3   [2016] ScotCS CSIH 84.

Unlawful or prohibited relationships

Full list

9.107 When are two people treated as **not** being a couple?

Despite any evidence that would otherwise point to a LTAMC relationship, two people cannot be treated as 'living together'[1] if:

(a)   their relationship would be a prohibited one for marriage or civil partnership purposes; or
(b)   it would be illegal for them to have sexual intercourse (ie one or both would be committing a crime).

The full list supplied by DMG at Appendix 1 to para 11082 is:

(1)   adoptive child
(2)   adoptive parent
(3)   child
(4)   former adoptive child
(5)   former adoptive parent
(6)   grandparent
(7)   grandchild
(8)   parent
(9)   parent's sibling
(10) sibling
(11) sibling's child
(12) child of former civil partner
(13) child of former spouse
(14) former civil partner of grandparent
(15) former civil partner of parent
(16) former spouse of grandparent
(17) former spouse of parent
(18) grandchild of former civil partner
(19) grandchild of former spouse.

'Sibling' includes half-siblings. No living together finding can be made where there is such a relationship. Whilst 'child' and 'grandchild' in this list go wider than the social security definition (ie a person under 16), it should be made clear too that all children under 16 are outside the reach of the living together rules; they cannot be partners.

[1] DMG, paras 11031–11032 (Chapter 11) and Appendix 1 to Chapter 11, and also paras E4061–E4062 (Chapter E4) and Appendix 1 to Chapter E4.

Running a cohabitation case against the DWP, HMRC or a local authority

How the DWP, HMRC and local authorities make adverse cohabitation decisions

9.108 The Single Fraud Investigation Service (SFIS) was introduced between July 2014 and March 2016. SFIS is a partnership between DWP Fraud Investigation Service, HMRC and local authorities. The DWP now conducts single welfare benefit fraud investigations to one set of policies and procedures[1].

Sometimes investigations relate to suspected fraud here it is assumed that the investigation of your client seeks to show a couple relationship exists so as to stop or reduce benefit payment.

[1] https://www.gov.uk/government/collections/single-fraud-investigation-service.

Pressure to withdraw

9.109 Investigations may include interviews under caution and, if so, your client will need your (or another practitioner's) advice from a criminal law perspective, including application of the PACE 1984 rules. Sometimes an investigation will result in the client being told there is evidence of fraud and that if they withdraw their claim and repay any overpayment to date, there will be no prosecution. That degree of pressure can escalate to the 'offer' of paying an administrative penalty to ward off a prosecution. Your advice in those circumstances needs to be preceded by very careful scrutiny of the case against the client to see if it has substance. If it appears unfounded, pressure to withdraw the claim should be resisted, and an appeal lodged against a subsequent decision to stop benefit, but the client is likely to want a high degree of confidence in your view that the allegation can be defended.

Types of evidence gathered by the departments

9.110 Evidence is gathered through:

(a) witness and neighbour reports;
(b) undercover observation;
(c) questioning neighbours;
(d) the benefit fraud hotlines;
(e) interviews under caution.

The validity of such evidence must be treated with caution insofar that there is scope for hearsay which, while arguably admissible at a tribunal, should not carry any significant weight. The unreliability of unhelpful evidence does need to be stressed to the tribunal. Where observations have been done by

9.110 *Cohabitation and Welfare Benefits*

investigators sitting in a car near the claimant's home for example, it is important to see the original record of those observations and to assess their shortcomings.

Visiting officers will record the claimant's answers to questions and will also ask to see the premises. Claimants do not have to accede to this, but if a glance at the bedroom arrangements will be enough to demonstrate separate bedrooms that is always a useful line of argument and the evidence of being shown the bedrooms can be conclusively favourable to the point that the department concedes without further ado.

Assuming that the matter is not so easily won, clients need to be advised to be careful with the personal and sometimes intimate information that they may be asked about. Helping clients to understand the admittedly quite opaque rules on living together is one way to ensure that they avoid giving a misleading impression about the relationship, or refrain from giving too much detail where they are unsure if it helps. Naturally they must also be advised that deliberately misleading the department would be wrong and perhaps fraudulent.

Also bear in mind the recent case of *AK v HMRC (TC)*[1] in which the claimant's claim for child tax credits was made and granted on the basis that she was a single woman only to be terminated on the grounds that she had been living with a 'Mr D' as husband and wife. This decision was made 'substanitially on the strength of Mr D's 'financial footprint' as revealed in reports from a credit reference agency, Equifax, together with HMRC's own records'. After some further contact between HMRC, the claimant appealed. The case came before the First-tier tribunal on 18 June 2014, unfortunately the claimant was late for the hearing. It is not clear from the decision whether the judge had already signed the decision notice before he was aware of the claimant's arrival, nor is it entirely clear whether he allowed the claimant to address him at all. The claimant did not give evidence, that much was clear. The appeal was refused, including on the basis that the claim was made as a single person but 'subsequent enquiries showed a paper trial linking Mr D to her address'. Whilst noting that there is was no doubt that the evidence obtained by HMRC raised a number of points for the claimant to answer, Judge Rowland stated:

> ' . . . what is striking about this case is the complete failure of HMRC to ask the necessary questions before making its decision. Realistically, that probably required HMRC to interview the claimant and put to her the inferences it drew from the Equifax reports, rather than ask questions in writing, but it scarcely attempted even the latter, seemingly expecting all the material answers to emerge from documentary evidence. As is now conceded, HMRC had an obligation to ask the material questions. This is clear from what Baroness Hale of Richmond, with whom the other members of the House of Lords agreed, said in *Kerr v Department for Social Development* [2004] UKHL 23; [2004] 1 WLR 1372, . . . The questions that need to be asked are sometimes ones that give guidance as to the evidence that is required.' (paragraph 6).

[1] [2016] UKUT 0098 (AAC).

Practical issues to address

CHECKLIST: WHAT TO DO IF YOUR CLIENT'S BENEFIT/TAX CREDITS ARE STOPPED

9.111 If your clients benefits are stopped you may:

(a) Challenge the decision via revision or appeal – within one month.
(b) Re-apply for benefit if circumstances change (eg contact with the alleged partner breaks down in some way) – even pending appeal.
(c) Apply for other benefits that might be payable instead.
(d) Prepare the appeal/revision request.
(e) Is there a fraud charge as well? Advise on, or refer, the criminal aspects of the case.

WHAT IS THE ALLEGATION?

9.112 The department must be clear about what is alleged. However, often the detail of the evidence on which they base their decision is hard to determine from the bald wording of the refusal letter. It is possible to ask for reasons for the decision, and this can be a useful first step in formulating the challenge.

However, it is often advisable to seek a reconsideration anyway, as the grounds do not need to be spelt out exhaustively at the point of making that application.

BURDEN OF PROOF

9.113 The department seeking to close or end an existing claim has the burden of showing that circumstances have changed so as to end the entitlement. On a first claim though, it is open to the department to refuse it because the claimant has failed to discharge their burden of showing that they are entitled.

IS IT ALSO AN OVERPAYMENT CASE?

9.114 Very often, the context in which the cohabitation question is aired is when the client has been told they must repay overpaid benefit that they received whilst claiming as a single person when in fact they were a member of a couple.

Overpayment cases have two distinct aspects:

- was the person overpaid? and
- if they were, is the overpayment recoverable by the benefit-paying agency?

It is the first of these questions that will raise the issue of whether they were living together. The legal burden, in an overpayment recovery case, is on the benefit-paying department to make out all aspects of their case. You should put them to proof as to the allegations they make; all the more since their case may consist in part of insinuations and vague assertions. The department must be

Is it also a benefit fraud case?

9.115 An indication that the benefit-paying department suspects a cohabitation fraud (ie they think that couple status is deliberately being concealed, perhaps so as to allow a lone-parent Income Support claim) is where the Benefit Fraud Investigation Service ask the claimant, and often the alleged partner too, to attend, separately, an interview under caution. These are subject to the same protections and safeguards as police interviews, under the interview codes to the Police and Criminal Evidence Act 1984. The interviewee may have their legal adviser present, for example, and may ask for breaks as needed. If your client is invited to attend such an interview, your, or a colleague's, knowledge of criminal law will form part of the advice they will likely need.

Penalties

9.116 One area that sits somewhere between criminal law and the administrative law of benefit entitlement is that of civil and administrative penalties. Your client may face one or both of these two charges.

He or she may find that in addition to being asked to repay an overpayment following a living together allegation, they are also required to pay a one-off £350 civil penalty[1]. It is only chargeable if there was indeed an overpayment – ie the living together arguments have been lost – and then only if they acted negligently or they failed without excuse to supply information or report a change. If you lose the living together argument on behalf of a client, consider whether it was nevertheless a scenario in which there was enough doubt about what kind of relationship they were in, that their failure or alleged negligence was justifiable. The imposition of the civil penalty is discretionary, and a key factor informing that discretion is the degree of blameworthiness; arguments should be focused on that.

Separately, the option of paying an administrative penalty can be 'offered' by the investigating benefit-paying agency as an alternative to prosecution[2]. These can be up to £5,000 and all too often a claimant who is in the middle of a living together case, already overwhelmed by the prospect of losing their appeal, will seize upon the penalty as a way of avoiding the further calumny of a fraud prosecution. Clearly, it should only be considered as an option in cases where the department has evidence likely to achieve a conviction. That is a matter to which your (or a colleague's) expertise in criminal law must be applied. It is not unknown for administrative penalties to be sought from, and duly paid by, claimants against whom the available evidence would have been unlikely to secure a conviction.

[1] Social Security Administration Act 1992, ss 115C-115D.
[2] Social Security Administration Act 1992, s 115A.

DECISIONS SUSCEPTIBLE TO CHALLENGE

9.117 It is now well-established that 'outcome decisions' attract an appeal right[1]. A decision whether a person is single or a member of a couple is of itself only one of the 'building block decisions' that go towards the outcome decision of whether the client is entitled and if so to how much. A 'building block' gives rise to appeal rights once it becomes part of the outcome. An outcome decision will broadly read something like 'Mr G is not entitled to Income Support as a lone parent from 1.1.2011 on the basis that he has been living together as a married couple with Ms F and is therefore a member of a couple'. Such a decision may be appealed.

Decisions as to entitlement further divide into those made on an initial claim, where the claimant has claimed benefit and not yet had any previous decision in the current circumstances, and those in which an on-going claim is stopped (this is usually a department-instigated supersession) because the department now take a different view on the cohabitation point. Either type of decision is appealable but it is fairly clear that the burden of establishing single status falls on the claimant upon lodging their claim, but the burden is on the department when it wishes to stop or reduce an existing live claim[2].

Another context in which decisions may need to be challenged though is where the client has received benefit in the past, but the department in question now seeks to recover that benefit on the basis that it was overpaid because it has supposedly come to light that the claimant was living together as a married couple with another person. Here the client may be arguing that they were not living together as a married couple – and therefore benefit was not overpaid – in order to resist recovery of the benefit.

[1] The question of the tribunal's jurisdiction and the triggering, or not, of appeal rights in this respect is dealt with at length in decisions CPC/3891/2004, CIS/1720/2004 and CIS/3655/2007, but practitioners will only rarely need to refer to these authorities. See also the application of these principles by Judge Wikeley in *Secretary of State for Work and Pensions v AM (IS)* [2010] 428 (AAC).
[2] CIS/317/1994; CIS/4156/2006.

Challenging the decision

9.118 'Well, here we go yet again'. These are the opening words of Judge Wikeley in *VO v HMRC (TC)*[1] in a fairly damning decision against HMRC, in which he went on to say:

> 'So, yes, in short this is yet another sorry tale of HMRC institutional incompetence and inefficiency which could well have led to injustice, were it not for the persistence of the Appellant.'

This followed Judge Wikeley's earlier decision in *NI v HMRC*[2] in which he used the phrase 'well, here we go again' with 'a sense of frustration, bordering on despair' in a case where he criticised HMRC for 'both its decision making processes and its conduct of appeal in relation to tax credits claims'. These decisions demonstrate the importance of challenging decisions where necessary.

9.118 Cohabitation and Welfare Benefits

The following is only a brief guide to the complex rules on decisions and appeals. It is governed by the Tribunals, Courts and Enforcement Act 2007 and the Social Security Act 1998; the finer detail is covered by the Social Security and Child Support (Decisions and Appeals) Regulations 1999 (SI 1999/991)[3].

The starting point is that the client receives a decision capable of challenge, ie:

(a) an outcome decision as to entitlement; or
(b) a decision to recover an overpayment.

Action should be taken as soon as possible; the deadline is:

(a) one month (for benefits); or
(b) 30 days (for tax credits)

from the date of the decision under challenge. This means the date of the letter or the postmark. Within one month (30 days for tax credits) the claimant must seek a **mandatory reconsideration**: this means asking the department to look again at their decision and to revise it in the client's favour.

If the outcome of the mandatory reconsideration is adverse, then the claimant may lodge an **appeal**. They have a further month (30 days for tax credits) to do this from the date of the outcome of the mandatory reconsideration.

Rules for Housing Benefit reconsiderations and appeals are slightly different but the pattern is similar.

The relevant action must be taken so that the request or appeal *arrives* at the relevant destination address within the one-month (30 days for tax credits) period. Merely posting it within the one month will not suffice.

Where the decision is favourably revised upon revision or appeal, then any backdating of benefit will go back usually to the date of the decision that has been challenged – or in the case of recovery of an overpayment, the overpayment is waived.

Decisions may be challenged outside the one month deadline by way of:

(a) late appeal or late revision request – where there are compelling good reasons for the delay – up to a maximum time-limit overall of 13 months;
(b) in a narrow range of cases involving mistake or error, the 'any time revision' route; or
(c) at any time at all, seeking a supersession: this means asking the department to reconsider outside the time limit but on the basis that if the decision is favourably revised, then any backdated benefit is only paid back to the date when the supersession was sought.

[1] [2017] UKHT 343 (AAC).
[2] [2015] UKIT 160 (AAC).
[3] For tax credits, see relevant sections of the Tax Credits Act 2002, the Tax Credits (Claims and Notifications) Regulations 2002 (SI 2002/2014) and the Tax Credits (Appeals) (No 2) Regulations 2002 (SI 2002/3196). For housing benefit, see Sch 7 to the Child Support, Pensions and Social Security Act 2000 and the Housing Benefit and Council Tax Benefit

(Decisions and Appeals) Regulations 2001 (SI 2001/1002). For universal credit see the Universal Credit, Personal Independence Payment, Jobseeker's Allowance and Employment and Support Allowance (Decisions and Appeals) Regulations 2013 (SI 2013/380).

Appeals procedure in 'living together' cases

LODGING THE APPEAL

9.119 The appeal should normally be lodged on the official form SSCS1 and usually should be sent to HMCTS. This is called direct lodgement. The appeal needs to state grounds. However, these do not have to be exhaustively set out at the initial stage. It is acceptable to add further arguments and amend or elaborate the grounds later in the process without formality or making any application. On the other hand, it assists the process if the grounds are set out as fully as the time-limit permits.

THE APPEAL HEARING

9.120 Living-together matters in welfare benefits and tax credits cases are heard by a single judge sitting in the Social Entitlement Chamber of the First-tier Tribunal. He or she will be a qualified lawyer or other person with equivalent legal experience. The hearing is usually fairly informal. Often there is nobody present from the decision-making department. But where there have been extensive investigations and/or an interview under caution it is common for the department to send a presenting officer, and sometimes an investigating officer as a witness. Appellants often appear unrepresented; the current ungenerous Legal Help climate does not ameliorate this situation. But for that reason, the proceedings are relatively informal and conducted in an inquisitorial style. There is often no formal examination and cross-examination of witnesses; the appellant may be the only witness.

Proceedings are governed by the Tribunal Procedure (First-tier Tribunal) (Social Entitlement Chamber) Rules 2008[1] which give considerable leeway to judges as to how to manage the hearing[2]. A typical living together hearing might last 30–90 minutes.

If the client is to appear unrepresented, consideration should be given to how they will present their case – or whether they will merely respond to the judge's questions, and if so, advice on predicting likely questions is useful. Clients may be advised that they will not have to stand up or make any formal submissions or speech. It is unlikely but not impossible that they will have to take an oath.

[1] SI 2008/2685.
[2] Case management powers are covered in r 5, and Chapter 2 (rr 27–31) contains provisions concerning the hearing.

WITNESS EVIDENCE AT THE TRIBUNAL

9.121 Oral evidence from your client does not need to be accompanied by a written witness statement – this is not required though it can sometimes help. Clients may ask if they can refer to such a statement while they give evidence.

9.121 *Cohabitation and Welfare Benefits*

If other witnesses such as the alleged partner cannot attend, a signed witness statement (even of the most informal kind) is acceptable. But attendance in person by the witness, if only to adopt and confirm the content of their statement, must inevitably add some weight. Other supporting letters eg from friends and family are perfectly admissible, but clients should not over-estimate the weight that will be placed on them.

Living together cases are a rare instance in social security matters when it is useful to call other witnesses; practitioners are advised to consider this, so that where helpful the alleged partner can appear, or sometimes the actual partner of the alleged partner (so as to vitiate the charge of couple status against your client). Witness orders are very rare but still possible in this jurisdiction. You can make an application to the Tribunal for a witness summons (eg in relation to the alleged partner) if you think this could help your client's case[1].

The recent decision of Judge Wikeley in *UA v HMRC (TC)*[2] highlights issues in relation to the Tribunal ordering the attendance of an alleged partner in a tax credits case, and the subsequent ambiguous 'adverse' inference drawn against the claimant when the alleged partner did not attend.

If you do not represent your client at the hearing because legal help will not cover this, or for any reason, remember that there will be no formal examination in chief; rather the tribunal judge is likely to ask the questions, and whilst these will not be strongly leading questions, they may be slightly more so than those that you might have asked. There is still a chance, in cases where the department investigated forensically, that a departmental presenting officer may attend, and they may cross-examine the client. You should advise your client as to the type of questions that could be asked, based on your own analysis of how the department might be expected to present their case.

Where investigating officers attend as witnesses for the benefit-paying department, you should try to ensure they are not allowed to make submissions as well. You may wish to prepare questions with which to cross-examine them too, especially if you think you can throw doubt on, for example, the reliability of covert observations.

[1] Tribunal Procedure (First-tier Tribunal) (Social Entitlement Chamber) Rules 2008, r 16.
[2] [2019] UKUT 113 (AAC).

CREDIBILITY OF THE EVIDENCE

9.122 It is necessary to be very rigorous as to what meaning is imputed to agreed evidence. In remitting case *CG v Secretary of State for Work and Pensions (IS)*[1] for rehearing Judge Wikeley advises prudence and care:

> '44. The tribunal should take particular care in making findings about the period over which there were incidents of domestic violence. If the tribunal takes the view that the documentary evidence on file is broadly accurate – namely that the police were involved in two such incidents in 2001 and 2002 and then again repeatedly from March 2008 – then that may well indicate that the couple were maintaining a common household throughout the relevant period (at least until late 2007 in any event). However, it is by no means conclusive. The tribunal must consider all the

relevant evidence in the light of all the factors that go to the issue of sharing a common household.

'45. So, for example, the tribunal will need to make findings about holidays. Do the photos seized by the DWP indicate shared and happy family holidays? Or does the tribunal believe the claimant's account of the reason for her accompanying her husband on holiday (namely that on one occasion, while under the influence of alcohol, he had managed to lose their disabled son when abroad)? These issues may not be straightforward. The tribunal might note that the receipt for the Ryanair flights booked in 2005 gives a contact address for the husband which is different from the claimant's. The tribunal might also note that the claimant was on holiday without her husband at the time of the police raid in 2007.

'46. Likewise the tribunal will need to decide what weight to attach to the letters sent by the claimant's husband when he was in prison. Do they show, as the DWP argue, that the couple were sharing a common household because of the nature of some of the issues being discussed (eg advice about works on the property?). Or, as the claimant's representative argues, do they demonstrate the manipulative nature of the claimant's husband? I simply observe that the representative's point that all the letters were from the claimant's husband to her, rather than vice versa, may not carry much weight, as it is plain from the letters that this was a two-way correspondence (eg "I got your letter . . . "). However, the evaluation of such evidence is a matter for the new tribunal.'

It is Mr Deputy Commissioner Wikeley (as he then was) too who elaborated what must be considered a definitive approach to claimant credibility, in *CIS/4022/2007*, which he later cited with approval specifically in the living-together context in *Secretary of State for Work and Pensions v AM (IS)*[2]:

'52. In my assessment the fundamental principles to be derived from these cases and to be applied by tribunals where credibility is in issue may be summarised as follows:
(1) there is no formal requirement that a claimant's evidence be corroborated – but, although it is not a prerequisite, corroborative evidence may well reinforce the claimant's evidence;
(2) equally, there is no obligation on a tribunal simply to accept a claimant's evidence as credible;
(3) the decision on credibility is a decision for the tribunal in the exercise of its judgment, weighing and taking into account all relevant considerations (eg the person's reliability, the internal consistency of their account, its consistency with other evidence, its inherent plausibility, etc, whilst bearing in mind that the bare-faced liar may appear wholly consistent and the truthful witness's account may have gaps and discrepancies, not least due to forgetfulness or mental health problems);
(4) subject to the requirements of natural justice, there is no obligation on a tribunal to put a finding as to credibility to a party for comment before reaching a decision;
(5) having arrived at its decision, there is no universal obligation on tribunals to explain assessments of credibility in every instance;
(6) there is, however, an obligation on a tribunal to give adequate reasons for its decision, which may, depending on the circumstances, include a brief explanation as to why a particular piece of evidence has not been accepted. As the Northern Ireland Tribunal of Commissioners explained in *R3/01(IB)(T)*, ultimately "the only rule is that the reasons for the decision must make the decision comprehensible to a reasonable person reading it".'

Credibility of the claimant's (your client's) evidence and to a large degree that of the alleged partner, if available, will be critical. There will be details which

9.122 Cohabitation and Welfare Benefits

no third party or documentary evidence can corroborate. Ask how plausible your client's account would be, to a reasonable but reasonably sceptical observer. Remember that credibility will be judged against the obvious backdrop of the financial motivation to lie, that a claimant might be susceptible to. Judge Jacobs entered a reminder about that possibility in *PP v Basildon District Council (HB)*[3]. The emphasis in social security law was, he warned, 'on the protection of public funds in a context where the parties have an incentive to conceal their true relationship'. That does not (and must not) amount to a presumption of course, but it can quite properly result in a tribunal judge's scepticism and may trigger[4] the judge's inclination to test it rigorously.

[1] [2011] UKUT 97 (AAC).
[2] [2010] UKUT 428 (AAC).
[3] [2013] UKUT 0505 (AAC).
[4] CJSA/2034/2005.

Representing your client at the hearing

9.123 If you represent the client be aware that the proceedings are less formal than most courts. You do not need to stand, nor should you present too formally. It is wise though to keep some separation between your examination in chief and your submissions, and to avoid giving evidence yourself, which you are not able to do. That said, lawyers are sometimes surprised at the extent to which the hearing of evidence can apparently intermingle with the making of submissions even at the judge's behest, and you should not be troubled by this, nor believe that it means there is no structure.

If you cannot represent

9.124 In these circumstances you should consider preparing a skeleton argument of no more than 4–6 pages, in support of your client's case. This can be done in much the same way as you would write it for any other court, but bearing in mind that it must substitute for your attendance in person, not supplement it.

Case law arguments

9.125 Even if (as is likely) none of the case law supports precisely your client's circumstances, consider nevertheless producing cases in which the appellant succeeded on facts which bear some resemblance to your client's case. However, do not make the mistake of arguing that the tribunal judge is bound by a given case where the facts are merely *similar*. They are patently not. Where judgments have produced an adverse result for the claimant in question, consider using those cases by distinguishing them convincingly. You should produce copies of the cases you wish to rely on, either in advance or on the day if they are few in number. Do not produce more than 3 or 4 judgments in any case. Most of the cases in this chapter can be found on one or other of the websites listed above at **9.6** above.

Checklist of issues to address in preparing the appeal

9.126 The following issues should be addressed in preparing the appeal:

(a) What is the DWP's/local authority's evidence?
(b) Can its reliability be attacked?
(c) What is the prima facie account of your client and of the alleged partner (and any other third parties)?
(d) If proven, will this win the case?
(e) Or are there points of law to be won as well?
(f) How credible is your client's account?
(g) What are its strengths and weaknesses?
(h) Does it disclose internal inconsistencies?
(i) Is it implausible? – examples include: sharing a bed at different times, never together; 'only one single instance of intercourse took place'; previous cohabitation has now changed completely though a single household is still shared. Address the implausibility.
(j) Are the client's and the alleged partner's accounts consistent with one another?
(k) Can the alleged partner assist? The importance of his/her witness evidence cannot be overstated. Very often this will be determinative.
(l) Was there an interview under caution? If so is its accuracy disputed at all by the interviewee (your client or the alleged partner)? What did your client concede in the interview?
(m) Can oral or witness statement evidence be corroborated with documentary evidence? Review for example Judge Wikeley's advice at para 43 et seq (cited above) of *CG v Secretary of State for Work and Pensions (IS)*[1]?
(n) Have DWP and local authority collaborated on the investigation? If so, is there inconsistency between either their arguments or their evidence?

[1] [2011] UKUT 97 (AAC).

Checklist of areas to cover in your arguments

9.127 Whether you are appearing in person for the client or not, you should make sure that the key areas of cohabitation law are addressed:

(i) The general relationship: describe its general 'flavour'.
(ii) Is there a shared household? Be clear as to where you stand on this but if arguing there is no shared household, prepare arguments in the alternative, which include minimising the household's importance.
(iii) Is there some reason (other than LTAMC) to explain the living together arrangement? Is anyone disabled, physically or mentally unwell/ill, vulnerable or dependent in some other way?
(iv) Does the claimant have any purpose, intention or motive as to the shared household that will help the case?
(v) Is there a sexual relationship? If not, what evidence can you adduce? If there is, how can you minimise its significance?
(vi) How stable is the relationship? How are you going to seek to define 'stability' for best advantage?

9.127 *Cohabitation and Welfare Benefits*

(vii) Are there children? What circumstances will diminish the adverse effect of this fact? Are the children the only reason the claimant and the alleged partner share a household?
(viii) What are the money arrangements in the relationship?
(ix) What evidence can the client give as to love, commitment, common purpose – or lack thereof?
(x) How do the claimant and the alleged partner lead separate lives?
(xi) If the relationship used to be one of cohabitation, marriage or civil partnership, why and how did it change?

Chapter 10
MISCELLANEOUS

Part A LAW AND PRACTICE

Change of name

10.1 A person can be called by whatever name he or she chooses[1]. No formalities are necessary, and a name can be acquired simply by habit and repute[2]. At some stage somebody is likely to require evidence of the change of name, and so it is usual practice to document a change of name by means of one of the more formal procedures, such as executing a deed or making a statutory declaration[3]. As far as children are concerned, where a residence order[4] or care order[5] is in force, nobody can cause the child to be known by a new surname without the leave of the court or the written consent of every person who has parental responsibility for the child[6]. Where a change of name deed is to be enrolled in the Central Office of the Supreme Court, the enrolment regulations distinguish between children who have attained the age of 16, and those who have not[7]. A child of 16 or over can either execute the deed poll himself or endorse his consent on the deed executed by his parent or guardian on his behalf[8]. Where a child is under 16 the deed poll must be executed by his parent or guardian, and the application for enrolment must be supported by an affidavit showing that the change of name is for the child's benefit[9].

[1] Provided he does not do so for any fraudulent purpose or in order to deceive and inflict economic loss on another (*Du Boulay v Du Boulay* (1869) LR 2 PC 430; *Cowley v Cowley* [1901] AC 450). See also, Nasreen Pearce *Name-changing: A Practical Guide* (Fourmat Publishing, 1990).
[2] *Dancer v Dancer* [1949] P 147.
[3] Other methods include Notarial Instrument, Royal Licence, and even a private Act of Parliament.
[4] Defined in CA 1989, s 8(1).
[5] Defined in CA 1989, ss 31(11) and 105(1).
[6] CA 1989, ss 13(1) and 33(7). And see **5.19**.
[7] Enrolment of Deeds (Change of Name) Regulations 1983 (SI 1983/680), reg 8.
[8] Enrolment of Deeds (Change of Name) Regulations 1983 (SI 1983/680), reg 8(3).
[9] Enrolment of Deeds (Change of Name) Regulations 1983 (SI 1983/680), reg 8(5). See also *Practice Direction of 24 May 1976* [1977] 1 WLR 1065.

Contractual licence

10.2 A contractual licence is permission granted by the owner of property allowing another person to be on or in the property. The licence need not

10.2 Miscellaneous

assume any particular form, and can be written or oral, but there must be an intention to create legal relations, and there must also be consideration[1]. For several years, landlords used the device of the contractual licence as a means of circumventing the operation of the Rent Acts. This contrivance was defeated by the decision of the House of Lords in *Street v Mountford*[2]. At the end of his judgment in that case Lord Templeman stated[3] that: 'henceforth the courts which deal with these problems will, save in exceptional circumstances, only be concerned to inquire whether as a result of an agreement relating to residential accommodation the occupier is a lodger or a tenant'.

It is submitted that a cohabitant sharing residential accommodation with his or her partner is usually neither a lodger nor a tenant, and would presumably fall within that residual category of 'exceptional circumstances'. Where a licensee shares accommodation with the licensor in his or her only or principal home, the licence is an excluded licence for the purposes of the Protection from Eviction Act 1977[4].

[1] *Horrocks v Forray* [1976] 1 WLR 230 at 236.
[2] [1985] AC 809.
[3] [1985] AC 809 at 827E.
[4] Protection from Eviction Act 1977, s 3A(2) (inserted by the Housing Act 1988, s 31).

Part B PRECEDENTS

10.3

Change of name deed: not intended for enrolment[1]

THIS CHANGE OF NAME DEED made on (*date*)

BY me (*forename(s) and new surname*) of (*address*) formerly known as (*forename(s) and old surname*)

WITNESS that:

1   I now completely renounce and abandon the use of my former surname (*old surname*).

2   I now adopt and assume the surname (*new surname*).

3   I ask and authorise all persons at all times to address, describe and identify me by using the surname (*new surname*).

4   From now onwards I will use and sign the name (*forename(s) and new surname*):

    (a)   in all deeds, documents, forms, records and other written instruments;

    (b)   in all actions and proceedings;

    (c)   in all dealings and transactions; and

    (d)   on all occasions.

SIGNED as a Deed by (*forename(s) and old surname*) in the presence of:

[1] See, generally, Nasreen Pearce *Name-changing: A Practical Guide* (Fourmat Publishing, 1990). For enrolment in the Central Office of the Supreme Court, see the Enrolment of Deeds

(Change of Name) Regulations 1983 (SI 1983/680).
A change of name deed is commonly referred to as a 'deed poll'. Historically, a deed was either 'indented' or 'poll'. A deed indented was made by more than one party; more than one copy was made; each copy was cut or indented so that its indentations corresponded with the indentations in the other copy or copies. A deed poll was made by only one party, and was 'polled' or cut evenly without any indentations. For a change of name deed made by a mother on behalf of her child, see 5.88 above.

10.4

Contractual licence[1]

THIS LICENCE is made on (*date*)

BETWEEN 'the parties' (1) (*name 1*) of (*address*) ('*name 1*') and (2) (*name 2*) (also) of (*address*) ('*name 2*').

IT IS AGREED that:

1 Recitals

1.1 The parties (intend to) live together at (*address*) ('the property').
1.2 The property is owned by (*name 1*) (and is mortgaged to (*lender*))[2].
1.3 The parties intend that this licence will be legally binding on them[3].
1.4 This licence is made in consideration of the mutual concessions it contains and for other good and valuable consideration, the sufficiency of which each of the parties acknowledges[4].

2 Licence

(Name 1) allows (name 2) to:

2.1 live with (him)/(her) in the property; and
2.2 use (his)/(her) furniture and fittings in the property; and
2.3 use the garage, parking space and garden belonging to the property.

3 Payment

On the first day of each month (*name 2*) will pay to (*name 1*) the sum of £ , or such other sum as the parties may from time to time agree, as a contribution towards (his)/(her) living and accommodation expenses.

4 Terms and conditions

(Name 2) will:

4.1 keep the property reasonably clean and tidy;
4.2 not intentionally damage the property or any part of it or any furniture and fittings in it;
4.3 not remove any of the furniture and fittings from the property;
4.4 not allow anyone else to stay overnight in the property without first obtaining the consent of (*name 1*);

10.4 *Miscellaneous*

4.5 consent to the sale of the property by (*name 1*), (his)/(her) personal representatives, trustee in bankruptcy or mortgagee, and vacate the property before completion of the sale;

4.6 not do anything that may annoy or cause a nuisance to (*name 1*) or the owners or occupiers of the premises nearby; and

4.7 not do anything that could render the insurance on the property void or voidable or could result in an increase in the insurance premium.

5 Licence revocable without notice

(*Name 1*) can revoke this licence at any time without having to give notice to (*name 2*) in advance if (*name 2*):

5.1 fails to pay (his)/(her) contribution towards (his)/(her) living and accommodation expenses when it is due; or

5.2 fails to comply with any of the terms and conditions of this licence.

6 Termination of licence

Subject to the above, this licence will come to an end when the first of the following events occurs:

6.1 the expiration of (one month's) written notice given by either party to the other; or

6.2 (*name 2*) vacates the property with the intention of never resuming residence in it; or

6.3 (2 months) after (*name 1's*) death; or

6.4 when the property is sold.

7 The nature of this licence

(*Name 2*) acknowledges that:

7.1 this licence is not a lease;

7.2 this licence does not create any kind of tenancy[5];

7.3 (he)/(she) has no exclusive right to occupy the property or any part of it;

7.4 (his)/(her) occupation of the property and use of its furniture and fittings will not give rise to joint ownership of the property or its furniture and fittings;

7.5 regardless of the contributions (he)/(she) makes towards (his)/(her) living and accommodation expenses (he)/(she) will not acquire any legal estate or beneficial interest in the property;

7.6 this licence is personal to (him)/(her) and cannot be transferred to anyone else; and

7.7 (he)/(she) understands the nature and effect of this licence and is entering into it freely and voluntarily after receiving legal advice on its provisions and implications.

SIGNED as a Deed by (*name 1*) in the presence of:

SIGNED as a Deed by (*name 2*) in the presence of:

[1] See, generally, Jean Warburton *Sharing Residential Property* (Sweet & Maxwell, 1990) at pp 24–35.
[2] The mortgagee will probably require the licensee to execute a deed postponing his or her rights in the property and undertaking not to assert an overriding interest against the mortgagee (*Williams & Glyn's Bank v Boland* [1981] AC 487).
[3] *Horrocks v Forray* [1976] 1 WLR 230 at 236, per Megaw LJ.
[4] *Horrocks v Forray* [1976] 1 WLR 230 at 236, per Megaw LJ.
[5] 'To consolidate a tenancy the occupier must be granted exclusive possession for a fixed periodic term certain in consideration of a premium or periodical payments' (*Street v Mountford* [1985] AC 809 at 818E, per Lord Templeman).

10.5

Separation agreement

THIS SEPARATION AGREEMENT is made on (*date*)

BETWEEN 'the parties' (1) (*name 1*) of (*address*) ('*name 1*') and (2) (*name 2*) of (*address*) ('*name 2*').

IT IS AGREED that:

1 Recitals

1.1 The parties lived together from (*date*) to (*date*).

1.2 The parties are now living apart.

1.3 The parties have (two) children, namely (*name 3*) who was born on (*date*) and (*name 4*) who was born on (*date*) ('the children').

1.4 Both of the parties have parental responsibility for the children.

1.5 The parties wish to effect an agreement which will dispose of any financial claims that either of them may have against the other and which will make provision for the future welfare and support of the children.

1.6 Each party has fully disclosed his or her financial situation to the other and each party is generally aware of the other's financial situation.

1.7 Each party is entering into this Agreement freely and voluntarily after receiving independent legal advice on its provisions and implications.

1.8 The parties intend that this Agreement will be legally binding on them.

2 Separation

The parties will (continue to) live separately and apart from each other.

3 Non-interference

Neither party will annoy or interfere with the other or his or her relatives, friends, colleagues or business contacts.

4 Confidentiality

Neither party will disclose, divulge or use to the detriment or disadvantage of the other any confidential information about the other's private life, family life, financial affairs or business interests which may have come to his or her knowledge during

10.5 *Miscellaneous*

the course of their relationship, unless such disclosure is required in legal proceedings or for the purpose of making a maintenance assessment under the Child Support Act 1991 ('a maintenance assessment').

5 Children

5.1 The provisions of this Clause will at all times be subject to the ascertainable wishes and feelings of the children themselves, considered in the light of their respective ages and understanding.

5.2 The children will live with (*name 2*).

5.3 The children will be entitled to spend at least (2 weekends) with (*name 1*) each month.

5.4 The children will be entitled to spend at least (2 weeks) with (*name 1*) during the summer holidays each year.

5.5 The children will be entitled to spend Christmas Eve, Christmas Day and Boxing Day with (*name 1*) each alternate year.

5.6 The children will be entitled to maintain contact with (*name 1's*) parents, brothers and sisters.

5.7 All major decisions affecting the children's education, upbringing, health, welfare and the administration of their property will be made by the parties jointly.

5.8 Neither party will cause or allow the children to be known by a new surname or removed from the United Kingdom without the consent of the other party or the leave of the court.

5.9 Each party is responsible for maintaining the children.

5.10 From the date of this Agreement (*name 1*) will pay to (*name 2*) for the benefit of both of the children the sum of £ a month or such other sum as the parties may from time to time agree.

5.11 (*Name 1*) will continue to pay maintenance to (*name 2*) for the children's benefit in accordance with the terms of this Clause until a maintenance assessment takes effect or until such time as a maintenance assessment, if it had been made, would cease to have effect.

5.12 Regardless of the terms of this Clause, either party can at any time apply to the Child Support Agency for a maintenance assessment to be made in respect of either or both of the children.

6 Property

6.1 Within a period of (4) weeks from the date of this Agreement (*name 1*) will transfer to (*name 2*) (his)/(her) legal estate and beneficial interest in the property known as (*address*) ('the property') subject to the mortgage in favour of (*lender*).

6.2 (*Name 2*) will be responsible for the payment of the mortgage and all the other outgoings on the property.

6.3 (*Name 2*) will ensure that all future accounts relating to the outgoings are addressed to (him)/(her).

7 Personal chattels

7.1 The parties have already divided between them all of the personal chattels which formerly belonged to them jointly.

7.2 Each party is now the absolute owner of the personal chattels in his or her possession free from any claim, right or title of the other.

8 Debts

8.1 The parties have divided between them all the debts for which they are jointly and severally liable.

8.2 (*Name 1*) has assumed responsibility for the payment of the following debts:

(name and address of creditor) (amount outstanding).

8.3 (*Name 2*) has assumed responsibility for the payment of the following debts:

(name and address of creditor) (amount outstanding).

8.4 Each party promises to pay the debts for which he or she has assumed responsibility and will indemnify the other against all costs, claims, proceedings and demands arising in respect of those debts.

9 Conciliation

Any difference, disagreement or dispute arising out of or in connection with this Agreement will be referred in the first instance to the Family Conciliation Service without prejudice to the right of either party subsequently to apply to the court for adjudication or to the Child Support Agency for a maintenance assessment to be made or reviewed.

10 Variation

This Agreement can only be varied by an instrument in writing executed as a Deed by both parties.

SIGNED as a Deed by (*name 1*) in the presence of:

SIGNED as a Deed by (*name 2*) in the presence of:

10.6

Family Law Protocol: Part 12 Cohabitation

[The kind permission of the Law Society to reproduce the following material is gratefully acknowledged.]

Solicitors should keep under review at all times the availability of public funding and the need to provide clients with costs information at the outset and on a regular basis.

12.1 Scope

12.1.1 English law does not yet recognise cohabitation as a defined legal status and so very few specific rights exist for cohabitants. This position is

10.6 Miscellaneous

becoming untenable as increasing numbers of the population (1 in 6 of all couples according to the 2001 census) live together without marrying or, if same-sex, entering into a civil partnership. The problems they face on relationship breakdown are similar to those faced by couples who have married or who are civil partners.

12.1.2 The lack of a single statute to deal with cohabitants can make the task of resolving their problems particularly complex. The Law Commission has acknowledged this and proposed reform of this area of law in 2007 (*Cohabitation: The Financial Consequences of Relationship Breakdown* (Cm 7182)). However, the government announced that it would postpone action until it had studied research findings following the implementation of the earlier Family Law (Scotland) Act 2006, which had introduced some specific remedies for cohabitants in that jurisdiction, and so failed to support Lord Lester's Cohabitation Bill in the House of Lords in 2009. Meanwhile, a bill has been introduced in Eire which would, inter alia, have the effect of introducing similar remedies for cohabitants in that country (the Civil Partnership Bill 2009). There are, of course, remedies for cohabitants in many other jurisdictions. Solicitors should be alert to prospective changes to the law and the need to advise clients accordingly.

12.1.3 Much of the Protocol applies equally to cohabiting couples as to married couples or civil partners. See in particular, the approach contained in the Main Protocol (see Part 1) and also Parts 5 and 6 (relating to children), Part 4 (domestic abuse) and Part 2 (mediation/alternative dispute resolution).

12.1.4 It is primarily in the area of finances that the options available to cohabitants on relationship breakdown differ greatly from those available to spouses or civil partners. This section of the Protocol deals mainly with those financial claims which arise on cohabitation breakdown. The key point for solicitors to remember in this area is that there is usually no discretion for the court to adjust the interests of the parties in order to achieve a fair outcome. The most that the court can do is to declare and enforce their existing interests, applying established principles of trust and property law.

12.1.5 Solicitors must be aware that same-sex couples who register their relationship under the Civil Partnership Act 2004 acquire rights equivalent to those of married couples and should not be treated as cohabitants.

12.1.6 Solicitors should bear in mind that it may occasionally be necessary to ascertain the beneficial interests in property in the case of even a married couple or civil partners where there is a third-party claim against the interest of one of them, eg following bankruptcy or the making of a charging order, and that in such circumstances the procedure outlined in 12.4–12.5 would apply.

12.2 Advice at the commencement of or during cohabitation

12.2.1 Experience shows that most clients are completely unaware of their legal position when they cohabit and that they usually have misconceptions as to their rights. Clients may consult solicitors either at the start of their relationship or during it and solicitors should use such opportunities to explain to clients their legal position.

12.2.2 Clients may seek advice at the commencement of a relationship. If so, they should be encouraged to consider entering into a formal cohabitation agreement, if such an agreement would be beneficial to them. Solicitors should have access to appropriate precedents for cohabitation agreements at all times (model cohabitation agreements can be obtained from Resolution and from a number of other sources (see Appendix Aj). Solicitors must advise clients that they can only act for one of the parties in drawing up such an agreement and that the other party must be separately represented.

12.2.3 Clients should be referred to the Advice Now website (see www.advicenow.org.uk/living-together) which is funded by the Ministry of Justice as part of its Living Together campaign. They may also wish to consider the 'Living Together Agreement' which is published on that website.

12.2.4 Clients will often consult solicitors when they are intending to purchase a property together. In such circumstances, careful consideration needs to be given as to how the property is to be held. Particular care is needed where the property is to be held in the name of only one of them or where they have made or are intending to make unequal contributions towards the purchase price. If legal title is to be held in their joint names, solicitors must discuss with them the implications of owning the property either as beneficial joint tenants or tenants in common and ascertain whether a declaration of trust is desirable and/or whether they wish to enter into a cohabitation agreement. To fail to give and record such advice in an appropriate case can lead to a claim for negligence.

12.2.5 Where cohabitants decide to prepare a declaration of trust at the time of purchase of a property, solicitors can act for both cohabitants in preparing the declaration only if it is clear that there is complete agreement from the outset as to all the terms of the declaration and there is no conflict of interest.

12.2.6 At all relevant times, solicitors should advise cohabitants about the importance of making wills, making pension and death-in-service benefit nominations, considering life assurance policies and the benefits of parental responsibility agreements. Solicitors should also advise as to what might occur in the event that these matters are not dealt with. Such advice should be recorded in writing.

12.2.7 Cohabitants should be warned that there is no equivalent to the spouse exemption for them on inheritance tax (IHT) and therefore that gifts made within 7 years of death will attract IHT. At the time of the making of a will, estate planning should be discussed. Practitioners should advise clients of the effect of the ruling in *Holland v IRC*[1] which confirmed that the lack of spouse exemption from IHT for cohabitants is not in breach of the Human Rights Act 1998. Unless there is a change in the law there will be no tax relief on any gifts between cohabitants other than in the normal way. Note that since the Civil Partnership Act 2004, there has been a tax exemption for registered civil partners equivalent to the spouse exemption for married couples.

12.2.8 Solicitors are reminded that they may need to liaise with conveyancing practitioners or third parties who are involved in any existing wills, trusts or settlements. They should obtain letters of authority from their client where appropriate. Solicitors must avoid giving investment advice unless authorised to do so.

12.3 Advice following relationship breakdown

12.3.1 At the first meeting or early on in the case, solicitors should consider and advise, where appropriate, on all the matters referred to in Part 1. The

10.6 *Miscellaneous*

sections relating to reconciliation and other support services apply equally to cohabitation.

12.3.2 The paragraphs relating to family dispute resolution, mediation and collaborative law in Part 2 are also equally applicable in cohabitation cases. Accordingly, solicitors must, at an early stage, unless it is clearly inappropriate to do so, explain the mediation process and advise clients on the benefits and/or limitations of mediation and/or collaborative law in their particular case as well as the role of solicitors in supporting the mediation process. The suitability of mediation should be kept under review throughout the case and clients should be referred to mediation when and where appropriate.

12.3.3 The rest of Part 1 will apply equally to cohabitation cases and should be referred to. It is important that solicitors screen appropriately for domestic abuse and consider whether there are any urgent issues to be dealt with.

12.3.4 Solicitors should check whether a client has made a will and, if so, consider with them whether it is still appropriate in the circumstances.

12.3.5 Solicitors should check how the property is held by obtaining office copies of the Land Registry title documentation. They should also consider obtaining a copy of the original conveyancing file relating to the property in question if, for example, there is likely to be any dispute as to original contributions or intentions at the date of purchase.

12.3.6 If the property is held as a joint tenancy, then consideration should be given to severing the joint tenancy and an appropriate notice prepared, signed by the client and served on the other property owner.

12.3.7 Solicitors should consider whether it is necessary to register a restriction at the Land Registry to protect a client's interest in a property. This is done by completion of Form RXI with a request for entry of a standard-form restriction, usually in Form A of Sch A to the Land Registration Rules 2003, SI 2003/1417. Reference may be had to Land Registry Practice Guide 24: Private Trusts of Land (2009) (at www.landregistry.gov.uk). Provided that the application is clearly worded and shows how and why the client's beneficial interest arose, this will be accepted by the Land Registry as evidence that the client has 'sufficient interest'. It should be noted that the Land Registry will give the (other) registered owner of the land notice of the application and an opportunity to object. If a dispute is identified at this stage, the matter may be referred to the Land Registry Adjudicator for determination, although in practice the adjudicator will usually direct one or other of the parties to commence court proceedings within a specified time-frame.

12.3.8 Solicitors should consider whether to advise a client to contact the mortgage company to place a dispute indicator on their records in order to prevent one party from drawing down on the mortgage if there is any flexibility to do so.

12.3.9 In certain cases it may be appropriate to write and request that the other side consent to the mortgage being converted to interest-only whilst the issues are sorted out, or if one person is paying a lot more, write and put them on notice that they may expect credit by way of equitable accounting. For example, an application under the Children Act (CA) 1989, Sch 1 would not provide for anything other than an interest-only mortgage, but if the father is meeting the mortgage on a repayment basis he is in effect adding to the mother's capital which is not permitted by Sch 1.

Precedents 10.6

12.3.10 Matters relating to children and the provision of information are equally applicable to cohabitation cases, although it is acknowledged that the availability of standard information for cohabitants is not as wide as for other family matters.

12.3.11 Under 1.5 of Part 1 it is important that solicitors should, at the end of the first meeting or at an early stage, outline the possible remedies that are available and the possible outcomes, as far as this is practical with the information available. It is important that clients are not given unrealistic expectations either of what can be achieved or of the time the matter may take to resolve.

12.3.12 Solicitors should advise clients that they might have claims in both property law and family law. Property law claims may be claims for a beneficial interest in a property by way of a resulting or constructive trust dealt with under the Trusts of Land and Appointment of Trustees Act (TLATA) 1996, or proprietary estoppel and/or equitable accounting. If a couple has children, a client may also have claims under CA 1989, Sch 1 and the Child Support Act 1991 (as amended). In exceptional cases these can extend effectively to support of the parent as well as the child.

12.3.13 Solicitors need to bear in mind that practice and procedure for property law and family law claims are very different, the former being governed by the Civil Procedure Rules 1998 (CPR) as amended, the latter by the Family Proceedings Rules (FPR) 1991, SI 1991/1247 and the Family Proceedings Courts (Children Act 1989) Rules (FPCR) 1991, SI 1991/1395 as amended. This is a developing area of law (see for example the cases of *Stack v Dowden*[2] and *Kernott v Jones*[3] and solicitors must ensure that they are aware of the latest case law and confident in their knowledge before offering advice in this area.

12.3.14 When dealing with property claims of cohabiting couples, solicitors should also check to see if they were engaged. Provided that less than 3 years has elapsed since any engagement was broken off, an application could also be made under the Married Women's Property Act (MWPA) 1882 for a declaration in respect of property (which would include chattels).

12.3.15 Although in general, engaged couples are treated in the same way as unmarried couples, solicitors should be aware of the Law Reform (Miscellaneous Provisions) Act (LR(MP)A) 1970, s 3(1) relating to gifts between engaged couples and also the Matrimonial Proceedings and Property Act (MPPA) 1970, s 37 allowing an entitled applicant to argue that he has a share, or an increased share, in property by virtue of substantial contributions to the improvement of that property. In practice, MPPA 1970, s 37 is rarely relied upon because such works would usually now form the basis of a constructive trust or proprietary estoppel claim. They would, however, be family proceedings and FPR 1991 would apply.

12.3.16 There are similar provisions relating to those who were in an agreement to enter into a civil partnership which has been terminated within the last 3 years (Civil Partnership Act 2004, s 74) – see s 65 for the equivalent to MPPA 1970, s 37; s 66 for MWPA 1882; and s 74(5) for LR(MP)A 1970.

12.3.17 The above provisions are particularly useful in relation to property other than real property. Claims concerning real property are better dealt with under the TOLATA 1996 as the court has a wider discretion and can, for example, delay sale.

12.3.18 Requirements for solicitors to provide costs information as outlined in the Main Protocol (see 1.8) apply equally to cohabitation cases. Clients

10.6 *Miscellaneous*

should be advised realistically as to likely costs and solicitors should be aware that contested applications are significantly more expensive than, for example, comparable ancillary relief proceedings. In addition, significant civil court fees are payable on issue, on allocation, on listing and for trial.

12.3.19 Public funding may be available where the proceedings relate to the ownership or possession of the client's home (Legal Services Commission Manual, para.3C-014). Applications under TOLATA 1996 are not 'family proceedings' within the meaning of the Courts and Legal Services Act 1990 and so they can be funded under a conditional fee agreement. If so, an appropriate funding notice must be served on the other party as any success fee would otherwise be unrecoverable under CPR 44.3B(I)(c).

12.3.20 Clients should be advised that, unlike most other 'family' proceedings, the court is likely to make a costs order in favour of whichever party is considered to have 'won' the case – since under CPR 44.3(2)(a) the general rule is that costs will follow the event.

12.3.21 The provisions within the Main Protocol as to communications with the other party (see 1.9) and the giving of notice of issue of proceedings (see 1.11) are both applicable to cohabitation cases.

12.3.22 Clients should be reminded at this early stage that cohabitation cases depend heavily on evidence. Consideration should be given as to how the case is to be pleaded and the evidence that will be necessary in order to prove that case. Witness statements should be taken from the client and any likely witnesses and clients should be advised of the necessity of keeping and producing relevant documentary evidence (eg bank statements, receipts and the like) as the case proceeds. Solicitors should seek to establish the strength of the client's case at this early stage and advise appropriately.

12.4 Prior to issuing proceedings for financial matters

Voluntary disclosure and ADR

12.4.1 Solicitors must consider and discuss the following with clients:

(1) The importance of pre-application disclosure and negotiation. An application must not be issued when settlement is a reasonable prospect. Solicitors are referred to the Pre-Application Protocol for Ancillary Relief (see 11.5). Making an application to the court should not be regarded as a hostile step or a last resort but rather as a way of starting the court timetable, controlling disclosure and endeavouring to avoid the cost of final hearing.

(2) The most appropriate form of dispute resolution for the case, based on clients' needs and individual circumstances, at an early stage. Solicitors must discuss alternative dispute resolution (ADR) with clients, except where it is inappropriate to do so, and advise on whether it is likely to be suitable to their case and, where appropriate, refer them to an appropriate individual (see Part 2).

Identifying the issues

12.4.2 Solicitors must seek to clarify the parties' claims and identify the issues between them as soon as possible. To achieve this the parties must provide, as soon as possible, a full, frank and clear disclosure of facts, information and documents which are material and sufficiently accurate to enable proper negotiations to take place in order to settle their differences. Openness in all dealings is essential.

Pre-action protocol

Civil Procedure Rules 1998, SI 1998/3132

12.4.3 Although there is no protocol specific to TOLATA 1996 cases, solicitors (or parties where unrepresented) will be expected to comply with Annex A of the Practice Direction (Pre-Action Conduct) which applies to all types of civil cases and therefore to cohabitants in proceedings under TOLATA 1996.

12.4.4 The common objectives of all the pre-action protocols are as follows:

(a) to encourage the early and full exchange of information between the parties about any dispute between them which might need resolution by a court;

(b) to enable the parties to avoid proceedings by agreeing a settlement of the claim before commencement of proceedings, either through negotiation directly between them, with or without the assistance of a mediator if appropriate, or negotiation between the solicitors; and

(c) to support the efficient management of proceedings where litigation cannot be avoided.

12.4.5 Under para A.2 of the Practice Direction, the court will expect the parties and their legal advisers to act reasonably in exchanging information and documents relevant to the claim and generally in trying to avoid the necessity for the commencement of proceedings (in accordance with the overriding objective and the matters referred to in CPR 1.1(2)). In view of the nature of family proceedings, the parties and their representatives should act in a conciliatory and constructive manner at all times.

Pre-action procedure for Trusts of Land and Appointment of Trustees Act 1996 claims

12.4.6 For TOLATA 1996 claims, solicitors (or unrepresented parties) should comply with the following key elements of pre-action procedure, if appropriate, unless there are very good reasons for not doing so. They should:

(1) Send an initial letter (referred to in the CPR as a 'letter of claim') setting out the following information in concise form:

(a) a clear summary of uncontroversial facts;

(b) the main allegations of fact including, where appropriate, a summary of what was said by the parties at the time;

(c) an indication of the exact financial claim;

(d) indications as to witnesses and a summary of their evidence;

(e) disclosure of any relevant documents supporting the claim.

Care should be exercised to ensure that the tone of the letter is non-threatening and sets out facts in a non-aggressive way. If addressed to a party who is not represented the letter must advise the party to seek legal advice and should enclose a second copy of the letter to facilitate this.

10.6 Miscellaneous

  (2) If possible and appropriate, refrain from issuing proceedings for 6 weeks, during which time full disclosure should be given and negotiations commenced.

  (3) If responding, give a preliminary reply within 2 weeks of receiving the initial letter of claim.

  (4) If responding, give a full reply within 4 weeks of receiving the letter of claim.

12.4.7 Preparation of the initial letter of claim will involve a substantial financial commitment from clients. Solicitors must give proper advice to ensure that the claim is framed in the correct way bearing in mind that the court will impose penalties if the case is later presented on a different basis.

12.4.8 Solicitors must consider and discuss with clients the fact that failure to comply with the pre-action protocol may lead to an order for indemnity costs and other financial penalties. CPR 43.3(5)(a) requires the court to consider the conduct of the parties before, as well as during, the proceedings and in particular the extent to which the party has followed the relevant protocol. If no letter is sent, then this will usually be regarded as unreasonable conduct and indemnity costs will be awarded against the claimant.

12.4.9 Solicitors must consider with clients whether the immediate issue of proceedings is required in order to obtain protection of assets. An injunction can be sought to restrain the disposal of an asset pending final hearing. Reference should be made to CPR Pt 25.

12.4.10 If matters between the parties are concluded without the issue of court proceedings, the outcome should be recorded in a formal deed.

12.5 Issue and conduct of proceedings

12.5.1 Applications for an order under TOLATA 1996, s 14 (usually brought under CPR Pt 8) will be issued on Form N208 with a claim form, a signed statement of truth and a witness statement from the claimant. They attract a court issue fee. The defendant has 14 days from receipt of the claim in which to file an acknowledgement of service and witness statement. In practice, 14 days will seldom be long enough and it would be usual to agree a voluntary extension.

12.5.2 Solicitors will be aware that the proceedings will offer only a declaration of an equitable interest in a property and a consequential order, for example an order for sale.

12.5.3 Solicitors should note that if there is to be a substantial question of fact or law raised within a case, eg a dispute as to whether a claimant has any beneficial interest in the property at all or as to the extent of that interest, it will be more appropriate to issue the proceedings under the CPR Pt 7 procedure with a claim in Form N201 supported by formal particulars of claim containing full details of the legal basis of the claim and remedies sought. Although a strict reading of CPR 64.3 and PD 64A, para I(1)(a)(iii) suggests that Pt 8 should be used for these applications, the court is unlikely in practice to raise any issue if the Pt 7 procedure is used, particularly if the parties have agreed to its use. Claims commenced under Pt 8 can be transferred to Pt 7 at an early stage under CPR 8.8 if the other party objects, or by the court itself under rule 8.1(3).

12.5.4 It should be noted that there are specific requirements for the contents of particulars of claim and reference should be made to CPR 16.4 and para 7 of the accompanying Practice Direction.

12.5.5 In all cases, further consideration should be given to mediation as the court will agree to stay the proceedings for a fixed period to enable the parties to attempt to settle the action either by negotiation or another form of ADR.

12.5.6 Most applications under Pt 7 will be allocated to the multi-track because they have a value of over £25,000 and/or the court considers that the trial will probably last longer than one day, as will usually be the case. Applications under Pt 8 are automatically treated as allocated to the multi-track, although a specific allocation is usually sought if the parties wish to ensure that the route of appeal is to the Court of Appeal (which is not available if the case is merely 'treated as' allocated to that track).

12.5.7 Solicitors should be aware that most interlocutory hearings in civil cases take the form of a telephone hearing, and that it is usually the responsibility of the applicant/claimant to arrange these. BT Legal Conferencing can be contacted on 0800 028 4194 in order to arrange such a hearing.

12.5.8 Although FPR 1991 do not apply to these claims, many courts are prepared to direct that a case management conference be conducted as if it were a financial dispute resolution (FDR) appointment in an ancillary relief application and an appropriate direction should be sought at allocation stage.

12.6 Directions

12.6.1 Directions which the court might be asked to make are:

(a) that the case be listed for a directions appointment for the purpose of assessing the parties' positions and for the purpose of discussion and negotiation;

(b) that the parties serve signed witness statements in advance;

(c) that the parties file:

(1) details of all offers;

(2) a position statement;

(3) an agreed statement of issues;

(d) that the parties shall attend personally;

(e) that the appointment shall be conducted on a without prejudice basis;

(f) in the event that the proceedings are not settled at the hearing the district judge hearing the appointment should not make any orders or directions that the case shall be listed for a case management conference.

12.6.2 Note that the court should be asked to list the appointment with a realistic time estimate (at least one hour) and the parties asked to attend one hour prior to narrow the issues.

12.6.3 Clients should be encouraged to make a reasonable offer of settlement and in most cases the procedure under CPR Pt 36 should be followed. The recipient has 21 days in which to accept the offer. If the claimant fails to beat a Pt 36 offer, then there are costs consequences.

10.6 Miscellaneous

12.6.4 Clients should be reminded that the trial of an application under TOLATA 1996 takes place in open court, to which the public are admitted. Advocates will usually be robed.

12.6.5 Solicitors are advised to carefully consider the provisions of the CPR when undertaking an application under TOLATA 1996, and if they feel that they are not sufficiently proficient in this area, should consider taking advice from a more experienced civil practitioner or transferring the file to another solicitor. Failure to comply with the CPR can lead to sanctions, including the automatic striking out of claims or defences at very short notice, if procedural steps are not taken in a timely fashion.

12.7 Claims under the Inheritance (Provision for Family and Dependants) Act 1975

12.7.1 Most firms distinguish between contentious probate work and claims under the Inheritance (Provision for Family and Dependants) Act (I(PFD)A) 1975. In some firms, I(PFD)A 1975 cases are dealt with by family lawyers.

12.7.2 Solicitors should not undertake without supervision any work which they know to be outside their area of expertise.

12.7.3 If a case appears complex or beyond the expertise of a practitioner they should consider whether the case should be passed to a member of the Association of Contentious Trust and Probate Specialists (ACTAPS). Solicitors are referred to the ACTAPS Practice Guidance Notes and Code of Conduct which can be found on the Association's website at www.actaps.com. Best practice pre-action procedures are contained in their Draft Pre-Action Protocol for the Resolution of Probate and Trust Disputes and failure to follow this Protocol can lead to costs penalties.

12.7.4 Solicitors must understand that claims brought under I(PFD)A 1975 are also governed by the CPR. In particular, CPR 57.16 clearly requires that claims under I(PFD)A, s 1 be issued under CPR Pt 8, even though the Pt 8 procedure is probably not appropriate if there are substantial disputed facts and the case is likely to be dealt with under Pt 7.

12.7.5 Particular care needs to be taken as to the persons who are to be parties to the proceedings as it would be usual to have the personal representatives and the beneficiaries of the estate as separate defendants. Solicitors should note that personal representatives have no power to compromise a claim under the I(PFD)A 1975 unless the beneficiaries instruct them to settle the claim. Note also that if any beneficiary is a minor, then the approval of the court will be needed for any settlement.

12.7.6 Solicitors must note that the time limit for issuing a claim is 6 months from the date of the issue of the grant of representation, for example the date of the grant of probate.

12.7.7 In the case of *Re Parnall (Deceased)*[4] the court confirmed that it was not appropriate in I(PFD)A 1975 cases to seek to prevent a grant from being issued while negotiating a claim by entering caveat.

12.7.8 Instead, to be put on notice of the issuing of a grant in an estate a request should be made to the Probate Registry for a standing search. The fee is currently £5.00 and covers a period of 6 months. Successive periods can be covered by making additional applications. If in that period a grant is issued the Registry will send notification of the person who has extracted the grant and solicitors can obtain a copy of the grant. It will therefore be possible to issue a claim within the time limits of the grant.

Precedents 10.6

12.7.9 In view of the time limit for issuing a claim, pre-issue negotiation is necessarily limited, but this may serve to focus the minds of those involved.

12.7.10 It is helpful to agree, wherever possible, that a directions hearing in an I(PFD)A 1975 case be treated similarly to an FDR hearing so that the judge gives an indication of his or her view of a case and an indication to the parties of the costs implications of continuing to a final hearing.

12.7.11 Solicitors requiring information on the subject of probate are referred to the Probate Practitioner's Handbook (6th edn, Law Society, 2010) which deals with both contentious probate and I(PFD)A 1975 claims.

12.7.12 Solicitors are reminded that the same civil costs rules apply to claims under I(PFD)A 1975 as to those under TOLATA 1996.

12.8 Financial issues relating to children

12.8.1 Solicitors are referred to Part 5 for guidance on acting in private children law cases, Part 9 for claims under CA 1989, Sch 1 and Part S for general child support issues (ie the Child Maintenance and Enforcement Commission (CMEC)).

12.9 Jurisdiction and in which court to commence proceedings

12.9.1 Before proceedings relating to disputes about property, money, other belongings and children are issued, solicitors must consider carefully where they should issue the application. Where proceedings about different issues are being conducted in relation to the same couple, all proceedings must, where possible, be heard in the same court. If there are applications under TOLATA 1996 and under CA 1989 they should be consolidated and heard together (*W v W (Joinder of Trusts of Land Act and Children Act Applications)*[5]).

12.9.2 The county court has unlimited jurisdiction under TOLATA 1996 although the application must be issued in the appropriate court for the area in which the defendant resides or in which the property is situated. The Principal Registry of the Family Division, which sits as a county court, has full jurisdiction to deal with applications under TOLATA 1996, s 14 and such claims can be issued out of the Principal Registry (see CPR PD 2B, para 3.2 and *Practice Direction (Family Division: Allocation of Cases: Costs)* [1999] 3 All ER 192).

12.9.3 Claims can be issued out of any District Registry of the High Court. Solicitors should be aware that proceedings may not be started in the High Court unless the value of the claim is more than £25,000 (CPR PD 7A, para 2.1). Subject to that limitation, if the financial value of the claim, the amount in dispute and/or the complexity of the facts, legal issues, remedies or procedures involved and/or the importance of the outcome of the claim to the public in general are such that solicitors believe that the claim ought to be dealt with by a High Court judge, then the case should be issued in the High Court. In any event, a claim with a value of less than £50,000 will generally be transferred to the county court (CPR PD 29, para 2.2).

12.9.4 Claims may be issued in either the Family Division or Chancery. The Family Division is likely to be the more appropriate where the parties were living together as a family unit, particularly if they have children or if there are to be linked family claims. The latter may be more appropriate if their relationship was more business-like.

10.6 Miscellaneous

1. [2003] WTLR 207.
2. [2007] UKHL 17.
3. [2010] EWCA Civ 578).
4. [2003] All ER (D) 40.
5. [2004] 2 FLR 321.

Index

A

Abduction of child
  custody rights **5.39–5.41**
  introduction **5.37**
  status of unmarried parent **5.38**

Acknowledgment of advice received
  cohabitation agreements, and **2.16**

Adoption
  applications by cohabitants **5.28**
  consent **5.31**
  court's discretion **5.35**
  dispensing with consent **5.32**
  introduction **5.26**
  one person, by **5.29**
  order, revocation **5.36**
  preliminaries **5.30**
  same-sex couples **5.28**
  status of unmarried father **5.33, 5.34**
  statutory basis **5.27**

Advance decisions
  content **6.98**
  introduction **6.97**
  legal status **6.99–6.101**

Advice to client
  cohabitation agreements, and **2.2**

After-acquired property
  cohabitation agreements, and **2.17, 2.18**

Agricultural relief
  inheritance tax, and **3.14**

Amount required to redeem mortgage
  definition clause **1.191**

Applications
  Children Act 1989, s 17, under **1.130**
  Children Act 1989, s 20, under **1.129**
  declaration of interest in trust property, for
    applicants **1.64**
    exercise of court's discretion **1.69–1.71**
    injunctions **1.73**
    introduction **1.62**
    issue **1.66**
    order **1.72**
    precedents **1.232**
    procedure **1.67, 1.68**
    relevant court **1.65**
    relief available **1.63**

Applications – *cont.*
  declaration of ownership of chattels, for
    court's approach **1.140**
    form of order **1.242**
    introduction **1.138**
    order **1.141**
    relevant court **1.139**
  family provision from deceased's estate
    checklist on first instructions **6.105**
    procedure generally **6.103**
  homelessness, and
    Children Act 1989, s 17, under **1.130**
    Children Act 1989, s 20, under **1.129**
    local authority, to **1.128**
  inheritance provision by children, for
    circumstances at date of hearing **6.71**
    court's approach **6.68–6.70**
    court's discretion **6.67**
    eligibility **6.60–6.62**
    ground for application **6.63**
    introduction **6.59**
    matters to be considered **6.64–6.66**
  inheritance provision by dependant, for
    court's discretion **6.58**
    eligibility **6.50–6.53**
    ground for application **6.54**
    introduction **6.49**
    matters to be considered **6.55–6.57**
  inheritance provision by surviving cohabitant, for
    court's discretion **6.48**
    eligibility **6.38–6.43**
    ground for application **6.44**
    introduction **6.37**
    matters to be considered **6.45–6.47**
  loan from social fund, for **1.131**
  local authority, to
    Children Act 1989, s 17, under **1.130**
    Children Act 1989, s 20, under **1.129**
    introduction **1.128**
  Married Women's Property Act 1882, under
    applicants **1.76**
    court's approach **1.81**
    hearing **1.80**
    injunctions **1.83**

Index

Applications – *cont.*
  Married Women's Property Act 1882, under – *cont.*
    introduction **1.74**
    order **1.82**
    procedure **1.78**
    relevant court **1.77**
    relief available **1.75**
    service **1.79**
  Matrimonial Proceedings and Property Act 1970, under **1.84**
  non-molestation orders, for
    hearing **4.10**
    issue **4.8**
    service **4.9**
  occupation orders, and
    hearing **4.43**
    issue **4.40**
    service **4.41**
  order of sale of chattels, for
    court's approach **1.140**
    form of order **1.242**
    introduction **1.138**
    order **1.141**
  order of sale of property, for
    applicants **1.64**
    exercise of court's discretion **1.69–1.71**
    injunctions **1.73**
    introduction **1.62**
    issue **1.66**
    legal background **1.145**
    order **1.72**
    precedents **1.232**
    procedure **1.67, 1.68, 1.146**
    relevant court **1.65**
    relief available **1.63**
  parental responsibility order **5.77**
  social fund loan, for **1.131**
  transfer of tenancy (CA 1989, Sch 1), for
    applicants **1.122**
    court's approach **1.126**
    exercise of court's discretion **1.125**
    introduction **1.120**
    issue **1.123**
    relevant court **1.121**
    service **1.124**
  transfer of tenancy (FLA 1996, Pt IV), for
    exercise of court's discretion **1.114**
    hearing **1.119**
    issue **1.115**
    order **1.118**
    precedents **1.237**
    relevant court **1.110**
    response **1.117**
    service **1.116**
    time limits **1.113**

Applications – *cont.*
  transfer of tenancy (FLA 1996, Pt IV), for – *cont.*
    transferable tenancies **1.112**
Applications without notice
  non-molestation orders, for **4.14**
  occupation orders, and **4.42**
Appointment of guardian
  generally **5.25**
  precedents **5.87**
Arbitration
  cohabitation agreements, and **2.52**
Arrest
  occupation order, court powers **4.86**
Artificial insemination by donor
  declaration of parentage, and **5.7**
Assault
  generally **4.65**
  procedure **4.66**
Assault and battery
  procedure **4.74, 4.75**
Assignment of tenancies
  assured tenancies **1.93**
  local authority housing **1.102**
  protected tenancies **1.97**
Associated persons
  non-molestation orders, for **4.5**
  occupation orders, and **4.17**
Assured tenancies
  assignment **1.93**
  introduction **1.90**
  security **1.92**
  succession **1.94**
  transfer
    Children Act 1989, Sch 1, under **1.120**
    Family Law Act 1996, Pt IV, under **1.110**
    introduction **1.109**
Attestation
  cohabitation agreements, and **2.20**
  property, and **1.200**
  wills, and **6.157**
Attorneyship
  cohabitation agreements, and **2.73**

B

Balance of harm test
  occupation orders, and
    s 33 applications **4.22**
    s 36 applications **4.32**
    s 38 applications **4.38**
Bank accounts
  cohabitation agreements, and **2.21, 2.22**
  termination **2.132**

Index

Bank accounts – *cont.*
  ownership of chattels, and **1.134**
Bankruptcy
  contingencies **1.205**
Battery
  generally **4.65**
  procedure **4.66**
Beneficial interests
  cohabitation agreements, and **2.23**
Beneficial joint tenants
  express declaration of beneficial trusts, and **1.19**
Bequest of chattels
  wills, and **6.126–6.129**
Bereavement damages
  fatal accident claims
    FAA 1976, under **6.90**
Binding effect
  cohabitation agreements, and **2.24**
Birth control
  cohabitation agreements, and **2.25**
Building society accounts
  cohabitation agreements, and **2.21, 2.22**
    termination **2.132**
  ownership of chattels, and **1.134**
Business interests
  cohabitation agreements, and **2.26**
Business reliefs
  inheritance tax, and **3.14**

C

Cancellation
  cohabitation agreements, and **2.27**
Capital gains tax
  introduction **3.7**
  private residence relief **3.8**
Careers
  cohabitation agreements, and **2.31**
Cars
  cohabitation agreements, and **2.28–2.30**
Caution against dealings
  generally **1.7, 1.8**
Change of name
  children, and
    applicant **5.22**
    court's discretion **5.24**
    generally **5.21**
    precedent deed **5.86**
    procedure **5.23**
  deed **10.3**
  generally **10.1**
Charge cards
  cohabitation agreements, and **2.46, 2.47**
    termination **2.133**

Chattels, ownership of
  applications for declarations
    court's approach **1.140**
    introduction **1.138**
    order **1.141**
    relevant court **1.139**
  bank accounts **1.134**
  cohabitation agreement **1.137**
  engaged couples **1.143**
  existing property **1.135**
  generally **1.133**
  gifts **1.136**
  injunctions **1.142**
  introduction **1.132**
Child
  family provision applicant **6.104**
  pension rights, for **7.17**
Child abduction
  custody rights **5.39–5.41**
  introduction **5.37**
  status of unmarried parent **5.38**
Child allowances
  income tax, and **3.5**
Child arrangements order
  generally **5.19**
  procedure **5.20**
Child care
  cohabitation agreements, and
    allocation of responsibility **2.32**
    support of care **2.33**
Child maintenance
  meaning **5.43**
Child maintenance agreement
  precedent **5.89**
Child periodical payments
  meaning **5.43**
Child support
  agreements and child maintenance **5.49**
  calculation **5.46**
  meaning **5.43**
  qualifying children **5.45**
  scheme for **5.44**
  top-up orders **5.48**
  variation, collection and enforcement **5.47**
Child support scheme
  enforcement of financial provision orders **5.67, 5.72**
  child maintenance **5.71**
  child maintenance arrears **5.68, 5.69**
  child periodical payments **5.70**
  Family Court procedures **5.73**
  Family Court, registration in **5.74**
  High Court procedures **5.73**
  other financial provision **5.68**
  termination by resumption of cohabitation **5.66**

Index

Child support scheme – *cont.*
  termination of payments 5.65
Child tax credit
  income tax, and 3.6
Child-rearing
  contingencies 1.208
Children
  adoption
    applications by cohabitants 5.28
    consent 5.31
    court's discretion 5.35
    dispensing with consent 5.32
    introduction 5.26
    one person, by 5.29
    order, revocation 5.36
    preliminaries 5.30
    same-sex couples 5.28
    status of unmarried father 5.33, 5.34
    statutory basis 5.27
  appointment of guardian
    generally 5.25
    precedents 5.87, 5.88
  artificial insemination by donor 5.7
  change of name
    applicant 5.22
    court's discretion 5.24
    generally 5.21
    precedent deed 5.86
    procedure 5.23
  child abduction
    custody rights 5.39–5.41
    introduction 5.37
    status of unmarried parent 5.38
  child arrangements order 5.19
    procedure 5.20
  child maintenance agreement
    precedent 5.89
  cohabitation agreements, and
    care 2.32
    recitals 2.109
    statement of intentions 2.34
    termination 2.140, 2.141
  death of cohabitant, and 6.13
  declaration of parentage
    artificial insemination by donor 5.7
    evidence 5.5
    introduction 5.3
    refusal to submit to testing 5.6
    statutory basis 5.4
  financial provision
    child support scheme 5.44–5.46, 5.48, 5.49, 5.65, 5.66
    introduction 5.42
    terminology 5.43
    variation, collection and enforcement 5.47

Children – *cont.*
  financial relief under CA 1989, Sch 1
    applicants 5.53
    available relief 5.51
    court's approach 5.60
    court's discretion 5.59
    interim orders 5.63
    introduction 5.50
    issue of application 5.55
      pre-application protocol 5.54
      procedure at first appointment 5.58
    service of application 5.56
    venue for proceedings 5.52
  guardianship 5.25
  inheritance provision claims, and
    circumstances at date of hearing 6.71
    court's approach 6.68–6.70
    court's discretion 6.67
    eligibility 6.60–6.62
    ground for application 6.63
    introduction 6.59
    matters to be considered 6.64–6.66
  introduction 5.1
  law and practice
    adoption 5.26
    appointment of guardian 5.25
    change of name 5.21
    child abduction 5.37
    child support scheme 5.44–5.46, 5.48, 5.49, 5.65, 5.66
    financial provision 5.42
    introduction 5.1
    parental responsibility 5.8
    paternity 5.3
    registration of births 5.2
    terminology 5.43
    variation, collection and enforcement 5.47
  lump sum orders
    applicants 5.53
    available relief 5.51
    court's approach 5.61
    court's discretion 5.59
    interim orders 5.63
    introduction 5.50
    issue of application 5.54, 5.55, 5.58
    service of application 5.56
  orders, application for 5.83
  parentage, declaration of
    artificial insemination by donor 5.7
    evidence 5.5
    introduction 5.3
    refusal to submit to testing 5.6
    statutory basis 5.4
  parental responsibility
    acquisition of 5.9

Index

Children – *cont.*
  parental responsibility – *cont.*
    adoption, by 5.26
    appointment as guardian 5.25
    child arrangements order, by 5.19
    introduction 5.8
    joint registration of birth 5.10
    parental responsibility agreement, by 5.11
    parental responsibility order, by 5.14
    residence order, by 5.19
  parental responsibility agreement
    duration 5.13
    generally 5.11
    precedent 5.84
    procedure 5.12
  parental responsibility order
    application 5.85
    court's discretion 5.16
    discharge 5.18
    duration 5.17
    generally 5.14
    procedure 5.15
  periodical payment orders
    applicants 5.53
    available relief 5.51
    court's approach 5.60
    court's discretion 5.59
    interim orders 5.63
    introduction 5.50
    issue of application 5.54, 5.55, 5.58
    service of application 5.56
    venue for proceedings 5.52
  precedents
    appointment of guardian 5.87
      informal appointment by one parent 5.88
    change of name deed 5.86
    child maintenance agreement 5.89
    financial statements for a financial remedy 5.92
    Form C1 5.83
    notice of an application for a financial remedy 5.90, 5.91
    parental responsibility agreement 5.84
    parental responsibility order 5.85
  registration of births
    generally 5.2
    joint 5.10
  transfer of property orders 5.51
    applicants 5.53
    court's approach 5.62
    court's discretion 5.59
    interim orders 5.63
    introduction 5.50
    issue of application 5.54, 5.55, 5.58

Children – *cont.*
  transfer of property orders – *cont.*
    service of application 5.56
    variation of orders 5.64
    venue for proceedings 5.52
Children Act 1989
  financial relief, and
    applicants 5.53
    available relief 5.51
    court's approach 5.60
    court's discretion 5.59
    interim orders 5.63
    introduction 5.50
    issue of application 5.55
      pre-application protocol 5.54
      procedure at first appointment 5.58
    service of application 5.56
    venue for proceedings 5.52
  homelessness, and
    s 17, under 1.130
    s 20, under 1.129
  occupation of the home, and 1.87
  service 1.124
  transfer of tenancy, and
    applicants 1.122
    court's approach 1.126
    exercise of court's discretion 1.125
    introduction 1.120
    issue 1.123
    relevant court 1.121
Civil partners
  cohabitation test
    welfare benefits for 9.17, 9.18
Civil partnership
  family provision on death 6.104
  parental responsibility as step-parent 5.78
  tenancy transfer of home 1.148, 4.71
Coercion
  cohabitation agreements, and 2.8
Cohabitant
  family provision application 6.104
  tenancy transfer by court 1.148, 4.71
Cohabitation
  disqualification, and 9.10, 9.11
  means test, and 9.9
  running case against DWP, HMRC or local authority 9.108–9.127
    appeals, checklist for 9.126, 9.127
    case law arguments 9.125
    representation at hearing 9.123, 9.124
  social security law, and 9.8, 9.9, 9.12
  'couple' 9.13–9.15
    living together 9.16–9.20
      additional factors 9.24
      alternative reasons 9.39, 9.42–9.44
      disability and care 9.40, 9.41

817

Index

Cohabitation – *cont.*
  social security law, and – *cont.*
    'couple' – *cont.*
      living together – *cont.*
        areas of relationship **9.21, 9.22**
          six signposts **9.23**
        children **9.81–9.86, 9.88, 9.89**
          birth certificate **9.87**
        civil partners **9.97–9.102**
        financial support **9.73–9.77, 9.80**
          child maintenance **9.79**
          property purchase **9.78**
        list of factors, importance of using **9.25**
        members of same household **9.26–9.29**
          different address **9.30, 9.31**
          separate households **9.34–9.36**
          staying overnight **9.32, 9.33**
        multi-partner scenarios **9.106**
        public acknowledgment **9.90–9.95**
        reasons
          sexual relationship **9.45–9.50**
            engaged to be married **9.52**
            faithfulness **9.64**
            no sex at material time **9.55**
            no sex ever **9.51, 9.53, 9.54**
            now ceased **9.59–9.63**
            sleeping arrangements **9.56–9.58**
          sharing degree of family life **9.37, 9.38**
          stability of relationship **9.65–9.72**
          temporary separations **9.103–9.105**
        unlawful relationships **9.107**
    disqualification **9.10, 9.11**
  tax credits law, and **9.8, 9.9, 9.12**
    'couple' **9.13–9.15**
      living together **9.16–9.20**
        additional factors **9.24**
        alternative reasons **9.39, 9.42–9.44**
          disability and care **9.40, 9.41**
        areas of relationship **9.21, 9.22**
          six signposts **9.23**
        children **9.81–9.86, 9.88, 9.89**
          birth certificate **9.87**
        civil partners **9.97–9.102**
        financial support **9.73–9.77, 9.80**
          child maintenance **9.79**
          property purchase **9.78**
        list of factors, importance of using **9.25**
        members of same household **9.26–9.29**
          different address **9.30, 9.31**

Cohabitation – *cont.*
  tax credits law, and – *cont.*
    'couple' – *cont.*
      living together – *cont.*
        members of same household **9.26–9.29** – *cont.*
          different address **9.30, 9.31** – *cont.*
          separate households **9.34–9.36**
          staying overnight **9.32, 9.33**
        multi-partner scenarios **9.106**
        public acknowledgment **9.90–9.95**
        reasons
          sexual relationship **9.45–9.50**
            engaged to be married **9.52**
            faithfulness **9.64**
            no sex at material time **9.55**
            no sex ever **9.51, 9.53, 9.54**
            now ceased **9.59–9.63**
            sleeping arrangements **9.56–9.58**
          sharing degree of family life **9.37, 9.38**
          stability of relationship **9.65–9.72**
          temporary separations **9.103–9.105**
        unlawful relationships **9.107**
    disqualification **9.10, 9.11**
  welfare benefits, and **9.8–9.12**
    'couple' **9.13–9.15**
      living together **9.16–9.20**
        additional factors **9.24**
        alternative reasons **9.39, 9.42–9.44**
          disability and care **9.40, 9.41**
        areas of relationship **9.21, 9.22**
          six signposts **9.23**
         children **9.81–9.86, 9.88, 9.89**
          birth certificate **9.87**
        civil partners **9.97–9.102**
        financial support **9.73–9.77, 9.80**
          child maintenance **9.79**
          property purchase **9.78**
        list of factors, importance of using **9.25**
        members of same household **9.26–9.29**
          different address **9.30, 9.31**
          separate households **9.34–9.36**
          staying overnight **9.32, 9.33**
        multi-partner scenarios **9.106**
        public acknowledgment **9.90–9.95**
        reasons
          sexual relationship **9.45–9.50**
            engaged to be married **9.52**
            faithfulness **9.64**
            no sex at material time **9.55**

Index

Cohabitation – *cont.*
  welfare benefits, and – *cont.*
    'couple' – *cont.*
      living together – *cont.*
        reasons – *cont.*
          sexual relationship 9.45–9.50 – *cont.*
            no sex ever 9.51, 9.53, 9.54
            now ceased 9.59–9.63
            sleeping arrangements 9.56–9.58
          sharing degree of family life 9.37, 9.38
          stability of relationship 9.65–9.72
          temporary separations 9.103–9.105
          unlawful relationships 9.107
Cohabitation agreements
  acknowledgment of advice received 2.16
  advising clients 2.2
  after-acquired property
    separate 2.17
    shared 2.18
  aims and expectations 2.19
  arbitration 2.52
  attestation 2.20
  attorneyship 2.73
  bank accounts
    separate 2.21
    shared 2.22
  beneficial interests 2.23
  binding effect 2.24
  birth control 2.25
  business interests 2.26
  cancellation 2.27
  careers 2.31
  cars
    one party providing for other 2.30
    separate 2.28
    shared 2.29
  checklist for
    contents 2.14
    drafting 2.12
    initial interview 2.11
    property and financial issues 2.15
    submission of draft, client to 2.13
  child care
    allocation of responsibility 2.32
    support of care 2.33
  children
    care 2.32
    recitals 2.109
    statement of intentions 2.34
  coercion 2.8
  cohabitant under 18 2.104

Cohabitation agreements – *cont.*
  commencement
    date 2.36
    generally 2.35
  conciliation 2.53
  confidentiality 2.37
  consideration
    clauses 2.38
    general 2.39
    generally 2.6
  contents
    checklist 2.14
    generally 2.10
  cooling-off
    counselling 2.40
    trial separation 2.41
  costs 2.42
    one party to pay all 2.43
    one party to pay for independent advice 2.44
  counselling 2.40
  covenants relating to property 2.45
  credit cards
    separate 2.46
    shared 2.47
  death-in-service benefits 2.95
  debts 2.48
  declaration of trust 2.49
  deed 2.50
  dispute resolution
    arbitration 2.52
    conciliation 2.53
    named mediator 2.54
  duration
    fixed term 2.56
    indefinite 2.55
  duress
    generally 2.8
    recitals 2.103
  dwelling
    joint tenancy 2.57
    sole owner 2.59
    tenancy in common 2.58
  enforceability
    coercion 2.8
    consideration 2.6
    duress 2.8
    equality of bargaining power 2.8
    intention to create legal relations 2.5
    introduction 2.4
    ousting court's jurisdiction 2.9
    uncertainty 2.7
  equality of bargaining power 2.8
  estate rights 2.60
  execution 2.61
  family provision 2.111

Index

Cohabitation agreements – *cont.*
  fiduciary duty 2.62
  financial disclosure 2.63
    both cohabitants, by 2.64
  forms
    joint account to pay housing costs 2.154
    keeping everything separate 2.151
    one party supporting the other 2.152
    personal chattels acquired jointly 2.153
    sharing everything (longer form) 2.150
    sharing everything (short form) 2.149
  further assurances 2.65
  gifts
    between cohabitants 2.66
    reservation of rights 2.67
    separate 2.68
  guests 2.69
  headings 2.70
  housekeeping allowance 2.71
  housework 2.72
  illness or incapacity
    attorneyship 2.73
    next of kin 2.74
    support 2.75
  income 2.76
    shared 2.77
  independent legal advice
    generally 2.81
    recitals 2.106
  inheritance provision 2.111
  intention not to create legal relations 2.101
  intention to create legal relations
    clause 2.78
    generally 2.5
    recitals 2.100
  interpretation 2.79
  introduction 2.1
  joint property
    joint tenancy 2.80
    tenancy in common 2.81
  joint tenancy
    dwelling 2.57
    property 2.80
  joint use 2.82
  law and practice
    advising clients 2.2
    contents 2.10
    enforceability of agreements 2.4
    introduction 2.1
    validity of agreements 2.3
  legal adviser's certificate 2.83
  life assurance 2.84
  living expenses
    defined areas of responsibility 2.89

Cohabitation agreements – *cont.*
  living expenses – *cont.*
    fixed percentages 2.87
    joint account 2.85
    one party pays all 2.88
    proportion to respective incomes 2.86
  marriage 2.90, 2.91
  medical insurance 2.92
  mortgage payments 2.93
  next of kin 2.74
  non-disclosure to third parties 2.94
  ousting court's jurisdiction 2.9
  ownership of chattels, and 1.137
  pension benefits 2.95
  personal information 2.108
  precedents
    clauses 2.16
    forms 2.149
    use 1.152
  present property and debts 2.97
  proper law 2.98
  property
    covenants 2.45
    joint tenancy 2.57, 2.80
    sole ownership 2.59
    tenancy in common 2.58, 2.81
  purpose 2.102
  recitals
    children 2.109
    cohabitant under 18 2.104
    cohabitation 2.99
    independent legal advice 2.106
    intention not to create legal relations 2.101
    intention to create legal relations 2.100
    legally binding recitals 2.105
    no duress or undue influence 2.103
    personal information 2.108
    purpose of agreement 2.102
    understanding nature and effect 2.107
  release of rights
    inheritance provision 2.111
    other's separate property 2.110
  religious upbringing of child 2.112
  remedies for breach 2.113
  rent 2.114
  review
    ad hoc 2.115
    generally 2.116
  revocation 2.117
  separate property 2.96
  separation 2.118
  severance 2.119
  sexual relations 2.120
  sole ownership 2.59

Cohabitation agreements – *cont.*
  support
    mutual support **2.121**
    no obligation **2.122**
    no promises made **2.123**
    reservation of right **2.124**
    waiver of rights **2.125**
  surname **2.126, 2.127**
  tenancy in common
    dwelling **2.58**
    property **2.80**
  terminating events
    death **2.130**
    end of relationship **2.128**
    injunctions **2.130**
    marriage **2.130**
    mutual agreement **2.130**
    notice **2.129**
    order **2.130**
    separation **2.130**
  termination consequences
    bank accounts **2.132**
    children **2.140, 2.141**
    credit and charge cards **2.133**
    dwelling **2.134**
    introductory **2.131**
    jointly owned goods and chattels **2.136**
    lump sum payment **2.138**
    marriage, on **2.142**
    miscellaneous cancellations **2.139**
    separate property **2.135**
    support **2.137**
  transfers between cohabitants **2.143**
  trial separation **2.41**
  uncertainty **2.7**
  understanding nature and effect **2.107**
  undue influence **2.103**
  validity **2.3**
  variation **2.144**
    deed **2.145**
  waiver of breach **2.146**
  whole agreement **2.147**
  wills **2.148**
Committal for contempt
  personal protection orders, and
    application **4.56**
    hearing of application **4.57**
    introduction **4.54**
    sentencing **4.58**
    venue for proceedings **4.55**
  protection from harassment, and **4.64**
Committal order
  breach of judgment or order, for **4.76–4.85**
    appeal **4.86**
    application procedure **4.76–4.85**

Committal order – *cont.*
  breach of judgment or order, for – *cont.*
    court **4.86**
    discharge **4.86**
    disposal powers **4.86**
    hearing **4.86**
    service **4.86**
  breach of undertaking, for **4.76–4.85**
  judgment or order enforced by **4.76–4.85**
Conciliation
  cohabitation agreements, and **2.53**
Conduct
  inheritance provision claims, and **6.35**
Confidentiality
  cohabitation agreements, and **2.37**
Consent
  adoption, and **5.31**
Consideration
  cohabitation agreements, and **2.39**
    clauses **2.38**
    generally **2.6**
Constructive trusts
  contribution **1.33–1.43**
  detrimental reliance **1.44**
  establishment **1.33–1.43**
  generally **1.32**
  quantification, and **1.45–1.52**
Contempt of court
  committal order
    disposal proportionate **4.86**
    discharge of contemnor **4.86**
  personal protection orders, and
    application **4.56**
    hearing of application **4.57**
    introduction **4.54**
    sentencing **4.58**
    venue for proceedings **4.55**
  protection from harassment, and **4.64**
Contingencies
  bankruptcy **1.205**
  child-rearing **1.208**
  death **1.204**
  disagreement as to sale **1.203**
  failure to pay share of mortgage **1.202**
  full-time education
    conversion of fixed shares into floating shares **1.210**
    mortgage payments treated as loan **1.209**
  improvement to property **1.206**
  incapacity to work **1.207**
  introductory **1.177**
  moving out before sale **1.213**
  other person permitted to reside **1.201**
  pregnancy **1.208**
  prior rights to sole ownership **1.211**

821

Index

Contingencies – *cont.*
  prior rights to sole ownership – *cont.*
    rules for determining 1.212
    repair to property 1.206
    separation after purchase 1.214
    unemployment 1.207
    wish to realise share 1.215
Contractual licence
  deed 10.4
  generally 10.2
Contribution
  constructive trusts 1.33–1.43
Contribution to repairs and improvements
  precedent 1.183
Cooling-off
  cohabitation agreements, and
    counselling 2.40
    trial separation 2.41
Co-owners
  definition clause 1.197
Costs
  cohabitation agreements, and 2.42
    one party to pay all 2.43
    one party to pay for independent advice 2.44
  declaration, and 1.187
  inheritance provision claims, and 6.87
Counselling
  cohabitation agreements, and 2.40
County court
  injunction
    harassment, restraining 4.72
    non-molestation 4.72
Covenants relating to property
  cohabitation agreements, and 2.45
  positive acts 1.185
  prohibited acts 1.184
Credit cards
  cohabitation agreements, and 2.46, 2.47
  termination 2.133
Criminal Injuries Compensation Scheme
  applicants 6.93
  introduction 6.92
  procedure 6.95
  time limits 6.94
Criminal liability
  protection from harassment, and 4.63

D

Damages
  bereavement
    fatal accident claims
      FAA 1976, under 6.90

Death *see also* Death and succession
  contingencies, and 1.204
  inheritance tax, and 3.15
  order for sale, and 1.181
  termination of cohabitation agreements, and 2.130
Death and succession
  advance decisions
    content 6.98
    introduction 6.97
    legal status 6.99–6.101
  children
    death of cohabitant, and 6.13
    inheritance provision 6.59
  contentious precedents
    claim forms 6.166, 6.167
    interim payment order 6.174
    order for provision from estate 6.175
    specimen directions 6.173
    witness statements 6.168–6.172
  Criminal Injuries Compensation Scheme
    applicants 6.93
    introduction 6.92
    procedure 6.95
    time limits 6.94
  death of cohabitant
    children 6.13
    effect of judicial separation or separation order 6.12
    fatal accident claims 6.89, 6.90
    inheritance provision 6.15
    intestacy 6.11
    introduction 6.9
    proprietary estoppel 6.14
    valid will 6.10
  donationes mortis causa 6.8
  fatal accident claims
    Criminal Injuries Compensation Scheme 6.92
    FAA 1976, under 6.89, 6.90
    LR(MP)A 1934, under 6.91
  illness or incapacity of cohabitant
    advance decisions 6.97
    introduction 6.96
    living wills 6.97
  inheritance provision for family and dependants
    applicants 6.17
    applications by children 6.59
    applications by dependant 6.49
    applications by surviving cohabitant 6.37
    available relief 6.16
    costs 6.87
    form of order 6.77
    ground for application 6.27

Index

Death and succession – *cont.*
  inheritance provision for family and dependants – *cont.*
    interim orders **6.83**
    interlocutory applications **6.81**
    introduction **6.15**
    orders available **6.72**
    parties to application **6.18**
    permission to apply out of time **6.22**
    preservation of property **6.85**
    procedure **6.20**
    reasonable financial provision **6.27**
    taxation **6.88**
    timing of application **6.21**
    transactions intended to defeat claims **6.79**
    variation of orders **6.78**
    venue for proceedings **6.19**
  inheritance provision for family and dependents *see also* Inheritance provision claims
  inheritance tax **6.2**
  intestacy **6.11**
  joint property **6.5**
  judicial separation or separation order, and **6.12**
  law and practice
    death of cohabitant **6.9**
    illness or incapacity of cohabitant **6.96**
    making provision for death **6.1**
  lifetime gifts
    donationes mortis causa **6.8**
    generally **6.7**
  living wills
    content **6.98**
    introduction **6.97**
    legal status **6.99–6.101**
  making provision for death
    introduction **6.1**
    joint property **6.5**
    lifetime gifts **6.7**
    nominations **6.6**
    wills **6.2**
  nominations **6.6**
  non-contentious precedents
    application for standing search **6.165**
    disinheriting codicil **6.159**
    request to pension trustees **6.158**
    will clauses **6.106, 6.107**
    will forms **6.160**
  precedents
    contentious **6.166, 6.167**
    non-contentious **6.106, 6.107**
  proprietary estoppel **6.14**
  wills
    cohabitation, and **6.4**

Death and succession – *cont.*
  wills – *cont.*
    description of cohabitant **6.3**
    generally **6.2**
    precedent clauses **6.106, 6.107**
Death-in-service benefits
  cohabitation agreements, and **2.95**
  occupational pensions, and **7.11**
Debts
  cohabitation agreements, and **2.48**
Declarations of beneficial interests
  accounting for occupation rent **1.60**
  applications for declaration of interest in trust property
    applicants **1.64**
    exercise of court's discretion **1.69–1.71**
    injunctions **1.73**
    introduction **1.62**
    issue **1.66**
    order **1.72**
    procedure **1.67, 1.68**
    relevant court **1.65**
    relief available **1.63**
  applications under MPPA 1970 **1.84**
  applications under MWPA 1882
    applicants **1.76**
    court's approach **1.81**
    hearing **1.80**
    injunctions **1.83**
    introduction **1.74**
    order **1.82**
    procedure **1.78**
    relevant court **1.77**
    relief available **1.75**
    service **1.79**
  beneficial joint tenants **1.19**
  checklist **1.151**
  constructive trusts
    detrimental reliance **1.44**
    establishment **1.33–1.43**
    generally **1.32**
    quantification, and **1.45–1.52**
  contentious precedents
    claim form **1.232**
    order **1.235**
    witness statement in support **1.233, 1.234**
  express declaration
    beneficial joint tenants **1.19**
    constructive trusts **1.32**
    introduction **1.18**
    no express declaration **1.23**
    proprietary estoppel **1.53–1.59**
    resulting trusts **1.27–1.29**
    severing joint tenancy **1.21, 1.22**
    tenants in common **1.20**

Index

Declarations of beneficial interests – *cont.*
  generally **1.4**
  implied trusts **1.25, 1.26**
  joint legal ownership **1.24**
  no express declaration **1.23**
  proprietary estoppel
    generally **1.53–1.59**
    illegality of purpose **1.61**
  resulting trusts
    generally **1.27–1.29**
    quantification, and **1.30, 1.31**
  severing joint tenancy **1.21, 1.22**
  sole legal ownership **1.24**
  tenants in common **1.20**
Declarations of ownership of chattels
  court's approach **1.140**
  introduction **1.138**
  order
    generally **1.141**
    precedent **1.242**
  relevant court **1.139**
Declarations of parentage
  artificial insemination by donor **5.7**
  evidence **5.5**
  introduction **5.3**
  refusal to submit to testing **5.6**
  statutory basis **5.4**
Declarations of trust
  cohabitation agreements, and **2.49**
  co-owners, by
    co-owner alone to pay mortgage **1.218**
    fixed shares (long form) **1.217**
    fixed shares (short form) **1.216**
    floating shares (long form) **1.220**
    floating shares (tabular form) **1.219**
  costs **1.187**
  person moving in after purchase, by **1.222**
  sole owner, by
    council house purchased with assistance of child **1.224**
    other person contributed to price **1.223**
  variation **1.225**
Deed
  cohabitation agreements, and **2.50**
Deeds of surrender
  person moving in after purchase, by **1.221**
Deferred trust of land
  precedent **1.164**
Dependants
  Criminal Injuries Compensation Scheme
    applicants **6.93**
    introduction **6.92**
    procedure **6.95**
    time limits **6.94**

Dependants – *cont.*
  fatal accident claims
    Criminal Injuries Compensation Scheme **6.92**
    FAA 1976, under **6.89**
    LR(MP)A 1934, under **6.91**
  inheritance provision claims, and
    court's discretion **6.58**
    eligibility **6.50**
      being maintained **6.53**
      immediately before the death **6.51, 6.52**
    ground for application **6.54**
    introduction **6.49**
    matters to be considered **6.55–6.57**
  occupational pensions, and **7.10**
Detrimental reliance
  constructive trusts, and **1.44**
Disability of parties
  inheritance provision claims, and **6.34**
Disagreement as to sale
  contingencies **1.203**
Discharge
  parental responsibility order, and **5.18**
  personal protection orders, and **4.4**
Discretion
  adoption, and **5.35**
  change of name, and **5.24**
  declaration of interest in trust property, and **1.69–1.71**
  inheritance provision claims, and
    children, by **6.67**
    dependant, by **6.58**
    surviving cohabitant, by **6.48**
  lump sum orders, and **5.59**
  non-molestation orders, and **4.7**
  occupation orders, and
    s 33 applications **4.23**
    s 36 applications **4.29–4.31**
    s 38 applications **4.37**
  orders of sale, and **1.69–1.71**
  parental responsibility order, and **5.16**
  periodical payment orders, and **5.59**
  TOLATA 1996, under **1.69–1.71**
  transfer of property orders, and **5.59**
  transfer of tenancy, and
    Children Act 1989, Sch 1, under **1.125**
    Family Law Act 1996, Pt IV, under **1.114**
  warrant of arrest, and **4.51**
Dispensing with consent
  adoption, and **5.32**
Dispute resolution
  cohabitation agreements, and
    arbitration **2.52**
    conciliation **2.53**

Index

Dispute resolution – *cont.*
  cohabitation agreements, and – *cont.*
    named mediator **2.54**
    occupation of home, and
      checklists **1.150**
    ownership of the home, and
      checklists **1.149**
    generally **1.17**
    Tomlin order **1.241**

Divorce
  tenancy, transfer of, on **1.148, 4.71**

Domestic Violence and Occupation of the Family Home (Law Commission, 1992)
  personal protection orders, and **4.1**

Donationes mortis causa
  lifetime gifts, and **6.8**

Duress
  cohabitation agreements, and
    generally **2.8**
    recitals **2.103**

Dwelling
  cohabitation agreements, and
    joint tenancy **2.57**
    sole owner **2.59**
    tenancy in common **2.58**
    termination **2.134**

E

Elderly married couples
  income tax, and **3.4**

Enforcement
  cohabitation agreements, of
    coercion **2.8**
    consideration **2.6**
    duress **2.8**
    equality of bargaining power **2.8**
    intention to create legal relations **2.5**
    introduction **2.4**
    ousting court's jurisdiction **2.9**
    uncertainty **2.7**
  committal for contempt
    application **4.56**
    hearing of application **4.57**
    introduction **4.54**
    sentencing **4.58**
    venue for proceedings **4.55**
  non-molestation orders, of
    committal for contempt **4.54**
    warrant of arrest **4.49**
  personal protection orders, of
    committal for contempt **4.54**
    warrant of arrest **4.49**
  protection from harassment, and
    contempt of court **4.64**

Enforcement – *cont.*
  protection from harassment, and – *cont.*
    criminal liability **4.63**
  warrant of arrest
    applicants **4.50**
    application **4.50**
    court's discretion **4.53**
    introduction **4.49**
    procedure **4.52**
    venue for proceedings **4.51**

Engaged couples
  ownership of chattels, and **1.143**

Entire agreement
  cohabitation agreements, and **2.147**

Equality of bargaining power
  cohabitation agreements, and **2.8**

Estate rights
  cohabitation agreements, and **2.60**

Evidence
  parentage, and **5.5**

Execution
  cohabitation agreements, and **2.61**

Execution in duplicate
  precedent **1.199**

Executors
  wills, and **6.115–6.117**

Existing property
  ownership of chattels, and **1.135**

Expectation of marriage
  wills, and **6.108, 6.109**

Express declaration of beneficial trusts
  beneficial joint tenants **1.19**
  constructive trusts
    detrimental reliance **1.44**
    establishment **1.33–1.43**
    generally **1.32**
    quantification, and **1.45–1.52**
  introduction **1.18**
  no express declaration **1.23**
  proprietary estoppel
    generally **1.53–1.59**
    illegality of purpose **1.61**
  resulting trusts
    generally **1.27–1.29**
    quantification, and **1.30, 1.31**
  severing joint tenancy **1.21, 1.22**
  tenants in common **1.20**

Extension of orders
  personal protection orders, and **4.4**

F

Failure to pay share of mortgage
  contingencies **1.202**

Index

Family Law Act 1996, Pt IV
  applicants **1.111**
  personal protection orders, and
    available relief **4.2**
    committal for contempt **4.54**
    discharge **4.4**
    enforcement **4.49**
    extension **4.4**
    introduction **4.1**
    non-molestation orders **4.5**
    occupation orders **4.17**
    relevant court **4.3**
    variation **4.4**
    venue for proceedings **4.1**
  rights of occupation, and **1.89**
  transfer of tenancy, and
    generally **1.110**
    precedents **1.237**
  use of chattels, and **1.144**
Family Law Act 1996, Part IV
  personal protection orders, and *see also* Personal protection orders
  transfer of tenancy, and *see also* Transfer of tenancy
Family Law Protocol
  cohabitation **10.6**
Family provision
  affidavit in answer **6.104**
  answer **6.104**
  appeal **6.104**
  applicants **6.104**
    cohabitant **6.104**
  cohabitation agreements, and **2.111**
  county court application **6.104**
    answer **6.104**
  defendants **6.104**
  documents on application **6.104**
  High Court application **6.104**
    affidavit in answer **6.104**
    application, form **6.104**
    parties **6.104**
  interim order **6.104**
  lump sum order **6.104**
  maintenance agreement, variation etc of **6.104**
  orders **6.104**
  periodical payments order **6.104**
  procedure for claim **6.103**
    checklist on first instructions **6.105**
  service **6.104**
  settlement, order for **6.104**
Fatal accident claims
  Criminal Injuries Compensation Scheme
    applicants **6.93**
    introduction **6.92**
    procedure **6.95**

Fatal accident claims – *cont.*
  Criminal Injuries Compensation Scheme – *cont.*
    time limits **6.94**
  FAA 1976, under **6.89, 6.90**
  LR(MP)A 1934, under **6.91**
Fiduciary duty
  cohabitation agreements, and **2.62**
Financial disclosure
  cohabitation agreements, and **2.63**
    both cohabitants, by **2.64**
Financial obligations and needs
  inheritance provision claims, and **6.31**
Financial provision for children
  child maintenance agreement precedent **5.89**
  child support scheme **5.44–5.46, 5.48, 5.49, 5.65, 5.66**
  Children Act 1989, Sch 1, under
    applicants **5.53**
    court's approach **5.60**
    court's discretion **5.59**
    interim orders **5.63**
    introduction **5.50**
    issue of application **5.55, 5.58**
      pre-application protocol **5.54**
    service of application **5.56**
    venue for proceedings **5.52**
  introduction **5.42**
  lump sum orders
    court's approach **5.61**
    generally **5.50**
    interim orders **5.63**
    variation **5.64**
  periodical payment orders
    court's approach **5.60**
    generally **5.50**
    interim orders **5.63**
    variation **5.64**
  terminology **5.43**
  transfer of property orders
    court's approach **5.62**
    generally **5.50**
    interim orders **5.63**
    variation **5.64**
  variation, collection and enforcement **5.47**
Financial relief order (for child)
  appeals **5.82**
  application for **5.81**
    High Court/county court, in **5.82**
  directions **5.82**
  interim **5.82**
  orders **5.82**
  respondents **5.82**
  service **5.82**
  types of order **5.82**

Fixed shares
advantages 1.10
disadvantages 1.11
fractions, percentages and ratios 1.14
generally 1.9
precedents
long form 1.217
short form 1.216
sale price and net proceeds of sale 1.15, 1.16
Floating shares
advantages 1.12
disadvantages 1.13
fractions, percentages and ratios 1.14
generally 1.9
precedents
long form 1.220
tabular form 1.219
sale price and net proceeds of sale 1.15, 1.16
Forced marriage protection order
enforcement 4.86
Fractions
shares in property, and 1.14
Full-time education
contingencies 1.209, 1.210
Funeral wishes
wills, and 6.114
Further assurances
cohabitation agreements, and 2.65

G

Gifts
cohabitation agreements, and
between cohabitants 2.66
separate 2.68
inheritance tax, and
gifts of other property 3.13
lifetime gifts 3.10
not intended to confer benefit 3.12
residence 3.11
ownership of chattels, and 1.136
Guardian
appointment
appeal 5.80
applicant 5.80
application 5.79
court and judge for 5.80
directions 5.80
form 5.80
order 5.80
procedure 5.79
respondents 5.80
service 5.80

Guests
cohabitation agreements, and 2.69

H

Harassment
injunction restraining 4.73
applicant 4.75
breach 4.75
committal for breach 4.86
interim injunction 4.75
procedure 4.72, 4.75
warrant for arrest 4.75
without notice 4.75
undertaking restraining 4.75
Headings
cohabitation agreements, and 2.70
Hearing of application
committal for contempt, and 4.57
non-molestation orders, and 4.10
occupation orders, and 4.43
HM Land Registry
Form FR1 1.231
Form JO 1.228
Form RX1 1.230
Form SEV 1.229
Homelessness
Children Act 1989, s 17, and 1.130
Children Act 1989, s 20, and 1.129
introduction 1.128
loan from social fund 1.131
Honeymoon agreement
nature of 8.36
Housekeeping allowance
cohabitation agreements, and 2.71
Housework
cohabitation agreements, and 2.72
Housing Act 1985
personal protection, and 4.67
Housing associations
occupation of the home, and 1.91

I

Illegality
proprietary estoppel, and 1.61
Illness or incapacity
advance decisions
content 6.98
introduction 6.97
legal status 6.99–6.101
ancillary relief, and 1.207
cohabitation agreements, and
attorneyship 2.73

Index

Illness or incapacity – *cont.*
  cohabitation agreements, and – *cont.*
    next of kin 2.74
    support 2.75
  introduction 6.96
  living wills
    content 6.98
    introduction 6.97
    legal status 6.99–6.101

Implied trusts
  determination of beneficial interests 1.25, 1.26

Improvement to property
  contingencies 1.206

Incidental selling costs
  definition clause 1.192

Income
  cohabitation agreements, and 2.76, 2.77

Income tax
  child allowances 3.5
  child tax credit 3.6
  elderly married couples 3.4
  introduction 3.2
  married couples 3.3
  universal credit 3.6
  working tax credit 3.6

Independent legal advice
  cohabitation agreements, and
    generally 2.81
    recitals 2.106

Inheritance provision claims
  applicants 6.17
  applications by children
    circumstances at date of hearing 6.71
    court's approach 6.68–6.70
    court's discretion 6.67
    eligibility 6.60–6.62
    ground for application 6.63
    introduction 6.59
    matters to be considered 6.64–6.66
  applications by dependant
    court's discretion 6.58
    eligibility 6.50
      being maintained 6.53
      immediately before the death 6.51, 6.52
    ground for application 6.54
    introduction 6.49
    matters to be considered 6.55–6.57
  applications by surviving cohabitant
    court's discretion 6.48
    eligibility 6.38, 6.39
      living in same household 6.40–6.42
      living together as spouse or civil partner 6.43
    ground for application 6.44

Inheritance provision claims – *cont.*
  applications by surviving cohabitant – *cont.*
    introduction 6.37
    matters to be considered 6.45–6.47
  available relief 6.16
  claim forms 6.166, 6.167
  cohabitation agreements, and 2.111
  conduct 6.35
  considerations
    conduct 6.35
    disability of parties 6.34
    financial resources and needs 6.31
    introduction 6.30
    mental disability of parties 6.34
    moral culpability 6.36
    nature of estate 6.33
    obligations and responsibilities 6.32
    other relevant matters 6.35
    physical disability of parties 6.34
    size of estate 6.33
  costs 6.87
  court's discretion
    applications by children 6.67
    applications by dependant 6.58
    applications by surviving cohabitant 6.48
  disability of parties 6.34
  eligibility
    applications by children 6.60–6.62
    applications by dependant 6.50
      being maintained 6.53
      immediately before the death 6.51, 6.52
    applications by surviving cohabitant 6.38–6.43
  financial resources and needs 6.31
  form of order 6.77
  ground for application
    applications by children 6.63
    applications by dependant 6.54
    applications by surviving cohabitant 6.44
  generally 6.27
  interim orders
    generally 6.83
    precedent 6.174
    procedure 6.84
  interlocutory applications
    generally 6.81
    procedure 6.82
  introduction 6.15
  lump sums 6.74
  maintenance agreements, and 6.16
  matters to be considered
    age of applicant 6.46

Inheritance provision claims – *cont.*
  matters to be considered – *cont.*
    applicant's contribution to welfare of family **6.47**
    applications by children **6.64–6.66**
    applications by dependant **6.55–6.57**
      assumption of responsibility **6.56, 6.57**
    applications by surviving cohabitant **6.45**
    conduct **6.35**
    disability of parties **6.34**
    financial resources and needs **6.31**
    introduction **6.30**
    length of cohabitation **6.46**
    mental disability of parties **6.34**
    moral culpability **6.36**
    nature of estate **6.33**
    obligations and responsibilities **6.32**
    other relevant matters **6.35**
    physical disability of parties **6.34**
    size of estate **6.33**
  mental disability of parties **6.34**
  moral culpability **6.36**
  nature of estate **6.33**
  nuptial settlements, and **6.16**
  obligations and responsibilities **6.32**
  order for provision from estate **6.175**
  orders available
    introduction **6.72**
    lump sum **6.74**
    periodical payments **6.73**
    transfer of property **6.75**
  parties to application **6.18**
  periodical payments **6.73**
  permission to apply out of time
    court's discretion **6.23–6.25**
    introduction **6.22**
    standing search **6.26**
  physical disability of parties **6.34**
  precedents
    claim forms **6.166, 6.167**
    interim payment order **6.174**
    order for provision from estate **6.175**
    specimen directions **6.173**
    witness statements **6.168–6.172**
  preservation of property
    generally **6.85**
    procedure **6.86**
  procedure **6.20**
  reasonable financial provision
    conduct **6.35**
    court's approach **6.29**
    disability of parties **6.34**
    financial resources and needs **6.31**
    introduction **6.27**

Inheritance provision claims – *cont.*
  reasonable financial provision – *cont.*
    matters to be considered **6.30**
    meaning **6.28**
    mental disability of parties **6.34**
    moral culpability **6.36**
    nature of estate **6.33**
    obligations and responsibilities **6.32**
    other relevant matters **6.35**
    physical disability of parties **6.34**
    size of estate **6.33**
  settlement of property **6.16**
  size of estate **6.33**
  specimen directions **6.173**
  standing search
    generally **6.26**
    precedent **6.165**
  striking out
    generally **6.81**
    procedure **6.82**
  taxation **6.88**
  timing of application **6.21**
  transactions intended to defeat claims
    generally **6.79**
    procedure **6.80**
  transfer of property
    generally **6.75**
    variation of settlement **6.76**
  variation of orders **6.78**
  venue for proceedings **6.19**
  wills, and **6.153**
  witness statements **6.168–6.172**
Inheritance tax
  agricultural relief **3.14**
  avoidance **3.15**
  business reliefs **3.14**
  gifts not intended to confer benefit **3.12**
  gifts of other property **3.13**
  gifts of residence **3.11**
  lifetime gifts **3.10**
  spouses, transfers between **3.9**
  unmarried couples, transfers between **3.9**
  wills, and **6.2**
Injunction
  breach **4.76–4.85**
  enforcement **4.86**
  personal protection **4.73, 4.75**
    application **4.75**
    urgent application **4.75**
  service **4.86**
Injunction to prevent service of notice to quit
  applicant's sworn statement in support **1.236**
Intention to create legal relations
  cohabitation agreements, and
    clause **2.78**

Index

Intention to create legal relations – *cont.*
cohabitation agreements, and – *cont.*
generally 2.5
recitals 2.100
Interim orders
financial relief, and 5.63
inheritance provision claims, and
generally 6.83
procedure 6.84
Interlocutory applications
inheritance provision claims, and
generally 6.81
procedure 6.82
Intestacy
death of cohabitant, and 6.11
Issue of application
lump sum orders, and 5.54, 5.55, 5.58
non-molestation orders, and 4.8
occupation orders, and 4.40

J

Joint legal ownership
beneficial interests 1.24
Joint property
cohabitation agreements, and
joint tenancy 2.80
tenancy in common 2.81
death of cohabitant, and 6.5
Joint tenancy
cohabitation agreements, and
dwelling 2.57
property 2.80
occupation of the home, and 1.104
Joint tenants
express declaration of beneficial trusts, and 1.19
severance, and 1.21, 1.22
Joint use
cohabitation agreements, and 2.82
Jointly owned goods and chattels
termination of cohabitation agreements, and 2.136
Judicial separation or separation order
death of cohabitant, and 6.12

L

Land Registry forms
generally 1.7, 1.8
precedents 1.227

Lasting powers of attorney
registration 6.102
types of 6.102
Legal advice
precedent 1.186
Legal adviser's certificate
cohabitation agreements, and 2.83
Licences
occupation of the home, and 1.86
Life assurance
cohabitation agreements, and 2.84
Lifetime gifts
donationes mortis causa 6.8
generally 6.7
Living expenses
cohabitation agreements, and
defined areas of responsibility 2.89
fixed percentages 2.87
joint account 2.85
one party pays all 2.88
proportion to respective incomes 2.86
Living in same household
meaning 6.40–6.42
Living together as married couple
definition, benefits law 9.1
Living wills
content 6.98
introduction 6.97
legal status 6.99–6.101
Local authority housing
assignment 1.102
introduction 1.100
security 1.101
succession 1.103
Lump sum orders
applicants 5.53
court's approach 5.61
court's discretion 5.59
interim orders 5.63
introduction 5.50
issue of application 5.54, 5.55
service of application 5.56
variation of orders 5.64
venue for proceedings 5.52
Lump sum payments
inheritance provision claims, and 6.74
termination of cohabitation, and 2.138
wills, and 6.133

M

Maintenance agreements
inheritance provision claims, and 6.16

Maintenance agreements – *cont.*
  variation of
    application 5.82
Marriage
  cohabitation agreements, and
    agreement ceases to apply on marriage 2.91
    consequences of termination 2.142
    generally 2.90
    terminating events 2.130
Marriage of co-owners
  recitals of intention, and 1.159
Married couple
  cohabitation test
    welfare benefits for 9.17, 9.18
Married couples
  income tax, and 3.3
Married Women's Property Act 1882
  applications
    applicants 1.76
    court's approach 1.81
    hearing 1.80
    injunctions 1.83
    introduction 1.74
    order 1.82
    procedure 1.78
    relevant court 1.77
    relief available 1.75
    service 1.79
Martin trust
  precedent 1.164
Matrimonial home
  tenancy, transfer of 1.148, 4.71
Matrimonial Proceedings and Property Act 1970
  ownership of the home, and 1.84
Means test
  cohabitation, and 9.9
Medical insurance
  cohabitation agreements, and 2.92
Mental disability
  inheritance provision claims, and 6.34
Mesher trust
  precedent 1.164
Molestation *see also* Non-molestation orders
  meaning 4.6
Moral culpability
  inheritance provision claims, and 6.36
Mortgage of property
  recitals of fact, and 1.155
Mortgage payments
  cohabitation agreements, and 2.93
  definition clause 1.195
  recitals of intention, and 1.158
Moving in after purchase
  declaration of trust 1.222

Moving in after purchase – *cont.*
  deed of surrender 1.221
Moving out before sale
  contingencies 1.213
Mutual agreement
  termination of cohabitation agreements, and 2.130
  wills, and 6.110

N

Nature of declaration
  precedent 1.198
Net income until sale
  general 1.178
  payments from grown-up children 1.180
  payments from lodgers 1.179
Net proceeds of sale
  definition clause 1.193
  shares in property, and 1.15, 1.16
Next of kin
  cohabitation agreements, and 2.74
Nominations
  death of cohabitant, and 6.6
Non-disclosure to third parties
  cohabitation agreements, and 2.94
Non-molestation orders
  applicants 4.5
  application in Form FL401 4.89
  applications
    hearing 4.10
    issue 4.8
    service 4.9
    without notice 4.14
  'associated persons' 4.5
  available relief 4.2
  breach
    criminal offence 4.86
    penalties 4.48
    person under 18 4.86
  checklists
    application steps 4.88
    initial instructions 4.87
  committal for contempt
    application 4.56
    hearing of application 4.57
    introduction 4.54
    sentencing 4.58
    venue for proceedings 4.55
  court's discretion 4.7
  discharge 4.4
  duration 4.13
  enforcement
    committal for contempt 4.54
    warrant of arrest 4.49

Index

Non-molestation orders – *cont.*
  extension 4.4
  form 4.11, 4.12
  hearing of application 4.10
  introduction 4.1
  issue of application 4.8
  legal background 4.68
  'molestation' 4.6
  power of arrest
    generally 4.15
    procedure 4.69
  relevant court 4.3
  service of application 4.9
  sworn statement in support of application 4.90, 4.91
  undertakings 4.16
  variation 4.4
  venue for proceedings 4.3
  warrant of arrest
    applicants 4.50
    application 4.50
    court's discretion 4.53
    introduction 4.49
    procedure 4.52
Notice
  termination of cohabitation agreements, and 2.129
Notice to quit
  generally 1.107
  injunction to prevent service
    applicant's sworn statement in support 1.236
    witness statement in support 1.235
Nuisance
  generally 4.65
  procedure 4.66
Nuptial settlements
  inheritance provision claims, and 6.16

O

Occupation of the home
  applications to local authority
    Children Act 1989, s 17, under 1.130
    Children Act 1989, s 20, under 1.129
    introduction 1.128
    loan from social fund 1.131
  assignment of tenancies
    assured tenancies 1.93
    local authority housing 1.102
    protected tenancies 1.97
  assured tenancies
    assignment 1.93
    introduction 1.90
    security 1.92

Occupation of the home – *cont.*
  assured tenancies – *cont.*
    succession 1.94
  Children Act 1989, Sch 1, under 1.120
  Family Law Act 1996, Pt IV, under 1.110
    introduction 1.109
  homelessness 1.127
  housing associations 1.91
  injunctions
    generally 1.108
    witness statement in support 1.235
  joint names tenancy 1.104
  licences 1.86
  local authority housing
    assignment 1.102
    introduction 1.100
    security 1.101
    succession 1.103
  mortgage default 1.85
  notice to quit 1.109
  owner-occupied home
    Children Act 1989, Sch 1 orders 1.87
    licences 1.86
    rights of occupation 1.85
  private sector tenancies
    assured tenancies 1.92
    introduction 1.90
    protected tenancies 1.95
  protected tenancies
    assignment 1.97
    introduction 1.95
    security 1.96
    succession 1.98, 1.99
  protection of cohabitant in occupation
    injunctions 1.108
    introduction 1.106
    notice to quit 1.107
  registered social landlords 1.91
  rented home
    generally 1.88
    rights of occupation 1.89
  rights of occupation
    owner-occupied home 1.85
    rented home 1.89
  security of tenancies
    assured tenancies 1.92
    local authority housing 1.101
    protected tenancies 1.96
  sole name tenancy 1.105
  succession to tenancies
    assured tenancies 1.94
    local authority housing 1.103
    protected tenancies 1.98, 1.99
  wills, and 6.124

Index

Occupation orders
  additional obligations
    s 33 applications **4.24, 4.25**
    s 36 applications **4.33**
  applicants **4.17**
  application in Form FL401 **4.89**
  application procedure
    hearing **4.43**
    issue **4.40**
    service **4.41**
  application without notice **4.42**
  'associated persons' **4.17**
  available relief **4.2**
  balance of harm test
    s 33 applications **4.22**
    s 36 applications **4.32**
    s 38 applications **4.38**
  checklists
    application steps **4.88**
    initial instructions **4.87**
  choice of proceedings **4.19**
  committal for contempt
    application **4.56**
    hearing of application **4.57**
    introduction **4.54**
    sentencing **4.58**
    venue for proceedings **4.55**
  discharge **4.4**
  discretion of court
    s 33 applications **4.23**
    s 36 applications **4.29–4.31**
    s 38 applications **4.37**
  enforcement
    committal for contempt **4.54**
    warrant of arrest **4.49**
  extension **4.4**
  hearing of application **4.43**
  introduction **4.1**
  issue of application **4.40**
  legal background **4.68**
  letter to mortgagee/landlord subject of application **4.92**
  power of arrest
    duration **4.46**
    enforcement **4.49**
    generally **4.45**
    procedure **4.47**
  procedure **4.69**
  relevant court **4.3**
  s 33 applications
    additional obligations **4.24, 4.25**
    applicants **4.20**
    application procedure **4.40**
    balance of harm test **4.22**
    court's discretion **4.23**
    court's powers **4.21**

Occupation orders – *cont.*
  s 33 applications – *cont.*
    duration **4.26**
  s 36 applications
    additional obligations **4.33**
    applicants **4.27**
    application procedure **4.40**
    balance of harm test **4.32**
    court's discretion **4.29–4.31**
    court's powers **4.28**
    duration **4.34**
  s 38 applications
    applicants **4.35**
    application procedure **4.40**
    balance of harm test **4.38**
    court's discretion **4.37**
    court's powers **4.36**
    duration **4.39**
  service of application **4.41**
  sworn statement in support of application **4.90, 4.91**
  undertakings **4.44**
  variation **4.4**
  venue for proceedings
    generally **4.18**
    introduction **4.1**
  warrant of arrest
    applicants **4.50**
    application **4.50**
    court's discretion **4.53**
    introduction **4.49**
    procedure **4.52**
    venue for proceedings **4.51**
Occupation rent, accounting for
  out of occupation owner, compensation for **1.60**
Occupation rights
  wills, and **6.124**
Occupational pensions
  introduction **7.9**
  lump sum death-in-service benefits **7.11**
  registered pension schemes **7.10**
  surviving dependants, for **7.10**
Open market value
  definition clause **1.194**
Option to purchase
  wills, and **6.125**
Order
  breach of, committal for **4.76–4.85**
Orders for sale, applications for
  applicants **1.64**
  circumstances in which order be made
    death **1.182**
    separation **1.181**
  exercise of court's discretion **1.69–1.71**
  injunctions **1.73**

833

Index

Orders for sale, applications for – *cont.*
  introduction **1.62**
  issue **1.66**
  legal background **1.145**
  order **1.72**
  precedents
    claim form **1.232**
    order **1.235**
    witness statements in support **1.233, 1.234**
  procedure **1.67, 1.68, 1.146**
  relevant court **1.65**
  relief available **1.63**
Ousting court's jurisdiction
  cohabitation agreements, and **2.9**
Owner-occupied home
  Children Act 1989, Sch 1 orders **1.87**
  licences **1.86**
  rights of occupation **1.85**
Ownership of chattels
  applications for declarations
    court's approach **1.140**
    form of order **1.242**
    introduction **1.138**
    order **1.141**
    relevant court **1.139**
  bank accounts **1.134**
  cohabitation agreement **1.137**
  engaged couples **1.143**
  existing property **1.135**
  generally **1.133**
  gifts **1.136**
  injunctions **1.142**
  introduction **1.132**
Ownership of the home
  accounting for occupation rent **1.60**
  applications for declaration of interest in trust property
    applicants **1.64**
    exercise of court's discretion **1.69–1.71**
    injunctions **1.73**
    introduction **1.62**
    issue **1.66**
    order **1.72**
    procedure **1.67, 1.68**
    relevant court **1.65**
    relief available **1.63**
  applications under MPPA 1970 **1.84**
  applications under MWPA 1882
    applicants **1.76**
    court's approach **1.81**
    hearing **1.80**
    injunctions **1.83**
    introduction **1.74**
    order **1.82**
    procedure **1.78**

Ownership of the home – *cont.*
  applications under MWPA 1882 – *cont.*
    relevant court **1.77**
    relief available **1.75**
    service **1.79**
  beneficial interests
    implied trusts **1.25, 1.26**
  beneficial joint tenants **1.19**
  constructive trusts
    common intention **1.33–1.43**
    detrimental reliance **1.44**
    establishment
      common intention **1.33–1.43**
    generally **1.32**
    quantification, and **1.45–1.52**
  declaration of beneficial interests
    applications for declaration **1.62**
    express declaration **1.18**
    generally **1.4**
  detrimental reliance **1.44**
  disputes as to ownership **1.17**
  duty of solicitor **1.2, 1.3**
  express declaration of beneficial trusts
    beneficial joint tenants **1.19**
    constructive trusts **1.32**
    introduction **1.18**
    no express declaration **1.23**
    proprietary estoppel **1.53–1.59**
    resulting trusts **1.27–1.29**
    severing joint tenancy **1.21, 1.22**
    tenants in common **1.20**
  express declaration of trust
    effect **1.6**
    generally **1.5**
  expression of share
    fixed shares **1.10**
    floating shares **1.12**
    fractions, percentages and ratios **1.14**
    generally **1.9**
    sale price and net proceeds of sale **1.15, 1.16**
  fixed shares
    advantages **1.10**
    disadvantages **1.11**
    generally **1.9**
  floating shares
    advantages **1.12**
    disadvantages **1.13**
    generally **1.9**
  introduction **1.1**
  Land Registry forms **1.7, 1.8**
  proprietary estoppel
    generally **1.53–1.59**
    illegality of purpose **1.61**
  resulting trusts
    generally **1.27–1.29**

Index

Ownership of the home – *cont.*
  resulting trusts – *cont.*
    quantification, and 1.30, 1.31
    severing joint tenancy 1.21, 1.22
    sole or joint legal ownership 1.24
    use of chattels 1.144

P

Parentage, declaration of
  artificial insemination by donor 5.7
  evidence 5.5
  introduction 5.3
  refusal to submit to testing 5.6
  statutory basis 5.4
Parental responsibility
  acquisition of 5.9
  adoption, by
    applications by cohabitants 5.28
    consent 5.31
    court's discretion 5.35
    dispensing with consent 5.32
    introduction 5.26
    one person, by 5.29
    order, revocation 5.36
    preliminaries 5.30
    same-sex couples 5.28
    status of unmarried father 5.33, 5.34
    statutory basis 5.27
  appointment as guardian
    generally 5.25
    precedents 5.87, 5.88
  child arrangements order 5.19
  introduction 5.8
  joint registration of birth 5.10
  parental responsibility agreement, by
    duration 5.13
    generally 5.11
    precedent 5.84
    procedure 5.12
  parental responsibility order, by
    application 5.85
    court's discretion 5.16
    discharge 5.18
    duration 5.17
    generally 5.14
    procedure 5.15
Parental responsibility agreement
  duration 5.13
  generally 5.11
  precedent 5.84
  procedure 5.12
Parental responsibility order
  appeal 5.78
  applicant 5.78

Parental responsibility order – *cont.*
  application 5.77, 5.78, 5.85
  court and judge 5.78
  court's discretion 5.16
  directions 5.78
  discharge 5.18
  duration 5.17
  form 5.78
  generally 5.14
  joinder 5.78
  order 5.78
  procedure 5.15, 5.77
  respondents 5.78
  service 5.78
Paternity
  artificial insemination by donor 5.7
  evidence 5.5
  introduction 5.3
  refusal to submit to testing 5.6
  statutory basis 5.4
Pecuniary legacy
  wills, and 6.130, 6.131
Pension benefits
  cohabitation agreements, and 2.95
Pension Protection Fund
  establishment 7.16
Pension rights
  advice, clients for 7.19
  automatic enrolment 7.15
  children 7.17
  civil partnerships 7.2
  death benefits 7.8, 7.13
  introduction 7.1
  National Employment Savings Trust
    (NEST) 7.15
  new scheme 7.6
  occupational pensions
    introduction 7.9
    lump sum death-in-service benefits 7.11
    registered pension schemes 7.10
    surviving dependants, for 7.10
  old scheme 7.5
  Pension Protection Fund 7.16
  pensionable age 7.4
  personal pension schemes
    introduction 7.12
    stakeholder pensions 7.14
  state retirement pension 7.3
  state single tier pension 7.6
  survivors' pensions 7.18
Pension trustees
  request by cohabitant, and 6.158
Percentages
  shares in property, and 1.14
Periodical payment orders
  applicants 5.53

835

Index

Periodical payment orders – *cont.*
  court's approach 5.60
  court's discretion 5.59
  interim orders 5.63
  introduction 5.50
  issue of application 5.54, 5.55
  service of application 5.56
  variation of orders 5.64
  venue for proceedings 5.52
Permission to apply out of time
  inheritance provision claims, and
    court's discretion 6.23–6.25
    introduction 6.22
    standing search 6.26
Personal information
  cohabitation agreements, and 2.108
Personal pension schemes
  introduction 7.12
Personal protection
  assault
    generally 4.65
    procedure 4.66
  battery
    generally 4.65
    procedure 4.66
  Family Law Act 1996, Pt IV, under
    enforcement 4.49
    introduction 4.1
    non-molestation orders 4.5
    occupation orders 4.17
  Family Law Act 1996, Part IV, under *see also* Personal protection orders
  Housing Act 1985, under 4.67
  introduction 4.1
  nuisance
    generally 4.65
    procedure 4.66
  Protection from Harassment Act 1997, under
    contempt of court 4.64
    criminal liability 4.63
    enforcement 4.63
    introduction 4.59
    procedure 4.62
    prohibition 4.61
    venue for proceedings 4.60
  tort, application in 4.72
  trespass to the person
    generally 4.65
    procedure 4.66
Personal protection orders
  available relief 4.2
  checklists
    application steps 4.88
    initial instructions 4.87

Personal protection orders – *cont.*
  committal for contempt
    application 4.56
    hearing of application 4.57
    introduction 4.54
    sentencing 4.58
    venue for proceedings 4.55
  discharge 4.4
  enforcement
    committal for contempt 4.54
    warrant of arrest 4.49
  extension 4.4
  introduction 4.1
  legal background 4.68
  non-molestation orders *see also* Non-molestation orders
    applicants 4.5
    applications 4.8
    applications without notice 4.14
    court's discretion 4.7
    duration 4.13
    enforcement 4.49
    form 4.11, 4.12
    hearing of application 4.10
    issue of application 4.8
    'molestation' 4.6
    power of arrest 4.15
    service of application 4.9
    undertakings 4.16
  occupation orders *see also* Occupation orders
    applicants 4.17
    application procedure 4.40
    application without notice 4.42
    choice of proceedings 4.19
    enforcement 4.49
    hearing of application 4.43
    issue of application 4.40
    power of arrest 4.45
    s 33 applications 4.20
    s 36 applications 4.27
    s 38 applications 4.35
    service of application 4.41
    undertakings 4.44
    venue for proceedings 4.18
  powers of arrest
    enforcement 4.49
    occupation orders 4.46
  procedure 4.69
  relevant court 4.3
  variation 4.4
  venue for proceedings 4.1
  warrant of arrest
    applicants 4.50
    application 4.50
    court's discretion 4.53

Index

Personal protection orders – *cont.*
  warrant of arrest – *cont.*
    introduction 4.49
    procedure 4.52
    venue for proceedings 4.51
Physical disability
  inheritance provision claims, and 6.34
Possession orders
  personal protection, and 4.67
Powers of arrest
  non-molestation orders
    generally 4.15
  occupation orders
    duration 4.46
    enforcement 4.49
    generally 4.45
    procedure 4.47
Pregnancy
  contingencies 1.208
Pre-nuptial agreements
  advising the client 8.34, 8.35
  ambit of reform 8.46–8.48
  case law 8.9–8.14
    Court of Appeal 8.15
    post-Radmacher 8.21–8.31
    Radmacher v Granatino 8.15–8.20
    Supreme Court 8.16–8.20
  checklist 8.43
  current position 8.4, 8.5
  development 8.8, 8.21–8.33
  enforceability 8.8
  essentials
    fairness 8.42
    free will 8.41
    generally 8.37
    independent legal advice 8.38
    material disclosure 8.39
    periodic review 8.40
  fairness 8.42
  free will 8.41
  future developments 8.59, 8.60
  gender balance 8.6, 8.7
  generally 8.4, 8.5
  honeymoon agreement 8.36
  human rights 8.32, 8.33
  independent legal advice 8.38
  Law Commission report 8.49, 8.50
  law of coverture 8.1
  material disclosure 8.39
  need for reform 8.58
  other jurisdictions 8.32, 8.33
  periodic review 8.40
  precedent 8.61
  professional liability limitation 8.44, 8.45
  Qualifying Nuptial Agreement
    examples for use of 8.51–8.55

Pre-nuptial agreements – *cont.*
  Qualifying Nuptial Agreement – *cont.*
    examples for use of – *cont.*
      avoiding equal sharing 8.55
      clean break 8.54
      family gifts, protection of 8.52
      specific property, protection of 8.53
    legal advice guidance 8.56
    overview 8.57
  reform 8.2, 8.3
  relevance 8.6, 8.7
  statutory reform 8.46–8.58
Preservation of property
  inheritance provision claims, and
    generally 6.85
    procedure 6.86
Prior rights to sole ownership
  contingencies 1.211, 1.212
Private residence relief
  capital gains tax, and 3.8
Private sector tenancies
  assured tenancies
    assignment 1.93
    introduction 1.90
    security 1.92
    succession 1.94
  introduction 1.90
  protected tenancies
    assignment 1.97
    introduction 1.95
    security 1.96
    succession 1.98, 1.99
Proper law
  cohabitation agreements, and 2.98
Property
  applications for declaration of interest in trust property
    applicants 1.64
    exercise of court's discretion 1.69–1.71
    injunctions 1.73
    introduction 1.62
    issue 1.66
    order 1.72
    procedure 1.67, 1.68
    relevant court 1.65
    relief available 1.63
  applications for declaration of ownership of chattels
    court's approach 1.140
    introduction 1.138
    order 1.141
    relevant court 1.139
  applications to court for order of sale
    death 1.182
    separation 1.181

Index

Property – *cont.*
  applications to local authority
    Children Act 1989, s 17, under **1.130**
    Children Act 1989, s 20, under **1.129**
    introduction **1.128**
    loan from social fund **1.131**
  applications under MPPA 1970 **1.84**
  applications under MWPA 1882
    applicants **1.76**
    court's approach **1.81**
    hearing **1.80**
    injunctions **1.83**
    introduction **1.74**
    order **1.82**
    procedure **1.78**
    relevant court **1.77**
    relief available **1.75**
    service **1.79**
  assignment of tenancies
    assured tenancies **1.93**
    local authority housing **1.102**
    protected tenancies **1.97**
  assured tenancies
    assignment **1.93**
    introduction **1.90**
    security **1.92**
    succession **1.94**
  attestation clause **1.200**
  beneficial joint tenants **1.19**
  checklists **1.149**
  Children Act 1989, Sch 1 orders **1.87**
  cohabitation agreements, and
    covenants **2.45**
    joint tenancy **2.57, 2.80**
    sole ownership **2.59**
    tenancy in common **2.58, 2.81**
  commencement clause **1.153**
  constructive trusts
    detrimental reliance **1.44**
    establishment **1.33–1.43**
    generally **1.32**
    quantification, and **1.45–1.52**
  contentious precedents **1.232**
  contingencies
    bankruptcy **1.205**
    child-rearing **1.208**
    death **1.204**
    disagreement as to sale **1.203**
    failure to pay share of mortgage **1.202**
    full-time education **1.209, 1.210**
    improvement to property **1.206**
    incapacity to work **1.207**
    introductory **1.177**
    moving out before sale **1.213**
    other person permitted to reside **1.201**
    pregnancy **1.208**

Property – *cont.*
  contingencies – *cont.*
    prior rights to sole ownership **1.211, 1.212**
    repair to property **1.206**
    separation after purchase **1.214**
    unemployment **1.207**
    wish to realise share **1.215**
  contribution to repairs and improvements **1.183**
  costs of declaration **1.187**
  covenants
    positive acts **1.185**
    prohibited acts **1.184**
  declaration of beneficial interests
    applications for declaration **1.62**
    express declaration **1.18**
    generally **1.4**
  declaration of trust by co-owners
    co-owner alone to pay mortgage **1.218**
    fixed shares (long form) **1.217**
    fixed shares (short form) **1.216**
    floating shares (long form) **1.220**
    floating shares (tabular form) **1.219**
    variation **1.225**
  declaration of trust by sole owner
    council house purchased with assistance of child **1.224**
    other person contributed to price **1.223**
    variation **1.225**
  definitions
    amount required to redeem mortgage **1.191**
    co-owners **1.197**
    incidental selling costs **1.192**
    mortgage payments **1.195**
    net proceeds of sale **1.193**
    open market value **1.194**
    repairs and improvements **1.196**
    sale price **1.190**
  detrimental reliance **1.44**
  disputes as to ownership
    generally **1.17**
    Tomlin order **1.241**
  duty of solicitor **1.2, 1.3**
  execution in duplicate **1.199**
  express declaration of beneficial trusts
    beneficial joint tenants **1.19**
    constructive trusts **1.32**
    introduction **1.18**
    no express declaration **1.23**
    proprietary estoppel **1.53–1.59**
    resulting trusts **1.27–1.29**
    severing joint tenancy **1.21, 1.22**
    tenants in common **1.20**

Index

Property – *cont.*
  expression of share
    fixed shares **1.10**
    floating shares **1.12**
    fractions, percentages and ratios **1.14**
    generally **1.9**
    sale price and net proceeds of sale **1.15, 1.16**
  fixed shares
    advantages **1.10**
    disadvantages **1.11**
    generally **1.9**
  floating shares
    advantages **1.12**
    disadvantages **1.13**
    generally **1.9**
  forms
    declaration of trust by co-owners **1.216**
    declaration of trust by sole owner **1.223**
    person who 'moves in' **1.221**
    variation of declaration of trust **1.225**
  general clauses
    application to court for order of sale **1.181**
    attestation clause **1.200**
    contingencies **1.177**
    contribution to repairs and improvements **1.183**
    costs of declaration **1.187**
    covenants **1.184**
    definitions **1.190**
    execution in duplicate **1.199**
    legal advice **1.186**
    nature of declaration **1.198**
    net income until sale **1.178**
    purpose of trust **1.156**
    sale costs **1.188**
    third party contributions **1.157**
    transfer of beneficial entitlement **1.189**
  homelessness
    introduction **1.127**
  housing associations **1.91**
  injunctions **1.108**
  joint names tenancy **1.104**
  Land Registry forms **1.7, 1.8**
  law and practice
    occupation of the home **1.85**
    ownership of chattels **1.132**
    ownership of the home **1.1**
    use of chattels **1.144**
  legal advice **1.186**
  licences **1.86**
  local authority housing
    assignment **1.102**
    introduction **1.100**
    security **1.101**

Property – *cont.*
  local authority housing – *cont.*
    succession **1.103**
    nature of declaration **1.198**
    net income until sale
      general **1.178**
      payments from grown-up children **1.180**
      payments from lodgers **1.179**
    non-contentious precedents
      commencement **1.153**
      contingencies **1.201**
      forms **1.216**
      general clauses **1.177**
      recitals **1.154**
      shares in property **1.165–1.169**
      trusts **1.160**
      use **1.152**
    notice to quit **1.109**
    occupation of the home
      homelessness **1.127**
      housing associations **1.91**
      joint names tenancy **1.104**
      local authority housing **1.100**
      owner-occupied home **1.85**
      private sector tenancies **1.90**
      protection of cohabitant in occupation **1.106**
      registered social landlords **1.91**
      rented home **1.88**
      sole name tenancy **1.105**
      transfer of tenancy **1.109**
    owner-occupied home
      Children Act 1989, Sch 1 orders **1.87**
      licences **1.86**
      rights of occupation **1.85**
    ownership of chattels
      applications for declarations **1.138**
      bank accounts **1.134**
      cohabitation agreement **1.137**
      engaged couples **1.143**
      existing property **1.135**
      generally **1.133**
      gifts **1.136**
      injunctions **1.142**
      introduction **1.132**
    ownership of home
      checklist **1.226**
    ownership of the home
      applications for declarations of interest **1.62**
      declaration of beneficial interests **1.4**
      disputes, and **1.17**
      duty of solicitor **1.2, 1.3**
      express declaration of beneficial trusts **1.18**
      express declaration of trust **1.5**

839

Index

Property – *cont.*
  ownership of the home – *cont.*
    expression of share **1.9**
    introduction **1.1**
    Land Registry forms **1.7, 1.8**
  precedents
    contentious **1.232**
    non-contentious **1.153**
    use **1.152**
  private sector tenancies
    assured tenancies **1.92**
    introduction **1.90**
    protected tenancies **1.95**
  proprietary estoppel
    generally **1.53–1.59**
    illegality of purpose **1.61**
  protected tenancies
    assignment **1.97**
    introduction **1.95**
    security **1.96**
    succession **1.98, 1.99**
  protection of cohabitant in occupation
    injunctions **1.108**
    introduction **1.106**
    notice to quit **1.109**
  purpose of trust **1.156**
  recitals of fact
    mortgage of property **1.155**
    purchase of property **1.154**
    purpose of trust **1.156**
    third party contributions **1.157**
  recitals of intention
    marriage of co-owners **1.159**
    mortgage payments **1.158**
    third party contributions **1.157**
  registered social landlords **1.91**
  rented home
    generally **1.88**
    rights of occupation **1.89**
  resulting trusts
    generally **1.27–1.29**
    quantification, and **1.30, 1.31**
  rights of occupation
    owner-occupied home **1.85**
    rented home **1.89**
  sale costs **1.188**
  security of tenancies
    assured tenancies **1.92**
    local authority housing **1.101**
    protected tenancies **1.96**
  severing joint tenancy **1.21, 1.22**
  shares
    average of two or more methods of calculation **1.175**
    fixed shares **1.165**

Property – *cont.*
  shares – *cont.*
    fixed shares – *cont.*
      expressed as fixed share of sale price **1.166**
      refund of original contributions **1.167–1.169**
    floating shares **1.170**
      calculation **1.171, 1.172**
        formulae **1.173**
        tabular form **1.174**
    gradual equalisation of shares **1.176**
  sole name tenancy **1.105**
  sole or joint legal ownership **1.24**
  succession to tenancies
    assured tenancies **1.94**
    local authority housing **1.103**
    protected tenancies **1.98, 1.99**
  third party contributions **1.157**
  transfer of beneficial entitlement **1.189**
  transfer of tenancy
    Children Act 1989, Sch 1, under **1.120**
    Family Law Act 1996, Pt IV, under **1.110**
    introduction **1.109**
  trusts
    deferred trust of land **1.164**
    joint tenants until severance **1.161**
    Martin trust **1.164**
    Mesher trust **1.164**
    shares of net proceeds differ from net income until sale **1.163**
    standard trusts **1.160**
    tenants in common until marriage **1.162**
  use of chattels **1.144**

Proprietary estoppel
  death of cohabitant, and **6.14**
  generally **1.53–1.59**
  illegality of purpose **1.61**

Protected tenancies
  assignment **1.97**
  introduction **1.95**
  security **1.96**
  succession **1.98, 1.99**
  transfer
    Children Act 1989, Sch 1, under **1.120**
    Family Law Act 1996, Pt IV, under **1.110**
    introduction **1.109**

Protection from Harassment Act 1997, orders under
  contempt of court **4.64**
  criminal liability **4.63**
  enforcement **4.63**
  introduction **4.59**
  procedure **4.62**

Index

Protection from Harassment Act 1997, orders under – *cont.*
  prohibition 4.61
  venue for proceedings 4.60
Purchase of property
  recitals of fact, and 1.154
Purpose of trust
  recitals of fact, and 1.156

R

Ratios
  shares in property, and 1.14
Reasonable financial provision
  conduct 6.35
  court's approach 6.29
  disability of parties 6.34
  financial resources and needs 6.31
  introduction 6.27
  lifestyle 6.28
  matters to be considered 6.30
  meaning 6.28
  mental disability of parties 6.34
  moral culpability 6.36
  nature of estate 6.33
  obligations and responsibilities 6.32
  other relevant matters 6.35
  physical disability of parties 6.34
  repayment of debts 6.28
  settlement of property 6.16
  size of estate 6.33
Recitals of fact
  mortgage of property 1.155
  purchase of property 1.154
  purpose of trust 1.156
  third party contributions 1.157
Recitals of intention
  marriage of co-owners 1.159
  mortgage payments 1.158
  third party contributions 1.157
Registered social landlords
  occupation of the home, and 1.91
Registration of births
  generally 5.2
  joint 5.10
Release of debt
  wills, and 6.132
Release of rights
  cohabitation agreements, and
    inheritance provision 2.111
    other's separate property 2.110
Religious upbringing of child
  cohabitation agreements, and 2.112
Remand
  county court/High Court power 4.86

Remedies for breach
  cohabitation agreements, and 2.113
Rent
  cohabitation agreements, and 2.114
Repairs and improvements
  contingencies 1.206
  definition clause 1.196
Residuary estate
  wills, and 6.134–6.144
Restriction
  generally 1.7, 1.8
  standard 1.7, 1.8
Resulting trusts
  generally 1.27–1.29
  quantification, and 1.30, 1.31
Retirement pensions
  advice, clients for 7.19
  civil partnerships 7.2
  death benefits 7.8, 7.13
  introduction 7.1
  new scheme 7.6
  occupational pensions
    introduction 7.9
    lump sum death-in-service benefits 7.11
    registered pension schemes 7.10
    surviving dependants, for 7.10
  old scheme 7.5
  pensionable age 7.4
  personal pension schemes
    introduction 7.12
  retirement age 7.3
  stakeholder pensions 7.14
  state retirement pension 7.3
  state single tier pension 7.6
  survivors' pensions 7.18
  taxation 7.7
Review of cohabitation agreements
  ad hoc 2.115
Revocation
  cohabitation agreements, and 2.117
Rights of occupation
  owner-occupied home 1.85
  rented home 1.88

S

Sale costs
  precedent 1.188
Sale price
  definition clause 1.190
  shares in property, and 1.15, 1.16
Sale, applications for order for
  applicants 1.64
  circumstances in which order be made
    death 1.182

841

Index

Sale, applications for order for – *cont.*
  circumstances in which order be made – *cont.*
    separation 1.181
  exercise of court's discretion 1.69–1.71
  injunctions 1.73
  introduction 1.62
  issue 1.66
  legal background 1.145
  order 1.72
  precedents
    claim form 1.232
    order 1.235
    witness statements in support 1.233, 1.234
  procedure 1.67, 1.68, 1.146
  relevant court 1.65
  relief available 1.63
Same-sex couples
  adoption, and 5.28
Scientific test
  application procedure 5.76
  legal background 5.75
Security of tenancies
  assured tenancies 1.92
  local authority housing 1.101
  protected tenancies 1.96
Sentencing
  committal for contempt, and 4.58
Separation
  cohabitation agreements, and
    generally 2.118
    termination 2.130
  contingencies, and 1.214
  order for sale, and 1.181
Separation agreement
  generally 10.2
  precedent 10.5
Service of application
  lump sum orders, and 5.56
  non-molestation orders, and 4.9
  occupation orders, and 4.41
  periodical payment orders, and 5.56
  transfer of property orders, and 5.56
Severance
  cohabitation agreements, and 2.119
Severing joint tenancy
  declaration of beneficial interest, and 1.21, 1.22
Sexual relations
  cohabitation agreements, and 2.120
Shares in property
  average of two or more methods of calculation 1.175
  declarations of trust by co-owners
    fixed shares (long form) 1.217

Shares in property – *cont.*
  declarations of trust by co-owners – *cont.*
    fixed shares (short form) 1.216
    floating shares (long form) 1.220
    floating shares (tabular form) 1.219
    variation 1.225
  fixed shares
    advantages 1.10
    disadvantages 1.11
    generally 1.9
    long form 1.217
    short form 1.216
  floating shares
    advantages 1.12
    disadvantages 1.13
    generally 1.9
    long form 1.220
    tabular form 1.219
  fractions, percentages and ratios 1.14
  gradual equalisation of shares 1.176
'Sharing Homes' (Law Commission)
  ownership of the home, and 1.1
Social security law
  cohabitation, and 9.8–9.12
  'couple' 9.13–9.15
    living together 9.16–9.20
      additional factors 9.24
      alternative reasons 9.39, 9.42–9.44
      disability and care 9.40, 9.41
      areas of relationship 9.21, 9.22
      six signposts 9.23
    children 9.81–9.86, 9.88, 9.89
      birth certificate 9.87
    civil partners 9.97–9.102
    financial support 9.73–9.77, 9.80
      child maintenance 9.79
      property purchase 9.78
    list of factors, importance of using 9.25
    members of same household 9.26–9.29
      different address 9.30, 9.31
      separate households 9.34–9.36
      staying overnight 9.32, 9.33
    multi-partner scenarios 9.106
    public acknowledgment 9.90–9.95
    reasons
      sexual relationship 9.45–9.50
      engaged to be married 9.52
      faithfulness 9.64
      no sex at material time 9.55
      no sex ever 9.51, 9.53, 9.54
      now ceased 9.59–9.63
      sleeping arrangements 9.56–9.58

Social security law – *cont.*
  cohabitation, and – *cont.*
    'couple' – *cont.*
      living together – *cont.*
        sharing degree of family life 9.37, 9.38
        stability of relationship 9.65–9.72
        temporary separations 9.103–9.105
        unlawful relationships 9.107

Sole legal ownership
  beneficial interests 1.24

Sole name tenancy
  occupation of the home, and 1.105

Sole ownership
  cohabitation agreements, and 2.59

Solicitor, duty of
  ownership of the home, and 1.2, 1.3

Stakeholder pensions
  cohabitants' rights 7.14

Stalking
  contempt of court 4.64
  criminal liability 4.63
  enforcement 4.63
  introduction 4.59
  procedure 4.62
  prohibition 4.61
  venue for proceedings 4.60

Stamp duty
  taxation, and 3.16

Standing search
  application 6.165
  generally 6.26

State retirement pension
  cohabitants' rights 7.3

State single tier pension
  cohabitants' rights 7.6

Step-parent
  parental responsibility 5.78

Striking out
  inheritance provision claims, and
    generally 6.81
    procedure 6.82

Succession to tenancies
  assured tenancies 1.94
  local authority housing 1.103
  protected tenancies 1.98, 1.99

Support between co-habitants
  mutual support 2.121
  no obligation 2.122
  no promises made 2.123
  reservation of right 2.124
  waiver of rights 2.125

Surname
  cohabitation agreements, and 2.126, 2.127

Survivorship
  wills, and 6.112, 6.113

T

Tax credit
  income tax, and 3.6

Tax credits law
  cohabitation, and 9.8–9.12
    'couple' 9.13–9.15
      living together 9.16–9.20
        additional factors 9.24
        alternative reasons 9.39, 9.42–9.44
          disability and care 9.40, 9.41
        areas of relationship 9.21, 9.22
          six signposts 9.23
        children 9.81–9.86, 9.88, 9.89
          birth certificate 9.87
        civil partners 9.97–9.102
        financial support 9.73–9.77, 9.80
          child maintenance 9.79
          property purchase 9.78
        list of factors, importance of using 9.25
        members of same household 9.26–9.29
          different address 9.30, 9.31
          separate households 9.34–9.36
          staying overnight 9.32, 9.33
        multi-partner scenarios 9.106
        public acknowledgment 9.90–9.95
        reasons
          sexual relationship 9.45–9.50
            engaged to be married 9.52
            faithfulness 9.64
            no sex at material time 9.55
            no sex ever 9.51, 9.53, 9.54
            now ceased 9.59–9.63
            sleeping arrangements 9.56–9.58
        sharing degree of family life 9.37, 9.38
        stability of relationship 9.65–9.72
        temporary separations 9.103–9.105
        unlawful relationships 9.107

Taxation
  inheritance provision claims, and 6.88
  retirement pensions 7.7

Taxation of unmarried couples
  agricultural relief 3.14
  business reliefs 3.14
  capital gains tax
    introduction 3.7
    private residence relief 3.8
  child allowances 3.5

Index

Taxation of unmarried couples – *cont.*
  child tax credit **3.6**
  elderly married couples **3.4**
  gifts
    lifetime **3.10**
    not intended to confer benefit **3.12**
    property **3.13**
    residence **3.11**
  income tax
    child allowances **3.5**
    child tax credit **3.6**
    elderly married couples **3.4**
    introduction **3.2**
    married couples **3.3**
    universal credit **3.6**
    working tax credit **3.6**
  inheritance tax **3.9**
    agricultural relief **3.14**
    business reliefs **3.14**
    death, on **3.15**
    gifts not intended to confer benefit **3.12**
    gifts of other property **3.13**
    gifts of residence **3.11**
    lifetime gifts **3.10**
  law and practice
    capital gains tax **3.7**
    income tax **3.2**
    introduction **3.1**
    stamp duty **3.16**
  married couples **3.3**
  private residence relief **3.8**
  stamp duty **3.16**
  universal credit **3.6**
  working tax credit **3.6**
Tenancies
  assignment
    assured tenancies **1.93**
    local authority housing **1.102**
    protected tenancies **1.97**
  assured tenancies
    assignment **1.93**
    introduction **1.90**
    security **1.92**
    succession **1.94**
  housing associations **1.91**
  joint names, in **1.104**
  local authority housing
    assignment **1.102**
    introduction **1.100**
    security **1.101**
    succession **1.103**
  notice to quit **1.109**
  private sector
    assured tenancies **1.92**
    introduction **1.90**
    protected tenancies **1.95**

Tenancies – *cont.*
  protected tenancies
    assignment **1.97**
    introduction **1.95**
    security **1.96**
    succession **1.98, 1.99**
  protection of cohabitant in occupation
    injunctions **1.108**
    introduction **1.106**
    notice to quit **1.109**
  registered social landlords **1.91**
  security
    assured tenancies **1.92**
    local authority housing **1.101**
    protected tenancies **1.96**
  sole name, in **1.105**
  succession
    assured tenancies **1.94**
    local authority housing **1.103**
    protected tenancies **1.98, 1.99**
  transfer
    Children Act 1989, Sch 1, under **1.120**
    Family Law Act 1996, Pt IV, under **1.110**
    introduction **1.109**
    transfer on divorce etc **1.148, 4.71**
    undertaking not to surrender **1.147, 4.70**
Tenancy in common
  cohabitation agreements, and
    dwelling **2.58**
    property **2.80**
  declaration of beneficial interest, and **1.20**
Termination of cohabitation
  consequences
    bank accounts **2.132**
    children **2.140, 2.141**
    credit and charge cards **2.133**
    dwelling **2.134**
    introductory **2.131**
    jointly owned goods and chattels **2.136**
    lump sum payment **2.138**
    marriage, on **2.142**
    miscellaneous cancellations **2.139**
    separate property **2.135**
    support **2.137**
  death **2.130**
  end of relationship **2.128**
  injunctions **2.130**
  marriage **2.130**
  mutual agreement **2.130**
  notice **2.129**
  order **2.130**
  separation **2.130**
Testimonium
  wills, and **6.156**

Index

Third party contributions
  recitals of fact and intention, and 1.157
Tomlin order
  compromise of property dispute 1.241
Tort
  personal protection injunction 4.72
Transfer between cohabitants
  cohabitation agreements, and 2.143
Transfer of beneficial entitlement
  precedent 1.189
Transfer of land
  generally 1.7, 1.8
  precedents 1.227
Transfer of property
  inheritance provision claims, and
    generally 6.75
    variation of settlement 6.76
Transfer of property orders
  applicants 5.53
  court's approach 5.62
  court's discretion 5.59
  interim orders 5.63
  introduction 5.50
  issue of application 5.54, 5.55
  service of application 5.56
  variation of orders 5.64
  venue for proceedings 5.52
Transfer of tenancy
  application 1.237
  Children Act 1989, Sch 1, under
    applicants 1.122
    court's approach 1.126
    exercise of court's discretion 1.125
    introduction 1.120
    issue 1.123
    relevant court 1.121
    service 1.124
Transfer of tenancy (FLA 1996, Pt IV)
  exercise of court's discretion 1.114
  hearing 1.118
  issue 1.115
  order 1.119
  precedents
    application 1.237
    orders 1.239, 1.240
    witness statements 1.238
  relevant court 1.110
  response 1.117
  service 1.116
  time limits 1.113
  transferable tenancies 1.112
Trespass
  generally 4.65
  procedure 4.66
Trial separation
  cohabitation agreements, and 2.41

Trust precedents
  deferred trust of land 1.164
  joint tenants until severance 1.161
  Martin trust 1.164
  Mesher trust 1.164
  shares of net proceeds differ from net
    income until sale 1.163
  standard trusts 1.160
  tenants in common until marriage 1.162
Trustees' powers
  wills, and 6.146–6.152
Trusts of Land and Appointment of Trustees
  Act 1996, applications under
  applicants 1.64
  circumstances in which order be made
    death 1.182
    separation 1.181
  exercise of court's discretion 1.69–1.71
  injunctions 1.73
  introduction 1.62
  issue 1.66
  legal background 1.145
  order 1.72
  precedents
    claim form 1.232
    order 1.235
    witness statements in support 1.233,
      1.234
  procedure 1.67, 1.68, 1.146
  relevant court 1.65
  relief available 1.63

U

Uncertainty
  cohabitation agreements, and 2.7
Undertaking
  breach of, committal for 4.76–4.85
  harassment protection, for 4.75
  non-molestation orders, and 4.16
  occupation orders, and 4.44
Undue influence
  cohabitation agreements, and 2.103
Unemployment
  contingencies 1.207
Universal credit
  income tax, and 3.6
Unmarried fathers
  adoption, and 5.33, 5.34
Unmarried parents
  child abduction, and 5.38
Urgent application
  personal protection injunction 4.75

Index

V

Validity
  cohabitation agreements, and 2.3
Variation
  cohabitation agreements, and 2.144, 2.145
  inheritance provision claims, and 6.78
  lump sum orders, and 5.64
  periodical payment orders, and 5.64
  personal protection orders, and 4.4
  transfer of property orders, and 5.64
Venue for proceedings
  financial relief for children, and 5.52
  inheritance provision claims, and 6.19
  non-molestation orders, and 4.3
  occupation orders, and 4.18
  protection from harassment, and 4.60
  warrant of arrest, and 4.51
Violence
  definition 4.6

W

Waiver of breach
  cohabitation agreements, and 2.146
Warrant of arrest
  applicants 4.50
  application 4.50
  county court/High Court power 4.86
  court's discretion 4.53
  introduction 4.49
  procedure 4.52
  venue for proceedings 4.51
Welfare benefits
  benefit fraud 9.5
  client 9.3
  cohabitation, and 9.8–9.12
    'couple' 9.13–9.15
      living together 9.16–9.20
        additional factors 9.24
        alternative reasons 9.39, 9.42–9.44
          disability and care 9.40, 9.41
        areas of relationship 9.21, 9.22
        six signposts 9.23
        children 9.81–9.86, 9.88, 9.89
          birth certificate 9.87
        civil partners 9.97–9.102
        financial support 9.73–9.77, 9.80
          child maintenance 9.79
          property purchase 9.78
        list of factors, importance of using 9.25
        members of same household 9.26–9.29

Welfare benefits – *cont.*
  cohabitation, and – *cont.*
    'couple' – *cont.*
      living together – *cont.*
        members of same household 9.26–9.29 – *cont.*
          property purchase 9.78 – *cont.*
            different address 9.30, 9.31
            separate households 9.34–9.36
            staying overnight 9.32, 9.33
        multi-partner scenarios 9.106
        public acknowledgment 9.90–9.95
        reasons
          sexual relationship 9.45–9.50
            engaged to be married 9.52
            faithfulness 9.64
            no sex at material time 9.55
            no sex ever 9.51, 9.53, 9.54
            now ceased 9.59–9.63
            sleeping arrangements 9.56–9.58
        sharing degree of family life 9.37, 9.38
        stability of relationship 9.65–9.72
        temporary separations 9.103–9.105
        unlawful relationships 9.107
  investigations, 'living together' cases 9.108–9.110
    appeals procedure 9.119–9.127
      case law arguments 9.125
      checklist 9.126, 9.127
      evidence 9.121, 9.122
      hearing 9.120
      lodging appeal 9.119
      representation 9.123, 9.124
    challenging decisions 9.118
    evidence 9.110
    practical issues 9.111–9.117
      allegations 9.112
      burden of proof 9.113
      client's benefits stopped 9.111
      decisions susceptible to challenge 9.117
      fraud 9.115
      overpayment cases 9.114
      penalties 9.116
  opponent 9.4
  range of 9.2
  using departmental guidance 9.7
  using social security case law 9.6
Whole agreement
  cohabitation agreements, and 2.147
Will
  Law Commission consultation 6.8

Wills
　clauses
　　attestation **6.157**
　　bequest of chattels **6.126–6.129**
　　'cohabits' **6.154, 6.155**
　　commencement **6.106, 6.107**
　　definitions **6.154, 6.155**
　　executor **6.115–6.117**
　　expectation of marriage **6.108, 6.109**
　　full discretionary trust **6.143**
　　funeral wishes **6.114**
　　gifts of dwelling **6.122, 6.123**
　　guardians **6.118, 6.119**
　　guardianship **6.120, 6.121**
　　inheritance provision claim statement **6.153**
　　lump sum to buy annuity **6.133**
　　mutuality declaration **6.110**
　　non-mutuality declaration **6.111**
　　occupation rights **6.124**
　　option to purchase **6.125**
　　pecuniary legacy **6.130, 6.131**

Wills – *cont.*
　clauses – *cont.*
　　release of debt **6.132**
　　residuary estate **6.134–6.144**
　　survivorship **6.112, 6.113**
　　testimonium **6.156**
　　trustees' powers **6.146, 6.148–6.152**
　　　investment **6.147**
　　two-year discretionary trust **6.144**
　cohabitation agreements, and **2.148**
　cohabitation, and **6.4**
　description of cohabitant **6.3**
　forms
　　childless couple **6.161**
　　couple with children **6.162**
　　older couple **6.163**
　　older unmarried couple **6.164**
　　single mother leaving estate to child **6.160**
　generally **6.2**

Working tax credit
　income tax, and **3.6**